BUSINESS & **SOCIETY**

Ethics

and Stakeholder

Management

Second Edition

Archie B. Carroll
Professor of Management
The University of Georgia

COLLEGE DIVISION South-Western Publishing Co.
Cincinnati Ohio

Sponsoring Editor: Randy G. Haubner
Production Editor: Shelley Brewer
Production House: The Book Company
Cover Designer: Tom Hubbard
Internal Designer: Russell Schneck Design
Cover Photographers: Kent Knudson, FPG © 1989
Gabe Palmer, The Stock Market © 1989
Pete Saloutos, The Stock Market © 1989
Marketing Manager: Scott D. Person

GO60BA
Copyright © 1993
by South-Western Publishing Co.
Cincinnati, Ohio

ALL RIGHTS RESERVED

The text of this publication, or any part thereof, may not be reproduced or transmitted in any form or by any means, electronic or mechanical, including photocopying, recording, storage in an information retrieval system, or otherwise, without the prior written permission of the publisher.

Library of Congress Cataloging-in-Publication Data

Carroll, Archie B.
    Business & society: ethics and stakeholder management / Archie B. Carroll.
      p.   cm.
    Includes bibliographical references and index.
    ISBN 0-538-82296-1
    1. Business ethics. 2. Social responsibility of business—United States. I. Title. II. Title: Business and society.
HF5387.C35   1992
658.4′08—dc20
                                       92-12942
                                       CIP

1 2 3 4 5 6 7 8 9 D 0 9 8 7 6 5 4 3 2

Printed in the United States of America

This book is printed on recycled, acid-free paper that meets Environmental Protection Agency standards.

CONTENTS

Preface xvii

PART ONE BUSINESS, SOCIETY, AND STAKEHOLDERS 1

1 The Business and Society Relationship 2

Business and Society 4
- Business: Defined 4
- Society: Defined 5

The Macroenvironment 6

Role of Pluralism 7
- Weaknesses and Strengths of Pluralism 8
- Business Versus Multiple Publics and Systems 8

Our Special-Interest Society 9

Business Criticism/ Corporate Response 10
- Factors in the Social Environment 11
- Criticisms: Use and Abuse of Power 16
- Response: A Changing Social Environment and Social Contract 19

Focus of this Book 20
- Managerial Approach 20
- Two Broad Classes of Social Issues 21
- The Ethics Theme 22
- The Stakeholder Management Theme 22

Structure of This Book 23

2 Corporate Social Responsibility, Responsiveness, and Performance 26

The Social Responsibility Issue 27
- Historical Perspective 29
- Social Responsibility: A Number of Viewpoints 31
- A Four-Part Definition 32

Arguments Against and for Social Responsibility 37
- Arguments Against Social Responsibility 37
- Arguments for Social Responsibility 38

Social Responsibility Versus Social Responsiveness 39
- Ackerman and Bauer's Action-Oriented View 40
- Sethi's Schema 40
- Frederick's CSR_1 and CSR_2 41
- Epstein's Processes 41

    Other Views   41
    Measurable Dimensions of Responsiveness   43
  Corporate Social Performance   43
    Factors in Selecting Areas of Social Involvement   44
    Aspects of the Corporate Social Performance Model   44
    Usefulness of the Model to Academics and Managers   46
    Nonacademic Research   49
  Social Responsibility and Financial Performance   53
    Socially Conscious Investing Movement   54

3 The Stakeholder Management Concept   58

  Origin of the Stakeholder Concept   59
    What Is a Stake?   60
    What Is a Stakeholder?   60
  Who Are Business's Stakeholders?   60
    Production, Managerial, and Stakeholder Views   61
    Primary and Secondary Stakeholders   62
  Strategic Versus Multifiduciary Views   62
  Stakeholder Management   66
    Who Are Our Stakeholders?   67
    What Are the Stakeholders' Stakes?   72
    What Opportunities and Challenges
      Are Presented to Our Firm?   75
    What Responsibilities Does Our Firm
      Have to Our Stakeholders?   76
    What Strategies or Actions Should Our Firm Take?   77
    Effective Stakeholder Management   80

PART TWO   Business Ethics and Management   83

4 Business Ethics Fundamentals   84

  Business Ethics and the Public   86
    The Gallup Poll   86
    Has Business Ethics Really Deteriorated?   90
    Are the Media Reporting Ethical
      Problems More Vigorously?   91
    Is It Society That Is Actually Changing?   91
  What Does Business Ethics Mean?   92
    The Conventional Approach   93
    Ethics Versus the Law   94

        Making Ethical Judgments 95
    The Important Ethics Questions 97
        What Is? 97
        What Ought to Be? 98
        How to Get from What Is to What Ought to Be 99
        What Is Our Motivation in All This? 99
    Three Types of Management Ethics 100
        Immoral Management 101
        Moral Management 102
        Amoral Management 104
        A Hypothesis 105
    Making Moral Management Actionable 107
    Developing Moral Judgment 108
        Levels of Moral Development 108
        Source of a Manager's Values 111
    Elements of Moral Judgment 114
        Moral Imagination 114
        Moral Identification and Ordering 114
        Moral Evaluation 115
        Tolerance of Moral Disagreement and Ambiguity 115
        Integration of Managerial and Moral Competence 115
        A Sense of Moral Obligation 116

5 Personal and Organizational Ethics 120

    Levels at Which Business Ethics May Be Addressed 121
        Personal Level 121
        Organizational Level 123
        Industry Level 123
        Societal and International Levels 124
    Managing Personal Ethics 124
        Approaches to Personal Ethical Decision Making 125
        Principles Approach to Ethics 125
        Ethical Tests Approach 132
    Managing Organizational Ethics 135
        Factors Affecting the Organization's Moral Climate 135
        Illustrative Cases 140
        Actions to Improve Ethical Climate 141

6 Ethical Issues in the Global Arena 159

    Eras in the Trend Toward Internationalization of Business 160
        The Post-World War II Decade (1945–1955) 161

The Growth Years (1955–1970) 161
The Troubled Years (1970–1980) 161
The New International Order (1980–Present) 162

MNCs and the Global Environment 162
Changed Scope and Nature of U.S.-Based MNCs 163
Underlying Problems of Operating
 in a Multinational Environment 163
MNC–Host Country Challenges 165

Ethical Problems in the Multinational Environment 168
Questionable Marketing and Safety Practices 168
Bribery and Questionable Payments 172
Doing Business in South Africa 176

Improving Global Ethics 180
Global Codes of Conduct 180
Ethics and Global Strategy 182
Suspension of Activities 182
Ethical Impact Statements 183
Fundamental International Rights 183
Seven Moral Guidelines 184
Guidelines for International Corporations 184

PART THREE External Stakeholders and the Management of Them 189

7 Business, Government, and Regulation 190

A Brief History of Government's Role 192

Understanding the Major Issues 194
A Clash of Ethical Belief Systems 194
Social, Technological, and Value Changes 195

Interaction of Business, Government, and the Public 196
Government-Business Relationship 196
Public-Government Relationship 197
Business-Public Relationship 197

Government's Nonregulatory Influences on Business 198
Industrial Policy 198
Privatization 201
Other Nonregulatory Governmental Influences 202

Government's Regulatory Influences on Business 203
Regulation: Defined 204
Reasons for Regulation 205
Types of Regulation 207

Issues Arising Out of Regulation 209

Deregulation 213
   Purpose of Deregulation 214
   Trend Toward Deregulation 214
   Dilemma with Deregulation 215

Regulatory Reform 216
   Approaches to Regulatory Reform 216
   Regulatory Revival 217

8 Business's Influence on Government and Public Policy 222

The Current Political Environment 223
   Growth in Government Activity 224
   Democratization of Congress 224
   Rise of Special-Interest Groups 224
   Decline in Voter Participation 225

Corporate Political Participation 226

Business Lobbying 227
   Organizational Levels of Lobbying 227
   Lack of Unity Among Umbrella Organizations 233

Political Action Committees 234
   Evolution of PACs 234
   Magnitude of PAC Activity 236
   Arguments for PACs 236
   Arguments Against PACs 238

Coalition Building 244

Strategies for Political Activism 245
   Regulatory Life Cycle Approach 245
   Contingency Approaches 245
   Corporate Political Entrepreneurship 246

9 Consumer Stakeholders: Information Issues and Responses 251

Consumer Orientation: The Paradox 252

The Consumer's Magna Carta 253

The Consumer Movement 254
   Ralph Nader's Consumerism 255
   Consumerism in the 1980s 257
   Consumerism in the 1990s 259

Product Information Issues 261
   Advertising 262
   Warranties 279
   Packaging and Labeling 280
   Other Product Information Issues 280
The Federal Trade Commission 281
   Activist Periods of the FTC 281
   Less Active Years of the FTC 282
   The FTC Reasserts Itself 282
Self-Regulation in Advertising 284
   Types of Self-Regulation 284
   The National Advertising Division's Program 284

10 Consumer Stakeholders: Product Issues and Responses 290

Two Central Issues 291
   The Issue of Quality 291
   The Issue of Safety 294
Consumer Product Safety Commission 300
Food and Drug Administration 303
Business's Response to Consumer Stakeholders 306
   Creating a Consumer Affairs Office 306
   Establishing a Product Safety Office 308

11 The Natural Environment as Stakeholder: Issues and Challenges 312

   The Natural Environment 314
   The Human-Environment Interface 316
Natural Environment Issues 319
   Ozone Depletion 320
   Global Warming 320
   Solid and Hazardous Wastes 321
   Marine Environments 323
   Freshwater Quality and Quantity 323
   Forests 324
   Land Degradation 324
   Biological Diversity 325
   Other Environmental Issues 325
Causes of the Environmental Crisis 329
   Natural Pollution and Depletion 329
   Human-Caused Pollution and Depletion 329

Environmental Perspectives 332
   The Optimistic Perspective 332
   The Pessimistic Perspective 333
   A Realistic Perspective? 333

12 Business and Stakeholder Responses to Environmental Challenges 337

Responsibility for Environmental Issues 338
   The NIMBY Problem 338
   Environmental Ethics 339

The Role of Governments in Environmental Issues 342
   Responses of Governments in the United States 342
   International Government Environmental Responses 347

Other Environmental Stakeholders 350
   Environmental Interest Groups 350
   Green Consumers, Employees, and Investors 351
   The Role of Women in Environmental Issues 354

Business Environmentalism 356
   Examples of Business Environmentalism 356
   Systematic Business Responses to the Environmental Challenge 359

The Future of Business: Greening and/or Growing? 365

13 Community Stakeholders 369

Community Involvement 370
   Various Community Projects 372
   Managing Community Involvement 375

Corporate Philanthropy/Business Giving 381
   A Brief History of Corporate Philanthropy 381
   Giving to the "Third Sector" 382
   Managing Corporate Philanthropy 394

Business and Plant Closings 399
   Nature and Magnitude of the Problem 399
   Reasons for Plant Closings 400
   What Should Business Do? 401

Decision Factors, Action, and Research Groups 410
   Plant-Closing Public Action Groups 411
   Plant-Closing Researchers and Action Specialists 411

PART FOUR Internal Stakeholders and the Management of Them 415

14 Employee Rights and Stakeholder Issues 416

Changes in the Workplace 417
- Increased Technological Hazards 418
- The Computer Invasion 418
- Professionals with Divided Loyalties 418
- Increased Mobility of Employees 419

The Employee Rights Movement 420

The Right to a Job/Not to Be Fired 421
- Employment-at-Will Doctrine 421
- Management's Response 423

The Right of Due Process and Fair Treatment 424
- Employee Constitutionalism 425
- Management's Response 426

The Right to Freedom of Speech 428
- Whistle-Blowing 429
- Consequences of Whistle-Blowing 431
- Government's Protection of Whistle-Blowers 431
- The Whistle-Blowers Protection Act of Michigan 433
- Management Responsiveness to Potential Whistle-Blowers 434

15 Employee Stakeholders: Privacy, Safety, and Health 439

The Right to Privacy 440
- Collection and Use of Employee Information by Employers 441
- Use of the Polygraph 442
- Honesty Testing 444
- Drug Testing 445
- Monitoring Employees on the Job 448
- Policy Guidelines on the Issue of Privacy 450

The Right to Safety 451
- The Workplace Safety Problem 451
- The Right-to-Know Laws 452
- The Troubles at OSHA 453
- Threats to Reproductive Health 455

The Right to Health in the Workplace 456
- Smoking in the Workplace 456
- AIDS in the Workplace 458

16 Protected Groups: Employment Discrimination and Affirmative Action   465

The Civil Rights Movement and Minority Progress   466
- The 1950s and 1960s   467
- The 1970s   467
- The 1980s   468
- The 1990s   468

Federal Laws Prohibiting Discrimination   469
- Title VII of the Civil Rights Act of 1964   469
- Age Discrimination in Employment Act of 1967   470
- Equal Pay Act of 1963   470
- Rehabilitation Act of 1973, Section 503   470
- The Americans with Disabilities Act   472
- Proposed Civil Rights Acts of 1990 and 1991   475
- Role of the EEOC   476

The Meaning of Discrimination   478
- Disparate Treatment   478
- Disparate Impact   478

Issues in Employment Discrimination   480
- Issues on Race, Color, and National Origin   480
- Issues on Sex Discrimination   482
- Issues on Age and Religion   489

Affirmative Action in the Workplace   489
- The Range of Affirmative Action Postures   490
- The Concept of Preferential Treatment   491
- The Concept of Reverse Discrimination   491
- Minority Opposition to Affirmative Action   492
- Supreme Court Decisions   493
- The Corporate View   498

17 Owner Stakeholders: Corporate Governance   503

Legitimacy and the Corporate Governance Problem   504
- The Issue of Corporate Governance   506
- Corporate Organization   507
- Ineffective Boards of Directors   509
- Managerial Self-Interest   515
- Consequences of the Merger, Acquisition, and Takeover Craze   518

Improving Corporate Governance   522
- Changes in the Boards of Directors   522
- Increased Role of Shareholders   529
- Federal Chartering of Corporations   541

PART FIVE Strategic Management for Social Responsiveness 547

18 Strategic Management and Corporate Public Policy 548

Understanding the Concept of Corporate Public Policy 549
- Corporate Public Policy: Defined 550
- Relationship of Corporate Public Policy to Strategic Management 550
- Relationship of Ethics to Strategic Management 551

The Strategy Levels 551
- Importance of the Four Strategy Levels 552
- Emphasis on Enterprise-Level Strategy 552

The Six-Step Strategic Management Process 557
- Goal Formulation 559
- Strategy Formulation 559
- Strategy Evaluation 561
- Strategy Implementation 561
- Strategic Control 562
- Environmental Analysis 565

19 Issues Management and Crisis Management 574

Issues Management 575
- Approaches to Issues Management 576
- The Changing Mix of Issues 578
- Issues Management Process 578
- Issues Development Process 589
- Issues Management in Practice 591

Crisis Management 593
- The Nature of Crises 593
- The Four Crisis Stages 594
- Managing Business Crises 595

20 Public Affairs Management 600

Evolution of Corporate Public Affairs 602

Public Affairs in the Early 1980s 603
- Results of the Broad Survey 603
- Results of the Case Studies of Four Firms 604

The Current View of Corporate Public Affairs 605
- Trends and Observations of the 1985 Survey 605
- International Public Affairs as a Growth Area 607
- Conclusions on PA Productivity, Evaluation, and Effectiveness 610

Public Affairs Strategy 611
  Design of the Corporate External Affairs Function and Corporate Social Performance 611
  Business Exposure to the Social Environment and the External Affairs Design 611
Incorporating Public Affairs into Every Manager's Job 613
  Make Public Affairs Truly Relevant 613
  Develop a Sense of Ownership of Success 614
  Make It Easy for Operating Managers 614
  Show How Public Affairs Makes a Difference 615

EPILOGUE

Challenges for the Future 617
Corporate Governance 619
Organizational Ethics 620
Business, Government, and Politics 620
Strategic Management 621
Multinational Perspective 622
Reconciling Economic and Social Goals 623

CASES

Case Studies 627
Guidelines for Analyzing Cases 628

1. The Main Street Merchant of Doom 629
2. The Body Shop International PLC 637
3. Control Data Corporation and the Norris Era 642
4. Lakewood Bank & Trust 647
5. The Bill Collector 653
6. Home of the Braves? 655
7. Thomas Brandt's Job Search 658
8. End of the Line 663
9. The High Cost of Principles 665
10. Well Logging, Inc. 667

11 What Should a Manager Do? 672

12 The Plastichem Corporation 674

13 Multitype Corporation: Doing Business in the Caribbean 680

14 The Early CPSC Gets the Worm Gett'r! 683

15 Lobbying Ethics 687

16 The Big Mac Attack 689

17 Product Performance and Warranties: Consumer and Producer Obligations 691

18 A View of the Alps 696

19 All-Terrain Vehicles and the Consumer Product Safety Commission 700

20 Hooker Chemical and Love Canal 705

21 Update of Hooker Chemical and Love Canal Case 714

22 Community-Corporate Relationships: When Companies Say "Good-Bye" 716

23 Employment-at-Will? 721

24 Was Due Process Rendered? 722

25 The Letter to the Editor 724

26 The Zellerbach Seven 726

27 The Case of the Questionable Order 728

28 E-Mail and Employee Privacy 729

29 You Owe Me a Smoke-Free Workplace 732

30 Discrimination Cases 734

31 Propmore Corporation 737

32 The "Swedish Bikini Team" and Sexual Harassment 744

33 Rethinking Corporate Governance 747

34 Mayday for Marine Life: The Wreck of the Exxon *Valdez* 749

35 The Chrysler Odometer Episode and Crisis Management 756

36 When *Push* Comes to Shove 758

37 The Gerber Glass Scare 763

Name Index 767

Subject Index 779

PREFACE

This second edition of *Business & Society: Ethics & Stakeholder Management* is intended for college and university courses that are variously entitled "Business and Society"; "Business and Its Environment"; "Business and Public Policy"; "Social Issues in Business"; "Business, Government, and Society"; or other similar titles. At some institutions, textbooks such as this are used for courses in business ethics. This book is appropriate either for a *required* course in fulfillment of the American Assembly of Collegiate Schools of Business (AACSB) requirement for a coverage of social, ethical, and political influences or for an *elective* course. It is intended primarily for undergraduate courses but could be supplemented with other materials to be appropriate for a graduate course.

COURSE OBJECTIVES OF THIS BOOK

Depending on the place of a course in the curriculum or the individual instructor's philosophy, this book could be used for a variety of objectives. The courses for which it is intended include a number of legitimate objectives such as the following:

1. Students should be made aware of the issues and demands emanating from stakeholders that are placed on business firms.
2. As prospective managers, students need to understand appropriate business responses and management approaches for dealing with social issues and stakeholders.
3. An appreciation of ethical issues and the influence these issues have on management decision making is important.
4. The whole question of business's legitimacy as an institution in society is at stake and must be addressed.
5. The increasing extent to which social, ethical, and public issues must be considered from a strategic perspective is critical in such courses.

Other relevant objectives might be added to this list.

APPROACH USED IN THIS BOOK

A managerial perspective is embedded within this book's dual themes of business ethics and stakeholder management. The ethics dimension is essential because it is becoming increasingly clear that ethical or moral considerations are woven into the fabric of the public issues that managements face. Economic and legal issues are inevitably present, too. However, these aspects are typically treated thoroughly in other business administration courses.

The stakeholder management dimension is essential because it requires managers to (1) identify the various groups or individuals who have a stake in the firm or its actions and decisions and (2) incorporate these stakeholders' concerns into the firm's strategic plans. Stakeholder management is an approach that increases the likelihood that decision makers will integrate ethical wisdom with management wisdom in all they do.

STRUCTURE OF THIS BOOK

Part 1 of this book provides an introductory coverage of pertinent topics and issues. Since most courses for which this book is intended evolved from the issue of corporate social responsibility, this concept is treated early on. It is documented and discussed how corporate social responsiveness evolved from social responsibility and how these two matured into a concern for corporate social performance. Also appropriate for early coverage is the stakeholder management concept.

Part 2 addresses business ethics specifically. In real life, business ethics cannot be separated from the full range of external and internal stakeholder concerns. For discussion purposes, Part 2 focuses on a number of business ethics fundamentals, personal and organizational ethics, and the all-important global arena. Ethical issues in the international sphere are among the most complex. Though we cannot resolve these issues, an early treatment of them will help to keep them fresh in our minds throughout the study of this book.

External stakeholders are the subject of Part 3. Vital topics here include business's relations with government, consumers, the environment, and the community. Two entirely new chapters on the natural or physical environment have been added for this second edition. The focus of Part 4 is internal stakeholders. Here we consider employees and the related issues of employee rights, employment discrimination, and affirmative action. Owner stakeholders are also treated in Part 4. The theme of corporate governance captures most owner stakeholder concerns.

Part 5 addresses strategic management for social responsiveness. The purpose of this section is to convey management considerations for dealing with the issues developed in the book. A strategic management perspective is vital because these issues have an impact on the total organization and have become all-consuming to many upper-level managers. Special treatment is given to corporate public policy, issues and crisis management, and public affairs management. Some instructors may elect to cover Part 5 earlier in their courses. Part 5 could easily be covered after Parts 1 or 2. This option would be most appropriate for those who desire to enhance the strategic management perspective. The book closes out, as many others do, with an epilogue containing a brief summary and glance at where we are headed.

CASE STUDIES

The 37 cases at the end of this book address a wide range of issues and decision situations. Some of them are brief, and some are long. They are all intended to provide the instructor and the students with a real-life context in which to interact with some of the issues and topics discussed throughout the text. The cases were intentionally placed at the end of the text material so that the instructor would feel freer to use the cases where he or she desired. Fourteen new cases have been added to this second edition. This edition also contains five more cases in total than the first edition.

Many of the cases in this book carry ramifications that spill over into a number of areas. Almost all of them may be used for different chapters. Also provided is a set of guidelines for analysis that the instructor may wish to use in place of or in addition to the questions that appear at the end of each case. The Instructor's Manual makes recommendations on which cases to use with each chapter.

THE INSTRUCTOR'S MANUAL

For each chapter in the text, the Instructor's Manual accompanying this edition of *Business & Society: Ethics & Stakeholder Management* contains the following:

1. A complete chapter outline
2. A restatement of chapter objectives
3. Teaching suggestions
4. Suggested answers and text-page references to the chapter discussion questions
5. Objective tests consisting of 20 true-false and 20 multiple-choice questions
6. Suggested responses to end-of-case questions
7. Selected transparency masters from the text

ACKNOWLEDGMENTS

There are many people to acknowledge for their contributions to and support of this book. First, I would like to express gratitude to the many members of the Social Issues in Management Division of the National Academy of Management. Over the years these individuals have meant a lot to me and helped provide a stimulating environment in which I could intellectually pursue these topics that we have in common. Many of these individuals are cited in this book quite liberally, and I appreciate their work.

Second, I would like to specifically thank the following people who reviewed the first edition and took the time to provide me with helpful critiques. My regret is that I did not have the time to incorporate all their recommendations. Many of their ideas and suggestions have been used for this second edition.

Craig P. Dunn
San Diego State University

John Gardner
Cleveland State University

Marc Lampe
University of San Diego

John Logan
University of South Carolina

Steven Wartick
University of Missouri-St. Louis

A special note of appreciation goes to Professor Mark Starik of George Washington University for his contribution of Chapters 11 and 12 on environmental issues.

At the University of Georgia, I especially want to thank our departmental secretaries without whose support I would not have been able to finish the book on time. This group includes Melanie Blakeman, Emily Duggar, Nancy Fajardo, Billie Najour, and Karen Turner. I also appreciate the help of graduate research assistants Robert Bennett and Karen Kelley. Professors James Ledvinka and Vida Scarpello kindly permitted me to use several cases from their personnel/human resources texts.

Finally, I wish to express appreciation to my wife, Priscilla, and my son, Bradley, for their patience, understanding, and support when work on the book altered the family's plans.

Archie B. Carroll

PART ONE BUSINESS, SOCIETY, AND STAKEHOLDERS

1 The Business-and-Society Relationship

2 Corporate Social Responsibility, Responsiveness, and Performance

3 The Stakeholder Management Concept

CHAPTER **ONE**

The Business and Society Relationship

CHAPTER OBJECTIVES

After studying this chapter, you should be able to:

- Define business and society and their interrelationship.

- Explain pluralism and identify its strengths and weaknesses.

- Explain how our pluralistic society has become a special-interest society.

- Discuss the major criticisms of business and characterize business's general response.

- Identify this textbook's themes: managerial approach, ethics, and stakeholder management.

- Describe the structure of this book.

Over the past several years, many news stories have portrayed social or ethical issues in the relationship between business organizations and segments of society. In many instances the situation was one in which a business organization was being criticized for its behavior, actions, or decisions. Major examples of this include (1) the accusation against General Dynamics of fraud in its dealings with the Pentagon; (2) the E. F. Hutton scandal in which this brokerage firm was accused of fraud and illegal cash management practices; (3) the action taken against A. H. Robins and its ill-fated Dalkon Shield; (4) the tragic accident at Union Carbide's plant in Bhopal, India; (5) the Exxon Valdez oil spill into Alaska's Prince William Sound; (6) the greed and mismanagement at Drexel Burnham Lambert, which partially resulted in the firm's bankruptcy; and (7) the massive Savings and Loan (S & L) scandal, which resulted in the conviction of hundreds of executives for criminal fraud. Public awareness of the S & L scandal began in 1988, but its repercussions have spilled over into the 1990s. The ultimate cleanup costs are still being calculated, though they already run into the hundreds of billions of dollars, which ultimately will be borne by U.S. taxpayers.

In addition to these specific incidents, many general issues that carry social or ethical overtones arise between business and society. Some of these general issues have included the role of corporations in South Africa, sexual harassment in the workplace, toxic waste disposal crises, use of lie detectors, minorities' rights, AIDS in the workplace, smoking in the workplace, drug testing, insider trading, whistle blowing, product liability crises, fetal protection, and use of political action committees by business to influence the outcome of legislation.

This sampling of both specific corporate incidents and general issues typifies the kinds of business and society cases one finds today on reading a daily newspaper or magazine or watching television. It is not our intent here to take a position on these issues. Rather, we offer these issues as illustrations of the widespread interactions between business and society that occur on an almost daily basis.

Most of these corporate episodes are situations in which the public or some segment of the public believes the firm has done wrong. Indeed, in some cases major laws were broken. In any event, they all contain questions of whether business firms behaved properly or not. Thus, ethical questions typically reside in these kinds of situations. In today's socially aware environment, a business firm frequently finds itself on the defensive—that is, it finds itself being criticized for some action it took or failed to take. Whether a business is right or wrong sometimes does not matter. Powerful groups of individuals can frequently exert enormous pressure on businesses and wield a significant influence on public opinion, causing the firms to take a particular course of action.

In other cases, like the general issues mentioned earlier, businesses are attempting to deal with broad societal concerns (such as the "rights" movement, smoking in the workplace, or AIDS in the workplace) in which there is no clearly acceptable position to everyone involved. Nevertheless, businesses must weigh the pros and cons of these issues and adopt the best posture, given the many and conflicting points of view on the issue that are being expressed. Although the correct response is not simple to identify, businesses must respond and be willing to live with the consequences.

At a broad level, what is at stake is the role of business in society. Abstract debates on this issue have taken place. In this book we will address some of these concerns—particularly the role of business versus government in our socioeconomic system. But the issues we mentioned earlier are anything but abstract. They require immediate attention and definite courses of action, which quite often become the next subject of debate on the role and responsibilities of business in society.

As the 1990s get underway, many economic, legal, ethical, and social questions and issues about business and society are under debate. This period is turbulent in the sense that it has been characterized by significant changes in the economy and in society. Against this continuing turbulence in the business and society relationship, we want to develop some ideas that are fundamental to an understanding of where we are and how we got here.

BUSINESS AND SOCIETY

This chapter will develop certain terms and concepts that are important in the continuing business and society debate. Among these concepts are pluralism, our special-interest society, business criticism, and corporate response. But, first, let us define and explain two key terms: *business* and *society*.

Business: Defined

Business is the collection of private, commercially oriented (profit-oriented) organizations that range in size from one-person proprietorships (for example, Roger's TV Sales and Service, Tony's Restaurant, or Pressley's Garage) to corporate giants (for example, General Electric, Procter & Gamble, AT&T, or Sears). Between these extremes, of course, are many medium-sized proprietorships, partnerships, and corporations.

When we speak of business in this comprehensive sense, we mean businesses of all sizes and in all types of industries. But as we embark on our discussion of business and society, we will, for a variety of reasons, doubtless find ourselves speaking more of *big* business in *selected* industries. Why? For one thing, big business is highly visible. Its products and advertising are more widely disseminated. Consequently, it is more frequently in the critical public eye. In addition, people in our society often associate bigness with power, and the powerful are given closer scrutiny. Although it is well known that small businesses in our society far outnumber the larger ones, the impact, pervasiveness, power, and visibility of large firms keep them on the front page much more of the time.

[margin note: Big business has extreme power.]

With respect to different industries, some are simply more conducive to the creation of visible social problems than are others. For example, many manufacturing firms by nature cause air and water pollution. Such firms, therefore, are more likely to be subject to criticism than, say, a life insurance company, which emits no obvious pollution. The auto industry is a particular case in point. Much of the criticism against General Motors (GM) and the other automakers is raised because of their high visibility as manufacturers, the products they make (which are the largest single source of air pollution), and the popularity of their products (nearly every family owns one or more cars). In the case of the auto industry, we have not yet worked out an ideal solution to the product-disposal problem, so we see unsightly pieces of metal and plastic on every roadside.

Some industries are highly visible because of the advertising-intensive nature of their products (for example, Alka-Seltzer, Clorox 2, Die Hard Batteries, Budweiser). Other industries (for example, cigarettes, toys, food products) are examined because of the possible effect of their products on health or because of their role in providing health-related products (pharmaceutical firms).

When we refer to business in its relationship with society, therefore, we may focus our attention too much on *large* businesses, in *particular* industries. But we should not lose sight of the fact that small- and medium-sized companies also are important. In fact, over the last decade, problems have arisen for small businesses because they have been subjected to many of the same regulations and demands as those imposed by government on large organizations. In many instances, however, smaller businesses do not have the resources to meet the requirements for more accountability on many of the social fronts that we will discuss.

Society: Defined

Society may be defined as a community, a nation, or a broad grouping of people having common traditions, values, institutions, and collective activities and interests. As such, when we speak of business and society relationships, we may in fact mean business and the local community (business and Los Angeles), business and the United States as a whole, or business and a group of people (consumers, minorities, stockholders).

When we refer to business and the entire society, we think of society as being composed of numerous interest groups, more or less formalized organizations, and a variety of institutions. These groups, organizations, and institutions are purposeful units of people who have banded together because they represent a common cause or share a set of common beliefs about a particular issue. Examples of interest groups or purposeful organizations are numerous: Friends of the Earth, Common Cause, chambers of commerce, National Association of Manufacturers, Mothers Against Drunk Driving, and Ralph Nader's activists.

THE MACROENVIRONMENT

The environment is a key concept in understanding business and society relationships. At its broadest level, the environment might be thought of in terms of a macroenvironment, which includes the total environment outside the firm. The macroenvironment is the total context in which the organization resides. In a sense, the idea of the macroenvironment is just another way of thinking about society. In fact, early business and society courses in business schools were sometimes, and some still are, entitled "business and its environment." The concept of the macroenvironment, however, evokes different images or ways of thinking about business and society relationships and is therefore useful in terms of framing or understanding the total business context.

The view of the macroenvironment as developed by Liam Fahey and V. K. Narayanan is useful for our purposes. They see the macroenvironment as being composed of four segments: social, economic, political, and technological.[1]

The *social* segment (or environment) focuses on demographics, life-styles, and social values of the society. Of particular interest here would be how shifts in these factors affect the organization and its functioning. The *economic* segment focuses on the nature and direction of the economy in which business operates. Variables of interest might include such indices as gross national product, inflation, interest and unemployment rates, foreign exchange fluctuations, and various other aspects of economic activity.

The *political* segment focuses on the processes by which laws get passed and officials get elected and all other aspects of the interaction between the firm and political processes. Of particular interest to business in this segment is the regulatory process and changes that occur over time in the state of regulation of business, various industries, and various issues. Finally, the *technological* segment is another relevant way of thinking about issues. The technological segment, or environment, represents that total set of technology-based advancements or progress taking place in society. Pertinent aspects of this segment include new products, processes, and materials, as well as the state of knowledge and scientific advancement in both a theoretical and applied sense. The process of technological change is of special importance here.[2]

Thinking of business and society relationships in terms of the macroenvironment provides us with a different but useful way of understanding the kinds of issues that constitute the broad milieu in which business functions. Throughout the book we will see evidences of these environmental segments in a state of turbulence and will come to appreciate what managers are up against as they strive to develop effective organizations. The many specific groups and organizations that make up our pluralistic society can typically be traced to one of these four environmental segments; therefore, it is helpful to appreciate at a conceptual level what they are.

ROLE OF PLURALISM

Our society's pluralistic nature makes for more interesting and novel business and society relationships than those in other societies. *Pluralism* is a condition in which there is diffusion of power among the society's many groups or organizations. Joseph W. McGuire's straightforward definition of a pluralistic society is extremely useful for our purposes: "A pluralistic society is one in which there is wide decentralization and diversity of power concentration."³

The key descriptive words in this definition are wide *decentralization* and *diversity* of power concentration. In other words, power is dispersed. Power is not in the hands of any single group (such as business, government, labor, or the military) or a small number of groups. Many years ago, in *The Federalist Papers*, James Madison speculated that pluralism was a virtuous scheme. He correctly anticipated the rise of numerous organizations in our society as a consequence of it. Some of the virtues of a pluralistic society are summarized in Figure 1-1.

FIGURE 1-1   The Virtues of a Pluralistic Society

A pluralistic society prevents power from being concentrated in the hands of a few.
A pluralistic society maximizes freedom of expression, action, and striking a balance between monism (social organization into one institution) on the one hand and anarchy (social organization into an infinite number of persons) on the other.[a]
In a pluralistic society the allegiance of the individuals to groups is dispersed.
Pluralism creates a wildly diversified set of loyalties to many organizations and minimizes the danger that a leader of any one organization will be left uncontrolled.[b]
Pluralism provides a built-in set of checks and balances, in that groups can exert power over one another with no single organization (business, government) dominating and becoming overly influential.

Sources: [a]Keith Davis and Robert L. Blomstrom, *Business and Society: Environment and Responsibility*, 3rd ed. (New York: McGraw-Hill, 1975), 63.
[b]Joseph W. McGuire, *Business and Society* (New York: McGraw-Hill, 1963), 132.

Weaknesses and Strengths of Pluralism

All societal systems have their weaknesses, and pluralism is no exception. One weakness in a pluralistic system is that it creates an environment in which the diverse institutions pursue their own self-interests, with the result that there is no central direction to unify individual pursuits. Another weakness is that groups or institutions proliferate to the extent that their goals tend to overlap, thus causing confusion as to which organizations best serve which functions. Pluralism forces conflict onto center stage because of its emphasis on autonomous groups, each pursuing its own objectives. In light of these concerns, a pluralistic system does not appear to be very efficient.

History and experience have demonstrated, however, that the merits of pluralism are considerable and that most people in our society prefer the situation that has resulted from it. Indeed, pluralism has worked to achieve equilibrium in the balance of power of the dominant institutions that constitute the American way of life.

Business Versus Multiple Publics and Systems

Knowing that society is composed of so many different semiautonomous and autonomous groups might cause one to question whether we can realistically speak of society in a broad sense that has any agreed-on meaning. We nevertheless do speak in such terms, knowing that unless we specify a particular societal subgroup or subsystem, we are referring to all those persons, groups, and institutions that constitute our society. This situation raises an important point: When we speak of business and society relationships, we usually refer either to particular segments or subgroups of society (consumerists, women, minorities, environmentalists, youth) or to business and some system in our society (politics, law, custom, religion, economics). These groups of people or systems may also be referred to in an institutional form (business and the courts, business and Common Cause, business and the church, business and the AFL-CIO, business and the Federal Trade Commission).

Figure 1-2 displays in pictorial form the points of interface between business and some of the multiple publics, or stakeholders, with which business has social relationships. Stakeholders are those groups or individuals with whom the organization interacts or has interdependencies. We will develop the stakeholder concept further in Chapter 3. Note that each of the stakeholder groups may be further divided into more specific subgroups.

If sheer numbers of relationships are an indicator of complexity, then we could easily argue that business's current relationships with different segments of society constitute a truly complex environment. And if we had the capacity to draw a diagram similar to Figure 1-2 that noted all the detail composing each of those points of interface, it would be too overwhelming to comprehend. Management of businesses today cannot sidestep this problem because management must live with these interfaces on a daily basis.

FIGURE 1-2   Business and Some of Its Stakeholder Relationships

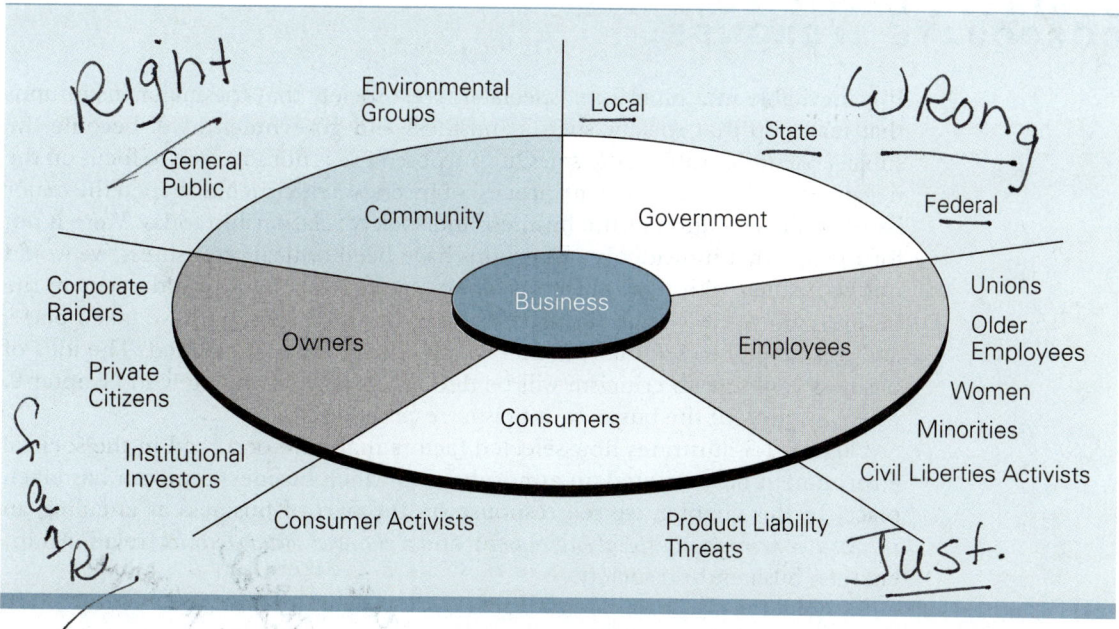

OUR SPECIAL-INTEREST SOCIETY

One could well argue that our pluralistic society has become a *special-interest society*. That is, we have carried the idea of pluralism to an extreme position in which we have literally tens of thousands of special-interest groups, each pursuing its own limited agenda. General-purpose interest organizations, such as Common Cause or the United States Chamber of Commerce, still exist. However, the last two decades have been characterized by increasing specialization on the part of interest groups representing all sectors of society—consumers, employees, communities, government, and business itself. One recent newspaper headline noted that "there is a group for every cause." Special-interest groups not only have grown in number at an accelerated pace but have become increasingly activist, intense, diverse, and focused on single issues. Such groups are increasingly committed to their causes.

The consequence of such specialization is that each of these groups has been able to attract a significant following that is dedicated to the group's goals. Increased memberships have meant increased revenues and a clearer focus as each of these groups has aggressively sought its limited purposes. The likelihood of these groups working at cross purposes and with no unified set of goals has made life immensely more complex for the major institutions, such as business, that have to deal with them.

BUSINESS CRITICISM/ CORPORATE RESPONSE

It is inevitable in a pluralistic, special-interest society that the major institutions that make up that society, such as business and government, will become the subject of considerable criticism. Our purpose here is not so much to focus on the negative as to illustrate how the process of business criticism has shaped the major issues in the evolution of the business and society relationship today. Were it not for the fact that individuals and groups have been critical of business, we would not be dealing with this subject in a book, and no changes would occur in the business and society relationship over time. But such changes have taken place, and it is helpful to see the role that business criticism has assumed. The idea of business response to criticism will be developed more completely in Chapter 2, where we present the business criticism/response cycle.

Figure 1-3 illustrates how selected factors that have occurred in the societal environment have created an atmosphere in which business criticism has taken place. In this chapter, we see response on the part of business as entailing an *increased concern for the social environment* and a *changed social contract* (relationship) between business and society.

FIGURE 1-3 Business Criticism and Response

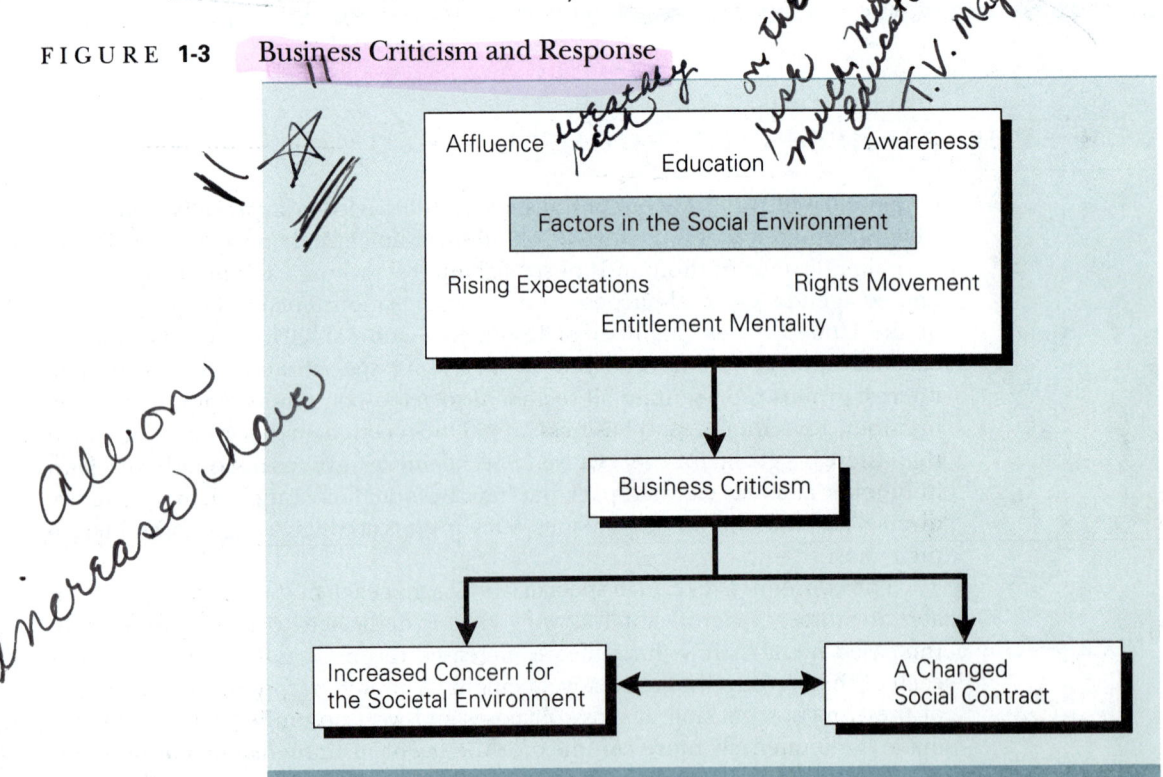

Factors in the Social Environment

Many factors in the social environment have created a climate in which criticism of business has taken place and flourished. Some of these are relatively independent, and some are interrelated with other factors. In other words, they occur and grow hand in hand.

Affluence and Education. Two factors that have developed side by side are *affluence* and *education*. As a society becomes more affluent and well educated, higher expectations of its major institutions, such as business, will follow.

Affluence refers to the level of wealth, disposable income, and standard of living of the society. Measures of our country's standard of living indicate that it has been rising for decades. Although some Americans perceive that U.S. living standards have stopped rising, recent data from the Conference Board indicate that life is better for most of us now than in the past and continues to be so in spite of the recession in the early 1990s and the contributing influence of the Persian Gulf War. The Conference Board concludes: "All told, the period 1970–1990 represents an era of substantial economic expansion and a marked improvement in the living standards of the average American."[4] They further observe that today's young adults are living nearly twice as well as their parents and that this improvement in American living standards will continue throughout this final decade of the twentieth century. A Gallup poll of Americans substantiated this perspective. Gallup found that most Americans see a better life for themselves on all fronts—finances, careers, and general quality of life.[5] Alongside an increased standard of living has been a growth in the average formal education of the populace. As people become more highly educated, their expectations of life generally rise. Combined, affluence and education form the underpinning for a climate in which societal criticism of major institutions, such as business, arises.

Awareness Through Television. Closely related to formal education is the high and growing level of public *awareness* in society. Although newspapers and magazines are still read by only a fraction of our population, a more powerful medium—television—is accessed by virtually our entire society. Through television, the citizenry gets a variety of information that contributes to a climate of criticism.

First, let us establish the power and prevalence of TV. Several statistics document the extent to which our society is dependent on TV for information. According to data compiled by the A. C. Nielsen Company, the daily average time spent viewing television per household rose from 4 1/2 hours in 1950 to a little over 7 hours in 1983. As one writer put it: "Think about it. A typical day for an American household now divides into three nearly equal parts: eight hours of sleep, seven hours of TV, and nine hours of work or school, including getting there and back."[6] Other statistics indicate that in 1990 there were 2.3 TVs in every home, that over 98 percent of homes in America have TV,[7] and that from ages 2 to 18 the average American spends 11,000 hours in school and over 20,000 hours in front of the TV.[8] Indeed, television is a powerful medium in our society.

Straight News and Investigative News Programs. There are at least three ways in which information that leads to criticisms of business appears on television. First, there are *news shows*, such as the evening news on the major networks, and *investigative news programs*. It is debatable whether the major news programs are treating business fairly or not, but in one major study, an overwhelming 73 percent of the executives surveyed indicated that business and financial coverage on TV news is prejudiced against business. TV pollster Lou Harris thinks that TV news has to deal with things too briefly and that, whenever a company makes the evening news, it is usually because the story is unfavorable.[9]

In another major study, chief executive officers of companies of all sizes reported overwhelmingly that newspapers and magazines report business and economic news with a negative bias. Of the total number of CEOs, 19 percent thought such coverage was *very negative;* 46 percent thought it was *negative;* 27 percent thought it was *neutral;* and only 7 percent thought it was *positive*.[10]

Although many business leaders believe that the news media are out to get them by exaggerating the facts and overplaying the issues, journalists see it differently. They counter that business executives try to avoid them, are evasive when questioned about major issues, and try to downplay problems that might reflect negatively on their companies. The consequence is an adversary relationship that perhaps helps to explain some of the unfavorable coverage.

Business has to deal not only with the straight news coverage problems but also with a growing number of investigative news programs like "60 Minutes" and "20/20" that seem to thrive on exposés of business wrongdoings or questionable practices. Whereas the straight news programs make some effort to be objective, the investigative shows are tougher on business. These shows are enormously popular and influential, and many companies squirm when reporters show up on their premises complete with a camera crew.

What is behind this apparent antagonism between business and the news media? There are many answers. One fundamental reason is that business executives and journalists differ considerably in their basic political ideology and attitudes on major business and economic issues of the day. With respect to political ideology, studies show that journalists are much more liberal than either CEOs of major corporations or the general public. Journalists overwhelmingly vote Democratic, whereas CEOs tend to vote Republican. Although journalists say they do not oppose the basic institutions of capitalism, they are much less likely than business executives to think that unregulated markets are consistent with the public interest, and they are considerably more likely to think that regulation is needed to protect the public.[11] Furthermore, it should be noted that some businesses do, indeed, engage in questionable practices that the news legitimately must cover.

Prime-Time Television Programs. The second way in which criticisms of business appear on TV is through *prime-time television programs*. Television's depiction of business people brings to mind the scheming J. R. Ewing of "Dallas," whose backstabbing shenanigans dominated prime-time TV for over a decade (1978–

1991) before it went off the air. In most cases the businessperson is portrayed as a smirking, scheming, cheating, and conniving "bad guy." A vice-president of the Chamber of Commerce of the United States puts it this way: "There is a tendency in entertainment television to depict many business people as wealthy, unscrupulous, and succeeding through less-than-honorable dealings. This is totally incorrect."[12]

A major research study on this issue has concluded that since 1945, most business people (usually men) depicted in television and serious literature are characterized as greedy, unethical, and immoral (or amoral). Another researcher has argued that there is a much higher ratio of "bad guys" among business people than among doctors or police officers.[13]

Another major study was conducted over an 8-week period by analyzing how business people were portrayed on major prime-time shows. Business people proved to be the major staple of prime-time shows, appearing in about half the shows studied. In this study, not one businessperson was of the working class or poor. Many resided in beautifully furnished estates, were pampered by servants, and sported expensive jewelry and clothing. How were they portrayed? Sixty percent were portrayed negatively. Of the 60 percent who were bad guys, 35 percent did something illegal; 32 percent were greedy or otherwise self-interested; 21 percent played the fool, mainly in sitcoms; and the remaining 12 percent were malevolent. In general, big-business people fared worse than small-business people. Business people were also shown to be at their worst when performing purely business functions, more so than when they were performing under purely personal circumstances.[14]

Any redeeming social values that business may have rarely show up on prime-time television. Rather, business people are cast as evil and greedy social parasites whose efforts to get more for themselves are justly condemned and usually thwarted.[15] There are many views as to why this portrayal has occurred. Some would argue that business is being characterized accurately. Others say that the television writers are dissatisfied with the direction our nation is taking and believe they have an important role in reforming American society.[16] Apparently they think that this treatment of business will bring about change.

Commercials. The third way in which television contributes to business criticism is through *commercials*. To the extent that business does not honestly and fairly portray its products on TV, it undercuts its own credibility. Commercials are a two-edged sword. On the one hand, they may sell more products in the short run. On the other hand, they may damage business's long-term credibility if they promote products deceptively.

One major study hints at how this occurs. In an investigation of how television commercials were reviewed by children, Harvard Business School researchers found considerable skepticism, tension, and anger among children because of misleading advertising. By age 11, the study concluded, "Most children have already become cynical—ready to believe that like advertising, business and other institutions are riddled with hypocrisy." About three-fourths of the 11- and 12-year-olds studied thought that advertising is sometimes designed to "trick" the consumer.[17]

Thus we see three specific settings—news coverage, prime-time programming, and commercials—in which a strained environment is being created and fostered by this "awareness" factor made available through the power and pervasiveness of television. We should make it clear that the media are not to blame for business's problems. If it were not for the fact that some of business's behavior is questionable, the media would not be able to create this kind of environment. The media, therefore, should be seen just as one major factor that contributes to the environment in which business finds itself.

Revolution of Rising Expectations. In addition to affluence, formal education, and awareness through television, there are other societal developments that have aided the climate in which business criticism has occurred. Growing out of these factors has been a *revolution of rising expectations.* This might be defined as an attitude or belief that each succeeding generation ought to get more than its predecessor and that its expectations of major institutions, such as business, would be greater also. Building on this line of thinking, one could argue that business has been criticized today because society's expectations of its performance have outpaced business's ability to meet these growing expectations. To the extent that this has occurred over the last 20 to 30 years or so, business finds itself with a larger problem. Figure 1-4 illustrates this larger "social problem" that business faces today versus years ago.

FIGURE 1-4 Society's Expectation Vs. Business's Social Performance

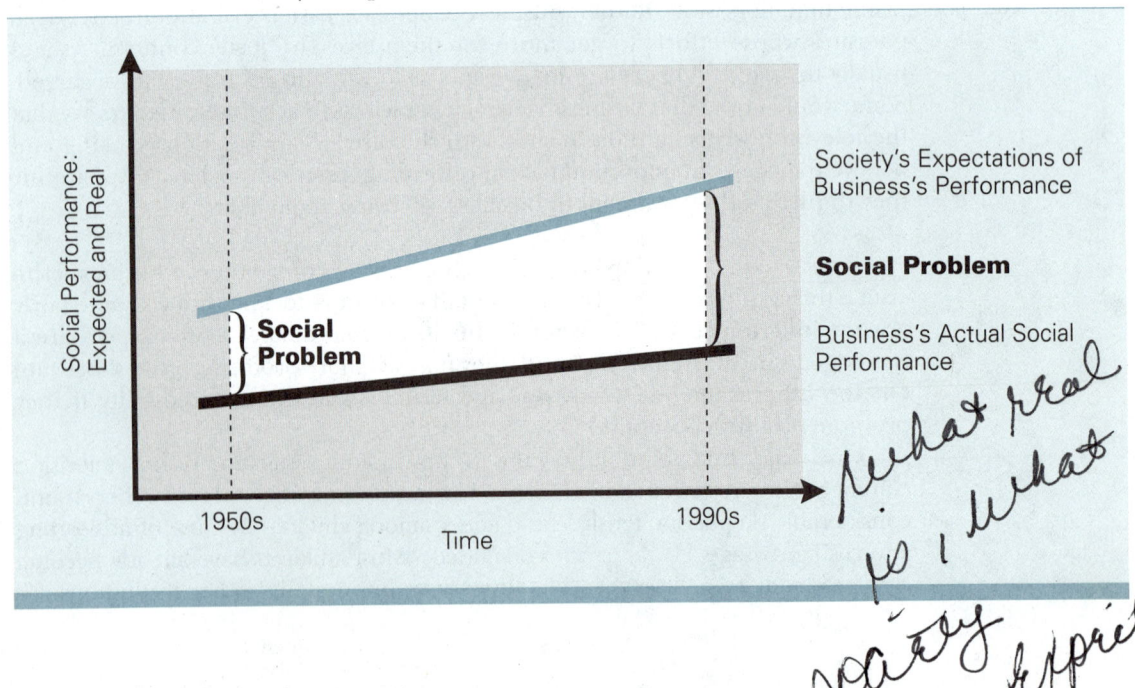

A *social problem* has been described as a gap between society's expectations of social conditions and the present social realities.[18] From the viewpoint of a business firm, the social problem might be the gap between society's expectations of its social performance and its actual social performance. The nature of rising expectations is that they typically outpace the responsiveness of institutions such as business, thus creating a constant condition that is conducive to criticism.

Although the general trend of rising expectations continues, there are signs that the revolution may have moderated in spite of citizens' expectations that their job situation, health, family life, and overall quality of life are expected to be better in the 1990s. The emergence of social problems such as crime, poverty, homelessness, AIDS, environmental pollution, and alcohol and drug abuse threaten to worsen during the decade and to moderate rising expectations.[19]

Rights Movement. All of the factors discussed so far have contributed somewhat to what might be termed the *rights movement* that is present in our country today. The Bill of Rights was attached to the United States Constitution almost as an afterthought and was virtually unused for more than a century. But in the past several decades, and at an accelerating pace, a rising tide of cases have come before the U.S. Supreme Court trying to establish for some groups various rights that perhaps never occurred to our Founding Fathers.[20] Some of these rights, such as the right to privacy and the right to due process, have been generic for all citizens.

In addition to these generalized rights has been pressure for rights for particular groups in our society. The modern movement began with civil rights cases in the 1950s. Many groups have been inspired by the success of blacks and have sought success by similar means. Thus, we have seen the protected status of minorities grow to include women, the handicapped, the aged, and other groups. At various levels—federal, state, and local—we have seen claims for the rights of homosexuals, smokers, nonsmokers, and AIDS victims.

There seem to be no limits to the notion of particular groups or individuals seeking "rights" in our society. And business, as one of society's major institutions, has been hit with an ever-expanding array of constraints and expectations as to how people want to be treated and dealt with, not only as employees but also as owners, consumers, and members of the community. The "rights" movement is interrelated with the special-interest society we discussed earlier and sometimes precedes an "entitlement" mentality among some people and sectors of society.

Entitlement Mentality. Several years ago, the Public Relations Society conducted a study of public expectations, with a particular focus on public attitudes toward the *philosophy of entitlement*. This philosophy is the general belief that someone is owed something (for example, a job) just because he or she is a member of society. The survey was conducted on a nationwide basis, and respondents were asked to categorize items they thought people (1) were entitled to have and (2) have now. A sampling of the findings shown in Figure 1-5 illustrates some interesting perspectives on what people think are due them.[21]

FIGURE 1-5   Findings on the Entitlement Mentality

Item	Entitled to Have	Have It Now
1. Steadily improving standard of living	88%	39%
2. A guaranteed job for all those willing and able to work	85%	34%
3. Products certified as safe and not hazardous to one's health if properly used	90%	54%

For each of the items studied, there was a yawning gap between those who thought that the public was entitled to a particular benefit and those who thought they had it now. The size of the differences boldly underscored what the pollsters had been telling business and government for years: *that society is not satisfied with the performance of these institutions.*

In summary, affluence and education, awareness through television, the revolution of rising expectations, the "rights" movement, and an "entitlement" mentality have formed a backdrop against which criticism of business has grown. To be sure, this list does not summarize all issues and trends that are present in the social environment. However, it does help to explain why we have an environment that is so conducive to criticism of business. In the next section we will see what some of the criticisms of business have been, and in the section after that we will discuss some of the general results of this criticism.

Criticisms: Use and Abuse of Power

Many criticisms have been leveled at business over the years: It's too big, it's too powerful, it pollutes the environment and exploits people for its own gain, it takes advantage of workers and consumers, it does not tell the truth, and so on. A catalog of business criticisms would occupy too much space to present here. If one were to identify a common thread that seems to run through all the complaints, it seems to be business's use and abuse of power. Before discussing business power in more detail, we should note that the major criticism seems to be that business often engages in questionable or unethical behavior with respect to its stakeholders.

Now, what is power? *Power* refers to the ability or capacity to produce an effect or to bring influence to bear on a situation. Power, in and of itself, may be either positive or negative. In the context of business criticism, however, power typically is perceived as abused. Business certainly does have enormous power, but whether it abuses power is an issue that needs to be carefully examined. We will not settle that issue here, but the criticism remains that business abuses power.

Levels of Power. To understand corporate power, one must recognize that it resides at several levels. Edwin M. Epstein identified four: the macro level, the intermediate level, the micro level, and the individual level.[22] The *macro level* refers to the corporate system—the totality of business organizations. Power here emanates from the sheer size and dominance of the corporate system. The *intermediate level* refers to groups of corporations acting in concert in an effort to produce a desired effect—raise prices, control markets, dominate a purchaser, promote an issue, or pass or defeat legislation. Prime examples are office equipment leaders, banks, OPEC, defense contractors, or the Conference Board. The *micro level* of power is the level of the individual firm. This might be any major corporation—GM, IBM, Procter & Gamble, Wal-Mart—exerting power. The final level is the *individual level*. This refers to the individual corporate leader—Lee Iacocca, the late Henry Ford II, Ted Turner, Donald Trump, Victor Kiam ("I liked the Remington shaver so much I bought the company").

The important point here is that, as one thinks of corporate power, one should think in terms of the different levels in which it is manifested. When this is done, it is not easy to conclude whether corporate power is excessive or has been abused.

Spheres of Power. There are not only levels of power to examine but also numerous different spheres in which this power resides. Figure 1-6 briefly portrays one way of looking at the levels Epstein identified and some of the spheres of power being referred to. Economic power and political power are two spheres that are referred to often, but business has other, more subtle forms of power also. These other spheres include social and cultural power, power over the individual, technological power, and environmental power.

Is business power excessive? Does business abuse its power? Obviously, a number of people think so. To provide a careful and fair answer to these questions, however, one must very carefully stipulate which level of power is being referred to and in which *sphere* the power is being employed. When this is done, it is not simple to arrive at a clear or fair answer.

Furthermore, the nature of power is such that it is only sometimes wielded intentionally. Sometimes it is consequential; that is, it is not wielded intentionally but rather arises even though no attempt is made to exercise it.[23] An example of this might be a large firm like IBM that purchases huge parcels of land in cities all across the United States to keep in its real estate inventory for possible use some day. IBM comes right out and says it has no definite plans to move to these various cities. But in spite of an attempt not to wield power, IBM still has enormous power with the various city councils and county commissions in which it has purchased land.

FIGURE 1-6   Levels and Spheres of Corporate Power

Spheres \ Levels	Macro Level (the business system)	Intermediate Level (several firms)	Micro Level (single firm)	Individual Level (executive)
Economic				
Social/Cultural				
Individual				
Technological				
Environmental				
Political				

Balance of Power and Responsibility. Whether business abuses its power or allows its use of power to get out of hand is a central issue cutting through all the topics we will be discussing in this book. But power cannot be viewed in isolation from responsibility, and this power-responsibility relationship is the foundation for calls for corporate social responsibility. Davis and Blomstrom articulated this major concern in what they called the *Iron Law of Responsibility:* "In the long run, those who do not use power in a manner which society considers responsible will tend to lose it."[24] Stated another way, whenever power and responsibility become substantially out of balance, forces will be generated to bring them into closer balance.

When power gets out of balance, a variety of forces come to bear on business to be more responsible and responsive to the criticisms being made against it. Some of these more obvious forces include governmental actions such as increased regulations or new laws. The investigative news media become interested in what is going on, and a whole host of special-interest groups bring pressure to bear.

This power-responsibility relationship holds true among other institutions, too. An example is the relationship between big-time intercollegiate athletics and the NCAA, which is its principal membership and regulatory association. Several years ago, a number of large university "football powers" became upset with the degree of power the NCAA wielded regarding rules about how often games could be televised. So a number of the football "power" schools embarked on their own to form the College Football Association (CFA) and began bargaining directly with the major networks for television scheduling. But this balancing action also works the other way. In the face of public criticism that big-time athletics has lost the perspective of academics, the NCAA has acted to raise admission standards for eligibility to play college sports. Thus, this issue of power-responsibility balance works in both directions and applies not only to business organizations but also to other institutions in our society.

Response: A Changing Social Environment and Social Contract

Growing out of criticisms of business and the idea of the power-responsibility equation has been an increased concern for the social environment and a changed social contract. Earlier we indicated that the *social environment* was composed of such factors as demographics, life-styles, and social values of the society. It may also be seen as a collection of conditions, events, and trends that reflect how people think and behave and what they value. As firms have sensed that the social environment and the expectations of business are changing, they are realizing that they have to change, too. The *social contract* is a set of two-way understandings that characterize the relationship between major institutions—in our case business and society. It is changing, and it is a direct outgrowth of the increased importance of the social environment.

The social contract between business and society is partially articulated through:

1. *Laws or regulations* that society has established as the framework within which business must operate
2. *Shared understandings* that prevail as to each group's expectations of the other

Figure 1-7 depicts the social contract graphically.

It is clear how laws or regulations spell out the "rules of the game" for business. Shared understandings, on the other hand, create more confusion and room for misunderstandings. In a sense, these shared understandings reflect mutual expectations regarding each other's roles, responsibilities, and ethics. These are the unspoken components of the relationship.

A parallel may be seen through the relationship between a professor and the students in his or her class. University regulations and the syllabus for the course spell out the formal aspects of the relationship. The shared understandings address those expectations that are generally understood but not necessarily spelled out formally. An example might be "fairness." The student expects the professor to be "fair" in making assignments, in the level of work expected, in grading, and so on. Likewise, the professor expects the student to be fair in evaluating him or her on teaching evaluation forms, to be fair by not passing off someone else's work as his or her own, and so on.

An editorial from *Business Week* magazine that dates back to over 20 years on the subject of the social contract summarizes well the modern era of business and

FIGURE 1-7 Elements in the Social Contract

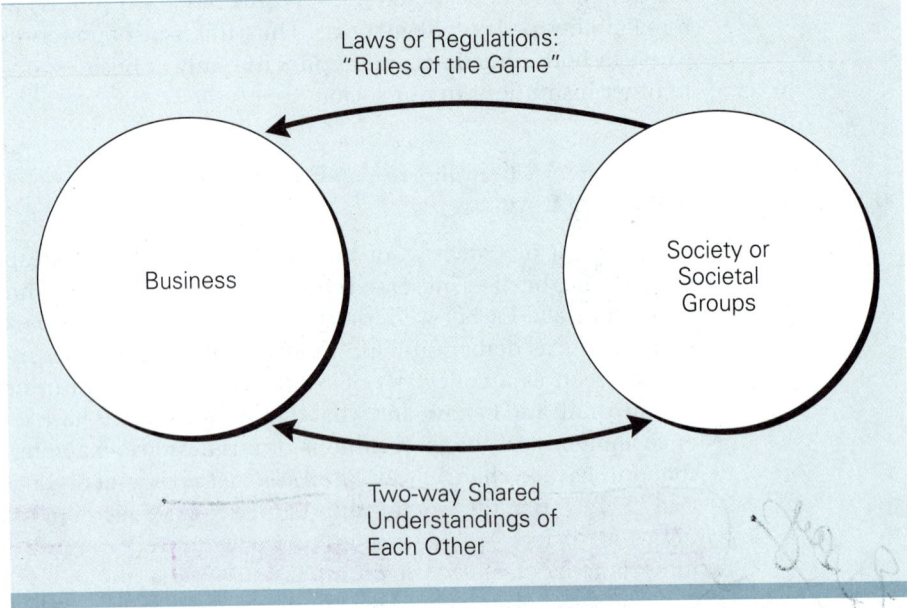

society relationships: "Today it is clear that the terms of the contract between society and business are, in fact, changing in substantial and important ways. Business is being asked to assume broader responsibilities to society than ever before, and to serve a wider range of human values.... Inasmuch as business exists to serve society, its future will depend on the quality of management's response to the changing expectations of the public."[25]

FOCUS OF THIS BOOK

This book takes a managerial approach to the business and society relationship. The managerial approach emphasizes two major themes that are important today: ethics and stakeholder management. First, let us discuss the managerial focus.

Managerial Approach

Managers, being the pragmatic beings that they are, have begun to deal with social concerns in ways similar to those they have used in dealing with traditional business functions—production, marketing, finance, and so forth—in a rational, systematic, and administratively sound fashion. By viewing issues of social concern from a managerial frame of reference, managers have been able to reduce seemingly unmanageable social concerns to ones that can be dealt with in a rational fashion.

A managerial approach to the business and society relationship confronts the individual manager continuously with questions such as these:

- What changes are occurring or will occur in society's expectations of business that mandate business's taking the initiative with respect to particular societal problems?
- Did business in general or our firm in particular have a role in creating these problems?
- What impact is social change having on the organization, and how should we best respond to it?
- Can we reduce broad social problems to a size that can be effectively addressed from a managerial point of view?
- On which social problems can we act most effectively?
- What are the specific problems, alternatives for solving the problems, and implications for management's approach to dealing with social issues?
- How can we best plan and organize for responsiveness to socially related business problems?

Two Broad Classes of Social issues

From the standpoint of urgency in managerial response, management is concerned with two broad classes of social issues. First, there are those issues that arise on the spur of the moment and for which management formulates a relatively quick response. These may be either issues that management has never faced before or issues it has faced but does not have time to deal with except on a short-term basis. A typical example might be a protest group that shows up on management's doorstep one day, arguing vehemently that the company should withdraw its sponsorship of a violent television show scheduled to air the next week.

Second, there are issues or problems that management has time to deal with on a more long-term basis. These might involve environmental pollution, employment discrimination, product safety, or occupational safety and health. In other words, these are issues that will be of concern to society for a long time and for which management must develop a reasonably sophisticated organizational response. It is true that issues of this type could also appear in the form of ad hoc problems necessitating an immediate response, but they should suffice to illustrate areas that have matured somewhat. Management must thus be concerned with both short-term and long-term capabilities to deal with social problems and the organization's social performance.

Our managerial approach, then, will be one that (1) clarifies the nature of the social or ethical issues that affect organizations and (2) suggests alternative managerial responses to these issues in a rational and systematic fashion. The test of success will be the extent to which we can improve an organization's social performance by taking the managerial approach rather than dealing with the issues on an ad hoc basis.

The Ethics Theme

As hard as we might try to extricate business from the major ethical issues of the day, it just cannot be done. The managerial focus attempts to take a practical look at the social issues and expectations business faces, but ethical questions inevitably come into play. *Ethics* basically refers to issues of right, wrong, fairness, and justice, and *business ethics* focuses on those issues that arise in the commercial realm. Ethical threads run through our discussion because questions of right, wrong, fairness, and justice, no matter how slippery they are to deal with, permeate business's behavior as it attempts to deal with major stakeholder groups: employees, customers, owners, government, and the community.

The inevitable task of management is not only to deal with the various stakeholder groups in an ethical fashion but also to reconcile the conflicts of interest that occur between the organization and the stakeholder groups. Implicit in this challenge is the ethical dimension present in practically all business decision making where stakeholders are concerned. In addition to the challenge of treating fairly the groups that business interacts with, management faces the equally important task of creating an organizational climate in which all employees make decisions with the interest of the public, as well as that of the organization, in mind. At stake is not only the firm's reputation but that of the business community generally.

The Stakeholder Management Theme

As we have alluded to throughout this chapter, *stakeholders* are individuals or groups with which business interacts who have a "stake," or vested interest, in the firm. They could be called "publics," but that term may imply that they are outside the business sphere and should be dealt with as external players rather than as integral components of the business-society relationship. As a matter of fact, stakeholders actually constitute the most important elements of that broad grouping known as *society*.

We deal with two broad groups of stakeholders in this text. First, we consider *external* stakeholders, which include government, consumers, and community members. We treat government first because it represents the public. It is helpful to understand the role and workings of government to best appreciate business's relationships with other groups. Consumers may be business's most important stakeholders. Members of the community are crucial, too, and they are concerned about a variety of issues. One of the most important is the physical environment. Two other major community issues include business giving (or corporate philanthropy) and plant closings. All these issues have a direct effect on the community.

The second broad grouping of stakeholders are the *internal* stakeholders. Business owners and employees are the principal groups of internal stakeholders. We live in an organizational society, and many people feel that their roles as employees are just as important as their roles as investors or owners. Both of these groups have legitimate claims on the organization, and management's task is to address their needs and balance these against the needs of the firm and of other stakeholder groups. We will develop the idea of stakeholder management more fully in Chapter 3.

STRUCTURE OF THIS BOOK

Part 1 of this book provides an overview of the business and society relationship; social responsibility, responsiveness, and performance; and the stakeholder management concept. These materials provide a crucial basis for understanding all discussions that follow.

Part 2 focuses entirely on business ethics. Business ethics fundamentals are established in one chapter, and the idea of managing business ethics is presented in another. A third chapter treats business ethics in the global or international sphere. Although ethical issues cut through and permeate many of our discussions in the book, this special treatment is warranted by a need to explore in some detail what is meant by the ethical dimension in management.

Part 3 treats the major external stakeholders of business. Government is dealt with first because it is an active player in all the groups to follow. First, we consider business-government relationships and government regulations. Then we discuss how business endeavors to shape and influence public policy. Consumer stakeholders, environmental issues, and community issues are then dealt with in turn.

In Part 4, internal stakeholders are addressed. These include employees and owners. We first deal with the growing employee rights movement and then focus on the special case of employment discrimination. Corporate governance is the chapter under which we discuss the business-ownership relationship.

In Part 5, we place our managerial and stakeholder perspective within the context of strategic management. We assume a knowledge and awareness of the issues at this point and focus on the more enduring management responses that are essential to a well-conceived managerial approach. In addition to conceptual materials on strategic management and social issues, we examine public affairs management, issues management, and crisis management. Here we are concerned with generalizable management and organizational response patterns that are proving effective in dealing with social issues. Part 5 of the book contains chapters and materials that could easily be covered after Part 1 or Part 2, should an even stronger strategic management perspective be desired. We close this book with an epilogue that addresses future issues.

Taken as a whole, this book strives (1) to take the reader through basic concepts and ideas that are vital to the business and society relationship and (2) to explore the nature of social issues and stakeholder groups with which management must interact. It considers the external and internal stakeholder groups in some depth and closes with a treatment of management issues and approaches to making the firm more responsive to the full range of societal expectations that are placed on it.

SUMMARY

The pluralistic business system in the United States has a number of advantages and some disadvantages. Within this context, business firms must deal with a multitude of stakeholders and an increasingly special-interest society. A major force that shapes the public's view of business is the criticism that business receives from a variety of sources. Factors in the social environment that have contributed to an atmosphere in which business criticism thrives include affluence, education, public awareness developed through the media (especially TV), the revolution of rising expectations, the rights movement, and a growing entitlement mentality. In addition, actual questionable practices on the part of business have made it a natural target. Not all firms are guilty, but the guilty attract attention to the total business community.

A major criticism of business is that it has abused its power. To understand power, you need to recognize that it may reside at four different levels: the business system, groups of companies acting in concert, the level of the firm, and the level of the individual corporate executive. Also, business power may be manifested in a number of different spheres: economic, political, technological, environmental, social, and individual. It is difficult to assess whether business is actually abusing its power, but it is clear that business has enormous power. Power evokes responsibility, and this is the central reason that calls for corporate responsiveness have been prevalent in recent years. These concerns have led to a changing social environment for business and a changed social contract.

DISCUSSION QUESTIONS

1. In discussions of business and society, why is there a tendency to focus on large rather than small- or medium-sized firms?
2. What are the single major strength and the single major weakness of a pluralistic society? Do these work for or against business?
3. Identify and explain the major factors in the social environment that create an atmosphere in which business criticism takes place and prospers.
4. Give an example of each of the four levels of power discussed in the chapter. Also give an example of each of the spheres of power that business has.

5. Explain in your own words the social contract. Give an example of a shared understanding between you as a consumer or employee and a firm you are doing business with or working for.

ENDNOTES

1. Liam Fahey and V. K. Narayanan, *Macroenvironmental Analysis for Strategic Management* (St. Paul: West, 1986), 28–30.
2. *Ibid.*
3. Joseph W. McGuire, *Business and Society* (New York: McGraw-Hill, 1963), 130.
4. Fabian Linden, "The American Dream," *Across the Board* (May, 1991), 7–10.
5. Linda DeStefano, "Looking Ahead to the Year 2000: No Utopia, but Most Expect a Better Life," *The Gallup Poll Monthly* (January, 1990), 18.
6. "Average American Family Watches TV 7 Hours Each Day," *Athens Banner Herald* (January 25, 1984), 23.
7. George Gallup, Jr. and Frank Newport, "Americans Have Love-Hate Relationship With Their TV Sets," *The Gallup Poll Monthly* (October, 1990), 5.
8. "Observations," *San Jose Mercury Times* (July 19, 1981), 19.
9. "Business Thinks TV Distorts Its Image," *Business Week* (October 18, 1982), 26.
10. "CEOs: Biz News is Negative," *USA Today* (February 27, 1987), 1B.
11. Fred J. Evans, "Management and the Media: Is Accord in Sight? View Four: The Conflict Surveyed," *Business Forum* (Spring, 1984), 16–23.
12. Eric Pace, "On TV Novels, the Bad Guy Sells," *The New York Times* (April 15, 1984).
13. *Ibid.*
14. Linda S. Lichter, S. Robert Lichter, and Stanley Rothman, "How Show Business Shows Business," *Public Opinion* (November, 1982), 10–12.
15. *Ibid.*, 12.
16. Nedra West, "Business and the Soaps," *Business Forum* (Spring 1983), 4.
17. Morton C. Paulson, "What Youngsters Learn on TV," *National Observer* (May 19, 1976), 10.
18. Neil H. Jacoby, *Corporate Power and Social Responsibility* (New York: Macmillan, 1973), 186–188.
19. DeStefano, p. 21.
20. Charlotte Low, "Someone's Rights, Another's Wrongs," *Insight* (January 26, 1987), 8.
21. Joseph Nolan, "Business Beware: Early Warning Signs for the Eighties," *Public Opinion* (April/May, 1981), 16.
22. Edwin M. Epstein, "Dimensions of Corporate Power: Part I," *California Management Review* (Winter, 1973), 11.
23. *Ibid.*
24. Keith Davis and Robert L. Blomstrom, *Business and Its Environment* (New York: McGraw-Hill, 1966), 174–175.
25. "The New 'Social Contract,'" *Business Week* (July 3, 1971).

CHAPTER **TWO**

Corporate Social Responsibility, Responsiveness, and Performance

CHAPTER OBJECTIVES

After studying this chapter, you should be able to:

- Explain how corporate social responsibility encompasses economic, legal, ethical, and voluntary components.

- Outline the pros and cons of the social responsibility issue.

- Differentiate between social responsibility and responsiveness.

- Elaborate on the concept of corporate social performance.

- Provide an overview of studies relating social responsibility to financial performance.

- Describe the socially conscious investing movement.

For the past two decades, business has been undergoing the most intense scrutiny it has ever received from the public. As a result of the many charges being leveled at it—charges that it has little concern for the consumer, cares nothing about the deteriorating social order, has no notion of acceptable ethical behavior, is indifferent to the problems of minorities and the environment—concern is increasingly expressed as to what responsibilities business has to the society in which it resides. These concerns have generated an unprecedented number of pleas for corporate social responsibility.

The basic issue can be framed in terms of two key questions: Does business have a social responsibility? If so, how much and what kinds? Although the questions seem simple and straightforward, answers to them must be phrased carefully. What is particularly paradoxical is that large numbers of business people have enthusiastically embraced the concept of social responsibility during the past two decades, but only limited consensus has emerged about what social responsibility really means.

In this chapter, therefore, we intend to explore a number of different facets of the social responsibility question and to provide some insights to the questions raised above. We say insights because the dynamics of social change preclude our obtaining general agreement on answers to these questions for any extended period. We are dedicating an entire chapter to the issue of social responsibility and concepts that have devolved from it because it is a core idea that underlies most of our discussions in this book.

THE SOCIAL RESPONSIBILITY ISSUE

In the previous chapter, we traced how criticisms of business led to increased concern for the social environment and a changed social contract. Out of these ideas grew the notion of corporate social responsibility, Before treating this topic in some depth and providing some historical perspective, let us provide an initial view on what corporate social responsibility means. Raymond Bauer presented an early view as follows: "Corporate social responsibility is seriously considering the impact of the company's actions on society."[1]

Another definition is helpful: "The idea of social responsibility . . . requires the individual to consider his (or her) acts in terms of a whole social system, and holds him (or her) responsible for the effects of his (or her) acts anywhere in that system."[2]

Both of these definitions provide preliminary insights into the idea of business responsibility that will help us appreciate some brief evolutionary history. Figure 2-1 illustrates how the concept of social responsibility grew out of the ideas introduced in Chapter 1—the increased concern for the social environment and the changed social contract. We further see in Figure 2-1 that the assumption of social responsibility by businesses led to increased corporate responsiveness and improved social performance—ideas that are developed more fully in this chapter.

FIGURE 2-1 Business Criticism/Social Response Cycle

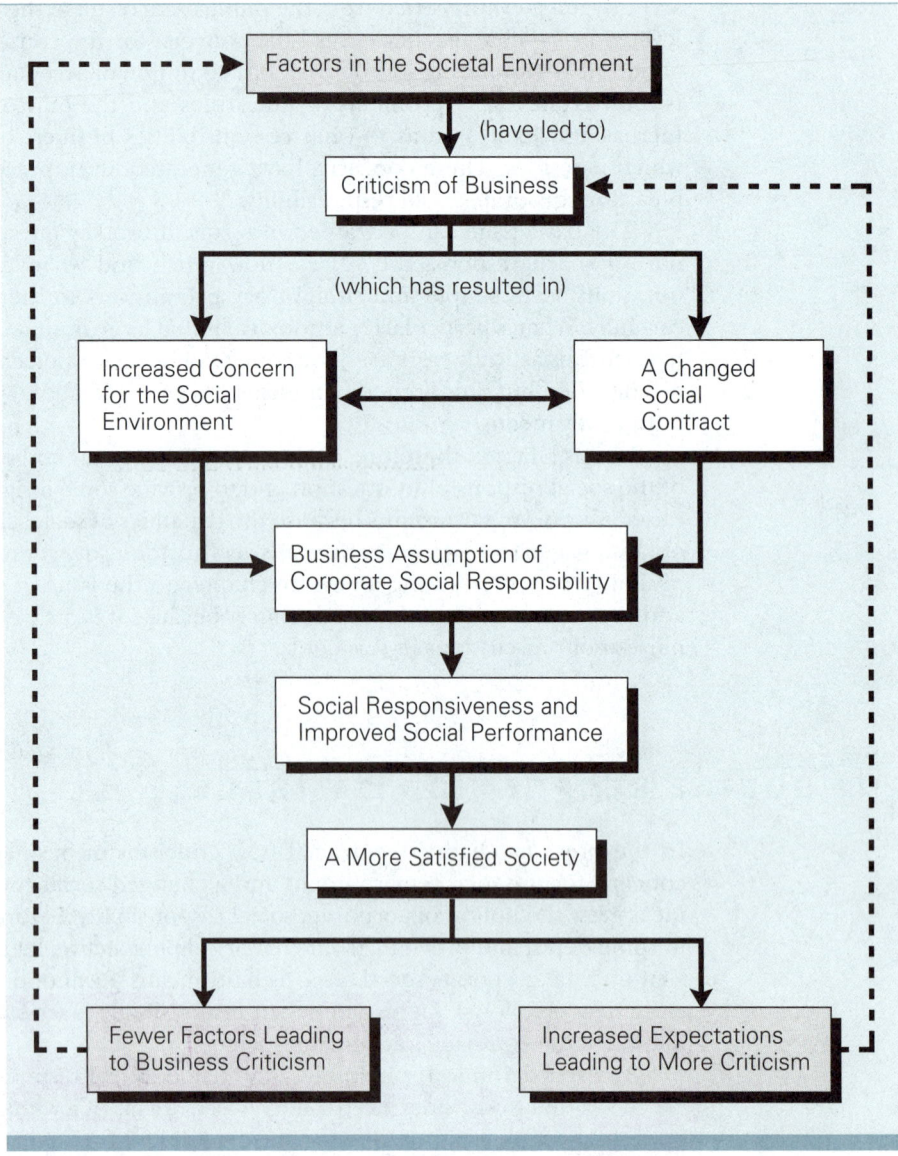

All of this has resulted in a more satisfied society. However, out of this satisfaction have come *fewer* factors leading to business criticism and, at the same time, *increased* expectations that perhaps lead to more criticism. The net result is that the overall level of business performance and societal satisfaction should increase with time in spite of this interplay of positive and negative factors. Should business not be responsive to societal expectations, it could conceivably enter a downward spiral, resulting in significant changes in the business-society relationship.

Historical Perspective

The concept of business responsibility that prevailed in the United States during most of our history was fashioned after the traditional or ***classical economic model.*** Adam Smith's concept of the "invisible hand" was its major point of departure. The classical view held that a society could determine its needs and wants through the marketplace. If business simply responds to this demand, society will get what it wants. If business is rewarded on the basis of its ability to respond to the demands of the market, the self-interest pursuit of that reward will result in society getting what it wants. Thus, the "invisible hand" of the market converts self-interest into societal interest. Unfortunately, although the marketplace did a reasonable job in deciding what goods and services should be produced, it did not fare as well in ensuring that business always acted fairly and ethically.

Somewhat later, when laws began to proliferate to constrain business's behavior, it might be said that a ***legal model*** prevailed. Society's expectations of business changed from being strictly economic in nature to encompassing aspects that had been previously at business's discretion.

In practice, although business subscribed early to the economic emphasis and was willing to be subjected to an increasing number of laws imposed by society, the business community later did not fully live by the tenets of even these early conceptions of business responsibility. As James W. McKie observed, "The business community never has adhered with perfect fidelity to an ideologically pure version of its responsibilities, drawn from the classical conception of the enterprise in economic society, though many businessmen have firmly believed in the main tenets of the creed."[3]

Modification of the Classical Economic Model. A modification of the classical economic model was seen in practice in at least three areas: philanthropy, community obligations, and paternalism.[4] Evidence exists that business people did engage in *philanthropy*—contributions to charity and other worthy causes—even during periods characterized by the traditional view. In addition, voluntary *community obligations* to improve, beautify, and uplift were evident. One example of this was the cooperative effort between the railroads and the YMCA immediately after the Civil War to provide community services in areas served by the railroads. Although these services economically benefited the railroads, they nevertheless were philanthropic at the same time.[5]

During the latter part of the nineteenth century and even into the twentieth century, *paternalism* appeared in many forms. One of the most visible examples was the company town. Although business's motives for beginning company towns (for example, the Pullman/Illinois experiment) were mixed, business had to do a considerable amount of the work in governing them. Thus, the company accepted a form of social responsibility.[6]

The emergence of large corporations during the late 1800s played a major role in hastening movement away from the classical economic view. As society evolved from the economic structure of small, powerless firms governed primarily by the marketplace to large corporations in which power was concentrated, questions of responsibility to society surfaced.[7]

Although the idea of social responsibility had not fully developed in the 1920s, managers even then had a more positive view of their role. Community service was in the forefront. The most visible example was the Community Chest movement, which received its impetus from business. Morrell Heald suggests that this was the first large-scale endeavor in which business leaders became involved with other nongovernmental community groups for a common, nonbusiness purpose, necessitating their contribution of time and money to community welfare projects.[8] Social responsibility, then, had received a further broadening of its meaning.

The 1930s signaled a transition from a predominantly laissez-faire economy to a mixed economy in which business found itself one of the constituencies monitored by a more activist government. From this time well into the 1950s, business's social responsibilities grew to include employee welfare (pension and insurance plans), concern for safety, medical care, retirement programs, and so on. McKie has suggested that these new developments were spurred both by governmental compulsion and by an enlarged concept of business responsibility.[9]

Neil J. Mitchell, in his book *The Generous Corporation*, presents an interesting thesis regarding how social responsibility evolved.[10] Mitchell's view is that the ideology of corporate social responsibility, particularly philanthropy, was developed by American business leaders as a strategic response to the antibusiness fervor that was beginning in the late 1800s and early 1900s. The antibusiness reaction was the result of specific business actions such as railroad price-gouging and public resentment of the emerging gigantic fortunes being made by late nineteenth-century moguls such as Andrew Carnegie and John D. Rockefeller.[11]

As business leaders came to realize that the government had the power to intervene in the economy and, in fact, was being encouraged to do so by public opinion, there was a need for an ideology that promoted large corporations as a force for social good. Thus, Mitchell argued, the businessmen (there were no businesswomen then) attempted to persuade those affected by business power that such power was being used appropriately. An example of this early progressive business ideology was reflected in Carnegie's 1889 essay, "The Gospel of Wealth," which asserted that business must pursue profits but that business wealth should be used for the benefit of the community. Philanthropy, therefore, became the most efficient means of using corporate wealth for public benefit. A prime example of this was Carnegie's funding and building of more than 2,500 libraries.

In a discussion of little-known history, Mitchell documents by way of specific examples how business developed this idea of the generous corporation and how it had distinct advantages: It helped business gain support from national and local governments; it helped to achieve in America a social stability that was unknown in the Europe of this period. In Ronald Berenbeim's review of Mitchell's book, he argues that motives for corporate generosity of the early 1900s were essentially the same as it is in the 1990s—to keep government at arm's length.[12]

Acceptance and Broadening of Meaning.

The period from roughly the 1950s to the present may be considered part of the modern era in which the concept of social responsibility gained considerable acceptance and broadening of meaning. During this time, the emphasis moved from an awareness of social and moral concerns to a period in which particular issues, such as product safety, honesty in advertising, employee rights, affirmative action, environmental protection, and ethical behavior, were emphasized. The issue orientation eventually gave way to the more recent focus on social responsiveness and social performance, which we will discuss later in this chapter. First, however, we can expand the modern view of social responsibility by examining various definitions or understandings of the term that have prevailed in recent years.

Social Responsibility: A Number of Viewpoints

Let's now return to the basic question: What does social responsibility really mean? To this point we have been operating with Bauer's definition of social responsibility: "Social responsibility is seriously considering the impact of the company's actions on society." Although this definition has inherent frailties, we will find that most of the definitions presented by others also have limitations. Part of the difficulty in deriving a definition on which we might get consensus is the problem of determining, operationally, what the definition implies for management. This poses an almost insurmountable problem because organizations vary in size, in the types of products they produce, in their profitability and resources, in their impact on society, and so on. Because this is the case, the ways they all embrace and practice social responsibility will vary, too.

One might ask: Why is this so? Are there not absolutes, areas in which all firms must be responsible? Yes, there are, and these are nearly equivalent to those expectations society has translated into legal aspects of the social contract. But as we will suggest here, social responsibility goes beyond simply (although it frequently is not so simple) abiding by the law. In the realm of activities over and above abiding by the law, the variables (size of the firm, types of products produced, and so on) become more relevant.

A second definition is worth looking at. Keith Davis and Robert Blomstrom defined social responsibility as follows: "Social responsibility is the obligation of decision makers to take actions which protect and improve the welfare of society as a whole along with their own interests."[13] This definition is somewhat more pointed. It suggests two *active* aspects of social responsibility—protecting and improving. To *protect* implies avoiding negative impacts on society. To *improve* implies creating positive benefits for society.

Like the first definition, the second contains a number of words that are perhaps unavoidably vague. For example, words from both definitions that might permit managers wide latitude in interpretation include *seriously, considering, protect, improve,* and *welfare* of society. The intention here is not to be critical of these good, general definitions but rather to show that business people and others are quite legitimately confused when trying to translate the concept of social responsibility into practice.

A third definition, by Joseph McGuire, is also quite general. But unlike the previous two, it places social responsibilities in context vis-à-vis economic and legal objectives. McGuire asserts: "The idea of social responsibility supposes that the corporation has not only economic and legal obligations, but also certain responsibilities to society which extend beyond these obligations."[14] Although this statement is not fully operational either, its attractiveness is that it acknowledges the primacy of economic objectives side by side with legal obligations, while it also encompasses a broader conception of the firm's responsibilities.

A fourth definition, set forth by Edwin Epstein, relates social responsibility to the growing concern on the part of managers with stakeholders and ethics. He asserts: "Corporate social responsibility relates primarily to achieving outcomes from organizational decisions concerning specific issues or problems which (by some normative standard) have beneficial rather than adverse effects upon pertinent corporate stakeholders. The normative correctness of the products of corporate action have been the main focus of corporate social responsibility."[15] Epstein's definition is useful because it concentrates on the outcomes, products, or results of corporate actions for stakeholders.

A Four-Part Definition

Each of the definitions of corporate social responsibility has value. At this point, we would like to present a four-part definition that focuses on the kinds or types of social responsibilities it might be argued business has. This four-part definition attempts to place economic and legal expectations of business in perspective by relating them to more social concerns.[16] These social concerns include ethical responsibilities and voluntary/discretionary or philanthropic responsibilities. In a sense, our definition, which includes four kinds of responsibilities, elaborates and builds on the definition proposed by McGuire.

Economic Responsibilities.
First, there are business's *economic* responsibilities. It may seem odd to call an economic responsibility a social responsibility, but this is, in effect, what it is. First and foremost, the American social system calls for business to be an economic institution. That is, it should be one whose orientation is to produce goods and services that society wants and to sell them at a fair price—a price that society thinks represents the value of goods and services delivered and that provides the business with adequate profit for its perpetuation, growth, and reward to its investors.

Legal Responsibilities.
Second, there are business's *legal* responsibilities. Just as society has sanctioned our economic system by permitting business to assume the

productive role mentioned above, as a partial fulfillment of the social contract, it has also laid down the ground rules—the laws—under which business is expected to operate. Legal responsibilities reflect a view of "codified ethics" in the sense that they embody basic notions of fairness as established by our lawmakers. It is business's responsibility to society to comply with these laws. If business does not agree with laws that have been passed or are about to be passed, our society has provided a mechanism through the political process for dissenters to be heard.

Ethical Responsibilities. Ethical responsibilities embrace those activities and practices that are expected or prohibited by societal members even though they are not codified into law. Ethical responsibilities embody the range of norms, standards, or expectations that reflect a concern for what consumers, employees, shareholders, and the community regard as fair, just, or in keeping with the respect for or protection of stakeholders' moral rights.[17]

In one sense, changing ethics or values precede the establishment of law because they become the driving force behind the very creation of laws or regulations. For example, the civil rights, environmental, and consumer movements reflected basic alterations in societal values and thus may be seen as ethical bellwethers foreshadowing and leading to later legislation. In another sense, ethical responsibilities may be seen as embracing and reflecting newly emerging values and norms that society expects business to meet even though they may reflect a higher standard of performance than that currently required by law. Ethical responsibilities in this sense are often ill-defined or continually under public scrutiny and debate as to their legitimacy and thus are frequently difficult for business to deal with.

Superimposed on these ethical expectations emanating from societal and stakeholder groups are the implied levels of ethical performance suggested by a consideration of the great ethical principles of moral philosophy such as justice, rights, and utilitarianism.[18]

Because ethical responsibilities are so important, we devote three chapters to the subject. For the moment, let us think of ethical responsibilities as encompassing those areas in which society expects a certain performance but for which it has not yet been able or willing to articulate and codify into law.

Voluntary/Discretionary or Philanthropic Responsibilities. Fourth, there are business's *voluntary, discretionary,* or *philanthropic* responsibilities. Perhaps it is a misnomer to call these responsibilities, for they are completely guided by business's discretion—its choice or desire. These activities are purely voluntary, guided only by business's desire to engage in social activities that are not mandated, not required by law, and not generally expected of business in an ethical sense. These might include having executive loan programs in the community, giving to charitable causes, providing day-care centers for working mothers, initiating adopt-a-school programs, and conducting in-house programs for drug abusers.

The distinction between ethical responsibilities and voluntary/discretionary or philanthropic responsibilities is that the latter are typically not expected in a moral or ethical sense. Communities desire business to contribute its money, facilities, and employee time to humanitarian programs or purposes, but they do not regard the firms as unethical if they do not provide the desired level. Therefore, these responsibilities are more discretionary, or voluntary, on business's part, though the societal expectation that they be provided is always present. This category of responsibility might be deemed "corporate citizenship."

The Four-Part Social Responsibility Model. In essence, then, our definition forms a four-part conceptualization of social responsibility that may be summarized as follows: The *social responsibility of business* encompasses the economic, legal, ethical, and discretionary expectations placed on organizations by society at a given point in time.

We suggest that this four-part definition provides us with categories within which to place the various expectations that society has of business. With each of these categories considered as one facet of the total social responsibility of business, we have a conceptual model that more completely describes what society expects of business. One advantage of the model is that it can accommodate those who have argued against social responsibility by characterizing an economic emphasis as separate from a social emphasis. This model offers these two facets along with others that collectively make up social responsibility. Figure 2-2 depicts the model as it might appear when superimposed on a scale denoting all of the social responsibilities of business.

Another helpful way of graphically depicting the four-part model is envisioning a pyramid composed of four layers. This Pyramid of Corporate Social Responsibility (CSR) is shown in Figure 2-3.[19]

The pyramid portrays the four components of CSR, beginning with the basic building block notion that economic performance undergirds all else. At the same time, business is expected to obey the law because the law is society's codification of acceptable and unacceptable behavior. Next is business's responsibility to be ethical. At its most fundamental level, this is the obligation to do what is right, just, and fair and to avoid or minimize harm to stakeholders (employees, consumers, the environment, and others). Finally, business is expected to be a good corporate citizen. This is captured in the voluntary/discretionary or philanthropic responsibility category wherein business is expected to contribute financial and human resources to the community and to improve the quality of life.

No metaphor is perfect, and the Pyramid of CSR is no exception. It is intended to portray that the total CSR of business is composed of distinct components that taken together make up the whole. Although the components have been treated as separate concepts for discussion purposes, they are not mutually exclusive and are not intended to juxtapose a firm's economic responsibilities with its other responsibilities. At the same time, a consideration of the separate components helps the manager to see that the different types of obligations are in a constant but dynamic tension with one another. The most critical tensions, of course, would be between economic and legal, economic and ethical, and economic and philanthropic. The traditionalist might see this as a conflict between a firm's "concern for profits" versus its "concern for society," but it is suggested here that this is an

FIGURE 2-2 Four-Part Model of Corporate Social Responsibility

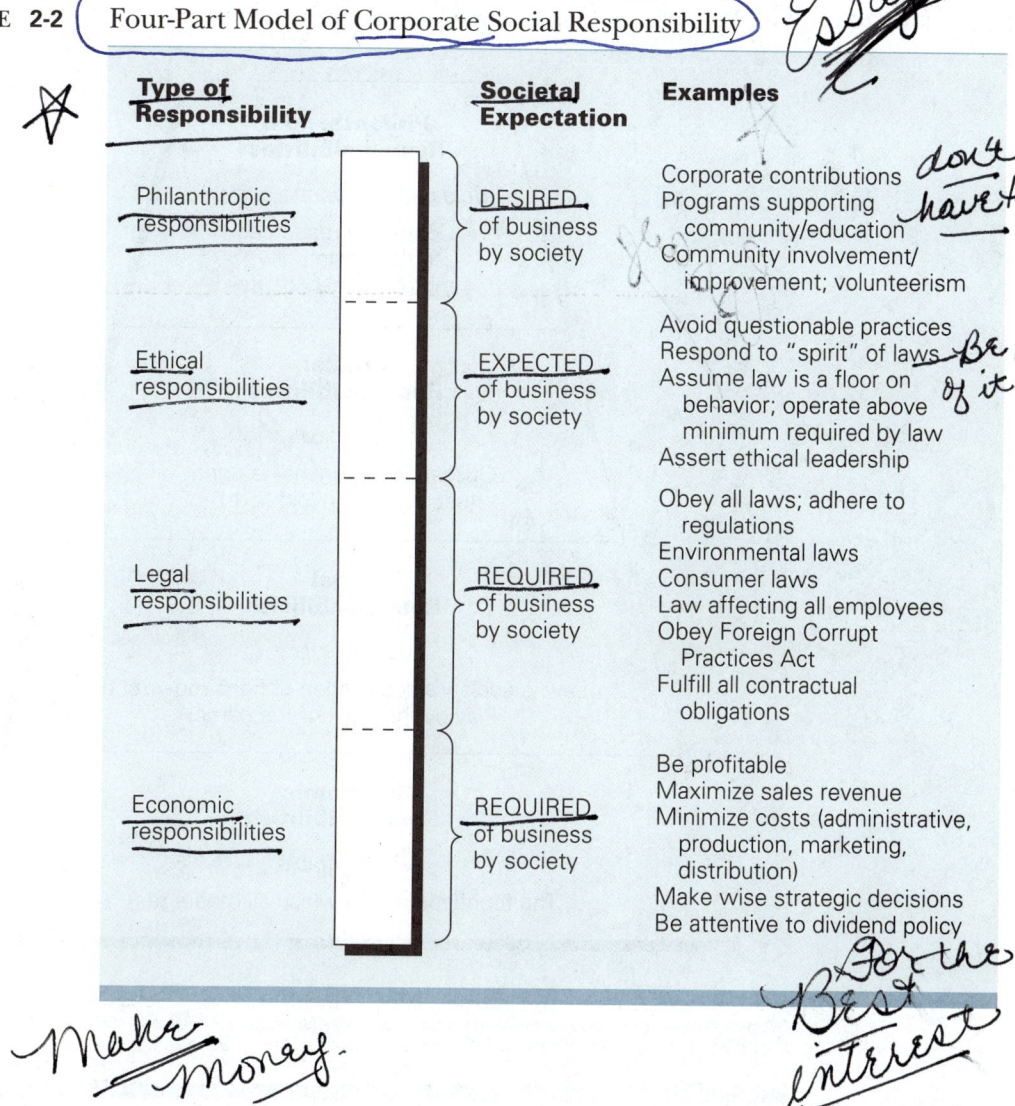

oversimplification. A CSR or stakeholder perspective would recognize these tensions as organizational realities but would focus on the total pyramid as a unified whole and how the firm might engage in decisions, actions, and programs that simultaneously fulfill all its component parts.

In summary, the total corporate social responsibility of business entails the simultaneous fulfillment of the firm's economic, legal, ethical, and philanthropic responsibilities. In equation form, this might be depicted as follows: Economic Responsibilities + Legal Responsibilities + Ethical Responsibilities + Philanthropic Responsibilities = Total Corporate Social Responsibility of Business. Stated in more pragmatic and managerial terms, the CSR firm should strive to make a profit, obey the law, be ethical, and be a good corporate citizen.

FIGURE 2-3 The Pyramid of Corporate Social Responsibility

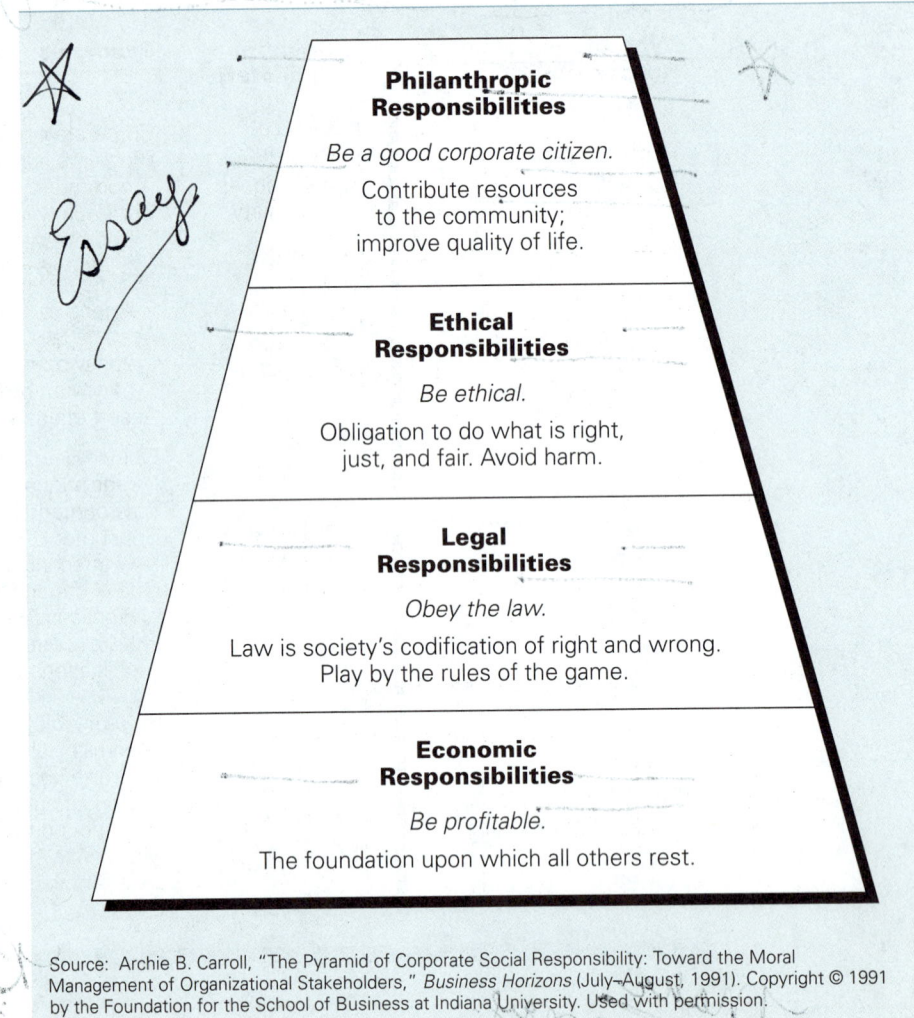

Source: Archie B. Carroll, "The Pyramid of Corporate Social Responsibility: Toward the Moral Management of Organizational Stakeholders," *Business Horizons* (July–August, 1991). Copyright © 1991 by the Foundation for the School of Business at Indiana University. Used with permission.

As we study the evolution of business's major areas of social concern, as presented in various chapters in Parts 2 and 3, we will see how our model's four facets (economic, legal, ethical, and philanthropic) provide us with a useful framework for conceptualizing the issue of social responsibility. The social contract between business and society is to a large extent formulated from mutual understandings that exist in each area of our basic model. But it should be noted that the ethical and philanthropic categories, taken together, more nearly capture the essence of what people generally mean today when they speak of social responsibility. Situating these two categories relative to the legal and economic obligations, however, keeps them in proper perspective.

ARGUMENTS AGAINST AND FOR SOCIAL RESPONSIBILITY

In an effort to provide a balanced view of the corporate social responsibility issue, we will consider the arguments that have been raised against and for it. We clearly should state at the outset, however, that those who argue against social responsibility are not using in their considerations the comprehensive social responsibility model presented above. Rather, it appears that the critics are viewing social responsibility more narrowly—as only the efforts of the organization to pursue social, noneconomic goals (our ethical and philanthropic categories). Some critics equate social responsibility with only the philanthropic category. We should also state that only a few business people and academics argue against the fundamental notion of social responsibility today. The debate among business people more often centers on the kinds and degree of social responsibility and on subtle ethical questions rather than on the basic question of whether business has it or not. As for academics, economists are probably the easiest group to single out as being against the pursuit of social goals. But even some economists no longer resist social responsibility on grounds of economic theory.

Arguments Against Social Responsibility

Let us now look at the arguments that have surfaced over the years from the "anti" school of thought. Most notable has been the classical economic argument. This traditional view holds that management has one responsibility: *to maximize the profits of its owners or shareholders.* This classical economic school, led by economist Milton Friedman, argues that social matters are not the concern of business people and that these problems should be resolved by the unfettered workings of the free market system.[20] Further, this view holds that if the free market cannot solve the social problem, then it falls on government and legislation to do the job. Friedman softens his argument somewhat by his assertion that management is "to make as much money as possible *while conforming to the basic rules of society, both those embodied in the law and those embodied in ethical customs.*"[21] When Friedman's entire statement is considered, it appears that he accepts three of the four categories of the four-part model—economic, legal, and ethical. The only item not specifically embraced is the voluntary or philanthropic category. In any event, it is clear that the economic argument views social responsibility more narrowly than we have in our conceptual model.

A second major objection to social responsibility is that business is not equipped to handle social activities. This position holds that managers are oriented toward economics and production and do not have the necessary expertise (social skills) to make social decisions.[22] Closely related to this argument is a third: If managers were to pursue social responsibility vigorously, it would tend to dilute the business's primary purpose.[23] The objection here is that social responsibility would put business into fields not related, as F. A. Hayek has stated, to their "proper aim."[24]

A fourth argument against social responsibility is that business already has enough power—economic, environmental, and technological—so why should we place in its hands the opportunity to wield additional power?[25] As it is, the influence of business permeates society. By giving decision-making opportunities in the social domain to business, would we not be aggravating the balance of power problem that already exists in our society?

One other argument that merits mention is that by pursuing social responsibilities we might be placing business in a deleterious position in terms of international balance of payments. One consequence of being socially responsible is that business must internalize costs that it formerly passed on to society in the form of dirty air, unsafe products, consequences of discrimination, and so on. The increase in the costs of products caused by including social considerations in the price structure would necessitate raising the price of products, making them less competitive in international markets. The net effect might be to dissipate the country's advantages gained previously through technological advances.

The arguments we have discussed constitute the principal claims made by those who oppose the social responsibility concept. Many of the reasons given appear quite rational. Value choices as to the type of society the citizen would like to have become, at some point, part of the total social responsibility question. Let us now examine some of the main arguments given in favor of this concept.

Arguments for Social Responsibility

It is worthwhile summarizing Thomas Petit's statement as our point of departure in discussing support of the social responsibility doctrine. Petit synthesizes the thoughts of such intellectuals as Elton Mayo, Peter Drucker, Adolph Berle, and John Maynard Keynes. He asserts that although their ideas on this matter vary considerably, they agree on two fundamental points: "(1) Industrial society faces serious human and social problems brought on largely by the rise of the large corporations, and (2) managers must conduct the affairs of the corporation in ways to solve or at least ameliorate these problems."[26]

This generalized justification of social responsibility is appealing. It actually comes close to what we might suggest as a first argument for social responsibility, namely, that it is in business's long-range self-interest to be socially responsible. This argument provides an additional dimension by suggesting that it was partially business's fault that these social problems arose in the first place and that, consequently, business should assume a role in remedying the problems. It might be inferred from this that deterioration of the social condition must be halted if business is to survive and prosper in the future.

The long-range self-interest view is basically that if business is to have a healthy climate in which to exist in the future, it must take actions now that will ensure its longer-term viability. Perhaps the reasoning behind this view is that society's expectations are such that if business does not respond on its own, its role in society may be altered by the public, for example, through government regulation or, more dramatically, through alternative systems for the production and distribution of goods and services.

It is frequently difficult for managers who have a short-range orientation to appreciate that their rights and roles in the economic system are determined by society. Business must be responsive to society's expectations over the long term if it is to survive in its present form or in a less restrained form.

Perhaps the most pragmatic reason for business assuming social responsibilities is to ward off future government intervention and regulation. Today there are numerous areas in which government intrudes with an expensive, elaborate regulatory apparatus to fill a void left by business's inaction. To the extent that business polices itself with self-disciplined guidelines, future government intervention can be somewhat forestalled. Later, we will discuss some areas in which business could have prevented intervention and simultaneously ensured greater freedom in decision making had it imposed higher standards of behavior on itself.

Keith Davis presents two arguments that deserve mention together: "Business has the resources" and "Let business try."[27] These two views maintain that because business has a reservoir of management talent, functional expertise, and capital and because so many others have tried and failed to solve general social problems, business should be given a chance. These arguments have some merit, as there are some social problems that can be handled, in the final analysis, only by business. Examples include avoiding discrimination, providing safe products, and engaging in fair advertising. Admittedly, government can and does assume a role in these areas, but business must make the final decisions.

Another view is that "proacting is better than reacting." This position holds that *proacting* (anticipating and initiating) is a more practical and less costly posture than that of simply reacting to problems once they have developed. Environmental pollution is a good example, particularly business's experience with attempting to clean up rivers, lakes, and other waterways that were neglected for years. In the long run, it would have been wiser not to allow the environmental deterioration to occur in the first place.

SOCIAL RESPONSIBILITY VERSUS SOCIAL RESPONSIVENESS

We have discussed the evolution of corporate social responsibility, a model for viewing social responsibility, and the arguments for and against it. It is now important to address a concern that has arisen in recent years over the use of the terms *responsibility* and *responsiveness*. We will consider the views of several writers to make our point.

Ackerman and Bauer's Action-Oriented View

A general argument that has been taking shape over the last decade or so states that the term *responsibility* is too suggestive of efforts to pinpoint accountability or obligation. Therefore, it is not dynamic enough to fully describe business's willingness—apart from obligation—to respond to social demands. For example, Robert Ackerman and Raymond Bauer criticized the term by stating, "The connotation of 'responsibility' is that of the process of assuming an obligation. It places an emphasis on motivation rather than on performance." They go on to say, "Responding to social demands is much more than deciding what to do. There remains the management task of doing what one has decided to do, and this task is far from trivial."[28] As the title of their book suggests, they then argue that "social responsiveness" is a more apt description of what is essential.

Their point is well made. **Responsibility**, taken quite literally, does imply more of a state or condition of having assumed an obligation, whereas **responsiveness** connotes a dynamic, action-oriented condition. We should not overlook, however, that much of what business has done and is doing has resulted from a particular motivation—an assumption of obligation—whether assigned by government, forced by special-interest groups, or voluntarily assumed. Perhaps business, in some instances, has failed to accept and internalize the obligation, and thus it may seem odd to refer to it as a responsibility. Nevertheless, some motivation that led to social responsiveness had to be there, even though in some cases it was not admitted to be a responsibility or obligation.

Sethi's Schema

S. Prakash Sethi takes a slightly different, but related, path in getting from social responsibility to social responsiveness. He proposes a three-stage schema for classifying corporate behavior in responding to social or societal needs: social obligation, social responsibility, and social responsiveness.

Social obligation, Sethi argues, is corporate behavior in response to market forces or legal constraints. Corporate legitimacy is very narrow here and is based on legal and economic criteria only. **Social responsibility,** Sethi suggests, "implies bringing corporate behavior up to a level where it is congruent with the prevailing social norms, values, and expectations."[29] He argues that whereas the concept of social obligation is proscriptive in nature, social responsibility is prescriptive in nature. **Social responsiveness,** the third stage in his schema, suggests that what is important is "not how corporations should respond to social pressure but what should be their long-run role in a dynamic social system."[30] He suggests that here business is expected to be "anticipatory" and "preventive." Note that his *obligation* and *responsibility* categories embody essentially the same message we were attempting to convey with our four-part conceptual model.

Frederick's CSR$_1$ and CSR$_2$

William Frederick has distinguished between corporate social responsibility, which he calls CSR$_1$, and corporate social responsiveness, which he terms CSR$_2$, in the following way:

> Corporate social *responsiveness* refers to the capacity of a corporation to respond to social pressures. The literal act of responding, or of achieving a generally responsive posture, to society is the focus. . . . One searches the organization for mechanisms, procedures, arrangements and behavioral patterns that, taken collectively, would mark the organization as more or less capable of responding to social pressures.[31]

Frederick further argued that advocates of social responsiveness (CSR$_2$) "have urged corporations to eschew philosophic questions of social responsibility and to concentrate on the more pragmatic matter of responding effectively to environmental pressures." He later articulated an idea known as CSR$_3$—corporate social rectitude, which addressed the moral correctness of actions taken and policies formulated, but that concept is outside of the scope of our immediate interest in social responsiveness.[32]

Epstein's Processes

Edwin Epstein discusses corporate social responsiveness within the context of a broader concept that he calls the corporate social policy process. In this context, Epstein emphasizes the process aspect of social responsiveness. He asserts that corporate social responsiveness focuses on the individual and organizational processes "for determining, implementing, and evaluating the firm's capacity to anticipate, respond, and manage the issues and problems arising from the diverse claims and expectations of internal and external stakeholders."[33]

Other Views

Several other writers have provided conceptual schemes that describe the responsiveness facet. Ian Wilson, for example, asserts that there are four possible business strategies: *reaction, defense, accommodation,* and *pro-action*.[34] Terry McAdam has likewise described four social responsibility philosophies that mesh well with Wilson's and describe the managerial approach that would characterize the range of the responsiveness dimension: "Fight all the way," "Do only what is required," "Be progressive," and "Lead the industry."[35] Davis and Blomstrom, too, describe alternative responses to societal pressures as follows: *withdrawal, public relations approach, legal approach, bargaining,* and *problem-solving*.[36] Finally, James Post has articulated three major social responsiveness categories: adaptive, proactive, and interactive.[37] Figure 2-4 summarizes the views of the above mentioned, along with several other conceptualizations, on a responsiveness continuum. Note that each

FIGURE 2-4   Social Responsiveness Categories

Categories	Authors
1. Reaction Defense Accommodation Proaction	Wilson[a]
2. Fight all the way Do only what is required Be progressive Lead the industry	McAdam[b]
3. Withdrawal Public relations approach Legal approach Bargaining Problem solving	Davis and Blomstrom[c]
4. Social obligation Social responsibility Social responsiveness	Sethi[d]
5. Reaction Stable-state Advocacy Cooperative	Tombari[e]
6. Adaptive Proactive Interactive	Post[f]
7. Preemptive Prescriptive Preventative Promotive	Fisher[g]
8. Reactive Informative Public Relations/Advocacy Coalitions	Keim[h]
9. Individualistic/adversarial Collaborative/problem solving	Miles[i]

Sources: [a]Ian Wilson, "What One Company Is Doing About Today's Demands on Business," in George Steiner (ed.), *UCLA Conference On Changing Business-Society Relationships* (Los Angeles: Graduate School of Management, UCLA, 1975).
[b]T.W. McAdam, "How to Put Corporate Responsibility into Practice," *Business and Society Review/Innovation* (Summer, 1973), 8–16.
[c]K. Davis and R.L. Blomstrom, *Business & Society: Environment and Responsibility*, 3d ed. (New York: McGraw-Hill, 1975), 85–86.
[d]S. Prakash Sethi, "Dimensions of Corporate Social Responsibility," *California Management Review* (Spring, 1975), 58–64.
[e]Henry A. Tombari, *Business and Society: Strategies for the Environment and Public Policy* (Chicago: The Dryden Press, 1984), 325.
[f]James E. Post, *Corporate Behavior and Social Change* (Reston, VA: Reston Publishing Co., 1978), 39.
[g]D. W. Fischer, "Strategies Toward Political Pressures: A Typology of Firm Responses," *Academy of Management Review* (January, 1983), 71–78.
[h]Gerry Keim, "Foundations for a Political Strategy for Business," *California Management Review* (Spring, 1981), 41–48.
[i]Robert H. Miles, *Managing the Corporate Social Environment* (Englewood Cliffs, NJ: Prentice-Hall, 1987), 8–11.

of these authors is addressing a different aspect of responsiveness and that the various response categories in the schemes are not all directly comparable.

Thus, the corporate social responsiveness dimension that has been discussed by some as an alternate focus to that of social responsibility is, in actuality, the action phase of management's responding in the social sphere. In a sense, the responsiveness orientation enables organizations to rationalize and operationalize their social responsibilities without getting bogged down in the quagmire of definition problems, which can so easily occur if organizations try to get an exact determination of what their true responsibilities are before they act.

Measurable Dimensions of Responsiveness

Very few efforts have been made to break down these responsiveness categories into specific, measurable dimensions. One major study by Robert Miles, however, sought to measure the corporate social responsiveness of a large sample of insurance companies. The dimensions he used are worth listing because they give us a feel for what responsiveness means in practice. His list included the following:

1. *Reliability of company executives:* The extent to which they stand by their commitments.
2. *Attentiveness of company executives:* The extent to which they listen and are receptive to information flowing from outside the company.
3. *Preparedness of company executives:* The extent to which they are aware of (have identified and analyzed for impact) potential public policy issues.
4. *Credibility of company statements:* The extent to which you can believe information communicated by the companies.
5. *Accessibility of company executives:* The extent to which they are available to you for responses and discussions.
6. *Perceived legitimacy of outsiders:* The extent to which company executives respect the purpose of outside critics.
7. *Communication with its publics:* The extent to which the company communicates its programs and interests to its various publics.
8. *Clarity of company interests:* The extent to which the company clearly defines its own interests in responding to public issues.
9. *Overall corporate responsiveness:* The extent to which the company has an effective overall process for learning about and adapting to changing societal norms, pressures, and public issues.[38]

One major finding of Miles's study was that some of these measures of social responsiveness were more powerful in terms of discriminating between best- and worst-rated corporate social performing insurance companies. The three most powerful were found to be (1) attentiveness of company executives, (2) preparedness of company executives, and (3) perceived legitimacy of outsiders.

CORPORATE SOCIAL PERFORMANCE

During the late 1970s, throughout the 1980s, and into the 1990s there has been a trend toward making the concern for social and ethical issues more and more pragmatic. The responsiveness thrust that we just discussed was a part of this trend. It is possible to integrate some of the concerns into a model of corporate social *performance.* The performance focus is intended to suggest that what really matters is what companies are able to accomplish—the results of their acceptance of social responsibility and adoption of a responsiveness philosophy. In developing a conceptual framework for corporate social performance, we not only have to specify the nature (economic, legal, ethical, philanthropic) of the responsibility, but we also need to adopt a particular philosophy or mode of responsiveness. Finally, we need to identify the stakeholder issues or topical areas to which these responsibilities are tied. One need not ponder the stakeholder issues that have evolved under the rubric of social responsibility to recognize how they have changed over time. The issues, and especially the degree of organizational interest in the issues, are always in a state of flux. As the times change, so does emphasis on the range of social issues that business must address.

Also of interest is the fact that particular issues are of varying concern to businesses, depending on the industry in which they exist as well as other factors. A bank, for example, is not as pressed on environmental issues as a manufacturer. Likewise, a manufacturer is considerably more absorbed with the issue of environmental protection than is an insurance company.

Factors in Selecting Areas of Social Involvement

Many factors come into play as a manager attempts to get a fix on which social or stakeholder issues should be of highest priority to the organization. A survey by Sandra Holmes illustrates this point quite well. In her survey of managers of large firms, she asked what factors were prominent in selecting areas of social involvement by their firms. The top five factors were:

1. Matching a social need to corporate need or ability to help
2. Seriousness of social need
3. Interest of top executives
4. Public relations value of social action
5. Government pressure[39]

That these disparate factors should show up in a response to a question of this kind suggests clearly that business executives do not have a consensus on what social issues should be addressed. Thus, we are left with a recognition that social issues must be identified as an important aspect of corporate social performance, but there is by no means agreement as to what these issues should be.

Aspects of the Corporate Social Performance Model

Figure 2-5 illustrates the *corporate social performance model* that brings together the three central dimensions we have discussed:

1. Social responsibility categories—economic, legal, ethical, philanthropic (discretionary)

FIGURE 2-5 Carroll's Corporate Social Performance Model

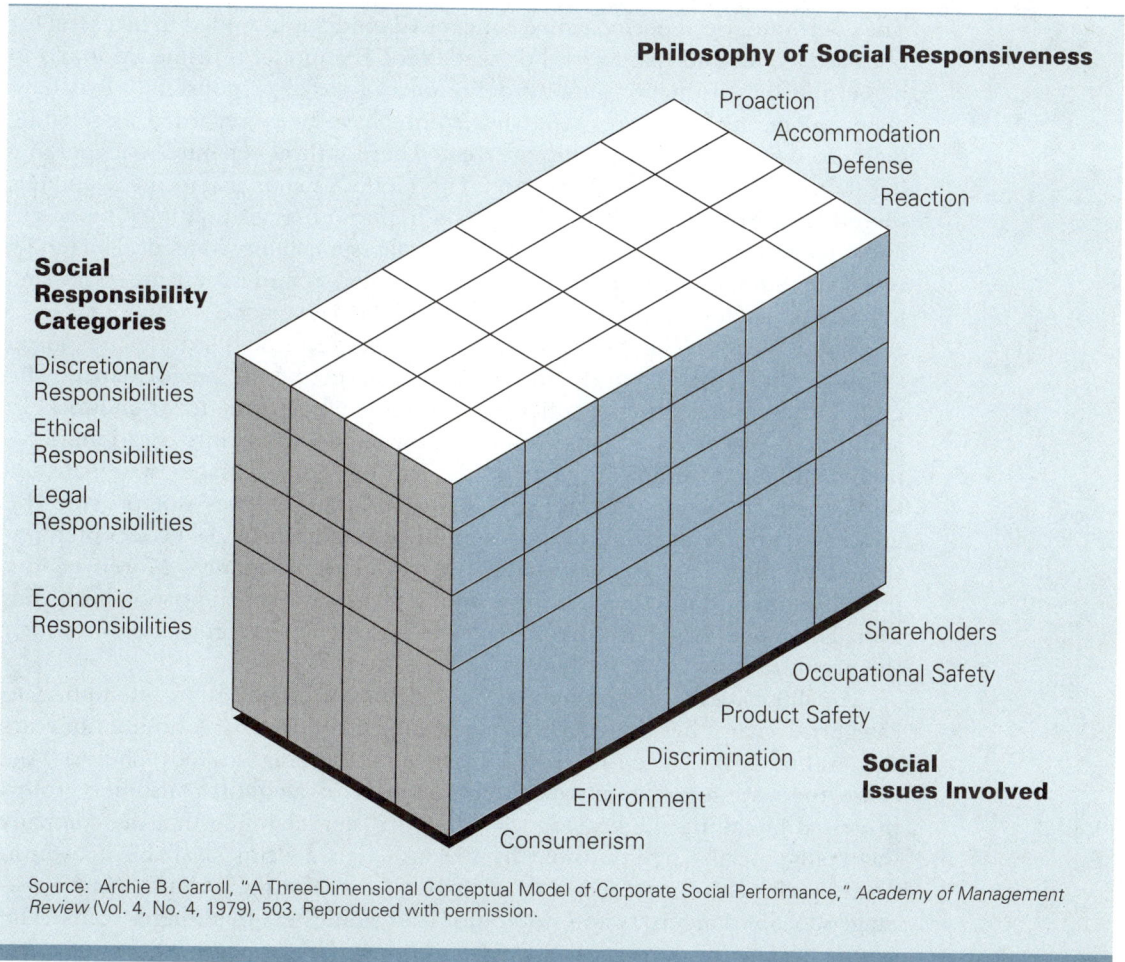

Source: Archie B. Carroll, "A Three-Dimensional Conceptual Model of Corporate Social Performance," *Academy of Management Review* (Vol. 4, No. 4, 1979), 503. Reproduced with permission.

2. Philosophy or mode of social responsiveness
3. Social issues involved

One aspect of the model pertains to all that is included in our definition of social responsibility—the economic, legal, ethical, and discretionary components. The second aspect concerns the range of social or stakeholder issues (for example, consumerism, environment, and discrimination) that management must address. Finally, there is a social responsiveness continuum. Although some writers have suggested that this is the preferable focus when one considers social responsibility, the model suggests that responsiveness is but one additional aspect to be addressed if corporate social performance is to be achieved.

Usefulness of the Model to Academics and Managers

The corporate social performance conceptual model is intended to be useful for both academics and managers. For academics, the model is primarily an aid to perceiving the distinction among definitions of social responsibility that have appeared in the literature. What heretofore have been regarded as separate definitions of social responsibility are treated here as three separate issues pertaining to corporate social performance. The model's major use to the academic, therefore, is in helping to systematize the important issues that must be taught and understood in an effort to clarify the social responsibility concept. The model is not the ultimate conceptualization. It is, rather, a modest but necessary step toward understanding the major facets of social performance.

The conceptual model can assist managers in understanding that social responsibility is not separate and distinct from economic performance. The model integrates economic concerns into a social performance framework. In addition, it places ethical and discretionary expectations into a rational economic and legal framework. The model can help the manager systematically think through major stakeholder issues. Although it does not provide the answer to how far the organization should go, it does provide a conceptualization that could lead to better-managed social performance. Moreover, the model could be used as a planning tool and as a diagnostic problem-solving tool. The model can assist the manager by identifying categories within which the organization can be situated.

An illustration will perhaps be helpful for an organization attempting to categorize what it has done (see the segments in Figure 2-5). A number of years ago, Anheuser-Busch test-marketed a new adult beverage called "Chelsea." Because the beverage contained a small amount of alcohol, consumer groups protested by calling the beverage "kiddie beer" and claiming that the company was being socially irresponsible by making such a drink available to youth. Anheuser-Busch's first reaction was defensive—attempting to claim that the beverage was not dangerous and would not lead youngsters to stronger drink. The company's later response was to withdraw the beverage from the marketplace and reformulate it so that it would be viewed as safe. The company concluded that this was the socially responsible action to take, given the criticism.

According to the social performance model in Figure 2-5, the company found itself in the consumerism segment of the model. The social responsibility category of the issue was ethical (the product being introduced was strictly legal because it conformed to the maximum alcoholic content standard). As it became clear that so much protest might be turning an ethical issue into an economic one (as threats of product boycotts surfaced), the company moved along the responsiveness dimension in the model from reaction and defense to accommodation.

This example shows how a business's response can be positioned in the social performance model. The average business firm faces many such controversial issues and might use the conceptual model to analyze its stance on these issues and perhaps to help determine its motivations, actions, and response strategies.

Managers would have a systematic framework for thinking through not only the social issues faced but also the managerial response patterns contemplated. The model could serve as a guide in formulating criteria to assist the organization in developing its posture on various stakeholder issues. The net result could be more systematic attention being given to the whole realm of corporate social performance.[40]

Before leaving our discussion of the corporate social performance model, it is important to examine extensions of the model. The initial version of the model employed "social issues" as the third aspect or dimension, which embraced such issues as consumerism, environment, and discrimination. That dimension is now referred to as stakeholder issues, to place it within our current framework. While it was still being referred to as social issues, however, Steven Wartick and Philip Cochran proposed that the dimension of social issues had, in fact, grown from simply an identification of the social issue categories in which companies must take action to a whole new management field known as social issues management. *Issues management*, which we will treat more fully in Chapter 18, entails such activities as issues identification, issues analysis, and response development.[41] Whether the third dimension is seen as social issues or stakeholder issues, the issues management approach is equally useful.

Wartick and Cochran extended the social performance model even further by proposing that the three dimensions be thought of as depicting *principles* (corporate social responsibilities, reflecting a philosophical orientation), *processes* (corporate social responsiveness, reflecting an institutional orientation), and *policies* (social issues management, reflecting an organizational orientation). These extensions are extremely useful because they help us to more fully appreciate complimentary aspects that were neglected in the original model. Figure 2-6 summarizes Wartick and Cochran's model extensions.

Recently, Donna Wood has elaborated and reformulated Carroll's model and Wartick and Cochran's extensions. Using Wartick and Cochran's extensions, she has produced a useful definition of corporate social performance:

> A business organization's configuration of principles of social responsibility, processes of social responsiveness, and policies, programs and other observable outcomes as they relate to the firm's societal relationships.[42]

Wood's proposal is (1) to think of social responsiveness as a *set* of processes rather than as a single process and (2) to think of Wartick and Cochran's policies as entailing *observable outcomes* of corporate and managerial actions. Wood takes this definition further by proposing that each of the three components—principles, processes, and outcomes—are composed of specific elements. Figure 2-7 presents Wood's corporate social performance model.

These extensions and reformulations to Carroll's corporate social performance model add significantly to our appreciation of what all is involved as we strive to think of corporate social performance as a dynamic and multifaceted managerial concept.

FIGURE 2-6 Wartick and Cochran's Corporate Social Performance Model Extensions

Principles	Processes	Policies
Corporate Social Responsibilities	Corporate Social Responsiveness	Social Issues Management
(1) Economic	(1) Reactive	(1) Issues Identification
(2) Legal	(2) Defensive	(2) Issues Analysis
(3) Ethical	(3) Accommodative	(3) Response Development
(4) Discretionary	(4) Proactive	
Directed at:	Directed at:	Directed at:
(1) The Social Contract of Business	(1) The Capacity to Respond to Changing Societal Conditions	(1) Minimizing "Surprises"
(2) Business as a Moral Agent	(2) Managerial Approaches to Developing Responses	(2) Determining Effective Corporate Social Policies
Philosophical Orientation	Institutional Orientation	Organizational Orientation

Source: Steven L. Wartick and Philip L. Cochran, "The Evolution of the Corporate Social Performance Model," *Academy of Management Review* (Vol. 10, 1985), 767.

FIGURE 2-7 Wood's Corporate Social Performance Model

Principles of corporate social responsibility:
- Institutional principle: legitimacy
- Organizational principle: public responsibility
- Individual principle: managerial discretion

Processes of corporate social responsiveness:
- Environmental assessment
- Stakeholder management
- Issues management

Outcomes of corporate behavior:
- Social impacts
- Social programs
- Social policies

Source: Donna J. Wood, "Corporate Social Performance Revisited," *Academy of Management Review* (October, 1991), 694.

Nonacademic Research

Considerable academic research on the subject of corporate social performance has been done over the last decade.[43] We should stress, however, that academics are not the only ones who are interested in this topic. Prominent organizations that report on social performance include *Fortune,* the Council on Economic Priorities, and the Business Enterprise Trust.

Fortune's Rankings of "Most Admired" and "Least Admired" Corporations.

For a number of years now, *Fortune* magazine has conducted rankings of "America's Most Admired Corporations" and has included among their "Eight Key Attributes of Reputation" the category entitled "Community and Environmental Responsibility." The rankings are the result of a poll of more than 8,200 senior executives, outside directors, and financial analysts. In this category, the most admired firms for 1991 were Merck, Johnson & Johnson, and DuPont; the least admired were Continental Airlines, Goldome, and Meritor Savings Bank.[44] It is not clear what impact, if any, the *Fortune* rankings have for these businesses, but surely it has some impact on the firm's general reputation. The important point to note here, however, is that the Community and Environmental Responsibility category is one indicator of corporate social performance and that it was included as a criterion by one of our country's leading business magazines.

Figure 2-8 summarizes the companies that received the best and worst ratings in the *Fortune* survey for the last 5 years for which information was available.

CEP's Rating of America's Corporate Conscience.

Another indication of the public's interest in corporate social performance was the 1986 publication of a new volume entitled *Rating America's Corporate Conscience,* which was compiled by the Council on Economic Priorities (CEP). The new book rates food products, health care products, hotels, automobiles, appliances, and dozens of other consumer goods companies according to various categories of social performance. The CEP issued what it calls the first comprehensive shopping guide for the socially conscious consumer, with the goal of "enhancing corporate performance as it affects society in critically important areas. . . ."[45] "This book," the authors write, "will help you cast an economic vote on corporate social responsibility when you shop—whether you're buying toothpaste, a typewriter, or an airline ticket."[46]

Rating America's Corporate Conscience, a 500-page volume, rates corporate social performance by analyzing comparable data and presenting them in a practical format. The authors chose seven issues on which to base their judgments of corporate social performance. These were:

1. Charitable contributions
2. Representation of women on boards of directors and among top corporate officers
3. Representation of minorities on boards of directors and among top corporate officers

FIGURE 2-8   Fortune's Most and Least Admired Corporations: Community and Environmental Responsibility Category

Three Most Admired by Year	Three Least Admired by Year
1987 1. Johnson & Johnson 2. IBM 3. Merck	**1987** 1. Manville 2. LTV 3. E. F. Hutton
1988 1. Johnson & Johnson 2. Eastman Kodak 3. Procter & Gamble	**1988** 1. Financial Corp. of America 2. Texas Air 3. Manville
1989 1. Johnson & Johnson 2. DuPont 3. Merck	**1989** 1. Financial Corp. of America 2. Texas Air 3. Gibraltar Financial
1990 1. Johnson & Johnson 2. Merck 3. DuPont	**1990** 1. Gibraltar Financial 2. Texas Air 3. LTV
1991 1. Merck 2. Johnson & Johnson 3. DuPont	**1991** 1. Continental Airlines 2. Goldome 3. Meritor Savings Bank

Source: Annual Rankings in *Fortune* Magazine, 1987–1991.

4. Disclosure of social information

5. Involvement in South Africa

6. Conventional weapons-related contracting

7. Nuclear weapons-related contracting[47]

Included in the book are product charts and company profiles that assess the firms and their products using criteria presented above. Figure 2-9 presents an example of their product chart for soft drinks, and Figure 2-10 on page 52 presents an example of their company profile, in this case Delta Air Lines, Inc.

Many could debate whether the criteria CEP chose were appropriate measures of corporate social performance and whether they were accurately applied. The important point, however, is that such a volume was produced in the first place and made commercially available to the public in bookstores. It demonstrated further the public's interest in the social performance of business. When the book

Chapter 2 ◆ Corporate Social Responsibility, Responsiveness, and Performance 51

FIGURE 2-9   Product Chart for Soft Drinks

Beverages — **Soft Drinks**

Size of Charitable Contributions	Women Directors and Officers	Minority Directors and Officers	Social Disclosure	Brand Name	Company (Profile Page)	Involvement in South Africa	Conv. Weapons–Related Contracts	Nuclear Weapons–Related Contracts	Authors' Company of Choice
$	♀♀	♀♀	✍✍✍	Coca-Cola, Fanta, Fresca, Mello Yello, Ramblin' Root Beer, Sprite, Tab	Coca-Cola	Yes B	No	No	
$$	No	♀	✍✍✍	Mountain Dew, Pepsi, Slice	PepsiCo	No	No	No	
$$	♀	♀♀	✍✍✍	7-Up	Philip Morris	No	No	No	
$$$	♀	♀♀	✍✍✍	Crush, Hires Root Beer	Procter & Gamble	No	No	No	✓
$$	♀♀	♀	✍✍	Gatorade	Quaker Oats	No	No	No	

* = See company profile
? = No information available
Single figure ($, ♀) = Minimal
Double figure ($$, ♀♀, ✍✍) = Moderate
Triple figure ($$$, ♀♀♀, ✍✍✍) = Substantial

No = No involvement or participation
Yes = Involvement or participation, A, B, C in the South African column reflect the degree of compliance with Sullivan Principles and/or involvement in strategic industries.

Source: Steven D. Lydenberg, Alice Tepper Marlin, Sean O'Brien Strub, and the Council on Economic Priorities, *Rating America's Corporate Conscience: A Provocative Guide to the Companies Behind the Products You Buy Every Day* (Reading, MA: Addison-Wesley Publishing Co., 1986), 67.

FIGURE 2-10   Company Profile for Delta Air Lines, Inc.

In an industry characterized by labor disputes and tough contract negotiations, the non-union and profitable Delta stands out for its long history of harmonious relations with its workers. According to the authors of *The 100 Best Companies to Work for in America,* "One of the most publicized corporate love affairs is between Delta employees and their airline."

Among its policies for employees is near total job security. The company boasts of having kept this promise through good times and bad for over 25 years. Pay scales and benefits at Delta are reportedly as good as or better than other airlines. The company's management works hard to keep communications open with workers and to promote the "family" feeling for which the airline is famous.

This family spirit has served the airline well. Delta remained profitable in the years first following deregulation of the industry in 1978, when other airlines were racking up huge losses. In 1982, when the company succumbed to industry-wide losses, its top executives took a pay cut and 80 percent of its workers contributed a portion of their paychecks to finance the acquisition of a new airplane.

The work force is 99 percent non-union, and the company likes it that way. Management attributes part of the airline's profitability to the flexibility in duties which its workers accept in return for good wages and job security.

The company's charitable contributions appear to be minimal ($346,000 in 1983—or 0.1 percent of pre-tax earnings—as reported in the Taft *Corporate Giving Directory*) and go entirely to educational institutions primarily in the southeastern United States. This figure is for the company's foundation only and may understate the company's total program.

The company did not respond to CEP's questionnaires.

DELTA AIR LINES, INC.											
	Women		Minorities				Contracts		PAC Contributions		
% to Charity	Directors	Officers	Directors	Officers	Social Disclosure	Sullivan Rating	% Military	Nuclear Weapons-Related	Dollar Amount	% to Republicans	% to Democrats
0.1%	1	0	1	1	F	None	None	None	$12,775	29%	71%

Source: Steven D. Lydenberg, Alice Tepper Marlin, Sean O'Brien Strub, and the Council on Economic Priorities, *Rating America's Corporate Conscience: A Provocative Guide to the Companies Behind the Products You Buy Every Day* (Reading, MA: Addison–Wesley Publishing Co., 1986), 251.

came out, it certainly got noticed by the business press, though some of the reviews were somewhat tongue-in-cheek.[48] On the whole, however, the reviews were quite positive, and many consumers may find the book to be a useful layperson's guide to corporate social performance.

The CEP publishes an annual volume that rates the corporate citizenship records of companies. In addition, it gives out annual Corporate Conscience Awards. Among the companies receiving awards in 1990 were AT&T for its program to stop using ozone-depleting chlorofluorocarbons; U.S. West for its support groups for minorities; Pitney Bowes for its affirmative-action, profit-sharing, and child-care-leave policies; Xerox for allowing employees with 3 years of service to take a leave with full pay to do community work; and Cummins Engine for giving 5 percent of its domestic pretax profits to charity.

Business Enterprise Trust Awards. A new organization, the Business Enterprise Trust, was created in 1989 to stimulate a national debate on responsible business behavior in the complex economy of the 1990s and beyond. The Trust was created by 17 prominent business leaders, including such notables as Warren Buffett (Berkshire Hathaway, Inc.), Norman Lear (Act III Communications), and James Burke (Johnson & Johnson). Kirk Hanson, a business ethics professor at Stanford University, was appointed the first president of the Trust. According to Hanson, one of the major activities of the Trust is an annual awards program that seeks to identify and promote acts of courage, integrity, and social vision in business. The Trust's Board hopes that the Business Enterprise Awards will become a kind of Pulitzer Prize for business. The Trust presented its first awards in 1991. James E. Burke, chairman of the Trust, provides a useful summary of the awards' purpose:

> The Business Enterprise Awards will stimulate and inspire businesspeople to the kind of behavior which reflects the simple truth—that business institutions have a responsibility to all of those in society who are dependent upon them—and that following this simple moral imperative turns out to be very good business.[49]

SOCIAL RESPONSIBILITY AND FINANCIAL PERFORMANCE

One issue that comes up frequently in considerations of corporate social responsibility is whether there is a demonstrable relationship between a firm's social responsibility and its financial performance. Unfortunately, attempts to measure this relationship are always hampered by measurement problems. Debates exist as to the appropriate performance criteria to measure financial performance and social responsibility. Furthermore, the measurement of social responsibility is fraught with definitional problems. Even if a definition of social responsibility could be agreed on, there still remains the complex task of operationalizing the definition.

Over the years, studies on the social responsibility–financial performance relationship have produced varying results. Whereas some studies concluded that a relationship existed, those that appeared to be most methodologically sound did not reach that conclusion. A thorough analysis of this issue gets into a level of research methodology that is beyond the scope of this book.

We should not be discouraged that we cannot consistently verify a statistical relationship between social responsibility and a firm's profitability. This is an extremely difficult issue to study. It may be that the merits of corporate social responsibility and performance do not always show up on the "bottom line." In any event, if we recall the central arguments set forth earlier on behalf of corporate social responsibility, there was no mention of an expected financial payoff that could be readily seen and measured. It could be that the intangible benefits of obeying the law, engaging in ethical behavior, and participating in philanthropic programs tend to evade scientific inquiry.

Socially Conscious Investing Movement

Not only are the media, academic, and special-interest groups interested in business's social performance, but apparently investors are also. The socially conscious or ethical investing movement arrived on the scene in the 1970s and has continued to grow and prosper.

Historically, social responsibility investing dates back to the early 1900s when church endowments refused to buy "sin" stocks—shares in tobacco, alcohol, and gambling companies. During the Vietnam War era of the 1960s and early 1970s, antiwar investors refused to invest in defense contracting firms. In the early 1980s, universities, municipalities, and foundations sold off their shares of companies that had operations in South Africa to protest apartheid. In the 1990s, self-styled socially responsible investment seems to be coming into its own.[50]

The Social Investment Forum, a trade-association in Minneapolis, says that socially conscious investments in pension funds, mutual funds, and municipal and private portfolios in 1990 totaled more than $500 billion, up from $40 billion in 1984. Managers of the socially conscious funds do not just use ethical or social responsibility criteria to screen what companies to invest in. They typically screen for a company's financial health before all else. And, there is a growing corps of brokers, financial planners, and portfolio managers available to help people evaluate investments for their social impacts.[51]

Among private individuals, mutual funds are the most popular outlet for investing in firms with good corporate social performance records. Different funds, however, specialize in emphasizing or screening for different social or ethical criteria. A few examples illustrate the types of funds available and criteria used. The Calvert Ariel Growth fund buys stocks of firms that are not involved in South Africa, weapons, or nuclear energy. The Calvert Ariel Appreciation Fund uses these same criteria but also employs an "intense" environmental screen that shuns polluters and actively seeks companies that take leadership roles in preserving and cleaning up the environment. The New

Alternatives fund invests in solar energy and energy conservation stocks, as well as other forms of alternative energy. The Dreyfus Third Century fund looks for emphasis in environmental protection, occupational safety and health, consumer protection, and equal opportunity.[52]

The financial performance of socially conscious funds shows that investors do not have to sacrifice profitability for principles. A new index, called the Domini Social Index (DSI), is made up of 400 common stocks that pass multiple ethical screens. In a test that compared the hypothetical monthly returns of the DSI and the S&P 500 from January 1986 to April 1990, the social index's performance almost never diverted from the S&P by more than 1 percent.

The Council on Economic Priorities indicates that there are at least five reasons why there has been an upsurge in social or ethical investing:

1. There is more reliable and sophisticated research on corporate social performance than in the past.

2. Investment firms using social criteria have established a solid track record, and investors do not have to sacrifice principles for gains.

3. The socially conscious 1960s generation is now making investment decisions.

4. The explosive situation in South Africa has prompted many firms and institutions to divest from firms doing business there.

5. The Reagan administration's cutbacks on social service programs and regulation has brought an increased public awareness of the need for new and innovative corporate initiatives.[53]

Socially conscious funds continue to be debated in the investment community. The fact that they exist, have grown, and have prospered, however, provides evidence that the idea is a serious one and that there truly are investors who take the social performance issue quite seriously.

SUMMARY

The corporate social responsibility concept has a rich history. It has grown out of many diverse views and even today does not enjoy a consensus of definition. A four-part conceptualization was presented that broadly conceives social responsibility as encompassing economic, legal, ethical, and philanthropic components.

The concern for corporate social responsibility has been expanded to include a concern for social responsiveness. The responsiveness focus suggests more of an action-oriented theme in which firms not only must address their basic obligations but also must decide on a basic mode of responding to these obligations. A social performance model was presented that brought the responsibility and responsiveness dimensions together into a framework that also identified realms of social issues that must be considered. The identification of social issues has blossomed into a field now called issues management.

The interest in corporate social responsibility extends beyond the academic community. On an annual basis, *Fortune* magazine polls executives on a variety of dimensions of corporate performance. One major dimension included is Community and Environmental Responsibility. The Council on Economic Priorities also recently published a volume entitled *Rating America's Corporate Conscience,* which further heightened public interest in the social and ethical domains of business performance. The Business Enterprise Trust now gives awards for exceptional social performance.

Finally, the socially conscious investing movement seems to be flourishing. This indicates that there is a growing body of investors who are sensitive to business's social, ethical, and financial performance. Studies of the relationship between social responsibility and economic performance do not yield consistent results, but social efforts are nevertheless expected and are of value to the firm and the business community.

DISCUSSION QUESTIONS

1. Identify and explain the four-part definition of corporate social responsibility. Provide several examples of each component of the definition.
2. In your view, what is the single strongest argument against the idea of corporate social responsibility? The single strongest argument in support of social responsibility? Briefly explain.
3. Differentiate social responsibility from social responsiveness. Give an example of each.
4. Of the social responsiveness categories summarized in Figure 2-4, which set of categories do you find most useful in terms of describing the responsiveness dimension? Explain.
5. Based on your understanding of corporate social responsibility developed in the chapter, classify each of the seven criteria used by the Council on Economic Priorities in their book *Rating America's Corporate Conscience* into the four CSR categories: economic, legal, ethical, or philanthropic.

ENDNOTES

1. John L. Paluszek, *Business and Society: 1976–2000* (New York: AMACOM, 1976), 1.
2. Keith Davis, "Understanding the Social Responsibility Puzzle," *Business Horizon* (Winter, 1967), 45–50.
3. James W. McKie, "Changing Views," in *Social Responsibility and the Business Predicament* (Washington, DC: The Brookings Institute, 1974), 22.
4. McKie, 22.
5. See Morrell Heald, *The Social Responsibilities of Business: Company and Community,* 1900–1960 (Cleveland: Case Western Reserve University Press, 1970), 12–14.
6. McKie, 23.
7. *Ibid.,* 25.
8. Heald, 119.
9. McKie, 27–28.

10. Neil J. Mitchell, *The Generous Corporation: A Political Analysis of Economic Power* (Yale University Press, 1989).
11. Ronald E. Berenbeim, "When the Corporate Conscience Was Born" [A review of Mitchell's book], *Across the Board* (October, 1989), 60–62.
12. *Ibid.*, 62.
13. Keith Davis and Robert L. Blomstrom, *Business and Society: Environment and Responsibility*, 3d ed. (New York: McGraw-Hill, 1975), 39.
14. Joseph W. McGuire, *Business and Society* (New York: McGraw-Hill, 1963), 144.
15. Edwin M. Epstein, "The Corporate Social Policy Process: Beyond Business Ethics, Corporate Social Responsibility and Corporate Social Responsiveness," *California Management Review*, (Vol. XXIX, No. 3, 1987), 104.
16. Archie B. Carroll, "A Three-Dimensional Conceptual Model of Corporate Social Performance," *Academy of Management Review* (October, 1979), 497–505.
17. Archie B. Carroll, "The Pyramid of Corporate Social Responsibility: Toward the Moral Management of Organizational Stakeholders," *Business Horizons* (July–August, 1991), 39–48.
18. *Ibid.*
19. *Ibid.*
20. Milton Friedman, "The Social Responsibility of Business Is to Increase Its Profits," *New York Times* (September, 1962), 126.
21. *Ibid.*, 33 (emphasis added).
22. Christopher D. Stone, *Where the Law Ends* (New York: Harper Colophon Books, 1975), 77.
23. Keith Davis, "The Case For and Against Business Assumption of Social Responsibilities," *Academy of Management Journal* (June, 1973), 312–322.
24. F. A. Hayek, "The Corporation in a Democratic Society: In Whose Interest Ought It and Will It Be Run?" in H. Ansoff (ed.), *Business Strategy* (Middlesex: Penguin, 1969), 225.
25. Davis, 320.
26. Thomas A. Petit, *The Moral Crisis in Management* (New York: McGraw-Hill, 1967), 58.
27. Davis, 316.
28. Robert Ackerman and Raymond Bauer, *Corporate Social Responsiveness: The Modern Dilemma* (Reston, VA: Reston Publishing Company, 1976), 6.
29. S. Prakash Sethi, "Dimensions of Corporate Social Performance: An Analytical Framework," *California Management Review* (Spring, 1975), 58–64.
30. *Ibid.*, 62–63.
31. William C. Frederick, "From CSR1 to CSR2: The Maturing of Business-and-Society Thought" (Graduate School of Business, University of Pittsburgh, 1978), Working Paper No. 279, 6.
32. William C. Frederick, "Toward CSR3: Why Ethical Analysis Is Indispensable and Unavoidable in Corporate Affairs," *California Management Review* (Winter, 1986), 131.
33. Epstein, 107.
34. Ian Wilson, "What One Company Is Doing About Today's Demands on Business," in G. A. Steiner (ed.), *Changing Business-Society Interrelationships* (UCLA, 1975).
35. T. W. McAdam, "How to Put Corporate Responsibility into Practice," *Business and Society Review/Innovation* (Summer, 1973), 8–16.
36. Keith Davis and Robert L. Blomstrom, *Business and Society: Environment and Responsibility*, 3d ed. (New York: McGraw-Hill, 1975).
37. James E. Post, *Corporate Behavior and Social Change* (Reston, VA: Reston Publishing Co., 1978), 39.
38. Robert H. Miles, *Managing the Corporate Social Environment: A Grounded Theory* (Englewood Cliffs, NJ: Prentice-Hall, 1987), 77.
39. Sandra L. Holmes, "Executive Perceptions of Corporate Social Responsibility," *Business Horizons* (Vol. 3, 1976), 34–40.
40. Carroll, 1979: 502–504.
41. Steven L. Wartick and Philip L. Cochran, "The Evolution of the Corporate Social Performance Model," *Academy of Management Review* (Vol. 10, 1985), 765–766.
42. Donna J. Wood, "Corporate Social Performance Revisited," *Academy of Management Review* (October, 1991), 691–718.
43. See, for example, Lee E. Preston (ed.), *Research in Corporate Social Performance and Policy*, Vols. 1–7 (Greenwich, CT: JAI Press, 1978–1985).
44. Edward C. Baig, "America's Most Admired Corporations," *Fortune* (January 19, 1987), 18–31.
45. Steven D. Lydenberg, Alice Tepper Martin, Sean O'Brien Strub, and the Council on Economic Priorities, *Rating America's Corporate Conscience: A Provocative Guide to the Companies Behind the Products You Buy Every Day* (Reading, MA: Addison-Wesley, 1986).
46. *Ibid.*, vii, 3.
47. *Ibid,.* 17.
48. Daniel Seligman, "The Case of the Ethical Ketchup," *Fortune* (February 16, 1987), 28; and Alan Murray, "New Book Rates Consumer Firms on Social Issues," *The Wall Street Journal* (January 16, 1987), 25.
49. *The Business Enterprise Awards for Courage, Integrity and Social Vision in Business: Request for Nominations*, 1990.
50. Joan Warner, "Putting Your Cash Where Your Conscience Is," *Business Week* (December 24, 1990), 74–75.
51. *Ibid.*
52. Kristin Davis, "Socially Conscious Funds: A Fresh Look," *Changing Times* (August, 1990), 57–60.
53. *Ibid.*

CHAPTER **THREE**

The Stakeholder Management Concept

CHAPTER OBJECTIVES

After studying this chapter, you should be able to:

◆ Define *stake* and *stakeholder* and describe the origin of these concepts.

◆ Differentiate among the production, managerial, and stakeholder views of the firm.

◆ Discuss the concept of stakeholder management.

◆ Identify and discuss the five major questions that capture the essence of stakeholder management.

At one time, life was simpler in business organizations. First, there were the investors who put up the money to get a business started. Of course, this was in the precorporate period, so there was only one person or a few at most who were financing the business. Next, the owners needed employees to do the productive work of the firm. Because the owners themselves were frequently the managers, another group—the employees—was needed to get the business going. Then the owners needed suppliers to make raw materials available for production and customers to purchase the products or services they were providing. All in all, it was a less complex period, with minimal expectations among the various parties.

It would take many books to describe how and why we got from that relatively simple period to the complex situation we face today in our society. Many of the factors we discussed in the past two chapters were driving forces behind this societal transformation. The principal factor, however, has been the recognition by the public, or society, that the business organization has evolved to the point that it is no longer the sole property of the founder, or the founder's family, or even a group of owner-investors.

The business organization today, especially the modern corporation, is the institutional centerpiece of a complex society. Our society today consists of many people with a multitude of interests, expectations, and demands as to what major organizations ought to provide to accommodate the people's life-styles. We have seen business respond to the many expectations placed on it. We have seen an ever-changing social contract. We have seen many assorted legal, ethical, and philanthropic expectations and demands being met by organizations willing to change as long as the economic incentive was there. What was once viewed as a specialized means of providing profit through the manufacture and distribution of goods and services has become a multipurpose social institution that many people and groups depend on for their livelihood and prosperity.

In a society conscious of an always-improving life-style, with more groups every day laying claims to their piece of the good life, business organizations today need to be responsive to individuals and groups that they once viewed as powerless and unable to make such claims on them. We call these individuals and groups *stakeholders.*

Business organizations must address stakeholders if they want to be profitable in the long run. Business must also address stakeholders because it is the ethical course of action to pursue. Stakeholders have claims, rights, and expectations that should be honored, and the stakeholder approach assists in that pursuit. It is for this reason that the stakeholder orientation is useful in the arena of business, society, and ethics.

ORIGIN OF THE STAKEHOLDER CONCEPT

The stakeholder concept is a central idea in understanding business and society relationships. The term grew out of the more familiar and traditional idea of *stockholders*—the investors in or owners of businesses. Just as a private individual might own his or her house, automobile, or video recorder, a stockholder owns a portion or a share of one or more businesses. Thus, a stockholder is also called a shareholder.

What Is a Stake?

To appreciate the concept of stakeholders, it helps to understand the idea of a stake. A *stake* is an interest or a share in an undertaking. If a group is attempting to go out to dinner and a show for the evening, each person in that group has a stake, or interest, in the group's decision. No money has yet been invested, but each member sees his or her own interest (preference, taste, priority) in the decision. A stake is also a claim. A *claim* is an assertion to a title or a *right* to something. A claim is a demand for something due or believed to be due. We can see clearly that an owner or a stockholder has an interest in and an ownership of a share of a business.

The idea of a stake, therefore, can range from simply an interest in an undertaking at one extreme to a legal claim of ownership at the other extreme. In between these two extremes is a right to something. This right might be a *legal* right to certain treatment rather than a legal claim of ownership such as that of a shareholder. Legal rights might include the right of due process (to get an impartial hearing) or the right to privacy (not to have his or her privacy invaded or abridged). The right might be thought of as a *moral* right, such as that expressed by an employee: "I've got a right not to be fired because I've worked here 30 years, and I've given this firm the best years of my life." Or a consumer might say, "I've got a right to a safe product after all I've paid for this."

As we have seen, there are a number of different types of stakes. Figure 3-1 summarizes what each means.

What Is a Stakeholder?

A *stakeholder*, then, is an individual or group that asserts to have one or more of the kinds of stakes in a business. Just as stakeholders *may be affected* by the actions, decisions, policies, or practices of the business firm, these stakeholders also *may affect* the organization's actions, decisions, policies, or practices. With stakeholders, therefore, there is a potential two-way interaction or exchange of influence. In short, a stakeholder may be thought of as "any individual or group who can affect or is affected by the actions, decisions, policies, practices, or goals of the organization."[1]

WHO ARE BUSINESS'S STAKEHOLDERS?

In today's business environment there are many individuals and groups who are business's stakeholders. From the business point of view, there are certain individuals and groups who have legitimacy in the eyes of management. That is, they have a

FIGURE 3-1   Types of Stakes

An Interest	A Right	Ownership
When a person or group will be affected by a decision, it has an *interest* in that decision.	*Legal Right:* When a person or group has a legal claim to be treated in a certain way or to have a particular right protected.	When a person or group has a legal title to an asset or a property.
Example: This plant closing will affect the community. This TV commercial demeans women, and I'm a woman.	*Example:* Employees expect due process, privacy; customers or creditors have certain legal rights.	*Example:* "This company is mine, I founded it, and I own it." Or, "I own 1,000 shares of this corporation."
	Moral Right: When a person or group thinks it has a moral right to be treated in a certain way or to have a particular right protected.	
	Example: Fairness, justice, equity.	

legitimate interest in or claim on the operations of the firm. The most obvious of these groups would be stockholders, employees, customers, and competitors. From the point of view of a highly pluralistic society, stakeholders might include not only those groups mentioned but other groups as well. These other groups might include the community, special-interest groups, and society or the public at large.

Production, Managerial, and Stakeholder Views

The growth of the stakeholder concept parallels the evolution of business. In what has been termed the traditional ***production view of the firm,*** owners viewed as stakeholders only those individuals or groups who supplied resources or bought products or services.[2] As time passed and we witnessed the growth of corporations and the resulting separation of ownership from control, business firms began to see the need for interaction with major constituent groups if they were to be managed successfully. Thus, we had the ***managerial view of the firm.*** Finally, as major internal and external changes occurred in business, managers were required to undergo a major conceptual shift in how they saw the firm and its multilateral relationships with constituent or stakeholder groups. The result was the ***stakeholder*** *view of the firm.*³ In actual practice, however, many managers have not yet come to appreciate the need for the stakeholder view. Figure 3-2 depicts the evolution from the production view to the managerial view, and Figure 3-3 on page 64 portrays the stakeholder view of the firm.

In the stakeholder view of the firm, management must see its stakeholders as not only those groups management thinks have some stake in the firm but also those groups that themselves think they have a stake in the firm. This must be the perspective management takes at the outset, at least until it has had a chance to very carefully weigh the legitimacy of the claims and the power of the stakeholders. We should note here that each stakeholder group is composed of subgroups.

Primary and Secondary Stakeholders

Management may also think in terms of whether the individuals or groups are *primary* stakeholders or *secondary* stakeholders. We must use these terms cautiously, however, because secondary stakeholders probably think of themselves as primary stakeholders and prefer to be treated as such. This primary and secondary distinction is needed to help management rank the legitimacy of the claims the groups have or are making. Figure 3-4 on page 65 portrays one possible ranking for a firm.

In this particular stakeholder classification, **primary stakeholders** are seen as those that have a formal, official, or contractual relationship with the firm, and all others are classified as **secondary stakeholders**.

Consequently, a secondary stakeholder can quickly become a primary one. This occurs often with the media or special-interest groups when the urgency of their claim (as in a boycott or demonstration) takes precedence over the legitimacy of their claim. In today's business environment, the media has the power to instantaneously transform a stakeholder's status with coverage on the evening news. Thus, it may be useful to think of primary and secondary classes of stakeholders for discussion purposes, but we should understand how easily and quickly those categories could shift.

STRATEGIC VERSUS MULTIFIDUCIARY VIEWS

One challenge embedded in the stakeholder approach is whether it should be seen primarily as a way to manage better those groups known as stakeholders or as a way to more ethically treat those groups known as stakeholders. Kenneth Goodpaster has addressed this issue by distinguishing between the "strategic" approach and the "multifiduciary" approach.⁴

FIGURE 3-2 The Production and Managerial Views of the Firm

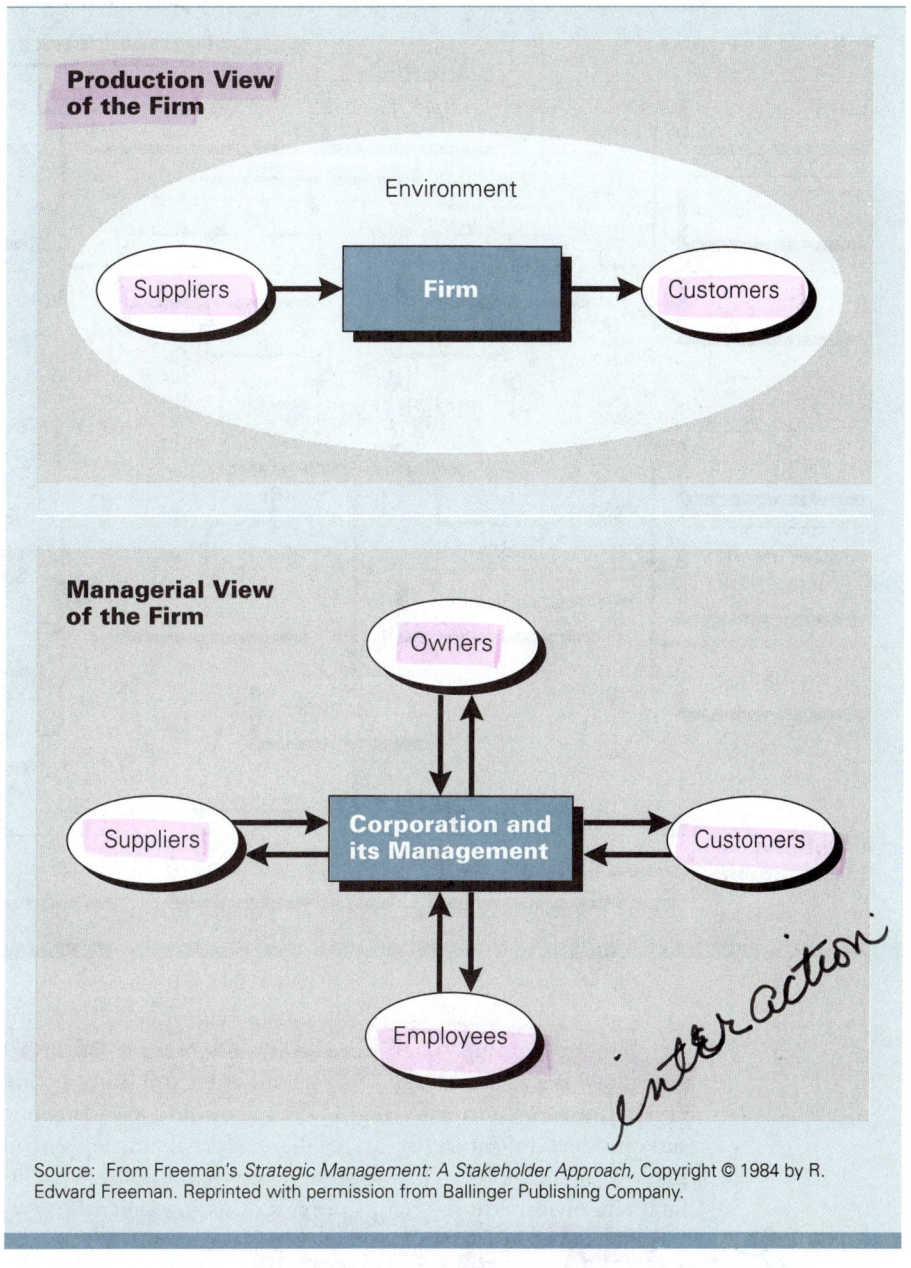

Source: From Freeman's *Strategic Management: A Stakeholder Approach*, Copyright © 1984 by R. Edward Freeman. Reprinted with permission from Ballinger Publishing Company.

FIGURE 3-3 The Stakeholder View of the Firm

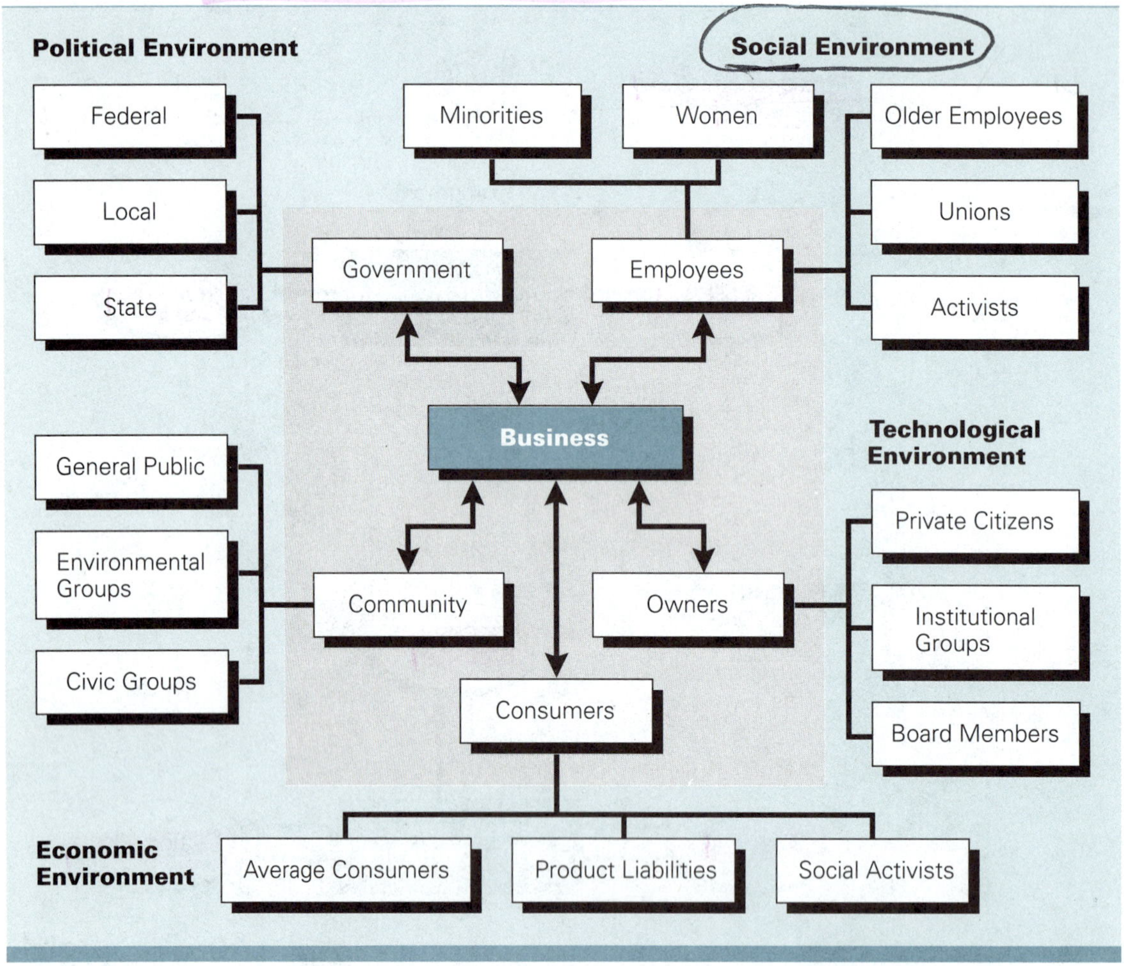

Political Environment
- Federal
- Local
- State
- General Public
- Environmental Groups
- Civic Groups

Social Environment
- Minorities
- Women
- Older Employees
- Unions
- Activists

Technological Environment
- Private Citizens
- Institutional Groups
- Board Members

Economic Environment
- Average Consumers
- Product Liabilities
- Social Activists

Central entities: Government, Employees, Business, Community, Owners, Consumers

The strategic approach views stakeholders as primarily factors to be taken into consideration and managed while the firm is pursuing profits for the shareholders. In this view, managers might take stakeholders into account because offended stakeholders might resist or retaliate (for example, through political action, protest, or boycott). This approach sees stakeholders as instruments that may facilitate or impede the firm's pursuit of its strategic objectives.

The "multifiduciary" approach views stakeholders as more than just people who can wield economic or legal power. This view holds that management has a fiduciary responsibility to stakeholders just as it has this responsibility to shareholders. Here, management's traditional fiduciary, or trust duty, is expanded to embrace stakeholders on a roughly equal footing with shareholders.

FIGURE 3-4 Primary Versus Secondary Stakeholder Groups

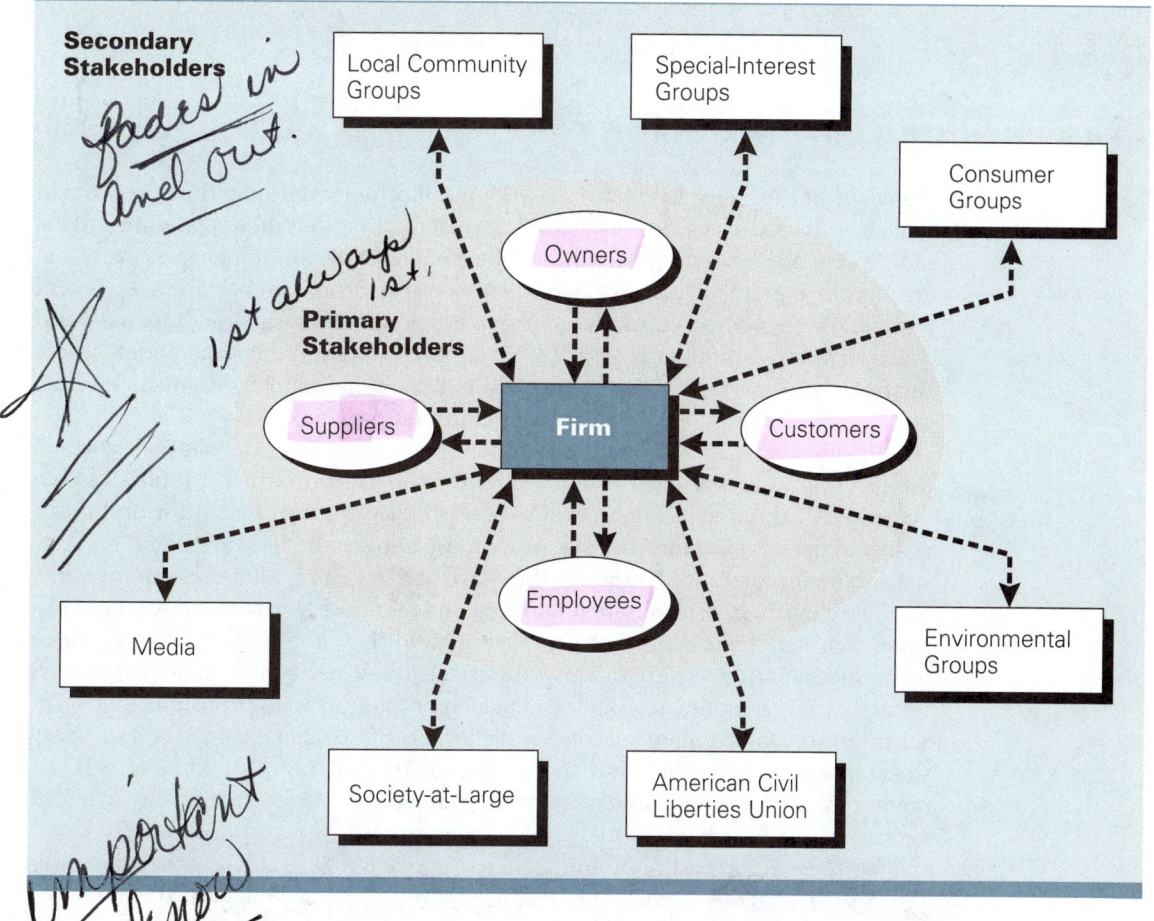

Thus, shareholders are no longer of exclusive importance as they would be under the strategic approach.

Goodpaster recommends that business organizations take neither of these extreme postures but rather pursue a new stakeholder synthesis. This new view holds that business does have moral responsibilities to stakeholders, but they should not be seen as part of a fiduciary obligation. Thus, management's basic fiduciary responsibility to shareholders is kept intact, but it is also expected to be implemented within a context of ethical responsibility. This ethical responsibility is its duty to not harm, coerce, lie, cheat, steal, and so on.[5]

As we continue our discussion of stakeholder management, it should be clear that we are pursuing it from a balanced perspective. This balanced perspective suggests that we are integrating the strategic view with the multifiduciary view such that they are both compatible. We should be managing strategically but morally at the same time. The stakeholder approach is not just a better way to manage—it should be an ethical way to manage at the same time.

STAKEHOLDER MANAGEMENT

Managers of a business firm have the responsibility for establishing the firm's overall direction (its goals, policies, strategies) and seeing to it that these plans are carried out. As a consequence, managers have some long-term responsibilities and many that are of more immediate concern. Before the social environment became as turbulent and rapidly changing as it is, the managerial task was relatively straightforward and the external environment was stable. As we have evolved to the stakeholder view of the firm, however, we see the managerial task as an inevitable consequence of the trends and developments we described in our first two chapters.

Stakeholder management has become important as managers have discovered the many groups that have to be relatively satisfied for the firm to meet its own objectives. Without question, we still see the primacy of and necessity for profits as a return to the stockholders' investments, but we also see the growing claims of other stakeholder groups and the success they have had in getting what they want.

The challenge of stakeholder management, therefore, is to see to it that the firm's primary stakeholders achieve their objectives and that other stakeholders are dealt with ethically and also satisfied. This is the classic "win-win" situation. It does not always occur, but it is a legitimate goal for management to pursue to protect its long-term self-interests. Management's second-best alternative is to meet the goals of its primary stakeholders, keeping in mind the important role of the owners-investors. Even among the primary stakeholders we must have acceptable levels of profits. Without economic viability, all other stakeholders' interests are lost.

With these perspectives in mind, let us approach stakeholder management with the idea that we can become successful stewards of the stakeholders' resources by gaining knowledge about stakeholders and using this knowledge to predict and deal with their behavior and actions. Ultimately, we should manage the situation in such a way that we achieve our objectives ethically and effectively. Thus, the important functions of stakeholder management are to describe, to understand, to analyze, and, finally, to manage.

Five major questions may be asked to capture the essential information we need for stakeholder management:

1. Who are our stakeholders?
2. What are their stakes?
3. What opportunities and challenges do our stakeholders present to our firm?
4. What responsibilities (economic, legal, ethical, philanthropic) does our firm have to all its stakeholders?

5. What strategies or actions should our firm take to best deal with stakeholder challenges and opportunities?[6]

Who Are Our Stakeholders?

To this point we have described the likely primary and secondary stakeholder groups for a business organization. To manage them effectively, each firm must ask and answer this question for itself: Who are our stakeholders? To answer this question fully, management must identify not only generic stakeholder groups but also the specific groups. A *generic stakeholder group* is simply a broad grouping such as employees, shareholders, environmental groups, or consumers. Within each of these generic categories there may be a few or many specific groups. Figure 3-5 illustrates just some of the generic and specific stakeholder groups of a very large organization.

Stakeholder Identification: Nestlé, S. A.
Two examples of stakeholder maps that have been developed to illustrate the process of stakeholder identification are useful. The first is the case of Nestlé, S. A., the Swiss conglomerate that at one time dominated the marketing of infant formula in the Third World, or less-developed countries (LDCs). Other companies also marketed infant formula in the LDCs, but Nestlé was the major company.

Beginning in about 1970, Nestlé became involved in a controversy over the morality of selling any infant formula in the Third World and of using specific promotional and marketing techniques considered immoral by some. The basic allegation against Nestlé and the others was that in these Third World countries, infant formula was likely to be misused and therefore might lead to malnutrition, diarrhea, and death. Also, it was claimed that Nestlé's aggressive marketing tactics encouraged women to choose bottle-feeding, thus resulting in a decline in breast-feeding, which is safer and more healthful, particularly in the Third World. Poor sanitation, impure water, inadequacy of water supplies, and inability to read, comprehend, and follow directions resulted in disease and malnutrition. Mothers who were poor (and most are in these countries) tried to save money and thus overdiluted the infant formula to make it go further.

The complete controversy over marketing infant formula in the Third World requires a longer discussion, and we will explore it in more depth in Chapter 6. Suffice it to say, however, that Nestlé fought its critics for years, and its array of stakeholder groups became numerous. Picture, if you can, what the stakeholder map of Nestlé might have looked like before the infant formula controversy. Most likely it was similar to the relatively simple managerial view of the firm shown in Figure 3-2. When Third World governments, social activist groups, and United Nations agencies got involved, the stakeholder map grew considerably. Figure 3-6 on page 69 illustrates what Nestlé's stakeholder map might have looked like after all these various groups got involved.

Do you think Nestlé had any idea that its persistence in wanting to sell infant formula would have resulted in a situation as complex as this? Perhaps if Nestlé had taken a stakeholder view of the firm before it got

FIGURE 3-5 Some Generic and Specific Stakeholders of a Large Firm

Owners	Employees	Governments	Customers
Trusts	Young employees	Federal	Business
Foundations	Middle-aged	• EPA	purchasers
Mutual funds	employees	• FTC	Government
Board members	Older employees	• OSHA	purchasers
Management	Women	• CPSC	Educational
owners	Minority groups	State	institutions
Employee pension	Handicapped	Local	Special-interest
funds	Special-interest		groups
Individual owners	groups		Consumers' union
	Unions		

Community	Competitors	Social Activist Groups
General fund	Firm A	PUSH (People
raising	Firm B	United to Save
United Way	Firm C	Humanity)
YMCA/YWCA		Friends of the
Middle schools		Earth
Elementary		MADD (Mothers
schools		Against Drunk
Residents who		Driving)
live close by		American Civil
All other residents		Liberties Union
Neighborhood		
associations		
Local media		
Chamber of		
Commerce		

embroiled in this controversy, it would have saved itself years of grief and lost reputation.

Stakeholder Identification: Hooker Chemical Company. The second example worth considering is the case of Hooker Chemical Company and Love Canal.[7] Love Canal was really just a partially dug canal in the southeast corner of the city of Niagara Falls, New York, in the late 1800s. Originally the canal was to be used for generating and transmitting hydroelectric power from the falls to the businesses in the city, but the project was abandoned.

FIGURE 3-6   Stakeholder Map of Nestlé During Infant Formula Controversy

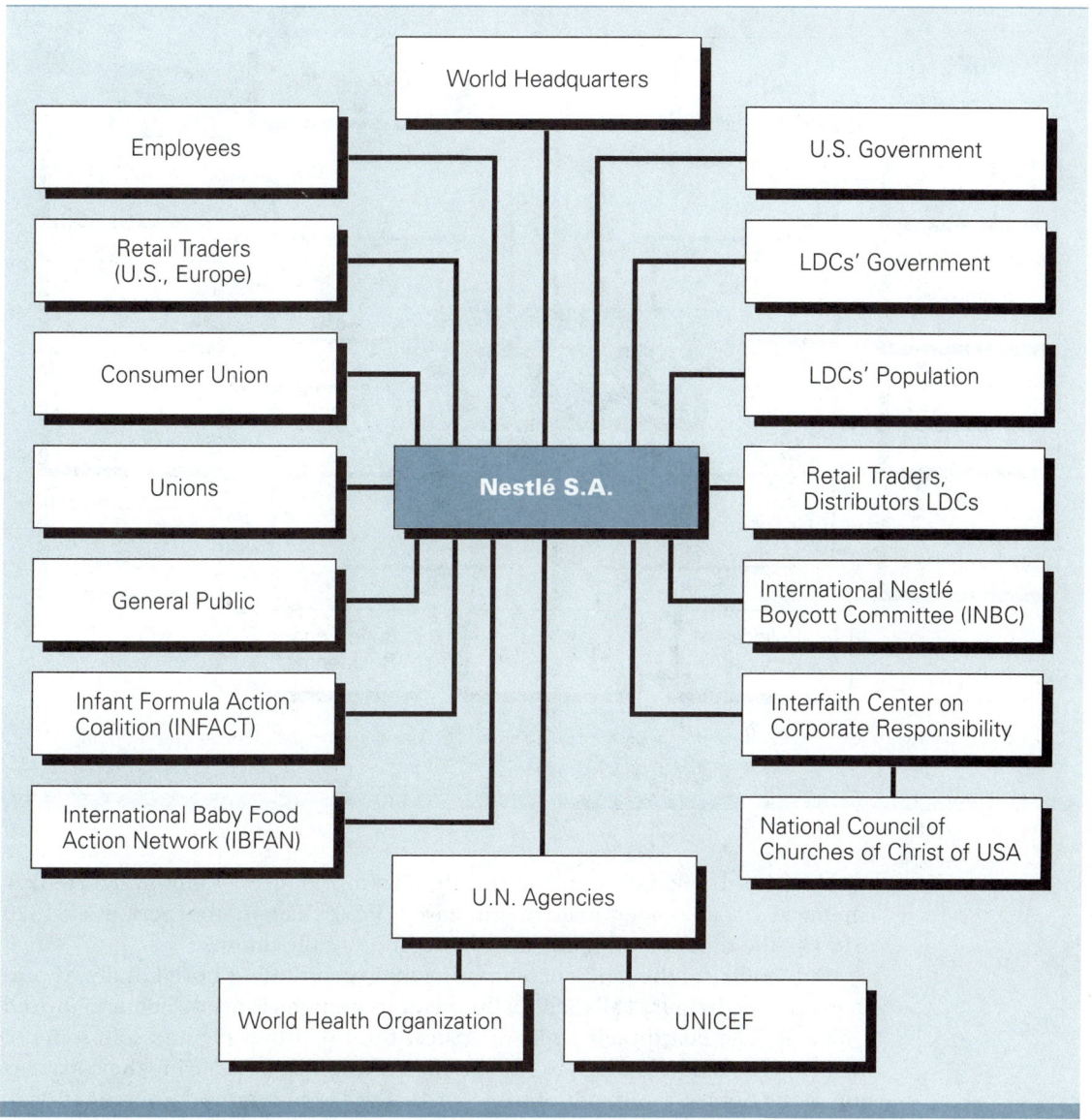

Hooker Chemical Company, now a subsidiary of Occidental Petroleum Company, built its first plant in the area in 1905. In the 1940s, the abandoned section of Love Canal became a toxic waste dump for a number of chemical companies. In 1942, Hooker received permission to use the site for chemical dumping. In 1947, Hooker purchased the Love Canal site from Niagara Power and Development Company. In 1953, the canal, filled with years of toxic waste accumulation,

FIGURE 3-7   Hooker Chemical's Stakeholder Map: 1920–1953

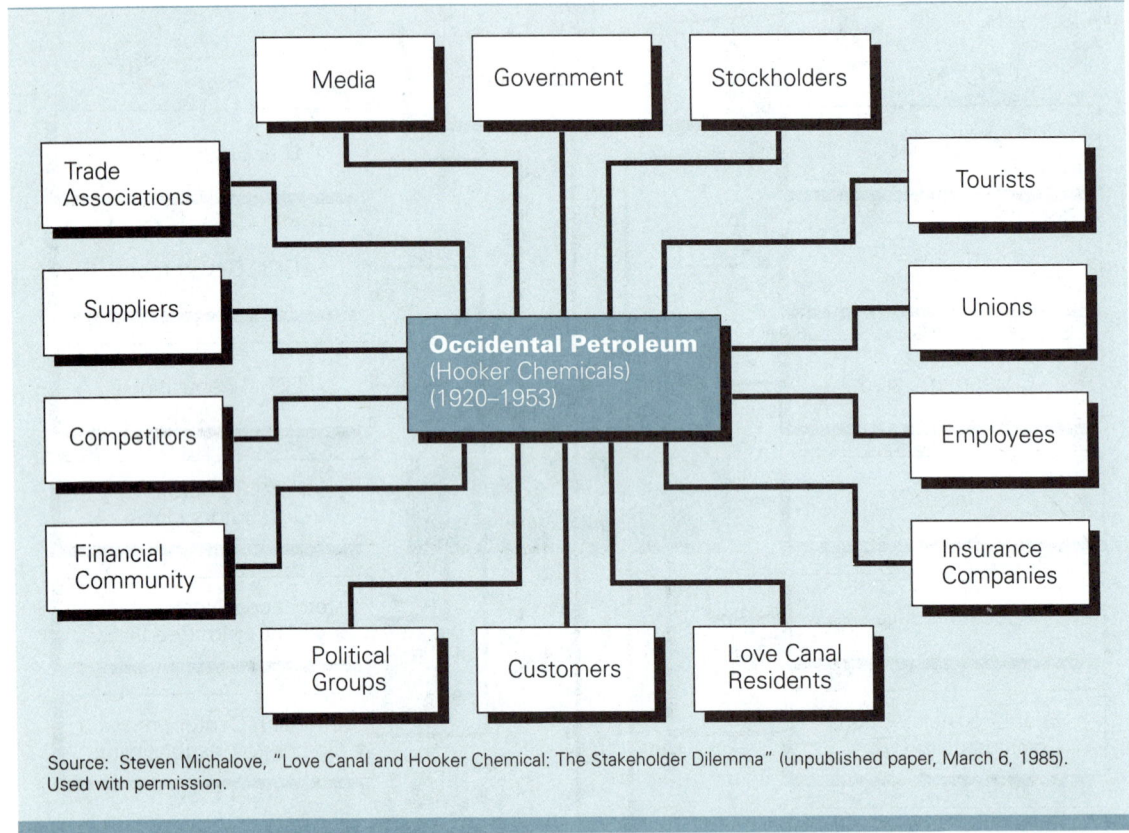

Source: Steven Michalove, "Love Canal and Hooker Chemical: The Stakeholder Dilemma" (unpublished paper, March 6, 1985). Used with permission.

was closed and sealed with an impermeable clay top. Figure 3-7 shows what Hooker Chemical's stakeholder map might have looked like in the period of 1920 to 1953—the time spanning the active operation of the dump.

Subsequently, the land encompassing and surrounding Love Canal was purchased by the Niagara Falls School Board, even though Hooker Chemical advised against it. The board built a school adjacent to the dump site and sold some of the property to developers, who then built a tract of homes. During the construction of the homes, thousands of cubic yards of soil were removed from the surface of the sealed canal. Figure 3-8 represents what Hooker's stakeholder map might have looked like during the period 1953 to 1971, which corresponds to the active settlement of the Love Canal area. Note that the first and second stakeholder maps indicate only slight changes of stakeholder interests in the Love Canal situation.

Apparently the construction work damaged the seal on the Love Canal dump. This, combined with water from heavy rains and snow, resulted in water seeping into the clay-lined basin, which eventually overflowed, causing toxic waste seepage

Chapter 3 ◆ The Stakeholder Management Concept 71

FIGURE 3-8 Hooker Chemical's Stakeholder Map: 1953–1971

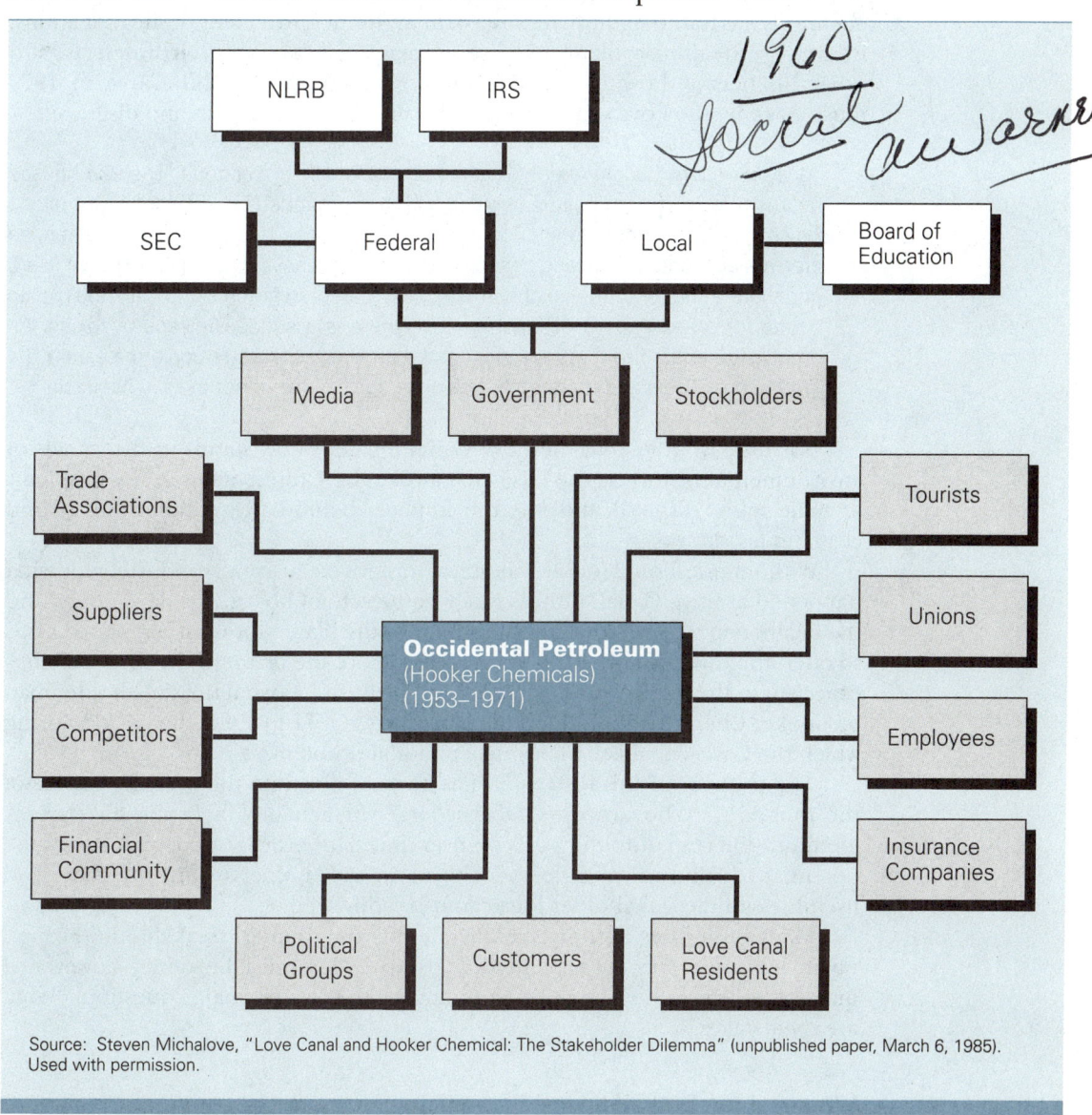

Source: Steven Michalove, "Love Canal and Hooker Chemical: The Stakeholder Dilemma" (unpublished paper, March 6, 1985). Used with permission.

into the homes and basements of nearby residents. By 1978, evidence of toxic chemicals was found in the living area of many homes. After lengthy investigations, a variety of health problems like liver damage, miscarriages, birth defects, and other ills began showing up. The following description of the area in 1979 illustrates why the Love Canal incident became a national crisis and disgrace:

> Today the Love Canal area of Niagara Falls looks like a war zone. The 235 houses nearest the landfill are boarded up and empty, surrounded by an 8-foot-high cyclone fence that keeps tourists and looters away. Still other houses outside the fenced area are also boarded up and deserted, their owners having fled the unknown. Here and there throughout the neighborhood, newly erected green signs mark the pickup points for emergency evacuation in case there is a sudden release of toxins. An ambulance and a fire truck stand by in the area as workers struggle to seal off the flow of chemicals and render the area once again safe—if not exactly habitable.[8]

It is little wonder that the Love Canal incident now stands in the annals of environmental history as the crisis that awoke the United States to the problems of toxic waste disposal and was the impetus behind the national Superfund clean-up legislation.

Without question, Hooker Chemical was not exclusively responsible for what happened at Love Canal. Others, such as the school board, the developers, and the health department must shoulder part of the blame for what happened. As is so often the case, however, the business firm bore the brunt of the responsibility, especially in the media. Figure 3-9 on page 73 illustrates what the stakeholder map of Hooker Chemical might have become during 1971 to 1982, the period during which the Love Canal issue became a national problem.

The purpose of this discussion has been to illustrate the evolving nature of the question, "Who are our stakeholders?" In actuality, a firm's stakeholder identification is an unfolding process over time. However, by recognizing early the potential of failure if one does not think in stakeholder terms, the value and usefulness of the stakeholder idea can be readily seen.

Many businesses do not carefully identify their generic stakeholder groups, much less their specific stakeholder groups. This must be done, however, if management is to be in a position to answer the second major question, "What are their stakes?"

What Are the Stakeholders' Stakes?

Once stakeholders have been identified, the next step is to determine the stakes of the various groups. Even groups in the same generic category frequently have different specific interests, concerns, perceptions of rights, and expectations. Management's challenge here is to identify the *nature/legitimacy* of a group's stake(s) and the *power* that the group possesses to affect the organization.

Chapter 3 ◆ The Stakeholder Management Concept 73

FIGURE 3-9   Hooker Chemical's Stakeholder Map
During Love Canal Issue: 1971–1982

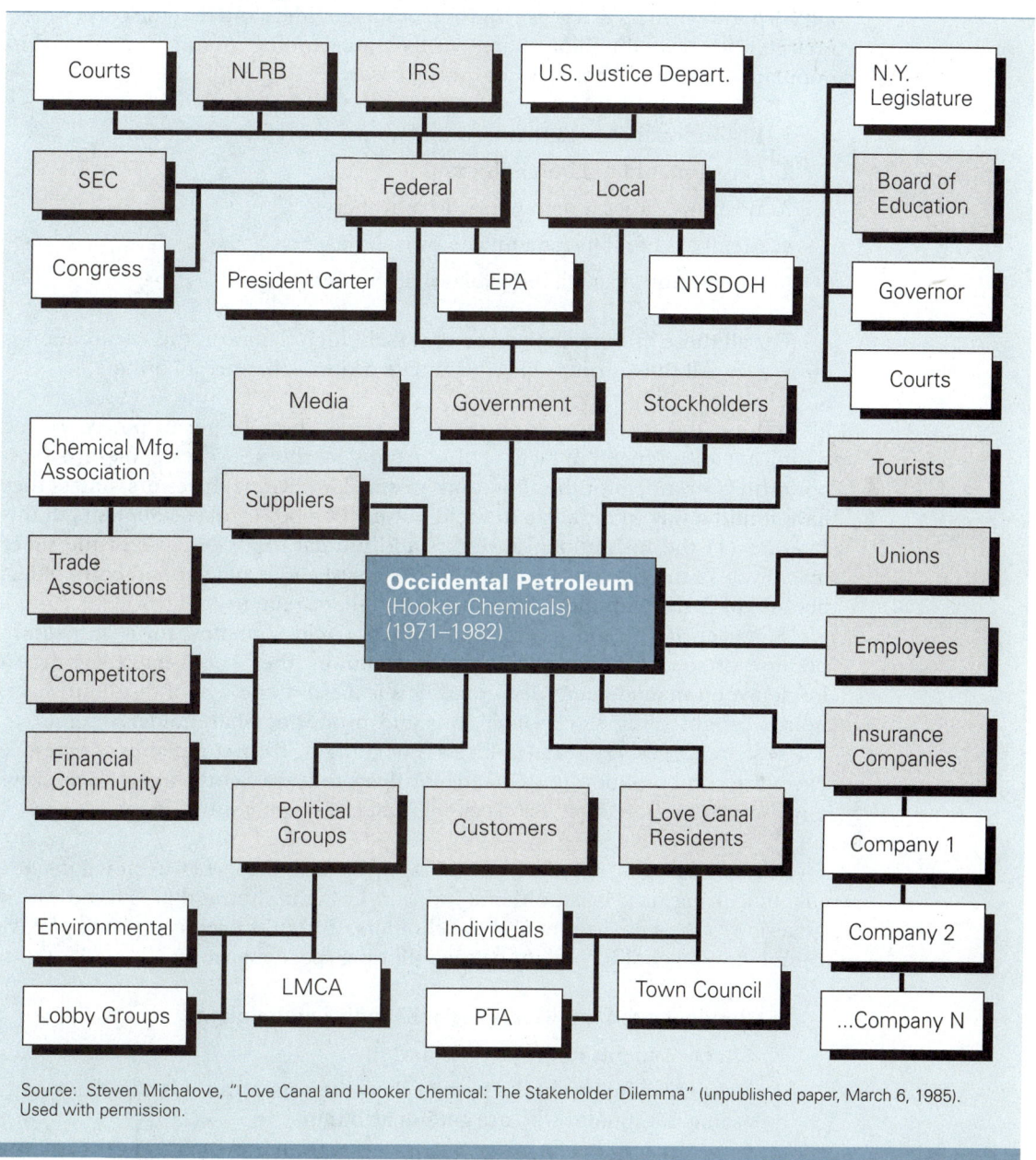

Source: Steven Michalove, "Love Canal and Hooker Chemical: The Stakeholder Dilemma" (unpublished paper, March 6, 1985). Used with permission.

Identifying the Nature/Legitimacy of a Group's Stakes. Let's consider an example of stakeholders who possess varying stakes. Assume that we are considering corporate owners as a generic group of stakeholders and that the corporation is large, with several million shares of stock outstanding. Among the ownership population are these more specific groups:

1. Institutional owners (trusts, foundations, churches, universities)
2. Large mutual fund organizations
3. Board of director members who own shares
4. Members of management who own shares
5. Thousands of small, individual shareholders

For all these groups, the nature of stakeholder claims on this corporation is ownership. All these groups have legitimate claims—they are all owners.

Identifying the Power of a Group's Stakes. When we get to power, we see significant differences. Which of the groups in the above example are most powerful? Certainly not the thousands of small, individual investors, unless they have found a way to organize to wield power. The powerful stakeholders in this case are (1) the institutional investors and mutual funds because of the sheer magnitude of their investments and (2) the board and management shareholders because of their dual roles of ownership and management (control).

However, if the individual shareholders could somehow form a coalition because of some interest they have in common, they could exert significant influence on management decisions. This is the day and age of dissident shareholder groups filing stockholder suits and proposing shareholder resolutions. These shareholder resolutions address issues ranging from complaints of excessive executive compensation to demands for firms to leave South Africa, to improve environmental protection, or to cease illegal campaign contributions.

Identifying Specific Groups Within a Generic Group. Let us now look at a manufacturing firm in an old-line industry in Pennsylvania that is faced with a generic group of environmental stakeholders. Within the generic group of environmental stakeholders might be the following specific groups:

1. Residents who live within a 10-mile radius of the plant
2. Other residents in the city
3. Residents who live in the path of the jet stream hundreds of miles away (some in Canada) who are getting acid rain
4. Environmental Protection Agency (federal)
5. Pennsylvania Environmental Protection Division (state)
6. Friends of the Earth (social activist group)

7. The Wilderness Society (social activist group)
8. Pennsylvanians Against Smokestack Emissions (PASE)

It would require some degree of care to identify the nature, legitimacy, and power of each of these specific groups. However, it could and should be done if the firm wants to get a handle on its environmental stakeholders. Furthermore, we should stress that companies have an ethical responsibility to be sensitive to legitimate stakeholder claims even if the stakeholders have no power or leverage with management.

What Opportunities and Challenges Are Presented to Our Firm?

In many respects, opportunities and challenges represent opposite sides of the coin when it comes to stakeholders. Essentially, the opportunities are to build good, productive working relationships with the stakeholders. Challenges, on the other hand, usually present themselves in such a way that the firm must handle the stakeholders well or be hurt in some way—financially (short term or long term) or in terms of its public image or standing in the community. Therefore, it is understandable why our emphasis is on challenges rather than on opportunities posed by stakeholders.

These challenges typically take the form of varying degrees of expectations or demands. In most instances, they arise because stakeholders think or feel that their needs are not being met adequately. The challenges also arise when stakeholder groups think that any crisis that occurs is the responsibility of the firm or that the firm caused the crisis in some way. In addition to the Nestlé and Hooker Chemical crises described earlier, examples of other stakeholder crises include:

- The 1980 Procter & Gamble (P&G) Rely tampon crisis, in which P&G withdrew the product from the marketplace in the midst of charges that the product was associated with the sometimes fatal disease called toxic shock syndrome.
- The 1982 Johnson & Johnson (J&J) Tylenol crisis, in which someone had replaced Tylenol Extra-Strength capsules with cyanide-laced capsules, resulting in the horrible deaths of seven unsuspecting purchasers.
- The 1984 Union Carbide tragedy in Bhopal, India, where a leak of the poisonous gas methyl isocyanate resulted in the death of more than 2,000 people and serious injury to an estimated 200,000 people.
- The 1989 Exxon Valdez oil spill disaster in which 11 million gallons fouled close to 2,600 miles of beaches in Alaska's Prince William Sound. Groups wanting Exxon to pay up included the state of Alaska, shareholders, environmentalists, consumers, and local businesses. This is regarded as America's worst environmental disaster.

If one looks at the business experiences of the past two decades, including the crises mentioned above, it is evident that there is a need to think in stakeholder terms to fully understand the potential threats that businesses of all kinds face on a daily basis.

Opportunities and challenges might also be viewed in terms of potential for cooperation and potential for threat. Savage, et al. have argued that such assessments of cooperation and threat are necessary so that managers might identify strategies for dealing with stakeholders.[9] In terms of potential for threat, Savage, et al. assert that managers need to consider the stakeholder's relative power and its relevance to a particular issue confronting the organization. In terms of potential for cooperation, the firm needs to be sensitive to the possibility of joining forces with other stakeholders for the advantage of all parties involved.

The authors cite how Ross Laboratories, a division of Abbott Laboratories, was able to develop a cooperative relationship with some critics of its sales of infant formula in Third World countries. Ross and Abbott convinced these stakeholder groups (UNICEF and the World Health Organization) to join them in a program to promote infant health. Other firms, such as Nestlé, did not develop the potential to cooperate and suffered from consumer boycotts.[10]

Figure 3-10 presents a list of the factors that Savage, et al. claim will increase or decrease a stakeholder's potential for threat or cooperation. By carefully analyzing these factors, managers should be able to better assess potentials for threat or cooperation.

What Responsibilities Does Our Firm Have to Our Stakeholders?

Once threats and opportunities of stakeholders have been identified and understood, a next logical question is, "What responsibilities does our firm have in our relationships with all stakeholders?" Responsibilities here could be thought of in terms of the concepts presented in Chapter 2. What economic, legal, ethical, and philanthropic responsibilities do we have to each stakeholder? Because most of the firm's *economic* responsibilities are principally to itself, the analysis really begins to focus on legal, ethical, and philanthropic questions. The most pressing threats present themselves as legal and ethical questions.

We should stress, however, that the firm itself has an economic stake in the legal and ethical issues it faces. For example, when J&J was faced with the Tylenol poisoning incident, it had to decide what the legal or ethical action to take was and what was in the firm's best economic interests. J&J probably judged that recalling the Tylenol products was not only the ethical action to take but also would ensure its reputation for being concerned about consumers' health and well-being. Figure 3-11 on page 78 illustrates the stakeholder/responsibility matrix management faces when assessing the firm's responsibilities to stakeholders.

FIGURE 3-10 Factors Affecting Potential for Stakeholder Threat and Cooperation

	Increases or Decreases Stakeholder's Potential for Threat?	Increases or Decreases Stakeholder's Potential for Cooperation?
Stakeholder controls key resources (needed by organization)	Increases	Increases
Stakeholder does not control key resources	Decreases	Either
Stakeholder more powerful than organization	Increases	Either
Stakeholder as powerful as organization	Either	Either
Stakeholder less powerful than organization	Decreases	Increases
Stakeholder likely to take action (supportive of the organization)	Decreases	Increases
Stakeholder likely to take nonsupportive action	Increases	Decreases
Stakeholder unlikely to take any action	Decreases	Decreases
Stakeholder likely to form coalition with other stakeholders	Increases	Either
Stakeholder likely to form coalition with organization	Decreases	Increases
Stakeholder unlikely to form any coalition	Decreases	Decreases

Source: Grant T. Savage, Timothy W. Nix, Carlton J. Whitehead, and John D. Blair, "Strategies for Assessing and Managing Organizational Stakeholders," *Academy of Management Executive* (May, 1991), 64.

What Strategies or Actions Should Our Firm Take?

Once responsibilities have been assessed, a business must pursue strategies and actions for dealing with its stakeholders. In every decision situation a multitude of alternative courses of action are available, and management must choose one or several that seem best. MacMillan and Jones state that management has before it a number of basic strategies or approaches in dealing with stakeholders. Important questions or decision choices are:

- Do we deal *directly* or *indirectly* with the stakeholders?
- Do we take the *offense* or the *defense* in dealing with the stakeholders?
- Do we *accommodate, negotiate, manipulate,* or *resist* stakeholder overtures?
- Do we employ a *combination* of the above strategies or pursue a singular course of action?[11]

Savage et al. argue that specific strategies may be developed based on classifying stakeholders according to the earlier presented concepts of potential for support and threat. If we use these two dimensions, four stakeholder types and

FIGURE 3-11 Stakeholder/Responsibility Matrix

	Types of Responsibilities			
Stakeholders	Economic	Legal	Ethical	Philanthropic
Owners				
Customers				
Employees		✓	✓	✓
Community				
Public at Large				
Social Activist Groups				
Others				

resultant strategies emerge.[12] Stakeholder Type 1—the supportive stakeholder—is high on cooperation and low on threat. This is the ideal stakeholder type. To a well-managed organization, supportive stakeholders might include its board, managers, employees, and customers. Others might be suppliers and service providers. The strategy here would be one of involvement. An example of this might be the strategy to involve employee stakeholders through participative management or decentralization of authority. Figure 3-12 presents this stakeholder classification.

Stakeholder Type 2—the marginal stakeholder—is low on both potential for threat and potential for cooperation. For large organizations, these might include professional associations of employees, consumer interest groups, or stockholders, especially those who are not organized. The strategy here is for the organization to monitor the marginal stakeholder. Monitoring is especially called for to make sure circumstances do not change. Careful monitoring could avert later problems.

Stakeholder Type 3 is termed the nonsupportive stakeholder. This group is high on the potential for threat but low on cooperative potential. Examples of this group could include competing organizations, unions, federal or other levels of government, and the media. The recommended strategy here is to defend against the nonsupportive stakeholder.

FIGURE 3-12 Diagnostic Typology of Organizational Stakeholders

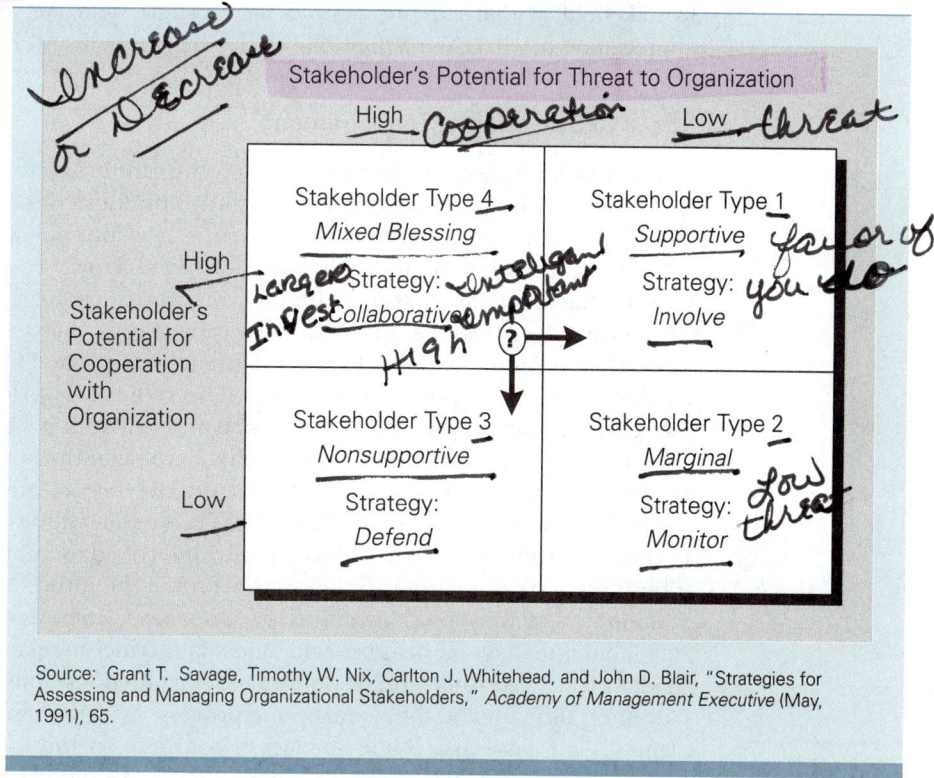

Source: Grant T. Savage, Timothy W. Nix, Carlton J. Whitehead, and John D. Blair, "Strategies for Assessing and Managing Organizational Stakeholders," *Academy of Management Executive* (May, 1991), 65.

Stakeholder Type 4—the mixed blessing stakeholder—is high on both potential for threat and potential for cooperation. Examples of this group, in a well-managed organization, might include employees who are in short supply, clients, or customers. A mixed blessing stakeholder could become a supportive or a nonsupportive stakeholder. The recommended strategy here is to collaborate with the mixed blessing stakeholder. By maximizing collaboration, the likelihood is enhanced that this stakeholder group will remain supportive.

The authors summarize their position regarding these four stakeholder types as follows:

> ... managers should attempt to satisfy minimally the needs of marginal stakeholders and to satisfy maximally the needs of supportive and mixed blessing stakeholders, enhancing the latter's support for the organization.[13]

The four stakeholder types and recommended strategies are what was referred to earlier in the chapter as the "strategic" view of stakeholders. By taking stakeholders' needs and concerns into consideration, we are improving our ethics. We must go beyond just considering them, however. Management still has an ethical responsibility to stakeholders that extends beyond the strategic view. We will develop a fuller appreciation of what this responsibility is in Chapters 5, 6, and 7.

Effective Stakeholder Management

Effective stakeholder management requires the careful assessment of the five core questions we have posed. To deal successfully with those who assert claims on the organization, we must understand these core questions at least at a basic level. It is tempting to wish that all of this was not needed. However, such wishing would require management to accept the production or managerial view of the firm. This is no longer possible. Business today cannot turn back the clock to a simpler period. Business has been and will continue to be subjected to careful scrutiny of its actions, practices, policies, and ethics. This is the real world in which management lives, and management must accept it and deal with it. Criticisms of business and cries for corporate social responsibility have been the consequence, and the stakeholder management approach to viewing the organization has become one needed response. To do less is to refuse to accept the realities of business's plight in the modern world and to fail to see the kinds of adaptations that are essential if businesses are to prosper in the present and in the future.

In fairness, we should also note that there are criticisms or limitations of the stakeholder management approach. One major criticism relates to the complexity of identifying, assessing, and responding to stakeholder claims, which becomes an extremely difficult and time-consuming process. Also, the ranking of stakeholder claims is no easy task. Some managers continue to think in *stockholder* terms because this is easier. To think in stakeholder terms increases the complexity of decision making, and it is overly taxing for some managers to determine which stakeholders' claims take priority in a given situation. Despite its complexity, however, the stakeholder management view is most consistent with the environment that business faces today.

SUMMARY

A stakeholder is an individual or a group that asserts to have one or more stakes in an organization. Stakeholders may affect the organization and, in turn, be affected by the organization's actions and decisions. The stakeholder approach extends beyond the traditional production and managerial views of the firm and warrants a much broader conception of the parties involved in the organization's functioning and success. Both primary and secondary stakeholders assume an important role in the eyes of management.

Five key questions aid managers in stakeholder management: (1) Who are our stakeholders? (2) What are the stakeholders' stakes? (3) What challenges or opportunities are presented to our firm by our stakeholders? (4) What responsibilities does our firm have to our stakeholders? (5) What strategies or actions should our firm take with respect to our stakeholders? Although the stakeholder management approach is quite complex and time consuming, it is a way of managing that squares with the complex environment that organizations face today.

DISCUSSION QUESTIONS

1. Explain the concepts of stake and stakeholder from your perspective as an individual. What kinds of stakes and stakeholders do you have? Discuss.
2. Differentiate between primary and secondary stakeholders in a corporate situation. Explain how you determine which individuals or groups are primary or secondary. Can there be movement between the primary and secondary categories? Explain.
3. Explain in your own words the differences among the production, managerial, and stakeholder views of the firm.
4. Choose any group of stakeholders listed in the stakeholder/responsibility matrix in Figure 3-11, and identify the four types of responsibilities that the firm has to that stakeholder group.
5. What do you see as the major problems or limitations to the stakeholder management approach? Discuss.

ENDNOTES

1. This definition is similar to that of R. Edward Freeman, *Strategic Management: A Stakeholder Approach* (Boston: Pitman, 1984), 25.
2. Freeman, 5.
3. Freeman, 24–25.
4. Kenneth E. Goodpaster, "Business Ethics and Stakeholder Analysis," *Business Ethics Quarterly,* Vol. 1, No. 1 (January, 1991), 53–73.
5. Ibid.
6. Similar questions are posed by Ian C. MacMillan and Patricia E. Jones, *Strategy Formulation: Power and Politics* (St. Paul, MN: West, 1986), 66.
7. The description of this incident comes from Martha W. Elliott and Tom L. Beauchamp, "Hooker Chemical and Love Canal" in Tom L. Beauchamp, *Case Studies in Business, Society and Ethics* (Englewood Cliffs, NJ: Prentice-Hall, 1983), 107–115; and Steve Michalove, "Love Canal and Hooker Chemical: The Stakeholder Dilemma," unpublished paper (March, 1985).
8. Thomas H. Maugh, II, "Toxic Waste Disposal a Growing Problem," *Science* 204 (May 25, 1979), 820.
9. Grant T. Savage, Timothy W. Nix, Carlton J. Whitehead, and John D. Blair, "Strategies for Assessing and Managing Organizational Stakeholders," *Academy of Management Executive,* Vol. V, No. 2 (May, 1991), 61–75.
10. Ibid., 64.
11. MacMillan and Jones, 66–70.
12. Savage, Nix, Whitehead, and Blair, 65.
13. Ibid., 72.

PART TWO BUSINESS ETHICS AND MANAGEMENT

4 Business Ethics Fundamentals

5 Personal and Organizational Ethics

6 Ethical Issues in the Global Arena

CHAPTER **FOUR**

Business Ethics Fundamentals

CHAPTER OBJECTIVES

After studying this chapter, you should be able to:

◆ Explain how the public regards business ethics.

◆ Provide a definition of business ethics and appreciate the complexities of making ethical judgments.

◆ Enumerate and discuss the four important ethics questions.

◆ Identify and explain three types of management ethics.

◆ Recognize the challenges in making moral management actionable.

◆ Describe the three levels in developing moral judgment.

◆ Identify and discuss the elements of moral judgment.

Because interest in the modern period in business ethics spans about 30 years, two conclusions may be drawn. First, interest in business ethics has heightened for each of the last three decades. Second, the interest in business ethics seems to be spurred by major headline-grabbing scandals. Certainly, there has been an ebb and flow of interest on society's part. But it has grown to a preoccupation and, some might say, to an obsession.

In the modern period, the interest in business ethics was stimulated by a number of cases in 1960 in which electrical equipment manufacturers were indicted for alleged conspiracy to fix prices and restrict competition. The following year, the United States Secretary of Commerce formed a Business Ethics Advisory Council, which had as its objective the voluntary improvement of business conduct.

In 1961, Raymond Baumhart published his now-classic work, "How Ethical Are Businessmen?"[1] Although his survey of 1,700 *Harvard Business Review* readers did not indicate a prevalence of unethical practices in the private sector, executives did admit and point out numerous generally accepted practices in their industries that they considered unethical.

A number of books and articles on the subject of business ethics were published in the middle and late 1960s, but preoccupation with ethical behavior did not set in again until 1974 with Watergate and its aftermath. Since that time, a profusion of headline stories has suggested a growing interest in the ethical behavior of business people.

In 1982, *U.S. News & World Report* published two important findings that caught the public eye. First, it found that of the 500 largest corporations in the United States, 115 had been convicted in the last decade of at least one major crime or had paid civil penalties for serious misbehavior. Second, it found that among the 25 biggest firms—with annual sales running from 15 to 108 billion dollars—the rate of documented misbehavior had been even greater.[2] The who's who of firms with convictions or civil penalties included the backbone of the American business system: Exxon, Mobil, GM, AT&T, IBM, Gulf, Sears, GE, K Mart, Bank of America, and others.[3]

Ethical scandals of the mid-1980s included E. F. Hutton (1985), which pleaded guilty to federal charges stemming from an elaborate check-kiting scheme. General Dynamics (1985), the second-largest U.S. defense contractor, was the target of a barrage of embarrassing revelations including a criminal indictment for conspiring to defraud the Pentagon. Morton Thiokol, manufacturer of the booster rocket in the 1986 space shuttle *Challenger* explosions was implicated for going along with NASA to launch the rocket though it knew the weather conditions were not appropriate. The famed 1986 Ivan Boesky insider-trading scandal called into question the fundamental integrity of the total financial system in the United States.

The mega-scandal of the late 1980s that spilled over into the 1990s was the Savings and Loan (S&L) industry debacle. The S&L scandal has been referred to as the nation's largest fiscal scandal and has resulted not only in the indictment and conviction of hundreds of S&L executives for fraud but the destruction of the industry as well. The most noteworthy figure of the S&L scandal was Charles Keating, former chairman of Lincoln Savings and Loan in Irvine, California. It is estimated that the S&L debacle could eventually cost Americans as much as $1 trillion dollars, as the U.S. government has to absorb the cost of failing S&Ls. By 1990, the Justice Department had convicted and sentenced over 300 S&L felons, well over half of whom were jailed.

To give the reader an appreciation of the kinds of issues we are discussing under the rubric of business ethics, Figure 4-1 on pages 87 and 88 presents an Inventory of Ethical Issues in Business compiled by the Josephson Institute. Here we see business ethics issues categorized based on stakeholder relationships.

Against this backdrop, we plan to discuss business ethics, specifically, in this chapter and the next two. In this chapter we will introduce business ethics fundamentals. In Chapter 5 we will consider personal and organizational ethics. In Chapter 6, our attention will turn to the international sphere when we discuss ethical issues in the global arena.

BUSINESS ETHICS AND THE PUBLIC

The public's view of business's ethics has never been very high. Anecdotal evidence suggests that many people see business ethics as essentially a contradiction in terms and that there is only a fine line between a business executive and a crook. It is useful for our discussion here, however, to look at some of the actual surveys of business ethics that have been taken.

The Gallup Poll

Perhaps the most reliable expression of public attitudes on business ethics may be found in the Gallup Poll, which regularly surveys public opinion of social and political issues. Gallup periodically quizzes the public about its feelings about the ethics of business executives as well as other professions. The latest data available are from the 1990 poll. According to this poll, business executives' honesty and ethical standards were rated as follows:[4]

High or Very High	25%
Average	55%
Low or Very Low	14%
No Opinion	6%

To place these findings into perspective, it is useful to compare them with previous periods. Figure 4-2 on page 89 presents these same statistics for a number of years since 1976. Over this time span, the combined categories of "Very High" and "High" have ranged from a low of 16 percent in 1988 to a high of 25 percent in 1990. Even in the best year, business executives get only a modest amount of

FIGURE 4-1   Inventory of Ethical Issues in Business

This checklist is designed to stimulate thought and discussion on important ethical concerns in your company and the larger business community.

**For each of the following issues indicate whether ethical problems are:
5 = Very serious; 4 = Serious; 3 = Not very serious;
2 = Not a problem; 1 = No opinion.**

Column I = In the business world in general   Column II = In your company

Employee–Employer Relations

____ ____ 1. Work ethic—giving a full day's work for a full day's pay
____ ____ 2. Petty theft (i.e., supplies, telephone, photocopying, etc.)
____ ____ 3. Cheating on expense accounts
____ ____ 4. Employee acceptance of gifts or favors from vendors
____ ____ 5. Distortion or falsification of internal reports
____ ____ 6. Cheating or overreaching on benefits (sick days, insurance, etc.)

Employer–Employee Relations

____ ____ 7. Sexual or racial discrimination in hiring, promotion, or pay
____ ____ 8. Sexual harassment
____ ____ 9. Invasions of employee privacy
____ ____ 10. Unsafe or unhealthy working conditions
____ ____ 11. Discouragement of internal criticism re: unfair, illegal, or improper activities
____ ____ 12. Unfair or insensitive handling of assignment changes or major re-organizations
____ ____ 13. Improper dealing with persons with AIDS
____ ____ 14. Failure to give honest, fair, and timely work appraisals
____ ____ 15. Recruiting for employee's replacement without telling employee being replaced
____ ____ 16. Using strategies or technical justifications to deny employees earned benefits
____ ____ 17. Dealing peremptorily or unfairly with employee complaints
____ ____ 18. Misleading employees about the likelihood of lay-offs, terminations, or job changes
____ ____ 19. Inadequate training or supervision to assure employee's success
____ ____ 20. Inadequate participation by qualified staff in major policy decisions
____ ____ 21. Unfair demands on or expectations of paid staff
____ ____ 22. Inadequate compensation
____ ____ 23. Inadequate recognition, appreciation, or other psychic rewards to staff

(continued)

FIGURE 4-1 (continued)

This checklist is designed to stimulate thought and discussion on important ethical concerns in your company and the larger business community.

**For each of the following issues indicate whether ethical problems are:
5 = Very serious; 4 = Serious; 3 = Not very serious;
2 = Not a problem; 1 = No opinion.**

Column I = In the business world in general   Column II = In your company

Employee–Employee Relations

____ ____ 24. Inappropriate blame-shifting or credit-taking to protect or advance personal careers
____ ____ 25. Unhealthy competition among employees about "turf," assignments, budget, etc.
____ ____ 26. Inadequate communication among departments and divisions for the wrong reasons
____ ____ 27. Inadequate mutual support and teamsmanship; individuals focus primarily on their own narrow jobs

Company–Customer Relations

____ ____ 28. Unfair product pricing
____ ____ 29. Deceptive marketing/advertising
____ ____ 30. Unsafe or unhealthy products
____ ____ 31. Unfair and/or legalistic handling of customer complaints
____ ____ 32. Discourtesy or arrogance

Company–Shareholder Relations

____ ____ 33. Excessive compensation/top management
____ ____ 34. Self protective management policies (golden parachutes, poison pills, greenmail)
____ ____ 35. Mismanagement of corporate assets or opportunities
____ ____ 36. Public reports and/or financial statements which distort actual performance

Company–Community/Public Interest

____ ____ 37. Injury to the environment
____ ____ 38. Undue influence on the political process through lobbying, PACs, etc.
____ ____ 39. Payoffs, "grease," or bribes to union or public officials
____ ____ 40. Payoffs, "grease," or bribes in foreign countries
____ ____ 41. Doing business in countries with inhumane or anti-American policies (e.g., South Africa, Iran)
____ ____ 42. Inadequate corporate philanthropy
____ ____ 43. Inadequate community involvement

Source: Reprinted with permission © Josephson Institute of Ethics, *Ethics: Easier Said Than Done*, Vol. 2, No. 1, 1989.

FIGURE 4-2 Ethics and Honesty—Trend
(Percent saying "very high" or "high")

	1976	1977	1981	1983	1985	1988	1990
Druggists/pharmacists	NA	NA	59%	61%	65%	66%	62%
Clergy	NA	61%	63	64	67	60	55
Medical doctors	56%	51	50	52	58	53	52
Dentists	NA	NA	52	51	56	51	52
College teachers	49	46	45	47	53	54	51
Engineers	49	46	48	45	53	48	50
Policemen	NA	37	44	41	47	47	49
Funeral directors	NA	26	30	29	32	24	35
Bankers	NA	39	39	38	38	26	32
TV reporters/commentators	NA	NA	36	33	33	22	32
Journalists	33	33	32	28	31	23	30
Business executives	20	19	19	18	23	16	25
Newspaper reporters	NA	NA	30	26	29	22	24
Senators	19	19	20	16	23	19	24
Lawyers	25	26	25	24	27	18	22
Local officeholders	NA	14	14	16	18	14	21
Building contractors	23	18	19	18	21	22	20
Congressmen	14	16	15	14	20	16	20
State officeholders	NA	11	12	13	15	11	17
Real estate agents	NA	13	14	13	15	13	16
Labor union leaders	12	13	14	12	13	14	15
Stockbrokers	NA	NA	21	19	20	13	14
Insurance salesmen	NA	15	11	13	10	10	13
Advertising practitioners	11	10	9	9	12	7	12
Car salesmen	NA	8	6	6	5	6	6

Source: *The Gallup Poll Monthly*, February 1990, 24.

support for high ethics. It is encouraging, however, to note that the 1990 ranking is the highest achieved since 1976.

It is also useful to compare the public's perception of business executives' ethics with those of other professionals. Such a comparison finds that business ranks about in the middle of the pack of those considered. Although business executives do not achieve the high rankings of such groups as pharmacists, clergy, doctors, and dentists, they do rank higher than senators, congressmen, and state office holders.[5] Such a contrast reveals some possible ethical problems in the political arena.

It is difficult to pinpoint the exact public sentiment on business ethics today. In general, however, it is safe to conclude that the public thinks business ethics is at least somewhat suspect and that it would like to see improvements. There is sentiment that business is only one of the major institutions that have questionable ethics today, but business is the focus of our attention here.

If we were to make judgments about the current state of business ethics by reading the daily newspapers or news magazines or watching "60 Minutes" or "20/20" on television, we might quickly reach the conclusion that it is in a shambles and that behind every business door an evil-minded individual is lurking. To be honest, we must ask three questions: (1) Has business ethics really deteriorated? (2) Are the media reporting ethical problems more frequently and vigorously? (3) Is it actually society that is changing so that once-accepted practices are now considered unacceptable by the public?

Has Business Ethics Really Deteriorated?

Unfortunately, there is no scientific way to determine whether business ethics has really deteriorated. Max Ways's description of a statistical analysis (the twentieth century's favorite kind of investigation), aimed at answering the question, "How widespread is corporate misconduct?" is enlightening. He says that to describe such a project would demonstrate its impossibility. He argues that the researcher would have to count the transgressions publicly exposed in a certain period of time. Then the total of known misdeeds would have to be correlated with the trillions and trillions of business transactions that occur daily. He concludes:

> If we assume (recklessly) that a believable estimate of total transactions could be made, then the sum of the publicly known malfeasances almost certainly would be a minute fraction of the whole. At this point the investigator would have to abandon the conclusion that the incidence of business misconduct is so low as to be insignificant.[6]

In fact, no such study has ever been attempted. Public opinion polls might be able to gather data about the current state of business ethics.

Are the Media Reporting Ethical Problems More Vigorously?

There is no doubt that the media are reporting ethical problems more frequently and fervently. Spurred on by Watergate in 1974 and the post-Watergate moral climate, the media have found business ethics and, indeed, ethics questions among all institutions a subject of sustaining interest.

Of particular interest in recent years has been the in-depth investigative reporting of business scandals as found on such TV shows as "60 Minutes," "20/20," "A Current Affair" and "PrimeTime Live." Such investigations keep business scandals in the public eye and make it difficult to assess whether public opinion polls are actually reflecting business ethics as they actually are or are just the reaction to the latest scandal.

Is It Society That Is Actually Changing?

We would definitely make this argument here as we did in Chapter 1. Many business managers subscribe to this belief. W. Michael Blumenthal, former United States Secretary of the Treasury and chief executive officer of the Bendix Corporation, is one of the leading advocates of this view. He argues:

> It seems to me that the root causes of the questionable and illegal corporate activities that have come to light recently . . . can be traced to the sweeping changes that have taken place in our society and throughout the world and to the unwillingness of many in business to adjust to these changes.[7]

He goes on to say: "People in business have not suddenly become immoral. What has changed are the contexts in which corporate decisions are made, the demands that are being made on business, and the nature of what is considered proper corporate conduct."[8]

Although it would be difficult to prove Blumenthal's thesis, it is an attractive one. You do not have to make a lengthy investigation of some of today's business practices to realize that a good number of what are now called unethical practices are ones that were at one time acceptable. Or it may be that the practices never really were acceptable to the public but that because they were not known, they were tolerated, thus causing no moral dilemma for the public.

Figure 4-3 illustrates how the ethical problem today may be more severe than it once was as a result of the public's expectations of business ethical behavior rising more rapidly than actual business ethics. Note that actual business ethics is assumed to be improving but not as quickly as public expectations are rising. The magnitude of the current ethical problem, therefore, is seen here as a function of rapidly rising societal expectations.

FIGURE 4-3 Business Ethics Today Versus an Earlier Period

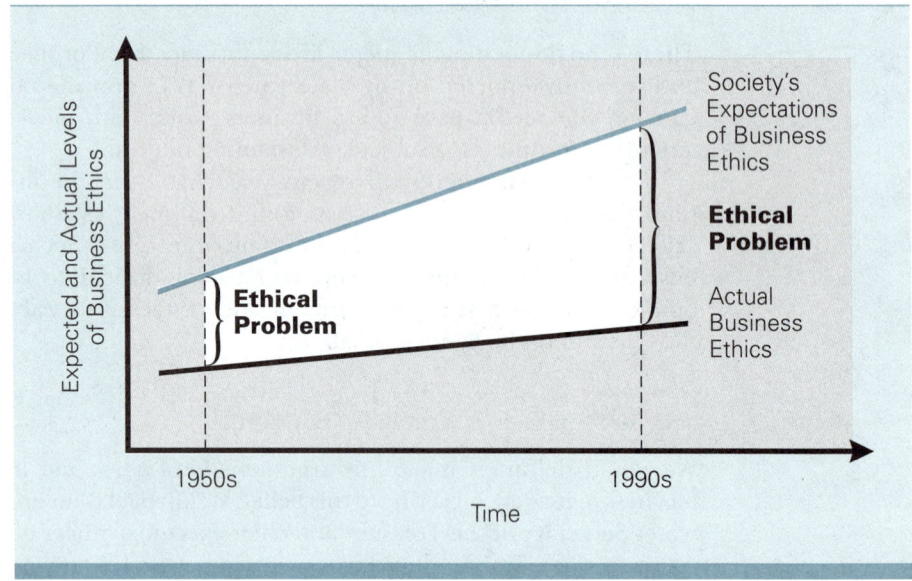

WHAT DOES BUSINESS ETHICS MEAN?

In Chapter 2 we discussed the ethical responsibilities of business as if we all knew exactly what that meant. To be sure, we all have a general idea of what business ethics means, but here we would like to probe the topic deeper. To understand business ethics we need to appreciate the relationship between ethics and morality.

Ethics is the discipline dealing with what is good and bad and with moral duty and obligation. Ethics can also be regarded as a set of moral principles or values. Morality is a doctrine or system of moral conduct. Moral conduct refers to that which relates to principles of right and wrong in behavior. In a sense, then, we can think of ethics and morality as being so similar to one another that we may use them interchangeably to refer to the study of right and wrong behavior.

Business ethics, therefore, is concerned with good and bad or right and wrong behavior that takes place within a business context. Concepts of right and wrong are increasingly being interpreted today to include the more difficult or subtle questions of fairness, justice, and equity.

Two key branches of moral philosophy, or ethics, are descriptive ethics and normative ethics. It is important to distinguish between the two because they each take a different perspective. *Descriptive ethics* is concerned with describing, characterizing, and studying the morality of a people, a culture, or a society. It also compares and contrasts different moral codes, systems, practices, beliefs, or values.[9] In descriptive business ethics, therefore, our focus is on learning what is occurring in the realm of behavior, actions, decisions, policies, and practices of business firms, managers or, perhaps, specific industries. Descriptive ethics focuses on "what is" or "what are" the prevailing ethical standards in the business community.

By contrast, *normative ethics* is concerned with supplying and justifying a coherent moral system. Normative ethics seeks to uncover, develop, and justify basic moral principles that are intended to guide behavior, actions, or decisions.[10] Normative business ethics, therefore, seeks to propose some principle or principles for distinguishing right from wrong in the business context. It deals more with "what ought to be" or "what ought *not* to be" in terms of business behavior. Normative ethics is concerned with establishing norms or standards by which business ethics might be guided or judged.

In our study of business ethics we need to be ever mindful of this distinction between descriptive and normative perspectives. It is tempting to observe the frequency of a particular practice in business (for example, padding expense accounts, deceptive advertising) and conclude that because so many are doing it (descriptive ethics), it must be acceptable behavior. Normative ethics would insist that a practice be justified on the basis of some ethical principle, argument, or rationale before being considered acceptable. Normative ethics demands a more meaningful moral anchor than just "everyone is doing it."

In this chapter and the next, we will discuss three major approaches to determining what ethical business conduct is: (1) the conventional approach, (2) the principles approach, and (3) the ethical tests approach. We will discuss the conventional approach to business ethics in this chapter and the other two approaches in Chapter 5.

The Conventional Approach

The conventional approach to business ethics is essentially an approach whereby we compare an act, decision, or behavior with the prevailing norms of acceptability. The major challenge with this approach is answering the questions "Whose norms do we use?" and "What norms are prevailing?" There is considerable room for variability on both of these issues. With respect to whose norms are used as the basis for ethical judgments, the conventional approach would consider as legitimate norms emanating from family, friends, the local community, one's employer, and so on. In addition, one's conscience, or the individual, would be seen by many as a legitimate source of ethical norms. A recent Frank and Ernest cartoon pokes fun at the use of conscience. A sign on the wall reads "Tonight's Lecture: Moral Philosophy." Then it shows Frank saying to Ernest—"I'd let my conscience be my guide, but I'm in enough trouble already!" Figure 4-4 illustrates some of the sources of norms that come to bear on the individual and which might be used in varying circumstances under the conventional approach.

In many circumstances, the conventional approach to ethics is useful and applicable. What does a person do, however, if norms from one source conflict with norms from another source? Also, how can we be sure that societal norms are really right or defensible? Culture in our society sends us many and often conflicting messages about what appropriate behavior is. We get these messages

FIGURE 4-4   Sources of Ethical Norms Communicated to Individuals

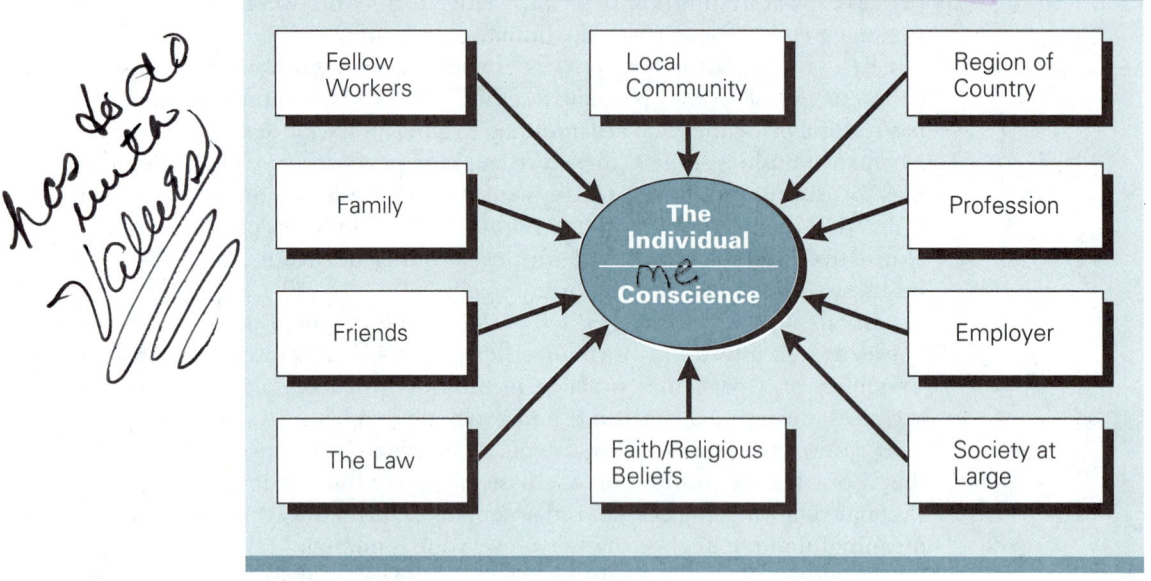

from television, movies, music, and other sources. An interesting example of the kind of message television sends occurred one night on "Dallas" when J. R. Ewing blurted out to a colleague this sage advice: "Once you give up integrity, the rest is a piece of cake!" We might call this tidbit of wisdom "J. R.'s Rule of Ethics." At first blush, this appears to most of us as humorous. It is just possible, however, that an impressionable young person might see this and hundreds of other references like it and conclude that dishonesty is really the standard in business.

Another example of the conflicting messages people get today from society occurs in the realm of sexual harassment in the workplace. On the one hand, today's television, movies, advertisements, and music are replete with sexual innuendo and treatment of women as sex objects. This would suggest that such behavior is normal. On the other hand, law and the courts are stringently prohibiting any kind of sexual gesture or innuendo in the workplace. As we will see in a later chapter, it does not take much sexual innuendo to constitute a "hostile work environment" and a sex discrimination charge under Title VII of the Civil Rights Act. Here we see a norm arising from society clashing with a norm evolving from employment law.

Ethics Versus the Law

We have made various references to ethics versus the law. In Chapter 2, we said that ethical behavior resides above behavior required by the law. This is the generally accepted view of ethics. We should make it clear, however, that in many respects the law and ethics overlap. To appreciate this, you need to recognize that the law embodies notions of ethics. That is, the law may be seen as a reflection of what society thinks are minimal standards of conduct and behavior. Both law and ethics have to do with what is deemed right or wrong, but law reflects society's *codified* ethics. Therefore, if a person breaks a law or violates a regulation, he or she is also behaving unethically. In spite of this overlap, we continue to talk about desirable ethical behavior as behavior that extends beyond what is required by law. Viewed from the standpoint of minimums, we would certainly say that obedience to the law is a minimum standard of behavior. In addition, we should make note of the fact that the law does not address all realms in which ethical questions might be raised.

Making Ethical Judgments

When decisions are made about what is ethical (right, just, fair), there is room for variability on several counts (see Figure 4-5). Three key elements go into the decision. First, we have the behavior or act that has been committed. Second, we compare the act with prevailing norms of acceptability—that is, society's or some other standard of what is right or wrong. Third, we must recognize that value judgments are being made by someone as to what really occurred (the actual behavior) and what prevailing norms of acceptability really are. This means that two different persons may look at the same behavior, compare it with their concept of what prevailing norms are, and reach different conclusions as to whether the behavior was ethical or not. This becomes quite complex as perceptions of what is ethical inevitably lead to the difficult task of ranking different values against one another.

If we can put aside for a moment the fact that perpetual differences about an incident do exist, and the fact that we differ among ourselves because of our personal philosophies of right and wrong, we are still left with the problematical task of determining society's prevailing norms of acceptability of business behavior. As a whole, members of society generally agree at a very high level of abstraction that certain behaviors are wrong. However, the consensus tends to disintegrate as we move from abstract to specific situations.

Let us illustrate with a business example. We might all agree with the general dictum that "You should not steal someone else's property." At a high level of abstraction (as a general precept), we would have consensus on this. But as we look at specific situations, our consensus tends to disappear. Is it acceptable to take home from work such things as pencils, pens, paper clips, paper, staplers, adding machines, and calculators? Is it acceptable to use the company telephone for personal long-distance calls? Is it acceptable to use company gasoline for private use or to pad expense accounts? What if everyone else is doing it?

What is interesting in this example is that we would likely get more consensus in principle than in practice. A number of people who would say these practices are not acceptable would privately engage in them. Furthermore, a person who would not think of shoplifting even the smallest item from a local store would take

FIGURE 4-5   Making Ethical Judgments

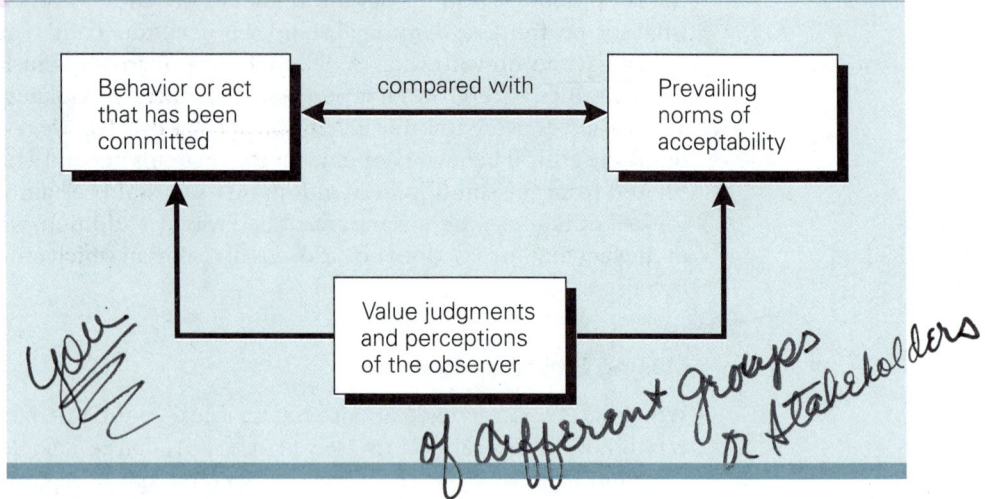

pencils and paper home from work on a regular basis. A cartoon depicting the "Born Loser" is related to this discussion. In the first panel the father admonishes his son Wilberforce in the following way: "You know how I feel about stealing. Now tomorrow I want you to return every one of those pencils to school." In the second panel, Father says to Wilberforce, "I'll bring you all the pencils you need from work." This is an example of the classic double standard.

Thus, determinations of what is ethical and what is not involve judgments being made on three counts:

1. What is the true nature of the event, act, or decision that occurred?
2. What are society's (or business's) prevailing norms of acceptability?
3. What value judgments are being made by someone about the event, and what are that person's perceptions of applicable norms?

The human factor in the situation thus introduces the problem of perception and values.

The conventional approach to business ethics can be valuable because we all need to be aware of and sensitive to the total environment in which we exist. It has limitations, however, and we need to be cognizant of these as well. The most serious danger is that of falling into an ethical relativism where we pick and choose which source of norms we wish to use based on what will justify our current actions or maximize our freedom. In the next chapter we will argue that a principles approach is needed to augment the conventional approach. The principles approach looks to the general guides to ethical decision making that come from moral philosophy.

THE IMPORTANT ETHICS QUESTIONS

It is hard to do justice to ethics discussions in such a short space, but we ought to provide some "big picture" perspective that could legitimately be asked of ethics in general or of business ethics in particular. Philosophers have concepts and terminology to make this sound more academic, but let us approach it, as Otto Bremer has done, by starting with four apparently simple but really different kinds of questions:

1. What is?
2. What ought to be?
3. How to get from what is to what ought to be?
4. What is our motivation in all this?[11]

These four questions capture the core of what ethics is all about. They force an examination of what *really is,* what *ought* to be, how we close the gap between what *is* and *ought* to be, and what our *motivation* is for doing all this.

Before we discuss each question briefly, let us suggest that these four questions may be asked at four different levels: the level of the individual (the personal level), the level of the organization, the level of the industry or profession, and finally the societal level. Figure 4-6 depicts a matrix of the four major questions and the four levels of business ethics at which the questions may or should be asked.

What Is?

This question forces us to face the reality of what is going on in an ethical sense in business. Ideally, it is a factual, scientific, or descriptive question. Its purpose is to help us understand the reality of the ethics we find before us. As we discussed earlier when we were describing the nature of making ethical judgments, it is not always easy to state exactly what the "real" situation is. This is because we are humans, and humans make mistakes when they "sense" what is happening. Also, we are conditioned by our personal beliefs, values, and biases, and these factors affect what we see or sense. Or we may see real conditions for what they are but fail to think in terms of alternatives or in terms of "what ought to be." Think of the difficulty you might have in attempting to describe "what is" with respect to business ethics at the personal, organizational, industry/professional, and societal levels, depicted in Figure 4-6. The questions then become:

- What are your personal ethics?
- What are your organization's ethics?
- What are the ethics of your industry or profession?
- What are society's ethics?

FIGURE 4-6   The Important Ethics Questions

Question / Level	1 What is?	2 What ought to be?	3 Getting from 1 to 2?	4 Motivation in all this?
Personal				
Organizational				
Industry or Professional				
Societal				

What Ought to Be?

This is quite a different question from the first question. It is certainly not a scientific question. It is a question that seldom gets answered directly, particularly in a managerial setting. Managers are used to identifying alternatives and choosing the best one, but seldom is this done with questions that entail moral content or the "rightness" of a decision. Examples of this question in a business setting might be:

- How *ought* we to treat our aging employees whose productivity is declining?
- How safe *ought* we to make this product, knowing fully well we can't pass all the costs on to the consumer?
- How clean an environment *should* we aim for?
- What *ought* we to do with this tender offer just made by a hostile takeover specialist?

At a corporate planning seminar several years ago, the leader suggested that if you are the president of a large corporation, the place to start planning is with a vision of society, not with where you want to be 5 or 10 years into the future. What kind of world do you want to have? How does your industry or your firm fit into that world?[12] An executive cannot just walk into the office one day and say, "I had a vision last night," and expect many adherents.[13] But that does not make the question or the vision invalid. It just suggests that we must approach the "What ought to be?" question at a more practical level. There are ample issues to which this question can be applied in the everyday life of a manager. Therefore, such lofty, visionary exercises are not necessary.

How to Get from What Is to What Ought to Be

This question represents the challenge of bridging where we are with where we ought to be. Therefore, it represents a real-world dimension. We may discuss endlessly where we "ought" to be in terms of our own personal ethics or the ethics of our firm, of our industry, or of society. And as we move further away from the individual, we have less control or influence over the "ought to be" question.

When faced with these ideas as represented by our "what ought to be" questions, we may find that from a practical point of view we cannot achieve our ideal. This doesn't mean we shouldn't have asked the question in the first place. Our "ought to be" questions become goals or objectives. They become benchmarks that help us to measure progress.

In all managerial situations we are faced with this challenge of balancing what we ought to do with what we must or can do. The notions of Leslie Weatherhead in his book *The Will of God* could be adapted to our discussion here. He refers to God's intentional will, circumstantial will, and ultimate will. Looked at from a managerial or ethics point of view, we might think in terms of what we intend to accomplish, what circumstances permit us to accomplish, and what we ultimately are able to accomplish. These ideas interject a measure of realism into our efforts to close the gap between where we are and where we want to be.

This is also the stage in which managerial skill, competence, and strategy come into play. The first step in managerial problem solving is identifying the problem (what "is"). Next comes identifying where we want to be (the "ought" question). Then comes the managerial challenge of closing the gap. "Gap analysis" sets the stage for concrete business action.

What Is Our Motivation in All This?

Pragmatic business people do not like to dwell on the motivation for being ethical because so often it reveals some manipulative or self-centered motive. At one level it is perhaps desirable not to discuss motivation because isn't it really actions that count? If someone makes a $100 contribution to a charitable cause, is it fair to ask whether he or she did it (1) because he or she really believes in the cause (altruistic motivation), or (2) because he or she just wanted a tax deduction (selfish motive)? Most of us would agree that it is better that the person made the contribution rather than not making it, regardless of motive.

Ideally, we would hope that people would be ethical because they intrinsically see that being ethical is a better way to live or manage. What kind of world (or organization) would you prefer to be in? One where people do good things (behave ethically) because there are selfish or instrumental reasons for doing so, or a world (or organization) where people really believe in what they are doing?

We will accept the former, but the latter is more desirable. We will be better off in the long run if "right" managerial practices are motivated by the knowledge that there is inherent value in ethical behavior.

This can be compared to the situation in organizations where managers are attempting to motivate their workers. If a manager is interested only in greater productivity and sees that being "concerned" about employees' welfare will achieve this goal, he or she had better be prepared for the fact that employees may see through the "game playing" and eventually rebel against the manager's effort. On the other hand, employees can see when management is genuinely concerned about their welfare, and they will be responsive to these well-motivated efforts. This is borne out in practice. You can look at two companies that on the surface appear to have identical personnel policies. In one company the employees know and feel they are being manipulated, and in the other company there is confidence that management really does care.[14]

THREE TYPES OF MANAGEMENT ETHICS

In attempting to understand the basic concepts of business ethics, it is useful to think in terms of some ethical models that might describe different types of management ethics.[15] These models should provide some useful base points for discussion and comparison. The media have focused so much on immoral or unethical business behavior that it is easy to forget or not think about the possibility of other ethical styles. For example, scant attention has been given to the distinction that may be made between those activities that are *immoral* versus those that are *amoral*; similarly, little attention has been given to contrasting these two forms of behavior with ethical or *moral* management.

Believing that there is value in developing descriptive models for purposes of clearer understanding, here we will describe, compare, and contrast what might be termed three types of ethical management: (1) immoral management, (2) amoral management, and (3) moral management. A major goal is to develop a clearer understanding of the full gamut of management styles in which ethics or morality is a major dimension. By seeing these styles come to life through description and example, managers are expected to be in an improved position to assess their own ethical styles and those of other organizational members (supervisors, subordinates, and peers). Of course, we presume that they would desire to do this in light of the increasingly important role that ethics is coming to assume in business, in the professions, and in other organizations today.

Another central objective is to identify more accurately the amoral management style—a style often overlooked in the human rush to classify things as good or bad, moral or immoral. In a later section we will discuss the elements of moral judgment that must be developed if the transition to moral management is to succeed. Figure 4-7 portrays these three styles of management.

FIGURE 4-7 Three Types of Management Ethics

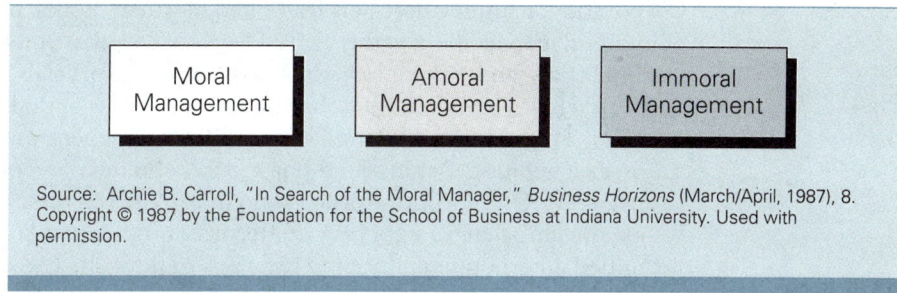

Source: Archie B. Carroll, "In Search of the Moral Manager," *Business Horizons* (March/April, 1987), 8. Copyright © 1987 by the Foundation for the School of Business at Indiana University. Used with permission.

A more detailed development of each management style is valuable in coming to understand the range of ethics that leaders may intentionally or unintentionally display. Let us consider the two extremes first—immoral and moral management—and then amoral management.

Immoral Management

Using *immoral* and *unethical* as synonyms, **immoral management** is a style that not only is devoid of ethical principles or precepts but also implies a positive and active opposition to what is ethical. Here management decisions, behaviors, or actions are discordant with ethical principles. This view holds that management's motives are selfish and that it cares only or principally about the company's gains. If management's activity is actively opposed to what is regarded as ethical, this implies that management knows right from wrong and chooses to do wrong. Thus, its motives are deemed greedy or selfish. According to this style, management's goals are profitability and organizational success at almost any price. Management does not care about others' claims to be treated fairly or justly.

What about management's orientation toward the law, considering that law is often regarded as an embodiment of minimal ethics? Immoral management regards legal standards as barriers that management must overcome to accomplish what it wants. Immoral management would just as soon engage in illegal activity as in immoral or unethical activity.

Operating Strategy. The operating strategy of immoral management is focused on exploiting opportunities for corporate or personal gain. An active opposition to what is moral would suggest that managers cut corners anywhere and everywhere it appears useful. Thus, the key operating question guiding management is, "*Can we make money with this action, decision, or behavior regardless of what it takes?*" Implicit in this question is that nothing else matters, or matters very little.

Illustrative Cases. Examples of immoral management abound. The Frigitemp Corporation, manufacturer of refrigerated mortuary boxes, provides an example of immoral management at the highest levels of corporate hierarchy. In litigation, criminal trials, and federal investigations, corporate officials including the president and chairman admitted to having made millions of dollars in payoffs to get business. They admitted taking kickbacks from suppliers, embezzling corporate funds, exaggerating earnings in reports to shareholders, and providing prostitutes to customers. One corporate official said that greed was their undoing. They were so busy stealing that they got caught. Records indicate that Frigitemp's executives permitted a corporate culture of chicanery to flourish. The company eventually went bankrupt because of management's misconduct.[16]

Brown & Root, Inc., which had been building a nuclear power plant for Texas Utilities, fired a quality control inspector in 1982. It fired two other inspectors during the next year. Evidence gathered by the government suggests that the inspectors may have been doing their jobs too well. The inspectors claimed that they were discharged after resisting orders from management to overlook flaws in the plant. The Nuclear Regulatory Commission (NRC) began conducting inquiries into the cases of dozens of inspectors who maintained that managers pressured them to ignore defects because the repairs might delay construction, thus incurring added costs and delays.[17]

The Securities and Exchange Commission (SEC) accused Southland Corporation, a convenience-store operator and independent gasoline retailer, of paying kickbacks to big buyers of its dairy products. According to the accusation, the company disregarded minimum pricing laws in about eight states and dispensed almost $2 million in what it called "dairy discounts." A number of the major customers received monthly kickback checks in the form of anonymous cashier's checks from a bank in Utah.[18]

All of the above are examples of immoral management where executives' decisions or orders were self-centered, actively opposed to what is right, and focused on achieving organizational success at whatever the cost and cutting corners where it was useful. These decisions were made without regard to the possible consequences of such concerns as safety or fairness to others.

Moral Management

At the opposite extreme from immoral management is moral management. **Moral management** conforms to standards of ethical behavior or professional standards of conduct. Although it is not always crystal clear what ethical standards prevail, moral management strives to be ethical in terms of its focus on ethical norms, professional standards of conduct, motives, goals, orientation toward the law, and general operating strategy.

In contrast to the selfish motives in immoral management, moral management aspires to succeed but only within the confines of sound ethical precepts—that is, standards predicated on such norms as fairness, justice, and due process. Management's motives, therefore, might be termed fair, balanced, or unselfish.

Organizational goals continue to stress profitability but only within the confines of legal obedience and sensitivity to ethical standards. Management, therefore, pursues its objectives of profitability, legality, and ethicalness as both required and desirable. Moral management would not pursue profits at the expense of the law and sound ethics. Indeed, the focus here would be not only on the letter of the law but on the spirit of the law as well. The law would be viewed as a minimal standard of ethical behavior, since moral management strives to operate at a level above what the law mandates.

Operating Strategy. The operating strategy of moral management would be to live by sound ethical standards, seeking out only those economic opportunities that the organization could pursue within the confines of ethical behavior. The company would assume a leadership position when ethical dilemmas arose. The central question guiding management actions, decisions, and behaviors would be, "*Is this action, decision, or behavior fair to us and all stakeholders involved?*"

Illustrative Cases. Moral management can be illustrated by companies in the toy industry. Such companies thoroughly test toys before releasing them for commercial production and sales. The toy industry has now adopted some of the strictest standards for flammability. Other standards have been set for toxicity, safety, and durability. The safety testing process at Hasbro-Bradley, Inc., for example, in one year eliminated nearly 2,000 toy concepts before the company chose the 100 toys it planned to produce. Toys also undergo psychological testing as companies attempt to screen out those toys that might have a lasting, negative emotional impact on children.[19]

We should stress at this time that all organizations engaging in moral management have not done so all along. These companies, including the toy industry, arrived at this posture after years or decades of rising consumer expectations, increased government regulations, lawsuits, and pressure from social and consumer activists. We must think of moral management, therefore, as a pragmatic posture that in many instances evolved over time. If we hold management to an unreasonable 100 percent historical moral purity test, then no management will fill the bill. Rather, we should consider moral those managements that now see the enlightened self-interest of responding in an ethical way.

An excellent example of moral management taking the initiative in displaying ethical leadership is provided by McCulloch Corporation, a manufacturer of chain saws. Chain saws are notoriously dangerous. The Consumer Product Safety Commission estimated that in 1981 there were 123,000 medically attended injuries involving chain saws, up from 71,000 in 1976. In spite of these statistics, the Chain Saw Manufacturers Association has fought mandatory safety standards. The association has claimed that the accident statistics were inflated and did not offer any justification for mandatory regulations. Manufacturers support voluntary standards, though some of them say that when chain brakes, a major safety device, are offered as an option, they do not sell. Apparently, consumers do not have adequate knowledge of the risks inherent in using chain saws.

McCulloch became dissatisfied with the Chain Saw Manufacturers Association's refusal to support higher standards of safety and withdrew from it in 1978. Chain brakes have been standard on McCulloch saws since 1975 and are mandatory for most saws produced in Finland, Britain, and Australia. A Swedish Company, Husqvarna, Inc., now installs chain brakes on saws it sells in the United States. Statistics from the Quebec Logging Association and Sweden demonstrate that kickback-related accidents were reduced by about 80 percent after the mandatory installation of safety standards, including chain brakes.[20]

McCulloch is an example of moral management. After attempting and failing to persuade its association to adopt a higher ethical standard that would greatly reduce injuries, it took a courageous action and withdrew from the association.

Amoral Management

In some respects, *amoral management* appears to be a hybrid between moral and immoral management. It is not just a middle position on the continuum, however. Conceptually it has been positioned between the other two, but it is different in kind from both. Actually there are two kinds of amoral management. First, there is *intentional amoral management.* Amoral managers of this type do not factor ethical considerations into their decisions, actions, and behaviors because they believe business activity resides outside the sphere to which moral judgments apply. These managers are neither moral nor immoral. They simply think that different rules apply in business than in other realms of life.

Second, there is *unintentional amoral management.* Like intentional amoral managers, these managers do not think about business activity in ethical terms. These managers simply are casual about, careless about, or inattentive to the fact that their decisions and actions may have negative or deleterious effects on others. These managers lack ethical perception and moral awareness; that is, they blithely go through their organizational lives not thinking that what they are doing has an ethical dimension to it. These managers are well intentioned but are either too insensitive or too egocentric to consider the affect of their behavior on others.

Amoral management pursues profitability as its goal but does not cognitively attend to moral issues that may be intertwined with that pursuit. If there is an ethical guide to amoral management, it would be the marketplace as constrained by law—the letter of the law, not the spirit. The amoral manager sees the law as the parameters within which business pursuits take place.

Operating Strategy. The operating strategy of amoral management is to not bridle managers with excessive ethical structure but to permit free rein within the unspoken but understood tenets of the free enterprise system. Personal ethics may periodically or unintentionally enter into managerial decisions, but it does not preoccupy management. Furthermore, the impact of decisions on others is an afterthought if it ever gets considered at all. Amoral management is a style in which the managers' ethical mental gears, to the extent they are present, are placed in neutral. The key management question guiding decision making is, "*Can we make money with this action, decision, or behavior?"* Note that the question does not imply an active or implicit intent to be either moral or immoral.

Figure 4-8 provides a visual summary of the major characteristics of amoral management and the other two styles that have been identified and discussed.

Illustrative Cases. There are perhaps more examples of amoral management than any other kind. When police departments stipulated that recruits must be 5'10" and 180 lb to qualify, this was an amoral decision. They did not consider the deleterious exclusion it would have for women, Hispanics, and others who do not, on average, attain that height and weight. When companies decide to use scantily clad young women to advertise autos, men's cologne, and other such products, these companies do not think of the degrading and demeaning characterization that may eventually come from their ethically neutral decision. When firms decided to do business in South Africa, this was neither a moral nor an immoral decision. But a major unanticipated consequence of these firms' decisions has been to appear to give capitalistic (or United States) approval to apartheid.

Nestlé's decision to market infant formula in Third World countries (see Chapter 3) could have initially been an amoral decision. Nestlé may not have considered the detrimental effects such a seemingly innocent business decision would have on mothers and babies in a land of impure water, poverty, and illiteracy.

The liquor, beer, and cigarette industries have not, according to generally accepted standards, been immoral in the making, advertising, and distributing of their products. But in recent years, severe moral issues have arisen that they did not think about or anticipate—at least not to an extent that it altered their decisions. Alcoholism, drunk driving deaths, lung cancer, deteriorating health, and offensive secondary cigarette smoke are among the negative impacts these product decisions have on society today.

When PepsiCo promoted Frito Corn Chips on television with its "Frito-Bandito" theme, it greatly offended Mexican-Americans, who put such pressure on the company that it dropped the ad campaign entirely. Surely PepsiCo was not thinking of the adverse stereotype it was creating when it entered into this campaign. The company just didn't think through the ethical consequences of its promotional campaign.

A Hypothesis

There are numerous other examples of amoral management, but the ones presented above should suffice to illustrate the point. A thorough study has not been conducted to ascertain precisely what proportions of managers each style represents in the total management population. A rough hypothesis is that the distribution might approximate a normal curve, with the amoral group occupying the large middle part of the curve and the moral and immoral categories occupying the smaller tails of the curve. A limited survey of managers revealed findings contrary to this hypothesis. In this study, managers estimated that among other managers, about 70 percent were moral, 20 percent were amoral, and 10 percent

FIGURE 4-8 Three Approaches to Management Ethics

Organizational Characteristics	Immoral Management	Amoral Management	Moral Management
Ethical Norms	Management decisions, actions, and behavior imply a positive and active opposition to what is moral (ethical). Decisions are discordant with accepted ethical principles. An active negation of what is moral is implied.	Management is neither moral nor immoral, but decisions lie outside the sphere to which moral judgments apply. Management activity is outside or beyond the moral order of a particular code. May imply a lack of ethical perception and moral awareness.	Management activity conforms to a standard of ethical, or right, behavior. Conforms to accepted professional standards of conduct. Ethical leadership is commonplace on the part of management.
Motives	Selfish. Management cares only about its or the company's gains.	Well-intentioned but selfish in the sense that impact on others is not considered.	Good. Management wants to succeed but only within the confines of sound ethical precepts (fairness, justice, due process).
Goals	Profitability and organizational success at any price.	Profitability. Other goals are not considered.	Profitability within the confines of legal obedience and ethical standards.
Orientation Toward Law	Legal standards are barriers that management must overcome to accomplish what it wants.	Law is the ethical guide, preferably the letter of the law. The central question is what we can do legally.	Obedience toward letter and spirit of the law. Law is a minimal ethical behavior. Prefer to operate well above what law mandates.
Strategy	Exploit opportunities for corporate gain. Cut corners when it appears useful.	Give managers free rein. Personal ethics may apply but only if managers choose. Respond to legal mandates if caught and required to do so.	Live by sound ethical standards. Assume leadership position when ethical dilemmas arise. Enlightened self-interest.

Source: Archie B. Carroll, "In Search of the Moral Manager," *Business Horizons* (March/April, 1987), 8. Copyright © 1987 by the Foundation for the School of Business at Indiana University. Used with permission.

were immoral.[21] Because this limited study polled just under 50 managers in a specific industry, we should not generalize the results.

Equally disturbing as the belief that the amoral management style is common in organizations today is an alternative hypothesis that, within the average manager, these three styles may operate at various times and under various circumstances. That is, the average manager may be amoral most of the time but slips into a moral or immoral style on occasion, based on a variety of impinging factors. This view cannot be empirically supported at this time, but it does provide an interesting perspective for managers to think about. This perspective would be somewhat similar to the situational ethics argument that has been around for some time.

The more serious social problem in organizations today seems to be this group of well-intended managers who for one reason or another subscribe to or live out the amoral ethic. These are managers who are driven primarily by the profitability or bottom-line ethos, which places economic success as the almost exclusive barometer of organizational and personal achievement. They are basically good people, but they see the competitive business world as essentially ethically neutral. Until this group of managers moves toward the moral ethic, we are going to continue to see American business and organizations criticized as they have been in the past two decades.

MAKING MORAL MANAGEMENT ACTIONABLE

The characteristics of immoral, moral, and amoral management discussed in this chapter should provide some useful base points for managerial self-analysis, since self-analysis and introspection will ultimately be the way in which managers move from the immoral or amoral ethic to the moral ethic. Numerous others have suggested management training for business ethics; therefore, this prescription will not be further developed here, although it has great potential. However, until senior management fully embraces the concepts of moral management, the transformation in organizational culture that is so essential for moral management to blossom, thrive, and flourish will not take place. Ultimately, senior management has the leadership responsibility to show the way to an ethical organizational environment by leading the transition from amoral to moral management, whether that is done by business ethics training and workshops, codes of conduct, corporate ombudsmen, tighter financial controls, more ethically sensitive decision processes, or leadership by example.

Underlying all these efforts, however, needs to be the fundamental recognition that amoral management exists and that it is a condition that can be certainly, if not easily, remedied. Most notably, we must acknowledge that amoral management is a morally vacuous condition that can be quite easily disguised as just an innocent, practical, bottom-line philosophy—something to take pride in. Amoral management is, however, and will continue to be, the bane of American management until recognized for what it really is and until managers undertake steps toward overcoming it. American managers are not all "bad guys" as so frequently portrayed, but the idea that managerial decision making can be ethically neutral is bankrupt and no longer tenable in the society of the 1990s and beyond.

DEVELOPING MORAL JUDGMENT

It is helpful to know something about how individuals, whether they are managers or employees, develop moral (or ethical) judgment. Perhaps if we knew more about this process we could better understand our own behavior and the behavior of those around us and those we manage. A good starting point is to come to appreciate what psychologists have to say about how we as individuals develop morally. The major research on this point is Kohlberg's levels of moral development.[22]

Levels of Moral Development

An American psychologist, Lawrence Kohlberg, has done extensive research into the question of moral development. He has concluded, on the basis of 20 years of research, that there is a sequence of three levels (each with two stages) through which people evolve in learning to think morally. Although his theory is not universally accepted, there is widespread practical usage of his levels of moral development, and this suggests a kind of broad consensus. Figure 4-9 portrays the three levels and the six stages.

Level 1: Preconventional Level.
At the *preconventional level of moral development*, which is typically descriptive of how we behave as infants and children, the focus is mainly on *self*. As an infant starts to grow, his or her main behavioral reactions are in response to punishment and rewards. Stage 1 is the reaction-to-punishment stage. If you want a child to do something (like stay out of the street) at a very early age, spanking or scolding is typically needed. The orientation at this stage is toward pain avoidance.

As the child gets a bit older, rewards start working. Stage 2 is the seeking-of-rewards stage. The child begins to see some connection between being "good" (that is, doing what Mom or Dad wants the child to do) and some reward that may be forthcoming. The reward may be parental praise or something tangible like candy, extra TV time, or a trip to the movies. At this preconventional level, children do not really understand the moral idea of "right" and "wrong" but rather learn to behave according to the consequences—punishment or reward—that are likely to follow.

FIGURE 4-9 Levels of Moral Development

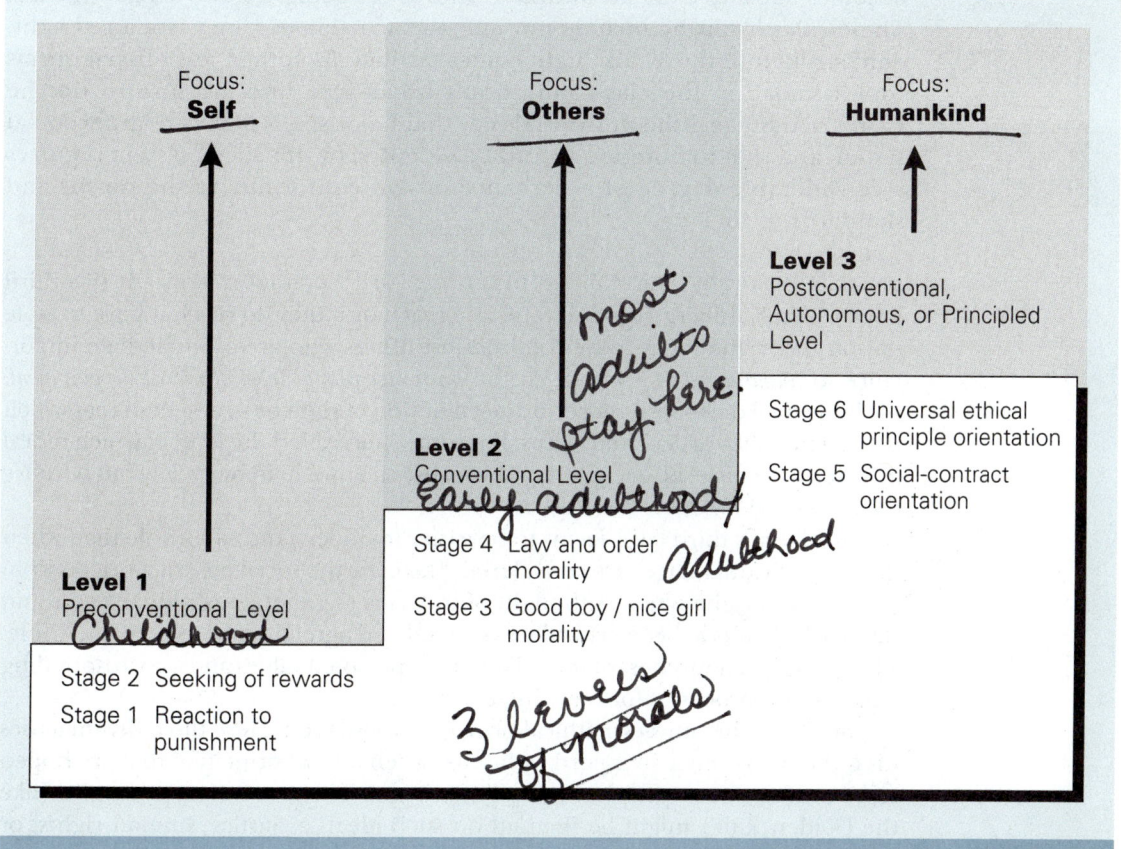

Level 2: Conventional Level. As the child gets older, he or she learns that there are *others* whose ideas or welfare ought to be considered. Initially, these others include family and friends. At the ***conventional level of moral development,*** the individual learns the importance of conforming to the conventional norms of society.

The conventional level is composed of two stages. Stage 3 has been called by some the "Good boy/Nice girl" morality stage. The child learns that there are some rewards (such as feelings of loyalty, warmth, acceptance, or trust) for living up to what is expected by family and peers. So the individual begins to conform to what is generally expected of a good son, daughter, sister, brother, friend, and so on.

Stage 4 is the law-and-order morality stage. Not only does the individual learn to respond to family, friends, the school, and the church as in Stage 3, but the individual now recognizes that there are certain norms in society (in school, in the theater, in the mall, in stores, in the car) that are expected or needed for society to function in an orderly fashion. Thus, the individual becomes socialized or acculturated into what being a good citizen means. These rules for living include not only the actual laws (don't run a red light, don't walk until the "Walk" light comes on) but also other, less official norms (don't smoke in the classroom, don't break into line, be sure to tip the waiter). At Stage 4 the individual sees that he or she is part of a larger social system and that to function in and be accepted by this social system requires a considerable degree of acceptance of and conformity to the norms and standards of society.

Level 3: Postconventional, Autonomous, or Principled Level. At this third level, which Kohlberg argues few people reach or if they do reach it have trouble staying there, the focus moves beyond just others who are of immediate importance to *humankind* as a whole. At the ***postconventional level of moral development,*** the individual develops a more advanced notion of right or wrong than that which is conventionally articulated. Thus, it is sometimes called the level at which moral principles become self-accepted, not because they are held by society but because the individual now sees them as "right."

Kohlberg's third level seems to be easier to understand as a whole than when the two individual stages are considered. Stage 5 is the social-contract orientation. At this stage, right action is thought of in terms of general individual rights and standards that have been critically examined and agreed on by society as a whole. There is a clear awareness of the relativism of personal values and a corresponding emphasis on processes for reaching consensus.

Stage 6 is the universal-ethical-principle orientation. Here the individual uses his or her conscience in accord with self-chosen ethical principles that are hoped to be universal, comprehensive, and consistent. These universal principles (like the Golden Rule) might be focused on such ideals as justice, human rights, or social welfare.

Kohlberg suggests that at Level 3, the individual is able to rise above the conventional level where "rightness" and "wrongness" are defined by societal institutions and that he or she is able to defend or justify his or her actions on some higher basis. For example, in our society the law tells us we should not discriminate against certain minorities. A Level 2 manager might not discriminate because to do so is to violate the law. A Level 3 manager might not discriminate but might offer a different reason—for example, it is wrong *not* to consider universal principles of human justice. Part of the difference between Levels 2 and 3, therefore, is traceable to our motivation for the course of action we take. This takes us back to our earlier discussion of motivation as one of the important ethics questions.

Our discussion to this point may have suggested that we are at Level 1 as infants, at Level 2 as youth, and, finally, at Level 3 as adults. There is some correspondence between chronological age and Levels 1 and 2, but the important point should be made again that Kohlberg thinks many of us as adults never get beyond Level 2. The idea of getting to Level 3 as managers is desirable because it would require us to think about people, products, and markets at a higher level of treatment than that used by conventional society. However, even if we never get there, Level 3 urges us to continually ask "What ought to be?" And the first two levels tell us a lot about moral development that should be useful to us as managers. If we state the issue in the following form, "Why do managers behave ethically?" we might derive conclusions from Kohlberg that look like those in Figure 4-10.

Source of a Manager's Values

In addition to considering the levels of moral development as an explanation of how and why people behave ethically, it is also useful to look at the source of a manager's values.

Ethics and values are intimately related. We referred earlier to ethics as the rightness or wrongness of behavior. More precisely, ethics is the set of moral principles or values that drives behavior. Thus, the rightness or wrongness of behavior really turns out to be a manifestation of the ethical beliefs held by the individual. **Values,** on the other hand, are the individual's concepts of the relative worth, utility, or importance of certain ideas. Values reflect what the individual considers important in the large scheme of things. One's values, therefore, shape one's ethics. Because this is so, it is important to understand the many different value-shaping forces that influence managers.

FIGURE 4-10 Why Do Managers Behave Ethically?

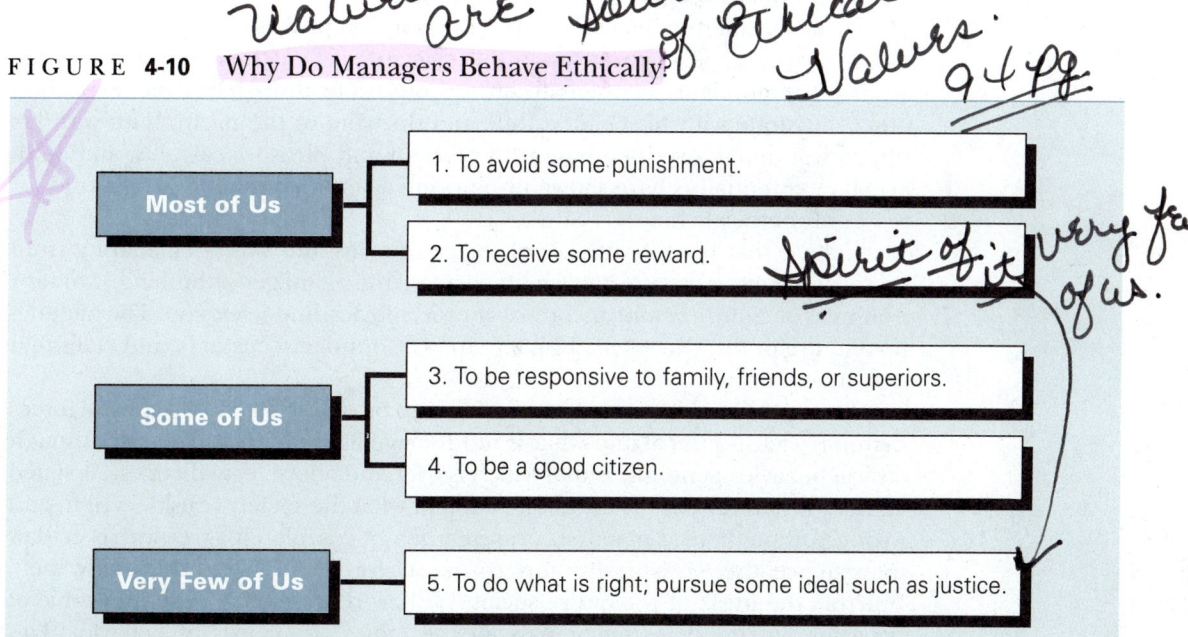

The increasing pluralism of the society in which we live has exposed managers to a large number of kinds of values, and this has resulted in ethical diversity. We can examine the source of a manager's values by considering both forces that come from outside the organization to shape or influence the manager and those that emanate from within the organization. This, unfortunately, is not as simply done as we would like, for some sources are difficult to pinpoint. It should lend some order to our discussion, however.

External Sources. By *external sources of a manager's values,* we refer to those broad sociocultural values that have evolved in society over a long period of time. Although current events (kickbacks, fraud, bribery cases) seem to affect these historic values by bringing specific ones into clearer focus at a given time, these values are rather enduring and change slowly.

George Steiner has stated that "every executive is at the center of a web of values" and that there are five principal repositories of values influencing business people. These five include *religious, philosophical, cultural, legal,* and *professional* values.[23]

Religion has long been a basic source of morality in American society, as in most societies. Religion and morality are so intertwined that William Barclay relates them for definitional purposes: "Ethics is the bit of religion that tells us how we ought to behave."[24] The biblical tradition of Judeo-Christian theology forms the core for much of what we believe today about the importance of work, the concept of fairness, and the dignity of the individual.

Philosophy and various philosophical systems are also an external source of the manager's values. Beginning with preachments of the ancient Greeks, philosophers have claimed to demonstrate that reason can provide us with principles or morals in the same way it gives us the principles of mathematics. John Locke argued that morals are mathematically demonstrable, though he never explained how.[25] Aristotle with his Golden Rule and doctrine of the mean, Kant with his categorical imperative, Bentham with his pain and pleasure calculus, and modern-day existentialists have shown us time and again the input of various kinds of reasons for ethical choice.

Culture, that broad synthesis of societal norms and values emanating from everyday living, has also had an impact on the manager's thinking. Modern examples of culture would encompass music, movies, and television. The melting-pot culture of the United States is a potpourri of norms, customs, and rules that defy summarization.

The *legal* system has been and continues to be one of the most powerful forces defining what is ethical and what is not for managers. This is true even though ethical behavior generally is that which is over and above legal dictates. As stated earlier, the law represents the codification of what the society considers right and wrong. Although we as members of society do not completely agree with every law in existence, there is typically more consensus for law than for ethics. Law, then, "mirrors the ideas of the entire society."[26] Law represents a minimum ethic of behavior but does not encompass all the ethical standards of behavior. Law addresses only the grossest violations of society's sense of right and wrong and thus is not adequate to completely describe all that is acceptable or unacceptable. Because it represents our official consensus ethic, however, its influence is most pervasive.

Professional values are those emanating, for the most part, from professional organizations and societies that represent various jobs and positions. As such, they presumably articulate the ethical consensus of leaders of those professions. For example, the Public Relations Society of America has a code of ethics that public relations executives have imposed on themselves as their own guide to behavior. The National Association of Realtors adopted its "Rules of Conduct" in 1913. Compliance with the code was first recommended for voluntary adoption and then made a condition of membership in 1924.[27] Professional values thus exert a more particularized impact on the manager than the four broader values discussed earlier.

In sum, a number of external sources of values bear on the manager. In addition to those mentioned, the manager is influenced by family, friends, acquaintances, and social events of the day. The manager thus comes to the workplace with a personal philosophy that is truly a composite of numerous interacting values that have shaped his or her view of the world, life, and business.

Internal Sources. The external forces described above constitute the broad background or milieu against which a manager or employee behaves or acts. They affect a person's personal view of the world and business and help to formulate what is acceptable and unacceptable. There are, however, a number of less remote factors that help to channel the individual's behavior, and these grow out of the specific organizational experience itself. These ***internal sources of a manager's values*** (within the business organization) constitute more immediate and direct influences on one's behavior and decisions.

When an individual goes to work for an organization, a socialization process takes place in which the individual assumes the predominant values of that organization. The individual learns rather quickly that, to survive and to succeed, certain norms must be perpetuated and revered. There are a number of norms that are prevalent in business organizations, including respect for the *authority structure, loyalty, conformity, performance,* and *results.* Each of these norms can assume a major role in a person who subordinates his or her own concept of ethics to those of the organization. In fact, we suggest that these internal sources play a much more significant role in shaping business ethics than do the host of external sources we considered first.

Respect for the authority structure, loyalty, conformity, performance, and results have been historically almost synonymous with survival and success in business. When these concepts are operating together, they form a composite ethic that is extremely persuasive in its impact on individual and group behavior. These values form the central motif of organizational activity and direction.

Underlying the first three norms is the focus on *performance* and *results.* Carl Madden referred to this as the "calculus of the bottom line."[28] One does not need to study business organizations for long to recognize that the bottom line—

profits—is the sacred value that seems to take precedence over all others. "Profits now" rather than later seems to be the orientation that spells success for managers and employees alike. Respect for authority, loyalty, and conformity become means to an end, although one could certainly find organizations and people who see these as legitimate ends in themselves. We will examine these internal sources in more detail in the next chapter.

ELEMENTS OF MORAL JUDGMENT

Managers must come to appreciate the key elements in making moral judgments. This is a central notion in moving from the amoral management condition to the moral management condition. According to Charles Powers and David Vogel, there are six major elements or capacities that are essential in making moral judgments: (1) moral imagination, (2) moral identification and ordering, (3) moral evaluation, (4) tolerance of moral disagreement and ambiguity, (5) integration of managerial and moral competence, and (6) a sense of moral obligation.[29]

Moral Imagination

Moral imagination refers to the ability to perceive that a web of competing economic relationships is, at the same time, a web of moral or ethical relationships. Developing moral imagination means not only becoming sensitive to ethical issues in business decision making but also developing the perspective of searching out subtle places where people are likely to be detrimentally affected by decision making or behaviors of managers. This is a necessary first step but is extremely challenging because of prevailing methods of evaluating managers on bottom-line results. It is essential before anything else can happen, however.

Moral Identification and Ordering

Moral identification and ordering refers to the ability to discern the relevance or nonrelevance of moral factors that are introduced into a decision-making situation. Are the moral issues real or just rhetorical? The ability to see moral issues as issues that can be dealt with is at stake here. Once moral issues are identified, they must be ranked, or ordered, just as economic or technological issues are in a decision. A manager must not only develop this skill through experience but also finely hone it through repetition. And it is only through repetition that this skill can be developed.

Several decision environments in which moral identification and ordering have become important in recent years include the issue of business or plant closings, the future of affirmative action programs, the status of employees' "right to know" what toxic chemicals they are being exposed to, and the question of how to deal with whistleblowers. In each of these instances the ability to identify and order moral issues is a key to their effective handling. To decide wrongly opens the firm up to extensive public criticism and the threat of endless lawsuits. Moral identification and ordering are vital skills that need to be developed when employing stakeholder management.

Moral Evaluation

Once issues have been identified and ordered, the question of making evaluations or judgments enters in. *Moral evaluation* is the practical phase and entails minimal skills, such as coherence and consistency, that have proved to be effective principles in other contexts. What managers need to develop here is the importance of clear principles, processes for weighing ethical factors, and the ability to identify what the likely moral as well as economic outcomes of a decision will be.

The real challenge in moral evaluation is in integrating concern for others into organizational goals, purposes, and legitimacy. In the final analysis, though, the manager may not know the "right" answer or solution, although moral sensitivity has been introduced into the process. This is the real key to our discussion because there are multiple right and wrong decisions, but the important point is that amorality has not prevailed or driven the decision process.

Tolerance of Moral Disagreement and Ambiguity

An objection managers often have to ethics discussions is the amount of disagreement generated and the volume of ambiguity that must be tolerated in thinking ethically. This must be accepted, however, for there is no other way. To be sure, managers need closure and precision in their decisions. But the situation is never clear in moral discussions any more than it is in many traditional but more familiar decision contexts of managers, such as introducing a new product based on limited test marketing, choosing a new executive for a key role, deciding which of a number of excellent computer systems to install, or making a strategic decision based on instincts. All of these are precarious decisions, but managers have become accustomed to making them in spite of the disagreements and ambiguity that prevail among those involved in the decision or within the individual himself or herself.

In a real sense, the *tolerance of moral disagreement and ambiguity* is just an extension of a managerial talent or facility that is present in practically all decision situations managers face. But managers are more unfamiliar with this special kind of decision because of the absence of practice.

Integration of Managerial and Moral Competence

The *integration of managerial and moral competence* underlies all we have been discussing. This kind of decision making is exempt from moral or social factors. The issue is whether the manager has chosen to deal with the factors. Moral issues in management arise not isolated and distinct from traditional business decision making but right smack in the middle of it. The scandals major corporations face today did not grow up apart from the companies' economic activities but were embedded in a series of decisions that were made at various points in time and culminated from the earlier decisions. Therefore, moral competence is an integral part of managerial competence. And managers are learning—some the hard way—that there is a significant corporate, and in many instances personal, price to pay for their amorality. The amoral manager sees ethical decisions as isolated and independent of managerial decisions and competence, but the moral manager sees every evolving decision as one in which an ethical perspective must be integrated. This kind of future-looking view is an essential executive skill.

A Sense of Moral Obligation

The foundation for all the capacities we have discussed is a *sense of moral obligation* and integrity. This sense is the key to the process but is the most difficult to acquire. This sense requires the intuitive or learned understanding that moral fibers—a concern for fairness, justice, and due process to people, groups, and communities—are woven into the fabric of managerial decision making and are the integral component that holds systems together.

These qualities are perfectly consistent with, indeed are essential requisites to, the free enterprise system as we know it today. One can go all the way back to Adam Smith and the foundation tenets of our system and not find references to immoral or unethical practices as being elements that are needed for the system to work. Our modern-day Adam Smith—Milton Friedman—even alluded to the importance of ethics when he stated that the purpose of business is "to make as much money as possible while conforming to the basic rules of society, both those embodied in the law and *those embodied in ethical custom*."[30] The moral manager, then, has a sense of moral obligation and integrity that is the glue that holds together the decision-making process in which human welfare is inevitably at stake.

Figure 4-11 summarizes the six elements of moral judgment identified by Powers and Vogel as they might be seen in amoral versus moral managers.

SUMMARY

Business ethics has become a serious problem for the business community over the past several decades. Polls indicate that the public does not regard the ethics of managers too highly. It is not easy to say whether business's ethics have declined or just seem to have done so because of the increased media coverage and the rising public standards against which ethics is being compared. Business ethics concerns the rightness or wrongness of management behavior, and these are not

FIGURE 4-11   Elements of Moral Judgment in Amoral vs. Moral Managers

Amoral Managers	Moral Managers
Moral Imagination	
See a web of competing economic claims as just that and nothing more. Are insensitive to and unaware of the hidden dimensions of where people are likely to get hurt.	Perceive that a web of competing economic claims is simultaneously a web of moral relationships. Are sensitive to and hunt out the hidden dimensions of where people are likely to get hurt.
Moral Identification and Ordering	
See moral claims as squishy and not definite enough to order into hierarchies with other claims.	See which moral claims being made are relevant or irrelevant; order moral factors just as economic factors are ordered.
Moral Evaluation	
Are erratic in their application of ethics, if it gets applied at all.	Are coherent and consistent in their normative reasoning.
Tolerance of Moral Disagreement and Ambiguity	
Cite ethical disagreement and ambiguity as reasons for forgetting ethics altogether.	Tolerate ethical disagreement and ambiguity while honestly acknowledging that decisions are not precise like mathematics but must finally be made nevertheless.
Integration of Managerial Competence and Moral Competence	
See ethical decisions as isolated and independent of managerial decisions and managerial competence.	See every evolving decision as one in which a moral perspective must be integrated with a managerial one.
A Sense of Moral Obligation	
Have no sense of moral obligation and integrity that extends beyond managerial responsibility.	Have a sense of moral obligation and integrity that holds together the decision-making process in which human welfare is at stake.

Source: Archie B. Carroll, "In Search of the Moral Manager," *Business Horizons* (March/April, 1987), 15. Copyright © 1987 by the Foundation for the School of Business at Indiana University. Used with permission.

easy judgments to make. Multiple norms compete to determine which standards business behavior should be compared with. Four important ethics questions are: (1) What is? (2) What ought to be? (3) How to get from what is to what ought to be? and (4) What is our motivation in this transition?

Specific ethical issues that chief executive officers expect will be a serious problem over the next five years were revealed in a Conference Board Survey. The five areas included (1) environmental issues, (2) product and workplace safety, (3) employee health screening, (4) security of company records, and (5) shareholder interests.[31]

Three types of management ethics include (1) immoral management, (2) moral management, and (3) amoral management. Amoral management is further classified into that which is intentional and that which is unintentional. A generally accepted view is that moral judgment develops according to the pattern described by Lawrence Kohlberg. His three levels of moral development include (1) preconventional, (2) conventional, and (3) postconventional/autonomous. Managers' ethics are affected by external sources of values and sources from within the organization. The latter category includes respect for the authority structure, loyalty, conformity, and a concern for financial performance and results. Finally, six elements in developing moral judgment were presented.

DISCUSSION QUESTIONS

1. Give a definition of ethical business behavior, explain the components involved in making ethical decisions, and give an example from your personal experience of the difficulties involved in making these determinations.

2. To demonstrate that you understand the three types of management ethics—moral, immoral, and amoral—give an example from your personal experience of each type. Do you agree that amorality is a serious problem? Explain.

3. Give an example from your personal experience of Kohlberg's Levels 1, 2, and 3. If you do not think you have ever gotten to Level 3, give an example of what it might be like.

4. Compare your motivations to behave ethically or unethically with those listed in Figure 4-10. Do the reasons square with your personal assessment? Discuss the similarities and differences between that listing and your personal assessment.

5. From your own personal experiences, give an example of a situation you have faced, or might face, that would require one of the six elements of moral judgment.

ENDNOTES

1. Raymond C. Baumhart, "How Ethical Are Businessmen?" *Harvard Business Review* (July-August, 1961), 6ff.
2. Orr Kelly, "Corporate Crime: The Untold Story," *U.S. News & World Report* (September 6, 1982), 25–29.
3. *Ibid.,* 26–27.
4. Gallup Opinion Index, "Honesty and Ethical Standards of Business Executives" (August, 1985), 17.
5. Gallup Opinion Index, "Americans Chide Counterparts for Dishonesty, Unethical Behavior" (May, 1986), 12–13.
6. Max Ways, "A Plea for Perspective," in Clarence C. Walton (ed.), *The Ethics of Corporate Conduct* (Englewood Cliffs, NJ: Prentice Hall, 1977), 108.
7. Michael Blumenthal, "Business Morality Has Not Deteriorated—Society Has Changed," *The New York Times* (January 9, 1977).
8. *Ibid.*
9. Richard T. DeGeorge, *Business Ethics,* 3rd ed. (New York: Macmillan, 1990), 14–15.
10. *Ibid.,* 15.
11. Otto A. Bremer, "An Approach to Questions of Ethics in Business," Audenshaw Document No. 116 (North Hinksey, Oxford: The Hinskey Centre, Westminster College, 1983), 1–12.
12. *Ibid.,* 7.
13. *Ibid.*
14. *Ibid.,* 10–11.
15. Most of the material in this section comes from Archie B. Carroll, "In Search of the Moral Manager," *Business Horizons* (March/April, 1987), 7–15.
16. Edward T. Pound and Bruce Ingersoll, "How Frigitemp Sank After It Was Looted by Top Management," *The Wall Street Journal* (September 20, 1984), 1.
17. Ron Winslow, "Regulators Investigate Harassing of Inspectors at New Nuclear Plants," *The Wall Street Journal* (November 7, 1984), 1.
18. Bruce Ingersoll and Edward T. Pound, "SEC Says Southland Was Involved in Questionable Payoffs in the 1970s," *The Wall Street Journal* (November 9, 1984), 1.
19. Pamela Hollie, "Seeking Safe Toys That Sell," *New York Times* (February 10, 1985), 4F.
20. Ray Vicker, "Rise in Chain-Saw Injuries Spurs Demand for Safety Standards, but Industry Resists," *The Wall Street Journal* (August 23, 1982), 17.
21. Archie B. Carroll, "Management Ethics in the Workplace: An Investigation," *Management Quarterly* (Fall, 1989), 40–44.
22. Lawrence Kohlberg, "The Claim to Moral Adequacy of a Highest Stage of Moral Judgment," *The Journal of Philosophy* (LXX, 1973), 630–646.
23. George A. Steiner, *Business and Society* (New York: Random House, 1975), 226.
24. William Barclay, *Ethics in a Permissive Society* (New York: Harper and Row, 1971), 13.
25. Marvin Fox, "The Theistic Bases of Ethics," in Robert Bartels (ed.), *Ethics in Business* (Columbus, OH: Bureau of Business Research, Ohio State University, 1963), 86–87.
26. Carl D. Fulda, "The Legal Basis of Ethics," in Bartels, 43–50.
27. H. Jackson Pontius, "Commentary on Code of Ethics of National Association of Realtors," in Ivan Hill (ed.), *The Ethical Basis of Economic Freedom* (Chapel Hill, NC: American Viewpoint 1976), 353.
28. Carl Madden, "Forces Which Influence Ethical Behavior," in Walton, 31–78.
29. Charles W. Powers and David Vogel, *Ethics in the Education of Business Managers* (Hastings-on-Hudson, NY: The Hastings Center, 1980), 40–45.
30. Milton Friedman, "The Social Responsibility of Business Is to Increase Its Profits," *New York Times* (September, 1962), 126. (Emphasis mine.)
31. Ronald E. Berenbeim, *Corporate Ethics* (New York: The Conference Board, 1987), 3.

CHAPTER **FIVE**

Personal and Organizational Ethics

CHAPTER OBJECTIVES

After studying this chapter, you should be able to:

- Understand the different levels at which business ethics may be addressed.

- Enumerate and discuss guides to personal ethical decision making and ethical tests.

- Identify the factors affecting an organization's moral climate and provide examples of these factors at work.

- Describe and explain actions or strategies that management may take to improve an organization's ethical climate.

The ethical issues on which managers must make decisions are numerous and varied. The news media tends to focus on the major ethical scandals involving well-known corporate names. Therefore, Exxon, General Motors, Union Carbide, Drexel, Burnham, Lambert, and other such high-visibility firms attract considerable attention. The consequence of this is that many of the everyday, routine ethical dilemmas that managers face are often overlooked.

A more typical situation for managers is to encounter day-to-day ethical dilemmas in such arenas as conflicts of interest, sexual harassment, inappropriate gifts to corporate personnel, unauthorized payments, affirmative action, and evaluation of personnel.

Unfortunately, managers face these ethical quandaries on a daily basis but have had no background or training in business ethics or ethical decision making to help them. A recent training program conducted by the author illustrates this point well. The training session was in a continuing education program, and the topic was business ethics. The 62 managers in attendance were asked how many of them had had formal business ethics training before—in college or in a company-sponsored program. Not one hand went up out of 62 managers.

The ethics problem in business is, indeed, a serious one, but what is a manager to do? A recent poll indicated that 71 percent of the managers surveyed responded that integrity was a major trait leading to success.[1] But how does one get personal integrity, and, as a manager, how do you instill it in your organization and create an ethical organizational climate? Indeed, these are significant challenges. How, for example, do you keep your own personal ethics focused in such a way that you avoid immorality and amorality? What principles or guidelines are available to help you to be ethical? What specific strategies or approaches might be emphasized to bring about an ethical culture in your company or organization?

LEVELS AT WHICH BUSINESS ETHICS MAY BE ADDRESSED

As individuals and as managers we experience ethical dilemmas in a variety of settings. These dilemmas occur on different levels. These levels include the individual or personal level, the organizational level, the industry level, the societal level, and the international level. Figure 5-1 illustrates one way of looking at these levels.

Personal Level

First, we have *personal level* ethical challenges. These include situations we face in our personal lives that are generally outside the work context. Questions or dilemmas that we might face at the personal level include:

FIGURE 5-1 Levels at Which Business Ethics May Be Addressed

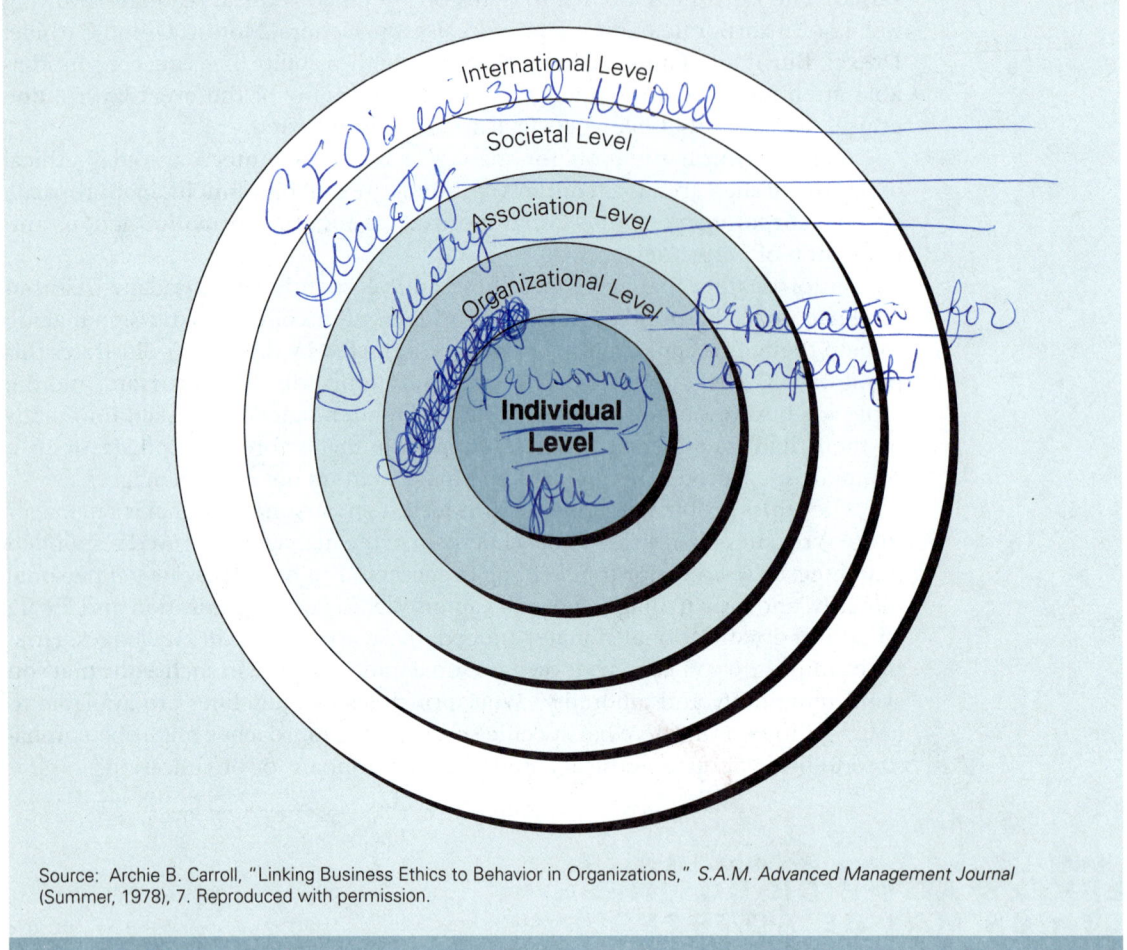

Source: Archie B. Carroll, "Linking Business Ethics to Behavior in Organizations," *S.A.M. Advanced Management Journal* (Summer, 1978), 7. Reproduced with permission.

- Should I call in sick and take a day off, knowing that if I don't use my sick leave soon, I'll lose it?
- Should I cheat on my income tax return by overinflating my charitable contributions?
- Should I return this extra pair of socks that the department store sent me by accident?
- Should I help my son with his research report when I know he is supposed to be working on his own?
- Should I notify my bank that it credited someone else's $500 to my checking account?

- Should I tell the cashier that she gave me change for a $20 bill when all I gave her was a $10 bill?
- Should I turn in this tape recorder that I found on my seat at the theater last week or keep it?

Organizational Level

We also confront ethical issues at the *organizational level* in our roles as managers or employees. Certainly, many of these issues are similar to those that we face personally. However, these issues carry significant consequences for the company's reputation and success in the community and also for the kind of ethical environment or culture that will prevail on a day-to-day basis at the office. The kinds of issues posed at the organizational level might include:

- Should I accept this gift or bribe that is being given to me to close a big deal for the firm?
- What kinds of values am I communicating to my peers and subordinates by my behavior?
- Should I set high production goals for my subordinates to benefit the organization even though I know it may cause them to cut corners to achieve such goals?
- Should I overlook the wrongdoings of my colleagues and subordinates in the interest of harmony in the company?
- Should I authorize a subordinate to violate company policy so that we can close the deal and both be rewarded?
- Should I make this product safer than I'm required by law to do, since I know the legal standard is grossly inadequate?
- Should I blow the whistle on the vice-president of purchasing for the shady practices I think he/she is employing?

A survey on corporate ethics by The Conference Board found widespread agreement that the following represented current ethical issues at the organizational level for business: employee conflicts of interest, inappropriate gifts to corporate personnel, sexual harassment, unauthorized payments, affirmative action, employee privacy, and environmental issues.

Industry Level

A third level at which a manager might influence business ethics is the *industry* of which he or she is a part. The industry might be stock brokerage, real estate, insurance, mobile homes, financial services, automobiles, or a host of others. Related to the industry might be the *profession* of which an individual is a member—accounting, engineering, pharmacy, medicine, or law. Examples of questions that might pose ethical dilemmas at this level include the following:

- Is this practice that we realtors have been using for years with prospective buyers really fair and in their self-interest?
- Is this safety standard we electrical engineers have passed really adequate for protecting the consumer in this age of do-it-yourselfers?
- Is this standard contract we mobile home sellers have adopted really in keeping with the financial disclosure laws that have recently been strengthened?
- As an accountant, is my profession really being honest with this new "generally accepted" principle, or are we just making it easy on ourselves and really neglecting the best interests of our clients?

Societal and International Levels

At the *societal* and *international levels* it becomes very difficult for the individual manager to have any *direct* effect on business ethics. However, managers acting in concert through their companies and trade and professional associations can definitely bring about constructive changes. Because the societal and industry levels are quite removed from the actual practicing manager, we will focus our attention in this chapter primarily on the personal and organizational levels. The manager's greatest impact can be felt through what he or she does personally or as a member of the management team.

We should also note that managers have an important role to play as *ethical role models* for society. To the extent that they successfully convey to the general public that they believe in the importance of integrity in business and throughout society, managers may have a significant impact on society's general level of ethics and on the future course of the free enterprise system. In Chapter 6, we will deal with global ethics—a crucial topic that will be of growing importance in the years to come.

MANAGING PERSONAL ETHICS

The point of departure for discussing the management of personal ethics is from the assumption that you want to behave ethically or to improve your ethical behavior. Keep in mind that you are a stakeholder of someone else. Someone else—a friend, a family member, an associate, or a businessperson—has a stake in your behavior; therefore, your ethics is important to them also. What we discuss here is aimed at those who desire to be ethical and are looking for help in doing so. All of the difficulties with making ethical judgments that we discussed in the last chapter are applicable.

Personal ethics, for the most part, entails making decisions. It typically confronts the individual with a conflict-of-interest situation. A conflict-of-interest situation is usually present when the individual has to choose between his or her interests and the interests of someone else or some other group (stakeholders). What it boils down to in the final analysis is answering the personal question, "*What shall I do in this situation?*"

In answering this question, more often than not it seems that individuals think about the situation briefly and then go with their instincts. There are, however, guides to ethical decision making that one could turn to if he or she really wanted to make the best ethical decision. What are some of these guides?

Approaches to Personal Ethical Decision Making

In Chapter 4 we indicated that there are three major approaches to ethics or ethical decision making: (1) the conventional approach, (2) the principles approach, and (3) the ethical tests approach. In Chapter 4 we discussed the conventional approach, which entailed a comparison of an act, decision, or behavior with prevailing norms of acceptability. In this chapter we discuss the other two approaches.

Principles Approach to Ethics

The principles approach to ethics or ethical decision making is based on the idea that managers need to compare their proposed actions, decisions, or behaviors with certain principles of ethics. This raises the question of what a principle of business ethics is and how might it be applied. A principle of business ethics is a guideline or rule that, if applied when you are faced with an ethical dilemma, will assist you in making an ethical decision.[2] There are many different principles of ethics in existence, but three of the most popular that have been articulated by ethicists and philosophers are the principles of utilitarianism, rights, and justice. We will discuss each of these and then examine a few other ethical principles.

Principle of Utilitarianism.
Many people hold that the rightness of an action can be determined by looking at its results or consequences. If the consequences are good, then the action or decision is considered good. If the consequences are bad, the action or decision is considered wrong. Utilitarianism is, therefore, a consequential principle. In its simplest form, *utilitarianism* asserts that "we should always act so as to produce the greatest ratio of good to evil for everyone."[3] Two of the most influential philosophers who advocated this consequential view were Jeremy Bentham (1748–1832) and John Stuart Mill (1806–1873).

The attractiveness of utilitarianism is that it forces us to think about the general welfare. It proposes a standard outside of self-interest by which to judge the value of a course of action. It also forces us to think in stakeholder terms: What would produce the greatest good in our decision, considering stakeholders such as owners, employees, customers, and others, as well as ourselves? Finally, it provides for latitude in decision making in that it does not recognize specific actions as inherently good or bad but rather allows us to fit our personal decision to the complexities of the situation.

A weakness of utilitarianism is that it ignores actions that may be inherently wrong. By focusing on the *ends* (consequences) of a decision or action, the *means* (the decision or action itself) may be ignored. Thus, we have the problematical situation where the end justifies the means. Therefore, the action or decision would be considered objectionable only if it leads to a lesser ratio of good to evil. Another problem with the principle of utilitarianism is that it may come into conflict with the idea of justice. Critics of this principle say that the mere increase in *total* good is not good in and of itself because it ignores the *distribution* of good, which is also an important issue. Another stated weakness is that, when using this principle, it is very difficult to formulate satisfactory rules for decision making. Therefore, utilitarianism, like most ethical principles, has its advantages and disadvantages.[4]

Principle of Rights. One major problem with utilitarianism is that it does not handle the issue of *rights* very well. That is, utilitarianism implies that certain actions are morally right when in fact they may violate another person's rights.[5] Moral rights are important, justifiable claims or entitlements. The right to life or the right not to be killed by others is a justifiable claim in our society. The Declaration of Independence referred to the rights of life, liberty, and the pursuit of happiness. John Locke earlier had spoken of the right to property. Today we speak of human rights. Some of these are legal rights and some are moral rights.

The basic idea behind the **principle of rights** is that rights cannot simply be overridden by utility. A right can be overridden only by another more basic right. Let us consider the problem if we apply the utilitarian principle. For example, if we accept the basic right to human life, we are precluded from considering whether killing someone might produce the greatest good for the greatest number. To use a business example, if a person has a right to equal treatment (not to be discriminated against), then we could not argue for discriminating against that person so as to produce more good for others.[6] However, some people would say that this is precisely what we do when we advocate affirmative action.

The rights principle expresses morality from the point of view of the *individual,* or groups of individuals, whereas the utilitarian principle expresses morality in terms of the *group* or *society as a whole.* The rights view forces us in our personal decision making to ask what is due each individual and to promote individual welfare. The rights view also limits the validity of appeals to numbers and to society's aggregate benefit.[7] However, a central question that is not always easy to answer is, "What constitutes a right, and what or whose rights take precedence over others?"

Figure 5-2 provides an overview of the types of rights that are being claimed in our society today. Some of these rights are legally protected today, whereas some of them are claimed as moral rights but are not legally protected. Managers are expected to be attentive to both legal and moral rights, but there are no clear

FIGURE 5-2 Legal Rights and Claimed Moral Rights in Society Today

Civil rights	Smokers' rights
Minorities' rights	Nonsmokers' rights
Women's rights	AIDS-victims' rights
Disabled persons' rights	Children's rights
Older persons' rights	Fetal rights
Religious affiliation rights	Embryo rights
Employee rights	Animals' rights
Consumer rights	Right to burn the American flag
Shareholder rights	Right of due process
Privacy rights	Gay rights
Right to safety	Right to an abortion
Right to life	Victims' rights
Criminals' rights	

[Handwritten annotations: "Could be both legal and moral Rights", "Moral rights", "helps prevent government regulations or laws!"]

guidelines available to sort out which claimed rights should be protected, to what extent they should be protected, and which rights take precedence over others.

Principle of Justice. Just as the utilitarian principle does not handle well the idea of rights, it does not deal well with *justice* either. One way to look at justice involves giving each person his or her due. But how do you decide what a person is due? People might be given what they are due according to their work, their effort, their merit, their need, and so on. Each of these criteria might be appropriate in different situations. At one time the view prevailed that married heads of households ought to be paid more than single males or women. Today, however, the social structure is different. Women have entered the work force in greater numbers, some families are structured differently, and a revised concept of what is due people has evolved. The just action now is to pay everyone more on the basis of equality than needs.[8]

To use the principle of justice, we must ask, "*What do we mean by justice?*" There are several kinds of justice. **Distributive justice** refers to the distribution of benefits and burdens. **Compensatory justice** involves compensating someone for a past injustice. ***Procedural justice*** refers to fair decision-making procedures, practices, or agreements.[9]

John Rawls provides what some have referred to as a comprehensive ***principle of justice***.[10] His theory is based on the idea that what we need first is a fair method by which we may choose the principles through which conflicts will be resolved. The two principles of justice that underlie his theory are as follows:

1. Each person has an equal right to the most extensive basic liberties compatible with similar liberties for all others.
2. Social and economic inequalities are arranged so that they are both (a) reasonably expected to be to everyone's advantage and (b) attached to positions and offices open to all.[11]

Under Rawls's first principle, each person is to be treated equally. The second principle is more controversial. It is criticized by both those who argue that the principle is too strong and those who think the principle is too weak. The former think that, as long as we have equal opportunity, there is no injustice when some people benefit from their own work, skill, ingenuity, or risks assumed. Therefore, such people deserve more and should not be required to produce benefits for the least advantaged. The latter group thinks that the inequalities that may result may be so great as to be clearly unjust. Therefore, the rich get richer and the poor get only a little less poor.[12]

Supporters of the principle of justice claim that it preserves the basic values—freedom, equality of opportunity, and a concern for the disadvantaged—that have become embedded in our moral beliefs. Critics object to various parts of the theory and would not subscribe to Rawls's principles at all. Utilitarians, for example, think the greatest good for the greatest numbers should reign supreme.

Other Principles. In addition to the three ethical principles that we have chosen to discuss in some detail, Figure 5-3 provides a brief sketch of a number of ethical principles that have evolved over the years.

The *Golden Rule* merits brief discussion because of its popularity as a basic principle of ethical living and decision making. A number of studies have found it to be the most powerful and useful to managers.[13] The Golden Rule—"Do unto others as you would have them do unto you"—is a fairly straightforward, easy to understand principle. Further, it guides the individual decision maker to behavior, actions, or decisions that she or he should be able to express as acceptable or not based on some direct comparisons with what she or he would consider ethical or fair.

The Golden Rule simply argues that, if you want to be treated fairly, treat others fairly; if you want your privacy protected, respect the privacy of others. The key is impartiality. According to this principle, we are not to make an exception of ourselves. In essence, the Golden Rule personalizes business relations and brings the ideal of fairness into business deliberations.[14]

Perhaps the reason the Golden Rule is so popular is that it is rooted in history and religious tradition and is among the oldest of the principles of living. Further, it is universal in the sense that it requires no specific religious belief or faith. Almost since time began, religious leaders and philosophers have advocated the Golden Rule in one form or another. It is easy to see, therefore, why Martin Luther could say that the Golden Rule is a part of the "natural law," because it is a moral rule that anyone can recognize and embrace without any particular religious teaching. In three different studies, when managers or respondents were asked to rank ethical principles according to their value to them, the Golden Rule was ranked first.[15]

FIGURE 5-3   A Brief Sketch of Ethical Principles

The **Categorical Imperative:** Act only according to that maxim by which you can at the same time "will" that it should become a universal law. In other words, one should not adopt principles of action unless they can, without inconsistency, be adopted by everyone else.

The **Conventionalist Ethic:** Individuals should act to further their self-interests so long as they do not violate the law. It is allowed, under this principle, to bluff (lie) and to take advantage of all legal opportunities and widespread practices and customs.

The **Disclosure Rule:** If the full glare of examination by associates, friends, family, newspapers, television, and so on, were to focus on your decision, would you remain comfortable with it? If you think you would, it probably is the right decision.

The **Golden Rule:** Do unto others as you would have them do unto you. It includes not knowingly doing harm to others.

The **Hedonistic Ethic:** Virtue is embodied in what each individual finds meaningful. There are no universal or absolute moral principles. If it feels good, do it.

The **Intuition Ethic:** People are endowed with a kind of moral sense with which they can apprehend right or wrong. The solution to moral problems lies simply in what you feel or understand to be right in a given situation. You have a "gut feeling" and "fly by the seat of your pants."

The **Market Ethic:** Selfish actions in the marketplace are virtuous because they contribute to efficient operation of the economy. Decision makers may take selfish actions and be motivated by personal gain in their business dealings. They should ask whether their actions in the market further financial self-interest. If so, the actions are ethical.

(continued)

FIGURE 5-3 (continued)

The **Means-Ends Ethic:** Worthwhile ends justify efficient means, i.e., when ends are of overriding importance or virtue, unscrupulous means may be employed to reach them.
The **Might-Equals-Right Ethic:** Justice is defined as the interest of the stronger. What is ethical is what an individual has the strength and power to accomplish. Seize what advantage you are strong enough to take without respect to ordinary social conventions and laws.
The **Organization Ethic:** The wills and needs of individuals should be subordinated to the greater good of the organization (be it church, state, business, military, or university). An individual should ask whether actions are consistent with organizational goals and what is good for the organization.
The **Professional Ethic:** You should do only that which can be explained before a committee of your peers.
The **Proportionality Principle:** I am responsible for whatever I "will" as a means or an end. If both the means and the end are good in and of themselves, I may ethically permit or risk the foreseen but unwilled side effects if, and only if, I have a proportionate reason for doing so.
The **Revelation Ethic:** Through prayer or other appeal to transcendent beings and forces, answers are given to individual minds. The decision makers pray, meditate, or otherwise commune with a superior force or being. They are then apprised of which actions are just and unjust.
The **Utilitarian Ethic:** The greatest good for the greatest number. Determine whether the harm in an action is outweighed by the good. If the action maximizes benefit, then it is the optimum course to take among alternatives that provide less benefit.

Source: T. K. Das, "Ethical Preferences Among Business Students: A Comparative Study of Fourteen Ethical Principles," Southern Management Association (November 13–16, 1985), 11–12, as adapted from George A. Steiner and John F. Steiner, *Business, Government and Society: A Managerial Perspective* (New York: Random House, 1980), 383–389. Adapted with permission of McGraw-Hill.

Figure 5-4 presents another list of ethical principles as developed by the Josephson Institute. This list of principles identifies those generic characteristics and values most people associate with ethical behavior.

There is no single principle we should recommend. As one gets into each principle, one encounters numerous problems with definitions, with measurement, and with generalizability. The more one gets into each principle, the more one realizes how difficult it would be for a person to use each principle consistently as a guide to decision making. On the other hand, to say that an ethical principle is imperfect is not to say that it has not raised important factors that must be addressed in personal or business decision making. The three major principles we discussed, for example, have raised to our consciousness the importance of the collective good, individual rights, and fairness.

FIGURE 5-4   Ethical Principles for Business Executives

This list of principles incorporates the characteristics and values most people associate with ethical behavior. Ethical decision making systematically considers these principles.

I. HONESTY. Ethical executives are honest and truthful in all their dealings and they do not deliberately mislead or deceive others by misrepresentations, overstatements, partial truths, selective omissions, or any other means.

II. INTEGRITY. Ethical executives demonstrate personal integrity and the courage of their convictions by doing what they think is right even when there is great pressure to do otherwise; they are principled, honorable and upright; they will fight for their beliefs. They will not sacrifice principle for expediency, be hypocritical, or unscrupulous.

III. PROMISE-KEEPING & TRUST-WORTHINESS. Ethical executives are worthy of trust, they are candid and forthcoming in supplying relevant information and correcting misapprehensions of fact, and they make every reasonable effort to fulfill the letter and spirit of their promises and commitments. They do not interpret agreements in an unreasonably technical or legalistic manner in order to rationalize noncompliance or create justifications for escaping their commitments.

IV. LOYALTY. Ethical executives are worthy of trust, demonstrate fidelity and loyalty to persons and institutions by friendship in adversity, support and devotion to duty; they do not use or disclose information learned in confidence for personal advantage. They safeguard the ability to make independent professional judgments by scrupulously avoiding undue influences and conflicts of interest. They are loyal to their companies and colleagues and if they decide to accept other employment, they provide reasonable notice, respect the proprietary information of their former employer, and refuse to engage in any activities that take undue advantage of their previous position.

V. FAIRNESS. Ethical executives are fair and just in all dealings; they do not exercise power arbitrarily, and do not use overreaching nor indecent means to gain or maintain any advantage nor take undue advantage of another's mistakes or difficulties. Fair persons manifest a commitment to justice, the equal treatment of individuals, tolerance for and acceptance of diversity, and they are open-minded; they are willing to admit they are wrong and, where appropriate, change their positions and beliefs.

(continued)

FIGURE 5-4 (continued)

This list of principles incorporates the characteristics and values most people associate with ethical behavior. Ethical decision making systematically considers these principles.

VI. CONCERN FOR OTHERS. Ethical executives are caring, compassionate, benevolent, and kind; they live the Golden Rule, they help those in need, and seek to accomplish their business objectives in a manner that causes the least harm and the greatest positive good.

VII. RESPECT FOR OTHERS. Ethical executives demonstrate respect for the human dignity, autonomy, privacy, rights, and interests of all those who have a stake in their decisions; they are courteous and treat all people with equal respect and dignity regardless of sex, race, or national origin.

VIII. LAW ABIDING. Ethical executives abide by laws, rules, and regulations relating to their business activities.

IX. COMMITMENT TO EXCELLENCE. Ethical executives pursue excellence in performing their duties, are well informed and prepared, and constantly endeavor to increase their proficiency in all areas of responsibility.

X. LEADERSHIP. Ethical executives are conscious of the responsibilities and opportunities of their position of leadership and seek to be positive ethical role models by their own conduct and by helping to create an environment in which principled reasoning and ethical decision making are highly prized.

XI. REPUTATION AND MORALE. Ethical executives seek to protect and build the company's good reputation and the morale of its employees by engaging in no conduct that might undermine respect, and by taking whatever actions are necessary to correct or prevent inappropriate conduct of others.

XII. ACCOUNTABILITY. Ethical executives acknowledge and accept personal accountability for the ethical quality of their decisions and omissions to themselves, their colleagues, their companies, and their communities.

Source: Reprinted with permission © Josephson Institute of Ethics, *Ethics: Easier Said Than Done*, Vol. 2, No. 1, 1989.

Ethical Tests Approach

In addition to the ethical principles approach to guide personal decision making, a number of *ethical tests* might be set forth, too. Whereas the principles have almost exclusively been generated by philosophers, the tests we discuss here are more practical in orientation and do not require the depth of thinking that the principles do. No single test is recommended as a universal answer to the question, "What action or decision should I take in this situation?" However, each person may find one or more tests that will be useful in helping to clarify the best course of action in a decision situation. To all students the notion of a test invokes the thought of questions posed that need to be answered. And, indeed, each of these tests for personal ethical decision making requires the thoughtful deliberation of a central question that gets to the heart of the matter.

Test of Common Sense. Here the individual simply asks, "*Does the action I am getting ready to take really make sense?*" When you think of behavior that might have ethical implications, it is logical to consider the practical consequences. If, for example, you would surely get caught engaging in a questionable practice, the action does not pass this test. Many unethical practices have come to light where one is led to ask whether a person really used his or her common sense at all. This test has severe limitations. For example, if you had concluded that you would not get caught engaging in a questionable practice, this test might lead you to think that the questionable practice is an acceptable course of action when in fact it is not. In addition, there may be other commonsense aspects of the situation that you have overlooked.

Test of One's Best Self. Each person has a self-concept. Most people could construct a scenario of themselves at their best. This test requires the individual to pose the question, "*Is this action or decision I'm getting ready to take compatible with my concept of myself at my best?*" This test addresses the notion of the esteem that we hold for ourselves and the kind of person we want to be known as. Naturally, this test would not be of much value to those who do not hold themselves in high esteem.

Test of Making Something Public. This is one of the most powerful tests.[16] It is similar to the disclosure rule mentioned in Figure 5-3. If you are about to engage in a questionable practice or action, you should pose the following questions: "*How would I feel if others knew I was doing this? How would I feel if I knew that my decisions or actions were going to be featured on the national evening news tonight for all the world to see?*" This test addresses the issue of whether your action can withstand public disclosure and scrutiny. How would you feel if all your friends, family, and colleagues knew you were engaging in this action? If you feel comfortable with this thought, then you are probably on solid footing. If you feel uncomfortable with this thought, then you ought to rethink your position.

The concept of public exposure is quite powerful. A number of years ago, a poll of managers was taken asking whether the recently passed Foreign Corrupt Practices Act would stop bribes abroad. Many of the managers said it would not. When then asked what would, most managers thought that public exposure would be most effective. "If the public knew we were accepting bribes, then this knowledge would have the best chance of being effective," they replied.

Test of Ventilation. The idea of ventilation is to expose your proposed action to others and get their thoughts on it. This test works best if you get opinions from people you know might not see things your way. The important point here is that you do not isolate yourself with your dilemma but seek others' views. After you have subjected your proposed course of action to other opinions, you may find that you had not been thinking clearly.

Test of the Purified Idea. An idea or action may be thought to be "purified," that is, made right, when a person with authority says it is appropriate. Such a person might be a supervisor, an accountant, or a lawyer. The central question here is, *"Am I thinking this action or decision is right just because someone with appropriate authority or knowledge says it is right?"* If you look hard enough, you can find a lawyer or accountant to endorse almost any idea if it is phrased right.[17] However, neither of them is the final arbiter of what is right or wrong. Similarly, just because a superior says an action or decision is ethical does not make it so. The decision or course of action may still be questionable or wrong even though someone else sanctified it with his or her approval. This is one of the most common ethical errors people make, and they must constantly be reminded that they themselves ultimately will be held accountable if the action is indefensible.

The Gag Test. This test was provided by a judge on the Louisiana Court of Appeals. He argued that a manager's clearest signal that a dubious decision or action is going too far is when you simply gag at the prospect of carrying it out.[18] Admittedly, this test can only capture the grossest of unethical behaviors, but there are some managers who may need such a general kind of test. Actually, this test is intended to be more humorous than serious, but a few might be helped by it.

None of the abovementioned tests alone offers a perfect way to question the ethicalness of a decision or act. If several tests are used together, especially the more powerful ones, they do provide a means for examining proposed actions before engaging in them. To repeat, this assumes that the individual really wants to do what is right and is looking for assistance. To the fundamentally unethical person, however, these tests would not be of much value.

Phillip V. Lewis conducted a 5-year study of ethical principles and ethical tests. Based on his findings, he asserted that there is high agreement on how a decision maker should behave when faced with a moral choice. He concludes:

> In fact, there is almost a step-by-step sequence. Notice: one should (1) *look* at the problem from the position of the other person(s) affected by a decision; (2) *try to determine* what virtuous response is expected; (3) *ask* (a) how it would feel for the decision to be disclosed to a wide audience and (b) whether the decision is consistent with organizational goals; and (4) *act* in a way that is (1) right and just for any other person in a similar situation and (2) good for the organization.[19]

Implicit in Lewis's conclusion is evidence of the Golden Rule, the Disclosure Rule, and Rawls's Principle of Justice.

MANAGING ORGANIZATIONAL ETHICS

To manage ethics in organizations, a manager must appreciate how the organization's ethical climate is just one part of its overall corporate culture. When McNeil Laboratories, a subsidiary of Johnson & Johnson, voluntarily withdrew Tylenol from the market immediately after the 1982 and 1986 reports of tainted, poisoned products, some people wondered why they made this decision as they did. An often cited response was "It's the J & J way."[20] This statement conveys a significant message about the firm's ethical climate. It also raises the question of how organizations and managers should deal with, understand, and shape business ethics through actions taken, policies established, and examples set. The organization's moral climate is a complex entity, and we can discuss only some facets of it in this section.

Figure 5-5 illustrates a number of levels of moral climate and the factors that may come to bear on the individual as he or she makes decisions. Our focus in this section is on the organization's moral climate. Two major questions that need to be considered are (1) What factors contribute to unethical behavior in the organization? and (2) What actions or strategies might management employ to improve the organization's ethical climate?

Factors Affecting the Organization's Moral Climate

For managers to be in a position to create an ethical climate, they must first understand the factors at work in the organization that influence whether managers or employees behave ethically or not. Over the past 25 years or so, a number of studies have been conducted that have sought to identify and to rank the source of ethical problems in organizations.

In 1961, Baumhart conducted a survey of over 1,500 *Harvard Business Review* readers (executives, managers). One of the questions asked was to rank-order a number of factors that the managers thought influenced or contributed to unethical behaviors or actions. The factors listed were:

1. Behavior of superiors
2. The ethical practices of one's industry or profession
3. Behavior of one's peers in the organization
4. Formal organizational policy (or lack thereof)
5. Personal financial need[21]

In 1977, Brenner and Molander replicated the 1961 study, using over 1,200 *Harvard Business Review* readers. They added one additional factor to the list: society's moral climate.[22] In 1984, Posner and Schmidt surveyed over 1,400 managers, again asking them to rank the list of six factors in terms of their

FIGURE 5-5 Factors Affecting the Morality of Managers

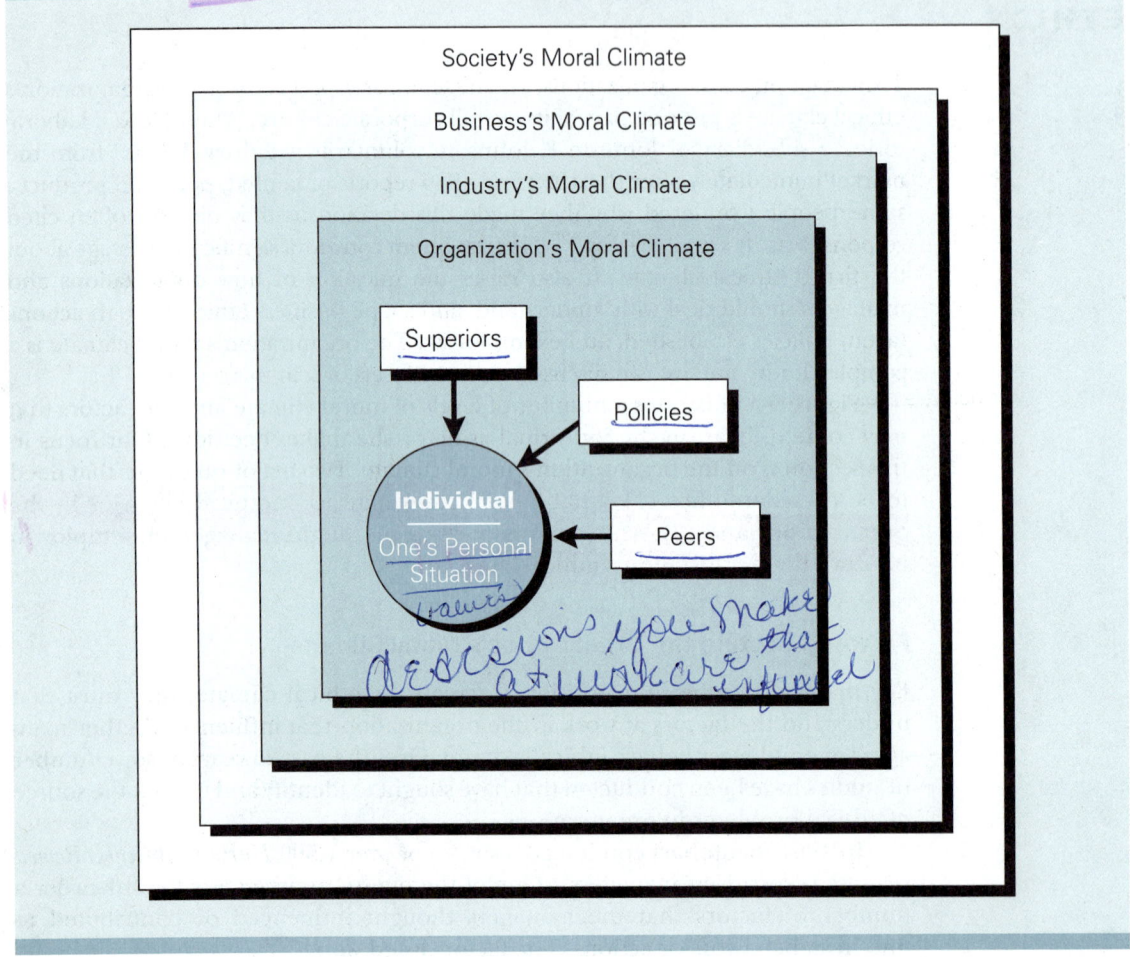

influence or contribution to unethical behavior.[23] Figure 5-6 presents the findings of the 1961, 1977, and 1984 studies.

Although there is variation in the rankings of the three studies, several findings are worthy of note:

1. *Behavior of superiors* was ranked as the number one influence on unethical behavior in all three studies.
2. *Behavior of one's peers* was ranked high in two of the three studies.
3. *Industry or professional ethical practices* ranked in the upper half in all three studies.
4. *Personal financial* need ranked *last* in all three studies.

FIGURE 5-6 Factors Influencing Unethical Behavior
Question: "Listed below are the factors that many believe influence unethical behavior. Rank them in order of their influence or contribution to unethical behaviors or actions by managers."[a]

Factor	1984 Study[b] (N=1443)	1977 Study[c] (N=1227)	1961 Study[d] (N=1531)
Behavior of superiors	2.17(1)	2.15(1)	1.9(1)
Behavior of one's organizational peers	3.30(2)	3.37(4)	3.1(3)
Ethical practices of one's industry or profession	3.57(3)	3.34(3)	2.6(2)
Society's moral climate	3.79(4)	4.22(5)	[e]
Formal organizational policy (or lack thereof)	3.84(5)	3.27(2)	3.3(4)
Personal financial need	4.09(6)	4.46(6)	4.1(5)

[a]Ranking is based on a scale of 1 (most influential) to 6 (least influential).
Sources: [b]Posner and Schmidt, *California Management Review*.
[c]Brenner and Molander, *Harvard Business Review*.
[d]Baumhart, *Harvard Business Review*.
[e]This item not included in 1961 study.

What stands out here from an organizational perspective is the influence of the behavior of one's superiors and peers. Also notable about these findings is that quite often it is assumed that society's moral climate has a lot to do with managers' morality, but this factor was ranked low in the two studies in which it was considered. Apparently, society's moral climate is a background factor that does not have a direct bearing on organizational ethics. Furthermore, it is interesting that personal financial need ranked so low.

Superiors' Pressures on Subordinates. One major consequence of the behavior of superiors and peers is pressure being placed on subordinates or other organizational members. In a national study conducted by the author of this text soon after the 1974 Watergate incident, managers were asked to what extent they agreed with the following proposition: "Managers today feel under pressure to compromise personal standards to achieve company goals." It is insightful to consider the management level of the 64.4 percent of the respondents who agreed with the proposition. The results were:[24]

Top management	50 percent agreed
Middle management	65 percent agreed
Lower management	85 percent agreed

This study revealed that the perceived pressure seems to be felt most by those in lower management, followed by those in middle management. In 1984, Posner and Schmidt also asked managers whether they sometimes had to compromise their personal principles to conform to organizational expectations. Twenty percent of the top executives agreed, 27 percent of the middle managers agreed, and 41 percent of the lower managers agreed.[25] In other words, the same pattern prevailed.

This author's study posed another proposition: "I can conceive of a situation where you have sound ethics running from top to bottom, but because of pressures from the top to achieve results, the person down the line compromises." The pattern of findings with this proposition was similar to that of the other two findings.[26]

What is particularly troublesome about these findings is the pattern of response. It seems that the lower a manager is in the hierarchy, the more that person perceives pressures toward unethical conduct. Although there are a number of plausible explanations for this phenomenon, one explanation seems particularly attractive because of its agreement with conversations this author has had with a number of different managers. This interpretation is that top-level managers do not know how strongly their subordinates perceive pressures to go along with their bosses. These varying perceptions at different levels in the managerial hierarchy suggest that higher-level managers may not be tuned in to how pressure is received at lower levels. There seems to be a gap in the understanding of higher managers and lower managers regarding the pressures toward unethical behavior that exist, especially in the lower echelons. This breakdown in understanding, or lack of sensitivity by top management to how far subordinates will go to please them, can be conducive to lower-level subordinates behaving unethically out of a real or perceived fear of reprisal, a misguided sense of loyalty, or a distorted concept of their jobs.

In addition to the studies that document the extent to which lower- and middle-level managers feel pressure to perform even if it leads to questionable activities, a number of actual business cases demonstrate the reality of cutting corners to achieve high production goals. In a glass container plant in Gulfport, Mississippi, for example, the plant manager began to fear that top management might close the aging facility because its output was falling behind that of other plants. So, the plant manager secretly started altering records and eventually inflated the value of the plant's production by 33 percent. Top management learned of this when a janitor acquired documents and reported this bogus information to company auditors. The plant manager was fired. He was not willing to discuss the matter, but his wife said her husband was under "constant pressure" to raise the plant's production and that he believed he and the other employees had a job as long as he was able to do so. The company's president said he had no intention of firing the plant manager for failing to meet the production goal.[27]

Another interesting case involved a big Chevrolet truck plant in Flint, Michigan. Here, three plant managers installed a secret control box in a supervisor's office so that they could override the control panel that governed the speed of the assembly line. The plant managers claimed they felt pressure to do this because top management was not understanding of the high absenteeism, conveyor breakdowns, and other problems that were causing them to not reach their goals. Once they began using the hidden controls, they began meeting their production goals and winning praise from their superiors. The plant managers claimed they thought top management knew that the plant managers were speeding up the line and that what the plant managers were doing was unethical. However, top management never said anything and therefore it was thought to be okay. The executives denied any knowledge of the secret box. The speedup was in violation of GM's contract with the United Auto Workers' union. Once it was exposed, the company had to pay $1 million in back pay to the affected UAW members.[28]

The motive behind superiors putting pressure on subordinates to perform even at the sacrifice of ethics seems to be driven by the "bottom-line" mentality that places economic success above all other goals. Subordinates frequently find themselves making compromises as a result of the pressure coupled with the socialization process that emphasizes compliance with the authority structure, the need to conform to their superiors' wishes, and the expectation of loyalty.

Other Behaviors of Superiors and/or Peers.
Other behaviors of one's superior and/or peers that create a questionable organizational atmosphere include:

1. *Amoral decision making.* This includes managers who themselves fail to factor ethical considerations into their actions, decisions, and behaviors. The result of this is a vacuous leadership environment.
2. *Unethical acts, behaviors, or practices.* Some managers simply are not ethical themselves, and this influence wears off onto others. Employees watch their superiors' behavior carefully and take cues from them as to what is acceptable.
3. *Acceptance of legality as a standard of behavior.* Some managers think that, if they are strictly abiding by the law, they are doing the most they ought to do.
4. *"Bottom-line" mentality and expectations of loyalty and conformity.* This focus places little value on doing what is right and on being sensitive to other stakeholders.
5. *Absence of ethical leadership.* This is a global indicator of sorts that includes some of the other points already mentioned. In addition, management never steps out ahead of the pack and assumes a leadership role in doing what is right.
6. *Objectives and evaluation systems that overemphasize profits.* If management sets unrealistic goals or does not take ethics into consideration in evaluating employees, then it is creating a potentially destructive environment.
7. *Insensitivity toward how subordinates perceive pressure to meet goals.* This is related to several of the previous points. Management must be constantly vigilant of the directives and expectations it is making on employees.

The manager might always ask, "How might this goal, directive, or expectation be misread or misunderstood in terms of how far I want people to go to achieve it?"

8. *Inadequate formal policies.* Problems here might include inadequate management controls for monitoring and compliance, unreasonable reimbursement/expense policies, and absence of a clear code of conduct.

Illustrative Cases

Being found guilty of legal and ethical violations can have a disastrous effect on companies that may require years to overcome. Two major cases effectively illustrate the impact ethical scandals can have on an organization's internal climate.

E. F. Hutton Case. The first case is that of E. F. Hutton, the giant retail brokerage firm. In 1985, Hutton pleaded guilty to federal fraud charges stemming from an elaborate scheme of writing checks against uncollected or nonexistent funds. Congress investigated the firm, many big customers stopped doing business with the firm, and federal and state regulators launched investigations to determine if any of the firm's employees should be barred from the securities business. The case was highly publicized and resulted in significant changes eventually being made at Hutton.[29]

The turmoil not only affected the bottom line for the firm but also raised questions about which employees ought to be suspended. The scandal had a detrimental effect on the firm's morale. The firm also had trouble attracting new securities dealers. One person said that headhunters were busily swarming around the firm attempting to attract away some of its best employees.

Although it is difficult to pinpoint responsibility for the scheme Hutton got involved in, it had been observed that the firm's former president encouraged aggressive cash management techniques.[30] It had also been observed that Hutton had a loose organizational climate and that this may have been an important factor in permitting the overdraft system to blossom. A new president was thereafter chosen to help put the firm back on solid footing.[31]

Wedtech Case. Wedtech was a South Bronx defense contractor that collapsed in the late 1980s under the weight of its own excessive greed and fraud. The company won government contracts through payoffs, lies, and hired political muscle. After Wedtech got $400 million worth of contracts, it used fraudulent accounting to expedite the influx of federal money. Much of the money went into the pockets of its top executives and political patrons. The company held itself out to be a showcase firm with its plans to replace the welfare state with entrepreneurship. It won the contracts under false pretenses. It claimed to be able to build the small engines required under the contract when, in fact, Wedtech had never produced any kind of engine much less one capable of meeting the Army's stringent standards. In addition, Wedtech won "minority enterprise" status by lying about its ownership structure to the Small Business Administration. In the end, the Wedtech scam was exposed, and observers began to understand the appalling unethical climate that had been created there. Over 25 people, including members of Congress and the Executive Branch, were convicted once the rampant fraud came to light.[32]

Actions to Improve Ethical Climate

The E. F. Hutton and Wedtech cases raise the serious question, "What actions can and should management take to improve the ethical climate of the organization?" Some actions to improve the moral atmosphere of the workplace are discussed below.

Providing Leadership from Top Management. It has become almost a cliché, but this premise must be established at the outset: *The moral tone of an organization is set by top management.* This is because all managers and employees look to the highest level for their cues as to what is acceptable. A former chairman of Bethlehem Steel Corporation stated it well: "Starting at the top, management has to set an example for all the others to follow."[33] Top management, through its capacity to set a personal example and to shape policy, is in the ideal position to provide a highly visible role model. The authority and ability to shape policy, both formal and implied, forms one of the vital characteristics of the leader's job in any organization.

An example of bad ethical leadership and one of good ethical leadership make these points clear. In one of his consulting experiences, this author encountered a situation in a small company where a long-time employee was identified as having embezzled about $20,000 over a 15-year period. When the employee was approached and questioned as to why she had done this, she explained that she thought it was all right because the president had led her to believe it was. She further explained that any time during the fall, when the leaves had fallen in his yard and he needed them raked, he would simply get company personnel to do it. When the president needed cash, he would take it out of the company's petty cash box or get the key to the soft drink machine and raid its coin box. When he needed stamps to mail his personal Christmas cards, he would take them out of the company stamp box. The woman's perception was that it was all right for her to take the money because the president did it frequently. Therefore, she thought it was an acceptable practice for her!

The example of positive ethical leadership is seen in the case of a firm that was manufacturing vacuum tubes. One day the plant manager called a hurried meeting to announce that a sample of the tubes had failed a critical safety test. This meant that the 10,000 tubes were of highly questionable safety and performance. The plant manager wondered out loud, "What the hell are we going to do now?" Ethical leadership was shown by the vice-president for technical operations, who looked around the room at each person and then declared in a low voice, "Scrap them!" According to a person who worked for this vice-president, that act set the tone for the corporation for years because every person present knew of situations where faulty products had been shipped under pressures of time and budget.[34]

Both of these cases provide vivid examples of how a leader's actions and behavior communicated important messages for others in the organization. In the absence of knowing what to do, many employees look to the leader's behavior for their cues as to acceptable conduct. In our second case, another crucial point is illustrated. When we speak of management providing ethical leadership, it is not just restricted to top management. Vice-presidents, plant managers, and, indeed, all managerial personnel carry the responsibility for ethical leadership.

In a period in which the importance of a sound corporate culture has been strongly advocated, management must stress the primacy of integrity and morality as vital components of the organization's culture. There are many different ways and situations in which management needs to do this. In general, management needs to create a climate of *moral consciousness*. In everything it does, it must stress the importance of sound ethical principles and practices. A former president and chief operating officer for Caterpillar Tractor Company suggested four specific actions for accomplishing this:

1. Create clear and concise policies that define the company's business ethics and conduct.
2. Select for employment only those people and firms whose character and ethics appear to be in keeping with corporate standards.
3. Promote people on the basis of performance and ethical conduct and beliefs.
4. Company personnel must feel the obligation and the opportunity to report perceived irregularities in ethics or in accounting transactions.[35]

Mark Pastin recommends a set of four principles that high-ethics firms employ to help develop a climate of moral consciousness. Figure 5-7 summarizes these four principles that provide organizational guidelines that focus on (1) stakeholders, (2) fairness, (3) individual responsibility, and (4) purpose. They are based on his research of 25 firms recognized for both ethical and economic performance.[36]

Another example of top management providing ethical leadership is provided by Robert D. Haas, Chairman and CEO of Levi Strauss & Co. The San Francisco-based apparel manufacturer has had a reputation since its founding in 1850 for successfully combining a commitment to strong commercial values with a commitment to strong social values. In 1987, Haas initiated the development of what came to be known as the Levi Strauss Aspirations Statement. The Aspirations Statement was a major initiative designed to identify and define the shared values that would guide management and the work force. Among the topics addressed

FIGURE 5-7 Principles for High-Ethics Firms

Principle 1	High-ethics firms are at ease *interacting with diverse internal and external stakeholder groups.* The ground rules of these firms make the good of these stakeholder groups part of the firm's own good.
Principle 2	High-ethics firms are *obsessed with fairness.* Their ground rules emphasize that the other person's interests count as much as their own.
Principle 3	In high-ethics firms, *responsibility is individual* rather than collective, with individuals assuming personal responsibility for actions of the firm. These firms' ground rules mandate that individuals are responsible to themselves.
Principle 4	The high-ethics firm sees its activities in terms of a *purpose.* This purpose is a way of operating that members of the firm value. And purpose ties the firm to its environment.

Source: Mark Pastin, *The Hard Problem of Management: Gaining the Ethics Edge* (San Francisco: Jossey-Bass, 1986), 221–225. Reproduced with permission.

in the statement were commitments to openness, diversity, ethical management practices, communications, and empowerment.

The section on ethical management practices calls for "Leadership that epitomizes the stated standards of ethical behavior." The section goes on to read "We must provide clarity about our expectations and must enforce these standards through the corporation.[37] The fact that Haas has been a champion for ethical and social values has been instrumental in Levi Strauss's exemplary corporate record on issues ranging from work-force diversity to benefits for workers dislocated by plant closings and technological change.

We should add, however, that the leader must infuse the organization's climate with values and ethical consciousness, not just run a one-person show. This point is made vividly clear by Steven Brenner, who concludes: "Ethics programs which are seen as part of one manager's management system, and not as a part of the general organizational process, will be less likely to have a lasting role in the organization."[38]

Management also carries a heavy burden in terms of providing leadership in the area of *effective communication.* We have seen the importance of communicating through acts, principles, and organizational climate. We will discuss further the communication aspects of setting realistic objectives, codes of conduct, and the decision-making process. Here, however, we want to stress the importance of communication principles, techniques, and practices.

Conveying the importance of ethics through communication includes both written and verbal forms of communication. In each of these settings, management should operate according to certain key ethical principles. *Candor* is one very important principle. Candor requires that a manager be forthright, sincere, and honest in communication transactions. In addition, it requires the manager to be fair and free from prejudice and malice in the communication. Related to this is the principle of fidelity. *Fidelity* in communication means that the communicator should be faithful to detail, should be accurate, and should avoid deception or exaggeration. *Confidentiality* is a final principle that ought to be stressed. The ethical manager must exercise care in deciding what information he or she discloses to others. Trust can be easily shattered if the manager does not have a keen sense of what is confidential in a communication.

Setting Realistic Objectives. Closely related to leadership being exercised from the top is the necessity that managers at all levels set realistic objectives or goals. A manager may quite innocently and inadvertently create a condition leading to unethical behavior on a subordinate's part. Take the case of a marketing manager setting a sales goal of a 25 percent increase for next year when a 15 percent increase is all that could be realistically expected, even with outstanding performance. In the absence of clearly established and communicated ethical norms, it is easy to see how a subordinate might feel that he or she should go to any lengths to achieve the 25 percent goal. With the goal having been set too high, the salesperson faces a situation that is conducive to unethical behavior in order to please the superior.

Fred T. Allen, a former executive, reinforces this point:

> Top management must establish sales and profit goals that are realistic—goals that can be achieved with current business practices. Under the pressure of unrealistic goals, otherwise responsible subordinates will often take the attitude that "anything goes" in order to comply with the chief executive's target.[39]

The point here is that there are ethical implications to even the most routine managerial decisions such as goal setting. Managers must be keenly sensitive to the possibility of innocently creating situations in which others may perceive a need or an incentive to do the wrong thing.

Making Ethical Decisions. Decision making is at the heart of the management process. If there is any act or process that is synonymous with management, it is decision making. Decision making usually entails a process of stating the problem, analyzing the problem, identifying the possible courses of action that might be taken, evaluating these courses of action, deciding on the best alternative, and then implementing the chosen course of action.

Decision making at best is a challenge for management. Many decisions management faces turn out to be ethical decisions or have ethical implications or consequences. Once we leave the realm of relatively ethical-free decisions (such as which production method to use for a particular product), decisions quickly become complex, and many carry with them an ethical dimension.

According to LaRue Hosmer, five important points should be made about the character and nature of ethics and decision making:

1. Most ethical decisions have extended consequences. First-level consequences are followed by a multitude of effects having impacts both within and outside of the organization that should be considered when decisions are made.
2. Most ethical decisions have multiple alternatives. Such decisions do not present themselves in simple yes or no form, such as "Do we pay a bribe or not?" The simple dichotomy makes for sharp contrasts but does not always capture the real complex alternatives presented.
3. Most ethical decisions have mixed outcomes. Like the second point, outcomes are mixed rather than occurring in any clear unambiguous fashion.
4. Most ethical decisions have uncertain consequences. Some consequences may occur that were not anticipated. Thus it is not always clear what consequences will follow a decision.
5. Most ethical decisions have personal implications. The ethical issues management faces are not all impersonal but often have very real individual benefits and costs for the decision maker.[40]

Ethical decision making is not a simple process but is punctuated by the characteristics previously described. It would be nice if a set of ethical principles were readily available for the manager to "plug in" and walk away from, with a decision to be forthcoming. That was not the case when we discussed principles that help personal decision making, however. And it is not the case when we think of organizational decision making. The ethical principles we discussed earlier are useful here, as are the principles for high-ethics firms that we presented in Figure 5-7. But there are no simple formulas.

Although it is difficult to portray graphically the process of ethical decision making, it is possible as long as we recognize that such an effort cannot totally capture reality. Figure 5-8 presents one conception of the ethical decision-making process. In this model, the individual is asked to identify the decision, action, or behavior that is being considered and then to articulate all dimensions of the proposed course of action. Then the individual is asked to subject the course of action to what we call an *ethics screen.* An ethics screen consists of a variety of standards against which the proposed course of action is to be compared. In the

FIGURE 5-8   A Process of Ethical Decision Making

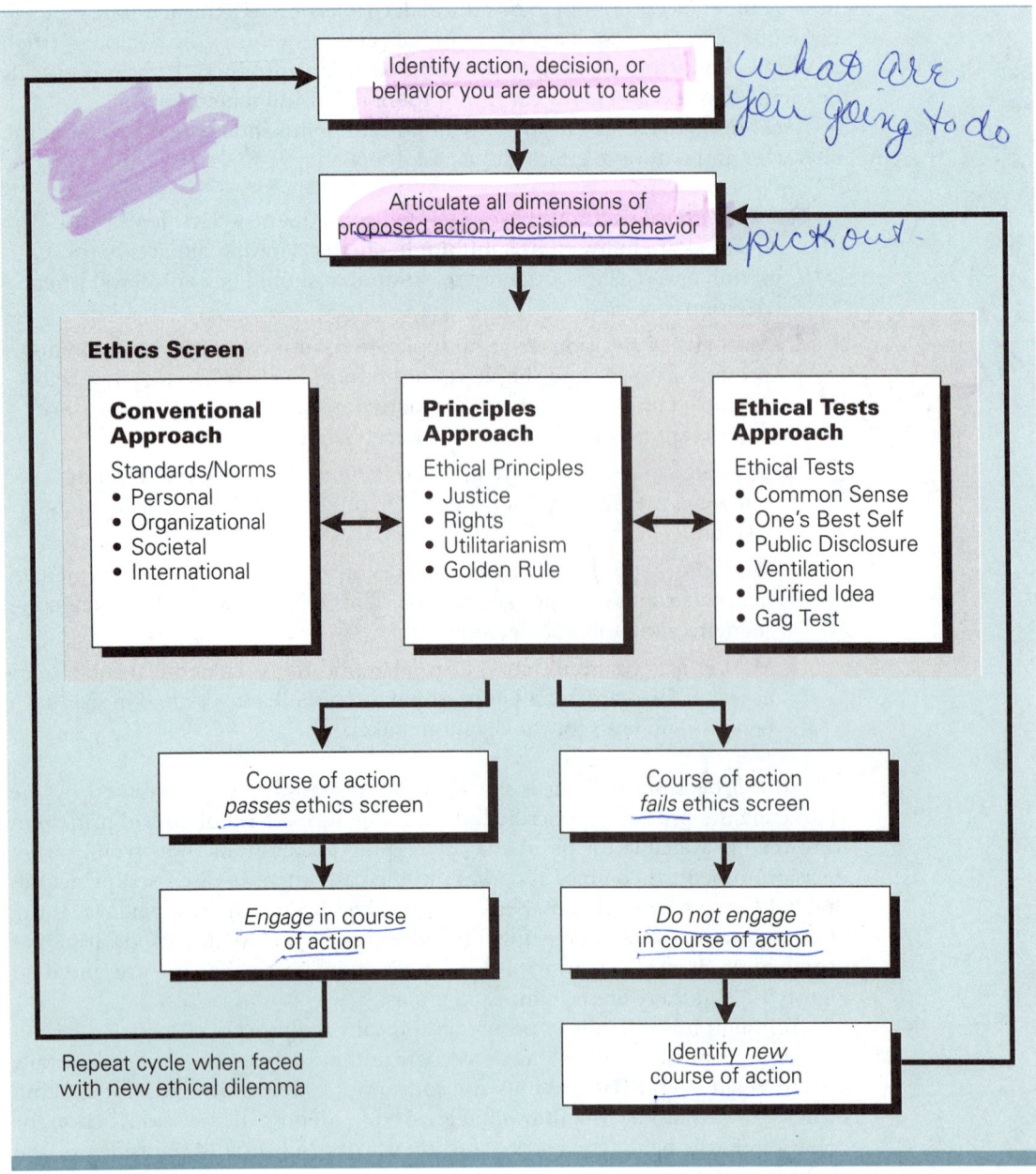

illustrated ethics screen, we reference our earlier discussion of the Conventional Approach (embodying standards/norms), the Principles Approach, and the Ethical Tests Approach to ethical decision making.

In this model, it is left up to the individual to determine what mix of guides to use as the ethics screen. Normally, some combination of the guidelines contained in the screen would be helpful to the individual who truly is attempting to make an ethical decision. If the proposed course of action fails the ethics screen, the decision maker should not engage in the course of action but should consider a new decision, behavior, or action and submit it to this same process. If the proposed course of action passes the screen (the decision maker has determined it to be an ethical course of action), he or she should engage in the action, decision, or behavior and then repeat the cycle only when faced with a new ethical dilemma.

Another useful approach to making ethical decisions is to systematically ask and answer a series of 12 questions that have been formulated by Laura Nash.[41] These questions are:

1. Have you defined the problem accurately?
2. How would you define the problem if you stood on the other side of the fence?
3. How did this situation occur in the first place?
4. To whom and what do you give your loyalties as a person and as a member of the corporation?
5. What is your intention in making this decision?
6. How does this intention compare with the likely results?
7. Whom could your decision or action injure?
8. Can you engage the affected parties in a discussion of the problem before you make your decision?
9. Are you confident that your position will be as valid over a long period of time as it seems now?
10. Could you disclose without qualms your decision or action to your boss, your CEO, the board of directors, your family, or society as a whole?
11. What is the symbolic potential of your action if understood? If misunderstood?
12. Under what conditions would you allow exceptions to your stand?

One final set of questions merits mention here because of its popularity in the book *The Power of Ethical Management* (1988). Kenneth Blanchard and Norman Vincent Peale propose the "ethics check" questions as follows:

1. *Is it legal?* Will I be violating either civil law or company policy?

2. *Is it balanced?* Is it fair to all concerned in the short term as well as the long term? Does it promote win-win relationships?
3. *How will it make me feel about myself?* Will it make me proud? Would I feel good if my decision was published in the newspaper? Would I feel good if my family knew about it?[42]

These questions are intended to produce a process of ethical inquiry that is of immediate use and understanding to a group of managers. Note that some of the items are similar to points raised earlier. The questions help ensure that ethical due process takes place. They cannot tell us whether our decisions are ethical or not, but they can help us be sure that we are raising the appropriate issues and genuinely attempting to be ethical.

Establishing Codes of Ethics. Top management has the responsibility for establishing standards of behavior and for effectively communicating these standards to all managers and employees in the organization. One of the classic ways by which managers have fulfilled this responsibility is through **codes of ethics**, or **codes of conduct**. Codes of ethics are a phenomenon of the 1970s and 1980s. Virtually all major corporations have them today, and the central questions in their usefulness or effectiveness revolve around managerial policies and attitudes associated with their use.

A survey of corporate officers by the Ethics Resource Center, a Washington, D.C.-based nonprofit organization, revealed a number of the values or results business organizations received as a result of their codes of ethics. The results achieved and the percentage of executives citing the reason give us insights into what companies really think they get from corporate ethics codes:

1. Legal protection for the company (78%)
2. Increased company pride and loyalty (74%)
3. Increased consumer/public goodwill (66%)
4. Improved loss prevention (64%)
5. Reduced bribery and kickbacks (58%)
6. Improved product quality (14%)
7. Increased productivity (12%)[43]

Through a code of ethics, management attempts to communicate to all organization members general precepts to guide decision making and actions. Figure 5-9 poses a number of important questions managers ought to ask while thinking about the *nature* of their codes of conduct.

The *content* of codes of ethics is another critical factor. A large-scale survey of ethical codes in 1983 revealed that codes covered a number of different policy areas. These policy areas were found to be in two general categories: (1) conduct on behalf of the firm and (2) conduct against the firm.

FIGURE 5-9   Questions Managers Might Ask to Evaluate Their Codes of Conduct

1. What is the basic purpose of your firm's code of conduct—to prevent employee corruption or to *extend* the firm's concept of business ethics to include corporate responsibility to society?

2. What do you feel your firm's reputation for integrity depends on—in order of priority? Where does the code of conduct stand in this ranking?

3. Do you feel that any improvement in the business ethics of your firm in the last five years was the result of voluntary or internal management actions, or was it due to changes imposed from outside (e.g., regulatory legislation, outside directions, SEC directives, etc.)?

4. Does your firm examine its ethical behavior through the eyes of its many beholders, as well as through the effectiveness of its own internal system to control employee behavior?

5. Do you feel that having a code of conduct and a strong surveillance system convinces the public that your firm can be depended upon to operate in the public interest?

6. Does your firm voluntarily look as carefully at controlling business conduct that is socially undesirable but profitable (e.g., marketing a dangerous product), as it does at conduct that is socially desirable but unprofitable (e.g., maintaining stable employment)?

7. Does your code of conduct speak as clearly on matters of profitability as related to responsibility to the public as it does to profitability as related to the shareowners?

8. At what point in your firm will pressure on employees to reach internal goals be so great as to overcome the code of conduct? How does your view of this problem compare with that of lower-level managers?

Source: Henry W. Tulloch and W. Scott Bauman, *The Management of Business Conduct* (Charlottesville, VA: Center for Applied Ethics, University of Virginia, 1981), 6–7. Reproduced with permission.

A major observation about the policy areas covered in the codes should be made. There did not appear to be any consensus among the topics covered in the codes. While over 15 areas were addressed in the codes, in only three areas were the items covered by at least two-thirds of the firms. These three areas were (1) relations with the United States government, (2) relations with customers and suppliers, and (3) conflicts of interest. This diversity of focus suggests an attempt by the firms to tailor the codes to their individual concerns.[44]

In a 1987 study of codes of ethics, Marilynn Cash Mathews of Washington State University found that her *Fortune 500* respondents included the following issues at least 75 percent of the time: (1) relations with the United States government, (2) customer/supplier relations, (3) political contributions, (4) conflicts of interest, and (5) honest books or records. She also found that companies tended not to address in their codes such issues as product safety, environmental affairs, product quality, and civic/community affairs.[45]

A 1990 study by the Ethics Resource Center of the content of corporate codes found the following to be among the most frequently addressed topics in corporate codes:

1. Conflicts of interest
2. Receiving gifts, gratuities, entertainment
3. Protecting company proprietary information
4. Giving gifts, gratuities, entertainment
5. Discrimination
6. Sexual harassment
7. Kickbacks
8. General conduct
9. Employee theft
10. Proper use of company assets[46]

More management groups seem to be successful in creating codes of ethics than in effectively managing or administering codes. In actuality, many managers make false assumptions about the use of codes in their firms. Figure 5-10 summarizes some of the false assumptions, and these merit careful study to assist in effective code administration.

Let us illustrate what all might be involved in creating and administering a code of ethics by looking at the experience of a major firm—Motorola, Inc. At Motorola, a Business Ethics Compliance Committee was created as a subcommittee of the Board of Directors. The three-person committee was composed of the chairman of the board, the chief financial officer, and the senior vice-president/general counsel. The committee was charged with the following responsibilities:

◆ Development, distribution, and periodic revision of a code of conduct
◆ Interpretation and clarification of the code to ensure that Motorola employees abide by these established principles
◆ Examination of specific cases of potential code violations with the authority to pass judgment and impose appropriate sanctions[47]

In promulgating its code, the committee reached the conclusion that the company's general principles had to be converted to detailed guidelines. It also decided to clarify the guidelines by including specific examples of prohibited practices. For example:

FIGURE 5-10 False Assumptions Managers May Make About Code of Ethics Administration

It would be ill-advised for any corporate executive to assume that in his/her company:

1. Adopting a company policy and control mechanisms on business conduct ensures against dishonesty.
2. Our managers read and understand the full intent of company policies on business conduct.
3. The company booklet on business conduct provides adequate guidance on all sensitive matters.
4. Another company's code of conduct and its communication program will nicely meet our own needs.
5. Managers down through our firm always weigh carefully, and understand fully, the recommendations of legal counsel on matters of conduct.
6. Our top-, middle-, and lower-level managers are regularly evaluated on their integrity.
7. Managers probe into the integrity of job applicants for high-level positions.
8. The pressure we exert on management for bottom-line results will not be able to bend their basic integrity.
9. All our managers in sensitive positions are no doubt honest; therefore, the risk of any major violation of company policy is so remote that the extra cost of a preventive program is not worth incurring.

Source: Henry W. Tulloch and W. Scott Bauman, *The Management of Business Conduct* (Charlottesville, VA: Center for Applied Ethics, University of Virginia, 1981), 9. Reproduced with permission.

- "Acceptance by Motorolans of presents from suppliers at Christmas as well as the acceptance by Motorolans of money, property, or services (e.g., free trips) from business associates is prohibited by the code."
- "Suppliers win Motorola business on the basis of product or service suitability, price, delivery, and quality. *There is no other basis.* Attempts to influence procurement decisions by any offers of any compensation, commission, kickback, paid vacation, special discount on a product or service, entertainment, or any form of gift or gratuity must be firmly rejected by all Motorolans."[48]

The committee also was responsible for *communicating* the code to the over 100,000 Motorola employees. The code has been disseminated throughout the world and translated into most European and Asian languages. When new workers are hired, they are familiarized with the code. Periodic seminars are conducted to remind employees of the company's continuing commitment to high ethical standards, and videotapes have been produced and distributed to this end.

In addition to the educational function, the Business Ethics Compliance Committee has an active and ongoing role in *interpreting* the code. Hundreds of requests per year are handled. The committee meets on an ad hoc basis six to eight times a year and issues statements clarifying relevant code provisions. Finally, the committee serves a judicial function in cases where not only an interpretation of the code but also a ruling on an individual's conduct is required.

The adjudicatory actions of the committee range from merely advice giving to demotion and economic penalties, discharge, civil pursuit of restitution, and recommendation of prosecution to law enforcement officials. The committee monitors adherence to the code by asking key personnel, along with all personnel in audit or control functions, to sign specific acknowledgments of the code to ensure that they are integrating its precepts into their daily routines. Entering its second decade of activity, the committee is regarded by the chairman as a highly successful and integral element in Motorola's commitment to ethics.[49]

There have been both successes and failures reported with organizational codes of ethics, but the acid test seems to be to make them "living documents," not just platitudinous public relations statements that are put into a file drawer on discrimination. Codes may not be a panacea for management but, when properly developed and administered, they serve to raise the level of ethical behavior in the organization by clarifying what is meant by ethical conduct and encouraging moral behavior. To be effective, codes of ethics must embody the thinking and policy beliefs that management and employees alike desire in the organization. As such, they should represent sincere communication efforts to guide employees' acts and behavior in questionable situations. If they are anything less than this, they tend to be symbolic gestures that are probably not worth having.

Disciplining Violators of Ethics Standards. To bring about an ethical climate that all organizational personnel will believe in, management must punish violators of its accepted ethical norms. A major reason the general public, and even employees in many organizations, have questioned business's sincerity in desiring a more ethical environment has been business's unwillingness to discipline violators. There are numerous cases of top management personnel who behaved unethically and were retained in their positions. At lower levels there have been cases of top management overlooking or failing to punish unethical behavior of subordinates. These evidences of inaction on management's or the board's part represent implicit approval of the individual's behavior.

Fred Allen argues that an organization should respond forcefully to the individual who is guilty of deliberately or flagrantly violating its code of ethics: "From the pinnacle of the corporate pyramid to its base, there can only be one course of action: dismissal. And should actual criminality be involved, there should be total cooperation with law enforcement authorities."[50]

Phillip Blumberg supports this general line of reasoning with his assertion that "there should be effective sanctions for violations so that there is no doubt that the code really represents corporate policy and that the effort is more than a public relations charade."[51] The effort has to be complete in communicating to all, by way of disciplining offenders, that unethical behavior will not be tolerated in the organization. It is management's tacit approval of violations that has seriously undermined efforts to bring about a more ethical climate in many organizational situations.

Creating an Ethics-Advocate Role. A creative proposal by Theodore Purcell is that each organization appoint or hire an ethical devil's advocate—a top-level corporate manager whose responsibility is to serve as an ethical catalyst for management by constantly asking probing questions regarding the organization's actions and posture. Whereas a strategic planner might ask with respect to a certain decision, "What would our market share be?" or "What would our discounted cash flow be?" the ethics advocate might ask, "How will this decision affect the rights of our employees versus the rights of the corporation?"[52]

One possible serious problem with this proposed organizational position is that managers might be inclined to delegate ethical concerns to the advocate and not worry about the ethical dimension themselves. This must be carefully guarded against. Very little experience exists to show whether the ethics advocate concept might work in practice; however, it does represent innovative thinking.

Businesses have not yet adopted this proposal of creating an ethics-advocate role. The closest firms have come to adopting such an idea is the use of an ethical ombudsman by a very small number of firms. A study by the Ethics Resource Center reports 3 percent of firms employing an ethical ombudsman, with no details provided as to what the ombudsman does. More typically, responsibility for monitoring and compliance of ethical behavior is given to supervisors, department/division heads, Human Resources Departments, Legal Departments, and Internal Audit Departments. A scant 4 percent of companies surveyed by the Ethics Resource Center even have a Corporate Ethics Office.[53]

Providing a Whistle-Blowing Mechanism. One problem that frequently leads to the covering up of unethical acts by persons in an organization is that they do not know how to react when they observe a questionable practice. An effective ethical climate is contingent on employees having a mechanism for (and top management support of) "blowing the whistle" on violators. Allen has summarized this point as follows: "Employees must know exactly what is expected of them in the moral arena and how to respond to warped ethics."[54]

It frequently occurs that unethical practices or crimes come to the attention of organization members several levels down in the organization's structure. John McCloy, who served as chairman of the Special Review Committee to study the use of corporate funds by Gulf Oil Corporation, found that some boards of directors of companies have "adopted and disseminated throughout their companies a policy which encourages any employee who observes a criminal act to report the incident to his or her superior. If the superior is not responsive, the employee then has direct access to the board, usually through its audit committee."[55] This would illustrate the functioning of a whistle-blowing mechanism. Extreme care should be exercised, however, in use of this approach, as there is considerable evidence of whistle-blowing that backfires.

Training Managers in Business Ethics. For several years there has been debate and controversy about whether managerial ethics can and should be taught. One school of thought assumes that ethics is personal, already embedded within the manager and, hence, not alterable or teachable. A growing school of thought, on the other hand, argues that instruction in business ethics should be made a part of business school education, management training, development programs, and seminars.

Professor Kirk Hanson has been teaching business ethics at the Stanford Business School for about 15 years. Whereas he agrees with some critics who say it is tough to infuse values in university students, he also thinks that there is a legitimate role for business ethics courses. Hanson believes that we can help most the fundamentally decent, well-intentioned student. He says:

> If we teach techniques and strategies for handling a wide variety of business decisions, we can do the same for predictable ethical decisions or challenges. Among those situations are: finding a match between a person's values and those of his or her employer; managing the pushback point where one's values are tested by peers, subordinates, or superiors; handling an unethical directive from one's boss; and coping with a performance system that gives strong incentives to cut ethical corners.[56]

In addition, in a number of organizations in the United States today, management training in business ethics is taking place. What might be the purposes or objectives of such ethics training? A number of purposes have been suggested:

1. To increase the manager's sensitivity to ethical problems
2. To encourage critical evaluation of value priorities
3. To increase awareness of organizational realities
4. To increase awareness of societal realities
5. To improve understanding of the importance of public image and public/society relations[57]

To this list we might add some other desirable goals:

6. To examine the ethical facets of business decision making
7. To bring about a greater degree of fairness and honesty in the workplace
8. To respond more completely to the organization's social responsibilities

Materials and formats typically used by firms in their ethics training include the following: ethics codes (as a training device), lectures, workshops/seminars, case studies, films/discussions, and articles/speeches.[58]

In terms of the effectiveness of ethics training, Thomas Jones discovered in his research that exposure to lengthy programs (for example, 10 weeks) resulted in significant improvements in moral development. Brief exposures to business ethics, however, yielded less encouraging results.[59] Questions remain, therefore, as to the ultimate and lasting value of ethics education.

There will doubtless be difficulties in training managers in such an amorphous subject as ethics. These difficulties, however, should not preclude serious attempts and experimentation with case studies, incidents, role playing, and discussion of crucial ethical issues. With respect to the teaching of ethics, John Adair has asserted, "A good teacher can help managers to become generally aware of their values and to compare them with the consensus of value judgments in a particular company, industry, or profession."[60] We believe, therefore, there is merit in management training and development in ethics as a viable aid to bringing about more ethical organizational behavior.

Figure 5-11 summarizes what the Ethics Resource Center has concluded about improving the ethical climate of organizations. These conclusions are based on its surveys of the actual practices of 2,000 U.S. corporations surveyed. This statement is not the definitive word on the subject, but it does give us keen insights into what major companies are doing today in actual practice.

Although we have not touched on all that can be done at the organizational level to improve or manage business ethics, the actions suggested can move management a long way toward improving the organization's ethical climate. By taking specific steps as suggested, many behaviors or decisions that might otherwise have been wrong have a greater chance of being in line with leadership's ethical standards. Thus, ethics can be managed, and managers do not have to treat value concerns as matters totally out of their control. On the contrary, managers can intercede and improve the organization's ethical climate.[61]

SUMMARY

The subject of business ethics may be approached at a number of different levels: personal, organizational, industry, societal, and international. This chapter focuses on the personal and organizational levels.

A number of different ethical principles serve as guides to personal decision making. Major philosophical principles include utilitarianism, rights, and justice. Six practical tests were proposed to assist the individual in making ethical decisions. These included the tests of common sense, one's best self, making something public, ventilation, and purified idea and the gag test.

FIGURE 5-11 Improving the Organization's Ethical Climate

Executives and managers seeking to improve the ethical climate of their organizations should consider the following conclusions from the present survey report:

Companies who see their ethics monitoring and enforcement methods as very effective share these characteristics: *Mission Statements*

- Written codes, policies, or guidelines;
- Distribution of policies to all employees, not just management;
- Reinforcement through communications, including videotapes, articles, posters, and public talks by company executives;
- Additional training geared towards application of policies to everyday work situations;
- Sources of information and advice, such as ombudsmen and hotlines; and
- Monitoring and enforcement through a Corporate Ethics Office and a Board of Directors Ethics Committee.

If companies' perceptions correlate with actual effectiveness, then companies that do not have the above elements are risking greater amounts of unethical conduct than companies that do.

Source: *Ethics Policies and Programs in American Business* (Washington, DC: Ethics Resource Center and Behavior Research Center, 1990). Used with permission.

At the organizational level, factors were discussed that affect the organization's moral climate. It was argued that the behavior of one's superiors and peers and industry ethical practices were the most important influences of a firm's ethical climate. Society's moral climate and personal needs were considered to be less important. A number of actions that could improve the firm's ethical climate include providing leadership from management, setting realistic objectives, infusing the decision-making process with ethical considerations, employing codes of ethics, disciplining violators, using ethics advocates, creating whistle-blowing mechanisms, and training managers in business ethics.

DISCUSSION QUESTIONS

1. From your own personal experience, give two examples of ethical dilemmas in your personal life. Give two examples of ethical dilemmas you have experienced as a member of an organization to which you belong.

2. Using the examples you provided for question 1, identify one or more of the guides to personal decision making or ethical tests that you think would have helped you resolve your dilemmas.
3. Assume that you are in your first real managerial position. Identify five ways in which you might provide ethical leadership. Rank-order them in terms of importance, and be prepared to explain your ranking.
4. What do you think about the idea of codes of ethics? Give three reasons why an organization ought to have a code of ethics, and give three reasons why an organization should not have a code of ethics. On balance, how do you regard codes of ethics?
5. A lively debate is going on in this country over the question of whether business ethics can or should be taught in business schools. Do you think business ethics can and should be taught? Be prepared to explain your reasons carefully.

ENDNOTES

1. Lisa Crowe, "Typical Top Exec: He's White, Male and Republican," *Atlanta Journal and Constitution* (February 2, 1987), 13-C.
2. Archie B. Carroll, "Principles of Business Ethics: Their Role in Decision Making and an Initial Consensus," *Management Decision* (Vol. 28, No. 28, 1990), 20–24.
3. Vincent Barry, *Moral Issues in Business* (Belmont, CA: Wadsworth, 1979), 43.
4. *Ibid.*, 45–46.
5. Manuel C. Velasquez, *Business Ethics: Concepts and Cases* (Englewood Cliffs, NJ: Prentice-Hall, 1982), 53–54.
6. Richard T. DeGeorge, *Business Ethics*, 2d ed. (New York: Macmillan, 1986), 79–80.
7. Velasquez, 61.
8. DeGeorge, 76.
9. *Ibid.*, 77.
10. John Rawls, *A Theory of Justice* (Cambridge, MA: Harvard University Press, 1971).
11. DeGeorge, 77.
12. *Ibid.*, 78.
13. Carroll, 22.
14. Barry, 50–51.
15. Carroll, 22.
16. Gordon L. Lippett, *The Leader Looks at Ethics*, 12–13.
17. "Stiffer Rules for Business Ethics," *Business Week* (March 30, 1974), 88.
18. Frederick Andrews, "Corporate Ethics: Talks with a Trace of Robber Baron," *New York Times* (April 18, 1977), C49–52.
19. Phillip V. Lewis, "Ethical Principles for Decision Makers: A Longitudinal Study," *Journal of Business Ethics* (Vol. 8, 1989), 275.
20. Cited in John B. Cullen, Bart Victor, and Carroll Stephens, "An Ethical Weather Report: Assessing the Organization's Ethical Climate," *Organizational Dynamics*, 1988, 50.
21. Baumhart, 1961.
22. Steve Brenner and Earl Molander, "Is the Ethics of Business Changing?" *Harvard Business Review* (January/February, 1977).
23. Barry Z. Posner and Warren H. Schmidt, "Values and the American Manager: An Update," *California Management Review* (Spring, 1984), 202–216.
24. Archie B. Carroll, "Managerial Ethics: A Post-Watergate View," *Business Horizons* (April, 1975), 75–80.
25. Posner and Schmidt, 211.
26. Carroll, 75–80.
27. George Getschow, "Some Middle Managers Cut Corners to Achieve High Corporate Goals," *The Wall Street Journal* (November 8, 1979), 1, 34.
28. *Ibid.*, 34.
29. Susan Dentzer, Carolyn Friday, and Elaine Shannon, "The Nightmare at Hutton," *Newsweek* (July 22, 1985), 45.
30. *Ibid.*
31. Roy Rowan, "E. F. Hutton's New Man on the Hot Seat," *Fortune* (November 11, 1985), 130–136.
32. William Sternberg and Matthew C. Harrison, *Feeding Frenzy: The Inside Story of Wedtech* (New York: Henry Holt and Co., 1989).

33. L. W. Foy, "Business Ethics: A Reappraisal," Distinguished Lecture Series, Columbia Graduate School of Business (January 30, 1975), 2.
34. Harvey Gittler, "Listen to the Whistle Blowers Before It's Too Late," *The Wall Street Journal* (March 10, 1986), 16.
35. Lee L. Morgan, "Business Ethics Starts with the Individual," *Management Accounting* (March, 1977), 14, 60.
36. Mark Pastin, *The Hard Problems of Management: Gaining the Ethics Edge* (San Francisco: Jossey-Bass, 1986), 221–225.
37. Robert Howard, "Values Make the Company: An Interview With Robert Haas," *Harvard Business Review* (September-October, 1990), 133–135.
38. Steven N. Brenner, "Influences on Corporate Ethics Programs" (San Diego, CA: International Association for Business and Society, March 16–18, 1990), 7.
39. Fred T. Allen, "Corporate Morality: Is the Price Too High?" *The Wall Street Journal* (October 17, 1975), 16.
40. LaRue T. Hosmer, *The Ethics of Management* (Homewood, IL: Richard D. Irwin, 1987), 12–14.
41. Laura L. Nash, "Ethics Without the Sermon," *Harvard Business Review* (November-December, 1981), 79–90.
42. Kenneth Blanchard and Norman Vincent Peale, *The Power of Ethical Management* (New York: Fawcett Crest, 1988), 20.
43. *Creating a Workable Company Code of Ethics* (Washington, D.C.: Ethics Resource Center, 1990), VIII-1.
44. Donald R. Cressey and Charles R. Moore, "Managerial Values and Corporate Codes of Ethics," *California Management Review* (Summer, 1983), 57–58.
45. Cited in Rick Wartzman, "Nature or Nurture? Study Blames Ethical Lapses on Corporate Goals," *The Wall Street Journal* (October 9, 1987), 31.
46. *Ethics Policies and Programs in American Business* (Washington, D.C.: Ethics Resource Center, 1990), 23–24.
47. "Motorola's Ethics Committee: Adding Teeth to the Corporate Code," *Ethics Resource Center Report* (Summer, 1986), 4–6.
48. *Ibid.*
49. *Ibid.*
50. Allen, 16.
51. Phillip I. Blumberg, "Corporate Morality and the Crisis of Confidence in American Business," *Beta Gamma Sigma Invited Essay* (St. Louis: Beta Gamma Sigma, January, 1977), 7.
52. Purcell, 47.
53. *Ethics Policies and Programs in American Business*, 35.
54. Allen, 16.
55. Myles L. Mace, "John J. McCloy on Corporate Payoffs," *Harvard Business Review* (July-August, 1976), 28.
56. Kirk O. Hanson, "What Good Are Ethics Courses?" *Across the Board* (September, 1987), 10–11.
57. Ron Zemke, "Ethics Training: Can We Really Teach People Right from Wrong?" *Training* HRD (May, 1977), 39.
58. *Ethics Policies and Programs in American Business*, 34.
59. Thomas M. Jones, "Can Business Ethics Be Taught? Empirical Evidence," *Business & Professional Ethics Journal,* (Vol. 8, 1989), 86.
60. John E. Adair, *Management and Morality: The Problems and Opportunities of Social Capitalism* (London: David & Charles, 1974), 143.
61. W. Edward Stead, Dan L. Worrell, and Jean Garner Stead, "An Integrative Model for Understanding and Managing Ethical Behavior in Business Organizations," *Journal of Business Ethics,* (Vol. 9, 1990), 223–242.

CHAPTER **SIX**

Ethical Issues in the Global Arena

CHAPTER OBJECTIVES

After studying this chapter, you should be able to:

- Identify and describe the four areas in the trend toward the internationalization of business.

- Explain the evolving role of and problems with multinational corporations in the global environment.

- Recognize the major ethical challenges of operating in the multinational environment.

- Discuss strategies for improving global ethics.

- Enumerate seven moral guideliness for improving multinational corporations' operations in the global sphere.

The rise of international business as a critical element in the world economy is one of the most significant developments of the past 40 years or more. This period has been characterized by the rapid growth of direct investment in foreign lands by the United States, by countries in Western Europe, by Japan, and by other industrialized countries as well. In the United States, domestic issues have been made immensely more complex by the rising international focus. At the same time, the internationalization of business has created unique problems of its own. It no longer appears that international markets can be seen as opportunities that may or may not be pursued. Rather, international markets should be seen as natural extensions of an ever-expanding marketplace that must be pursued if firms are to remain competitive. Peter Drucker has termed this expanded marketplace the *transnational economy.* He further goes on to say that, if business expects to establish and maintain leadership in one country, it must also strive to hold a leadership position in all developed markets worldwide. This apparent need helps explain the worldwide boom in transnational investments.[1]

The complexity introduced by the internationalization of business is seen clearly in cases in which ethical issues arise. At best, business ethics is difficult when we are dealing with one culture. Once we bring two or possibly more cultures into consideration, it gets extremely complicated. We have to deal not only with differing customs, protocol, and ways of operating but also with differing concepts of law or notions of what is acceptable or unacceptable behavior in an ethical sense. All of this is then exacerbated by the fact that world political issues become intertwined. For example, what might be intended as a corporate attempt to simply bribe an official of a foreign government, in keeping with local custom, could explode into major international political tension between two countries.

International business is an extremely broad topic. We can expose only the tip of the iceberg here, and, because we must limit our discussion to ethical and social issues, we can examine only one small facet of that exposed tip. Nevertheless, we do need to briefly consider some of the challenges introduced in business ethics at an international level, and that will be our major purpose in this chapter.

ERAS IN THE TREND TOWARD INTERNATIONALIZATION OF BUSINESS

Depending on which international business expert you read, the period from 1945 to the present may be divided into three or four general eras in the growth of the international economy. We do not need to consider these eras in detail, but it is helpful to note some of the major changes that occurred during this time to help us appreciate the modern situation.

The Post-World War II Decade (1945–1955)

Immediately after World War II, the United States was the dominant country as Western Europe and Japan underwent a period of reconstruction. According to Richard D. Robinson, this *postwar decade* is the first era in international development.[2]

The Growth Years (1955–1970)

By 1955, Japanese and European reconstruction was essentially completed and we entered the *growth years*. Both Japanese and European firms began to seek global markets more aggressively. Also, during this time the United States got bogged down in Vietnam. As the United States built up massive balance-of-payments deficits, the dollar came under increasing pressure. A number of the larger U.S.-based international firms became multinational in that they moved toward globally integrated production and marketing systems that necessitated central control.

Because of the development of international communication systems and technology, jet air travel, and increased international expertise, such centralized control became possible.[3] It was one thing to just sell products in a foreign land. But with the increasing prevalence of multinational corporations (MNCs)—first in the United States, then in Western Europe, and then in Japan—the sensitivities of host governments became heightened. A **multinational corporation** is a firm whose operations extend beyond the boundaries of its home country by having one or more subsidiaries in countries other than that in which it is chartered (its home country). Production and distribution systems are still significantly owned by the companies of a home country but are located in a host country where they have become a vital element in that country's economy.

The 1955–1970 period saw a strong rise in MNCs, with U.S. firms dominating. The growth of U.S.-based MNCs was followed by rapid expansion of Western European MNCs and then by expansion of Japanese MNCs, particularly during the 1970s. The United States felt the Japanese expansion as well. Practically everyone in the United States today recognizes such names as Sony, Toyota, Honda, and Mitsubishi as they would such U.S. names as GE, Ford, or General Motors.

The Troubled Years (1970–1980)

The 1970s—the *time of trouble*—is Robinson's third era in international business development.[4] During this time, the persistent balance-of-payments deficit forced the United States to drop the fixed exchange rate system, and the value of the dollar declined significantly, especially in relation to the Japanese yen and the German mark. During this time, the political power of the MNC was finally recognized. The worldwide oil crisis and the high visibility of OPEC also occurred during this period.

The New International Order (1980–Present)

The *new international order* (1980 and beyond) is Robinson's fourth era.[5] By the mid- to late 1970s, the entire sphere of international business was being heavily politicized, both at home and abroad. There was mounting government regulation in many countries as public concerns intensified with regard to pollution, natural resource allocation, income and wealth distribution, consumer protection, and energy. All this was made more complex by internal-country conflict, lack of clear national policies, and the increasingly strong voice of special-interest groups. Some of these groups—whether they were religious, ethnic, political, economic, or professional—have been establishing international linkages and loyalties that are quite distinct from the traditional nation-state loyalties. Efforts to create new international agencies based on common interest (consumers, labor, the poor, conservationists, business) became commonplace. Many of these groups wanted to create a new international order in their own image. The upshot of these developments has been a complex multiactor era.[6]

The most significant occurrence in international business over the past 20 years has been the diminishment of the United States as a world economic power. Whereas it once dominated global markets, this is no longer the case. The new international order, therefore, is one in which the United States no longer occupies the almost monopolistic position it once did. It is still a major actor, but it now shares the stage with Japan, Western Europe, and the developing countries. Perhaps it has been this diminishment of status in the world that has made the push toward better business ethics at the international level a bitter pill to swallow for many business people. The United States has definitely lost some of its economic status and is scrambling to become competitive again. Yet, at the same time, it is getting increased pressures to be a world leader in the ethics arena. In this environment, the MNC is the focal point for much of the tension. Therefore, the MNC is worth examining closely.

MNCs AND THE GLOBAL ENVIRONMENT

All problems of operating in a global environment are not attributable to MNCs. However, MNCs have become the symbolic heart of the problem because they represent the prototypical international business. We will focus on U.S.-based MNCs, but we should remember that the MNCs of other countries experience these same environmental circumstances, too. In fact, the presence of MNCs from various countries makes for a complex operating environment for all firms.

Changed Scope and Nature of U.S.-Based MNCs

Over the years, both the scope and the nature of U.S.-based MNCs have changed. In the early 1900s, the United Fruit Company was growing bananas in Central America and achieving a degree of notoriety for its "invasion" of Honduras. Another wave of MNCs was in the extractive industries (oil, gas, gems). Today, financial institutions, chemicals, drugs, manufacturers, and service firms represent the kinds of enterprises that may be found operating in the multinational environment.

The investment of U.S.-based MNCs has been phenomenal over the past three decades or more, growing from $20 billion to well over $250 billion.[7] We should also note that the most controversial situation for MNCs is when they are operating in so-called emerging nations, or *less-developed countries (LDCs)*, where charges of exploitation seem more plausible. These situations are ripe for charges of American imperialism in struggling economies.

Underlying Problems of Operating in a Multinational Environment

It has been argued that there are at least two underlying and related problems as firms attempt to operate in a multinational environment. One problem is that of *corporate legitimacy* as the MNC seeks a role in a foreign society. The other problem is the fundamentally *different philosophies* that may exist between the firm's home country and the host country in which it seeks to operate.[8] These two problems set the stage for understanding how ethical problems arise in the global environment.

Corporate Legitimacy. For a MNC to be perceived as legitimate in the eyes of a host country, it must fulfill its social responsibilities. As we discussed earlier, these include economic, legal, ethical, and voluntary responsibilities. Larger firms, in particular, are seen as outsiders, and the expectations on them are greater than on smaller, less visible firms. Further, the similarities and differences between the cultures of the two countries affect the perceived legitimacy. For example, an American firm operating in Canada is not likely to experience major problems. An American or Western firm in Iran, however, could be perceived as quite alien.[9] Differences between the life-styles of managers who live in the two countries could pose serious legitimacy problems. If a host country finds the life-style repugnant—as many LDCs may well find the materialistic life-styles of American managers—then legitimacy may be difficult to achieve.

Another, perhaps more basic, barrier to achieving legitimacy is the inherent conflict that may exist between the interests of the MNC and those of the host country. The MNC is seeking to optimize globally, while host governments are seeking to optimize locally. This may pose little difficulty for an MNC operating in a developed country where macroeconomic or regulatory policies are sophisticated and appropriate. But it may pose serious problems in the LDCs where there is often the perception that MNCs are beyond the control of local governments. In these latter situations, especially, it is not uncommon to see the local government impose various control devices such as *indigenization* laws requiring majority ownership by locals, exclusion of foreign firms from certain industries, restrictions on foreign personnel, or even expropriation.[10]

Part of the reason MNCs have difficulty achieving legitimacy is a reaction to the real or perceived conflicts between the interests of the firm and those of the host country or government that place the MNC in a "no-win" situation. If a MNC tries to bring in the latest labor-saving technology, this may conflict with the perceived need for labor-creating technology in high unemployment-prone LDCs. If the MNC repatriates large parts of its profits, this may be seen as depriving the local economy of new wealth. If the MNC reinvests the profits locally, this may be perceived as furthering its control over the economy. If the MNC pays market rate wages, this may be seen as exploiting labor with low wage rates. If the MNC pays a premium for labor, this may be seen as skimming the cream of the local labor supply and thus hurting local businesses that cannot afford to pay a premium. Consequently, whatever it does, the MNC is a convenient target for criticism from some faction or stakeholders. In this sometimes hostile environment, legitimacy can be a fleeting idea—difficult to get and harder to keep.[11]

Differing Philosophies. Closely related to the legitimacy issue is the dilemma of MNCs that have quite different philosophical perspectives from those of their host countries. The philosophy of Western industrialized nations, and thus their MNCs, focuses on economic growth, efficiency, specialization, free trade, and comparative advantage. By contrast, LDCs, for example, have quite different priorities. Other important objectives for them might include a more equitable income distribution or increased economic self-determination. In this context, the industrialized nations may appear to be inherently exploitative in that their presence may perpetuate the dependency of the poorer nation. This is evident in relations not only between Western-based MNCs and LDCs but also between market-oriented Western-based MNCs and planning-oriented communist countries.[12]

These philosophical differences build in an environment of tension that sometimes results in stringent actions being unilaterally taken by the host country. During the 1970s, for example, the environment for MNCs investing in LDCs became much more harsh. Some of these harsh actions initiated by the host countries included outright expropriation (as occurred in the oil industry) and creeping expropriation (as occurred in the manufacturing industries when foreign subsidiaries were required to take on some local partners). Other restrictions included limits on profits repatriation.[13] As a result of the dilemmas that the MNCs face, it is easy to understand why philosopher Richard DeGeorge has argued that "First World MNCs are both the hope of the Third World and the *scourge* of the Third World."[14]

Thus, MNCs increasingly find themselves in situations where their very legitimacy is in question and their philosophical perspective is radically different from that of their host countries. Added to this are the normal problems of operating in a foreign culture with different types of governments, different languages, different legal systems, diverse stakeholders, and different social values. One could well argue that ethical problems are built into this environment. MNCs are attempting to bridge the cultural gaps between two peoples; yet, as they attempt to adapt to local customs and business practices, they are assailed at home for not adhering to the standards, practices, laws, or ethics of their home country. Indeed, there are ethical dilemmas for MNCs. Figure 6-1 portrays the dilemma of MNCs caught between the characteristics and expectations of a home country and those of one or more host countries.

MNC–Host Country Challenges

There are so many issues characterizing the challenges between MNCs and host countries that it is almost impossible to draw limits on them. However, we must limit our focus in this chapter. Before discussing a few select ethical issues in the next section, we will here attempt to at least identify what some of these broader challenges are. The issues we will touch on here include the cultural aspects of global business, business-government interactions of global operations, management and control of resources in global operations and, finally, exploration of global markets.[15]

FIGURE 6-1 The Dilemma of the Multinational Corporation

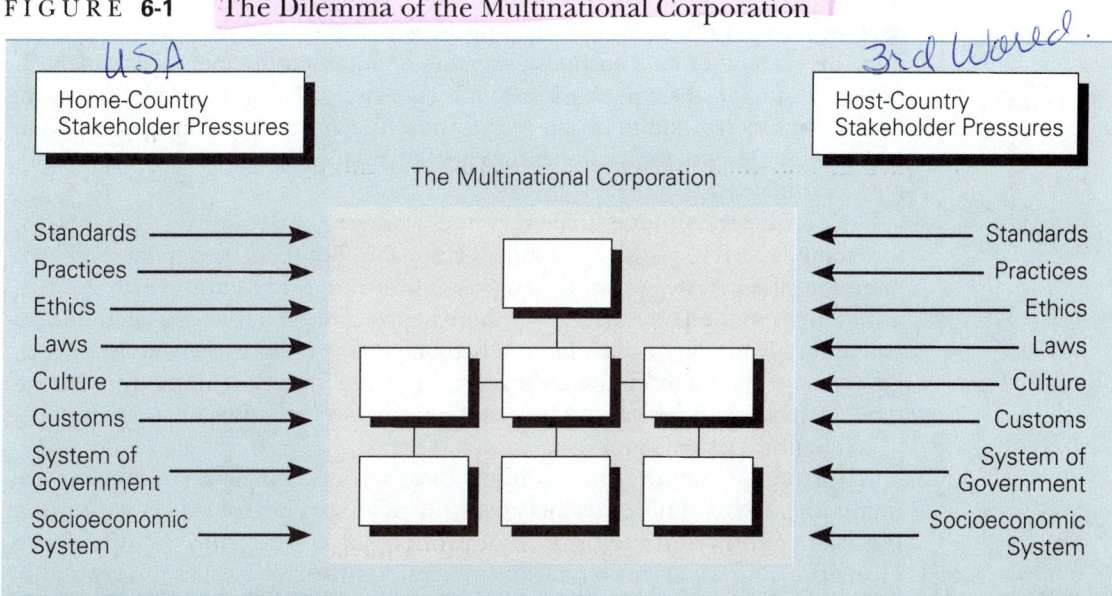

It has been argued that the most significant reason why MNC managers fail is their inability to cope with the foreign environment. Managers and companies experience culture shock when they are faced with cultures and languages that are significantly different from their own. Culture becomes one of the most critical make-or-break factors in successful multinational corporate operations. Culture, customs, language, attitudes, and institutions vary from country to country, and these differences pose sometimes insurmountable obstacles to success for MNCs.

Many humorous stories are told of how changing cultural contexts have created problems for MNCs. The following brief excerpt from Senator Paul Simon illustrates this point well:

> *Body by Fisher,* describing a General Motors product, came out "Corpse by Fisher" in Flemish, and that did not help sales. . . . *Come Alive With Pepsi* almost appeared in the Chinese version of the *Reader's Digest* as "Pepsi brings your ancestors back from the grave." A major ad campaign in green did not sell in Malaysia, where green symbolizes death and disease. An airline operating out of Brazil advertised that it had plush "rendezvous" lounges on its jets, unaware that in Portuguese, "rendezvous" implied a room for making love.[16]

If these kinds of problems arise because of language, customs, or symbols, it is interesting to speculate what issues are likely to result from contrasting ethical standards.

Beyond the differences that stem from cultural variables, the interaction of the business and government sectors poses challenges that MNC executives must deal with. Depending on the region of the world and industry under consideration, the extent of the business-government interactions may vary widely. In worldwide financial services, for example, heavy regulation was typical until the 1980s, when deregulation began in the United States and spread to other countries as well. Deregulation came fast to world banking, yet now some reregulation is occurring.

Government continues to be very important in some countries. "Japan, Inc.," for example, refers to the close-knit relationship between the Japanese government and the private sector. By contrast, government and business are more at arms length in the United States. In Korea, government has always been influential, and only in recent years has the banking sector been privatized. In Europe, government has been intimately involved in business and banking from time to time. Many key industries have been nationalized in Great Britain, depending on which political party is in power.[17]

It is not uncommon for conflicts to arise between host country governments and MNCs. These conflicts typically relate to control over operations in the host country and the division of profits that accrue from the operations. Host governments are also typically interested in such issues as the regulation of technology transfer and transfer prices used by MNCs for conducting intrafirm trade.[18]

Two issues are worthy of mention under a consideration of the management and control of global operations. One issue is organizational structure and design, and the other issue is human resource management. MNCs must employ a multiplicity of organizational approaches in its markets. This is in significant part due to host government regulations. MNC management becomes complex when the firm licenses in country A, joint ventures in country B, and countertrades in country C. In each environment the firm faces different challenges. A second major topic that needs to be addressed is the proper use of human resources. In the arena of staffing, a question arises concerning the tactical use of home versus host country nationals. Use of each implies different costs and benefits for the firm. Other critical human resource issues include selection and training.[19]

Finally, in this section, we will mention exploring global markets as a vital MNC–host country challenge. Although U.S. MNCs dominated world markets for a period of time, this is no longer the case. Today, we have a world of intense competition from firms all over the globe. In the past 20 years there has been a remarkable resurgence not only from Japan and the European economies but from some other countries as well. One major issue in this general topic is the question of strategic alternatives that may be used by MNCs considering expansion into new foreign markets. A number of different strategies involving products and promotions are possible. Relevant factors in such strategic planning include the product function or need satisfied, conditions of product use, consumers' ability to buy, and communications strategy.[20]

Another major issue surrounds the pursuit of underdeveloped Third World markets. Marketing concepts for Asia, Africa, and some countries in Latin America may differ markedly from those we have become accustomed to in the United States. This category of issue is quite important in connection with our discussion of global ethics, because less developed countries pose significant temptations to MNCs to exploit and cut corners. International expert Richard D. Robinson suggests we need to be sensitive to the long-run national interests of such countries. He advocates three levels of sensitivity. First, management of MNCs should be sensitive to the need to *modify* or *redesign products* so that they will be appropriate for their intended markets. An example of this was a truck manufacturer that modified its truck design to accommodate the rough roads, extreme heat, and high elevations found in Turkey. Second, management must be sensitive to the *impact of products,* especially in terms of their impacts on the long-term interests of non-Western markets. For example, luxury products and those of a fundamentally labor-saving nature would not necessarily be appealing under all circumstances to a development-conscious foreign government. Third, MNC managers should be sensitive to the extent to which their product is *politically vulnerable.* Products that are politically vulnerable may lead to labor agitation, public regulation (for example, price fixing, allocation quotas), nationalization, or political debates. Examples of products that in the past have led to political debates and action include sugar, salt, kerosine, gasoline, tires, and medicines.[21]

The need to be sensitive to marketing in other countries provides an appropriate transition to our discussion of ethical issues. It should be clear from this discussion that ethical issues or conflicts might easily arise from cultural conditions that are not anticipated by the MNCs. Further, even though we will examine in more detail quite interesting and glamorous issues such as marketing practices, questionable payments, and doing business in South Africa, we should be ever-vigilant of the fact that such ethical dilemmas can also arise in such realms as production management, financial management, and global strategic management.

ETHICAL PROBLEMS IN THE MULTINATIONAL ENVIRONMENT

For many companies, most of the ethical problems that arise in the international environment are the same as those that arise in their domestic environments. These ethical issues reside in all of the functional areas of business—production, marketing, finance, and management. These issues concern the fair treatment of stakeholders—employees, customers, the community, and competitors. These issues involve product safety, advertising, environmental problems, and so on.

The ethical problems seem to be somewhat fewer in developed countries, but they exist there as well. The ethical problems seem to be worse in the underdeveloped countries or the LDCs because these countries are at a different stage of economic development. This situation creates an environment in which there is a temptation to adhere to lower standards, or perhaps no standards, because no government regulation or activist groups exist to protect the stakeholders' interest. In the LDCs, the opportunities for business exploitation and the engagement in questionable (by developed countries' standards) practices are abundant.

We will illustrate some prominent examples of ethical problems in the multinational sphere to provide some appreciation of the development of these kinds of issues for business. First, we will treat two leading ethical issues that have arisen with regard to questionable marketing and safety practices. Second, we will consider the special problem of bribery and questionable payments, which has been an ethical issue in the United States for about 20 years. Third, we will look at the issue of doing business in South Africa, for few issues have been more prominent throughout the 1980s than this one. From these examples we should be able to develop an appreciation of the ethical issues that confront MNCs and others doing business abroad.

Questionable Marketing and Safety Practices

An example of a questionable marketing practice is the infant-formula controversy that spanned most of the 1970s and continues on in the 1990s. The plant-safety issue is best illustrated by examining the Union Carbide Bhopal crisis that began in late 1984 and continues even today.

The Infant-Formula Controversy. The infant-formula controversy appropriately illustrates the ethical questions that can arise while doing business abroad. We will briefly refer to James Post's observations about this now-classic case. For decades, physicians working in tropical lands (many of which are LDCs) realized that there were severe health risks posed to infants from bottle-feeding as opposed to breast-feeding. Such countries typically have neither refrigeration nor sanitary conditions. Water supplies are not pure, and, therefore, infant formula mixed with this water contains bacteria that would likely lead to disease and diarrhea in the bottle-fed infant. Because these LDCs are typically poor, this condition encourages mothers to overdilute powdered formula, thus diminishing significantly the amount of nutrition the infant receives. Once a mother begins bottle-feeding, her capacity for breast-feeding quickly diminishes. Poverty also leads the mother to put in the bottle substitute products that are less expensive. These products, such as powdered whole milk and corn starch, are not acceptable substitutes—they are inadequate nutritionally and unsatisfactory to the baby's digestive system.

By the late 1960s, it was apparent that in the LDCs there was increased bottle-feeding, decreased breast-feeding, and a dramatic increase in malnourished and sick babies. Bottle-feeding was cited as one of the major reasons.[22] The ethical debate began when it was noted that a number of the infant-formula companies, aware of the environment just described, were promoting their products and, therefore, promoting bottle-feeding in a very intense way. Such marketing practices as mass advertising, billboards, radio jingles, and free samples became commonplace. These promotional devices typically portrayed the infants who used their products as healthy and robust, in sharp contrast with the reality that was brought about by the conditions mentioned.

One of the worst marketing practices entailed the use of "milk nurses"—women dressed in nurses' uniforms who walked the halls of maternity wards urging mothers to get their babies started on formula. In reality, these women were sales representatives employed by the companies on a commission basis. Once the infants were hooked on formula, the mothers' capacity to breast-feed diminished.[23]

Although a number of companies were engaging in these questionable marketing practices, the Swiss conglomerate Nestlé was singled out by a Swiss social activist group when it published an article in 1974 entitled "Nestlé Kills Babies." At about the same time, an article appeared in Great Britain entitled "The Baby Killers."[24] From this point on, a protracted controversy developed with Nestlé and other infant-formula manufacturers on one side and a host of organizations on the other side filing shareholder resolutions and lawsuits against the company. Among the groups that were actively involved in the controversy were church groups such as the National Council of Churches and its Interfaith Center on Corporate Responsibility (ICCR), UNICEF, the World Health Organization (WHO), and the Infant Formula Action Coalition (INFACT). Nestlé was singled out because it had the largest share of the world market and because it aggressively pushed sales of its infant formula in developing countries even after the World Health Organization developed a sales code to the contrary.[25]

In 1977, INFACT and ICCR organized and led a national boycott against Nestlé that continued for almost 7 years. More than 70 American organizations representing churches, doctors, nurses, teachers, and other professionals participated in the boycott. These groups mounted an international campaign aimed at changing these objectionable marketing practices in the LDCs.[26] In 1984, after spending tens of millions of dollars resisting the boycott, Nestlé finally reached an accord with the protesters. The company agreed to four changes in its business practices:

1. It would restrict the distribution of free samples.
2. It would use Nestlé labels to identify the benefits of breast-feeding and the hazards of bottle-feeding.
3. It promised to help ensure that hospitals use its products in accordance with the WHO code.
4. It agreed to drop its policy of giving gifts to health professionals to encourage them to promote infant formula.

The protesters, in return, agreed to end their boycott but to continue monitoring Nestlé's performance.[27]

The infant-formula controversy continued on through the 1980s and into the 1990s. In 1991, Nestlé (which controls more than 40 percent of the world-wide market) and American Home Products (which controls about 15 percent of the world-wide market) announced that after decades of boycotts and controversy, they planned to discontinue the practice of providing free and low-cost formula to developing countries.

The action by Nestlé was its most aggressive ever in an attempt to quell the protracted criticism that it had defied WHO's marketing restrictions by dumping huge quantities of baby milk on Third World hospitals. The distribution of supply had been a lingering concern in the infant-formula controversy. Until this announcement, Nestlé had supplied formula on a request basis but over the next several years plans to distribute formula only on a request basis to children "in need" as outlined in the WHO guidelines. The pledges by Nestlé and American Home Products, the world's two biggest formula makers, are regarded as a watershed in the bitter infant-formula controversy.[28]

The infant-formula controversy is rich with examples of the actions and power of social activist groups, government, and the various strategies that might be employed by MNCs. For our purposes, however, it illustrates the character of questionable business practices of firms pursuing what might be called normal practices were it not for the fact that they were being pursued in foreign countries where circumstances made them questionable.

The Bhopal Tragedy. The Union Carbide Bhopal tragedy in late 1984 brings the dilemma of multinationals operating in a foreign, particularly less developed, environment into sharp focus. At this writing, the issues surrounding this event have not been resolved and probably will not be for years to come. On December

3, 1984, a leak of methyl isocyanate gas caused what many have termed the "worst industrial accident in history." The gas leak killed 2,000 people and injured 200,000 more. The tragedy has raised numerous legal, ethical, social, and technical questions for MNCs.[29]

Interviews with experts just after the accident revealed a belief that the responsibility for the accident had to be shared between the company and the Indian government. According to Union Carbide's own inspector, the Bhopal plant did not meet U.S. standards and had not been inspected in over 2 years. The Indian government allowed thousands of people to live very near the plant, and there were no evacuation procedures.[30]

Many different issues have been raised by the Bhopal disaster. Among the more important of these issues are:

1. To what extent should MNCs maintain identical standards at home and abroad, regardless of how lax laws in the host country are?
2. How advisable is it to locate a complex and dangerous plant in an area where the entire work force is basically unskilled and where the populace is ignorant of the inherent risks posed by such plants?
3. How wise are laws that require plants to be staffed entirely by local employees?
4. What is the responsibility of corporations and governments in allowing the use of otherwise safe products that become dangerous because of local conditions? (This question addresses the infant-formula controversy also.)
5. After reviewing all the problems, should certain kinds of plants be located in developing nations?[31]

At the heart of these issues is the question of differing standards in different parts of the world. This dilemma arose in the 1970s when American firms continued to export drugs and pesticides that had been restricted in the United States. Pesticides, such as DDT and others that had been associated with cancer, were shipped to and used in LDCs by farmers who did not understand the dangers or the cautions that were needed in their use of these products. Not surprisingly, poisonings did occur. In 1972, hundreds to thousands of Iraqis died from mercury-treated grain from the United States. In 1975, Egyptian farmers were killed and many made ill from a U.S.-made pesticide. Asbestos and pesticide plants that violated American standards were built in a number of countries. These companies typically broke no laws, but many experts are now saying that the Bhopal tragedy has taught us that companies have a moral responsibility to enforce high standards, especially in developing countries not yet ready or able to regulate these firms.[32]

One major problem that some observers say contributed to the Bhopal explosion and, indeed, applies to MNCs generally, is the requirement that firms be significantly owned by investors in the host country. Union Carbide owned only 50.9 percent of the Bhopal, India, subsidiary. It has been observed that this situation may have reduced Union Carbide's motivation and/or capacity to ensure adequate industrial and environmental safety at its Bhopal plant, mainly by diluting the degree of parent control and reducing the flow of technical expertise into that plant. If developing countries continue to insist on a dilution of MNC control over plants, this may also diminish the MNC's motivation and incentive to transfer environmental management and safety competence. As Gladwin and Walter conclude, "The painful realities of this tradeoff may turn out to be a key lesson of the world's worst industrial accident."[33] Other observers have said that this is a contrived excuse that firms use to obfuscate the issue and evade responsibility.

Another major problem highlighted by the Bhopal explosion is the fact that the people of developing countries are often not aware of the dangers of new technology. As one expert observed, countries such as India have not "internalized the technological culture."[34] On the one hand, the LDCs want technology because they see it as critical to their economic development, but their ability to understand and manage the new technology is in serious doubt.

Back in the United States, the Union Carbide Corporation is fighting for its life. The litigation brought on by the poison gas leak threatens to wipe out the company. One lawyer said the litigation could be the "largest and most lucrative civil case in the history of the world." The wave of lawsuits ranges from $15 to $50 billion. Legal experts are saying that the outcome of the litigation not only will dictate Union Carbide's future but also could influence future relationships among U.S.-based MNCs and foreign subsidiaries, populations, and governments.[35]

The lessons from the Bhopal disaster are many and continue to be debated. Figure 6-2 summarizes a number of these lessons. In companies around the globe, the Bhopal disaster has sparked new enthusiasm in the debate about operating abroad. To be sure, ethical and legal issues are central to the discussions. What is at stake, however, is not just businesses' practices abroad but the very question of businesses' presence abroad. Depending on the final outcome of the Union Carbide experience, MNCs may decide that the risk of doing business abroad is too great. As Professor Jack Behrman stated, "You aren't going to invest in situations that are going to jeopardize the whole company."[36]

Bribery and Questionable Payments

Certainly, bribes and questionable payments occurred prior to the 1970s. It was in the mid-1970s, however, when evidence of widespread questionable corporate payments to foreign government officials, political parties, and other influential persons became widely known. Such major corporations as Lockheed, Gulf Oil, Northrop, Carnation, and Goodyear are among those firms admitting to such payments. Huge sums of money have been involved. Gulf, for example, admitted paying $4.2 million to the political party of Korean President Park. Gulf also created a subsidiary in the Bahamas that was then used as a conduit for unlawful political contributions. Lockheed acknowledged payments of $22 million, mostly to officials in the Middle East.[37]

FIGURE 6-2 Lessons from the Bhopal Disaster

- Hazardous facilities often pose added risks in developing nations, where skilled labor and public understanding are often lacking. Special training is needed to compensate for these extra risks.
- Public education is critical in developing countries, where people often do not understand the hazards of toxic substances. Repeated drills and clear warning signals are needed.
- The more rural areas of the developing world should not be used to test complex new technology.
- A sense of urgency about all safety problems and attention to worst-case possibilities—routine in industrial countries but often not transferred to developing countries—should be part of worker training, especially in plants with a high turnover of personnel.
- The company headquarters should audit its plants in developing countries frequently, perhaps more often than it audits plants at home.
- Sophisticated backup safety systems, often installed in industrial nations, are needed to compensate for lapses in training and staff in developing nations, where they are needed more.
- Company executives should be technically—not just administratively—trained in businesses that use toxic materials; such training can compensate for a lack of technical know-how in the local plant staff.
- Many areas of the developing world are growing rapidly and are without zoning laws. Suitable buffers should be placed around the factory to prevent dangers of crowding.
- Cultural differences between foreign and host countries should be considered. If preventive maintenance is a new concept, it should be more thoroughly taught.
- Host governments should closely and continually inspect hazardous factories and their managements, enforcing strict and quick sanctions for safety lapses.
- In making agreements with multinational companies, the governments of developing countries should consider only those technologies that can be safely handled in the long run. It may be necessary to change laws that mandate turning factories over to local control completely.

Source: Stuart Diamond, "The Disaster in Bhopal: Lessons for the Future," *New York Times* (February 5, 1985), 1. Copyright © 1985 by The New York Times Company. Reprinted by permission.

One of the most notorious cases was that of Lockheed giving $12.5 million in bribes and commissions in connection with the sale of $430 million worth of TriStar airplanes to All Nippon Airways. The president of Lockheed defended the payments, claiming that it was common practice and it was expected to give bribes in Japan. The news of the payments rocked Japan more than it did the United States because Prime Minister Kakuei Tanaka and four others were forced to resign and stand trial. Another important point made about this case is that Lockheed did not offer a bribe, but rather the Japanese negotiator demanded it. This point raises the continuing question in matters of this kind: "Are those who accede to bribery equal in guilt to those who demand bribes?"[38]

Arguments for and Against Bribery. Arguments typically given *in favor* of permitting bribery include the following: (1) It is *necessary* for profits in order to do business; (2) *everybody* does it—it will happen anyway; (3) it is *accepted practice* in many countries—it is normal and expected; and (4) bribes are forms of commissions, taxes, or compensation for conducting business between cultures.[39]

Arguments frequently cited *against* giving bribes include (1) bribes are inherently wrong and cannot be accepted under any circumstances; (2) bribes are illegal in the United States and, therefore, unfair elsewhere; (3) one should not compromise his or her own beliefs; (4) we should not deal with corrupt governments; (5) such demands, once started, never stop; (6) one should take a stand for honesty, morality, and ethics; (7) those receiving bribes are the only ones who benefit; (8) bribes create dependence on corrupt individuals and countries; and (9) bribes deceive stockholders and pass on costs to customers.[40]

The Foreign Corrupt Practices Act. Many of the payments made by U.S.-based MNCs were not illegal prior to the passage of the 1977 Foreign Corrupt Practices Act (FCPA). Even so, firms could have been engaging in illegal activities depending on whether and how the payments were reported to the IRS. With the passage of the FCPA, however, it became a criminal offense for a representative of an American corporation to offer or give payments to the officials of other governments for the purpose of getting or maintaining business. The FCPA specifies a series of fines and prison terms that can result if a company or management is found guilty of a violation.[41] The legislation was passed not only for ethical reasons but also out of a concern for the image of the United States abroad.

The FCPA has been controversial, to say the least. The law does not prohibit so-called grease payments, or minor payments to officials, for the primary purpose of getting them to do whatever they are supposed to do anyway. Such payments are commonplace in many countries. The real problem is that some forms of payments are prohibited (for example, bribes), but other payments (for example, grease payments) are not prohibited. The law is ambiguous on the distinctions between the two. The language of the FCPA suggests that *the duties performed by the person receiving payment,* not the intent of the payor, is the key factor in determining legality.[42] Figure 6-3 presents what we think are the distinctions between bribes

FIGURE 6-3 Bribes Versus Grease Payments

Definitions	Examples
Grease Payments Relatively small sums of money given for the purpose of getting someone to • do what they are *supposed to be doing*. • do what they are supposed to be doing *faster or sooner*. • do what they are supposed to be doing *better* than they would otherwise.	Money given to minor officials (clerks, attendants, customs inspectors) for the purpose of expediting. This form of payment helps get goods or services through red-tape or administrative bureaucracies.
Bribes Relatively *large amounts* of money given for the purpose of *influencing* someone to *make a decision or take an action* that he/she *otherwise* might not take. If the person considered the merits of the situation only, he/she might take some other action.	Money given, often to high-ranking officials. Purpose is often to get these persons to purchase goods or services from the bribing firm. May also be used to avoid taxes, forestall unfavorable government intervention, secure favorable treatment, etc.

(which are prohibited) and grease payments (which are not prohibited) based on the FPCA. Even with these general definitions, it is unclear exactly where the line would be drawn in a given situation.

Impact of the FCPA. Since the passage of the FCPA, which prohibited bribery for U.S.-based MNCs, the major criticism against the act has been that it is unilateral; that is, it affects U.S. firms but not foreign competitors. U.S firms often claim that they cannot compete successfully if they are prohibited from giving bribes but others are not. The consequence, it is argued, would be a decline in U.S. exports. However, several studies suggest that there is no appreciable impact on U.S. competitiveness by the antibribery law.

Barry Richman studied 65 major U.S. corporations, many of which were in industries in which there was a high incidence of companies that had disclosed questionable payments. In cases where bribing companies stopped giving the payments, the loss of business seemed modest. In only six cases did he find that the loss of business amounted to more than 0.5 percent of total consolidated sales. Where payments were effective, they often seemed to have transferred orders from one American company to another. Richman argues that if both companies had followed the same standards that govern competition at home, no payments would have been necessary.[43]

In the 2 years following the enactment of the FCPA, U.S. exports did not decrease but rather increased by 11 percent. This is not proof-positive, but an exhaustive 1984 study by John L. Graham at the University of Southern California concluded that the FCPA has not had a negative effect on U.S. exports. Graham noted that "no differences in United States market share were to be discovered in nations where the FCPA is reported to be an important disincentive, both in terms of total trade with each country, as well as for sales of individual product categories."[44]

In a 1981 study by the General Accounting Office (GAO) entitled "Impact of the FCPA on U.S. Business," 250 U.S. firms were surveyed as to their experience with the FCPA. The Securities and Exchange Commission (SEC), while commenting on the GAO's findings, observed that "the GAO's survey data indicate that while there have been some lost opportunities, it has been a much less serious problem than many had assumed. Indeed, less than 1 percent of the 250 American businesses questioned reported any serious loss of business."[45]

Finally, in a major 1987 study of the impact of the FCPA on the international competitiveness of U.S. firms, Kate Gillespie found that the restrictions placed on U.S. firms in 1977 have not had an adverse effect on sales to the Middle East. In addition, she found that the FCPA restrictions were consistent with the efforts of a number of countries to reduce corruption in their own countries.[46]

The problem of foreign bribery and questionable payments remains real despite the passage of the FCPA. Efforts were begun by at least one legislator in 1986 to emasculate the FCPA through amendments. The evidence, however, seems to indicate that the act has not created the problems originally anticipated. Therefore, it may well be serving to some extent as an effective self-policing instrument.[47]

Doing Business in South Africa

South African *apartheid* (racial segregation, separateness) has been an ethical and human rights issue for decades. As civil rights laws have been passed in the United States and as American and European societies have been increasingly sensitized to the mistreatment and discrimination against racial minorities, pressure has built on American and other world firms to disengage from doing business in South Africa. Later in this section we will see some of the dramatic changes that have taken place in South Africa beginning in 1990.

U.S. MNCs have received significant pressure from activist groups to withdraw from their South African operations, especially since the early to mid-1980s. The pressure on U.S. firms has taken a number of forms. Shareholders have filed resolutions calling for their firms to discontinue operating in South Africa to protest that country's discriminatory racial policies. Some states, school systems, and universities have passed legislation prohibiting the investment of public or pension funds in U.S. companies continuing to do business in South Africa. The U.S. government publically opposed South Africa's human rights policies.

The issue of U.S. firms doing business in South Africa escalated in 1975 when a group of black leaders approached the Reverend Leon Sullivan, a civil rights activist and board member of General Motors Corporation, and asked him to devise a code of conduct or set of principles for American businesses operating in South Africa. He finished the code in 1977, and it became known as the *Sullivan Principles,* which are summarized in Figure 6-4.

The Sullivan Principles played a significant role in helping black South Africans to gain workplace rights in many businesses and have been helpful in the efforts of black industrial labor unions in winning official recognition. Reverend Sullivan began a signatories program in which he asked major corporations to comply with the Sullivan Principles. Over 150 of the several hundred major firms doing business in South Africa became signatories to the principles and even agreed to pay up to $7,000 a year to take part in the program and have their performance monitored and assessed by the accounting firm of Arthur D. Little. Reverend Sullivan did not expect that the principles alone would end apartheid, but he did think the program would be helpful toward improving the plight of black South Africans.

A major impact of U.S. society's pressure on American firms was that many of them began withdrawing (disinvestment) from South Africa, especially during the 1980s. The U.S government expedited this withdrawal by the significant sanctions it began leveling against the South African government in 1985. In that year, President Reagan issued an executive order banning new loans and military sales

FIGURE 6-4 The Sullivan Principles for American Companies Doing Business in South Africa

- Nonsegregation of the races in all eating, comfort, locker room, and work facilities.
- Equal and fair employment practices for all employees.
- Equal pay for all employees doing equal or comparable work for the same period of time.
- Initiation and development of training programs that will prepare blacks, coloreds, and Asians in substantial numbers for supervisory, administrative, clerical, and technical jobs.
- Increasing the number of blacks, coloreds, and Asians in management and supervisory positions.
- Improving the quality of employees' lives outside the work environment in such areas as housing, transportation, schooling, recreation, and health facilities.

to the South African government. In 1986, Congress passed the Comprehensive Anti-Apartheid Act, which banned most new direct investment, air transport, and imports of coal, steel, uranium, textiles, and farm products from South Africa. The U.S. sanctions, along with those also levied by other countries, had a significant impact on the South African economy. Many believe that the actions played a significant role in bringing about the reforms in South Africa in the early 1990s.

Throughout the 1980s, especially the mid- to late 1980s, doing business in South Africa became a hot ethical issue for firms. A number of major firms withdrew from South Africa in the mid-1980s. Among them were such household names as Coca-Cola, IBM, General Motors, Honeywell, General Electric, Bell and Howell, Procter and Gamble, and Phillips Petroleum. According to the Washington-based Investor Responsibility Research Center, 117 U.S. firms were still in business in South Africa in 1990, but this was down from 284 in 1984. Another contributing factor was that in 1987, Reverend Sullivan called for the withdrawal of U.S. firms from South Africa, and he eventually disassociated himself from the formal administration of the Sullivan Principles because at that point he believed the only effective course of action was withdrawal.

Many U.S. firms left South Africa, and many U.S. firms stayed in South Africa. The firms operating in South Africa faced a real dilemma because, no matter what they did, there were pros and cons to their actions. Each course of action could be justified on some reasonable grounds. Figure 6-5 summarizes some of the reasons why business people have chosen to stay or leave, and, if they stayed, what their positions might be toward apartheid.

Radical changes began occurring in South Africa on the election of F. W. De Klerk as president. De Klerk stunned his country in 1989 and 1990 by his pledge to end apartheid. His early decisions included opening formerly segregated beaches, releasing political prisoners, lifting the ban on the African National Congress and other political groups, and releasing black leader Nelson Mandela after 27 years of imprisonment. De Klerk began holding formal talks with black leaders to negotiate a new nonracial constitution. In 1991, De Klerk announced repeal of the Land Acts, which barred blacks from owning land outside of specially designated homelands, and the Group Areas Act, which segregates black and white residential areas. He unveiled a plan to phase out the infamous Population Registration Act, which forced South Africans to register by racial group for political and economic purposes. This latter act was seen by many as being the final pillar of apartheid. Most of these actions taken by the South African government were conditions that had to be met before the United States and other countries lifted economic sanctions against South Africa.

The actions taken by South Africa to dismantle apartheid are to be applauded, but they have created significant conflicts within that country and only time will tell whether discrimination against blacks will in actuality be eliminated. The debate in the United States over discrimination has not yet ended even though 30 years has elapsed since the passage of the Civil Rights Act. Therefore, it would be premature to conclude that the apartheid system that has characterized South Africa since its beginning will be quickly and easily eliminated. Even in the early

FIGURE 6-5   U.S. Reasons for Staying or Leaving and Posture Toward Apartheid in South Africa

1. Reasons for *staying* in South Africa

- We are making money—we are profitable.
- We've been here a long time and we have managers and employees who depend on us.
- We are helping the economy of South Africa.
- We can work to improve conditions in South Africa by adhering to the Sullivan Principles.
- We account for 20 percent of South Africa's foreign investment.

2. Reasons for *leaving* South Africa

- By staying we show approval for apartheid.
- By staying it hurts our image and the human rights policy of the United States government.
- South African operations account for only 1 percent of total U.S. foreign investment.
- It would be better to divest and enter into licensing agreements or sell to local management.
- The black community wants us out.

3. *Postures* toward apartheid if staying in South Africa

- Apartheid is morally repugnant, and we'll do only what we have to do to accommodate it.
- We will accept it; it is part of the culture.
- We will subscribe to the Sullivan Principles and work toward fair treatment of blacks.
- We will actively fight apartheid.

1990s, some activist groups in the United States are continuing to push for U.S. business divestment, while others are displaying a renewed interest in returning to South Africa as the sanctions are lifted. By all accounts it appears that the question of U.S. firms doing business in South Africa will continue with us for some time. It is an issue fraught with moral, political, and economic dimensions and should continue to serve as a significant touchstone for global business ethics for years to come.

We have by no means covered all the areas in which ethical problems in the multinational environment reside. The topics treated have been major ones subjected to extensive public discussion. Examples of other issues that have become important recently and will probably increase in importance include the issues of international competitiveness, protectionism, industrial policy, and political risk analysis. These issues are of paramount significance in discussions of business's relations with international stakeholders. Other issues that include an ethical dimension are national security versus profit interests in selling to the Soviet Bloc, the use of internal transfer prices to evade high taxes in a country, and mining of the ocean floor. Space does not permit us to discuss these issues in detail.

IMPROVING GLOBAL ETHICS

The most obvious observation to extract from the cases we have discussed up to this point is that business ethics is more complex at the global level than at the domestic level. The complexity arises from the fact that varied value systems, stakeholders, cultures, forms of government, socioeconomic conditions, and standards of ethical behavior exist across the world. Recognition of diverse standards of ethical behavior is important, but if we assume that U.S. firms should more closely operate according to U.S. standards than foreign standards, then the strategy of ethical leadership in the world is a challenging one. Because the United States, and hence U.S.-based MNCs, have played such a leadership role in world affairs—usually espousing fairness and human rights—our firms have a heavy responsibility, particularly in underdeveloped countries and LDCs. The power-responsibility equation also argues that U.S. firms have a serious ethical responsibility in global markets. That is, our larger sense of ethical behavior and social responsiveness derives from the enormous amount of power we have.

Gene Laczniak and Jacob Naor recommend four actions that seem to be desirable and reasonable courses of action for conducting business in foreign environments: (1) develop worldwide codes of conduct, (2) factor ethics into global strategy, (3) suspend activities when faced with unbridgeable ethical gaps, and (4) develop periodic "ethical impact statements."[48]

Thomas Donaldson has set forth 10 fundamental international rights that pick up on the principle of rights discussed in the last chapter. These are worthy of consideration as are Richard DeGeorge's seven "moral guidelines" that provide guidance for MNCs. Finally, we will consider the ethical guidelines for international corporations identified in a Vesper International sponsored multi-stakeholder consultation. First, let us consider Laczniak's and Naor's four recommended actions.

Global Codes of Conduct

In the previous chapter we discussed codes of conduct, and that discussion applies in the global sphere as well. While operating in the global sphere, MNCs have been severely criticized for operating with divergent ethical standards in different countries, thus giving the impression that they are attempting to exploit local circumstances. When in doubt, the course of action that manifests ethical leadership is to adhere to higher rather than lower standards. A growing number of MNCs, such as Caterpillar Tractor, Allis Chalmers, Johnson's Wax, and Rexnord, have developed and used codes geared at worldwide operations.[49]

One of the first and most well known of the codes is that of Caterpillar Tractor Company, issued in 1974 by the chairman of the board, entitled "A Code of Worldwide Conduct." The code goes into considerable detail and has major sections that cover the following vital areas: ownership and investment, corporate facilities, relationships with employees, product quality, sharing of technology, accounting and financial records, different business practices, competitive conduct, observance of local laws, business ethics, relationships with public officials, and international business. The purpose of the code is clearly set forth in the introduction to the code:

> This revised "Code of World Wide Business Conduct" is offered under the several headings that follow. Its purpose continues to be to guide us, in a broad and ethical sense, in all aspects of our worldwide business activities. Of course, this code isn't an attempt to prescribe actions for every business encounter. It *is an attempt to capture basic, general principles to be observed by Caterpillar people everywhere*.[50]

Other companies do not have comprehensive codes addressing their international operations but rather have a code containing a section that addresses foreign practices. For example, in its "General Dynamics Standards of Business Ethics and Conduct," General Dynamics has a section entitled "International Business." One excerpt from this section is encouraging and illustrates the point we have been developing:

> Our policy is to comply with all laws which apply in the countries where we do business. In countries where common practices might indicate acceptance of standards of conduct lower than those to which we aspire, we will follow our own Standards as outlined in this booklet.[51]

As another example, Lockheed makes a more pointed reference to the FCPA: "Lockheed will comply with terms of the Foreign Corrupt Practices Act prohibiting the tendering of money and items of value to a foreign official for the purpose of obtaining or retaining business. Any action that might be construed as soliciting or extending a bribe is forbidden." Lockheed's code also asserts that "ethical conduct is the highest form of loyalty to Lockheed."[52]

At the global level in the late 1980s, the United Nations (U.N.) drafted a Code of Conduct for Transnational Corporations. The code was intended to address ethics and corporate responsibility issues using a trilateral model, involving MNCs, host countries, and home countries. The U.N. code addressed numerous topics including the following: sovereignty of the host country, host country national goals, negotiating contracts in good faith, respect for social and cultural values of host country, human rights, political activities, corrupt practices, financial transfers, consumer protection, environmental protection, and so on.

The major problem with the code included the perception that it was too abstract and lacked precision, especially because of the process of compromise. Another major problem was its difficulty of implementation. A common problem with almost all U.N. resolutions and decisions is the absence of any real enforcement mechanism. New complexities have entered the process as unprecedented political changes have taken place in the Soviet Union and Eastern Europe. Perhaps with time and experience, such U.N. efforts will be more successful.[53]

Ethics and Global Strategy

The major recommendation here is that the ethical dimensions of multinational corporate activity should be considered as significant inputs into top-level strategy formulation and implementation.[54] Carroll, Hoy, and Hall have argued even more broadly that corporate social policy should be integrated into strategic management.[55] At the top level of decision making in the firm, corporate strategy is established. At this level, commitments are made that will define the underlying character and identity that the organization will have. The overall moral tone of the organization and all decision making and behavior are set at the strategic level, and management needs to ensure that social and ethical factors do not get lost in the preoccupation with market opportunities and competitive factors.

If ethics does not get factored in at the strategic formulation level, it is doubtful that ethics will be considered at the level of operations where strategy is being implemented. Unfortunately, much current practice has tended to treat ethics and social responsibility as residual factors. We cannot overemphasize that a more proactive stance is needed for dealing with ethical issues at the global level. Strategic decisions that may be influenced by ethical considerations in the global sphere include, but are not limited to, product/service decisions, plant location, manufacturing policy, marketing policy and practices, and personnel or human resources management policies.

Suspension of Activities

Laczniak and Naor note that a MNC may encounter unbridgeable gaps between the ethical values of its home country and those of the host country. When this occurs, and reconciliation does not appear in sight, the MNC should consider suspending activities in the country. Examples of firms that have taken this course of action are those that decided to divest their South African operations or to leave that country. IBM and Coca-Cola suspended their activities in India because of that country's position on the extent of national ownership and control.[56] Suspension of business in a foreign country is not a decision that can or should be taken precipitously, but it must be regarded as a viable option for those firms that desire to travel on the higher moral road.

Each country is at liberty to have its own standards, but this does not mean that U.S. firms must do business in that country. What does ethical leadership mean if it is not backed up by a willingness and ability to take a firm stand when the occasion merits?

Ethical Impact Statements

MNCs should be constantly aware of the impacts they are having on society, particularly foreign societies. One way to do this is to periodically assess the company's impacts. Companies have a variety of impacts on foreign cultures, and ethical impacts are only one of these. The impact statement idea probably derived, in part, from the practice of environmental impact statements that the U.S. Environmental Protection Agency pioneered in the early 1970s. These statements are similar to the corporate social audit, a concept we will discuss more fully in Chapter 18. Social auditing is "a systematic attempt to identify, analyze, measure (if possible), evaluate, and monitor the effect of an organization's operations on society (that is, specific social groups) and on the public well-being."[57] ***Ethical impact statements*** would be an attempt to assess the underlying moral justifications for corporate actions and the consequent results of those actions. The information derived from these actions would permit the MNCs to modify or change their business practices if the impact statement suggested that such changes would be necessary or desirable.

Fundamental International Rights

Thomas Donaldson has set forth 10 fundamental international rights that he argues should be honored and respected by all international actors, including nation-states, individuals, and corporations. He argues that these rights serve to establish a moral minimum for the behavior of all international economic agents. Donaldson's 10 fundamental rights are as follows:[58]

1. The right to freedom of physical movement
2. The right to ownership of property
3. The right to freedom from torture
4. The right to a fair trial
5. The right to nondiscriminatory treatment (freedom from discrimination on the basis of such characteristics as race or sex)
6. The right to physical security
7. The right to freedom of speech and association
8. The right to minimal education
9. The right to political participation
10. The right to subsistence

Such a list of rights is somewhat general and still leaves considerable room for interpretation. However, it serves to establish a beginning point for MNCs as they contemplate what responsibilities they have in international markets.

Seven Moral Guidelines

According to Richard DeGeorge, a business ethicist, MNCs should apply seven moral guidelines in their international operations. Some of these are rather straightforward, but they do summarize a useful perspective that might well improve MNC operations in the global sphere.

1. MNCs should do no intentional direct harm.
2. MNCs should produce more good than bad for the host country.
3. MNCs should contribute by their activities to the host country's development.
4. MNCs should respect the human rights of its employees.
5. MNCs should pay their fair share of taxes.
6. To the extent that local culture does not violate moral norms, MNCs should respect the local culture and work with it, not against it.
7. MNCs should cooperate with the local government in the development and enforcement of just background institutions (for example, tax system, health and safety standards).[59]

DeGeorge does not present these seven guidelines as a panacea. He does suggest that if they were brought to bear on the dilemmas that MNCs face, the companies could avoid the moral stings of their critics. The spirit of these seven guidelines, if adopted, would go a long way toward improving MNC–host country relations.

Guidelines for International Corporations

In 1990, Vesper International and the Hinksey Centre of Oxford, England, held a Conference in San Francisco entitled "Just Profits: Wending Our Way Through the Moral Maze." The conference was billed as a "multi-stakeholder consultation" because it was composed of representatives from many groups such as management, labor, consumer groups, academics, and religious organizations. Both domestic and international representatives participated. The objective of the conference was to explore the relationship between values and decision making in MNCs. One major outcome of the 3-day conference was the creation of a set of guidelines designed to assist MNCs in their international decision making. The guidelines evolved into a format that specified the responsibilities of international corporations in 12 areas. Figure 6-6 presents the guidelines decided on by the group.

FIGURE 6-6   Guidelines for International Corporations

International corporations have a responsibility to:

- Commit to a long tertm relationship when investing in a community and to operate in cooperation with the host community to seek beneficial impacts

- Act in ways that respect and protect fundamental human rights

- Make full and fair disclosure of all information relevant to the well-being of stakeholders and the general public

- Protect the ecosystem by specifically meeting identified environmental standards and conserving natural resources through efficient use

- Produce products and services which meet adequate standards of safety within a healthy workplace environment

- Recognize the rights of employees to organize and bargain collectively

- Seek to promote employee welfare through fair terms of employment, job security, a safe and non-discriminatory workplace and a commitment to retraining in order to mitigate the impact of layoffs or a plant closure

- Seek long term profitability by providing quality goods and services at a fair price

- Identify and involve stakeholders at appropriate levels and phases of the decision-making process

- Provide management leadership and resources to develop and implement internal ethical guidelines

- Respect local practices and customs or adhere to the coporations's own ethical guidelines, whichever is most beneficial for the local community

- Respect international law and support the development and implementation of codes of conduct for international business which achieve broad international consensus

Sources: Vesper International, 311 MacArthur Blvd., San Leandro, CA 94577, USA, (1-510-633-0666).
The Hinsky Centre, Westminster College, Oxford OX2 9AT, United Kingdom, (44-865) 247-644

Like the other lists presented, the guidelines can only serve as general principles for managers who are aspiring to make ethical decisions in the global arena. They do, however, provide the consensus thinking of a host of stakeholder representatives as to what responsibilities international corporations have.

SUMMARY

Ethical dilemmas pose difficulties, in general, for businesses, and those arising in connection with doing business in foreign lands are among the most complex. A cursory examination of major issues that have arisen in global business ethics over the past two decades shows that they rank right up there with the most well-known news stories. The infant-formula controversy, the Bhopal tragedy, the Lockheed payments to high-ranking Japanese government officials, the seemingly never-ending turmoil in South Africa, and the continuing concern about the exploits of MNCs in Third World countries have all provided an opportunity for business critics to assail corporate ethics in the international sphere. These problems arise for a multiplicity of reasons, but differing cultures, value systems, forms of government, socioeconomic systems, and underhanded and ill-motivated business exploits have all been contributing factors.

Global codes of conduct, the integration of ethical considerations into corporate strategy, the option of suspending activities, the use of ethical impact statements, and the adherence to moral guidelines offer some hope that conditions can be better managed. Current trends do not point to the diminishment of business activity in the transnational economy, and therefore these issues will become more rather than less important in the future. Indeed, it could easily be argued that business's greatest ethical challenges in the future will be at the global level.

DISCUSSION QUESTIONS

1. Drawing on the notions of moral, amoral, and immoral management introduced in Chapter 4, categorize your impressions of (a) Nestlé, S. A., in the infant-formula controversy, and (b) Union Carbide in the Bhopal tragedy.
2. Of the lessons learned from the Bhopal tragedy presented in Figure 6-2, identify the single lesson you think is most important and explain why.
3. Differentiate between a bribe and a grease payment. Give an example of each.
4. Identify what you consider to be the single most important of the six Sullivan Principles. Briefly explain.
5. Of DeGeorge's seven moral guidelines, identify which single guideline you think is of most practical value for a MNC. Briefly explain.

ENDNOTES

1. Peter F. Drucker, "The Transnational Economy," *The Wall Street Journal* (August 25, 1987), 38.
2. Richard D. Robinson, "Background Concepts and Philosophy of International Business from World War II to the Present," in William A. Dymsza and Robert G. Vambery (eds.), *International Business Knowledge: Managing International Functions in the 1990s* (New York: Praeger, 1987), 3–4.
3. *Ibid.*
4. *Ibid.*, 5–6.
5. *Ibid.*, 6.
6. *Ibid.*
7. W. Michael Hoffman, Ann E. Lange, and David Fedo (eds.), *Ethics and the Multinational Enterprise* (Lanham, MD: University Press of America, 1986), xix.
8. John Garland and Richard N. Farmer, *International Dimensions of Business Policy and Strategy* (Boston: Kent Publishing Company, 1986), 166–173.
9. *Ibid.*, 167–168.
10. *Ibid.*, 169.
11. *Ibid.*, 170–171.
12. *Ibid.*, 172.
13. *Ibid.*
14. "Ethical Dilemmas of the Multinational Enterprise," *Business Ethics Report*, Highlights of Bentley College's Sixth National Conference of Business Ethics (Waltham, MA: The Center for Business Ethics at Bentley College, October 10 and 11, 1985), 3.
15. James C. Baker, John C. Ryans, Jr., and Donald G. Howard, *International Business Classics* (Lexington, MA: Lexington Books, 1988), 73–367.
16. Paul Simon, *The Tongue Tied American* (New York: Continuum Press, 1980), 32.
17. Baker, Ryans, and Howard, 127–138.
18. Alan M. Rugman, Donald J. Lecraw, and Laurence D. Booth, *International Business: Firm and Environment* (New York: McGraw-Hill, 1985), 293.
19. Baker, Ryans, and Howard, 245–246.
20. *Ibid.*, 314–315.
21. Richard D. Robinson, "The Challenge of the Underdeveloped National Market," in Baker et al., 347–356.
22. James E. Post, "Assessing the Nestlé Boycott: Corporate Accountability and Human Rights," *California Management Review* (Winter, 1985), 115–116.
23. *Ibid.*, 116–117.
24. Rogene A. Buchholz, William D. Evans, and Robert Q. Wagley, *Management Response to Public Issues* (Englewood Cliffs, NJ: Prentice Hall, 1985), 80.
25. *Ibid.*, 81–82.
26. Oliver Williams, "Who Cast the First Stone?" *Harvard Business Review* (September-October, 1994), 155.
27. "Nestlé's Costly Accord," *Newsweek* (February 6, 1984), 52.
28. Alix M. Freedman, "Nestlé to Restrict Low-Cost Supplies of Baby Food to Developing Nations," and "American Home Infant-Formula Giveaway to End," *Wall Street Journal* (February 4, 1991), B1.
29. Stuart Diamond, "The Disaster in Bhopal: Lessons for the Future," *New York Times* (February 5, 1985), 1.
30. Stuart Diamond, "Disaster in India Sharpens Debate on Doing Business in Third World," *New York Times* (December 16, 1984), 1.
31. Diamond, 1984, 1.
32. *Ibid.*
33. Thomas M. Gladwin and Ingo Walter, "Bhopal and the Multinational," *The Wall Street Journal* (January 16, 1985), 1.
34. Diamond, 1984, 1.
35. James B. Stewart, "Suits Against Union Carbide Raise Issues for Lawyers, Multinationals," *The Wall Street Journal* (December 17, 1984), 37.
36. "For Multinationals, It Will Never Be the Same," *Business Week* (December 24, 1984), 57.
37. Dwight R. Ladd, "The Bribery Business," in Tom L. Beauchamp (ed.), *Case Studies in Business, Society and Ethics* (Englewood Cliffs, NJ: Prentice-Hall, 1983), 251.
38. Richard T. DeGeorge, *Business Ethics* (New York: Macmillan, 1982), 53.
39. Ian I. Mitroff and Ralph H. Kilmann, "Teaching Managers to Do Policy Analysis: The Case of Corporate Bribery," *California Management Review* (Fall, 1977), 50–52.
40. *Ibid.*
41. Ladd, 256.
42. Garland and Farmer, 183.
43. Barry Richman, "Stopping Payments Under the Table," *Business Week* (May 22, 1978), 18.
44. Cited in Thomas Goldwasser, "Don't Make Foreign Bribery by U.S. Firms Easier," *The Wall Street Journal* (October 1, 1986), 32.
45. *Ibid.*
46. Kate Gillespie, "The Middle East Response to the U.S. Foreign Corrupt Practices Act," *California Management Review* (Summer, 1987), 9–30.
47. Goldwasser, 32.
48. Gene R. Laczniak and Jacob Naor, "Global Ethics: Wrestling with the Corporate Conscience," *Business* (July-September, 1985), 3–10.
49. Laczniak and Naor, 7.
50. "A Code of Worldwide Business Conduct," in Frederick D. Sturdivant (ed.), *The Corporate Social Challenge: Cases and Commentaries* (Homewood, IL: Richard D. Irwin, 1985), 159–169.

51. "General Dynamics Standards of Business Ethics and Conduct" (August, 1985), 17.
52. "The Lockheed Way" (May 2, 1977).
53. G. R. Bassiry, "Business Ethics and the United Nations: A Code of Conduct," *SAM Advanced Management Journal* (Autumn, 1990), 38–41.
54. Laczniak and Naor, 7–8.
55. Archie B. Carroll, Frank Hoy, and John Hall, "The Integration of Corporate Social Policy into Strategic Management," in S. Prakash Sethi and Cecilia M. Falbe (eds.), *Business and Society: Dimensions of Conflict and Cooperation* (Lexington, MA: Lexington Books, 1987), 449–470.
56. Laczniak and Naor, 8.
57. David H. Blake, William C. Frederick, and Mildred S. Myers, *Social Auditing: Evaluating the Impact of Corporate Programs* (New York: Praeger, 1976), 3.
58. Thomas Donaldson, *The Ethics of International Business* (New York: Oxford University Press, 1989), 81.
59. Richard T. DeGeorge, "Ethical Dilemmas for Multinational Enterprise: A Philosophical Overview," in Hoffman, Lange, and Fedo (eds.), 39–46.

PART THREE EXTERNAL STAKEHOLDERS AND THE MANAGEMENT OF THEM

7 Business, Government, and Regulation

8 Business's Influence on Government and Public Policy

9 Consumer Stakeholders: Information Issues and Responses

10 Consumer Stakeholders: Product Issues and Responses

11 The Natural Environment as Stakeholder: Issues and Challenges

12 Business and Stakeholder Responses to Environmental Challenges

13 Community Stakeholders

CHAPTER **SEVEN**

Business, Government, and Regulation

CHAPTER OBJECTIVES

After studying this chapter, you should be able to:

◆ Articulate a brief history of government's role in its relationship with business.

◆ Appreciate the complex interactions among business, government, and the public.

◆ Identify and describe government's nonregulatory influences, especially the concepts of industrial policy and privatization.

◆ Define government regulation and explain the major reasons for regulation, the types of regulation, and issues arising out of regulation.

◆ Provide a perspective on regulation versus deregulation along with accompanying trends.

◆ Describe major types of regulatory reform and their characteristics.

Few issues seem to excite business people as much as government's role in society. This became especially true when government began playing a more active role in the 1960s and 1970s. Over the past 20 years, the depth, scope, and direction of government's involvement in business have made the business-government relationship one of the most hotly debated issues of modern times. In addition, government's role, particularly in the regulation of business, has assured its place among the major stakeholders with which business must establish an effective working relationship if it is to survive and prosper.

Business has never been fond of government's increasingly activist role in establishing the ground rules under which it operates. Business has almost always been against an increased role for government, especially the federal government. The public, on the other hand, has gone through periods when it has thought the federal government had too much power, and at other times it has thought government should be more activist. The public's desire for government intervention in business has been cyclical. President Ronald Reagan came into office in 1980 when the public was growing somewhat weary of an active federal role. President Reagan's favorite saying was that "government isn't the solution; it's the problem." He seemed to hit a responsive chord with the public at that particular point in time. In 1982, 38 percent of a Gallup poll sample indicated the federal government had too much power. By 1986, this figure had fallen to 28 percent, with 41 percent of the public sample now indicating the federal government should use its power more vigorously.[1]

Throughout the decade of the 1980s, the federal government played less and less of a role, especially in terms of monitoring and regulating business. It was not without reason, therefore, that in late 1989 *Time* magazine ran a cover story entitled "Is Government Dead?"[2] This article was not limited to government's role vis à vis business but criticized government's lack of initiative and responsiveness on a host of problems facing the United States—the unprecedented opportunity to promote democracy in Eastern Europe, the spreading plague of drugs, the plight of the underclass, and the dire need for educational reform. In essence, the Reagan Revolution of an inactive federal government had left the public with a desire for government to become active again. It was against this backdrop that George Bush was elected president in 1988.

In this chapter we will examine the relationship between business and government, although the general public will assume an important role in the discussion as well. A central concern in this chapter is the government's role in influencing business. Exploring this relationship carefully will give you an appreciation of the complexity of the issues surrounding business-government interactions. From the prospective manager's standpoint, one needs a rudimentary understanding of the forces and factors that are involved in these issues before one can begin to talk intelligently about strategies for dealing with them. Unfortunately, more is known about the nature of the problem than about the nature of solutions, as is common when dealing with complex social issues. In the next chapter, we will discuss how business attempts to influence government and public policy.

A BRIEF HISTORY OF GOVERNMENT'S ROLE

In the early days of the United States, the government supported business by imposing tariffs to protect our fledgling industries. In the second half of the 1800s, government gave large land grants as incentives for private business to build railroads. Since a number of the railroads had grown large and strong because of mergers, people began to use them because their service was faster, cheaper, and more efficient. This resulted in a decline in the use of alternative transportation forms such as highways, rivers, and canals. Many railroads began to abuse their favored positions. For example, railroads that had a monopoly on service to a particular town charged unfairly high rates for the service. Competitive railroads sometimes agreed among themselves to charge high but comparable rates. Higher rates were charged for shorter hauls, and preference was shown to large shippers over smaller shippers.

Public criticism of what were perceived as abusive practices led to the passage of the Interstate Commerce Act of 1887 which was intended to prevent discrimination and abuses by the railroads. This act marked the beginning of extensive federal government regulation of interstate commerce. The act created the Interstate Commerce Commission, which became the first federal regulatory agency and a model for future agencies.[3]

Many large manufacturing firms and mining firms also began to abuse consumers during the late 1800s. Typical actions included the elimination of competition and the charging of excessively high prices. A number of large firms during this period formed organizations known as trusts. A trust was an organization that brought all or most competitors under a common control that then permitted them to eliminate most of the remaining competitors by price cutting, an act that forced the remaining competitors out of business. Then, the trusts would restrict production and raise prices. As a response, Congress passed the Sherman Antitrust Act in 1890, which became the first in a series of actions intended to control monopolies in various industries. The Sherman Act outlawed any contract, combination, or conspiracy in restraint of trade, and it also prohibited the monopolization of any market. In the early 1900s, the act was used by the federal government to break up the Standard Oil Company, the American Tobacco Company, and several other large firms that had abused their economic power.[4]

The Clayton Antitrust Act was passed in 1914 to augment the Sherman Act. It addressed other abusive practices that had arisen. It outlawed price discrimination that gave favored buyers preference over others and forbid anticompetitive contracts whereby a company would only agree to sell to a supplier who agreed not to sell the products of a rival competitor. The act also prohibited an assortment of other anticompetitive practices. Also in 1914, Congress formed the Federal Trade Commission, which was intended to maintain free and fair competition and to protect consumers from unfair or misleading practices.[5]

Another great wave of regulation occurred during the Depression and the subsequent New Deal of the 1930s. Significant legislation included the Securities Act of 1933 and the Securities and Exchange Act of 1934. These laws were aimed at curbing abuses in the stock market, stabilizing markets, and restoring investor confidence. Significant labor legislation during this same period signaled government involvement in a new area. Several examples were the 1926 Railway Labor Act, the 1932 Norris-LaGuardia Act, and the 1935 Wagner Act.

During the New Deal period in the 1930s, government also took on a new dimension in its relationship with business, as it actively assumed responsibility for restoring prosperity and promoting economic growth through public works programs. In 1946, this new role of government was formalized with the passage of the Full Employment Act.

This brings us to the present period in which government has passed considerable legislation, involving itself deeply in the affairs of business. Prior to the mid-1950s, most congressional legislation affecting business was economic in nature. Since that time, however, legislation has had social goals as well. Much legislation of the last three decades has been concerned with the quality of life.[6] Several illustrations of this include the Civil Rights Act of 1964, the Water Quality Act of 1965, the Occupational Safety and Health Act of 1970, the Consumer Product Safety Act of 1972, and the Warranty Act of 1975.

Just as the areas in which government has chosen to initiate legislation have changed, the multiplicity of roles that government has assumed has increased the complexity of its relationship with business. A number of the varied roles that government has assumed in its relationship with business are worth looking at because they suggest the influence, interrelationships, and complexities that are present. These roles indicate that government:

1. Prescribes the rules of the game for business.
2. Is a major purchaser of business's products and services.
3. Uses its contracting power to get business to do things it wants.
4. Is a major promoter and subsidizer of business.
5. Is the owner of vast quantities of productive equipment and wealth.
6. Is an architect of economic growth.
7. Is a financier.
8. Is the protector of various interests in society against business exploitation.
9. Directly manages large areas of private business.
10. Is the repository of the social conscience and redistributes resources to meet social objectives.[7]

After examining and assessing these various roles, you can perhaps begin to appreciate the crucial interconnectedness between business and government and the difficulty both business and the public have in fully understanding (much less prescribing) what government's role ought to be in relation to business.

UNDERSTANDING THE MAJOR ISSUES

We do not intend to philosophize in this chapter on the proper role of government in relation to business because this is outside our stakeholder frame of reference. However, we will strive for an understanding of current major issues as they pertain to this vital relationship. For effective management, government, as a stakeholder, must be understood.

The fundamental question underlying our entire discussion of business-government relationships is, *"What should be the respective roles of business and government in our socioeconomic system?"* This question is far easier to ask than to answer, but as we explore it, some important basic understandings begin to emerge.

The issue could be stated in a different fashion: Given all the tasks that must be accomplished to make our society work, which of these should be handled by government and which should be handled by business? This poses the issue clearly, but there are other questions that remain to be answered. If we decide, for example, that it is best to let business handle the production and distribution roles in our society, the next question pertains to how much autonomy we are willing to allow business. If goals were simply the production and distribution of goods and services, we would not have to constrain business severely. In modern times, however, other goals have been added to the production and distribution functions: for example, a safe working environment for those engaging in production, equal employment opportunities, fair pay, clean air, safe products, employee rights, and so on. With these goals superimposed on the basic economic goals, the task of business becomes much more complex and challenging.

Because these latter, more socially oriented goals are not automatically factored into business decision making and processes, it often falls on government to ensure that those goals that reflect concerns of the public interest be achieved. Thus, whereas the marketplace dictates economic production decisions, government becomes one of the citizenry's designated representatives to articulate and protect the public interest.

A Clash of Ethical Belief Systems

A clash of emphases partially forms the crux of the antagonistic relationship that has evolved between business and government over the years. This problem has been termed "a clash of ethical systems." The two ethical systems (systems of belief) are the *individualistic* ethic of business and the *collectivistic* ethic of government. Figure 7-1 summarizes the characteristics of these two philosophies.[8]

FIGURE 7-1 The Clash of Ethical Systems Between Business and Government

Business Beliefs	Government Beliefs
• Individualistic ethic	• Collectivistic ethic
• Maximum concession to self-interest	• Subordination of individual goals and self-interest to group goals and group interests
• Minimizing the load of obligations society imposes on the individual (personal freedom)	• Maximizing the obligations assumed by the individual and discouraging self-interest
• Emphasizes inequalities of individuals	• Emphasizes equality of individuals

[handwritten note: Government must treat Everyone Equally!]

The clash of these two ethical systems partially explains why the current business-government relationship is adversarial in nature. In elaborating on the adversarial nature of the business-government relationship, Jacoby offered the following comments:

> Officials of government characteristically look upon themselves as probers, inspectors, taxers, regulators, and punishers of business transgressions. Businessmen typically view government agencies as obstacles, constraints, delayers, and impediments to economic progress, having much power to stop and little to start.[9]

The business-government relationship not only has become adversarial but also has been deteriorating. The goals and values of our pluralistic society have become more complex, more numerous, more interrelated, and, consequently, more difficult to reconcile. The result has been increasing conflicts among diverse interest groups, with trade-off decisions becoming harder to make. In this process it has become more difficult to establish social priorities, and consensus has in many cases become impossible to achieve.[10]

Social, Technological, and Value Changes

As we attempt to understand why all this has happened, it is only natural to look to changes in the social and technological environments for some explanations. According to Daniel Bell, since World War II four major changes have had a profound impact on American society in general and on the business-government relationship in particular. First, out of local and regional societies a truly national one has arisen.[11] Second, we have seen a "communal society" arise, characterized by a great emphasis on public goods and the internalization of external costs. Third, the revolution of rising expectations has brought with it the demand for "entitlements"—good jobs, excellent housing, and other amenities. Fourth, a rising concern has emerged for an improved "quality of life."[12]

In addition to these, six other societal value changes have shaped the course of business-government relations. These are the youth movement, the consumer protection movement, the ecology movement, the civil rights movement, the women's liberation movement, and the egalitarian movement.[13]

In a sense, this last movement—the egalitarian movement—embraces all of the others, as it represents an effort to create an equitable balance of all facets of what is good in life in the United States. Thus, the value changes that have taken place "have multiplied the number of political decisions that have to be made relative to the number of decisions made in markets."[14] And to the extent that these political decisions affect business—and they do to a great extent—we can understand the basic conflict arising once again in a clash between individualist and collectivist belief systems. Government's responses to changes taking place in society have put it directly in opposition to business's philosophy and mode of operating.

INTERACTION OF BUSINESS, GOVERNMENT, AND THE PUBLIC

A brief examination is offered of the influence relationships among business, government, and the public. This should be helpful in understanding both the nature of the process by which public policy decisions are made and the current problems that characterize the business-government relationship. Figure 7-2 illustrates the influence relationships.

You might rightly ask at this point, "Why include the public? Isn't the public represented by government?" In an ideal world, perhaps this would be true. To help us appreciate that government functions somewhat apart from the public, we have depicted it separately in the diagram. In addition, the public has its methods of influence that need to be singled out.

Government-Business Relationship

Government influences business through regulation and other forms of persuasion that we will consider in more detail in the next section. Business, likewise, has its approaches to influencing government, which we will deal with in Chapter 8. Lobbying, in one form or another, is business's primary process of influencing government.

FIGURE 7-2 Interaction Among Business, Government, and the Public

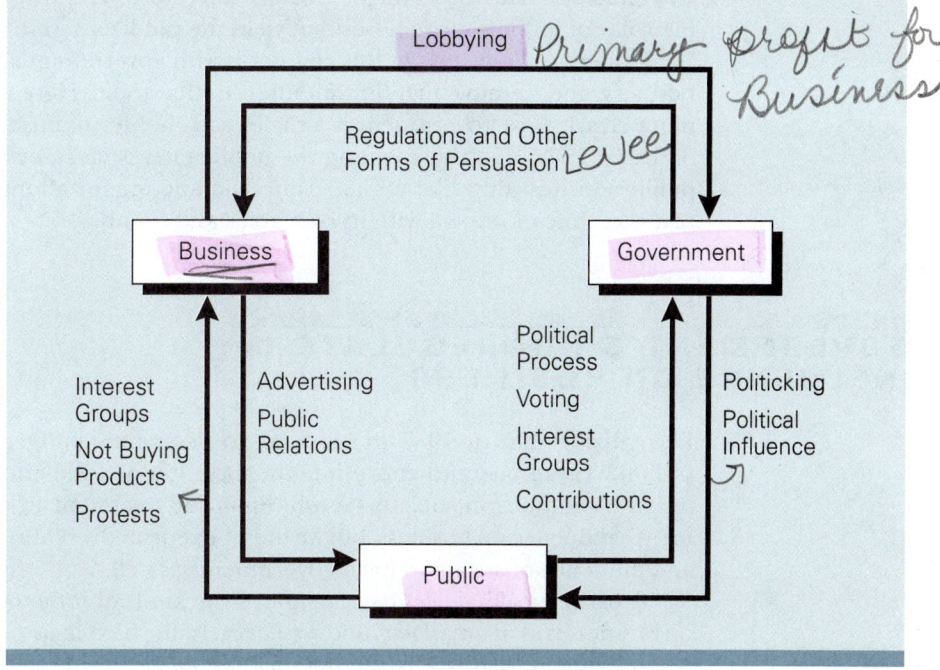

Public-Government Relationship

The public uses the political processes of voting and electing officials (or removing them from office) to influence government. It also does this by forming into special-interest groups (farmers, small-business people, educators, senior citizens, truckers, manufacturers) to wield more targeted influence. Government, in turn, uses politicking, public policy formation, and other political influences to have an impact on the public.

Business-Public Relationship

Business influences the public through advertising, public relations, and other forms of communication. And the public influences business through the marketplace or by forming special-interest groups (for example, People United to Save Humanity, American Association of Retired Persons, Friends of the Earth, American Civil Liberties Union) or protest groups.

Earlier we raised the question of whether government really represents the public. This question may be stated another way: "Who determines what is in the public interest?" In our society, determining the public interest is not a simple matter. Whereas government may be the official representative of the public, we should not assume that representation occurs in a straightforward fashion. As we saw from Figure 7-2, the public takes its own initiatives both with business and with government. The three major groups, therefore, are involved in a dynamic interplay of influence processes that yield the public interest.

Our central concern in this chapter is with government's role in influencing business, and we now turn our attention to that topic. Here we will begin to see more clearly how government is a major stakeholder of business. Government's official priority is in representing the public interest as it sees and interprets the public's wishes. But, like all large bureaucratic organizations, government also takes on a life of its own with its own goals and agenda.

GOVERNMENT'S NONREGULATORY INFLUENCE ON BUSINESS

Recognizing that in 1987 the federal government's budget first exceeded $1 trillion, we can begin to appreciate the magnitude of the effect government has on all institutions in society. We will limit our treatment to the federal government's influence on business, but we must be repeatedly reminded of the presence and influence of state and local governments as well.

Broadly speaking, we may categorize the kinds of influence government has on businesses as *nonregulatory* and *regulatory*. In the next major section we will focus on government regulation, but here let us consider the wide range of nonregulatory influences.

Two major issues merit consideration before we examine some of the specific policy tools or mechanisms government uses to influence business. These two major issues are (1) industrial policy and (2) privatization. Industrial policy is concerned with the role that our government plays in the world of international trade, and privatization zeroes in on the question of whether current public functions (for example, public education, public transit, social security, fire service) should be turned over to the private (business) sector. Both of these issues have important implications for the business-government relationship, although at the time of this writing they are not being strongly advocated. They are both important, however, because they seem to come into and out of popularity on a fairly regular basis.

Industrial Policy

Important initial questions include, *"What does industrial policy mean, and why has it become such a hotly debated issue?"* An **industrial policy** may be defined as follows: "Any selective government measure that prevents or promotes changes in the structure of an economy."[15]

This very broad definition by itself does not give us enough focus to understand the concept. Let us elaborate. One school of thought thinks of industrial policy as some variation of the British model wherein government provides help for older, declining industries. Therefore, if steel company executives in the United States argue for tax breaks and tariffs that would enable them to better survive and compete with foreign competition, they are asking for an industrial policy.[16]

Another school of thought is exemplified by Robert Reich in his book *The Next American Frontier*, wherein he argues for a national industrial policy that attempts to identify *winning* (or sunrise) industries and foster their growth. As for *losing* (or sunset) industries, industrial policy should have as its goal redirecting resources into growth fields.[17]

Variations of these themes could yield a variety of industrial policy schools of thought. Five schools of thought include the following: the accelerationists, the adjusters, the targeters, the central planners, and the bankers.[18] The **accelerationists** would try to pinpoint industries that promise to become strong international competitors and position them to move rapidly into world markets. Their goal would be to accelerate changes already signaled by the marketplace. The **adjusters** would offer adjustment assistance to declining industries in return for commitments that they would slim down, modernize, and help their employees relocate and train for new skills and jobs.

The **targeters** would target a select group of sectors or industries (for example, high tech, agriculture, energy, finance, health care equipment) to turn them into engines for growth. The **central planners** would advocate growth-oriented macroeconomic policies that would come close to comprehensive planning. Finally, the **bankers** would advocate a federally backed industrial development bank that would provide "patient capital"—money that could be sunk into a high-risk venture for 5 to 10 years or longer.

The modern debate over industrial policy became more active on publication of Reich's *The Next American Frontier* in 1983 and the realization of our drab economic performance during the 1979–1982 period when the United States lost significant ground to Japan as the world leader in industrial expansion. Many experts see the very survival of the U.S. economy at stake in the face of subsidized foreign competition from Japan and other industrialized countries. Indeed, in 1987 a trade confrontation arose between the United States and Japan over the significant trade imbalances arising out of these issues.

An example of an industrial policy proposal that was circulating in 1991 was the proposed Critical Technologies Act of 1991, which was targeted to support U.S. producers of the components used in machine tools—steel, gears, bearings, semiconductors, fasteners, software, and so on. Under the bill, foreign investors or importers that "impair or threaten to impair" U.S. producers considered critical to machine tool manufacturing would face an array of sanctions. The president could negotiate a quota with the offending nation or he could propose a tariff on the import.[19] Supporters of this bill see it as vital to U.S. interests. Critics prefer that foreign markets remain open to the United States. There are good arguments on both sides.

Arguments for an Industrial Policy. Proponents of an industrial policy (more active role of government in the business sector) cite a variety of reasons for pursuing it. First, of course, is the declining competitiveness of the United States in world markets. A second argument is the use of industrial policy, by other world governments, most notably Japan. Also mentioned are West Germany, Britain, France, and Italy. A third major argument is that the United States already has an industrial policy, but it is the haphazard result of unplanned taxes, tariffs, regulatory policies, and research and development policies. Others have called our current system an ad hoc industrial policy because the United States has, in fact, intervened in many specific industries as emergencies have arisen. Protection schemes have been used in the apparel, auto, and steel industries to deal with foreign competition. The federal government's decision in 1979 to provide loan guarantees to Chrysler Corporation and Chrysler's early repaying of its $1.2 billion loan is cited by many advocates as an example of how federal intervention can benefit companies, employees, and communities at no net cost to the United States Treasury.

Arguments Against an Industrial Policy. Critics of industrial policy also have significant reasons for their opposition. Critics say that government interference reduces the market's efficiency. How do you keep politics out of what ought to be economic decisions? Some politicians, as well as experts, think the United States should focus on rescuing steel and other "sunset" industries. Others argue we ought to promote emerging "sunrise" industries such as high-technology electronics.

Those who oppose industrial policy say that foreign success with it has been very overrated. It is argued that Japan, for example, has had as many failures as successes with its government's development agency, Ministry of International Trade and Industry (MITI). MITI is generally credited with helping to build Japan's computer, semiconductor, and steel industries, but efforts to promote aluminum-refining, petrochemicals, shipping, and commercial-aircraft industries are viewed as failures.[20]

Finally, current efforts at industrial policy have been criticized as being irrational and uncoordinated and composed largely of "voluntary" restrictions on imports, occasional bail-outs for near-bankruptcy companies, and a wide array of subsidies, loan guarantees, and special tax benefits for particular firms and industries. Thus, such efforts have constituted an industrial policy by default.[21] One could argue that the United States is incapable of developing a successful and planned industrial policy, given its past experience and the composition of the public policy process that has characterized past decision making. However, there are some who believe that despite the current administration's opposition to a large-scale federal effort, the United States is adopting an industrial policy piece by piece. This is because of dozens of federal and state programs aimed at assisting manufacturers in improving their technology and efficiency so that they might compete with foreign companies. In addition, many in Congress would like to expand the current programs.

There is an ebb and flow of interest in the concept of industrial policy. And because many of the problems that initially started the current debate on industrial policy in the 1980s are still with us, especially the trade conflicts with

Japan, it is easy to believe that it could continue to be a business-government debate for years to come. This is particularly true given the increasing international competitiveness.

Privatization

Whereas industrial policy is a macro policy issue more oriented toward international trade and world markets, privatization is more focused on the domestic scene. Privatization threatens to displace "partnerships" as the primary buzzword when people talk about the contribution business can make to the solution of problems that beset the public and government. **Privatization,** generally speaking, refers to the process of "turning over to" the private sector (business) some function or service that was previously handled by some government body. To understand privatization, we need to differentiate two functions government might perform: (1) *producing* a service and (2) *providing* a service.[22]

Producing Versus Providing a Service. A city government might *provide* security if it employed a private firm to work at the coliseum when the state basketball playoffs are taking place. This same city government would be *producing* a service if it had its own police force to provide security at the same basketball tournament. The federal government would be *providing* medical care to the aged with a national Medicare program. The "production" of medical care would be coming from private physicians. The government would be providing *and* producing medical care if it employed its own staff of doctors as, for example, the military does. The terminology can be very confusing, but the distinction must be made because sometimes government provides a service (has a program for and actually pays for a service) and other times it also produces a service (has its own employees who do it).[23]

The Tennessee Valley Authority (TVA) was once widely regarded as a model for how electric power should be produced and distributed. Now there is talk of proposals to sell TVA to the private sector to increase its efficiency. Conrail, Amtrak, the postal service, public housing, and even public lands are federal enterprises that some are arguing should be sold to the private sector.

A Worldwide Movement. Privatization is a worldwide movement. In Great Britain the government sold major publicly owned companies in aerospace, automobiles, and telecommunications. It is thinking about selling British Airways, Rolls-Royce, British Gas, and others. Spain's socialist government, elected in 1982, nationalized a major private company but since then has returned it to the private sector along with other state companies. France is now running strongly toward privatization.[24]

Private Firm- Versus Government-Provided Services. In a recent study, eight government services provided by local governments were compared to those same services provided by private firms. The services studied were street sweeping, janitorial operations, refuse collection, payroll administration, traffic signal maintenance, repairs to asphalt surfaces, tree trimming, and lawn care. In seven out of eight services, the private firms showed a savings of 37 to 96 percent over the government-provided services.[25]

Proponents of privatization suggest that the work of entire bureaucracies be contracted out to the private sector. They maintain that government at all levels is involved in thousands of businesses in which it has no real comparative advantage and no basic reason for being involved.[26] Proponents also argue that publicly owned enterprises are less efficient and less flexible than competitive private firms.[27]

These two issues—industrial policy and privatization—are largely unresolved. They continue to be discussed and experimented with, however. They could have significant implications for the business-government relationship for years to come. We should now return to our discussion of the ways in which government uses various policies and mechanisms for influencing business.

Other Nonregulatory Governmental Influences

Government has a significant impact on business by virtue of the fact that it has a large payroll and is a *major employer* itself. At all levels, government employs millions of people who, as a consequence of being government employees, see things from the government's perspective. This influence is felt by business throughout society. Government is also in the position of being a standard setter: the 8-hour work day began in the federal government. When the Reagan administration broke the air traffic controller's strike in 1981, this ushered in wage restraints in the private sector.

Government is one of the largest *purchasers* of goods and services produced in the private sector. Some key industries, such as aerospace, electronics, and ship-building, are very dependent on government purchasing. Government can exert significant influence over the private sector by its insistence that minorities be hired, depressed areas be favored, small businesses be favored, and so on. For some firms in narrow markets like defense, the government dominates and controls whether they have a good year or not—indeed, whether they survive or not.[28]

Government influences business's behavior through the use of *subsidies* in a variety of ways. Generous subsidies are made available to industries such as agriculture, fishing, transportation, nuclear energy, and housing and to groups in special categories such as minority-owned enterprises and businesses in depressed areas. Quite often these subsidies have special qualifications attached.

Government also influences business, albeit indirectly, by virtue of its *transfer payments*. Government provides money for social security, welfare, and other entitlement programs that total hundreds of billions of dollars every year. These impacts are indirect, but they do significantly affect the market for business's goods and services.[29]

Government is a major *competitor* of business. Organizations like the TVA compete with private suppliers of electricity, the Government Printing Office competes with private commercial publishers and printing firms, and the United States Postal Service competes with private delivery services. In areas such as health, education, recreation, and security, the competition between government and private firms run the gamut of levels—federal, state, and local.

Government loans and *loan guarantees* are sources of influence as well. Government loans money directly for small businesses, housing, farmers, and energy companies. Often such loans are made at lower interest rates than those of private competitors. Loan guarantee programs, such as the one provided to Chrysler, is another way in which government's influence is felt.[30]

Taxation, through the Internal Revenue Service, is another example of a government tool. Tax deductibility, tax incentives, depreciation policies, and tax credits are all at the disposal of the government. *Monetary policy,* although it is administered through the Federal Reserve System, can have a profound effect on business. Although the Federal Reserve System is technically independent of the executive branch, it often responds to presidential leadership or initiatives.

Finally, *moral suasion* is a tool of government.[31] This refers to the government's attempts, usually through the president, to "persuade" business to act in the public interest by taking or not taking a particular course of action. These public-interest appeals might include a request to roll back a price hike, show restraint on wage and salary increases, or exercise "voluntary" restraints of one kind or another.

In sum, government is quite active in the economy and in a number of ways brings its influence to bear on business to achieve national goals. Figure 7-3 depicts these influence methods in graphic form.

GOVERNMENT'S REGULATORY INFLUENCES ON BUSINESS

For the past two decades, government regulation has been the most controversial issue in the business-government relationship. This is so because it has affected virtually every aspect of business functions. It has affected the terms and conditions under which firms have competed in their respective industries. It has touched almost every business decision ranging from the production of goods and services to their packaging, distribution, marketing, and service. Most people agree that some degree of regulation has been necessary to ensure that consumers and employees are treated fairly and are not exposed to unreasonable hazards and that the environment needs to be protected. However, they also think that government regulation has often been too extensive in scope, too costly, often unreasonable, and inevitably burdensome in terms of paperwork requirements and red tape. Business people, more than the general public, have felt these disadvantages and have borne the frustration of attempting to live up to government's expectations.

FIGURE 7–3 Nonregulatory Influences of Government on Business and the Business System

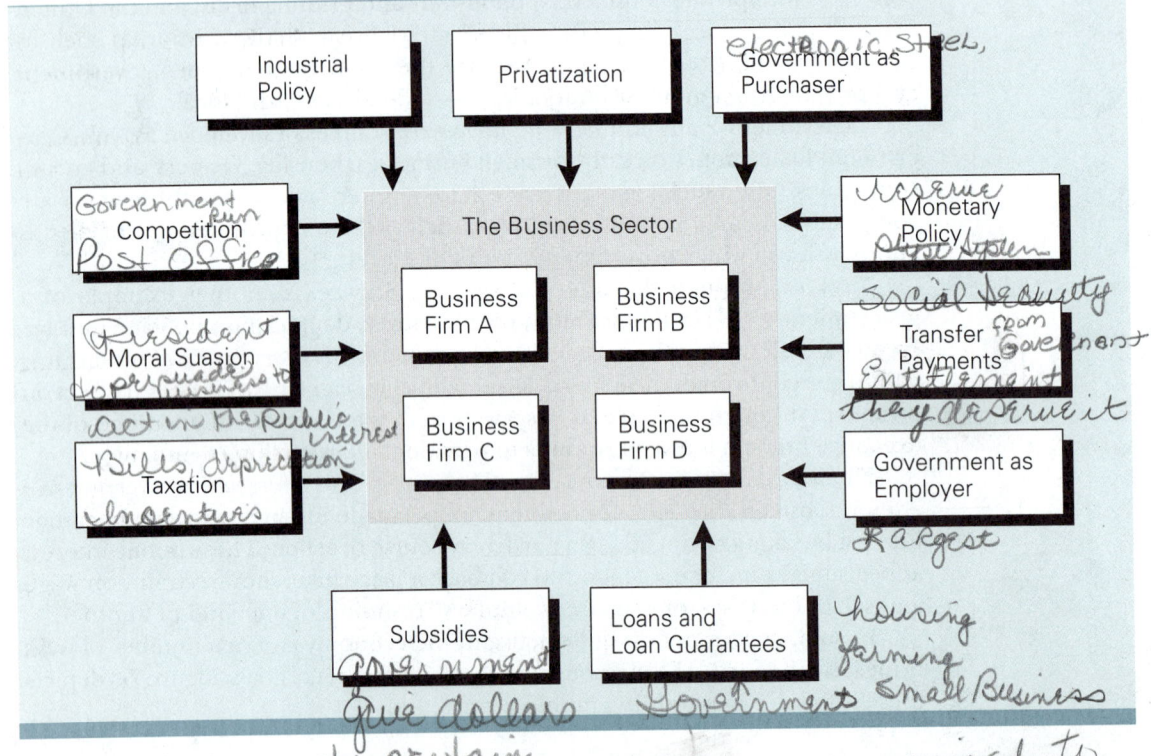

Regulation: Defined

Generally, *regulation* refers to the act of governing, directing according to rule, or bringing under the control of law or constituted authority. Although there is no universally agreed on definition of federal regulation, we can look to the definition of a federal regulatory agency proposed by the Senate Governmental Affairs Committee in 1977. It described a federal regulatory agency as one that:

1. Has decision-making authority.
2. Establishes standards or guidelines conferring benefits and imposing restrictions on business conduct.
3. Operates principally in the sphere of domestic business activity.
4. Has its head and/or members appointed by the president (generally subject to Senate confirmation).
5. Has its legal procedures generally governed by the Administrative Procedures Act.[32]

Chapter 7 ♦ Business, Government, and Regulation   205

The commerce clause of the U.S. Constitution grants to the government the legal authority to regulate. Within the confines of a regulatory agency as outlined above, the composition and functioning of regulatory agencies differ. Some are headed up by an administrator and are located within an executive department, for example, the Federal Aviation Administration (FAA). Others are independent commissions composed of a chairman and several members located outside the executive and legislative branches such as the Interstate Commerce Commission (ICC), the Federal Communications Commission (FCC), and the Securities and Exchange Commission (SEC).³³

Reasons for Regulation

Regulations have come about over the years for a variety of reasons. Some managers probably think that government is just sitting on the sidelines looking for reasons to butt into their business. There are a number of legitimate reasons why government regulation has evolved, although these same business people may not entirely agree with them. For the most part, however, government regulation has arisen because some kind of market defect or market failure has occurred and government, intending to represent the public interest, has chosen to take corrective action. We should make it clear that many regulations have been created primarily because of the efforts of special-interest groups that have lobbied successfully for them. The governmental decision-making process in the United States is characterized by congressional regulatory response to the pressures of special-interest groups.

Four major reasons or justifications for regulation are typically offered: (1) controlling natural monopolies, (2) controlling negative externalities, (3) achieving social goals, and (4) other reasons.

Controlling Natural Monopolies. One of the earliest circumstances in which government felt a need to regulate occurred when a natural monopoly existed. A *natural monopoly* exists in a market where the economics of scale are so great that the largest firm has the lowest costs and thus is able to drive out its competitors. Such a firm can supply the entire market more efficiently and cheaply than several smaller firms. Local telephone service is a good example because parallel sets of telephone wires would involve waste and duplication that would be much more costly.

Monopolies such as this may seem "natural" but when left to their own devices could restrict output and raise prices. This potential abuse justifies the regulation of monopolies. As a consequence, we see public utilities, for example, regulated by a public utility commission. This commission determines the rates that the monopolist may charge its customers.³⁴

Controlling Negative Externalities. Another important rationale for government regulation is that of controlling *negative externalities* (or spillover effects) that result when the manufacture or use of a product gives rise to unplanned or unintended side effects on others (other than the producer or the consumer). Examples of these negative externalities are air pollution, water pollution, and improper disposal of toxic wastes. The consequence of negative externalities is that neither the producer nor the consumer of the product directly "pays" for all the "costs" that are created by the product. The costs may be experienced by the public as an unpleasant or foul atmosphere, illness, and even health care. Some have called these "social" costs because they are absorbed by society rather than being truly incorporated into the cost of making the product.

Preventing negative externalities is enormously expensive, and few firms are willing to voluntarily pay for these added costs. This is especially true in an industry that produces an essentially undifferentiated product, such as steel, where the millions of dollars needed to protect the environment would only add to the cost of the product and provide no benefit to the purchaser. In situations like this, therefore, government regulation is reasonable because it requires all firms competing in a given industry to operate according to the same rules (costs).

Just as companies do not voluntarily take on huge expenditures for environmental protection, individuals often behave in the same fashion. For example, automobile emissions are one of the principal forms of air pollution. But how many private individuals would voluntarily request an emission control system if it were offered as optional equipment? In situations like this, a government standard that requires everyone to adhere to the regulation is much more likely to address the public's concern for air pollution.[35]

Achieving Social Goals. Government not only employs regulations to address market failures or negative externalities but also seeks to use regulations to help achieve certain social goals it deems are in the public interest. Some of these social goals are related to negative externalities in the sense that government is attempting to correct problems that might also be viewed as negative externalities by particular groups. An example of this might be the harmful effects of a dangerous product or the unfair treatment of minorities resulting from employment discrimination. These externalities are not as obvious nor as visible as air pollution, but they are just as real.

Another important social goal of government is to keep people informed. One could argue that *inadequate information* is a serious problem and that government should use its regulatory powers to require firms to reveal certain kinds of information to consumers. Thus, the Consumer Product Safety Commission requires firms to warn consumers of potential product hazards through labeling requirements. Other regulatory mandates that address the issue of inadequate information include grading standards, weight and size information, truth-in-advertising requirements, product safety standards, and so on.

Other important social goals that have been addressed include preservation of national security (deregulation of oil prices to lessen dependence on imports), considerations of fairness or equity (employment discrimination laws), protection of those who provide essential services (farmers), allocation of scarce resources (gasoline rationing), and protection of consumers from excessively high price increases (natural gas regulation).[36]

Other Reasons. There are several other reasons for government regulation. One is to *control "excess profits."* The claim for regulation here would be aimed at transferring income for purposes of economic fairness. For example, as a result of the Arab oil embargo between 1973 and 1980, oil stocks went up suddenly by a factor of 10. One argument is that the extra profit occurring to these producers is somehow undeserved and the result of plain luck, not wise investment decisions. So, in situations such as this in which profits are drastically, suddenly, and perhaps undeservedly increased, an argument can be made for government regulation.[37]

Another commonly advanced rationale for regulation is to *deal with "excessive competition."* The basic idea behind this rationale is that excessive competition will lead to prices being set at unprofitably low levels. This action will force firms out of business and ultimately result in products that are too costly because the remaining firm will raise its prices to excessive levels, leaving the public worse off then before.[38]

These "other" reasons for regulation are not cited much anymore, and arguments against them could be set forth. They are mentioned primarily to round out our discussion of various rationales that have been given for regulation.

Types of Regulation

Broadly speaking, government regulations have been used for two central purposes: achieving certain *economic* goals and achieving *social* goals. Therefore, it has become customary to identify two different types of regulation: economic regulation and social regulation.

Economic Regulation. The classical or traditional form of regulation that dates back to the 1800s in the United States is *economic regulation.* This type of regulation is best exemplified by old-line regulatory bodies such as the Interstate Commerce Commission (ICC), which was created in 1887 by Congress to regulate the railroad industry; the Civil Aeronautics Board (CAB), which was created in 1940; and the Federal Communications Commission (FCC), which was established in 1934 to consolidate federal regulation of interstate communications and, later, radio, telephone, and telegraph.

These regulatory bodies were designed primarily along industry lines and were created for the purpose of regulating business behavior through the control of or influence over economic or market variables such as prices (maximum and minimum), entry to and exit from markets, and types of services that can be offered. It is estimated that as of the late 1960s, the industries subject to economic regulations by federal and state agencies accounted for about 10 percent of the gross national product.[39]

Later we will discuss deregulation, a trend that significantly affected the old-line form of economic regulation that dominated business-government relations for the last 100 years.

Social Regulation. The 1960s ushered in a new form of regulation that for all practical purposes became what regulation means to modern-day business managers. This new form of regulation has come to be known as **social regulation,** for it has had as its major thrust the furtherance of societal objectives quite different from the earlier focus on markets and economic variables. Whereas the older form of regulation focuses on markets, the new social regulation focuses on business's *impacts on people*. The emphasis on people essentially addresses needs of people in their roles as employees, consumers, and citizens.

Two major examples of social regulations having a specific impact on people as *employees* were (1) the Civil Rights Act of 1964 that created the Equal Employment Opportunity Commission (EEOC) and (2) the creation of the Occupational Safety and Health Administration (OSHA) in 1970. The goal of the EEOC is to provide protection against discrimination in all employment practices on the basis of race, color, religion, sex, or national origin. The goal of OSHA is to assure that the nation's workplaces are safe and healthful.

An example of major social regulation protecting people as *consumers* was the 1972 creation of the Consumer Product Safety Commission (CPSC). This body's goal is to protect the public against unreasonable risks of injury associated with consumer products. An example of a major social regulation to protect people as *citizens* and residents of communities was the 1970 creation of the Environmental Protection Agency (EPA). The goal of EPA is to coordinate a variety of environmental protection efforts and to develop a unified policy at the national level.

Figure 7-4 summarizes the nature of economic versus social regulation along with pertinent examples.

Whereas the older form of economic regulations was aimed primarily at companies competing in *specific* industries, the new form of social regulation addresses business practices affecting *all* industries. In addition, there are social regulations that are industry-specific such as the National Highway Traffic Safety Administration (automobiles) and the Food and Drug Administration (food, drugs, medical devices, cosmetics). The consequence of social regulations beginning in the 1960s has been a matrix effect where many firms get hit by industry-specific regulations and also the newer form of social regulations. Figure 7-5 on page 210 summarizes the major U.S. independent regulatory agencies along with their dates of establishment. In addition to these, we should remember that there are a number of regulatory agencies that exist within executive departments of the government. Examples of this latter category include the following:

Agencies	Within the
Food & Health Administration	Department of Health & Human Services
Antitrust Division	Department of Justice
Drug Enforcement Administration	Department of Justice
Occupational Safety & Health Administration	Department of Labor
Federal Highway Administration	Department of Transportation

FIGURE 7-4 Comparison of Economic and Social Regulations

	Economic Regulations	Social Regulations
Focus	Market conditions, economic variables (entry, exit, prices, services)	People in their roles as employees, consumers, and citizens
Industries affected	Selected (railroads, aeronautics, communications)	Virtually all industries and selected industries
Examples	Interstate Commerce Commission (ICC) Civil Aeronautics Board (CAB) Federal Communications Commission (FCC)	Equal Employment Opportunity Commission (EEOC) Occupational Safety and Health Administration (OSHA) Consumer Product Safety Commission (CPSC) Environmental Protection Agency (EPA)
Trend	From regulation to deregulation	Stable—No significant increase or decrease in agencies

The new wave of government regulation brought about in the past 20 years through use of the social regulatory model has had sweeping effects on society. It has signaled a new and seemingly increasing role for government in the affairs of business. As a consequence, no manager today, whether he or she operates a small neighborhood grocery store or manages a Fortune 500 firm, is exempt from the many and varied standards, guidelines, and restrictions that the government imposes. Close attention must be paid to these issues just as close attention needs to be paid to making traditional managerial decisions. To better appreciate the impact that government regulation is having on business, it is helpful to consider some of the issues that have arisen as a direct outgrowth of government regulations.

Issues Arising Out of Regulation

It is important to consider some of the issues that have arisen out of the increased governmental role in regulating business. In general, managers have been concerned with what might be called "regulatory unreasonableness."[40] We can expect that business would just as soon not have to deal with these regulatory bodies.

FIGURE 7-5 Major United States Independent Regulatory Agencies

Agency	Year Established
Interstate Commerce Commission	1887
Federal Reserve System (Board of Governors)	1913
Federal Trade Commission	1914
International Trade Commission	1916
Federal Home Loan Bank Board	1932
Federal Deposit Insurance Corporation	1933
Farm Credit Administration	1933
Federal Communications Commission	1934
Securities and Exchange Commission	1934
National Labor Relations Board	1935
Small Business Administration	1953
Federal Maritime Commission	1961
Council on Environmental Quality	1969
Cost Accounting Standards Board	1970
Environmental Protection Agency	1970
Equal Employment Opportunity Commission	1970
National Credit Union Administration	1970
Occupational Safety and Health Review Commission	1971
Consumer Product Safety Commission	1972
Commodity Futures Trading Commission	1974
Council on Wage and Price Stability	1974
Nuclear Regulatory Commission	1974
Federal Election Commission	1975
National Transportation Safety Board	1975
Federal Energy Regulatory Commission	1977
Office of the Federal Inspector for the Alaska Natural Gas Transportation System	1979

Therefore, some of business's reactions are simply related to the nuisance factor of having to deal with a complex array of restrictions. There are other legitimate issues that have arisen over the past few years that also need to be addressed.

Benefits of Regulation. To be certain, there are many benefits of government regulation. Employees are treated more fairly and have safer work environments. Consumers are able to purchase safer products and receive more information about them. Citizens in all walks of life have cleaner air to breathe and cleaner water in lakes and rivers where they go for recreational purposes. These benefits are real, but their exact magnitude is difficult to measure.

One study to determine the benefits of regulation was done in 1980 by the Center for Policy Alternatives at MIT. This study claimed that billions of dollars were saved each year as a direct result of federal regulation. The study found that effective health, safety, and environmental regulations reduced death and injury rates in jobs, resulted in increased productivity, fostered the development of new and better products and processes, and decreased environmental abuse.[41] The specific benefits identified include the following:

- Air pollution control benefits ($5 billion–$58 billion annually)
- Avoidance of lost workday accidents and deaths during a 2-year period ($15 billion reduced)
- Water pollution cleanup resulting in a $9 billion gain due to increased recreational (camping, fishing, vacationing) use
- Crib safety standards resulting in reduced injuries to infants (44 percent injury reduction over 6 years)[42]

Of course, the above are estimates, and the study is somewhat dated, but they do serve to remind us of the fact that benefits are derived from government regulations.

Costs of Regulation. Costs are difficult to measure. Let us consider in more detail what some of these costs are. Weidenbaum has argued that the costs that result from government regulation may be grouped into three categories: direct, indirect, and induced.[43]

Direct Costs. The *direct costs of regulation* are most visible when we look at the number of new agencies created, aggregate expenditures, and growth patterns of the budgets of federal agencies responsible for regulation. There were 14 major regulatory agencies prior to 1930, over two dozen in 1950, and 57 in the early 1980s. The most rapid expansion came in the 1970s.[44] Figure 7-6 illustrates overall trends in federal regulatory spending for economic and social regulations, as well as the total for the period 1970 to 1991.

FIGURE 7-6 Trends in Regulatory Spending

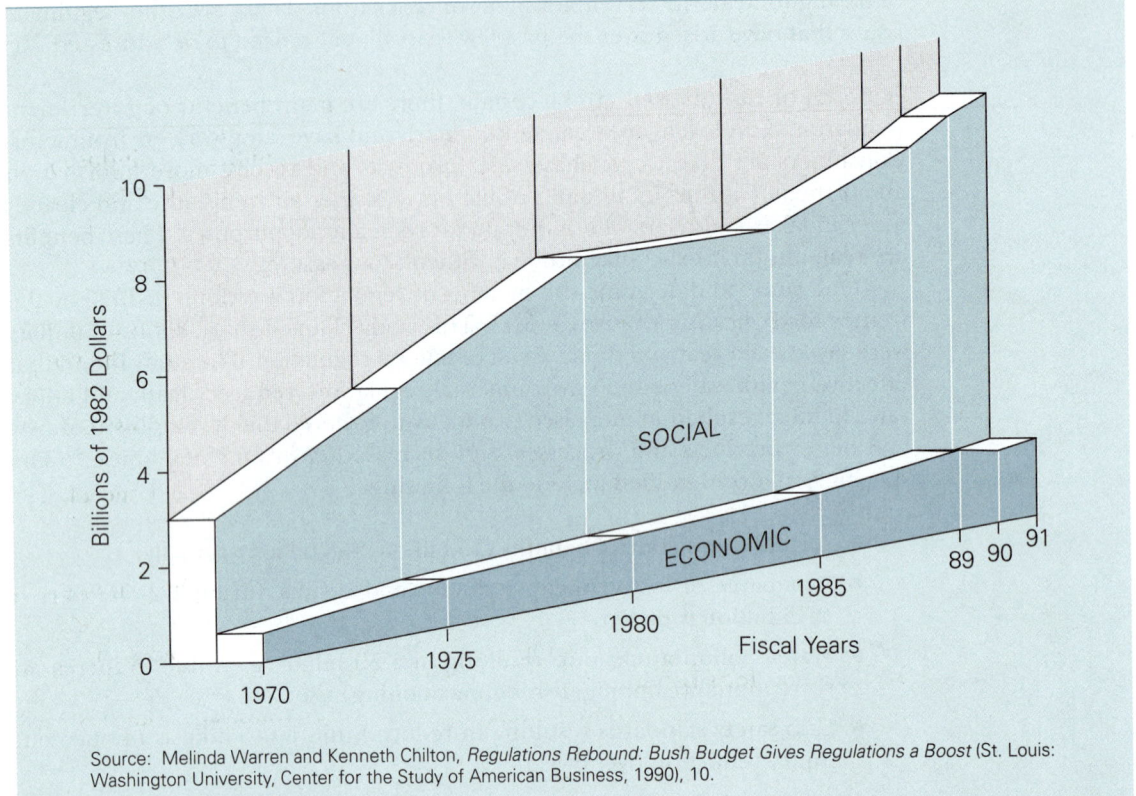

Source: Melinda Warren and Kenneth Chilton, *Regulations Rebound: Bush Budget Gives Regulations a Boost* (St. Louis: Washington University, Center for the Study of American Business, 1990), 10.

Indirect Costs. In addition to the direct costs of administering the regulatory agencies, there are *indirect costs of regulation* that need to be identified. The costs of government regulation get passed on to the consumer in the form of higher prices that constitute a "hidden tax" of government. Each year billions of dollars are added to the costs of goods and services because of regulation. One estimate is that, on average, each dollar Congress appropriates for regulation results in an additional $20 in costs imposed on the private sector.[45] One part of these added costs is the paperwork burden that business must absorb. There is an endless flow of forms, reports, and questionnaires that business must complete to satisfy the requirements of the regulatory agencies.

Induced Costs. The *induced effects of regulation* are diffuse and elusive, but they constitute some of the most powerful consequences of the regulatory process. In a real sense, then, these induced effects have to be thought of as costs. Three effects are worthy of elaboration:[46]

1. *Innovation is affected.* When corporate budgets must focus on "defensive research," certain innovation does not take place. To the extent that firms must devote more of their scientific resources to meeting government requirements, fewer resources are available to dedicate to new product and process research and development and innovation. One industry affected in this way is the drug industry. Economists estimate that stringent FDA regulations seriously hinder innovation in the drug industry. The consequences are a slowed pace and a decreased number of new drugs arriving on the marketplace for consumer use.

2. *New investments in plant and equipment are affected.* To the extent that corporate funds must be used for regulatory compliance purposes, these funds are diverted from more production uses. One estimate is that environmental and job safety requirements diminish by one-fourth the potential annual increase in productivity. It should also be pointed out that uncertainty about future regulations has an adverse effect on the introduction of new products and processes.[47]

3. *Small business is adversely affected.* Although it is not intentional, most federal regulations have a disproportionately adverse effect on small firms. Large firms have more personnel and resources and are therefore better able to get the work of government done than are small firms. In one study of small-business owner-managers, responses were solicited as to what they expected of government. Out of a list of nine choices, tax breaks for small firms was listed first and relief from government regulation was a close second.[48] More than any other group, small business seems to feel keenly affected by government regulation.

In addition to these induced effects, several others affect managers especially. These include stress on managers, modified decision processes, and alterations of corporate structure. To be sure, these kinds of effects are seen and experienced by managers as costs of government regulation, although they are typically overlooked in most calculations.

DEREGULATION

Quite frequently, trends and countertrends overlap with one another. Such is the case with regulation and its counterpart, deregulation. There are many reasons for this, but typically they include both the economic and the political. From an economic perspective, there is a continual striving for the balance of freedom and control for business that will be best for society. From a political perspective, there is an ongoing interplay of different societal goals and means for achieving these goals. The outcome is a mix of economic and political decisions that seem to be in a constant state of flux. Thus, in the economy at any point in time, trends that appear counter to one another can easily coexist. These trends are the natural result of competing forces seeking some sort of balance or equilibrium.

This is how we can explain the trend toward deregulation that evolved in a highly regulated environment. Deregulation represented a counterforce aimed at keeping the economy in balance. It also represented a political philosophy that was prevailing during the period of its origin and growth.

Deregulation may be thought of as one kind of regulatory reform. But because it is quite unique and unlike the regulatory reform measures discussed earlier, we will treat it separately. Deregulation has taken place primarily with respect to economic regulations, so this, too, helps to explain its separate treatment.

Purpose of Deregulation

The basic idea behind deregulation has been to remove certain industries from the old-line economic regulations of the past. The purpose of this deregulation, or at least the reduced level of regulation, has been to increase competition with the expected benefits of greater efficiency, lower prices, and enhanced innovation. These goals have not been uniformly received, but it is still undecided whether deregulation will work as a method of maximizing society's best interests.

Deregulation of certain industries has been basically a phenomenon of the last decade, although some big steps toward deregulation took place in the late 1960s and throughout the 1970s. Most of the landmark decisions in the move toward deregulation have occurred in the following fields: telecommunications (for example, breakup of AT&T), finance (for example, interest rate ceilings phased out), energy (for example, decontrol of gas/petroleum products), and transportation (for example, deregulation of trucking, railroad, and airline industries).

Trend Toward Deregulation

The trend toward deregulation, most notably exemplified in the financial industry, the telecommunications industry, and the transportation (trucking, airlines, railroads) industry represents business's first major redirection in 50 years.[49] The result seems to be a mixed bag of benefits and problems. On the benefits side, prices have fallen in many industries, and better service has appeared in some industries along with increased numbers of competitors and innovative products and services.

A number of problems have arisen also. Though prices have fallen and many competitors have entered some of these industries, more and more it appears that these competitors are unable to compete against the dominant firms. Thus, they are failing, going bankrupt, or being absorbed by the larger firms. Experts are now seeing that entry barriers into some industries are enormous and have been greatly underestimated. This has shown to be the case in airline, trucking, railroad, and long-distance telephone service.[50] In addition, many of the problems that have arisen with savings and loan associations and banks have been attributed to deregulation.

Concerns are being expressed about what appears to be growing anticompetitive side effects as key industries increasingly are dominated by a few firms. This trend is very obvious in transportation, where the major companies in railroads, airlines, and trucking boosted their market share considerably between 1978 to 1986. The top six railroads went from about 56 percent of market share to about 90 percent during this time. The top six airlines went from about 75 percent of market share to about 85 percent. The top 10 trucking firms went from about 38 percent of market share to about 58 percent. In long-distance telephone service, AT&T still enjoys an 82 percent share of the domestic market and a virtual monopoly of the huge toll-free, big business, and overseas markets.[51]

To guard against the growing concentration in these major industries, greater vigilance will be needed in the antitrust area. Many of the experts who advocated deregulation during the 1970s knew that anticompetitive side effects would be likely. However, they expected the regulatory agencies to do a better job of actively supervising the transition to free markets. If this close supervision does not take place, the regulatory pendulum could readily swing back toward the other direction.[52]

Dilemma with Deregulation

The intent of deregulation was to deregulate the *industries,* thus allowing for freer competition. The intent was not to deregulate health and safety requirements. The dilemma with deregulation is how to enhance the competitive nature of the affected industries without losing the applicable social regulations. This is the second major problem with deregulation that needs to be discussed. Unfortunately, the dog-eat-dog competition unleashed by economic deregulation forces many companies to cut corners in ways that endanger the health or safety of their customers. This pattern, which seems to occur in any deregulated industry, is increasingly obvious in the trucking and airline industries.[53]

Problems in the Trucking Industry.
The evidence seems clear that to survive in a deregulated industry, many truckers are delaying essential maintenance and are spending too many hours behind the wheel, sometimes on drugs. The growing safety problem in trucking highlights the perils of deregulation. Unlike other transportation industries, such as railroads and airlines, trucking attracts thousands of entrants. The larger firms are better managed and stay on top of their drivers and maintenance. But the thousands of others, all hustling to do enough business to keep ahead of their bills, pose serious hazards. Price competition has forced hundreds of firms out of business. The smaller firms and independent truckers that took their place have to hustle to make money. In today's competitive climate, many hard-pressed drivers have ample incentive to spend excessive hours at the wheel and to overlook expensive maintenance requirements.

According to some industry experts, as many as one-third of the long-haul drivers turn to illegal drugs to help them cope with the grueling hours on the road. Accident statistics show a sharp increase in the number of truck accidents from 1980 to 1986, and roadside inspections in one recent year turned up serious problems in 30 to 40 percent of the trucks inspected. The industry's economic woes continue to build with no expectation of improved truck safety in sight.[54]

Problems in the Airline Industry. The picture in the airline industry is not quite as dismal as trucking, but changes in the industry have a number of experts concerned. Numerous accidents over the past 10 years have been traceable to poor maintenance or increased congestion at airports. While the major airlines have historically maintained safety and maintenance standards higher than the minimum prescribed by the FAA, continuous price wars are forcing the best and largest firms to cut costs by abandoning previous standards. FAA-imposed fines for safety violations increased 20-fold over a recent 3-year period. Other cost-cutting measures that have been shown to be associated with safety include widespread use of unapproved parts and a reduction in the number of flight attendants.[55]

Some experts think that a backlash against deregulation is well underway. Time will tell whether current efforts and decisions will prove to be the best ones; however, it is hard to forget that regulations came about in the first place because of many market failures arising out of basically deregulated markets. Is the pendulum merely swinging in the direction of deregulation now, only to be redirected in the future?

REGULATORY REFORM

The 1970s witnessed a surge of regulatory initiatives unprecedented in the history of the United States. Ironically, at almost the same time, or at least during the same decade, a surge of second thoughts about the wisdom of these initiatives occurred. Many questions began to be asked: Had we gone too far? Had our best intentions got the better of us? Had our idealism reached beyond the bounds of practicality?[56]

By the mid-to-late 1970s, the calls for regulatory reform were begun by President Gerald Ford and quickly embraced by President Jimmy Carter. President Ronald Reagan interpreted his 1980 election as a mandate to further the efforts at reform and to get the government off the backs of the people. Thus far, President George Bush has reactivated some of the attentiveness the regulatory agencies have given toward their missions.

Approaches to Regulatory Reform

Three broad kinds of regulatory reform proposals surfaced during the late 1970s and 1980s. One approach was to *streamline the process* and to *review justifications* for existing and proposed rules. The idea here was that a rule should not be developed unless its benefits clearly outweighed its costs. President Carter promoted this idea with Executive Order 12044. This order required agencies to justify new rules with cost-benefit analysis. President Reagan embraced the cost-benefit idea enthusiastically, as did many members of Congress.

A second approach to regulatory reform advocated that *regulators be more accountable* to Congress, the courts, and the executive branch. In this connection, the controversial legislative veto was proposed that would allow Congress to void proposed rules. The courts would be given power to review regulations under another proposal. The president's powers would be expanded under another proposal. Picking up on this, the Reagan administration sought and received from Congress the authority to enlarge the Office of Management and Budget's (OMB) review over independent regulatory commissions.

A third approach to regulatory reform held that these procedural reforms were superficial and what was needed was a *broad-based attack on the regulations* themselves and the statutes that gave the agencies power. This approach was brought up during the lengthy controversy over renewal of the *Clean Air Act* and the reauthorization of several regulatory commissions.[57]

Figure 7-7 summarizes regulatory reform proposals that have been advocated or used at various times.

No single approach to regulatory reform is likely to cure all the problems we have with government regulations. The important consideration is that policy makers be sensitive to the problems that bring about regulatory failure and be prepared to address these problems when regulations are proposed and, later, when it is evident that reform is necessary. In some cases, generic reforms will be adequate. In other cases, a regulation-by-regulation examination may be necessary.

Regulatory Revival

In late 1986 and 1987, there was some evidence that a regulatory revival was beginning. A *Wall Street Journal*/NBC poll showed that 38 percent of the public still believed there was too much government regulation of the economy, 32 percent thought there was about the right amount, and 23 percent said there was not enough. These results indicate a major swing in public opinion in favor of regulation since polls taken in the early 1980s.[58] Earlier in the chapter we also cited a Gallup poll calling for more vigorous use of its power by the federal government.

Although President Reagan pursued a deregulation strategy during the period 1980–1985, in his second term he allowed modest growth in regulatory agencies' budgets and staff. Similarly, President Bush appears to be more inclined to allow the federal agencies to increase their budgets and staff levels. Economists from the Center for the Study of American Business at Washington University conclude that regulation is rebounding as the Bush budget is giving it a boost. The 1991 budget, which was President Bush's first, showed spending levels at the federal regulatory agencies reaching a record high both in current dollars and in

FIGURE 7-7   Approaches to Regulatory Reform

Approach	Brief Explanation
"Sunset" legislation	Metaphorically speaking, the sun would set on regulatory agencies (they would go out of business) automatically on a certain date unless a specific action was taken to continue or renew them. This would put the burden of proof for effectiveness on the shoulders of those who wanted the regulatory body or regulation continued.
Legislative veto	This would permit the Senate or the House of the U.S. Congress to disapprove a proposed regulation before it becomes effective.
Regulatory budget	Would require a budget of the maximum allowable regulatory compliance costs in a given year along with the regular budget to be prepared and submitted to Congress. The purpose would be to give each agency a set amount which it can impose on private firms for meeting its regulations.
Cost-benefit analysis	Would require agencies to conduct analyses of costs and benefits associated with regulations to ascertain that benefits do, indeed, exceed costs. Both costs and benefits are difficult to assess, but this would require a logical and good-faith effort on the agency's part.
Case-by-case analysis	This approach would avoid generic solutions and focus on a careful case-by-case analysis of regulatory agencies over the course of several years on predetermined terms.

Source: Timothy B. Clark, Marvin H. Kosters, and James C. Miller, III (eds.), *Reforming Regulation* (Washington, DC: American Enterprise Institute for Public Policy Research, 1980), 1. Reproduced with permission.

real terms. President Bush seems to be less skeptical about the role of federal regulators in the economy, and his first budget would suggest a growth trajectory similar to the budget trends from the Carter years, just prior to Reagan.[59]

In addition to stepping up enforcement of existing regulations and expanding budgets and staffing of the regulatory agencies, recent costly laws have been passed by Congress that will increase the focus on regulation. In 1990, Congress passed two significant pieces of legislation—the Clean Air Act amendments and the Americans with Disabilities Act. Some estimates are that the new air pollution laws may turn out to be the costliest regulations in the nation's history. Estimates of the annual costs of the law range from $25 billion to $40 billion. This sum would amount to about a $300 to $400 cost to each U.S. household per year. Economists are alarmed because of the fear that these regulatory expenditures threaten needed U.S. economic expansion and could lead to a diminishment of productivity, an undermining of competitiveness, and significant numbers of lost jobs in the U.S. work force.[60]

Another significant factor that may have brought about a public concern for more regulation was the stock market crash in October 1987. It is clear that the public was greatly unsettled by this event. Moreover, this event could likely precipitate renewed interest in tighter government regulations. To this must be added the Savings and Loan Association bail-out by the federal government and the increasing numbers of bank failures, both of which are at least in part attributable to careless or inadequate government regulation.

Professional economists may debate the pros and cons of government regulation, but in the final analysis the outcome of the political process will prevail. It can be readily seen by these trends, countertrends, and examples that the public does, indeed, see government as the mediator of its relationship with business. This is how the system works, and the changes we continue to see and sense in the business-government-public relationship are constantly changing and evolving; they cannot be pinned down for any significant period. The best judgment at this point, however, is that there will be some renewed interest in social regulation but that the trend toward economic deregulation will not be reversed any time soon. Part of the reason, of course, is that the economic decisions are of such a larger magnitude and, once made, are not easily changed.

SUMMARY

Business cannot be discussed without considering the paramount role played by government. Although the two institutions have opposing systems of belief, they are intertwined in terms of their functioning in our socioeconomic system. In addition, the public assumes a major role in a complex pattern of interactions among business, government, and the public. Government exerts a host of nonregulatory influences on business. Two influences with a macro orientation include industrial policy and privatization. A more specific influence is the fact that government is a major employer, purchaser, subsidizer, competitor, financier, and persuader. These roles permit government to affect business significantly.

One of government's most controversial interventions in business is direct regulation. Government regulates business for a number of legitimate reasons, and in the past two decades social regulation has been more dominant than economic regulation. There are many benefits and a number of direct, indirect, and induced costs of government regulation.

A trend of the 1980s was deregulation. However, bad experiences in key industries, such as trucking, airlines, savings and loans, and banks have caused many to wonder whether the government has gone too far in that direction. Although regulatory reform has been a central issue throughout the 1980s, there has been some amount of talk about *reregulation*. This has occurred for a variety of reasons, but the stock market crash in October of 1987 made the general public quite anxious about the private sector and its stability. Obviously, these perceptions of the business sector come and go, but they often assume a much more important weight in determining government's role than theoretical economic arguments.

DISCUSSION QUESTIONS

1. Briefly explain how business and government represent a clash of ethical systems (belief systems). Go through the list of characteristics of each belief system in Figure 7-1. With which do you find yourself identifying most? Explain. With which would most business students identify? Explain.

2. Explain why the public is treated as a separate group in the interactions among business, government, and the public. Doesn't government represent the public's interests? How should the public's interests be manifested?

3. What is regulation? Why does government see a need to regulate? Differentiate between economic and social regulation. What social regulations do you think are most important and why? What social regulations ought to be eliminated? Explain.

4. Outline the major benefits and costs of government regulation. In general, do you think the benefits of government regulation exceed the costs? In what areas, if any, do you think the costs exceed the benefits?

5. The airline and trucking industries were cited as examples of problems with deregulation. What is the current mood of the country regarding deregulation? What evidence can you present to substantiate your opinion?

ENDNOTES

1. "Wanted: More Action," *Newsweek* (November 17, 1986), 7.
2. "Is Government Dead?" *Time* (October 23, 1989).
3. "Antitrust Laws," *The World Book Encyclopedia* (Chicago: World Book, 1988), Vol. 1, 560; see also "The Interstate Commerce Act," Vol. 10, 352–353.
4. *Ibid.*
5. *Ibid.*
6. Alfred L. Seelye, "Societal Change and Business-Government Relationships," *MSU Business Topics* (Autumn, 1975), 5–6.
7. George A. Steiner, *Business and Society*, 2d ed. (New York: Random House, 1975), 359–361.
8. L. Earle Birdsell, "Business and Government: The Walls Between," in Neil H. Jacoby (ed.), *The Business-Government Relationship: A Reassessment* (Santa Monica, CA: Goodyear, 1975), 32–34.
9. Jacoby, 167.
10. *Ibid.*, 168.
11. For a view somewhat counter to this, see Kevin Phillips, "The Balkanization of America," *Harper's* (May, 1978), 37–47.
12. Daniel Bell, "Too Much, Too Late: Reactions to Changing Social Values," in Jacoby, 17–19.
13. Seelye, 7–8.
14. Jacoby, 168.
15. Arthur T. Denzau, "Will an 'Industrial Policy' Work for the United States?" (St. Louis: Center for the Study of American Business, Washington University, September, 1983), 1.
16. *Ibid.*, 2.
17. Robert B. Reich, *The Next American Frontier* (New York: Penguin Books, 1984).
18. "Industrial Policy: Is It the Answer?" *Business Week* (July 4, 1983), 55–56.
19. Paul Magnusson, "Critical Technology: A New Way to Say Industrial Policy," *Business Week* (June 10, 1991), 37.

20. Monroe W. Karmin, "Industrial Policy: What Is It? Do We Need One?" *U.S. News & World Report* (October 3, 1983), 47.
21. Ira C. Magaziner and Robert S. Reich, *Minding America's Business: The Decline and Rise of the American Economy* (New York: Vintage Books, 1983), 255.
22. Ted Kolderie, *"What Do We Mean by Privatization"* (St. Louis: Center for the Study of American Business, Washington University, May, 1986), 2–5.
23. Kolderie, 3–5.
24. Gary S. Becker, "Why Public Enterprises Belong in Private Hands," *Business Week* (February 24, 1986), 20.
25. "Privatization Increases at Local, State and Federal Levels," *What's Next: A Newsletter of Emerging Issues and Trends* (Washington, DC: Congressional Clearinghouse on the Future, Summer, 1985), 1, 5.
26. *Ibid.*, 5.
27. Becker, 20.
28. Murray L. Weidenbaum, *Business, Government and the Public*, 3d ed. (Englewood Cliffs, NJ: Prentice-Hall, 1986), 5–6.
29. *Ibid.*, 6–8.
30. *Ibid.*
31. *Ibid.*, 10–11.
32. *Congressional Quarterly's Federal Regulatory Directory*, 5th ed., 1985–1986, 2.
33. *Ibid.*, 2–3.
34. *Ibid.*, 9.
35. *Ibid.*, 10–11.
36. *Ibid.*, 12.
37. Stephen Breyer, *Regulation and Its Reform* (Cambridge, MA: Harvard University Press, 1982), 21–22.
38. *Ibid.*, 31–32.
39. Weidenbaum, 1986, 178–179.
40. Graham K. Wilson, *Business and Politics: A Comparative Introduction* (Chatham, NJ: Chatham House, 1985), 39.
41. *Congressional Quarterly's Federal Regulatory Directory*, 1985–1986, 30.
42. *Ibid.*, 30.
43. Murray L. Weidenbaum, *Costs of Regulation and Benefits of Reform* (St. Louis: Center for the Study of American Business, Washington University, November, 1980), 3.
44. *Ibid.*, 3.
45. Weidenbaum, *Costs of Regulation and Benefits of Reform*, 6–11.
46. *Ibid.*, 12–14.
47. *Ibid.*, 12.
48. James J. Chrisman and Fred L. Fry, "How Government Regulation Affects Small Business," *Business Forum* (Spring, 1983), 25–28.
49. "Deregulating America," *Business Week* (November 28, 1983), 80–89.
50. Is Deregulation Working?" *Business Week* (December 22, 1986), 50–55.
51. *Ibid.*, 52.
52. *Ibid.*, 55.
53. Frederick C. Thayer, "The Emerging Dangers of Deregulation," *New York Times* (February 23, 1986), 3.
54. Kenneth Labich, "The Scandal of Killer Trucks," *Fortune* (March 30, 1987), 85–87.
55. Thayer, 3.
56. Timothy B. Clark, Marvin H. Kosters, and James C. Miller, III (eds.), *Reforming Regulation* (Washington, DC: American Enterprise Institute, 1980), 1.
57. *Congressional Quarterly's Federal Regulatory Directory*, 5th ed., 1985–1986, 59–60.
58. Laurie McGinley, "Federal Regulation Rises Anew in Matters That Worry the Public," *The Wall Street Journal* (April 21, 1987), 1.
59. Melinda Warren and Kenneth Chilton, *Regulation's Rebound: Bush Budget Gives Regulation a Boost* (St. Louis: Center for the Study of American Business, May, 1990), 1–2.
60. Carolyn Lochhead, "Economists Say Federal Rules May Choke U.S. Productivity," *Insight* (November 19, 1990), 42–43.

CHAPTER **EIGHT**

Business's Influence on Government and Public Policy

CHAPTER OBJECTIVES

After studying this chapter, you should be able to:

- Identify the four major changes that are shaping the current political environment of business.

- Describe the evolution of corporate political participation.

- Differentiate among the different levels at which business lobbying occurs and explain the lack of unity among the umbrella organizations.

- Explain the phenomenon of political action committees (PACs) in terms of their historical growth, their magnitude of activity, and the arguments both for and against them.

- Define coalitions and describe the critical role they now assume in corporate political involvement.

- Outline the principal strategic approaches that firms are employing for political activism.

It is obvious from our discussion of business-government relationships and government regulation that government is a central stakeholder of business. Government's interest, or stake, in business is broad and multifaceted, and its power is derived from its legal and moral right to represent the public in its dealings with business.

Significant challenges for business are posed by government as business finds government not only in the role of establishing the rules of the game for business functions but also as a competitor, financier, purchaser, supplier, watchdog, and so on. Opportunities for the mutual pursuit of common goals with government are somewhat present, but the major opportunity is in developing strategies for effectively working with government in such a way that business's objectives are achieved. In doing this, business has the responsibility of obeying the laws of the land and of being ethical in its response to government expectations and mandates. To do otherwise raises the specter of abuse of political power, a criticism the corporate community has had enough of over the years. As the regulatory environment has become more intense and complex and as other changes have taken place in society, businesses have had little choice but to become more politically active.

It should be emphasized at the outset of this chapter that attempts of business to influence government is a major part of the public policy process in the United States. The U.S. political system is driven by the active participation of interest groups striving to achieve their own objectives. The business sector is, therefore, behaving in a normal and expected fashion when it assumes an advocacy role for its interests. Other groups, whether they be labor organizations, consumer groups, farmers groups, doctors' organizations, real estate operators, military groups, women's rights organizations, environmental groups, church groups and so on, all strive to pursue their special interests with government. Today's new pluralism requires that all of these groups seek to influence government. The public interest in this process is that some semblance of a balance of power be maintained and that the activities and practices of these organizations remain legal and ethical.

THE CURRENT POLITICAL ENVIRONMENT

In the early 1970s, business was at a low point as far as its political fortunes were concerned because of a hostile public mood that had grown in the 1960s. In response to a set of perceived national crises including product safety, employment discrimination, energy shortages, environmental problems, foreign bribery, and domestic political payoffs, business was hit with a wave of legislation that left it in an environment of reduced autonomy and sharply curtailed prerogatives.

By the 1980s, it was becoming clear that changes in four key areas over the past 25 years were shaping a political environment in which business's participation in the political process would be greatly affected. According to Gerald Keim, these four changes included (1) a growth in the volume of government activity, (2) the democratization of Congress, (3) the rise of special-interest groups, and (4) a decline in voter participation in the United States.[1]

Growth in Government Activity

In the last chapter we chronicled the growth in government activity. Some other statistics that document this growth include the rise in the number of recorded votes in both houses of Congress and the increase in the number of regulatory acts that became law. In 1960, there were 310 recorded votes in both houses of Congress. This number grew to 861 in 1972 and jumped to 1,349 in 1976. It fell back to 683 in 1984. In the 1950s, fewer than 30 regulatory bills were passed. In the 1960s, there were fewer than 60. In the 1970s, more than 120 new regulations were passed. While all these increases have taken place, the number of elected officials handling this work has remained the same.[2] The pattern over the past decade has reflected a continuation of this growth in government activity.

Democratization of Congress

Another important change in the political environment has been the "democratization" of Congress. Beginning in about 1970, a number of incremental changes began altering the structure of Congress in ways that decentralized power in both houses, made the legislative process more open to public scrutiny, reduced the importance of seniority, and increased the opportunity for more junior members of Congress to have an impact on legislative proceedings.

In 1970, the *Legislative Reorganization Act* made roll call votes in committees and votes on floor amendments a matter of public record. The result was less secrecy. The influence of senior members was diluted as more subcommittees were created and given more autonomy. Junior members' opportunities to chair important subcommittees increased. Senior members were restricted in how many leadership positions they could hold. The net result of these changes was to open up Congress, lessen party discipline, and increase member independence from traditional party lines. This independence was increased when many states moved from party caucuses to primary elections as the means to choose candidates for the general election. The party no longer provided all the financial and personnel backing. Organized special-interest groups began playing important roles in getting candidates elected. Contributions by political action committees became significantly more important.[3]

Rise of Special-Interest Groups

Still another change was taking place in the realm of special-interest groups. They began to increase in number and in political activism. In fact, a nationwide outburst of public-interest group activity grew out of the 1960s. This growth was related to the social changes and events that produced significant protest movements that were at first dedicated to fostering black civil rights and opposing the Vietnam War. These movements stimulated the growth of related reform groups concerned with the environment, nuclear power and weaponry, feminism, gay rights, and other causes.[4] An important contribution these groups made to their members was low-cost information about current political issues, thus making it easier for group members to be informed about key issues. As we will see later, groups that are organized will have more political power than those that are not organized.[5] Thus, the rise in special-interest groups constitutes an important change in the political landscape.

The 1980s became a period in which politics was often defined in terms of special-interest groups, and this trend continued into the 1990s. During the Reagan years of the 1980s, conservative groups began appearing on the scene and joined the liberal interest groups as powerful actors in Washington. Formerly unorganized groups got together and began having a significant impact on American politics. Significantly, special interest groups began to replace political parties as the dominant organizations of the American political system. This new era of a sharp decline of political parties and a related rise of interest groups articulating political demands has continued unabated on the national and state levels.[6] It is not a surprising consequence that the business sector perceived a need for greater political participation.

Decline in Voter Participation

The growth of special-interest groups occurred in tandem with a decline in voter participation in the United States, which fell from about two-thirds to less than one-half of the eligible voting population.[7] Thus, it seems that 25 percent is enough votes to determine who gets elected to Congress.

Furthermore, voters who are members of organized groups tend to be the most knowledgeable about issues; therefore, candidates have to pay special attention to them. The rest of us have less information about specific issues and are likely to vote on the basis of more general information.[8] Consequently, as a decline in voter participation continues, organized special-interest groups will capture the attention of Senate and House members because these groups have specific, formalized expectations that must be addressed.

In summary, these four changes in the political environment create a situation that business must be aware of when it interacts with government. First, the growth of regulations creates a need for business response. Second, the new openness of Congress makes it more approachable. Third, the rise and success of special-interest groups makes it clear that business, too, must get organized and more involved. Fourth, the decline in voter participation permits these interest groups to be more powerful. Against this backdrop, it is not surprising that we have seen increased and growing corporate political participation.

CORPORATE POLITICAL PARTICIPATION

Political involvement is broadly defined as participation in the formulation and execution of public policy at various levels of government. As decisions about the current and future shape of society and the role of the private sector shift from the marketplace to the political arena, corporations, like all interest groups, find it imperative to increase their political involvement and activity.[9]

Historically, companies entered into debates in Washington only on an issue-by-issue basis and with no overall sense of purpose, goals, or strategy. Furthermore, companies tended to be reactive; that is, they dealt with issues only after the issues had become threats. This approach became obsolete as the kinds of changes we have described occurred. Today, in many industries, success in Washington is just as important as success in the marketplace. Just as business has learned that it must develop competitive strategies to succeed, it has also learned that political strategies are essential as well.[10]

Corporate political involvement greatly increased in the 1970s. Between 1968 and 1978, the number of corporations with offices in Washington quintupled to more than 500. Washington office staff sizes grew, and companies created or expanded public affairs/government relations units in their corporate staffs. Significant efforts were made by many companies to mobilize constituent groups, such as past and present stockholders and employees, into grassroots lobbying networks.

As campaign finance laws changed, a dramatic increase of companies participating in federal elections through the political action committees (PACs) occurred. The increased political participation resulted in a number of important business victories in the 1970s, such as the defeat of a proposed consumer protection agency, reformed labor law, and reduction in the capital gains tax rate. Business came to play a very significant role in the legislative process in Congress. By the mid-1980s, there were signs that business was working harder at lobbying Congress but enjoying it less. The easy victories had been won, and the problems remaining were proving to be intractable.[11] To more fully appreciate business's participation in the process of public policy formation in the United States, it is necessary to understand the techniques that business uses to influence the government stakeholder. We will focus only on the following major approaches: (1) lobbying, (2) PACs, and (3) coalition building. At this point, our approach will be largely descriptive as we seek to understand these techniques, their strengths and weaknesses, and business's successes and failures with them. At the same time, however, we must be constantly vigilant of possible abuses of power or violations of sound ethics.

BUSINESS LOBBYING

Lobbying is the process of influencing public officials to promote or secure the passage or defeat of legislation. Lobbyists are intensely self-interested. Their goals are to promote legislation that is in their organization's interests and to defeat legislation that runs counter to their organization's interests. As the changes we described earlier have taken place, groups representing all kinds of special interests have increased their lobbying efforts. Business interests, labor interests, ethnic and racial groups, professional organizations, and those simply pursuing some ideological goal they believe is in the public interest are lobbying at the federal and state levels today. Our focus is on business lobbying at the federal level, although we must remember that this process is also occurring daily at the state and local levels.

H. R. Mahood defines lobbying as the professionalization of the art of persuasion.[12] Lobbying serves a number of purposes. It is not just a technique for gaining legislative support or institutional approval for some objectives such as a policy shift, a judicial ruling, or the modification or passage of a law. Lobbying may also be directed toward the reinforcement of established policy or the defeat of proposed policy shifts. Lobbying also targets the election or defeat of national, state, or local legislators. A lobbyist may be a lawyer, a public relations specialist, a former head of a public agency, a former corporate executive, or a former elected official. In this sense, there is no typical lobbyist.[13] It is clear, however, that more and more businesses, as well as other special-interest groups, are turning to lobbyists to facilitate their involvement in the public policy process. A cartoon depicts the increasing stature of lobbyists. The teacher asks the class "Who runs America?" She then gives her students the following choices: "the president, the Supreme Court, or Congress?" An astute class member responds, "Lobbies."[14]

Organizational Levels of Lobbying

The business community engages in lobbying at a variety of organizational levels. At the broadest level are **umbrella organizations** that represent the collective business interest in the United States. The best examples of umbrella organizations are the Chamber of Commerce of the United States and the National Association of Manufacturers (NAM). Out of these have grown organizations that represent some subset of business in general, such as the Business Roundtable, which was organized to represent the largest firms in America, and the National Federation of Independent Business, which represents smaller firms.

At the next level are *trade associations* composed of many firms in a given industry or line of business. Examples include the National Auto Dealers Association, the National Association of Home Builders, the National Association of

Realtors, and the Tobacco Institute. Finally, there are individual *company lobbying* efforts. Here, firms such as BellSouth, Ford, ARCO, or Delta lobby on their own behalf. Typically they use their own personnel, establish a Washington office for the sole purpose of lobbying, or hire a professional lobbying firm or consultant located in Washington.

We will consider each of these levels further, beginning with the efforts of individual firms and the use of professional lobbyists.

Company Lobbying. Lobbyists, sometimes derisively referred to as "influence peddlers," operate under a number of formal titles and come from a variety of backgrounds. Officially they are lawyers, government-affairs specialists, public relations consultants, or public affairs consultants. Some are on the staffs of large trade associations based in Washington. Others represent specific companies that have Washington offices dedicated to the sole purpose of representing those companies in the capital city. Still others are professional lobbyists who work for large law firms or consulting firms in Washington that specialize in representing clients to the lawmakers.

The new breed of lobbying consultant in Washington most often is a former government official. Some are ex-congressional staff members or ex-members of Congress. Others are former presidential staff assistants or other former highly placed government officials. Many of these individuals are legally prohibited from discussing private business matters with anyone in the White House for 1 year after leaving office. However, 1 year is a relatively short apprentice period for someone who will likely increase his or her former salary manyfold. Someone once said that influence peddling is one of the biggest growth industries around, and the increase in the number of lobbyists from 3,498 to 8,000 in the period 1976 to 1986 bears this out.[15] Examples of former government officials who left positions to represent private interests include Michael Deaver (former Reagan deputy chief of staff), Richard Allen (former national security adviser), and Richard Schweiker (former secretary of Health and Human Services).

What do business lobbyists accomplish? Lobbyists offer a wide range of services that include drafting legislation, creating slick advertisements and direct-mail campaigns, and, most important, getting access to lawmakers. *Access,* or connections, seems to be the central product that the new breed of lobbyist is selling—the returned phone call, the tennis game with a key legislator, or the golf outing with the Speaker of the House. With so many competing interests in Washington today, the opportunity to get your point across in any format is a significant advantage. Lobbyists also play the important role of showing busy legislators the virtues and pitfalls of complex legislation.[16] Figure 8-1 summarizes some of the various activities that business lobbyists accomplish for their clients.

Grassroots Lobbying. In addition to lobbying directly through the use of professional lobbyists, firms use what is called **grassroots lobbying**, which refers to the process of mobilizing the "grassroots" toward political action. The grassroots are those specific citizens and individuals in communities who might be most

FIGURE 8-1 What Business Lobbyists Do for Their Clients

- Get access to key legislators (connections)
- Monitor legislation
- Establish communication channels with regulatory bodies
- Protect firms against surprise legislation
- Draft legislation, slick ad campaigns, direct-mail campaigns
- Provide issue papers on anticipated effects of legislative activity
- Communicate sentiments of association or company on key issues
- Influence outcome of legislation (promote helpful legislation, defeat harmful legislation)
- Assist companies in coalition building around issues that various groups may have in common
- Help Congress people get reelected
- Grassroots organizing

directly affected by legislative activity. Grassroots lobbying is also used by trade associations and the umbrella organizations.

The better corporate grassroots lobbying programs usually flow from a company that recognizes that people are the firm's most potent political resource. Although people cannot be directed or required to become politically involved, they can be persuaded and encouraged. The major features of grassroots programs include:

1. Regular newsletter communications with large numbers of employees, shareholders, retirees, and other stakeholder groups
2. Objective discussion of pros and cons of policy issues in constituent newsletters and other communications
3. Nonpartisan political education for corporate constituents so that they can understand the importance of feedback from the grassroots to legislators
4. Regular meetings to hear elected officials or company executives discuss relevant political issues[17]

Trade Association Lobbying. Most major companies are members of trade associations that lobby on their behalf. A ***trade association*** is an organization that represents firms in a *specific* industry. The association receives its funds from firms in the industry that join and pay dues. According to the *Encyclopedia of Associations,* which lists all the registered national and international associations, there are over 23,000 registered in the United States today. Of these, a significant portion are classified as "Trade, Business, and Commercial."[18]

A central issue facing trade associations today is the question of representing specific industry needs versus general business needs. Trade associations are best equipped to represent the narrow interests of their members, but by doing so they may come into conflict with other associations or fail to support broader business interests that are also important to them. This point is illustrated by the experience of the National Association of Wholesalers. Until the late 1970s, this group was a sleepy organization that focused on the narrow issues affecting its members. Then it broadened its outlook, and its power and influence grew. One member of the organization said, "We realized that we could do a masterful job on parochial issues, but unless the big problems were worked out it wouldn't make any difference."[19]

Much to their dismay, trade associations sometimes find themselves in the undesirable role of battling with each other in their attempts to lobby Congress. A prominent example of this battle occurred in 1991 as two huge transit associations—the American Trucking Association and the Association of American Railroads—locked horns over the issue of whether triple-trailer trucks would be permitted on American highways. The railroad association was lobbying against the use of triple-trailer trucks because of their belief that such use cuts into railroad transport profits and that they are dangerous. Publicly, the railroad association ran commercials on television designed to play on motorists' fear of big trucks. The television ad apparently worked, as it generated thousands of telephone calls from private citizens, and the bill that was passed represented a railroad victory.[20]

Umbrella Organizations. The umbrella organizations are associations, too. But unlike the trade associations, they have a broad base of membership that represents businesses in a number of different industries and of varying sizes. Historically, the two major umbrella organizations in the United States have been the Chamber of Commerce of the United States and the National Association of Manufacturers. Each of these groups has political action as one of its central objectives.

Chamber of Commerce of the United States. The national Chamber of Commerce was founded in 1912 as a federation of businesses and business organizations. In addition to firms, corporations, and professional members, the Chamber has thousands of local, state, and regional chambers of commerce, American chambers of commerce abroad, and several thousand trade and professional associations. Its diversity of membership indicates why it is referred to as an umbrella organization.

The U.S. Chamber of Commerce is the largest and most broadly represented business association in Washington. It has dozens of committees that study and initiate policy positions in diverse areas such as antitrust, taxation, environment, labor relations, agribusiness, governmental relations, and community affairs. The members of the committees are representatives of the member companies and organizations that belong to the Chamber, and they are assisted by a paid professional staff. The Chamber seeks to influence the legislative process by way of congressional testimony, by lobbying in conjunction with the Washington representatives of its member organizations, and through grassroots efforts of the local and state chambers.

The Chamber specializes in grassroots political action. Such indirect lobbying involves frequent communication with members and others, urging them to write or phone key legislators. One example of the Chamber's main techniques for mobilizing its membership on an issue is the distribution of what it terms an "action call." An ***action call*** is essentially a memorandum outlining the Chamber's position on an issue and urging members to contact their lawmakers. Action calls are typically sent to a district or state where the representative or senator is thought to hold a key vote on the pending legislation.[21]

Historically, the U.S. Chamber of Commerce has been a legislative powerhouse in its ability to influence public policy. Although many think its power is waning, there is continuing evidence of the Chamber's clout. During the life of the 98th Congress, for example, the Chamber—responding to its members' needs—presented views on 106 issues due for congressional action. The results: 57 victories, 25 losses, and 24 partial wins. Chamber representatives met more than 2,000 times with members of the 98th Congress or their staffs for lobbying purposes or to answer requests for information. Chamber testimony was presented 166 times to committees and subcommittees. Witnesses included chamber directors, staff experts, and business people serving on chamber policy committees. Congress also heard from thousands of chamber members in businesses, associations, and state and local chambers around the country who were mobilized to write or phone.[22]

National Association of Manufacturers (NAM). The NAM is organized similar to the U.S. Chamber of Commerce but represents a more specialized grouping of businesses. It was founded in 1895. The membership of the NAM has historically been tilted toward the larger smokestack industry firms, whereas the Chamber's membership includes small firms, retailers, and service industries. Today the NAM is more diverse with large, small, old-line, and high-tech manufacturers.

Historically the NAM has been thought of as staunchly conservative and dominated by Republicans, just like the Chamber. In fact, in 1922 the NAM withdrew from the Chamber because it disliked the Chamber's unwillingness to denounce all Democrats and all forms of government interference in the economy.[23]

Significant changes occurred in the NAM late in 1979 when two Democrats were installed in key positions. Alexander Trowbridge, who had been secretary of commerce during the Lyndon Johnson administration, was named president. He chose as the number two person Jerry Jasinowski, an assistant secretary of state in

Jimmy Carter's administration. When Trowbridge and Jasinowski took over the helm, the NAM took a decidedly different direction. Some of the new policy directions included an advocacy of industrial policy (arguing for a new federal program to subsidize robotics) and a movement toward protectionist trade policies. Both views had been traditionally opposed by business organizations.[24]

The NAM did not shift to the radical left as some feared but rather became more moderate. One CEO said, "Too moderate, if you ask me." However, this executive had to admit that he was generally impressed with the NAM's lobbying efforts.[25] On Capitol Hill, the NAM gets mixed ratings. One legislator says the NAM is far less effective and influential than it once was, but others praise the NAM for its more practical, accommodationist approach to politics. One top legislative aide argued, "Compared to the Chamber of Commerce, which is the Model T of the Washington scene, the NAM looks like a Ferrari." Others also say that of the two, the NAM is better.[26]

Not surprisingly, the changes at the NAM have split the Washington business community on a growing number of issues. This is a significant factor because the NAM and the Chamber have settled on opposite sides of some major issues, and members of Congress tend to write off the business community when it is divided.[27]

Business Roundtable. Formed in 1972, the Business Roundtable is often regarded as an umbrella organization, although, like the NAM, its membership is restricted. It is composed of the chief executive officers (CEOs) of 200 major corporations. The Roundtable's success could be attributed to its two unique premises: (1) the CEOs themselves lobby in Washington, and (2) the group focuses on large public policy matters and not on narrow business interests.[28]

During the early years of the Business Roundtable, a handful of corporate CEOs came to dominate Washington's relationship with business. Especially prominent were Irving Shapiro (DuPont), Reginald Jones (GE), John deButts (AT&T), and Thomas Murphy (GM). These corporate superstars (as they were sometimes called) pioneered an unusual era of business involvement in government affairs, and they spoke in unison for the collective concerns of business. They were heard and listened to by everyone in Washington who counted, from the president on down.[29]

The decline of the Washington superstar era ended when these four leaders all retired between 1979 and 1981 and President Ronald Reagan arrived on the scene in 1980 with his pro-business philosophy and administration. The exodus of the four corporate giants left a vacuum in leadership atop U.S. businesses. But there was no real need for other leaders to emerge because the Reagan administration seemed to embrace business's views wholeheartedly.

The broad issues of the 1970s on which the Business Roundtable was successful gave way to a whole new set of issues in the 1980s. With the Reagan administration dominating the 1980s, business was not involved in the general lobbying that characterized the Roundtable's efforts in the 1970s. The concerns of the 1980s— growth of global competition, trade policy, and the after-effects of a worldwide recession—left business people confused and often at odds with one another. For example, some of the troubled smokestack industries raised calls for protectionist measures, while those in high tech waved the flag for free trade. With this disunity, it has become difficult for anyone to speak clearly for the business community.[30]

Lack of Unity Among Umbrella Organizations

With the passage of the 1981 tax bill, a unified business community celebrated one of its most impressive legislative victories in decades. By 1987, the business alliance had shattered. The long fierce debates over the 1986 tax reform bill produced deep divisions and much bitterness. According to Irving Shapiro, one of its former leaders, the leadership of the Roundtable split on the tax issue. Leaders in the business community are trying to recover the unity they once had, but so far their efforts have been futile. It no longer seems possible to come up with an effective business consensus that the diverse groups can support. The decline in effectiveness, ironically, comes at a time when business is investing more than it ever has in political campaigns.

Reasons for Lack of Unity.
There are several reasons why business lobbying efforts have become splintered. First, the power of the large umbrella groups, such as the Chamber, the NAM, and the Roundtable, has diminished because of their inability to reach a consensus on important issues. Second, the traditional heavy industry clique that used to dominate has declined in power as service firms, high-technology firms, and mid-sized firms have become increasingly active. Third, the nature of business lobbying has changed. Business lobbyists could once cut deals with a few powerful legislators but, as power in Congress became more dispersed, they have had to work with more and different people. According to Raymond Hoewing of the Public Affairs Council, "The old-boy network just doesn't work very well anymore."[31]

Different Needs of Specialized Groups.
Business lobbying is changing as the call for increasingly specialized lobbying arises to meet the needs of specialized groups. Trade problems and the budget deficit are examples of two issues in which lobbying groups are coming down on opposite sides of the fence. One example of the specialized kind of organization that has grown up and prospered in the new environment is the American Business Conference. Started in 1981, this group consists of 100 CEOs of medium-sized, fast-growing companies. To be a member, this group requires double-digit growth each year. By aggressively promoting itself and its members' interests as growth companies, it is on the upward slope of the power curve in Washington.[32]

Need to Strengthen Business's Collective Interest.
Some experts have expressed concern over the increasingly fragmented business community and dwindling power of the umbrella organizations. Ian Maitland, for example, has argued that the fragmented form of current political involvement by the business community has

resulted in each business interest lobbying separately for its own parochial goals. The outcome has been a free-for-all in which business's collective interest has been the real loser. Maitland argues that if business is to avoid the self-defeating consequences of much of today's lobbying, it must find a way to strengthen its collective institutions such as the Chamber of Commerce, the NAM, and the Business Roundtable. He thinks these umbrella organizations need to define a public agenda that transcends the interests of different sections of their membership if business is to be successful.[33]

POLITICAL ACTION COMMITTEES

To this point, our discussion of lobbying has focused on interpersonal contact and powers of persuasion. We now turn our attention to *political action committees (PACs)*, the principal instrument through which business uses financial resources to influence government. PACs should be thought of as one part of lobbying. However, because they have become such an influential phenomenon, they deserve separate treatment in this text.

Evolution of PACs

PACs have been around for years, but their influence has been most profoundly felt in the past decade. This is perhaps because the bottom line in politics, as well as in business, is most often measured in terms of money—who has it, how much they have, and how much power they are able to bring to bear as a result. This has been often referred to as the *Golden Rule of Politics:* "He who has the gold, rules."[34]

Business PACs appeared on the scene in the early 1970s as a direct result of the 1974 amendments to the *Federal Election Campaign Act* (FECA). Under this law, organizations of like-minded individuals (such as business, labor, or other special-interest groups) may form together and create a PAC for the purpose of raising money and donating it to candidates for public office. PACs may contribute $5,000 per candidate per election—primary, runoff, general, or special. There are no aggregate limits on how much a PAC may contribute to numerous candidates nor on how much money a candidate may accept from all sources. The $5,000 limit is less restricting than that placed on individuals, who are limited to donating $1,000 per federal candidate per election and to donating an aggregate $25,000 in total annual contributions. Under the 1976 amendments to FECA, individuals may contribute up to $5,000 per year to PACs.[35]

The 1974 amendments to FECA grew out of an unprecedented number of companies being indicted for illegal campaign contributions in the 1972 presidential election campaign. In 1974, after Watergate, PACs offered corporations an organized, centralized, safe route for campaign participation. Labor organizations had managed to be politically active using PACs since the 1930s, but it was not until the 1970s that business PAC activity took off.

Figure 8-2 illustrates the explosive growth in numbers of PACs for the period 1974 to 1988.

In 1975, the Federal Election Commission announced a landmark ruling involving Sun Oil Company's PAC: SunPAC. The company was given permission to solicit stockholders and employees for contributions, to establish a separate political giving program among employees using payroll deduction, and to use general treasury funds to create and administer the PAC and solicit contributions. Labor, displeased with the SunPAC decision, campaigned to have the rules amended in 1976, whereby corporate solicitation among employees was restricted to twice a year. In 1979, other amendments were passed, eliminating much of FECA's paperwork and red tape. The net effect was that political involvement via PACs was encouraged.[36]

FIGURE 8-2 Explosive Growth in the Number of PACs

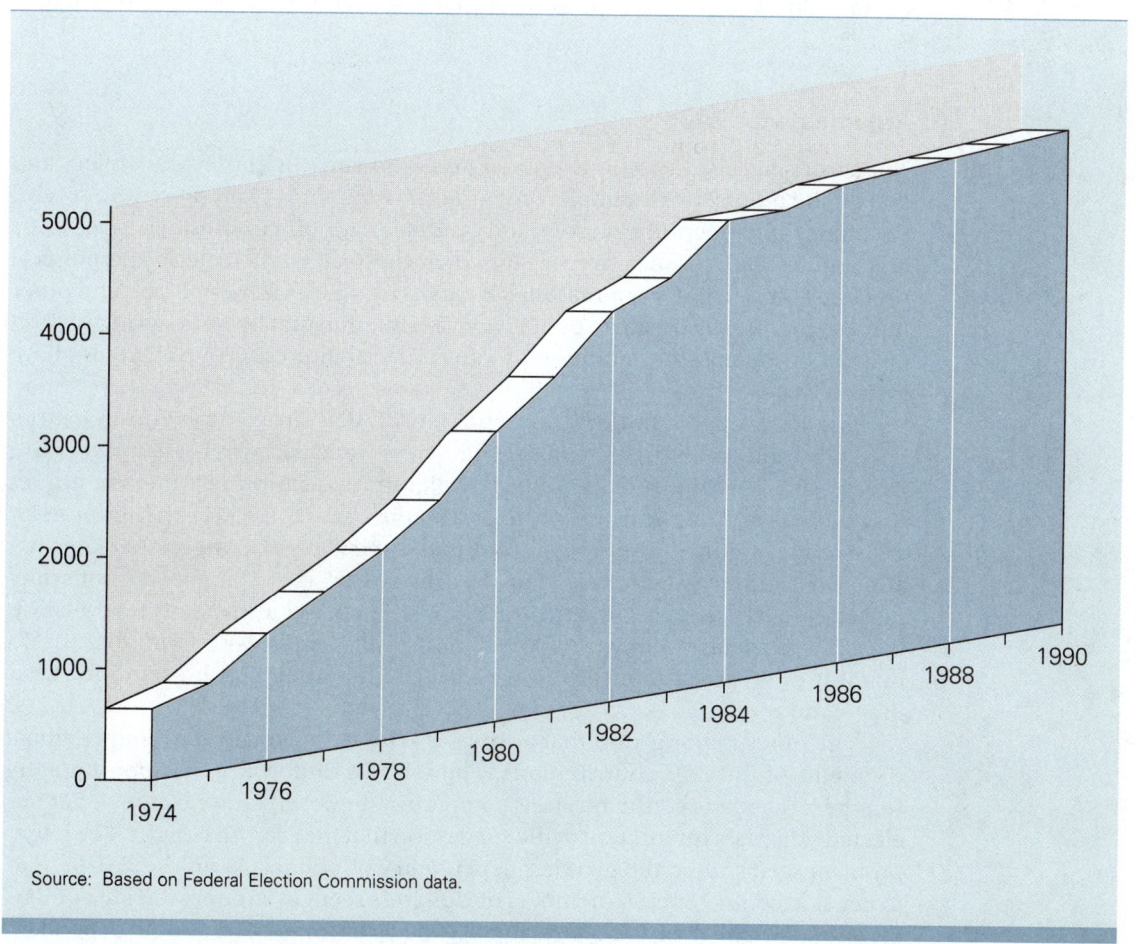

Source: Based on Federal Election Commission data.

Attitudes toward PACs may be grouped into opposing camps. Supporters of PACs laud the process as pluralism in action and point to the large numbers of people who are brought into the political process, thereby making government more responsive. Critics see PACs as a powerful catalyst for corruption and favoritism. They accuse candidates for office, as well as incumbents, of adjusting their positions on issues in order to maximize their own special-interest dollars.[37] We will discuss these two extreme positions more fully later.

Magnitude of PAC Activity

One reason PACs have drawn so much attention in recent years is the amount of money they control. Over 4,800 PACs were officially registered at the end of the 1988 election year (the last presidential election held as of this writing), and 3,300 of these actually contributed funds to federal candidates. Their total contributions to Senate and House of Representative candidates in 1988 were about $160 million. This represented an increase of 14% over the 1986 election year.[38]

Arguments for PACs

Not surprisingly, those who support PACs are primarily those who collect and donate the money (for example, the business community) and those who receive the money (members of Congress and candidates for office). Businesses see PACs as a positive and constructive way by which they can participate in the political process. They see PACs as a reasonable means by which business, labor, and other interest groups may organize their giving. They argue that business giving is offset by labor giving and the multitude of other special-interest groups that also have formed PACs.

The business community contends that PAC contributions do not influence the political process unfairly or "buy" votes. Lloyd Unsell, executive vice-president of the Independent Petroleum Association of America, argues that there is nothing sinister in the correlation between PAC contributions by automobile, medical, and dairy interests and the votes of Congresspersons that affect these interests. He says that the "discovery" that Congresspersons supported by such groups voted favorably for them is not a scandalous revelation but only confirms an obvious expectation.[39] The business community thinks that it is only logical that they would contribute to people who stand for what they stand for.

The other major group that advocates PACs are many of the Congressional recipients of the PAC contributions. There is less uniformity of support among Congress than among the business community, however. One reaction from our elected officials is resentment at the suggestion that they can be bought. The larger problem seems to be the growing dependency of politicians on the PAC money to get elected. In general, members of Congress seem to support the idea of PAC contributions, as their campaign financing has become increasingly dependent on it. It may be that some Congress members are against the PACs or see the need for reform but just can't bring themselves to do it. With each passing year, however, the need for reform of the PAC laws is becoming apparent to many politicians. Figure 8-3 somewhat indicates the amounts that are at stake by listing the contributions made by the top 20 PACs for the past election.

FIGURE 8-3   Political Action Committee (PAC) Contributions, 1988

Rank	PAC Sponsor	Total	Principal Category
1	National Assn of Realtors*	$3,047,269	Real Estate
2	Teamsters Union*	$2,925,164	Transport Union
3	American Medical Assn*	$2,664,202	Doctors
4	National Education Assn*	$2,151,029	Teachers Union
5	National Assn of Retired Federal Employees*	$1,986,400	Govt Union
6	Assn of Trial Lawyers of America*	$1,962,058	Lawyers
7	United Auto Workers*	$1,955,099	Manuf Union
8	National Assn of Letter Carriers*	$1,758,742	Postal Union
9	American Federation of State-County/Munic Employees	$1,658,386	Govt Union
10	Machinists/Aerospace Workers Union*	$1,524,780	Manuf Union
11	National Assn of Home Builders*	$1,462,756	Resid Constr
12	Marine Engineers Union*	$1,430,771	Seamen Union
13	Carpenters & Joiners Union*	$1,409,395	Constr Union
14	American Bankers Assn*	$1,345,083	Comml Banks
15	National Assn of Life Underwriters	$1,329,150	Life Insurance
16	AT&T	$1,305,112	Long Distance/Defense
17	Intl Brotherhood of Electrical Workers*	$1,237,170	Misc Union
18	Air Line Pilots Assn	$1,209,500	Transport Union
19	AFL-CIO*	$1,207,232	Labor Unions
20	National Auto Dealers Assn	$1,202,420	Auto Dealers

*Contributions came from more than one PAC affiliated with this sponsor
Source: Federal Election Commission data.

Arguments Against PACs

Some of the most vocal opposition to PACs and the role they are currently playing comes from members of Congress themselves. Consider the following comments:

- Senator Robert Dole (R-Kansas): "When these political action committees give money, they expect something in return other than good government. It is making it much more difficult to legislate. We may reach a point where if everybody is buying something with PAC money, we can't get anything done." He worries about differing treatment of the rich and the poor: "Poor people don't make campaign contributions. You might get a different result if there were a Poor-PAC up here."[40]
- Representative Richard Bolling (D-Missouri) on retiring after 34 years: "The proliferation of special-interest money has created a political 'stench.'"[41]
- Representative Jim Leach (R-Iowa): "A government of the people, by the people, and for the people cannot be a government where influence is purchasable through substantial campaign contributions. It is simply a fact of life that when big money in the form of group contributions enters the political arena, big obligations are entertained."[42]
- Representative William Brodhead (D-Michigan) on announcing that he would not seek reelection, responding to the question, "Why do you find raising campaign funds so offensive?": "When my opponent can spend $500,000, I need funds to counter him. Where am I going to get it? I can get it from these PACs. But we're not fleecing these people, they're investing. Human nature being what it is, if you take their money, you feel obligated to them. Then you get dependent on the money. It's like being addicted to a drug. And if you haven't delivered—if the realtors have given you $5,000 and you've voted against all their bills—then you're out of it. All of a sudden, people have got their hooks in you. . . . People (Congressmen) are getting corrupted. They're not voting their districts. They're not voting their consciences. They're not even playing politics anymore. They're just out for the bucks."[43]

Figure 8-4 presents a 1991 letter from consumer advocate Ralph Nader, founder of Public Citizen, criticizing PAC contributions.

Two major criticisms come through in these comments and in criticisms of PACs by others. First, it is argued that PACs are buying votes with their contributions. Second, it is argued that members of Congress have become too dependent on PAC money for election and reelection.

PACs and the Vote-Buying Controversy.
A serious allegation about PACs is that their contributions "buy" votes of Congress people. Many studies have been done to

FIGURE 8-4   Nader Letter Regarding PACs

Ralph Nader

Dear Member:

When a city official takes cash from a contractor, it's called <u>bribery</u>. When a Senator has breakfast with a special interest lobbyist, accepts a check for $2,000, then votes in favor of that group on a measure that may award them billions of dollars in government contracts, it's called <u>honoraria</u>.

When a health inspector takes cash from a restaurant owner whose establishment doesn't meet standards, it's called <u>bribery</u>. When an industry pollutes our environment, yet escapes prosecution and fines because the law is changed after influence money is given to congressional campaigns, it's called a <u>contribution</u>.

When a police officer takes cash from a drug dealer to look the other way, it's called <u>bribery</u>. When congressional members receive millions in dollars from Savings & Loan owners to permit risky investments and the looting of an entire industry, it's called a political campaign <u>donation</u>.

Honoraria. Contribution. Donation. These words are only Washington doublespeak for one thing -- <u>legalized bribery.</u>

The corrupting influence that special interest political action committees (PACs) and lobbyists hold over our elected officials in Washington is intolerable. With few honorable exceptions, your representatives and senators no longer represent you and me -- they represent the lobbyists that pad their pockets and campaign coffers with hundreds of millions of dollars.

We must break the hold that these special interest groups have on our government. This summer, we have a chance to pass some meaningful reforms. After their self-serving pay raise, huge deficit, the S&L bailout, and many other scandals, Congress is under intensifying citizen pressure to do something about this corruption.

Please read the enclosed information, then offer your additional support to a campaign that has made a difference -- the Public Citizen "Clean Up Congress" campaign.

Only as citizens, united together, can we stand up to the highly-organized, big money lobbies that run Washington today.

Sincerely,

Ralph Nader

calculate correlations between PAC giving and congressional voting. The major problem is that correlations do not necessarily prove causation. But many of the correlations do appear convincing and are used by PAC critics to fullest advantage.

Several political analysts have been able to conduct studies using more sophisticated statistical techniques than simple correlation. These studies have been able to control variables, such as party ideology and past voting records, to determine what independent effects the contributions have. W. P. Welch studied the effect of 1974 dairy PAC contributions on the following year's vote for milk price supports. His finding was that the PAC gifts had a relatively small effect on the vote. It seemed that voting for Congresspersons was determined more by how important dairy production was in each legislator's home district than by ideology and party affiliation. However, Welch also established that dairy price support voting was clearly related to contributions made in the next election as the PACs offered "reward" money.[44]

The American Trucking Association's PAC. John Frendreis and Richard Waterman investigated the United States's Senate vote on deregulation of the trucking industry in 1980. This was an issue of considerable importance to the American Trucking Association (ATA). The ATA's PAC made contributions to 54 senators and 319 representatives in 1979–1980. This study showed a strong linkage between congressional votes and PAC contributions. Indeed, this relationship was stronger than that between votes and party ideology and constituency, and it was strongest for those senators whose seats were up for grabs in the 1980 election.[45]

The National Automobile Dealers Association's PAC. Perhaps one of the most egregious examples of the power of PACs occurred in 1982 as the National Automobile Dealers Association's (NADA) PAC attempted to defeat a Federal Trade Commission (FTC) proposal that would have required used-car dealers to reveal any known defects on cars. This was a motherhood issue for consumers.[46] The House vetoed the FTC rule. Of the 286 House members who supported the veto resolution, 242 had previously received donations from NADA's PAC. The simple correlation was only suggestive. But when other variables, such as ideology and party, were statistically controlled, an independent relationship between the PAC money and the vote still existed. In the case of those whose ideology matched the PAC's views, the money only marginally enhanced the probability of voting the NADA viewpoint. For those who were decidedly more liberal or conservative than NADA, the contributions substantially raised the probability they would vote with NADA. Also, a vote for the NADA position resulted in more generous gifts in the 1982 reelections. There were 251 legislators who voted for the veto and ran again in 1982. Eighty-nine percent received money, averaging more than $2,300, from NADA. Just 22 percent of the 125 legislators who voted against the NADA position received money in 1982, which averaged only about $1,000 per person.[47]

Center for Public Integrity Study. A 1991 study released by the Washington-based Center for Public Integrity reported the results of tracking contributions from 1981 to 1990 and found that money appeared to be a factor in a number of votes. The center concluded that "patterns do emerge when votes are compared with campaign contributions."[48] A sampling of the study's findings include the following:

- Eighty-five percent of the senators who received $15,000 or more from sugar interests voted against curtailing the sugar support program in 1990. The support program costs consumers $3 billion annually in higher prices.
- Insurance industry contributions averaged $44,030 to Judiciary Committee members who backed the industry on a key vote. Those who voted against the industry averaged $16,294.
- The auto industry gave $44,000 to key lawmakers in an 11-day period between two Senate procedural votes on a bill to raise auto mileage standards. Two of the senators who received contributions switched from opposing the industry position against raising the requirements to supporting it. The industry won by just three votes the second time and was able to kill the bill.[49]

The study cites a number of other specific examples where it appears contributions by PACs influenced the outcome of voting.

What conclusion can we reach about the charge that PAC contributions buy votes? The opinion of Larry Sabato appears most reasonable:

> The best answer based on the available evidence seems to be that PAC contributions do make a difference, at least on some occasions, in securing access and influencing the course of events on the House and Senate floors. But those occasions are not nearly as frequent as Anti-PAC spokesmen, even Congressmen themselves, often suggest.

It has also been observed by Sabato that PAC contributions appear to be most effective when certain conditions prevail.[50] These conditions include the following:

1. *The less visible the issue.* PAC funds are more likely to be effective while the issue being debated is less visible, that is, not yet in the full glare of the public and the media.
2. *During the early stages of the legislative process.* When agenda setting and subcommittee work is being done, the public, press, and "watchdog" groups are not as attentive.
3. *When the issue is narrow, specialized, or unopposed.* PAC contributions are more effective on specialized or unopposed issues than on broad national issues.
4. *When PACs are allied together.* When "PACs travel in packs" and work together, they can wield considerable power.

5. *When PACs adapt lobbying techniques to their contribution strategy.* Successful PACs also employ grassroots lobbying with contributions.

PACs and Campaign Financing. Because PAC money is easy to come by, it is clear why PACs have so much influence with their contributions. When this fact is combined with the ever-escalating sums of money that legislators need to get and stay elected, the result is quite powerful.

The increasing dependency on PAC contributions is driven partly by the rising costs of getting elected and partly by the ease of getting PAC money. In 1977, the cost of a campaign averaged about $600,000. By 1987, a decade later, it averaged $3 million.[51] Representative Al Swift of Washington state easily won his fifth term in the House in the fall of 1986. Rather than resting on his laurels, he went out soliciting funds for his 1988 campaign and said, "I've had one fund-raiser, we're working on another, and it's only mid-March (1987). It's outrageous."[52]

Recent episodes have cast the current process in a very negative light. Chairman of the Senate Finance Committee, Lloyd Bentsen, offered 200 Washington lobbyists and PACs the opportunity to join him for breakfast once a month and become part of his Chairman's Council. The arrangement quickly became a popular joke in Washington: What is yellow and white and costs $10,000? Answer: Egg McBentsen! The Texas Democrat withdrew the offer.[53]

Not only has the dependency on PAC money become a serious problem, but it is growing increasingly evident that the majority of the money is going to incumbents. Common Cause, a citizen's lobby, studied the giving patterns of PACs. According to their research, in 1984, PACs contributed $4.60 to incumbents for every $1 given to challengers. By 1986, the ratio had grown to $6-to-$1. In 1986, the average incumbent received 44 percent of his or her campaign money from PACs.[54] In 1988, this percentage grew to 46 percent.[55]

One problem with this trend is that it indicates the extent to which congressional elections have become special-interest affairs. Another problem is that incumbents have an advantage over challengers that arises from their preferred ability to raise PAC funds. In 1986, the average incumbent raised 44 percent of campaign funds from PACs. The corresponding figure for challengers was 22 percent. According to Common Cause, 98 percent of all challengers lost. Political analysts think the ability to amass huge sums of money have a "totem effect"—a tendency to scare off political challengers.[56]

Not only are citizen lobby groups and a growing number of legislators becoming alarmed at the effects of PACs, but the general public, too, distrusts PACs and considers them harmful to the nation's political process. S. Prakash Sethi and Nobuaki Namiki find that the negative reaction is independent of socioeconomic and demographic factors, political ideology, and party affiliation. They found in a national survey that (1) PACs are a good thing (17.6 percent), (2) PACs are a bad thing (43.1 percent), (3) PACs have a great deal of influence (35.6 percent), and (4) PACs have some influence (45.8 percent). Sethi and Namiki conclude that "business must undertake substantive and communications-related measures to improve public perception of PAC activities if it is to maintain societal legitimacy in its involvement in the political process."[57]

Campaign Financing Reform Proposals. For several years, proposals have been surfacing to reform the method by which legislators raise funds. As far back as 1977, proposals were introduced and then defeated that sought to provide public funds for congressional campaigns and to restrict the amount candidates could accept from PACs. It is becoming more evident, however, that money is dominating to such a degree that even supporters of PACs now think that reform is necessary.[58]

A major scandal erupted in 1990. It became known as "the Keating Five Scandal." Five U.S. congressional leaders were investigated because they had all been recipients of campaign contributions by Charles H. Keating, who owned Lincoln Federal Savings and Loan Association of California. The five senators were accused of intervening with federal regulators on behalf of Keating during the late 1980s. Four of the senators were found by the Senate Ethics Committee to have used poor judgment. Senator Alan Cranston of California was found to have engaged in "improper conduct." Mr. Keating and his associates had made $1.4 million in campaign contributions to the five senators' campaign committees and related political organizations. The Keating Five Scandal represented one of the most recent events to help push Congress toward campaign finance reform.[59]

There appears to be such a dire need for campaign financing reform that some members of Congress are even saying that it is one of the principal reasons Congress has such a poor reputation these days. Many observers think the most significant single action Congress could take to improve its standing with the public is to change the way campaigns for Congress are financed. Former senator Thomas Eagleton observed: "I don't care what ethics bills you pass, if you don't do anything about campaign-spending reform, you haven't done anything at all." Former Nevada senator Paul Laxalt adds: "There's far too much emphasis on money and far too much time spent collecting it. It's the most corrupting thing on the congressional scene."[60]

Ideas being suggested for campaign financing reform include federal funding, caps on campaign spending, routing campaign funds through political parties instead of to individuals, limiting the terms of legislators and taxing PACs. No action is expected to take place, however, until a stable and reasonable alternative source of campaign funds can be identified.[61]

Reform of the current system seems more likely than ever to take place. However, experience has shown the political process to be unpredictable, and it requires legislators to finally change a system under which many, if not all, of them have been beneficiaries. In addition, there is a growing public sentiment that the current PAC contributions-campaign funds system must be reformed if it is to survive. The relationship between business and government in this connection is coming under increasing scrutiny.

COALITION BUILDING

An important and growing mechanism of political involvement in the public policy process is through the creation and use of coalitions to influence government processes. A *coalition* is formed when distinct groups or parties realize they have something in common that might warrant their joining forces, at least temporarily, for joint action. More often than not, an issue that various groups feel similarly about creates the opportunity for a coalition.

Historically, businesses have been reluctant to form coalitions for the purpose of getting political advantage, but this is changing. Coalition formation is becoming a standard practice for firms interested in accomplishing political goals or influencing public policy. If a company or association wants to pass or defeat particular legislation, it needs to seek support of any individual or organization that has a similar position on the issue.[62]

The success of such efforts has been seen in a variety of instances, such as the defeat of the Common Situs picketing bill several years ago. This accomplishment resulted from a coalition of builders, retailers, manufacturers, oil companies, and representatives of minority workers. The central feature these groups had in common was their opposition to this bill.[63] Other coalitional successes include the defeat of the bill for a consumer protection agency and the defeat of expanded union power through labor law reform.[64] One long-time Washington lobbyist put this new political strategy into context when he observed, "My job used to be booze, broads, and golf at Burning Tree. Now it is organizing coalitions and keeping information flowing."[65]

Since coalitions tend to form around issues, an astute political strategist should analyze past, present, and likely coalitions so that coalitional behavior can be anticipated and managed. To do this, MacMillan and Jones recommend the following steps:

1. Manage the sequence in which issues are addressed. This kind of control can dictate priorities and emphasis and result in the proper channeling of effort to suit the organization's interests.

2. Increase the visibility of certain issues. By doing this, the strategist can focus attention in such a way that his or her goals are met.

3. Unbundle issues into smaller subissues. The strategist may be able to successfully reach his or her goals by slowly but surely accomplishing a small step at a time. The net result may be more success for the entirety.[66]

Raymond Hoewing of the Public Affairs Council in Washington thinks that the rise of specialized coalitions has undermined the power and influence of the major umbrella groups such as the national Chamber of Commerce, the NAM, and the Business Roundtable. With ad hoc coalitions continually forming and disbanding, many companies are wondering about the value of membership in umbrella organizations. Hoewing says, "I hear Washington representatives of corporations asking what the value of an association is if you have to run around finding coalitions all the time."⁶⁷ Clearly, coalition development and use has become a popular and effective technique for business in its effort to achieve its political goals.

STRATEGIES FOR POLITICAL ACTIVISM

We have discussed some of the principal approaches by which business has become politically active—lobbying, PACs, and coalitions. There are other approaches, but these are the major ones. In our discussion we have unavoidably made reference to using these approaches as part of a strategy. To develop the idea of strategy, it is important to understand that we must not only identify useful approaches but also address when and under what conditions these various approaches should be used or would be most effective. We do not want to carry this idea too far because it is beyond the scope of this book. On the other hand, some discussion of strategy is necessary to help us fulfill our stakeholder frame of reference.

Regulatory Life Cycle Approach

Several fairly sophisticated attempts to link corporate political strategies with key issues or variables have been set forth. Arieh Ullman has developed a relationship between the *regulatory life cycle* and the *use of political strategies*. He argues that there are various stages in the **regulatory life cycle**—formation, formulation, implementation, administration, and modification—that require or demand that the firm adjust its political strategy contingent on the stage that an issue has reached. He concludes, for example, that capturing key bureaucrats is meaningful only in the later stages, while corporate grassroots campaigns are advantageous only during the early stages.⁶⁸

Contingency Approaches

Similarly, Gerald Keim and Carl Zeithaml have developed a **contingency approach of corporate political strategy** and legislative decision making. Their model considers two major variables: (1) the number of salient issues in a legislative district and (2) the amount of information a legislator possesses concerning voter preferences on these issues. Keim and Zeithaml then argue that knowledge of these two contingencies is useful in the selection of effective corporate political strategies for specific issues. If the corporation can identify the set of legislators who will be the key to important decisions, then the task is (1) to determine the salience of the issue under consideration to each legislator's constituency and (2) to identify the expected position(s) of voters on the issue. This will permit a prediction of the probable position of each legislator and facilitate the company's selection of an appropriate political strategy (for example, lobbying, constituency building, making campaign contributions through a PAC).[69]

S. Prakash Sethi proposes a more straightforward approach to developing political strategy. His approach takes the position that the political activities (campaign financing, direct lobbying, coalition building) of a company are contingent on (1) the various modes of corporate responses the firm determines are appropriate for the environment it finds itself in, (2) its internal corporate conditions, and (3) its anticipated political risks.[70] The three modes a firm may find itself in are (1) the defensive mode, (2) the accommodative mode, or (3) positive activism.

The *defensive mode* is characterized by a situation where a company sees its objectives as completely legitimate, thinks that anyone opposing these objectives is an adversary, and generally operates by itself in the political arena. The major company goal in this situation is to maintain the status quo in terms of political climate, legislative makeup, and regulatory environment. The strategies suggested are typically ad hoc and reactive. In this mode, of course, the firm would see the external environment and internal corporate conditions as conducive to such a defensive posture.[71]

The *accommodative mode* is one in which the firm thinks its political objectives are contingent on its ability to co-opt other groups to its viewpoint. Here the firm would be willing to form coalitions that are likely to become the norm. This mode does not require a radical departure from traditional goals and strategies but is more responsive and adaptive to a changing political environment and structure. The accommodative mode would appear to be minimally required in today's environment.

Positive activism is a mode in which the focus moves from responding to external pressures to the *initiation* and *development* of a national agenda and a more progressive role in the public policy process. Firms become active leaders for social and political change rather than just responding to external factors. This mode is proactive in nature, and its goal is to anticipate and shape future events.[72]

In today's environment, the politically successful firm needs to take an accommodative mode at a minimum and a positive activism mode ideally. There may be situations where the defensive mode would yet be appropriate; however, these situations are rapidly fading from the scene. For the firm or industry that finds itself in an increasingly competitive environment, positive activism would be the strategy of choice. Furthermore, it is the strategy that is most compatible with innovative, aggressive, and professional management that truly understands the broader role of business in society and what it takes to be successful today.

Corporate Political Entrepreneurship

One final strategy is worthy of discussion as we think about firms becoming active in the arena of political strategy. This is the concept of *corporate political entrepreneurship*. David Yoffie and Sigrid Bergenstein assert that political entrepreneurs have risen to prominence in the same way that public-interest entrepreneurs, such as Ralph Nader, rose to prominence. Political entrepreneurs have created political advantage by leveraging their resources, taking political risks, and using the tools that have been successful for business entrepreneurs. Political entrepreneurs, like business entrepreneurs, need to be opportunity driven. That is, they need to exploit opportunities in rapidly changing environments without being constrained by existing resources. They need to act quickly and speak with one, unified, authoritative voice. They need to use the resources of other firms in their quest and not be constrained by the boundaries of established trade associations or interest groups.[73]

The usefulness of an entrepreneurial strategy can be seen through the example of American Express (AmEx). Until the late 1970s, American Express was just another company with a small Washington office. Information gathering was its principal activity, and virtually no lobbying was done. In 1975, James Robinson was made chairman and CEO, and he appointed a veteran of the Washington environment, Harry Freeman, to take charge of political activities. Robinson's strategy was to aggressively convert AmEx into an integrated service company. After several failures, the goal became one of being a premier *financial* services company. The decision to move into the financial sphere made government a much more important stakeholder because AmEx now had to interact with a number of government agencies even though deregulation was underway.[74]

AmEx created some political advantages for itself when it reorganized its business-government relations. Its Washington office was expanded. It opened other offices in New York, London, and Ottawa. Harry Freeman began reporting directly to Robinson so that political and business strategy could be most effectively coordinated. AmEx then decided to take what had been a relatively dormant issue—trade in services—and champion it with a high-profile strategy. Several companies had tried to make this into an important trade agenda item, but the issue did not become salient until AmEx took it on. Robinson made speeches, attended important meetings, testified at hearings, and was eventually made chairman of a committee that advised the U.S. government on trade in service issues.

Robinson drew more attention to the area by engaging his own top executives in a "strategy of illumination" in which hundreds of speeches were given advocating a new trade initiative in services. By 1982, *Fortune, The New York Times,* and other major publications were quoting company officials almost weekly. AmEx created ad hoc coalitions with other companies on the issue. Finally, the U.S. Special Trade Representative, William Brock, declared trade in services to be a top agency agenda item. Trade in services was made into AmEx's issue and became a central U.S. issue because of its efforts and success.[75]

Yoffie and Bergenstein conclude:

> By developing an issue which had broad political appeal, and fit into the agendas of key politicians, American Express went from an unimportant political player in Washington to a company with access to key decision makers on a wide range of

issues. its efforts built political capital for itself that extended well beyond the area of trade in services to other critical areas for its business strategy.[76]

Corporate political entrepreneurship, as a political strategy, seems particularly well suited to the environment businesses find themselves in today. Not every company could execute the strategy quite as well as AmEx did, but the incentives are so enormous that companies should seriously consider some variety of political entrepreneurship that may mesh well with their needs, resources, and skills.

SUMMARY

The current political environment has been characterized by a growth in government activity, the democratization of Congress, the rise of special-interest groups, and a decline in voter participation. These factors have created a situation in which corporate political participation has flourished. Lobbying is the principal approach for influencing government and the public policy process. Lobbying is now done at the company level, at the trade association level, and through large umbrella organizations such as the U.S. Chamber of Commerce and the National Association of Manufacturers. Lobbying has become increasingly specialized, and one major consequence of this trend has been the diminishment of power of the broad-based umbrella organizations.

Political action committees (PACs) are the major force in raising and distributing monies to legislators. There has been an explosion in the growth and power of PACs over the past decade, and their influence has caused a heated debate. Supporters claim that PACs represent pluralism in action. Critics claim that PACs buy votes and have assumed too large a role in campaign financing. A number of reform proposals are currently before Congress.

Coalition building is one of the most successful strategies for exercising influence over the public policy process. Other important strategies for political activism include the regulatory life cycle approach, contingency approaches, and corporate political entrepreneurship.

DISCUSSION QUESTIONS

1. Of the four major changes that have occurred in the current political environment, in your opinion which has been most significant, and why?
2. Explain *lobbying* in your own words. Describe the different levels at which lobbying takes place. Why is there a lack of unity among the umbrella organizations?

3. What is a PAC? What are the major arguments in favor of PACs? What are the major criticisms of PACs? In your opinion, are PACs a good approach for business to influence the public policy process? What changes would you recommend for PACs?
4. Explain the regulatory life cycle approach to political activism. Differentiate it from contingency approaches.
5. What is meant by corporate political entrepreneurship? Briefly discuss.

ENDNOTES

1. Gerald D. Keim, "Corporate Grassroots Programs in the 1980s," *California Management Review* (Fall, 1985), 111–116.
2. *Ibid.*, 111.
3. *Ibid.*, 112–114.
4. Seymour Martin Lipset, "The Sources of Public Interest Activism," *Public Relations Quarterly* (Fall, 1986), 9–13.
5. Keim, 114–115.
6. Ronald J. Hrebenar and Ruth K. Scott, *Interest Group Politics in America*, 2d ed. (Englewood Cliffs NJ: Prentice-Hall, 1990), vii–viii.
7. Lipset, 10.
8. Keim, 115–116.
9. S. Prakash Sethi, "Corporate Political Activism," *California Management Review* (Spring, 1982), 32.
10. David B. Yoffie and Sigrid Bergenstein, "Creating Political Advantage: The Rise of the Corporate Political Entrepreneur," *California Management Review* (Fall, 1985), 124.
11. Ian Maitland, "Self-Defeating Lobbying: How More Is Buying Less in Washington," *Journal of Business Strategy* (Fall, 1986), 67–68.
12. H. R. Mahood, *Interest Group Politics in America* (Englewood Cliffs, NJ: Prentice-Hall, 1990), 52.
13. *Ibid.*, 53–54.
14. Dick Lochner, Editorial Cartoon, *U.S. News & World Report* (September 19, 1983), 63.
15. Evan Thomas, "Peddling Influence," *Time* (March 3, 1986), 27.
16. *Ibid.*, 33.
17. Keim, 116–117.
18. *Encyclopedia of Associations* (Detroit, MI: Gale Research Co., 1987).
19. Alan Murray, "Lobbyists for Business Are Deeply Divided, Reducing Their Clout," *The Wall Street Journal* (March 25, 1987), 1, 22.
20. Don Phillips, "King of the Road," *The Washington Post National Weekly Edition* (June 24–30, 1991), 15.
21. *The Washington Lobby*, 3d ed. (Washington, DC: Congressional Quarterly, October, 1979), 113–117.
22. "Keeping America Growing," *Nation's Business* (May, 1985), 65–68.
23. Walter Olson, "A Malleable Manufacturer's Lobby," *The Wall Street Journal* (October 10, 1984), 32.
24. *Ibid.*
25. Marilyn Wilson, "The New Look at NAM," *Dun's Business Monthly* (April, 1984), 44.
26. *Ibid.*, 50.
27. Olson, 32.
28. Leslie Wayne, "The New Face of Business Leadership," *The New York Times* (May 22, 1983), F3, F8, F9.
29. *Ibid.*
30. *Ibid.*
31. Cited in Murray, 1.
32. *Ibid.*, 22.
33. Maitland, 67, 73.
34. Larry J. Sabato, "PAC-Man Goes to Washington," *Across the Board* (October, 1984), 16.
35. Herbert E. Alexander and Mike Eberts, "Political Action Committees: A Practical Approach," *Business Forum* (Winter, 1984), 6.
36. Andria Sagedy, "Why We Have PACs," *Business Forum* (Winter, 1984), 8.
37. Alexander and Eberts, 6.
38. Larry Makinson, *Open Secrets: The Dollar Power of PACs in Congress* (Washington, DC: Congressional Quarterly, 1990), 16.
39. Lloyd N. Unsell, "Business PACs: Do They Sway Votes?" *The Wall Street Journal* (September 29, 1982), 32.
40. Albert R. Hunt, "Special Interest Money Increasingly Influences What Congress Enacts," *The Wall Street Journal* (July 26, 1982), 1.
41. *Ibid.*
42. Randy Huwa, "Political Action Committees: Creating a Scandal," *Business Forum* (Winter, 1984), 13.
43. "The Fun Is All Gone, Process Gets Corrupt," *USA Today* (October 6, 1982) (Interview with *USA Today's* Chris Collins).
44. Cited in Sabato, 21–22.
45. *Ibid.*, 22.

46. Norman C. Miller, "The Pernicious Influence of PACs on Congress," *The Wall Street Journal* (February 17, 1983), 30.
47. *Ibid.*, 22–23.
48. "Contributions from Special Interests Buy Attention in Congress, Study Finds" (The Associated Press), *The Atlanta Journal* (July 2, 1991), A3.
49. *Ibid.*
50. Sabato, 23.
51. Bill Whalen, "Hill May Be Ready to Place a Lid on Campaign Spending," *Insight* (April 13, 1987), 18.
52. *Ibid.*, 18.
53. *Ibid.*
54. John J. Fialka, "House Incumbents Increasingly Depend on PAC Funds, Study Says," *The Wall Street Journal* (April 8, 1987), 70.
55. Makinson, 3.
56. *Ibid.*
57. S. Prakash Sethi and Nobuaki Namiki, "The Public Backlash Against PACs," *California Management Review* (Spring, 1983), 133.
58. David Shribman and Brooks Jackson, "Conservative Support Adds Momentum to a Move by Congress to Limit PACs Influence in Elections," *The Wall Street Journal* (November 22, 1985), 64.
59. Tom Price, "Keating Scandal Spurs Reforms," *The Atlanta Journal* (May 12, 1991), A6.
60. David S. Broder, "Take It from Those Who Know Best: Congress Is a Wreck," *The Washington Post National Weekly Edition* (January 14–20, 1991), 24.
61. Norman Ornstein, "If They Can't Be Banned, Make Them Pay—Tax PACs! *The Washington Post National Weekly Edition* (April 1–7, 1991), 24.
62. Gerald D. Keim, "Foundations of a Political Strategy for Business," *California Management Review* (Spring, 1981), 45.
63. *Ibid.*
64. S. Prakash Sethi, "Corporate Political Activism," *California Management Review* (Spring, 1982), 41.
65. "New Ways to Lobby a Recalcitrant Congress," *Business Week* (September, 1979), 140–149.
66. Ian C. MacMillan and Patricia E. Jones, *Strategy Formulation: Power and Politics,* 2d ed. (St. Paul, MN: West, 1986), 68.
67. Cited in Murray, 22.
68. Arieh A. Ullman, "The Impact of the Regulatory Life Cycle on Corporate Political Strategies," *California Management Review* (Fall, 1985), 140–154.
69. Keim and Zeithaml, 828–841.
70. Sethi, 1982, 34.
71. *Ibid.*
72. *Ibid.*
73. David B. Yoffie and Sigrid Bergenstein, "Creating Political Advantage: The Rise of the Political Entrepreneur," *California Management Review* (Fall, 1985), 124.
74. *Ibid.*, 126–128.
75. *Ibid.*, 129–130.
76. *Ibid.*, 130–131.

CHAPTER **NINE**

Consumer Stakeholders: Information Issues and Responses

CHAPTER OBJECTIVES

After studying this chapter, you should be able to:

◆ Recite the consumer's Magna Carta and explain its meaning.

◆ Chronicle the evolution of the consumer movement.

◆ Identify the major abuses of advertising and discuss specific controversial advertising issues.

◆ Enumerate and discuss other product information issues that present problems for consumer stakeholders.

◆ Describe the role and functions of the FTC.

◆ Discuss the strengths and weaknesses of regulation and self-regulation of advertising.

How important are consumers as stakeholders? An argument could be made that consumers, or customers, rank at or very near the top when it comes to stakeholder priorities. Their importance may be seen in a variety of ways. While discussing the fundamental question of business purpose, the esteemed management expert, Peter Drucker, emphasized the centrality of consumers with his assertion that there is only one valid definition of business purpose: *to create a customer.* The customer is the foundation of a business and keeps it in existence.[1] When Steven Brenner and Earl Molander surveyed executives as to which stakeholder groups were owed the most by business, the results were rank-ordered as follows:

1. Customers (consumers)
2. Stockholders
3. Employees
4. Local community environment[2]

Businesses cannot exist, much less survive and prosper, without customers. Customer satisfaction, therefore, is a central objective of all organizations, large and small alike. The business-consumer relationship is of utmost concern to all of us, since we are all consumers of the products and services provided by the business community.

Ironically, consumers seldom seem completely satisfied with their exchange relationships with business in spite of the fact that business cannot exist without them. A survey of 2,400 metropolitan household consumers revealed that one in five (20 percent) purchases of products and services resulted in consumer dissatisfaction with something other than price, and about one in three of the complaints made by those surveyed ended with an unsatisfactory resolution of the problem.[3]

It is no surprise that the issue of business and the consumer stakeholder is at the forefront of discussions about business and its relationships with and responsibility to the society in which it exists. Products and services are the most visible manifestations of business in society. For this reason, the issue of business and its consumer stakeholders deserves a careful examination. We devote two chapters to it. In this chapter, we focus on the evolution and development of the consumer movement and product information issues, most notably, advertising. In Chapter 10 we consider product issues, especially product safety and liability, and business's response to its consumer stakeholders.

CONSUMER ORIENTATION: THE PARADOX

If one studies the history of business in America, one sees how business has evolved through different eras in the evolution of marketing. It has been said that recent changes in business practices could be characterized as a revolution in marketing.[4]

Basically, this revolution stems from the idea that the customer, not the company, is the focus of business. The focus, in other words, has shifted from problems of production to problems of marketing. The product business can make is no longer as important as the product the consumer *wants* business to make. Robert Keith, using the Pillsbury Company as a model, asserts that this company went through four eras—which he suggests also typifies American business in general. The first era was that of manufacturing in which the company philosophy was product-oriented. The second era was sales-oriented, where the focus was on having a first-rate sales organization that could dispose of all the products (in Pillsbury's case, flour) that could be made. The third era was marketing-oriented. During this era the philosophy was, "We make and sell products for consumers." The fourth era followed a philosophy of marketing control, articulated as, "We are moving from a company that has the marketing concept to a marketing company."[5] This emphasis is confirmed by Regis McKenna in a recent article in which he argues that "marketing is everything." He further asserts the timeliness and importance of this business-consumer stakeholder relationship by his assertion that "the 1990s will belong to the customer."[6]

The consumer orientation, which prevails today, is at the heart of the marketing concept.[7] However, the paradox of the marketing concept is that in a period when practically all marketing theorists and practitioners proclaim a consumer orientation, we see a concomitant rise in the voice of the consumer exclaiming that business does not care about the consumer. Indeed, the consumer movement of the last two decades or so, marching under the banner of "consumerism," seems to contradict the marketing concept. *Business Week* magazine expressed this concern a number of years ago when it asserted, "In the very broadest sense, consumerism can be defined as the bankruptcy of what the business schools have been calling the 'marketing concept.'"[8]

We will return to the subject of consumerism later. At this point, we should look at a number of fundamental questions that have already emerged. The most important of these questions is, "*What does business owe the consumer stakeholder?*" Or, stated differently, "*What does the consumer stakeholder have a right to expect from business?*"

THE CONSUMER'S MAGNA CARTA

Many marketing experts have chosen to suggest what business owes the consumer by reciting what Holloway and Hancock termed the "consumer's Magna Carta," or the four basic consumer rights spelled out by President John F. Kennedy in his 1962 Special Message on Protecting the Consumer Interest.[9] Those rights were the right to safety, the right to be informed, the right to choose, and the right to be heard.

The ***right to safety*** is concerned with the fact that many products (insecticides, foods, drugs, automobiles, appliances) are dangerous. The ***right to be informed*** is intimately related to the marketing and advertising function. Here the consumer's right is to know what a product really is, how it is to be used, and what cautions must be exercised in using it. This right also includes the whole array of marketing: advertising, warranties, labeling, and packaging. The *right to choose*, although perhaps not as great a concern as the first two rights, refers to the assurance that competition is effectively working. The fourth right, the **right to be heard**, was proposed because of the view of many consumers that they cannot effectively communicate to business their desires and, especially, their grievances.[10] Considerable evidence exists, including the study cited at the beginning of this chapter, that the business environment is not receptive to consumer complaints and their rectification, although in recent years this has been changing.

Although these four basic rights do not embody all the responsibilities that business owes to consumer stakeholders, they do capture the fundamentals of business's social responsibilities to consumers. They provide an excellent first approximation of those responsibilities.

A more encompassing statement of business's responsibilities to the consumer stakeholder evolved from a Business Values Seminar that was held at the C. W. Post Center of Long Island University. Figure 9-1 summarizes the major points made in that seminar.

THE CONSUMER MOVEMENT

For decades, there have been outcries that the consumer has been mistreated.[11] The contemporary wave of criticism, however, started to build in the late 1950s, took form in the 1960s, matured in the 1970s, and continues even today though in different form. The following definition of consumerism captures the essence of the consumer movement: "*Consumerism* is a social movement seeking to augment the rights and powers of buyers in relation to sellers."[12] Henry Assael elaborates by saying that consumerism is a "set of activities of independent consumer organizations and consumer activists designed to protect the consumer. Consumerism is concerned primarily with ensuring that the consumer's rights in the process of exchange are protected." He also clarifies that it is somewhat misleading to use the term "consumer movement" unless we understand it to be referring to the conglomeration of groups' efforts rather than any single unified organization of consumers.[13]

Although the consumer movement is often said to have begun in the 1960s with the 1965 publication of Ralph Nader's criticism of General Motors in *Unsafe at Any Speed*,[14] the impetus for the movement was actually a complex combination of circumstances. With respect to consumerism, Philip Kotler asserts:

> The phenomenon was not due to any single cause. Consumerism was reborn because all of the conditions that normally combine to produce a successful social movement were present.[15] These conditions are structural conduciveness, struc-

FIGURE 9-1 What Does Business Owe the Consumer Stakeholder?

A customer/consumer is entitled to receive:

1. *Fair value* for the money he or she spends.
2. A product that will satisfy *reasonable* expectations.
3. A *full disclosure* of the product's specifications.
4. A product/service which will have been *advertised in a truthful and honest manner*.
5. A product which is *safe*. *Safety testing* will be done which is *reasonable* in relation to the foreseeable possibility of injury. Consumers will be warned of dangers—both the obvious and the not so obvious.
6. If later information reveals serious questions about the product's safety, it should be removed from the market or other action should be taken which is appropriate.

Source: Summarized from *Criteria for Decision Making* (New York: C. W. Post Center, Long Island University, 1979), 10. Reproduced with permission.

---

tural strains, growth of a generalized belief, precipitating factors, mobilization for action, and social control.[16]

Kotler argues that consumerism is, indeed, a beneficial movement and that it promises to deliver real gains in the long run—both to business and to the consumer. It will force business to reexamine its role in society, challenge business people to scrutinize problems that are easily ignored, and challenge managers to look at ends as well as means.[17]

Ralph Nader's Consumerism

We cannot overstate the contribution that Ralph Nader made to the birth, growth, and nurturance of the consumer movement. It is now over 25 years since Nader arrived on the scene, but he is still the acknowledged father of the consumer movement. Figure 9-2 summarizes some interesting information on Nader that surfaced when he was honored after 20 years of contributions.

Consumer complaints did not disappear with Ralph Nader's activism. On the contrary, they intensified. Someone once said that Nader made consumer complaints respectable. Indeed, consumer complaints about business proliferated. It is impossible to catalog them all, but Figure 9-3 on page 257 lists examples of the major problems consumers worry about with business.

FIGURE 9-2 Ralph Nader: Father of the Consumer Movement

> In November, 1985, friends, admirers, and colleagues of Ralph Nader gathered to honor him on the 20-year anniversary of *Unsafe At Any Speed,* the auto safety expose that made him king of the consumer movement. His book (1) led to the passage of federal safety legislation, (2) gave rise to the era of consumer activism (consumerism), and (3) propelled Nader into the national limelight.
>
> *Unsafe At Any Speed* described the auto industry and, specifically, General Motors, as businesses that put style and profit ahead of lives and safety. The GM Corvair was the object of his criticism. The legislation that resulted helped lead to safety belts, padded dashboards, stronger door latches, head restraints, shatter-proof windshields, and collapsible steering columns. Nader said: "My strongest memories [of the book] are people writing me saying their lives were saved, or their children's lives were saved, because they were wearing seatbelts."
>
> In 1966, GM couldn't figure out what motivated Nader so they put a couple of detectives on his trail in an effort to discredit the 32-year-old crusader. GM denied Nader's charges that the company used women as "sex lures" as part of its inquiry. The company did apologize to him at a Congressional hearing and paid him $480,000 for invasion of privacy.
>
> Nader put the money into his emerging consumer protection empire. His zealous legion of idealistic muckrakers became known as "Nader's Raiders." His organization now has in excess of 80 "Raiders" and a budget in excess of $1.6 million. His crusading and exposes helped pass a number of laws such as the *Wholesome Meat Act of 1967,* the *Radiation Control for Health and Safety Act of 1968,* the *Clean Water Act of 1972,* and the *Toxic Substance Act of 1976.*

Source: UPI, "Raiders Gather to Honor Nader 20 Years after Car Safety Expose," *The Atlanta Constitution* (November 21, 1985). Reprinted with permission of United Press International. Copyright © 1985.

Nader and the consumer movement were the impetus for consumer legislation being passed in the 1970s. The 1980s, however, did not turn out to be a consumer decade. One observer noted how uncontroversial Nader had become, not only because of the climate of the times but also because most of the significant gains that were to be made had been made.[18] In the deregulatory Reagan environment that characterized most of the 1980s, the consumer movement changed significantly. Consumer activists such as Nader believed that consumers were then being ignored. Regarding the Reagan administration, Nader has argued, "This Administration is out to destroy the rule of law as it applies to corporations."[19]

FIGURE 9-3 Examples of Consumer Problems with Business

- The high prices of many products.
- The poor quality of many products.
- The failure of many companies to live up to claims made in their advertising.
- The poor quality of after-sales service.
- Too many products breaking or going wrong after you bring them home.
- Misleading packaging or labeling.
- The feeling that it is a waste of time to complain about consumer problems because nothing substantial will be achieved.
- Inadequate guarantees and warranties.
- Failure of companies to handle complaints properly.
- Too many products that are dangerous.
- The absence of reliable information about different products and services.
- Not knowing what to do if something is wrong with a product you have bought.

Consumerism in the 1980s

Years after a conservative administration opposed to regulation came into power, consumer organizations are still adjusting to changes in the political environment. For two decades they influenced policies on issues ranging from auto safety to food additives. In the 1980s, they waged an essentially defensive struggle to hold onto earlier gains. Many groups make up the loose confederation known as the consumer movement, and Figure 9-4 enumerates some of the leading ones. These groups, however, are not likely to regain anytime soon the power and influence they enjoyed in the 1970s,[20] even though the early 1990s and the George Bush administration seem to be much more supportive of consumer concerns and enforcement of consumer protection laws.

The consumer movement has partially become a victim of its own success. Many groups can legitimately take credit for facilitating the passage of such legislation as the *Freedom of Information Act* and the Clean Air and Clean Water amendments and for applying pressures leading to closer scrutiny of food, drugs, and children's clothing. But, with many of these important battles largely won, they have trouble finding issues that consumers will rally around. Nader thinks this situation is only a

FIGURE 9-4   Leading Consumer Activist Groups

Action for Children's Television
Action on Smoking and Health
American Consumer's Association
Americans for Better Care
Automotive Consumer Action Program
Council on Economic Priorities
Center for Auto Safety
Center for Corporate Public Involvement
Center for Science in the Public Interest
Coalition of Consumer Justice
Conference of Consumer Organizations
Consumer Alert
Consumer Federation of America
Consumers Union of the United States
Health Research Group
Interfaith Center on Corporate Responsibility
Nursing Home Information Service
Product Safety Association
Public Citizen
The National Consumer League

pause in the progress brought about by the Reagan administration.[21] Some conservatives, however, think that consumer activist groups have worn out their welcome with the public through their loud, constant warnings about perceived perils in everyday life.

Michael Pertschuck, a former consumerist who was Federal Trade Commission (FTC) chairman, believes that consumer expectations of business behavior are higher now largely because of attitudes created by consumer interest groups.

He said, "Today, people expect products to be safe, and they expect to be heard." He also believes that the consumer movement will remain an important force, though its role will not likely be as dramatic. He observes that the old concept of controlling national policy based on the "iron triangle" of interest groups, congressional supporters, and the bureaucracy has given way to a more complicated model that now includes the news media, scientists or policy experts, and other powerful forces.[22]

It is tempting for managers to think that consumer stakeholders are no longer important, given the fact that consumer activist groups are not as powerful as they once were and that there has been virtually no new major consumer legislation passed in over a decade. Part of the problem seems to be that some executives view consumerism as the expression of what is wanted by consumer activists but not consumers as a whole. The problem may also be one of focusing too much on the legislative scorecard to assess the strength of the movement. That is, when the score declined, that is, fewer laws were passed, it was assumed that consumerism had spent its momentum.

According to E. Patrick McGuire, who conducted a major study for the Conference Board, it would be a mistake to assume that the movement is dead because of these trends. He concludes that the movement is healthy, influential, and here to stay.[23] Adding to this view, Paul Bloom and Stephen Greyser asserted that consumerism will continue to have an impact in the years ahead but that, like any social movement, it is maturing. They see the consumer movement as having entered a more advanced stage of its life cycle. As a consequence, it has experienced a considerable degree of market fragmentation. They believe that consumers will rely less on national consumer groups and take more initiative on their own to address consumer problems.[24]

Consumerism in the 1990s

In the late 1980s and early 1990s, consumer groups, along with environmental groups, began showing a resurgence of social activism. Although they were virtually ignored during the Reagan years (1980–1988), these groups have achieved some specific victories by returning to grassroots activism. Consumer victories were won over insurance underwriters, cigarette and food companies, and producers of racy television shows.[25] An interesting and specific example of 1990s-style consumerism occurred when a 66-year-old Omaha millionaire, Phil Sokolof, began a crusade against fat-laden tropical oils typically found in cookies, cereals, and many fast foods. He not only pleaded with food companies to eliminate these ingredients, which had been linked to heart disease, but he then sent out 11,000 letters and bought a full-page, $200,000 ad in national newspapers with offending Hydrox cookies and Cracklin Oat Bran cereal depicted over the strong headline "The Poisoning of America." Kellogg's initial defense of its cereal was to label the ad as irresponsible. Within a month, however, the food-processing giant made the decision to eliminate coconut oil from its products. Soon thereafter, most of the food industry's major firms as well as some fast-food chains followed their lead.[26]

Some have argued that the new wave of consumer protests, boycotts, and activism that we are witnessing in the 1990s represents a backlash against the Reagan administration's deregulation of industries such as airlines and broadcasting and the budget cuts in the staffs of such agencies as the Federal Trade Commission and the Consumer Product Safety Commission. These protests are likely in response to the greedy tendencies of corporate leaders and Wall Streeters during the 1980s. Specific corporate misdeeds also likely eroded public confidence in business. Ivan Boesky and a ring of Wall Streeters traded on insider information. Managers at Beech-Nut attempted to pass off flavored water to consumers as apple juice. Uniroyal was using the suspected carcinogen Alar to ripen apples and keep them fresh. They finally took Alar off the market. Highly visible industrial accidents such as the deadly chemical explosion in Bhopal, India, ground water contamination at Colorado's Rocky Flats nuclear weapons plant, and the oil slick from the Exxon *Valdez* all suggested a lack of business sensitivity toward safety.[27]

One of the most recent manifestations of 1990s-style consumer activism has been the publication and use of consumer or shopping guides to socially responsible companies. By purchasing products only from socially responsible companies (as identified by these guides), consumers can cast a vote for or against the corporate efforts in such arenas as environmental protection, philanthropy, advancement of women and minorities, animal testing, community outreach, and so on. A major example of a book promoting firms sensitive to environmentalism (the "green" movement) is *The Green Consumer Market Guide* (1991).[28] Another guide, *Shopping for a Better World: A Quick and Easy Guide to Socially Responsible Supermarket Shopping* (1989), was published by the Council on Economic Priorities (CEP) and rates numerous products and companies on a host of social responsibility criteria.[29] Figure 9-5 summarizes the criteria used by the CEP.

The consumer movement came somewhat as a shock to many business people, for they believed that, because they had created the most advanced and productive economic machinery known, they were beyond consumer criticism. Some business people still express disbelief that the movement continues despite all they have done for the consumer and the world. But the consumer movement has not gone away and neither have business's problems with consumer issues. The increased competitiveness brought about by the Japanese and other major producing nations has seen to that.

Before we consider more closely the corporate response to the consumer movement and the consumer stakeholder, it is fruitful to look in more detail at some of the issues that have become prominent in the business-consumer relationship and the role that the major federal regulatory bodies have assumed in addressing these issues. Broadly, we may classify the major kinds of issues into two groups: *product information* and the *product itself*. As stated earlier, in this chapter we focus on product information issues such as advertising, warranties, packaging, and labeling. The next chapter will focus on the product itself. Throughout our discussion of products, the reader should keep in mind that we are referring to services also.

FIGURE 9-5   Becoming a Socially Responsible Consumer

> The Council on Economic Priorities' *Shopping for a Better World: A Quick and Easy Guide to Socially Responsible Supermarket Shopping* (Ballantine Books, 1989) strives to assist consumers in becoming more socially responsible in their purchasing by evaluating specific products and companies on a variety of social criteria. The products evaluated range from alcoholic beverages to yogurt. The social criteria used by the CEP to evaluate the product and firms include the following:

- Giving to charity
- Women's advancement
- Advancement of people of color
- Military contracts
- Animal testing
- Disclosure of information
- Community outreach
- Nuclear power involvement
- South Africa
- Environment
- Family benefits

PRODUCT INFORMATION ISSUES

Why have issues been raised about business's social and ethical responsibilities in the area of product information? Most consumers know the answer. Consider, for a moment, the following actual cases:

♦ An ad for *Lysol* disinfectant spray carries a tempting inducement: "Buy one, get one free." The photo in the ad shows two same-sized cans of the stuff. But the small print gives the details: You buy a 12- or 18-ounce can and get a coupon for a free 6-ounce can.[30]

- Hanes Hosiery has made a lot of pantyhose buyers angry. The label on the package of *Summeralls* promises a cash refund and notes "purchase proofs required—see details inside." The details inside require proofs of purchase all right, but for *other* types of Hanes pantyhose, not for *Summeralls*.[31]
- "Free waterbed" said the newspaper ad for Harry Smith Woodworking, in Hellam, Pennsylvania. There *was* one catch: You had to buy a fill-and-drain kit ($3 value) for $159.[32]
- Getting a $2.50 rebate on an aerosol can of *Polycel* insulating sealant isn't impossible, but it's a nuisance. You're supposed to send in, among other things, the small rigid-plastic actuator from the can. A person tried to do that, but the post office returned the letter. It was marked "Return to sender—unmailable. Rigid articles not accepted in letter-style envelopes."[33]
- On the front of the package of *Tyson Chick'n Quick* patties, a highlighted message reads, "Ideal for Microwaves." Turn the package over, and the instructions on the back recommend using a conventional oven "for best results."[34]

These cases are actual examples of the questionable use of product information. It is estimated that the public is exposed to as many as 500 to 1,500 similar advertisements or product communications each day. It is not clear whether the firms that created the aforementioned communications were intending to deceive or not, but one might reasonably conclude that some effort to deceive might have been present. Whether the motive was there or not, business has a legal responsibility, and in many cases an ethical responsibility, to fairly and accurately provide information on its products or services.

The primary issue with product or service information falls in the realm of advertising. Other information-related areas include warranties or guarantees, packaging, labeling instructions for use, and the use of sales techniques by direct sellers.

Advertising

The debate over the role of advertising in society has been going on for decades. Most observers have concentrated on the economic function of advertising in our market system, but opinions are diverse as to whether advertising is beneficial or detrimental as a business function. Critics charge that it is a wasteful and inefficient tool of business and that our present standard of living would be even higher if we could be freed from the negative influence of advertising. These critics argue that advertising raises the price of products and services because it is an unnecessary business cost whose main effect is to circulate a lot of superfluous information that could better and more cheaply be provided on product information labels or by salespersons in stores. The result is that significant amounts of money are spent that produce no net consumer benefit.[35]

In response, others have claimed that advertising is a beneficial component of the market system and that the increases in the standard of living and consumer satisfaction may be attributed to it. They argue that, in general, advertising is an efficient means of distributing information because there is such an enormous and ever-changing array of products that consumers need to know about. Advertising is an effective and relatively inexpensive way to inform consumers of new and improved products.36

The debate over whether advertising is a productive or wasteful business practice will undoubtedly continue. As a practical matter, however, advertising has become the lifeblood of the free enterprise system. It stimulates competition and makes available information that consumers can use in comparison buying. It also provides competitors with information with which to respond in a competitive way and contains a mechanism for immediate feedback in the form of sales response. So, despite its criticisms, advertising does provide social and economic benefits to the American people.

With the thousands of products and their increasing complexity, the consumer today has a real need for information that is *clear, accurate,* and *adequate.* **Clear information** is that which is direct and straightforward and on which neither deception nor manipulation relies. **Accurate information** communicates truths, not half-truths. It avoids gross exaggeration and innuendo. **Adequate information** provides potential purchasers with enough information to make the best choice among the options available.37

Whereas providing information is one legitimate purpose of advertising in our society, another legitimate purpose is *persuasion*. Most consumers today expect that business advertises for the purpose of persuading them to buy their products or services, and they accept this as a part of the system. Indeed, many people enjoy companies' attempts to come up with yet another interesting way to sell their products. It is commonplace for people to talk with one another about the latest interesting or clever advertisement they have seen. Thus, awards for outstanding or interesting advertisements have appeared on the scene. Awards for bad advertisements have become popular also.

Ethical issues in advertising usually arise as companies attempt to inform and persuade consumer stakeholders. The frequently heard phrase "the seamy side of advertising" alludes to the economic and social costs that derive from advertising abuses, such as those mentioned earlier in the chapter, and for which the reader is probably able to supply ample examples.

Abuses of Advertising. William Shaw and Vincent Barry have proposed four types of advertising abuses in which ethical issues reside. These include situations in which advertisers *are ambiguous, conceal facts, exaggerate,* or *employ psychological appeals.*38 These four types cover most of the general criticisms leveled at advertising.

Ambiguous Advertising. One of the more gentle ways that companies deceive is through **ambiguous advertising**, which means that something about the product or service has not been made clear because it may mean several different things.

There are a number of ways an ad may be ambiguous. One way is to make a statement that leaves to the viewer the opportunity to *infer* the message by using **weasel words**. These are words that are inherently vague and for which the company could always claim it was not misleading the consumer. An example of a weasel word is "help." Once an advertiser uses the qualifier "help," almost anything could follow and the company could claim that it wasn't intending to deceive. We see ads that claim to "help us keep young," "help prevent cavities," or "help keep our houses germ free." Think how many times you have seen expressions in advertising such as "helps stop," "helps prevent," "helps fight," "helps you feel," "helps you look," or "helps you become."[39] Other weasel words include "like," "virtually," and "up to" (for example, stops pain "up to" 8 hours). Their use in ads is clearly ambiguous. Other vague terms that are ambiguous include "big" savings, "low" prices, "mild" cigarettes, and "sporty" cars.

Concealed Facts. A type of advertising abuse called **concealing facts** refers to the practice of not telling the whole truth or deliberately not communicating information the consumer ought to have access to in making an informed choice. Another way of stating this is to say that "a fact is concealed when its availability would probably make the desire, purchase, or use of the product less likely than its absence."[40] This is a difficult area, for few would argue that an advertiser is obligated to tell "everything" even if that were humanly possible. For example, a pain reliever company might claim the effectiveness of its product in superlative terms without stating that there are dozens of other products on the market that would be just as effective. Or, an insurance company might promote all the forms of protection that a given policy would provide without enumerating all the situations where the policy does *not* provide coverage.

Few of us would really expect that business would inform us of all of the facts. As consumers, it is up to us to be informed about factors such as competitors' products, prices, and so on. Ethical issues arise when a firm, through its advertisements, presents facts in such a selective way that a false belief is created. Of course, there is judgment involved here as to what has created a false belief or not. This makes the whole realm of deceptive advertising difficult to deal with.

Three examples in which facts were clearly concealed so as to create an inaccurate impression were the Colgate-Palmolive ad for Rapid Shave and, more recently, a Campbell Soup ad and a Volvo ad. Colgate concealed that the "sandpaper" in an ad was actually Plexiglass and that real sandpaper had to be soaked in Rapid Shave for over an hour before it came off with a razor stroke. A Campbell ad showed a bowl of vegetable soup appearing to be rich and thick. It was later discovered that the company had placed clear glass marbles in the bottom of the bowl, thus lifting up the vegetables and making the soup appear richer and thicker than it actually was.[41] In 1990, Volvo Cars of North America admitted that it had reinforced the roof of a Volvo station wagon so that it could withstand the weight of a huge truck that was driven over it in an ad. With its rigged demonstration, Volvo put at risk its long-standing reputation as "a car you can believe in." The company was required to run corrective ads in 19 Texas newspapers where the ad had appeared. That we mention these examples here is proof that such advertising abuses are not quickly forgotten by consumers.

Exaggerated Claims. Companies can also mislead consumers by exaggerating their products and services. ***Exaggerated claims*** are claims that simply cannot be substantiated by any kind of evidence. An example of this would be a pain reliever that is "50 percent stronger than aspirin" or that is "superior to any other on the market."

A frequent mistake by advertisers is making claims that are too broad. This is what happened to Carnation, which promoted its New Breed dog food as better than all other brands. When a small competitor was able to demonstrate that its dog food was actually preferred by dogs to New Breed, Carnation was forced by the FTC to modify its ads. Its new claim was that New Breed is the best of the "leading brands."[42]

Another kind of exaggeration is known as ***puffery***, a euphemism for hyperbole or exaggeration that usually refers to the use of general superlatives. Was Eastern Airlines truly "America's favorite way to fly"? Its bankruptcy in 1991 suggests that it wasn't. Does Ford Motor Company make "the best-built American cars and trucks"? Is Bud really the "King of Beers"? Is Wheaties the "Breakfast of Champions"? Is Dial soap "the most effective deodorant soap you can buy"? Is Buck's Barbecue the "best money can buy"? Most people are not too put off by puffery because the claims are so general and so frequent that any consumer would know that the firm is exaggerating and simply doing what many do by claiming their product is best. It has been argued, however, that such exaggerated product claims (1) induce people to buy things that do them no good, (2) result in loss of advertising efficiency as companies are forced to match puffery with puffery, (3) drive out good advertising, and (4) generally result in consumers losing faith in the system because they get so used to companies making claims that exceed their products' capabilities.[43]

Psychological Appeals. In advertising, ***psychological appeals*** are those designed to persuade on the basis of human emotions and emotional needs rather than reason. There is perhaps as much reason to be concerned about ethics in this category as in any other category. One reason is that the products can seldom deliver what the ads promise. What they promise is power, prestige, sex, masculinity, femininity, approval, acceptance, and other such psychological satisfactions.[44] Throughout advertising today, there is an increasing emphasis on "emotional" commercials in which the consumer is exposed to an endless series of nonverbal gratification promises associated with the product inferentially. Love, friendship, acceptance, sex, and the other promises cited above are routine.[45] Many other specific emotional appeals—fear, hope, flattery, humor—are also used.

Subliminal advertising is a variety of psychological appeal that has also been criticized. It refers to advertising that communicates at a level that is beneath our psychological awareness. Vance Packard was one of the first popular writers to address the technological manipulation that can result from subliminal advertising. In his enormously popular book, *The Hidden Persuaders,* he explained that it was about

> ... the way many of us are being influenced and manipulated—far more than we realize—in the patterns of our everyday lives. Large-scale efforts are being made, often with impressive success, to channel our unthinking habits, our purchasing decisions, and our thought processes by the use of insights gleaned from psychiatry and the social sciences. Typically, these efforts take place beneath our level of awareness.[46]

Packard argued that consumers were becoming creatures of conditioned reflex rather than rational thought and that much of this manipulation was done at a subconscious level. Wilson Bryan Key carried this line of thought further, arguing that subliminal messages can be and are concealed within advertisements themselves. For example, he claims to have found the word *sex* baked into the surface of Ritz crackers.[47]

Specific Controversial Advertising Issues. We have considered four major kinds of deceptive advertising—ambiguous advertising, concealed facts, exaggerated claims, and psychological appeals. There are many other variations on these themes, but these are sufficient to make our point. Later in the chapter we will discuss the FTC's attempts to keep advertising honest. But even there we will see that the whole issue of what constitutes deceptive advertising is an evolving and amorphous concept, particularly when it comes to the task of proving deception and recommending some appropriate remedial action. This is why the role of business responsibility is so crucial if it sincerely attempts to deal with its consumer stakeholders in a fair and honest manner.

We will now consider six specific advertising issues that have become particularly controversial in recent years: comparative advertising, use of sex and women in advertising, advertising to children, advertising of alcoholic beverages, cigarette advertising, and health and environmental claims.

Comparative Advertising. One advertising technique that has become controversial and threatens to affect advertising negatively, in general, is *comparative advertising*. This refers to the practice of directly comparing a firm's product with the product of a competitor. Some examples are AT&T long-distance service versus MCI or Sprint; Coke versus Pepsi; Whopper versus Big Mac; Sprite versus 7-Up; Avis versus Hertz.

At one time the idea of naming your competitor or competitor's product in an ad was taboo. For years the television networks did not allow it, so companies had to be content with referring to their competition as "the other leading brand" or "Brand X." In about 1972, the FTC began to accept the direct comparison approach because it thought this approach would provide more and better information to the consumer. The networks cooperated by lifting their ban. Thus, we entered the new era of comparative advertising.

Some companies and large advertising agencies were reluctant to use this new form of advertising because they predicted that the temptation for name-calling and mudslinging would be high. The networks were not too excited either because they had to make the decisions about which ads to air. They saw this leading to larger legal staffs and other costly experts. In retrospect, we must say that these fears were not unfounded. Comparative advertising has led to considerable litigation and negative publicity.[48]

One estimate is that comparative ads have become so popular that they now account for 35 percent of all television commercials. This has resulted in stiff competition between traditional rivals. How would you feel about Ford's claim of "the best-built American cars and trucks" if you were Chrysler or GM? This is a case where specific competitors are not named; this may be thought of as a backhanded way of engaging in comparative advertising. One reason companies have gone to these more vague approaches is because of the trouble they have gotten into and the response they have evoked by naming competitors.

Whether out of pride or general business interest, more and more companies are fighting back when they think the competition has gone too far. Companies may take their adversaries to court, before the FTC, or before voluntary associations, such as the National Advertising Division of the Council of Better Business Bureaus, that attempt to resolve these kinds of disputes.[49]

The weapons used in comparative ad battles are getting increasingly sophisticated. Companies are turning to elaborate scientific tests and consumer surveys to prove their assertions. For example, to challenge Mars Inc.'s claim that Three Musketeers candy bars offer "more of what you buy chocolate for," another candy company provided the Better Business Bureau with a perception test showing that most people interpret the Mars phrase to mean that Three Musketeers has more chocolate than other products—which it does not. Mars agreed to discontinue using the slogan. AMF Inc. ran television ads declaring that an independent study proved that tennis players "overwhelmingly preferred" its new Head racket. Chesebrough-Pond's challenged the test, claiming that its Prince rackets had not been strung to the correct tension for the test. AMF denied the charge but withdrew the ads before the case was settled.[50]

It is unclear what the future of comparative advertising will be. However, it has become one of a few controversial advertising issues that have the potential for more detrimental effects. Any practice that is likely to evoke more criticism from consumer stakeholders, as well as from competitors, should be carefully examined by management to determine if it is a legitimate practice that should be used in the future.

Bruce Buchanan suggests that there are a number of questions that should be asked by both those who are victims of comparative ads and those who are contemplating using them. For example, were consumers actually asked to compare one brand with another? Was the sample of consumers representative of product users? Could the subjects being studied really discriminate between the products being compared?[51] Questions such as these are essential if companies are to develop sound research methods on which to base comparative ads. To do otherwise is to invite criticism from the public and consumers alike.

Use of Sex and Women in Advertising. The use versus abuse of sex and women in advertising has been an issue that has essentially grown in importance as the women's movement has grown in power and influence. Although it does not seem to be a burning issue with women in general today, women's special-interest groups increasingly are taking it on as a concern.

Perhaps the first time the use of sex became a big issue was in the early 1970s when several women's groups were offended by a series of television commercials sponsored by National Airlines. In 1971, National introduced its provocative "I'm Cheryl, Fly me" campaign. After that ad, National enjoyed a reported 23 percent increase in passengers, nearly twice the increase for the industry as a whole. This commercial was so successful that National followed it with even more suggestive ones. One commercial showed stewardesses looking seductively at the viewers, saying "I'm going to *fly* you like you've never been flown before." The viewer might think that the message had a double meaning. It was reported in *Time* magazine that the stewardesses were coached "to say it like you're standing there stark naked."[52]

Professor Lee Reed's analysis of the above commercial explains how the National ad series also illustrates the subliminal effect we described earlier. In the ad, the *unconditional* stimulus (sexual invitation) evokes the response (heightened excitement, desire, and so on). This is paired with the *conditional* stimulus (National Airlines) and evokes a response. After repeated showings of the "Fly me" commercial, the advertiser gets its payoff when the businessman goes into the travel agent's office, sees the National Airlines ad, and decides to fly National (Cheryl) instead of Eastern or United. At the conscious level, the consumer is not likely to consider that sex will be the end product of his choice. At the unconscious or subliminal level, however, the National ad influences his choice of airlines. This effect has been called "learning without awareness."[53]

Use of sex in advertising has become commonplace. The beautiful woman perched on the hood of the sports car suggests at a minimum that your sex life will improve if you buy this one. Handsome members of both sexes promote shaving cream, cologne, lipstick, and other cosmetics. Product names and shapes add to the allure. Interestingly, the FTC, which is the principal regulatory body for advertising, does not seem to be concerned about the use of sex or the exploitation of women in ads. Women's groups are concerned, and the major TV networks have shown some concern, although it is not always evident.

One feminist group that is quite concerned with how women are portrayed in ads is Women Against Pornography (WAP). Each year WAP gives awards to those companies whose ads portray positive images for women in ads. WAP also "zaps" companies that "stereotype, dehumanize, and degrade women" by awarding them plastic pigs. Several years ago, Gillette was zapped with a plastic pig by this group. Gillette's ad for its Daisy shaver featured a leggy policewoman, in hot pants, being admired by coworkers. Two years later, Gillette ads portrayed a newly married couple on a moped with a spotlight on the bride's legs. Gillette denied that receiving the plastic pig caused it to cancel its policewoman campaign. Some companies that receive the feminist group's booby prize dismiss the awards as insignificant. But other companies have admitted that their ads were insensitive and have since changed them.[54]

The major television networks also make an effort to screen commercials for taste and deceptiveness, though this effort may not be readily apparent to the viewer. Product ads are carefully screened for sexual innuendo, offensive words, or camera angles. Network editors sift through thousands of commercials a week, searching for the swimsuit that is too brief or the ad that is otherwise too seductive. Often the changes the editors suggest are subtle. One agency had to put wedding rings on a man and woman in a cologne commercial. Chicken marketer Frank Perdue could lounge around in a swimming pool with several attractive women but only if they wore one-piece suits instead of bikinis. The famous model Christie Brinkley's bathing suit was deemed to be too skimpy in one Anheuser-Busch commercial.[55]

Whether sex and the role of women will become a major advertising issue with staying power remains to be seen. However, it is interesting to note that we live in a day and age when exploitation of women as sex objects is rampant on television commercials and advertisements, and yet at the same time there is very little public response to the issue outside of the efforts of a limited few women's organizations. The irony of this is that there is significant opposition to stereotyping women or to even subtle forms of sex discrimination or sexual harassment in the workplace while exploitation of women as sex objects remains relatively unabated in advertisements and commercials. Astute companies that want to be sensitive to their stakeholders will monitor this situation very carefully so that they do not step across the line separating the appropriate from the unacceptable.

Advertising to Children. A hotly debated issue over the past several decades has been advertising to children, specifically on television. A typical afternoon or Saturday morning in America finds millions of kids sprawled on the floor, glued to the TV. On one station, the Teenage Mutant Ninja Turtles are triumphing over the forces of evil; on another, Slimer and Ghostbusters are doing the same. On yet another station, you find animated Gumby figures. Interspersed are commercials for Circus Fun Cereal featuring chocolate-covered marshmallow animals and Snicker bars. As Claudia Mills has observed, "It's hard to resist the conclusion that commercial children's TV is a wasteland."[56] In spite of this, it is estimated that children age 6 to 11 watch an average of 27 hours of TV a week, or a total of 1,400 hours a year. Preschoolers watch more.[57]

A National Science Foundation Study estimated that, on average, children are exposed to about 20,000 commercials per year, mostly for toys, cereals, candies, and fast-food restaurants. The report goes on to say that children under 8 years old have great difficulty in differentiating between commercials and programs.[58] This problem has become more severe as a number of companies have begun making full-length programs based on toy characters that they promote for sale.

Examples of this include Teenage Mutant Ninja Turtles, Masters of the Universe, Muppet Babies, Wuzzles, Super Mario Brothers, Kissyfur, Care Bears, Gummi Bears, Punky Brewster, and a host of others that are easily identified in *TV Guide* during the hours of 7:00 A. M. to noon on Saturday morning and other days of the week as well.

A question can be raised as to how much harm is done to children watching commercials aimed at selling them products that are packed with sugar or that present products (mostly toys) in a context that misrepresents what they actually are or what they actually do. Over the years this issue has been the subject of considerable debate as to what is fair and ethical. It even resulted in the creation by parents of a special-interest group in the early 1970s known as Action for Children's Television (ACT).

The investigations by the FTC into the controversial children's advertising issue in the mid-1970s became known as "kid-vid." One of the early issues that ACT and other groups were concerned about was the prevalence of advertisements promoting sugared cereals. All kinds of attractive characters—elves, Easter bunnies, and the like—sang praises of products that had doubtful nutritional value and may have been potentially harmful. Experts testified to the dental hazards, heart disease, high blood pressure, and diabetes likely to result from sugared snacks and cereals.

On the other side of the issue, it was easy for broadcasters and companies to turn the kid-vid issue into a question involving the abridgment of the first amendment. If advertising to children were censored, where else would the federal government encroach on citizen rights? Meanwhile, the FTC was being ridiculed for trying to be the "national nanny," usurping the parental role of monitoring and controlling what children see and hear on TV.[59]

Efforts of the FTC to create a kid-vid rule to regulate children's advertising failed. In 1983, the FTC ruled against ACT's long-standing petition for reforms that would have required all stations to broadcast a minimum of 14 hours of children's programming each week and would have banned all advertisements on children's programs.[60] The climate in the Reagan administration and in Congress throughout most of the 1980s has not been conducive to moving in a regulatory sense against children's advertisers. But the issue does not go away. It is one that companies must carefully monitor lest it come up again in a more favorable public environment.

Although government regulations have not addressed the whole issue of children's advertising, this does not mean that voluntary actions have not taken place. As far back as 1972, the Council of Better Business Bureaus, a voluntary association, issued Children's Advertising Guidelines designed to encourage truthful and accurate advertising that is sensitive to the special nature of children. In 1974, a Children's Advertising Review Unit (CARU) of the National Advertising Division of the Council of Better Business Bureaus was established to respond to public concerns. CARU revised its "Self-Regulatory Guidelines for Children's Advertising" in 1975, 1977, 1983, and 1990. Figure 9-6 summarizes the five basic principles from those guidelines.

FIGURE 9-6 Principles for Advertising to Children

Five basic principles underlie these guidelines for advertising directed to children:

1. Advertisers should always take into account the level of knowledge, sophistication, and maturity of the audience to which their message is primarily directed. Younger children have a limited capability for evaluating the credibility of what they watch. Advertisers, therefore, have a special responsibility to protect children from their own susceptibilities.

2. Realizing that children are imaginative and that make-believe play constitutes an important part of the growing up process, advertisers should exercise care not to exploit that imaginative quality of children. Unreasonable expectations of product quality or performance should not be stimulated either directly or indirectly by advertising.

3. Recognizing that advertising may play an important part in educating the child, information should be communicated in a truthful and accurate manner with full recognition by the advertiser that the child may learn practices from advertising which can affect his or her health and well-being.

4. Advertisers are urged to capitalize on the potential of advertising to influence social behavior by developing advertising that, wherever possible, addresses itself to social standards generally regarded as positive and beneficial such as friendship, kindness, honesty, justice, generosity, and respect for others.

5. Although many influences affect a child's personal and social development, it remains the prime responsibility of the parents to provide guidance for children. Advertisers should contribute to this parent-child relationship in a constructive manner.

Source: *Self-Regulatory Guidelines for Children's Advertising*, 3d ed., Children's Advertising Review Unit, National Advertising Division, Council of Better Business Bureaus, Inc. (1983), 4–5. Reproduced with permission.

Figure 9-7 summarizes some specific guidelines for product presentations and claims in advertisements for children.

The function of the guidelines is to delineate those areas that need particular attention to help avoid deceptive advertising messages to children. The basic activity of CARU is the review and evaluation of child-directed advertising in all media. When advertising to children is found to be misleading, inaccurate, or inconsistent with the guidelines, CARU seeks changes through the voluntary cooperation of advertisers. Figure 9-8 illustrates two toy commercials that had been called to CARU's attention, what the basis for the inquiry was, and the voluntary resolution that resulted. In 1989, CARU developed voluntary *Guidelines for the Advertising of 900/976 Teleprograms to Children*. These were developed with the cooperation and input of teleprogram

FIGURE 9-7 Product Presentations and Claims Guidelines in Advertising to Children

Children look at, listen to, and remember many different elements in advertising. Therefore, advertisers need to examine the total advertising message to be certain that the net communication will not mislead or misinform children.

1. Copy, sound, and visual presentations should not mislead children about product or performance characteristics. Such characteristics may include, but are not limited to, size, speed, method of operation, color, sound, durability, and nutritional benefits.

2. The advertising presentation should not mislead children about perceived benefits from use of the product. Such benefits may include, but are not limited to, the acquisition of strength, status, popularity, growth, proficiency, and intelligence. Social stereotyping and appeals to prejudice should be avoided.

3. Care should be taken not to exploit a child's imagination. Fantasy, including animation, is appropriate for younger as well as older children. However, it should not create unattainable performance expectations nor exploit the younger child's difficulty in distinguishing between the real and the fanciful.

4. The performance and use of a product should be demonstrated in a way that can be duplicated by the child for whom the product is intended.

5. Products should be shown used in safe environments and situations.

6. What is included and excluded in the initial purchase should be clearly established.

7. The amount of product featured should be within reasonable levels for the situation depicted.

8. Representation of food products should be made so as to encourage sound usage of the product with a view toward healthy development of the child and development of good nutritional practices. Advertisements representing mealtime in the home should clearly and adequately depict the role of the product within the framework of a balanced diet.

9. Portrayals of violence and presentations that could unduly frighten or provoke anxiety in children should be avoided.

10. Objective claims about product or performance characteristics should be supported by appropriate and adequate substantiation.

Source: *Self-Regulatory Guidelines for Children's Advertising*, 3d ed., Children's Advertising Review Unit, National Advertising Division, Council of Better Business Bureaus, Inc. (1983), 4–5. Reproduced with permission.

producers, television representatives, telephone companies, and government agencies, together with the CARU Academic Advisory Panel and the CARU Business Advisory Panel.[61] We will consider further the activities of the National Advertising Division at a later point in the chapter.

FIGURE 9-8   Two National Advertising Division Toy Cases and Their Resolution

LJN TOYS, LTD.
Photon Electronic Phaser Target Game
Harvey Herman Associates, Inc.

Basis of Inquiry: A television commercial appearing during children's programming on independent stations featured an electronic game that included a phaser gun, helmet, and chest target. The commercial opened with a boy lying in bed. A voice-over stated: "You have been chosen to be the ultimate laser warrior. First choose wisely. Choose the only laser that really works." Throughout the remainder of the commercial, the phaser appeared to shoot red beams. A small video disclosure stated: ". . . Red Beam for Illustration Only." The Children's Advertising Review Unit (CARU) questioned whether children would expect the toy to shoot light beams.

The Self-Regulatory Guidelines for Children's Advertising advise that copy, sound, and visual presentations should not mislead children about product or performance characteristics. In addition, CARU noted that disclosures should not contradict advertising messages.

Resolution: The advertiser stated that the commercial in question had been permanently discontinued, and it would consider CARU's concerns in future advertising. (#2471)

MATTEL, INC.
Masters of the Universe Action Figures/Monstroid
Ogilvy & Mather

Basis of Inquiry: A commercial appearing during children's programming on independent stations featured a wind-up monster figure whirling other action figures in its claws. The advertisement stated: "Now—A raging terror grabs hold of the universe. Monstroid. When Monstroid gets wound up, it grabs . . ." The product appeared to pick up other figures automatically. The Children's Advertising Review Unit (CARU) asked for clarification of the toy's method of operation.

Resolution: In response, the advertiser submitted a sample of the toy. CARU determined that in real play the action figures must be placed manually into Monstroid's claws. The advertiser explained that the commercial in question was filmed to show an action figure being placed in the claws. CARU maintained that the depiction was unclear and drew the advertiser's attention to the section of the Self-Regulatory Guidelines for Children's Advertising that states "copy, sound, and visual presentations should not mislead children about product or performance characteristics."

The advertiser did not share CARU's view regarding the apparent performance and play value of the toy. However, it advised that the commercial in question had completed its run, and that in future advertising for Masters of the Universe products, the advertiser would continue to take CARU's concerns into consideration. (#2472)

Source: *National Advertising Division Case Report* (New York: Council of Better Business Bureaus, February 16, 1987), 3. Reproduced with permission.

4. *Advertising Alcoholic Beverages.* Special issues about advertising to adults also exist. One that has become quite controversial is alcoholic beverages advertisements, specifically for beer and wine, on television. This issue got its most significant support beginning in 1985, when a coalition was formed operating under the banner of Project SMART (Stop Marketing Alcohol on Radio and Television). The coalition was spearheaded by the Washington-based Center for Science in the Public Interest, a Nader-style health advocacy group. Other members of the coalition include the 5.5 million members of the National Parent-Teacher Association, the National Council on Alcoholism, and scores of other civic and religious organizations.[62]

The coalition, which mounted a lobbying campaign in Congress, planned to gather one million signatures on a petition demanding that Congress either ban advertisements of alcoholic beverages or allow equal time for countermessages on the dangers of alcohol. The group cited as its cause for alarm the statistics that over 25,000 traffic deaths per year and half of all homicides are alcohol related.[63] Estimates are that alcohol contributes to over 100,000 deaths and $120 billion in economic losses each year.[64]

Furthermore, a *Business Week*/Harris Poll found that 57 percent of Americans want beer and wine ads banned from the airwaves. Even if a total ban is not achieved, congressional insiders predict that the industry may have to accept a code restricting it from using sports and entertainment figures, rock stars, and youthful models in its ads.[65] This is because of the coalition's major fear that these types of promoters glamorize alcohol to youths. Already, Project SMART has claimed some credit for Congress's decision to withhold federal highway funds from states that did not raise their drinking age to 21 by 1986.[66]

A 1991 study commissioned by the alcoholic beverage industry group known as the Century Council found that despite the industry's efforts to improve its image, "the vast majority of Americans still believe the booze business is irresponsible and unethical and that its ads encourage teenagers to drink." The study also found that the public holds the industry in low esteem and believes that it is moving in the wrong direction. A particularly troubling finding to the industry was that 73 percent of the people polled either "strongly" or "somewhat" agreed that alcohol advertising is "a major contributor" to underage drinking.[67]

The brewing industry has not been sitting idly by. Beer and wine companies spend over $750 million a year for advertising. The networks are concerned because they receive the bulk of the money, and major sports organizations like the National Football League gets well over half of that. And they are aware that a ban on advertising is not without precedent. In 1971, cigarette ads were banned from television, and the ban was upheld by the courts.[68]

The president of the U.S. Brewers Association said, "We take this threat seriously."[69] Determined to stave off government regulations, beverage-industry officials and nervous broadcasters have been taking a number of actions to tighten up standards on their own. Their first line of defense has been that advertising just enhances market share; it does not convert or encourage new drinkers.

Specific actions have been voluntarily taken, however. For example, NBC strengthened its standards for beer and wine commercials, while ABC and CBS argued that they were more stringently applying and adhering to existing standards. NBC rejected a wine commercial that featured a Michael Jackson look-alike because of its blatant appeal to the youth market. Adolph Coors pulled an ad for its light beer that contained the refrain "beer after beer," fearing it could be misinterpreted as encouraging excessive use. The U.S. Brewers Association revised its voluntary code to warn members not to include scenes involving inebriation or denigration of academic study. The Wine Institute, a trade association of California growers, bars the use of athletes and other youth heroes from its wine ads.[70]

The newly created Century Council, which claims to be an independent anti-alcohol abuse organization even though it was founded and funded by alcohol companies, believes that its new code of conduct for advertising will help the problem. The code, which was scheduled to go into use in October 1991, dictates that alcoholic beverages should not be "actively promoted" at events where most of the audience is underage. A footnote to the code exempts professional sports events and signs already in place in stadiums and arenas. Marketing to underage drinkers at college events is also prohibited, but campus marketing is okay if it does not violate the college's rules. The council further asserts that perceptions will change because of the code, even though it argues that "most" alcohol companies are already working within the guidelines. As of this writing, there is a bill pending in Congress that would put warning messages in alcohol advertisements.[71]

Like the issues of comparative ads, use of sex, and ads for children, the advertising of alcoholic beverages serves as a constant reminder to the business community that it cannot generalize about consumer stakeholders. Rather, consumer stakeholders are composed of many special interests, each having the capacity to change the rules of the game for business if it is not responsive. Business's challenge is to monitor and be sensitive to these threats and expectations if it is to prosper and survive.

5. *Cigarette Advertising.* It is difficult to determine whether alcoholic beverages or cigarette advertising is most under attack today. As a recent *Time* magazine article concluded, cigarette makers are "under fire from all sides."[72] Two particularly questionable issues dominate the current debate about cigarette advertising. First, there is the general opposition to promoting a dangerous product. As Louis Sullivan, U.S. Secretary of Health and Human Services, has put it, "Cigarettes are the only legal product that when used as intended cause death."[73] As a result of offensive and dangerous secondary smoke, cigarettes are now severely restricted in workplaces, governmental buildings, restaurants, and air flights.

The second issue concerns the ethics of the tobacco industry's advertising to young people and, in particular, to less-educated consumer markets. Related to this is the industry's target-marketing of specific groups. Two examples illustrate this latter concern. R. J. Reynolds (RJR) was publically taken to task by several consumer groups for its advertising of Dakota, a new cigarette aimed at women, and Uptown, a new cigarette targeted at blacks. The antismoking group, the Advocacy Institute, released copies of an RJR marketing plan to target Dakota (known in the company documents as Project VF, for virile female) to a specific group of young women. The prototype woman was characterized as an entry-level factory worker, 18 to 20 years old, who enjoys drag racing and tractor-pulls and aspires to get married in her early 20s and raise a family. Women's groups and health experts criticized RJR for exploiting uninformed young women and targeting them for death. It was pointed out that lung cancer among women now surpasses breast cancer as the leading cause of death. Over the past 20 years, lung cancer among women has increased over five times, and the percentage of women smoking has only decreased from about 40 percent to 30 percent over the period 1965 to 1988, whereas the rate for men has decreased from 60 percent to 30 percent over the same period.[74] In a related issue, the director of Consumer Affairs for New York City, Mark Greene, strongly argued that RJR should discontinue its "Smooth Dude" Camel cigarette advertisements, which he asserted were a thinly veiled attempt to lure children to start smoking.[75]

Louis Sullivan was also instrumental in condemning RJR for its promotion of Uptown cigarettes, which were targeted at blacks. Sullivan called for "an all-out effort to resist the attempts of tobacco merchants to earn profits at the expense of the health and well-being of our poor and minority citizens." Uptown billboards in the inner city were also the target of a shadowy figure, known only as "Mandrake," who secretly stalked the inner city of Chicago and whitewashed billboards that promoted cigarettes and beer to young people. Mandrake was reportedly a middle-aged black professional who had had enough of ads that encourage youth to smoke and drink. The efforts of Sullivan, Mandrake, and a host of other grassroots supporters were undoubtedly instrumental in RJR's decision to cease its test-marketing of Uptown cigarettes.[76]

The manufacture and advertising of cigarettes and tobacco products, such as "smokeless tobacco," raise a number of interesting ethical issues worth contemplating. Is it fair to criticize a company that is promoting a legal product? Should these products remain legal given that we know they are addictive and are linked to serious health problems and death-causing diseases? Are some of the companies' marketing practices appropriate whereas others are questionable? Is it fair to criticize tobacco companies for target marketing when all business school students know that market segmentation is taught as a way of business life? Would discontinuing the advertising of cigarettes and alcoholic beverages be an acceptable and desirable solution to current problems? Given the health consciousness trends of the 1990s and the political strength of the manufacturers of these products, these issues will likely be with us for some time.

6. *Health and Environmental Claims.* An assortment of practices are under criticism today for advertising and labeling that entail health-related and environmentally safe claims for products. One major reason the issues have come to the forefront is the renewed enforcement activities of the Food and Drug Administration (FDA), Federal Trade Commission (FTC), and states' attorneys general in cracking down on misleading claims. In the health- and environmentally conscious 1990s, these issues have taken on major importance. Given consumers' desires for products that are healthy and protect the environment, it is not too surprising that these issues have gained so much attention.

John Calfee claims that the modern era of using health claims to promote foods actually began in 1984 when ads and labels for Kellogg's All-Bran recounted the National Cancer Institute's message on fiber and cancer. Health claims spread quickly to ingredients such as saturated fats, calcium, and beta carotene, and such illnesses as heart disease, osteoporosis, and gum disease. One major positive outcome of the All-Bran high-fiber cereal example is that the competitors quickly brought out their own versions of the product, and in a short 3 years, the breakfast market was transformed to one where cereals were much higher in fiber yet lower in fat and salt.[77]

By 1991, the FDA was on the attack again against companies that it claimed "misled" consumers with untrue or deceptive advertising health claims. A *Time* magazine cover story asserted that "by launching a holy war against misleading claims, the government could clear up some of the confusion on supermarket shelves and help Americans become healthier consumers." *Time* cited the following as illustrations of how shoppers are shamelessly deceived:[78]

- There is no real fruit—just fruit flavors—in Post Fruity Pebbles.
- Honey Nut Cheerios provides less honey than sugar and more salt than nuts.
- Mrs. Smith's Natural Juice Apple Pie contains preservatives. The word "natural" refers to the fruit juice used to make the pie.
- Diet Coke contains more than the one heavily advertised calorie per can (so does Diet Pepsi).
- Budget Gourmet Light and Healthy Salisbury Steak—which is labeled "low fat"—derives 45 percent of its total calories from fat.

Several high-profile incidents have communicated to the business community that the FDA is serious. The FDA wrote letters to Procter and Gamble (P&G) about its advertising use of the word "fresh" on Citrus Hill packages because the orange juice is made from concentrate. Despite long meetings between the agency and the company, it would not voluntarily back down and remove the offending word. The meetings apparently ended with P&G convinced that the FDA would not take action. They were wrong. Within days, the FDA seized a shipment of Citrus Hill, and an embarrassed P&G quickly agreed to alter its labels. Weeks later, P&G was forced to delete the words "no cholesterol" and a small heart insignia off its packaging for Crisco corn oil. For its part, P&G set up a new worldwide organization for handling regulatory issues, and it believes it will have some success in Washington.[79]

The FDA is in the process of developing new guidelines for health and nutritional advertising and labeling. Three major areas of abuse are being targeted for label and advertising abuse: deceptive definitions, hazy health claims, and slipping serving sizes. The FDA is in the process of developing standard definitions to be used in each of these three areas. There is some evidence that the FDA plans to take on the drug industry next.[80] In addition to the FDA, the states have also begun to crack down on misleading health and food claims. Examples of the states' successes include the following: nine states got Nestlé's Carnation unit to stop claiming that its Good Start formula is hypoallergenic; Campbell Soup was pressured by state officials to stop broad ads that promote its soups as sources of calcium and fiber; and Texas is suing Quaker Oats over a claim that some of its cereals significantly reduce the risk of heart attacks. In the late 1980s, a task force of attorneys general from 10 states formed a joint effort to protect consumers from misleading food ads and claims.[81]

Another major controversial advertising practice in the 1990s is companies claiming that their products or their product's packaging is environmentally friendly or safe. As recently as 1989, studies found that consumers balked at environmentally friendly packaging and advertisements. Convenience seemed to win out over environmentalism.[82] By 1991, what has come to be known as "green marketing" seemed destined to dominate the near future. *Fortune* magazine captured the new trend well: "Manufacturers eager to appear ecologically correct are frantically relabeling, repackaging, and repositioning products, often in the face of fast-changing and inconsistent state laws." One research study found that in 1990, 26 peercent of all new household items advertised that they were ozone-friendly, recyclable, biodegradable, compostable, or some other form of "green." At the same time, another research firm found that nearly 47 percent of consumers dismiss environmental claims as mere gimmickry.[83]

Because of the ease with which environmental claims might be deceptive or misunderstood, it is not surprising that in 1991 states' attorneys general from 10 states issued a report entitled "The Green Report II: Recommendations for Responsible Environmental Advertising," intended to identify how "environmental claims can be made in a manner that is most likely to be consistent with state laws." The Green Report was built on the basic premise that "as more and more manufacturers turn to environmental claims to market their products, the need for federal standards to control and regulate these claims is more important than ever."[84]

The realms of health claims and environmental claims, when added to the controversial topics of alcohol- and tobacco-related advertising, create a growth field in terms of potential advertising abuses. Consumer groups are likely to continue their attacks where they seem warranted, and federal and state regulators are expected to assume ever-larger roles if companies do not initiate reforms on their own.

Warranties

From the glamorous realm of advertising, we now move to the less glamorous issues of warranties. Although *warranties* were initially used by manufacturers to limit the length of time they were expressly responsible for products, they came to be viewed by consumers as devices to protect the buyer against a faulty or defective product. Most consumers have had the experience of buying a hair dryer, stereo, refrigerator, automobile, washing machine, chain saw, or one of thousands of other products only to find that it did not work properly or did not work at all. Then, when the buyer read the fine print on the warranty, it was found to include so many qualifications and exceptions as to make the manufacturer's promise to remedy the defect useless.

Much of this was changed with the passage of the *Magnuson-Moss Warranty Act of 1975*. This act was aimed at clearing up some misunderstandings about manufacturers' warranties—especially whether a *full warranty* was in effect or whether certain parts of the product or certain types of defects were excluded from coverage. Also at issue was whether the buyer had to pay shipping charges when a product was sent to and from the factory for servicing a defect.[85]

The warranty law sets standards for what must be contained in a warranty and the ease with which consumers must be able to understand it. If a company, for example, claims that its product has a full warranty, it must contain certain features, including repair "within a reasonable time and without charge."[86] The law holds that anything less than this unconditional assurance must be promoted as a *limited warranty*.

There was some speculation in the business community that calling attention to an unwillingness to offer a full warranty might scare off buyers. A midwestern producer of auto replacement parts, for example, was so afraid that a warranty labeled "limited" would be counterproductive that it dropped warranties from its entire product line.[87] Similarly, Fisher-Price toy makers dropped written warranties on music boxes rather than use the word "limited."[88] Many products, on the other hand, need the warranty as an aid to sales (as in the case of big-ticket items), and thus companies like General Electric and Whirlpool continue to offer full warranties.

Catalog companies, in particular, find that warranties or guarantees are essential when marketing by mail. Few companies, however, go to the lengths L. L. Bean has gone with its "100% guarantee." L. L. Bean asserts, "All our products are guaranteed to give 100% satisfaction in every way. Return anything purchased from us at any time if it proves otherwise. We will replace it, refund your purchase price or credit your credit card, as you wish. We do not want you to have anything from L. L. Bean that is not completely satisfactory."[89]

Warranties continue to be an important product information issue to consumer stakeholders, even though many consumers believe they are not adequate. Warranties and guarantees are not at the top of the list of consumer concerns, but they have been an enduring issue. The public wants warranties to be both understandable and adequate. This concern has had an impact on the marketplace and is likely to be the focus of increased consumer demands if business does not remain responsive to this consumer expectation.

Packaging and Labeling

Like warranties, packaging and labeling have not, until recently, been leading issues. Abuses in the packaging and labeling areas were fairly frequent until the passage of the *Federal Packaging and Labeling Act of 1967*. The purpose of this act was to prohibit deceptive labeling of certain consumer products and to require disclosure of certain important information. This act, which is administered by the Federal Trade Commission, requires the FTC to issue regulations regarding net contents disclosures, identity of commodity, and name and place of manufacturer, packer, or distributor. The act authorizes additional regulations when necessary to prevent consumer deception or to facilitate value comparisons with respect to declaration of ingredients, slack fill of packages, "downsizing" of packaging, use of "cents off," or lower-price labeling and package size. The act gives the FTC responsibility for consumer commodities and cosmetics, which are regulated by the Food and Drug Administration.[90] As we mentioned in an earlier section, packaging and labeling is drawing renewed interest because of health and environmental claims.

Other Product Information Issues

It is difficult to catalog all the consumer issues in which product information is a key factor. Certainly advertising, warranties, packaging, and labeling constitute the bulk of the issues. In addition to these, however, we must briefly mention several others. Sales techniques in which direct sellers use deceptive information must be mentioned. Other laws that address information disclosure issues include the following;

1. *Equal Credit Opportunity Act*, which prohibits discrimination in the extension of consumer credit
2. *Truth-in-Lending Act*, which requires all suppliers of consumer credit to fully disclose all credit terms and to permit a 3-day right of rescission in any transaction involving a security interest in the consumer's residence (for example, in the case of home equity loans)
3. *Fair Credit Reporting Act*, which ensures that consumer reporting agencies provide information in a manner that is fair and equitable to the consumer
4. *Fair Debt Collection Practices Act*, which regulates the practices of third-party debt collection agencies

THE FEDERAL TRADE COMMISSION

We have discussed three main areas of product information—advertising, warranties, and packaging/labeling. Both the FTC and the FDA are actively involved in these issues. It is important now to look more closely at the federal government's major instrument, the FTC, for ensuring that business lives up to its responsibilities in these areas. Actually, the FTC has broad and sweeping powers, and it delves into a number of other areas that we will refer to throughout the book. The Consumer Product Safety Commission and the Food and Drug Administration are major regulatory agencies, too, but we will consider them more carefully in the next chapter.

Some history and evolution of the FTC is helpful in gaining a better appreciation of governmental activism and its relationship to the political parties in power in Washington at various points in time. The FTC is one of the oldest of the federal agencies charged with responsibility for overseeing commercial acts and practices. It was created in 1914, originally as an antitrust weapon, and broadened in 1938 to permit the agency to pursue "unfair or deceptive acts or practices in commerce."[91] Over the years, Congress has given the FTC enforcement responsibility in a number of consumer-related fields, including the important *Truth-in-Lending Act, Fair Packaging and Labeling Act, Fair Credit Reporting Act,* and *Equal Credit Opportunity Act*. Congress gave the FTC broad power because of fear that any specification of a list of prohibitions might lead business to reason that it could do anything *not* on the list. Figure 9-9 presents an overview statement of the role of the FTC. The FTC has the following major divisions: advertising practices, credit practices, enforcement, marketing practices, and service industry practices.

Activist Periods of the FTC

The FTC actually did relatively little from 1941 to 1969, a period Thomas G. Krattenmaker called the "decades of neglect." But 1970 to 1973 were the "years of promise" for the FTC.[92] The agency became "activist" when President Richard Nixon appointed Miles Kirkpatrick chairman. Kirkpatrick and his staff of eager young lawyers put the FTC on the map, so to speak, and the agency became so aggressive that it created "an escalating struggle" between itself and business.[93] The source of the struggle was the FTC's zealousness, its fuzzy and broad powers, its lack of consistency in its own administration, and its concept of what constitutes proper business conduct.

The FTC's activism continued when Michael Pertschuk became chairman in 1977. His directorship spanned the late 1970s and early 1980s and encompassed the "kid-vid" period that we discussed earlier in the chapter. Although many of the controversial initiatives preceded his appointment, he became identified with all of them. Yet Pertschuk was accurately identified with the initiatives because for 12 years prior to his chairmanship he was staff director and chief counsel for the Senate Commerce Committee. He had nurtured and drafted practically all the

FIGURE 9-9   Role of the FTC

Overview Statement

The role of the Federal Trade Commission, as defined by Congress, is to enforce a variety of Federal antitrust and consumer protection laws. Under these laws, the Commission seeks to ensure that the nation's markets are free from undue governmental as well as private restrictions. The Commission also seeks to improve the operation of the marketplace by eliminating deceptive and "unfair" practices, with emphasis on those practices that may unreasonably restrict or inhibit the free exercise of informed choice by consumers. The Commission's economic analyses support this law enforcement effort and contribute generally to the economic policy deliberations of the Congress, the Executive Branch, and the public.

Source: Federal Trade Commission, *Fiscal Year 1988 Program Budget* (Washington, DC: FTC, 1987), i.

major consumer legislation that was passed, including the *Magnuson-Moss Warranty Act*. Unfortunately, Pertschuk developed a reputation for being antibusiness. This hurt his relationship with the business community so much that he never overcame it.[94]

Less Active Years of the FTC

Succeeding Pertschuk as chairman was James C. Miller III, appointed by President Reagan. As with so many agencies on the election of a new administration, the FTC shifted its focus to the Reagan approach to regulation. Miller was dubbed by some in the press as Reagan's "deregulation czar," and he took the FTC off into another, less active direction. Miller characterized the FTC's activism on behalf of consumers during the 1970s as "excesses" and embarked on a course that was much more in keeping with the Reagan doctrine.[95] The same general approach to regulation continued under Miller's successor, Daniel Oliver. Miller and Oliver gained reputations as deregulators who willingly slashed the FTC's budget and staff.

The FTC Reasserts Itself

After almost a decade of Reagan-era deregulation that saw the FTC's work force cut in half and its enforcement efforts greatly reduced or redirected, the FTC seems to be reasserting itself in the early 1990s. Its chairperson became Janet D.

Steiger, and under Steiger the FTC has come back to life. It has not returned to its heyday of the 1970s, but through a series of highly visible cases it has reasserted itself. According to one observer, the FTC now looks more like the FTC of the pre-Reagan administration rather than the seemingly toothless agency it became in the 1980s.[96]

Among the high-profile cases the FTC has recently pursued, it has won headlines by cracking down on Nintendo, the videogame maker, for price-fixing; moving in on "900" telephone numbers for advertisements aimed at children; and accusing major colleges and Capital Cities-ABC for conspiring to limit the market for televised college football games. It has announced plans to investigate advertisers' claims that their products benefit the environment. It is also considering taking action against cigarette and liquor advertising, especially in the area previously discussed—that of marketing aimed at youth.[97]

Several observers have commented that the FTC has become much more activist but that it has taken on a less ideological and more practical posture. The FTC seems to be pursuing more of a middle-of-the-road agenda, enforcing existing consumer protection and antitrust laws rather than interpreting the laws from a particular political philosophy. The enforcement of laws that have been virtually ignored for the best part of a decade, however, conveys an image that somewhat belies Steiger's free enterprise philosophy. She claims that she is not all that different from her predecessors: "Everything we do here is based on a shared belief that free markets work. I regard our job as allowing them to do so . . . with the aim of trying to prevent consumer injury." Steiger believes the course is set for the FTC in the decade of the 1990s: to design a program "that does provide strong national consumer protection in a changing environment, without unduly interfering with what is a dynamic marketplace . . . our job is trying to keep the playing field level, not stop the game."[98] Such a mission sounds quite reasonable, and only time will tell what the "new" FTC will accomplish.

In spite of its apparent early successes, one major consumer group, the Center for Science in the Public Interest, has released a survey that reveals that the FTC is lagging behind the efforts of state officials in squelching false and misleading claims by national advertisers. The Washington-based consumer group gives the FTC credit for improvements over the "do-nothing" Reagan years but complains that the agency stops fewer deceptive ads and television commercials than do states' attorneys general, and is less likely to extract monetary penalties out of violators.[99] Indeed, the states' attorneys general have been quite aggressive and successful in prosecuting misleading advertising, and they should be acknowledged as a significant source of consumer regulation.

While we are giving credit to groups other than the FTC, we would be remiss if we did not also mention the renewed activism at the FDA. According to New York City consumer affairs commissioner Mark Green, the FDA has "metamorphosed from a lap dog into a watchdog." The FDA's early successes in cracking down on food advertisers have brought applause from consumer groups and Capitol Hill.[100]

SELF-REGULATION IN ADVERTISING

Cases of deceptive or unfair advertising in the United States are handled primarily by the FTC. In addition to this regulatory approach, however, self-regulation of advertising has become an important business response, primarily in the last two decades. Under the regulatory approach, advertising behavior is controlled through various governmental rules that are backed by the use of penalties. *Self-regulation*, on the other hand, refers to the control of business conduct and performance by business itself rather than by government or by market forces.[101]

J. J. Boddewyn has identified the various strengths and weaknesses of advertising regulation and self-regulation, as summarized in Figure 9-10. These strengths and weaknesses are presented within the context of six tasks that must be performed if "good" advertising behavior is to be obtained. These tasks are (1) developing standards, (2) making them widely known and accepted, (3) advising advertisers beforehand about gray areas, (4) pre- or postmonitoring of compliance with the norms, (5) handling complaints from consumers and competitors, and (6) sanctioning "bad" behavior in violation of the standards, including the publicity of wrongdoings and wrongdoers.[102]

Types of Self-Regulation

Business self-regulation of advertising may take on various forms. One is **self-discipline**, where the *firm* itself controls its own advertising. Another is **pure self-regulation**, where the *industry* itself (one's peers) controls advertising. A third type is **co-opted self-regulation**, where the industry, on its own volition, involves nonindustry people (for example, consumer or public representatives) in the development, application, and enforcement of norms. A fourth type is **negotiated self-regulation**, where the industry voluntarily negotiates the development, use, and enforcement of norms with some outside body (for example, a government department or a consumer association). Finally, a fifth type is **mandated self-regulation** (which may sound like a contradiction of terms), where the industry is ordered or designated by the government to develop, use, and enforce norms, whether alone or in concert with other bodies.[103]

The National Advertising Division's Program

The most prominent instance of self-regulation in the advertising industry is the program sponsored by the National Advertising Division (NAD) of the Council of Better Business Bureaus, Inc. The NAD and the National Advertising Review Board (NARB) were created in 1971 by the American Advertising Federation, the American Association of Advertising Agencies, the Association of National Advertisers, and the Council of Better Business Bureaus to help sustain high standards of truth and accuracy in national advertising.

FIGURE 9-10 Respective Strengths and Weaknesses of Advertising Regulation and Self-Regulation

Advertising-Control Tasks	Regulation	Self-Regulation
Developing standards	+ Greater sensitivity and faster response to emerging public concerns − Difficulty in elaborating standards in areas of taste, opinion, and public decency − Difficulty in amending standards	− Greater lag in responding to emerging concerns + Greater ability to develop and amend standards in areas of taste, opinion, and public decency
Making standards widely known and accepted	+ Everybody is supposed to know the law − Compulsory nature of the law generates more hostility and evasion	− Difficulty in making the public aware of the industry's standards and consumer-redress mechanisms + Greater ability to make industry member respect both the letter and the spirit of voluntarily adhered to codes and guidelines
Advising advertisers about grey areas before they advertise	− This service is usually not provided by government	+ This service is increasingly being promoted and provided by industry—sometimes for a fee
Monitoring compliance	± Routinely done but often with limited and even relatively declining resources	± Increasingly done by the industry although restricted by available financial resources
Handling complaints	+ Impartial treatment + Extensive capability to handle many complaints − Slower and more expensive − Cannot put the burden of proof on advertisers in criminal cases	− Treatment may be perceived as partial − Limited capability to handle many complaints + Faster and cheaper + Usually puts the burden of proof on the incriminated advertiser
Sanctioning bad behavior including the publicity of wrongdoings and wrongdoers	+ Can force compliance − Generates hostility, foot dragging, appeals, etc. − Limited publicity of judgments unless picked up by the press	− Problem of the noncomplier but the media will usually refuse to print or broadcast incriminated ads or commercials + More likely to obtain adherence to decisions based on voluntarily accepted standards + Greater publicity of wrongdoings and—to a lesser extent—of wrongdoers

Source: J. J. Boddewyn, "Advertising Self-Regulation: Private Government and Agent of Public Policy," *Journal of Public Policy and Marketing* (1985), 129. Reproduced with permission.

FIGURE 9-11 Sources of Advertising Issues Considered by NAD/NARB and Their Resultant Decisions

	1986 #	1986 %	1985 #	1985 %
Sources				
NAD monitoring	29	27	38	37
Competitor challenges	46	43	43	41
Local BBB's	16	15	10	10
Consumer complaints	13	12	11	11
Other (i)	3	3	1	1
Total	107	100%	103	100%
Decisions				
Substantiated	26	24	31	30
Modified/discontinued	80	75	70	68
Referred to NARB (ii)	1	1	2	2
Total	107	100%	103	100%

Notes: (i) Three cases in 1986 resulted from challenges by trade organizations.
(ii) Two additional NARB panels were held in 1986. One appeal concerned a 1985 referral to the NARB. The second panel was held as the result of an appeal of an NAD decision by a competitor challenger.
Source: *NAD Case Report* (January 19, 1987), 1. Reproduced with permission.

The NAD initiates investigations, determines the issues, collects and evaluates data, and makes the initial decision whether it can agree that an advertiser's claims are substantiated. When the NAD is unable to agree that substantiation is satisfactory, the advertiser is asked to undertake modification or permanent discontinuance of the advertising. If the NAD fails to resolve a controversy, appeal can be made to the NARB, which has a reservoir of over 50 men and women representing national advertisers, advertising agencies, and the public sector. The chairman of the NARB selects an impartial panel of five members for each appeal. The parties involved submit briefs expressing their views for discussion at an oral hearing, after which the panel issues a public report.[104]

Figure 9-11 summarizes for 2 years the sources of advertising issues considered by the NAD and the NARB and the decisions arrived at in the cases. We earlier reviewed two cases heard by the Children's Advertising Review Unit of NAD, and those cases illustrate the typical kind of case that the NAD considers.

SUMMARY

Among stakeholder groups, consumers rank at the top. In a consumption-driven society, business must be especially attentive to the issues that arise in its relationships with customers. It is a paradox that consumerism arose during the very period that the business community discovered the centrality of the marketing concept to business success. The consumer's Magna Carta includes the rights to safety, to be informed, to choose, and to be heard. Consumers expect more than this, however, and thus the consumer movement, or consumerism, was born. Ralph Nader was the father of this movement and made consumer complaining respectable.

Product information issues compose a major area in the business-consumer stakeholder relationship. Foremost among these is advertising. Many issues have arisen because of perceived advertising abuses such as ambiguity, concealed facts, exaggerations, and psychological appeals. Specific controversial spheres have included, but are not limited to, comparative advertising, use of sex and women in advertising, advertising to children, advertising of alcoholic beverages, advertising of cigarettes, and health and environmental claims. Other product information issues include warranties, packaging, and labeling. The major body for regulating product information issues has been the FTC. The FDA and the states' attorneys general have become especially active recently. On its own behalf, however, business has initiated a variety of forms of self-regulation.

DISCUSSION QUESTIONS

1. In addition to the basic consumer rights expressed in the consumer's Magna Carta, what other rights or expectations do you think consumer stakeholders have of business?
2. What is your opinion of the consumerism movement? Is it "alive and well" or dead? Provide evidence for your observations.
3. Give an example of the major abuses of advertising from your own observations and experiences. How do you feel about this as a consumer?
4. Which of the kinds of controversial advertising issues are you most concerned with? Explain.
5. Of the various strengths and weaknesses of advertising self-regulation presented in Figure 9-10, which do you think are the most important ones? Explain.

ENDNOTES

1. Peter F. Drucker, *Management: Tasks, Responsibilities, Practices* (New York: Harper & Row, 1973), 61.
2. Steven N. Brenner and Earl A. Molander, "Is the Ethics of Business Changing?" *Harvard Business Review* (January-February, 1977).
3. Allen R. Andreasen and Arthur Best, "Consumers Complain—Does Business Respond?" *Harvard Business Review* (July-August, 1977), 93.
4. Robert J. Keith, "The Marketing Revolution," *Journal of Marketing* (January, 1960).
5. *Ibid.*
6. Regis McKenna, "Marketing Is Everything," *Harvard Business Review* (January-February, 1991), 65.
7. Martin L. Bell and C. William Emory, "The Faltering Marketing Concept," *Journal of Marketing* (October, 1971).

8. "Business Responds to Consumerism," *Business Week* (September 4, 1969), 95.
9. Robert J. Holloway and Robert S. Hancock, *Marketing in a Changing Environment,* 2d ed. (New York: John Wiley & Sons, 1973), 558–565. For additional discussion, see Robert M. Estes, "Consumerism and Business," *California Management Review* (Winter, 1971), 5–12.
10. *Ibid.,* 565–566.
11. Robert O. Herrmann, "Consumerism: Its Goals, Organizations, and Future," *Journal of Marketing* (October, 1970), 55–60.
12. Philip Kotler, "What Consumerism Means for Marketers," *Harvard Business Review* (May-June, 1972), 48–57.
13. Henry Assael, *Consumer Behavior and Marketing Action,* 3d ed, (Boston: Kent, 1987), 667.
14. Ralph Nader, *Unsafe at Any Speed* (New York: Grossman Publishers, 1965).
15. Kotler, 50.
16. Kotler states that these conditions were proposed by Neil J. Smelser, *Theory of Collective Behavior* (New York: The Free Press, 1963).
17. Kotler, 53.
18. Robert J. Samuelson, "The Aging of Ralph Nader," *Newsweek* (December 16, 1985), 57.
19. "Let the Buyers Beware: Consumer Advocates Retrench for Hard Times," *Time* (September 21, 1981), 22–23.
20. Jeanne Saddler, "Consumer Groups Try to Keep Earlier Gains as Their Power Wanes," *The Wall Street Journal* (December 21, 1986), 1.
21. *Ibid.*
22. Cited in *Ibid.*
23. E. Patrick McGuire, "Consumerism Lives! . . . and Grows," *Across the Board* (January, 1980), 57.
24. Paul N. Bloom and Stephen A. Greyser, "The Maturing of Consumerism," *Harvard Business Review* (November, 1981), 130.
25. Ronald Grover, "Fighting Back: The Resurgence of Social Activism," *Business Week* (May 22, 1989), 34–35.
26. *Ibid.,* 34–35.
27. Christine Gorman, "Listen Here, Mr. Big!" *Time* (July 3, 1989), 38–40.
28. Joel Makower and John Elkington, *The Green Consumer Supermarket Guide* (New York: Penguin Books, 1991).
29. Ben Corson, Alice Tepper Marlin, Jonathan Schorsch, Anitra Swaminathan, and Rosalyn Will, *Shopping for a Better World: A Quick and Easy Guide to Socially Responsible Supermarket Shopping* (New York: Ballantine Books, 1989).
30. "Upon Closer Look," *Consumer Reports* (August, 1986), 551.
31. "Taking a Hosing," *Consumer Reports* (August, 1986), 551.
32. "This Offer Is All Wet," *Consumer Reports* (June, 1986), 423.
33. "Mission Impossible," *Consumer Reports* (August, 1986), 551.
34. "Dept. of Doublespeak," *Consumer Reports* (August, 1986), 551.
35. William Leiss, Stephen Kline, and Sut Jhally, *Social Communication in Advertising* (Toronto: Methuen, 1986), 13.
36. *Ibid.*
37. William Shaw and Vincent Barry, *Moral Issues in Business,* 4th ed. (Belmont, CA: Wadsworth, 1989), 389–414.
38. *Ibid.,* 403.
39. *Ibid.,* 404.
40. *Ibid.*
41. *Ibid.,* 405.
42. John Koten, "More Firms File Challenges to Rivals' Comparative Ads," *The Wall Street Journal* (January 12, 1984), 27.
43. Eli P. Cox, "Deflating the Puffer," *MSU Business Topics* (Summer, 1973), 29.
44. Barry, 406–407.
45. O. Lee Reed, "The Next 25 Years of Advertising Regulations," *Collegiate Forum* (Fall, 1981), 2.
46. Vance Packard, *The Hidden Persuaders* (New York: D. McKay, 1957), 1.
47. Wilson Bryan Key, *Subliminal Seduction* (New York: Signet, 1972) and *Media Sexploitation* (New York: Signet, 1976).
48. Bruce Buchanan, "Can You Pass the Comparative Ad Challenge?" *Harvard Business Review* (July-August, 1985), 109.
49. Koten, 27.
50. *Ibid.*
51. Buchanan, 106.
52. *Time* (June 24, 1974), 76, Col. 2.
53. O. Lee Reed, Jr., "The Psychological Impact of TV Advertising and the Need for FTC Regulation," *American Business Law Journal* (Vol. 13, 1975), 176–177.
54. Diane Petzke, "Five Advertisers Will Soon Get a Plastic Pig," *The Wall Street Journal* (Febuary 28, 1985), 31.
55. Bill Abrams, "The Networks Censor TV Ads for Taste and Deceptiveness," *The Wall Street Journal* (September 30, 1982), 3.
56. Claudia Mills, "Children's Television," *Report from the Center for Philosophy and Public Policy* (College Park, MD: University of Maryland, Summer, 1986), 11.
57. *Ibid.*
58. Marie Winn, *The Plug-in-Drug* (Middlesex: Penguin, rev. ed., 1985).
59. Susan J. Tolchin and Martin Tolchin, *Dismantling America: The Rush to Deregulate* (Boston, MA: Houghton Mifflin, 1983), 153–161.
60. Mills, 14.
61. *1989 Annual Report: Council of Better Business Bureaus* (Arlington, Virginia), 3.

62. Michael F. Jacobsen and Ronald Collins, "Blitz Against Beer Commercials: Ads Glamorize Alcohol, Hide Dangers," *New York Times* (April 21, 1985), 2F.
63. Robert Friedman, "Beer and Wine Industry Girds for Battle as Campaign to Ban Ads Gathers Steam," *The Wall Street Journal* (January 30, 1985), 9.
64. Jacobsen and Collins, 21.
65. Brenton Welling, "What If the Airwaves Can't Hold Their Beer?" *Business Week* (March 11, 1985), 112.
66. *Fortune* (January 21, 1985), 84.
67. Joanne Lipman, "Sobering View: Alcohol Firms Put Off Public," *The Wall Street Journal* (August 21, 1991), B1.
68. Friedman, 9.
69. *Fortune*, 84.
70. Friedman, 9.
71. John E. Gallagher, "Under Fire From All Sides," *Time* (March 5, 1990), 41.
72. *Ibid.*
73. *Ibid.*
74. Mark Green, "Luring Kids to Light Up," *Business and Society Review* (Spring, 1990, No. 73), 22–26.
75. Marcus Mabry, "Fighting Ads in the Inner City," *Newsweek* (February 5, 1990), 46; Ben Wildavsky, "Tilting at Billboards," *The New Republic* (August 20 and 27, 1990), 19.
76. *Ibid.*
77. John E. Calfee, "FDA Underestimates Food Shoppers," *The Wall Street Journal* (May 29, 1991), A10.
78. Christine Gorman, "The Fight Over Food Labels," *Time* (July 15, 1991), 52–53; Zachary Schillar and John Carey, "Procter & Gamble: On a Short Leash," *Business Week* (July 22, 1991), 76, 78.
79. Gorman, 55–56.
80. John Carey, "Snap, Crackle, Stop: States Crack Down on Misleading Food Claims," *Business Week* (September 25, 1989), 42–43.
81. Alecia Swasy, "For Consumers, Ecology Comes Second," *The Wall Street Journal* (August 23, 1989), B1.
82. Jerry Taylor, "Bossy States Censor Green Ads," *The Wall Street Journal* (August 8, 1991), A12.
83. Jaclyn Fierman, "The Big Muddle in Green Marketing," *Fortune* (June 3, 1991), 91.
84. Taylor, A12.
85. "The Guesswork on Warranties," *Business Week* (July 15, 1975), 51; "Marketing: Anti-Lemon Aid," *Time* (February, 1976), 76.
86. *Ibid.*
87. *Time* (February, 1976), 76.
88. *Ibid.*
89. *L.L. Bean Catalog* (Freeport, Maine: Fall, 1991), 3.
90. Federal Trade Commission, *Fiscal Year 1988 Budget* (Washington, DC: Federal Trade Commission, 1987), B-6.
91. "The Escalating Struggle Between the FTC and Business," *Business Week* (December 13, 1976), 52.
92. Thomas G. Krattenmaker, "The Federal Trade Commission and Consumer Protection," *California Management Review* (Summer, 1976), 94–95.
93. *Business Week* (December 13, 1976), 52–59.
94. Tolchin and Tolchin, 147–149.
95. James C. Miller, III, "Revamping the Federal Trade Commission" (St. Louis: Center for the Study of American Business, December, 1984), 3.
96. Mark Potts, "What's Gotten Into the FTC?" *The Washington Post National Weekly Edition* (June 17–23, 1991), 32.
97. *Ibid.*
98. *Ibid.*
99. Bruce Ingersoll, "FTC Lays Far Behind States in Fighting Misleading Ads, Consumer Group Says," *The Wall Street Journal* (April 8, 1991), A6.
100. Malcolm Gladwell, "A Fresh Approach at the FDA," *The Washington Post Weekly Edition* (May 13–19, 1991), 32.
101. J. F. Pickering and D. C. Cousins, *The Economic Implications of Codes of Practice* (Manchester, England: University of Manchester Institute of Science and Technology, Department of Management Sciences, 1980), 17.
102. J. J. Boddewyn, "Advertising Self-Regulation: Private Government and Agent of Public Policy," *Journal of Public Policy and Marketing* (1985), 129.
103. *Ibid.*, 135.
104. *NAD Guide for Advertisers and Advertising Agencies* (New York: Council of Better Business Bureaus, 1985), 1–2.

CHAPTER **TEN**

Consumer Stakeholders: Product Issues and Responses

CHAPTER OBJECTIVES

After studying this chapter, you should be able to:

◆ Describe and discuss the two major product issues: quality and safety.

◆ Explain the role and functions of the Consumer Product Safety Commission and the Food and Drug Administration.

◆ Enumerate and discuss the reasons for the growing concern about product liability and differentiate strict liability, absolute liability, and market share liability.

◆ Outline business's response to consumer stakeholders to include the consumer affairs office and product safety office.

If product information has historically been a pivotal issue between business and consumer stakeholders, more recently product and service issues such as *quality* and *safety* have occupied center-stage. It is not so much that product information issues have declined in importance as that quality and safety have risen in significance. In this chapter, we will limit our discussion to product quality and safety issues. In connection with safety, we consider the product liability issue and the calls for tort reform. The Consumer Product Safety Commission and the Food and Drug Administration are also covered. Finally, we will discuss business's response to consumer stakeholders regarding the issues introduced both in Chapter 9 and in this chapter.

TWO CENTRAL ISSUES

The two central issues we are concerned with in this chapter represent the overwhelming attention that has been given to product issues over the past decade: *quality* and *safety*.

The Issue of Quality

There are several particularly important reasons for the recent obsession with product quality. First, a concern for quality has been driven by the fact that the average consumer household has experienced a rise in family income and consequently demands more. As more and more American homes are characterized by both husband and wife working outside the home, they become more demanding of a higher life-style. In addition, no one has surplus time to hang around repair shops or wait home all day for the service representative to show up. This results in a need for products to work as they should, to be durable and long lasting, and to be easy to maintain and fix. A recent Time/CNN survey showed that consumers were less interested in technical innovation and attractive designs than they were in the product's ability to function as promised, its durability, and its ease of maintenance and repair.[1]

Closely related to rising household expectations is the global competitiveness issue. Increasingly, American manufacturers have found themselves taking second or third place in terms of quality to European, Japanese, or other Asian competitors. Throughout most of the 1980s and into the 1990s, U.S. firms have been struggling to match the quality that has come from other countries just so they could remain competitive in world markets. Recent evidence suggests that the U.S. efforts are paying off. The Time/CNN poll found that 52 percent of the adult consumers surveyed said the quality of U.S. products has improved in the past 5 years. Additionally, the United States was ranked first among foreign competitors for its major appliances, clothing, telephones, and small appliances.[2] A Gallup poll also found that 51 percent of those surveyed thought the United States has gained ground relative to competitors such as Japan, South Korea, Taiwan, and

Hong Kong. In addition, 68 percent thought the United States will continue to gain ground in the next few years.[3] Although the struggle remains for international competitiveness, it is encouraging to see that U.S. efforts have had some effect.

Consideration of a specific case helps us to see how payoffs can be achieved when firms redirect their efforts toward consumers and quality. Xerox was in serious jeopardy in the early 1980s. Xerox, whose name is synonymous with copying machines, began losing business to Japan's Ricoh, Canon, and other competitors. Their world market share plummeted from 86 percent in 1974 to just 16.6 percent in 1984. A careful study of its competition makes it clear that Japan's secret was close adherence to quality standards. Xerox chairman David Kearns was appalled at his firm's sloppiness and inefficiency and in 1983 launched a quality program. Using employee teams to encourage problem solving and innovation and tough new standards for every phase of its operations, Xerox cut manufacturing costs and product defects in half. Customer satisfaction increased 38 percent. Xerox recaptured the lead in moderately priced copiers. Kearns observed, "At Xerox we define quality as meeting customer requirements. It's an axiom as old as business itself. Yet much of American business lost sight of that. Xerox was one of those companies. But by focusing on quality, we have turned that around." In 1989, President Bush singled out Xerox's copier division for one of two Malcolm Baldridge National Quality Awards, named after the former secretary of commerce, who died in 1987. The awards were created by Congress to recognize U.S. companies. They have become highly sought-after prizes in American industry.[4] It should come as no surprise that the following cartoon appeared in *The New Yorker* magazine in 1983. It depicted an executive commenting to several other executives sitting around a conference table: "Unless I'm misinterpreting the signs, gentlemen, we are approaching the end of the golden age of shoddy merchandise." This cartoon is an excellent summary of what has been happening in the world of quality products.

It should be made clear that our discussion of quality here includes *service* as well as products. We have clearly become a service economy in the United States, and poor quality of service has become one of the great consumer frustrations of all time.

In 1987, *Time* magazine made poor service one of its cover stories. Consumers today seem to swap horror stories about poor service as a kind of ritualistic, cathartic exercise. Consider the following examples: repeated trips to the car dealer, poor installation of refrigerator ice makers resulting in several visits from repair persons, returned food to the supermarket resulting in brusque treatment, fouled-up travel reservations, poorly installed carpeting, no clerk at the shoe department of your favorite department store, and on and on. Tom Peters, coauthor of *In Search of Excellence*, summarizes: "In general, service in America stinks."[5]

There is evidence that U.S. firms are becoming increasingly sensitive to service quality now. In the early 1990s it became clear that service companies were attempting to satisfy consumers through service guarantees. If you were unhappy with your hotel room, Hampton Inn would refund your money. If you were transferred from phone to phone while seeking an answer to an insurance question, Delta Dental Plan of Massachusetts would send you $50. If your luncheon pizza took more than 5 minutes to be served, Pizza Hut would give you a free one. Banks, auto-service outlets, restaurants, and other service firms have embraced a quality emphasis as market growth has slowed.[6]

The rising clamor about service quality suggests that there may be something fundamentally wrong in the U.S. service sector. Sloppy service has the potential to become more than just a consumer annoyance. Some economists warn that diminishing quality standards could cost the United States more of its international competitive standing in services and thus worsen existing trade problems. For example, Japanese banks have already made inroads into the U.S. market.[7]

With respect to quality, it is not clear whether American business has fully appreciated the spectrum of meanings that quality takes on for the consumer stakeholder. As David Garvin has expressed, there are at least eight critical dimensions of product or service quality that must be understood if business is to respond strategically to this variable.[8] These eight dimensions include (1) performance, (2) features, (3) reliability, (4) conformance, (5) durability, (6) serviceability, (7) aesthetics, and (8) perceived quality.

Performance refers to a product's primary operating characteristics. For an automobile, this would include such items as handling, steering, and comfort. *Features* are the "bells and whistles" of products that supplement their basic functioning. *Reliability* reflects the probability of a product malfunctioning or failing. *Conformance* is the extent to which the product or service meets established standards. *Durability* is a measure of product life. *Serviceability* refers to the speed, courtesy, competence, and ease of repair. *Aesthetics* is a subjective factor that refers to how the product looks, feels, tastes, and so on. Finally, *perceived quality* is a subjective inference that the consumer makes based on a variety of tangible and intangible product characteristics. To address the issue of product or service quality, a manager must be astute enough to appreciate these different meanings of quality and the subtle and dynamic interplays among them.

An important question is whether quality is a social or ethical issue or just a competitive factor that business needs to emphasize to be successful in the marketplace. Business must be attentive to the competitive factor for economic reasons. Beyond that, firms would want to do what is fair and right in terms of consumer expectations, and this is where the ethical dimension enters the picture. In the last chapter we discussed that consumers expect *fair value* for money spent, a product that will satisfy *reasonable expectations,* and a product that reflects the representations that were made for it in advertising. Each of these considerations embodies notions of fairness. Perhaps most important here is that consumers expect and deserve quality that is at least commensurate with the price paid for the product. Thus, Sears would be expected to produce a higher quality sparkplug wrench for its Craftsman line and its $8.95 price than Wal-Mart would be expected to sell at its $3.95 price. Quality, therefore, could easily be thought of as a concept embodying ethical norms.

The Issue of Safety

Business clearly has a responsibility to consumer stakeholders to sell them safe products. The concept of safety, in a definitional sense, means "free from harm or risk" or "secure from threat of danger, harm, or loss." In reality, however, the use of virtually any consumer product entails some degree of risk or some chance that the consumer may be harmed by the product.

In the 1800s, the legal view that prevailed was "caveat emptor," *let the buyer beware*. The basic idea behind this concept was that the buyer had as much knowledge of what he or she wanted as the seller and, in any event, the marketplace would punish any violators. In the 1900s, caveat emptor gradually lost its favor and rationale, as it was frequently impossible for the consumer to have complete knowledge about manufactured goods. Today, manufacturers are held responsible for all products placed on the market.[9]

Through a series of legal developments as well as changing societal values, business has become significantly responsible for product safety. Court cases and legal doctrine now hold companies financially liable for harm to consumers. Yet this still doesn't answer the difficult question, "How safe are manufacturers obligated to make products?" It is probably not possible to make products totally "risk free," as past experience has shown that consumers seem to have an uncanny ability to injure themselves in novel and creative ways, many of which cannot be anticipated. The challenge to management, therefore, is to make products as safe as possible while at the same time making them affordable and useful to consumers.

The public today is concerned, perhaps even to the point of paranoia, about a variety of hazards such as pesticide residues in food, living near toxic waste dumps or nuclear plants, and so on. Supermarkets in some states (for example, California and New York) now compete by advertising that their produce is free of pesticides. In 1989, consumers halted their consumption of red apples, apple juice, and other apple products for fear of residues from the chemical Alar. During this same period, all fruit previously imported from Chile was suspended because two grapes were found to have been injected with cyanide.[10]

As for manufactured products, these create hazards of harm not only in product design but also in the realm of inadequate information for the consumer to be aware of the hazards associated with using the product. Consequently, it is not surprising in product liability claims to find that the charges are based on one or more of the following allegations. First, it may be charged that the product was *improperly manufactured*. Here the producer failed to exercise due care in the product's production, and this failure caused the accident or injury. Second, if the product was manufactured properly, its *design* could be defective in that alternate designs, or devices, if used at the time of manufacture, may have prevented the accident. Third, it may be charged that the producer failed to provide *satisfactory instructions and/or warnings* and that the accident or injury could have been prevented if such information had been provided. Fourth, it may be charged that the producer *failed to foresee a reasonable and anticipated misuse* of the product and warn against such misuse.[11]

Figure 10-1 presents estimates of hospital emergency room treated injuries associated with the use of certain consumer products and gives us an overall perspective on the product categories associated with injuries.

Whether we are dealing with consumer products where the potential for harm due to accidents or misuse occurs or with food products where not-so-visible threats to human health may exist, the field of product safety is a significant responsibility and a growing challenge for the business community. It seems that no matter how careful business is with respect to these issues, the threat of product liability lawsuits has become an industry into itself and becomes intimately linked with discussions of product safety. Therefore, we will now turn our attention to this vital topic.

Product Liability. Product liability has become a monumental consumer issue in the United States for a variety of reasons.

Reasons for the Growing Concern About Product Liability. First, product liability has become such a major issue because of the *sheer numbers of cases* where products have resulted in illness, harm, or death. We documented some of these statistics in Figure 10-1. Second, we have become an *increasingly litigious society*. More citizens are responding "I'll sue!" when faced with a situation they are unhappy about. Lawsuits of all shapes and sizes have been piling up in the nation's courts. More than 20 million civil and criminal cases are filed each year in state and local courts. This represents one lawsuit for about every 1.2 persons. Furthermore, many of the lawsuits are for unusual reasons.[12] The litigation explosion in the United States has definitely affected the number of product liability suits filed.

Closely paralleling the rise in lawsuits in the United States has been the *growing size of the financial awards* given by the courts. Perhaps the path-breaking award in the product liability category was the $128.5 million awarded in 1978 to a 19-year-old, who at age 13 was severely injured. He was riding with a friend in a Ford Pinto car that was struck from behind. The Pinto's gas tank ruptured, filling the passenger compartment with flames that killed his friend and severely burned him over 90 percent of his body. The badly scarred teenager underwent more than 50 operations. Ford was required by the jury to pay $666,280 to the dead driver's family, $2.8 million to the survivor in compensatory damages, and a whopping $125 million in punitive damages to the survivor.[13] It is now estimated that each year over $100 billion flows through the liability system from companies to claimants and lawyers.[14]

Since the Pinto case, multimillion dollar lawsuits have become commonplace. Some major companies have been hit so hard by lawsuits that they have filed for protection under Chapter 11 of the federal bankruptcy law. One example of this is the Johns Manville Corporation, which faced an avalanche of asbestos-related lawsuits that totaled 16,500 suits demanding over $12 billion. Manville sought Chapter 11 protection in 1982.[15] A second example is that of A. H. Robins, which filed for protection in 1985. Robins faced over 5,000 product liability lawsuits in which women charged that its Dalkon Shield, an intrauterine contraceptive

FIGURE 10-1 Estimates of Hospital Emergency Room Treated Injuries Associated with the Use of Certain Consumer Products October 1, 1988–September 30, 1989

Product Group	Total	Under 5	Age Group 5–24	25–64	65 and Over
1. Child Nursery Equipment and Supplies	91,530	77,965	6,749	5,339	1,477
2. Toys	152,173	75,428	60,860	14,708	1,076
3. Sports and Recreational Activities and Equipment	3,266,173	174,527	2,346,816	714,492	29,986
4. Home Communication, Entertainment and Hobby Equipment	103,217	28,351	34,527	30,900	9,439
5. Personal Use Items	469,530	161,802	173,499	110,052	24,178
6. Packaging and Containers for Household Products	287,449	49,353	111,448	109,726	16,804
7. Yard and Garden Equipment	218,780	11,403	56,333	123,692	27,351
8. Home Workshop Apparatus, Tools and Attachments	280,865	12,727	81,739	163,168	23,130
9. Home and Family Maintenance Products	110,782	36,264	27,409	40,218	6,789
10. General Household Applicances	136,533	33,259	34,070	55,119	13,983
11. Space Heating, Cooling and Ventilating Appliances	121,929	39,486	34,935	40,557	6,951
12. Housewares	665,171	58,108	253,990	321,289	31,746
13. Home Furnishings and Fixtures	1,521,665	494,125	387,903	424,940	214,347
14. Home Structures and Construction Materials	2,716,902	459,072	965,959	937,353	354,054
15. Miscellaneous	181,913	40,286	87,156	42,973	11,454

Source: Natonal Electronic Injury Surveillance System (NEISS); Consumer Product Safety Commission, 1989 Annual Report.
Note: NEISS data indicate that a product was associated with an injury but not necessarily that the product caused the injury.

device, had injured them.[16] Other companies encountering large lawsuits include Union Carbide with its Bhopal, India, poison gas explosion; Dow Chemical with its Agent Orange defoliant; and Merrill Dow with its Bendectin morning sickness drug, which allegedly causes birth defects.[17] In discussions aimed at settling the dispute between Union Carbide and the country of India, a figure in excess of $500 million has been most commonly mentioned as the final settlement.

The fourth major reason that product liability has become such a prominent issue is the *creation of an insurance crisis* that has emerged from the escalating lawsuits and awards we just discussed. A couple of examples will illustrate this:

- William H. Brine of Milford, Massachusetts, is one of only two makers of lacrosse equipment. In 1984, Brine paid $8,000 annually for $25 million worth of product-liability insurance. In 1986, he learned that his premium was going up to $200,000 for just $1 million of protection.[18]
- Oliver Machinery Co. of Grand Rapids, Michigan, designs saws, lathes, and other woodworking equipment. Oliver's product-liability premiums quadrupled from $72,000 to $282,000.[19]

These cases of product-liability insurance skyrocketing are matched by liability premiums for other organizations and professions: municipalities, voluntary organizations, directors of corporations, physicians, day care schools, truckers, and others. The net result is characterized properly by *Business Week* when it said, "Now everyone is in a risky business."[20] As the insurance crisis has occurred, virtually everyone, directly or indirectly (through escalating consumer prices), is being affected. This makes the product-liability problem an issue of urgent proportions for everyone. Later, we will discuss the calls for product-liability reform that have become increasingly frequent as a result of the issues just mentioned.

The final reason we will discuss here for product liability becoming such an issue is the ***doctrine of strict liability*** and the expansion of this concept in the courts. In many ways the doctrine of strict liability is behind the issues we have discussed up to this point. In its most general form, the doctrine of strict liability holds that the manufacturer of a product is liable for harm caused to the user if the product as sold was unreasonably dangerous because of its defective condition.[21] In other words, there is no legal defense for placing on the market a product that is dangerous to a consumer because of a known or knowable defect. The courts have carried the interpretation of the strict-liability rule to extreme lengths, creating a major problem for business. For example:

- A worker in Texas won $50,000 in damages from a bench-saw maker for injuries received while using a saw that had been originally delivered, complete with safety equipment, to the U.S. Navy in 1942. After buying the saw as surplus, a dealer rebuilt it and resold it without the safety guard to a private operator. The original manufacturer was held liable.[22]

◆ The Fifth U.S. Court of Appeals held that a jury could find that a single-control shower faucet is unreasonably dangerous because, if one turns it all the way to one side, it will allow only hot water to spray, which could burn the occupant of the shower.[23]

Extensions of the Strict-Liability Rule. As if the strict-liability rule were not enough, recent expansions of the rule have been causing enormous problems for business in the product-liability area. Courts in several states are establishing a standard that is much more demanding than strict liability. This new concept is being called **absolute liability**. The most important case establishing this new concept was handed down by the New Jersey Supreme Court in *Beshada* v *Johns Manville Corporation* (1982). The plaintiffs in Beshada were employees of Manville and other companies who had developed asbestos-related diseases due to exposure in the workplace.[24] The court ruled in this case that a manufacturer could be strictly liable for failure to warn of a product hazard, even if the hazard was *scientifically unknowable* at the time of the manufacture and sale. Therefore, a company cannot use as its defense the assurance that it did its best according to the state of the art in the industry at that time. Under this ruling, the manufacturer is always liable for damages, even if it had no way of knowing that the product could cause a problem later.

The absolute-liability rule frequently involves cases in which chemicals or drugs are involved. For example, a drug producer might put a drug on the market (with government approval) thinking that it is safe, based on current knowledge. Under the doctrine of absolute liability, the firm could be held liable for side effects or health problems that develop years, or even decades, later. The result is that a large, and to some firms unacceptable, amount of uncertainty is injected into the production process.[25]

Another extension of strict liability is known as **market share liability**. This concept has evolved out of **delayed manifestation cases,** or those situations where delayed reactions to such products as asbestos, drugs, Agent Orange, and formaldehyde appear years later after consumption or exposure to the product.[26] An example of market share liability was seen in a California case where a group of women claimed their mothers had taken the drug DES while pregnant years earlier. The women could not name the company that made the pill that their mothers took. But in 1980 the California Supreme Court upheld a ruling that the six drug firms that made DES would be responsible in proportion to their market share of DES unless they could prove that they had not made the actual doses the women took.[27]

Product Tampering and Product Extortion. Two other problems that have contributed to the product-liability crises are *product tampering* and *product extortion.* Consider the Tylenol cases, first in 1982 when seven people died from tainted Extra-Strength Tylenol capsules in Chicago, and again in 1986 when cyanide-laced bottles of Tylenol were found in New York and one woman died. James Burke, chairman of Johnson & Johnson, dramatically characterized the case as "terrorism, pure and simple."[28] In 1991, two persons were killed after they had taken some Sudafed that had been poisoned. We earlier mentioned the disclosure of Chilean grapes that had been poisoned, apparently en route to the United States. Adulterated and poisoned products stretch beyond such national brands as Tylenol, and the targets include more than national drug companies.

Product extortion schemes emerged in the late 1970s and at first received only local publicity. In a typical situation, an adulterated product was sent to the manufacturer along with a note demanding money, in exchange for disclosure of other locations where poisoned or drugged products had been put on retail shelves. A variation of this scheme was the Vlasic pickles case in 1980, when retail stores in Atlanta were told of the location of one adulterated product and warned that they would not be told of other similarly poisoned products if they did not pay. On several occasions in the 1970s, the national press investigated and decided not to publish stories on the growing extortion menace. The Tylenol disaster in 1982 revealed the problem, however.[29] Product tampering and extortion have had significant implications for product packaging as well as product liability.

Product-Liability Reform. The major problems discussed up to this point have combined to create a need for ***product-liability reform***. Experts of all persuasions are attempting to pinpoint blame for the massive problems we now have and identify the guilty parties. Some experts point to corporations that produce dangerous products. But other reasons are singled out, too: for example, abuses by lawyers, activist liberal judges, overly generous juries, the insurance industry, and the "system" itself. It is a complex issue, and there seems to be blame enough to spread around to everyone.

However, not everyone agrees that reform is needed. On one side are business groups, medical associations, local and state governments, and insurance companies that want to change the system that they claim gives costly and unfair advantage to plaintiffs in liability suits. On the other side are consumer groups and trial lawyers who defend the present system as one that protects the constitutional rights of wrongfully injured parties.[30]

The criticisms of the business community to the current system illustrate some of the aspects of the controversy. Currently we have a patchwork of state laws. Business wants a uniform federal code. Currently there are no statutory limits on punitive damages in most states. Business argues for no punitive damages unless the plaintiff meets tougher standards of proof. Currently, meeting government standards is no defense in most states. Business thinks it should have an absolute shield against punitive damages for drugs, medical devices, and aircraft that meet government regulations. Currently, victorious plaintiffs in about 30 states can collect full damages from any defendant, even if the company is only partly at fault. Business wants victorious plaintiffs to be able to recover damages to the extent defendants are liable. Consumer groups have argued that the current system is better because the threat of lawsuits and megaverdicts forces companies to make safer products.[31]

The law governing liability for injury is known as *tort law,* and it has traditionally been left to the courts and to the states. In the last 25 years product-liability law has become a separate branch of tort law according to Dorsey Ellis, dean of the Washington University School of Law. According to Dean Ellis, this separate branch possesses unique characteristics. The most salient feature of product liability is "strict liability," as contrasted to the fault-based liability concept found in other areas of tort law. The "litigation explosion," the "insurance crisis," and the skyrocketing verdicts have all combined to focus attention on product-liability law. Consequently, in the past decade we have seen almost every state legislature consider, and some have adopted, tort reforms. In the past 5 years, bills have been introduced in Congress to reform product-liability laws.[32]

As of this writing, the most recent bill to be introduced in Congress was the "product-liability fairness" bill, which seemed to have bipartisan support because it claimed to reflect both business and consumer interests. Four key provisions were as follows: (1) The bill would require the defendant to pay only that portion of a pain-and-suffering award for which it is actually responsible, rather than making the "deepest pocket" pay for everything; (2) it would require that punitive damages—intended to punish a defendant—be permitted only when it is proved "by clear and convincing evidence" that the conduct showed a "conscious, flagrant indifference to public safety"; (3) it would protect drug and medical device manufacturers against punitive damages for products that had been approved by the FDA; and (4) it would preserve a plaintiff's right to sue until an injury is discovered, rather than permitting some states to limit lawsuits after some designated number of years. Many consumer groups are against this proposed legislation and plan to lobby against it.[33]

The debate over product-liability law is likely to continue unabated. Business claims the current system is inherently inefficient, raises the costs of litigation, and imposes a hidden tax on consumers, as it inhibits innovation and dampens competitiveness. Consumer groups argue that the current system has forced companies to make safer products. Recent studies show that both sides have valid arguments: The laws have spurred some safety improvements but they have also hampered innovation.[34] It is expected that product liability will remain a vital issue and that as businesses increasingly internalize the notion of product safety, the entire business-consumer relationship will be well served.

At this point, we should consider two major government agencies that are dedicated to product safety: the Consumer Product Safety Commission and the Food and Drug Administration.

CONSUMER PRODUCT SAFETY COMMISSION

The Consumer Product Safety Commission (CPSC) is an independent regulatory agency that was created by the Consumer Product Safety Act in 1972. The commission began its work in 1973 and it is composed of five commissioners. The commissioners are appointed to 7-year terms by the president and are confirmed by the Senate. The commission's statutory purposes are to:

1. Protect the public against unreasonable risks of injury associated with consumer products
2. Assist consumers in evaluating the comparative safety of consumer products
3. Develop uniform safety standards for consumer products and minimize conflicting state and local regulations
4. Promote research and investigation into the causes and prevention of product-related deaths, illnesses, and injuries[35]

Figure 10-2 spells out in more details the kinds of activities the CPSC has been involved in since its formation.

The CPSC was created at the zenith of the consumer movement as a result of initiatives taken in the late 1960s. President Lyndon Johnson established a National Commission on Product Safety in 1968, and this commission recommended

FIGURE 10-2 Introduction to the CPSC

Seeking to protect consumers from unreasonable risks of injury associated with consumer products, Congress passed the Consumer Product Safety Act in the fall of 1972. The U.S. Consumer Product Safety Commission began formal operations on May 14, 1973.

Over the past 17 years, the Commission has pursued a multifaceted approach to consumer injuries by:

- Cooperating and working with industry to develop voluntary safety standards;
- Issuing and enforcing mandatory standards where appropriate;
- Banning products for which no reasonable standard would adequately protect the public;
- Securing the recall and repair of consumer products that present substantial or imminent hazards to users;
- Researching potential hazards of products in the marketplace; and
- Conducting information programs to alert consumers about potential product hazards and how to use products safely.

Some 15,000 types of consumer products fall under the agency's jurisdiction.

In addition to exercising the authority granted it by the Consumer Product Safety Act of 1972, the Commission also regulates products covered by the Flammable Fabrics Act, the Federal Hazardous Substances Act, the Poison Prevention Packaging Act of 1970, and the Refrigerator Safety Act.

Source: Consumer Product Safety Commission, *1989 Annual Report*, 1.

the creation of a permanent agency. The commission justified its recommendation by its finding that an estimated 20 million Americans were injured annually by consumer products. President Richard Nixon took office while the proposed agency was still being debated and supported the agency's creation, but not as an independent agency. Congress gave the agency an unusually high degree of independence and required that it open its proceedings to the public to address the often-heard criticism of regulatory agencies that then become captives of the industries they regulate. Congress's intent was to keep business at arm's length and to involve consumers as primary participants in the agency's decision making.[36]

The CPSC experienced ups and downs as various administrations came into office. The agency grew in the 1970s, became controversial in the late 1970s, and was significantly reduced in power after the 1980 election of Ronald Reagan as president. The Reagan years of the CPSC (1980–1988) were marked by drastic budget cuts, massive staff reductions, and eventual paralysis of the agency. The agency survived several attempts to dismantle it. As one indication of the downturn it took during the Reagan years, its budget steadily declined from $40.6 million in 1980 to $32.6 million in 1988 before experiencing an upturn.[37]

Like most of the regulatory agencies in the post-Reagan environment, the CPSC has been demonstrating renewed activism. For its part, the CPSC claims it conducts "a viable product safety program to protect the public against unreasonable risks of injury associated with consumer products." In its 1989 annual report, the CPSC identified a number of products that were subjects of recent investigations and actions. These products included lawn darts, all-terrain vehicles (ATVs), containers for prescription drugs and over-the-counter medicines, cigarette lighters, and hand-held hair dryers. Major surveillance and monitoring activities of the commission recently included water coolers, hair dryers, fireworks, toys and children's products, bunk beds, toy premiums (for example, in cereal boxes), and ATVs.[38]

Consumer-group critics of the CPSC think the agency is doing an inadequate job of regulating product safety and that the agency could be doing much better if it had more money and more power. The CPSC has struggled in its legal battles to actually take conclusive action against products and companies and frequently finds itself in protracted litigation and appeals. In addition, some critics claim the agency takes on products and companies that represent only a very limited set of hazards or trivial risks. Some economists now think that simply providing information to the public about hidden product hazards may be a more useful role for the commission to assume given the difficulty of taking on major product standards with so many technical issues involved.[39]

As the CPSC enters the 1990s, one observer said "It vaguely resembles an etherized patient reviving on the operating table." The new chair of the CPSC, Jacqueline Jones-Smith, appointed by President Bush to serve a 7-year term that expires in 1996, has said that she wants to restore good relations between the agency and Congress and to fulfill the agency's mandate. She plans to rely on voluntary standards but will litigate if necessary. There has been renewed support for the CPSC by Congress. The CPSC is expected to pursue a moderate course in the 1990s, less controversial than before but perhaps more effective. Because a limited budget is a major obstacle, the agency will be expected to go after violators on a more selective and cost-effective basis.[40]

FOOD AND DRUG ADMINISTRATION

The health and food safety concerns of Americans reached a new height in the late 1980s as a result of two incidents. First, an apparent terrorist injected Chilean grapes with cyanide and an anonymous phone call in 1989 warned that the grapes were en route to the United States. Food and Drug Administration (FDA) Commissioner James S. Young decided to impose a controversial embargo on all fruit imports from Chile after inspectors discovered two cyanide-tainted grapes among a boatload that unloaded in Philadelphia. The embargo was suspended after 5 days, but by then consumer worries were already firmly established.

During the same period as the grape incident, a private Washington, DC environmental group, the National Resources Defense Council (NRDC), stirred up a massive public outcry with a report on Alar, a crop preservative frequently sprayed on apples. Alar was branded a carcinogen by the Environmental Protection Agency (EPA). The Food and Drug Administration got involved when Commissioner Young joined with other top government officials to assure the public that U.S.-grown apples were safe to eat. By then, public outcry over Alar forced its maker to withdraw it from the market, and the EPA banned it.[41]

As a result of the two tainted grapes and the Alar threat triggering a panic about what we eat, along with a slowly growing public concern about food and drug safety, it is not surprising that *Newsweek* and *Time* solidified public concern with their March 27, 1989 cover stories: "How Safe Is Your Food?" and "Is Anything Safe?"[42] It is against this backdrop that we describe briefly the Food and Drug Administration, an agency that has become much more high-profile in the past 5 to 10 years.

The FDA grew out of experiments with food safety by one man—Harvey W. Wiley—chief chemist for the Agricultural Department in the late 1800s. Wiley's most famous experiments involved feeding small doses of poisons to human volunteers. The substances fed to the volunteers were similar to those found in food preservatives at the time. The volunteers became known as the "Poison Squad," and their publicity generated a public awareness of the dangers of eating adulterated foods. The Food and Drug Act of 1906 was a direct result of the publicity created by Wiley's experiments. The act was administered by Wiley's Bureau of Chemistry until 1931, when the name Food and Drug Administration first was used. The Food and Drug Act called for the protection of the public from potential health hazards presented by adulterated or mislabeled foods, drugs, cosmetics, and medical devices. Later laws the FDA became responsible for included Food, Drug, and Cosmetics Act of 1938; the Public Health Service Act of 1944; the 1968 Radiation Control for Health & Safety Act; the Fair Packaging and Labeling Act of 1966; and the 1984 Drug Price Competition and Patent Restoration Act. In response to these major laws and others, the FDA regulates foods, drugs, cosmetics, and medical devices found in interstate commerce.[43] Figure 10-3 summarizes just some of the major responsibilities of the FDA.

The powers of the FDA were expanded as a result of other laws and amendments. The 1958 *Delaney Amendment* to the Food, Drug, and Cosmetic Act was especially notable. The Delaney Amendment requires the FDA to ban any food or color additive that has been shown to cause cancer in laboratory test animals. In 1962, amendments were passed to require drug manufacturers to prove the effectiveness as well as the safety of their products before marketing. In addition, the FDA was authorized to order the withdrawal of dangerous products from the market. In 1976, Congress passed legislation requiring the regulation of complex medical products and diagnostic devices.

The FDA is composed of a commissioner and seven associate commissioners, and the agency resides within the Health and Human Services Department. The FDA engages in three broad categories of activity: analysis, surveillance, and correction. Under President Reagan, throughout most of the 1980s, the themes emphasized were the cutting of bureaucratic delays and red tape, the speeding-up of agency decisions, and the elimination of unnecessary regulation. A major blow occurred to the agency during the 1980s when it was disclosed that four FDA employees were accused of taking cash payoffs and illegal gifts from a major generic drug company in return for favored treatment. Major challenges the FDA faced early in the Bush administration included the AIDs epidemic, regulation of medical devices, food safety, fat substitutes, nutritional labeling, and over-the-counter drug review.[44]

In 1991, under a new commissioner, David Kessler, the FDA embarked on an aggressive crackdown on deceptive product labels, which created a fair amount of controversy. In early 1991 the FDA targeted two highly visible products and companies to make its point. It seized Procter and Gamble's Citrus Hill "Fresh Choice" orange juice and a few days later Ragu "Fresh Italian" pasta sauce, the nation's leading tomato sauce brand. In both cases the FDA forced the companies to remove the term "fresh" from their products because they thought the companies were inaccurately applying the words to their products.

The point of the FDA was clear. It was no longer going to pursue the practice that had become commonplace throughout the 1980s of companies suspected of violations stretching out negotiations with the agency for years while engaging in an endless back-and-forth of proposals and counterproposals. The FDA was reasserting itself as an agency that was planning to take swift action against violators. In addition to the two cases cited, the FDA sent

FIGURE 10-3 Major Responsibilities of the Food and Drug Administration

- Regulates the composition, quality, safety and labeling of food, food additives, colors and cosmetics and carries out some research in these areas.
- Monitors and enforces regulations through the inspection of food and cosmetic producers' facilities, surveillance of advertising and media reports, and by researching consumer complaints.
- Regulates the composition, quality, safety, efficacy and labeling of all drugs for human use and establishes, in part through research, scientific standards for this purpose.
- Requires pre-market testing of new drugs and evaluates new drug applications and requests to approve drugs for experimental use.
- Develops standards for the safety and effectiveness of over-the-counter drugs.
- Develops guidelines on good drug manufacturing practices and makes periodic inspections of drug manufacturing facilities in the United States and overseas.
- Monitors the quality of marketed drugs through product testing, surveillance, and compliance and adverse reaction reporting programs.
- Conducts recalls or seizure actions of products found to violate federal laws and pose hazards to human health.
- Conducts research and establishes scientific standards for the development, manufacture, testing, and use of biological products.
- Inspects and licenses manufacturers of biological products.
- Requires pre-market testing of new biological products and evaluates the claims for new drugs that are biologics.
- Tests biological products, often on a lot-by-lot basis.
- Collects data on medical device experience and sets standards for medical devices.
- Regulates the safety, efficacy, and labeling of medical devices and requires pre-market testing of medical devices categorized as potentially hazardous.

Source: Food and Drug Administration.

warning letters to the manufacturers of Listerine, Plax, and Viadent mouthwash brands, Weight Watchers and Kraft brands cholesterol-free mayonnaise, and Fleischmann's reduced-calorie margarine, among other products. The agency thinks these products have misrepresented claims about the features of these products.[45]

What is particularly controversial about zealously pursuing these kinds of cases is the belief by some that they represent the FDA getting into the realm of policing competition among the food companies rather than dealing directly with health and safety specifically.[46] In its defense, the FDA's Kessler asserts that "consumers have a right to expect the FDA to make sure that food labels accurately and fairly reflect what is in the product." Kessler adds, "The purpose of the FDA's review of food labels is to make sure that all food companies are competing on a level playing field."[47]

BUSINESS'S RESPONSE TO CONSUMER STAKEHOLDERS

Business's response to consumerism and consumer stakeholders has been mixed. It has ranged from poorly conceived public relations ploys at one extreme to well-designed and implemented departments of consumer affairs at the other. The history of business's response to consumers parallels its perceptions of the seriousness, pervasiveness, effectiveness, and longevity of the consumer movement. When the consumer movement first began, business's response was casual, perhaps symbolic, and hardly effective. An early study of the communication systems between management and consumers, for example, showed that whereas such communication did exist, it was not used for managerial decision-making purposes.[48]

Today the consumer movement has matured, and formal interactions with consumer stakeholders have become more and more institutionalized. Business has realized that consumers today are more persistent than in the past, more assertive, and more likely to use or exhaust all appeal channels before being satisfied.[49] Armed with considerable power, consumer activists have been a major stimulus to more sincere responses on behalf of business. These responses have included the creation of toll-free hot lines and consumer service representatives, the integration of consumer input into marketing decisions, the designation of specific consumer affairs officers, and the creation of specific company departments to handle consumer affairs.

Two particular efforts on the part of business are worthy of mention because they typify the growing corporate response to the consumer interest: (1) the consumer affairs office, and (2) the product safety office.

Creating a Consumer Affairs Office

There are various ways of organizing the corporate response to consumers. Two ways might be to appoint a consumer affairs officer or create a consumer affairs task force or committee. A more sophisticated way is to establish a consumer affairs office or department. To be sure, the establishment of such a formalized unit is not a substitute for a consumer-relations focus on the part of all members of the organization. But it does provide a hub around which a dedicated consumer affairs thrust might be built.

Basic Mission. The basic mission of a consumer affairs office is to heighten management responsiveness to consumer stakeholders. In accomplishing this mission, consumer affairs professionals have to execute two roles: one is the role of consumer advocate in the company, and the other is the role of consumer specialist making managerial recommendations about corporate practices that mesh well with the needs of consumers and the company. Some companies may take one or the other of these two postures, and others use both approaches. There are potential conflicts in the two roles, but they need not create conflicts if the consumer affairs professional and management have a sympathetic understanding of each other's goals.[50]

Essential Functions. Mary Gardner Jones, former vice-president for consumer affairs at Western Union Telegraph and former federal trade commissioner, suggests there are four essential functions of an effective consumer affairs office:

1. *Establish a comprehensive, complete, and accurate data base* that assesses the level of consumer satisfactions and dissatisfactions with the company's products and services in all important areas involving consumers, such as billing and collection practices, repair services, guarantee policy and practice, handling of complaints, quality of products and services, and pricing.
2. *Audit the company's programs* to determine how adequate they are in responding to consumer complaints and interests. Use company records, special task forces, outside consultants, and consumer groups.
3. *Recommend specific consumer programs, policies, and practices* in all areas where needed.
4. *Establish programs to ensure effective communication* between the company and consumers to build public confidence and understanding of company policy and practice.[51]

Jones goes on to argue that there are four principal factors that will determine the success or failure of consumer affairs offices. These are essential if the office is to be able to accomplish its two central objectives of raising consumer satisfaction and improving long-term company profitability:

1. The office should be located close to that of the chief executive of the company.
2. The office should have access to all relevant information in the company about consumers and must be given authority to create effective mechanisms to get it.
3. Information about consumers should be quantified to the extent feasible. This is necessary to make intelligent decisions/trade-offs.

4. These managers should be skilled in designing effective performance measurement tools with which to evaluate what people throughout the company are doing. (Cliché: People will do what is inspected, not expected.)[52]

In general, the appropriate response of a company to consumer stakeholders is to ensure an understanding of the movement throughout the organization, especially at top management levels, where it is easy for executives to get isolated from company activities. Managers would do well to remember one of the key findings argued in *In Search of Excellence:* Stay close to the customer. Managers should also remember that Peters and Waterman concluded the excellent firms are those that are obsessed with *service* and *quality*.[53]

Establishing a Product Safety Office

Obviously, a consumer affairs office could be divided into parts, one of which might focus on product safety. In a growing number of firms, however, product safety offices are being established independently. This is quite logical, given what we documented earlier as the product safety and product-liability problems.

Three particular issues contribute to the need for greater organization in handling the product safety issue. First, there is the *complexity of most current products*. Products today may be made of exotic materials and incorporate complex and sensitive control devices. They are often built up from subsystems that themselves might be quite complex, for example, the modern automobile. Second, there is the *subtlety of the hazards that can be generated during product use*. People often use products in novel and strange ways, not for their intended purpose. Complexity contributes to an impatience with reading the instructions, and this can lead to subtle hazards, too. Third, there are *coordination problems in large, multidivision manufacturing organizations* that inhibit communications among departments, and structures are frequently set up wherein top management is insulated from discovering safety problems. The net effect of these three factors working together is to create a need for some sort of product safety organization.[54]

Levels at Which to Locate a Product Safety Office. The most important locations for product safety offices in organizations, according to a study by George Eads and Peter Reuter, are at the division level and the corporate level. The division responsible for the product is a logical location because the interaction of processes such as manufacturing, quality control, and packaging can best be perceived at this level. The division is also likely to know the most about the product's basic technology and conditions for use. Finally, the division's financial performance might be directly linked to the product's success, and, therefore, the division has the strongest incentive to ensure the product's safety.

Whereas a product safety office at the divisional level would have greatest operational responsibility, one at the corporate level could also be critical. At the corporate level, the product safety officer would most likely serve in a liaison role with the divisions. Activities that the product safety officer might perform include performing safety education and training, auditing against corporate design and safety policies, transmitting and reinforcing top management commitment to safety, and acting as a court of appeals when safety issues arise. A corporate-level product safety officer has greater organizational access to key decision makers, and this is an important factor, too.[55]

Other Functions of a Product Safety Office. Other important functions of a product safety office include the following:

- Setting the tone for the firm's product safety effort
- Structuring and helping to enforce financial and nonfinancial rewards and penalties
- Developing links to other safety- and quality-related activities in the firm
- Helping with product safety-related litigation
- Helping with regulatory liaison[56]
- Setting up product safety committees
- Performing periodic safety audits and tests
- Designing a contingency plan for product recalls[57]

Of all the product issues management faces, product safety has become one of the most important. Some companies produce high-hazard products and might need to incorporate all the ideas we have discussed, plus more. Other companies produce products in which the hazard is much lower. In any event, the product safety issue has become a "front-burner" consumer issue, and there is no sign of this changing. Because human health and safety are involved, product safety is justified as a central concern on its own merit. Trends in litigation, jury awards, and insurance premiums offer other practical reasons why the consumer stakeholder must be carefully considered when management is planning its responsiveness efforts with the groups with which it interacts.

SUMMARY

In recent years, consumer stakeholders have been extremely concerned with product quality and safety. On the quality front, U.S. firms seem to have declined from a leadership position in the world to one of competing to survive with other world producers. The situation has been no different with services. Although we are now a service-dominated economy, consumer dissatisfaction with service quality is at an all-time high. One major challenge is considering all the different dimensions of the quality issue. Today, quality may mean performance, features, reliability, conformance durability, serviceability, aesthetics, perceived quality, or some combination of these dimensions.

An extremely important legal and ethical issue is the consumer's right to safety. Product safety has become perhaps the most crucial consumer issue to firms. The product-liability crisis is an outgrowth of business's lack of attention to this issue. Other reasons contributing to the product-liability crisis include the sheer numbers of harmful-product cases, our increasingly litigious society, the growing size of financial awards given by the courts, and the insurance crisis. A major consequence of these occurrences has been cries for tort reform. Product tampering and product extortion have also become safety-related issues. In recent years, the health and safety issues related to foods, drugs, and medical devices have propelled the Food and Drug Administration into a prominent role.

Two major responses to consumer stakeholder issues have been the creation of consumer affairs offices and product safety offices in corporations. Although these two institutional responses do not solve the problems, they have the potential for addressing the problems in a significant way if they are properly formulated and implemented. In addition to these responses, a consumer focus and orientation needs to permeate management decision making if the consumer is to be handled effectively. In today's business environment, consumers have many choices. Consequently, companies have no alternative but to internalize this focus if they are to succeed.

DISCUSSION QUESTIONS

1. Identify the eight dimensions of quality. Give an example of a product or service in which each of these characteristics would be important.
2. Identify the principal reasons why we have a product-liability crisis. Have any reasons been omitted? Discuss.
3. Differentiate the doctrine of strict liability from the doctrine of absolute liability. What implications do these views have for the business community and future products or services that might be offered?
4. What type of company would most need a product safety office? Explain.
5. Given the current business and consumer climate, what do you anticipate the future to be like for the CPSC and the FDA? What role will politics play in your answer?

ENDNOTES

1. Janice Castro, "Making It Better," *Time* (November 13, 1989), 78–80.
2. *Ibid.*, 80.
3. Jay Schmiedeskamp, "Most Americans Optimistic That Product Quality Will Be Improved," *The Gallup Poll Monthly* (November, 1990), 32–33.
4. Castro, 78–79.
5. Stephen Koepp, "Pul-eese! Will Somebody Help Me?" *Time* (February, 1987), 48–55, 49.
6. Daniel Pearl, "More Firms Pledge Guaranteed Service," *The Wall Street Journal* (July 17, 1991), B1.
7. Koepp, 50.
8. David A. Garvin, "Competing on the Eight Dimensions of Quality," *Harvard Business Review* (November-December, 1987), 101–109.
9. Yair Aharoni, *The No Risk Society* (Chatham, NJ: Chatham House Publishers, 1981), 62–63.

10. Lester B. Lave, *How Safe Is Safe Enough? Setting Safety Goals* (St. Louis: Center for the Study of American Business, Washington University, January, 1990), 1.
11. E. Patrick McGuire, "Product Liability: Evolution and Reform" (New York: The Conference Board, 1989), 6.
12. Ted Gest, "Order in the Court—and Weirdness, Too," *U.S. News & World Report* (March 2, 1987), 24.
13. "Ford's $128.5 Million Headache," *Time* (February 10, 1978), 65.
14. Michele Galen, "The Class Action Against Product-Liability Laws," *Business Week* (July 29, 1991), 74.
15. Andrew Hacker, "The Asbestos Nightmare," *Fortune* (January 20, 1986), 121.
16. Francine Schwadel, "Robins and Plaintiffs Face Uncertain Future," *The Wall Street Journal* (August 23, 1985), 4.
17. Clemens P. Work, "Why It Isn't Easy to Settle Huge Claims," *U.S. News & World Report* (April 7, 1986), 52.
18. George J. Church, "Sorry, Your Policy Is Canceled," *Time* (March 24, 1986), 17.
19. *Ibid.*, 23.
20. "The Insurance Crisis: Now Everyone Is in a Risky Business," *Business Week* (March 10, 1986), 88–92.
21. Roger Leroy Miller, "Drawing Limits on Liability," *The Wall Street Journal* (April 4, 1984), 28.
22. Paul C. Hood, "Product Liability: It'll Raise Prices, But . . . Let the Seller Beware," *The National Observer* (February 12, 1977), 1, 12.
23. Miller, 28.
24. Terry Morehead Dworkin and Mary Jane Sheffet, "Product Liability in the 1980s," *Journal of Public Policy and Marketing* (1985), 71.
25. Miller, 28.
26. Dworkin and Sheffet, 69.
27. Clemens P. Work, "Product Safety: A New Hot Potato for Congress," *U.S. News & World Report* (June 14, 1982), 62.
28. "Tampering with Buyer's Confidence," *U.S. News & World Report* (March 3, 1986), 46.
29. Priscilla S. Meyer and Jay Gissen, "The Poison Problem," *Forbes* (December 20, 1982), 34.
30. Peter Waldman and Eileen White, "Battle Rages Over Damages, Insurance Rates: States Are Debating Sweeping Changes in Tort Laws," *The Wall Street Journal* (April 15, 1986), 5.
31. Galen, 74.
32. Dorsey D. Ellis, Jr., "Introduction," in Kenneth Chilton (ed.), *Product Liability Reform: Debating the Issues* (St. Louis: Center for the Study of American Business, Washington University, April, 1990), 1.
33. Arthur S. Hayes and Stephanie Simon, "Product Liability Law Gains Momentum," *The Wall Street Journal* (July 29, 1991), B6.
34. "The Defects in Product-Liability Laws," *Business Week* (July 29, 1991), 88.
35. "Consumer Product Safety Commission," *Federal Regulatory Directory*, 6th ed. (Washington, DC: Congressional Quarterly, 1990), 46.
36. *Ibid.*, 46–47.
37. *Ibid.*, 48–54.
38. *1989 Annual Report, Consumer Product Safety Commission*, 2–13.
39. Carolyn Lochhead, "A Risky Walk on the Safe Side," *Insight* (December 18, 1989), 8–17.
40. *Federal Regulatory Directory*, 52.
41. "Food and Drug Administration," *Federal Regulatory Directory* (Washington, DC: Congressional Quarterly, 1990), 297.
42. "How Safe Is Your Food? A Newsweek Guide," *Newsweek* (March 27, 1989) and "Is Anything Safe?" *Time* (March 27, 1989).
43. *Federal Regulatory Directory*, 290–292.
44. *Ibid.*, 292.
45. Malcolm Gladwell, "A Fresh Approach at the FDA," *The Washington Post Weekly Edition* (May 13–19, 1991), 32.
46. "The Food Crusades" (editorial), *The Wall Street Journal* (August 12, 1991), A10.
47. Gladwell, 32.
48. D. Cohen (ed.), *Communication Systems Between Management and the Consumer in Selected Industries* (Hofstra University Yearbook of Business, 1969).
49. Sarah Cash, "With Complaints: Consumer Now More Effective," *Atlanta Journal* (January 19, 1977), B-3.
50. Mary Gardner Jones, "The Consumer Affairs Office: Essential Element in Corporate Policy and Planning," *California Management Review* (Summer, 1978), 63.
51. *Ibid.*, 64–69.
52. *Ibid.*, 70–72.
53. Thomas J. Peters and Robert H. Waterman, Jr., *In Search of Excellence: Lessons from America's Best-Run Companies* (New York: Harper & Row, 1982), 156–199.
54. George Eads and Peter Reuter, "Designing Safer Products: Corporate Response to Product Liability Law and Regulation," *Journal of Products Liability* (Vol. 7, 1984), 265–267.
55. *Ibid.*, 268–271.
56. *Ibid.*, 285–289.
57. Rajan Chandran and Robert Linneman, "Planning to Minimize Product Liability," *Sloan Management Review* (Fall, 1978), 36.

CHAPTER **ELEVEN**

The Natural Environment as Stakeholder: Issues and Challenges

CHAPTER OBJECTIVES

After studying this chapter, you should be able to:

- Identify what makes up the natural environment.
- Discuss why natural environment issues are complex.
- Describe eight major natural environment issues.
- Recognize the causes of environmental problems.
- Characterize two differing perspectives on these issues.

The term "environment" means many things to many people—trees in the backyard, a family's favorite vacation spot, a mare and her colt in a pasture, a trout stream in the mountains, a view of Earth from outer space. This and the following chapter focus on the natural environment, specifically, what it is, why it is important, how it has become a major concern, and what businesses and other organizations have done both to and for it. This chapter identifies what we mean when we use the term "environment" and why it has become one of the most significant societal issues of our time. The next chapter describes the variety of responses human organizations, including businesses, have developed to address this issue. Throughout both chapters, we will emphasize two themes: (1) that humans are a part of their natural environments and (2) that the environment itself, as well as the issues and human responses related to it, is extremely complex, defying simple analyses.

To assist you in making business environmental decisions in the future, we will be presenting a number of facts and figures, some technical and scientific, related to environmental issues and responses. These are included to help you understand the complexities involved in today's business and public environmental issues. Ten years ago, for instance, most students and business executives had never heard of the words "chlorofluorocarbon" or "entropy." Yet today, because of the influence of progressive business, government, and environmental interest groups and individuals, the media and, increasingly, business and society texts discuss these and many other technical terms and concepts. Environmental literacy, whether for wise business, government, or individual decision making, requires, at minimum, some rudimentary knowledge for effective decisions. Without at least basic technical information, would-be stakeholder managers abdicate their responsibility to make prudent choices potentially crucial to the survival of their organizations, as well as to the survival of human and other species in the natural environment.

We present this technical information not only to support the claims and conclusions we make throughout these chapters but also to increase your GPA, that is, your Green Point Average. A 1991 Roper Survey found that the average American scored only a 33 out of 100 on a 10-question quiz about air, water, and land quality.[1] Although two chapters on a topic this broad and deep will not make you an environmental expert, we hope that the environmental issues and responses we present will prompt you to think twice about how you interact with your environment and pique your interest so that you explore these topics further in future courses and throughout your career.

Concern about the current and future states of the world's natural environment is evident in nearly every aspect of organizational life. Businesses are forming environmental associations, holding environmental conferences, supporting environmental organizations, publishing environmental newsletters, beginning

---

This chapter was contributed by Professor Mark Starik of George Washington University.

pollution prevention and cleanup programs, and including environmental concerns in their advertising. Business schools and other educational institutions are increasingly focusing on the natural environment as an important subject for preparing students to succeed in their careers. Growing out of a cooperative effort between a number of major U.S. businesses and a large U.S. environmental group, the Management Institute for Environment and Business was established in 1990 to develop curriculum materials for business school faculty to begin to incorporate environmental issues into courses as diverse as accounting, strategic management, production and operations, marketing, and finance. Political parties (including "green" political parties in the United States and elsewhere), governments, unions, civic groups, religious institutions, health centers, and athletic organizations all have recently intensified their efforts to contribute to resolving perceived environmental problems. The evidence appears overwhelming that the decade of the 1990s deserves the title "The Decade of the Environment."

The U.S. federal government is treating business environmental violations more seriously than ever. For instance, whereas in 1985, at the federal level, there were 37 guilty pleas and environmental criminal fines totaling $600,000, these amounts jumped to 107 guilty pleas and $13 million by 1989, including 53 years of jail sentences. For every business indicted under these laws, four corporate officials were also charged.[2] The aspiring and prudent business executive would do well not to ignore this increasingly important subject.

On the more positive side, opportunistic businesses have identified the recent concern for the environment as good for business. U.S. recycling businesses, for instance, did $6 billion of business in 1989 and were projected to grow as a group at between 25 to 30 percent per year through 1994.[3] Environmental consultants in the United States brought in revenues in 1989 between $10 and $15 billion and also had projected growth rates in the 30 percent per year range.[4] Other environment-related businesses projected to have significant increases in worldwide sales in the next few years range from pollution testing and control equipment suppliers to ecotourism firms. The environmentally sensitive entrepreneurial manager is advised to treat each complaint by polluting businesses about the high costs of complying with environmental regulations as an advertisement of yet another opportunity to "clean up."[5]

The Natural Environment

As busy people, we often take nature for granted. For instance, did you consider that this page you are reading required a number of natural resources for its production, as did the energy for the light in the room and the chair and building in which you are sitting? When we take nature for granted, we fail to appreciate the amazing complexity of the world around us. One amazing but typically forgotten characteristic about the natural world is that we constantly *interact* with it. From this point of view, Earth and everything else in the universe make up our environment and can be considered our continuous ever-present stakeholders (and we theirs).

For our purposes, we will consider the Earth, together with the energy and matter it receives from and returns to space, as our relevant environment. Earth is a water planet; that is, two-thirds of its surface is covered by water, which can be found in oceans, lakes, glaciers, aquifers, rivers, bays, creeks, human-made containers, the air, and all plants and animals. The Earth's core is a mixture of molten metals. The closer to the surface from the core, the more likely it is that these metals will have formed crusts on ocean bottoms and land masses, such as continents and islands. Surrounding both land and water is the atmosphere, layered gases of mostly nitrogen and oxygen that circulate around the globe. Finally, on the land and in the water are plants and animals so numerous that, after centuries of natural science development, we are still trying to identify and count them all. A recent estimate puts the overall number of Earth species—plants, animals, and microbes—somewhere between 2 million and 20 million.[6]

Although such a listing of components is a useful start to understanding our environment, those who study and appreciate ecology go well beyond list making. They are in awe of the "extraordinary motion, complexity, and interaction of the ecosphere. A confusion of birth and death, sex and violence, organic construction and decay, . . . a perception of the ecosphere as a scene of almost incredible living activity in contrast to the staticness that abounds (in the rest of the universe)."[7] The *interaction* of species under certain time, place, chemical, and physical conditions is what drives this complexity. Consider just one aspect of nature, the habitat, or the location where a species spends most if its life. Habitats can be hundreds of miles up in the atmosphere, deep within the ocean, several inches in the soil, or in the intestines of human beings. Some species' habitats, such as those of a number of shorebirds, bacteria, and insects, include working the interface among two or more of these phenomena.

Interaction can, but does not always, take place among these and other species, adding the element of chance to the complex webs we call ecosystems. Further, consider the intricacy of just two, perhaps adjoining, habitats: a meadow and a pond. Any number of rooted meadow plants from short grasses to towering trees and their surrounding soil could provide habitats for a vast variety of microorganisms, insects, reptiles, birds, and mammals. Ponds also contain some rooted aquatic plants, numerous types of algae, green bacteria, and green protozoa, and their surroundings might provide shelter and food energy for an entirely different set of animals, including amphibians and fish. This tremendous variety of habitats and inhabitants, and their interactions are but a fraction of what continues to astound ecologists about the natural environment.

Ongoing attempts to unravel nature's many perplexing mysteries produce findings that are surprising and potentially very useful. For instance, while land masses such as meadows appear to be prolific producers of plant and animal mass, watery environments such as ponds have been found to produce 2,000 times more "biomass" than meadows because of differences in the metabolism of the plants and animals found in each.[8] This fact may have significant implications for how a hungry human world, running out of good topsoil, can be fed most efficiently in the future.

As we mentioned earlier, the topic of the environment is so all-encompassing and potentially overwhelming, we are only introducing it here. In addition, we call your attention to Figure 11-1, which identifies a few of the most important environmental concepts that might be helpful to you now and in the future.

The Human-Environment Interface

Humans interact with their natural environments in numerous ways. The air we breathe, the water we drink, and the food we eat all originate in nature, and eventually all return to nature. Other significant human needs provided by the natural environment include materials for shelter, clothing and energy for temperature control, and transportation. In fact, nature's materials, whether in liquid, solid, or gaseous form, provide the base of every human product and service. Indeed, every physical human activity has its beginnings and ends in the physical environment, which is a very strong argument for including nature as a consideration in many human organizational decisions and actions.

Humans and the natural environment are intricately connected because *humans are part of nature.* As biological entities composed of organic and inorganic natural substances, humans, as individuals and as collections in organizations, depend on nature's physical resources and processes for survival and development. As we mentioned, we humans often take this dependency for granted. However, by continuously reminding ourselves that we, too, are part of nature, individuals and organizations, including businesses, might begin to develop a closer conceptual connection with the natural environment. Environmental protection could then be thought of as human protection, a concept most of us can easily support. One perspective on considering that we humans, too, are part of nature is that, how we *interact* with one another may be an important aspect of our overall environmental sensitivity. In this view, ensuring that human stakeholders, such as employees and customers, and even competitors, are treated with respect is one way to advance natural environment goals.

Unfortunately, that businesses have played a major role in contributing to natural environment pollution and depletion is beyond debate. Virtually every sector of business in every country is responsible for consuming significant amounts of materials and energy, causing waste accumulation and resource degradation. For instance, raw materials processing companies, such as uranium, coal, oil, and forestry firms, have caused major air, water, and land pollution problems in their extraction, transportation, and processing stages. Manufacturing firms, such as those in steel, petrochemicals, and paper products, have long been identified as major air and water pollution sources.

Figure 11-2 on page 318 illustrates that most major industry sectors contribute significant levels of pollution. The figure identifies the top 10 polluting manufacturing industries reporting the release of some 5.7 billion pounds of 320 chemicals and compounds into the air, water, and lands. Figure 11-3 on page 319 identifies those U.S. companies that released the greatest amounts of these polluting substances in 1989. Even service businesses, such as dry cleaners, grocery and

FIGURE 11-1 Glossary of Important and Helpful Environmental Terms

Environment:	Broadly, anything that is external or internal to an entity. For humans, the environment can include external living, working, and playing spaces and natural resources, as well as internal physical, mental, and emotional states.
Carrying Capacity:	The volume and intensity of use by organisms that can be sustained in a particular place and at a particular time without degrading the environment's future suitability for that use. A resource's carrying capacity has limits that need to be respected for continued use.
Entropy:	A measure of disorder of energy, indicating its unavailability for recycling for the same use. Energy tends to break down into lower quality with each use. For instance, a kilowatt of electricity, once it is produced and consumed, can never be used as electricity again, and, if stored, will allow far less than 1 kilowatt to be consumed.
Ecosystem:	All living and nonliving substances present in a particular place, often interacting with others.
Niche:	The role organisms play in their natural communities, including what they eat and the conditions they require for survival. Habitats and niches are interrelated concepts.
Cycle:	The continuous looplike movement of water, air, and various nutrients, such as nitrogen, phosphorous, and sulfur, through the environment. Such cycles can be impaired in performing their evolutionary roles, such as purification and sustenance, by excessive human-caused pollution and depletion.
Threshold:	The point at which a particular phenomenon, previously suppressed, suddenly begins to be activated. For instance, when a population's carrying capacity threshold is exceeded, populations tend to decrease or even crash due to increased morbidity and mortality.
Pollution:	The existence of material or energy that has gone through a transformation process and is perceived as unwanted or devalued in a particular place at a particular time.
Irreversibility:	The inability of humans and nature to restore environmental conditions to a previous state within relevant timeframes. Human environment-related actions that appear irreversible are the destruction of a rainforest or wilderness area and the extinction of a species.
Sustainability:	The characteristic of an entity, such as an economic or environmental system, related to its ability to remain viable over an acceptably long period of time.

FIGURE 11-2 Toxic Releases Inventory Releases and Transfers by Industry, 1989: Top Ten U.S. Industries

Industry	Rank	Pounds	Percent of Total
Chemicals	1	2,745,768,071	48.12
Primary metals	2	756,808,577	13.26
Multiple industries	3	437,278,275	7.66
Paper	4	313,254,241	5.49
Transportation	5	245,316,145	4.30
Fabrication metals	6	207,383,999	3.63
Plastics	7	194,502,619	3.41
Electrical	8	145,758,174	2.55
Petroleum	9	103,136,599	1.81
Machinery	10	74,922,470	1.31

Source: Environmental Protection Agency, *Toxics in the Community*. Washington, DC: U.S. Government Printing Office, 1991, 62.

retail stores, and auto repair shops, use nonnegligible amounts of energy and materials, which can be associated with hazardous wastes and urban sprawl. As a major consumer of the world's energy and materials, and as a large producer of waste and degraded ecosystems, business definitely affects the natural environment. Therefore, businesses that profess to practice good stakeholder management need to play a leading role in finding and implementing solutions to our environmental problems.

While manufacturing and operations processes are the most visible contributors to air, water, and land pollution, virtually every other department within a business potentially plays some role in affecting the natural environment. Research labs and engineering departments, for instance, could be producing their own nonnegligible amounts of environmental contaminants and forwarding to their manufacturing departments products they have designed that are toxic and nonrecyclable. Finance departments, using inadequate accounting department data, could be recommending decisions based on short-term criteria that have not incorporated the full costs to the environment of potentially damaging projects. Human resources departments could be neglecting to incorporate environmental concerns in their personnel recruitment, selection, and development decisions, potentially advancing indi-

FIGURE 11-3   Ten Companies with the Largest Toxic Releases Inventory Total Releases and Transfers, 1989

Company	Rank	Pounds	Percent of Total
DuPont	1	349,275,844	6.12
Monsanto	2	293,833,577	5.15
American Cyanamid	3	202,092,889	3.54
BP America	4	123,971,863	2.17
Renco Group	5	119,079,722	2.09
3M Co.	6	108,727,958	1.91
Vulcan Chemicals	7	92,349,716	1.62
General Motors	8	90,279,073	1.58
Eastman Kodak	9	79,258,257	1.39
Phelps Dodge	10	77,423,843	1.36

Source: Environmental Protection Agency, *Toxics in the Community.* Wasington, DC: U.S. Government Printing Office, 1991, 66.

viduals within the organization who do not share the organization's environmental values. Finally, marketing departments could be advertising and selling environmentally dubious products and services, with or without their customers' knowledge of this fact.

NATURAL ENVIRONMENT ISSUES

The latest wave of environmentalism has paralleled a growing public perception that global environmental problems are severe and worsening with time. The United Nations (UN) and many governmental bodies at several levels generally support this perception. For instance, the executive director of the United Nations Environment Programme (UNEP) made this statement in 1990 about world environmental problems: "Never has humanity faced so crucial a decade as the 1990s. The decisions—and, even more important, the actions—taken over these ten short years will determine the shape of the world for centuries. The very fate of life hangs upon them."[9] The UN has identified the following eight key global natural environment problems.

- Ozone depletion
- Global warming
- Solid and hazardous wastes
- Marine environment protection
- Freshwater quality and quantity
- Forest management
- Land degradation
- Biological diversity

We will discuss each of these environmental problems briefly to give the reader a sense of the complexity and urgency with which these issues are increasingly viewed.

Ozone Depletion

Ozone is an oxygen-related gas that is harmful to life near the Earth's surface but is vital in the stratosphere in blocking dangerous ultraviolet radiation from the sun. Every year in the southern hemisphere in the spring, a huge hole that has grown to be four times as large as the United States opens up over Antarctica. This hole is growing annually and is thought to be caused by human-produced chemicals—chlorofluorocarbons (CFCs), used in refrigeration, and halons, used in fire extinguisher systems. In addition, the northern hemisphere ozone layer is thinning. These ozone reductions put at risk thousands of humans and uncounted numbers of other animals to blinding cataracts and increases in skin cancer. Ozone depletion has also been identified as a cause of plant stunting, including food crops and widespread killing of phytoplankton, which are the base of ocean food chains.[10]

Global Warming

According to a number of reputable sources, the Earth's atmosphere is in danger of heating up. Human production of carbon dioxide, primarily through the burning of fossil fuels in power plants and automobile engines, has been identified as a probable contributor to this "greenhouse effect," that is, the prevention of solar heat absorbed by our atmosphere from returning to space. One estimate has been made that the amount of global carbon dioxide has increased by 25 percent since the Industrial Revolution[11] and continues to increase 0.4 percent per year.[12] A number of researchers estimate that this increased carbon dioxide production has raised the global average air temperature at the Earth's surface by 1°F over the last century.[13] Global sea surface temperature has increased about the same amount just since 1982.[14]

These recent temperature increases are about half of the entire warming of the Earth that has occurred in the last 10,000 years. Some atmospheric prediction models indicate that, with continued global warming of from 3 to 7°F, coastal flooding from glacier melting might result and forests, farm belts, wildlife habitats, and deserts would shift significantly. Both the severity and the effects of these shifts are unknown, as are the adaptability of ecosystems and living species, including humans, to these effects.[15,16] We do not yet know if we have crossed a threshold in which many of these projected effects will begin to be more substantially, perhaps threateningly, realized. Figure 11-4 identifies the gases and countries that are the primary contributors to global warming.

Solid and Hazardous Wastes

The most visible evidence that much of the world has become a garbage-making machine can be found at the local dump, landfill, or incinerator. These disposal sites, which are quickly being outstripped by the sheer volume of primarily the "developed" world's garbage, annually accumulate billions of tons of wastes of all kinds. However, because recordkeeping of waste is inadequate, no one knows exactly how much trash is produced by people everyday. Estimates have been made for Western "developed" nations, however. The United States produces about 10 billion metric tons of solid waste each year with about two-thirds of this categorized as nonhazardous. While U.S. households create about 140 million metric tons of municipal solid waste each year (or 3.5 pounds per person daily), the overwhelming bulk of solid waste in the United States is generated by industry.[17] Because these industrial wastes are

FIGURE 11-4   Global Warming Gases and Country Producers

Greenhouse Gas	Percentage Contribution	Country Producers	Percentage Contribution
Carbon dioxide	49	United States	21
Methane	18	Soviet Union	14
Chlorofluorocarbons	14	Europe	14
Nitrous oxide	6	China	7
Other gases	13	Brazil	4
Total	100	India	4
		Rest of the world	36
		Total	100

Source: Environmental Protection Agency, *Meeting the Environmental Challenge*. Washington, DC: U.S. Government Printing Office, 1990, 12.

disposed of primarily in private facilities, little is known about their content. Figure 11-5, however, identifies the composition of U.S. municipal waste by source. Every year Americans discard about 1 billion foil-lined fruit juice boxes, 25 billion styrofoam cups, 1.6 billion disposable pens, and 16 billion disposable diapers.[18] In comparison to the United States, the European Community discards an estimated 2 billion metric tons of waste each year, or about 20 percent as much.

The production of hazardous global wastes, that is, those requiring special handling to protect humans and the environment, has been estimated at between 375 and 500 million tons,[19] about 90 percent of which is produced in industrialized countries. These hazardous wastes include pesticides, petrochemicals, other organic chemicals such as dioxin and PCBs, and heavy metals. The United States produces more than a ton of these hazardous wastes per person per year. Unfortunately, many of these substances were not identified as hazardous until the 1970s, and consequently, their disposal up to that point is cause for great concern today, since many of these older disposal sites are unlined and are located within leaching distance of various bodies of water, especially underground aquifers.[20] In addition, because of tightening site controls in some areas, hazardous wastes are being transported away from their sources with greater frequency in recent years, both within countries and between countries, often to sites with weaker controls. For instance, in 1983, Western European countries sent Eastern European countries between 200,000 and 300,000 metric tons of hazardous waste.[21] One report suggests that this amount has tripled in the last several years.[22]

FIGURE 11-5   Composition of U.S. Municipal Wastes

Waste Category	Percentage of Composition
Paper/Paperboard	41
Yard waste	18
Metals	9
Glass	8
Food waste	7
Plastics	7
Other	10

Source: Environmental Protection Agency, *Meeting the Environmental Challenge*. Washington, DC: U.S. Government Printing Office, 1990, 14.

Marine Environments

Water is both literally and figuratively our lifeblood. We evolved from it, we are made of it, we need it for drink and food. Yet, humans often treat this precious source as just another garbage dump. Municipal sewage, industrial wastes, urban runoff, agricultural runoff, atmospheric fallout, and overharvesting all contribute to the degradation of the world's oceans and their most productive areas, the coastal waters within 700 miles of land. While the marine environment problem is global, consider just the effects of businesses and cities in the United States. Each year roughly 4 trillion gallons of American sewage and 5 trillion gallons of industrial waste are dumped into marine waters. These and other pollutants, such as oil and plastics, have been associated with significant damage to a number of coastal ecosystems, including salt marshes, mangroves, estuaries, and coral reefs. The result has been local and regional shellfish bed closures, declining fish populations, seafood-related illnesses, and reduced shoreline protection from floods and storms.[23] The U.S. Council on Environmental Quality (CEQ) reports that over 4 million acres of shellfish beds off the East Coast and the Gulf of Mexico were closed in 1990, about the same total amount as in 1985.[24]

Freshwater Quality and Quantity

Although three-quarters of the Earth's surface is water, 97.4 percent is salt water, and most of the remaining fresh water is inaccessible because of its underground or polar locations. Although so little fresh water is available, humans have acted as though the supply is limitless by overusing, polluting, or otherwise mismanaging this vital resource. Fresh water is used for numerous important human activities, including drinking, bathing, agriculture, manufacturing, transportation, recreation, and waste disposal.

Because global fresh water is unequally distributed, supplies are already overtaxed in shortage areas. Dam sedimentation, deforestation, overgrazing, overirrigation, and various sources of pollution are reducing the quality of fresh water available for necessary human purposes. The associated result has been drought, desertification, and water-borne diseases in the developing world, and river, lake, bay, and accessible groundwater contamination on a large scale in developed countries. For instance, one EPA study estimated that 10 percent of the U.S. surface waters were significantly polluted,[25] while another study estimated groundwater contamination at 25 percent of the total U.S. groundwater available for human consumption.[26]

One organization known for its global environmental studies has identified a number of large areas around the world where water scarcity has become a health-threatening problem. These water-shortage areas include rapidly shrinking water tables in China, the loss of two-thirds of the Aral Sea in the Soviet Union, and the overappropriation of about half the rivers in the American West.[27] However, the U.S. Council on Environmental Quality reported that same year that the trend in the United States was toward decreasing water demand, greater waste water treatment, and great water quality control efforts.[28] This discrepancy in information is a common condition in the discussion of environmental issues, contributing further complexity to the environmental manager's task.

Forests

In a previous era, environmentalists were once derided as "treehuggers," referring to their concern for forests and other woodlands. After the decimation of the world's tree species in the 1980s, an era that has been called "The Decade of Destruction," such concern appears justified. Although humans depend on forests for building materials, fuel, medicine, chemicals, food, employment, and recreation, the world's forests are quickly being depleted by a number of human factors. More than 50 million acres of trees fall each year worldwide, most of which is tropical rain forest. Two-thirds of Western Europe's natural forests and 95 percent of the virgin forests in the United States have been felled,[29] leaving worldwide less than 1 percent of the original (precivilization) forests still standing.[30]

If human activities, such as overharvesting, land clearing, and the production of tree-weakening air pollution, do not change, forests could continue to diminish, to the extent that the developing world's remaining forests may be gone by the end of this decade.[31] While the impact on humans of forest depletion would likely be tragic, the effect on other species and on ecosystems could be devastating. Forests are homes to millions of animal and plant species. Tropical rain forests in particular are prolific habitats, but thousands of its species are doomed for extinction before the year 2000, as these forests are cut down at the rate of 85 acres a minute.[32]

In addition, deforestation adds to soil erosion problems and is a major cause of the greenhouse effect, since felled trees are no longer able to absorb carbon dioxide and are sometimes burned for land clearing and charcoal, thereby releasing rather than absorbing carbon dioxide. Moisture and nutrient ecosystem cycles can also be severely damaged in deforesting activities, negatively affecting adjacent land and water ecosystems.

Land Degradation

Another disturbing environmental issue human populations face in the 1990s is the continuing and increasing problem of soil erosion and spoilage. "Every year the world has about 80 million more mouths to feed and over 20 billion tons less topsoil on which to grow food."[33] Productive, nutrient-rich soil is blown away by winds and carried away by rains when unprotected. Deforestation, acid rain, waterlogging, ozone depletion, and overgrazing all contributed to a loss of 240 billion tons of topsoil in the 1980s.[34] World grain production has fallen 14 percent since 1984, and famine, drought, overpopulation, and distribution inequities have annually been responsible for 40 to 60 million human deaths from hunger and hunger-related disease.[35] While many of these land degradation problems are regionalized in Third World countries, developed nations, too, have experienced land productivity difficulties. The United States may be losing more than 3 billion tons of topsoil each year,[36] stripping 170 million acres annually.[37] Loss of topsoil productivity costs Canada an estimated $1 billion per year.

Biological Diversity

Of all the environmental issues related to human individual and organizational activity, protecting and preserving the plant and animal species with which we share this planet is perhaps the most pressing. Biological diversity protection is important because many ecosystems are very fragile webs of interconnected and interdependent plant and animal species, so that affecting one species can set off a kind of chain reaction effect, requiring too-quick adaptations by other species with which it interacts. The irony is that several traditionally important human activities, such as hunting, fishing, agriculture, and livestock raising, as well as construction for human settlements, have seriously threatened many of these species. Their endangerment now threatens humans, either as individuals or as a species, through global warming, soil erosion, and the loss of botanical medicines on which many humans depend.

To put the problem in perspective, although there may be some 20 million species on Earth today, perhaps 100 are lost every single day, a rate of extinction many times greater than was thought to exist before the Industrial Revolution.[38] In addition to the depletion of large mammal species, such as the elephants and black rhinos of Africa, and birds such as the California condor and mosquito-catcher, there are some 20,000 endangered species of animals around the world, many in trouble because of overhunting and poaching. Ecosystem and habitat destruction through agricultural and urban development activities and, of course, pollution has put at risk not only wildlife but many species of very beneficial plants as well. Up to half of all human medicines are derived from plants, yet, in especially productive areas such as the world's rain forests, excesses in individual and organizational activity are responsible for significant and tragic ecosystem and species degradation.

Other Environmental Issues

In addition to the eight major environmental issues identified by the UN, a number of other concerns have arisen around the world that appear to threaten human health and other aspects of the natural environment. *Air pollution,* both outside buildings and inside, often rates high in concern, according to public opinion polls. While several industrialized countries have experienced decreases in a number of outdoor, or ambient, air pollutants in the past two decades, many metropolitan areas in these nations still experience severe problems with sulphur dioxides, nitrogen oxides, and particulates. The burning of some fossil fuels for energy production, car and truck emissions, and a combination of these two sources are the main culprits for ambient air problems, which are increasing in many urban areas.[39] In Mexico City, for instance, nearly 3 million motor vehicles making nearly 30 million trips every day are being blamed for the city's worsening ozone smog problem, contributing to the unfortunate fact that 125 days each year the city's air quality is considered dangerous to people's health.[40] In the Soviet Union, 68 cities were said to have the highest degrees of atmospheric pollution in 1988, with the capitals of each of the republics experiencing the severest problems in meeting the maximum permissible concentrations of air pollutants.[41] Figure 11-6 identifies these and other air pollutants and their associated human health concerns.

In addition to causing human health problems, ambient air pollution is also responsible for a condition called "*acid rain*," which has caused a number of significant negative impacts on the natural environments of a number of countries. Figure 11-7 defines this condition and lists some of its effects. Damage from this fossil fuel-caused problem to date appears to have hit Europe the hardest, being blamed for sterilizing up to 80 percent of the lakes and streams in Norway, damaging 64 percent of British forests, and destroying more than 40 percent of coniferous forests in central Switzerland.[42] Acid rain has caused significant deterioration to both the natural environment and human structures in other areas of the world, including Pennsylvania; Nova Scotia; Agra, India; Tokyo; Central Africa; and Sao Paulo, Brazil.[43]

Indoor air pollution is becoming an increasing concern, primarily in industrialized countries. Asbestos in schools and other buildings was used as an insulator for many years in the United States, for instance, but has been identified with causing asbestosis, an incurable lung disease afflicting those who inhale asbestos

FIGURE 11-6 Health Effects of Several Air Pollutants

Pollutants	Health Concerns
Ozone	Respiratory tract problems such as difficult breathing and reduced lung function. Asthma, eye irritation, nasal congestion, reduced resistance to infection, and possible premature aging or lung tissue
Particulates	Eye and throat irritation, bronchitis, lung damage, and impaired visibility
Carbon monoxide	Ability of blood to carry oxygen-impaired, cardiovascular, nervous, and pulmonary systems affected
Sulfur dioxide	Respiratory tract problems, permanent harm to lung tissue
Lead	Retardation and brain damage, especially children
Nitrogen dioxide	Respiratory illness and lung damage

Source: Environmental Protection Agency. *Meeting the Environmental Challenge.* Washington, DC: U.S. Government Printing Office, 1990, 10.

FIGURE 11-7 Acid Rain Definition and Effects

"Acid rain" refers to all acid deposition which occurs in the form of rain, snow, fog, dust, or gas. Manmade emissions of SO_2 and NO_x are transformed into acids in the atmosphere, where they may travel hundreds of miles before falling as acid rain. Acid rain has been measured with a pH of less than 2.0— more acidic than lemon juice. The political implications of the problem are important because the pollutants may originate in one jurisdiction but affect another.

EPA research has increased scientific understanding of the effects of acid rain, including the sterilization of lakes and streams, reproductive effects on fish and amphibians, possible forest dieback, and deterioration of manmade structures. These effects have been most obvious in the eastern United States and Canada and in western and eastern Europe.

Source: Environmental Protection Agency, "Progress and Challenges: Looking at EPA Today." *EPA Journal* (September/October, 1990), 17.

fibers. Other serious indoor air pollutants include radon, tobacco smoke, formaldehyde, pesticide residues, and perchloroethylene (associated with dry cleaning). The use of particular construction materials and other household products, such as certain paints, carpeting, and gas furnaces, is primarily responsible for these contaminants, which are associated with a number of human health problems, from nausea to cancer.[44]

A third environmental problem, one that received significant attention in the 1970s and is once again garnering major interest in the 1990s, is *energy inefficiency,* or the wasting of precious nonrenewable energy. Nonrenewable energy sources, such as coal, oil, and natural gas, were formed millions of years ago under unique conditions of temperature, pressure, and biological phenomena (hence the term "fossil" fuels). Once these are used up, they will apparently be gone forever. An overreliance on these nonrenewable energy sources causes them to be consumed faster than otherwise, and because of their hydrocarbon nature, fossil fuels cause a number of pollution and depletion problems identified later in this chapter. In addition, because these fuels are not equally distributed around the world, they are the cause of significant power imbalances worldwide, with associated armed conflicts, the latter of which are typically disastrous for both humans and the natural environment in general.[45]

Although none of the environmental problems mentioned above appear easy to resolve (with the possible exception of the cessation of tobacco smoking), part of the answer to the nonrenewability problem is to use as little as possible of these energy supply sources through implementation of sound energy conservation practices. In addition, shifting to renewable energy supply sources, such as solar, wind, hydro, and biomass, is an increasingly attractive option for both industrial and agricultural societies. Although a number of technologies to tap these renewable, low-polluting energy sources are becoming economically competitive with nonrenewable sources,[46,47] continued subsidies and systems promoting nonrenewable energy development continue to hamper this transition.[48]

Another environmental problem that is interconnected with those mentioned above deserves special attention because of its potential for harm: the production of *toxic substances*, whether as constituents of an intended end-product or as an unwanted by-product. Toxic substances, defined by the EPA as "a chemical or mixture that may present an unreasonable risk to injury to health or the environment,"[49] can include pesticides, herbicides, solvents, fuels, and radioactive substances, among many other possibilities. Whether considered waste or not, toxic substances can pose significant negative impacts on humans and on the natural environment in general. The problem with materials such as benzyl chloride, hydrogen cyanide, and methyl isocyanate is that very small amounts are incompatible with living tissue, destroying cell functions and eventually causing total system shutdown.[50]

Although extreme care may be exercised if society decides it needs to manufacture such substances, which is a questionable prospect, two problems remain. First, we are not always aware of the effects, especially long-term and *interactive* effects, of exposure to the thousands of chemicals produced every year. The U.S. EPA, for instance has no information on the toxicity of 80 percent of the 48,500 chemicals it has listed, and it has tested less than 10 percent of these for long-term effects.[51] Even in those instances where the toxicity of a chemical is known and is banned for sale in a country, such as the pesticide DDT in the United States, the substance can still be manufactured in that country and exported, only to return again when products that have been exposed to these substances are imported.

Second, toxic substances can be associated with industrial accidents, causing unforeseen widespread biological damage. The 1984 Bhopal, India, chemical plant leak, the 1986 Chernobyl nuclear power plant meltdown in the Soviet Union, and the 1989 Exxon *Valdez* 11-million-gallon oil spill in Alaska are three well-known environmental disasters involving toxic substances. Not so well known are the 20,000 toxic chemical accidents in the United States that occurred between 1980 and 1985, the more than 30,000 nuclear power plant mishaps that occurred in the United States between the 1979 Three Mile Island disaster and 1989, or the 91 million gallons of oil that were spilled in U.S. waters between 1980 and 1986.[52] Consider, for example, that just one oil storage tank farm and pipeline complex in New York state, run by Amoco and Mobil, is responsible for leaking an estimated 17 million gallons of fuel into the surrounding groundwater.[53] The world seems awash in toxic substances, and this and the other environmental issues mentioned in this section lead us to ask about the core causes of this perceived crisis.

Several other types of pollution that have received more attention in the past than recently are *radon, noise*, and *aesthetic pollution*. Radon is a radioactive gas that has been found in an increasing number of residential structures, resulting from the natural radioactive decay of certain materials either found in the soil or used in construction materials. After tobacco smoking, radon has been identified as the leading cause of lung cancer in the U.S.[54] Noise pollution can exist anywhere unwanted sounds are heard but most often result from heavy machinery operating within limited areas. Factories, construction sites, and airports are frequently identified noise pollution areas. Severe noise pollution can cause hearing impairment in humans and habitat disruption in other species. Aesthetic pollution occurs when visual tastes are violated and typically center around construction, signage, and land appearance. Commercial building facades, outdoor billboards, and litter, respectively, were significant local issues in the past. We mention these pollution sources to illustrate that environmental issues change with time and can vary from place to place, arguing for a flexible approach to environmental management.

CAUSES OF THE ENVIRONMENTAL CRISIS

Natural Pollution and Depletion

In assessing environmental quality, one needs to start with the fact that even nature isn't perfect. That is, the natural environment is responsible for a significant amount of pollution and degradation itself. Sometimes called "background" or "natural" levels of destructive materials and processes, these pollution and depletion sources are numerous and significant. For instance, everyday and everywhere on Earth, our planet's surface receives a huge dose of various forms of harmful radiation from the Earth's subsurface, our sun, and the rest of the cosmos. "Natural disasters" here on Earth can be considered environmental problems, as was evidenced by the Mount Saint Helens volcanic eruption and resultant air pollution in Washington state in 1980. The Earth's core is continuously polluting many bodies of water and airsheds with a full range of toxic heavy metals, some of which, such as uranium-238, are especially toxic because they are radioactive.

Viral and bacterial diseases, whether plant or animal, can also be considered natural pollution or degradation. Species have been going extinct since life first evolved, and ecosystems, such as lakes, streams, and glaciers, die "natural" deaths continuously. Species overpopulation (such as locusts and other insects) has led to pollution and habitat degradation necessitating huge die-offs and mass migrations. Nature, indeed, is its own destroyer, continuously dying and giving rebirth in a long-term cycle of creation and destruction of life.

Human-Caused Pollution and Depletion

If nature is a big polluter and humans have survived as a species for thousands of years while nature has been destroying itself, what's the problem? Won't humans continue to survive as a species for thousands more years as nature continues to degrade? The answer to these questions is that humans have "put the pedal to the metal" and drastically increased the levels and kinds of pollution and depletion, threatening numerous ecosystems and many species. This human intensification of pollution and depletion, if not immediately endangering Homo sapiens as a species, has at least contributed to the perception of a lower quality of life for many individuals worldwide, now and in the future.

Consider, for instance, that, prior to the Industrial Revolution, one plant or animal species went extinct every 300 years. Since that time, the rate of species extinction has increased to perhaps a hundred species a day. In category after category, human-caused environmental pollution and degradation has increased manifold in the last 200 years, at a constantly increasing rate. Human population, settlements, production, consumption, and waste are continuing to rise and are increasingly identified as causes of environmental destruction. Rain forests and other wilderness areas around the world are fast disappearing, directly as a result of this increased human activity.

The difference between natural and human-caused destruction is that nature has evolved over billions of years to blend this destruction with creation or construction but at a much slower pace than most comparatively frenetic human activity. Natural pollution and depletion allow habitats and niches time to re-emerge and cycles to regenerate.

However, human-caused pollution and depletion can occur with such swiftness, destruction, and staying power, that its addition to the natural or background levels can overwhelm nature's capacity to adapt to this heightened pace of degradation. Nowhere is this more the case than in the world's rain forests, which take hundreds of years to grow back and less than a fraction of that to burn or chop down. Once destroyed, rain forests have been planted with crops, harvested, and grazed until little, if any, life-giving nutrients remain in its soil. A second obvious example is long half-life radioactive waste, which can take seconds to manufacture and thousands of years to decay to safe biological levels.

Although the scope of this text does not allow us to discuss all of the ways humans contribute to environmental deterioration, we can focus on one critical resource that illustrates the human, and mostly business, potential for environmental destruction—*energy*. Humans need energy as much as water for their existence. We need food energy, typically produced by our agricultural systems, to maintain our internal life support functions, and we need energy to provide heat for most human shelters and for food preparation. In addition, we humans use energy to transport ourselves and our goods at high speeds, to cool our living spaces and perishable food supplies, to perform labor-saving household chores, and to manufacture many goods and provide many services desired by human society.

The problem with current energy use by humans at home and in business is that all of these benefits, whether physically necessary or simply desirable, have environmental costs. Much of our current agricultural production is based on increasing usage of petroleum-based herbicides and pesticides and petroleum-based on-farm fuel usage. For instance, the world used nearly 2 billion barrels of oil in agriculture in 1985, up 3.4 percent from 1980.[55] Food processing, both preconsumer and afterward, currently uses significant amounts of natural gas and electricity. Residential, commercial, and industrial buildings consume large amounts of these same fossil fuels for space, water heating, and cooling. Power plants that produce electricity using fossil fuels do so with an efficiency rate of only about one-third, illustrating the entropy idea that energy with a high capacity for work is capable of doing much less work each time it is transformed. In the United States, about a quarter of the energy consumed in 1990 was used in transportation,[56] with about three-eighths used in the industrial sector for the production of goods and services. Overall, the per capita use of energy is once again increasing in the United States, nearing preenergy crisis levels.[57]

What happens when all this primarily fossil fuel energy is consumed? More fossil fuel burning releases more carbon dioxide (up worldwide more than 120 percent since 1960).[58] More herbicides and pesticides typically result in more water pollution and soil degradation. More utility generated electricity may mean more acid rain, smog, and airborne heavy metals.[59] More gasoline-burning passenger and freight vehicles also contribute to increased acid rain, smog, and carbon dioxide problems. One fossil fuel, petroleum, is also the base of a number of consumer products, and, as illustrated in Figure 11-8, the manufacture and consumption of these products also produces negative environmental impacts.

Settlement patterns, too, play a role in energy consumption. The current approach to organization in most developed countries, and increasingly adopted by cities in developing countries, requires significant amounts of energy to transport people and goods into the city and people, goods, and wastes out of the city.[60] In addition, the quest for single-family dispersed housing, the development of strip shopping malls, and the never-ending building of highways and car parking lots encourage even greater use of fossil fuels.[61] Indeed, just considering this one natural resource, energy, it is clear that human activity, mostly business-related activity, is the current major factor in environmental degradation.

FIGURE 11-8 Selected Petroleum Products and Associated Hazardous Wastes

Petroleum Product	Associated Hazardous Waste
Plastics	Organic chlorine compounds, organic solvents
Pesticides	Organic chlorine compounds, organic phosphate compounds
Paints	Heavy metals, pigments, solvents, organic residues
Oil, gasoline, and other petroleum products	Oil, phenols, and other organic compounds, heavy metals, ammonia, salt acids, caustics

Source: Environmental Protection Agency, *Meeting the Environmental Challenge*. Washington, DC: U.S. Government Printing Office, 1990, 10.

The key for ecosystem protection and the halting or slowing of the deterioration in human quality of life is to reduce the negative impacts of human individual and organization activity and to ensure that any necessary impacts are as environmentally benign as possible. We need to allow nature to return to its role as environmental purifier, creator, and destroyer.

ENVIRONMENTAL PERSPECTIVES

In the mid-1970s, a small paperback book, called *Ecotopia*,[62] appeared in bookstores throughout the United States, offering a vision of a modern society based on ecological values. This novel, which has received renewed interest in recent years, describes a nation in which the norm is for people to "walk lightly on the land," and in which recycling, renewable (solar, wind, hydro, and biomass) energy development, and nonautomobile transport are commonplace. However, even in this idealized econation, issues related to how humans interact with their environment are continuously debated. In our world, environmental issues, similar to other issues that capture the public's attention, have generated their share of heated disputes and multiple perspectives. Questions such as "How serious are environmental issues?" "Who is responsible for taking action to reduce the negative effects of air, water, and land pollution?" and "What should be done to preserve endangered species?" have arisen once again with the resurgence of environmentalism in the late 1980s and early 1990s, with no overwhelming consensus of opinion. However, viewpoints have tended to polarize into at least two camps: the optimists and the pessimists. This chapter closes with these two alternate perceptions of the current situation and probable futures of these environmental issues and whether these perspectives can be reconciled.

The Optimistic Perspective

One view of environmental issues takes a decidedly optimistic approach and is widely supported by traditional business interests. This view holds, first, that environmental problems may not be as bad as environmentalists have made them out to be. Global warming and other ecological issues are not a significant, current reality in this perspective but require further study and measured action, if absolutely necessary. According to this perspective, technology will be developed in time to handle many air, land, and water pollution problems. Capitalist economies will, if allowed, allocate capital, labor, entrepreneurship, information, and natural resources efficiently to develop the demand and supply for these technologies (at the right time, place, and level). These technologically oriented "free" economies will also simultaneously provide a high material standard of living in these economies. In this view, human demands on natural resources are not significant problems; rather, these phenomena are identified as central solutions to problems of economic development and environmental improvement.

One proponent of this view has proposed a perspective that looks "optimistically upon people as a resource rather than as a burden—a vision of receding limits, increasing resources and possibilities, a game in which everyone can win ... (a perspective in which) creation, building excitement, and the belief that persons and firms, acting spontaneously in the search of the their individual welfare, regulated only by rules of a fair game, will produce enough to maintain and increase economic progress and liberty. (This) view leads to hope and progress, in the reasonable expectation that the energetic efforts of humankind will prevail in the future, as they have in the past to increase worldwide our numbers, our health, our wealth, and our opportunities."[63]

The Pessimistic Perspective

A completely different perspective has been advanced in both of the more recent waves of environmentalism in the West. This view is far less optimistic about either the near- or long-term prospect for humans and their organizations to deal with what are perceived by these environmental advocates as intractable, urgent issues of survivability and quality of life. Here the argument is made that the full extent of our environmental problems is either not known because of their complexity and our current limits of understanding or that what we do know reveals a daunting global problem that will require unprecedented levels of human individual and organization effort and cooperation for their resolution. Proponents of these arguments tend to focus to a far greater extent on nonhuman aspects of the natural environment and on the problems of air, land, and water degradation and species endangerment than do the optimists. Population and human material and energy production, consumption, and waste are often identified as the sources of the ecological crises they perceive, and, therefore, calls for resolving these dilemmas usually entail significant decreases in either population growth rates or material and energy demand or both.

After describing his position on a number of population and production issues, one advocate of this view stated, "We have wasted two critical decades. If we miss this chance, we face unprecedented peril. The processes of environmental abuse are as destructive as nuclear war and far less easy to avert—for they are already well advanced and gaining momentum. A gigantic task looms ahead."[64]

A Realistic Perspective?

How can these two contrasting views of human interaction with the natural environment be reconciled? Again, perhaps there are two answers to this question. The first is that a middle ground can be found—that, basically, humans, through their businesses and other institutions, can design systems that advance both material (and energy) growth and protection of the environment. This view is advanced by some progressive business organizations and the more conservative political parties and environmental groups. If these middle-of-the-road advocates are correct, environmental issues become just administrative details that will be worked out over time. Although some species will be lost and some level of pollution will need to be tolerated, this view does not require either wondrous technologies or radical social changes.[65]

The second answer is that the optimistic and pessimistic perspectives cannot be reconciled. Advocates in either camp would likely argue that the rosy technological solution and the stark social change solution are mutually exclusive. Society needs to decide to go down one path or the other, for, the respective advocates might argue, technological creativity can be hamstrung by "excessive" regulation, while significant social change toward greater environmental consciousness can be hindered by people waiting for a savior technology that is "right around the corner." As in most business and society issues, the individual manager may need to devote a considerable amount of time, energy, and concern to resolving these complex environmental issues to develop his or her own "realistic perspective."

SUMMARY

The natural environment can be considered all of the physical phenomena that surround us. This all-encompassing concept is one that we as humans can appreciate but typically do not understand and often take for granted. A number of environmental issues have captured our attention recently, and we are just beginning to become aware of their scope and interrelatedness and our role in contributing to them. These issues include ozone depletion, global warming, solid and hazardous wastes, marine environments, freshwater quality and quantity, forests, land degradation, and biological diversity. Other environmental issues, such as ambient and indoor quality, acid rain, energy inefficiency, and toxic substances, also apparently need to be addressed. Although we know nature itself plays some role in these conditions, human activity, including agricultural, manufacturing, transportation, and consumption activities, appears to be intensifying these problems, which is leading to widespread concern about the future of our environment. At least two perspectives on environmental issues have been identified, and students of business are advised to be alert to, collect, and attempt to process information from a number of sources to help decide which of these two perspectives is appropriate for their future environmental management decisions.

DISCUSSION QUESTIONS

1. What is the natural environment?
2. Should businesses be concerned about the natural environment? Why or why not?
3. What are several of the most important environmental issues that are receiving worldwide attention?
4. What are some of the causes of environmental pollution and depletion?
5. What is the future outlook for the natural environment?

ENDNOTES

1. Gutfeld, R., "Americans Flunk Test On Environment," *The Wall Street Journal* (November 8, 1991), B3F.
2. Whitley, J. D., "Avoiding Criminal Penalties for Environmental Mishaps," *Environmental Outlook* (Vol. 2, No. 2, 1990), 1.
3. Nulty, P., "Recycling Becomes a Big Business," *Fortune* (August 13, 1990), 82.
4. Geewax, M., "Cleaning Up the Environment Is Big Business," *The Atlanta Journal-Constitution* (June 18, 1989), E1.
5. Nazario, S. L., "Green Field: Environmental Engineers Command High Pay, Choice Assignments," *The Wall Street Journal* (October 21, 1991), B1.
6. Arthur, W., *The Green Machine* (Oxford, UK: Basil Blackwell, 1990), 13.
7. *Ibid.*, 5–6.
8. Odum, E. P., *Ecology and Our Endangered Life-Support Systems* (Sunderland, MA: Sinauer Association, 1990), 44.
9. *UNEP Profile* (Kenya, Nairobi: United Nations Environment Programme, 1990), 2.
10. *Ibid.*, 4.
11. *Ibid.*, 6.
12. Brown, L. R., "The New World Order," in Brown, L. R. et al., *State of the World, 1991* (New York: Norton, 1991), 7.
13. Hansen J., "I'm Not Being an Alarmist about the Greenhouse Effect," *The Washington Post* (February 11, 1989), A23.
14. Brown, L. R., Flavin, C., and Postel, S., "Outlining a Global Action Plan," in Brown, L.R. et al., *State of the World, 1989* (New York: Norton, 1989), 178.
15. United Nations Environment Programme, 6, 7.
16. Corson, W. H. (ed.), *The Global Ecology Handbook* (Boston: Beacon Press, 1990) 231–233.
17. *Ibid.*, 267.
18. Hirschhorn, J. S. and Oldenburg, K. U., *Prosperity Without Pollution* (New York: Van Nostrand Reinhold, 1991), 14.
19. Corson, 247.
20. United Nations Environment Programme, 8.
21. *Ibid.*
22. United Nations Environment Programme, *UNEP North American News* (April, 1989) reporting on a Green-Peace study.
23. Corson, 137.
24. Council on Environmental Quality, *Environmental Quality* (Washington, DC: U.S. Government Printing Office, 1990), 303.
25. International Rivers Network, *World Rivers Review* (July/August, 1989), 4.
26. Draper, E., "Groundwater Protection," *Clean Water Action News* (Fall, 1987), 4.
27. Postel, S., "Saving Water for Agriculture," in Brown, L. R. et al. *State of the World, 1990* (New York: Norton, 1990), 49.
28. Council on Environmental Quality, 303.
29. United Nations Environment Programme, 16.
30. Postel, 75.
31. United Nations Environment Programme, 17.
32. *Ibid.*
33. United Nations Environment Programme, 14.
34. Postel, 60.
35. Corson, 68.
36. *Ibid.*
37. Council on Environmental Quality, 338.
38. United Nations Environment Programme, 18.
39. Seager, J. (ed.), *The State of the Earth Atlas* (New York: Simon & Schuster, 1990), 110.
40. Cody, E., "In Mexico City, There's Fear in the Air," *The Washington Post* (November 24, 1991), A27.
41. Richman, B., "The Changing Face of Environmentalism in the Soviet Union," *Environment* (Vol. 32, No. 2, 1990), 28.
42. Seager, 116.
43. Naar, J., *Design for a Livable Planet* (New York: Harper & Row, 1990), 101.
44. Environmental Protection Agency, *Meeting the Environmental Challenge* (Washington, DC: U.S. Government Printing Office, December 1990), 11.
45. Mathews, J., "Acts of War and the Environment," *The Washington Post* (April 8, 1991), A17.
46. Lippman, T. W., "Future of Wind Power Gets a Lift," *The Washington Post* (November 17, 1991), H1.
47. Coffin, T. (ed.), "A Look at Alternative Energy," *The Washington Spectator* (Vol. 16, No. 18, 1991), 1–3.
48. Brower, M., "Energy Favoritism: Why Renewable Sources Are Not Being Developed Fast Enough," *Nucleus* (Union of Concerned Scientists) (Vol. 11, No. 3, 1989), 3.
49. Environmental Protection Agency, *Glossary of Environmental Terms and Acronym List* (Washington, DC: U.S. EPA, 1989), 18.
50. Naar, 38.
51. Naar, 39.
52. Naar, 39, 63, 159.
53. Rackleff, R. B., "The Oozing of America," *The Washington Post* (September 15, 1991), C5.
54. Environmental Protection Agency, *Meeting the Environmental Challenge*, 10.
55. Brown, L. R., "Sustaining World Agriculture," in Brown, L. R. et al., *State of the World, 1987* (New York: Norton), 131.

56. Council on Environmental Quality, 287.
57. Council on Environmental Quality, 298.
58. Flavin, C., "Slowing Global Warming," in Brown, L. R., *State of the World, 1990* (New York: Norton, 1990), 19.
59. Postel, S., "Stabilizing Chemical Cycles," in Brown, L. R. et al., *State of the World, 1987* (New York: Norton, 1987), 170.
60. Brown, L. R. and Jacobsen, J., "Assessing the Future of Urbanization," in Brown, L. R. et al., *State of the World, 1987* (New York: Norton, 1987), 51.
61. Cook, T., "Sprawl vs. Greenbelt," *Land Use Patterns*. Presented at the First International Ecology City Conference (Berkeley, CA, March, 1990).
62. Callenbach, E., *Ecotopia* (New York: Bantam Press, 1975).
63. Simon, J. L., "Population Growth Is Not Bad," *Phi Kappa Phi Journal* (Winter, 1990), 12–16.
64. Tolba, M. K., "Introduction," *UNEP Profile* (1990), 2–3.
65. Olson, R. L., "The Greening of High Tech," *The Futurist* (Vol. 25, No. 3, 1991), 29.

CHAPTER **TWELVE**

Business and Stakeholder Responses to Environmental Challenges

CHAPTER OBJECTIVES

After studying this chapter, you should be able to:

- Describe the NIMBY environmental problem.
- Explain the concept of environmental ethics.
- Discuss the role governments play in environmental issues.
- Identify various environmental stakeholders and their impact.
- Catalog a variety of business responses to these stakeholders.
- Examine business eco-responses with several decision models.
- Focus on the root cause of environmental dilemmas.

The previous chapter identified the nature of the environmental challenge. Air, water, land, ecosystem, and species devastation appear to be both ubiquitous and increasing. Therefore, the obvious question arises: Who should be responsible for this situation and what should be done about it? Environmental damage apparently continues unabated day after day, slightly but inexorably decreasing the quality of life both for us and for future generations. Should something be done, and, if so, what, who, how, how much, and when? Although these questions are being asked with increasing frequency, the answers are less than clear and no consensus has emerged. Is the environment the responsibility of governments? If so, which ones and to what extent? Is the environment the responsibility of environmental groups and the general public? What responsibility do businesses and other organizations have in addressing the environmental challenge? If there is no consensus on these questions, what should society do to prevent serious reductions in human quality of life and in the health or robustness of the natural environment?

RESPONSIBILITY FOR ENVIRONMENTAL ISSUES

Problems such as smog, toxic waste, and acid rain can be described as "wicked problems," that is, those with characteristics, such as interconnectedness, complexity, uncertainty, ambiguity, conflict, and societal constraints.[1] Affixing responsibility for such messy situations is problematic because solutions to wicked problems are seldom complete and final, and, therefore, credit for these solutions is seldom given or taken. Chlorofluorocarbons (CFCs), for example, were once thought to be safe alternatives to other more toxic refrigerants, which is why these ozone destroyers are so ubiquitous in our society's equipment.

The NIMBY Problem

One example of this question of responsibility has arisen recently in a number of environmental areas and has been labeled the NIMBY, or Not In My Back Yard, phenomenon. This acronym, which can be found on bumperstickers and conference agendas and in newspaper articles, college courses, and many other communication vehicles, is the human denial of responsibility for the use of the environment. An example of NIMBY is the community that uses ever-increasing amounts of electricity but decides it does not want a power plant that produces that electricity to locate nearby. Another is a company that generates increasing

---

This chapter was contributed by Professor Mark Starik of George Washington University.

amounts of waste but is unwilling to pay the full cost of proper disposal. Essentially, NIMBY is an attitude/behavior set based on avoiding or denying responsibility. When applied to the field of environmental management, NIMBY spells big trouble.

The obvious difficulty with the NIMBY syndrome is that the entity (human individuals, organizations, or both) causing environmental pollution or degradation is not identified as the problem source, and, therefore, no action is taken to reduce the problem. The NIMBY phenomenon avoids or denies the root cause of the damage and addresses only the symptoms with an attitude of nonresponsibility, characterized by an approach of "I'll create an environmental problem, but I want to have as little as possible to do with taking care of it." One popular cartoon characterizing the NIMBY problem pictures a stream of polluting, honking cars along a highway as they pass a huge billboard that reads "Honk if you love the environment!"

Environmental Ethics

"Behind all the studies, the figures, and the debates, the environment is a moral issue. We can and should be nature's advocate." President George Bush.[2]

"There is something fundamentally wrong in treating the Earth as if it were a business in liquidation." Herman Daly, Economist, World Bank.[3]

Another way to view business-environment issues is through the perspective of ethics, which as you will recall from Chapter 4, is "an act, decision, or behavior (which) . . . is consonant (in agreement) with prevailing norms or standards of society." Environmental ethics, then, might be considered to be those acts, decisions, or behaviors related to the natural environment that agree with society's norms. In addition, the principles of justice, rights, and utilitarianism might serve as moral anchors for society's norms, as we discussed in Chapter 5. This definition of environmental ethics brings up similar issues as those raised in Chapter 4, namely (1) Are these norms absolute or relative? and (2) Who sets these norms?

As we described in Chapter 11, nature itself is a polluter and destroyer. Given this fact, what does *absolute* human environmental sensitivity mean? Humans must consume at least some plants and water to survive. If humans and their organizations need to pollute and destroy at least some of nature for their survival, what is the *relative* level of degradation that is ethical? Do nonhuman species have any "rights," and if so, what are these, and how can they be reconciled with human rights? Concerning human rights and the environment, how do we assess the claims of indigenous cultures for the use of their respective environments? Is there any connection between the domination of humans by humans (say, for example, the domination of women by men or dark-skinned persons by light-skinned persons), and the domination of nature by humans?

The second problem with ethics, in general, and environmental ethics, in particular, is, whose standards will determine what is or is not ethical? Although numerous public opinion polls in the late 1980s and early 1990s have indicated that most citizens in many countries (such as the United States) support the concept of environmental protection,[4] how much the public will do itself or insist that governments and businesses do to protect the environment is still an unanswered question. How clean does the public's air and water need to be, and how much are they willing to pay to meet these standards? As in our earlier discussion of business ethics, values play a major role and can be highly variable in breadth and depth across perspectives, time, and situations.

What are some environmental values? According to one source associated with the "green movement," many environmentalists hold four beliefs as fundamental values: (1) Life on Earth should continue; (2) human life on Earth should continue; (3) natural justice should be done; and (4) nonmaterial qualities of life are worth pursuing.[5] These four principles form the base of a dozen integrated attitudes and behaviors identified in Figure 12-1. They are summed up in the statement, "Overall the Green goal is to allow everyone the opportunity to live a fulfilling life, caring and sharing with each other,

FIGURE 12-1 One Listing of "Green" Values

Put Earth first: respect nature's life support systems.
Live within limits: unlimited expansion is self-defeating.
Think in terms of sufficiency: "enough" must replace "more."
Tread lightly: seek productive coexistence not domination.
Defend diversity: promote variety of environment and culture.
Respect our descendants' rights: save for future generations.
Design with nature: respect long-term, stable patterns.
Keep things in proportion: human scale for human-made systems.
Balance rights and responsibilities: society has value.
Decentralize and democratize: localism and participation.
Tread carefully: technology can have unforeseen results.
Bad means produce bad ends: how is as important as what.

Source: S. Irvine and A. Pouton, *A Green Manifesto* (London: Optima, 1988), 14–16.

future generations and other species, while living sustainably within the capacities of a limited world.[6]

Another attempt at defining environmental values was undertaken by a pair of sociologists from Washington State University. In 1978, these researchers developed a 12-question scale to measure the strength of what they called the "New-Environmental Paradigm" or NEP. This scale contains eight questions that are intended to indicate environmental sensitivity, such as "Mankind is severely abusing the environment," and four questions that are reverse-scored and are associated with what the authors call the "Dominant Social Paradigm," or DSP, a set of values, beliefs, and attitudes that are more traditional perspectives of humans and nature, such as, "Mankind was created to rule over the rest of nature." This questionnaire has been administered many times to numerous groups since its development. In general, these researchers have found a surprisingly high level of agreement among the general public for the NEP and, as might be expected, an even higher level among individuals associated with environmental interest groups.[7]

Following the ethical models provided earlier in Chapters 4 and 5, environmental issues can be added to develop a better idea of what environmental ethics is and how it can be practiced. Kohlberg's model of moral development, for instance, can be used to identify environmentally related attitudes and behaviors by development level. At the preconventional (infant) level in environmental ethics, humans and human organizations can be perceived as being concerned only with self or with its own species and habitats. A conventional (adolescent) level might entail some appreciation of nature but only when and where such appreciation is commonplace or "in." A postconventional (adult) environmental ethic might include more mature attitudes and behaviors that are more universal (including all species and habitats), long-term (including unborn generations), and more consistent (If we humans have a right to survive as a species, why don't all species have that right?). Similarly, the moral principle of utilitarianism, the greatest good for the greatest number, could be expanded in environmental ethics to the greatest good for the greatest number of species and ecosystems. The Golden Rule could read "Do unto other species as you would have them do unto you." Finally, the "best self" ethical test could include the question, "Is this action or decision related to the natural environment compatible not only with my concept of myself at my best but also with my concept of myself as a human representing my species at its best?"

Environmental ethics is an important and intriguing subtopic of business ethics and is gaining attention both in academics and in business. However, the prudent business environmentalist is advised to be cautious to prevent becoming self-righteous in either his or her own individual environmental ethics or that of his or her organization. Not only is the concept of "ecological correctness" a very slippery issue (since both nature and humans and their technology are so varied around the planet and are constantly changing), it can also be an obstacle to others who might wish to become more environmentally sensitive but are put off by a "more-ecological-than-thou" attitude.

To return to the question of who sets environmental norms, the answer may be similar to the question as to who sets society's norms—we all do, in part. This analysis implies that, as in ethical questions in general, the best approach to environmental ethics may be to practice tolerance, to see the world through others' perspectives, and to continue to question your own and the environmental values of others.

THE ROLE OF GOVERNMENTS IN ENVIRONMENTAL ISSUES

As we mentioned earlier, governments have played a major role in environmental issues since their inception. Governments have procured, distributed, and developed habitable land and other resources; have protected, taxed, and zoned natural environment-based areas; and, more recently, have exercised regulatory control over how these environments could be used. In this section, we will look at how governments in the United States have dealt with environmental challenges and then identify what is done in several other countries and at the international level.

Responses of Governments in the United States

Although the U.S. federal government has influenced environmental policy since at least 1899, with its permit requirement for discharge into navigable waters, the major entrance of the U.S. government into environmental issues took its form in 1970 with the signing of PL 91-190, the National Environmental Policy Act (NEPA). The second section of this act spells out its purposes "to declare a national policy which will encourage productive and enjoyable harmony between man and his environment; to promote efforts which will prevent or eliminate damage to the environment and biosphere and stimulate the health and welfare of man; and to enrich the understanding of the ecological systems and natural resources important to the Nation."[8]

In addition to these broad policy goals, this legislation placed on federal agencies a requirement to prepare environmental impact statements (EIS) for any "proposals for legislation and other major federal action significantly affecting the quality of the human environment." An EIS is a report of a study explaining and estimating the impacts on the environment, irreversible uses of resources, and detailed reasonable alternatives to the action.

Business is affected by NEPA in several ways. First, the federal government annually pays private consultants to conduct over $40 billion worth of EISs. Second, because the federal government is the largest landholder in the United States, private businesses wishing to secure licenses and permits to conduct timber, grazing, mining, and highway dam and nuclear construction operations likely will be parties to the completion of an EIS. Third, private businesses working under federal government contracts are typically obliged to participate in EISs. Fourth, the federal NEPA has been used as a model by many state governments in the United States, and, therefore, businesses heavily involved in significant state and local government contracts are likely to be involved in an EIS.

Also in 1970, the U.S. Environmental Protection Agency (EPA) was created as an independent agency to research pollution problems, help state and local government environmental efforts, and administer many of the federal environmental laws. These laws can be categorized into three areas: air, water, and land, even though pollution and degradation, such as acid rain, often overlap two or more of these categories.

Air Quality Legislation. The key federal air quality legislation is called the Clean Air Act and was recently and significantly amended in 1990. The overall approach used is similar to other areas of federal regulation, such as safety and health legislation, in that standards are set and a timetable for implementation is established. In the Clean Air Act, there are two kinds of standards: primary, which are designed to protect human health, and secondary, which are intended to protect property, vegetation, climate, and aesthetic values. As of this writing, the EPA has set primary and secondary standards for a number of air pollutants, including lead, particulates, hydrocarbons, sulfur dioxide, and nitrogen oxide. Businesses directly producing these substances (such as electric utilities) and those whose products when used cause these substances to be produced, such as automobiles, must reduce their emissions to these standard levels within a certain time frame.[9,10]

State governments are responsible for filing plans with the EPA on how these standards will be met. Depending on the business and the pollution emitted, firms invest in various state-of-the-art control technologies to meet these standards. For instance, the 1990 Clean Air Act requires coal-burning electric power plants to cut their acid rain-related sulfur dioxide emissions roughly in half by the year 2000, so many utilities are installing new scrubbers and electrostatic precipitators to achieve this goal.

One emerging but controversial concept that has recently been included in the Clean Air Act is the *bubble concept*. This approach is intended to reduce a particular pollutant over an entire industrial region by treating all emission sources as if they were under one bubble. Thus, a business could increase its emissions of sulfur dioxide in one part of a plant or region if it reduces its sulfur dioxide pollution by as much or more in another part of the plant or region. In addition, and as an extension of this bubble concept, businesses that reduce their emissions can trade these rights to other businesses that want to increase their emissions. Proponents of the bubble concept and emissions credit trading hail these as "free market environmentalism," while opponents ridicule them as "licenses to pollute." Early returns indicate a mixed success for this new policy tool, with some firms, especially utilities, taking advantage of the concepts, and others, such as 3M, refusing to use their credits to pollute further and, in effect, "retiring" their credits so that no other firm can use their credits to produce more pollution.

One type of air pollution that is increasing in importance but that is not yet regulated by the Clean Air Act is indoor air pollution. Tobacco smoke, paints, products, furnace exhaust, and outgassing products of many kinds have been identified as potential indoor air pollutants, causing business employees and housing residents to complain about a variety of health problems. Apparently, businesses are left to regulate themselves in this area, unless local ordinances establish restrictions. Many businesses have decided, for instance, to establish no-smoking areas on their premises.

Water Quality Legislation. U.S. government involvement in water quality issues has followed a pattern similar to air quality issues. The Clean Water Act (also known as the Federal Water Pollution Control Act) was passed in the early 1970s with broad environmental quality goals and an implementation system involving both the federal and state governments designed to attain those goals. The one purpose of the Clean Water Act was to achieve water quality allowing for fish, shellfish, and wildlife protection and for human recreation in and on the water. The second goal was to eliminate pollution discharges into navigable waters, which includes most U.S. rivers, streams, and lakes. These goals were to be accomplished through a pollution permit system, called the National Pollutant Discharge Elimination System, which specifies a maximum permissible discharge level and often a timetable for using state-of-the-art pollution control equipment. Another act, the Marine Protection, Research, and Sanctuaries Act of 1972, sets up a similar system for discharges into coastal ocean waters within U.S. territory. A third water quality law administered by the EPA, the Safe Drinking Water Act of 1974, establishes maximum contaminant levels for drinking water.[11,12]

One significant water quality problem is virtually unregulated—non-point source water pollution. Runoff from city streets, construction sites, farm- and rangelands, and animal feedlots can cause significant nutrient and toxic substance buildup in the bodies of water receiving these pollutants, thereby damaging the usability of the resource for plants, animals, and humans alike. Again, similar to the indoor air quality issue, businesses regulate their own non-point source pollution. Many farmers, for instance, have adopted voluntary planting and tillage practices that limit soil erosion and runoff and the use of harmful chemical herbicides and pesticides.

Land-Related Legislation. Land pollution and degradation differs from air and water quality issues, since land by definition is far less fluid and, therefore, somewhat more visible and more amenable to local or regional problem-solving approaches. Consequently, the U.S. federal government, in the Solid Waste Disposal Act of 1965, recognized that regional, state, and local governments should have the main responsibility for nontoxic waste management. The EPA's role in this area is limited to conducting research and providing technical and financial assistance to these other governmental levels. However, a 1976 amendment to this act, called the Resource Conservation and Recovery Act, set up a federal regulatory system of tracking and reporting of the generation, transportation, and eventual disposal of *hazardous* wastes by businesses responsible for creating these wastes.

Concerning *toxic* wastes, however, the U.S. government has staked out a much larger role for itself. The 1976 Toxic Substances Control Act requires manufacturing and distribution businesses in the chemical industry to identify any chemicals that pose a "substantial risk" of human or other natural environment harm. The act also requires chemical testing before commercialization and the possible halting of its manufacture if the associated risks are unreasonable. Because there are over 70,000 chemicals already in use in the United States and more than 1,000 new chemicals introduced every year, the EPA has prioritized those substances that must be tested to focus on those that might cause cancer, birth defects, or gene mutations.

The other major U.S. government activity in toxic wastes is known as Superfund, or more formally, the Comprehensive Environmental Response, Compensation, and Liability Act of 1980 (CERCLA). Superfund is an effort to clean up over 2,000 hazardous waste dumps and spills around the country, some dating back to the previous century. Funded by taxes on chemicals and petroleum, this program has established a National Priorities List to focus on the most hazardous sites and affixes legal and financial responsibility for the proper remediation of these sites on the appropriate parties. In addition, CERCLA also requires that unauthorized hazardous waste spills be reported and can order those responsible to clean up the site.

One of the most recent and perhaps most important amendments to the Superfund law, the Emergency Planning and Community Right-to-Know Act of 1986, requires manufacturing companies to report to the federal government annually all of their releases into the environment of more than 300 toxic chemicals and 20 categories of chemical compounds. These reports are accumulated and then made available to the public, with the intention that an informed public will pressure manufacturers to reduce these toxic releases.[13,14]

Other Environment-Related Legislation in the United States. The U.S. government's role in the natural environment is not restricted to activities of the EPA. Although this agency and the major laws mentioned that it administers are the most visible, nearly every major department in the federal government has some actual or potential impact on environmental quality. Figure 12-2 is a brief list of these departments and one assessment of their actual or potential environmentally related activities.

One particular legislative effort of national governments worthy of attention by business managers is the protection of endangered species by law. Costa Rica, for instance, has set aside fully one-quarter of its territory and 80 percent of wilderness outside of this area, restricting industrial development in these regions. Wilderness areas are also set aside in the United States through several programs;

the U.S. federal legislation that perhaps most directly affects business activity is the Endangered Species Act. This federal law assigns the responsibility of preventing harm to species considered "endangered," that is, facing extinction, or "threatened" (likely to become endangered). Since the law was passed in 1973, 606 species have been so listed, and another 3,500 animals and plants are being considered.[15] While protecting species sometimes means moving them to safe areas when their original habitats are destroyed by human activities, often species protection involves preventing these activities, such as mining, construction, and fishing, before such habitat deprivation occurs. This restriction of business activi-

FIGURE 12-2 U.S. Government Departments and Actual or Potential Environmentally Related Activities

Department	Environmentally Related Activities
Agriculture	Forest management wilderness preservation, soil and water conservation Water bank (wetlands) management Range (livestock grazing) management
Commerce (NOAA)	Ocean radioactive dumping monitoring Environmental monitoring
Defense (Corps of Engineers)	Inland waterways dredging/pollution Dam building Toxic waste sites
Energy	Energy efficiency, renewable energy, fossil fuels, nuclear power development
Nuclear Regulatory Commission	Radioactive waste, nuclear reactors regulation
Interior	Endangered species, oil and gas leases, mining reclamation, national parks, wildlife refuges, fish hatcheries, dam building, livestock grazing, coastal protection
Justice	Environmental law enforcement
State	Global environmental negotiations Debt for nature swaps Ocean protection
Transportation	Energy efficiency, air pollution control
Treasury	Debt for nature swaps

Source: T. A. Comp (ed.), Blueprint for the Environment (Salt Lake City: Howe Brothers, 1989).

ties can be expected to continue as the extinction rate of nonhuman species climbs, resulting in sometimes intense political conflicts between these business interests and environmental groups.

One recent Endangered Species Act case involved the protection of the Northern spotted owl, a harmless, nocturnal bird native to the ancient forests in the Pacific Northwest, whose numbers had been reduced by human logging activity to 2,000 known pairs. In 1990, the U.S. Interior Department decided to declare the owl "threatened." The subsequent restriction of logging by forestry firms, whose heavy cutting activity had involved 70,000 acres per year in the region, was estimated by the department to jeopardize 28,000 timber and related jobs by the year 2000.[16] Forestry firms complained that this action would entail $1 billion in lost wages for the U.S. Northwest economy and force unnecessary hardship on smaller loggers, while environmentalists argued that more jobs would be lost by the forestry industry's ongoing efforts to replace labor with technology and that the owl was an "indicator" species that needed to be protected so that the entire ancient forest ecosystem in the region could be conserved.

In the United States, state governments have been given increased responsibility for environmental protection, since the "New Federalism" effort of the Reagan administration, which attempted to decentralize nondefense domestic programs. One independent organization that tracks state government environmental activities, Renew America, published several "State of the States" reports in the late 1980s, assessing and ranking state governments on various environmental effort criteria. Overall, although this study found some excellent state programs in areas such as air, water, and land quality protection, the level of federal funding assistance for many of these programs fell precipitously during the 1980s, and many states experienced cutbacks of their own. The result of this greater state burden for environmental protection with diminishing financial resources, according to Renew America, was fragmented, inconsistent, inadequate, and waste-producing institutional policies. For instance, while water consumption had increased by 51 percent in the United States since 1960, contributing to significant local and regional shortages, only six states had water conservation programs.[17] Figure 12-3 identifies eight areas of environmental concern, identifying the state government program perceived as a leader in the nation in that particular area.

International Government Environmental Responses

Although the United States is the focus of many environmental issues because of its high profile in causing and responding to environmental problems, the global nature of many natural environment issues has meant that international institutions have also played important roles. Certainly, one international institution that has led the way in identifying global environmental problems and in working toward their resolution has been the United Nations Environment Programme (UNEP). Since its creation in 1972, this agency has been at the forefront in each of eight major environmental areas mentioned in the previous chapter. As early as 1977, UNEP was studying the ozone problem and began to lay the groundwork for the 1987 Montreal Protocol, in which most of the CFC-producing and -consuming nations around the world agreed to a quick phase-out of these ozone-destroying substances. UNEP is also conducting research and assisting in information exchange on global warming problems, with the hopes of a Montreal-like multination agreement in 1992.

Concerning wastes, UNEP has been instrumental in encouraging countries to reduce the amount and toxicities of their wastes and to dispose of them in environmentally sound ways. Its office on Industry and the Environment has been

FIGURE 12-3 Environmental Areas of U.S. State Governments' Concern and Model Programs

Environmental Area	State Government Program
Forest management	Washington's cooperative agreement among many parties, including timber producers, to lengthen application comment period and identify critical environmental priority areas for special attention.
Solid waste recycling	Oregon's Opportunity to Recycle Act requiring community drop off centers or curbside recycling programs. Programs to encourage market development via tax credits.
Drinking water	Maine's use of computer tracking and training and certification for maintaining water quality and monitoring schedules.
Land-use planning	Oregon's integrated land-use planning program requiring establishment of urban boundaries and zones for environmental protection.
Surface water	North Carolina's significant efforts at controlling agricultural and urban runoff, using in part, a cost sharing program with farmers.
Pesticides	California's Birth Defects Prevention Act allowing the state to refuse to register pesticides for which there is a less environmentally damaging alternative available.
Indoor air	New Jersey's protection of areas by prohibiting smoking in "restaurants, workplaces, government buildings, public transportation, and health facilities."
Energy efficiency	Massachusetts' policies promoting energy conservation, least-cost electricity planning, appliance efficiency standards, and building code upgrades.

Source: Renew America. *The State of the States*, 1989. Washington, DC: Renew America.

promoting reduced-waste technology since 1977. This pattern of UNEP research, information sharing, and negotiation networking has also been used in addressing marine environment, water and land quality, forests, and biological diversity problems with some success.[18]

Another major UN effort directed at dealing with global environmental problems is the United Nation's Conference on the Environment and Development (UNCED), held in Rio de Janeiro in June 1992. This conference is the official worldwide environmental summit, following up on the 1972 UN Conference on the Human Environment, the first UN meeting explicitly recognizing that environmental protection was a global issue. UNCED's six-point agenda included a charter of principles; sustainable development in the twenty-first century; climate change; technology transfer; financial mechanisms; and institutions.

One especially controversial issue at the conference was the international trade in hazardous and toxic wastes. The transport and disposal of municipal wastes, such as sewage and industrial wastes containing heavy metals such as mercury and lead, is generally supported by waste-producing industrialized nations, but its receipt is being stringently regulated and banned outright by an increasing number of less-industrialized nations. For instance, since 1986, 83 nations have prevented the import of wastes, and the European Economic Community has banned the export of hazardous wastes to 67 African, Caribbean, and Pacific nations.

Other international institutions involved in business environmentalism issues include the World Bank, the Inter-American Development Bank, the Asian Development Bank, and the African Development Bank, sometimes categorized together under the title Multilateral Development Banks (MDBs). These institutions make low-interest loans to countries interested in further developing their respective economies. Some environmentalists have charged MDBs as being insensitive, at best, to ecological problems in their borrowing client countries, and as contributing to the environmental problems in these nations, at worst. Protests by GreenPeace and others have centered on MDB loans made to rainforest nations, which have been used for development projects, potentially contributing to deforestation in these countries. For example, in 1982, the World Bank loaned money to a company owned and managed by the Brazilian government to finance two dozen industrial projects dependent on charcoal for heat in one region of Eastern Amazonia. The required 1.1 million tons of charcoal per year were produced using a significant portion of the region's virgin tropical rainforest reserves. In addition to financing these forest-denigrating projects, MDBs have been charged with favoring energy supply rather than energy efficiency projects, with neglecting conservation-oriented efforts such as low-pesticide agriculture and solar cookstove and bicycle manufacturing, and with not including local communities adequately in the formulation and implementation of the projects financed by their loans.[19-21]

OTHER ENVIRONMENTAL STAKEHOLDERS

Environmental Interest Groups

Perhaps no force in today's society is more responsible for the "greening" of nations around the world than the many interest groups making up what has come to be known as "the environmental movement." These nonprofit, membership and think-tank organizations, such as GreenPeace and the World Resources Institute, respectively, have been credited with moving the world's governments and businesses, as well as publics, in the direction of environmental responsibility through a host of activities, including demonstrations, boycotts, public education, lobbying, and research.

The history of the environmental movement is instructive. While a few U.S. groups (the National Audubon Society, the Izaak Walton League, and the Sierra Club) were formed in the early 1900s during the first green wave of the century, many of the largest national or international environmental groups, such as the Environmental Defense Fund (EDF), GreenPeace, and the National Resources Defense Council (NRDC), were created during the second environmental wave, during the late 1960s and early 1970s. Since that time, all of the groups mentioned above and hundreds of other smaller, more locally focused environmental organizations have grown in size and clout. The century's third wave of environmentalism, beginning in the late 1980s, gave many of these groups the power and legitimacy to become credible players in environmental policy-making around the globe.

That environmental interest groups have grown in size and resources is undisputed. Since 1988, the number of members and the amount of revenues of the largest groups have increased significantly, for some doubling and tripling in just 3 years. GreenPeace, one of the more "radical" environmental groups, is one of the fastest growing organizations, with received information requests increasing from 1,000 per month to 1,000 per day during that time period[22] and membership increasing from 600,000 in 1987 to more than 1.8 million in 1989.[23] Another indication of the popularity of environmental groups is the subscription base and revenue generation capacity of the periodicals published by those involved in public education campaigns. Even in the face of new entrants in the environmental publications field, environmental group publications were one of the few periodical segments to weather the recession of 1990–1991.[24]

That environmental interest groups have more clout than ever in the early 1990s is also difficult to dispute. At this writing, the former president of the Conservation Law Foundation and World Wildlife Fund, William Reilly, is President Bush's Environmental Protection Agency administrator. Much of the Environmental Defense Fund's work on emissions trading was incorporated into the 1990s Clean Air Act. GreenPeace has scored a number of international environmental victories, including stopping French nuclear testing in the atmosphere, reducing toxic waste dumping and illegal whaling, and advancing the Antarctica protection cause.[25] The National Resources Defense Council forced the EPA, through a lawsuit settlement, to work for the Montreal Protocol, the international accord to phase out the use of CFCs faster than the administration originally had planned.[26]

Environmental interest groups have also been instrumental in significantly influencing business environmental policy in this third wave. EDF has coresearched and coplanned a comprehensive Waste Reduction Plan with the McDonald's Corporation, with the ultimate goal of reducing corporate-wide waste by 80 percent. The Conservation Law Foundation has worked with the Massachusetts-based Northeast Utilities to develop a far-reaching energy conservation program, and this has inspired dozens of state and local environmental organizations to become involved in what has become known as Least Cost Utility Planning efforts, which are multiparty negotiations at the state level that typically encourage utility energy conservation programs.

Other environmental interest group and business stakeholder relationships have included corporate selection of environmental group representatives for corporate boards and top management positions; mutual participation in environmental cleanup projects; and corporate donations of time and money to environmental groups for their environmental conservation programs. This trend toward cooperation between otherwise political adversaries is a characteristic of the third wave, which sets it apart from the two previous environmental eras. The chairman of the Sierra Club has identified three kinds of major U.S. environmental organizations based on this criterion of cooperation with business. He has labeled several groups as "radicals," characterized by confrontational behaviors; "mainstreamers," as groups that seek pragmatic reform through a combination of confrontation and cooperation; and "accommodators," who avoid confrontation and are more trusting of corporations. These categories and details of several of the groups in each are listed in Figure 12.4.

However, businesses and governments may want to consider that decisions to avoid engaging in such cooperative negotiation efforts with environmental groups in the 1990s may result in unproductive adversarial relationships with these organizations and their increasing constituencies. Toxic and hazardous waste producers, such as the nuclear power and petrochemical industries, respectively, appear especially vulnerable to "direct action," and other potentially embarrassing and costly situations, as do mineral and forest products and waste management firms. Managers in these high environmental exposure firms may want to consider improving their stakeholder relationships involving environmental organizations.

Green Consumers, Employees, and Investors

In addition to environmental groups, businesses are paying more attention to the latest green wave because of at least three other stakeholder groups—green consumers, employees, and investors. So-called "green" consumers are actual and potential customers of retail firms, usually in the industrialized countries, who express a preference for products, services, and companies that are perceived to be more "environment friendly" than other competitive products, services, and firms. Marketing research firms in these countries have identified a range of green consumerism, often segmenting these consumers into four or five roughly equal groups, based on the strength of these preferences and reported consumer purchases. These studies show that nearly half of all consumers surveyed say they purchase products specifically because the products or the companies are perceived to be "green."[27] Based on these survey results and the evidence that the media has picked up on this trend with increasing frequency, prudent business managers are advised not to ignore that many of their current and potential customers prefer "environment-friendly" products, services, and companies. The popularity of books such as *The Green Consumer* and a newsletter by the same name, the development of ecolabeling programs such as Blue Angel in Germany and Green Seal and Green Cross in the United States, and a flurry of new environmental catalogs led by the Vermont firm Seventh Generation attest to the emerging business reality that green consumerism is an important economic and social trend.

A second stakeholder group with which most businesses are concerned are employees. Although the popular press has not focused as much attention on "green" employees as it has on "green" consumers, there is some evidence that employees are playing a major role in promoting environmentalism at work. In

FIGURE 12-4   One View of U.S. Environmental Groups

Group Name	Founding Year	No. of Members	Budget
Radicals			
Environmental Action	1970	20,000	$1.2 Mil
Friends of the Earth	1969	50,000	$3.2 Mil
GreenPeace USA	1971	1,800,000	$50.1 Mil
Mainstreamers			
Environmental Defense Fund	1967	150,000	$15.0 Mil
National Resources Defense Fund	1970	160,000	$13.5 Mil
Sierra Club	1892	545,000	$28.0 Mil
National Wildlife Federation	1936	5,800,000	$79.0 Mil
Accommodators			
Nature Conservancy	1951	550,000	$109.0 Mil
World Wildlife Fund	1961	1,000,000	$50.0 Mil

Source: M. E. Kriz, "Shades of Green," *National Journal* (July 28, 1990), 1828.

addition to union and general employee environmental concerns with plant, warehouse, and office safety and health, employees in many companies have assisted management in going beyond these traditional concerns into areas such as pollution prevention, recycling, energy and environmental audits, and community environmental projects. Successful "Green Teams" have been operating at such diverse businesses as Goldman Sachs, Ace Hardware, Eastman Kodak, and Apple Computer.[28]

The 3M company in 1991 rewarded several employees for a number of environmental projects including the establishment of a public park for the preservation of a northern Minnesota waterfall and the development of a system to track hazardous solvent inventories in its St. Paul laboratories. Gail Mayville, an employee of Ben & Jerry's Homemade, Inc. Vermont-based frozen dessert company, was recognized with a Business Enterprise Trust award for beginning recycling programs in most departments throughout the company. Of course, employees in environmental units, which are increasing in number in major Western corporations, play a vital role in transforming their respective organizations into "greener" firms. A 3M corporation-wide Technical Forum on Environmentally Compatible Products and Processes in 1991 was initiated not by management but by technical specialists throughout the company. Environmental specialists of this kind are in very high demand, especially in the United States, with entry-level salaries at far higher levels in the early 1990s than was the case in the late 1980s.[29]

Alliances between organized labor and environmental groups are receiving increasing attention in the third green wave. Ecolabor coalitions have been forged in two areas especially: proposals for a workers' superfund and environmentally oriented international trade agreements. Both groups support the general idea of a workers' superfund, which would encourage corporations to fund a pool of money to finance workers who need to be retrained or relocated because of company responses to environmental regulations. The second issue, international trade, revolved around the question of whether high environmental standards are considered barriers to free trade. Both unions and environmental groups want to see high standards maintained in any international trade agreements (such as GATT and the North American Free Trade Agreement talks), to prevent job flight and cross-border pollution.[30]

Another important business stakeholder involved in environmental issues is the "green" investor. Similar to investors interested in advancing social causes, individuals and organizations sometimes want to "put their money where their environmental values are," by identifying and using financial instruments that are associated with environmentally oriented companies. For instance, in 1990, there were 14 mutual funds in the United States that had some type of environmental characteristics, eight of which dealt exclusively with this issue. In addition, a growing number of stock and bond offerings, as well as money market funds and other financial instruments, have included environmental components in recent years. Each of these investment options offers its clients the opportunity to advance one or more environmental

Chapter 12 ♦ Business and Stakeholder Responses to Environmental Challenges 353 interests (for example, recycling or solar energy development), without being penalized with lower-than-average financial returns.

Although this growing trend appears to be the perfect combination of ideals and practicality, there is one problem with these instruments. No commonly acceptable set of criteria yet exists for establishing whether a company financed by these investments is or is not environmentally beneficial. For example, some environmental mutual funds invest in Waste Management, Inc. because this firm is the largest collector of recyclables in the United States, while others shun Waste Management because of its millions of dollars of environmental, criminal, and antitrust violations.[31]

After the Exxon *Valdez* oil spill, a number of environmental, labor, and social investor groups developed a preamble and a set of 10 policy statements called the Valdez Principles, which have been advanced as models for business to express and practice environmental sensitivity. Excerpts from these principles are listed in Figure 12-5 and have been adopted by such companies as Ben & Jerry's Homemade, Inc., the Herman Miller Company, and Earth Care Paper.

The Role of Women in Environmental Issues

Women, both as individuals and as organization leaders and members, may have the opportunity to play a significant role in advancing global environmental values. This opportunity gained significant attention just before, during, and after the UNEP World Women's Congress for a Healthy Planet held in Miami in November 1991. This conference identified more than 200 important and successful environmental projects initiated by women around the globe. The projects included the establishment of scientifically trained ecocounselors throughout Europe, ecotourism co-ops in Greece, an environmental literacy campaign in Mexico, and an organic gardening project in the San Francisco County Jail.

A number of writers on the environment have suggested that women are more environmentally sensitive than men and that this observation can be accounted for by both biological and socioeconomic factors. Regarding the biological factor, women are most deeply affected by environmental contaminants such as radiation and toxic chemicals that affect their ability to bear and nurse healthy children. Concerning the social and economic factors, women in industrialized countries are still more likely to have family responsibilities for consumer purchasing and for maintaining a hygienic and safe home environment, while women in the less-industrialized world must often gather food and fuel for heating and cooking and pump the water for drinking and cleaning purposes. Whatever the rationale, most polls taken during the third green wave have shown women to be more environmentally conscious than men in general and to favor government, business, and individual practices that are more safety- and health-oriented.[32,33]

By adopting these principles, we publicly affirm our belief that corporations and their shareholders have a direct responsibility for the environment. We believe that corporations must conduct their business as responsible stewards of the environment and seek profits only in a manner that leaves the Earth healthy and safe. . . . We intend to make consistent, measurable progress in implementing these principles and to apply them wherever we operate throughout the world.

1. Protection of the Biosphere: We will minimize and strive to eliminate the release of any pollutant that may cause environmental damage to the air, water, or earth or its inhabitants. . . .

2. Sustainable Use of Natural Resources: We will make sustainable use of renewable natural resources, such as water, soils and forests. . . . We will protect wildlife habitat, open spaces and wilderness, while preserving biodiversity.

3. Reduction and Disposal of Waste: We will minimize the creation of waste, especially hazardous waste, and wherever possible recycle materials. We will dispose of all wastes through safe and responsible methods.

4. Wise Use of Energy: We will make every effort to use environmentally safe and sustainable energy sources to meet our needs. We will invest in improved energy efficiency and conservation in our operations. . . .

5. Risk Reduction: We will minimize the environmental, health and safety risks to our employees and the communities in which we operate by employing safe technologies and operating procedures and by being constantly prepared for emergencies.

6. Marketing of Safe Products and Services: We will sell products or services that minimize adverse environmental impacts and that are safe as consumers commonly use them. . . .

7. Damage Compensation: We will take responsibility for any harm we cause to the environment by making every effort to fully restore the environment and to compensate those persons who are adversely affected.

8. Disclosure: We will disclose to our employees and to the public incidents relating to our operations that cause environmental harm or pose health or safety hazards. . . .

9. Environmental Directors and Managers: We will commit management resources to implement the Valdez Principles, to monitor and report upon our implementation efforts, and to sustain a process to ensure that the Board of Directors and Chief Executive Officer are kept informed of and are fully responsible for all environmental matters. . . .

10. Assessment and Annual Audit: We will conduct and make public an annual self-evaluation of our progress in implementing these Principles and in complying with all applicable laws and regulations throughout our worldwide operations. . . .

Source: CERES, *Valdez Principles* (Boston: The Social Investment Forum, 1989).

FIGURE 12-5 Valdez Principles 1990

BUSINESS ENVIRONMENTALISM

Coping with environmental challenges is nothing new to businesses and other organizations in both the industrialized and less-industrialized worlds. Indeed, if agriculture and agricultural product trading are seen as early human business activities, one could argue that human organizations have needed to develop and implement responses to environmental challenges since very early in their evolution. Sun, wind, rain, soil, and pests posed significant environmental demands on early human organizations. Unwise farming practices and overgrazing of livestock were two early business-caused environmental challenges. The industrial and postindustrial revolutions, however, wrought manifold increases in human-related pollution and degradation. In addition, the pressure of human population and urbanization, the latter associated with real estate, commercial, and financial organizations, increased the challenges of natural disasters, through human settlements of floodplains, along hurricane and volcanic eruption paths, in structures ill-equipped to withstand tornados and other dangerous weather conditions, and, generally, in encroachment on "wild" wilderness areas.

The responses to these environmental challenges by business and related organizations were relatively limited until very recently. In the United States, before 1970, most of this response was either voluntary, characterized by participation in antilitter campaigns and support for a limited number of "outdoors" organizations such as the Boy Scouts, or in response to court cases originating out of nuisance and tort common law. With the enactment of the National Environmental Policy Act and similar legislation at the state levels, regulation and the threat of regulation became increasingly important as motivation of business responses. The 3M company in 1975 was one of the earliest large U.S.-based businesses to adopt an environmental policy and program.

Examples of Business Environmentalism

With the third and latest wave of environmentalism to wash over the industrialized world in this century, the dam of business environmentalism burst forth. By late 1991, it was common for multinational corporations to appear to be involved in some voluntary environmentally related activity. Of course, many businesses in the United States and other developed nations need to comply with a number of laws at various levels designed to protect some aspect of the natural environment. In addition, however, several business organizations have developed programs that have progressed well beyond mere compliance with environmental regulation.

The 3M company is perhaps the best-known multinational company to have adopted a comprehensive, beyond compliance, environmental policy and program. Begun in 1975, 3M's Pollution Prevent Pays program is a manufacturing multiproduct and multiprocess approach that has saved more than $500 million for the company by reducing various pollutants at their source. Through product reformulation, process modification, equipment redesign, and waste recycling, 3M has prevented thousands of tons of air, water, and land pollutants from being produced and subsequently discharged. 3M gives the credit (and financial reward) for these environmental successes to its employees, who developed more than 2,500 subprojects under this program. In 3M's innovative fashion, the firm has begun a new program—3P-Plus—which set new goals to reduce its hazardous and nonhazardous air, water, and land releases by 90 percent more and limit its waste generation 50 percent more by the year 2000. An interim goal focusing on a 70 percent reduction in air pollutants, 3M's most common pollution problem, was pegged for 1993.[34]

Other good examples of business environmentalism have been identified by four awards programs, focusing on outstanding environmental efforts by business. The first of these awards programs, the Business Enterprise Trust, is an organization that highlights businesses and individuals in businesses who make substantial social contributions and are selected as examples for the business community to follow. In 1991, two of the several business winning awards included Merck & Co. for donating one of its drugs to combat an African blindness disease caused by insects, and an employee at Ben & Jerry's Homemade who single-handedly started a companywide recycling program for this frozen dessert maker and its franchisees.[35]

The second awards program, designed and implemented by Renew America (mentioned earlier), makes announcement awards to both profit and nonprofit organizations. In 1991, this program identified several dozen U.S. businesses with some kind of business environmentalism program. Figure 12-6 identifies a number of these business award winners.

A third awards program, this one sponsored by the President's Council on Environmental Quality (CEQ), identified several business organizations' meeting their environmental criteria, including the *LA Times*, for its 50 percent-plus recycled paper content; Pacific Gas & Electric, for its energy conservation programs; and the Environmental Media Association of Culver City, California, for its public environmentalism awareness programs.[36]

A fourth business environmentalism awards program, the Better Environment Awards for Industry program, promoted by the Confederation of British Industry and the Financial Times, gave recognition to Imperial Chemicals Industries for its development of water pollution technology to handle chlorine discharges, British Petroleum Chemicals for its development of an environment-friendly airport runway deicer, and the Body Shop for its incorporation of environmental concern throughout its personal care products operations.[37]

In addition to these awards programs, the list of organizations identified as "green businesses" is an ever-lengthening one. Paul Shrivastava, an authority on business environmentalism, identified GM's efforts at fuel efficiency and auto pollution control, DuPont's 35 percent waste reduction, McDonald's intention to use recycled products in restaurant construction and remodeling, and Chevron's industry-leading low oil-spill rate as further examples of this movement toward addressing the environmental challenge by big business.[38]

The Green Lights program, a voluntary, nonregulatory program administered by the EPA to encourage major U.S. corporations to install energy-efficient lighting, had, by the end of 1990, already enlisted 22 companies, including Amoco, Eli Lilly, and Polaroid to participate. Industry associations, as diverse as the American Bakers Association to the American Paper Institute, have begun working with rather than against the U.S. EPA in developing environmental legislation and regulations.[39] One association, the Chemical Manufacturers' of America, has developed a set of 10 environmental principles called the Responsible Care program, which has been adopted by a number of large chemical firms. Although this environmental policy set falls far short of the Valdez Principles in scope and specificity, it does include an affirmation to "participate with government and others in creating responsible laws, regulations and standards to safeguard the community, workplace and environment."[40]

Small businesses, too, are promoting "green" products and services. Body-wares, a two-store personal care products company based in Washington, DC, mixes and sells skin moisturizers and cleansers that are made from nonsynthetic bases and are not tested on animals. In addition, this retailer encourages its customers to return its plastic product bottles for refills and discounts. Another

FIGURE 12-6 Examples of Corporate Environmental Policies and Programs

Company	Environmental Action
AT&T	Will eliminate all CFC emissions by 1994
Whirlpool	Recycles CFCs used in its freezers and refrigerators
DuPont	Voluntarily withdrew a fungicide from farm use because of health risks to farmers
Monsanto	Will reduce its toxic air emissions by 90% by 1992
Boeing	Increased the amount of waste it recycles in-house to 50%
Bankers Trust	Assisted in a debt-for-nature swap in the Philippines
KSSN Radio (Arkansas)	Established a promotional campaign with a theme of good land stewardship
Potomac Electric Power	Reintroduction of fish species on its marsh-like property; involvement in shoreline erosion control of Chesapeake Bay
Valvoline Oil	Established more than 300 used motor oil recycling centers.

Source: *Environmental Success Index*, Washington, DC: Renew America, 1991.

environmental entrepreneurial effort, Ecotech Autoworks in McLean, Virginia, offers one of the few "green" auto repair shops in the United States. Ecotech recycles all car fluids, especially CFC-containing air conditioning fluid, and uses recycled auto parts at customer request. In addition, this innovative service uses recycled-tire shop floor mats and carbon monoxide-absorbing hanging spider plants and offers a full range of environmental magazines in the customer waiting room.[41]

The "greening" of business has certainly not been limited to corporations based in the Unites States and Great Britain. Japanese and continental European firms, too, have begun to preach and practice a more environmentally conscious attitude in the third green wave. More than 300 large Japanese corporations had environmental planning departments in 1991, and, also in that year, a network of 40 Japanese companies, the Nippon Eco Life Center, was formed to facilitate the exchange of information on the natural environment and on green businesses. In addition to Toyota's campaign to produce a solar-powered car and Mitsubishi's Malaysian rainforest reforestation effort, one prominent environmental program established by a Japanese firm is the environmental credit card of the Daiei Supermarket group. This program, which was designed by two well-known Japanese environmental groups, allows the grocery consumer who uses one of these cards to direct 0.5 percent of the grocery bill to any one of 20 different environmental causes.[42] Other examples of Japanese business environmentalism programs include businesses such as Sanyo's plans to use recycled paper instead of plastic foam as packing material and the Japanese Automobile Manufacturers' Association's establishment of standards to mark plastic car parts for easy classification and dismantling for later recycling.[43]

Business environmentalism is also blossoming on the European continent. In Germany, a multi-industry recycling association made up of 95 companies and trade associations has been formed to accept and recycle a variety of packages that will be returned for deposit. The Swiss chemical company Ciba-Geigy has adopted an environmental policy statement, called Vision 2000, which gives equal weight to economic, social, and environmental responsibilities and has put into practice its Oekogenda (Eco-Agenda), providing environmental goals for each department and individual supervisor. The French steel company Usinor Sacilor S.A. is studying the environmental effects of steel cans and car bodies. Several European carmakers are attempting to design their cars for easy recyclability.

Systematic Business Responses to the Environmental Challenge

Business, as the major economic sector in most developed economies, has begun to address environmental issues in a number of ways. These responses have been categorized by several business/environment writers. As shown in Figure 12-7, two of these response classification schemes are similar to that used on the corporate social responsiveness axis of the three-dimensional corporate social performance model, presented in Chapter 2. The message this figure indicates is that businesses can be categorized on environmental responsiveness dimensions, so the prudent business manager is advised to determine how he or she wants his or her business to be perceived by others before selecting an environmental management strategy.

A number of management tools are available in selecting or constructing an environmental strategy. These include several management approaches that will be discussed in more general terms in other chapters and a few that are specific to natural environment issues. In the first group are crisis management, issues management, and stakeholder management. Because these topics are more fully addressed in later chapters, only their applicability to environmental management will be discussed here. In the second group of decision-making tools are cost-benefit analysis, risk management, and strategic environmental management, which will be discussed more fully in this chapter.

Generic Management Decision-Making Tools. Managers can use crisis management in the environmental area by focusing on two factors: prevention and contingency plans. As can be seen in the Exxon *Valdez* case, neither Exxon, Alyeska, nor the federal or state governments apparently paid enough attention to preventing the 1989 Alaskan oil spill disaster or to implementing the inadequate

FIGURE 12-7 Environmental Management Classification Schemes

Wilson's Social Responsiveness Categories	Mathew's Green, Inc.	Hunt & Auster's Environmental Management
Reactive	Exploit the green fad while it lasts	Beginner: Environmental management is unnecessary Fire Fighter: Address environmental issues only as necessary
Defensive	Environmentalism can sometimes be good for business	Concerned Citizen: Environmental management is a worthwhile function
Accommodative	Environmentalism is here to stay	Pragmatist: Environmental management is an important business function
Proactive	The environment is a strategic business opportunity	Proactivist: Environmental management is a priority item

Sources: 1. Wilson, 1975. "What one company is doing about today's demands on business." In G. Steiner, (ed.), UCLA Conference on Changing Business-Society Relationships. Los Angeles: Graduate School of Management; J. Mathews, 1991. "Green, Inc.," *The Washington Post*, March 15, A23; and C. B. Hunt and E. R. Auster, 1990. "Proactive Environmental Management: Avoiding the Toxic Trap," *Sloan Management Review* (Winter), 9.

contingency plan to recover the oil once it was spilled. Although some attention was paid to the vulnerability of the Alaskan natural environment to a small potential oil spill, this appeared to be understated and generally ignored. That Exxon or Alyeska assessed their own vulnerability to a spill of any size appears doubtful. Finally, the lack of coordination between the two companies in immediately addressing the spill indicated a response plan that was only a paper tiger, never really put into practice. Had the businesses and governments followed basic crisis management principles, including vulnerability assessments and simulation drills, the outcome may have been different for both these organizations and for Prince William Sound.

Issues management can be employed to track public interest in natural environment issues and to develop and implement plans to attempt to ensure that the scope of environmental problems is minimized and that the firm develops effective responses at each stage in the life cycle of environmental issues. Environmental issues can be developed as part of the environmental impact statement process or as part of the strategic planning macroenvironmental analysis process.

Similarly, stakeholder management applies to environmental management in that environmental stakeholders and their stakes can be identified, including the environmental public, environmental regulators, environmental groups, and various entities (human and nonhuman) in the entire natural environment. The follow-up stages of stakeholder management, that is, planning for and interacting with stakeholders, can then be conducted, so that each important environmental stakeholder is given adequate attention after it is identified.

While crisis management, issues management, and stakeholder management can be used as generic approaches to environmental management, several more traditional management approaches that have been used in the past specifically to decide natural environment issues include cost-benefit analysis and risk management.

Cost-Benefit Analysis. Although the first cost-benefit analysis has been used in other areas, especially those related to public and private capital budgeting and investment, it has also received an extraordinary amount of attention in natural environmental policy decisions. For instance, most environmental impact statements, required by the National Environmental Policy Act, have one or more cost-benefit analyses as the basis for many of the environmental decisions resulting from these studies. The idea behind cost-benefit analysis is that, in a rational planning situation, an organization wants to ensure that an environmental project is worth the investment. Costs are totaled and compared to overall benefits; if benefits are sufficiently greater than costs, the project is given the go-ahead. If not, it is shelved, revised, or scrapped. Decision makers in many dam projects, other water reclamation projects, and land development projects in the United States have used cost-benefit analysis to determine the value of these environmentally oriented projects.

Although this approach sounds straightforward, a number of problems have been identified. First, measuring all costs and all benefits of a proposed action is often very difficult. What will the costs be to an ecosystem if a species is pressured into extinction? What is the benefit or value of wilderness? Second, comparing costs and benefits has been problematic, since these are not always in the same units. How does one compare the advantages of a commercial or light industrial development with the loss of scenic beauty and wildlife habitats? Finally, costs can accrue to one party, while another party receives the benefits. For instance, a real estate firm wishing to develop residential property may be prevented from earning profits (an opportunity cost), while an ecosystem and its species accrue the benefit of continued existence (or vice versa). One typical way to handle this generic inequality has been through side payments to right the balance. However, humans have not yet devised a system for "paying back" the natural environment for problems they have caused.

Given these significant weaknesses, how can the prudent manager use cost-benefit analysis as a tool in addressing the environmental challenge? First, attempting to identify and measure costs and benefits can be helpful in using other decision methodologies, for instance, stakeholder management. Costs and benefits in this way can be thought of as negative and positive stakes. Second, if any costs and benefits can be compared, the trade-off between these can in some cases serve to simplify the often complex decisions involved in environmental management. However, the shortcomings of cost-benefit analysis appear to warrant continuous attention and require the use of additional environmental decision methods.

Risk Management. Risk management is a second managerial decision-making tool currently being employed by organizations attempting to address the environmental challenge. This approach is similar to cost-benefit analysis in that quantified trade-offs are made to decide whether an environmental project or program is worth developing and implementing. The difference with this method, however, is that risk of environmental damage (to ecosystems, nonhuman species, or humans) is substituted for either costs or benefits. In this scheme, the relevant decision questions are, "How much should be invested to reduce the risk of environmental damage from our business activity?" or "How much environmental risk is acceptable to receive the benefits of an economic development activity?" The difficulties with this decision technique are similar to those of cost-benefit analyses; that is, how can risk (especially long-term risks) be measured, and how can it be appropriately compared to costs or benefits? For instance, even if the risk of a nuclear meltdown could be measured and found to be a small probability, would this risk assessment matter to community residents who would be neighbors of the proposed nuclear power plant? Again, the caveats are suggested that the disadvantages of using this method in environmental decisions are best kept in mind and that additional criteria be incorporated into decision frameworks involving the natural environment.

Because they are quantification-oriented methodologies, both cost-benefit analyses and risk management appear inappropriate for many environmental decisions. Science often lacks the quantified data that would allow us to estimate carrying capacities, thresholds, and long-term effects to work into our cost-benefit or risk calculations. "Wicked" problems, such as the effects of global warming or the adequacy of nuclear waste storage, often require qualitative data from a wide spectrum of perspectives for their "resolution." Exclusive reliance on either approach, quantitative or qualitative, appears unwise in environmental decision making.

Strategic Environmental Management. The final managerial approach to addressing the business environmental challenge presented here is a well-known organization effectiveness tool that has been adapted by the authors to assist managers in developing and implementing overall approaches to natural environment issues. This model is called Strategic Environmental Management (SEM) and is forwarded as one way organizations can readily respond to their environmental challenges and integrate a wide range of responses for environmental effectiveness.

As can be seen in Figure 12-8, this method uses the McKinsey 7S framework, in which seven typical organizational components necessary for success are identified and integrated, and several "green" suggestions are given for each "S." Businesses can build environmental components into their superordinate goals, strategies, structures, and so on, in order to develop an organization-wide environmental response. Superordinate goals can include an emphasis on environmental protection in a company's mission statement, for instance, while one of its strategies can be developing or acquiring environmentally sensitive businesses. The key to using this model is for managers to identify opportunities for developing environmental responses in each of the "S" categories and to ensure that each of these responses is compatible with the others.

Using this approach, the environmental manager can incorporate concern for the environment and take environmentally sensitive actions in all organization departments and at all organizational levels. For instance, the *shared value of waste minimization* can translate into the low-cost *strategy*, enhanced by environmental quality circles *structures*, energy conservation *systems* in manufacturing facilities, and environmentally skilled *staff* personnel who are motivated by incentives for meeting personal environmental objectives and by managers exhibiting an environmentally sensitive *style*. As mentioned in the previous chapters, all organizational departments can play a role in the organization's interaction with the natural environment. Research and development departments can work with manufacturing personnel to alter their products and processes to limit pollution and depletion. Finance and accounting personnel can develop effective environmental auditing systems and cost out the potential for environmentally damaging projects, with the aim to reduce this as much as possible. Human resources managers can begin to incorporate environmental concerns in their recruitment and training programs, attempting to build an "environmental culture" in the

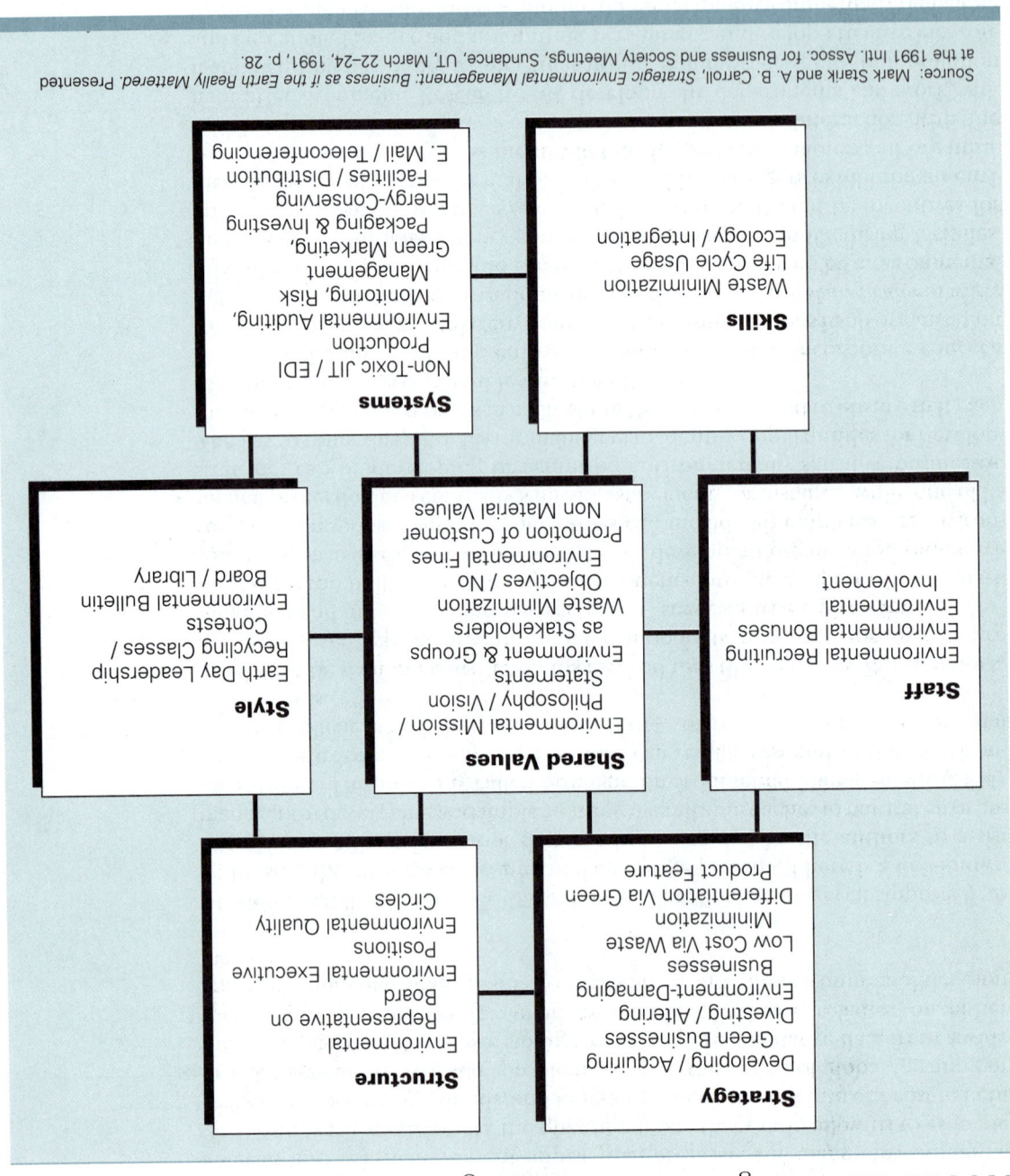

FIGURE 12-8 Strategic Environmental Management (SEM)

Source: Mark Stark and A. B. Carroll, Strategic Environmental Management: Business as if the Earth Really Mattered. Presented at the 1991 Int'l. Assoc. for Business and Society Meetings, Sundance, UT, March 22–24, 1991, p. 28.

THE FUTURE OF BUSINESS: GREENING AND/OR GROWING?

Although the movie *Wall Street* focused on the ethical problem of insider trading, it also highlighted the salient environmental question we all may need to address in the future: "How much is enough?" A common business and public policy goal in most human societies has been economic growth. Typically, businesses and societies have needed increasing amounts of either material or energy or both to achieve that economic growth. Limits to growth, similar to limits to human reproduction, at either the macro or micro level, have not been widely popular. One potential problem with unrestrained economic growth worldwide is that, unless technology or people change significantly within a generation, environmental problems could change in degree from significant to severe.

World population is projected to continue to increase, potentially requiring greater demands on world food and fuel resources. Both industrialized and less-industrialized nations may contribute to this dilemma. The West and Japan continue to use increasing amounts of materials and energy to maintain highly consumptive life-styles, while the rest of the world continues to use these developed nations as models for their own development. Given that the typical industrialized country resident uses 15 times more paper, 10 times more steel, and 12 times as much fuel as a typical Third World resident,[44] one can see the looming problem on the horizon. Combined with the Third World's population increase (approximately one billion more humans by the end of this decade), this quest

organization. Marketers can identify their customers' "real needs," as opposed to their frivolous (and potentially environmentally damaging) desires for products and services, and adjust their distribution systems in transportation, packaging, and labeling to promote environmental sensitivity.

The authors identified two well-known organizations that appear to have come closest to developing this strategic view of the environmental challenge: 3M with its 3P-Plus policy statement and programs mentioned earlier in this chapter, and the Body Shop, which builds its entire business around environmental protection and conservation, from using bicycles for delivery to allowing employees to volunteer for environmental projects on company time. The limitations of the SEM approach are similar to those of the McKinsey 7S model itself. These include a decidedly internal orientation (nonorganization stakeholders or forces are not explicitly emphasized) and a potential for much complexity. The prudent manager, once again, is advised to remember these weaknesses and to supplement this method with others mentioned in this section. The stakeholder management approach, with its external focus, might be a good match for the more internal SEM focus. Indeed, an eighth "S" that could be added to this model is "stakeholders," which could include environmentally oriented suppliers, customers, investors, and regulators, as well as the natural environment itself.

SUMMARY

In this chapter and the last, we have explored a number of environmental challenges and several actual and potential responses to these issues. What themes appear to be woven throughout these chapters that can be especially helpful to prospective managers? First, many scientists, policymakers, public interest groups, individuals, and businesses recognize that the natural environment is crucial for human survival and that a number of complex and interconnected human-induced actions may be threatening this environment. Problems such as deforestation, pollution, and expanding populations are potentially endangering nonhuman species and ecosystems and reducing quality of life for humans. Individuals and their organizations, including businesses, were found to be directly or indirectly responsible for this situation.

Second, there are significant differences of opinion on how these problems will develop in the future and what should be done to resolve these issues. The facts that nature continues to evolve and human knowledge and actions regarding nature also continuously change argue against an "ecological correctness" approach. Instead, individuals and organizations, including businesses, concerned about reducing environmental degradation might adopt a flexible and prudent approach to keeping themselves informed and taking actions, no matter how small, in the direction of "walking lightly on the Earth." A minimum baseline of not increasing human-caused pollution and depletion may be a potential start for consensus building and environmental consciousness.

This chapter began with a discussion of environmental responsibility, identifying the NIMBY problem of nonresponsibility as a significant factor in human individual and organizational decision making. We discussed the meaning of environmental ethics and several different sets of environmental values. The role of governments in the United States and elsewhere regarding environmental problems was explored, and the necessity for involving other environmental stakeholders, such as environmental interest groups, consumers, employees, and investors, was advised. We presented numerous examples of business environmentalism and several generic and specific models managers might use in making more effective environmental management decisions. Finally, we raised the issue of continued economic growth and suggested that managers continue to explore environmental issues and to consider reducing negative environmental impacts related to their organizations.

DISCUSSION QUESTIONS

1. Who has responsibility for addressing environmental issues?
2. How can ethics be applied to responses to environmental issues?
3. How have nonbusiness organizations responded to environmental challenges?
4. What are some examples of business environmentalism and decision models for addressing environmental concerns?
5. Should businesses and societies continue to focus on unlimited economic growth?

ENDNOTES

1. Mason, R. O. and Mitroff, I. I., *Challenging Strategic Planning Assumptions* (New York: Wiley, 1981), 12–13.
2. Council on Environmental Quality, *Environmental Quality* (Washington, DC: U.S. Government Printing Office, 1990), XV.
3. Editors, "A Heretic Amid Economic Orthodoxy," *Science* (June 17, 1988), 1611.
4. Dunlap, R. E., "Public Opinion in the 1980s: Clear Consensus, Ambiguous Commitment," *Environment* (Vol. 33, No. 8, 1991), 10–15, 32–37.
5. Irvine, S. and Ponton, A., *A Green Manifesto* (London: Optima, 1988), 14–16.
6. Ibid., 16.
7. Dunlap, R. E. and VanLiere, K. D., "The New Environmental Paradigm," *The Journal of Environmental Education* (Vol. 9, No. 4, 1978), 10–19.
8. Public Law 91-190 (1969), 42 U.S.C. Section 4331 et seq.
9. McAdams, T., *Law, Business, and Society*, 3d ed. (Homewood, IL: Irwin, 1992), 779–783.
10. Reed, O. L., *The Legal Environment of Business* (New York: McGraw-Hill, 1987), 697–703.
11. McAdams, 784–787.
12. Reed, 704–706.
13. McAdams, 788–792.
14. Reed, 709–712.
15. Foster, D., "Endangered Species," *The Associated Press* (April 12, 1991), 0020.
16. Egan, T., "U.S. Declares Owl to Be Threatened by Heavy Logging," *The New York Times* (June 23, 1990), 10.
17. Renew America, *The State of the States, 1989* (Washington, DC: Renew America, 1989), 2, 29.
18. United Nations Environment Programme, *UNEP Profile* (Nairobi, Kenya: United Nations Environment Programme, 1990), 4–20.
19. Postel, S. and Flavin, C., "Reshaping the Global Economy," in Brown, L. R. et al., *State of the World, 1991* (New York: Norton, 1991), 75.
20. Corson, E. H. (ed.), *The Global Ecology Handbook* (Boston: Beacon Press, 1990), 58.
21. Rich, B. M., "The 'Greening' of the Development Banks: Rhetoric and Reality," *The Ecologist* (Vol. 19, No. 2, 1989), 44–52.
22. Weisskopf, M., "From Fringe to Political Mainstream," *The Washington Post* (April 19, 1990), A1.
23. Sterne, D., "Many Environmental Groups Slow to React to Growth, Some Critics Say," *The NonProfit Times* (Vol. 4, No. 1, 1990), 1, 16–17.
24. Thompson, A., "Environmental Magazines Defy Slump," *The Wall Street Journal* (September 10, 1991), B1, 4.
25. Naar, J., *Design for a Livable Planet* (New York: Harper & Row, 1990), 264–265.
26. Weisskopf, A16.
27. Gutfeld, R., "Eight of 10 Americans Are Environmentalists, At Least They Say So," *Wall Street Journal* (Vol. 228, No. 24, 1991), A1.
28. Makower, J., "Green Teams," *The Green Business Letter* (November 6, 1991), 1.
29. Nazario, S. L., "Green Field: Environmental Engineers Command High Pay, Choice Assignments," *Wall Street Journal* (October 21, 1991), B1.
30. Ahlberg, B., "Green Around the Blue Collar?" *Utne Reader* (July/August, 1991), 44–45.
31. Rose, R. A., "Environmental Investing," *Garbage* (September/October, 1990), 48–53.
32. DiPerna, P., "Truth vs. Facts," *Ms* (Vol. 11, No. 2, 1991), 21–26.
33. Dean, T., "Environment: Global Assembly of Women Offers Success Stories," *Inter Press Service* (November 4, 1991).
34. *3M's Pollution Prevention Pays: An Initiative for a Cleaner Tomorrow* (St. Paul, MN: 3M Company, 1991).
35. James O'Toole, "Do Good, Do Well: The Business Enterprise Trust Awards," *California Management Review* (Spring, 1991), 9–24.

36. Staff Writer, "Bush Gives Times a Medal for Environmental Work," *Los Angeles Times* (November 1, 1991).
37. Hunt, J., "Winners Announced Today," *Financial Times* (March 13, 1991), IV.
38. Shrivastava, P., "Corporate Self-Greenewal: Strategic Responses to Environmentalism," Presented at the Eleventh Annual International Strategic Management Society Conference, Toronto (October 23–26, 1991).
39. Staroba, K., "Environment: Truth, Outrage, and the American Way," *Association Management* (September, 1991), 39–41.
40. Chemical Manufacturers' Association. *Responsible Care: Guiding Principles* (Washington, DC: CMA, 1991).
41. Sadler, J., "Going for the Green," *The Wall Street Journal* (November 22, 1991), R13.
42. Porter, D., "A Greening Corporate Image—Japan Business Survey," Advertising supplement to the *Wall Street Journal* (September 23, 1991), B12.
43. Porter, D., "Recycling Is a New Resource," Advertising supplement to the *Wall Street Journal* (September 23, 1991), B12.
44. Durning, A., "Asking How Much Is Enough," in Brown, L. R. *State of the World, 1991* (New York: Norton, 1991), 161.
45. Lippman, T. W., "Energy That Both Develops and Depletes the World," *Washington Post National Weekly Edition* (January 28, 1991), 18.

CHAPTER THIRTEEN

Community Stakeholders

CHAPTER OBJECTIVES

After studying this chapter, you should be able to:

- Identify and discuss two basic ways of business giving.

- Describe reasons for community involvement, various types of community projects, and management of community stakeholders.

- Explain the pros and cons of corporate philanthropy, provide a brief history of it, and explain why and to whom companies give.

- Differentiate between strategic philanthropy and cause-related marketing.

- Characterize the nature, magnitude, and reasons for the plant-closing issue.

- Address steps that business might take before a plant-closing decision is made.

- Identify strategies that business might employ after a plant-closing decision is made.

COMMUNITY INVOLVEMENT

Perhaps one of the best explanations of why business should be interested in its community is given by Robert Cushman, president of Norton Company in Worcester, Massachusetts. He asserts in one of his company's employee manuals:

When we speak of a community, we usually mean the immediate locale—the town, city, or state—in which a business resides. In our modern age of instantaneous communication and speedy travel, however, the region, the nation, or even the world can become the relevant community. After Union Carbide experienced its 1984 Bhopal disaster, corporate executives felt that Bhopal suddenly became part of their world. This feeling has lingered for years. As global competition increasingly characterizes the nature of business activities, the corporate stake in community involvement will broaden and intensify. Traditional geographical boundaries will be eclipsed by communication technology and travel. The community of the near future, therefore, will encompass the world.

When we think of business and its community stakeholders, two major kinds of relationships come to mind. One is the positive contributions business can make to the community. Examples of these positive contributions include volunteerism, company contributions, and support of programs in education, culture, urban development, the arts, civic activities, and other health and welfare endeavors. On the other hand, business can cause harm to community stakeholders. It can pollute the environment, close a plant, abuse its power, and exploit consumers and employees.

Issues regarding business's community stakeholders could legitimately be discussed in depth. In this chapter we will concentrate on community involvement and corporate philanthropy as community stakeholder concerns. In addition, we will discuss business and plant closings as a community stakeholder issue. This coverage should provide us with an opportunity to explore both the positive and the detrimental effects that characterize business and community relationships.

In addition to being profitable, obeying the law, and being ethical, a company may create a positive impact in the community by giving in basically two ways: (1) donating the time and talents of its managers and employees and (2) making financial contributions. The first category manifests itself in a wide array of voluntary activities in the community. The second category involves corporate philanthropy. We should note that there is significant overlap between these two categories because companies quite frequently give their resources, time, and talents to the same general projects. First, we will discuss community involvement and the various kinds of ways that companies enhance the quality of life in their communities.

Business does not operate in a vacuum, but as a social institution interacting with other social institutions. What business does affects its community; in turn, the people's goodwill and trust are essential for business to fulfill its primary role, which is to provide goods and services. . . . Therefore, business must—not only for a healthier society, but for its own well-being—be willing to give serious consideration to human needs as it does to the needs for production and profits.[1]

Beyond this general statement, Cushman enumerates six reasons for business involvement in the community:

1. Business people are efficient problem solvers.
2. Employees gain satisfaction and improved morale from involvement in community programs.
3. A positive image in your community helps in hiring.
4. Often a company gains prestige and greater acceptance in a community when it gets actively involved.
5. Social responsibility in business is the alternative to government regulation.
6. Business helps itself by supporting those institutions that are essential to the continuation of business.

Obviously, it is practical for business to be involved in the community. It is quite appropriate for business to help itself in the process of helping others. This dual objective of business efforts clearly illustrates that profits and social concerns are not mutually exclusive endeavors. Other rationales for business involvement in community affairs could be given, but they would not add much to what has been said. As we look at business motives for corporate giving, additional insights will be suggested.

When we think about business involvement with the community, we cannot help but wonder what business really *ought* to be doing in the community. One view addressing this question is presented in Figure 13-1.

It is clear from the statement in Figure 13-1 that business has a public responsibility to build a relationship with the community and be sensitive to its impacts in the community. An example of a corporation that is publicly pursuing this philosophy is NCR. In 1987, NCR began running a series of ads in *Fortune* that focused on its relationships with its stakeholders. In each of the ads, the following statement was set forth: "NCR's Mission: Create Value for Our Stakeholders." Following this was specific mention of communities, employees, shareholders, and suppliers as stakeholder groups. In the community ad, NCR stated, "We are committed to being caring and supportive corporate citizens within the worldwide communities in which we operate."

Chapter 13 ◆ Community Stakeholders 371

Various Community Projects

To provide an appreciation of the kinds of community projects that businesses get involved in, Figure 13-2 summarizes the wide spectrum of activities reported as most frequently pursued by firms in the insurance industry. It is difficult to gather this kind of information from business in general. Thus, we report what insurance companies are doing because they have for years systematically gathered these kinds of statistics through the Center for Corporate Public Involvement, sponsored by the American Council of Life Insurance and the Health Insurance Association of America. We will get a better appreciation of what business, in general, is doing when we examine statistics on business giving that closely parallels community projects. It is worth noting in Figure 13-2 that, in the types of projects reported, there is a remarkable stability over a period of years.

Literacy Programs. Several other community involvement projects illustrate the range and variety of business voluntarism in the community. *Literacy programs* have become a popular corporate cause in the past decade. As evidence of the degree to which American adults are functionally illiterate becomes increasingly available, companies have begun dedicating personnel and money to the growing problem. The U.S. Department of Education estimates that 25 million American adults—one in seven—are functionally illiterate. They cannot read such simple instructions as "In an emergency, pull lever." It is estimated that about 2.3 million people a year are added to the list of the functionally illiterate.[2]

FIGURE 13-1 The Business-Community Relationship

> A corporation has a responsibility to be sensitive to the needs of the community within which it exists. It should foster communication with the community's representatives, coordinating with them decisions that affect the community as a whole. It should contribute to the betterment of the social and cultural life of each community in which the corporation has a presence by encouraging employee participation in community activities, making resources available to the community, and in general taking an interest in community affairs. A community that wishes to attract and retain business has a reciprocal obligation to provide, through such means as honest government and adequate community services, a political and social environment that business enterprises and their employees will find hospitable.

Source: *Criteria for Decision Making* (New York: C. W. Post Center, Long Island University, 1979), 12. Reproduced with permission.

FIGURE 13-2 Types of Community Projects Supported by Insurance Companies: Percent of Reporting Companies Involved, 1990

Types of Projects	Total
Education	87%
Arts and Cultural Programs	78
Youth Activities	73
Local Health Programs	72
Neighborhood Improvement Programs	61
Minority Affairs	58
AIDS Education/Treatment	57
Drug or Alcohol Abuse Programs	53
Programs for Handicapped	51
Programs for Hunger/Homeless	50
Activities for Senior Citizens and Retired Persons	44
Safety Programs	34
Day-Care Programs	32
Housing Programs	32
Environmental Programs	31
Hard-to-Employ Programs	29
Crime Prevention	28
Prenatal and Well-Baby Care	25
Health Promotion/Low-Income & Minority Populations	16
Transportation Programs	16
Other	17

Number of Companies Reporting (167).
Source: *1991 Social Report of the Life and Health Insurance Business* (Washington, DC: Center for Corporate Public Involvement, 1991), 4.

Businesses see the illiteracy problem as directly related to their successful functioning. For example, an insurance company authorized a payment of $22.00 on a dental claim, but the patient received a check for $2,200. The reason: The clerk who made out the payment did not understand the meaning of the decimal point.[3] As technology advances, companies need more competent entry-level employees who can read, do math, and solve problems. Ironically, the whole problem is made worse by the fact that, at the same time functional illiteracy is on the increase, business is needing workers with higher levels of basic skills.

Companies are tackling the functional illiteracy problem head-on by (1) aiding current programs to improve literacy, (2) training employees, and (3) working with the public schools. Dayton Hudson's B. Dalton Bookseller is a good example of a firm that not only is pouring money into existing programs but also is encouraging its executives and other employees to participate in local programs both as board members and tutors. It has also promised to recruit other companies for the campaign with the goal of producing 50,000 volunteer tutors.[4] Employee training programs range from those that use workers to tutor other employees on a one-to-one basis at Aetna and United Technologies, to a large-scale training program at New York Telephone that seeks to boost the education of barely literate employees to 9th or 10th grade levels.

In terms of working with the public schools, Texas Instruments' employees now go into classrooms to talk about why tough math courses are stepping-stones to achievement later in life. In addition, company employees work with fourth and fifth grade math students in Dallas, helping them discover the excitement of the subject instead of learning by rote.[5] Another company effort to promote literacy is PepsiCo's Pizza Hut offer of free pizza to students who meet reading goals set by their teachers.[6]

There is a growing emphasis on public schools directed largely at low-income and minority pupil populations. For example, 16 corporations created a tuition-free grammar school in a low-income area of Chicago. In addition to investing $2 million in the project, the groups announced plans to open similar schools in other poor neighborhoods in other cities. Corporate sponsors hope the schools will serve as models for the future.[7]

Executive Loan Programs. Another popular way business may help meet community needs is through *executive loan programs*—the loaning of corporate personnel to assist local governments. This technique was used in the 1970s to stave off bankruptcy in New York City and Cleveland. Now, dozens of state and local governments are benefiting from similar arrangements. In Montana, a task force of 30 executives donated 12 weeks of their time studying every detail of state government operations. In Birmingham, Alabama, a team of financial and accounting executives from Sonat, Inc. helped the city straighten out its budget. Baltimore saved $700,000 on its school bus operation through changes initiated by business experts. In Tyler, Texas, GE loaned an expert from its local plant to help the school system tighten its purchasing operations.[8] Figure 13-3 briefly summarizes some other examples of company involvement in community projects.

Managing Community Involvement

For discussion purposes we are separating our treatment of managing community involvement from managing corporate philanthropy. We should be aware, however, that the reality of this separation is impossible to achieve. There are significant overlaps between these two areas. Corporate philanthropy involves the giving of financial resources. Community involvement focuses on other issues in the business-community relationship, especially the contribution of managerial and employee time and talent. This section addresses these broader community issues; a later section of this chapter deals with the narrower issue of managing corporate philanthropy.

FIGURE 13-3 Company Involvement in Community Projects

- National Life Insurance Company of Montpelier, VT, took the lead in an effort by Vermont businesses to raise money to help families of National Guard members weather financial hardships while the troops were in the Middle East during Operation Desert Storm.

- Kansas City Life Insurance Co. is joining forces with the Kansas City Royals baseball team and law enforcement agencies to sponsor a baseball collector card program. The effort will bring anti-drug and -crime messages, along with health and safety tips, to area youngsters.

- To interrupt the cycle of violence, abuse and neglect affecting very young people in Boston, John Hancock will help underwrite the cost of developing City Bound, which is a residential program for 25 "virtually homeless" students, ages 11–15, who will live for up to a year on a privately owned island in Boston Harbor.

- The Prudential has joined a consortium of seven national foundations to commit $62.5 million to spur neighborhood renewals in America's poorest inner city communities.

- CIGNA employee volunteers in Connecticut are serving as tutors to young children who come from families which are mostly on welfare. CIGNA's program is one of the largest of its kind in the country. The goal is to improve reading and math skills.

Source: Center for Corporate Public Involvement, *Response* (Washington, DC), July, 1991.

Business Stake in the Community. When one talks with corporate executives in the fields of community and civic affairs and examines community-affairs manuals and other corporate publications, one sees a broad array of reasons companies need to keep abreast of the issues, problems, and changes expressed as community needs. One reason is directly related to *self-interest* and *self-preservation*. For example, companies usually have a significant physical presence in the community and want to protect that investment. Issues of interest to them are zoning regulations, threat of neighborhood deterioration, corporate property taxes, the community tax base, and availability of an adequately trained work force.[9]

A second reason companies need to stay abreast of community needs and problems is that certain issues involve some *direct* or *indirect* benefit to them. Examples here would include health services, social services, community services, a healthy physical environment, the appearance of the community, and the overall quality of life. A third reason has to do with the company's *reputation* and *image* in the community. For example, companies want to be thought of as responsible corporate citizens by residents, employees, and competitors. Companies may have expertise that can help solve community problems, and they want to build a reserve of community goodwill.[10]

Development of a Community Action Program. The motivation for developing a community action program is evident when one considers the stake a firm has in the community. Likewise, the community represents a major stakeholder of business. Therefore, business has an added incentive to be systematic about its relationship with the community. The four steps in developing a community action program, as articulated by the Norton Company, provide a framework for approaching the community from a managerial frame of reference. These four steps include (1) knowing the community, (2) knowing the range of company resources available, (3) selecting a project, and (4) monitoring the project. These steps may be useful whether the company is considering specific community projects or is attempting to build a relationship with community stakeholders.

Knowing the Community. A key to developing worthwhile community involvement programs is knowing the community in which the business resides. This is a research step that requires management to assess the characteristics of the local area. Every locale has particular characteristics that can help shape social programs of involvement. Who lives in the community? What is its ethnic composition? What is its unemployment level? Are there inner-city problems or pockets of poverty? What are other organizations doing? What are the really pressing social needs of the area? What is the community's morale?

Knowing the leadership in the community is another factor. Is the leadership progressive? Is leadership cohesive and unified, or is it fragmented? If it is fragmented, the company may have to make difficult choices about which groups to work with. If the community's present approach to social issues is well led, all that may be necessary is "jumping on the bandwagon." If the community's leadership is not well organized, the company may want to provide an impetus and an agenda for restructuring or revitalizing the leadership. Figure 13-4 on pages 378 and 379[16] presents a checklist of items that companies might include in conducting a community needs assessment.

Knowing the Company's Resources. To effectively address various community needs, an inventory and assessment of the company's resources and competencies are needed. What is the variety, mix, and range of resources—personnel, money, meeting space, equipment, and supplies? Many companies are willing to give employees time to engage in and support community projects. This may be in the form of managerial assistance, technical assistance, or personnel. A wide spectrum of abilities, skills, interests, potentials, and experience exists in most organizations. To put any of these resources to work, however, it is necessary to know what is available, to what extent it is available, on what terms it is available, and during what time it is available.

Selecting Projects. The selection of community projects for the company to be involved in grows out of the matching of community stakeholders' needs with company resources. Frequently, because there are a number of such good matches, the company must be selective in choosing among them. Sometimes companies develop and refine policies or guidelines to help in the selection process. These policies are extremely useful because they further delineate areas in which the company may be involved and provide perspective for channeling the organization's energies.

George Steiner identified several social policies that could be extremely useful to management in its attempts to inject rationality into its selection of community projects. These policies are illustrative of those an organization might develop:

1. It is the policy of this company "to concentrate action programs on areas strategically related to the present and prospective economic functions of the business."

2. It is the policy of this company "to begin action programs close to home before spreading out in far distant regions."

3. It is the policy of this company "to facilitate employee actions which can be taken as individuals rather than as representatives of the company."[11]

Frank Koch has spelled out guidelines for developing a strategy for community involvement. The following list summarizes some of these guidelines:

1. Community involvement must be planned and organized with the same care and energy devoted to other parts of the business.

2. Community projects should meet the same measure of cost-effectiveness expected from money invested in research, marketing, production, or administration.
3. The corporation should capitalize on its talents and resources. Those responsible should get involved in things they understand. The company should look at social problems that affect its realm of operations.
4. Employees should be involved in community programs. The program should focus on some of the things that affect and interest employees.
5. The corporation should get involved in the communities it knows, the people it knows best, and the needs that have the best chance of being fulfilled and are important goals of the community.

FIGURE 13-4 A Checklist of Items Companies Might Include in a Community Needs Assessment

Demographics
- Basic descriptions (sex, level of education)
- Racial mix
- Poverty and unemployment
- Neighborhood characteristics
- Implications of the above for crime rate; percent elderly; racial discrimination; and so on

Environment and Land Use
- Housing stock (including restoration and preservation)
- Commercial and industrial space
- Open space planning; recreation
- Quality of water, air, land

Infrastructure and Physical Services
- Condition of roads, bridges
- Traffic patterns and parking space
- Utilities
- Sanitation
- Communications

Leadership
- Business
- Government
- Civic groups
- Community groups

(continued)

Leisure
- Parks and indoor recreational facilities
- Cultural and art facilities (museums, libraries, galleries)
- Shopping facilities
- Restaurants

Local Economy
- Tax base and rates
- Cost of living
- Economic development plans and agenda
- Employment and labor-force characteristics
- Aid to small business

Local Education
- Primary and secondary
- Vocational
- Colleges and universities

Local Government
- Structure (e.g., mayor, city manager)
- Municipal finance
- Crime and safety capabilities

Local Health and Human Services
- Social- and family-service capabilities
- Hospitals, ambulance service, emergency care facilities
- Degree of community problems relating to above (e.g., alcohol and drug abuse)

Source: Kathryn Troy, *Studying and Addressing Community Needs: A Corporate Case Book* (New York: The Conference Board, 1985), 8. Reproduced with permission.

FIGURE 13-4 (continued)

6. All action should not originate in company headquarters. Effective programs should occur wherever business is done.
7. Corporate policy should allow continuing support to established causes while finding some new initiatives.
8. The best kind of support is that which helps others to help themselves.[12]

Policies and guidelines such as those just presented go a long way toward rationalizing and systematizing business involvement with the community. Such policy statements should be developed and articulated throughout the organization to help provide a unified focus for company efforts.

An excellent example of a community project that was carefully chosen and likely meets most of the guidelines discussed above would be the Ronald McDonald Houses sponsored by McDonald's Corporation. These houses, which provide shelter and solace for a half a million people a year whose children are seriously ill, were first begun in 1974. By 1990, there were 129 houses all over the United States and in Canada, England, Holland, Germany, and Australia. McDonald's employs the same pattern in all the communities in which the houses are located. Each is operated by a nonprofit corporation and is staffed by volunteers, except for a paid manager. Each house is located near a hospital treating children, and families are charged $5 to $15 a day if they can afford it and nothing if they can't. The families may remain for as long as their child is undergoing treatment.

Another interesting example of community involvement is that of Amoco, the petroleum giant, as it attempts to pump life into needy neighborhoods. The hands-on program Amoco has used in downtown neighborhoods in the city of Atlanta in the early 1990s is illustrative. Amoco has created the Amoco Fund for Neighborhood Economies, and it works closely with community leaders. In one neighborhood, Amoco funded a $6,000 feasibility study for converting a dilapidated school into a community center. In another neighborhood, Amoco helped to organize resources to build and renovate homes, acquire school property, establish a neighborhood crime watch, and implement a program for teens. In a neighborhood near the planned Olympic Village for the 1996 Olympics to be held in Atlanta, Amoco helped fund and develop a master plan for revitalizing the area near the planned stadium. Amoco has held workshops with community leaders in which it has stressed its approach: (1) candidly diagnosing the strengths and weaknesses of neighborhoods, (2) organizing short-term projects that would get a lot of people involved and have an excellent chance for success, (3) finding a theme for the neighborhoods (for example, one was "Together We're Strong"), and (4) tailoring long-range plans to meet the neighborhoods' needs. An Atlanta City Council member boasted about Amoco: "Many corporations in their well-intentioned philanthropy give money and don't see it through. Amoco's involvement is structured so that they get the most bang for the buck."[13]

Monitoring Projects. Monitoring company projects involves review and control. Follow-up is necessary to ensure that the projects are being executed according to plans and on schedule. Feedback from the various steps in the process provides the information management needs to monitor progress. In later chapters we will elaborate on the managerial approach to dealing with various social issues. The guidelines previously listed, however, provide some insights into the development of business-community stakeholder relationships. As we stated earlier, community involvement is a discretionary activity in our corporate social performance model. It is also an extremely costly area of endeavor. Our stance is that it should be carefully managed, just as other business functions are, so that rationality and effectiveness can be maintained in what otherwise might become just an expensive arena of corporate "do-goodism."

Let us now examine business giving by way of financial contributions.

CORPORATE PHILANTHROPY/ BUSINESS GIVING

The dictionary defines *philanthropy* as "a desire to help mankind as indicated by acts of charity; love of mankind."[14] Robert Payton argues that philanthropy is defined as three related activities: voluntary service; voluntary association, and voluntary giving for public purposes.[15] He goes on to state that it includes "acts of community to enhance the quality of life and to insure a better future."[16] These definitions of philanthropy suggest a broad range of activities. One more restricted contemporary usage of the word is "business giving." In this section we will concentrate on the voluntary giving of financial resources as composing philanthropy. One problem with the dictionary definition is that the motive for the giving is characterized as charitable, benevolent, or generous. In actual practice, it is difficult to assess the true motives behind businesses—or anyone's—giving of themselves or their financial resources.

A Brief History of Corporate Philanthropy

Business philanthropy of one kind or another can be traced back many years. It was in the 1920s that the most significant effort to "translate the new social consciousness of management into action" emerged in the form of organized corporate philanthropy. Before World War I, steps had been taken toward establishing systematic, federated fund-raising for community services. The early success of the YMCA and the wartime chests, welfare federations, Community Chests, colleges and universities, and hospitals provided impetus for these groups to organize their solicitations. The business response to the opportunity to help community needs was varied. At one extreme, large enterprises such as the Bell Telephone system, with branches, offices, and subsidiaries in thousands of communities, contributed to literally thousands of civic and social organizations. Smaller firms, such as the companies in small mill towns of North Carolina, supported schools, housing, religious activities, and community welfare with a degree of enthusiasm that exceeded most nineteenth-century paternalism.[17]

Corporate giving in the period 1918 to 1929 was dominated by the Community Chest movement. In the period 1929–1935, there was an attempt to allow business to deduct up to 5 percent of its pretax net income for its community donations. The years 1935 to 1945, marked by the Depression and World War II, did not show an expansion of business giving. The period 1945 to 1960 saw new horizons of corporate responsibility, and the period since about 1960 can truly be called a period in which social responsibility has flourished and goes beyond simple corporate giving. But because we are focusing on corporate contributions to the community, we will exclude those broader endeavors that began in the 1960s. The debate continues about whether businesses should give away money. The evidence shows that they are doing so, and they probably will continue to do so in the future.

Giving to the "Third Sector"

Philanthropist John D. Rockefeller, III has argued that business giving is necessary to support what has been called the *third sector*—the nonprofit sector. The first two sectors, business and government, have support through profits and taxes. But the third sector (which includes hundreds of thousands of churches, museums, hospitals, libraries, private colleges and universities, and performing arts groups) depends on philanthropy for support. Philanthropy gives these institutions the crucial margin that assures them of their most precious asset—their independence.[18]

Business giving in 1989, the latest year for which data were available, was estimated to be in excess of $5.6 billion. It was believed that corporate giving exceeded $6 billion in 1990.[19] Figure 13-5 on pages 383 and 384 presents all corporate contributions and corporate income before and after taxes, 1936 to 1989, as compiled by the Conference Board.

Historically, corporate giving has averaged about 1 percent of income before taxes. It can be seen from Figure 13-5, however, that this average increased during the decade of the 1980s. This increase may have been in response to President Reagan's cutbacks in federal support for social programs in the early 1980s and his appeals to the corporate sector to take up the slack.[20]

Why Do Companies Give? Perhaps it would be more worthwhile to know why companies give to charitable causes rather than *how much* they give. There are a number of ways to approach this question. We get initial insights when we consider the five categories of corporate contribution programs identified by the *National Directory of Corporate Charity*, as shown in Figure 13-6 on page 385.[21] The motivations that come through in these categories range from pure self-interest to a desire to be a good corporate citizen by supporting both traditional and innovative programs in the community.

A more straightforward assessment of the reasons for undertaking contributions activities was provided in a survey conducted by the Conference Board. In a study of Fortune 500 companies, with 417 chairmen and presidents responding, they identified the reasons for supporting specific contributions activities, as reported in Figure 13-7 on page 386.

From the data in Figure 13-7, we see that the major reasons for undertaking the specific activities varied slightly but constituted an identifiable pattern overall. Quite often, in surveys of this kind, altruistic motives for corporate contributions are indicated. Several studies have been conducted, however, that suggest a profit motive for corporate contributions. Block and Goodman, for example, designed two fund-gathering strategies to ascertain why companies give. One was aimed at the motive of giving for the less fortunate in the community (altruism), and the other was aimed at self-interest of the firms. The researchers' conclusion was that the approach appealing to the giver's self-interest was more effective in motivating the giving than the approach emphasizing the interest of others.[22] In another

FIGURE 13-5 All Corporate Contributions and Corporate Income Before and After Taxes, 1936 to 1989[1]

Year	Contributions ($ millions)	Income[4] Before Taxes ($ millions)	Contributions as Percent of Income Before Taxes	Income[4] After Taxes ($ millions)	Contributions as Percent of Income After Taxes
1936	$30	$ 7,900	0.38%	$ 4,900	0.61%
1937	33	7,900	0.42	5,300	0.62
1938	27	4,100	0.65	2,900	0.93
1939	31	7,200	0.43	5,700	0.54
1940	38	10,000	0.38	7,200	0.53
1941	58	17,900	0.32	10,300	0.56
1942	98	21,700	0.45	10,300	0.95
1943	159	25,300	0.63	11,200	1.42
1944	234	24,200	0.97	11,300	2.07
1945	266	19,800	1.34	9,100	2.92
1946	214	24,800	0.86	15,700	1.36
1947	241	31,800	0.76	20,500	1.18
1948	239	35,600	0.67	23,300	1.03
1949	223	29,200	0.76	19,000	1.17
1950	252	42,900	0.59	25,000	1.01
1951	343	44,500	0.77	21,900	1.57
1952	399	39,800	1.01	20,200	1.96
1953	495	41,200	1.20	20,900	2.37
1954	314	38,700	0.81	21,100	1.49
1955	415	49,200	0.84	27,200	1.53
1956	418	49,600	0.84	27,600	1.51
1957	419	48,100	0.87	26,700	1.57
1958	395	41,900	0.94	22,900	1.72
1969	482	52,800	0.92	28,900	1.67
1960	482	49,800	0.97	27,100	1.78
1961	512	49,700	1.03	26,900	1.90
1962	595	55,000	1.08	31,100	1.91
1963	657	59,600	1.10	33,400	1.97
1964	729	66,500	1.10	38,500	1.89
1965	785	77,200	1.02	46,300	1.70

(continued)

FIGURE 13-5   (continued)

Year	Contributions ($ millions)	Income[4] Before Taxes ($ millions)	Contributions as Percent of Income Before Taxes	Income[4] After Taxes ($ millions)	Contributions as Percent of Income After Taxes
1966	$ 805	$ 83,000	0.97	$ 49,400	1.63
1967	830	79,700	1.04	47,200	1.76
1968	1,005	88,500	1.13	49,400	2.03
1969	1,055	86,700	1.22	47,200	2.24
1970	797	75,400	1.06	41,300	1.93
1971	865	86,600	1.00	49,000	1.76
1972	1,009	100,800	1.00	58,900	1.71
1973	1,174	125,800	0.93	76,600	1.53
1974	1,200	136,700	0.88	85,100	1.41
1975	1,202	132,100	0.91	81,500	1.47
1976	1,487	166,300	0.89	102,500	1.45
1977	1,791	200,400	0.89	127,400	1.41
1978	2,084	233,500	0.89	150,000	1.39
1979	2,288	257,200	0.89	169,200	1.35
1980	2,359	237,100	0.99	152,300	1.55
1981	2,514	226,500	1.11	145,400	1.73
1982	2,906	169,600	1.71	108,500	2.73
1983	3,627	207,600	1,75	130,400	2.78
1984	4,057	240,000	1.69	146,100	2.78
1985	4,472	224,300	1.99	127,800	3.50
1986	5,179[2]	221,600	2.34	115,300	4.49
1987	4,980	275,300	1.81	142,000	3.51
1988	5,400(est.)[3]	316,700	1.71	168,900	3.20
1989	5,800(est.)[3]	307,700	1.82	161,000	3.48

[1]Reflects total consolidated corporate income before and after taxes.
[2]The IRS figure includes some 1987 gifts reported in 1986 to take advantage of the more favorable provisions of the tax law prevailing before the Tax Reform Act of 1986.
[3]From Council for Aid to Education.
[4]The income figures on this table have been adjusted to coincide with recently updated data issued by the Department of Commerce. Thus, some of the figures in the income columns, and the ratios based upon them, will differ slightly from those published here previously.
Note: Figures in this table reflect contributions and income of *all* U.S. corporations. Figures in all other tables in this report are based solely on responses by survey participants.
Sources: Department of Commerce, Internal Revenue Service, Council for Aid to Education
Anne Klepper, *Corporate Contributions, 1989* (New York: The Conference Board, 1990), 23.

FIGURE 13-6 Categories of Corporate Contribution Programs

1. The Nondonor—This is a firm for which no evidence of charitable giving was found.

2. The "What's In It For Us" Donor—With this firm, most contributions relate to the company's direct interest or to the welfare of its employees.

3. The "Company President Believes in Art Support" Donor—With this firm, most contributions relate to the company's direct interest, employees' welfare, or management's interest.

4. The "We Are a Good Citizen" Donor—Here a substantial portion of the company's giving provides support for traditional nonprofit institutions.

5. The "We Care" Donor—Here some funds go to newer organizations and established organizations that deal with nontraditional issues.

study, Fry, Keim, and Meiners found that corporate contributions are motivated by profit considerations that influence both advertising expenditures and corporate giving. They concluded that corporate giving is a complement to advertising and is, therefore, a profit-motivated expense.[23]

As economic pressures and increased international competitiveness force companies to be more careful with their earnings, we should not be surprised to see the profit motive coexisting with loftier goals in corporate contributions programs. Indeed, in a later section of this chapter, we argue that philanthropy *should* be "strategic," which means that corporate giving should be more directly related to the firm's economic or profitability objectives.

To Whom Do Companies Give? During the course of any budget year, companies receive numerous requests for contributions from a wide variety of applicants. Companies must then weigh both quantitative and qualitative factors to arrive at a decision regarding the recipients of their gifts. By looking at the beneficiaries of corporate contributions, we can estimate the value business places on various societal needs in the community. Figure 13-8 on pages 387 and 388 reports a large number of recipient categories of corporate contributions based on a survey of 1,600 companies. This listing provides an excellent picture of the array of programs that are supported by the contributions of American corporations.

Figure 13-9 on page 389 shows where corporate contributions went for the years 1988 and 1989 (the latest available at this writing), based on five major categories: (1) education, (2) health and human services, (3) civic and community activities,

FIGURE 13-7 Reasons for Undertaking Contribution Activities (responses of 417 chairmen and presidents)

Possible Reasons for Undertaking Contribution Activities	Specific Activities[a]		
	United Funds	Higher Education	The Arts
Corporate citizenship: practice good corporate citizenship	74%	49%	48%
Business environment: protect and improve environment in which to live, work, and do business	68%	46%	43%
Employee benefits: realize benefits for company employees (normally in areas where company operates)	47%	31%	31%
Public relations: realize good public relations value	34%	20%	32%
Pluralism: preserve a pluralistic society by maintaining choices between government and private-sector alternatives	28%	40%	10%
Commitment: of directors or senior officers to particular causes, involvement	23%	31%	28%
Pressure: from business peers, customers, and/or suppliers	12%	8%	17%
Altruism: practice altruism with little or no direct or indirect company self-interest	10%	8%	16%
Manpower supply: increase the pool of trained manpower or untrained manpower or access to minority recruiting	5%	63%	2%
No contributions or activities in this area	2%	2%	7%

[a]Adds to more than 100% because multiple responses were requested.
Source: James F. Harris and Anne Klepper, *Corporate Philanthropic Public Service Activities* (New York: The Conference Board, 1976), 16. Reproduced with permission.

(4) culture and art, and (5) other. These are from data that the Conference Board gathers on an annual basis. A brief discussion of each of these five categories will help explain the nature of business's involvement in philanthropy.

Education. Most of the corporate contributions in this category went to higher education—colleges and universities. The major educational recipients were capital grants (including endowments), unrestricted operating grants, depart-

FIGURE 13-8 Number and Percent of 1,600 Profiled Companies Giving According to Category (listed in descending order of popularity)

Category	Number	Percent
Private Colleges	1,517	94.8%
General Education	1,491	93.2%
United Way	1,019	63.7%
Fine Arts Institutes	839	52.3%
Cultural Institutes	803	50.2%
Civic Programs	789	49.3%
Minority Programs	781	48.8%
National Organizations	688	43.0%
Youth Service	676	42.3%
Federated Campaigns	533	33.3%
General Arts	530	33.1%
International	519	32.4%
Public Colleges	506	31.6%
Scholarships	501	31.3%
Music	478	29.9%
Urban Problems	475	29.7%
Theater	470	29.4%
General Health Care	456	28.5%
Economic Education	454	28.4%
Economic Development	443	27.7%
Welfare Programs	425	26.6%
Environmental	364	22.8%
Dance	358	22.4%
Hospitals	356	22.3%
Community Arts	348	21.8%
Rural Issues	347	21.7%
Medical Research	337	21.1%
Elem./Secondary Ed.	320	20.0%
Job Development	316	19.8%
Public Broadcasting	307	19.2%

(continued)

mental and research grants, scholarships and fellowships, and employee matching gifts. Also included in this category would be educational groups (for example, United Negro College Fund, the Council for Financial Aid to Education) and primary and secondary schools.

As we saw earlier, business's most frequently reported reason for supporting higher education was to increase the pool of trained personnel. This has obvious credibility, as higher education institutions do, indeed, form the resource base from which business fills its managerial and professional positions.

FIGURE 13-8 (continued)

Category	Count	Percent
General Charitable	305	19.1%
Children's Programs	280	17.5%
Women's Programs	269	16.8%
Vocational Ed.	251	15.7%
Legal Services	210	13.1%
Justice/Ex-offenders	173	10.8%
Film	152	9.5%
Science	141	8.8%
Handicapped/Disabled	121	7.6%
Political	121	7.6%
United Way Agencies	118	7.4%
Legal Advocacy	116	7.3%
Community Organizing	114	7.1%
Equal Rights	109	6.8%
Scientific Research	74	4.6%
Continuing Education	63	3.9%
Science Education	63	3.9%
Neighborhood Based	58	3.6%
Senior Citizens	50	3.1%
Religious/Non-sect.	46	2.9%
Religious/Sectarian	46	2.9%
Writing and Poetry	33	2.1%
Family Life	32	2.0%
Humanities	31	1.9%
Redevelopment	26	1.6%
Alcohol/Drug Treatment	23	1.4%
Occupational Health	15	.9%
Sports	6	.4%
Veteran Programs	4	.3%
Non Tax-Exempt	3	.2%
Gay/Lesbian Programs	2	.1%

Source: Sam Sternberg, *National Directory of Corporate Charity* (San Francisco: Regional Young Adult Project, 1984), 8.

Although contributions to educational institutions rank high in business giving (38.4 percent of all business contributions in 1989), companies do not always give blindly and expect nothing in return. In the last several years there has been some controversy about whether business should give to educational institutions that do not support the free enterprise values so important to business. The basic issue is whether support of education should be "with strings attached" or "without strings attached."

FIGURE 13-9 Distribution of the Contributions Dollar, 1988 and 1989

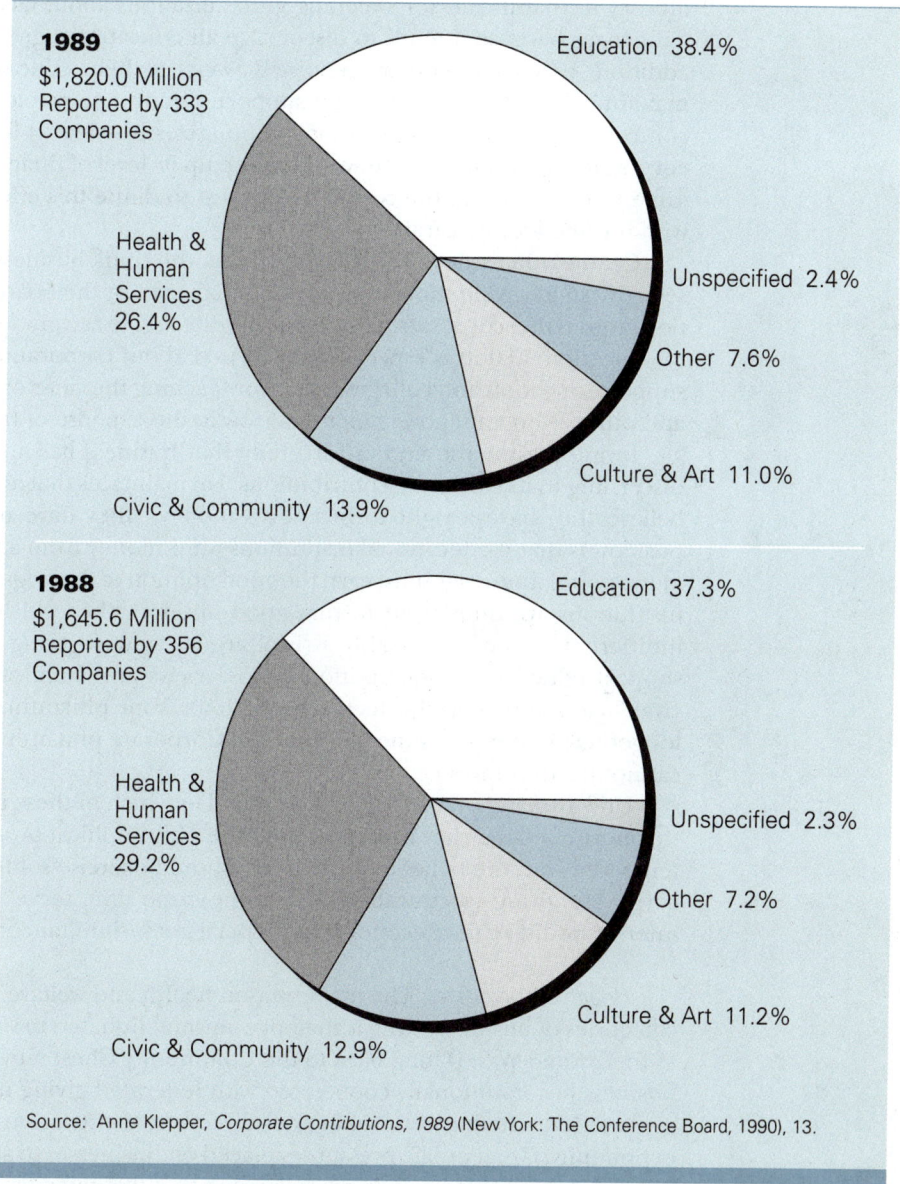

Source: Anne Klepper, *Corporate Contributions, 1989* (New York: The Conference Board, 1990), 13.

Those who argue that business should give to education without strings attached think that attempts to dictate to educational institutions will create conflict between the institutions and industry. Louis W. Cabot, chairman of the board of Cabot Corporation, argues that it is neither wise nor advantageous for business to limit its gifts to institutions that support free enterprise. His belief is that the corporate self-interest criterion is both illusory and dangerous. It is illusory in that it calls for sweeping generalizations about faculty members; it is dangerous because it tends to discourage all educational giving. He believes, in addition, that if a company genuinely wants to help education function with maximum effectiveness, it should support schools as a whole rather than try to control the use of its funds. Cabot summarizes his view as follows: "It is in the corporate community's self-interest to step up its level of financial support. At the same time, it is *not* in the corporate interest to dilute this effort by burdening it with uncalled-for constraints."[24]

On the other side of the issue are those who think business ought to be more selective in its giving. Robert H. Malott, chairman of the board of FMC Corporation, argues that corporate self-interest ought to serve as a guide for business giving to education. Malott is especially concerned about corporations giving financial support to schools and colleges that favor teaching the views of radical economists and others who want government to grow at the expense of free enterprise.[25]

Irving Kristol also argues forcefully that business has a responsibility to be discerning in its corporate contributions. He maintains that although universities believe they have a right to business's money, "they have no such right." His position is that if educational institutions want money from a particular segment of the population, they must earn the good opinion of that segment. If educational institutions are indifferent to that good opinion, they will have to learn to be indifferent to the money also. Kristol argues against giving business money to support educational organizations whose views are "inimical to corporate survival." He summarizes his feelings as follows: Your philanthropy must serve the longer-term interests of the corporation. Corporate philanthropy should not be, cannot be, disinterested.[26]

Unfortunately, there are no data to tell us which of these extreme positions is the most effective; they represent opposite philosophical postures. A philosophy tempered with the belief that managers should exercise some control over their corporate giving to education and at the same time serve the company's self-interest would achieve economic and social goals simultaneously.

Health and Welfare. The major reason health and welfare is one of the largest categories of business giving is the huge amount donated to such federated drives as the United Way. Dating back to the Community Chest movement cited earlier, business has traditionally cooperated with federated giving mechanisms. Money given to federated drives usually goes directly to assist various agencies in a local community. Great public pressure is placed on businesses to actively support such federated campaigns, so it is not surprising that this category is one of the largest beneficiaries. Business hopes, just as the community does, that such consolidated efforts will lend some order to the requests of major recipients in the community that business has chosen to support.

In addition to federated drives, major recipients in this category are hospitals, youth agencies, and other local health and welfare agencies. Hospitals represent an obviously important need in most communities. They receive financial support for capital investments (new buildings and equipment), operating funds, and matching employee gifts. Youth agencies include such groups as the YMCA, Boy Scouts, Girl Scouts, and Boys Clubs. Because a great part of the country's turmoil of the late 1960s and 1970s had its source in the dissatisfaction of young people, many of whom were antagonistic toward large corporations, it is quite logical for business to include youth as a prominent part of its health and welfare contributions.

Civic Activities. This category of business giving represents a wide variety of philanthropic activities in the community. Dominant among these are support for community improvement activities, environment and ecology, research organizations other than academic (for example, Brookings, Committee for Economic Development, Urban League), and neighborhood renewal. Because community improvement receives the largest share of this category, several examples will help illustrate the wide variety of ways in which business is involved in community endeavors.

One interesting example is the Community Relations Committee of Salem, New Jersey, established by the Anchor Hocking Corporation. The purpose of this program was to relieve racial tensions and to involve a large number of citizens in identifying and solving community problems. Those who met and identified positive factors affecting community life were representatives of city government; civic, social, and other organizations; and citizens at large. Negative factors were identified later, followed by group problem-solving sessions and assignment of project groups for in-depth investigation and implementation of solutions. Future plans called for training more citizens in the techniques of leading groups in problem solving, in an effort to transfer leadership to private citizens and community groups rather than rely so heavily on business leadership.

Anchor Hocking identified a number of indices of success, including the fact that there had been no riots or civil disturbances in this community of 10,000, although rioting had taken place in communities within 20 miles. Also, the first community swimming pool had been built, a day care center had been expanded and improved, and playground and recreational facilities had been created.[27]

Another interesting example of a business involved in community improvement was the "Spring Cleaning" program of the Citizens and Southern National Bank of Georgia. The purpose of this program was to spruce up the approaches to Savannah, Georgia, so tourists would stop and stay in Savannah rather than go on to Florida. In conjunction with the Savannah Visitors Center—and other banks in the community, Citizens and Southern sponsored a big "work day" to show the community that business was supporting efforts to help develop tourist trade.[28]

Eli Lilly and Company's "Big Brother and Big Sister" programs exemplify civic involvement with youth as the focus. In attempting to establish a "Big Brother" program at a nearby inner-city high school in Indianapolis, Indiana, 37 male employees from the company volunteered to work with a group of disadvantaged students. They tried to discover something they had in common with the students that would encourage further communication, thereby providing each student with a mature friend and sounding board. The volunteers entertained the students at professional sporting events, vocational field trips, and family outings. The "Big Sister" program was very similar, aimed at economically underprivileged female students. Women employees of Eli Lilly exposed the young persons to cultural, educational, vocational, and entertainment activities.[29]

Corning, Inc. is more than the biggest employer in Corning, New York. It is also a benefactor, landlord, and, some say, social engineer. In the past, Corning, New York, has been a company town with Corning, Inc. being involved in providing affordable housing, day care, and new business development. Now, its efforts are more focused. The company plans to convert a remote, insular town into a place that will appeal to professionals. Their goal is a place that offers social options for young singles, support for new families, and cultural diversity for minorities. Among its activities, Corning bought the run-down bars in one section of town because they didn't fit in with the company's redevelopment plans. Employing a $5,000 payment and continuous lobbying, the firm got the dump owner to move. Corning is even trying to develop a region that will be less dependent on its headquarters and 15 factories. The company also purchased and revitalized an auto-racing track and also convinced a supermarket chain to locate there. Corning continuously works to attract new business to the region, and it built the local Hilton Hotel, the museum, and the city library.[30]

Culture and Arts. Support for culture and the arts has been a favorite and prestigious outlet for business philanthropy for some time. Indeed, Richard Eells wrote an entire book entitled *The Corporation and the Arts*.[31] Business's support of the arts is interesting because there has never been any pressure from government to do so; business's efforts have been purely voluntary.

Of the various cultural beneficiaries of business support, museums tend to be the most frequent, followed in order by radio and television (especially public broadcasting), music (for example, symphony orchestras), arts funds or councils, and theaters. But as our data show, culture and the arts ranked behind health and welfare, civic and community, and education in total business giving.

Perhaps the most prominent organized effort on the part of business to give to the arts is the Business Committee for the Arts (BCA). Formed in the mid-1960s, the BCA is a private nationwide group that was designed to "unite corporate money with artistic need."[32] According to BCA data, when the group was formed, corporate giving to the arts amounted to $22 million. This grew to $90 million in 1968 and $110 million in 1970.[33] The amount was probably about $150 million in 1976 and exceeded $200 million in 1990. Business also takes pride in pointing out that it gives about the same amount to the arts as does government but that none of its money goes for administration.[34]

It is interesting to consider why business gives to the arts. There seems to be no direct benefit to business, as is the case with donations to education. As with other philanthropic categories, businesses claim various motives for their giving. There are those who argue altruistically that the reason for business's largesse is that it recognizes that art contributes to the kind of vitality and creativity that is important to society. The object of the BCA awards, given each year to companies that support the arts, is to "stimulate and encourage independent assistance of the arts" by business people.[35]

On the other hand, there are business executives who say openly that their support for the arts is at least in part a reflection of self-interest. Paul H. Eliker, president of SCM Corporation, argues for giving to the arts to gain recognition or visibility and for general image building.[36] He claims this is no different than the reasons the great patrons of the Renaissance—the Medicis and Pope Julius II—supported culture and the arts: to associate themselves with the grandeur of the times.

Eliker tells the story of a reporter who once asked George Weissman, vice-chairman of Phillip Morris, why his company supported such exhibitions as American Folk Art. Mr. Weissman is reported to have responded, "It's a lot cheaper than taking out ads saying how great we think we are."[37]

Although no one can peer into an executive's mind to find out why business really gives to the arts, at least one sociologist suggests that the motive is really self-interest, not altruism and social responsibility as claimed by businesses. This may not sound too startling, given the public admission of some executives that it is true. But M. David Ermann sees the giving efforts as part of an extremely selfish scenario. Citing gifts from major corporations totaling $12 million per year to the Public Broadcasting System (PBS), Ermann argues that such contributions are intended to create a less hostile social climate and thus mute the critics of business. In his words, the purpose of the corporate charity was to favorably "influence the social milieu . . . to ensure rewards and reduce penalties and uncertainty for the company."[38]

Recipients of business donations to the arts are not likely to turn down such contributions because the giver's motives may not be pure. Business giving, whatever the intent, does benefit the giver and the receiver, as well as the general public. Although Paul Eliker's earlier comments suggested an economic motive, he fully recognizes that his company is not the sole beneficiary. He concludes, "We do it because it's good for the arts, it's good for the millions of people who get pleasure viewing great works of art, and—not least—it's good for SCM Corporation."[39]

Other Activities. Figure 13-9, presented earlier, shows that, of the companies reporting, about 10 percent of their donations went to "other activities" or unspecified." It is not clear what all these other activities were, but some were identified as groups devoted to economic education (for example, Joint Council on Economic Education, Junior Achievement), groups whose purpose is to aid other countries, groups engaged in religious activities, and support for special sports or patriotic events (such as the Olympics and the renovation of the Statue of Liberty).

Managing Corporate Philanthropy

As performance pressures on business continue and intensify, companies are more and more having to turn their attention to managing corporate philanthropy. Despite increasing corporate expenditures on charity and the growing acceptance of corporate philanthropy as a legitimate corporate activity by shareholders, managements have been slow to subject their contributions programs to the same kind of rigorous analysis given to plant and equipment, inventory, product development, marketing, and the host of other business decisions they deal with daily.

In the mid-1980s all this began to change. Because of the federal cutbacks in the early 1980s, there was a need for continuing contributions. At the same time, however, the economy struggled through its worst recession in 50 years. Demands that business become more competitive became the authoritative view on corporate survival. It became increasingly clear that business had to reconcile its economic and social goals, for both were essential.[40] The term that arose to characterize this new concern for getting an economic "bang" out of its corporate giving was *strategic philanthropy*.

Strategic Philanthropy. We should make it clear that strategic philanthropy was not *discovered* in the mid-1980s. For at least a decade, and perhaps longer, the idea was evolving that business should apply its management knowledge to aligning its economic and social thrusts. In the 1980s it became clear that the need for this alignment was pressing. This need, combined with the experiments and experiences of a number of leading companies, brought this issue to a head.

How might we explain strategic philanthropy? **Strategic philanthropy** is an approach by which corporate giving or philanthropic endeavors of a firm are designed in a way that best fits with the firm's overall mission, goals, or objectives. This implies that the firm has some idea of what its overall strategy is and that it is able to articulate its missions, goals, or objectives. One goal of all firms is profitability. Therefore, one requirement of strategic philanthropy is to make as direct as possible a contribution to the economic goals of the firm. Philanthropy has long been thought to be in the long-range economic interest of the firm. Strategic philanthropy, on the other hand, presses for a more direct or immediate contribution to the firm's economic success.

Another important way in which philanthropy can be strategic is the extent to which it brings the contributions program into alignment with the business endeavors of the firm. This means that each firm would pursue those social programs that have a direct bearing on its success rather than an indirect bearing. Thus, a local bank would logically pursue people-oriented projects in the community in which it resides, whereas a manufacturer might pursue programs having to do with environmental protection or technological advancement.

A third way philanthropy can be made strategic is by ensuring that it is planned or managed rather than handled haphazardly and without direction. When a program is planned, this implies that it has clearly delineated goals, is properly organized and staffed, and adheres to certain established policies for its administration. Figure 13-10 presents one company's views as to what constitutes an effective, strategic corporate contributions program.

Timothy Mescon and Donn Tilson elaborate on the need for managing the philanthropic function:

> A professionally run contributions program requires a set of strategic plans, goals, and objectives which are reviewed regularly; a set of guidelines for determining how much money will be allocated to it; criteria for making and evaluating grants; and either an in-house staff or access to competent consultants.[41]

An example of a firm that turned its philanthropic program around by making it more strategic is Burger King. For years, Burger King was an average corporate good citizen, quietly dribbling out $200,000 to the United Way along with small contributions to arts organizations and a scattering of other causes. At the same time, McDonald's, its major competitor, was gaining a reputation for strong social programs through its strategically focused Ronald McDonald Houses for children with terminal cancer. Then, suddenly, Burger King woke up and turned its

FIGURE 13-10 Characteristics of an Effective Strategic Corporate Contributions Program

An effective strategic corporate contributions program will have most of these characteristics:

1. It will be based on the longer-term, strategic self-interest of the company.
2. It will have a clearly stated strategy, agreed to by top management.
3. It will have clear, well-defined guidelines.
4. By definition, strategic giving will be planned. But all planned giving programs are not necessarily strategic.
5. The effective strategic corporate contributions program will be based on objective criteria which all concerned should understand.
6. It will be actively managed and evaluated for results.
7. It will focus on programs, not on capital or endowments. (Strategies change.)
8. It will be recognized as another function or tool in the entire public affairs process—not simply as a measure of corporate conscience.

Source: Gerald S. Gendell, manager, public affairs division, Procter & Gamble. Excerpted from his talk at the Public Affairs Council's conference on strategic uses of philanthropy in public affairs. Diane R. Shayon, "Strategic Philanthropy Beginning to Take Hold," *Impact* (October, 1984), 2. Reproduced with permission.

corporate image around with a contributions strategy that sought to make a social statement. This Pillsbury subsidiary began pumping $4 million a year into highly focused programs that help students, teachers, and schools. Much of Burger King's philanthropy now consists of scholarships to its own teen work force, designed to reduce the high turnover rate among those workers. One direct result of the education focus has been a turnover rate that dropped by more than half during the first 6 months of its national effort.[42]

Richard Morris and Daniel Biederman provide further recommendations for "giving away money intelligently." Some of their suggestions, all compatible with the strategic thrust we have been discussing, include:

1. Align your gifts with your product and goals.
2. Choose the right organizational structure for your needs.
3. Pick a manager to give money away.
4. Treat grant seekers like customers.
5. Set a long-term budget for contributions.
6. Don't run your contributions program as a public relations exercise.
7. Don't try to please everyone.
8. Take a chance on an unconventional cause.[43]

James Rosebush has recommended other ways a company can make the contributions program more directly affect the bottom line:

1. Determine the level of exposure you want with your contributions program.
2. Examine the placement of the contributions program within your company. Does it report to the logical area to fulfill corporate objectives?
3. Integrate the public affairs, community relations, corporate marketing, and communications goals of your company with your contributions program.
4. Make contributions work for your company. Determine the public relations value of each potential grant.
5. Develop a strategic list of questions to ask each grantee. Make sure the grantee fulfills your requirements.
6. Use executive-on-loan, donated equipment, and marketing-gift programs to enhance your employee relations and procurement program.[44]

All of these recommendations have one purpose in common—professionalizing the corporate contributions function so that it is more effective and more efficient. Now let us turn our attention to a special kind of strategic philanthropy that has become quite prevalent in recent years: cause-related marketing.

Cause-Related Marketing. There is some debate as to whether cause-related marketing is really philanthropy or not, but it does represent the tightest of linkages between a firm's profits and corporate contributions. Therefore, we will treat it here as one form of strategic philanthropy. Cause-related marketing represents a unique joining of business and charity with the potential for great benefit for each. Stated in its simplest form, *cause-related marketing* is the direct linking of a business's product or service to a specified charity. Each time the consumer uses the service or buys the product, a donation is given to the charity by the business.[45]

"Cause-related marketing" was coined as a term by the American Express Company to describe a program it began in 1983 in which it agreed to contribute a penny to the restoration of the Statue of Liberty every time one of its credit cards was used to make a purchase. The project generated $1.7 million for the statue restoration and a substantial increase in usage of the American Express card.[46] Since that time, American Express has employed this same approach to raise millions of dollars for a wide variety of local and national causes.

In 1985, American Express began "Project Hometown America" with a goal of raising $3 million as seed money for new kinds of hometown projects initiated and run by local volunteers. American Express agreed to make a specific contribution to this fund each time its cardholders used their cards, purchased American Express Travelers Cheques, or purchased a travel package worth more than $500 at one of its travel service offices. The money would then be administered by major charitable organizations such as the United Way, the National Urban League, and the Girl Scouts.[47]

Cause-related marketing has been used by General Foods, Scott Paper, and many other large firms. One of General Foods' major campaigns linked the interest group Mothers Against Drunk Driving (MADD) with the promotion of Tang, a powdered, orange-flavored breakfast drink. In promoting Tang, General Foods staged a 4-month walk across America that raised $100,000 for MADD. The company spurred its own sales by distributing cents-off coupons to consumers and promising to give 10 cents to MADD for every Tang proof-of-purchase seal that consumers sent in. Cause-related marketing has received its most visible publicity in recent years as companies have attached themselves to part of fund-raising extravaganzas such as Hands Across America and Live Aid, the glitzy bicontinental rock concert held in 1985 that raised $83 million for famine-stricken Africa.[48]

Other notable examples of cause-related marketing have been conducted by Reebok, Nike, and Ralston Purina. Reebok created the Reebok Foundation to underwrite the Human Rights Now!, a world concert tour organized by Amnesty International. Nike is concerned with inner-city issues because its products are coveted by inner-city youth. The company funds programs that deal with drug and gang problems and donates its proceeds to inner-city youth. For example, in one program, Nike donated $1,000 to the Boys Club for every point scored by Michael Jordan during an NBA All Star Game. Ralston Purina sponsored a program called Pets for People that helped senior citizens adopt pets. For each coupon redeemed, the company donated $0.20, or up to $1 million, to the Humane Society.[49]

Proponents of cause-related marketing argue that everyone is a winner. Business enhances its public image by being associated with a worthy cause and increases its sales at the same time. Nonprofit organizations get cash needed for their programs, as well as enhanced marketing and public visibility made possible by business's expertise.

Critics of cause-related marketing suggest there are issues raised that make the approach controversial. For nonprofit organizations who participate, one issue is the "taint of commercialism" that cause-related marketing may bring. The direct link between the nonprofit organization and the product being marketed may appear to be a promotional effort on the part of the nonprofit, and some may see this as compromising the organization's image, which is supposed to be dedicated to altruistic purposes. Other critics fear that if cause-related marketing becomes widespread, it could undermine the very basis of philanthropy. Others fear that some corporations may use cause-related marketing as a substitute for regular corporate contributions rather than as a supplement. The consequence of this would be no net increase in the amount of funds available.[50]

From the corporate perspective, cause-related marketing looks attractive. Indeed, it is often viewed as a marketing strategy, not a strategy for corporate giving. Quite often, in fact, funds for these programs are drawn from advertising and marketing budgets. The primary purpose of this approach for many businesses is to increase sales, first, and to provide resources for charity, second.[51] Nevertheless, we continue to see companies bask in the recognition they inevitably receive from supporting charity. From the corporate perspective, we can expect cause-related marketing to increase, although a saturation point may eventually be reached.

Global Philanthropy. One of the recent additions to corporate contributions programs are formal international philanthropy efforts as part of global business strategies. DuPont sent 1.4 million waterjug filters to eight nations in Africa. The fabric in the filters removes debilitating parasitic worms from drinking water. The cost to DuPont was $400,000. Alcoa teamed up with local authorities in Brazil to build a $112,000 sewage plant to serve 15,000 rural residents. H. J. Heinz spent $94,000 to fund infant nutrition studies in China and Thailand. IBM donated $60,000 in computer equipment and expertise to Costa Rica's National Parks Foundation to develop strategies for preserving rain forests.[52]

Increasingly, multinational corporations are helping foreign communities. As foreign markets begin to assume a larger role in the earnings outlook, companies are striving to be good corporate citizens all over the world. In 1989, 333 of the largest U.S. firms gave only $117 million overseas, just 6 percent of their total $1.8 billion in donations, according to the Conference Board. More recent data are not available. Such companies as Alcoa, DuPont, and Hewlett-Packard have plans to spend much more in the years to come. IBM, the world's largest corporate giver, spent $50 million overseas in 1991.

It is not just U.S. multinationals that are creating the trend toward global philanthropy. It is estimated that in 1991, Japan gave $500 million in foreign contributions. It is expected that all global philanthropy will grow in the future as international markets become more important to business.[53]

BUSINESS AND PLANT CLOSINGS

It is useful to shift our focus now and address what has become one of the most important business-community issues of the past decade: business and plant closings. In the previous sections, we considered the ways in which business firms might have a positive and creative impact on community stakeholders. Firms might also have detrimental impacts on communities. We see a most pervasive example of this negative effect when a business or plant closes and its management does not carefully consider the stakeholders affected. Firms can have a negative impact on communities in ways other than closings. For example, firms can pollute, abuse natural resources, create congestion by use of land and zoning, and take advantage of their power. Because business and plant closings have been identified as such a critical problem, we will spend our time and space looking at this issue in some detail.

In the balance of this chapter, we will examine the nature and magnitude of the plant-closing problem, identify some reasons for these occurrences, and consider some actions and strategies that business might employ to minimize the negative impact on community stakeholders. We will also look at the status of plant-closing legislation and the role of public action groups and researchers in helping us to understand the problem.

Nature and Magnitude of the Problem

Business shutdowns may be looked at from a number of different perspectives. Managers often see them as economic or business decisions that must be made just like any other business decision. The employees and communities affected, as well as social activists, see ethical issues involved, too. One writer stated this point of view: "In deciding whether or not to relocate a manufacturing operation, a company has moral obligations to its employees and to the community in which the operation is located."[54]

Throughout the United States, anger on the part of employees, unions, and communities over plant and business closings has reached unprecedented heights in the past decade. Resistance to plant closings ranges from community protests and employee marches on headquarters of national firms to union demands that plants be kept open with negotiated concessions on wages, work rules, and benefits.[55] One estimate by Bluestone and Harrison, authors of *The Deindustrialization of America*, is that 32 to 38 million jobs were lost during the 1970s alone because of business and plant closings.[56] One of the most interesting findings to come out of the analyses of job losses is that business closings are not confined to the old industrial Frostbelt and thus must be considered a national phenomenon.[57] Plant shutdowns have continued on into the 1980s and 1990s.

Reasons for Plant Closings

There is no single reason why so many businesses and plants have closed over the past decade, although the recession of the early 1980s provided a major catalyst. Some companies are in declining industries, some have outdated facilities or technology, some move to the less unionized regions of the country, others seek access to new markets, and others are victims of the merger/acquisition frenzy.

One major survey was conducted among public affairs executives to ascertain why they thought business closings were occurring. Figure 13-11 summarizes the reasons that were cited. The major reasons included economic recessions, consolidation of company operations, outmoded technology/facilities, changes in

FIGURE 13-11 Reasons Cited for Business/Plant Closings

Reasons	Frequency of Mention	Percent
Economic recession	67	48.9
Consolidation of company operations	64	46.7
Outmoded technology/facilities	41	29.9
Changes in corporate strategy	39	28.5
Unmet corporate objectives	39	28.5
Firms in declining industry	32	23.4
Foreign competition	31	22.6
Domestic competition	20	14.6
Search for lower labor costs	18	13.1
State/local attitudes toward business	11	8.0
Costly regulations	10	7.3
Other	8	5.8
Automation	6	4.4
Poor long-term planning	5	3.6
Inadequate capital investment	4	2.9
Quality of life	1	0.7

Note: This question was answered only by 137 firms that had experienced shutdowns in the last five years. Frequency of mention includes all of the times the reason was cited as one of top four factors. It also includes multiple reasons cited by some respondents. Source: Archie B. Carroll, Elizabeth I. Gatewood, James J. Chrisman, "Plant Closings: PAOs Respond to a Survey on an Increasingly Troublesome Issue," *Public Affairs Review*, Copyright ø 1984, Public Affairs Council, 64. Reproduced with permission.

corporate strategy, and unmet corporate objectives.[58] It is clear from these findings and other studies that the primary reason a company decides to close down a plant is economics.[59]

What Should Business Do?

By all appearances, the business-closing issue is evolving much like many of the other social issues business has had to address during the last 20 years. The recession of the early 1980s gave the issue dramatic impetus. Although it is difficult to assess where public opinion on the issue will eventually come to rest, a strong case could be made for a positive or proactive response, given the magnitude of the problem and the activism it has generated. In addition to the desire to circumvent more government regulation and a continued hostile relationship with labor, responsive corporate action could be justified on the grounds of maintaining a long-run enlightened self-interest, preserving business as a viable institution in society, preventing further social problems, and creating a favorable public image for the corporation.[60]

Although the right to close a business has long been regarded as a management prerogative, the business shutdowns since 1970—especially their dramatic effects—call attention to the question of what rights and responsibilities business has in relation to employee and community stakeholders. The literature of business social responsibility and policy has documented corporate concern with the detrimental impact of its actions. Indeed, business's social response patterns over the past 15 years have borne this out. No less a business advocate than Peter Drucker has suggested the business position regarding social impacts of management decisions:

> Because one is responsible for one's impacts, one minimizes them. The fewer impacts an institution has outside of its own specific purpose and mission, the better does it conduct itself, the more responsibly does it act, and the more acceptable a citizen, neighbor, and contributor it is.[61]

The question is raised, therefore, whether business's responsibilities in the realm of plant closings and their impacts on employees and communities are any different than the host of responsibilities that have already been assumed in areas such as employment discrimination, employee privacy and safety, honesty in advertising, product safety, and concern for the environment. From the perspective of the employees affected, their role in plant and business closings might be considered an extension of the numerous employee rights issues that many corporate social policy experts think will dominate employer-employee relations throughout the next decade.

A number of executives have spoken on this issue, and several have indicated that there is an obligation to employees and to the community when a business opens up or decides to close. As D. Kenneth Patten, president of the Real Estate Board of New York, illustrates:

A corporation has a responsibility not only to its employees but to the community involved. It's a simple question of corporate citizenship. Just as an individual must conduct himself in a way relating to the community, so must a corporation. As a matter of fact, a corporation has an even larger responsibility since it has been afforded even greater advantages than the individual. Just as a golfer must replace divots, a corporation must be prepared at all times to deal with hardships it may create when it moves or closes down.[62]

Others have also argued that there is a moral obligation at stake in the business-closing issue. In an extensive consideration of plant closings, philosopher John Kavanagh has asserted that companies are not morally free to ignore the impact of a closing on employees and the community. His argument is similar to those that have been given on many other social issues, namely, that business should minimize the negative externalities (unintended side effects) of its actions.[63]

There is some debate over business's responsibility in the plant-closing question. Figure 13-12 summarizes the views of executives surveyed on this issue. First, the executives were asked their opinions regarding public expectations. Nearly 90 percent agreed that the public expects business to be responsive to employee and community needs in closedown situations. When asked to evaluate their responsibilities to their employees, to the community, and to their own stockholders, the respondents provided some rather interesting—and in one case quite surprising—answers. Eighty-five percent agreed that they had a greater responsibility to their employees than to the community.

That the executives did not feel more strongly about the primacy of responsibility to shareholders vis-à-vis employees and the community was quite surprising. Although more agreed than disagreed, over a third chose not to take sides. This would seem to indicate that these executives have a fairly balanced view of their obligations to stakeholder groups.

To other questions, almost 60 percent of the executives responding agreed that the media sometimes exaggerate business's responsibilities in shutdown situations, and over 80 percent believed that unions also have a responsibility to minimize the impacts of a closedown. In neither case, however, was the sentiment strong.[64]

Business essentially has two opportunities to be responsive to employee and community stakeholders when a possible shutdown occurs. It may take certain actions *before* the decision to close is made and then again *after* the decision to close is made.

Before the Decision to Close Is Made. Before a company makes a decision to close down, it has a responsibility to itself, its employees, and its community to thoroughly and diligently study whether the closing is the only option available. A decision to leave should be preceded by in-depth discussions with community leaders (testing their willingness to cooperate in meeting the difficulties faced)

FIGURE 13-12 Executive Evaluations of Business Responsibility in Plant-Closing Issue

ISSUES	FREQUENCY AND PERCENTAGE					
	Strongly Agree	Agree	Neither A nor D	Disagree	Strongly Disagree	
Public Expectations	1	2	3	4	5	Mean
The public expects business to be responsive to employee and community needs	30 (14%)	154 (73%)	20 (10%)	2 (1%)	4 (2%)	1.97
Business Responsibility						
Business has a responsibility to employees to minimize negative impacts of a closedown	81 (39%)	113 (54%)	8 (4%)	2 (1%)	1 (.5%)	1.68
Business has more of an obligation to employees than to the community	58 (28%)	120 (57%)	21 (10%)	7 (3%)	4 (2%)	1.89
Business has a responsibility to the community to minimize the negative impacts of a closedown	40 (19%)	126 (50%)	32 (15%)	8 (4%)	1 (.5%)	2.05
Businesses' responsibilities to stockholders should take precedence over employees and the community	24 (11%)	64 (31%)	78 (37%)	36 (17%)	4 (2%)	2.67
Business has a responsibility to take positive steps to smooth displaced workers' transition to new employment	33 (16%)	131 (62%)	28 (13%)	15 (7%)	3 (1%)	2.12
Media Views						
The media exaggerate businesses' responsibility in closedown situations	41 (20%)	82 (39%)	68 (32%)	14 (7%)	5 (2%)	2.27
Union Responsibility						
Unions have a responsibility to avoid or minimize the impacts of a closedown	38 (19%)	131 (62%)	30 (14%)	6 (3%)	2 (1%)	2.05

Totals do not equal 100% due to non-response to items and rounding. Source: Archie B. Carroll, Elizabeth J. Gatewood, James J. Chrisman, "Plant Closings: PAOs Respond to a Survey on an Increasingly Troublesome Issue," *Public Affairs Review,* Copyright ø 1984, Public Affairs Council, 66. Reproduced with permission.

and by a critical and realistic investigation of economic alternatives. This would include a study of long-term productivity and cost estimates, of the employee base and the nature of skills available, and of the likelihood that identical problems might recur in a different location.

After a careful study has been made, it may be concluded that finding new ownership for the plant or business is the only feasible alternative. Two basic options exist at this point: (1) find a new owner, or (2) explore the possibility of employee ownership.[65]

New Ownership. Malcolm Baldrige, former chairman of Scoville Manufacturing Co., argued that the first obligation a company has to its employees and the community is to try to sell the business as a going unit instead of shutting down. This may not always be possible, but it is an avenue that should be explored to its fullest extent.[66] Quite often, the most promising new buyers of a firm are residents of the state who have a long-term stake in the community and are willing to make a strong commitment.

For example, when Viner Brothers, a shoe manufacturer in Bangor, Maine, filed for bankruptcy in 1980, its three plants presented an attractive investment opportunity for area shoe companies. Within several weeks, Wolverine, the maker of Hush Puppies, was the new owner. Part of the multimillion dollar sale agreement was that Wolverine hire at least 60 percent of the laid-off workers. About 90 percent of the 900 workers who were laid off were eventually rehired.[67]

Employee Ownership. The idea of the company selling the plant or business to the employees as a way of avoiding a closedown is appealing at first glance. Hundreds of U.S. companies with at least 10 workers each are employee-owned. Most of these arrangements are the result of last-ditch efforts to stay in business. According to the National Center for Employee Ownership, over 50,000 workers have saved their jobs by taking over companies. In the last decade, such national firms as General Motors, National Steel, Sperry Rand, and Rath Packing Co. have sold plants to employees that would have been closed otherwise. The experience of many of these firms has not been extremely favorable, however.[68] In numerous cases, employees have been forced to take significant wage-and-benefit reductions to make the business profitable. In other cases, morale and working conditions have not been satisfactory under the new method of ownership and management.

Before Ford Motor Co. closed its Sheffield, Alabama, plant, it offered to sell the plant to the employees. The only way for this to work, according to Ford officials, would be for the employees to agree to 50 percent wage-and-benefit reductions. Union officials and employees declined the offer. One individual who had worked at the plant for 18 years summed up the thinking of many: "If Ford can't make the plant pay, I can't see me making it pay."[69]

In a rather dramatic case in 1983, however, negotiators worked out an agreement whereby the employees of National Steel's Weirton (West Virginia) mill would purchase the mill. This new company became the nation's largest employee-owned enterprise, as well as its eighth largest producer of steel. Experts gave the mill a surprisingly good chance of succeeding, though Weirton's workers had to take about a 32 percent cut in pay. But as the mill's union president argued, "32 percent less of $25 an hour is a whole lot better than 100 percent of nothing."[70]

After a decade as owners of Weirton Steel, employees in 1991 became extremely frustrated and angry that employee ownership did not guarantee them that they would not lose their jobs. In 1991, Weirton Steel had eliminated 1,000 of its 8,200 jobs, furloughed another 200 workers, and had plans to cut 700 more jobs. As demand sank in 1990 for the sheet steel it produces, Weirton found itself in the unenviable position of having to actually lay off employee-owners. One employee posed the question many were asking: "How can we be laid off if we own the company?" The reality of the situation, however, is that the company must still take whatever actions it must if it is to remain solvent and profitable. One of the major pitfalls of worker ownership is that it doesn't rewrite the laws of capitalism—the bottom line is still the bottom line.[71]

For the employee ownership option even to have a chance, a long lead time between the announcement and the actual closing is needed to organize employees while they are still on the site. In addition, time is necessary to conduct complete and detailed feasibility studies. These studies need to assess such factors as:

- Employee readiness for ownership
- Union attitudes
- Management/entrepreneurial skills present among employees
- Company's products and its markets
- Technology
- Proposed organization structure
- Potential funding sources[72]

The National Center for Employee Ownership has found that most employee-owned firms have a good chance of survival.[73] Figure 13-13 summarizes one excellent view of the role of business in a business-closing situation.

After the Decision to Close Is Made. There are a multitude of actions that business can take once the decision has been made that a closedown or relocation is unavoidable. The overriding concern is that the company seriously attempts to mitigate the social and economic impacts of its actions on employees and the community. Regardless of the circumstances of the move, some basic planning can help alleviate the disruptions felt by those affected. Possible actions that management can take include (1) conducting a community-impact analysis; (2) providing advance notice to the employees/community; (3) providing transfer, relocation, and outplacement benefits; (4) gradually phasing out the business; and (5) helping the community attract replacement industry.[74]

FIGURE 13-13 Business Responsibility in a Plant-Closing Decision

> The interests of both corporation and community are best served by recognizing the mutual advantages of the corporation's remaining in the community. There are many incentives to remain, among them a skilled labor pool, a tradition of goodwill and cooperation, and the claims of local citizenship. A decision to leave should be based only on compelling reasons and arrived at only after a thorough consideration of the profitability of the operation and the personal and social consequences of such a move. It should be preceded by extensive communication with community leaders, testing their willingness to cooperate in meeting the difficulties that have developed, and by a critical and realistic examination of economic alternatives, including longterm productivity and cost estimates, the employee base and the nature of the skills available, and the likelihood that the same problems will recur in a new location.
>
> If relocation is concluded to be necessary, a responsible corporation will exercise every effort to mitigate the social and economic impact of its move on the community by adequate notice, gradual phasing out of operation, affording reasonable and realistic opportunities for employees to transfer, and cooperating with the community in attracting other industry to utilize the old facilities.

Source: *Criteria for Decision Making.* Copyright Long Island University, 1979. (New York: C. W. Post Center, Long Island University, 1979), 12. Reproduced with permission.

Community-Impact Analysis. If management is responsible for its impacts on employees and the community, as Drucker stated, a thorough community-impact analysis of a decision to close down or move would be beneficial. The initial action would be to realistically identify those aspects of the community that would be affected by the company's plans. This would entail asking such questions as:

- What groups will be affected?
- How will they be affected?
- What is the timing of initial and later effects?
- What is the magnitude of the effect?
- What is the duration of the impact?
- To what extent will the impact be diffused in the community?[75]

Once these answers are provided, management is better equipped to modify its plans so that negative impacts can be minimized and favorable impacts, if any, can be maximized.

A community-impact analysis was proposed as a part of the Corporate Democracy bill introduced in Congress by Representative Benjamin Rosenthal (D-New York) in 1980. The bill was the outgrowth of some of the work inspired by Ralph Nader and Mark Green. Although it failed to pass, it provides further evidence of the kinds of considerations that have been discussed in an effort to increase corporate accountability.[76] It seems much more reasonable that companies conduct such impact analyses on their own volition than to have government involved in yet another aspect of business.

Because it is inevitable that management is going to be drawn into economic-action teams that will be formed in the community, initiatives should convey a spirit of cooperation in facilitating community action. For example, once National Steel decided it had to close its Weirton mill, its attempt to assess community impact led to management joining with union members, local business people, and government leaders to raise the money needed for the expensive studies and sophisticated investment advice that eventually led to employee ownership.

Advance Notice. Perhaps one of the most often discussed responsibilities in business- or plant-closing situations is the provision of advance notice to workers and communities. As discussed earlier, political pressures mounted for a law that would mandate such notice before firms close down. A 2-year advance notice was one of the key provisions in the *Corporate Democracy Act of 1980,* which failed to pass but was included in legislation created in Wisconsin and Maine.[77]

Finally, an advance-notice law was passed in 1988. It was called the Worker Adjustment and Retraining Notification Act (WARN), and it went into effect in February of 1989. WARN requires those firms employing 100 or more workers to provide 60 days advance notice to employees before shutting down or conducting substantial layoffs. A major problem is that most businesses are not large enough to be affected by the law. With WARN, the United States joins many other nations in mandating advance notice. Canada requires 1 to 16 weeks, depending on the case. Great Britain requires 60 to 90 days, depending on the case, and Japan requires "sufficient advance notice."[78]

The advantages of advance notice accrue primarily to the affected employees and their communities. Workers are given time to prepare for the shutdown both emotionally and financially. Advance notice makes it easier for employees to find new jobs because research has shown that employees have an improved chance at reemployment while they are still employed. Advance notice is motivational in that, once one joins the ranks of the unemployed, there is a tendency to coast until benefits start to be exhausted. Also, the company is in a better position to provide references, retraining, or counseling during the advance-notice period.[79]

The disadvantages of advance notice, particularly that which extends over a longer time period, accrue principally to the business firm. Once word leaks out in the community, financial institutions may be reluctant to grant credit, customers become worried about items purchased or promised, and the overall level of business activity can decline rapidly. One of the major disadvantages of a lengthy notice is the task of motivating workers who know they are going to lose their jobs. Declines in employee morale, pride in work, and productivity can be expected. Absenteeism may increase as workers begin to seek other employment. In addition, there is the likelihood of vandalism, pilferage, and neglect of property as employees lose interest or attempt to strike back against the employer's decision.

A Bureau of Labor Statistics survey showed that only 10 percent of collective bargaining agreements contained advance-notice provisions. The notifications typically run from a week to 6 months. It is expected that such provisions will increasingly appear in labor contracts, but the question of what the appropriate period of time is will continue to be the subject of much discussion.[80]

Transfer, Relocation, and Outplacement Benefits. Enlightened companies are increasingly recognizing that the provision of separation or outplacement benefits are in the long-range best interest of all parties concerned. Everyone is better off if disruptions are minimized in the lives of the firm's management, the displaced workers, and the community. Outplacement benefits have been used for years as companies have attempted to remove redundant or marginal personnel with minimum disruption and cost to the company and maximum benefit to the individuals involved. Increasingly these same benefits are beginning to be used in plant shutdowns.

The efforts of two British companies to ease the pain of plant closings by providing outplacement benefits offer some creative alternative positive social responses. Tate and Lyle, faced with a need to switch from imported cane to domestic beets, had to close three of its sugar refineries and sharply reduce production between 1977 and 1979. The company knew of the devastating impact this would have and decided to assume responsibility for finding alternative jobs for its displaced workers, most of whom were middle-aged with an average of 20 to 25 years of experience. Its most successful effort was to act as a merchant banker, prepared to invest in existing viable companies that needed capital to expand and that would give first refusal for jobs to former Tate and Lyle workers. In one case, a small electrical engineering firm moved to the economically weakened area and created 150 new jobs in return for financing from Tate and Lyle.[81]

In another case, British Steel Corporation set up BSC, Ltd., a subsidiary whose purpose was to find jobs for approximately 50,000 displaced workers. The subsidiary assists small firms willing to rent space in its old plants, with the objective of creating new jobs. The results of the firm's persistence are quite impressive. In 1979, BSC met its target of 3,000 jobs; in 1980, 5,000 jobs were created; and, in 1981, it hoped to develop 10,000 jobs. As seen in the cases presented, outplacement benefits can include assisting the displaced workers in finding new jobs, severance pay, insurance coverage, and a host of other separation benefits.

Gradual Phaseouts. Another management action that can significantly ameliorate the effects of a business shutdown is the gradual phasing out of the business. The gradual phaseout buys time for employees and the community to adjust to the new situation and to solve some of its problems.

The American Hospital Supply (AHS) Company provides a useful model of a socially responsive firm. AHS announced its intent to sell its medical manufacturing company of about 275 employees in October 1979.[82] A meeting of all employees was held to communicate the rationale for the decision. Although AHS received numerous inquiries from outside firms, the business did not sell. In preparing for this possible outcome, department heads prepared termination lists specifying those employees essential to the phaseout. In December 1979, another all-employee meeting was held, and it was announced that the business would be gradually phased out. A retention/outplacement program was prepared and explained in detail immediately following the meeting.

At AHS, terminated employees with no specific skills or with unique situations (such as illnesses) were identified early so that special outplacement support could be provided. The first group of terminated employees included all of the sales department, half of research and development, all of marketing, and various others not crucial to the wind-down. The outplacement activities resembled a college placement office. Over 25 firms visited to conduct on-site interviews. Resumés were drafted by the employees, reviewed and proofed by the personnel department, and typed on the company's word-processing equipment. The volume of outplacement correspondence was so high that additional word-processing capability and clerical support had to be acquired. Final survey results showed that one-fourth of the outplaced employees received "similar" compensation packages and another 65 percent received "superior" compensation packages as compared to their previous positions.

In addition, severance pay was offered, and a benefits plan was created for the employees. The benefits plan provided for 100 percent vesting in the company incentive program, retirement and profit-sharing plans, 3 months' basic benefit coverage (medical, dental, life insurance) beyond the date of termination, and various other extensions (maternity, orthodontia) as considered necessary.[83]

The Olin Corporation case gives us another good example of a gradual phaseout combined with benefits to the community being left. The Olin Corporation decided it had to close down its operations in Saltville, Virginia. Among the reasons for this decision was that it could not meet new water quality standards being required by the Virginia Water Control Board and the federal EPA. Olin attempted to lessen its impact on the employees and community by taking a number of actions. For its employees, it set up a generous severance plan and relocation assistance service. Another major decision it faced was the disposal of its plant, property, and equipment after the operations had closed. The company made several attempts to attract replacement industry but had little success. Finally, Olin approached the town of Saltville with an offer to donate the plant, 3,500 acres of property with mineral rights, and all remaining tangible property in the town over a period of several years. The company also gave the town $30,000 to hire experts to mark all the equipment with its probable market value, $150,000 to compensate the town for lost tax revenues over the next 3 years, and $450,000 to be used for planning, developing, and rehabilitating over the next 4 years.[84]

Of course, the closedown at Saltville represented such a massive economic upheaval that the townspeople were not completely satisfied with what the company did for them. In addition to its large donations, Olin Corporation received sizable tax writeoffs that eased its own financial burden. Nevertheless, what the company did for the community and the people over a period of several years represented a genuine attempt to help.

Helping to Attract Replacement Industry. The principal responsibility for attracting new industry falls on the community, but the management of the closing firm can provide cooperation and assistance. The closing company can help by providing inside information on building and equipment characteristics and capabilities, transportation options based on its past experience, and contacts with other firms in its industry that may be seeking facilities. Helping the community attract replacement industry has the overwhelming advantage of rapidly replacing large numbers of lost jobs. Also, because attracted businesses tend to be smaller than those that closed, this strategy enables the community to diversify its economic base while gaining the jobs.[85]

DECISION FACTORS, ACTION, AND RESEARCH GROUPS

A number of factors go into helping a business decide the extent to which it should assist displaced employees and communities. Some of these factors include the following:

1. General size of the negative impact the closedown is creating
2. The extent of commitment its employees and the communities displayed over the years to the firm
3. How large an employer the firm was relative to the total economic base
4. The length of time the firm was in the community
5. The length of time employees had worked in the firm
6. The economic options available to the firm to assist
7. The firm's overall sense of corporate responsibility or corporate social policy

Any one or several of these factors, along with other issues, assume a major role in dictating the responses of management and the firm.

One major study found that executives felt the following corporate actions were preferable once a business-closing decision had been made: severance pay, outplacement benefits, insurance benefits, advance notice, employee retraining and transfer/relocation benefits.[86]

If the state of the economy, and particularly the manufacturing sector, is a principal force in plant closings, there is perhaps little that business can do to exercise any appreciable degree of control over shutdowns. Over the longer term, however, careful strategic planning can assume an important role in reducing or ameliorating the plant-closing problem.

Plant-Closing Public Action Groups

An important phenomenon associated with the plant-closing issue is the growth and development of new *plant-closing public action groups.* Examples of these include the Ohio Public Interest Campaign, the Pennsylvania Public Interest Coalition, the Illinois Public Action Council, and the Oregon Plant Closure Organizing Committee. These groups continue to focus public attention on the plant-closing issue.

Plant-Closing Researchers and Action Specialists

Concomitant with increased legislative activity and the emergence of public-interest groups concerned with plant shutdowns has been the development of an active network of plant-closing researchers and action specialists. Prominent among these activists are those documenting the impact of job losses due to plant closings on mental health. Such impact has resulted in increases in suicides, spouse beatings, and other problems.[87] As data are gathered on the psychological impacts of plant closings, more compelling cases for additional legislation may be forthcoming. Although the future for these efforts is uncertain, the community of plant-closing researchers and activists could be creating the foundation for more intensive efforts in the years ahead.

We are only now beginning to define the stakeholders involved in the issue, the impacts that business closings have on employees and communities, the public's reaction to the problem, and types of actions that managements might take. From observing other social issues that have achieved the kind and degree of attention that business closings have, it is necessary that positive steps be taken if business is to be responsive to its employees and communities and if further state and federal legislation is to be avoided. It appears that business closings and their adverse consequences will have to be a front-burner issue with business in the future, lest yet another public problem culminate in new laws or a knotty regulatory apparatus.[88]

SUMMARY

Community stakeholders are extremely important to companies. Companies may have a positive impact on the community in two basic ways: donating time and talent of managers and employees and making financial contributions. Because business has a vital stake in the community, it engages in a variety of community projects. Examples include literacy programs and executive loan programs. Community action programs are a key part of managing community involvement. Important components of such efforts include knowing the company's resources, selecting projects to pursue, and monitoring corporate efforts.

Business also contributes to community stakeholders through philanthropy. The third sector, or nonprofit sector, depends on business's support. Companies give for a variety of reasons—some altruistic, some self-interested. Major recipients of business giving include education, health and welfare, civic activities, and culture and the arts. As companies attempt to manage their philanthropy, two concepts have developed: (1) strategic philanthropy, which seeks to improve the overall fit between corporate needs and charitable programs, and (2) cause-related marketing, which tightens the linkage between a firm's profits and its contributions. Cause-related marketing represents a unique joining of business and charity with the potential for great benefits for each.

Just as firms have beneficial effects on community stakeholders, they may have detrimental effects as well. Business or plant closings are a prime example of these detrimental effects. Plant closings have a pervasive influence in the sense that a multitude of community stakeholders are affected—employees, local government, other businesses, and the general citizenry. Business closings have become a serious problem in the United States over the past decade. There is no single reason why the closings have occurred, but among the major reasons are economic conditions, consolidation of company operations, outmoded technology or facilities, and changes in corporate strategy.

Before the decision to close a facility is made by management, it has a responsibility to itself, its employees, and the community to thoroughly study whether closing is the only or the best option. Finding a new owner for the business or pursuing the possibility of employee ownership are reasonable and desirable alternatives. After the decision to close has been made, possible actions include a community-impact analysis, advance notice, transfer, relocation or outplacement benefits, gradual phaseout, and help in attracting replacement industry. Companies have an added incentive to be responsive on the business-closing issue because state and federal governments are closely watching the manner in which firms are handling this problem. Nevertheless, companies that are sensitive to community stakeholders will want to fashion a socially responsive posture in dealing with their stakeholders.

DISCUSSION QUESTIONS

1. Outline the essential steps involved in developing a community action program.
2. Take the social policies attributed to George Steiner and explain how a firm with which you are familiar might apply them in a community.
3. Differentiate between strategic philanthropy and cause-related marketing. For each type, provide an example that is not discussed in the chapter.
4. What are the major reasons that business closings have become so prevalent in the past decade? Discuss.

5. In your opinion, why do businesses have a responsibility to community stakeholders in a business-closing decision? Enumerate what you think are the major reasons.
6. Identify and discuss briefly what you think are the major trade-offs that firms face as they think about a possible plant closing, and their responsibility to their employees and the community.
7. Describe what you think are a firm's social responsibilities in a plant- or business-closing situation. What factors influence the degree of responsibility you think management has?

ENDNOTES

1. "Community Action Manual" (Worcester, MA: Norton Company, April, 1978), 1–2.
2. "How Business Is Joining the Fight Against Illiteracy," *Business Week* (April 16, 1984), 94.
3. Ibid.
4. Ibid., 98.
5. Ibid.
6. "Literacy Programs Become a Popular Corporate Cause," *The Wall Street Journal* (August 14, 1986), 1.
7. Dirk Johnson, "Companies Create 'Model School' for Urban Poor," *New York Times* (October 26, 1988).
8. James M. Hildreth, "When Business Comes to Cities' Rescue," *U.S. News & World Report* (August 9, 1982), 42–43.
9. Kathryn Troy, *Studying and Addressing Community Needs: A Corporate Case Book* (New York: The Conference Board, 1985), 1.
10. Ibid.
11. George A. Steiner, "Social Policies for Business," *California Management Review* (Winter, 1972), 22–23.
12. Frank Koch, "A Strategy for Corporate Giving and Community Involvement," *Management Review* (December, 1977), 7–13.
13. John A. Conway, "Giving a Hand: The Eagles Score a Touchdown with Ronald McDonald Houses," *The Wall Street Journal* (April 26, 1990), B-2; Michelle Hiskey, "Amoco Pumps Life Into Needy Neighborhoods," *Atlanta Constitution* (September 9, 1991), B1 & B6.
14. *Webster's New World Dictionary* (Cleveland: World Publishing Company, 1964), 1098.
15. Robert L. Payton, *Philanthropy: Voluntary Action for the Public Good* (New York: Macmillan, 1988), 32.
16. Robert L. Payton, "Philanthropy in Action," in Robert L. Payton, Michael Novak, Brian O'Connell, Peter Dobkin Hall, *Philanthropy: Four Views* (New Brunswick: Transaction Books, Inc.), 1.
17. Morrell Heald, *The Social Responsibilities of Business: Company and Community 1900–1960* (Cleveland: Case Western Reserve University Press, 1970), 112.
18. John D. Rockfeller, III, "In Defense of Philanthropy," *Business and Society Review* (Spring, 1978), 26–29.
19. Anne Klepper, *Corporate Contributions, 1989* (New York: The Conference Board, 1990), 7.
20. Archie B. Carroll, "Corporate Social Responsibility: Will Industry Respond to Cutbacks in Social Program Funding?" *Vital Speeches of the Day* (July 15, 1983), 604–608.
21. Sam Sternberg, *National Directory of Corporate Charity* (San Francisco: Regional Young Adult Project, 1984), 14.
22. J. R. Block and Norman Goodman, "Why Companies Give," *Journal of Advertising Research* (October, 1976), 59–63.
23. Louis W. Fry, Gerald D. Keim, Roger E. Meiners, "Corporate Contributions: Altruistic or For-Profit?" *Academy of Management Journal* (March, 1982), 94–106.
24. Louis W. Cabot, "Corporate Support of Education: No Strings Attached," *Harvard Business Review* (July-August, 1978), 139–144.
25. Robert H. Malott, "Corporate Support of Education: Some Strings Attached," *Harvard Business Review* (July-August, 1978), 133–138.
26. Irving Kristol, "On Corporate Philanthropy," *The Wall Street Journal* (March 21, 1977), 18.
27. *The Handbook of Corporate Social Responsibility*, 110–111.
28. Ibid., 143–144.
29. Ibid., 223.
30. Keith H. Hammonds, "Corning's Class Act," *Business Week* (May 13, 1991), 68–76.
31. Richard Eells, *The Corporation and the Arts* (New York: Macmillan, 1967).
32. John B. Forbes, "Corporate America Giving More to the Arts," *New York Times* (May 15, 1977), F-19.
33. Ibid.
34. "Where Art and Business Meet," *Forbes* (February 1, 1977), 6.
35. Ibid.

36. Paul H. Eliker, "Why Corporations Give Money to the Arts," *The Wall Street Journal* (March 31, 1978), 15.
37. Ibid.
38. Cited in Robert Toth, "PBS Corporate Gifts Selfish?" *Atlanta Journal* (September 11, 1977), F-7.
39. Eliker, 15.
40. James J. Chrisman and Archie B. Carroll, "Corporate Responsibility: Reconciling Economic and Social Goals," *Sloan Management Review* (Winter, 1984), 59–65.
41. Timothy S. Mescon and Donn J. Tilson, "Corporate Philanthropy: A Strategic Approach to the Bottom-Line," *California Management Review* (Winter, 1987), 50.
42. Avery Hunt, "Strategic Philanthropy," *Across the Board* (July/August, 1986), 27.
43. Richard J. Morris and Daniel A. Biederman, "How to Give Away Money Intelligently," *Harvard Business Review* (November-December, 1985), 151–159.
44. James Rosebush, "Well-Planned Charity Helps Giver and Receiver," *The Wall Street Journal* (January 26, 1987), 22.
45. Patricia Caesar, "Cause-Related Marketing: The New Face of Corporate Philanthropy," *Business and Society Review* (Fall, 1986), 16.
46. Martin Gottlieb, "Cashing in on a Higher Cause," *New York Times* (July 6, 1986), 6F.
47. *For Members Only: A Newsletter for American Express Cardmembers* (October, 1985), 1–2.
48. Monci Jo Williams, "How to Cash in on Do-Good Pitches," *Fortune* (June 9, 1986), 76.
49. Cynthia D. Giroud, "Cause-Related Marketing: Potential Dangers and Benefits," in James P. Shannon (ed.), *The Corporate Contributions Handbook* (San Francisco: Jossey-Bass, 1991), 144–146.
50. Caesar, 17–18.
51. Ibid., 18–19.
52. Michael Schroeder and Jonathan Kapstein, "Charity Doesn't Begin at Home Anymore: Multinationals Are Discovering the Value of Global Philanthropy," *Business Week* (February 25, 1991), 91.
53. Ibid.
54. John P. Kavanagh, "Ethical Issues in Plant Relocation," *Business and Professional Ethics Journal* (Winter, 1982), 22.
55. Archie B. Carroll, "When Business Closes Down: Social Responsibilities and Management Actions," *California Management Review* (Winter, 1984), 125.
56. Barry Bluestone and Bennett Harrison, *The Deindustrialization of America* (New York: Basic Books, 1982), 29.
57. Ibid., 31.
58. Archie B. Carroll, Elizabeth J. Gatewood, James J. Chrisman, "Plant Closings: PAOs Respond to a Survey on an Increasingly Troublesome Issue," *Public Affairs Review* (1984), 64.
59. Cooper and Lybrand, *Closing Plants: Planning and Implementing Strategies* (Morristown, NJ: Financial Executives Research Foundation, 1986), 2.
60. Carroll, 129.
61. Peter F. Drucker, *Management: Tasks, Responsibilities, Practices* (New York: Harper & Row, 1974), 327–328.
62. Quoted in "A Firm's Obligations: To Employees, Community," *Atlanta Journal* (September 19, 1977), 4-C.
63. Kavanagh, 21–33.
64. Carroll, Gatewood, and Chrisman, 65.
65. Carroll, 131.
66. Quoted in *Atlanta Journal* (September 19, 1977), 4-C.
67. Jeff Strout, "Viner Shoe Expected to Be in Full Swing Soon," *Bangor News* (January 21, 1981), 9.
68. Terri Minsky, "Gripes of Rath: Workers Who Bought Iowa Slaughterhouse Regret That They Did," *The Wall Street Journal* (December 2, 1981), 1.
69. Robert L. Simison, "Ford Motor to Close Facility in Alabama," *The Wall Street Journal* (November 11, 1981), 5.
70. "A Steel Town's Fight for Life," *Newsweek* (March 28, 1983), 49.
71. Maria Mallary, "How Can We Be Laid Off If We Own the Company?" *Business Week* (September 9, 1991), 66.
72. Cornell University Workshop Report, *The Economic Crisis and Self-Managed Alternatives* (Ithaca, NY: Cornell University, June 6–8, 1980), 8, cited in Northeast-Midwest Institute, *Shutdown: A Guide for Communities Facing Plant Closings* (Washington, DC: 1981), 17.
73. Cory Rosen, *Employee Ownership; An Alternative to Plant Closings* (Arlington, VA: National Center for Employee Ownership, February, 1982), 1.
74. Carroll, 132.
75. Grover Starling, *The Changing Environment of Business* (Boston: Kent, 1980), 319–320.
76. Mark Green, "The Case for Corporate Democracy," *Regulation* (May/June, 1980), 23–24.
77. Green, 26.
78. Paul D. Staudohar, "New Plant Closing Law Aids Workers in Transition," *Personnel Journal* (January, 1989), 87–90.
79. Robert B. McKersie, "Advance Notice," *The Wall Street Journal* (February 25, 1980), 20.
80. Ibid.
81. "Plant Closings: Easing the Pain," *Management Review* (August, 1981).
82. Philip D. Johnston, "Personnel Planning for a Plant Shutdown," *Personnel Administrator* (August, 1981), 53–57.
83. Ibid.
84. Robert J. Litschert and Edward A. Nicholson, "Olin's Pullout from Saltville: A Company's Responsibility to the Community," *The Corporate Role and Ethical Behavior* (New York: Petrocelli/Charter, 1977), 102–115.
85. Northeast-Midwest Institute, 28–30.
86. Carroll, Gatewood, and Chrisman, 65–70.
87. Terry F. Buss and F. Stevens Redburn, *Mass Unemployment: Plant Closings and Community Mental Health* (Beverly Hills, CA: Sage, 1983).
88. Carroll, Gatewood, and Chrisman, 71–72.

PART FOUR INTERNAL STAKEHOLDERS AND THE MANAGEMENT OF THEM

14 Employee Rights and Stakeholder Issues

15 Employee Stakeholders: Privacy, Safety, and Health

16 Protected Groups: Employment Discrimination and Affirmative Action

17 Owner Stakeholders: Corporate Governance

CHAPTER **FOURTEEN**

Employee Rights and Stakeholder Issues

CHAPTER OBJECTIVES

After studying this chapter, you should be able to:

◆ Identify the major changes that are occurring in the work force today.

◆ Explain the employee rights movement and its underlying principles.

◆ Describe and discuss the employment-at-will doctrine and its role in the employee's right to a job or not to be fired.

◆ Discuss the right to due process and fair treatment.

◆ Elaborate on the freedom-of-speech issue and whistle-blowing.

Society's changing values are having a great impact on the workplace. Although external stakeholders such as the government, consumers, the environment, and the community continue to be major facets of business's concern for the social environment, considerable attention is now being given to employee stakeholders—their status, their treatment, their rights, and their satisfaction. This should come as no surprise when you consider that most adult Americans spend the bulk of their hours during the day at work. It was only a matter of time until citizens as employees would express the same kind of concern for their work lives as they have expressed for external, more remote social issues.

Although we cannot give a complete historical account of this development, it has been a direct outgrowth of the kinds of social changes that have brought other societal issues into focus. The history of work has been one of steady improvements for employees. In recent years, issues have emerged that are quite unlike the old bread-and-butter concerns advocated by labor unions—more pay, shorter hours, more job security, and better working conditions. These desires still exist, but they have given way to other, more complex expectations and issues.

Changes in the workplace in the past decade or so have created what is now called the *employee rights movement*. Because this topic is so extensive, we dedicate two chapters to it. In this chapter, we will include a discussion of changes in the workplace, the employee rights movement, the right to a job—or at least not to be fired without just cause—the right to due process or fair treatment, and the right to freedom of speech in the workplace. The next chapter will treat related issues—the right to privacy and the right to safety and health. These two chapters should be seen as a continuous discussion of employee stakeholders.

CHANGES IN THE WORKPLACE

The concern for workplace rights did not arise in a vacuum. Many of the societal changes we described earlier in this book—education, awareness, affluence, rising expectations, and so on—directly affected this issue. They caused employees to be more assertive about their treatment and what was owed them as employees. Other, more specific changes have occurred, however. Because these changes have had a more focused effect on the workplace, it is worthwhile discussing them before we proceed. According to David W. Ewing, a noted authority in workplace issues, four trends, in particular, have occurred in the workplace: (1) an increase in technological hazards to employees, (2) the invasion of the computer into the workplace, (3) the divided loyalties of professionals, and (4) the increased mobility of employees.[1]

Increased Technological Hazards

Over the past 30 years, employees have been subjected to an amazing number of new technologies and chemicals in the workplace. These include nuclear power, complex electronic control devices, and chemicals such as polychlorinated biphenyls (called PCBs). Productivity has been enhanced by the new technologies, but so have the hazards to which employees are being exposed. Control failures can cause an automatic subway train to crash. Careless packing can cause toxicity. Signs of the latent perils of modern chemistry—emergency showers in corridors, "Danger" signs, masks, and protective clothing—are evident in many manufacturing operations.[2]

People are concerned about the dark side of technology. A major poll found that the vast majority of Americans still say that science and technology do more good than harm, but the margin fell from 83 percent in 1983 to 72 percent in 1986. Furthermore, almost one-fourth of those surveyed thought that technology would do more harm than good for the human race over the next 20 years. *U.S. News & World Report* termed the problem "high tech anxiety."[3] Technological hazards in the workplace create a constant low-level anxiety among employees as they begin to think about how the next workplace disaster may somehow affect them.

The Computer Invasion

The computer invasion not only has contributed to workplace anxiety but also has turned the classic balance of privacy upside down. There was a time when privacy invasion was restricted to what a supervisor could see or hear or what information was collected by personnel offices. Today, a whole new array of computer-based or electronic devices that monitor employees are present in the work environment. Examples include listening devices, polygraphs, closed-circuit television monitors, computer-based information systems, and drug-testing devices. Most companies are careful about this newly found power, but employees still worry about abuses and privacy invasions.[4] We will discuss this issue more fully in the next chapter.

Professionals with Divided Loyalties

One of the most significant trends occurring in the workplace is the dramatic growth in numbers of professional and technical employees. According to the Census Bureau, the number of professional and technical employees in the work force doubled between 1960 and 1980.[5]

The increased number of professionals has improved organizations, but it has also altered attitudes and values in the workplace. Especially affected has been loyalty to the employer. Professionals such as scientists, engineers, accountants, computer specialists, and others find it hard to subscribe to the traditional philosophy, "my corporation, right or wrong." Their codes of conduct require that they use their knowledge and skill for the public welfare. In fact, it is a growing conviction among professionals that acts of dissidence, honestly and thoughtfully taken in the public interest, are not only permissible but obligatory.[6]

Conventional management wisdom used to be that, once management reached a decision, all employees were to assume that the decision was right and were to support it fully. Professionals, on the other hand, feel a compulsion to question what they think is wrong because of their duty to their professional codes. More and more this brings them into conflict with their employers.[7]

There is evidence that loyalty to employers is diminishing for other reasons as well. Younger workers, who are generally better educated, have higher expectations about their jobs and are more likely to feel dissatisfied when their ambitions are not met. Also, a wave of mergers and acquisitions that has resulted in significant reductions in professional and managerial jobs over the past decade has convinced many employees that companies will not return their loyalty anymore. Cutbacks and closings, as well as general cynicism about the workplace, have also resulted in diminished employee loyalty and an increase in concern about employee rights.[8]

A recent book describes how job security, particularly among white-collar professional jobs, which was so prevalent back in the 1950s, has disappeared. The book *The Death of the Organization Man,* by Amanda Bennett, describes how the perk-padded paradise for executives described in William H. Whyte's 1956 bestseller *The Organization Man* "went to hell in the 1980s." Managers who had staked everything on their loyalty to a major corporation all of a sudden found themselves out on their own. Their jobs, and their loyalty, were lost to meet cutback quotas forced by Japanese competition, postraid reorganizations, and other such unexpected events.[9] Consequently, the loyalty that corporate managements routinely expected from professionals was gone, and a new era of workers with divided loyalties had begun. This new era has continued on into the 1990s.

Increased Mobility of Employees

Another trend of the past 30 or 40 years is the increased mobility of employees. At one time people lived in one or a few places all their lives. This is no longer the case. Today we live in a corporate society where being transferred or moving to another employer to get a quick raise and a promotion has become commonplace. It has been half-jokingly said that IBM stands for "I've been moved."

As regional lines continue to diminish, one is as likely to find a New Englander living in the Southeast as a Midwesterner living on the West Coast. Employees move geographically, between functions, and between levels of responsibility. One major unintended result of this interchange is that it produces uncertainty in employee relationships. Employees no longer know exactly what to expect from their employers or supervisors. Anxiety, tension, and even conflict can arise as employment relationships become less stable and more transient. Employees in this kind of environment feel vulnerable.[10]

These four kinds of changes in workplace relationships have enhanced the professional environment in business organizations today. Productivity improvements have followed. For employees, however, these changes have had important downside consequences. These conditions have created an environment in which employees have felt more anxious and less secure, indeed, vulnerable to real or perceived detrimental management decisions. In this kind of environment, it should not be surprising to find employees increasingly sensitive and attentive to what rights they have in their employment roles.

THE EMPLOYEE RIGHTS MOVEMENT

To appreciate the background of the employee rights issues (especially the rights of freedom of speech and due process), it is useful to consider the underlying public sector-private sector dichotomy that society faces. The public sector is subject to constitutional control of its power. The private sector generally has not been subject to constitutional control because of the concept of private property. The ***private property*** notion holds that individuals and private organizations are free to use their property as they desire. As a result, private corporations historically and traditionally have not had to recognize employee rights because society honored the corporation's private property rights. The underlying issues then become *why* and *to what extent* the private property rights of business should be diluted.

Although Americans have enjoyed civil liberties for nearly two centuries, these same rights have not been afforded in most companies, government agencies, and other organizations where Americans work. David W. Ewing states the matter quite strongly:

> Once a U.S. citizen steps through the plant or office door at 9 a.m., he or she is nearly rightless until 5 p.m., Monday through Friday. The employee continues to have political freedoms, of course, but these are not the significant ones now. While at work, the important relationships are with bosses, associates, and subordinates. Inequalities in dealing with these people are what really count for an employee.[11]

Although there are increasing exceptions to Ewing's rather strong statement, it does call attention to the importance of the issue. Ewing goes on to state, "The employee sector of our civil liberties universe is more like a black hole, with rights so compacted, so imploded by the gravitational forces of legal tradition, that, like the giant black stars in the physical universe, light can scarcely escape."[12]

A brief comment on the role of labor unions is appropriate here. In general, although labor unions have been quite successful in improving the material conditions of work life—pay, fringe benefits, and working conditions—they have not been as interested in pursuing civil liberties. Unions must be given credit, however, for the gains they have made in converting what were typically regarded as management's rights or prerogatives into issues in which labor could participate. For nonunion workers, however, rightlessness continues to be a problem.

Many managers find the movement toward employee rights disturbing. Management prerogatives are being challenged at an unprecedented rate, and the traditional model of employee loyalty and conformity to the wishes of management is rapidly fading from the scene. The traditional model seems to be disappearing as a concept more than as a reality, however. Although managers indicate strong support for wider employee rights when responding to questionnaires, practice does not show employee rights prevailing extensively in business today. Indeed, although managers support the concept in principle, they sometimes express an ambivalence about employee rights and their costs. A survey of managers showed a higher concern for instability in our society (confusion about sexual standards, attitudes toward drugs, treatment of criminals, respect for the family and authority, breakdown of law and order, and disintegration of the work ethic) than for obstacles to individuality in the workplace.[13] Thus, while managers sympathize with the need for privacy, due process, and free speech in the workplace, they seem to be more concerned with general social trends and their impact.

The job-related rights that are mentioned often enough to merit discussion here include the following: (1) the *right to a job*, or at least the right *not to be fired without just cause*; (2) the *right to due process* and *fair treatment*; and (3) the *right to freedom*, particularly freedom of expression or freedom of speech. In Chapter 15 we will consider the rights to privacy, safety, and health in the workplace.

THE RIGHT TO A JOB/ NOT TO BE FIRED

We are not suggesting that employees have a *right* to a job. We are attempting, however, to assert that current trends in employment practices, if extended to their logical conclusion, may be signaling a belief on the part of workers that they have such a right. Currently, writings have begun to appear that raise the issue of the right to a job, the right to participation, and the right to meaningful work.[14] One recent book contains the "Right to Meaningful Work" as one of its major sections.[15]

It may be, given the entitlement mentality that prevails in our country today, that a significant proportion of Americans think they are entitled to a job. Our discussion, however, addresses this issue from another direction. There is growing evidence that Americans think they have *a right not to be fired without just cause*. Depending on how one defines *just cause*, we may be seeing a trend toward a right to keep a job once you have it or, perhaps, even a right to a job.

Employment-at-Will Doctrine

The central issue in this move to protect workers' jobs surrounds changing views of the **employment-at-will doctrine.** This doctrine is the long-standing, common-law principle that the relationship between employer and employee is a voluntary one and can be terminated at any time by either party. Just as employees are free to quit a company any time they choose, this doctrine holds that employers can discharge employees for any reason, or no reason, as long as they do not violate union contracts, federal discrimination laws, or state laws. What this doctrine means is that if you are not protected by a union contract (about 80 percent of the work force is not) or by one of the discrimination laws, then your employer is free to let you go anytime, for any reason.

The employment-at-will doctrine is being eroded by court decisions, however. The courts have ruled with increasing frequency that employers have responsibilities to employees that, from the standpoint of fairness, restrict management's former prerogative to fire at will. Into the vocabulary of employment relationships has thus entered new expressions, such as *unjust dismissals* or *wrongful discharge*. Three broad categories of issues are illustrative of the legal challenges that are arising regarding employment-at-will discharges: (1) public policy exceptions, (2) contractual actions, and (3) breach of good faith actions.

Public Poicy Exceptions. For a wide variety of reasons, the courts are beginning to hold that employees who previously were unprotected are now protected. One emerging major exception to the long-standing employment-at-will doctrine is the ***public policy exception.*** This exception protects employees from being fired because they refuse to commit crimes or because they try to take advantage of privileges to which they are entitled by law.[16] The courts have held that management may not discharge an employee who, for example, refuses to commit an illegal act (say, refusing to participate in a price-fixing scheme). In another case a company had to reinstate an X-ray technician fired for refusing to perform a medical procedure that, under state law, could be performed only by a physician or registered nurse. Another public policy exception is that employees cannot be dismissed for performing a public obligation, such as serving on a jury or supplying information to the police. Increasingly the courts are protecting whistle-blowers—those who report company wrongdoings—from being fired.

There have been so many claims of public policy exceptions in recent years that the majority of courts have had to establish standards for plaintiff employees. For example, an employee must specify a "clear public policy mandate," embodied in a statute, regulation, or court decision, that allegedly has been violated by his or her discharge. In addition, the plaintiff employee must show a direct causal linkage between that public policy and the discharge.[17] However, the *implied* existence of public policy actions is increasingly being accepted by state courts as a basis for successful employee lawsuits.[18]

Contractual Actions. The courts are also protecting workers who they believe had a **contract** or an ***implied contract*** with their employer. The courts are holding employers to promises the company did not even understand it had made. For example, statements in employee handbooks or personnel manuals, job-offer letters, and even oral assurances about job security are now being interpreted as implied contracts that management is not at liberty to violate.[19] One employee was protected because he proved in court that he was told "Nobody gets fired around here without a good reason." Another quoted a line in an employee handbook that read, "You will not be fired without just cause."[20] Still another employee successfully argued that, when the company used the term *permanent employee* to mean an employee past the 6-month probationary period, it had implied *continuous employment*.

Breach of Good Faith Actions.
The courts are beginning to recognize that employers are expected to hold themselves to a standard of fairness and good faith dealings with employees. This concept is probably the broadest restraint on employee-at-will terminations. The good faith principle suggests that employers may run the risk of losing former employee lawsuits if they fail to show that unsatisfactory employees had every reasonable opportunity to improve their performance before being fired. The major implication of this trend for companies is that they may need to introduce a grievance-type review procedure for employees.[21] We will discuss such due process mechanisms later in the chapter.

Management's Response

Management needs to be aware of the following important points: (1) It is now good stakeholder management to treat workers fairly and to dismiss them only for justifiable cause, and (2) the law today protects workers who do not get fair treatment. Therefore, management has an added incentive not to get embroiled in complex legal entanglements over unfair dismissals for wrongful discharges.

Four specific steps management might take on this issue include the following:

1. *Stay on the right side of the law.* It is management's responsibility to know the law and to obey it. This is the clearest, best, and most effective position to take. The company that conducts itself honestly and legally has the least to fear from disgruntled employees.

2. *Investigate any complaints fully and in good faith.* Well-motivated complainers in organizations are likely to first report a problem or concern to someone within the company. Therefore, employee complaints about company activities should be checked out. If there is substance to the problem, management will have time to make corrections internally, with a minimum of adverse publicity.

3. *Deal in good faith with your employees.* Honor commitments made, including those made in writing and those the employees have a reasonable right to expect as matters of normal policy, behavior, and good faith. Employees have won court cases when it was determined that the company acted in bad faith.

4. *When you fire someone, make sure it is for a good reason.* This is the best advice possible. Also, make sure the reason is supported by sound records and documentation. Effective performance appraisals, discipline procedures,

dispute-handling procedures, and employee communications are all keys to justifiable discharges. Management needs to be attentive to abusive or retaliatory firings that are supported by thin technicalities. If the need arises to fire someone, it should not be difficult to document sound reasons for doing so.[22]

Before an employee is terminated, management should ask the supervisor, "If you had to appear before a jury, why would you say the employee should be discharged?" Management should also ask the supervisor if the action being taken is consistent with other actions and whether the employee was aware that certain conduct would result in discharge. Finally, management should assume that litigation might result from the firing and that the supervisor making the decision to fire might not be with the company when the case goes to court. Therefore, documentation for the termination should be assembled immediately for each event leading to the termination.[23]

THE RIGHT OF DUE PROCESS AND FAIR TREATMENT

One of the most frequently discussed employee rights issues in the last decade has been the right to due process. Basically, **due process** is the right to receive an impartial review of one's complaints and to be dealt with fairly. In the context of the workplace, due process is thought to be the right of an employee to have any decision that adversely affects him or her to be reviewed by an objective, impartial third party.

One major obstacle to the due-process idea is that it may be contrary to the employment-at-will principle discussed earlier. It is argued, however, that due process is consistent with the democratic ideal that guarantees the universal right to fair treatment. It could be argued that without due process an employee does not receive fair treatment in the workplace. Furthermore, as the employment-at-will principle is being eroded by the courts, this might be an indication that the principle is basically not fair. If this is true, the due-process concept makes more sense. Werhane contends that, procedurally, due process should state, "Every employee has a right to a public hearing, peer evaluation, outside arbitration, or some other open and mutually agreed-upon grievance procedure before being demoted, unwillingly transferred, or fired."[24]

Sometimes the employee is treated unfairly in such a subtle way that it is difficult to know that unfair treatment has taken place. What do you do, for example, if your supervisor thinks you are so good that he or she refuses to recommend you for promotion or permit you to transfer because he or she does not want to lose you? How do you prove that a manager has given you a low performance appraisal because you resisted sexual advances? The issues over which due-process questions may arise can be quite difficult and subtle.

Only in the last 25 years have some leading companies given special consideration to employees' rights to due process. Historically, managements have had almost unlimited freedom to deal with employees as they wished. In many cases, unfair treatment was not intentional but was the result of an inept or distracted supervisor inflicting needless harm on subordinates.[25]

Employee Constitutionalism

David Ewing, an authority on the question of employee civil liberties, has argued that employee due process should be regarded as but one part of employee constitutionalism. He suggests that *employee constitutionalism* "consists of a set of clearly defined rights, and a means of protecting employees from discharge, demotion, or other penalties imposed when they assert their rights." He goes on to list the main requirements of a due-process system in an organization:

1. It must be a procedure; it must follow rules. It must not be arbitrary.
2. It must be visible and well-known enough that potential violators of employee rights and victims of abuse know about it.
3. It must be predictably effective.
4. It must be institutionalized—a relatively permanent fixture in the organization.
5. It must be perceived as equitable.
6. It must be easy to use.
7. It must apply to all employees.[26]

Ewing has gone on to define *corporate due process* in the following way:

A fair hearing procedure by a power mediator, investigaor, or board with the complaining employee having the right to be represented by another employee, to present evidence, to rebut the other side's charges, to have an objective and impartial hearing, to have the wrong corrected if proved, to be free from retaliation for using the procedure, to enjoy reasonable confidentiality, to be heard reasonably soon after lodging the complaint, to get a timely decision, and so forth.[27]

Ewing's concept of corporate due process represents an ideal and it is doubtful that many corporate due-process systems meet all his requirements. However, there are many due-process systems or mechanisms in use by companies today as they strive to treat their employees fairly. In the next section we will briefly discuss some of these approaches.

Management's Response

There are a number of different ways companies can and do provide due process for their employees. The techniques described below have been employed over the past 20 years.

Common Techiques. One of the most often-used mechanisms is the ***open-door policy.*** This approach typically relies on a senior-level executive who asserts that his or her "door is always open" for those who think that they have not been treated fairly. Another technique is to assign to a *personnel department executive* the responsibility for investigating employee grievances and either handling them or reporting them to higher management. Closely related to this technique would be assigning this same responsibility to an *assistant to the president.*[28] From the employee's standpoint, the major problems with these approaches are that (1) the process is closed, (2) one person is reviewing what happened, and (3) there is a tendency in organizations for one manager to support another manager's decisions. The process is opened up somewhat by companies that use a ***hearing procedure,*** which permits employees to be represented by an attorney or other person, with a neutral company executive deciding the outcome based on the evidence. Similar to this approach is the use of a ***management grievance committee,*** which may involve multiple executives in the decision process.

The Ombudsperson. A due-process mechanism that has become popular in the past decade is the use of a corporate ombudsperson. **Ombudsman,** the word from which *ombudsperson* is derived, is a Swedish word that refers to one who investigates reported complaints and helps to achieve equitable settlements. The ombudsperson approach has been used in Sweden since 1809 to curb abuses by government against individuals. In the United States, the corporate version of the ombudsperson was first experimented with in 1972, when the Xerox Corporation named an ombudsperson for its largest division. General Electric and the Boeing Vertol division of Boeing were quick to follow.[29]

The operation of the ombudsperson program at Xerox is generally representative of ombudsperson programs. The ombudsperson began as an *employee relations manager* on the organization chart in Xerox's Information Technology Group (ITG). Everyone soon knew that the ombudsperson's function was to ensure fair treatment of employees. This person reported directly to the ITG president, who was the only one who could reverse the ombudsperson's decisions. During the early years of the program, none of the ombudsperson's decisions were overturned—a point signifying the power and effectiveness of the one holding the job.

Under the Xerox system, the employee was expected to try to solve his or her problem through an immediate supervisor or the personnel department before submitting a complaint to the ombudsperson. At this point, the ombudsperson studied the complaint and the company file on the case. Then the ombudsperson discussed both items with a personnel department representative and then with the employee. Subsequently, the ombudsperson's recommended solution was passed on to the personnel department, which presented it as its own idea to the manager involved. Only if the manager declined to go along did the ombudsperson reveal his or her identity and put his or her authority behind the recommendation.[30]

The ombudsperson approach to ensuring due process is not without problems. Managers may feel threatened when employees go to the ombudsperson, who must be willing to anger executives in order to get the job done. There is also the fear that employees might experience retribution for going to the ombudsperson in the first place. Despite these potential problems, once in place and understood, the system has worked. A positive and unexpected result of the Xerox experience was that even supervisors went to the ombudsperson for advice on personnel problems. Thus, in some cases, issues were referred to the ombudsperson even before managerial decisions were made.[31]

The Peer Review Panel.
The *peer review panel* is another innovative due-process mechanism being experimented with at a number of large companies today. Control Data Corporation (CDC) is one of the pioneers in the use of the peer review process. Over 30 years ago, Control Data was one of the first nonunion companies in the United States to introduce an employee grievance system. It was a system whereby an aggrieved employee could appeal all the way up the line through six management levels. The company tried to make the system work, but many times the grievance either died because of the cumbersome process or was "kicked upstairs" for some higher level of management to handle. Rulings in favor of the worker were rare. The company determined that this approach was not fair, so in 1983 it added a peer review process to the system.[32]

The peer review process requires the same initial steps as the traditional grievance system. The employee is to talk first with his or her manager, then to the human resources manager, and then to one higher executive in the management chain. If the employee is still not satisfied that due process has prevailed, he or she is entitled to request a peer review board. The central feature of the board is a panel of two randomly chosen "peers" of the aggrieved employee, along with one disinterested executive from a different division. *Peers* are defined as fellow workers in the same job family at a grade level equal to or higher than that of the grievant.[33]

Managers on the losing side sometimes complain because they feel that outsiders are deciding on local issues they are not intimately knowledgeable about. The company's position is that a manager not only has to convince himself or herself and local superiors that a personnel action is right but also must have it measured as right against a companywide policy. The success of the system depends on (1) having the clear support of top management for fair treatment to employees and (2) being seen as a permanent fixture. The people who operate the system must have sufficient respect and stature to make the process credible in the eyes of even the most authoritarian line manager.[34]

The trend to broaden employee rights through peer review boards is now supported by over 100 major companies. Among the users of this approach are Federal Express Corporation, Digital Equipment Co., General Electric, Borg-Warner, and Citicorp. These companies say that the peer boards build an open, more trusting atmosphere; help deter union organizing; and stem the rising number of costly lawsuits that claim wrongful discharge and discrimination. Although many of their managers have initially resisted or objected to the approach, most of them now accept the procedure as policy. In fact, now they more carefully adhere to company disciplinary policy than in the past.[35]

Whether it is the peer review board, the ombudsperson approach, or some other technique, many enlightened companies today are attempting to make due process a reality. As Ewing has indicated, "Due process is a way of fighting institutionalized indifference to the individual—the indifference that says that productivity and efficiency are the goals of the organization, and any person who stands in the way must be sacrificed."[36] Increasingly, companies are acknowledging due process to be not only an employee right but also a sound management practice in keeping with the wishes and expectations of employees.

In his book, *Justice on the Job,* David Ewing lists a number of companies that today employ either investigator-type or board-type due process or employee grievance procedures. These companies and their systems' names are as follows:[37]

Investigator-Type Systems

Company	Due-Process System Name
Bank of America	"Let's Talk"
CIGNA	"Speak Easy"
IBM	The "Open Door"
NBC	Counselor System

Board-Type Systems

Company	Due-Process System Name
Citicorp	Problem Review Procedure
Control Data	Review Board
Federal Express	Guaranteed Fair Treatment Procedure
General Electric	Grievance Review Panel
Honeywell	Management Appeals Committee
John Hancock	Employee Relations Committee
Polaroid	The Employees Committee

THE RIGHT TO FREEDOM OF SPEECH

In letters written to and published in newspapers, a chemical researcher stated that the cosmetics industry (of which his employer was a member) was charging unconscionably high prices caused by exorbitant advertising expenses. After he was fired, he sued his employer, alleging that his right to free speech had been infringed on and that he was due damages. The court affirmed his right to free speech but not to a job in private industry. The company did not need a reason for firing him as long as it did not violate employment laws regarding sex and race. In another case with different results, an engineer in a California company alleged that a new computer console developed by his employer failed to meet state safety codes. He voiced his objections to management, even though management did not want to hear him. He was fired, went to court, and was awarded damages by the Superior Court in Santa Clara.[38]

Unfortunately for employees who believe they have a legitimate right to speak out against a company engaging in an illegal or unethical practice, the resolution of the first case above is more common than that of the second. Nevertheless, the willingness to challenge management is typical of a growing number of employees today, and increasingly these individuals are receiving some protection from the courts.

Whistle-Blowing

As stated earlier, the current generation of employees has a different concept of loyalty to and acceptance of authority than do those of years past. The result is an unprecedented number of employees "blowing the whistle" on their employers. A whistle-blower has been called a "muckraker from within, who exposes what he considers the unconscionable practices of his own organization."[39]

What constitutes whistle-blowing? For our purposes, we define a **whistle-blower** as "an individual who reports to some outside party (for example, media, government agency) some wrongdoing (illegal or unethical act) that he or she knows or suspects his or her employer of committing." Thus, there are four elements in the whistle-blowing process: the whistle-blower, the act or complaint the whistle-blower is concerned about, the party to whom the complaint or report is made, and the organization against which the complaint is made.[40] Although our definition indicates that whistle-blowing is to some outside party, there are many cases where whistle-blowers just report their concerns to some member of management and yet are treated as though they went to an outside party.

What is at stake is the employee's right to speak out in cases where he or she thinks the company or management is engaging in an unacceptable practice. This is contrary to our cultural tradition that an employee does not question his or her superior's decisions and acts, especially not in public. The traditional view holds that loyalty, obedience, and confidentiality are owed the corporate employer solely. The emerging view of employee responsibility holds that the employee has a duty not only to the employer but also to the public and to his or her own conscience. Whistle-blowing, in this latter situation, becomes a legitimate option for the employee should management not be responsive to expressed concerns. Figure 14-1 presents these two situations.

FIGURE 14-1 Two Views of Employee Responsibility in a Potential Whistle-Blowing Situation

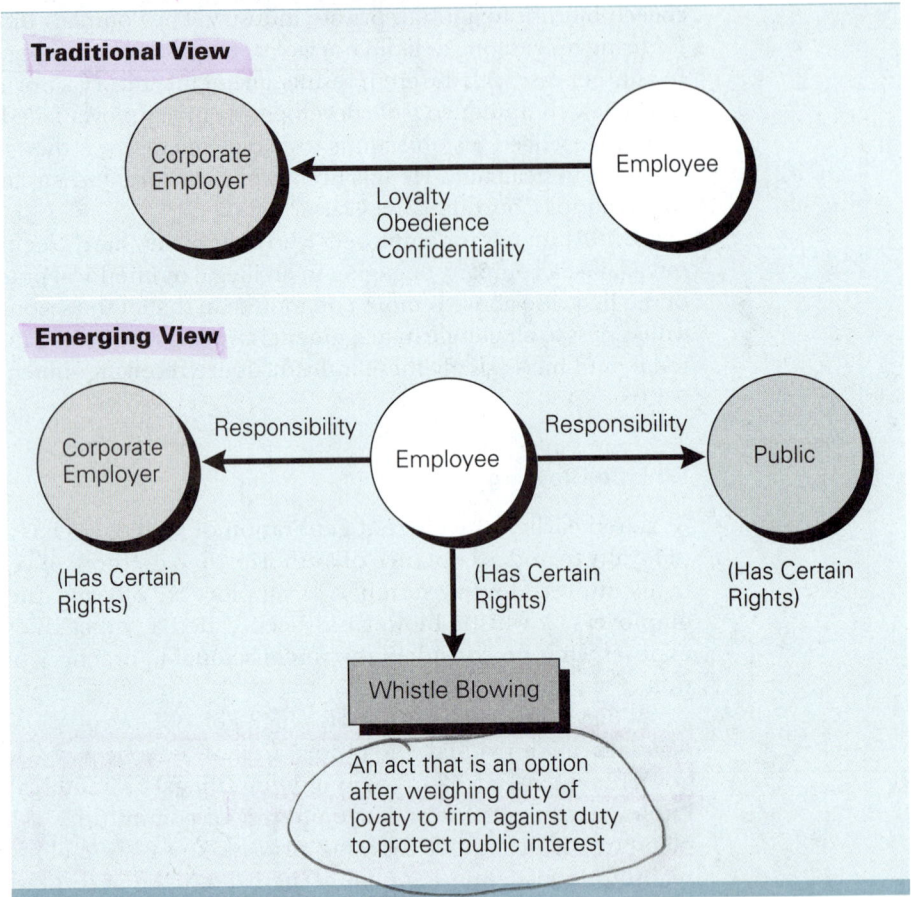

Most whistle-blowers seem to be engaging in the act out of a genuine or legitimate belief that the organization is wrong and that they are doing the right thing. They may have learned of the wrongful act because they were requested or coerced to participate in it. Or, they may have gained knowledge through observation or examination of company records. The genuinely concerned employee may initially express concern to superiors or someone else in the organization.[41] Other potential whistle-blowers may be planning to engage in the act to strike out or retaliate against the company or a manager for some reason. This motive is illegitimate. A recent survey of 233 whistle-blowers disclosed that the average whistle-blower is not an oddball, "loose cannon," or disgruntled employee. The average whistle-blower turned out to be a family man, in his mid-40s, who was motivated by conscience, or what might be termed "universal moral values."[42]

Consequences of Whistle-Blowing

What happens to employees when they blow the whistle? Unfortunately, whistle-blowers are not rewarded for their perceived contributions to the public interest. Although they are more often getting some form of protection from state courts, in general they have paid dearly for their lack of loyalty to the firm. Short of being fired, the following are some examples of corporate retaliation made against whistle-blowers:

- Their work was more stringently criticized.
- They received less desirable work assignments.
- They were pressured to drop charges against the company.
- They received a heavier workload.
- They lost perquisites (for example, telephone, parking privileges).
- They were excluded from meetings previously attended.[43]

One example of what happens to whistle-blowers as a consequence of their actions is the case of Charles Atchison. At age 40, Atchison stood up before regulators and told them about numerous safety violations at the Commanche Peak nuclear plant in Glen Rose, Texas. Atchison was a quality control inspector for Brown & Root, the construction company that built the plant for the Texas Utilities Electric Company. Atchison claimed he couldn't get anyone to fix the problems. Atchison lost his job and ended up in debt. Although Atchison was proud of the stance he had taken, he indicated he often felt psychic scars from the experience. "The whistle-blower today is probably the most discriminated against individual in the country," Atchison exclaimed.[44]

Another example is the case of Anne Livengood, a 51-year-old medical office worker, who claimed she was fired from a physical therapy clinic in Fremont, California, after she had notified management that its accounting system billed insurance companies for services that were not performed. Livengood was escorted out of her building by the company accountant. Her response to the experience: "You feel so alone and intimidated."[45]

Famous cases of whistle-blowing include Ernest Fitzgerald, the Air Force employee who blew the whistle on billions in cost overruns at Lockheed in 1968, and the Morton Thiokol engineers who tried to halt the launch of the space shuttle *Challenger* because of frozen o-rings. All of these whistle-blowers were fired.[46]

Figure 14-2 identifies what Donald Soeken refers to as the seven stages of life of a whistle-blower.

Government's Protection of Whistle-Blowers

Just as employees are beginning to get some protection from the courts through the public policy exception to the employment-at-will doctrine, the same is true for whistle-blowers. The federal government was one of the first to attempt to

FIGURE 14-2 The Seven Stages of Life of a Whistle-Blower

Based on extensive research into the life experiences of whistle-blowers, Donald Soeken has identified what he calls the "seven stages of life" of a typical whistle-blower. The seven stages are as follows:[a]

1. Discovery of the abuse
2. Reflection on what action to take
3. Confrontation with superiors
4. Retaliation (against the whistle-blower)
5. Long haul of legal action
6. Termination of the case
7. Going on to a new life

In terms of *personal effects,* Soeken found through a survey of 233 whistle-blowers that (a) 90% lost their jobs or were demoted; (b) 26% sought psychiatric and medical care; (c) 15% divorced in the aftermath of the episode; (d) 10% attempted suicide; and (e) 8% went bankrupt.

[a]Cited in Ana Radelat, "When Whistle-Blowing Ruins Your Life," *Public Citizen* (September/October, 1991), 18-19.

protect whistle-blowers in the federal service. A highlight of the 1978 *Civil Service Reform Act* was protection for federal employees who expose illegal, corrupt, or wasteful government activities. Unfortunately, this effort has had only mixed results since its creation.[47] It is difficult to protect whistle-blowers against retaliation because so often the reprisals are subtle. An added boost for federal employees came in 1989 when Congress passed the *Whistle-Blower Protection Act* and President Bush signed it into law. The effect of the act was to reform the Merit System Protection Board and the Office of General Counsel, the two offices that protect federal employees. Early results show that about one-third of the whistle-blowers had their complaints upheld, whereas less than 5 percent were being upheld, prior to the new legislation.[48]

Most state courts recognize a public policy exception; therefore, whistle-blowers have some limited protection. The normal remedy for wrongfully discharged employees is reinstatement with back pay, with compensatory damages for any physical suffering sometimes being given by sympathetic juries.[49]

The problem with most laws that are intended to protect whistle-blowers is that they are quite spotty. Some environmental laws and workplace safety regulations have whistle-blower protection provisions, but many states remain reluctant to interfere with employment-at-will contracts. Protection is intended to mean that employers are prohibited from firing or otherwise retaliating against the employee, but practically speaking, they typically mean that the employee may file suit for harassment or wrongful discharge. Currently, private-sector employees are not protected by whistle-blowing laws, but the Government Accountability Project, an independent, nonprofit organization in Washington, DC, plans to sponsor legislation that would protect private-sector jobs.[50] Their challenge will be in getting Congress's cooperation and action.

The Whistle-Blowers Protection Act of Michigan

Few states have gone as far as Michigan did by actually creating specific whistle-blower protection. The *Michigan Whistle-Blowers Protection Act of 1981* became the first state law designed to protect any employee in private industry against unjust reprisals for reporting alleged violations of federal, state, or local laws to public authorities. The burden is placed on the employer to show that questionable treatment is justified on the basis of proper personnel standards or valid business reasons.[51]

When the bill was proposed in Michigan, employer groups were opposed to it because they feared it would result in a flood of litigation and harassing actions by employees who were fired for valid reasons. The bill was amended to address employer concerns, and the final law carried the following requirements for employees to be protected under the law:

1. Employees must prove they had filed or were about to file a complaint at the time of dismissal.
2. The complaint must be made to public authorities, not the media.
3. Reports must not be found to be false or malicious.[52]

Alan Westin thinks that a major flaw in the bill was that it did not require the whistle-blower, before going public, to first use a company's own internal procedures for complaint.[53] Generally speaking, when the courts are attempting to decide whether a whistle-blower should be protected, they are interested in (1) the whistle-blower's motives, (2) whether internal channels were first used, (3) whether the whistle-blower's allegations were true or false, and (4) the degree of care exercised by the whistle-blower in gathering the information on which the charges were based. These requirements are reasonable safeguards to protect companies against negligent dissenters.

The Michigan act was expected to spur similar laws in other states. Another likely impact of the law will be on company personnel practices and policies. Well-managed companies will need to be sure they have effective and fair procedures or systems to deal with potential whistle-blowers.[54] Time has shown, however, that few states have followed Michigan's aggressive lead.

Although we see more and more cases of employees wanting the right to question management and to speak out, David Ewing argues that there are some forms of speech that should not be protected:

1. Employees should not have the right to divulge information about legal and ethical plans, practices, operations, inventions, and other matters that must be kept confidential if the organization is to do its job in an efficient manner.
2. Employees should not have the right to make personal accusations or slurs that are irrelevant to questions about policies and actions that seem illegal or irresponsible.
3. Employees should not be entitled to disrupt an organization or damage its morale by making accusations that do not reflect a conviction that wrong is being done.
4. Employees should not be entitled to rail against the competence of a manager to make everyday work decisions that have nothing to do with the legality, morality, or responsibility of management actions.
5. Employees should not be entitled to object to discharge, transfer, or demotion, no matter what they have said about the organization or how they said it, if management can demonstrate that unsatisfactory performance or violation of a code of conduct was the reason for its actions.[55]

In the final analysis, an employee should have a right to dissent, but this right may be constrained or limited by the kinds of reasons just given and perhaps others as well.

Management Responsiveness to Potential Whistle-Blowers

How can an organization work with its employees to reduce their need to blow the whistle? Kenneth Walters has suggested five procedures that might be kept in mind:

1. The company should assure employees that the organization will not interfere with basic political freedoms.
2. The organization's grievance procedures should be streamlined so that employees can obtain a direct and sympathetic hearing for issues on which they are likely to blow the whistle if their complaints are not heard quickly and fairly.
3. The organization's concept of social responsibility should be reviewed to make sure it is not being construed as merely corporate giving to charity.
4. Organizations should formally recognize and communicate a respect for the individual consciences of employees.

5. The organization should realize that dealing harshly with a whistle-blowing employee could result in needless adverse public reaction.[56]

Companies are learning that whistle-blowing can be averted if visible efforts are made on the part of management to listen to and be responsive to the employees' concerns. One specific technique is the use of an ombudsperson, which we discussed earlier, as a due-process mechanism. The ombudsperson can also be used to deal with employee grievances against the company. The Corporate Ombudsman Association, which includes such firms as Anheuser-Busch, Control Data, McDonald's, and Upjohn, even goes so far as to prepare training materials that include likely whistle-blowing scenarios. According to one report, the national grapevine among corporate ombudspersons is constantly buzzing with rumors of front-page scandals that they have averted. The companies that have put money into such programs say they are well worth the investment.[57]

Whether an ombudsperson is used or not, management should respond in a positive way to employee objectors or dissenters. At a minimum, companies that want to be responsive to such employees should engage in the following steps:

1. Listen. Management must listen very carefully to the employee's concern. Be particularly attentive to the employee's valid points and acknowledge them and show that you have a genuine respect for the employee's concerns. Ewing recommends that you attempt to "draw out the objector's personal concerns."
2. Delve into why the employee is pursuing the complaint or issue. Determining the objector's motives may give you important insights into the legitimacy of the complaint and how it should best be handled.
3. Look for solutions that will address the interests of both the objector and the company.
4. Attempt to establish an equitable means to judge future actions. Objective tests or criteria that are agreeable to both sides are superior to perseverance or negotiation as a means of resolving an impasse.[58]

Employees' desire to speak out is increasingly becoming a right in their eyes and in the eyes of the courts as well. Although the courts differ from state to state, it is likely that whistle-blowers and employees' rights to free expression will increase in the future. This being the case, management needs to carefully assess where it stands on this vital issue. It is more and more apparent that respecting an employee's right to publicly differ with management may indeed serve the longer-term interests of the organization. We should also remember, however, that companies need and deserve protection from employees who do not perform as they should. Thus, "in the end, nothing could be more contrary to public policy than providing judicially imposed job tenure for those who least deserve it."[59]

SUMMARY

Employee stakeholders today are more sensitive about employee rights issues for a variety of reasons. Underlying this new concern are four changes that have occurred in the workplace: increased technological hazards, the computer invasion, professionals with divided loyalties, and increased mobility of employees. Central among the employee rights issues that are treated in this chapter include the right to a job or the right not to be fired without just cause, the right of due process and fair treatment, and the right to freedom of speech.

The basis for the argument that we may be moving toward an employee's right to a job, or not to be fired, is the erosion by the courts of the employment-at-will doctrine. More and more the courts are making exceptions to this long-standing common law principle. Three major exceptions are the public policy exception, the idea of an implied contract, and breach of good faith.

The right to due process is concerned primarily with fair treatment. A number of common techniques for management responding to this concern include the open door policy, use of personnel specialists, grievance committees, and hearing procedures. The ombudsperson approach has been used successfully in the past, and recently the peer review panel seems to have become a popular due-process mechanism. A special case in which due process is needed is for employees who choose to speak out against management or blow the whistle on unethical or illegal actions. In spite of government efforts to protect whistle-blowers, these individuals face severe reprisals for taking actions against their employers. Managements should be very attentive to dealing with employees' rights in this realm if they wish to avert major scandals and prolonged litigation. A stakeholder approach that emphasizes ethical relationships with employees would dictate this attention and concern.

DISCUSSION QUESTIONS

1. Rank the various changes that are occurring in the workplace in terms of their importance to the growth of the employee rights movement. Briefly explain your ranking.
2. Explain the employment-at-will doctrine and describe why it is being eroded. Do you think its erosion is leading to a healthy or unhealthy employment environment in the United States? Justify your reasoning.
3. In your own words, explain the right to due process. What are some of the major ways managements are attempting to ensure due process in the workplace?
4. If you could only choose one, would the ombudsperson approach or the peer review panel be your choice as the most effective approach to employee due process? Explain.
5. How do you feel about whistle-blowing now that you have read about it in the chapter? Are you more sympathetic or less sympathetic to whistle-blowers now? Explain.

ENDNOTES

1. David W. Ewing, "Due Process: Will Business Default?" *Harvard Business Review* (November-December, 1982), 115–116.
2. *Ibid.*, 115.
3. "Living Dangerously," *U.S. News & World Report* (May 6, 1986), 19–21.
4. Ewing, 115.
5. *Ibid.*
6. *Ibid.*, 116.
7. *Ibid.*
8. Thomas F. O'Boyle, "Loyalty Ebbs at Many Companies as Employees Grow Disillusioned," *The Wall Street Journal* (July 16, 1985), 27.
9. Amanda Bennett, *The Death of the Organization Man* (Morrow, 1990); Raymond Sokolov, "Troubles in the Corporation and on Campus," *The Wall Street Journal* (April 16, 1990), A11.
10. Ewing, 116.
11. David W. Ewing, *Freedom Inside the Organization: Bringing Civil Liberties to the Workplace* (New York: McGraw-Hill, 1977), 3.
12. *Ibid.*, 5.
13. David W. Ewing, "What Business Thinks About Employee Rights," *Harvard Business Review* (September-October, 1977), 81–94.
14. Patricia H. Werhane, *Persons, Rights and Corporations* (Englewood Cliffs, NJ: Prentice-Hall, 1985), 27.
15. Gertrude Ezorsky (ed.), *Moral Rights in the Workplace* (Albany, NY: State University of New York Press, 1986), 1–34.
16. T. J. Condon, "Fire Me and I'll Sue: A Manager's Guide to Employee Rights" (Alexander Hamilton Institute, 1984–1985), 4.
17. Linda D. McGill, "Public Policy Claims in Employee Termination Disputes," *Employment Relations Today* (Spring, 1988), 46–47.
18. Axel R. Granholm, *Handbook of Employee Termination* (New York: John Wiley & Sons, 1991), 21.
19. Andrew M. Kramer, "The Hazards of Firing at Will," *The Wall Street Journal* (March 9, 1987), 22.
20. Richard Greene, "Don't Panic," *Forbes* (August 29, 1983), 122.
21. Granholm, 24–25.
22. Condon, 12.
23. Kramer, 22.
24. Werhane, 110.
25. Ewing, 1977, 10.
26. *Ibid.*, 11.
27. David W. Ewing, *Justice on the Job: Resolving Grievances in the Nonunion Workplace* (Boston: Harvard Business School Press, 1989), 324.
28. Ewing, *Harvard Business Review*, 1977.
29. "Where Ombudsmen Work Out," *Business Week* (May 3, 1976), 114–116.
30. "How the Xerox Ombudsman Helps Xerox," *Business Week* (May 12, 1973), 188–190.
31. *Ibid.*, 190.
32. Fred C. Olson, "How Peer Review Works at Control Data," *Harvard Business Review* (November-December, 1984), 58.
33. *Ibid.*, 58–59.
34. *Ibid.*, 58, 64.
35. Larry Reibstein, "More Firms Use Peer Review Panel to Resolve Employee Grievances," *The Wall Street Journal* (December 3, 1986), 29.
36. Ewing, *Freedom Inside the Organization*, 172–173.
37. Ewing, 1989, v.
38. David W. Ewing, "Multiple Loyalties," *The Wall Street Journal* (May 1, 1978), 16.
39. Charles Peters and Taylor Branch (eds.), *Blowing the Whistle: Dissent in the Public Interest* (New York: Praeger, 1972), 4.
40. Janet P. Near and Marcia P. Miceli, *The Whistle-Blowing Process and Its Outcomes: A Preliminary Model* (Columbus, OH: The Ohio State University, College of Administrative Science, Working Paper Series 83-55, September, 1983), 2.
41. Nancy R. Hauserman, "Whistle-Blowing: Individual Morality in a Corporate Society," *Business Horizons* (March-April, 1986), 5.
42. Ana Radelat, "When Blowing the Whistle Ruins Your Life," *Public Citizen* (September/October, 1991), 16–20.
43. Janet P. Near, Marcia P. Miceli, Tamila C. Jensen, "Variables Associated with the Whistle-Blowing Process" (Columbus, OH: Ohio State University, College of Administrative Science, Working Paper Series 83-11, March, 1983), 5.
44. N. R. Kleinfield, "The Whistle-Blowers' Morning After," *New York Times* (November 9, 1986), 1-F.
45. Joan Hamilton, "Blowing the Whistle Without Paying the Piper," *Business Week* (June 3, 1991), 139.
46. *Ibid.*, 138.
47. Joann S. Lublin, "Watchdog Has Hard Time Hearing Whistles," *The Wall Street Journal* (October 17, 1980), 30.
48. Radelat, 20.
49. Michael W. Sculnick, "Disciplinary Whistle-Blowers," *Employment Relations Today* (Fall, 1986), 194.
50. Hamilton, 138–139.
51. Alan F. Westin, "Michigan's Law to Protect the Whistle Blowers," *The Wall Street Journal* (April 13, 1981), 18.
52. *Ibid.*
53. *Ibid.*

54. *Ibid.*
55. Ewing, *Freedom Inside the Organization,* 109–110.
56. Kenneth D. Walters, "Your Employees' Right to Blow the Whistle," *Harvard Business Review* (July-August, 1975), 161–162.
57. Michael Brody, "Listen to Your Whistle-Blower," *Fortune* (November 24, 1986), 77–78.
58. David W. Ewing, "How to Negotiate with Employee Objectors," *Harvard Business Review* (January-February, 1983), 104.
59. Charles C. Bakaly, Jr. and Joel M. Grossman, "Does First Amendment Let Employees Thwart the Boss?" *The Wall Street Journal* (December 8, 1983), 30.

CHAPTER **FIFTEEN**

Employee Stakeholders: Privacy, Safety, and Health

CHAPTER OBJECTIVES

After studying this chapter, you should be able to:

- ◆ Articulate the concerns surrounding the employee's right to privacy in the workplace.

- ◆ Identify the advantages and disadvantages of polygraphs, honesty tests, and drug testing as management instruments for decision making.

- ◆ Discuss the right to safety in the workplace, and summarize the role and responsibilities of OSHA.

- ◆ Define right-to-know laws, and identify the status of workplace threats to reproductive health.

- ◆ Elaborate on the right to health in the workplace, with particular reference to the recent concerns about smoking in the office and AIDS.

Employee stakeholders are concerned not only with the issues we discussed in the previous chapter but also with several other issues. These other issues should be thought of as extensions to the concept of employee rights developed in Chapter 14. In particular, in this chapter we are concerned with the employee's right to privacy, the right to safety, and the right to a healthy work environment. The right to privacy addresses the psychological dimension, while the rights to health and safety address the physical dimension. To reiterate our point made in the previous chapter, however, the distinction between the issues discussed there and here are made for discussion purposes. With that in mind, let us continue our consideration of social and ethical issues that have been important to employee stakeholders in recent years. If managers are to be successful in dealing with employees' needs and to treat them fairly as stakeholders, they must address these concerns now and in the future.

THE RIGHT TO PRIVACY

In New York in 1986, an employee returned to work after a prolonged illness. His supervisor was concerned about the possibility of a relapse, so the supervisor asked the company physician to talk with the employee's doctor. When the employee found out about this, he filed an invasion of privacy suit. During the same year, managers at a New Mexico newspaper got a tip from undercover investigators that the night production crew was using drugs. Complete with roaring cars and whirring helicopters, the company's security force moved in. They lined up 27 employees for urine tests. Later, 17 were fired for failing the test or refusing to take it. Several privacy invasion suits were filed.[1]

Both of these cases typify the growing number of privacy suits being filed against employers in recent years. According to Jury Verdict Research, Inc., as many as 5,000 such suits have hit the courts in the past 5 years. In the first case, a federal court upheld the employer's action, saying the supervisor was legitimately interested in the employee's health and, therefore, did not commit "an outrageous act of privacy invasion." In the second case, a lower court also found in favor of the employer's action because reasonable cause for suspicion existed.[2] In this age of increased sensitivity to invasion of privacy, however, the outcome of such cases is not always in the employer's favor. The number of cases of privacy invasion are increasing in numbers in recent years, and Eric H. Joss, a corporate lawyer, predicts that workplace privacy will be "the hottest employment-law topic of the 1990s."[3]

There are no clear legal definitions of what constitutes privacy or privacy invasion, but everyone seems to have an opinion of when it has happened to him or her. Most experts say that *privacy* means the right to keep personal affairs to yourself and to know how information about you is being used.[4] Patricia Werhane opts for a broader definition. She says privacy includes (1) the right to be left alone, (2) the related right to autonomy, and (3) the claim of individuals and groups to determine for themselves when, how, and to what extent information about them is communicated to others.[5]

Defining privacy in this way, however, does not settle the issue. In today's world, achieving these ideals is extremely difficult and fraught with judgment calls about our own privacy rights versus other people's rights. This problem is exacerbated by the increasingly computerized, technological world in which we live. We gain great efficiencies from computers and new technologies, but we also pay a price. Part of the price is that information about us is stored in dozens of places, including federal agencies (the Internal Revenue Service and the Social Security Administration), state agencies (courts and motor vehicle departments), and many local departments and businesses (school systems, credit bureaus, banks, life insurance companies, and direct mail companies).

In the realm of employee privacy, which is our central concern here, five important issues stand out as representative of the major privacy issues of the past decade: (1) collection and use of employee information in personnel files; (2) use of the polygraph, or lie detector, in making employee decisions; (3) honesty testing; (4) drug testing; and (5) monitoring of employee work and conversations by electronic means. There are other issues where privacy protection or invasion enters in, but these five capture the majority of concerns today. Therefore, they merit separate consideration.

Collection and Use of Employee Information by Employers

Our focus here is not on the collection, use, and possible abuse of information at a global or societal level. However, this is a serious public policy issue that warrants close scrutiny. Government data bases today form a cohesive web of information on individuals as some 15 agencies mix and match data. Ostensibly, as citizens we are protected by such laws as the *Privacy Act of 1974*, which requires consent of individuals before a federal agency collects and uses data for a purpose other than that for which it was originally intended.[6] In the private sector, however, very few laws exist to protect individuals.

According to privacy-expert David F. Linowes, "Most Americans have no idea of the scope of record-keeping by corporations."[7] Linowes, who has conducted major studies on the privacy issue, warns that this information is being used to decide job promotions, grant credit, sell insurance, and help marketers and political groups tailor commercial or political solicitations. A couple of examples are illustrative of the kinds of practices going on. Linowes cites a case where an executive was passed over for promotion because his personnel file reported "larcenous tendencies." It turns out that his file had been poorly summarized, and the report referred to a ninth-grade prank that had occurred. In another instance, an executive was denied a promotion because his file included an investigator's report of marijuana use years earlier and because of a report that he and his wife had seen a marriage counselor.

The collection and use of information by employers is our major concern here. The overriding principle that should guide corporate decision making is to collect only that information from employees that it absolutely needs. Companies should be careful that they do not misuse this information by employing it for purposes for which it was not intended. For example, information collected during a medical exam for insurance purposes should not be used by a supervisor in making an evaluation for a promotion. A recent study, however, revealed that over 60 Fortune 500 companies use medical data in making "employment-related" decisions. The companies defend this practice by referring to high medical costs and substance-abuse problems.[8]

Another important principle is that the employer understand that information collected from employees is not a commodity that can be exchanged, sold, or released in the marketplace.[9] Thus, the release of information to a landlord, credit grantor, or any other third party without the employee's consent may be seen as an invasion of privacy.

A final important principle pertains to employees' access to information about themselves in company personnel files or other record-keeping systems. Employees should have some way of knowing what information is being stored about them, and they should have the opportunity to correct or amend inaccurate information. A study by David Linowes revealed that 87 percent of companies allow employees to look at their personnel files, but only 27 percent give the employees access to supervisors' files, which often contain the most subjective information.[10]

Use of the Polygraph

In the privacy arena, few issues have generated as much controversy as the use of the polygraph, or lie detector, in business. The following brief scenario typifies the type of employee experience that led up to the *Employee Polygraph Protection Act of 1988*, which banned most private-sector uses of the lie detector. A polygraph machine was perched on a makeshift table in a tiny storage area. The examiner, hired by the employer, connected electrodes to 28-year-old Sandra Kwasniewski and then started interrogating her. "Have you ever shoplifted anything? Who do you live with? Where does your boyfriend live? What are your dating practices? Do you drink?" Ms. Kwasniewski, manager of a gas station convenience store in the eastern United States, maintained that nothing had been stolen or even reported missing, but two days after the lie detector test she was fired.[11]

The notion of a "lie detector," historians tell us, is nothing new. The Bedouins of Arabia knew that certain physiological changes, triggered by guilt and fear, occurred when a person lied. The outstanding change that they observed was for a liar to stop salivating. They developed a simple test: a heated blade was passed across the tongue of a suspected liar. If innocent, he would be salivating normally and his tongue would not be burned; if he was lying, his tongue would be scorched. The ancient Chinese used dry rice powder. Someone suspected of lying was forced to keep a handful of rice powder in his mouth. If it was soggy when he spat it out, he was telling the truth; if it was dry, he was lying.[12]

Critics of lie detectors today may well argue that the modern devices are not much more advanced than these ancient techniques. The polygraph machine, as it is known today, was developed by John Larson in 1929, though others trace it to an earlier date. It measures changes in blood pressure, respiration, and perspiration, sometimes called galvanic skin response. The theory behind polygraphy is that the act of lying causes stress, which in turn is manifested by observable physiological changes. The examiner, or machine operator, then interprets the subject's physiological responses to specific questions and makes inferences about whether the subject's answers indicate the presence or absence of deception.[13]

Although the 1988 Employee Polygraph Protection Act banned most uses of the lie detector, it is easy to sympathize with businesses' desire to protect themselves against serious losses. A recent figure is that companies suffer annual losses in excess of $40 billion because of employee theft. Recent studies have shown that 75 percent of the employees who handle money steal some of it. In addition, one must add to these numbers the losses due to employee sabotage, industrial espionage, and other misconduct that costs businesses large sums.[14]

It is little wonder, therefore, that businesses turned to the polygraph as a method to help screen out dishonest employees or to catch employees suspected of thefts. Prior to the 1988 law, companies used the lie detector primarily in three types of situations: (1) to examine current employees concerning specific incidences of theft or misconduct, (2) to periodically examine current employees concerning nonspecific conduct, and (3) to screen potential employees in a preemployment situation.[15]

Because lie detectors are still legal in very restricted circumstances, it is useful to note what are seen as their strengths and weaknesses. Proponents of lie detectors argue that employers have a right to protect their property and that lie detectors are more reliable and less expensive than alternatives. They cite the polygraph industry's claim of 95 to 100 percent accuracy in detecting deception. Proponents further argue that although employees and job applicants may sacrifice some privacy, a properly administered test only gets into information the company has a legitimate right to know.[16] Critics of lie detectors cite studies indicating inaccurate diagnoses in 50 percent of cases. Critics also object to testing that entails broad probes into certain zones of privacy that are too personal and not related to the job. Examples of these personal zones include questions about a worker's sexual practices, union sympathies, finances, and political and religious beliefs.[17]

Regulations on Use of Polygraphs. Because of the increasing number of complaints about polygraph abuse and the growing patchwork of state restrictions on polygraph use, Congress passed the *Employee Polygraph Protection Act of 1988*. The legislation reflected, in part, Congress's concern over the scientific evidence supporting the validity of lie detectors and the sometimes demeaning tactics employed during the administration of lie detector tests.[18]

In general, the 1988 law prohibited all use of lie detector tests by private employers to examine current or prospective employees. The two major exceptions are (1) a test may be administered to existing employees in the course of an employer's ongoing investigation of economic loss, and (2) under certain circumstances employers in the private security and drug manufacturing industries may conduct preemployment polygraph examinations of applicants. Except in these restricted situations, employers may not directly or indirectly require, request, suggest, or cause any employee or applicant to take a polygraph test. Nor may they use, accept, refer to, or inquire concerning the results of any polygraph test that an employee or an applicant may have taken.[19]

The 1988 act defined the term "lie detector" to include "a polygraph, deceptograph, voice stress analyzer, psychological stress analyzer, or any similar device (whether mechanical or electrical) that is used, or the results of which are used, for the purpose of rendering a diagnostic opinion regarding the honesty or dishonesty of an individual." Because the act was intended to cover mechanical or electronic devices, it does not apply to written psychological tests intended to reveal honesty.[20]

Honesty Testing

As criticism was growing concerning the use of lie detectors, many companies anticipated an eventual elimination of lie detector use and began experimenting with paper-and-pencil honesty tests, sometimes called "integrity" tests. David Nye, a former human-resources executive, now a college professor, dubbed the tests "son of the polygraph."[21] There is a certain irony in this title, for already honesty tests are being subjected to the same kinds of criticisms that led to lie detectors being severely restricted.

Honesty-type tests typically pose 80 to 90 statements with which the employee or applicant is asked to agree or disagree. Some test questions are framed as yes-or-no or multiple-choice options. Examples include the following: "Would you tell your boss if you knew of another employee stealing from the company?" or, "What percent of employee thieves are never caught?" or, "What is the dollar value of cash or merchandise you have stolen from past employers?"[22]

Honesty tests are quick to administer, easy to grade, and cost only $6 to $15 each. This compares favorably with lie detector tests, which cost $25 to $75 each. Perhaps the tests have attracted less attention than polygraphs because they come across as less intrusive or intimidating than the lie detector tests, which hooked the examinee up to wires and sensors. The test comes across more like red tape or a job application to be filled out rather than an interrogation.[23]

In 1990, it was estimated that 2 to 3 million honesty tests were given, and the number is growing. Faced with the elimination of the polygraph, companies wanted to find a substitute, and honesty tests seemed to be a convenient alternative. Critics of the tests claim they are intrusive and invade privacy by the nature of their inquiries. Critics also say that they are unreliable and that employers use the tests as the sole judge of the fitness of an applicant. Even when the tests are properly administered, opponents charge that employers end up rejecting many honest applicants just to screen out the dishonest ones. Management and testing companies claim the tests are very useful in weeding out potentially dishonest applicants. They claim that each question asked has a specific purpose.

Psychologists disagree widely on the validity and effectiveness of the tests, and the American Psychological Association is preparing a major report for release. Much of the current research has been done by the test publishers themselves. The future for the tests is uncertain, but it is anticipated that honesty tests will probably face the same kinds of legal and ethical hurdles that affected polygraph and drug tests.[24]

Drug Testing

Drug testing in the workplace has some of the same characteristics as the lie detector and honesty test issues. Companies say they need to do it to protect themselves, but opponents claim the tests are not accurate and invade the employee's privacy.

A poll of American companies by the American Management Association indicated that the majority said they do not test workers or job applicants for drug or alcohol abuse. The reasons reported are shown in Figure 15-1.[25]

FIGURE 15-1   A Poll on Why Firms Do Not Engage in Drug Testing

Reason	Percent Reporting
Moral issue/privacy	68
Inaccuracy of tests	63
Negative impact on morale	53
Tests show use, not abuse	43
High cost	28
Management opposition	17
Employee opposition	16
Union opposition	7

On the other hand, a 1990 Conference Board report found that 55 percent of 681 companies surveyed now have drug-testing programs.[26] Part of the discrepancy may be due to definitional problems. Some companies do a routine urinalysis and may not consider that to be drug testing. Regardless, an increasing number of major companies, including corporate giant IBM, have begun testing job applicants or current employees for drug abuse.

Before getting to the specific arguments for and against drug testing, we should make it clear that drug testing in corporate America today is a direct result of substance abuse (primarily drugs and alcohol) in the workplace. As two experts on this problem have indicated, "Until drugs are out of the workplace—and there seems to be little chance of that happening soon—drug testing, as unpleasant as it may be for all sides, will be there too."[27] The problem seems to be of such magnitude, that drug testing will continue in one form or another unless it is restricted by federal or state law. Legitimate questions then arise as to what types of drug testing should be used in what types of situations.

Arguments for Drug Testing. Proponents of drug testing argue that the costs of drug abuse on the job are staggering. The consequences range from accidents and injuries to theft, bad decisions, and ruined lives. According to one estimate, drug abuse cost the U.S. economy $60 billion in 1983, nearly 30 percent more than in 1980.[28] More recent estimates are significantly higher but difficult to pin down. The greatest concern is in industries where mistakes can cost lives, for example, railroads, airlines, the space program, nuclear power plants, or hazardous equipment or chemicals. Edwin Weihenmayer, vice-president at Kidder, Peabody, a New York-based investment banking firm, believes drug testing is essential in his industry "where the financial security of billions of dollars is entrusted to us by clients."[29]

Arguments Against Drug Testing. Opponents of drug testing see it as both a due-process issue and an invasion-of-privacy issue. The due process relates to the questionable accuracy of the drug tests. Although one test manufacturer claims a 95 percent accuracy rate, some doctors disagree. For example, Dr. David Greenblatt, chief of clinical pharmacology at Tufts New England Medical Center, claims that "false positives can range up to 25 percent or higher. The test is essentially worthless."[30] Some legal experts argue that, even if the tests were foolproof, they would still be an invasion of employee privacy. They claim that tests represent an unconstitutional attempt on the part of companies to control employees' behavior at home because the tests can yield positive results days and even weeks after at-home drug use.[31]

Many questions arise on the drug-testing issue. Do employers have a right to know if their employees use drugs? Are employees performing on the job satisfactorily? Obviously, some delicate balance is needed as both corporate employers and employees alike have legitimate interests that must be protected. This issue is a fairly new one for business, but it is apparent that it will not go away. Therefore, if companies are going to engage in some form of drug testing, they should think carefully about developing policies that not only will achieve their intended goals but also will be fair to the employees and minimize any possible invasion of privacy. Such a balance will not be easy to achieve but must be sought. To do otherwise will guarantee decreased employee morale, more lawsuits, and new government regulations. Figure 15-2 presents guidelines for drug tests.

State and Federal Legislation. Some states and cities have enacted or are considering laws to restrict workplace drug testing. Generally, these laws restrict the scope of testing by private and public employers and establish privacy protections and procedural safeguards. The laws do not completely ban drug testing but typically restrict the circumstances (for example, for reasonable cause) in which tests may be used. States which have passed drug-testing laws include Vermont, Iowa, Minnesota, Montana, Connecticut, and Rhode Island. These states restrict drug testing to reasonable suspicion and place limits on the disciplinary actions employers may take. Other states are considering such legislation.[32]

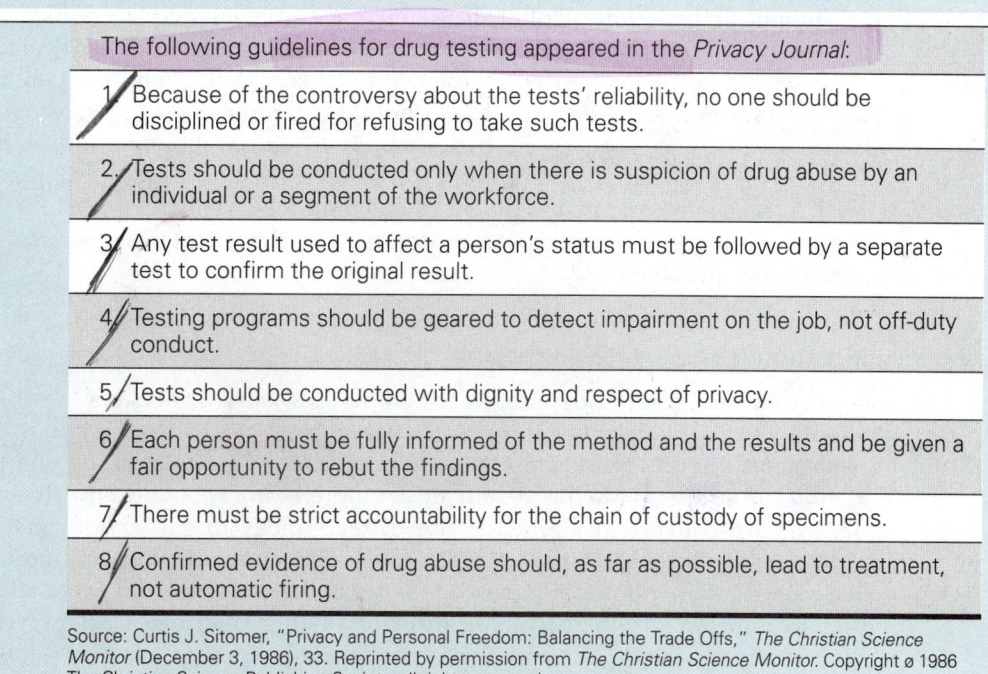

FIGURE 15-2 Guidelines for Drug Tests

The following guidelines for drug testing appeared in the *Privacy Journal*:

1. Because of the controversy about the tests' reliability, no one should be disciplined or fired for refusing to take such tests.
2. Tests should be conducted only when there is suspicion of drug abuse by an individual or a segment of the workforce.
3. Any test result used to affect a person's status must be followed by a separate test to confirm the original result.
4. Testing programs should be geared to detect impairment on the job, not off-duty conduct.
5. Tests should be conducted with dignity and respect of privacy.
6. Each person must be fully informed of the method and the results and be given a fair opportunity to rebut the findings.
7. There must be strict accountability for the chain of custody of specimens.
8. Confirmed evidence of drug abuse should, as far as possible, lead to treatment, not automatic firing.

Source: Curtis J. Sitomer, "Privacy and Personal Freedom: Balancing the Trade Offs," *The Christian Science Monitor* (December 3, 1986), 33. Reprinted by permission from *The Christian Science Monitor*. Copyright ø 1986 The Christian Science Publishing Society, all rights reserved.

At the federal level, few restrictions to drug testing are in place. The *Drug-Free Workplace Act of 1988*, in fact, provides that all businesses contracting with the federal government must certify that they have in place policies directed toward the creation and maintenance of a drug-free workplace. The act does not require the employer to provide evidence of success in attaining a drug-free workplace, but that it provide a good-faith effort to do so. The government, however, does strongly recommend that the employers create and use Employee Assistance Programs (EAPs), which provide counseling and rehabilitation.[33]

Employee Assistance Programs. One of the most significant strategies undertaken by corporate America to deal with the growing alcohol and drug abuse problem in the workplace has been Employee Assistance Programs (EAPs). EAPs originated, for the most part, in the 1940s, 1950s, and 1960s to deal with alcoholism on the job.[34] By the 1980s and 1990s, EAPs had extended into other employee problems as well, such as compulsive gambling, financial stress, emotional stress, marital difficulties, aging, legal problems, AIDs, and other psychological, emotional, and social difficulties.

EAPs are employer-provided programs that are operated either in-house, with corporate staff, or by an outside contractor to the firm. Generally, they are designed for two major objectives—to prevent problems that interfere with an employee's ability to do his or her job and to rehabilitate those employees who are experiencing problems that are interfering with their job performance.[35]

In spite of the serious alcohol, drug, and other problems employers must deal with, EAPs represent a positive and proactive step companies may take to deal with these serious problems. EAPs are designed to be confidential and nonpunitive, and they affirm three important propositions: (1) Employees are valuable members of the organization, (2) it is better to help troubled employees rather than disciplining or discharging them, and (3) recovered employees are better employees.[36] It is encouraging that in an era when employees are increasingly exerting their workplace rights, companies are offering EAPs in an effort to help them solve their mutual problems.

Monitoring Employees on the Job

In the old days, supervisors monitored employees' work by peeking over their shoulders and judging how things were going. Next came cameras and listening devices whereby management could keep track of what was going on from remote locations. With the advent of computers, workers and civil liberties activists are concerned about the use of technology to gather information about workers on the job. For example, many large companies already monitor the records of telephone calls in order to discourage wasteful and personal use and to improve productivity. The director of the American Civil Liberties Union's Project on Privacy and Technology speculates that, "not only will they see who's calling dial-a-porn, but also who's calling a union organizer or the newspaper."[37]

The *Electronic Communications Privacy Act* was signed into law by President Reagan, and for the first time restrictions were placed on government for intruding into individual privacy by technological means. This law, among other things, made it illegal to eavesdrop on electronic mail, computer-to-computer transmissions, private video conferences, and cellular car phones.[38] It becomes immediately obvious how difficult it would be to enforce this legislation.

Civil liberties groups argue, however, that the use of computers to monitor the efficiency and productivity of workers raises a growing concern related to privacy invasion.[39] In virtually any job in which computer terminals are used by workers today, the machines now have the capability of monitoring worker productivity. The consequence is that millions of workers today are laboring under the relentless gaze of electronic supervision.[40]

What Can Be Monitored? It is estimated that over 13 million Americans use computer terminals in their jobs and that as many as one-third of these people are being scrutinized as they work. Monitoring requires the installation of special software (called AUDIT by one firm), which is installed into the central computer to which terminals are attached. The programs are able to measure, record, and tabulate dozens of kinds of information about workers: how slow or fast they are, when they take breaks, how long phone calls take, how much time passes before a next order is processed, what number was called, how many keystrokes per hour an operator is typing, when machines are idle, and so on.

In addition to the monitoring of those at computer terminals, there is increasing surveillance by management of employees in other work settings. The monitoring of telephone conversations is a significant arena for electronic eavesdropping. Workers in such industries as telecommunications, mail order houses, airlines reservations, and brokerage firms are especially hard hit. Not only do supervisors frequently listen in on their conversations, but computers also gather and analyze data about their work habits. One major firm also claims that it uses tiny fish-eye lenses installed behind pinholes in walls and ceilings to watch employees suspected of crimes. Another firm actually uses special chairs for their employees that measure wiggling. The assumption is that employees who wiggle too much are not working. Other firms use long-distance cameras to monitor employees round the clock. It is little wonder that some privacy experts are likening the current situation of high-tech snooping to an "electronic sweatshop."[41]

Effects of Being Monitored. Possible invasion of privacy is one issue. Another is fair treatment. Employees working under such systems complain about stress and tension and the expectation that workers are to be more productive because their efforts can now be measured. The pressure of being constantly monitored is also producing low morale in a number of places. The director of a national group of working women declares that, "the potential for corporate abuse is staggering. It puts you under the gun in the short run and drives you crazy in the long run." The *New York Times* installed a software program to track the performance of its clerks who were taking classified ads over the phone. Some of the employees started wearing buttons that read, "BIG BROTHER IS WATCHING."[42]

As with lie detectors, the controversy over technology and its use seems to bring the company's rights into conflict with the employees' rights. The big difference between these two issues seems to be whether a corporate desire to maintain and improve productivity is as important a goal as a desire to protect against theft. Given the impact this issue is having on employee morale, wise managements may want to carefully consider it from the standpoint of a desirable management practice, as well as from the perspective of protecting worker privacy. This issue currently is not as controversial as lie detectors or drug testing, but the potential is definitely there as technology continues to outpace our ability to effectively monitor its social consequences.

Legislative Momentum. Since about the mid-1980s, employee advocacy groups have been pushing for legislation that would restrict bosses from snooping on workers. Although a number of states have various restrictions, little has happened at the federal level to protect private-sector employees. In 1987, the telemarketing industry lobbied heavily against and defeated a bill that would have mandated an audible beep when employers were listening in on employees. In 1990, two federal bills that were once considered dead had been receiving renewed interest. One would ban phone bugging without a warrant unless all parties to the call consented. Another would require employers to notify workers with a visual or aural signal when they are being monitored with computers, cameras, or taping machines.[43] In 1991, Senate hearings began on legislation to restrict employers from electronically monitoring employees. This is the farthest point any proposed legislation has reached, and there is growing sentiment that a bill might be passed soon.[44]

Policy Guidelines on the Issue of Privacy

As we have discussed various privacy issues, we have indicated steps that management might consider to be responsive to its employee stakeholders. As a final recommendation, we should consider four policy guidelines that touch on a number of the issues we have discussed. Robert Goldstein and Richard Nolan assert that organizations should:

1. *Prepare a "privacy impact statement."* This would require the firm to analyze the potential privacy implications that all systems (especially computerized ones) should be subjected to.
2. *Construct a comprehensive privacy plan.* The purpose of such planning would be to make sure that the necessary privacy controls are integrated into the design of a system at the very beginning.

3. *Train employees who handle personal information.* Be sure they are aware of the importance of protecting privacy and the specific procedures and policies to be followed.

4. *Make privacy a part of social responsibility programs.* Companies need to acknowledge that they have an internal responsibility to their employees and not fail to consider this when designing and implementing corporate social efforts.[45]

THE RIGHT TO SAFETY

The safety issue grew up like so many other issues we have discussed, complete with the eventual creation in 1970 of a federal agency—the Occupational Safety and Health Administration (OSHA). Unfortunately, OSHA became one of the most controversial and, some would argue, most ineffectual of the federal regulatory agencies. The controversy arose despite the fact that, with increasing emphasis on the quality of life, workplace health and safety has been and continues to be a legitimate concern of employees. OSHA's goals seemed quite appropriate: inspections in the workplace; development of safety standards, especially those relating to health; training of employers and employees to develop self-inspection programs; approval of state plans to provide job safety and health; and administration of programs for federal employees.[46]

The Workplace Safety Problem

Two events, among many, stand out in the past decade as symbols of the workplace safety problem. One is the dramatic and catastrophic poisonous gas leak at the Union Carbide plant in Bhopal, India, in 1984. The death toll topped 2,000, and tens of thousands more were injured. People around the globe were startled and shocked at what the results of one major industrial accident could be. The company is still reeling today from the aftermath of this industrial accident in which lawsuits seeking damages quickly exceeded the net worth of the company.[47] In 1991, India's Supreme Court upheld a $470 million settlement that Union Carbide had already paid, but it lifted the immunity from criminal prosecution that it granted the company in 1989.

The second event was considerably less publicized but nevertheless ranks among the landmark cases on job safety. In Elk Grove Village, Illinois, Film Recovery Systems operated out of a single plant that extracted silver from used hospital X-ray and photographic film. To extract the silver, the employees first had to dump the film into open vats of sodium cyanide and then transfer the leached remnants to another tank. On February 10, 1983, employee Stefan Golab staggered outside and collapsed, unconscious. Efforts to revive him failed, and he was soon pronounced dead from what the local medical examiner labeled "acute cyanide toxicity."[48]

An intensive investigation by attorneys in Cook County, Illinois, revealed a long list of incriminating details: (1) Film Recovery workers seldom wore even the most rudimentary safety equipment; (2) workers were laboring in what amounted to an industrial gas chamber; and (3) company executives played down the dangers of cyanide poisoning and removed labeling that identified it as poisonous. The prosecutors took action under an Illinois homicide statute that targets anyone who knowingly commits acts that "create a strong probability of death or serious bodily harm."[49] In 1985, three executives at Film Recovery Systems—the president, the plant manager, and the foreman—were convicted of the murder of Stefan Golab and sentenced to 25 years in prison. Their convictions marked the first time that managers had been convicted of homicide in a corporate matter such as an industrial accident.[50] The Film Recovery Systems case marked a new era in managerial responsibility for job safety.

A number of other prosecutions of managers have followed the Film Recovery Systems case. What this clearly signals is not only that employees have a moral right to a safe working environment but also that managers face prosecution if they do not ensure that employees are protected.

The Right-to-Know Laws

Prompted by the Union Carbide tragedy in Bhopal and other less dramatic industrial accidents, workers have been demanding to know more about the thousands of chemicals and hazardous substances they are being exposed to daily in the workplace. Experts are now arguing that employers have a duty to provide employees with information on the hazards of workplace chemicals *and* to make sure that workers understand what the information means in practical terms. By 1985, 20 states had passed *right-to-know laws* and expanded public access to this kind of information by employees and even communities.[51] Since that time, several other states have passed such laws. One point of view is that the states have moved in and taken such actions because of the federal nonenforcement of occupational safety and environmental laws.[52]

Whereas the states have taken the initiative on the right-to-know front, it is inaccurate to say that OSHA has done nothing. In 1983, OSHA created a Hazard Communication Standard that took effect in 1985. The standard requires covered employers to identify hazardous chemicals in their workplaces and to provide employees with specified forms of information on such substances and their hazards. Specifically, manufacturers, whether they are chemical manufacturers or users of chemicals, must take certain steps to achieve compliance with the standard. These steps include the following:

1. Update inventories of hazardous chemicals present in the workplace.
2. Assemble material safety data sheets (MSDSs) for all hazardous chemicals.

3. Ensure that all containers and hazardous chemicals are properly labeled.
4. Provide workers with training on the use of hazardous chemicals.
5. Prepare and maintain a written description of the company's hazard communication program.
6. Consider any problems with trade secrets that may be raised by the standard's disclosure requirements.
7. Review state requirements for hazard disclosure.[53]

Some managers have scoffed at the new state and federal right-to-know laws, arguing that they will not work or will cost too much. It appears clear, however, that legal and regulatory pressures for the disclosure of workplace hazard information will not abate in the near future. Employees as well as the public will want more, not less, information, disclosure, and rules governing the use of hazardous substances in the work environment. A *Business Week* editorial argues that the $600 million for industry to start up on the new OSHA rule and the $160 million a year compliance costs will be greatly exceeded by the benefits. Furthermore, this editorial provides the following advice for companies:

> They would be well advised to comply with the spirit as well as the letter of the regulations. Tell people the hazards, and tell them simply, in plain English. The point is to save lives and preserve health, and any effort is worth making that will encourage workers to use respirators and protective clothing, for example. In matters such as these, playing it straight is the only way to play it.[54]

The Troubles at OSHA

The time was right for an occupational, safety, and health agency such as OSHA, but the effort that followed was not exactly what OSHA or its designers had in mind. OSHA was troubled from the very beginning by the sheer size of its task—to monitor workplace safety and health in millions of workplaces with only several thousand inspectors to cover them all.[55]

Nitpicking Rules. In the early years, OSHA added to its own troubles by promulgating rules and standards that seemed quite trivial when compared to the larger issues of health and safety. It was not until 1978 that OSHA decided to purge itself of some of these nitpicking rules. Some of its standards were senseless, like the one that said, "Piping located inside or outside of buildings may be placed above or below the ground." That, of course, covered just about every possibility. Or, consider one that went too far in specifying product design: "Every water closet (toilet) should have a hinged seat made of substantial material, having a nonabsorbent finish. Seats installed or replaced shall be of the open front type."[56]

Another example follows: The telephone company was instructed that it could only provide linemen "belts that have pocket tabs that extend at least 1½ inches down and 3 inches back of the inside of the circle of each D-ring for riveting on plier or tool pockets. . . . There may be no more than 4 tool loops on any belt."[57] Such nuisance rules and standards created serious credibility problems for OSHA. Although at least 928 such rules were rescinded in 1978, many times that number are still on the books.

Court decisions of the last several years have ruled that OSHA must consider economic feasibility in its regulatory activities. This decision was a victory for business, which had long argued that many of OSHA's rules would not exist if a cost-benefit analysis were done.[58] In one decision, OSHA backed away from a proposed 85-decibel noise standard for workplaces because of the high cost involved in meeting such a standard.[59]

Spotty Record. Although OSHA has seriously tried to have an impact on health and injury statistics, over the years its record has been spotty. The year 1984 saw injuries, illnesses, and deaths in the workplace begin to climb again after a number of years of decline.[60] There are a number of reasons for this reversal and they cannot all be attributed to OSHA. During the recession of the early 1980s, companies sharply reduced their spending on health and safety. With the economic recovery, many employers hired inexperienced workers, which further contributed to accident statistics. The Reagan administration deemphasized the writing and enforcement of safety rules, and employers put greater emphasis on competitiveness, often at the expense of safety and health.[61]

A Rejuvenated OSHA. Like so many of the federal agencies we have discussed—FTC, FDA, CPSC—OSHA experienced a new boost of energy and enthusiasm in the post-Reagan period of the late 1980s and early 1990s. The renewed energy came at an appropriate time because the Bureau of Labor Statistics announced in 1988 that the trend in increased injury rates had been continuing since about 1983. Officials admitted that some of the increases had come from more accurate reporting.

With a new administrator and an increased budget, OSHA began taking significant actions against high-visibility employers. For example, in 1989 it hit USX Corporation with a $7.3 million fine, which was the largest ever. It charged USX with 58 "willful" hazards it claimed the company knew about but did not address. The company is appealing.[62]

OSHA continues to suffer from what it claims to be an inadequate budget and staff to do what Congress and the public expects it to do. One observer pointed out that the EPA's budget is more than 21 times that of OSHA. In some states, too, there are conflicts between OSHA and state inspectors as to who has responsibility for workplace safety. In 1991, a major accident in North Carolina illustrated this point. A major fire in a poultry processing plant led to the deaths of 25 workers. This occurred because the plant's management kept the emergency exits padlocked to deter pilfering. Employees said there were no fire exits, sprinkler system, or fire drills. It was discovered that no government agency had conducted a safety inspection at that plant for 11 years. Some blamed state authorities; others blamed OSHA.[63] In any event, there simply are not enough inspectors to handle all businesses, and, therefore, a heavy responsibility falls on business for safety in the workplace.

Threats to Reproductive Health

Another current issue on the job safety front is how companies ought to respond to threats to workers' ability to reproduce, brought about by exposures to hazards in the workplace. In 1983, pregnant women working at a Digital Equipment Corporation plant in Massachusetts experienced an unusual number of miscarriages. The company commissioned a study, which found that the miscarriage rate for women working in so-called "clean rooms" where computer chips were etched with acids and gases was 39 percent, nearly twice the national average.[64]

Corporate responses to the discovery that exposure to workplace hazards may be affecting reproductive processes have been varied. AT&T removed all pregnant women from several computer chip production jobs. Digital Equipment Corporation "strongly urged" pregnant women to leave such positions. National Semiconductor Corporation and others expressed no opinion on the report, leaving decisions about transferring to the women themselves. These different responses highlight the dilemma companies face today with one of the most sensitive job safety issues. Estimates have been that over 15 major employers have "fetal protection" policies in place.

Some evidence shows that exposure to a variety of chemicals and even video display terminals may be posing health risks, but it is not conclusive and there is little corporate consensus on what action to take. Some companies have designed policies to address the problem, such as banning pregnant or fertile women from certain jobs, but the result has been controversy and discrimination lawsuits.[65] Some women's groups, in particular, think the schemes are simply designed to displace women.

The controversy over corporate "fetal protection" policies raged throughout the 1980s. In 1991, however, a case known as *Automobile Workers* v. *Johnson Controls, Inc.* reached the U.S. Supreme Court. The Supreme Court ruled that fetal protection policies, which exclude women from certain high-risk jobs because of the potential harm to unborn babies, were illegal. The high court concluded that such fetal protection policies were tantamount to sex discrimination and, therefore, were contrary to Title VII of the Civil Rights Act of 1964.[66] We will discuss this case further in Chapter 16 under the topic of sex discrimination.

For employers who continue to be concerned about the safety of their female employees, a dilemma still remains. Two equally unpleasant choices are to (1) comply with the law and permit women to continue to be exposed to potentially harmful substances, risking lawsuits over damage to unborn babies, or (2) reduce the use of dangerous chemicals in the workplace, thus driving up costs and incurring an international competitive disadvantage. One of the major problems businesses face is that scientists have not yet been able to figure out what a safe fetal-exposure level is.[67]

THE RIGHT TO HEALTH IN THE WORKPLACE

In the health-conscious 1990s, it is not surprising that companies in the United States have become much more sensitive about health issues. In efforts to control runaway health costs, which are rising an estimated 10 percent per year, these companies are taking drastic steps, some of which have become controversial. Two controversial health issues in the workplace merit special attention. Because health reasons seem to be behind both issues, we have chosen to treat them here. Like other issues we have examined, however, they both contain employee rights, privacy, and due-process ramifications. The two issues are (1) smoking in the workplace and (2) AIDS in the workplace. Unfortunately, these issues pit non-smokers and companies against smokers and those who are HIV infected.

Smoking in the Workplace

The issue of smoking in the workplace grew out of the 1980s, especially in the second half of the decade. The idea that smoking ought to be curtailed or restricted in the workplace is a direct outgrowth of the antismoking sentiment that has been taking place in society generally. Much of the antismoking sentiment crystallized in 1984 when U.S. Surgeon General C. Everett Koop called for a smoke-free society. In 1986, he proclaimed that smokers were hurting not only themselves but also the nonsmoking people around them who were being harmed by the breathing of secondary, or passive, smoke. He argued that the evidence "clearly documents that nonsmokers are placed at increased risks for developing disease as the result of exposure to environmental tobacco smoke."[68] To substantiate his point, a National Academy of Science study estimated that in 1 year, passive smoke was responsible for 2,400 lung cancer deaths in the United States.[69] This finding is bolstered by public opinion. A 1990 Gallup poll found that 96 percent of the population think that cigarette smoking is harmful to your health.[70]

As the antismoking fervor hit the nation, effects could be felt everywhere in society. Over 40 states have now restricted smoking in public places; 33 prohibit it outright in trains, buses, streetcars, or subways; and 17 forbid it in offices and other workplaces. There are also an estimated 800 local ordinances against smoking.[71] This number is growing.

Corporate Responses. Although companies did not act until considerable public sentiment developed against smoking, they have begun developing policies restricting smoking. A Bureau of National Affairs study found that over 35 percent of all U.S. companies restrict smoking, although only 2 percent ban it outright. An additional 20 percent of companies are still studying the issue. Firms are becoming increasingly aware of the costs—higher insurance expenses and higher absenteeism—of having smokers on staff.[72]

Companies were initially slow in restricting workplace smoking. One explanation for this pattern was offered by the executive director of New Jersey's chapter of GASP (Group Against Smoking Pollution), a nonprofit advocacy organization. She said there are three stages in most smoking policies. First, managers are very apprehensive at the start. Second, the program goes over more smoothly than they anticipated. Finally, managers are flooded with positive responses from their employees.[73]

Companies that have developed smoking policies have generally tried to do so without alienating smokers. (Smokers represent about a third of the population.) Such policies are aimed at restricting smoking to designated areas in the office. A recent study conducted by the Administrative Management Society found that companies with smoking policies currently ban smoking in the following areas:

Meeting rooms	22%
Storage areas	20%
Reception areas	19%
Hallways, aisles	18%
Open office areas	15%
Cafeterias	14%
All areas	8%[74]

There was initial objection in the workplace to such policies, but much of that has dissipated. Sometimes a firm adopted a policy because of the top executives' attitudes toward smoking. One study of the executives running the country's 100 largest corporations found that 78 percent of them were nonsmokers.[75] This may help explain some of the absence of objections.

Other more serious policies, however, have created more controversy. One company has adopted the policy that employees may be dismissed if they do not stop smoking. Newspaper classified ads now frequently specify "nonsmokers only." One of the first questions asked of job applicants in one firm is, "Do you smoke?" If the answer is yes, the interview is over. This course of action is legal as long as the employer does not break any of the federal discrimination laws.[76] It has also been found that smoking is growing more and more hazardous to careers in business, as some employees believe that nonsmokers are being favored in selection and promotion decisions.[77]

The USG Ban. The corporate smoking policy debate grew more heated in 1987 when the USG Corporation announced a ban on employee smoking at work *and* at home. The company claimed that the protection of the company against future disability claims was at issue. Critics say this is a preposterous policy and that it represents a serious invasion of privacy. A spokesperson for the Tobacco Institute asserted, "The idea that any corporation has the right to reach beyond company gates, to what you could even describe as the bedroom of the employee, is ridiculous."[78] So far, no one has successfully challenged the USG ban. Attorneys say that constitutional rights to privacy apply only to actions by the state and not to actions by the private sector. On legal grounds, firms may face more of a threat from nonsmokers. Among these threats are disability claims from those who say they are injured by smoke and charges that the employer has not provided a safe or healthy workplace.[79]

One kind of response that companies have made to the smoking issue and other "unhealthy life-style conditions" that may cause their health care costs to rise has been the creation of what are being called "life-style policies." In general, these policies would require that those employees who participate in unhealthy activities such as smoking, substance abuse, skydiving, mountain climbing, or excessive eating (as monitored by weight guidelines) would receive monthly surcharges on their health insurance or have their activities otherwise restricted. For example, in 1991, Texas Instruments invoked a $10 health insurance surcharge for employees who smoke. ICH in 1991 invoked a $15 a month discount off medical contributions for employees who had not smoked in 90 days and who met a weight guideline. U-Haul International invoked a biweekly surcharge on health insurance for employees who smoke, chew tobacco, or exceed weight guidelines. Privacy expert Alan F. Westin worries that if such life-style discrimination continues, we could become a two-class society—"one that is perceived as fit and healthy and the [unhealthy] rest who would be unemployed or marginally employed."[80] Companies defend their policies on the basis of the adverse illnesses, chronic diseases, health costs, and impacts on performance of certain life-style conditions. The companies continue to support their decisions based on the significant cost savings, running into the millions of dollars, for such policies and wellness programs they have instituted.[81]

The smoking-in-the-workplace issue and related concerns are bound to stir debates for years to come as conflicts continue about company rights and individual rights. The most reasonable course of action seems to be for managers to consider carefully all employee stakeholders' claims in this issue and then develop reasonable policies that are gradually introduced, while employee feedback is continually monitored. Indeed, some companies have gotten the employees themselves into developing the policies. This democratizes the decision-making process and provides management with a more solid foundation for taking particular policy stances.

AIDS in the Workplace

Few public issues have as much potential to create severe problems for business as the widespread incidence of acquired immune deficiency syndrome (AIDS) in the United States. Estimates vary as to the precise statistics about AIDS-infected people. Some scientists predict a total of 271,000 diagnosed cases in the United States at a medical care cost to the nation of $66.4 billion annually by 1991—and a million AIDS cases by the year 2000.[82] AIDS has, indeed, become an epidemic problem in the United States and has the potential for becoming one of the most serious health and safety issues that business faces.

Not only is it a health and safety issue, but it also has due process, fair treatment, and privacy implications.

For business as well as for society at large, AIDS poses enormous problems because it is a frightening disease. It could be well argued that "no four-letter word inspires more fear or carries a greater social and moral stigma than AIDS."[83] Despite almost a decade of intense research, the disease continues to be shrouded in rumor, fear, and misinformation. Some say that it cannot be transmitted by casual contact. Nevertheless, this seems to be little consolation for employees who have to think through the consequences of working side by side with AIDS-infected coworkers. Figure 15-3 presents an informative ad that the American Red Cross began publishing in major magazines in 1987 as a public service announcement.

There are two distinct groups of employees for whom AIDS in the workplace has become a problem. The first group includes those persons who run some risk of contracting AIDS through contact with the bodily fluids of AIDS patients. This would include such groups as physicians, nurses, lab workers, paramedics, and police officers. The second group includes those employees who have AIDS victims among their coworkers. While experts claim this second group is in no danger of contracting AIDS from a coworker, the fear that AIDS generates among employees and their families can give rise to personnel problems. Consequently, for employers two major issues are raised. One is the liability risk they experience with AIDS-infected employees. The other is morale and productivity implications of AIDS victims in the workplace.[84]

Corporate Responses. In the summer of 1986, the business community received information about what they could legally do with AIDS victims. By 1987, however, that information was no longer completely valid. In 1986, the Justice Department ruled that some employers may legally fire AIDS victims if their motive was to protect other workers. Thereafter, business had good reason to think that AIDS victims were not protected as handicapped persons as defined under the *Rehabilitation Act of 1973*.[85] This view was effectively reversed in March of 1987, however, when the U.S. Supreme Court ruled that victims of contagious diseases are covered by the same law that protects handicapped workers from workplace discrimination. The case before the court involved a schoolteacher in Florida who had tuberculosis, but everyone, including the justices, knew that the ruling would also likely address the AIDS dilemma.[86]

Companies in the United States have only begun to deal with the AIDS crisis. A *Business Week*/Harris poll of 600 human resources executives in major firms found that only 10 percent of the firms had an AIDS policy in place and that 92 percent of them have had their policies for 2 years or less. Although the vast majority of companies do not have AIDS policies in place, a handful do. They include Syntex, Bank of America, AT&T, Eaton, Transamerica, and Pacific Telesis. Other companies, like Control Data, have decided to treat AIDS like any other fatal disease. More and more companies each day are adding AIDS policies to help deal with this issue.

FIGURE 15-3 An Informative Ad on AIDS

The American Red Cross addresses the most often asked questions about AIDS and the workplace:

CAN AN EMPLOYEE WITH AIDS INFECT OTHER EMPLOYEES?

The AIDS virus cannot be spread by normal everyday contact in the workplace.

CAN THE AIDS VIRUS BE SPREAD BY USING A TELEPHONE OR WATER FOUNTAIN?

No. The AIDS virus is not spread through air, water, or on surfaces, such as telephones, door knobs, or office machines. The virus is spread mainly through an exchange of body fluids during sexual activity, or the exchange of blood as occurs through sharing contaminated IV drug needles.

SHOULD I PROVIDE OR DESIGNATE SEPARATE BATHROOM FACILITIES FOR EMPLOYEES WITH AIDS?

There is no need to. The AIDS virus is not spread through ordinary use of toilets, sinks, or other bathroom facilities.

CAN I TELL IF SOMEONE IS INFECTED WITH THE AIDS VIRUS?

There are many *carriers* of the virus who do not have the symptoms or signs of the disease and may or may not develop the disease. A carrier of the AIDS virus can infect other people but not through ordinary workplace contact.

WHAT IF I TOUCH A COWORKER WITH AIDS WHO HAS A BLEEDING CUT?

All blood and other body fluids should be considered potentially infectious. Whether a person has AIDS or not, all open, bleeding cuts should be taken care of by observing good health and hygiene practices.

HOW SHOULD EMPLOYEES WITH AIDS BE TREATED?

On a day-to-day basis, treat them normally. You and your employees should learn about AIDS, and when dealing with their problem, use compassion and understanding.

Above all, remember...

AIDS IS HARD TO CATCH.

This information is based upon data from the U.S. Public Health Service. For more information, call your local health department, the National AIDS Hotline (1-800-342-AIDS) or your local Red Cross chapter.

Or, if you're interested in an educational program about AIDS for your company, call your local health department or your local Red Cross chapter.

WE WANT YOU TO KNOW AS MUCH ABOUT AIDS AS WE DO.

SHOULD YOU WORRY ABOUT AIDS AND THE WORKPLACE?

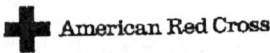 American Red Cross

Developed by J. Walter Thompson for the American Red Cross. Used with permission of the American Red Cross.

The most frequently identified element to date in corporate AIDS policies has been the presence of AIDS education programs. AIDS education programs help avoid panic reactions on the part of employees. Points that are typically made in such corporate education efforts include the following:[87]

1. AIDS is generally not transmittable in the workplace.
2. AIDS victims are legally entitled to handicap protection.
3. The employer provides many economic benefits to AIDS victims and their families.
4. Medical records are confidential.
5. Voluntary disclosure of AIDS enables victims to get better treatment and hold their jobs longer.
6. Employees will not be subject to mandatory AIDS testing.
7. AIDS victims deserve compassion, not punishment.
8. The employer's AIDS policies and procedures will be public information.

Other Ramifications of the AIDS Problem. What to do with AIDS victims is one issue business faces, but there are other dimensions of the problem, too. The expectation of privacy is present. AIDS patients have been known to resign rather than face the unpleasant task of telling their managers they have the disease. On one occasion an employee of a telephone company told his superior he had AIDS, and the supervisor allegedly told several coworkers. Some of them left threatening messages for the AIDS-infected employee, so he sued, charging that the phone company violated his privacy.[88] With virtually no privacy laws available in the private sector, however, it is doubtful whether he could win such a case.

Another major issue business faces is whether to test prospective employees to see if they have antibodies against the AIDS virus—which means they have been exposed to AIDS but are not necessarily infected. Some companies are testing in limited cases, for example, screening food service workers.[89] At this time, however, it appears that business opposes a policy of requiring an AIDS test for all job applicants.

What should be the corporate response to employee stakeholders on the AIDS issue? Companies should definitely adopt a humane approach to its employees who develop AIDS. The law now seems to make it clear that such employees are protected as long as they are performing their work satisfactorily. But companies need to go beyond just treating AIDS like any other disease. Companies need to sponsor educational programs such as those described so that all workers can understand that AIDS cannot be transmitted by casual contact. Management will never be able to overcome fear and hostility if it does not engage in a thorough and ongoing educational program.[90]

Companies also need to be extremely sensitive to the privacy and due-process aspects of AIDS. This is why it is very important that companies adopt policies in dealing with AIDS cases *before* they arise. Managers need to be trained and educated in how to handle AIDS cases. Policies on AIDS should not be developed in an ad hoc, spur-of-the-moment fashion but as part of an overall strategy for dealing with workplace health and safety, privacy, and employee rights.

SUMMARY

Critical employee stakeholder issues include the right to privacy and the rights to safety and health. These issues should be seen as extensions of the rights outlined in Chapter 14.

Workplace privacy issues that are especially important include management's collection and use of employee information and the use of the polygraph. Despite management's apparent justification in employing the polygraph because of employee theft and dishonesty, its abuse and lack of reliability have raised serious questions about its legitimacy as a decision-making tool. Most private-sector use of the polygraph was banned with the passage of the Employee Polygraph Protection Act of 1988. Many companies have begun using honesty tests, which seem to be less intrusive but still raise questions of privacy to which managements must be attentive.

Of equal, if not more, importance to employee stakeholders are the issues of safety and health. The workplace safety problem led to the creation of OSHA. In spite of its difficulties, OSHA is still the federal government's major instrument for protecting workers. State-promulgated right-to-know laws, as well as federal efforts, have been passed in recent years to provide employees with an added measure of protection, especially against chemicals and toxic substances. The Supreme Court's 1991 decision to ban corporate fetal protection policies created continuing dilemmas for business.

Two major health issues in the business-employee relationship today include smoking in the workplace and AIDS. The smoking issue is less severe, but currently it is more pervasive as a problem. AIDS has become the most serious health issue that business or our society has ever faced. Wise managements will begin now to develop policies for dealing with these issues, both of which have privacy and due-process implications.

DISCUSSION QUESTIONS

1. In your own words, describe what privacy means and what privacy protection companies should give employees.
2. Enumerate the strengths and weaknesses of the polygraph as a management tool for decision making. What are legitimate polygraph uses? What are illegitimate polygraph uses?

3. What are the two major arguments for and against honesty testing by employers? Under what circumstances could management most legitimately argue that honesty testing is necessary?
4. Which two of the four guidelines on the issue of privacy presented in the chapter do you think are the most important? Why?
5. Identify the privacy, health, and due-process ramifications of both the workplace smoking issue and the AIDS issue.

ENDNOTES

1. Barbara Wagner, "Privacy in the Workplace," *World* (April/June, 1987), 48.
2. *Ibid.*
3. Cited in Jeffrey Rothfeder and Michele Galen, "Is Your Boss Spying On You?," *Business Week* (January 15, 1990), 74.
4. "Big Brother, Inc. May Be Closer Than You Think," *Business Week* (February 9, 1987), 84.
5. Patricia H. Werhane, *Persons, Rights, and Corporations* (Englewood Cliffs, NJ: Prentice-Hall, 1985), 118.
6. *Business Week* (February 9, 1987), 84.
7. Cited in Jolie Solomon, "As Firm's Personnel Files Grow, Worker Privacy Falls," *Wall Street Journal* (April 19, 1989), B1.
8. *Ibid.*
9. Joseph R. DesJardins, "Privacy in Employment" in Gertrude Ezorsky (ed.), *Moral Rights in the Workplace* (Albany, NY: State University of New York Press, 1987), 133.
10. Solomon, B1.
11. Raymond Bonner, "Lie Detectors as Corporate Tools," *The New York Times* (February 13, 1983), 4F.
12. Kenneth F. Englade, "The Business of the Polygraph," *Across the Board* (October, 1982), 21–22.
13. James H. Coil, III and Barbara Jo Call, "Congress Targets Employers' Use of Polygraphs," *Employment Relations Today* (Spring, 1986), 23.
14. James H. Coil, III, "The Polygraph Protection Act Becomes Law," *Employment Relations Today* (Autumn, 1988), 181.
15. Coil and Call, 1986, 24.
16. *Ibid.*, 25.
17. Benjamin Kleinmuntz, "Lie Detectors Fail the Truth Test," *Harvard Business Review* (July-August, 1985), 36–42.
18. Coil, 1988, 181.
19. *Ibid.*, 184.
20. *Ibid.*
21. David Nye, "Son of the Polygraph," *Across the Board* (June, 1989), 21.
22. *Ibid.*
23. Ed Bean, "More Firms Use Attitude Tests' to Keep Thieves Off the Payroll," *The Wall Street Journal* (January 27, 1987), 41.
24. Elizabeth M. Cosin, "Tests to Spot the Pinocchios May Fail the Honest Abes," *Insight* (July 30, 1990), 42–43.
25. "Why Firms Don't Test for Drugs," *USA Today* (February 18, 1987), 7B.
26. Randall Poe and Emily L. Baker, "Fast Forward," *Across the Board* (May, 1990), 7.
27. Peter M. Stein and Peter S. Gray, "Truth in Drug Testing," *Across the Board* (May, 1988), 52.
28. "Battling the Enemy Within: Companies Fight to Drive Illegal Drugs Out of the Workplace," *Time* (March 17, 1986), 53.
29. Michael Waldholz, "Drug Testing in the Workplace: Whose Rights Take Precedence?" *The Wall Street Journal* (November 11, 1986), 39.
30. "The Many Tests for Drug Abuse," *New York Times* (February 24, 1985), F17.
31. *Ibid.*
32. John Fay, *Drug Testing* (Boston: Butterworth-Heinemann, 1991), 22.
33. *Ibid.*, 23–24.
34. Sarah F. Mullady, "The Champion Paper Company EAP and Major Issues for Employee Assistance Programs in the 1990s—Managed Care and Aging," *Employee Assistance Quarterly* (Vol. 6, No. 3, 1991), 37–50.
35. *Employee Assistance Programs: Drug, Alcohol and Other Problems* (Chicago: Commerce Clearing House, 1986), 7.
36. Fay, 20.
37. "The Boss That Never Blinks," *Time* (July 28, 1986), 47.
38. Curtis J. Sitomer, "Privacy and Personal Freedoms: The Impact of Technology," *The Christian Science Monitor* (December 5, 1986), 1.
39. *Ibid.*
40. *Time* (July 28, 1986), 46.
41. Rothfeder and Galen, 74.
42. *Ibid.*
43. Rothfeder and Galen, 75.

44. Michael Allen, "Legislation Could Restrict Bosses from Snooping on Their Workers," *The Wall Street Journal* (September 24, 1991), B1.
45. Robert C. Goldstein and Richard L. Nolan, "Personal Privacy Versus the Corporate Computer," *Harvard Business Review* (March-April, 1975), 62–70.
46. John L. Paluszek, *Will the Corporation Survive?* (Reston, VA: Reston Publishing Company, 1977), 120.
47. "Union Carbide Fights for Its Life," *Business Week* (December 24, 1984), 52–56.
48. Joseph P. Kahn, "When Bad Management Becomes Criminal," *Inc.* (March, 1987), 47.
49. Ibid.
50. David R. Spiegel, "Enforcing Safety Laws Locally," *New York Times* (March 23, 1986), 11F.
51. James T. O'Reilly, "What's Wrong with the Right to Know," *Across the Board* (April, 1985), 24.
52. Elizabeth Holtzman, "States Step in Where OSHA Fails to Tread," *The Wall Street Journal* (March 31, 1987), 36.
53. Peter A. Susser, "Chemical Hazard Disclosure Obligations," *Employment Relations Today* (Winter, 1986–1987), 301–302.
54. "Talk Straight on Chemical Hazards," *Business Week* (December 9, 1985), 142.
55. "Now OSHA Must Justify Its Inspection Targets," *Business Week* (April 9, 1979), 64.
56. "OSHA's Nitpicking Rules Die," *Athens Banner Herald* (November 24, 1978), 5.
57. Ibid.
58. "A Court Orders OSHA to Consider Economics," *Business Week* (October 3, 1977), 46–47.
59. "OSHA's Deaf Ear to Tighter Noise Control," *Business Week* (March 26, 1979), 30.
60. Robert L. Simison, "Job Deaths and Injuries Seem to Be Increasing After Years of Decline," *The Wall Street Journal* (March 18, 1986), 1, 25.
61. Ibid., 1.
62. Steven Waldman, "Danger on the Job," *Newsweek* (December 11, 1989), 44.
63. Scott Bronstein, "They Treated Us Like Dogs, Say Workers at Plant Where 25 Died," *The Atlanta Journal* (September 5, 1991), A6.
64. Barry Meier, "Companies Wrestle with Threats to Workers' Reproductive Health," *The Wall Street Journal* (February 5, 1987), 23.
65. Ibid.
66. Marc Hequet and Julie Johnson, "Weighing Some Heavy Metal," *Time* (April, 1991), 60.
67. Joann S. Lublin, "Decision Poses Dilemma for Employers," *The Wall Street Journal* (March 21, 1991), B1.
68. Otto Friedrich, "Where There's Smoke," *Time* (February 23, 1987), 23.
69. Lois Therrien, "Warning: In More and More Places, Smoking Causes Fines," *Business Week* (December 29, 1986), 40.
70. George Gallup, Jr. and Dr. Frank Newport, "Many Americans Favor Restrictions on Smoking in Public Places," *The Gallup Monthly* (July, 1990), 20.
71. Freidrich, 22.
72. Barbara Rudolph, "Thou Shalt Not Smoke: Companies Restrict the Use of Tobacco in the Workplace," *Time* (May 18, 1987), 56.
73. Dexter Hutchins, "The Drive to Kick Smoking at Work," *Fortune* (September 15, 1986), 43.
74. Larry Reibstein, "Forced to Consider Smoking Issue, Firms Produce Disparate Policies," *The Wall Street Journal* (February 2, 1987), 41.
75. Randall Poe, "Fast Forward," *Across the Board* (July/August, 1986), 3.
76. Rudolph, 58.
77. Alix M. Freedman, "Cigarette Smoking Is Growing Hazardous to Careers in Business," *The Wall Street Journal* (April 23, 1987), 1.
78. Carolyn Lochhead, "Banning Employee Smoking Beyond the Company Gates," *Insight* (March 2, 1987), 40–41.
79. Ibid., 41.
80. Cited in Zachary Schiller and Walecia Konrad, "Lifestyles: If You light up on Sunday, Don't Come to Work on Monday," *Business Week* (August 26, 1991), 68–72.
81. Sheri Caudron, "The Wellness Payoff," *Personnel Journal* (July, 1990), 55–60.
82. Gordon Witkins, "AIDS: A Job-Rights Victory," *Newsweek* (March 16, 1987), 11.
83. "AIDS Research: Where the Battle Stands," *Business Week* (March 23, 1987), 128.
84. Donald Klingner and Nancy G. O'Neill, *Workplace Drug Abuse and AIDS: A Guide to Human Resource Management Policy and Practice* (New York: Quorem Books, 1991), 100.
85. "AIDS in the Workplace," *Newsweek* (July 7, 1986), 62.
86. "A Victory for AIDS Victims," *Newsweek* (March 16, 1987), 33.
87. Klingner and O'Neill, 1991, 127–128.
88. "The AIDS Epidemic and Business," *Business Week* (March 23, 1987), 123.
89. Ibid., 124.
90. "Business Should Help Battle AIDS," *Business Week* (March 23, 1987), 174.

CHAPTER **SIXTEEN**

Protected Groups: Employment Discrimination and Affirmative Action

CHAPTER OBJECTIVES

After studying this chapter, you should be able to:

- Chronicle the civil rights movement and minority progress for the past 30 years.

- Outline the essentials of the federal discrimination laws, in particular Title VII of the *Civil Rights Act of 1964*.

- Provide two different meanings of discrimination and give examples of how each might be committed.

- Elaborate on issues in employment discrimination relating to race, color, national origin, sex, age, religion, and the handicapped.

- Define different postures with respect to affirmative action, explain the concept of reverse discrimination, and provide an overview of the Supreme Court's decisions on affirmative action.

- Articulate the corporate view on affirmative action.

A particular subgroup of employee stakeholders are those whose job rights are protected by way of federal, state, and local laws on discrimination. In the previous two chapters we considered employee rights issues that affect virtually everyone in the workplace. In this chapter we focus on that smaller grouping whose rights are protected by discrimination laws. In general, these *protected groups* include minorities, women, older people, handicapped people, and people with religious affiliations that might affect their conditions of employment. Many of the issues we treat in this chapter grew out of the general notion that employees have certain workplace rights that ought to be protected.

It is difficult to believe that our country is over 200 years old but has only made a serious and concerted effort to protect employees' rights for about 30 years. On the other hand, some would argue that we have come a long way in the past three decades. Actually, federal antidiscrimination laws date back to the U.S. Constitution, in particular, the First, Fifth, and Fourteenth Amendments, which were designed to forbid religious discrimination and deprivation of employment rights without due process. There were also the Civil Rights Acts of 1866, 1870, and 1871, which were based on these amendments. None of these acts were ever effective, however. Most authorities agree that the Civil Rights Act of 1964 was the effective beginning of the employee protection movement, particularly for those special groups that we will be discussing in this chapter.

Civil rights issues among protected groups are highly debated and controversial. Although there is basic acceptance of the idea of groups' workplace rights being protected, the extent of this protection and the degree to which governmental policy should go to accelerate the infusion of minorities and women into the work force and into higher paying jobs remains a topic of considerable debate, even in the 1990s. One issue of significant magnitude has framed the debate in the early 1990s. There has been considerable difference of opinion over a proposed 1990 Civil Rights Act. President Bush vetoed this act, fearing it would lead to quotas. The bill was resubmitted under the title of the Civil Rights Act of 1991 and was passed, but the debate over it continues. We will examine this bill more closely later, but at this point we should note that time has not quickly settled these issues.

THE CIVIL RIGHTS MOVEMENT AND MINORITY PROGRESS

It would take volumes to trace the history that led ultimately to passage of the first significant piece of civil rights legislation—the Civil Rights Act of 1964. William Glueck and James Ledvinka have provided a brief analysis of these events. They have argued that the act grew out of conflict which had been apparent for years but that erupted in the 1950s and 1960s in the form of protests and boycotts.[1]

The 1950s and 1960s

Behind the American dream had historically been the belief that merit rather than privilege is the means of getting ahead. Equal opportunity was everyone's birthright. Blacks and other minorities, however, had not shared fully in this American dream. In the 1950s and 1960s, the disparity between American ideals and American realities became quite pronounced for minorities. Americans became aware of it, not because they suddenly awoke to the realization that equal opportunity was not available to everyone but because of individuals who had the courage to stand up for what they believed were their rights.

It began on December 1, 1955, when Mrs. Rosa Parks, a black department store worker, was arrested for refusing to yield her seat on a bus to a white man. Out of that previously unthinkable act grew yet another—a bus boycott by blacks. One of the leaders of the boycott was a young minister, Dr. Martin Luther King, Jr. After the bus boycott came years of demonstrations, marches, and battles with police. Television coverage depicted scenes of civil rights demonstrators being attacked by officials with cattle prods, dogs, and fire hoses. Along with the violence that grew out of confrontations between protestors and authorities came the stark awareness of the *economic inequality* that existed in the United States at that time.[2]

In the voluminous data gathered by the Bureau of the Census, a few notable statistics documented the point quite well. Unemployment figures for blacks were double those for whites and higher still among nonwhite youth. Blacks accounted for only 10 percent of the labor force but represented 20 percent of total unemployed and nearly 30 percent of long-term unemployed. In 1961, only about one-half of black men worked steadily at full-time jobs, whereas nearly two-thirds of white men did so. Tracing the statistics to the 1970s, we saw some improvements among blacks and other minorities, but for the period prior to the passage of the Civil Rights Act, the numbers were clearly unfavorable to minorities. Against this backdrop of blacks and other minorities not being able to share in the American ideal of equal opportunity in employment, it should have been no surprise that Congress finally acted in a dramatic way in 1964.

The 1970s

As we entered the 1970s, blacks were making strong gains in employment and earnings. From the 1973 to 1975 recession on, however, rampant unemployment for blacks was discouraging. As the decade of the 1970s ended, the following statistics profiled the situation blacks faced:

- The unemployment rate was about 12 percent for blacks compared to 5 percent for whites.
- Black men were dropping out of the labor force at record rates; many could not get jobs.
- Real weekly earnings for blacks rose faster than for whites until 1973 and then stalled for both groups.[3]

The women's movement also began in the 1970s. Women's groups began to see that their workplace situation was little better than that of blacks and other minorities. Despite the fact that the labor participation rate for women was growing, women were still being kept in low-paying jobs. Some small gains were being made into management and professional jobs, but progress was very slow. Women, for the most part, were still in the lower-paying "women's jobs" such as bank teller, secretary, waitress, nurse's aid, and laundry worker.[4]

The 1980s

In the 1980s the plight of blacks and women improved, but women, in general, made greater progress in the workplace than blacks. From 1983 to 1986, the unemployment rate for all whites fell from 8.4 percent to 6.1 percent. During this same time, the unemployment rate for blacks fell from 19.5 percent to 15.1 percent. For women it fell from 6.9 percent to 5.4 percent.[5] From these statistics we can see that unemployment represented a major problem for blacks but was not a major problem for women. Indeed, the unemployment rate for blacks remained more than twice that of whites.

As the mid to late 1980s arrived, the problem of inequality in the work force remained a serious problem. Blacks continued to have lower participation rates in the work force, and undoubtedly some of this was traceable to racial discrimination. Women did not have the labor participation rate problem of blacks but continued to feel excluded from higher-paid managerial jobs. Also problematic were pay inequities between men and women performing essentially the same jobs.

Employment discrimination began essentially as a racial issue. Before long it became apparent that sex discrimination was a significant problem, too. We have focused on these two issues because they have historically constituted the bulk of the problem. The civil rights movement was aimed primarily at improving the status of blacks, though it later openly embraced the plight and cause of other minorities and women. Out of the civil rights movement grew a concern for fair treatment of older people and the handicapped and a belief that a person's religion should not affect his or her employment status.

The 1990s

In the early 1990s, the progress of blacks in America has been mixed. There have been notable gains on the educational front, but their incomes continue to trail those of whites. In 1990, nearly 80 percent of blacks aged 35 to 44 had completed 4 years of high school, compared with 63 percent in 1980. For the same period, 89 percent of whites completed high school, compared with 80 percent in 1980. In terms of attending college, the rate for black females steadily increased from 24 percent in 1970 to 31 percent in 1988. For black males, the percent attending college declined from 29 percent in 1970 to 25 percent in 1988. The poverty rate for black Americans in 1990 remained virtually the same as it has been for the past 20 years—nearly one-third.[6]

Within the group of black Americans, more were getting wealthier during the past decade but more also got poorer. Black ghetto poverty deepened during the past decade, with a 49 percent increase in the number of blacks living in poverty in cities. However, there were twice as many black families earning $50,000 or more in 1989 than a decade earlier. In addition, although the annual income for blacks is only 56 percent of the income for whites, the average income for college-educated black married couples is 93 percent of what comparable white couples earn. According to Kelvin M. Pollard, a demographer who wrote the report "African Americans in the 1990s," these trends "suggest the increasing segmentation of the African American community, and that will continue." The Pollard study also refers to the increasing number of black children born out of wedlock and the increasing number of black families headed by females as part of the economic problems they face.[7]

Perhaps one of the most significant issues coming to a head in the 1990s is the changing work force composition. To read most headlines, one would think the public debate is just about the role and progress of blacks. However, today's discrimination laws and affirmative action policies also cover 48 million white women, 10 million Hispanics, and 3 million Asians, in addition to 13 million blacks. Combined, they all make up 54 percent of the labor force. From 1980 to 1990, the percent of the work force composed of women has grown from 42 to 45 percent; for blacks, from 9.4 to 10.1 percent; for Hispanics, from 5.6 to 7.5 percent; and, for Asians, from 1.0 to 2.6 percent. The black, Hispanic, and Asian populations are all growing at a much faster pace than the white population. As competition for jobs continues in the 1990s, it is expected that affirmative action policies may pit these groups against each other.[8]

As the numbers of workers protected by discrimination laws increase in the 1990s, according to present trends, it is expected that civil rights issues will continue to be a front-burner topic.

FEDERAL LAWS PROHIBITING DISCRIMINATION

The following section provides an overview of the major laws that have been passed to protect workers against discrimination. We will focus our treatment on legislation at the federal level that has been created since the 1960s and will discuss issues arising from these particular forms of discrimination in more detail later in the chapter. Our purpose in this section is to provide an *overview* of the laws and the major federal agencies that enforce the laws.

Title VII of the Civil Rights Act of 1964

Title VII of the Civil Rights Act of 1964, as amended, *prohibits discrimination* in hiring, promotion, discharge, pay, fringe benefits, and other aspects of employment on the basis of *race, color, religion, sex, or national origin*. Title VII was extended to cover federal, state, and local employers and educational institutions by the *Equal Employment Opportunity Act of 1972*. This amendment to Title VII also gave the Equal Employment Opportunity Commission (EEOC) the authority to file suit in federal district court against employers in the private sector on behalf of individuals whose charges were not successfully conciliated. In 1978, Title VII was amended to include the *Pregnancy Discrimination Act*, which requires employers to treat pregnancy and pregnancy-related medical conditions the same as any other medical disability with respect to all terms and conditions of employment, including employee health benefits.[9] Figure 16-1 summarizes some details regarding the application of Title VII. Figure 16-2 on page 472 provides details on filing a charge and remedies that are available under Title VII.

Age Discrimination in Employment Act of 1967

This law protects workers 40 years old and older from arbitrary age discrimination in hiring, discharge, pay, promotions, fringe benefits, and other aspects of employment. It is designed to promote employment of older persons on the basis of ability rather than age and to help employers and workers find ways to meet problems arising from the impact of age on employment.[10]

Like the provisions of Title VII, the *Age Discrimination in Employment Act* does not apply where age is a ***bona fide occupational qualification* (*BFOQ*)**—a qualification that might ordinarily be argued as being a basis for discrimination but for which a company can legitimately argue that it is job related and necessary. Neither does the act bar employers from differentiating among employees based on reasonable factors other than age.[11] Figure 16-3 on page 473 provides other details regarding the Age Discrimination in Employment Act.

Equal Pay Act of 1963

As amended, this act prohibits sex discrimination in payment of wages to women and men who perform substantially equal work in the same establishment. Passage of this landmark law marked a significant milestone in helping women, who are the chief victims of unequal pay, achieve equality in their paychecks.[12] Figure 16-4 on page 474 summarizes other details about the *Equal Pay Act of 1963*.

Rehabilitation Act of 1973, Section 503

This law, as amended, prohibits job discrimination because of a handicap. It applies to employers holding federal contracts or subcontracts. In addition, it requires these employers to engage in affirmative action to employ the handicapped, a concept we will discuss later in the chapter. Related to this act is the *Vietnam Era Veterans Readjustment Assistance Act of 1974*, which also prohibits discrimination and requires affirmative action among federal contractors or subcontractors.[13]

FIGURE 16-1 Under Title VII of the Civil Rights Act

Employment discrimination by any of these groups having 15 or more employees is prohibited:

- private employers
- state and local governments
- educational institutions
- labor organizations

Employment discrimination by any of these groups also is prohibited:

- the federal government
- private and public employment agencies
- joint labor-management committees for apprenticeship and training

It is unlawful for an employer to discriminate with regard to:

- job advertisements
- recruitment
- testing
- hiring and firing
- compensation, assignment or classification of employees
- transfer, promotion, layoff, or recall
- use of company facilities
- training and apprenticeship programs
- fringe benefits such as life and health insurance
- pay, retirement plans, and disability leave
- causing or attempting to cause a union to discriminate
- other terms and conditions of employment

It is unlawful for employment agencies to discriminate with regard to:

- its own employees on the basis of race, color, religion, sex, or national origin
- receiving, classifying, or referring applications for employment
- job advertisements

It is unlawful for labor unions to discriminate with regard to:

- applications for membership
- segregation or classification of members
- referrals for employment
- training and apprenticeship programs
- other discriminatory conduct, including causing or attempting to cause an employer to discriminate
- job advertisements

It is unlawful for employers, employment agencies, and labor unions to retaliate against individuals who oppose unlawful employment practices or attempt to exercise their rights under the statute.

Source: "Title VII: Enforces Job Rights" (Washington, DC: The U.S. Equal Employment Opportunity Commission, Office of Communications, October, 1988), 1–3.

FIGURE 16-2 Title VII: Filing a Charge and Remedies Available

FILING A CHARGE

You must file an employment discrimination charge within 180 days of the alleged discriminatory act. Where there is a State or Local Fair Employment Practices Agency in your area, you have up to 240 days, and in some cases you may have up to 300 days to file your charge with the Commission. A charge may be filed either by or on behalf of an aggrieved individual or "class." A charge may be filed in person or by mail with any of EEOC's field offices.

If you are a FEDERAL EMPLOYEE, you must file a complaint of discrimination with your own agency. Your EEO counselor generally must be contacted within 30 days of the alleged discriminatory act.

REMEDIES AVAILABLE UNDER TITLE VII

Remedies under Title VII are tailored to specific findings of discrimination by EEOC or by the federal district courts. These remedies may include requiring an employer to end discriminatory practices and systems, institute equal employment practices and systems, and in some cases, provide specific make-whole compensation for victims of discrimination.

Remedies may involve reinstatement, hiring, reassignment, promotion, training, seniority rights, backpay, and other compensation and benefits. (Backpay awards under Title VII cannot accrue from a date more than two years prior to filing of a charge.)

Source: "Title VII: Enforces Job Rights" (Washington, DC: The U.S. Equal Employment Opportunity Commission, Office of Communications, October, 1988), 3–4.

The Americans with Disabilities Act

The most significant labor and employment statute to be enacted in 15 years was the 1990 passage of the *Americans with Disabilities Act* (ADA). Although passed in July 1990, the act became effective for most businesses in July 1992, after the Equal Employment Opportunity Commission had published regulations for its implementation. The ADA prohibits discrimination based on physical or mental disabilities in private places of employment and public accommodation, in addition to requiring transportation systems and communication systems to facilitate access for the disabled. The ADA is modeled after the Rehabilitation Act of 1973, which applies to federal contractors and grantees.[14]

Essentially, the ADA gives civil rights protections to individuals with disabilities, similar to those provided to individuals on the basis of race, sex, national origin, and religion. ADA applies not only to private employers but also to state and local governments, employment agencies, and labor unions. In July 1992, when the act went into effect, employers of 25 or more employees were covered. In 1994, the act will apply to employers of 15 or more employees.[15]

FIGURE 16-3 The Age Discrimination in Employment Act

WHAT IT DOES: Protects workers aged 40 to 70 from arbitrary age discrimination in hiring, discharge, pay, promotions, fringe benefits, and other aspects of employment.
   The law is designed to promote employment of older persons on the basis of ability rather than age and to help employers and workers find ways to meet problems arising from the impact of age on employment.

HEALTH INSURANCE BENEFITS: Employers must offer employees aged 65 to 70 the same health coverage under the same conditions as is offered to employees under age 65.

COVERAGE: Private employers of 20 or more workers; federal, state, local governments, and employment agencies; and labor organizations with 25 or more members or that operate a hiring hall or a hiring office which recruits potential employees or obtains job opportunities.

EXCEPTIONS: The law does not apply where age is a bona fide occupational qualification. It also does not bar employers from differentiating among employees based on reasonable factors other than age, or from observing the terms of a bona fide seniority system or any bona fide employee benefit plan (e.g., retirement, pension, or insurance plan), except that no such seniority system or employee benefit plan will excuse mandatory retirement and/or refusal to hire up to age 70.

PRIVATE SUITS: A charge of unlawful age discrimination must be filed with EEOC within 180 days of the alleged violation. In states having discrimination laws, this is extended to 300 days of the alleged violation or 30 days after termination of proceedings by the state enforcement agency, whichever is earlier. Individuals may file suit on their own behalf but not until 60 days after filing their charge of unlawful discrimination with EEOC and, where there is a state age discrimination law, with the state agency. Should EEOC take legal action, however, the individual may not file a private suit.

PENALTIES FOR EMPLOYER VIOLATION: Payment of damages, interest, liquidated damages, attorney's fees, and court costs.
   Recognizing the need for flexibility in fashioning conciliation agreements, the Commission's policy is to seek full and effective relief for each victim of employment discrimination, whether it is sought in court or in conciliation agreements reached before litigation.

RETALIATION: Employers, employment agencies, and labor organizations are prohibited from retaliation against any person who files a charge, participates in an investigation, or opposes an unlawful practice.

Source: "Age Discrimination Is Against the Law" (Washington DC: The U.S. Equal Employment Opportunity Commission, Office of Communications, January, 1986), 2–4.

FIGURE 16-4   The Equal Pay Act

WHAT IT DOES: Protects women and men who perform substantially equal work against pay discrimination based on sex. Passage of this landmark law in June 1963 marked a significant milestone in helping women, who are the chief victims of unequal pay, to achieve equality in their paychecks.

COVERAGE: Protects most private employees whose employers are covered by the Fair Labor Standards Act, including executive, administrative, professional, and outside sales employees who are exempt from the minimum wage and overtime provisions. Most federal, state, and local government workers also are covered under the Act.

BASIC PROVISIONS: (1) Prohibits sex discrimination in the payment of wages to women and men performing substantially equal work in the same establishment; (2) prohibits employers from reducing wages of either sex to comply with the law; (3) prohibits labor organizations from causing employers to violate the law.

EXCEPTIONS: The law does not apply to pay difference based on factors other than sex (e.g., seniority, merit, or systems that reward worker productivity).

STATE AND LOCAL LAWS: No provision of the Equal Pay Act justifies not complying with state or local laws setting higher standards; likewise, compliance with state or local laws does not justify noncompliance with the Equal Pay Act.
  State or local laws regulating job conditions for employees of one sex will not make otherwise equal work unequal or justify an otherwise prohibited wage rate difference.

PENALTIES FOR EMPLOYER VIOLATION: Payment of back wages, interest, liquidated damages, attorney's fees, and court costs. Criminal penalties also may apply.
  In pursuing its mission of eradicating discrimination in the workplace, the Commission intends that its enforcement be predictable, provide effective relief for those affected by discrimination, allow remedies designed to correct the sources of discrimination, and prevent its recurrence.

RETALIATION: Employers are prohibited from retaliating against any employee who files a complaint or participates in an investigation.

Source: "Equal Work, Equal Pay" (Washington, DC: The U.S. Equal Employment Opportunity Commission, Office of Communications, January 1986), 1–3.

The ADA prohibits discrimination in all employment practices, including job application procedures, hiring, firing, advancement, compensation, training, and other terms, conditions, and privileges of employment. Under the act, employment discrimination is prohibited against "qualified individuals with disabilities." These include persons who have a physical or mental impairment that substantially limits one or more major life activities such as seeing, hearing, speaking, walking, breathing, performing manual tasks, learning, caring for oneself, and working. According to the Justice Department, the ADA is intended to protect persons with AIDS and HIV disease from discrimination.[16]

During 1991 and 1992, the Equal Employment Opportunity Commission was conducting hearings on the ADA with the intent of giving employers and other interested parties an opportunity to provide comment on proposed regulations. Some of the thorniest problems are expected to include defining terms, such as "disability" and "major life activity"; determining the essential functions of a job; and determining what constitutes "reasonable accommodation" on the part of employers.[17] In the years ahead, it is expected that meeting the requirements of the ADA will pose significant challenges for private-sector employers.

Proposed Civil Rights Acts of 1990 and 1991

In both 1990 and 1991, civil rights bills were debated in Congress. The proposed Civil Rights Reform Act of 1990 was aimed primarily at restoring and strengthening civil rights laws and interpretations that banned discrimination in employment, many of which were overturned by recent U.S. Supreme Court rulings. President George Bush vetoed this bill because he argued that it would lead directly to quota hiring systems. The Senate failed to override the president's veto.

The bill, with some modifications, was reintroduced as the Civil Rights Act of 1991. Throughout 1991, a partisan debate between Democrats and Republicans continued on the proposed civil rights legislation. Supporters of the legislation argued that it would not mandate hiring quotas, but detractors believed quotas would be necessitated in its implementation. In November 1991, President Bush suddenly reversed his position on the proposed bill and announced support for it. It was speculated that President Bush's reversal on the legislation was due to political pressures he had received. It became apparent that President Bush may not have enough votes to sustain another veto. In addition, the president was getting pressure from women's groups that had been angered by the White House's attempts to discredit the testimony of Anita Hill, who had charged sexual harassment against then-Supreme Court nominee Clarence Thomas. Thomas was eventually confirmed on the Supreme Court, but women's groups were still upset at the president.

The Civil Rights Act of 1991 was passed, and it makes it easier for women to collect financial awards for intentional discrimination. Before the bill, women could only collect back pay. The new legislation permits women to collect punitive damages as well, ranging from $50,000 to $300,000, for sexual harassment. The 1991 Civil Rights Act also contained provisions that would make it easier for plaintiffs charging discrimination against employers. The bill would put the burden on employers to prove that their hiring policies were not discriminatory. In many places the 1991 act is so vague that it will be left up to the courts for final interpretation. One anticipated business response is to continue using quotas to avoid lawsuits.

The laws we have just discussed constitute the backbone of federal efforts to prevent employment discrimination. Several executive orders issued by the president of the United States also prohibit discrimination. However, because the executive orders also contain provisions for affirmative action, we will reserve our discussion of them until our treatment of affirmative action later in the chapter.

Role of the EEOC

As the major federal body created to administer and enforce job bias laws, the Equal Employment Opportunity Commission (EEOC) deserves special consideration. Several other federal agencies also are charged with enforcing some aspect of the discrimination laws and executive orders, but we will restrict our discussion to the EEOC.

The EEOC has five commissioners and a general counsel appointed by the president and confirmed by the Senate. The five-member commission is responsible for making equal employment opportunity policy and approving all litigation the commission undertakes. The EEOC staff receives and investigates employment discrimination charges/complaints. If the commission finds reasonable cause to believe that unlawful discrimination has occurred, its staff attempts to conciliate the charges/complaints. When conciliation is not achieved, the EEOC may file lawsuits in federal district court against employers. Private employers may be sued under Title VII, but only the Justice Department may sue a state or local government for a violation of Title VII.[18] Figure 16-5 provides additional information about the EEOC, including its official mission.

Like other federal regulatory bodies we have discussed such as the EPA, FTC, and OSHA, the EEOC has had mixed success over the years. Its fortunes, successes, and failures have been somewhat dictated by the times, the administration in office, and the philosophy and zeal of its chairperson. Over the course of its existence, the EEOC has at various times been criticized for mismanagement, overspending, leniency, zealousness, ineptness, inefficiency, and an assortment of other charges. During the late 1970s it was thought that the EEOC was on a "witch hunt," looking for violations so it could punish business for its past wrongs. Business thought this was unfair because it believed it had made more progress on the EEO front than in any other sector in which federal regulations existed.[19]

In 1983, Clarence Thomas, a black man, was named head of the EEOC by President Ronald Reagan. He remained in his job until 1990, when he was confirmed for a seat on the U.S. Court of Appeals for the District of Columbia. What makes Clarence Thomas a notable figure is that in 1991 President Bush nominated Judge Thomas to replace the retiring Thurgood Marshall on the Supreme Court. Many of Thomas's critics for his appointment to the Supreme Court based their objections on Thomas's philosophy and record while he headed the EEOC.

When Thomas was appointed to the EEOC, he initially resisted President Reagan's avowed goal to eliminate all hiring quotas in discrimination and affirmative action proceedings. Soon thereafter, however, Reagan made it clear to

FIGURE 16-5 The EEOC

EEOC'S MISSION: To ensure equality of opportunity by vigorously enforcing federal legislation prohibiting discrimination in employment through investigation, conciliation, litigation, coordination, regulation in the federal sector, and through education, policy research, and provision of technical assistance.

THE COMMISSION'S POLICY: In pursuing its mission of eradicating discrimination in the workplace, the Commission intends that its enforcement be predictable, provide effective relief for those affected by discrimination, allow remedies designed to correct the sources of discrimination, and prevent its recurrence.

THE COMMISSION'S MEETINGS: Commission policy, litigation, and related matters are discussed and approved at weekly meetings. The Commission generally meets twice each week: an open session on Tuesdays at 9:30 a.m., which the public may attend and at which general policy statements are considered, and a closed session on Mondays at 2 p.m., at which the Commission discusses litigation strategy and approves recommendations for litigation.

Commission agenda items are announced at least one week before each meeting. The public may call (202) 634-6748 to find out what items will be discussed at the open session.

STRUCTURE: In 1983, the Washington, DC, headquarters structure was reorganized to reflect a commitment to efficient public service through effective management and administration. Functions were streamlined and integrated into nine headquarters' offices. In 1984, field office operations were restructured to facilitate thorough and timely charge processing nationwide, reflecting the Commission's policy of vigorously enforcing the laws against employment discrimination.

Source: "Commission Enforces EEO Laws" (Washington, DC: The U.S. Equal Employment Opportunity Commission, Office of Communications, November, 1988), 1–3.

Thomas that the government should "speak with one voice," and Thomas accepted the administration's directives. By the time Thomas left the EEOC in 1990, the agency had (1) eliminated the use of minority hiring goals and timetables used by employers to correct racial and ethnic disparities; (2) largely abandoned class-action lawsuits that relied on statistical evidence to prove widespread discrimination at large companies; and (3) yielded the EEOC's once-dominant role on civil rights initiatives to the Justice Department. Thomas's philosophy was to direct and support lawsuits on behalf of only those individuals who could show that they had been personally hurt by discrimination.[20]

It is indeed ironic that Thomas's philosophy and practices, which seemed to be consistent with the majority of public opinion throughout the 1980s, would come back to haunt him in 1991 as he was vying for a seat on the Supreme Court. It should be made clear, however, that his primary critics were those who were significantly committed to the policy of affirmative action to solve society's ills in the realm of employment discrimination. Consequently, Thomas's views were actually more consistent with many voter's beliefs that "civil rights advocates are pressing for special, preferential benefits instead of such goals as equal opportunity."[21]

THE MEANING OF DISCRIMINATION

Over the years, it has been left to the courts to define the word "discriminate" because it was not defined in Title VII. Over time, it has become apparent that two specific kinds of discrimination have been used. These two kinds are known as disparate treatment and disparate impact.

Disparate Treatment

The initial usage of the word "discrimination" meant using race, color, religion, sex, or national origin *as a basis for treating people unequally.* This form of discrimination was referred to as *unequal treatment,* or **disparate treatment**. Examples of disparate treatment might include refusing to consider blacks for a job, paying women less than men for the same work, or supporting any decision rule with a racial or sexual premise or cause.[22] According to this common sense view of discrimination, the employer was allowed to impose any criteria so long as they were imposed *on all groups alike.*[23] This view of discrimination equated nondiscrimination with color-blind decision making. In other words, it meant that all groups or individuals had to be treated equally, without regard for color, sex, or other characteristics.[24]

Disparate Impact

Congress's intent in prohibiting discrimination was to eliminate practices that contributed to economic inequality. What it found was that, although companies could adhere to the previous definition of discrimination, this did not eliminate all of the economic inequalities it was intended to address. For example, a company could use two neutral, color-blind criteria for selection: a high school diploma and a standardized ability test. Blacks and whites could be treated the same under the criteria, but the problem arose when it became obvious that the policy of equal treatment resulted in *unequal consequences* for blacks and whites. Blacks were less likely to have a high school diploma, and blacks who took the test were less likely than whites to pass it. Therefore, a second, more expanded idea of what constituted discrimination was thought to be needed.

The Supreme Court had to decide whether an action was discriminatory if it resulted in unequal consequences in the *Griggs* v. *Duke Power Company* case in 1971.[25] In this case, the court said that it was the *consequences* of an employer's actions, not the employer's intentions, that determined whether discrimination had taken place. If any employment practice or test had an adverse or differential effect on minorities, then it was a discriminatory practice. An unequal impact, or *disparate impact,* as this new kind of discrimination came to be known, simply meant that fewer minorities were included in the outcome of the test or the hiring or promotion practice than would be expected by their numerical proportion. The court also held that a policy or procedure with a disparate impact would be permissible if the employer could demonstrate a business necessity for it or job-relatedness. In the Duke Power case, for example, a high school diploma and good scores on a general intelligence test were *not* shown to have a clearly demonstrable relationship to successful performance on the job under consideration.[26]

The definition of "unequal impact" is quite significant because it runs counter to so many traditional employment practices. There are many other examples. The minimum height and weight requirements of some police departments have unequal impact and have been struck down by courts because they tend to disproportionately screen out women, Orientals, and Hispanics.[27] The practice of discharging employees who have had their wages garnished to pay off debts has also been struck down because it falls heavily on minorities.[28] A number of Supreme Court rulings have addressed the issue of the kind of evidence needed to document or prove discrimination.

With at least two different ways in which to commit discrimination, managers have to be extremely careful because practically any action they take may possibly have discriminatory effects. Figure 16-6 summarizes the characteristics of disparate treatment and disparate impact.

FIGURE 16-6 Two Kinds of Employment Discrimination

Definition 1 Disparate Treatment	Definition 2 Disparate Impact
Direct discrimination	Indirect discrimination
Unequal treatment	Unequal consequences or results
Decision rules with a racial/sexual premise or cause	Decision rules with racial/sexual consequences or results
Intentional discrimination	Unintentional discrimination
Prejudiced actions	Neutral, color-blind actions
Different standards for different groups	Same standards, but different consequences for different groups

Source: James Ledvinka and Vida G. Scarpello, *Federal Regulation of Personnel and Human Resource Management*, 2d ed. (Boston: PWS-Kent, 1991), 48.

ISSUES IN EMPLOYMENT DISCRIMINATION

We have identified the essentials of the major laws on discrimination and seen the evolution of the concept of discrimination. Now it is useful to elaborate briefly on different issues that are related to the types of discrimination we have discussed. It is also important to indicate some of the particular problems that have arisen in each of the different issues.

Issues on Race, Color, and National Origin

Discrimination on the basis of race, color, or national origin was prohibited by Title VII, as we discussed earlier. Traditionally, most of the discrimination issues in this category have affected blacks. This kind of discrimination continued to be a major problem. Indeed, many are arguing that racial discrimination is still a serious problem. Statistics indicate that fewer blacks are going to college and graduate school and that discrimination against blacks on the nation's campuses remains a serious problem after 20 years. Others argue that the problem is not racial discrimination at all but rather a whole host of issues surrounding the black experience in America.

Abject Poverty of the Black Underclass. Part of the problem with blacks not advancing more rapidly in the workplace is attributable to the fact that many of them have not been able to escape *poverty*. While the black middle class is growing, millions of blacks are falling further behind in a seemingly hopeless underclass. The emergence of this underclass within black America has even been referred to as a "nation apart." These are the blacks who live in abject poverty. They are a seemingly irreducible core of inner-city poor who are trapped in an unending cycle of joblessness, broken homes, welfare, and often, drugs and violence. This group is estimated to be at about 2 million to 3.5 million, or about one-third of all poor blacks.[29] The statistics dramatically tell the story of what it is like for a black youngster growing up today:

- One in two lives in poverty.
- One in two grows up without a father.
- Nearly one in three teenagers is out of work.
- One out of four births is to a teenager.
- One in every 21 young black men winds up murdered.[30]

So, while many blacks are succeeding and moving ahead, poverty hangs over many others and gives the appearance that progress is not being made. Civil rights leaders, politicians, and academics debate fiercely the causes and possible solutions to the problem. Even black leadership is fractured into at least two camps—

those representing the "old guard" who hold that lingering racism and cramped economic opportunities are the problem, and a new breed of conservatives who say that race is no longer the critical factor but point to declining family values, the ghetto culture, and the need for blacks to help themselves.[31]

A controversial but highly respected book by Charles Murray entitled *Losing Ground: American Social Policy 1950–1980* made the case that welfare programs and government policy have hurt the poor by undermining their incentive to work and thus climb out of poverty. Murray proposed that the government dismantle all its benefit programs for working-age people but admitted that this action is politically impossible. He hopes, however, that his book will stimulate new thinking on U.S. social policy.[32] Murray's view is supported in a book by Walter Williams that argues that continuing discrimination against blacks is not the reason blacks have not caught up with whites in various statistical measures of well-being.[33] Despite these books, and others like them, the debate rages on.

From Civil Rights to Social Benefits. Another issue affecting people's perception of the racial discrimination problem is the belief of some people that civil rights have expanded to mean social benefits. Chester E. Finn, Jr. makes this argument. Where it was once the federal government's responsibility to make sure that a person was not turned away by a landlord because of color, age, or religion, now states are charged with providing housing for those who cannot afford it. The right to purchase a loaf of bread from the grocer soon was transformed into an entitlement for food stamps. The right to equal opportunity by a prospective employee evolved into a right to preferential treatment to hiring on account of one's color or gender. In short, Finn argues that civil rights organizations have lost their perspective and devote too much attention to income transfer and social service programs. The transformation of all social policy issues into "civil rights" issues results in a blurring of distinctions that fails to address the real problem.[34]

The Case of Hispanics. The growth rate among Hispanics in the United States exceeds the growth rate among blacks. Hispanics now account for about 7 percent to 8 percent of the U.S. work force, and this number is increasing. Hispanics hold only about 4 percent of white-collar jobs and frequently tend to be found in agricultural, janitorial, and other types of menial labor. Hispanics face a different set of problems than blacks. For many Hispanics, language is a barrier to good jobs. Another problem is employers' fear of hiring illegal immigrants. Although affirmative action has given Hispanics a higher profile, discrimination against them is still considered to be a critical problem. In some states, such as California, tensions among Hispanics and blacks over jobs is an increasingly frequent problem.[35]

Asian Image of Superminority. Other groups also experience discrimination on the basis of race, color, or national origin. Asian-Americans represent a growing issue in the United States. Asian-Americans represent about 3 percent of the U.S. work force. Some people point to Asian-Americans as a group that faced many of the same barriers as blacks but overcame them. This group enjoys the highest median family income of any ethnic group in the country.[36] Asian-Americans have not suffered the same magnitude of workplace discrimination as blacks, but a 1986 report by the Commission on Civil Rights concluded: "Anti-Asian activity in the form of violence, vandalism, harassment, and intimidation continues to occur across the nation."[37] In the 1990s, Asian-Americans started relying more on the courts to battle discrimination and hate crimes. This seems to signal a growing realization by Asian-Americans that their past reluctance to apply pressure through the legal system has placed them at a disadvantage.[38]

It has been argued that many of the problems of Asian-Americans stem from their image as a "superminority." They embrace discipline, hard work, and education. This image has a downside, however, because quiet achievement can be interpreted as passivity. The Asian-American response to this is to avoid confrontation and simply work harder. It is estimated that the presence of Asian-Americans will double to 10 million by the end of the century, so this will continue to be an issue for years to come.

Issues on Sex Discrimination

Issues surrounding sex discrimination are quite different from issues on race, color, and national origin. Statistics show that women are flooding the job market, boosting economic growth, and helping to reshape the economy dramatically. Women have seized two-thirds of the jobs created in the past decade. They are pushing harder than ever for equal pay and scoring some impressive gains. In 1973, women earned about 57 percent of what men earned. This figure grew to 60 percent in 1980 and about 64 percent by 1985.[39] By 1990, the median annual income for white females was close to 75 percent of the median annual income of white males.[40]

The major issues for women today include (1) getting into professional and managerial positions and out of traditional female-dominated positions, (2) achieving pay commensurate to that of men, (3) eliminating sexual harassment, and (4) being able to take maternity leave and get their old jobs back. Significant progress is being made on most of these fronts.

Moving into Professional/Managerial Positions. Statistics show that women are moving quickly into formerly male-dominated professional and managerial jobs. They are making progress into professional jobs for which education is a major prerequisite. In 1972, only about 4 percent of MBA graduates were women. Now this figure is over 33 percent. Similarly, in 1972, women occupied 20 percent of management and administrative jobs. This figure grew to more than 37 percent.[41] In a short time, women will be much more prevalent in the managerial ranks than they are now. In spite of this progress, many women and women's groups feel that progress is not being made fast enough, that women are hitting a "glass ceiling" in their jobs, and that women are not able to penetrate the upper echelons of management as soon as they should.

One study sought to identify the barriers that women and minorities face in their efforts to advance to upper management. The eight obstacles identified were as follows:[42]

1. The "comfort" factor as white male bosses tend to promote people like themselves
2. Absence of performance feedback
3. Lack of mentoring
4. Little formal career guidance
5. Exclusion from country clubs and social settings
6. Stereotyping
7. Harassment
8. Erroneous assumptions about assignments women will accept

Comparable Worth. As indicated earlier, women are making tremendous strides in closing the gap between male and female salaries and wages. The movement that has created some controversy in this sphere is the notion of comparable worth. This concept goes beyond the *Equal Pay Act of 1963*, which requires that men and women be paid the same for doing the same job. **Comparable worth** holds that pay should be the same for jobs that require comparable skills, efforts, and responsibilities. Thus, female secretaries or nurses might earn the same as male truck drivers if these jobs were judged to be comparable.[43]

The idea of comparable worth was born in the public sector. Advocates of comparable worth—mostly women's groups and unions—argue that differences in seniority and education alone cannot explain the fact that women generally earn only about two-thirds what men do. They argue that certain jobs are paid less just because they are traditionally held by women.[44] Others argue that companies should value more highly the responsibilities and skills associated with typically female jobs.

Opponents of comparable worth make several arguments. Some are opposed on philosophical grounds because it would mean replacing market forces with regulation by government wage-setting boards. One female economist says, "Trying to repeal supply and demand by using comparable worth systems instead of market values would lead to radical distortions in the economy."[45] Others are more pragmatic and contend that comparable worth is easier to apply in the public sector where civil service pay categories are fixed by legislation. Employers also say that making wage structures more equitable would disrupt the entire economic system of our country.[46]

The current state of comparable worth in the United States suggests very limited growth and acceptance. The progress that has been made has been restricted to the public sector and has been more in the form of pay equity adjustments rather than full-blown comparable worth programs. The states of Washington and Minnesota have experienced some success with efforts to close the salary gap between male and female jobs. One expert points to the state of Minnesota as the most successful institution of pay equity in state and local government. Minnesota not only was among the first to achieve pay equity for its own employees, but it then adopted legislation requiring all jurisdictions within the state—cities, counties, school boards—to report plans for implementation by 1985 and to have completed implementation by 1991. Some localities, such as San Jose and Alameda counties in California and also San Francisco, have been successful with pay equity plans, but their route to success required a coalition of women's organizations combined with a powerful labor union to achieve results. Such efforts as those described have failed to penetrate the private sector as state and federal laws have relied on more traditional means to achieve equity and have not resorted to comparable worth legislation.[47]

Sexual Harassment. It is difficult to document the extent to which sexual harassment is a problem in American business today. With the large increases of women in the work force, however, it is understandable why **sexual harassment** has become a much-debated issue.

The EEOC (December, 1990) defines sexual harassment in the following way:

> Unwelcome sexual advances, requests for sexual favors, and other verbal or physical conduct of a sexual nature constitute sexual harassment when submission to or rejection of this conduct explicitly or implicitly affects an individual's employment, unreasonably interferes with an individual's work performance or creates an intimidating, hostile or offensive work environment.

Implicit in this definition are two broad types of sexual harassment. First is what has been sometimes called *quid pro quo* harassment. This is a situation where something is given or received for something else. For example, a boss may make it explicit or implicit that a sexual favor is expected if the employee wants a pay raise or a promotion. Second is what has been referred to as *hostile work environment* harassment. In this type, nothing is given or received, but the employee perceives a hostile or offensive work environment by virtue of uninvited sexually oriented behaviors or materials being present in the workplace. Examples of this might include sexual teasing or jokes or sexual materials such as pictures or cartoons being present in the workplace.

To help us further understand what sexual harassment is, consider these uninvited sexually oriented behaviors, which were categorized by the Federal Merit System Protection Board as "Less Severe" and "Severe:"

Less Severe
- Pressure for dates
- Sexually suggestive looks or gestures
- Sexual teasing, jokes, remarks, or questions

Severe
- Letters, phone calls, or materials of a sexual nature
- Pressure for sexual favors
- Touching, leaning over, cornering, or pinching[48]

Sexual harassment has been a high-profile issue for years. The controversy heated up in 1991, however, after Supreme Court Justice nominee Clarence Thomas was charged with sexual harassment by a former employee of the EEOC. The country witnessed days of televised Senate hearings over the issue, and the event created a springboard for many women coming forward and publicly admitting they had been sexually harassed by coworkers in the past.

Figure 16-7 chronicles the kinds of experiences women are typically talking about when they say they have been sexually harassed.

One indicator of the severity of the sexual harassment problem is the number of charges filed at the EEOC. According to EEOC figures, complaints of sexual harassment filed with the agency rose from 4,046 in 1986 to 5,572 in 1990. Lawyers who specialize in such cases indicate that these numbers reflect only a small percentage of the actual violations.[49] Prior to 1986, sexual harassment was not a specific violation of federal law. In a landmark case, however, the Supreme Court ruled in 1986 in *Meritor Savings Bank* v. *Vinson* that sexual harassment was a violation of Title VII. In this case, the court ruled that the creation of a "hostile environment" through sexual harassment violates Title VII, even in the absence of economic harm to the employee or a demand for sexual favors in exchange for promotions, raises, or the like. Remedies available to the victims include back pay, damages for emotional stress, and attorney's fees.[50] We should also note that sexual harassment can be committed by women against men. To date, however, this situation has not been as prevalent as sexual harassment against women.

In the future it is expected that companies seeking to avoid sexual harassment lawsuits may have to redress behaviors many males never notice. In a landmark 1991 ruling, the influential Ninth U.S. Circuit Court of Appeals in San Francisco ruled that sexual harassment must be judged not by the prototypical "reasonable man" rule, which has been a legal convention for over 150 years, but by the standards of a "reasonable woman." Thus, women's claims of sexual harassment should be interpreted from the perspective of whether the alleged harassment would offend a "reasonable woman."[51] This new standard, if upheld by other and higher courts, should make sexual harassment easier to prove and thus more problematic for companies. Already, companies such as Corning, Honeywell, CBS, and DEC, just to name a few, are taking steps to raise the corporate consciousness about sexual harassment. Their efforts include letters from the CEO, hiring of sexual harassment consultants to conduct workshops, policies highlighted in company handbooks, worker orientation programs, films, and role-playing exercises.[52]

Sexual harassment is against the law, and responsive companies should take steps to ensure that harassment is ended. Following are some suggested company guidelines:

- Educate employees as to prohibited conduct.
- Reexamine, revise, and reissue written policy statements on the subject.
- Make employees aware of how to obtain redress if harassed.

FIGURE 16-7 Sexual Harassment: Count the Ways

What kinds of experiences are these women talking about when they say they've been sexually harassed? A woman who works in a production area reports that she and other women employees are constantly subjected to suggestive remarks and propositions as they go about their jobs. She added that supervisors participate in this and frequently send women on unnecessary errands through the area just to give the men another opportunity to act this way. Another woman writes that a great deal of sexual innuendo and joking goes on in her office and everyone feels obligated to contribute or tolerate it. "It is very uncomfortable to me," she says, "so I consider it a kind of harassment." A clerical worker says her boss stands touching her while she works. When his "buddies" stop by his desk, he makes remarks that imply that she cooperates sexually with him. He offers to share her "services" with his buddies, in a tone and manner that make clear it is not clerical services he's talking about. Suggestive looks and gestures often accompany the joking and remarks. One woman, for example, says that her fellow employees make obscene gestures and remarks to and about her. Her supervisor thinks it's funny and does nothing about it.

Deliberate touching and cornering is cited by a large number of women. A supervisor stands so close to a female subordinate while giving instructions or looking over her work that he touches her—and while so doing makes suggestive body movements. "The last time the Regional Director was here," writes another victim, "the head secretary had to come to my rescue as the Director was practically breathing down my shirt."

Many women find materials of a sexual nature bothersome. One woman dislikes the way her male co-workers pass around and put up pornographic cartoons in work spaces. When she objects, her boss tells her she's too sensitive.

Pressures for dates and sexual favors are also cited by women. Their descriptions indicate that their experiences not only were bothersome, but sometimes had serious consequences. One woman says when she ignored her boss's advances, he began to treat her cruelly; for example, he made her take four hours of dictation, made her stay late to transcribe it, then in her presence threw it all away because "He didn't need it." Another woman's boss kept pestering her for dates and for favors and kept making personal remarks. When she would not change her mind and play around with him, he had her transferred to a less desirable job. During her first week on the job, reports a temporary trainee, her supervisor kept rubbing her back and shoulders while she typed and filed. Later he made a point blank advance, which she refused. Within a week she was let go on the grounds that she could not adapt to the office.

From the report of the Merit System Protection Board on sexual harassment in the federal workplace.

Source: "Federal Cases," *Across the Board* (October, 1981), 5. Copyright ø The Conference Board. Reproduced with permission.

- Introduce, or update, training programs.
- Make certain that environmental harassment ("hostile environment") is absent from the workplace.
- Get input from women employees and union leaders.[53]

Figure 16-8 presents facts about sexual harassment published by the EEOC.

FIGURE 16-8 Facts About Sexual Harassment

Sexual harassment is a form of sex discrimination that violates Title VII of the Civil Rights Act of 1964.

Unwelcome sexual advances, requests for sexual favors, and other verbal or physical conduct of a sexual nature constitute sexual harassment when submission to or rejection of this conduct explicitly or implicitly affects an individual's employment, unreasonably interferes with an individual's work performance or creates an intimidating, hostile or offensive work environment.

Sexual harassment can occur in a variety of circumstances, including but not limited to the following:

- The victim as well as the harasser may be a woman or a man. The victim does not have to be of the opposite sex.
- The harasser can be the victim's supervisor, an agent of the employer, a supervisor in another area, a co-worker, or a non-employee.
- The victim does not have to be the person harassed but could be anyone affected by the offensive conduct.
- Unlawful sexual harassment may occur without economic injury to or discharge of the victim.
- The harasser's conduct must be unwelcome.

It is in the victim's best interest to directly inform the harasser that the conduct is unwelcome and must stop. The victim should use any employer complaint mechanism or grievance system available.

When investigating allegations of sexual harassment, EEOC looks at the whole record: the circumstances, such as the nature of the sexual advances, and the context in which the alleged incidents occurred. A determination on the allegations is made from the facts on a case-by-case basis.

Prevention is the best tool to eliminate sexual harassment in the workplace. Employers are encouraged to take steps necessary to prevent sexual harassment from occurring. Employees should be informed of their rights, a complaint or grievance process should be established and immediate and appropriate action should be taken when an employee complains.

Source: EEOC (December, 1990).

Maternity Leave. For some time, maternity leave has been an issue for women. In 1987, the Supreme Court upheld a California law that grants pregnant workers 4 months of unpaid maternity leave and guarantees them their old jobs back. Justice Thurgood Marshall argues, "By taking pregnancy into account, California's statute allows women, as well as men, to have families without losing their jobs."[54] Actually, the Pregnancy Discrimination Act of 1978, an amendment to Title VII, required employers to treat pregnancy and pregnancy-related medical conditions the same as any other medical disabilities with respect to all terms and conditions of employment. Although the EEOC had been empowered to protect women against discrimination in pregnancy, it was not until 1991 that it won a significant case that caught public attention. In 1991, after 13 years of litigation, the EEOC announced a $66 million settlement with AT&T to compensate 13,000 employees for job discrimination during pregnancy. The settlement came as a result of AT&T discriminating against women by restricting their maternity leaves beyond that permitted by law. Women's groups claim that discrimination of this kind continues even today but that the 1991 settlement with AT&T will force companies to look carefully at their corporate culture and how they are treating pregnant workers.[55]

Fetal Protection Policies. In 1991, a new form of sex discrimination was identified as the Supreme Court ruled that fetal protection policies constituted sex discrimination. The decisive case was *UAW* v. *Johnson Controls, Inc.* Johnson Controls, like a number of other major firms, developed a policy of barring women of child-bearing age from working in sites in which they, and their developing fetuses, might be exposed to such harmful chemicals as lead, which could cause damage to unborn fetuses. Johnson Controls believed it was taking an appropriate action in protecting the women from exposure to chemicals. In 1984, a class action lawsuit was brought against Johnson Controls by eight current and former employees, along with the United Auto Workers (UAW) union, arguing that the policy was discriminatory and illegal under Title VII of the Civil Rights Act. A U.S. District Court ruled in the company's favor, and the Chicago-based U.S. Court of Appeals for the Seventh Circuit affirmed that decision. The U.S. Supreme Court in 1991, however, reversed the appellate court, arguing that the policy was on its face discriminatory and that the company had not shown that women were more likely than men to suffer reproductive damage from lead.[56]

Even though the Supreme Court gave its opinion that injured children, once born, would not be able to bring lawsuits against the company, a number of experts think that there will likely be litigation in the future because of this ruling. One expert said, "A mother can waive her own right to sue, but she can't waive the right of a child to bring suit. So, five or ten years down the line you might see children born with cognitive disabilities, and they could independently sue businesses." The UAW does not dispute this possibility but asserts that it should provide a major impetus for companies to make workplaces safer.[57]

Issues on Age and Religion

Issues surrounding discrimination on the basis of age and religion are significantly fewer than the others we have discussed. With respect to age discrimination, two trends should be noted. First, with an aging work force we should expect that age discrimination cases would be on the rise in this changing job market.[58] Second, recent court decisions seem to indicate that employers who are faced with age discrimination cases have little reason for optimism. Age discrimination cases continue to follow a pro-plaintiff trend.[59]

The major issue with religious discrimination today concerns the extent to which an employer is required to accommodate employees who claim that their religious affiliations interfere with some aspect of their work, such as scheduling. The various circuit courts in the United States seem to be headed in diverse directions. For example, the Second Circuit Court has insisted that Title VII gives precedence to an employee's preferred mode of accommodation if it does not constitute undue hardship. On the other hand, the Ninth Circuit Court decided that precedence is given to the employer's preferred accommodation if it "reasonable" preserves the employee's employment status. Sooner or later the Supreme Court will have to resolve these conflicts.[60]

AFFIRMATIVE ACTION IN THE WORKPLACE

As a *Time* magazine article recently put it, "Affirmative action to benefit blacks and other minorities has become one of the most bitterly controversial social policies in the U.S."[61] Some whites have been against affirmative action from the very beginning. Others initially accepted the notion that social justice could be advanced by affirmative action but now are arguing that racial preferences have gone on long enough and are wondering whether minorities expect special treatment in perpetuity. Indeed, some observers believe there has emerged a white backlash against the policies that have been in effect for over 25 years.[62] The debate in Congress and the public arena over the 1990 and 1991 proposed Civil Rights bills and the confirmation hearings on Clarence Thomas for the Supreme Court have brought affirmative action back into the limelight of public controversy. Another writer summed it up well when he said that America has a love-hate relationship with affirmative action.[63]

Affirmative action is the idea of taking positive steps to hire and promote persons from groups previously discriminated against. The concept of affirmative action was formally introduced to the business world in 1965 when President Lyndon B. Johnson signed Executive Order 11246. The purpose of this order was to require that all firms doing business with the federal government would engage in affirmative actions to accelerate the movement of minorities into the work force. Many companies today have affirmative action programs because they do business with the government, have begun the plans voluntarily, or have entered into them through collective bargaining agreements with labor unions.

The Range of Affirmative Action Postures

The meaning of affirmative action has changed since it was first introduced. It originally referred only to special efforts to ensure *equal opportunity* for members of groups that had been subject to discrimination. More recently, the term also refers to some degree of *definite preference* for members of these groups in determining access to positions from which they were formerly excluded.[64]

Daniel Seligman has identified four postures that define the range that affirmative action may take:

1. *Passive nondiscrimination.* This involves a willingness in hiring, promotion, and pay decisions to *treat the races and the sexes alike.* This posture fails to recognize that past discrimination leaves many prospective employees unaware of or unprepared for present opportunities.
2. *Pure affirmative action.* This posture involves a *concerted effort to enlarge the pool of applicants* so that no one is excluded because of past or present discrimination. At the point of decision to hire or promote, however, the company selects the most qualified applicant without regard to sex or race.
3. *Affirmative action with preferential hiring.* Here, the company not only ensures the maximum labor pool but *systematically favors minorities and women in the actual decisions.* This could be thought of as a "soft" quota system.
4. *Hard quotas.* In this posture, the company *specifies numbers or proportions of minority group members that must be hired.*[65]

Over the past 25 to 30 years, much confusion has surrounded the concept of affirmative action because it was never clear which of the aforementioned views was being advocated by the government. In hindsight, we can now see that the government was advocating positions based on whichever posture it thought would work, or based on the particular candidate and political party in office at the time. Early on, "soft" or "weak" affirmative action (postures 1 or 2) was advocated. It became apparent, however, that these postures were not effective in getting the results desired. Therefore, "hard" or "strong" affirmative action (postures 3 and 4) was later advocated. The real controversy over affirmative action began with the use of "goals" and "preferential" hiring (posture 3) and hard quotas (posture 4). Today, when we speak of affirmative action, we are typically referring to some degree of preferential hiring as in postures 3 and 4. Related to this, President George Bush's opposition to the proposed 1990 and 1991 civil rights bills was because he believed they would take the country back to the use of hard "quotas" and that this degree of preferential treatment was not appropriate.

The Concept of Preferential Treatment

Let us briefly consider the arguments that have been set forth for and against the concept of preferential treatment. The underlying rationale for preferential treatment is the ***principle*** of ***compensatory justice,*** which holds that whenever an injustice is done, just compensation or reparation is owed to the injured parties.[66] Many people concur that groups discriminated against in the past (women, blacks, North American Indians, and Mexican-Americans) should be recompensed for these injustices by positive affirmative action. Over the years, deliberate barriers were placed on opportunities for minorities—especially blacks. These groups were prevented from participating in universities, business, law, and other desirable institutions. Additionally, when official barriers were finally dropped, matters frequently did not improve. Inequalities were built into the system, and although mechanisms for screening and promotion did not intentionally discriminate *against* certain groups, they did *favor* other groups. Thus, the view that we can and should restore the balance of justice by showing preferential treatment became established as a viable option for moving more quickly toward economic equality in the workplace and in our society.[67]

There are those who claim that such compensatory measures are unjust. They assert that no criteria exist for measuring compensation, that the extent of present discrimination is minor, and that none of those actually harmed in the past are available now to be compensated. They further argue that attempting reparations for all oppressed groups (women and blacks being just two among many) would compound initial injustices with a vastly complex system of further injustices.[68]

It has been further argued that strong affirmative action is objectionable because it is inefficient and unfair and damages self-esteem. The degree of inefficiency depends on how strong a role racial or sexual preferences played in the selection process. If people with lower qualifications are selected, performance or productivity might logically suffer. The principal objection to affirmative action by most people is that it is unfair. Finally, it is argued that affirmative action damages the self-esteem of the person who was chosen on the basis of preferential treatment. The idea here is that even those minorities who might have been selected because of their qualifications are called into suspicion for *why* they got the job.[69] We will explore this idea more in a later section.

The Concept of Reverse Discrimination

Without question, the principal objection to affirmative action and the reason it has become and remained controversial is due to ***reverse discrimination.*** This concept holds that when any sort of preference is given to minorities and women, discrimination may occur against those in the majority—usually white males. For well over a decade now, white males who have been passed over because of a preference shown for minorities or women have been filing reverse discrimination suits. They argue that Title VII prohibits discrimination based on race, color, and sex, and that includes reverse discrimination against them as well.

All of this has created a public policy dilemma that has been raging for well over a decade now. How can you show preferential treatment for minorities and women and at the same time not discriminate against white males? It is very difficult, if not impossible, to do. The next question then becomes a matter of public priority: Should we as a nation pursue affirmative action, even if it means that some opportunities for white males will have to be sacrificed in the process? Obviously, there are opinions on both sides.

Minority Opposition to Affirmative Action

Although it is clear that affirmative action is one of the major pillars of the mainstream civil rights agenda, during the past decade a growing and more visible number of blacks have begun to speak out against such policies. Three arguments, in particular, have been made. First, it has been argued that the very existence of preference programs may be aggravating racial tensions. Second, it has been argued that preferential advancement of blacks casts doubt on the credentials of all blacks both by white onlookers and in the minds of black achievers themselves. Third, it has been argued that the primary beneficiaries of affirmative action, from college admissions to corporate advancements, have been middle-class blacks rather than members of the underclass, who may need it most. Thus, according to this view, "affirmative action has succeeded at getting more black people into better jobs but has often failed to achieve the goal of a more equal society."[70]

Three prominent black critics of affirmative action include Dr. Thomas Sowell, Professor Stephen L. Carter, and columnist William Raspberry. Dr. Sowell has argued that blacks would be better served in the long run if affirmative action programs as we now know them were abolished.[71] Stephen L. Carter, a law professor at Yale University, who admits that his race helped him get into college, wrote a widely read and reported book entitled *Reflections of an Affirmative Action Baby* (1991).[72] Mr. Carter's concern seems to be with the effects of affirmative action on those whom the policy was intended to help. According to Carter, affirmative action sets up a dichotomy between "best" and "best black." Carter recalls how, over and over, his teachers told him he was the "best black" they had enrolled. The "best black" syndrome holds that, however accomplished a black person might be, he or she is likely to be categorized as "first black," "only black," or "best black," or measured by a different, most likely inferior, standard.[73] Carter apparently does not want to eliminate all types of affirmative action immediately. He supports some degree of racial consciousness, particularly in admission to college or professional school, but thinks that at some point the preferences must fall away entirely. He is against turning affirmative action into a tool for representing the "points of view" of excluded groups.[74]

National columnist William Raspberry argues that affirmative action doesn't sell in many parts of the white community because it misrepresents the civil rights problem in the United States today. He believes that white Americans, as reflected in a survey commissioned by the Leadership Conference on Civil Rights, see black leadership as no longer concerned with fairness but only with group advantage.

Further, he argues that many of these whites do not see themselves as racists or as opponents of equal opportunity and fundamental fairness. Raspberry argues that blacks say we want to be judged by the "content of our character" but our agenda is based on the color of our skin. According to Raspberry, the problems most critically affecting black America are "the joblessness and despair of our young people, the academic indifference of our children, the dissolution of our families, the destruction (by crime and drug trafficking) of our neighborhoods, the economic marginality of our people," and affirmative action policies won't solve these problems.[75]

Supreme Court Decisions

It would be too lengthy a venture to fully discuss the Supreme Court's views and decisions on affirmative action over the past decade or more. Whole books have been written on this topic for those who wish a more detailed accounting.[76] There is some merit, however, in providing a brief overview of selected significant actions and decisions of the high court.

Regents of the University of California v. Bakke, 1978.

The country hoped for a definite opinion regarding the legality of affirmative action in the celebrated Bakke case. Bakke, a white male, had been denied admission to medical school while a special admissions program for minorities was in effect. He charged that, because the admissions programs gave preference to less qualified minorities, this constituted discrimination again him. The Supreme Court, in a less than definitive decision, ruled that Bakke should be admitted, that strict racial quotas were illegal, but that race could continue to be "taken into consideration" in admissions.[77] After the Bakke decision straddled the issue of acceptability of affirmative action, the EEOC issued a new set of guidelines that said, in effect, the agency would not support charges that companies are violating the civil rights of white men in cases where "reasonable" affirmative action programs favor minorities or women. They interpreted "reasonable" to mean that some attention to race or sex was permissible even if hard quotas were not.

Kaiser Aluminum and Chemical Corporation v. Weber, 1979.

This case, being a somewhat more definitive decision, had the effect of smoothing the way for affirmative action programs. Brian Weber, a white man, charged that he was illegally discriminated against by being denied a position in a quota-based training program at Kaiser Aluminum. His case was upheld by the lower courts. If Weber's charge of reverse discrimination had been upheld by the Supreme Court, it would have represented a major setback to the concept of affirmative action. As it turned out, however, the Supreme Court in 1979 overturned the lower courts and ruled that employers *could* give preference to minorities and women in hiring and promotion for "traditionally segregated job categories." The majority opinion, written by Justice William Brennan, relied on what he determined was the "spirit" of the job-bias provisions of the Civil Rights Act of 1964. He argued:

It would be ironic indeed if a law triggered by a nation's concern over centuries of racial injustice and intended to improve the lot of those who had been victims of discrimination constituted the first legislative prohibition of all voluntary, private race-conscious efforts to abolish traditional patterns of racial segregation and hierarchy.[78]

The majority opinion made it clear that a racial preference in private employment is permissible whenever there are "manifest racial imbalances" in traditionally segregated job categories. The Weber decision, in essence, gave the green light to employers who had wanted to set up affirmative action programs but feared to do so because of possible reverse discrimination suits by white males.

Memphis Fire Department v. *Shotts,* 1984. In 1980, the city of Memphis made a settlement in a class-action suit in federal district court. The settlement called for an affirmative action program for the hiring of blacks in the fire department. In 1981, the city announced that budget deficits made it necessary to lay off some city employees under a "last hired, first fired" rule that was part of the city's seniority plan. The district court ordered the city to modify its layoff plans so as to protect black firefighters hired or promoted by affirmative action.[79] The case went to the Supreme Court.

The major issue in the case was whether the district court had exceeded its authority in requiring the city to modify its seniority plan in order to protect affirmative action. The Supreme Court decided that the district court *had* exceeded its powers. The reason was that Title VII permits employers to apply a seniority plan to employees, even if such application discriminates against minorities, as long as the seniority plan is not a result of intentional racial discrimination. The seniority plan was considered to be a bona fide plan.[80] The upshot of the Memphis firefighters' case was that seniority systems may not be disrupted to save newly hired blacks.

The Memphis firefighters' case was very important for the Reagan administration. The Justice Department declared that the Shotts decision squarely supported its view that Title VII prohibits a court from authorizing any preferential treatment to anyone other than the actual victims of proven discrimination. In 1985, Attorney General Edwin Meese proposed that Executive Order 11246 be revised to (1) eliminate employment goals, and (2) prohibit the Office of Federal Contract Compliance Programs (OFCCP) from using statistical measures to assess a contractor's compliance with the order.[81]

The Reagan administration had held for some time that numerical goals and timetables amounted to discriminatory quotas or reverse discrimination and should be eliminated. Therefore, they saw some hope in this decision that perhaps the Supreme Court was now leaning in their direction. However, the Shotts decision referred to *layoffs*, though it was being more broadly interpreted by the Reagan administration to mean that all goals and quotas were outlawed. The Meese proposals were roundly criticized by many in Congress, which threatened to adopt legislation to counter such moves. The Supreme Court's decisions in 1986 and 1987, however, clarified how the court felt about affirmative action.[82]

Wygant v. Jackson Board of Education, 1986. In this case, the Supreme Court again upheld seniority when it ruled that laying off more experienced white teachers violates the constitutional guarantee of equal protection. The decision also contained good news for proponents of affirmative action. The court said that preferential treatment of minorities is not always unconstitutional.[83]

Local 93, International Association of Firefighters v. City of Cleveland, 1986. This case involved the legality under Title VII of race-conscious promotional goals. In this case, the Supreme Court emphatically rejected the rationale the Reagan administration had been urging as the basis for its all-out assault on racial goals and quotas. The court held that trial judges may approve voluntary pacts between unions and public employers to give minorities hiring preferences.[84]

Local 28, Sheetmetal Workers International Association v. EEOC, 1986. This case answered the question left open in the Cleveland Firefighters case: Under Title VII, can a court *order* race-conscious affirmative action that may benefit individuals who are not identified victims of unlawful discrimination? By a narrow 5–4 margin, the Supreme Court decided that, in certain instances, a court could order such race-conscious relief.[85] Two important rules emerged from this case. First, a court may order a union to use quotas to overcome a history of "egregious discrimination." Second, black and Hispanic applicants can benefit even if they themselves were not victims of past union bias.[86] The court decisions in 1986 were clearly considered victories from the pro-affirmative action point of view.

Alabama State Police, 1987. In this case, the Supreme Court voted 5–4 to uphold a promotion quota for Alabama state troopers. A judge's order that the state promote one black for each white until blacks held 25 percent of top ranks was upheld by the court and justified on the basis of a "shameful record of delay and resistance."[87]

Johnson v. Transportation Agency, Santa Clara County, California, 1987. This case was a significant one because, for the first time, the Supreme Court ruled on an affirmative action case *directly involving a woman*. When a dispatcher job opened up in the Santa Clara County Transportation Agency, Paul Johnson and Diane Joyce both applied. Both were rated well qualified for the job. In applicant interviews, Johnson scored 75 and Joyce scored 73. The county agency had a voluntary affirmative action plan that allowed an applicant's sex to be considered when making promotions in job areas where women were significantly underrepresented. There were no women among the 238 skilled craft positions in the department, so managers decided this was the time to give a woman the job. Diane Joyce got the job. Johnson sued, claiming reverse discrimination.[88] The Supreme Court rejected Johnson's claim. It ruled that the affirmative action system for employees in Santa Clara County that allowed a woman, Diane Joyce, to be promoted to crew dispatcher over a man who had more on-the-job experience and who scored marginally higher in an oral interview was justified and approved.

This case was important because for the first time the high court ventured into approval of sex preferences—getting more women into nontraditional jobs—for pure social engineering. Justice William Brennan in a majority opinion wrote, "As long as there is a manifest imbalance in the ethnic or sexual composition of a work force, an employer may adopt a plan even when the disparity is not so striking."[89] The Johnson ruling upheld the idea that a plan can stay in effect until the percentage of women or minority group members matches that in the labor market as a whole.[90]

City of Richmond v. *J. A. Crosen Co.,* 1989. In this case, the Supreme Court ruled that the Constitution limits the power of state and local governments to reserve a percentage of their business for minority contractors. This decision forced 36 states and 190 cities and counties to review their programs. Changes in these programs may be required if they include racial quotas or if the programs are not correcting well-documented past cases of discrimination.[91]

Martin v. *Wilkes,* 1989. In this case, the Supreme Court ruled that court-approved affirmative action settlements can be reopened when white male employees allege reverse discrimination.[92]

Footnotes to the Supreme Court's Decisions. From the Bakke case in 1978 to the cases in 1989, the Supreme Court has come a long way in defining the legality and acceptability of affirmative action. In a case-by-case fashion, the high court has been systematically answering questions about when affirmative action might be used.

The court rulings from 1978 to 1987 were largely supportive of affirmative action programs. The cases cited from 1989 indicated some limitations being placed on such programs. These recent cases culminate over a decade of efforts by the court to decide just how far judges can go to remedy discrimination without stepping on the white majority's rights. In general, it is expected that companies will continue to use affirmative action programs regardless of these fine-tuning decisions made by the Supreme Court. Figure 16-9 summarizes the key Supreme Court decisions on affirmative action.

One economist, Gary S. Becker, provides an interesting footnote to the Supreme Court decision supporting women in affirmative action plans. He argues that this decision is fine, but women's groups will be disappointed when they see that decisions such as this will not have much impact on the economic position of the vast majority of women in the United States because changes in the earnings and occupations of women are much more closely related to changes in their productivity than to government action. Becker presents statistics, research, and the experience of other countries to show that the higher productivity of employed women is mainly responsible for the progress they have achieved. As more and more women go to business school and get more career-oriented schooling,

FIGURE 16-9   A Decade of Key Supreme Court Decisions on Affirmative Action (AA)

Date	Case	Setting	General Finding
1978	*Bakke*	Admission to university medical school	Mildly supportive of affirmative action (AA)
1979	*Weber*	Quota-based training program of private employer (Kaiser)	Supportive of AA
1984	*Shotts*	City fire department (Memphis)	Minor setback for AA; qualified seniority plans OK for layoffs
1986	*Wygant*	Jackson, Michigan, Board of Education-school teachers	Mixed finding; seniority system upheld; preferential treatment not always wrong
1986	*Firefighters*	Municipality (City of Cleveland Fire Dept.)	Supportive of AA; minorities may be given hiring preferences
1986	*Sheet Metal Workers*	Labor Union	Strongly supportive of AA; Court can order AA for those who were not specific victims of discrimination
1987	*Alabama State Police*	State police force	Strongly supportive of AA; Court can order promotion quotas
1987	*Johnson*	County transportation department (Santa Clara)	Strongly supportive of AA; AA can promote women to remedy their historical exclusion from certain job categories
1989	*Richmond* v. *Crosen*	City government	Mild limitation to AA
1989	*Martin* v. *Wilkes*	Setting unknown	Supportive of reverse discrimination charges

training, and experience, their economic positions will improve. Becker concludes that although affirmative action decisions by the courts will help the advancement of women working for governments and large publicity-conscious companies, the progress for most women will continue to depend on the quieter forces that encourage women to stay in the work force.[93]

The Corporate View

It is not easy generalizing about how the corporate community feels about affirmative action. Initially, business was opposed to the idea. As time passed, however, and as business leaders gained experience with affirmative action programs, their views changed somewhat. It is clear that the corporate sector is not adamantly opposed to affirmative action. However, it is also clear that business would prefer to be free of government mandates.

A 1985 survey of Fortune 500 chief executive officers was taken at the time that the Reagan administration was deciding to eliminate goals and timetables to assess affirmative action plans. Ninety-five percent of the executives said they would continue to use numerical objectives to track the progress of minorities and women regardless of what the government does. Furthermore, more than 90 percent said that the numerical objectives in their affirmative action programs were established partly to satisfy corporate objectives unrelated to government regulation.[94]

A survey of business leaders in 1991 by *Business Week* magazine gives us an opportunity to see how corporate America more recently feels about these issues.[95] In this survey, 65 percent of the senior executives responded that business, on its own, would hire and train minorities and women and give them the chance to get ahead without affirmative action laws. Thirty-one percent of the executives thought that such laws were needed. The reason given for the majority viewpoint was that the marketplace was already forcing companies to end discrimination. The executives pointed to the shifting composition of the labor supply and the benefits of a diverse work force as bigger spurs to affirmative action than fears of government enforcement or private lawsuits.

The survey also revealed that 53 percent of the respondents thought that business needs to do a better job of hiring, training, and promoting minorities, and 44 percent were not satisfied with their progress in hiring, training, and promoting women. Another interesting finding was that 53 percent of those surveyed thought that the whole area of affirmative action has been "not much trouble" for their companies, while 39 percent said it has been "some but not a lot" of trouble.[96]

The business community seems to now accept affirmative action programs as "good business policy." Some executives see goals and timetables as simply a good way of measuring progress, and others see them as a way to stave off expensive discrimination suits later. For some employers, affirmative action has practical business value in customer relations, especially for makers of consumer goods or providers of consumer services. Most large companies have an entrenched affirmative action program, and they think that tinkering with it now might draw wrath from women and minorities. Many executives think that if affirmative action is necessary and the law requires it, then a systematic program that has the government's approval is an effective way of going about it.[97]

Based on the Supreme Court decisions that we have discussed and the extent to which the business community has embraced the concept for a variety of practical reasons, the future of affirmative action looks bright. The message to business seems clear: Women and minority stakeholders have the backing of the highest court in the land, and it is therefore only logical that responsive management adhere to these public-policy decisions and attempt to fashion a program that will meet the letter and spirit of the law. At the same time, management should do all it can to eliminate or ameliorate the situations in which reverse discrimination might occur. As we have already seen, however, this is extremely difficult to do. Therefore, it is likely that this debate will rage for years to come in spite of what positions the high court takes.

SUMMARY

This chapter addresses several subgroups of employee stakeholders whose job rights are protected by law. The United States got serious about the problem of discrimination by enacting the Civil Rights Act of 1964, which prohibited discrimination on the basis of race, color, religion, sex, or national origin. Laws covering age and handicap were passed later. The EEOC was created to assume the major responsibility for enforcing the discrimination laws. Like other federal agencies, the EEOC has had problems. However, on balance it has done a reasonable job of monitoring the two major forms of discrimination: disparate treatment and disparate impact. Discrimination issues discussed in the chapter touch on abject poverty and the black underclass; the movement from civil rights to social benefits; the plight of Asian-Americans, Hispanics, and women moving into professional/managerial positions; comparable worth; sexual harassment; and fetal protection policies.

Affirmative action was one of the government's answers to the problem of discrimination. Although originally intended to broaden the applicant pool so that everyone would have an equal employment opportunity, it quickly became a form of preferential treatment, up to and including actual numerical goals and quotas. Considerable controversy has surrounded the question of how far affirmative action should go. One of the most serious problems has been the extent to which affirmative action has created *reverse discrimination*. The Supreme Court has addressed this issue slowly but surely, and the weight of recent evidence seems to come down on the side of affirmative action. The Supreme Court's votes have frequently been close, however, and a newly appointed justice could possibly sway the court in the other direction. Corporations have undertaken affirmative action by building their human resource management policies on affirmative action principles, and they will likely continue these practices in the future. To do otherwise at this point might evoke criticism from minorities, women, and others who have benefited from government policies. Furthermore, sound stakeholder management requires companies to continue to be fair in their employment practices.

DISCUSSION QUESTIONS

1. List the major federal discrimination laws and indicate what they prohibit. Which agency is primarily responsible for enforcing these laws?
2. Based on your reading of the chapter, what is a BFOQ? Give an example where age is a BFOQ and where sex is a BFOQ.
3. Give two different definitions of discrimination, and provide an example of each.
4. What do you think are the advantages and disadvantages of the concept of comparable worth? Do you think we should institute such a national policy? Explain.
5. Explain the dilemma between practicing affirmative action and reverse discrimination. Do you think the Supreme Court is headed in the right direction for handling this issue? Explain.

ENDNOTES

1. William F. Glueck and James Ledvinka, "Equal Employment Opportunity Programs," in William F. Glueck, *Personnel: A Diagnostic Approach*, rev. ed. (Dallas, TX: Business Publications, 1978), 593–633.
2. *Ibid.*, 597–599.
3. "Equal Opportunity: A Scorecard," *Dun's Review* (November, 1979), 107.
4. *Ibid.*, 108.
5. *The World Almanac and Book of Facts–1987* (New York: World Almanac, 1986), 129.
6. McKay Jenkins, "Despite Education Gains, Blacks Still Trailing Whites in Income," *The Atlanta Journal* (September 20, 1991), A16.
7. Cited in Lynne Duke, "Hard Data: The Black Money Gap Grows," *The Washington Post National Weekly Edition* (August 19–25, 1991), 37.
8. Paula Dwyer, "The 'Other Minorities' Demand Their Due," *Business Week* (July 8, 1991), 62.
9. "Title VII: Enforces Job Rights" (Washington, DC: The U.S. Equal Employment Opportunity Commission, Office of Communications, October 1988), 1.
10. "Age Discrimination Is Against the Law" (Washington, DC: The U.S. Equal Employment Opportunity Commission, Office of Communications, April 1988), 1.
11. *Ibid.*, 2.
12. "Equal Work, Equal Pay" (Washington, DC: The U.S. Equal Employment Opportunity Commission, Office of Communications, October 1988), 1.
13. "Equal Employment Opportunity is . . . The Law" (Washington, DC: The U.S. Equal Employment Opportunity Commission, Office of Communications, 1986), 1.
14. Henry H. Perritt, Jr. *Americans with Disabilities Act Handbook* (New York: John Wiley & Sons, 1990), vii.
15. U.S. Department of Justice, Office on the Americans with Disabilities Act, *The Americans with Disabilities Act: Questions and Answers* (Washington, DC: Government Printing Office, 1991), 1.
16. *Ibid.*
17. Barbara B. Brown, "Federal Regulations Update," *Employment Relations Today* (Spring, 1991), 109–110.
18. "Commission Enforces EEO Laws" (Washington, DC: The U.S. Equal Employment Opportunity Commission, Office of Communications, November 1988), 1.

19. Bob Tarmarkin, "Is Equal Opportunity Turning into a Witch Hunt?" *Forbes* (May 29, 1978), 29–31.
20. Bill McAllister, "Civil Rights: What Happened at the EEOC When Thomas Was There?" *The Washington Post Weekly Edition* (September 16–22, 1991), 31.
21. Thomas B. Edsall, "A Civil Rights Reality Check," *The Washington Post National Weekly Edition* (March 18–24, 1991), 38.
22. James Ledvinka, *Federal Regulation of Personnel and Human Resource Management* (Boston: Kent, 1982), 37.
23. Glueck and Ledvinka, 304.
24. Ledvinka, 37–38.
25. *Griggs v. Duke Power Company*, 401 U.S. 424, 1971.
26. Theodore Purcell, "Minorities, Management of and Equal Employment Opportunity," in L. R. Bittel (ed.), *Encyclopedia of Professional Management* (New York: McGraw-Hill, 1978), 744–745.
27. *Smith v. City of East Cleveland*, 502 F. 2d 492, 1975.
28. *Wallace v. Debron Corp.*, 494, F. 2d 674, 8th Cir., 1974.
29. "A Nation Apart," *U.S. News & World Report* (March 17, 1986), 18.
30. *Ibid.*
31. *Ibid.*
32. Charles Murray, *Losing Ground: American Social Policy, 1950–1980* (New York: Basic Books, 1984).
33. Walter Williams, *The State Against Blacks* (New York: New Press, McGraw-Hill, 1982).
34. Chester E. Finn, Jr., "From Civil Rights to Special Interests," *The Wall Street Journal* (March 22, 1983), 32.
35. Dwyer, 62.
36. Gregory A. Fossedal, "Black Progress and Government Intervention," *The Wall Street Journal* (March 22, 1982), 14.
37. "A Superminority Tops Out," *Newsweek* (May 11, 1987), 48.
38. Arthur S. Hayes, "Asian Americans Go to Court to Fight Bias," *The Wall Street Journal* (September 3, 1991), B5.
39. "Women at Work," *Business Week* (January 28, 1985), 80.
40. "Race in the Workplace: Is Affirmative Action Working?" *Business Week* (July 8, 1991), 53.
41. "Corporate Women: They're About to Break Through to the Top," *Business Week* (June 22, 1987), 75.
42. Carol Hymowitz, "One Firm's Bid to Keep Blacks, Women," *The Wall Street Journal* (February 16, 1989), B1.
43. "Why Can't a Woman's Pay Be More Like a Man's?" *Business Week* (January 28, 1985), 82.
44. Cathy Trost, "Pay Equity, Born in Public Sector, Emerges as an Issue in Private Firms," *The Wall Street Journal* (July 8, 1985), 15.
45. *Ibid.*
46. Lee Smith, "The EEOC's Bold Foray into Job Evaluation," *Fortune* (September 11, 1978), 58.
47. Alice H. Cook, "Current State of Comparable Worth in the United States," *Labor Law Journal* (August, 1990), 525–531.
48. "Federal Cases," *Across the Board* (October, 1981), 2.
49. Ruth Marcus, "When Is Flirting at Work Sexual Harassment?" *The Washington Post National Weekly Edition* (February 25–March 3, 1991), 32.
50. Marilyn Machlowitz and David Machlowitz, "Hug by the Boss Could Lead to a Slap from the Judge," *The Wall Street Journal* (September 25, 1986), 20.
51. Arthur S. Hayes, "Courts Concede the Sexes Think in Unlike Ways," *The Wall Street Journal* (May 28, 1991), B5.
52. "Ending Sexual Harassment: Business Is Getting the Message," *Business Week* (March 18, 1991), 98–99.
53. Machlowitz and Machlowitz, 20.
54. Beth Brophy, "Supreme Court Gives Motherhood Its Legal Due," *U.S. News & World Report* (January 26, 1987), 12.
55. Isabel Wilkerson, "AT&T Settles Bias Suit for $66 Million," *New York Times* (July 18, 1991), A16.
56. "Under a Civil Rights Cloud, Fetal Protection Looks Dismal," *Insight* (April 15, 1991), 40–41.
57. *Ibid.*
58. Victor Schachter and Joanne Dellaverson, "The Older Worker vs. The Company," *San Francisco Examiner* (February 10, 1985), 1–2.
59. Alan M. Koral, "Age Discrimination Cases Continue Pro-plaintiff Trend," *Employment Relations Today* (Summer, 1986), 105–113.
60. Alan M. Koral, "Religion in the Workplace: Mixed Signals from the Courts," *Employment Relations Today* (Summer, 1986), 100.
61. William A. Henry, III, "What Price Preference?" *Time* (September 30, 1991), 30.
62. *Ibid.*
63. James E. Ellis, "Up From Affirmative Action," *Business Week* (September 23, 1991), 20.
64. Thomas Nagel, "A Defense of Affirmative Action," *Report from the Center for Philosophy and Public Policy* (College Park, MD: University of Maryland, Fall, 1981), 6–9.
65. Daniel Seligman, "How 'Equal Opportunity' Turned into Employment Quotas," *Fortune* (March, 1973), 160–168.
66. Tom L. Beauchamp and Norman E. Bowie (eds.), *Ethical Theory and Business*, 2d ed. (Englewood Cliffs, NJ: Prentice Hall, 1983), 477–478.
67. *Ibid.*, 478.
68. Robert Simon, "Preferential Hiring," in Beauchamp and Bowie, 492–495.
69. Nagel, 6–7.
70. Henry, 30.
71. Tony Mecia, "Sowell Blasts Affirmative Actions Harmful Effects," *Campus* (Fall, 1991), 6–7.

72. Stephen L. Carter, *Reflections of an Affirmative Action Baby* (Basic Books, 1991).
73. Ernest Holsendolph, "Affirmative Action: Book Takes a Hard Look," *Atlanta Journal* (September 20, 1991), 1G [Book Review].
74. Linda Chavez, "An Insider's Account of Affirmative Action," *The Wall Street Journal* (September 6, 1991, A7 [Book Review]. See also James E. Ellis, "Up From Affirmative Action," *Business Week* (September 23, 1991), 20 [Book Review].
75. William Raspberry, "Why Civil Rights Isn't Selling," *The Washington Post National Weekly Edition* (March 18–24, 1991), 31.
76. See, for example, Melvin I. Urofsky, *A Conflict of Rights: The Supreme Court and Affirmative Action* (Scribner's, 1991) and Michel Rosenfeld, *Affirmative Action and Justice* (New Haven: Yale University Press, 1991).
77. "Bakke Wins, Quotas Lose," *Time* (July 10, 1978), 8–20.
78. Urban C. Lehner and Carol H. Falk, "Beyond Bakke: High Court Approves Affirmative Action in Hiring, Promotion," *The Wall Street Journal* (June 28, 1979), 1, 30.
79. Robert N. Corley and O. Lee Reed, *Instructor's Manual to Accompany the Legal Environment of Business,* 7th ed. (New York: McGraw-Hill, 1987) 432.
80. *Ibid.*
81. James H. Coil, III, "Affirmative Action Reaches a Crossroads—Not a Dead End," *Employment Relations Today* (Fall, 1986), 211–212.
82. *Ibid.*
83. "Affirmative Action—with Some Exceptions," *Newsweek* (April 6, 1987), 59.
84. *Ibid.*
85. Coil, 214.
86. *Newsweek* (April 6, 1987), 59.
87. Ted Gest, "Supreme Court Rules: A One-White for One-Black Quota for Promotions," *U.S. News & World Report* (March 9, 1987), 8.
88. "Use This Decision to End Discrimination," *USA Today* (March 31, 1987), 8A.
89. Charlotte Low, "Caveats Reversed in Workplace Equality," *Insight* (April 27, 1987), 8.
90. *Ibid.*
91. Paula Dwyer, "The Blow to Affirmative Action May Not Hurt That Much," *Business Week* (July 3, 1989), 61.
92. *Ibid.*
93. Gary S. Becker, "Productivity Is the Best Affirmative Action Plan," *Business Week* (April 27, 1987), 18.
94. Anne B. Fisher, "Businessmen Like to Hire by the Numbers," *Fortune* (September 16, 1985), 28.
95. "*Business Week*/Harris Executive Poll: Corporate America Grades Its Efforts," *Business Week* (July 8, 1991), 63.
96. *Ibid.*
97. *Ibid.*, 26–30.

CHAPTER **SEVENTEEN**

Owner Stakeholders: Corporate Governance

CHAPTER OBJECTIVES

After studying this chapter, you should be able to:

- Link the issue of legitimacy to corporate governance.

- Identify the major criticisms of boards of directors.

- Describe the general problems with greenmail, golden parachutes, and insider trading.

- Identify the major changes in boards of directors that are being employed to improve corporate governance.

- Discuss the principal ways in which shareholder activism is exerting pressure on corporate managements to improve governance.

- Summarize what companies are doing to become more responsive to owner stakeholders.

The giant corporation in the United States is in trouble. Indeed, it could be said that the American system of doing business is in trouble. When companies receive severe and unrelenting criticism from a group that historically has been their number one stakeholder (corporate owners or shareholders), then it is time to assess how American industry got to this point and what needs to be done to correct the problem.

What are some of the manifestations of the problem? The one that stands out above the rest is the increased shareholder activism of the past 20 years, especially in the 1980s and 1990s. Shareholder groups have become increasingly critical of how management groups and boards of directors run the firms. They complain about management's lack of accountability, ineffective and complacent boards, excessive managerial compensation, and a general lack of focus on the importance of shareholders relative to management. This latter criticism means that management is looking out for number one, but the number one it is protecting frequently is themselves, *not* their owners.

One possible view is that management groups have gotten so caught up in addressing the needs of other stakeholder groups—employees, customers, communities, and vocal activist groups—that the owner/stakeholder has been neglected. This may be partially true. Another view is that management has become so preoccupied with its own status, position, and rewards that it is no longer making corporate decisions in the interests of owners and other stakeholders but rather in its own interests. This may be partially true also. Whatever the actual nature of the problem, one point is clear: Corporate governance has become a major issue as shareholders, legal experts, and others are asking, "Who governs the giant corporation, and for whom is it governed? The shareholders? The management? The directors? Others?"

To address these concerns and explore recommendations that have been set forth, we need to cover two broad issues. First, we need to examine the components of the corporate governance problem. Second, we need to discuss what actions are being taken and may be taken to address these problems.

LEGITIMACY AND THE CORPORATE GOVERNANCE PROBLEM

To understand corporate governance, it is useful to understand the idea of *legitimacy*. Legitimacy is a somewhat abstract concept, but it is vital in that it helps explain the importance of the relative roles of a corporation's charter, shareholders, the board of directors, management, and employees—all of which are components of the modern corporate organization.

Let us start with a slightly modified version of Talcott Parsons' definition of legitimacy. "Organizations are legitimate to the extent that their activities are congruent with the goals and values of the social system within which they function."[1] From this definition, we see **legitimacy** as a *condition* that prevails when there is a congruence between the organization's activities and society's expectations. Thus, while legitimacy is a condition, **legitimation** is a dynamic process by which business seeks to perpetuate its acceptance. The dynamic process dimension should be emphasized because society's norms and values change, and business must change if legitimacy is to be continued. It is also useful to consider legitimacy at both the *micro,* or company, level and the *macro,* or business institution, level.

At the *micro* level, we refer to individual business firms maintaining legitimacy by conforming with societal expectations. According to Epstein and Votaw, companies seek legitimacy in several ways. First, a company may adapt its methods of operating to conform to what it perceives to be the prevailing standard. For example, a company may discontinue door-to-door selling if that marketing approach comes to be viewed in the public mind as a shoddy sales technique.[2] Or, a pharmaceutical company may discontinue offering free drug samples to medical students if this practice begins to take on the aura of a bribe. Second, a company may try to change the public's values and norms to conform to its own activities by advertising and other techniques. Avon was successful at this with its door-to-door marketing of cosmetics.

Finally, an organization may seek to enhance its legitimacy by identifying itself with other organizations, persons, values, or symbols that have a powerful legitimate base in society.[3] This occurs at several levels. At the national level, companies proudly announce appointments of celebrities, former politicians, or famous persons to managerial positions or to the board of directors. At the community level, the winning local football coach may be asked to endorse a company by sitting on its board or promoting its products.

The macro level of legitimacy is the level with which we are most concerned in this chapter. Here we refer to the corporate system—the totality of business enterprises. It is difficult to talk about the legitimacy of business in pragmatic terms at this level. American business is such a potpourri of institutions of different shapes, sizes, and industries that saying anything definite about it is difficult. Yet this is precisely the level at which business needs to be concerned about its legitimacy. What is at stake is the existence and form of business as an institution in our society. William Dill has suggested that business's social (or societal) legitimacy is a fragile thing:

> Business has evolved by initiative and experiment. *It never had an overwhelmingly clear endorsement as a social institution* (emphasis added). The idea of allowing individuals to joust with one another in pursuit of personal profit was an exciting and romantic one when it was first proposed as a way of correcting other problems in society; but over time, its ugly side and potential for abuse became apparent.[4]

Quite a bit of the excitement and romanticism has long since worn off; business must face up to its fragile mandate. It must realize that its legitimacy is constantly subject to ratification. And it must realize that it has no inherent right to exist—it exists solely because society has given it that right.

In comparing the micro view of legitimacy with the macro view, one may observe that, while specific business organizations try to perpetuate their own legitimacy, the corporate or business system as a whole rarely addresses the issue at all. This is unfortunate because the spectrum of powerful issues regarding business conduct clearly indicates that such institutional introspection is needed if business is to survive. If business is to continue to justify its right to exist, then the question of legitimacy and its operational ramifications cannot be ignored.

The Issue of Corporate Governance

The issue of corporate governance is a direct outgrowth of the question of legitimacy. For business to be legitimate and to maintain its legitimacy in the eyes of the public, its governance must correspond to the will of the people.

Corporate governance refers to the method by which a firm is being governed, directed, administered, or controlled and to the goals for which it is being governed. Corporate governance is concerned with the relative roles, rights, and accountability of such stakeholder groups as owners, boards of directors, managers, employees, and others. Not since the early days of the New Deal has the field of corporation law been so astir with proposals to reform the corporation.[5] Indeed, the subject has become a favorite preoccupation of congresspersons, SEC commissioners, legal scholars, shareholders, and Naderites.[6]

The issue has not arisen in a vacuum. Questions about how corporations govern themselves and to whom they are accountable are a direct consequence of their failure to perform to society's satisfaction—or at least to the satisfaction of many of society's most vocal activists and opinion leaders, including owners/stakeholders. Business corporations have grown large and powerful and so have the people who manage them. We do not argue that their power is irreparably socially destructive. Yet, despite the many economic and financial successes of modern business, a number of incidents have raised questions about management's performance in noneconomic spheres. Because many corporate giants have been tarnished by charges of malfeasance, there are demands for closer scrutiny of large corporations and for more accountability for their actions. As the public learns of corporate directors who claim to have no knowledge of admitted bribes, unlawful political contributions, and other chicanery, the question being raised time and again is, "Who governs the corporation?" The issue is stated by some in this way: "Is corporate management really responsible to anyone except itself?"[7] As company executives have become insulated from effective control by directors and shareholders—to whom they are legally responsible—they become even further removed from the influence of customers, employees, community groups, and others who have an interest in how the company performs.[8] The corporate governance issue, then, comes back to the question, "Who governs the giant corporation, and for whom is it governed? The shareholders? The management? The directors? Other stakeholders? The government?"

Corporate Organization

To appreciate the legitimacy and corporate governance issues, it is important that we understand the major groups that make up the corporate form of business organization, for it is only by so doing that we can appreciate how the system has failed to work according to its intended design.

Roles of Four Major Groups. The four major groups we need to mention in setting the stage are the shareholders, the board of directors, the management, and the employees. Overarching these groups is the **charter** issued by the state, giving the corporation the right to exist and laying down the basic terms of its existence. Figure 17-1 presents these four groups, along with the state charter, in a hierarchy of corporate authority.

Under American corporate law, **shareholders** are the owners of a corporation. As owners, they should have ultimate control over the corporation. This control is manifested primarily in the right to select the board of directors of the company. The degree of each shareholder's right is determined by the number of shares of stock owned. The individual who owns 100 shares of Mattel Toy Company, for example, has 100 "votes" when electing the board of directors. By contrast, the large public pension fund that owns 5 million shares likewise has 5 million "votes."

Because large organizations may have hundreds of thousands of shareholders, they elect a smaller group, known as the **board of directors,** to govern and oversee the management of the business. Traditionally, the board has been composed of individuals whose principal employment was with some other company. In the twentieth century, however, the practice of appointing **inside directors**—individuals serving as managers of the very companies that employ them—has become prevalent. Current trends are back toward more outside directors.

The third major group in the authority hierarchy is **management**—that group of individuals hired by the board to run the company and manage it on a daily basis. Along with the board, top management establishes overall policy. Middle- and lower-level managers carry out this policy and conduct the daily supervision of the operative employees. *Employees* are those hired by the company to perform the actual work. Managers are employees, too, but in this discussion we use the term *employees* to refer to nonmanagerial employees.

Separation of Ownership from Control. The social issues that have evolved in recent years focus on the *intended* versus *actual* roles, rights, responsibilities, and accountability of these four major groups. The major issue embedded in the structure of modern corporations that has contributed to the corporate governance problem has been *the separation of ownership from control.* In the precorporate period, owners were frequently the managers themselves. Thus, the system worked the way it was intended; the owner also controlled the business. Even when firms grew larger and managers were hired, the owners were on the scene to keep the management group accountable. For example, if a company got in trouble, the Carnegies or Mellons or Morgans were always there to fire the president.[9]

FIGURE 17-1 The Corporation's Hierarchy of Authority

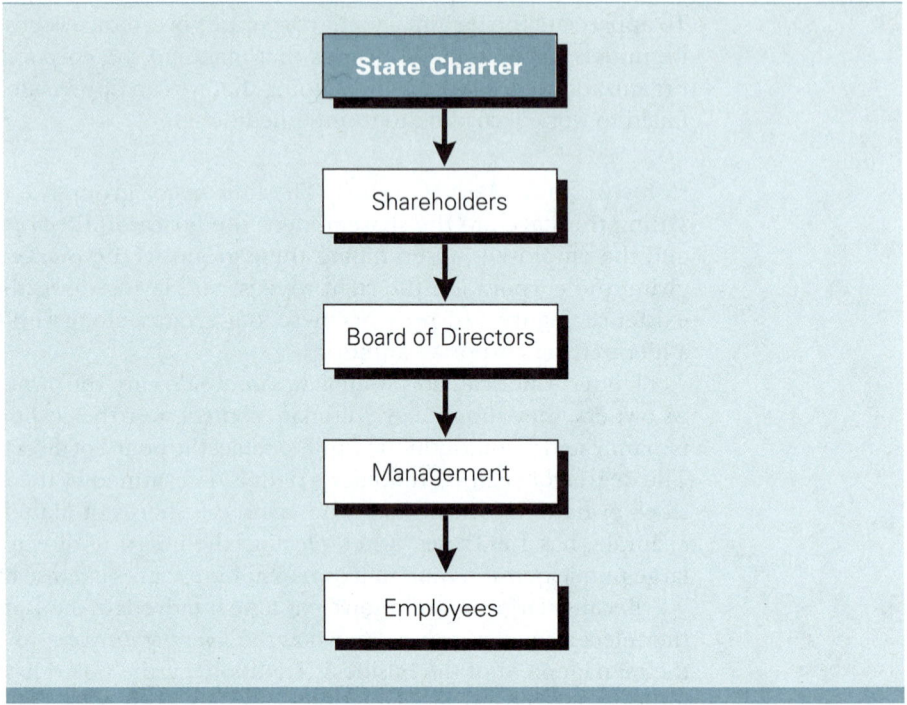

As the public corporation grew and stock ownership became dispersed, a separation of ownership from control became the prevalent condition. Figure 17-2 illustrates the precorporate and corporate periods and the separation of ownership from control problem. The dispersion of ownership into hundreds of thousands or millions of shares meant that essentially no one or no one group owned enough shares to exercise control. This being the case, the most effective control that owners could exercise was the election of the board of directors. As we will see in the next section, boards of directors became groups beholden to management and, thus, management came to control the board of directors rather than vice versa.

The upshot of this evolution was that authority, power, and control rested with the group that had the most concentrated interest at stake—management. The corporation did not function according to its designed plan with effective authority, power, and control flowing *downward* from the owners. The shareholders were owners in a technical sense, but most of them saw themselves as *investors* rather than owners. If you owned 100 shares of Texaco and there were 10 million shares outstanding, you would see yourself as an investor rather than an owner. With just a telephone call making a sell order to your stockbroker, your "ownership" stake is gone. Furthermore, with stock ownership so dispersed, no conscious, intended supervision of corporate boards was possible.

FIGURE 17-2   Pre-Corporate vs. Corporate Ownership and Control

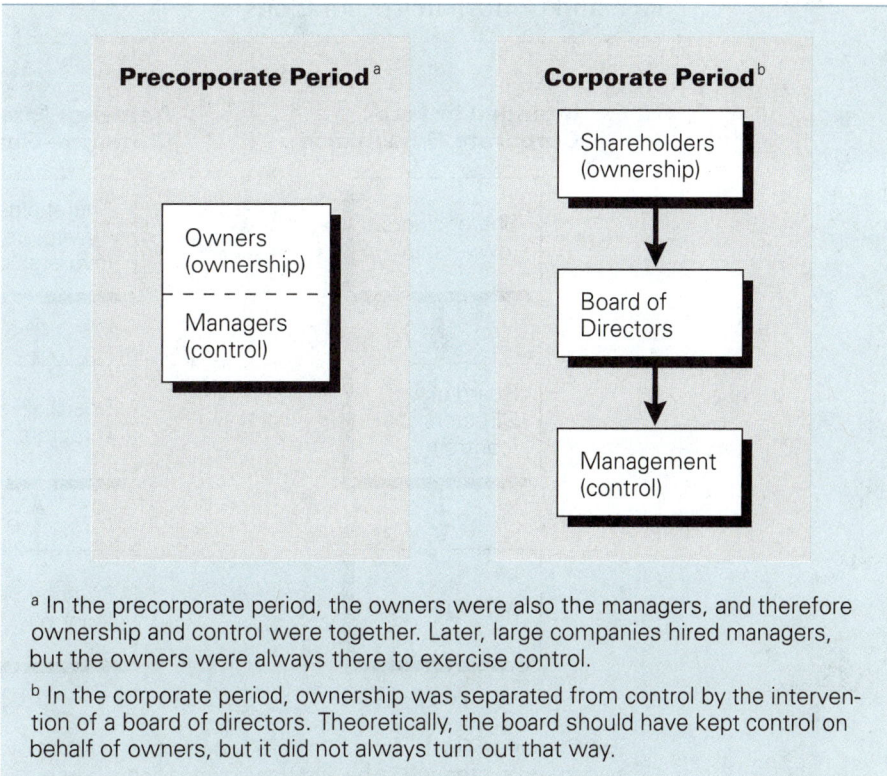

^a In the precorporate period, the owners were also the managers, and therefore ownership and control were together. Later, large companies hired managers, but the owners were always there to exercise control.

^b In the corporate period, ownership was separated from control by the intervention of a board of directors. Theoretically, the board should have kept control on behalf of owners, but it did not always turn out that way.

The other factors that added to management's power were the corporate laws and traditions that gave the management group control over the *proxy machinery*—the method by which the shareholders elect boards of directors. Over time it was not difficult for management groups to create boards of directors of like-minded executives who would simply collect their fees and defer to management on whatever it wanted. The result of this process was that power, authority, and control flowed *upward from management* rather than downward from the shareholders. Figure 17-3 contrasts the traditional, intended, legal flow of authority and control with what became the actual or effective flow of authority or control. Figure 17-4 on page 511 depicts many of the questions about corporate governance and the various rights and responsibilities of the major component groups.

Ineffective Boards of Directors

It is clear from the preceding discussion that a potential governance problem is built into the corporate system because of the separation of ownership from control. It is equally clear that the board of directors is intended to oversee

FIGURE 17-3 Intended vs. Actual Flows of Authority, Power, and Control in Corporations

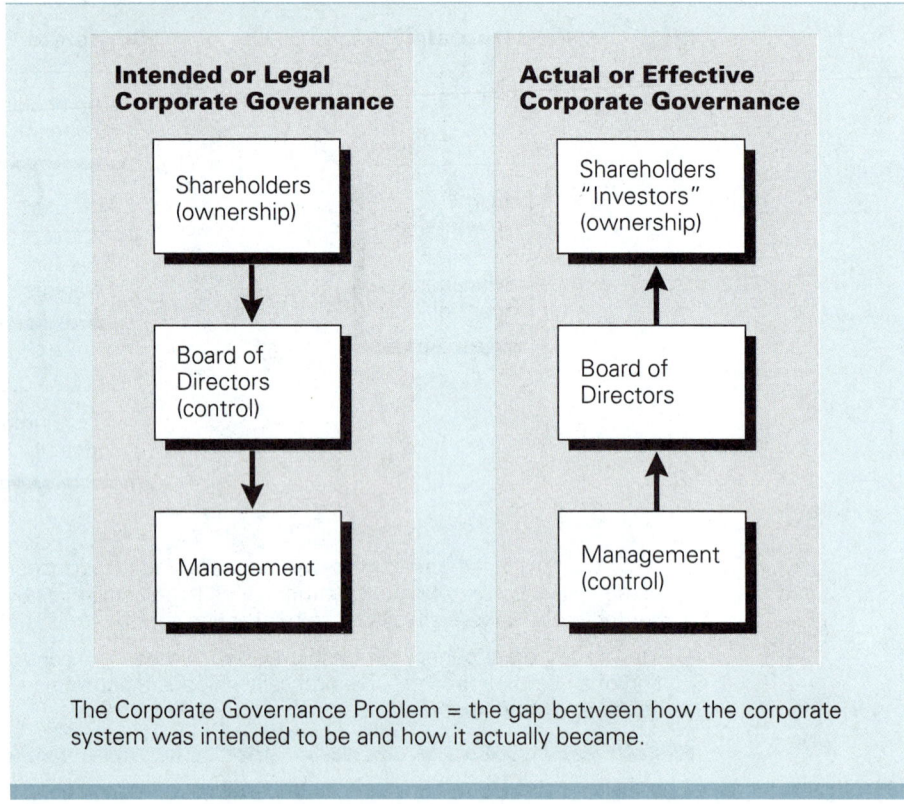

The Corporate Governance Problem = the gap between how the corporate system was intended to be and how it actually became.

management on behalf of the shareholders. However, this is where the system has broken down, and it could well be argued that corporate governance will never function as it is intended unless and until the board of directors becomes an effective, potent body that is carrying out its roles and responsibilities to supervise managements as intended.

Murray Weidenbaum approaches the problem by saying that we need to contrast what directors are *supposed to do* with what they *actually do* or have done.[10] This is a useful approach worth developing. First, what should directors do? From a formal or legal standpoint, corporate boards exist to fulfill the legal requirements imposed by state chartering authorities. Boards are given the authority and responsibility to direct management. This is quite a broad charge, and attempts have been made to flesh out that role by focusing on the board's primary function. The American Bar Association has asserted that the board's primary function is as follows: "The fundamental responsibility of the individual corporate director is to represent the interests of the shareholders

FIGURE 17-4 The Major Corporate Groups and Questions That Are Being Asked at Each Level

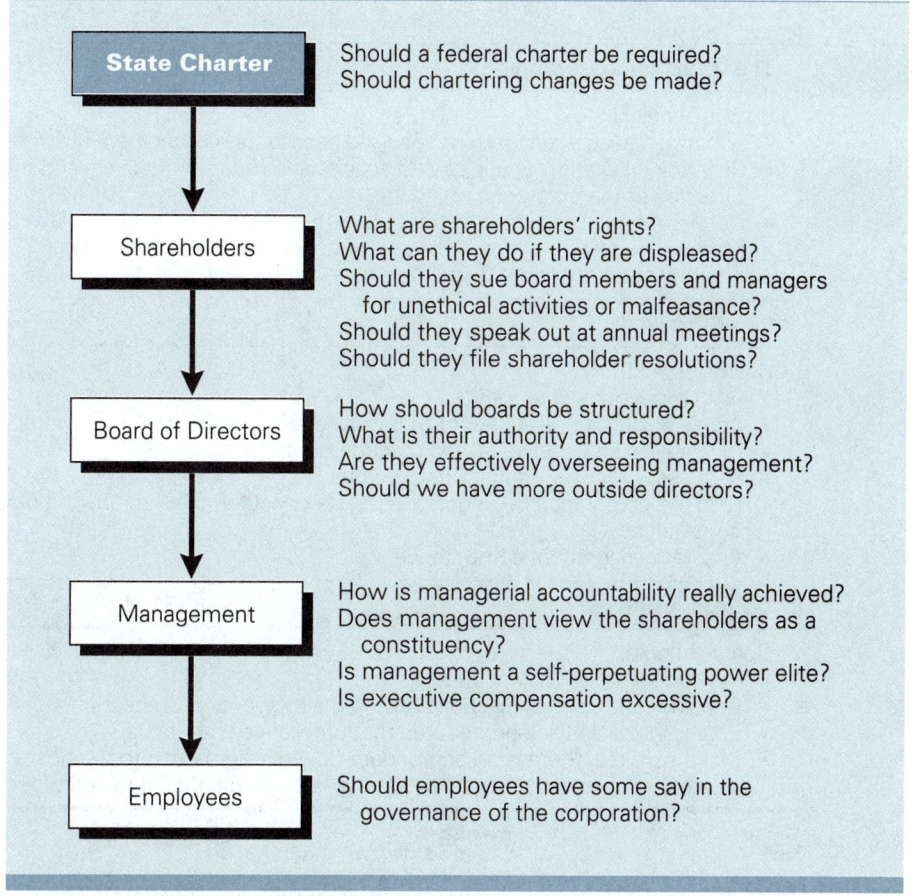

as a group, as the owners of the enterprise, in dealing with the business and affairs of the Corporation within the law."[11]

Others have attempted to state more completely what all this means, as shown in Figure 17-5. It is clear that the purpose of boards of directors is to oversee management and to ensure that the shareholders' interests are represented and protected.

Are boards doing what they are supposed to be doing? According to an increasing number of observers, they are not. Two executives summarize the views of many. David J. Dunn, chairman of Prime Computer, says that the governance problems we face today reflect "the failure of boards to do what they are supposed to do—represent the interest of stakeholders." The problems he is alluding to include lawsuits against directors, the inability of directors to handle unfriendly takeovers, and the pressures

FIGURE 17-5 What Boards of Directors Ought to Do: Three Viewpoints

The American Assembly[a]

Boards should:
- Appraise management performance and provide for management/board succession.
- Determine significant policies and actions and future profitability and the strategic direction of the enterprise.
- Determine policies and procedures to obtain compliance with the law.
- Monitor the totality of corporate performance.
- Interpret for management society's expectations and standards.

Peter Drucker[b]

Boards should:
- Ask crucial questions.
- Act as a conscience, a keeper of human and moral values.
- Give advice and counsel to top management.
- Serve as a window on the outside world.
- Help the corporation be understood by its constituencies and by the outside community.
- Assure management competence.

George A. Steiner[c]

Boards should:
- Provide for management succession.
- Consider decisions and actions having major economic impacts.
- Establish policies and procedures for compliance with the law.
- Make sure that there is an appropriate flow of information to the board and that internal policies and procedures are capable of responding to board decisions.

Sources: [a]*Corporate Governance in America* (New York: The American Assembly, 1978), 6.
[b]Peter Drucker, "The Bored Board," *Wharton Magazine* (Fall, 1976), 31.
[c]George A. Steiner, *The New CEO* (New York: Macmillan, 1984), 69.

from management that directors cannot handle.[12] Harold Geneen, retired CEO of ITT, has stated this same view with greater vehemence:

> Among the boards of directors of Fortune 500 companies, I estimate that 95% are not fully doing what they are legally, morally, and ethically supposed to do. . . . The board's primary function is to oversee and evaluate the performance of management . . . if that performance is not satisfactory, to do something about it. . . . That is what is supposed to happen . . . but it doesn't.[13]

There are three major, interrelated criticisms of boards: (1) the board is a rubber stamp of management's decisions, (2) the board is dominated by the CEO, and (3) the board is plagued with conflicts of interests.[14] These three criticisms are not applicable for every firm, but they do represent the historical problems with most boards.

The Board Is a Rubber Stamp.
This long-standing criticism of boards of directors probably evolved from the fact that managements have historically controlled the proxy machinery by which directors to the board are elected. Furthermore, boards have for many years been dominated by *inside* directors. So, if boards have been composed primarily of members of management along with carefully chosen outsiders, it is not surprising that they have turned into a "rubber stamp."

Historically, board memberships have been cushy, well-paid positions with lots of perks, embedded in a country club atmosphere where nobody rocks the boat. As Frederick Sturdivant characterized boards, they are cozy groups of insiders—"members of top management, an attorney from the corporation's outside law firm, the president from the company's bank, and a few of the chief executive officer's personal friends."[15] Can anyone imagine such a board challenging top management?

The Board Is Dominated by the CEO.[16]
This criticism is closely related to the first. In one survey, it was found that in 77 percent of the corporations the chairman of the board was also the firm's CEO.[17] What this means is that the board chairman/CEO controls both the agenda of the board meetings and the daily performance of the company. One cannot help but recall the old saying about the "fox guarding the chicken coop." In an environment in which the board chairmanship is also held by the CEO over whom the board is ostensibly exercising direction, it is not surprising that allegations of no accountability are being leveled against boards of directors.

The Board Is Plagued with Conflicts of Interest.
In addition to the conflict of interest wherein the CEO also serves as chairman of the board, another is created with inside directors. The inside director is a subordinate of the CEO, who controls the director's salary, career, and future in the company. Courtney Brown, an experienced director who served on many boards, says that he never saw a subordinate officer serving on a board dissent from the position taken by the CEO.[18] Figure 17-6 summarizes some interesting insights into the position of inside director of a board.

Another realm in which a conflict of interest is manifested is in the process of deciding on executive compensation. A board committee typically sets the CEO's salary. One researcher recently claims to have found an interesting correlation. Apparently, the higher the fees paid to directors, the higher the CEO's pay. The researcher's implication is that CEOs, who typically recruit board members (who get elected because management controls the proxy process), buy loyalty with high fees for directors. An example often cited is when the ITT Corporation board doubled the pay of its chairman in 1990 despite the company's ragged financial performance. The board members got $51,000 in basic fees that year plus $40,000 more in extras.[19]

FIGURE 17-6 Insights Provided by Executives Who Have Served as Inside Directors

The following comments were given in interviews about serving as an inside member of the board:

- "I don't really believe much in inside board members. I've been one and I've been an outside board member. I think an inside board member is captive. There are too many constraints on internal board members. I look at them not as board members but as advisers to the board."

- "I think that certain men in the organization who are officers ought to attend meetings strictly on questions that apply to their work so that they can answer questions and give their views. I think they should not be members of the board."

- "Inside board members are slowly but surely going to be a thing of the past. Insiders may be advisory members of the board or participants in board meetings but without voting. The Chief Operating Official or Chief Financial Officer or Legal Counsel are there to advise and should not be voting board members."

- "The relationships of the CEO with inside board members are entirely different from the relationships with outside board members. Inside board members are in a position of agreeing with the CEO or resigning."

- "There is a special burden on the CEO to involve inside directors in board deliberations and get the value of their information and input."

- "Many of the subjects coming to the board would have been discussed in the course of normal operations with the inside board members. The important influence of the inside board members will be in those executive discussions preceding the board meeting and not in their votes as members of the board."

- "My one major experience was that an inside controlled board was horrible for the company. It did not result in a board that made judgments independent of the company management because the board was dominated by the inside members."

- "If you have substantial internal owner board members, that constitutes a unique relationship for the CEO. They are essentially board members because of ownership. The relationship of the CEO to these owners/employees will be influenced significantly by the relative amount of stock owned by him and by them. That is not the typical inside board member situation, especially in large companies."

Source: Armand Stalmaker, *The Board of Directors and the Chief Executive Officer* (St. Louis: Washington University, Center for the Study of American Business, June, 1986), 40–41. Reproduced with permission.

There are also conflict-of-interest situations created by outside directors of companies who do business with the companies on whose boards they serve. For example, a commercial banker/director may insist that the company on whose board he or she is serving restrict itself to using the services of his or her own firm. Another example is seen in the "back scratching" that may be done by board members serving on the compensation committee when they are determining the compensation package for the CEO and other top management officials. The possible conflict arises when the board members are sympathetic to generous compensation for management because they know that the counterpart committees of their boards are considering what to do about their compensation. It could be argued that their own self-interest is being voted as they remain quite sensitive to likely actions to be taken by their own boards.[20]

We have touched on some of the major criticisms of boards of directors. As we examine other issues that have contributed to the corporate governance crisis today, we find that they all come back to the board of directors. The board of directors has the principal oversight responsibility on these issues. And if the board is falling prey to the rubber stamp role, to subordinates of the CEO/board chairman, or to conflicts of interest, it cannot effectively address these issues. Later in the chapter we will discuss changes that could strengthen the board.

Managerial Self-Interest

Many of the board characteristics we have described up to this point could be called managerial self-interest because they reflect situations in which the top management group has maximized its own autonomy. However, the allegations of managerial self-interest go beyond what we have described. Ann Crittenden has argued that we have entered an age of "me-first" management. This age is characterized by disproportionate salaries and bonuses paid to CEOs, a failure of corporate stewardship, and a preoccupation of executives with keeping their own jobs and maximizing their own personal financial rewards. Examples of the stampede of self-interests are easy to find. A handful of top auto executives received bonuses of more than $50 million. This raised eyebrows and angry comments because the executives, citing weak car sales, had won $4 billion in wage concessions from Ford and GM workers, had laid off thousands of other employees, and had won protectionism from Japanese imports that cost consumers millions of dollars in higher auto prices. An earlier example involves the Charter Company. It filed for bankruptcy, but its top five officers voted themselves special incentive bonuses of $250,000 each.[21]

The issue of executive pay has become one of the principal elements in "me-first" management. *Business Week* publishes an annual survey of executive compensation, and the last several years have documented enormous increases in executives' pay, often in spite of lackluster corporate performance.

In 1991, *Business Week* reported the top five highest paid CEOs as follows:[22]

1. Stephen M. Wolf	UAL	$18,301,000
2. John Sculley	Apple Computer	$16,730,000
3. Paul B. Fireman	Reebok International	$14,822,000
4. Dean L. Buntrock	Waste Management	$12,290,000
5. Leon C. Hirsch	U.S. Surgical	$11,676,000

Particular mention was made of Reebok's chairman, Paul Fireman, as his compensation rose from $11.4 million in 1988 to $14.8 million in 1990 in spite of two consecutive years in which the company experienced a loss of the number one spot in sneakers to Nike and a puny 1 percent rise in profits the next year. Two special cases of executive compensation cited by *Business Week* included Steven J. Ross of Time Warner, who received a $75 million bonus on top of his 1990 pay due to Time's merger with Warner Communications, and Donald A. Pel's spectacular $186 million windfall when his company, LIN Broadcasting, merged with another.[23] It is little wonder that *Business Week* subtitled its story on this topic as follows: "Investors, Employees and Academics Are Asking, How Much Is Enough?"

Of particular note during this era of rapidly escalating executive compensation is the observation that executive pay seems to rise despite poor or tenuous financial performance of the firms under question. The president of Institutional Shareholder Services recently observed, "When a CEO does badly, his pay almost never goes down." One compensation expert conducted a study in which it was found that 96 percent of CEO pay "has nothing, absolutely nothing, to do with the company's performance." In 1990, the UAL chairman made $18.3 million while profits fell 71 percent. Eagle-Picher Industries gave their CEO a 38 percent increase in compensation, although profits fell 25 percent and the company filed for Chapter 11 bankruptcy protection in 1991.[24]

Of special note in recent CEO compensation trends is the growing gap between CEOs and others (for example, engineers and factory workers), which began in 1960 and continues today. The most dramatic gap between these groups began in 1980. In 1980, the average CEO made 42 times the pay of the ordinary factory worker. By 1990, CEOs were earning 85 times what the average factory worker was earning.[25] Serious questions are being raised as to how this growing gap can be justified.

It was earlier suggested that there may be some linkage between CEO and executive compensation and board members. Therefore, it should not be surprising that director's pay is fast escalating and becoming an issue too. In 1990, the average director got retainer and meeting fees of $32,352 for 92 hours of work. Some companies are much more generous. For example, Pepsico paid $78,000 to their directors, Philip Morris paid $54,675, Coca-Cola paid $53,400 and Sara Lee paid $52,500.[26]

Companies claim they pay directors well in order to secure the best available. For their part, however, CEOs know that good pay and perks help to buy director loyalty. An example of this expectation was the free-spending F. Ross Johnson, former CEO of RJR Nabisco. Concerning the lavish care of his directors, Johnson once said, "If I'm there for them, they'll be there for me." They were there for him until his greed got out of hand as he tried to buy the company through a leveraged buyout.[27]

The "pampered, protected, and perked" life that CEOs enjoy prompted *Business Week* to publish a cover story in 1991 on what it termed "CEO disease." *Business Week* argued that the prerequisites and deferences afforded CEOs create a kind of protective cocoon, if not full-fledged fantasy world, in which CEOs begin to take on a level of self-importance that far exceeds reality. Not only is the CEO disease characterized by high pay and perks, but it also features such telltale signs as the following: the CEO refuses to concede any mistake; the CEO spends excessive time on boards of other companies and civic groups, playing the role of statesman; the CEO is surrounded by sycophants who "yes" the boss's every whim; the CEO wants to make every decision but doesn't bother to find out all the details; the CEO always tries to be one up on counterparts in salary, headquarters, and aircraft; the CEO relishes media attention; and the CEO hangs onto the job too long.[28]

A *Business Week* editorial argues that only a strong, independent board of directors can take corrective action against CEO disease, but often the board postpones corrective action until it is too late. Steps boards need to take include a thorough and objective review of the CEO's performance at regular intervals. Also, the board needs to rein in the outside activities of CEOs as they cannot handle their responsibilities while sitting on other boards and participating excessively in charitable and civic activities.[29]

It is clear from the data available on executive compensation and CEO disease that managerial self-interest is a serious problem. The traditionally cozy relationship between CEOs, who also frequently serve as board chairman, and the board itself suggests some of the problems with current corporate governance. When golden parachutes, which we will discuss in the next section, are added in, it is easy to get the impression that executive teams are looking out for themselves first and the shareholders and others second. These issues raise ethical questions of enormous proportions. The average small shareholder or person on the street has no effective means for effecting change. It is not surprising, therefore, that large institutional investors such as pension funds are becoming a significant factor in monitoring the corporate decision-making process. This concern recently has been articulated by the chief executive of the California Public Employees Retirement System, one of the largest U.S. pension-fund managers: "Our CEOs are being treated like pharaohs. Shareholders are beginning to question who's minding the store."[30]

Consequences of the Merger, Acquisition, and Takeover Craze

The merger, acquisition, and hostile takeover craze of the 1980s brought out many issues related to corporate organization, the separation of ownership from control, the functioning of boards of directors, and managerial self-interests. These factors had been around for years, but the economic prosperity of the 1980s coupled with other factors brought these issues out like never before in recent times. In the 1980s, complacent companies with undervalued assets became the targets for "takeover artists" or "corporate raiders" as they were variously called. The most notable of these raiders were T. Boone Pickens, Carl Icahn, and Saul Steinberg. The mere mention of these names could strike fear in the hearts of most CEOs. These corporate raiders became the business celebrities of the 1980s, and their names were more well known than the names of the corporate giants such as IBM, AT&T, GM, and GE.

The merger, acquisition, and takeover frenzy in the 1980s was characterized by hostile takeovers, financed with junk bonds, and LBOs (leveraged buyouts). Many corporate CEOs and boards went to great lengths to protect themselves from these takeovers. One major criticism of CEOs and boards during this period was that they were overly obsessed with self-preservation rather than making optimal decisions on behalf of their owner stakeholders. The takeover era generated a colorful vocabulary of its own—*raiders, poison pills, shark repellents, white knights, junk bonds, insider trading, greenmail,* and *golden parachutes.*[31]

Two of the most questionable top management practices to come out of the hostile takeover wave have been greenmail and golden parachutes. We will consider each of these and see how they fit into the corporate governance problem we have been discussing. Then we will examine the outburst of insider trading scandals that flourished during the takeover period.

Greenmail. Named after blackmail, **greenmail** is the repurchase of stock from an unwanted suitor at a higher-than-market price. Companies pay the greenmail to end the threat of a takeover.[32] For example, assume that Corporate Raider A quietly purchases a 5 percent stake in the ABC Corporation. It threatens to launch an all-out hostile takeover of ABC. ABC's management sees this as a threat to their jobs and agree to pay greenmail (buy back) for the shares from Corporate Raider A at a premium price. This example is somewhat simplified, but it basically describes the process.

Two classic cases of greenmail are worth mentioning. First, consider Saul Steinberg's pass at Walt Disney. Steinberg quickly earned $59 million when Disney bought back his 11.1 percent share of the company for $12 a share more than ordinary stockholders could get at the time. Second, consider the Bass brothers' run on Texaco. The Bass brothers earned $280 million for holding just under 10 percent of the oil company for 49 days! The corporate raider wins big in these transactions, and management gets to keep its jobs and perks. The shareholders of the target company are left sitting with shares whose underlying value has been eroded.³³ However, a number of big companies have now passed corporate bylaws that prohibit greenmail.

Another popular action has been for companies to adopt a "poison pill" defense. A *poison pill* is a shareholder rights plan aimed at discouraging or preventing a hostile takeover. Typically the poison pill provides that when a hostile suitor acquires more than a certain percentage of a company's stock, other shareholders receive share purchase rights designed to dilute the suitor's holdings and make the acquisition prohibitively expensive. Some poison pills adopted by companies, however, have been ruled illegal by the courts.³⁴ Congress has held hearings, and the Financial Accounting Standards Board has now considered rules that make greenmail less profitable.

Golden Parachutes. Whereas greenmail is designed to prevent hostile takeovers and help a firm's top executives keep their jobs, golden parachutes are a key instrument in providing the executives with financial security should they lose their jobs. A *golden parachute* may be defined as a contract in which a corporation agrees to make a payment to a key officer, or officers, in the event of a change in the control of the corporation.³⁵ In the last several years, golden parachutes have become extremely controversial and have been assailed by shareholders and others as totally unfair and a "flagrant waste of corporate assets." Some acquiring companies are refusing to honor them, and the battle over their validity is increasingly being fought in the courts.³⁶

The rapid increase in golden parachutes parallels the rapid growth in hostile takeovers. In 1981, only 15 percent of the 250 largest companies provided golden parachutes. By 1985, this figure had grown to almost 33 percent. The size of golden parachutes has been staggering. William M. Agee, chairman of the Bendix Corporation, pocketed $4 million in 1983 after selling his company to Allied. Outsiders expressed shock at the size of his payment. Two years later, parachutes of many times that amount were common. In 1985, Michel C. Bergerac, Revlon's former chairman, departed some $35 million richer when Pantry Pride acquired Revlon.³⁷

The original intent of golden parachutes was to prevent top executives involved in takeover battles from putting themselves before their shareholders. With the huge flurry of hostile takeovers in the mid-1980s, corporate boards hoped golden parachutes would serve three purposes: (1) make their companies less palatable to a potential corporate raider because of what it would cost to pay off the executives, (2) ensure that key executives did not jump ship during negotiations, and (3) reward the executives handsomely for their loyalty. Corporate leaders, however, were hard pressed to prove that the payments serve anyone's interests other than their own.³⁸

Cochran and Wartick offer a number of arguments against golden parachutes. They argue that executives are already being paid well to represent the company and that getting another reward constitutes "double dipping." They also argue that these executives are, in essence, being rewarded for failure. The logic here is that if the executives have managed their companies in such a way that the company's stock price is low enough to make the firm attractive to takeover specialists, then the executives are being rewarded for failure. Another argument is that executives, to the extent that they control their own boards, are giving themselves the golden parachutes. This represents a conflict of interest.[39]

An alarming trend is the extent to which offers of golden parachutes are being made down the management hierarchy. Union Carbide, which successfully defeated a hostile takeover attack by GAF recently, provided $28 million worth of golden parachutes for 42 managers. RCA installed golden parachutes worth $62 million. Beneficial Corporation extended the contracts to 500 of its 8,000 employees.[40] These offers clearly were not in keeping with the original intent of golden parachutes.

In 1984, Congress imposed severe tax penalties on firms that violated a provision of the *Deficit Reduction Act,* which placed limits on the size of golden parachutes. Companies found ways to get around these limits, and some of them were willing to exceed the limits and then pay the tax penalties.[41]

To most people, golden parachutes seem blatantly unfair. Shareholder groups are increasingly filing suits against corporate boards that grant them. Members of the public who hear about them are astounded. It should come as little surprise that golden parachutes have created an enormous amount of criticism for corporate managements who appear to be interested primarily in their own jobs and financial welfare. In this environment, calls for improved corporate governance will never cease. In a real sense, greenmail and golden parachutes provided the one-two punch that guarantees corporate governance will remain a vital and controversial issue.

Insider Trading Scandals. The insider trading scandals of the 1980s were a direct outgrowth of the takeover flurry that characterized U.S. business during that decade. Trading on inside information was not discovered just then, but in the merger and acquisition frenzy of the mid- to late 1980s it was raised to new and unprecedented heights. We could just as easily have treated the insider trading scandals in the chapter on business ethics, but it seemed appropriate here because it is entwined with the debate over corporate governance. Although it does not illustrate managerial selfishness as greenmail or golden parachutes do, it is a direct outgrowth of the accelerated takeover activity. In the environment of takeover and buyout, of offer and counteroffer, insider trading of astounding magnitude took place. The American public still remembers this period well, so a brief coverage of these events is useful.

Insider trading refers to the practice of a person obtaining critical information from someone inside a company and then using this information for his or her own personal financial gain. For example, an individual may hear from a corporate insider that the insider's firm is about to sell out to another firm at $10 per share above current market price; the individual then buys stock at the current price and later sells it for a profit at the higher price. The 1987 movie "Wall Street" had insider trading as one of its major themes, and the public became much more aware of this practice when the movie became popular.

Insider trading was once thought of as a minor problem that often resulted from someone casually picking up information at lunch or a cocktail party and then buying or selling stock at a profit based on this information. The 1980s scandal began in 1986 when the Securities and Exchange Commission (SEC) filed a civil complaint against Dennis B. Levine, a former managing partner of the Drexel Burnham Lambert investment banking firm, and charged him with illegally trading in 54 stocks. Levine then pleaded guilty to four criminal charges and gave up $10.6 million in illegal profits—the biggest insider trading penalty up to that point.[42] He also spent 17 months in prison.

Levine's downfall set off a chain reaction on Wall Street. His testimony led directly to the SECs $100 million judgment against Ivan Boesky, one of Wall Street's most frenetically active individual speculators. In a *consent decree,* Boesky agreed to pay $100 million, which was then described as by far the largest settlement ever obtained by the SEC in an insider trading case. Boesky, it turns out, made a career of the high-rolling financial game known as **risk arbitrage**—the opportunistic buying and selling of companies that appear on the verge of being taken over by other firms.[43] The Boesky settlement set off a flurry of litigation as dozens of private and corporate lawsuits were filed arising from the disclosures.[44]

Ivan Boesky then fingered Martin Siegel, one of America's most respected investment bankers at Kidder Peabody. Apparently Siegel and Boesky began conspiring in 1982, and over the next 2 years Siegel leaked information about upcoming takeovers to Boesky in exchange for $700,000 cash. Siegel pleaded guilty and began cooperating with investigators, and then he himself proceeded to finger two former executives at Kidder Peabody and one at Goldman Sachs.[45]

The insider trading scandals rocked Wall Street as accusations reached the upper levels of the financial industry's power and salary structure. New arrests seemed to occur weekly, and one of the most frequently asked questions was "Who's next?"[46]

In 1987, Ivan Boesky was sentenced to 3 years in prison. However, Boesky helped prosecutors reel in the biggest fish of all—junk bond king, Michael Milkin. The Securities and Exchange Commission accused Milkin and his employer, Drexel Burnham, of insider trading, stock manipulation, and other violations of federal securities laws. Drexel agreed in 1988 to plead guilty to six felonies, settle SEC charges, and pay a record fine of $650 million. A year later, the junk bond market crashed and Drexel filed for bankruptcy. In 1990, Milkin agreed to plead guilty to six felony counts of securities fraud, market manipulation, and tax fraud. He agreed to pay a personal fine of $600 million and later was sentenced to 10 years in prison.[47]

In a 1991 book, *Inside Out: An Insider's Account of Wall Street,* Dennis Levine made it clear that the insider trading scandals grew out of the takeover craze of the 1980s. Without question, the takeover period provided the opportunity. What took over next was human greed. Levine's legitimate income rose to $2 million a year,. but he kept breaking the law. He rationalized his crimes by asserting that everyone was doing it and that he really didn't think he would get caught. Levine called himself an "insider trading junkie" who couldn't stop.[48]

In the 1990s, the hostile takeovers have virtually disappeared. Replacing them are a growing number of legitimate mergers and consolidations that are free of the junk bond financing of the 1980s. Only time will tell whether the consolidations, mergers, and strategic alliances that are characterizing the early 1990s will succeed.[49]

Without question, the revelations and repercussions of the Wall Street scandal will be with us for years. The scandal was a direct outgrowth of takeover activity, which raised anew the corporate governance problem. The issues are quite complex, and solutions are not easily forthcoming. Unfortunately, the scandals have created the biggest "black eye" for the financial industry on Wall Street it has had in over 50 years. Not only are shareholders suspicious of what has been going on unbeknownst to them, but also the small investors and the general public have had their faith rocked in what they thought was the stable and secure financial industry. In spite of all the adverse publicity and law enforcement activity by the SEC, insider trading is still thought to be running rampant and constituting an epidemic.[50]

Many groups in the United States are concerned about the breakdown of managerial and board of director accountability to owner-stakeholders. Obviously, the owners themselves are most concerned, and their activism has reached unprecedented levels. We will discuss their actions in more detail later when we consider strengthening the role of shareholders. Even legislators, lawyers, educators, and other general social activist groups must be concerned. Although this breakdown in accountability has been discussed ever since Adolph Berle and Gardiner Means first wrote about the problem in 1932,[51] the height of this debate has come in the past 10 years. At this point it is appropriate to consider some of the actions that have been or should be made to improve management's accountability to its owners and, hence, the overall status of corporate governance. Managements are responsible to a host of stakeholder groups in today's society. But it is clear that their relationship with shareholders has never been worse.

IMPROVING CORPORATE GOVERNANCE

Efforts to improve corporate governance may be classified into three major categories. First, changes could be made in the structure and functions of boards of directors. Second, shareholders on their own initiative or on the initiative of management or the board could assume a more active role in governance. Third, changes in the chartering of corporations could be made at the state level, or federal chartering of corporations could be instituted. Each of these broad groupings deserves closer examination.

Changes in the Boards of Directors

It is quite logical that boards of directors be the initial focus for improving corporate governance. Boards are the specific groups assigned the responsibility of holding managements accountable, and, therefore, more changes have been seen and proposed here than anywhere else. As we indicated earlier, boards have historically been ineffective bodies that attended meetings; enjoyed the honor, distinction, and perquisites of being a board member; collected nice fees; and hoped to be appointed to other such cushy positions. One board member expressed it well: "If you get five of them (board memberships), it is total heaven, like having a permanent hot bath."[52] Another outside director of a large corporation recalls his introduction to the board room in the 1960s. He said he was told by the senior director the following rules: "After 10 years you can second a motion. After 15 years, you can make a motion. But you never get to vote 'no.'"[53]

Board memberships were once positions that everyone wanted. It was not uncommon for senior executives, CEOs, lawyers, bank presidents, or retired government officials to sit on 5 to 10 such boards and enjoy the accumulated benefits of all of them. However, in the past decade or so, changes have begun to be made in boards of directors. These changes have occurred because of the growing belief that CEOs and executive teams need to be made more accountable to shareholders and other stakeholders. Here we will discuss several of these changes and some other recommendations that have been set forth for improving board functioning.

Composition of the Board. Prior to the 1960s, boards were composed primarily of inside directors. It was not until the 1960s that pressure from Washington and Wall Street began to emphasize the notion of *outside directors*—individuals who were not currently members of management. Examples of the occupations of outside directors are CEOs or executives of other firms, academicians, retired executives of other firms, attorneys, or former government officials. Some boards use major shareholders, investment bankers, or "professional" directors.[54] By the 1970s, outsiders had become a majority on the boards of many, if not most, corporations.

This trend toward outside directors dominating the board has long been a recommendation for improving corporate governance. It was believed that outside directors would be more likely to carefully monitor management than inside directors. From about the mid-1970s on, the trend has been toward an increase in the proportion of outsiders on boards.[55] It was estimated that by 1980, 87 percent of boards had outside directors.[56] The percentage of boards of major corporations that are now composed of outsiders is much higher. A 1991 study of 100 major firms confirmed that only 5 percent still had a majority of inside directors. The study concluded that these changes were coming about because of pressure from large institutional investors and from a belief that the turbulent business environment that confronts directors today, from stiff global competition to takeover threats to difficult restructurings, necessitates these changes.[57]

Not only has it been recommended that outside directors be appointed to boards but also that they be independent outside directors—individuals who have no business relationship to the company they serve. Examples of independent outside directors are executives of unrelated companies, former government officials, college professors, "professional" directors, or representatives of consumer, environmental, or civil rights groups. Unfortunately, today many outside directors are not very independent. An outside director may be the company's banker, lawyer, management consultant, or a close friend of the company's CEO.[58] Figure 17-7 provides a summary of the advantages and disadvantages of outsider-dominated and insider-dominated boards.

FIGURE 17-7 Outsider-Dominated Versus Insider-Dominated Boards of Directors

CHARACTERISTICS OF OUTSIDER-DOMINATED BOARDS

Advantages

1. Outside directors provide a bridge between shareholders and professional managers.
2. Extra layer of review to confirm major decisions.
3. Independent resolution of inherent insider conflicts—compensation, performance review, etc.
4. Prominent directors enhance corporate image.

Disadvantages

1. Outside directors spend too little time on board matters.
2. They show little interest in the company except in times of crisis.
3. They lack good knowledge of the company and are not competent to make key decisions.
4. Independence may be an illusion.

CHARACTERISTICS OF INSIDER-DOMINATED BOARDS

Advantages

1. Intimate familiarity with company operations.
2. Substantial time devoted to board matters.
3. Unanimity of purpose.
4. Policymakers are responsible for execution and success of policy.

Disadvantages

1. Lack of independent perspective.
2. May fail to detect changes in external environment.
3. Possibility of self-dealing and excessive compensation.
4. Cannot independently judge their own performance.

Source: Murray L. Weidenbaum, *Strengthening the Corporate Board; A Constructive Response to Hostile Takeovers* (St. Louis: Washington University, Center for the Study of American Business, September, 1985), 4–5. Reproduced with permission.

In addition to a move toward independent outside directors, it also has been recommended that companies create boards with a broader diversity of backgrounds.[59] In the 1970s, there was a definite trend toward appointing minorities, women, and academics to boards.[60] We should note, however, that most boards have only a very small representation from these groups, if any at all. In 1991, a major executive search firm, Heidrick and Struggles, Inc., reported that among all boards the composition was as follows: 82.2 percent white males, 6.9 percent white females, 3.1 percent black females, 2.6 percent black males, 2.6 percent Hispanic females, 2.0 percent Asian/other males, 0.5 percent Hispanic males, and 0.1 percent Asian/other females.[61]

In the mid to late 1980s, not many wanted the board director position. Concerned about increasing legal hassles emanating from stockholder, customer, and employee lawsuits, directors were quitting their jobs or not accepting them in the first place. Although courts rarely hold directors personally liable in the hundreds of shareholder suits filed every year, there have been a few cases in the last several years where directors have been held personally and financially liable for their decisions. The Trans Union Corporation case involved directors agreeing to sell the company for a price the owners later decided was too little. A suit was filed, and the court ordered that the board members be held personally responsible for the difference between the price the company was sold for and a later-determined "fair value" for the deal. Depending on what the courts determined to be a fair value, each director could be responsible for millions of dollars in damages.[62] In addition to the Trans Union case, Cincinnati Gas and Electric reached a $14 million settlement in a shareholder suit that charged directors and officers with improper disclosure concerning a nuclear power plant.[63]

As lawsuits against directors have escalated, the cost of companies' liability insurance for directors and officers has skyrocketed or become unavailable. The cost of liability insurance for directors jumped 10-fold in the 2-year period of 1985 to 1986.[64] As a consequence, there has been a mass resignation of outsiders from many boards as some companies have been forced to drop their insurance coverage. The outcome has been a trend toward smaller boards.

Use of Stronger Board Committees. When the American Assembly studied the corporate governance problem in the late 1970s, it not only recommended that a majority of board members be true outsiders but also concluded that boards make more use of committees. In particular, the American Assembly recommended that the following four strong committees be established: audit, nominating, compensation, and public issues.[65] The last decade has seen the use of such committees as a definite trend, though not all corporations have used them effectively.

The *audit committee* is typically responsible for assessing the adequacy of internal control systems and the integrity of financial statements. It is seen as the primary watchdog committee of the full board.[66] The Securities and Exchange Commission has placed much emphasis on this committee, and the New York Stock Exchange mandates such a committee, composed of independent outside directors, for the firms listed with it. Charles Anderson and Robert Anthony, authors of *The New Corporate Directors: Insights for Board Members and Executives,* argue that the principal responsibilities of an audit committee are as follows:

1. To ensure that published financial statements are not misleading
2. To ensure that internal controls are adequate
3. To follow up on allegations of material, financial, ethical, and legal irregularities
4. To ratify the selection of the external auditor[67]

A major report by the Conference Board concluded that the audit committee should also have a broader mandate. The report argued that audit committees should have more authority and responsibility, more impact in improving financial controls reporting, and a growing role in strengthening auditors' independence and should become a major force in boosting board effectiveness.[68]

According to Arjay Miller, a board member and former president of Ford Motor Company, there should be at least one meeting per year between the audit committee and the firm's *internal auditor.* The internal auditor should be scheduled to meet alone with the committee and always be instructed to speak out whenever he or she believes something should be brought to the committee's attention. The committee should also meet with the *outside* auditor in a setting in which members of management are not present. Three major questions should be asked of the outside auditor by the audit committee:

1. Is there anything more that you think I should know?
2. What is your biggest area of concern?
3. In what area did you have the largest difference of opinion with company accounting personnel?[69]

The **nominating committee,** which should be composed of outside directors or a majority of outside directors, has the responsibility to see that competent, objective board members are selected. The American Assembly recommended that this committee be composed entirely of independent outside directors. The purpose of this committee is to nominate candidates for the board and for senior management positions. In spite of the suggested role and responsibility of this committee, in most companies the CEO continues to exercise a powerful role in the selection process of board members.

The **compensation committee** of the board has the responsibility of evaluating executive performance and recommending terms and conditions of employment. Ideally, this committee is composed of outside directors or a majority of outsiders. Although most large companies have compensation committees, one might ask how objective these board members will be when it is likely that the CEO played a significant role in their being elected to the board.

Finally, the American Assembly recommended that boards have a *public issues committee,* or public policy committee. Although it is recognized that most management structures have some sort of formal mechanism for responding to public or social issues, this area is important enough to warrant a board committee that would become sensitive to these issues, provide policy leadership, and monitor management's performance on these issues. Most major companies today have public issues committees that typically deal with such issues as affirmative action, equal employment opportunity, environmental affairs, employee health and safety, consumer affairs, political action, and other areas in which public or ethical issues are present. Debate continues over the extent to which large firms really use such committees, but the fact that they have institutionalized this concern by way of a corporate committee is encouraging. The American Assembly also recommended that firms develop evaluation systems to help them monitor the social performance of their corporate executives, but the evidence does not show that companies are doing this.[70]

Changing the composition of the board of directors to make it more independent and using strong committees are the two most often-mentioned suggestions for improving corporate governance. Other suggestions have also been set forth. For example, it has been suggested that the CEO should not simultaneously occupy the position of chairman of the board. Another suggestion is that boards be smaller and better paid.[71] Still another suggestion is that boards be given more authority and that directors be chosen from among major constituencies such as consumers, civil rights activists, environmentalists, and so on.[72]

A popular move during the late 1980s and early 1990s was for corporations to place environmentalists on their boards. A prominent example of this was Exxon, which placed an environmentalist on its board soon after its 1989 Alaskan oil spill. Other major oil companies have followed a similar course or at least seriously considered it. The goal is to help make the firm more responsive to environmental issues and impacts. Many have raised legitimate questions about such decisions. For example, will environmentalist directors be able to reconcile profit with their social agenda? Would a board member who voted for profit retain credibility as an environmentalist? Will environmentalist board members have enough influence to change corporate behavior, or will they end up being lonely voices for the wilderness? Richard J. Mahoney, chief executive of Monsanto, the chemical/pharmaceutical manufacturer, argues that environmentalists can help business people think differently about issues and, therefore, are valuable.[73]

Different Roles for Board Members. The changes for boards just discussed must continue to be addressed if corporate governance and responsiveness to stakeholders are to be achieved. A broader view is that boards need to alter the fundamental role that they assume in the corporation. William R. Boulton has suggested that corporate boards typically move through three stages in which they assume different roles:

1. The *legitimizing role*. Here boards do the minimum—sign the papers and adopt resolutions required by law. At this stage the board is truly a rubber stamp, and there is no role in decision making.
2. The *auditing role*. At this stage, the board recommends specific actions to improve the functioning of the management control or auditing process. The appearance of audit committees assumes an important role in the transition to the auditing role. The auditing role, however, must not be seen as the final role but rather as just a stage in the transition of the board to an even more active role—that of directing.
3. The *directing role*. Here the board assures that the executive functions are carried out over time in an appropriate and ethical manner. In this final role, boards actively assert their leadership. They do not just wait for management to make a decision and then react to it.[74]

In the case of many companies, the boards seem stalled in the legitimizing role. It seems clear from our discussion, however, that the auditing role is the minimum that is acceptable and that, ideally, boards should aim for the directing role. The complexities of today's business environment demands this broader view of an active board of directors.

Getting Tough with CEOs. It has always been a major responsibility of board directors to monitor CEO performance and to get tough if the situation dictates. Historically, however, chief executives have been pampered and protected. Changes are occurring that are now resulting in CEOs being taken to task, or even fired, for reasons that heretofore did not create a stir in boardrooms. These changes include the tough, competitive economic times; the rising vigilance of outside directors; and the increasing power of large institutional investors.

Examples of recently fired CEOs include Tom Barrett, chairman and CEO of Goodyear Tire and Rubber. Barrett quit under the pressure of his directors' increased dissatisfaction with how he was managing the troubled tiremaker. The board of General Public Utilities pressured its CEO out after it learned he was having an affair with a married vice-president. The CEO of Greyhound was ousted partly because of his differences with some creditors. Other recently ousted chiefs represented Data General Corporation, Grumman Corporation, Circle K Corporation, and Abbot Laboratories.[75]

Although there is no wholesale move against CEOs, their jobs are not as insulated as they once were. Many boards are getting tougher and are taking the actions they should take against CEOs. Jay Lorsch, a Harvard Business School professor, argues that boards take too long to act and that there are too many impediments in their way. Critics also contend that directors act only when they are under intense heat from regulators, shareholders, or the media.[76]

Other suggestions have been proposed for creating effective boards of directors and for improving board members' abilities to monitor executive teams to ensure that crises do not occur undetected. Figure 17-8 summarizes some of these recommendations.

Increased Role of Shareholders

Prior to the 1980s, civil rights activists, consumer groups, and other social activist pressure groups insisted that companies join their causes. The typical corporate response was, "Our job is to maximize returns to the legal owners of our corporation, the shareholders. We have no right to use their assets to promote social goals, no matter how worthy." Today, however, the typical corporate response is similar to that of the chairman of Avon Products, Inc., Hicks B. Waldron: "We have 40,000 employees and 1.3 million representatives around the world. We have a number of suppliers, institutions, customers, and communities. They have much deeper and much more important stakes in our company than our shareholders."[77]

The above situation appears to be an innocent shift in perspective from viewing shareholders as the sole stakeholders to viewing shareholders as just one group among many stakeholders and not necessarily the most important one. Why this seeming about-face? It may be because management is now under increasing attack from shareholders.[78] The shareholders now run the gamut from shareholder-raiders who want to seize control of the company to those who simply want to make management more accountable to the owners. Other shareholders seem to desire a larger role in decision making, while others just want to embarrass management at annual meetings.

The problem seems to be that shareholders feel like a neglected constituency. They are attempting to rectify this condition through a variety of means. They are demanding effective power. They want to hold managements accountable. They want to make changes, including changing management if necessary. Like companies' earlier responses to other stakeholder activist groups, many managements are resisting. The result is a battle between managers and shareholders for corporate control.[79]

Recent examples of this battle between managers and shareholders include the experiences at Time Warner and at Sears. At Time Warner, the world's largest communications company, a shareholder revolt against management led to the firm dropping a plan to issue 34.5 million new shares of stock.[80] At Sears, the battle took place between the company's management and shareholder activist Robert A. G. Monks, who was vying for a seat on Sears' board. Edward A. Brennan, chairman and CEO of Sears, spent $5.6 million to make sure Monks did not win the seat on Sears' board.[81]

Our discussion of an increased role for shareholders centers around two perspectives: (1) the perspective of shareholders themselves asserting their rights on their own initiative and (2) initiatives being taken by companies to

FIGURE 17-8 Improving Boards and Board Members

Building a Better Board[a]

- Don't overload it with too many members.
- Don't meet too often.
- Don't think you need high-profile CEOs or famous academics.
- Keep directors on for at least 5 years.
- Encourage directors to buy large quantities of stock.
- Pay directors with stock options, not with restricted stock.

Sharpening the Board's Sensors[b]

- Insist that board members become educated about their company.
- Insist that information-gathering systems deliver quickly the right information from the bottom to the top.
- Insist that board members understand board decision-making processes and not operate by consensus.
- Insist that the company undergo periodic audits of corporate activities and results.

Board of Director's Actions[c]

- Directors should evaluate the CEO's performance regularly against established goals and strategies.
- Evaluations of the CEO should be done by "outside directors."
- Outside directors should meet alone at least once a year.
- Directors should set qualifications for board members and communicate these expectations to shareholders.
- Outside directors should screen and recommend board candidates who meet the established qualifications.

Sources: [a]Graef S. Crystal, "Do Directors Earn Their Keep?" *Fortune* (May 6, 1991), 79.
[b]Richard O. Jacobs, "Why Boards Miss Black Holes," *Across the Board* (June, 1991), 54.
[c]The Working Group on Corporate Governance, "A New Compact for Owners and Directors, *Harvard Business Review* (July-August, 1991), 142–143.

make shareholders a true constituency. The shareholder initiatives will dominate our discussion because they clearly constitute the bulk of the activity underway.

Shareholder Initiatives. These initiatives may be classified into three major, overlapping areas: (1) rise of shareholder activist groups, (2) filing of shareholder resolutions and annual meetings, and (3) filing of shareholder lawsuits.

Rise of Shareholder Activist Groups. One major reason that relations between managements and shareholders have heated up is that shareholders are discovering the benefits of organizing and wielding power. Shareholder activism is not a new phenomenon. It goes back over 60 years to 1932 when Lewis Gilbert, then a young owner of 10 shares, was appalled by the absence of communication between New York-based Consolidated Gas Company's management and its owners. Supported by a family inheritance, Gilbert decided to quit his job as a newspaper reporter and "fight this silent dictatorship over other people's money." He resolved to devote himself "to the cause of the public shareholder."[82]

The history of shareholder activism is too detailed to report fully here, but Gilbert's efforts planted a seed that grew, albeit slowly. The major impetus for the movement came in the 1960s and early 1970s. The early shareholder activists were an unlikely conglomeration—corporate gadflies, political radicals, young lawyers, an assortment of church groups, and a group of physicians.[83] The movement grew out of a period of political and social upheaval—civil rights, the Vietnam War, pollution, and consumerism.

The watershed event for shareholder activism was *Campaign GM* in the early 1970s, also known as the Campaign to Make General Motors Responsible. Among those involved with this effort was Ralph Nader. The shareholder group did not achieve all its objectives, but it won enough to demonstrate that shareholder groups could wield power if they worked hard enough at it. Two of Campaign GM's most notable accomplishments were that (1) the company created a Public Policy Committee of the board, composed of five outside directors, to monitor social performance, and (2) GM appointed the Reverend Leon Sullivan as its first black director.[84]

One direct consequence of the success of Campaign GM was the growth of *church activism*. Church groups were the early mainstay of the corporate social responsibility movement and were among the first shareholder groups to adopt Campaign GM's strategy of raising social issues with corporations. Church groups began examining the relationship between their portfolios and corporate practices such as minority hiring and companies' presence in South Africa. Church groups remain among the largest group of institutional stockholders willing to take on management and press for what they think is right. In December 1972, the Investor Responsibility Research Center (IRRC) was formed "to provide timely and impartial analysis concerning corporate social responsibility issues."[85] The IRRC became a central organization that served as a resource for shareholder activism. Another group—the Interfaith Center on Corporate Responsibility—became a clearinghouse for church and other organizations and individuals concerned about the social impact of corporations.

In the mid to late 1980s, two groups characterized the new breed of shareholder activism. One was the Council of Institutional Investors (CII). Institutional investors (pension funds, church groups, foundations) now dominate the marketplace and thus wield considerable power because of their enormous shares of stock. Among the institutional groups, pension funds are the largest. They now own a third of the equity of all publicly traded companies in the United States and 50 percent or more of the equity of the large companies.[86] Institutional investors, many of whom are members of CII, are shaping this new world of shareholder activism and are the strongest fighters against "poison pills." They do not believe that managements should be able to adopt such antitakeover defenses without shareholder approval. In the takeover boom of the 1980s, institutional investors earned notable returns by offering their shares to outsiders. This chance of a large payoff put them squarely at odds with managements wanting to erect takeover defenses.[87]

The second group of shareholder activists is the United Shareholders Association (USA), which was founded in August 1986, by T. Boone Pickens. USA claims to be the first nonprofit organization designed to effectively represent the rights of America's 47 million shareholders. USA's goal is to restore American competitiveness by increasing management accountability to shareholders. One of Pickens's first actions was to set forth a shareholder rights platform, shown in Figure 17-9.

It remains to be seen how effective USA will be under the leadership of Pickens, but his goal is to make USA the most effective grassroots citizens' lobby in Washington, DC. According to Pickens, "Shareholders are unorganized, intimidated, and treated like second-class citizens."[88]

The CII and other groups representing large institutional investors, and the USA backing the average small investors, look like a one-two punch of shareholder activism. These groups lobby in Washington, speak out in corporate annual meetings, propose shareholder resolutions against managements, file shareholder lawsuits, and, generally speak out in favor of increased accountability for managements and increased rights for shareholders.

Filing of Shareholder Resolutions and Annual Meetings. One of the major vehicles by which shareholder activists communicate their concerns to management groups is through use of *shareholder resolutions,* or shareholder proposals. An example of such a resolution is, "The company should discontinue business in South Africa." To file a resolution, a shareholder or a shareholder group must obtain a stated number of signatures to require management to place the resolution on the proxy statement where it can be voted on by all the shareholders. Resolutions that are defeated (fail to get a majority vote) may be resubmitted provided they meet the following SEC requirements for such resubmission:

FIGURE 17-9 Platform of United Shareholders' Association (USA)

USA's goal is to restore American competitiveness by increasing management accountability to shareholders. The USA Shareholder Rights Platform guarantees shareholders a voice in the companies they own.
All shareholders are entitled to:

- A one share, one vote guarantee.
- A confidential vote in corporate elections.
- A proxy process free of conflicts of interest between management and institutional investors.
- A simplified proxy statement with a summary of major items.
- An executive compensation plan tied to stock performance.
- A pledge from management that it will not pay greenmail.
- Managers who encourage employee ownership.
- A right to vote on poison pill plans and other management entrenchment devices.
- An independent board of directors, each member of which has a substantial stake in the company.

USA members are encouraged to scrutinize companies in which they currently hold stock, or plan to purchase stock, to determine how many of these rights the company provides. Managements, recognizing the central role of shareholders in our corporate governance system, must adopt the shareholders platform.

Source: *USA Advocate* (June, 1987), 1. Reproduced with permission.

1. To be placed on the proxy again, the resolution should receive 5 percent of the votes cast the first time it is voted on, 8 percent the next year, and 10 percent in years thereafter.
2. The shareholder submitting the resolution should own $1,000 worth of the company's stock for at least 1 year.
3. A shareholder is limited to one proposal per company.
4. Proposals are excluded on company operations relating to less than 5 percent of a company's assets, earnings, and sales.

The purpose of these SEC provisions was to eliminate some abuses of the shareholder proposal process that had been taking place in past years. These provisions were meant to ensure that only legitimate voices be heard in the resolution process.[89]

The shareholder groups behind these proposals are usually socially oriented—that is, they want to exert pressure to make the company in which they own stock more socially responsive. Although an individual could initiate a shareholder resolution, he or she probably would not have the resources or means to obtain the required signatures to have the resolution placed on the proxy. Thus, most resolutions are initiated by large institutional investors who own large blocks of stock or by other activist groups who own a few shares of stock but have financial backing from some group. Foundations, religious groups, universities, and other such large shareholders are in an ideal position to initiate resolutions. Religious groups prominent in this endeavor include the Episcopal Church, the United Church of Christ, the Lutheran Church in America, the United Methodists, the United Presbyterian Church, and the American Jewish Congress.

The issues on which shareholder resolutions are filed vary widely, but they typically concern some aspect of a firm's social performance. In the aftermath of the revelations of illegal campaign contributions in the 1972 national elections, resolutions were filed on that issue. In 1979, corporate investments and loans in South Africa were the primary issue in terms of number of shareholder resolutions submitted. Corporate pay, perquisites, and governance were close behind. The Three Mile Island nuclear accident in Pennsylvania generated heated discussions at annual meetings. In the 1980s, popular resolutions related to plant closings, involvement in South Africa, the world debt crisis, drug lobbying in the Third World, hostile takeovers, and "poison pills." Figure 17-10 summarizes some of the major social issues on which shareholder resolutions were filed during 1991.

Because most shareholder resolutions never pass, one might ask why groups pursue them. The main reason is that they gain national publicity, which is part of what the protesting group is out to achieve. Increasingly, companies are negotiating with groups to settle issues before a resolution ever comes up for a vote. Several years ago, in a rare reversal of attitude, Exxon Corporation's management recommended that shareholders vote in favor of a resolution calling for the company to provide reams of data on its strip-mining operations. Exxon had agreed ahead of time to the request of the United Presbyterian Church and several Catholic groups, which sponsored the resolution, but the groups wanted the resolution to go all the way to a vote, and the company acquiesced. What happened at Exxon reflects subtle changes as managements, increasingly sensitive to public criticism, are more willing to sit down before annual meetings and work out agreements on shareholder resolutions.

Closely related to the surge in shareholder resolutions has been the increased activism at *corporate annual meetings* in the last decade. Professional "corporate gadflies" purchase a small number of shares of a company's stock and then attend its annual meetings to put pressure on managers to explain themselves. An example of the kind of social activism that can occur during an annual meeting was when GM shareholders sought explanations for a series of embarrassing controversies surrounding the automaker. Some shareholders wanted to know why the company substituted Chevrolet engines in cars sold by some of its other

FIGURE 17-10 Sample Corporate Responsibility Shareholder Resolutions: Spring, 1991

Corporation	Issue	Sponsors
American Cyanamid	Director attendance at stockholder meetings	Church groups
	Sign Valdez Principles	Church groups
American Express	Complete withdrawal from South Africa	TIAA/CREF, Church groups
American Home Products	End free infant formula supplies	Church groups
	Terminate South Africa relationships	Church groups
Amoco	Establish environmental committee	Carpenters Union
Bank America	International lending criteria	Church groups
Bristol-Myers Squibb	End free infant formula supplies	Church groups
	Halt animal testing	People for the Ethical Treatment of Animals
	Integrate board of directors	Church groups
Castle & Cooke	Third World employment practices	Church groups
Chevron	End oil sale to South African police & military	New York City Pension Funds
	Sever South African ties	Church groups
	Sign Valdez Principles	Church groups
Control Data	Terminate South African relationships	Church groups
Exxon	Alaska Oil spill cleanup	Church groups
	Reduce carbon monoxide emissions	Friends of the Earth
Ford Motor Co.	Fuel efficiency	Church groups
	Implement MacBride Principles	Churches
	Sign Valdez Principles	Church groups
General Electric	Equal employment opportunity report	Church groups
	Nuclear pollution	Church groups, GE Stockholder Alliance Against Nuclear Power & Weapons

(continued)

FIGURE 17-10 (continued)

Corporation	Issue	Sponsors
Helene Curtis	Report on animal testing	People for the Ethical Treatment of Animals
Johnson & Johnson	Halt animal testing	People for the Ethical Treatment of Animals
	Poor & minority communities	Church groups
Kimberly-Clark	Sign Valdez Principles	Church groups
	Tobacco free by the year 2000	Church groups
K-Mart	War toys	Church groups
McDonald's	Accelerate elimination of CFCs	Church groups
	Poor & minority communities	Church groups
	Wage equity review	Church groups
Southern Company	Sign Valdez Principles	Church groups
Time Warner	Affirmative Action in the media	Church groups
	Terminate South Africa relationships	Church groups
Toys-R-Us	War toys	Church groups
Wal-Mart	War toys	Church groups
	Affirmative action, women & minority purchasing	ACTWU (union)

Source: *The Corporate Examiner* (Interfaith Center on Corporate Responsibility) Vol. 18, No. 8-9, 1990, 2–8.

divisions, a move that infuriated many consumers who were not notified of the changes.[90] More recently, corporate executives have been asked to explain dealings in South Africa, high executive compensation packages, positions on hostile takeover attempts, plant closings, greenmail, golden parachutes, and environmental issues.

The motives for bringing up these issues at annual meetings are similar to those for shareholder resolutions: to put management "on the spot" and publicly demand some explanation or corrective action. Activism at annual meetings is one of the few methods shareholders have to demand explanations and obtain accountability from top management.

Being able to defend a company at annual meetings has become such an important task of top management that a number of consulting firms now publish an annual booklet of shareholder questions that are likely to be asked. The booklet is intended to help management and directors anticipate and plan for what they

FIGURE 17-11 Examples of Shareholder Questions at Annual Meetings

Voting and Proxy Issues

- Were any proposals submitted to management for inclusion in the proxy statement omitted? If so, who sponsored the proposals that were omitted? Why were they omitted?
- What anti-takeover measures have been adopted (considered) by the company?

Corporate Governance Issues

- Why is the board of directors composed primarily of inside directors?
- Were there any instances in which the board disagreed with management decisions? If so, what were the decisions and why?

Corporate Conduct

- Is the company presently under investigation by any federal or state regulatory agency? If so, what are the issues involved?
- Does the company have a PAC? If so, how does the PAC solicit contributions from employees? Who were the recipients of the PAC contributions this past year?

Executive Compensation

- Given the downturn in the company's earnings, why has compensation to officers and executives not been frozen or cut?
- Do you feel that "golden parachute" contracts are in the best interests of the company and its shareholders?

Source: Peat, Marwick, Mitchell, & Co., *Shareholders' Questions*, 1985, 1–28. Reproduced with permission.

---

might be quizzed on at annual meetings. Figure 17-11 provides a sampling of the types of questions that executives and directors might get at an annual meeting of shareholders. Figure 17-12 presents a list of questions that James E. Heard of the Investor Responsibility Research Center in Washington proposed as a "Quiz for Management" for the annual meeting season. He also offered a brief elaboration on each question.

Filing of Shareholder Lawsuits. We earlier made reference to the Trans Union case wherein shareholders sued the board of directors for approving a buyout offer that the shareholders argued should have had a higher price tag. Their suit charged that the directors had been negligent in failing to secure a third-party opinion from experienced investment bankers. The case went to trial and resulted in a $23.5 million judgment against the directors.[91] The Trans Union case may be one of the largest successful shareholder suits, but it does not stand alone. One estimate is that the number of shareholder rights suits quadrupled over the

FIGURE 17-12 A Quiz for Management During the Annual Meeting Season

Now, Mr. Officer and Mr. Director:
1. *Would you favor a confidential ballot for shareholder voting?* Private voting is virtually nonexistent in corporate America. Confidential voting would be important to stock fund managers, who may fear your company's pension fund being moved if they vote their consciences, as well as bank trust officers who may fear losing your company's banking business.
2. *Would the company pay greenmail to stave off a hostile bidder?* If the directors say they wouldn't, then ask them to submit an amendment to the corporate charter that would prohibit the payment of greenmail. It could be voted on at the next annual meeting. Greenmail wouldn't exist if executives, scared of losing their jobs, couldn't pay.
3. *Would the company adopt a poison pill to prevent being taken over?* If the directors say they wouldn't, ask them if they would submit a charter amendment providing that shareholders must approve any measure to make a takeover more difficult. If yours is one of the more than 400 companies that already has a pill in place, ask if you can vote to remove it.
4. *Would the company adopt another measure, besides a poison pill, to prevent a "hostile" takeover?* Most *Fortune* 500 companies have adopted some kind of antitakeover defense, including discriminatory voting plans, supermajority voting requirements, and staggered boards. Many have multiple defenses. Work to dismantle them. They protect management while working against shareholders' interests.
5. *What severance agreements have been worked out with top executives?* While certain agreements may help align the interests of management with those of shareholders, others provide huge payoffs (golden parachutes) for rightfully fired executives. Many such pacts allow an executive to quit and collect when control of the company changes.
6. *What is the value of the perquisites (perks) received by top management?* Investigations have found executives indiscriminately putting corporate assets, such as jets, to personal use, while the board's supposedly independent outside directors did nothing to halt the abuse—and occasionally indulged in it themselves. Of course, it's you who ultimately pays.

(continued)

1977–1987 decade.[92] The large number of shareholder suits being filed today makes you think that almost every decision a company makes is subject to a shareholder suit. As these suits proliferate, many wonder whose interests are really being served. Quite often, the shareholders' attorneys walk away with more money than the protesting shareholders.

FIGURE **17-12** (continued)

> 7. *What are the potential dilutive effects on your stock of executive stock option plans?*
> You may also want to know if pyramiding of options is allowed, if options are granted at below-market prices (both cash giveaways, not stock incentives), and if the company has canceled any outstanding options and issued lower-priced options in their place.
>
> 8. *How much in bonuses was awarded to top executives in 1986?*
> While you're asking, find out the formula the company uses to compute executive bonuses. Bonuses should be used to reward outstanding performance, not as a payoff for simply being on the team. And bonuses certainly shouldn't be awarded if your dividend is reduced.
>
> 9. *Do outside directors receive benefits apart from their fees for serving on the board?.*
> If they're to do their job of monitoring management, outside directors will have to be fairly compensated. Yet, if they are to remain independent, they shouldn't be overcompensated. Ask about consulting fees and perks which could compromise their independence.
>
> 10. *Does the company lend money to officers and directors?*
> It shouldn't. Like stock options at below market prices and bonuses for nonperformance, lending money at below interest rates (sweetheart loans) are cash giveaways, pure and simple. Your company should have a policy against these handouts.
>
> 11. *Did the company engage in "opinion shopping" for its independent auditor?*
> If your company interviewed several outside auditors until it could find one who would give the company an unqualified endorsement of its financial statements, you may want to sell your stock.
>
> 12. *Are all the company's directors and senior officers present?*
> An annual meeting is for the directors and managers to meet the owners. The company's representatives all should be there, and they all should be prepared to answer your questions. Ask questions. Find out who's looking out for your interests and who's just looking out for his own.

Source: James E. Heard, "Quiz for Management," *USA Advocate* (April, 1987), 45. Reproduced with permission.

Shareholder suits are easy to file but difficult to defend. One study estimated that 70 percent of the suits are settled before going to trial. Therefore, charges of corporate wrongdoing are seldom resolved. Quite often the lawsuits are seen as legitimate protests by shareholders against management actions, and the threat of litigation does deter corporate misbehavior. From the company's viewpoint, however, the lawsuits are an expensive nuisance. Some experts argue that management's quick willingness to settle before going to trial invites more suits. In spite of this, companies give in because the downside risks of trials and adverse publicity are just too great.[93]

The threat of lawsuits by shareholders has never been greater. Shareholders have discovered what other stakeholder groups before them have—that the legal system must sometimes be used in order to protect their rights. The litigation explosion has forced liability insurance rates up for corporate officers and directors, and, if nothing else, this will get management's attention. Shareholder suits will probably remain an active weapon of the owners for some time to come.

Company Initiatives. The need of companies to reestablish a relationship with their owners/stakeholders is somewhat akin to parents having to reestablish relations with their children once the children are grown up. Over the years the evidence suggests that corporate managements have neglected their owners rather than making them a genuine part of the family. As share ownership has dispersed, there are a number of legitimate reasons why this separation has taken place. But there is also evidence that management groups have been too preoccupied with their own self-interest. In either case, corporations need to realize that they have a responsibility to their shareholders that cannot be further neglected. Owners are demanding accountability, and it appears they will be tenacious until they get it.

Public corporations have obligations to their shareholders and to potential shareholders. Full disclosure is one of these responsibilities. Disclosure should be at regular and frequent intervals and should contain information that might affect the investment decisions of shareholders. This information might include the nature and activities of the business, financial and policy matters, tender offers, and special problems and opportunities in the near future and in the longer term.[94] Of paramount importance are the interests of the investing public, not the interests of the incumbent management team. Board members should avoid personal conflicts of interest with the interests of shareholders. Company executives and directors have an obligation to avoid taking personal advantage of information that is not disclosed to the investing public and to avoid any personal use of corporation assets and influence.

With regard to corporate takeovers, fair treatment to both sets of shareholders indicates the need for special safeguards. These might include (1) candor in public statements on the offer made, (2) full disclosure of all information, (3) absence of undue pressure, and (4) sufficient time for a shareholder to make a considered decision. A constructive purpose, not a predatory one, should be served by takeovers. The firm's major stakeholders are its owners. They are interdependent with other stakeholders, and, therefore, management should carry out its obligations to other constituency groups within the context of shareholder concern.[95]

Part of management's challenge is to have and maintain a constructive attitude toward shareholders. Some firms view shareholders with scorn, whereas others view them with sensitivity. Sun Company illustrates this latter position. According to one Sun Company executive, "Shareholders are our business partners. It's helpful to us if management gets an insight on what they think of us." Sun is concerned about getting its point across, even to the smallest stockholder. Each new stockholder gets a welcoming note from the chairman. Each dividend check contains a folksy newsletter prepared by the shareholder relations department. The department randomly selects about 100 shareholders six or eight times a year and invites them to a dinner at which a top company executive speaks. Sun makes company news available to shareholders on a toll-free telephone line. Shareholders are invited to call the shareholder relations department whenever they have questions or something bothers them. The whole focus is one of active interest rather than the ambivalence or bare tolerance shown by some corporate managements.[96]

Another way some companies are attempting to integrate shareholders into the corporate family is by getting them involved in political activities on behalf of the firm. One study found that shareholders often agree with company views on political issues. To the extent this is true, companies can form grassroots networks of shareholders to call or write Congressional representatives. Not everyone agrees with the strategy of using shareholders in this way, but it works for some firms. Sun Company has allowed shareholders to contribute to its PAC by automatically withholding part of their quarterly dividends, and this has been a successful program for them.[97]

Berkshire Hathaway Corporation set up a program whereby shareholders are allowed to determine the recipients of the several million dollars in charitable contributions the firm gives each year. For each share owned, a shareholder can instruct the firm to send $3 to a designated charity. Warren E. Buffett, chairman, told shareholders: "Your charitable preferences are as good as mine." Shareholders have sent Mr. Buffett many letters praising the idea. Buffett hopes that the shareholder designation program will foster what he calls "an owner mentality" in the shareholders and that it will strengthen shareholder loyalty.[98]

All of these shareholder programs do not substitute for keeping shareholders foremost in the minds of managements and boards when economic decisions are being made. However, the programs do demonstrate an attempt on management's part to give some serious consideration to corporate-shareholder relations. Taken together, these programs help the corporate governance problem because they show the shareholders that they matter and that they are important to the firm.

Federal Chartering of Corporations

Although corporations do business in many states and often in foreign countries, all they need to do business anywhere in the world is secure one charter from one state. The trouble with such charters, many argue, is that the states are either unable or unwilling to place restrictions on corporations for fear they will cease to attract them or will cause confusion by enacting tougher standards than other states. Indeed, Bayless Manning, former dean of Stanford Law School, said that state corporate statutes are "towering skyscrapers, internally welded together and containing nothing but wind."[99]

William L. Cary, a former chairman of the SEC and later a professor, worked for years to develop federal standards for corporation law. Suggestions for reform range from federal chartering of corporations at one extreme—a position advocated by Ralph Nader—to a "minimal standards act," which would merely create corporate accountability, at the other extreme. One reason the federal chartering proposal is so attractive is that it would most effectively eliminate the leniency of the state statutes. Cary has been quoted as saying that the problem with existing corporation law is, in a word, Delaware. He argues that the state of Delaware "has a laissez-faire attitude toward the fiduciary role and responsibility of management to its shareholders." He goes on to say that most state legislatures have engaged in a competitive race, recklessly outbidding each other in efforts to offer management "maximum freedom from restrictions."[100]

Most states have followed Delaware's lead in a nationwide surge toward permissiveness, tending to create a Gresham's Law effect—bad corporation law drives out the good. It should come as no surprise, therefore, that well over half of the top 500 industrial corporations have incorporated in the state of Delaware. Donald Schwartz has tempered the attack somewhat by pointing out that the issue is not Delaware but state law. He has stated that "state courts do not seem capable of achieving a balanced corporation law."[101]

Proposals for federal chartering of corporations would result in sweeping changes in current corporate law. The objectives—making the corporation more accountable, correcting management's neglect of shareholders, opening the decision-making process to accommodate community input, and requiring public disclosure on many matters for which it is not now required—are quite noble. There are many, however, who question what the true impact of federal chartering would be and who hesitate at the thought of such radical proposals. Because federal chartering is the most comprehensive concept offered for controlling big business—or "taming the giant corporation," as Nader, Green, and Seligman[102] choose to call it—many believe that it attempts to do too much too quickly when the potential impact is so uncertain. In fact, some think federal chartering is "an idea well worth forgetting."[103]

Marcus and Walters state a major problem in justifying federal chartering:

> In order to support the federal chartering proposal, one would have to conclude that the large corporation is the root of most social and economic evil ... that the existing widespread network of regulatory agencies of the federal and state governments is not working, and that the behavior of large corporations would be radically transformed by tying their right to continue in business to their "good behavior."[104]

In sum, there are both pros and cons to the idea of federal chartering, and the likelihood of its occurring is slim. What may happen is that particular parts of federal chartering proposals may be implemented in piecemeal fashion. However, we should not completely rule out federal chartering because it may well represent the model of the future for controlling large corporations.

SUMMARY

To remain legitimate, corporations must be governed according to the intended and legal pattern. We have had a major crisis in the United States over corporate governance because there has been a widespread belief that corporations are not being governed the way they were intended. One of the major criticisms is that managements have taken effective control away from boards of directors and are running the corporations in their own self-interests. Another related criticism is that corporate boards have been remiss and have not functioned the way they should. It has been claimed that boards are rubber stamps for management groups, that they are dominated by the CEOs, and that they are riddled with conflicts of interest. The wave of mergers, acquisitions, and hostile takeovers that occurred in the 1980s has brought to light other major problems—for example, greenmail, golden parachutes, and insider trading.

Over the years a number of suggestions for improving corporate governance have been made. Most of them have centered on the role, composition, and function of the board of directors. It has been recommended that boards (1) be recomposed to include more independent, outside directors; (2) use stronger committees; and (3) assume a more active role in governance and direction. In addition to board changes, suggestions for reform have focused on an increased role for shareholders and federal chartering of corporations. Increased shareholder activism has become a reality as groups speak out at annual meetings, file and negotiate shareholder resolutions, and file lawsuits. For their part, company managements have taken the initiative on a number of fronts to reestablish relations with owner stakeholders.

QUESTIONS FOR DISCUSSION

1. Explain the corporate governance problem. Why has it occurred?
2. What are the major criticisms of boards of directors? Which single criticism do you find to be the most important? Why?
3. Explain how mergers, acquisitions, takeovers, greenmail, golden parachutes, and insider trading are related to the corporate governance issue.
4. Outline the major suggestions that have been set forth for improving corporate governance. In your opinion, which suggestions have the greatest chance of being effective? Why?

5. In what ways have companies taken the initiative in becoming more responsive to owners/stakeholders? Discuss.

ENDNOTES

1. Cited in Edwin M. Epstein and Dow Votaw (eds.), *Rationality, Legitimacy, Responsibility: Search for New Directions in Business and Society* (Santa Monica, CA: Goodyear Publishing Co., 1978), 72.
2. *Ibid.*, 73.
3. *Ibid.*
4. William R. Dill (ed.), *Running the American Corporation* (Englewood Cliffs, NJ: Prentice-Hall, 1978), 11.
5. Sumner Marcus and Kenneth Walters, "Assault on Managerial Autonomy," *Harvard Business Review* (January-February, 1978), 56–66.
6. Victor H. Palmieri, "Officers of the Board?" *The Wall Street Journal* (August 14, 1978).
7. "Corporate Governance—New Heat on Outside Directors?" *Forbes* (October 1, 1977), 33.
8. Dill, 2.
9. Carl Icahn, "What Ails Corporate America—And What Should Be Done," *Business Week* (October 17, 1986), 101.
10. Murray L. Weidenbaum, *Strengthening the Corporate Board: A Constructive Response to Hostile Takeovers* (St. Louis: Washington University, Center for the Study of American Business, September, 1985), 4–5.
11. *Corporate Director's Guidebook* (Chicago: American Bar Association, 1978), 12.
12. David J. Dunn, "Directors Aren't Doing Their Jobs," *Fortune* (March 16, 1987), 117.
13. Harold G. Geneen, "Why Directors Can't Protect the Shareholders," *Fortune* (September 17, 1984), 28.
14. Weidenbaum, 11–16.
15. Frederick D. Sturdivant, *Business and Society* (Homewood, IL: Richard D. Irwin, 1981), 341.
16. Weidenbaum, 13.
17. Lester B. Korn and Richard M. Ferry, *Twelfth Annual Board of Directors Study* (New York: Korn/Ferry International, 1985), 4.
18. Weidenbaum, 15–16.
19. Rich Thomas and Larry Reibstein, "The Pay Police," *Newsweek* (June 17, 1991), 45.
20. *Ibid.*, 14.
21. Ann Crittenden, "The Age of 'Me-First' Management," *New York Times* (August 19, 1984), 1, 12.
22. John A. Byrne, "The Flop Over Executive Pay," *Business Week* (May 6, 1991), 90.
23. *Ibid.*
24. Thomas and Reibstein, 44–45.
25. Byrne, 95.
26. Judith H. Dobrzynski, "Director's Pay Is Becoming an Issue Too," *Business Week* (May 6, 1991), 94.
27. *Ibid.*
28. Jon Byrne, William C. Symonds, Julia Flynn Siler, "CEO Disease," *Business Week* (April 1, 1991), 52–60.
29. "The Rx for CEO Disease: An Alert Board," *Business Week* (April 1, 1991), 92.
30. Janice Castro, "How's Your Pay? CEOs: No Pain, Just Gain," *Time* (April 15, 1991), 40–41.
31. Ed Leefeldt, "Greenmail, Far from Disappearing, Is Doing Quite Well in Disguised Forms," *The Wall Street Journal* (December 4, 1984), 15.
32. *Ibid.*
33. Ruth Simon, "Needed: A Generic Remedy," *Forbes* (November 5, 1984), 40.
34. James B. Stewart and Daniel Hertzberg, "Life Becomes Easier for Corporate Raiders," *The Wall Street Journal* (August 22, 1986), 6.
35. Philip L. Cochran and Steven L. Wartick, "Golden Parachutes: Good for Management and Society?" in S. Prakash Sethi and Cecilia M. Falbe (eds.), *Business and Society: Dimensions of Conflict and Cooperation* (Lexington, MA: Lexington Books, 1987), 321.
36. Steven E. Prokesch, "Too Much Gold in the Parachutes?" *New York Times* (January 26, 1986), 3–1, 28F.
37. *Ibid.*
38. *Ibid.*
39. Cochran and Wartick, 325–326.
40. Prokesch, 28F.
41. *Ibid.*
42. George Russell, "The Fall of a Wall Street Superstar," *Time* (November 24, 1986), 71.
43. *Ibid.*
44. Donald Baer, "Getting Even with Ivan and Company," *U.S. News & World Report* (March 2, 1987), 46.
45. Anthony Bianco and Gary Weiss, "Suddenly the Fish Get Bigger," *Business Week* (March 2, 1987), 29–30.
46. "New Arrests on Wall Street: Who's Next in the Insider Trading Scandal?" *Newsweek* (February 23, 1987), 48–50.
47. James B. Stewart, "Scenes from a Scandal: The Secret World of Michael Milkin and Ivan Boesky," *The Wall Street Journal* (October 2, 1991), B1.
48. Dennis B. Levine with William Hoffer, *Inside Out: An Insider's Account of Wall Street* (Putnam, 1991). Reviewed by John Greenwald, "Bad Trades," *Time* (September 23, 1991); see also Joe Queenan, "Wall Street Scoundrel," *The Wall Street Journal* (September 10, 1991), A18.

49. "The Age of Consolidation," *Business Week* (October 14, 1991), 86–93; "The Dealers Return," *Time* (September 16, 1991), 46–47.
50. "The Epidemic of Insider Trading," *Business Week* (April 29, 1985), 78–92.
51. Adolph Berle and Gardiner Means, *The Modern Corporation and Private Property* (New York: Macmillan, 1932).
52. Leo Herzel, Richard W. Shepro, and Leo Katz, "Next-to-Last Word on Endangered Directors," *Harvard Business Review* (January-February, 1987), 38.
53. Neil Budde, "Shareholders and Raiders Stir Directors," *USA Today* (June 12, 1987), 1B.
54. "Who Sits on America's Corporate Boards," *The Atlanta Journal* (April 14, 1991), P1.
55. Leslie Wayne, "Who's Playing the Board Game?" *New York Times* (October 9, 1983), 18F.
56. Lawrence Ingrassia, "Outsider-Dominated Boards Grow, Spurred by Calls for Independence," *The Wall Street Journal* (November 3, 1980), 33.
57. Timothy D. Schellhardt, "More Directors Are Recruited from Outside," *The Wall Street Journal* (March 20, 1991), B1.
58. Ibid., 56.
59. Weidenbaum, 20.
60. Wayne, 18F.
61. "Who Sits on America's Corporate Boards," 1991.
62. "A Landmark Ruling That Puts Board Members in Peril," *Business Week* (March 18, 1985), 56–57.
63. Laurie Baum and John A. Byrne, "The Job Nobody Wants: Outside Directors Find That the Risks and Hassles Just Aren't Worth It," *Business Week* (September 8, 1986), 57.
64. Ibid., 56.
65. Donald E. Schwartz, "Corporate Governance," in Thorton Bradshaw and David Vogel (eds.), *Corporations and their Critics* (New York: McGraw-Hill, 1981), 227–228.
66. Arjay Miller, "A Director's Questions," *The Wall Street Journal* (August 18, 1980), 10.
67. Charles A. Anderson and Robert N. Anthony, *The New Corporate Directors: Insights for Board Members and Executives* (New York: John Wiley & Sons, 1986), 141.
68. Jeremy Bacon, *The Audit Committee: A Broader Mandate* (New York: The Conference Board, Research Report No. 914, 1988).
69. Miller, 10.
70. Schwartz, 228.
71. Dunn, 118.
72. Weidenbaum, 24, 31.
73. Cited in Michael Parrish, "Greening of the Boardroom," *Los Angeles Times* (July 11, 1989), Section IV, 1.
74. William R. Boulton, "The Evolving Board: A Look at the Board's Changing Roles and Information Needs," *Academy of Management Review* (October, 1978), 827–836.
75. Joann S. Lublin, "More Chief Executives Are Being Forced Out by Tougher Boards," *The Wall Street Journal* (June 6, 1991), A1.
76. Lorsch cited in *Ibid.*
77. "Shareholders Should Exercise Their Rights," *Business Week* (May 18, 1987), 168.
78. Ibid.
79. Bruce Nussbaum and Judith Dobrzynski, "The Battle for Corporate Control," *Business Week* (May 18, 1987), 102–109.
80. "Time Warner Feels the Force of Shareholder Power," *Business Week* (July 29, 1991), 58.
81. "Bolting the Boardroom Door at Sears," *Business Week* (May 13, 1991), 86.
82. Lauren Tainer, *The Origins of Shareholders Activism* (Washington, DC: Investor Responsibility Research Center, July, 1983), 2.
83. Ibid., 1.
84. Ibid., 12–22.
85. Ibid., 28–44.
86. Peter F. Drucker, "A Crisis of Capitalism," *The Wall Street Journal* (September 20, 1986), 32.
87. Christopher Power and Vicky Cahan, "Shareholders Aren't Just Rolling Over Anymore," *Business Week* (April 27, 1987), 32–33.
88. Unpublished press release, August 26, 1986.
89. Philip R. O'Connell, "The Tightening of Proxy Rules: Legitimate Voices Will Still Be Heard," *New York Times* (September 4, 1983), 2F.
90. Leonard Apcar and Terry Brown, "GM Reputation Is Defended by Chairman Under Barrage of Shareholder Questions," *The Wall Street Journal* (May 23, 1977), 17.
91. Thomas J. Neff, "Liability Panic in the Board Room," *The Wall Street Journal* (November 10, 1986), 22.
92. Julie Amparano, "A Lawyer Flourishes by Suing Corporations for their Shareholders," *The Wall Street Journal* (April 28, 1987), 1.
93. Richard B. Schmitt, "Attorneys Are Often Big Winners When Shareholders Sue Companies," *The Wall Street Journal* (June 12, 1986), 31.
94. "The Responsibility of a Corporation to Its Shareholders," *Criteria for Decision Making* (C. W. Post Center, Long Island University, 1979), 14.
95. Ibid., 14–15.
96. "Executives' View of Small Holders Ranges from Sensitivity to Scorn," *The Wall Street Journal* (April 8, 1981), 31.
97. Paul A. Gigot, "Some Corporations Trying to Turn Shareholders into a Political Force," *The Wall Street Journal* (January 19, 1982), 31.
98. Bill Richards, "Berkshire Hathaway Pleases Shareholders by Letting Them Earmark Corporate Gifts," *The Wall Street Journal* (April 26, 1983), 26.
99. "New Fire in the Drive to Reform Corporate Law," *Business Week* (November 21, 1977), 98.

100. William L. Cary, "Federalism and Corporate Law: Reflections upon Delaware," *Yale Law Journal* (March, 1974), 663.
101. Donald E. Schwartz, "'The Case for Federal Chartering of Corporations," in Robert L. Heilbroner and Paul London (eds.), *Corporate Social Policy: Selections from Business and Society Review* (Reading, MA: Addison-Wesley, 1975), 325–331.
102. Ralph Nader, Mark Green, and Joel Seligman, *Taming the Giant Corporation* (New York: W. W. Norton, 1976).
103. Peter H. Aranson, "Federal Chartering of Corporations: An Idea Well Worth Forgetting," in Heilbroner and London (eds.), 332–337.
104. Sumner Marcus and Kenneth Walters, "Assault on Managerial Autonomy," *Harvard Business Review* (January-February, 1978), 57–66.

PART FIVE STRATEGIC MANAGEMENT FOR SOCIAL RESPONSIVENESS

18 Strategic Management and Corporate Public Policy

19 Issues Management and Crisis Management

20 Public Affairs Management

CHAPTER **EIGHTEEN**

Strategic Management and Corporate Policy

CHAPTER OBJECTIVES

After studying this chapter, you should be able to:

- Define the concept of corporate public policy and relate it to strategic management.

- Articulate the four major strategy levels and explain enterprise-level strategy.

- Enumerate and briefly describe how a concern for social and ethical issues fits into the six-step strategic management process.

- Relate the notion of social audits to strategic control.

- Identify and discuss the four major stages in environmental analysis.

Understanding the multitude of external and internal social issues that impinge on business is not enough. Nor is it enough to appreciate the evolution of business's changing social role; the notions of corporate social responsibility and responsiveness, business ethics, and stakeholder management; and the intricacies of the complex business-government relationship. This knowledge only provides a frame of reference for the formulation of corporate public policy and the implementation of corporate social action.

In this chapter and the next two, we more closely examine how management has responded and should respond, in a managerial sense, to the kinds of social and ethical issues we have been discussing up to this point. Although we have mentioned in previous chapters how business has or should respond to stakeholder groups with various efforts and programs, we now want to consider how the traditional processes of management have been affected by business's acceptance of the social environment as a legitimate influence in decision making and corporate action.

In this chapter, we provide a broad overview of how social and ethical issues fit into the general strategic management processes of the organization. We use the term "corporate public policy" to describe that component part of management decision making that addresses these issues. The overriding goal of this chapter is to focus on planning for the turbulent social environment, and this encompasses the strategic management process and environmental analysis.

UNDERSTANDING THE CONCEPT OF CORPORATE PUBLIC POLICY

The impact of the social environment on business organizations is becoming more pronounced each year. It is an understatement to suggest that the social environment has become tumultuous, and a brief reminder of a few actual cases points out the validity of this claim quite dramatically. Procter & Gamble and its Rely Tampon recall, Firestone and its radial tire debacle, Ford Motor Company and its disastrous Pinto gas tank problem, and Johnson & Johnson and its Tylenol capsules are reminders of how social issues can directly affect a firm's offerings. In addition, there are many examples in which social issues have had a major impact on firms at the general management level.[1] Bank of Boston's involvement in money laundering, E. F. Hutton's high-level check-kiting scheme, General Electric's and General Dynamics' fraudulent overcharges on defense contracts, Exxon's catastrophic *Valdez* oil spill, and Drexel Burnham's involvement with junk bonds and securities fraud are all examples of the impact of top-level decisions that entail ethical ramifications.

What started as an awareness of social issues and social responsibility in the 1960s matured to a focus on the management of social responsiveness in the 1970s. Now it looms on the horizon as an emphasis, if not preoccupation, with corporate public policy in the 1990s and beyond. The term" corporate public policy" is an outgrowth of an earlier term, "corporate social policy," that has been in circulation for 20 years. The two concepts have essentially the same meaning, but we will use "corporate public policy" because it is more in keeping with terminology used in business today. Apparently, the word "social" has connotations that the business community wants to get away from; therefore, we will use the language that is more fitting to actual business practice.

Corporate Public Policy: Defined

What is meant by corporate public policy? Let us set forth and use the following definition: *Corporate public policy* is a firm's posture, stance, or position regarding the public, social, or ethical aspects of stakeholders and corporate functioning. Businesses encounter many situations in their daily operations that involve highly visible public or ethical issues. Some of these issues are the subject of intensive public debate for a specific period of time. Examples of such issues include AIDS in the workplace, affirmative action, product safety, and employee privacy. Other issues are more basic, more enduring, and more philosophical. Examples here might include the broad role of business in society, the corporate governance question, and the relative balance of business versus government direction that is best for our society.

The idea of corporate public policy is that a firm must give specific attention to issues in which basic questions of right, wrong, or fairness reside. The dynamic social environment of the past 25 to 30 years has necessitated that management apply a policy perspective to these issues. At one time, the social environment was thought to be a relatively constant backdrop against which the real work of business took place. Today these issues are center stage, and managers at all levels must address them. Corporate public policy is the process of management addressing these heretofore neglected concerns.

Relationship of Corporate Public Policy to Strategic Management

Where does corporate public policy fit into a concern for strategic management? First, let us discuss strategic management briefly. **Strategic management** refers to the overall management process that focuses on relating a firm to its environment. A basic way in which the firm relates to its environment is through the products and services it produces and the markets it chooses to address. Strategic management is also seen as a kind of overall organizational management by the firm's top-level executives. In this sense it represents the overall leadership function in which the sense of direction of the organization is decided on and implemented.

Top management groups must address many issues as a firm is positioning itself relative to its environment. The more traditional issues involve product/market decisions—the principal decision thrust of most organizations. Other decisions relate to competition, marketing, finance, accounting, personnel, production, research and development, and so on. Corporate public policy is seen as that part of the overall strategic management of the organization that focuses specifically on public or ethical issues embedded in the functioning and decision processes of the firm. Therefore, just as a firm needs to develop policy on personnel, production, marketing, or finance, it also must develop a corporate public policy to deal with the whole host of issues we have been discussing throughout this book.

Relationship of Ethics to Strategic Management

Although a consideration of ethics is implicit in corporate public policy discussions, we would like to make this relationship more explicit by special mention here. Over the years a growing number of writers have stressed this point. Kenneth R. Andrews, for example, is well known for his emphasis on the moral component of corporate strategy. In particular, he highlights the leadership challenge of determining future strategy in the face of rising moral and ethical standards. He argues that coming to terms with the morality of choice may be the most strenuous undertaking in strategic decision making. This is particularly stressful in the inherently amoral corporation.[2]

The challenge of linking ethics and strategy has been moved center stage by R. Edward Freeman and Daniel R. Gilbert, Jr. in their book *Corporate Strategy and the Search for Ethics*. The authors argue that if business ethics is to have any meaning beyond pompous moralizing, then it must be linked to business strategy. Their view is that we can revitalize the concept of corporate strategy by linking ethics to strategy. This linkage would permit the most pressing management issues of the day to be addressed in ethical terms. They suggest the concept of enterprise strategy as the idea that best links these two vital notions together, and we will examine this concept in more detail in the next section.[3]

The concept of corporate public policy and the linkage between ethics and strategy are better understood when we think about (1) the various levels of strategy and (2) the steps in the strategic management process.

THE STRATEGY LEVELS

Since organizations are hierarchical, it is not surprising to find that strategic management is hierarchical, too. That is, there are a number of different levels at which the strategy process is occurring in the firm. These levels range from the broadest or highest levels (where goals, decisions, and policies entail higher risks and are characterized by longer time horizons, more subjective values, and uncertainty) to the lowest levels (where planning is done for specific functional areas, where time horizons are shorter, where information needs are less complex, and where uncertainty is less).

Importance of the Four Strategy Levels

The broadest level is known as societal-level strategy, or ***enterprise-level strategy***, as it has come to be known. Enterprise-level strategy is the overarching strategy level that poses the basic question, *"What is the role of the organization in society?"* Enterprise-level strategy, as we will discuss in more detail later, encompasses the development and articulation of corporate public policy. It is the first and most important level at which ethics and strategy are linked. Until fairly recently, the ***corporate-level strategy*** was thought to be the broadest strategy level. In a limited, traditional sense this is true, for it addresses what is often posed as the most fundamental question for a firm, *"What business(es) are we in or should we be in?"* It is easy to see how the ***business-level strategy*** is a natural follow-on because this strategy level is concerned with the question, *"How should we compete in a given business or industry?"* Finally, the ***functional-level strategy*** addresses the questions, *"How should a firm integrate its various subfunctional activities and how should these activities be related to changes taking place in the various functional areas (finance, marketing, production)?"*[4]

The importance of the four strategy levels is to demonstrate that corporate public policy is a part of enterprise-level strategy, which, in turn, is but one level of strategic decisions that occur in organizations. Figure 18-1 illustrates how enterprise-level strategy is the broadest level and that the other levels are narrower concepts that flow from it.

Emphasis on Enterprise-Level Strategy

The terms "enterprise-level strategy" and "societal-level strategy" may be used interchangeably. The reader needs to be alert to the fact that neither of these terms is used with any degree of regularity in the business community. While many firms do address the issues that enterprise-level strategy is concerned with, the terminology as of this writing is restricted to the academic community. The terminology arose to describe the level of strategic thinking that an increasing number of observers believe is necessary to be fully responsive to today's complex and dynamic social environment.

Igor Ansoff visualized this strategy level as one in which the political legitimacy of the organization is addressed.[5] Ansoff later discussed this same concern for legitimacy under the title "Societal Strategy for the Business Firm."[6] Hofer and others described this level as the societal level.

According to Ed Freeman, enterprise-level strategy needs to be thought of in such a way that it would more closely align "social and ethical concerns" with traditional "business concerns."[7] In setting direction for a firm, a manager needs to understand the impact of changes in business strategy on the underlying values of the firm and the new stakeholder relations that will emerge and take shape as a result. Freeman proposes that enterprise-level strategy address the overriding question, "What do we stand for?" Thus, at the enterprise level the task of setting direction involves understanding the role of a particular firm

FIGURE 18-1   The Hierarchy of Strategy Levels

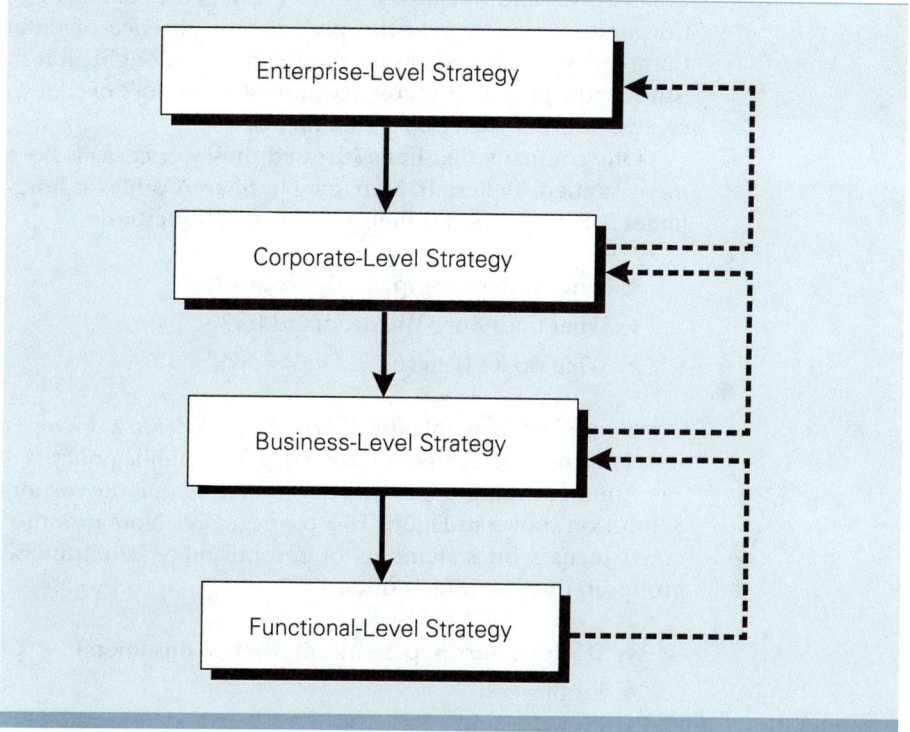

as a whole and its relationships to other social institutions. The appropriate questions then become:

- What is the role of our organization in society?
- How is our organization perceived by our stakeholders?
- What principles or values does our organization represent?
- What obligations do we have to society at large?
- What are the implications for our current mix of business and allocation of resources?[8]

Many firms have addressed some of these questions—perhaps in part, perhaps in an ad hoc way. The point of enterprise-level strategy, however, is that the firm needs to specifically and intentionally address these questions in such a way that a corporate public policy is forthcoming.

How have firms addressed these questions? What are the manifestations of enterprise-level thinking and corporate public policy? The manifestations show up in a variety of ways in different companies—for example, how a firm responds when faced with public issue crises. Does it respond to its stakeholders in a positive, constructive, and sensitive way or in a negative, defensive, and insensitive way? Corporate actions reveal the presence or absence of enterprise-level strategy. Companies also demonstrate the degree of thought that has gone into public issues by the presence or absence and use or nonuse of codes, conducts, corporate creeds, or other such policy statements.

One company that has addressed these concerns is Borg-Warner. In a document entitled "Believe It: Managing by Shared Values at Borg-Warner," Chairman James F. Bere poses and then answers these questions:

- What kind of company are we anyway?
- What does Borg-Warner stand for?
- What do we believe?

Figure 18-2 presents the *Beliefs of Borg-Warner,* a document that clearly manifests enterprise-level strategy and corporate public policy.

Another example of enterprise-level strategy is the corporate creed of Johnson & Johnson shown in Figure 18-3 on page 556. Note how the Johnson & Johnson creed focuses on statements of responsibility by enumerating its stakeholder groups in the following sequence:

- Doctors, nurses, patients, mothers (consumers)
- Employees
- Communities
- Stockholders

The "core values" program implemented at the Aluminum Company of America (Alcoa) by its chairman Paul H. O'Neill is another excellent illustration of an enterprise-level strategy. O'Neill had been chairman of Alcoa less than 3 months in 1987 when he began making decisions that seemed to reflect a new way of thinking at Alcoa. Four years later, it became apparent that Alcoa's six "core values" would provide the guiding direction for a new corporate conscience at the firm.[9]

The six "core values" at Alcoa were identified and articulated by O'Neill, company president C. Fred Fetterolf, and 10 senior executives during 100 hours of discussions and reflections in 1988. The core values program, known as "Visions, Values and Milestones," set forth a new ethics agenda built around the following six core values:

- Integrity
- Safety and health
- Quality of work
- Treatment of people

FIGURE 18-2 The Beliefs of Borg-Warner: To Reach Beyond the Minimal

Any business is a member of a social system, entitled to the rights and bound by the responsibilities of that membership. Its freedom to pursue economic goals is constrained by law and channeled by the forces of a free market. But these demands are minimal, requiring only that a business provide wanted goods and services, compete fairly, and cause no obvious harm. For some companies, that is enough. It is not enough for Borg-Warner. We impose upon ourselves an obligation to reach beyond the minimal. We do so convinced that by making a larger contribution to the society that sustains us, we best assure not only its future vitality, but our own.

This is what we believe.

We believe in the dignity of the individual.
However large and complex a business may be, its work is still done by people dealing with people. Each person involved is a unique human being, with pride, needs, values, and innate personal worth. For Borg-Warner to succeed, we must operate in a climate of openness and trust, in which each of us freely grants others the same respect, cooperation, and decency we seek for ourselves.

We believe in our responsibility to the common good.
Because Borg-Warner is both an economic and social force, our responsibilities to the public are large. The spur of competition and the sanctions of the law give strong guidance to our behavior, but alone do not inspire our best. For that we must heed the voice of our natural concern for others. Our challenge is to supply goods and services that are of superior value to those who use them; to create jobs that provide meaning for those who do them; to honor and enhance human life; and to offer our talents and our wealth to help improve the world we share.

We believe in the endless quest for excellence.
Though we may be better today than we were yesterday, we are not as good as we must become. Borg-Warner chooses to be a leader—in serving our customers, advancing our technologies, and rewarding all who invest in us their time, money, and trust. None of us can settle for doing less than our best, and we can never stop trying to surpass what already has been achieved.

We believe in continuous renewal.
A corporation endures and prospers only by moving forward. The past has given us the present to build on. But to follow our visions to the future, we must see the difference between traditions that give us continuity and strength, and conventions that no longer serve us—and have that courage to act on that knowledge. Most can adapt after change has occurred; we must be among the few who anticipate change, shape it to our purpose, and act as its agents.

We believe in the commonwealth of Borg-Warner and its people.
Borg-Warner is both a federation of businesses and a community of people. Our goal is to preserve the freedom each of us needs to find personal satisfaction while building the strength that comes from unity. True unity is more than a melding of self-interests; it results when values and ideals also are shared. Some of ours are spelled out in these statements of belief. Others include faith in our political, economic, and spiritual heritage; pride in our work and our company; the knowledge that loyalty must flow in many directions, and a conviction that power is strongest when shared. We look to the unifying force of these beliefs as a source of energy to brighten the future of our company and all who depend upon it.

Source: Company document. Borg-Warner Corporation. Reproduced by permission.

FIGURE 18-3 Johnson & Johnson Credo

Our Credo

We believe our first responsibility is to the doctors, nurses and patients,
to mothers and fathers and all others who use our products and services.
In meeting their needs everything we do must be of high quality.
We must constantly strive to reduce our costs
in order to maintain reasonable prices.
Customers' orders must be serviced promptly and accurately.
Our suppliers and distributors must have an opportunity
to make a fair profit.

We are responsible to our employees,
the men and women who work with us throughout the world.
Everyone must be considered as an individual.
We must respect their dignity and recognize their merit.
They must have a sense of security in their jobs.
Compensation must be fair and adequate,
and working conditions clean, orderly and safe.
We must be mindful of ways to help our employees fulfill
their family responsibilities.
Employees must feel free to make suggestions and complaints.
There must be equal opportunity for employment, development
and advancement for those qualified.
We must provide competent management,
and their actions must be just and ethical.

We are responsible to the communities in which we live and work
and to the world community as well.
We must be good citizens — support good works and charities
and bear our fair share of taxes.
We must encourage civic improvements and better health and education.
We must maintain in good order
the property we are privileged to use,
protecting the environment and natural resources.

Our final responsibility is to our stockholders.
Business must make a sound profit.
We must experiment with new ideas.
Research must be carried on, innovative programs developed
and mistakes paid for.
New equipment must be purchased, new facilities provided
and new products launched.
Reserves must be created to provide for adverse times.
When we operate according to these principles,
the stockholders should realize a fair return.

Johnson & Johnson

Source: Reprinted courtesy of Johnson & Johnson.

- Accountability
- Profitability

In part, O'Neill and Fetterolf placed values at the center of their corporate culture out of deep personal religious conviction. They argued that biblical principles such as truthfulness, compassion, and stewardship should not stop at the factory gate. On another level, they say they are attempting to reshape the company into the kind of unified, harmonious enterprise that will be needed to survive and compete in the global marketplace of the future.[10]

In terms of implementation, Alcoa began in 1989 disseminating the core values to its employees. Follow-up was done with films, training seminars, and departmental meetings. Recently, the company has begun evaluating employees to see how well they have been applying the core values in their work. Although Alcoa has faced some tough economic times, like all large metalmakers, O'Neill argues that whether business is good or bad, the firm is committed to its ethics program. O'Neill argues, "I don't think it's necessary to compromise your values to succeed economically."[11]

Other manifestations of enterprise-level strategic thinking in corporations might include the extent to which firms have established board or senior management committees. Such committees might include the following: public policy/issues committee, social audit committee, corporate philanthropy committee, and ad hoc committees to address specific public issues. The firm's public affairs function can also indicate enterprise-level thinking. Does the firm have an established public affairs office? To whom does the director of corporate public affairs report? What role does public affairs play in corporate-level decision making? Do public affairs managers play a formal role in the firm's strategic planning?

Another indicator of enterprise-level strategic thinking might be the extent to which the firm attempts to identify social or public issues, analyze them, and integrate them into its planning processes.

THE SIX-STEP STRATEGIC MANAGEMENT PROCESS

To understand how corporate public policy is but one part of the larger system of management decision making, it is useful to provide an overview of the major steps that make up the strategic management process. There are a number of acceptable ways to conceptualize this process, but we will use the six-step process identified by Hofer and Schendel. The six steps are (1) goal formulation, (2) strategy formulation, (3) strategy evaluation, (4) strategy implementation, (5) strategic control, and (6) environmental analysis.[12] Figure 18-4 graphically portrays an expanded view of this process. Note that the environmental analysis component collects information on trends, events, and issues that are occurring in the

FIGURE 18-4   The Strategic Management Process and Corporate Public Policy

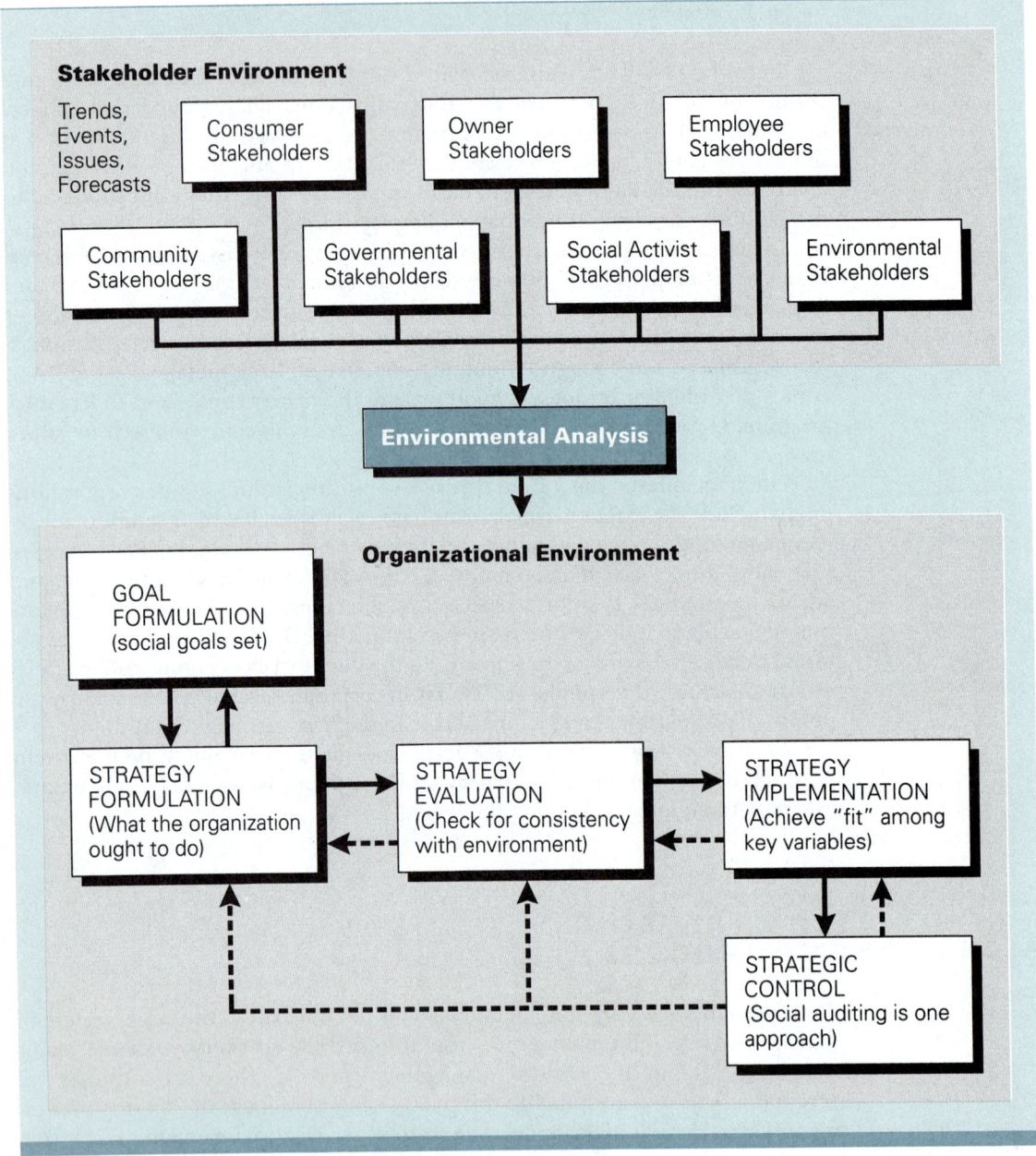

stakeholder environment, and this information is then fed into the other stages of the process. Note also that, although the tasks or steps are discussed sequentially in this chapter, they are in fact interactive and do not always occur in a neatly diagrammed pattern or sequence.

Goal Formulation

The *goal formulation* process of an organization is a complex task. It involves both the establishment of goals and the setting of priorities among goals. Often a politically charged process, goal formulation involves the personal values, perceptions, attitudes, and power of the managers and owners involved in the process. Economic or financial goals typically dominate the goal-formulation process. It is being increasingly recognized, however, that goal setting as it pertains to the public domain of the firm is in dire need of more attention.[13] Typical areas in which social goals might be set include equal employment opportunity, consumer product safety, occupational safety and health, corporate philanthropy, and environmental protection. Furthermore, it is becoming clear that economic and social goals are not necessarily at odds with each other and that the two can be reconciled in such a way that the firm's best interests, as well as the best interests of the stakeholders, are simultaneously served.[14]

We should note that the steps in the strategic management process could be activated for each of the four levels of strategy discussed earlier. Therefore, the strategic management process entails a system of decisions in which goals are successively more refined—moving from broad to specific—just as we illustrated in Figure 18-1. The result is a hierarchy of goals that addresses the various domains that have been identified.

Strategy Formulation

Once goals have been identified, the *strategy formulation* process becomes important. It is difficult to neatly factor out the formulation, evaluation, implementation, and control aspects of the process, for in real life they are intimately related and interdependent. For purposes of discussion, however, we will treat them as though they are distinct steps.

As shown in Figure 18-5, Kenneth Andrews argues that there are four major determinants of the *strategy formulation* decision: (1) identification and appraisal of the firm's *strengths and weaknesses,* (2) identification and appraisal of *opportunities* and *threats* in the environment, (3) identification and appraisal of personal *values* and *aspirations of the management group,* and (4) identification and appraisal of *acknowledged obligations to society.*[15]

Components 1 and 2 are the most fundamental, for they require a firm to carefully examine its own capabilities—strengths, weaknesses, resources—and think in terms of a match with opportunities, threats, and risks present in the market environment. Another way of stating this is that management must compare what the firm *can do* with what it *might do.* Components 3 and 4 are also vital. Realistically,

FIGURE 18-5 Four Components of Strategy Formulation

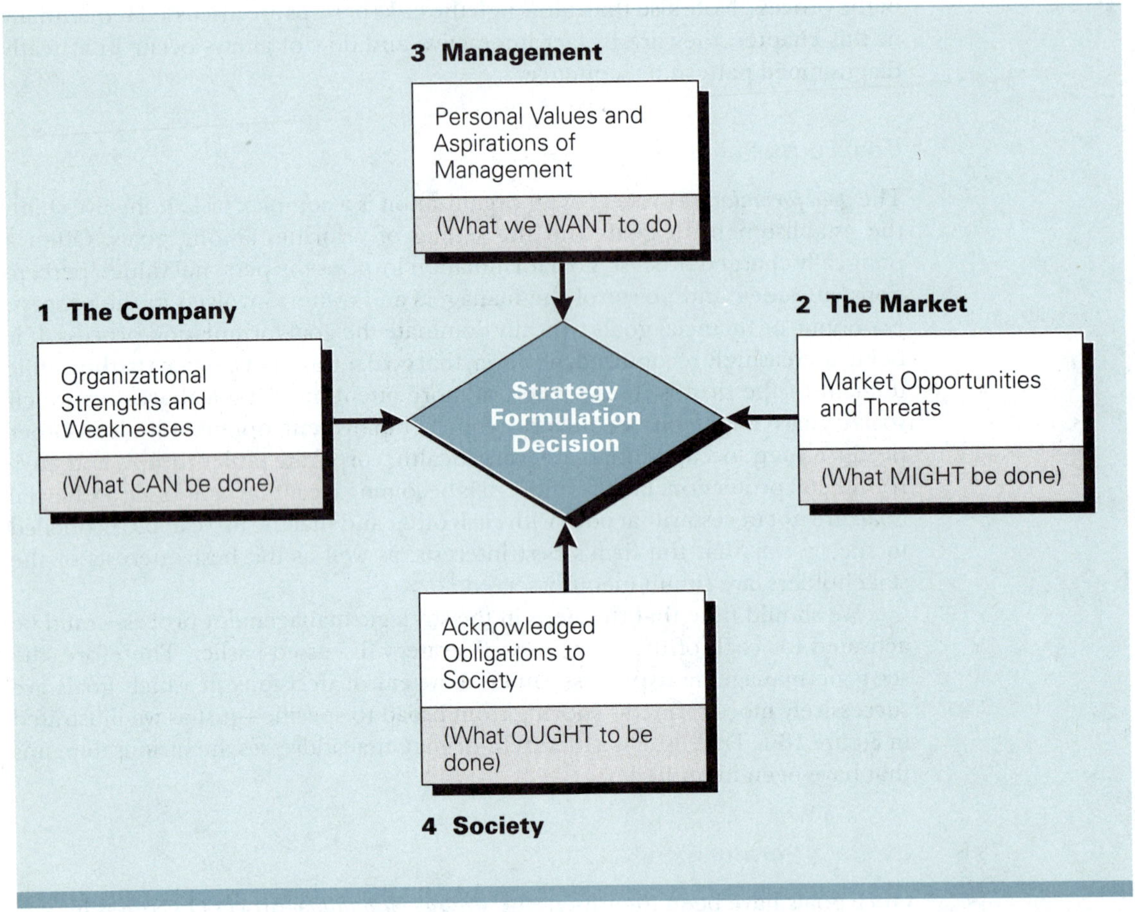

3 Management
Personal Values and Aspirations of Management
(What we WANT to do)

1 The Company
Organizational Strengths and Weaknesses
(What CAN be done)

Strategy Formulation Decision

2 The Market
Market Opportunities and Threats
(What MIGHT be done)

4 Society
Acknowledged Obligations to Society
(What OUGHT to be done)

attention needs to be paid to the personal values and aspirations of the management group. These sometimes subjective influences are real and, therefore, must be factored into the strategy formulation process. Thus, component 3—what management *wants to do*—is a key factor. Finally, strategic choice has a social or ethical aspect that can no longer be ignored. Component 4—what the firm *ought to do* in terms of its acknowledged obligations to society—should be factored in as well.[16]

Component 4 is the corporate public policy component in strategy formulation. It is not the most urgent factor, for a firm that does not have an acceptable matching of organizational characteristics with market characteristics (components 1 and 2) will not survive. However, in today's business environment, the successful firm will blend these components in such a way that the needs or issues arising out of each will be properly addressed. A careful consideration of how these public or ethical issues will be defined is discussed more fully in the section on environmental analysis in this chapter, as well as in the next two chapters.

Strategy Evaluation

In some conceptualizations of the strategic management process, *strategy evaluation* occurs in conjunction with strategic control, after implementation has taken place. We are treating it as the third step in the strategic management process because, in an ongoing organization, it can also be viewed as an integrative process that takes place in conjunction with goal formulation and strategy formulation. In an ongoing organization that already has a strategy, strategy evaluation entails a continuing assessment of the firm's current goals and strategy relative to proposed goals and strategic alternatives. At least six criteria for evaluating strategy have been set forth in question form:

1. Is the strategy internally consistent?
2. Is the strategy consistent with the environment?
3. Is the strategy appropriate in view of available resources?
4. Does the strategy involve an acceptable degree of risk?
5. Does the strategy have an appropriate time frame?
6. Is the strategy workable?[17]

Each of these criteria is important in strategy evaluation. Perhaps the most important, in terms of corporate public policy, is the strategy's consistency with the environment. The social environment is complex and dynamic, and the strategy that was once successful may no longer be. Careful attention to this criterion, then, should be the hallmark of a successful public policy.

Strategy Implementation

No strategy design, however grand, will benefit an organization if it is left on the drawing board. In its simplest form, *strategy implementation* means putting the plans (goals, strategies) that have been developed into effect. It means working the plan with the aim of achieving desired results. At a more complex level, implementation means that many different organizational processes must be activated and coordinated in such a way that the implementation is successful.

The McKinsey 7-S framework is a straightforward identification of seven key variables that must be skillfully coordinated for successful strategy implementation to occur. These seven variables are strategy, structure, systems, style, staff, skills, and shared values.[18]

The 7-S framework was originally conceived as a way of broadly thinking about the problems of effective organizing, but it also provides an excellent vehicle for thinking about the elements that must be successfully coordinated in strategy implementation. Of particular note to the idea of corporate public policy is the "shared values" element. Although these shared values do not refer to shared ethical or social responsiveness values in the original 7-S framework, we can easily see how they might be expanded to mean more than "corporate culture" as it has most frequently been conceived.

The key to the successful use of the 7-S framework is achieving *fit,* or congruence, among all of the elements. ***Fit*** is a process, as well as a state, in which there is a dynamic search that seeks to align an organization with its environment and to arrange internal resources in such a way that the alignment is supported. It is argued that "minimal fit" is needed for survival in a competitive environment and a "tight fit" is needed for long-term effectiveness.[19]

Strategic Control

As a management function, **strategic control** seeks to ensure that the organization stays on line and achieves its goals and strategies. The elements we have discussed to this point—goal formulation, strategy formulation, and strategy evaluation—are part of the overall planning that is essential if firms are to succeed. Planning is not complete without control, however, because control aims to keep management activities in conformance with plans.

Traditionally, control has subsumed three essential steps: (1) setting standards against which performance may be compared, (2) comparing actual performance with what was planned (the standard), and (3) taking corrective action to bring the two back into alignment.[20] It has been argued that a planning system will not achieve its full potential unless at the same time it monitors and assesses the firm's progress along key strategic dimensions. Furthermore, there is a need to control the "strategic momentum" by focusing on a particular strategic direction while at the same time coping with environmental turbulence and change.[21]

Development of the Social Audit.
In the context of corporate social performance or corporate public policy, the idea of a **social audit,** or social performance report, as a technique for providing control has been experimented with for a number of years. Although the term "social audit" has been used to describe a wide variety of activities, in this text we refer to it as a systematic attempt to identify, measure, monitor, and evaluate an organization's performance with respect to its social efforts, goals, and programs. Implicit in this definition is the idea that planning has already taken place. And although we discuss the social audit here as a control mechanism, it could just as easily be thought of as a planning-control technique.[22]

In the context of strategic control, the social audit could assume a role much like that portrayed in Figure 18-6. This figure is similar to the diagram of the strategic management process and corporate public policy shown in Figure 18-4 but is modified somewhat to focus on social goals, corporate social performance, the social audit, and the first three steps in the strategic control process.

Although the corporate social audit is not in widespread use in U.S. industry today, it is worth considering in more detail because of its potential for serving as a planning and control mechanism. Again, the components of the social audit include *identification, measurement, monitoring,* and *evaluating.* The identification

FIGURE 18-6 The Social Audit in the Context of Strategic Control

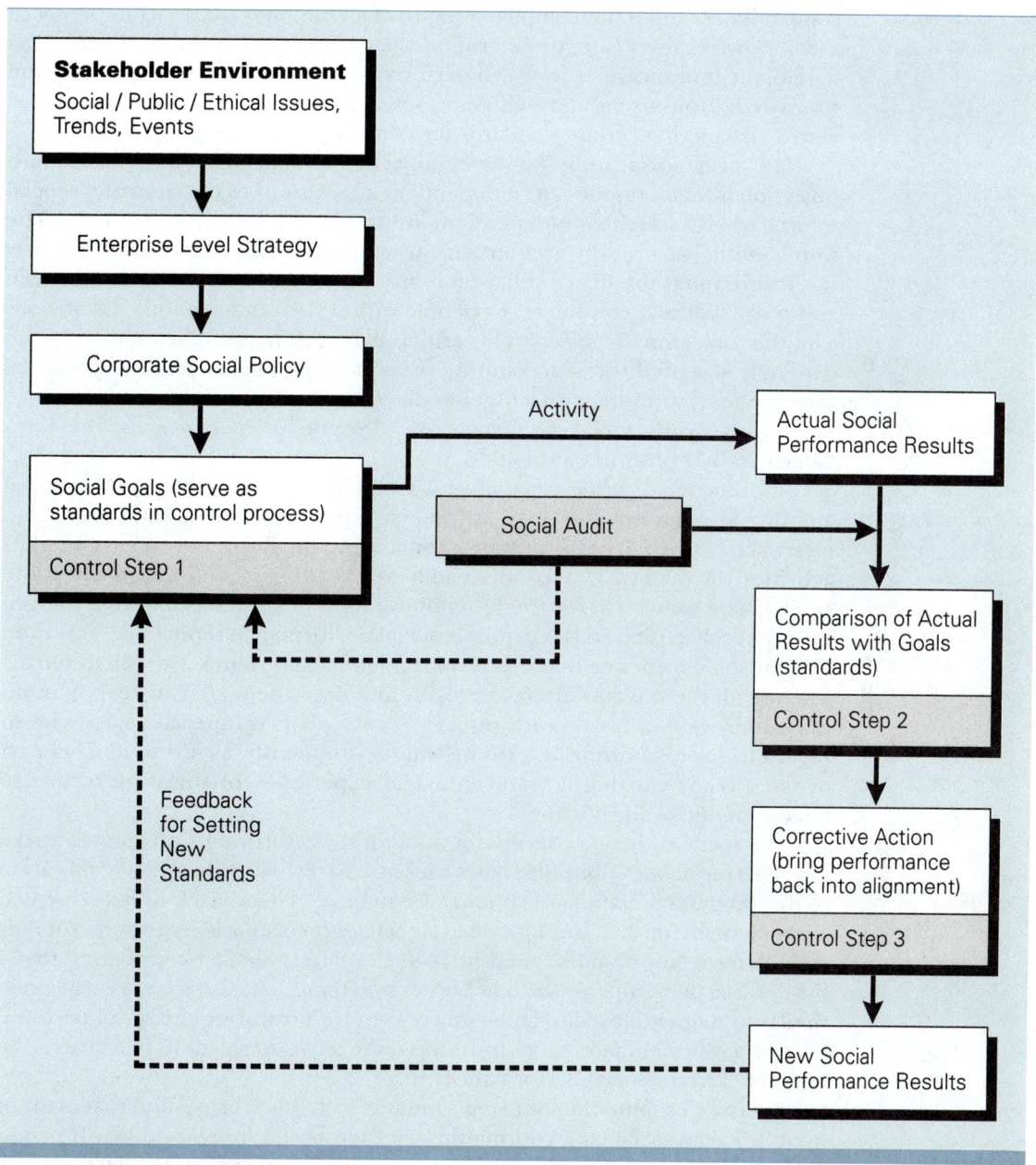

function is included as a part of the definition because experience has shown that companies are often not completely aware of all that they are doing in the social arena. Any serious effort to determine what a company is doing requires the development of measures by which performance can be reported, analyzed, and compared. Monitoring and evaluating stress that the effort is continuous and aimed at achieving certain standards the company may have in mind.

The term "social audit" has been subjected to some criticism. The foremost objection is that it implies an "independent attestation" to the company's social efforts, whereas such an independent attestation typically does not exist. The word "audit," as used by accountants, usually means that some outside party has verified that the firm's situation is as it has been reported. Because social audits are typically conducted by people within the organization, it is obvious why this objection is raised. The criticism is also made that there exist no generally accepted social accounting principles, no professionally recognized independent auditors, and no generally agreed-on criteria against which to measure a firm's social performance.[23] Despite these concerns, the term "social audit" continues to be used.

Another term, *social accounting,* is frequently used in reference to social auditing and has been defined as follows: "The measurement and reporting, internal or external, of information concerning the impact of an entity and its activities on society."[24] We can readily see that these definitions are quite similar. The only term for the function we have been describing that has not been severely criticized is "corporate social performance reporting." However, there is some evidence that this term is no longer in vogue. We will, nevertheless, use all these terms interchangeably and urge the reader to keep in mind the points we have made with respect to each. This is especially necessary in regard to social auditing, a term we will use frequently, as it is so much a part of the already existing literature on and experience of social performance measurement and reporting.

The social audit as a concept for monitoring, measuring, and appraising the social performance of business dates back at least to 1940.[25] In a 1940 publication of the Temporary National Economic Committee, Theodore J. Kreps presented a monograph entitled *Measurement of the Social Performance of Business.*[26] Not only was the term "social audit" used in 1940 (a remarkable fact considering that a firm's social performance was hardly discussed then), but also it was used in a vein similar to that employed today—as a concept for measuring the social performance of business. In fact, Kreps introduced the term "socialaudit" in a chapter he entitled "Tests of Social Performance."[27]

On close examination of Kreps's monograph, however, we find that many of what he called social issues during this late Depression/pre-World War II period were closer to what we would refer to today as economic issues. For example, the measurements he used were employment, production, payroll, dividends, and interest.[28] In contrast to current social audits, the Kreps audit involved more economic-type issues, represented a governmental evaluation of business's social performance, and was to be used by society to assess business performance.

Another landmark in the development of social audits came in 1953 in a book by Howard R. Bowen.[29] Bowen's concept was that the social audit would be a high-level, independent appraisal conducted about every 5 years by a group of disinterested auditors. The auditor's report would be an evaluation with recommendations intended for internal use by the directors and the management of the firm audited. Some of the areas Bowen proposed auditing were similar to those of Kreps, but Bowen also included more socially oriented activities.

In contrast to these earlier landmark models, the social audit as it came of age in the early 1970s attempted to focus on such social performance categories as minority employment, pollution/environment, community relations, consumer issues, and philanthropic contributions. The audits have been undertaken for a variety of purposes and for the most part have been used internally by the organization. Figure 18-7 presents in broad terms an overview and comparison of the Kreps, Bowen, and modern social audits.

Use of the Social Audit. Very few companies initially undertook social audits as control mechanisms. To use a device as a control mechanism implies that there are some goals or standards against which to compare actual performance. Initially, social audits were employed by companies to examine what the company was actually doing in selected areas, appraise or evaluate social performance, identify social programs that the company thought it ought to be pursuing, or just inject into the general thinking of managers a social point of view.[30] During this early time, companies had not developed enterprise-level strategy or corporate social policy. As firms began to plan for the social environment and to set social goals, the social audit was better used as a control mechanism.

As firms develop enterprise-level strategy and corporate public policy, the potential for social audits remains high. Social auditing is best seen not as an isolated attempt to periodically assess social performance but rather as an integral part of the overall strategic management process as it has been portrayed here. Because the need to improve planning and control will remain as long as management desires to evaluate its corporate social performance, the need for strategic control through techniques such as the social audit will likely be with us for some time, too. The net result of continued experimentation should be improved corporate social performance and enhanced credibility of business in the eyes of the public.

Environmental Analysis

To this point we have described the strategic management process without dwelling on where the information that management uses in its goal formulation, strategy formulation, and other processes comes from. Now we should discuss environmental analysis, the process by which this information is assembled. *Environmental analysis* is the linking pin between the organization, which is the managerial setting for the strategic management process, and the stakeholder environment from which information is being gathered.

FIGURE 18-7 Three Landmark Models of the Social Audit

Subject	Kreps's 1940 Audit	Bowen's 1953 Audit	Today's Audit
Definition	Acid test of business performance	Evaluation of the performance of business from a social point of view	Measurement of companies' progress toward social goals
Purpose	Government evaluation of business's social performance	The firm's evaluation of its social performance	The firm's evaluation of its social performance
Apparent motives	Establish criteria for future evaluations. Establish the technique for society to influence business performance	Bring social point of view to management	1. Satisfying the corporate conscience 2. Improving financial wisdom of social programs 3. Public relations 4. To enhance credibility of the business firm
Nature of issues audited	Quantifiable areas: 1. Employment 2. Production 3. Consumer effort commanded 4. Consumer funds absorbed 5. Payrolls 6. Dividends and interest	Company policy toward: 1. Prices 2. Wages 3. Research and development 4. Advertising 5. Public relations 6. Human relations 7. Community relations 8. Economic stabilization	Company performance in: 1. Minority employment 2. Pollution/environment 3. Working conditions 4. Community relations 5. Philanthropic contributions 6. Consumerism issues
Use	By society to assess business performance	By management to assess its performance	Divided between two schools of thought. One group feels it should be only for management's use. Another group feels it should be a public document.
Methodology	Evaluation of public information employing economic indices	Judgmental appraisal of company policy	Monitor, measure, and appraise all aspects of social performance using various techniques — cost vs. benefit, accounting, etc.
By whom conducted	A government bureau	Internal personnel or an industry agency	Internal personnel or a consultant

Source: Archie B. Carroll and George W. Beiler, "Landmarks in the Evolution of the Social Audit," *Academy of Management Journal* (September, 1975), 598. Reproduced with permission.

Before we describe environmental analysis, let us briefly discuss the idea of the stakeholder environment portrayed in Figure 18-4. One popular conception is to see the environment of business in terms of three levels: (1) the **task environment,** which is that set of customers, suppliers, competitors, and others with which a firm interacts on an almost daily basis; (2) the **competitive or industry environment,** which comprises those firms functioning in the same markets or industry; and (3) the **general environment,** or **macroenvironment,** which includes everything else "out there" that influences the organization. The macroenvironment is sometimes referred to as the *political economy*.[31]

Another way of conceptualizing the environment of business is in terms of the *component subsystems,* or *segments,* that compose it. The standard scheme here is that the environment is composed of social, economic, political, and technological components, or subenvironments. Because the environment is complex, these four components are highly interdependent and sometimes indistinguishable from one another. In addition, the environment is seen as having other dimensions that must be acknowledged and recognized. Some of these other dimensions are simplicity-complexity, homogeneity-heterogeneity, and stable-dynamic.[32]

In keeping with our general theme, we will refer to the environment of business, which possesses all these attributes described, as the **stakeholder environment.** As a basis or resource for information gathering, we should also observe that this environment is composed of trends, events, issues, and forecasts that may have a bearing on the strategic management process.

One further point needs to be made before we describe the environmental analysis process. In this chapter we are striving to convey the idea that a concern for enterprise-level strategy and corporate public policy is just one part of the more comprehensive strategic management process. Therefore, we are concerned with all four components of the business environment—economic, technological, political, and social. In other words, we are just as interested in such economic or technological trends as interest rates, the balance of payments, the international competitiveness problem, changes in computer technology, and trends in research-and-development expenditures as we are with ethical or other public issues. In the next chapter, however, we will focus on a set of techniques that share a common heritage with environmental analysis but are more concerned with public or ethical issues. These techniques are known as *issues management* and *crisis management.*

Narayanan and Fahey's conceptualization of the environmental analysis stage in the strategic management process is best suited for our purposes. They posit that four analytical stages in the process exist: (1) *scanning* the environment to detect warning signals, (2) *monitoring* specific environmental trends, (3) *forecasting* the future direction of environmental change, and (4) *assessing* current and future environmental changes for their organizational implications.[33]

Scanning the Environment. The *environmental scanning stage* focuses on identifying precursors or indicators of potential environmental changes and issues. The purpose of this stage is to alert management to potentially significant events, issues, or trends before they have fully formed or crystallized.[34] Early on, companies did their scanning in an informal, irregular, and ad hoc way. Executives simply read newspapers, magazines, institutional reports, polls, and surveys. As the environment became more turbulent, firms began engaging in periodic or continuous scanning rather than irregular scanning. As companies got more serious about scanning the environment, their techniques became more sophisticated, and a whole industry opened up to supply managers with professionally obtained information. Examples include the Yankelovich "Corporate Priorities" service and various newsletters and services provided by John Naisbitt, author of the book *Megatrends*. Figure 18-8 portrays three major types of environmental scanning along with a description of the characteristics of each.

Monitoring Environmental Trends. Whereas environmental scanning entails an open-ended viewing of the environment to identify early signals, the *environmental monitoring stage* focuses on the tracking of specific trends and events with an eye toward confirming or disconfirming trends or patterns. Monitoring often involves following up on indicators or signals that were detected during the scanning stage. The goal here is to gather and assemble sufficient data to discern patterns. Three outputs of scanning are useful: (1) specific descriptions of environmental patterns that may then be forecast, (2) the identification of other trends that need to be continually monitored, and (3) the identification of patterns requiring future scanning.[35] We should note that many of the sources of information that are employed in scanning, such as the professional services mentioned, are also used in monitoring.

Forecasting Environmental Changes. Scanning and monitoring are restricted to the past and the present. Information also needs to be obtained as to the likely future state of events, trends, or issues. The *environmental forecasting stage* is the future-oriented stage and is concerned with the development of plausible and realistic projections of the direction, scope, speed, and intensity of environmental change.[36] Forecasting of the economic, technological, social, and political components of the environment are needed, and this information base then forms the premises on which goal formulation, strategy formulation, and other strategic planning are developed.

Economic forecasting is the most frequently addressed area in this process. Only in the past two decades or so have firms begun formal attempts to forecast the technological, social, and political environments. A technique known as *sociopolitical forecasting* emerged at General Electric. Ian Wilson, an early proponent of this new technique, was one of the first to call to our attention the need to leave behind our two-sided approach to planning, which dwelt on economic and technological forecasts, and to adopt a "four-sided framework," which also included social and political forecasting.[37]

FIGURE 18-8 Three Types of Environmental Scanning

	Irregular	Periodic	Continuous
Impetus for scanning	Crisis-initiated	Problem-solving decision or issue-oriented	Opportunity finding and problem avoidance
Scope of scanning	Specific events	Selected events	Broad range of environmental systems
Temporal nature 1. Time frame for data 2. Time frame for decision impact	Reactive Retrospective Current and near-term future	Proactive Current and retrospective Near term	Proactive Current and prospective Long term
Types of forecasts	Budget-oriented	Economic- and sales-oriented	Marketing, social, legal, regulatory, cultural, and so on
Media scanning and forecasting	*Ad hoc* studies	Periodically updated studies	Structured data collection and processing systems
Organization structure	1. *Ad hoc* teams 2. Focus on reduction of perceived certainty	Various staff agencies	Scanning unit, focus on enhancing uncertainty-handling capacity
Resource allocation to activity	Not specific (perhaps periodic as fads arise)	Specific and continuous but relatively low	Specific, continuous, and relatively substantial
Methodological sophistication	Simplistic data analyses and budgetary projections	Statistical forecasting-oriented	Many futuristic forecasting methodologies
Cultural orientation	Not integrated into mainstream of activity	Partially integrated as a stepchild	Fully integrated as crucial for long-range growth

Source: Reprinted with permission from *Long Range Planning Journal* (April, 1982), L. Fahey, W. R. King, and V. K. Narayanan, "Environmental Scanning and Forecasting in Strategic Planning: The State of the Art," Copyright ø 1982, Pergamon Journals Ltd.

Kenneth E. Newgren conducted a major study of the state of social forecasting, and he found that it was most likely to have been formalized in companies that already practiced long-range planning. Also, the forecasts tended to be developed in conjunction with other external forecasts, and the techniques used most frequently were qualitative in nature, such as the pooled opinion of executives, trend analysis, surveys of interest groups, and industry-sponsored activities. Newgren conceptualized social forecasting as entailing (1) commitment by management, (2) identification of social trends and attitudes, (3) analysis for relevance to the organization, and (4) integration with other forecasts.[38]

Several observations are in order. First, Newgren defined social forecasting more broadly than we have been discussing it here. Second, he defined social forecasting as a process extending over a time period of at least 5 or more years into the future. Third, although his study was conducted some years ago, it does represent one of the most comprehensive efforts to survey what companies have actually been doing. As the social environment has become more complex and rapidly changing, companies are turning to shorter time spans and approaches such as issues management, which we will treat in the next chapter.

Assessment for Organizational Implications. Scanning, monitoring, and forecasting are done to enable the use of current and projected environmental information and changes for setting new goals and formulating strategies. The assessment stage of environmental analysis shifts the attention away from gathering and projecting and to the task of understanding what the information means to management. The central question now is, "What are the implications of our analysis of the environment for our organization?"[39] The key at this stage is to develop the ability to sift through all the information that has been generated and to determine what is relevant to management. Relevance may be thought of in terms of two key dimensions: (1) the probability that the event, trend, or forecast will occur and (2) the impact that the event, trend, or forecast will have on the organization. These two dimensions make it possible to create what is known as a probability-impact matrix, as shown in Figure 18-9. Note that the matrix permits management to categorize issues according to priorities that then can be used as a framework for assessment, comparison, and discussion.

The strategic management process provides an excellent framework for thinking about stakeholder management. The processes of environmental analysis, goal formulation, strategy formulation, strategy evaluation, strategy implementation, and strategic control describe what managers must do in their leadership roles. Furthermore, the strategic management process provides a comprehensive context in which we can better appreciate where enterprise-level strategy and corporate public policy fit into the total array of managerial challenges and responsibilities. Only by seeing public and ethical issues emanating from the stakeholder environment and having to compete with economic, technological, and political factors can we fully appreciate what it means to be a manager in today's climate.

SUMMARY

Corporate public policy is a firm's posture or stance regarding the public, social, or ethical aspects of stakeholders and corporate functioning. It is a part of strategic management, particularly enterprise-level strategy. Enterprise-level strategy is the

FIGURE 18-9   A Probability-Impact Matrix

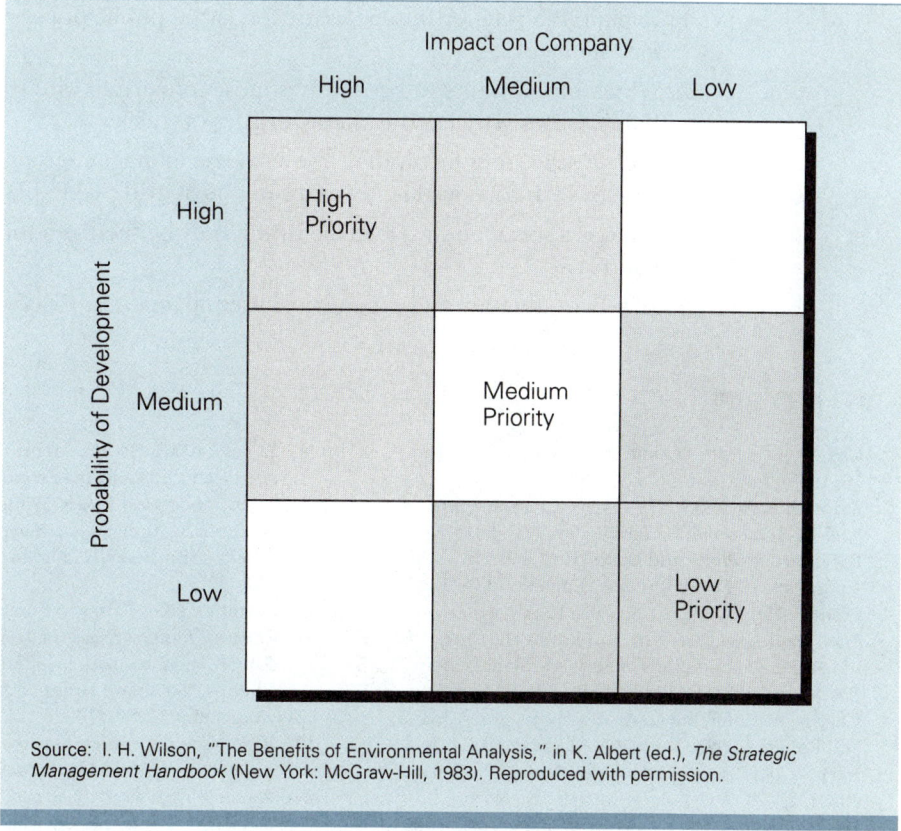

Source: I. H. Wilson, "The Benefits of Environmental Analysis," in K. Albert (ed.), *The Strategic Management Handbook* (New York: McGraw-Hill, 1983). Reproduced with permission.

broadest, overarching level of strategy, and its focus is on the role of the organization in society. Other questions that help flesh out enterprise-level strategy include the following: How is our organization perceived by our stakeholders? What principles or values does our organization represent? What obligations do we have to society at large? Enterprise-level strategy is manifested by way of corporate creeds, codes of ethics, "core values," public issues committees, and the degree of formalization of the public affairs function. The other strategy levels include the corporate level, business level, and functional level.

The strategic management process entails six stages, and a concern for social, ethical, and public issues may be seen at each stage. The stage at which public issues are most addressed for planning purposes is the environmental analysis stage. Vital components of environmental analysis include scanning, monitoring, forecasting, and assessing. In the overall environmental analysis process, social, ethical, and public issues are considered along with economic, political, and technological factors.

DISCUSSION QUESTIONS

1. Explain the relationship between corporate public policy and strategic management.
2. Which of the four strategy levels is most concerned with social, ethical, or public issues? Discuss the characteristics of this level.
3. Identify the steps involved in the strategic management process. In which step is a concern for social issues planning most evident? Explain.
4. What is a social audit? Describe how it may be seen as a tool for strategic control.
5. What are the four stages in environmental analysis? Briefly explain each stage.

ENDNOTES

1. Charles Alexander, "Crime in the Suites," *Time* (June 10, 1985), 56–57.
2. Kenneth R. Andrews, *The Concept of Corporate Strategy*, 3d ed. (Homewood, IL: Irwin, 1987), 68–69.
3. R. Edward Freeman and Daniel R. Gilbert, Jr., *Corporate Strategy and the Search for Ethics* (Englewood Cliffs, NJ: Prentice-Hall, 1988), 20. See also R. Edward Freeman, Daniel R. Gilbert, Jr., and Edwin Hartman, "Values and the Foundations of Strategic Management," *Journal of Business Ethics* (7, 1988), 821–834.
4. Charles W. Hofer, Edwin A. Murray, Jr., Ram Charan, and Robert A. Pitts, *Strategic Management: A Casebook in Policy and Planning*, 2d ed. (St. Paul, MN: West, 1984), 27–29.
5. H. Igor Ansoff, "The Changing Shape of the Strategic Problem," Paper presented at a Special Conference on Business Policy and Planning Research: The State of the Art, Pittsburgh, May, 1977.
6. H. Igor Ansoff, *Implanting Strategic Management* (Englewood Cliffs, NJ: Prentice-Hall, International, 1984), 129–151.
7. R. Edward Freeman, *Strategic Management: A Stakeholder Approach* (Boston: Pitman, 1984), 90.
8. *Ibid.*, 90–91.
9. Laura Sessions Stepp, "Industrial-Strength Ethics, Being Tested in the Crucible of Reality," *The Washington Post National Weekly Edition* (April 8–14, 1991), 22–23.
10. *Ibid*, 22–23.
11. *Ibid*, 23.
12. Hofer and Schendel, 52–55.
13. Archie B. Carroll, "Setting Operational Goals for Corporate Social Responsibility," *Long Range Planning* (April, 1978), 35.
14. James J. Chrisman and Archie B. Carroll, "Corporate Responsibility: Reconciling Economic and Social Goals," *Sloan Management Review* (Winter, 1984), 59–65.
15. Kenneth R. Andrews, *The Concept of Corporate Strategy*, 3d ed. (Homewood, IL: Irwin, 1987), 18–20.
16. *Ibid.*
17. Seymour Tilles, "How to Evaluate Corporate Strategy," *Harvard Business Review* (July-August, 1963), 111–121.
18. Robert H. Waterman, Jr., Thomas J. Peters, Julien R. Phillips, "Structure Is Not Organization," *Business Horizons* (June, 1980), 14–26.
19. R. Miles and C. Snow, *Environmental Strategy and Organization Structure* (New York: McGraw-Hill, 1978) 1.
20. Archie B. Carroll, *Business and Society: Managing Corporate Social Performance* (Boston: Little, Brown, 1981), 381.
21. Peter Lorange, Michael F. Scott Morton, Sumantra Ghoshal, *Strategic Control Systems* (St. Paul, MN: West, 1986), 1, 10.
22. David H. Blake, William C. Frederick, Mildred S. Myers, *Social Auditing: Evaluating the Impact of Corporate Programs* (New York: Praeger, 1976), 3.
23. *Ibid.*
24. Ralph Estes, *Corporate Social Accounting* (New York: John Wiley, 1976), 3.
25. Archie B. Carroll and George W. Beiler, "Landmarks in the Evolution of the Social Audit," *Academy of Management Journal* (September, 1975), 589–599.
26. Theodore J. Kreps, *Measurement of the Social Performance of Business*, Monograph No. 7, "An Investigation of Concentration of Economic Power for the Temporary National Economic Committee" (Washington, DC: U.S. Government Printing Office, 1940).
27. Kreps cited in Carroll and Beiler, 590–591.
28. Kreps, 3–4.

29. Howard R. Bowen, *Social Responsibilities of the Businessman* (New York: Harper & Row, 1953).
30. John J. Corson and George A. Steiner, *Measuring Business's Social Performance: The Corporate Social Audit* (New York: Committee for Economic Development, 1974), 33.
31. Liam Fahey and V. K. Narayanan, *Macroenvironmental Analysis for Strategic Management* (St. Paul, MN: West, 1986), 25.
32. *Ibid.*, 28–30.
33. V. K. Narayanan and Liam Fahey, "Environmental Analysis for Strategy Formulation," in William R. King and David I. Cleland (eds.), *Strategic Planning and Management Handbook* (New York: Van Nostrand Reinhold, 1987), 156.
34. *Ibid.*
35. *Ibid.*, 159–160.
36. *Ibid.*, 160.
37. Ian H. Wilson, "Socio-Political Forecasting: A New Dimension to Strategic Planning," in Archie B. Carroll (ed.) *Managing Corporate Social Responsibility* (Boston: Little, Brown, 1977), 159–169.
38. Kenneth E. Newgren, "Social Forecasting: An Overview of Current Business Practices," in Archie B. Carroll (ed.), *Managing Corporate Social Responsibility* (Boston: Little, Brown, 1977), 189.
39. Narayanan and Fahey, 162.

CHAPTER **NINETEEN**

Issues Management and Crisis Management

CHAPTER OBJECTIVES

After studying this chapter, you should be able to:

- ◆ Distinguish between the conventional and strategic management approaches to issues management.

- ◆ Identify and briefly explain the stages in the issues management process.

- ◆ Describe the major components in the issues development process and some of the factors that have characterized issues management in actual practice.

- ◆ Define a crisis and identify the four crisis stages.

- ◆ List and discuss the major stages in managing business crises.

Throughout this text we have referred to major social and ethical issues that have become controversies in the public domain. Some have been serious events or crises that continue to serve as recognizable code words for business—Love Canal, Three Mile Island, the Tylenol poisonings, the Pinto gas tank explosions, the insider trading scandals, the Union Carbide Bhopal tragedy, the Exxon *Valdez* oil spill, and the AIDS crisis. Other issues—employee rights, product safety, workplace safety, smoking in the workplace, affirmative action, deceptive advertising, and so on—have not been characterized by crisis proportions. Nevertheless, to business they represent considerable social issues that have evolved over time and must be dealt with.

Managerial decision-making processes known as issues management and crisis management are two ways in which business has responded to these situations. These two approaches symbolize the extent to which the environment has become turbulent and the public has become sensitized to business's response to the issues that have emerged from this turbulence. In the ideal situation, issues management and crisis management might be seen as the natural and logical by-products of a firm's development of enterprise-level strategy and overall corporate public policy. That is not always the case, however. Some firms have not thought seriously about public and ethical issues; for them these approaches represent first attempts to come to grips with the practical reality of a threatening social environment. Many of these firms have been fortunate that a major issue has not emerged to stun them as it did in the Johnson & Johnson Tylenol poisonings, the Union Carbide Bhopal explosion, or the Procter and Gamble Rely tampon crisis. Thus, they have lived in a vicarious way with a major business crisis but did not have to experience it themselves. Such firms should now be concerned with issues management and crisis management.

Like all planning processes, issues management and crisis management have many characteristics in common. There are differences, however, and we have chosen to treat them separately for discussion purposes. One common thread that should be mentioned at the outset is that both processes should be focused on improving stakeholder management and enabling the organization to be more ethically responsive to stakeholders' expectations. There is a temptation for managers to think of these approaches as being manipulative in nature, and this temptation must be resisted. Issues and crisis management, to be effective, must have as their ultimate objective the organization becoming more socially responsive.

ISSUES MANAGEMENT

Issues management refers to a process by which organizations identify issues in the stakeholder environment, analyze and prioritize these issues in terms of their relevance to the organization, plan responses to these issues, and then evaluate and monitor the results. It is helpful to think of issues management in connection with concepts we introduced in the previous chapter such as the strategic management process, enterprise-level strategy, corporate public policy, and environmental analysis. The process of strategic management and environmental analysis refers to an overall way of management thinking that includes economic, technological, social, and political issues. Enterprise-level strategy and corporate public policy, on the other hand, focus on public or ethical issues.

Approaches to Issues Management

Thinking about the concepts mentioned above requires us to make some distinctions. A central consideration seems to be that issues management has been thought of in two major ways: narrowly, in which public issues are the primary focus, and broadly, in which strategic issues and the strategic management process are the focus. Liam Fahey provides a useful sorting of these two approaches. He refers to (1) the conventional approach, and (2) the strategic management approach.[1] The *conventional approach to issues management* has the following characteristics:

- Issues fall within the domain of public policy or public affairs management.
- Issues typically have a public policy/public affairs orientation or flavor.
- An issue is any trend, event, controversy, or public policy development that might affect the corporation.
- Issues originate in social/political/regulatory/judicial environments.[2]

The *strategic management approach to issues management* has evolved in a small number of companies and is typified by the following:

- Issues management is typically the responsibility of senior line management or strategic planning staff.
- Issues identification is more important here than in the conventional approach.
- Issues management is seen as an approach to anticipate and manage external and internal challenges to the company's strategies, plans, and assumptions.[3]

The strategic approach to issues management has also been advocated by such authorities as H. Igor Ansoff[4] and William R. King.[5] Figure 19-1 portrays strategic issues management as seen by Ansoff. Note the "strategic" characteristics—threats/opportunities and strengths/weaknesses—that we alluded to in the previous chapter.

At the risk of oversimplification, the principal distinctions between the two approaches to issues management are that the conventional approach is restricted to public/social issues, whereas the strategic approach is inclusive of all issues. In

FIGURE **19-1** Strategic Issue Management

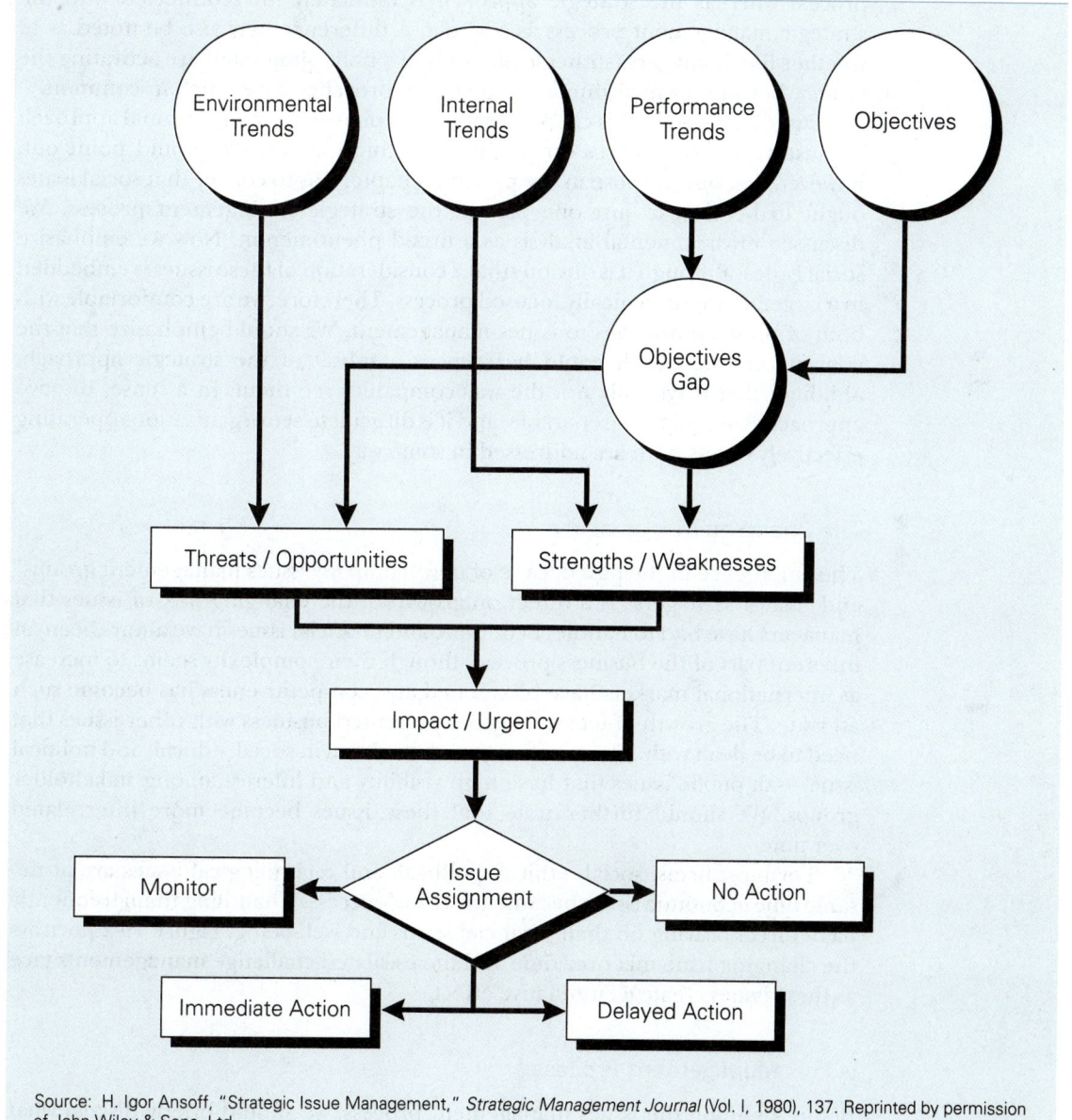

Source: H. Igor Ansoff, "Strategic Issue Management," *Strategic Management Journal* (Vol. I, 1980), 137. Reprinted by permission of John Wiley & Sons, Ltd.

addition, the conventional approach can be used as a "stand alone" decision process whereas the strategic approach is intimately interconnected with the strategic management process as a whole. A difference may also be noted as to whether line managers/strategic planners or public affairs staff are activating the system. Beyond these distinctions, the two approaches have much in common.

Our discussion in this chapter tends to emphasize the conventional approach because this book focuses on public and ethical issues. We should point out, however, that our purpose in the previous chapter was to convey that social issues ought to be seen as just one part of the strategic management process. We discussed environmental analysis as a broad phenomenon. Now we emphasize social issues, although it is obvious that a consideration of these issues is embedded in a larger, more strategically focused process. Therefore, we are comfortable with both of these approaches to issues management. We should emphasize that the conventional approach could be seen as a subset of the strategic approach, although that is typically not the way companies see them. In a sense, the two approaches are highly inseparable, and it is difficult to see organizations operating effectively unless both are addressed in some way.

The Changing Mix of Issues

The emergence in the past decade of new "company issues management groups" and "issues managers" is a direct outgrowth of the changing mix of issues that managers have had to handle. Economic and financial issues have always been an inherent part of the business process, though their complexity seems to increase as international markets have broadened and competitiveness has become such an issue. The growth of technology has presented business with other issues that need to be dealt with. The greatest growth has been in social, ethical, and political issues—all public issues that have high visibility and interest among stakeholder groups. We should further note that these issues become more interrelated over time.

For most firms, social, ethical, political, and technological issues are at the same time economic issues because the firms' success in handling them frequently has a direct bearing on their financial status and well-being. Figure 19-2 portrays the changing issue mix over time and the escalated challenge managements face as these issues create a cumulative effect.

Issues Management Process

Before defining the issues management process, we should briefly discuss what constitutes an issue and what assumptions we are making about issues management. An *issue* may be thought of as a matter that is in dispute between two or more parties. The dispute typically evokes a debate or controversy that needs to be resolved. At some point the organization needs to make a decision on the unresolved matter, but that does not mean the issue is resolved. Once issues become public and subject to public debate and media exposure, their resolution

FIGURE **19-2** The Changing Issue Mix Over Time

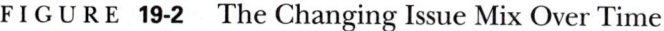

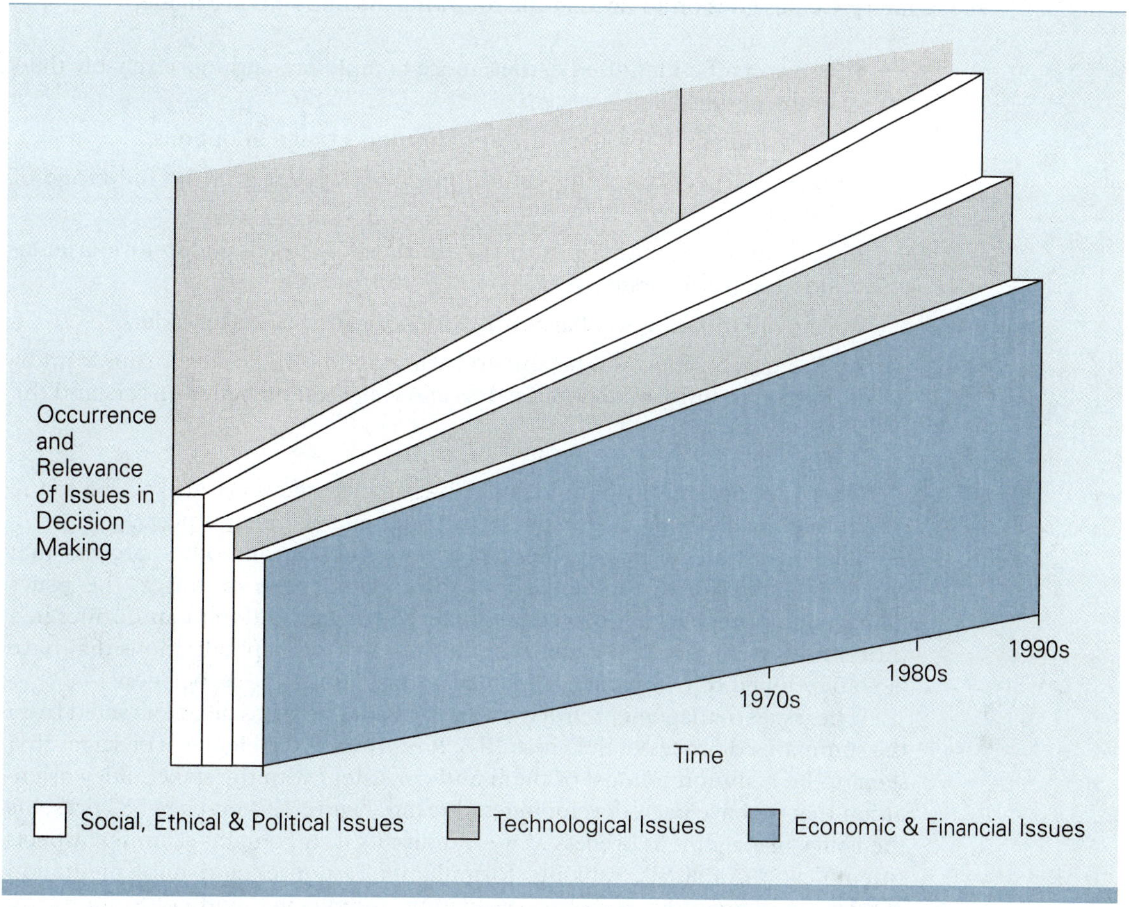

becomes exceedingly difficult. One of the features of issues, particularly those arising in the social or ethical realm, is that they are ongoing and therefore require an ongoing response.

Coates identifies the following characteristics of an "emerging issue":

- The terms of the debate are not clearly defined.
- It deals with matters of conflicting values and interest.
- It does not lend itself to automatic resolution by expert knowledge.
- It is often stated in value-laden terms.
- Trade-offs are inherent.[6]

Thus, we can see that resolution of issues is not easy.

What about the assumptions we make when we choose to use issues management? Coates goes on to say that the following assumptions are made:

- Issues can be identified earlier, more completely, and more reliably than in the past.
- Early anticipation widens the organization's range of options.
- Early anticipation permits study and understanding of the full range of issues.
- Early anticipation permits the organization to develop a positive orientation toward the issue.
- The organization will have earlier identification of stakeholders.
- The organization will be able to earlier and more positively supply information to influential publics, thus allowing them to better understand the issue.[7]

These are not only assumptions of issues management but also *benefits* to the extent that the company is effective in its issues management process.

Like the strategic management process or almost any other process that entails a multitude of sequential and interrelated steps or stages, the issues management process has been conceptualized by many different authorities in a variety of ways. Figure 19-3 summarizes a variety of conceptualizations that have been developed by companies, academics, consultants, and associations.

The issues management process we will discuss here has been extracted from the summarized processes in Figure 19-3. It represents the elements or stages that seem to be common to most of them and consistent with the stakeholder orientation that we have been developing and using. Figure 19-4 on page 583 presents the issues management process as we will discuss it. It contains planning aspects (identification, analysis, ranking, formulating response) and implementation aspects (implementing response, evaluating, monitoring, and controlling). Although we will discuss the stages in the issues management process as though they were discrete, we should recognize that in reality they overlap with one another.

Identification of Issues. Many names have been given to the process of issue identification. At various times, the terms "social forecasting," "futures research," "environmental scanning," and "public issues scanning" have been used. Similarly, many techniques have been used. All of these approaches and techniques are similar, but each has its own unique characteristics. Common to all of them, however, is the need to scan the environment and to identify emerging issues that might later be determined to have some relevance to the organization.

Issue identification, in its most rudimentary form, involves the assignment of some *individual* in the organization to continuously read a range of publications—newspapers, magazines, specialty publications—and to develop a comprehensive list of issues. Often this same person is assigned to review public documents,

FIGURE 19-3 Conceptualizations of the Issues Management Process

Chase & Chase [a]
- Issue Identification
- Issue Analysis
- Issue Change Strategy Options
- Issue Action Program
- Continuing Evaluation

Coates and Staff [b]
- Issue Identification
- Scanning
- Analysis
- Priority Setting
- Monitoring or Tracking
- Policy Implementation (0–4 years)
- Strategic Planning (5–10 years)

King [c]
- Issue Identification
- Issue Assessment
- Issue Analysis
- Development of Issue-Related Strategy
- Strategy Implementation
- Measuring Results-Monitoring Issue

Buchholz [d]
- Issue Identification
- Prioritization of Issues
- Analysis of High Priority Issues
- Formulation of Position on Issues
- Implementation of Specific Programs
- Evaluation of Results

Shell Oil Company [e]
- Identify and Assess Issues and Impacts
- Establish Priorities; Allocate Resources
- Plan Strategy and Tactics
- Implement Tactics and Plans

(continued)

FIGURE 19-3 (continued)

PPG Industries[f]
• Issue Identification • Impact Assessment • Position Formulation • Action Plan Development and Implementation • Communications
Public Affairs Council[g]
• Monitoring Environment • Analyzing and Evaluating Impact of Issues • Establishing Priorities Among Issues • Effecting Responses

Sources: [a]W. Howard Chase and Thomas Howard Chase, "Social and (Other) Issue Management" in S. P. Sethi and C. M. Falbe (eds.), *Business and Society: Dimensions of Conflict and Cooperation* (Lexington Books, 1987), 52.
[b]Joseph F. Coates, Vary T. Coates, Jennifer Jarratt, Lisa Heinz, *Issues and Management* (Mt. Airy, MD: Lomond Publications, 1986), 29.
[c]William R. King, "Strategic Issue Management," in William R. King and David J. Cleland (eds.), *Strategic Planning and Management Handbook* (New York: Van Nostrand Reinhold Co., 1987), 256.
[d]Rogene A. Buchholz, "Education for Public Issues Management: Key Insights from a Survey of Top Practitioners," *Public Affairs Review* (1982), 68.
[e]James K. Brown, *This Business of Issues: Coping with the Company's Environment* (New York: The Conference Board, 1979), 5.
[f]Ibid.
[g]Ibid.

congressional hearings, and other such sources of information. One result of this scanning is an internal report or newsletter that is circulated throughout the organization. A next step in this evolution may be for the company to subscribe to a *trend information service* or *newsletter* that is prepared and published by a private individual or consulting firm that specializes in environmental or issue scanning.[8]

Two of the most popular trend-spotting services today include (1) the Washington-based Naisbitt Group, which was founded by John Naisbitt, who was thrust into public recognition by his best-seller *Megatrends*, and (2) Yankelovich, Skelly, and White, a New York-based social research firm. For fees that range from $10,000 to $30,000 per year and more, firms pay these professionals to provide them with materials they have assembled.[9] Among the services offered are newsletters, short weekly or monthly reports, telephone bulletins, and quarterly visits to discuss what the trends mean. Trend spotters do not claim clairvoyance, but they do say they have less psychological resistance than their clients in seeing impending change.[10]

The Naisbitt Group claims to be different from many trend-spotters. The 30 or so professionals in that group do not scan national magazines but rather scan the local news in local newspapers. Their approach, which is controversial, is that

FIGURE 19-4   The Issues Management Process

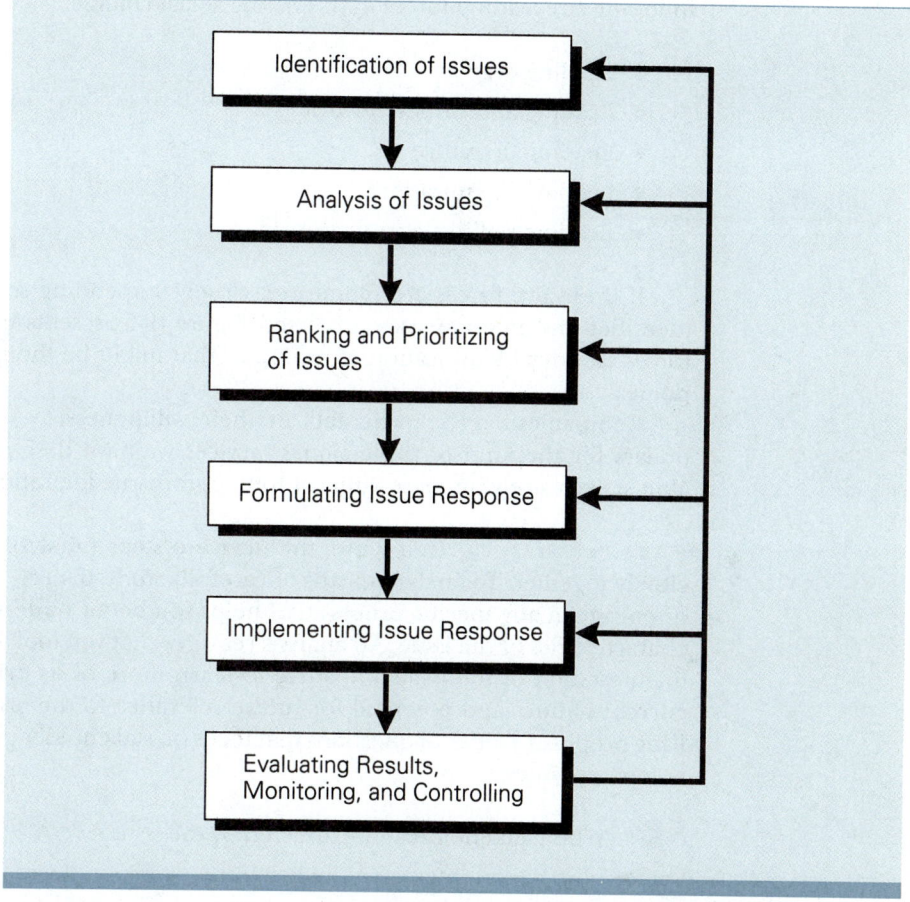

trends start with isolated local events. As Naisbitt states it, "The really important things that happen always start somewhere in the countryside. Taken together, what's going on locally is what's going on." Thus, according to Naisbitt, it is what people are *doing*, not what they are *saying*, that provides a more reliable picture of issues.

Yankelovich, Skelly, and White (YSW), on the other hand, pursue a diametrically opposed strategy. Years ago, through long interviews, YSW identified 35 widespread social trends, such as rejection of authority and female careerism. They then developed a survey made up of questions that assess the strength of these trends, and each year they administer the questionnaire to 2,500 people. YSW tracks the waxing and waning of these trends and claims to predict the trends' relative strength for the next 5 years. For $20,000 or more yearly, the service's 140 sponsors get the survey's results, a videocassette on the meaning of the results, a book discussing the implications of the results, and individual consulting.[11]

T. Graham Molitor, who is also a consultant on social issues, has advocated the following five leading forces in predicting social change:

- Leading events
- Leading authorities/advocates
- Leading literature
- Leading organizations
- Leading political jurisdictions[12]

If these five forces are monitored closely, impending social change can be identified and, in some cases, predicted. Figure 19-5 presents Molitor's five leading forces and our identification of examples that might be thought to illustrate his points.

Companies vary considerably in their willingness to spend thousands of dollars for the kind of professional services we have described, but some rely almost exclusively on these kinds of sources for issue identification.

Analysis of Issues. In a sense, the next two steps (analyzing and ranking) go closely together. To analyze means to carefully study, dissect, break down, group, or engage in any specific process that helps you better understand the nature or characteristics of the issue. An analysis requires that you look beyond the obvious manifestation of the issue and strive to learn more of its history, development, current nature, and potential for future relevance to the organization. William King proposes a series of questions that focus on stakeholder groups in attempting to analyze issues:

- Who (stakeholders) are affected by the issue?
- Who has an interest in the issue?
- Who is in a position to exert influence on the issue?
- Who has expressed an opinion on the issue?
- Who ought to care about the issue?[13]

In addition to these questions, a consulting firm—Human Resources Network—proposes the following three key questions to help with the issue analysis:

- Who started the ball rolling? (Historical view)
- Who is now involved? (Contemporary view)
- Who will get involved? (Future view)[14]

Answers to these questions place management in a better position to rank or prioritize the issues so that it will have a better feel for the urgency with which the issues need to be addressed.

FIGURE 19-5 Examples of Forces Leading Social Change

Leading Forces	Examples	Public Issue Realm
Events	Three Mile Island/Chernobyl nuclear plant explosions	Nuclear plant safety
	Bhopal explosion	Plant safety
	Earth Day	Environment
	Tylenol poisonings	Product tampering
	Love Canal	Toxic waste—environment
	Rely tampons	Product safety
	Ivan Boesky scandal	Insider trading abuses
	Thomas Hearings	Sexual harassment
	Valdez oil spill	Environment
Authorities/Advocates	Ralph Nader	Consumerism
	Rachel Carson	Pesticides—environment
	Rev. Martin Luther King	Civil rights
	Rev. Jesse Jackson	Blacks' rights
	Rev. Leon Sullivan	Doing business in South Africa
Literature	*Silent Spring*	Pesticide—environment
	Unsafe at Any Speed	Automobile safety
	Megatrends (John Naisbitt)	Issues identification
Organizations	Friends of the Earth	Environment
	Sierra Club	Environment
	Action for Children's Television (ACT)	Children's advertising
	Mothers Against Drunk Driving (MADD)	Highway safety/alcohol abuse
Political jurisdictions	State of Michigan-Whistle Blowers Protection Act	Employee freedom of speech
	State of Delaware	Corporate governance

Ranking or Prioritizing of Issues. Once issues have been carefully analyzed and understood, it is necessary to rank them in some form of a hierarchy of importance to the organization. We should note that some issues management systems place this step before analysis. This would especially be done if one's goal was to initially screen out those issues that are obviously not relevant and deserving of further analysis.

The prioritizing stage may range from a simple grouping of issues into categories of urgency to a more elaborate or sophisticated scoring system. Two company examples illustrate the grouping technique. Xerox categorizes issues

FIGURE 19-6   A Probability-Impact Matrix

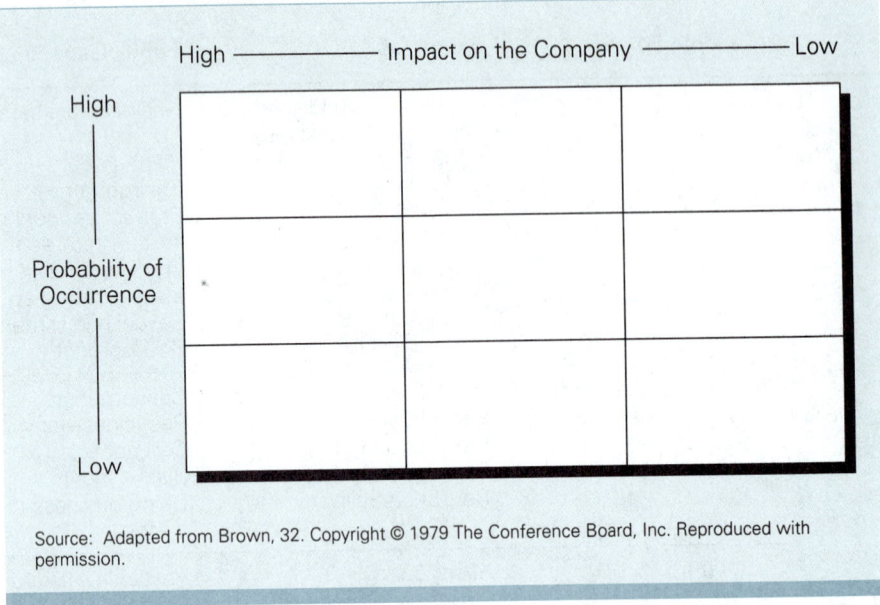

Source: Adapted from Brown, 32. Copyright © 1979 The Conference Board, Inc. Reproduced with permission.

into three classifications: (1) *High priority* (we must be well informed on these); (2) *Nice to know* (interesting but not critical or urgent); and (3) *Questionable* (not sure they are issues unless something else happens). PPG Industries groups issues into three priorities: *Priority A* (critical, warrants executive action and review); *Priority B* (warrants division general manager/staff surveillance); and *Priority C* (issue has potential impact and warrants public affairs department monitoring).[15]

A somewhat more sophisticated approach would be to use a probability-impact matrix requiring management to assess the *probability of occurrence* of the issue (high, medium, low) on one dimension with an assessment of the *impact on the company* (high, medium, low) on the other dimension. Figure 19-6 presents one view as to what this matrix might look like. Management could then place the issue in the appropriate sector of the matrix, and this would help the prioritization process.

As a variation on this theme, management could rank the issues by considering the mathematical product of their impact (for example, on a 10-point scale) multiplied by the probability of their occurrence (on a scale from 0 to 1). Figure 19-7 presents what an analysis and ranking of six issues might look like.

King provides a somewhat more elaborate issues-ranking scheme. He recommends that issues be screened on five filter criteria: strategy, relevance, actionability, criticality, and urgency.[16] Once each issue has been scored on a 10-point scale according to each criterion, issues are then ranked according to their resulting point total. Figure 19-8 on page 588 illustrates this filtering/ranking process. Other techniques that are often used in issues identification, analysis, and prioritization include

FIGURE 19-7 Issue Ranking Using Assessment of Impact and Probability of Occurrence

Issue	Probability Issue Will Occur[a]	Assessment of Impact[b]	Probability X Assessment	Issue Ranking
A	0.5	4.5	2.25	3
B	0.8	8.5	6.80	1
C	0.2	7.0	1.40	4
D	0.2	5.0	1.00	5
E	0.9	6.0	5.40	2
F	0.4	2.0	0.80	6

[a]On a scale of 0–1.
[b]On a scale of 1–10, where 10 is the highest impact. Source: Adapted from the procedure presented in Brown, 32. Copyright ø 1979. The Conference Board, Inc. Reproduced with permission.

polls/surveys, expert panels, content analysis, the Delphi technique, trend extrapolation, scenario building, and the use of precursor events or bellwethers.[17]

Earlier we described the issues identification process as involving an individual in the organization or a subscription to a newsletter or trend service. The analysis and ranking stages can be done by an individual, but more often the company has moved up to a next stage of formalization. This next stage involves assigning the issue management function to a *group of people,* often as part of a public affairs department, who begin to specialize in the issues management function. This group of specialists can provide a wide range of issues management activities, depending on the commitment of the company to the process.

Many companies today have created issues management units to alert management to emerging trends and controversies and to help mobilize the companies' resources to deal with them. Firms such as Arco, Monsanto, and Sears are among those that have created such units. At Monsanto, an issues manager organized a committee of middle managers to help do the work. At Arco, the group monitored hundreds of publications, opinion polls, and think-tank reports. It then prepared its own daily publication called *Scan,* which summarized considerable data for over 500 company middle managers and top executives. The group tracked over 140 issues in all.[18]

Formulating and Implementing Response. These two steps in the issues management process are grouped together here because we do not intend to discuss them extensively. Also, we should observe that the formulation and implementation stages in the issues management process are quite similar to the discussion

FIGURE 19-8 The Filtering and Ranking of Issues

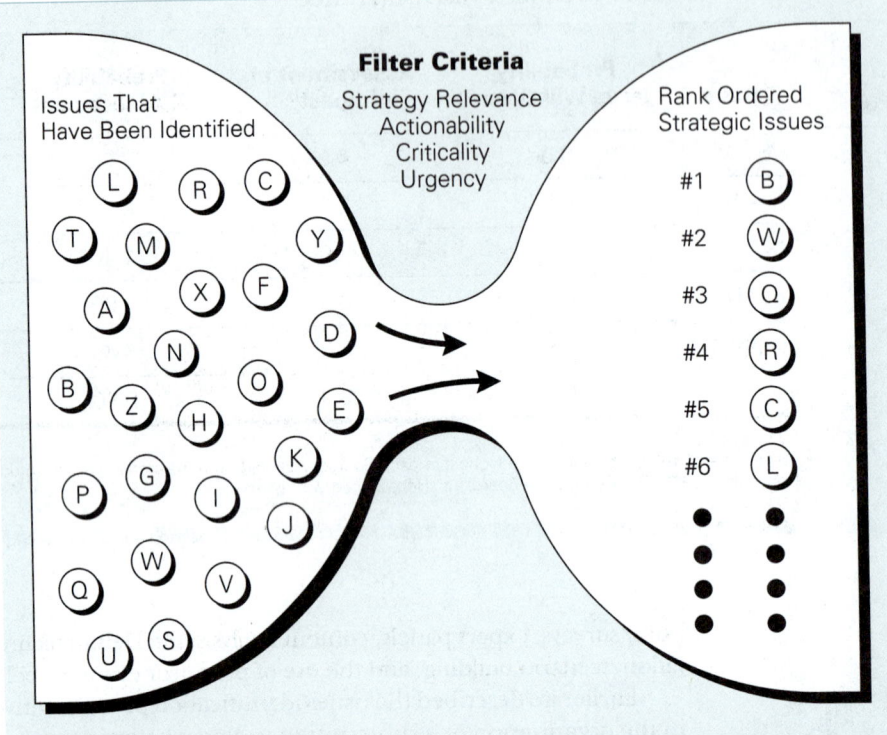

Source: William R. King, "Strategic Issue Management," in William R. King and David I. Cleland (eds.), *Strategic Planning and Management Handbook* (New York: Van Nostrand Reinhold Co., 1987), 257. Reproduced with permission.

we developed in the previous chapter, where these two stages pertained to the strategic management process as a whole.

Formulation refers to the response design process. Based on the analysis conducted, we now identify options that might be pursued in dealing with the issues, in making decisions on these options, and in implementing them. Strategy formulation refers not only to the content of what the firm intends to do but also to the overall strategy of aggressiveness in pursuing that strategy. Options might include aggressive pursuit, gradual pursuit, or selective pursuit of goals, plans, processes, or programs.[19] All of these more detailed plans are part of the strategy formulation process.

Once plans are formulated for dealing with issues, implementation becomes the focus. There are many organizational aspects that need to be addressed in the implementation process. Some of these include the clarity of the plan itself, resources needed to implement the plan, top management support, organizational structure, technical competence, and timing.[20] For additional considerations, refer to our discussion of the McKinsey 7-S framework in Chapter 18.

Evaluating, Monitoring, and Controlling. These recognizable steps in the issues management process were also treated as steps in the strategic management process in Chapter 18. The focus here is to continually evaluate the results of the company's response to the issue and to ensure that actions are kept on track. In particular, this stage requires a careful monitoring of stakeholders' opinions. A form of stakeholder audit—something derivative of the social audit discussed in Chapter 18—might be used. The information that is gathered during this final stage in the issues management process is then fed back to the earlier stages in the process so that changes or adjustments might be made as needed. Evaluation information may be useful at each stage in the process.

We have presented the issues management process as a kind of complete system. In actual practice, companies apply the stages in various degrees of formality/informality as needed. Some stages are truncated to meet the needs of different firms in different industries, as issues management is more important in some situations than in others. In addition, some firms are more committed to issues management than others. Those firms that are committed are probably members of the Issues Management Association, which was founded in 1981. Today, this association has hundreds of member firms.

Issues Development Process

A vital attribute of issues management is that issues tend to develop according to a pattern. This pattern might be thought of as a developmental or growth process or, as some have called it, a life cycle. It is important for managers to have some appreciation of this development process so that they can recognize when something becomes an issue and also because it might affect the strategy the firm employs in dealing with the issue. Companies may take a variety of courses of action depending on the stage of the issue in the process.

One view is that issues tend to follow an 8-year curve, though it is very difficult to generalize about the time frame. For the first 5 years or so, nascent issues emerge in local newspapers, are enunciated by public-interest organizations, and are detected through public opinion polling. According to Margaret Stroup, director of corporate responsibility at Monsanto, the issue is low-key and flexible at this stage.[21] During this time, the issue may reflect a felt need, receive media coverage, and attract interest-group development and growth. A typical firm may notice the issue but take no action at this stage. John Mahon's view is that more issues-oriented firms may become more active in their monitoring and in their attempts to shape or help "define the issue."[22] Active firms have the capacity to prevent issues from going any further, through either effective response to the issue or effective lobbying.

In the fifth or sixth year of the cycle, national media attention and leading political jurisdictions (for example, cities or states) may address the issue. Issues managers have identified a number of "precursor" or bellwether states where national issues frequently arise first. A number of experts think these include California, Oregon, Florida, Michigan, and Connecticut.[23] Quite often, federal government attention is generated in the form of studies and hearings; legislation, regulation, and litigation follow. Figure 19-9 presents one view of what this issue development life cycle process might look like.

We should note that the stages in the process, especially the early stages, might occur in a different sequence or in an iterative pattern. Further, not all issues complete the process; some are resolved before they reach the stage of legislation or regulation. Thomas G. Marx takes the view that issues go from a *social expectation*, to becoming a *political issue*, to *legislation*, and then to *social control*.

Marx illustrates this evolution through two examples. First, consider the issue of environmental protection. The social expectation was manifested in Rachel Carson's book *Silent Spring* (1963); it became a political issue in Eugene McCarthy's political platform (1968); it resulted in legislation in 1971–1972 with

FIGURE 19-9 Issue Development of Life Cycle Process

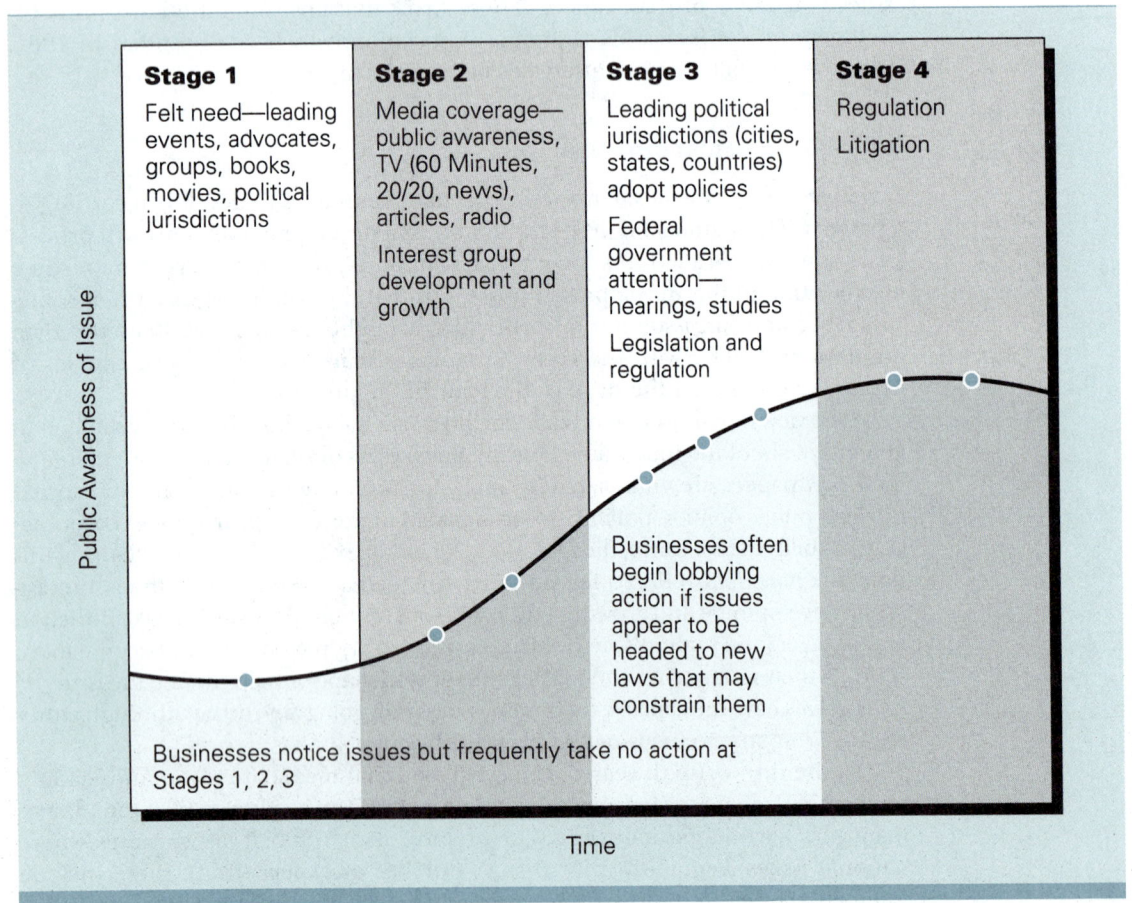

the creation of the EPA; and it was reflected in social control by emission standards, pollution fines, product recalls, and environmental permits. The second example is product/occupant safety. The social expectation was manifested in Ralph Nader's book *Unsafe at Any Speed* (1964); it became a political issue through the *National Traffic Auto Safety Act* and Motor Vehicle Safety hearings (1966); it resulted in legislation in 1966 with the passage of the *Motor Vehicle Safety Act* and mandatory seat belt usage laws passed in four states (1984); and it was reflected in social control through the ordering of seat belts in all cars (1967), defects litigation, product recalls, and driver fines.[24]

Issues Management in Practice

Few studies have been conducted on actual issues management programs as they are being implemented in companies. One study that has provided some interesting insights, however, was conducted by Steven Wartick and Robert Rude. They studied eight companies that were selected based on discussions with representatives of the Issues Management Association and the Public Affairs Council. They then interviewed the major issues management manager at each of the companies. The interviews focused on three major areas: (1) administration and organization, (2) activities and approach, and (3) success factors.[25]

Administration and Organization.
While discussing administration and organization, that is—*where* issues management fits into the organization structure and *what* resources are available to support it—Wartick and Rude found that the companies fell into two groups of four. In Group A were four companies in which issues management was a separate unit. Group B consisted of four companies in which issues management was a part of the public affairs/public relations function.

In Group A the separate units saw issues management as a broad function. The staff sizes ranged from two to six people, and each staff person had access to top management either through a direct reporting channel or through a board committee. The Group A managers did not make actual decisions as to how the company would respond to an issue but rather made alternative recommendations to top management.

In Group B, issues management had a much lower profile, and the companies' activities were tied to a particular task such as advertising. Various roles were played by Group B managers—one sought to increase managerial proaction, one served as an environmental scanner, one generated alternative responses on an ad hoc basis, and one was just beginning an issues management program that was to be integrated with the public relations function. Wartick and Rude observed that in all of the Group B companies, each emphasized only one aspect of the issues management process such as issues identification, evaluation, or response.[26]

Activities and Approach. When activities and approach were studied among the eight companies, there were similarities and differences. The similarities centered around tools and techniques. Position papers, issue briefs, pamphlets, scenarios, and topic reports were the common tools used in both groups. Three sets of differences were observed. First, Group A companies took a more active role in setting the issues agenda than did Group B companies. Second, at Group A companies the managers' focus was external and strategic. The Group B companies focused more on internal communication and on being responders rather than initiators. Third, Group A managers saw the corporation as a whole as the unit of analysis, while Group B managers focused more on departments.[27]

Success Factors. When the two groups considered success factors, they both agreed that there were four key factors in successful issues management implementation: (1) top management support *and* involvement are necessary, (2) field *and* related departments must be involved, (3) issues management must fill *a void* in decision making and must adapt to the firm's culture, and (4) *output*, not process, must be emphasized.[28]

Wartick and Rude think that the future of issues management is bright if the field can successfully address two key problems. First, issues management has an identity problem. Issues managers need to "carve out" what they think the field is capable of contributing to organizational success. Second, they must work toward minimizing the conflict between filling a void on one hand and pursuing professionalism on the other. Professionalizing the field is not a substitute for filling a decision void in the organization. A real contribution must be made if professionalism is to be meaningful.[29]

Issues management faces a serious challenge in business today. From the standpoint of what is happening in the stakeholder environment, there is no question that it is needed. To become a permanent part of the organization, however, issues management will have to continuously prove itself. We can conceptually talk about the process with ease, but the field still remains somewhat nebulous and is struggling to become more scientific and legitimate. Managers in the real world want results, and if issues management cannot deliver these results, then it will be destined to failure as a management process.

Some companies have claimed specific successes from their issues management programs. S. C. Johnson & Sons, the maker of floor waxes and other chemicals, claims it removed environmentally chancy fluorocarbons from its aerosol sprays 3 years before federal action required the industry to do so. Sears claims it spotted the flammable-nightwear controversy early and got nonflammable goods into its stores before government action mandated it. Bank of America claims it was alerted early by its issues managers about a practice known as "redlining" and took action to change its lending policies 2 years before Congress required banks to disclose whether they were barring all loans in certain parts of a city. According to the bank, its early action reduced its eventual cost of compliance significantly and spared it "a lot of grief and antagonism from cities and public-interest groups."[30] In the final analysis, specific successes such as these will ensure the future of issues management.

CRISIS MANAGEMENT

If issues management is considered a newcomer in terms of management processes, **crisis management** is still in the infancy stage. In fact, crisis management as a management term is largely a product of the mid-1980s. This was the era of the megacrisis: Union Carbide's Bhopal disaster, Johnson & Johnson's Tylenol poisonings, and Procter & Gamble's Rely tampon crisis. Other significant crises included the following:

1. Star-Kist Foods was charged with shipping rancid and decomposing tuna.
2. General Dynamics was indicted for its fraudulent billing practices.
3. Texaco was slammed with a $10.5 billion judgment, after which it considered filing for Chapter 11 bankruptcy protection.
4. E. F. Hutton was embarrassed by an overdraft scandal.
5. First National Bank of Boston pleaded guilty to charges of failure to report $1.2 billion in transactions with international banks.
6. Chrysler Corporation was indicted for disconnecting odometer cables on new cars, using the cars, and then selling them as new.
7. Jalisco cheese was accused of containing deadly bacteria, resulting in the deaths of dozens of people.

The Nature of Crises

There are many kinds of crises. Those we have just mentioned have all been associated with major stakeholder groups and have achieved high-visibility status. Hurt customers, hurt employees, hurt stockholders, and unfair practices are the concerns of modern crisis management. Not all crises involve such public or ethical issues, but these kinds of crises almost ensure front-page status. Major companies can be seriously damaged by such episodes.

What is a crisis? Webster's dictionary states that a *crisis* is a "turning point for better or worse," an "emotionally significant event," or a "decisive moment." We all think of crises as being emotion-charged. However, we do *not* always think of them as a turning point for *better* or for *worse*. The implication here is that a crisis is a decisive moment that, if handled one way, could make things worse but, if handled another way, could make things better. Choice is present, and how the crisis is handled *can* make a difference.

Consider, for a moment, the case referred to earlier wherein Star-Kist Foods, a subsidiary of H. J. Heinz Co., faced a management crisis. Gerald Clay, age 43, was appointed general manager of the Canadian subsidiary and was given the mandate to develop a 5-year business strategy for the firm. Just after his arrival in Canada, the crisis hit: Canadian Broadcasting Corporation accused his company of shipping 1 million cans of rancid and decomposing tuna. Dubbed "tunagate" by the media, the crisis dragged on for weeks. With guidance from Heinz, Clay chose to keep quiet even as the Canadian prime minister ordered the tuna seized. The silence cost plenty. According to Clay's boss, "We were massacred in the press." The company, which used to have half the Canadian tuna market, watched revenues plunge by 90 percent. Clay's boss observed that the company's future was in doubt.[31]

Being prepared for crises has become a primary activity in a growing number of companies today. Part of being prepared entails knowing something about the nature of crises. Steven Fink has conducted a major survey of Fortune 500 firms on the subject and has written one of the first books available on crisis management. Fink's survey disclosed that a staggering 89 percent of those who responded agreed that "a crisis in business today is as inevitable as death and taxes," but 50 percent of the executive respondents admitted that they did not have a prepared crisis plan. Of those who reported as already having had a crisis, 42 percent *still* did not have any sort of crisis management plan in preparation for another crisis.[32]

The following situations were identified in which the executives felt they were vulnerable to crisis: industrial accidents, environmental problems, union problems/strikes, product recalls, investor relations, hostile takeovers, proxy fights, rumors/media leaks, government regulatory problems, acts of terrorism, and embezzlement.[33] We have discussed practically all these situations in this book. The majority of them emanate from the major stakeholder groups: consumers, employees, communities, and shareholders. Of the major crises the companies had recently experienced, the majority reported the following outcomes: the crises escalated in intensity, were subjected to close media and government scrutiny, interfered with normal business operations, and damaged the company's bottom line.[34]

The Four Crisis Stages

According to Fink, a crisis may consist of as many as four distinct stages: (1) prodromal crisis stage, (2) acute crisis stage, (3) chronic crisis stage, and (4) crisis resolution stage.[35]

The *prodromal crisis stage* is the warning stage. ("Prodromal" is a medical term that refers to a previous notice or warning.) This warning stage could also be thought of as a symptom stage. While it could be called a "precrisis" stage, this presupposes that one knows that a crisis is coming. Perhaps management should adopt this perspective: *Watch each situation with the thought that it could be a crisis in the making.* Early symptoms might be quite obvious, such as a case where a social activist group tells management it will boycott if a certain problem is not addressed. Or the symptom may be more subtle, as in the case where defect rates on a particular product a company makes start edging up over time.

The *acute crisis stage* is the stage in which the crisis actually occurs. There is no turning back; the incident has occurred. Damage has been done at this point, and it is now up to management to handle or contain the damage. If the prodromal stage is the precrisis stage, the acute stage is *the* crisis stage. The crucial decision point in which things may get worse or better has been reached.

The *chronic crisis stage* is the lingering period. It may be the period of investigations, audits, or in-depth news stories. Management may see it as a period of recovery, self-analysis, or self-doubt. In Fink's survey of major companies, he found that crises tended to linger as much as two and a half times longer in firms without crisis management plans than in firms with such plans.

The *crisis resolution stage* is the final stage. This is the goal of all crisis management efforts. Fink argues that when an early warning sign of a crisis is noted, the manager should seize control swiftly and determine the most direct and expedient route to resolution. If the warning signs were missed in the first stage, the goal is to speed up all phases and reach the final one.

Figure 19-10 presents one way in which these four stages might be portrayed. Note that the phases overlap and that each phase varies in intensity and duration.

Other views of a crisis are possible. Gerald C. Meyers, former chairman of American Motors Corp., and others lay out the scenario for a *poorly managed crisis*, which typically follows a predictable pattern. The pattern is as follows:

- Early indications that trouble is brewing occur.
- Warnings are ignored/played down.
- Warnings build to a climax.
- Pressure mounts.
- Executives are often overwhelmed or can't cope effectively.
- Quick-fix alternatives look appealing. Hasty moves create trouble.
- Clamming up versus opening up options present themselves.
- Most firms choose the former.
- A siege mentality prevails.[36]

Visualizing a model or pattern of a poorly managed crisis is valuable because it illustrates how *not* to do it—a lesson that many managers might find quite valuable.

Managing Business Crises

There are many suggestions for managing a crisis, though they cannot be reduced to a cookbook recipe. Fink argues there are three vital stages: identifying the crisis, isolating the crisis, and managing the crisis. All should be done *quickly*.[37] Another view is that a series of steps must be taken. Each of these steps is discussed next and summarized in Figure 19-11 on page 597.

Identifying Areas of Vulnerability. This is considered the first step. Some areas of vulnerability are obvious, such as potential chemical spills. Others are more subtle. The key seems to be in developing a greater consciousness of how things

FIGURE 19-10 Four Stages in a Management Crisis

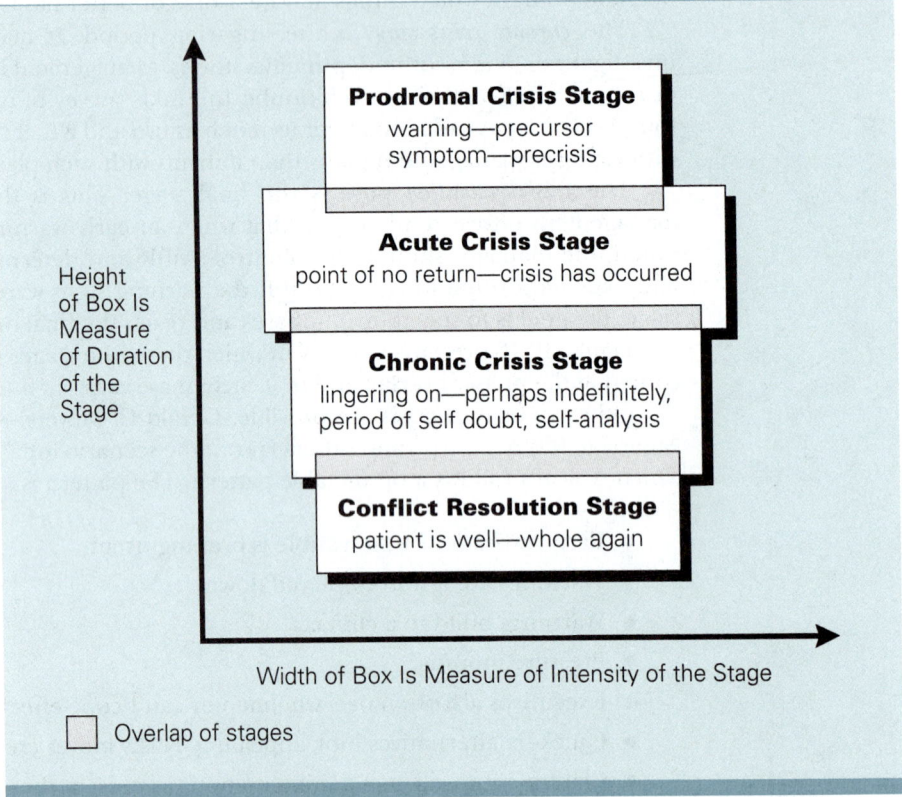

can blow up. At Heinz, after the "tunagate" incident, a vice-president set up brainstorming sessions. He said, "We're brainstorming about how we would be affected by everything from a competitor who had a serious quality problem to a scandal involving a Heinz executive."[38]

Developing a Plan. A plan for dealing with the most serious crisis threats is a logical next step. One of the most crucial issues is *communications planning*. After a Dow Chemical railroad car derailed near Toronto, forcing the evacuation of 250,000 people, Dow Canada prepared information kits on the hazards of its products so that executives would be knowledgeable enough to respond properly if a similar crisis arose in the future. Dow Canada also trained executives in interviewing techniques. This effort paid off several years later when an accident caused a chemical spill into a river that supplied drinking water for several nearby towns. The company's emergency-response team arrived at the site almost immediately and established a press center that distributed information about the chemicals. In addition, the company recruited a neutral expert to speak on the hazards and how to deal with them. Officials praised Dow for its handling of this crisis.[39]

FIGURE **19-11** Steps in Crisis Management

1. Identifying areas of vulnerability
   A. Obvious areas
   B. Subtle areas

2. Developing a plan for dealing with threats
   A. Communications planning is vital
   B. Training executives in product dangers and dealing with media

3. Forming crisis teams
   A. Vital to successful crisis management
   B. Identifying executives who can work well under stress

4. Simulating crisis drills
   A. Experience/practice is helpful
   B. "War rooms" serve as a gathering place for team members

5. Learning from experience
   A. Assess effectiveness of crisis strategies
   B. Move from reaction to proaction

Forming Crisis Teams. Another step that can be taken as part of an overall planning effort is the formation of *crisis teams*. Such teams have played key roles in many well-managed disasters. A good example is the team formed at Procter & Gamble when its Rely tampon was linked with the dreaded disease toxic shock syndrome. The team was quickly assembled, a vice-president was appointed to head it, and after 1 week the decision was made to remove Rely from marketplace shelves. The quick action earned the firm praise, and it paid off for P&G in the long run.

Another task for assembling crisis teams is identifying managers who can cope effectively with stress. Not every executive can handle a fast-moving, high-pressured, ambiguous decision environment like that created by a crisis. Early identification of executives who can handle this is important. We should also note that it is not always the CEO who can best perform in such a crisis atmosphere.

Simulating Crisis Drills. Some companies have even gone so far as to simulate crisis drills just for the experience of creating highly stressful situations in which managers might "practice" what they might do in a real crisis. United Airlines, for example, uses such drills. It has created a simulation that one of its planes had crashed. The executives, who carry beepers, are then rushed to a "war room" where strategy is decided.[40]

Learning from Experience. A final stage of crisis management is learning from experience. At this point, managers need to ask themselves what exactly they have learned from past crises and how that knowledge may be used in the future. Part of this stage entails an assessment of the effectiveness of the firm's crisis-handling strategies and an identification of areas where improvements in capabilities need to be developed. Without a crisis management system of some kind in place, the organization will find itself reacting to crises after they have occurred. If learning and preparation for the future is occurring, however, the firm may engage in more proactive behavior.[41]

SUMMARY

Crisis management, like issues management, is not a panacea. In spite of well-intended management efforts, all crises will not be worked out in the company's favor. Nevertheless, being prepared for the inevitable makes sense, especially in today's world of instantaneous communications and obsessive media coverage. Whether we are talking about the long term, the intermediate term, or the short term, managements need to be prepared to handle the turbulent public environment.

A range of management approaches is available to impose some order on these decision processes. At the macro level, enterprise-level strategy and corporate public policy are essential underpinnings. Environmental analysis is a vital component of the strategic management process, and issues management helps a firm deal with those current issues that affect the firm's immediate and future stakeholder environments. Finally, crisis management is there standing ready for those traumatic "surprises" that firms today inevitably face. Taken together, all these processes provide a bundle of approaches that all managers should be acquainted with for dealing with the turbid and fluid stakeholder environment. Effective management does not just recommend these kinds of approaches but mandates them. To do less is not to live up to a sound code of stakeholder management professionalism.

DISCUSSION QUESTIONS

1. Which of the major stages in the issues management process do you think is the most important? Why?

2. What is your opinion of Naisbitt's belief that the major issues start as isolated, local events? Give an example you are aware of that supports or appears to refute his hypothesis.

3. Using Figure 19-5 as your basis, identify one example, other than the ones listed there, of each of the leading force categories: events, authorities/advocates, literature, organizations, and political jurisdictions.

4. Identify a crisis that has occurred in your life or in the life of someone you know, and briefly explain it in terms of the four crisis stages: prodromal, acute, chronic, and resolution.

5. One of the steps suggested in crisis management is the development of a crisis management team. List the kinds of personal and managerial characteristics you think are important in someone who might serve on such a team.

ENDNOTES

1. Liam Fahey, "Issues Management: Two Approaches," *Strategic Planning Management* (November, 1986), 81, 85–96.
2. *Ibid.*, 81.
3. *Ibid.*, 86.
4. Igor Ansoff, "Strategic Issue Management," *Strategic Management Journal* (Vol. I, 1980), 131–148.
5. William R. King, "Strategic Issue Management," in William R. King and David I. Cleland (eds.), *Strategic Planning and Management Handbook* (New York: Van Nostrand Reinhold, 1987), 252–264.
6. Joseph F. Coates, Vary T. Coates, Jennifer Jarratt, and Lisa Heinz, *Issues and Management* (Mt. Airy, MD: Lomond Publications, 1986), 19–20.
7. *Ibid.*, 18.
8. *Ibid.*, 32.
9. Myron Magnet, "Who Needs a Trend-Spotter?" *Fortune* (December 9, 1985), 51–56.
10. *Ibid.*, 52.
11. *Ibid.*, 56.
12. T. Graham Molitor, "How to Anticipate Public Policy Changes," SAM *Advanced Management Journal* (42, 1977), 4.
13. King, 259.
14. James K. Brown, *This Business of Issues: Coping with the Company's Environment* (New York: The Conference Board, 1979), 45.
15. *Ibid.*, 33.
16. King, 257.
17. Coates et al., 46.
18. Earl C. Gottschalk, Jr., "Firms Hiring New Type of Manager to Study Issues, Emerging Troubles," *The Wall Street Journal* (June 10, 1982), 33, 36.
19. I. C. MacMillan and P. E. Jones, "Designing Organizations to Compete," *Journal of Business Strategy* (4, 1984), 13.
20. Roy Wernham, "Implementation: The Things That Matter," in King and Cleland, 1987: 453.
21. Gottschalk, 3.
22. John Mahon, "Issues Management: The Issue of Definition," *Strategic Planning Management* (November, 1986), 81–85.
23. Gottschalk, 33.
24. Thomas C. Marx, "Integrating Public Affairs and Strategic Planning," *California Management Review* (Fall, 1986), 145.
25. Steven L. Wartick and Robert E. Rude, "Issues Management: Fad or Function," *California Management Review* (Fall, 1986), 134–140.
26. *Ibid.*, 130–131.
27. *Ibid.*, 131–132.
28. *Ibid.*, 132.
29. *Ibid.*, 136–139.
30. Gottschalk, 21.
31. "How Companies Are Learning to Prepare for the Worst," *Business Week* (December 23, 1985), 74.
32. Steven Fink, *Crisis Management: Planning for the Inevitable* (New York: Amacom, 1986).
33. *Ibid.*, 68.
34. *Ibid.*, 69. See also, Sharon H. Garrison, *The Financial Impact of Corporate Events on Corporate Stakeholders* (New York: Quorem Books, 1990).
35. *Ibid.*, 20.
36. *Business Week* (December 23, 1985), 74–75.
37. Fink, 70.
38. *Business Week* (December 23, 1985), 76.
39. *Ibid.*
40. *Ibid.*
41. Ian Mitroff, Paul Shrivastava, and Firdaus Udwadia, "Effective Crisis Management" *The Academy of Management Executive* (November, 1987), 285.

CHAPTER **TWENTY**

Public Affairs Management

CHAPTER OBJECTIVES

After studying this chapter, you should be able to:

- Describe the evolution of the public affairs function in organizations.

- Identify the major functions of public affairs departments.

- Highlight trends that have been identified with respect to the public affairs function.

- Characterize the elements of an international public affairs effort.

- Link public affairs strategy with organizational characteristics.

- Indicate how public affairs might be incorporated into every manager's job.

"*Corporate public affairs*," or "*public affairs management*," is an umbrella term used by companies to describe the management process we have been discussing in Part 5 of this book. The public affairs function is a logical and increasingly frequent outcome of the overall strategic management process, which we introduced in Chapter 18. As an overall concept, it embraces corporate public policy, which we also introduced in Chapter 18, and issues management, which we treated in Chapter 19. Indeed, many issues and crisis management programs either begin in public affairs departments or intimately involve public affairs professionals.

It is easy to get confused at this point by all the different terms that are used to describe management's efforts to address the social environment. Part of the confusion arises from the fact that companies use different titles for the same functions. For example, the terms that are often interchangeably used by firms are "public affairs/external affairs," "public policy/corporate social responsibility," and "public issues management/public affairs management." Some companies create public affairs departments without even addressing the strategic management issue or enterprise-level strategy.

In a comprehensive system, which we have been describing in Part 5 of this book, the overall flow of activity would be as follows. A firm would engage in *strategic management,* and part of that would be *enterprise-level strategy,* which poses the question, "What do we stand for?" The answers to this question should help the firm to form a *corporate public policy,* which might be a more specific posture on the public, social, or stakeholder environment. Some firms call this a **public affairs strategy**. Two important planning aspects of corporate public policy include *issues management* and, often, *crisis management.* These two planning aspects frequently derive from or are related to environmental analysis, which we covered in Chapter 18. Some companies refer to these processes as the **corporate public affairs** function. These processes are typically housed, from a departmental perspective, in a public affairs department. Figure 20-1 helps illustrate likely relationships among these processes.

Our focus in this chapter will be on the organizational aspects of the public affairs management function. We will consider how public affairs has evolved in business firms, what issues public affairs currently faces, and how public affairs thinking might be incorporated into the operating manager's job. This latter issue is important because public affairs, to be most effective, must be thought of as an indispensable part of every manager's job, not as an isolated department that alone is responsible for the public issues of the firm.

FIGURE 20-1 Relationships Among Key Corporate Public Affairs Concepts

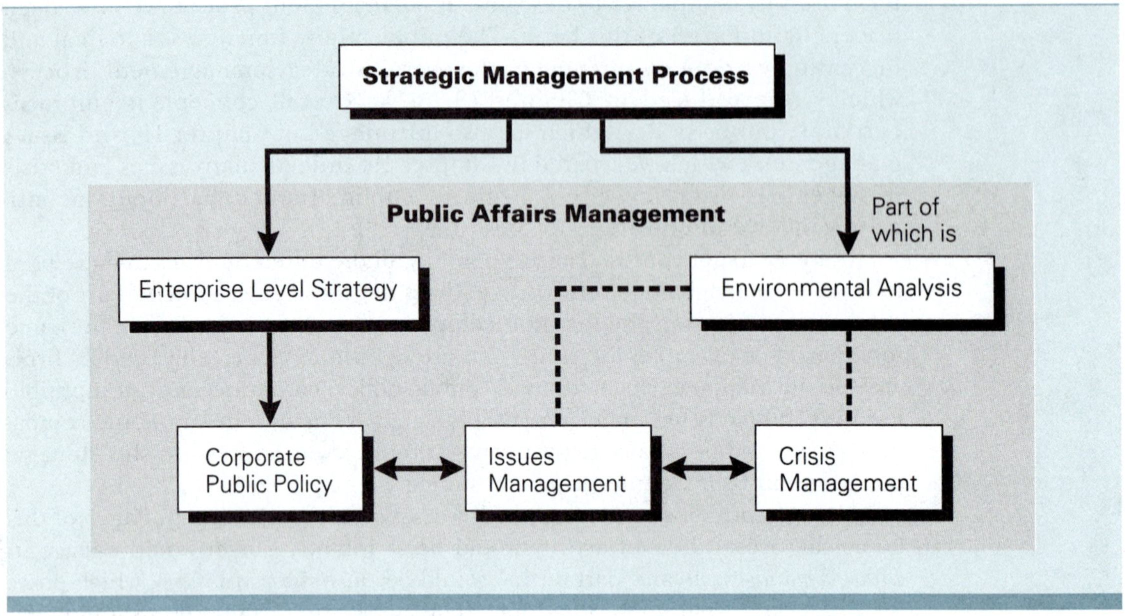

```
                    Strategic Management Process
                              |
        ┌─────────────────────┴─────────────────────┐
        |         Public Affairs Management          | Part of
        |                                            | which is
   Enterprise Level Strategy            Environmental Analysis
        |                                            |
        ↓                                            ↓
   Corporate          Issues              Crisis
   Public Policy ←→   Management  ←→      Management
```

EVOLUTION OF CORPORATE PUBLIC AFFAIRS

A comprehensive history of the public affairs function is not needed for our purposes, but it is helpful to understand some of its beginnings. One report traces a public affairs department back to a company organization chart in the early 1950s, but that is an isolated case. A 1980 study found that 60 percent of 400 large companies that then had public affairs departments had created them within the previous decade.[1] Thus, the public affairs function as we know it today was an outgrowth of the social activism of the 1960s. Just as significant federal laws were passed in the early 1970s to address such issues as discrimination, environmental protection, occupational health and safety, and consumer safety, corporations responded with a surge of public affairs departments. Public affairs, therefore, is clearly a product of the 1970s and 1980s.

Public affairs as a management function evolved out of isolated company initiatives to handle such diverse activities as community relations, corporate philanthropy and contributions, governmental affairs, lobbying, grassroots programs, corporate responsibility, and public relations. In some firms the public relations people handled issues about communication with external publics, so it is not surprising that public affairs partially grew out of public relations. Part of the confusion between public relations and public affairs is traceable to the fact that some corporate public relations executives changed their *titles,* but not their *functions,* to public affairs.

Richard Armstrong, for many years president of the Public Affairs Council, has addressed the distinctions between **public relations (PR)** and *public affairs* (PA) in terms of their relative emphasis, interest, and direction. He submits that the terminology is very important. The principal distinctions he makes are as follows: (1) Whereas PR deals with government as one of many publics, PA professionals are *experts* on government, and (2) whereas PR has many communication responsibilities, PA deals with issues management and serves as a corporate conscience.[2]

In spite of these sharp differences, the two functions still overlap or crisscross in some companies. Some PR practitioners see PA as a growth opportunity in which to invest their skills. This is because the practice of PA requires all the skills of the PR discipline, plus it gives the PR practitioners an opportunity to increase the importance of their roles and to become closer to, if not a part of, top management.[3] Many PR executives would argue that their roles are already substantive, as well as stylistic, and that the differences between the two groups are not all that great in actual practice.

PUBLIC AFFAIRS IN THE EARLY 1980S

The major study that provided the first comprehensive baseline information on the public affairs function in corporations was a 1981 survey of 1,001 large- and medium-size companies by a research group at Boston University. Their study included virtually all of the Fortune 500 companies and the Fortune 50s in financial services, retailing, and utilities. The remainder of the sample was chosen from the *Business Week* 1000. In addition to their broad survey, they conducted in-depth case studies of four firms: a utility, a commercial bank, a computer company, and a chemical company.

Results of the Broad Survey

The public affairs broad survey revealed that more than one-half of all PA units were created during the 1970s and that one-third were created since 1975. Budgets and professional staffs grew during this period, and the researchers concluded that the growth represented both a major new cost center for business and the most significant change in professional management since the 1970s when strategic planning flourished. The study also revealed that 60 percent of the PA departments reported directly to the corporate chairman, president, and/or CEO, thus providing them with access to top management on a regular basis. Most companies seemed to be moving toward an expanded public affairs function at that time.[4]

The broad survey also addressed the *scope of activities* that were part of the public affairs function. The majority of the firms, with the noted percentages, indicated that the following activities were considered PA responsibilities:

- Community relations (85 percent)
- Government relations (84 percent)
- Corporate contributions (72 percent)
- Media relations (70 percent)

Other activities reported, along with the share of firms engaging in the activity, included:

- Stockholder relations (49 percent)
- Advertising (40 percent)
- Consumer affairs (39 percent)
- Graphics (34 percent)
- Institutional investor relations (34 percent)
- Customer relations (24 percent)

Three major functions—social and political intelligence, external action programs, and internal communications—were addressed in each of these activity categories.[5]

Results of the Case Studies of Four Firms

In-depth case studies by the same research group found that there were wide variations among the firms in terms of how they handled certain aspects of public affairs. The differences showed up most dramatically in four areas: (1) structuring PA offices, (2) handling government relations, (3) relating external relations to planning and operations, and (4) public issues management.

The Boston University research group was able to make a number of generalizations based on their studies. Two categories stand out: (1) internal influence of PA and (2) external influence of PA. *Internally,* PA has its greatest influence:

1. When it focuses on matters that have short-term implications for line managers. Influence wanes with a longer-term orientation unless immediate relevance to line managers could be made known.
2. When PA develops in parallel with the firm's strategic planning system.
3. When firms are centrally organized. In centralized firms where PA offices are typically located at headquarters, PA officers can exercise greater influence than when decision making is geographically decentralized.[6]

Externally, influence is most dramatically felt when corporate efforts are present in Washington. Companies that use long-range strategic planning of a qualitative nature are more influential before Congress and regulatory agencies than firms that do not.[7]

THE CURRENT VIEW OF CORPORATE PUBLIC AFFAIRS

The Public Affairs Council, a major Washington-based professional association, has defined the current view of what constitutes corporate public affairs as follows:

> The management function responsible for monitoring and interpreting the corporation's non-commercial environment and managing the company's response to those factors.[8]

This definition is consistent with how we have been viewing the public affairs management function. The council has also stated what it views to be the functions of a public affairs department. These are presented in Figure 20-2.

In comparing this list of functions with those used in the Boston University survey, we should note that this current list does not include activities such as advertising and graphics. The modern view of a public affairs department is clearly one in which management functions are stressed.

In 1985, the Boston University research group conducted another survey with the aim of providing additional insights into the public affairs function as it had evolved since their 1981 study. James E. Post, director of the public affairs research program, has provided some initial impressions of the study's results. He indicates that the dominant issue now seems to be that of *productivity* of the PA function—how to ensure that good value is being received for PA dollars spent.[9] Raymond L. Hoewing, vice-president of the Public Affairs Council, observed that the turbulent environment of the 1980s included the following forces: technological change, international competition, deregulation, changing concepts of corporate responsibility, mergers and buyouts, plant closings, write-offs, joint ventures, overseas sourcing, ceaseless personnel cutbacks, and early retirements.[10] This has hardly been a positive environment for public affairs growth, and these trends have continued into the 1990s.

Trends and Observations of the 1985 Survey

The 1985 survey of public affairs professionals revealed the following trends and observations, most of which are still valid today.

1. The public affairs management profession has continued its growth.

FIGURE 20-2 Functions of a Public Affairs Department

What are the functions normally conducted by a public affairs department? Here is a quick way to view the responsibilities of the typical public affairs department:

Political Action
- Political action committees
- Political education
- Grassroots activities
- Communications on political issues

Community Involvement/Corporate Responsibility
- Community relations
- Philanthropy
- Social responsibility programs
- Volunteerism

International Public Affairs
- Monitoring international sociopolitical developments
- Host-country government relations
- Risk assessment/responses

Issues Management
- Issues identification
- Issues analysis
- Responses

Government Relations
- Federal
- State
- Local

Strategic Planning
- Sociopolitical monitoring
- Identification of emerging issues
- Inputs to business and strategic plans

Communications
- Media relations
- Employee communications
- Public relations

Source: *The Public Affairs Council,* Annual Report, 1991 (Washington, DC: The Public Affairs Council, 1991), 4. Reproduced with permission.

2. More firms have PA units than 5 years prior, and PA is seen as an increasingly legitimate part of all that top managers do.
3. The complexity of the internal public affairs mission is increasing, and the shift is more toward a coordinated or integrated PA system and away from a "running our own show" approach.
4. The complexity of the environment has required PA officers to focus more on management and less on PA specialty work such as lobbying.
5. The number of PA professionals appears to be stable to slightly increasing.
6. Budgets have not grown quite as rapidly as in the past.
7. There is a sharper focus to the PA mission than was present in the earlier study. Specifically, government relations is a function in 90 percent of the firms and community relations in about two-thirds of the firms.
8. Reductions were found in media relations and corporate contributions.
9. There is a heightened emphasis on those PA activities that are more closely tied to the corporate mission.
10. Two growth areas are issues management and international public affairs.[11]

James E. Post and Patricia C. Kelley provide an excellent summary of the public affairs function in organizations today. They submit:

> The public affairs function serves as a window: Looking out, the organization can observe the changing environment. Looking in, the stakeholders in that environment can observe, try to understand, and interact with the organization.[12]

Viewed in this way, it is easy to understand how Post and Kelley can conclude that the "product" of the public affairs department is the smoothing of relationships with external stakeholders and the management of company-specific issues.

A significant challenge today for public affairs professionals is to conduct these functions in an ethical fashion. There are many opportunities for questionable practices, especially in such arenas as political action, government relations, and communications. Therefore, it is encouraging to know that a code of conduct or set of ethical guidelines has been established for individuals working in public affairs. These ethical guidelines are set forth in Figure 20-3. They deserve careful scrutiny.

International Public Affairs as a Growth Area

It is important at this point to provide some additional comments on the international PA area. In 1983, the Public Affairs Council identified the international PA area as a new corporate function and formed a task force to investigate this area. Three points seemed to emerge time and again. First, it became obvious that more and more significant public affairs challenges and problems are occurring in the

FIGURE 20-3 Ethical Guidelines for Public Affairs Professionals

ETHICAL GUIDELINES

The public affairs professional . . .
. . . maintains professional relationships based on honesty and reliable information, and therefore:

1. Represents accurately his or her organization's policies on economic and political matters to government, employees, shareholders, community interests, and others.
2. Serves always as a source of reliable information, discussing the varied aspects of complex public issues within the context and constraints of the advocacy role.
3. Recognizes the diverse viewpoints within the public policy process, knowing that disagreement on issues is both inevitable and healthy.

The public affairs professional . . .
. . . seeks to protect the integrity of the public policy process and the political system, and he or she therefore:

1. Publicly acknowledges his or her role as a legitimate participant in the public policy process and discloses whatever work-related information the law requires.
2. Knows, respects and abides by federal and state laws that apply to lobbying and related public affairs activities.
3. Knows and respects the laws governing campaign finance and other political activities, and abides by the letter and intent of those laws.

The public affairs professional . . .
. . . understands the interrelation of business interests with the larger public interests, and therefore:

1. Endeavors to ensure that responsible and diverse external interests and views concerning the needs of society are considered within the corporate decision-making process.
2. Bears the responsibility for management review of public policies which may bring corporate interests into conflict with other interests.
3. Acknowledges dual obligations—to advocate the interests of his or her employer, and to preserve the openness and integrity of the democratic process.
4. Presents to his or her employer an accurate assessment of the political and social realities that may affect corporate operations.

Source: The Public Affairs Council (Washington, DC).

international arena, with greater impact on the company. Second, the number of firms with effective international PA capacities is small and growing very slowly. Third, the task force found that serious internal and external challenges often make an international PA program more difficult than a domestic program.[13] Figure 20-4 presents the elements that are commonly found in an international public affairs program.

FIGURE 20-4   Elements of an International Public Affairs Program

Environmental assessment/issue identification and management

- Identify, track, and assess issues and trends
- Achieve systematic internal issues awareness and coordination
- Assess political, social, and cultural elements of risk in projects, products, investments, and operations
- Issue research and analysis
- Emerging issue forecasting

Government relations activities

- Washington, DC
- Foreign-country level
- Regional level: EEC, OECD, ASEAN, etc.
- International level: UN, ILO, WHO, WIPO, etc.

Community action/involvement

- Community outreach
- Assess company impact on communities where located
- Philanthropy
- Corporate social responsibility activities
- Development activities
- Political involvement

Corporate public affairs training and constituency development

- Public affairs staff development
- Relations with line managers and other staff groups
- Employee relations
- Shareholder relations
- Media relations
- Academic relations
- Interest group relations
- External constituency group relations, e.g., suppliers

Corporate policy and strategy development

- External factor assessment in strategy planning and management decision-making
- Effect change in corporate strategy and policy to minimize risk and/or maximize opportunity
- Cost/benefit analyses of policy options based on external factors
- Assess impact/compliance with codes of conduct and company ethical standards

Source: "International Public Affairs: A Preliminary Report by a PAC Task Force" (Washington, DC: Public Affairs Council, April, 1983), 3. Reproduced with permission.

International public affairs, to function properly, must balance externally and internally focused activities. Externally, the central challenge is to manage the company's relations with various host countries where business is conducted. Requirements here include understanding and meeting host-country needs and dealing with diverse local constituencies, audiences, and governments. Internally, international PA programs must establish and coordinate external programs, educate company officials on PA techniques, and assist wherever possible the company's efforts to improve operations, activities, and image.[14] Companies that have been noted for having well-developed international public affairs programs include IBM, Avon, Standard Oil of California, and Dow Corning Corporation.

Despite the significant and growing challenges to international business, most multinational firms responded with only a limited improvement in their international PA efforts, according to a study conducted by the Conference Board. The survey of PA officers found that very few thought their firm's current involvement was "strong," and 60 percent thought their programs were "less than adequate." Only about one-fourth of the respondents noted a "marked" increase in some aspect of their international PA during the past 5 years.[15] Apparently there is a real need for growth in the international arena, but movement has been slow and unimpressive.

Conclusions on PA Productivity, Evaluation, and Effectiveness

Post drew a number of different observations and conclusions as he analyzed the data from his study in the areas of productivity, evaluation, and effectiveness. Here are some of his conclusions:

1. PA officers are continually (a) reassessing what activities are vital to them and (b) setting priorities.
2. PA officers are constantly reexamining their assumptions by asking such questions as, "What do we do and why?" and "How do we do it and why?"
3. PA officers are constantly rethinking their mission in an effort to keep PA aligned with overall corporate strategy.
4. PA officers are striving to reduce nonessential costs.
5. PA officers are using outside contractors more to perform certain PA functions—for example, lobbying or communications.
6. PA officers are using information systems technology more in efforts enhance their productivity.[16]

PUBLIC AFFAIRS STRATEGY

We do not plan to cover the issue of public affairs strategy extensively, but we do want to report the findings of a major research project that was undertaken by Robert H. Miles, which resulted in a book entitled *Managing the Corporate Social Environment: A Grounded Theory*. As very little work has been done in this area, Miles's work deserves mention even though we cannot do it complete justice here. Miles's study focused on the insurance industry, but many of his findings may be applicable to other businesses. A few of his findings follow.[17]

Design of the Corporate External Affairs Function and Corporate Social Performance

Miles studied the external affairs strategy (also called the public affairs strategy) of major insurance firms in an effort to see what relationships existed between the strategy and design of the corporate external affairs function and corporate social performance. He found that the companies that ranked best in corporate social performance had a top management philosophy that was *institution-oriented*. That is, top managements saw their corporations as a social institution that had a duty to adapt to a changing society and had a collaborative/problem-solving external affairs strategy. The ***collaborative/problem-solving strategy*** was one in which firms emphasized long-term relationships with a variety of external constituencies and a broad problem-solving perspective on the resolution of social issues affecting their business and industry.[18] Note how similar this is to the stakeholder management view.

Miles also found that the companies with the worst social performance records employed a top management philosophy of operating as an independent economic franchise. This was in sharp contrast with the social institution perspective of the best social performers. In addition, these worst social performers employed an ***individual/adversarial external affairs strategy***. In this posture, the executives denied the legitimacy of social claims on their businesses and minimized the significance of challenges they received from external critics. Therefore, they tended to be adversarial and legalistic.[19]

Business Exposure to the Social Environment and the External Affairs Design

On the subject of the organization's external affairs unit within firms, Miles found that a contingency relationship existed between what he called *business exposure to the social environment* and four dimensions of the external affairs design: breadth, depth, influence, and integration. High business exposure to the social environment means that the firm produces products that move them into the public arena because of such issues as their availability, affordability, reliability, and safety. In general, consumer products tend to be more exposed to the social environment than do commercial or industrial products.[20]

Breadth, depth, influence, and integration refer to dimensions of the external affairs unit that provide a measure of *sophistication* versus *simplicity*. Units that are high on these dimensions are sophisticated, whereas units low on these dimensions are simple. Miles found, basically, that firms with high business exposure to the social environment require more sophisticated units, whereas firms with low business exposure to the social environment could manage reasonably well with simple units.[21]

It is tempting to overgeneralize Miles's study, but we must note it as a significant advance in the realm of public affairs strategy and organizational design research. The bottom line seems to be that a firm's corporate social performance (as well as its industry legitimacy and viability and economic performance) is a function of business exposure, top management philosophy, external affairs strategy, and external affairs design. Figure 20-5 presents Miles's theory of corporate social performance.

FIGURE 20-5 Miles's Theory of Corporate Social Performance

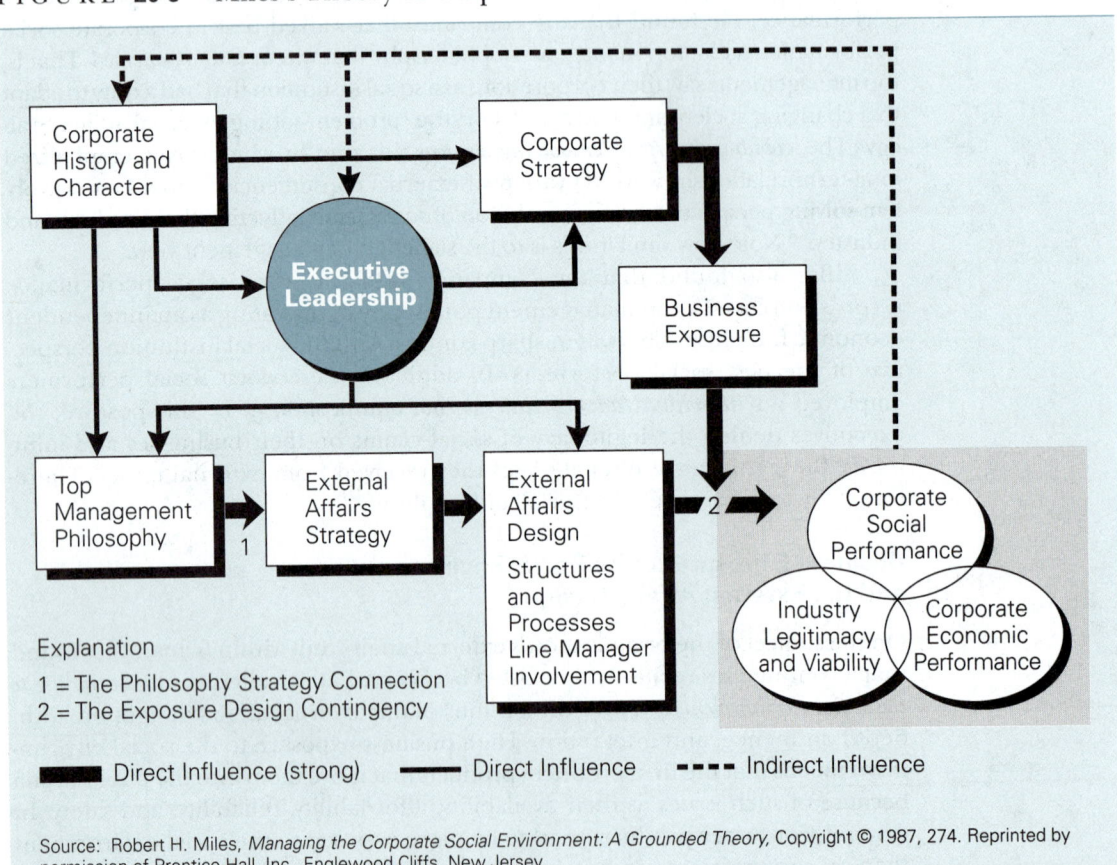

Source: Robert H. Miles, *Managing the Corporate Social Environment: A Grounded Theory*, Copyright © 1987, 274. Reprinted by permission of Prentice-Hall, Inc., Englewood Cliffs, New Jersey.

INCORPORATING PUBLIC AFFAIRS INTO EVERY MANAGER'S JOB

In today's highly specialized world, it is easy for line managers or operating managers to let public affairs departments worry about government affairs, community relations, issues management, or any of the numerous other PA functions. Public affairs people are concerned about this attitude. PA departments do have the central leadership role in getting their functions accomplished; in most cases, however, it is extremely helpful if line managers or operating managers are able to develop sensitivities or skills that can be useful to PA specialists.

David H. Blake has taken the position that we ought to incorporate public affairs into every operating manager's job. He argues that operating managers are vital to a successful PA function, especially if they can identify the public affairs consequences of their actions, be sensitive to the concerns of external groups, act to defuse or avoid crisis situations, and know well in advance when to seek the help of the PA experts. There are no simple ways to do this, but he proposes four specific strategies that may be helpful: (1) make public affairs truly relevant, (2) develop a sense of ownership of success, (3) make it easy for operating managers, and (4) show how public affairs makes a difference.[22] Each of these strategies is discussed below.

Make Public Affairs Truly Relevant

Operating managers often need help in seeing how external factors can and do affect them. A useful mechanism is to *analyze the manager's job* in terms of the likely or potential impacts his or her decisions might have on the social environment and possible developments in the environment that may affect the company or the decision maker. One procedure for doing this might be to list the manager's various impacts, the interested or affected strategic stakeholder groups, the potential actions of the groups, and the effects of groups on jobs or the company.

Another mechanism is to *link achievement of the manager's goals to public affairs*. A plant manager, for example, could be shown how failure to pay attention to community groups could hinder plant expansion, increased output, and product delivery. Failure to address the affected stakeholders could be shown to be related to extensive delays as these neglected groups seek media attention or pressure local officials.

Still another way to make PA relevant is to *use the language of the operating manager*. Instead of the jargon of public affairs, every effort should be made to use language and terms that the manager is familiar with. Thus, terms like *environment* to mean local community and *stakeholder* to mean employees and residents might be avoided.[23]

Another way to make public affairs relevant is to demonstrate to operating managers that a number of operations areas are affected by public affairs issues. John E. Fleming has argued that some of these areas include marketing, manufacturing, and human resources. Some of the specifics he provides in the manufacturing arena include product safety and quality, energy conservation, water pollution, air pollution, transportation, and raw materials. Fleming goes on to suggest that public affairs should be linked with corporate planning. If such a linkage is made, the operating manager should see more clearly how these issues are relevant to management decision making.[24]

Develop a Sense of Ownership of Success

It is helpful for operating managers if they have participated in planning and goal setting and are thus allowed to develop a sense of ownership for the public affairs endeavor. Operating managers may be formally or informally enlisted in these planning efforts. At PPG Industries, Inc., operating managers have been given the responsibility for coordinating all actions concerning a specific issue. As issue managers, they are asked to see to it that issue and environmental monitoring occurs, that strategy is developed, and that actions are implemented at various governmental levels.[25]

At Kroger, Inc., regional public affairs executives have worked with the individual operating divisions as they developed their business plans. A public affairs section was included in each operating division's plan. It was the *division's* plan, however, and not the PA department's plan. As a result of these efforts, the divisions now feel *they* have "ownership" of the PA goals in *their* plans.[26] This approach seems to work much better than PA executives simply imposing goals or expectations on the operating units.

Make It Easy for Operating Managers

Operating managers have experience meeting goals and timetables in their own realms. The PA area, however, can often appear nebulous, fuzzy, or inconclusive. Further, operating managers have neither the time nor the interest in setting up systems or strategies for PA initiatives. This is where the PA professionals can assist them by making their tasks easier. Any procedures, data collecting systems, or strategies that PA can supply should be used.

Training in public affairs can be helpful, too. Operating managers can better see the relevance and importance of PA work if carefully chosen topics are put on the agendas of their periodic training sessions. If PA effectiveness is to be monitored, measured, and made a part of performance evaluation systems, care should be taken to make sure that such systems are fair and straightforward or, at least, understandable. If PA does not make a careful effort to make its expectations reasonably met, then resistance, resentment, and failure will surely follow.[27]

Show How Public Affairs Makes a Difference

Part of what professional PA staff need to do is to keep track of public affairs successes in such a way that operating managers can see that their specific actions or efforts led to identifiable successes for the company. A scorecard approach where the operating managers can see that their efforts helped to avoid problems or prevent serious problems is useful. The scorecard may be used to reinforce managers' efforts and to help other managers see the potential of the PA function. It should explicitly state the achievements, the problems avoided, or the friends made for the company.

Obviously, such a scorecard would be of a qualitative nature, but this needs to be done to clearly describe what has been accomplished. Operating managers need to be shown that there are specific payoffs to be enjoyed from their public affairs efforts. It is up to the PA professionals to document these achievements. If no payoff is demonstrable from PA efforts, then operating managers are likely to use their time elsewhere.[28]

Public affairs is not just a specialized set of management functions to be performed by a designated staff. The nature of the tasks and challenges that characterize public affairs work is such that participation by operating managers is essential. To be sure, PA departments will continue to serve as the backbone of corporate systems, but true effectiveness will require that operating managers be integrated into the accomplishment of these tasks. The mutual interdependence of these two groups—professionals and line managers—will result in optimal effort.

SUMMARY

Public affairs might be described as the management function responsible for monitoring and interpreting a corporation's noncommercial environment and managing its response to those factors. Public affairs is intimately linked to corporate public policy, environmental analysis, issues management, and crisis management. The major functions of public affairs departments today include the following: government relations, political action, community involvement/responsibility, issues management, international public affairs, and strategic planning. Public affairs has gained widespread acceptance, and today a vital concern is with the productivity of this function. Two growth areas include issues management and international public affairs.

In terms of public affairs strategy, a collaborative/problem-solving strategy has been shown to be more effective than one that is individualistic/adversarial. Research has shown that a firm's corporate social performance, as well as its industry legitimacy, viability, and economic performance, is a function of business exposure, top management's philosophy, external affairs strategy, and external affairs design. In addition to being viewed as a staff function, public affairs is important for line managers. Four specific strategies are set forth for incorporating public affairs into operating managers' jobs: make it relevant, develop a sense of ownership, make it easy, and show how it can make a difference.

DISCUSSION QUESTIONS

1. How would you distinguish between public relations and public affairs? Why has there been confusion between these two concepts?
2. Why do you think issues management and international public affairs are the two major growth areas? Give specific reasons for your answer.
3. What factors will influence the growth of the public affairs function in the future? Briefly discuss.
4. Differentiate between a collaborative/problem-solving strategy and an individual/adversarial strategy. Which seems to be more effective in corporate public affairs?
5. What are the major ways in which public affairs might be incorporated into every manager's job? Rank-order them in terms of what you think their impact might be.

ENDNOTES

1. James C. Bowling, "Managing Public Affairs: New Dimensions" (Remarks before Public Affairs Conference of the Conference Board, January 15, 1981), 2.
2. Richard A. Armstrong, "Public Affairs vs. Public Relations," *Public Relations Quarterly* (Fall, 1981), 26.
3. Michael Cooper, "Public Affairs," *Public Relations Journal* (March, 1983), 28–29.
4. James E. Post, Edwin A. Murray, Jr., Robert B. Dickie, and John F. Mahon, "Managing Public Affairs: The Public Affairs Function," *California Management Review* (Fall, 1983), 135.
5. *Ibid.*, 138–139.
6. *Ibid.*, 147.
7. *Ibid.*, 148.
8. *Public Affairs Council* (Washington, DC, 1983), 5.
9. James E. Post, "Doing More with Less in Public Affairs: Today's Challenges," in Wesley Pederson (ed.), *Cost-Effective Management for Today's Public Affairs* (Washington, DC: Public Affairs Council, 1987), 4.
10. Raymond L. Hoewing, "Introduction," in Wesley Pederson (ed.), *Cost-Effective Management for Today's Public Affairs* (Washington, DC: Public Affairs Council, 1987), 2.
11. *Ibid.*, 6.
12. James E. Post and Patricia C. Kelley, "Lessons from the Learning Curve: The Past, Present and Future of Issues Management," in Robert L. Heath and Associates, *Strategic Issues Management* (San Francisco: Jossey-Bass, 1988), 352.
13. "International Public Affairs: A Preliminary Report by a PAC Task Force" (Washington, DC: Public Affairs Council, April, 1983), 2.
14. "Effective Management of International Public Affairs" (Washington, DC: Public Affairs Council, April, 1985), 1.
15. *Ibid.*, 4.
16. Post, 9–11.
17. Robert H. Miles, *Managing the Corporate Social Environment: A Grounded Theory* (Englewood Cliffs, NJ: Prentice-Hall, Inc., 1987).
18. *Ibid.*, 8.
19. *Ibid.*, 9–10, 111.
20. *Ibid.*, 2–3.
21. *Ibid.*, 11, 113.
22. David H. Blake, "How to Incorporate Public Affairs into the Operating Manager's Job," *Public Affairs Review* (1984), 35.
23. *Ibid.*, 36–38.
24. John E. Fleming, "Linking Public Affairs with Corporate Planning," *California Management Review* (Winter, 1980), 42.
25. Blake, 38–39.
26. Jack W. Partridge, "Making Line Managers Part of the Public Affairs Team: Innovative Ideas at Kroger," in Pederson (ed.), 67.
27. *Ibid.*, 39–40.
28. *Ibid.*, 40–41.

EPILOGUE

Challenges for the Future

As we conclude this book, it seems appropriate to consider briefly what the future will hold for the business and society relationship. There are many ways this could be done. We could predict the future in terms of the various issues or topics we covered in this book; however, our predictions could be obsolete before the ink is dry on the paper. We could report from surveys and polls what managers expect the future of business-stakeholder relations to be. Finally, we could provide an extensive discussion of the changes we expect to face in the economic, social, political, and technological spheres in the years ahead.

A problem with these methods is defining the future in terms that would be useful for the soon-to-be practicing manager. With each passing year, it seems that the future comes closer to the present than it was previously thought to be. Some make the point, only somewhat jokingly, that the future is later today or tomorrow. In this age of crisis management, there is considerable truth in this view. The next phone call or the next person to walk into your office—or into your life—could be the bearer of information that may significantly shape your personal, managerial, or organizational life for years to come. Talks with managers from Union Carbide, Johnson & Johnson, A. H. Robins, Bank of Boston, E. F. Hutton, Manville Corporation, Exxon, or a host of others would surely substantiate this point. Consequently, to be practical we need to think of the future as a period extending out a few years, probably less than 5.

It would appear that a useful way of considering the future is to summarize the five critical areas of challenge, conflict, and controversy identified by Lee Preston, who has been researching social issues in management for two decades. These areas include corporate governance, organizational ethics, business in politics, strategic management, and the multinational perspective.[1] Each of these areas has been discussed extensively or alluded to throughout this book. We will also briefly discuss the reconciling of economic and social goals.

It is tempting to add to this list of topics that of corporate social performance. This author and many others have argued that "corporate social performance" is the broad collective term under which all these topics might be organized. Donna Wood articulated this view recently:

> Despite the great diversity of topics studied under the banner of business and society, or social issues in management, the field takes on coherence and direction when seen within the framework of corporate social performance.[2]

Rather than treat this broad, encompassing concept as a separate topic to be discussed in this epilogue, we will refer the reader to Wood's recent articles in which she reviews the evolution of the corporate social performance model and extends it with both theoretical and practical implications.[3]

Our goal in this epilogue is not to add something new to what has been already said but to identify and isolate these particular themes or challenges as critical or urgent in the realm of business and society or business and stakeholder relations in the present and near future. These areas represent core concerns that parallel the pressing issues we developed in this book. We should further observe that embedded in each of these themes are ethical issues and stakeholder management challenges, both of which have been central features of this book.

CORPORATE GOVERNANCE

The central question Preston posed was, "How should the contemporary large corporation be governed?"[4] This issue has become very topical since the 1980s, largely because of the wave of hostile takeovers and the questionable responses of some management groups to these takeovers. The underlying question, however, has been a concern for decades. Implicit in the question are issues we discussed in Chapter 17, such as *who* will govern the corporation and *for whom* it will be governed.

Clearly, stakeholder and ethical issues are involved here. The stakeholder issue gets at the heart of the *for whom* question. In an organizational society such as ours, the American people think that their roles as employees and customers rank right up there with their roles as owners. Because more of us are employees and customers than are owners, it should not be surprising that this shifting of priorities has kept the *for whom* question at center stage. This problem has been exacerbated by a growing belief, with evidence to substantiate it, that management groups often think the *for whom* is themselves. Further, shareholder groups, particularly large institutional groups, have been attempting to reassert the idea of the owner as the principal stakeholder, which is the basic tenet on which our economic system was built.

The question of governance evokes thoughts of accountability, a theme that has run through social responsibility discussions for years. Barry Mitnick, in an important address given in 1986, argued that the governance idea ought to extend beyond the corporation and be applied to the broad realm of organization-environment relationships.[5] Such a view would cause one to think of accountability to external stakeholders in perceived failures of governance such as neglect or abuse of constituent groups, the physical environment, or the law.

In a real sense, the governance perspective is the glue that holds the corporation and society together. When these relationships are in a state of perceived balance, the system is functioning ethically, as it should. This is a value judgment, but that should not concern us because, in the final analysis, most important decisions are just that. When business-society relationships are out of balance, as some suggest is the case when governance is not working the way it was intended, problems arise and forces move to bring the system back into balance. The ethics question in all this has to do with the rightness or fairness of the relative roles of all the stakeholders in the governance relationship. To be sure, there appears to be no definitive, absolute prescription as to what corporate governance ought to be, but the public's acceptance and apparent satisfaction are the guiding indicators.

ORGANIZATIONAL ETHICS

The concern for organizational ethics cuts through practically all of the issues we have been discussing. Observers are split on the state of business ethics today, but it seems clear that this will continue to be an issue in the foreseeable future. Public opinion polls consistently have shown in the past decade that the public continues to rank business ethics in the questionable category. Some consider these low rankings as unacceptable. To others, however, they are seen as praiseworthy because they focus public attention on business practices. Robert Bartley, an editor of *The Wall Street Journal,* said recently that "we do not live in an age of moral collapse . . . we more nearly live in an age of moral zealotry."[6] This helps to explain the current preoccupation with business ethics.

The organizational ethics pressure is not on business alone. It is falling on other institutions in our society as well—government, education, and the military, for example. In a cover story, *U.S. News and World Report* noted that "government officials dissemble. Scientists falsify research. Workers alter career credentials to get jobs. What's going on here? The answer, a growing number of social critics fear, is an alarming decline in basic honesty."[7]

Many are turning to the nation's business schools to determine if business ethics can be improved by actions taken there. Opinions differ greatly as to whether business schools can and should teach business ethics. Critics say they cannot. Many B-schools say they can and they must.[8] The teaching of ethics at business schools became a primary topic when departing Securities and Exchange Commission chairman John Shad gave the Harvard Business School a $30 million gift to fund a business ethics program.[9]

How are a concern for ethics and a concern for stakeholders related? They are related in the sense that practically all business ethics questions involve a conflict of interests (stakes) among stakeholders. Most of the ethical dilemmas managers face require a resolution that forces them to prioritize the interests of different stakeholders—shareholders, employees, customers, residents in the community, or management itself. The importance of various stakeholders' interests changes over time in the minds of the public, and this keeps the ethical question "What is fair?" at the top of the list.

BUSINESS, GOVERNMENT, AND POLITICS

Central to any discussion about the future of the business and society relationship is the need to comment on business, government, and the political process. Throughout the 1980s, government regulation of business eroded as budget cuts undermined the power of the regulatory agencies to do their business effectively. In the 1990s there has been a resurgence of interest in regulatory activity, especially in such arenas as environmental protection, product safety, equal employment opportunity, and worker health and safety.

The challenge of business-government relations is to fashion a system that achieves the required degree of competitiveness to help American industry succeed but at the same time protects the interests of stakeholders—particularly customers and employees. This challenge is made more complex by the fact that our lawmakers are not in a system in which they can independently do what they think is in the best interests of the country. Increasingly they must be responsive to special-interest groups that can yield tremendous power but do not necessarily reflect the majority opinion. Added to this is the growing role that political action committees (PACs) play in congressional campaign funding. Over a decade (1977–1986), PAC contributions as a percentage of campaign funding rose from 17 percent to 28 percent and is still rising. A legitimate question is raised by *Business Week:* "Is Congress ready to bite the hands that feed it?"[10] In the 1990s, Congress seems to realize that it cannot continue on a "business as usual" basis. However, it seems paralyzed when it comes to taking steps that would bring the special-interest political contributions problem under control.

Ethics ("What is fair?") and stakeholder interests are clearly critical dimensions of business, government, and the political process. Since our country was founded, government has assumed an important role in the workings of the economic system, and there is no expectation that this will change. Many managers get caught up in the process of influencing public policy, not because they believe it is something they ought to be spending their time on but as a practical necessity. Public affairs management, therefore, will continue to be a crucial function in the years to come.

STRATEGIC MANAGEMENT

Companies are having to face the problem of novelty in the environment with greater frequency today. Alvin Toffler, in *The Adaptive Corporation* (1985), argued that the "management of surprise" has grown out of the rising levels of novelty in the firm's external and internal environments. The days of the stable or familiar environment are gone. On the business scene we now see firms facing a novel and fast-changing environment in which the problems and situations they face are themselves novel and fast-changing.[11] This kind of environment will continue to demand innovation not only in terms of products and technologies but also in terms of new ways of looking at people and social problems from a managerial perspective.

There is great potential for dealing with this novelty by moving toward the integration of corporate social policy into strategic management.[12] The first step in this integration is the recognition that enterprise-level strategy must be articulated by top-level management. In addition, the phases in the strategic management process must be infused with a consideration of public policy. Only by weaving public policy considerations into strategic management will companies be able to handle the novel challenges that will hit it with increasing frequency.

Growing out of this integration process will be a context in which issues management and crisis management will comfortably survive and prosper.[13] Regardless of how well the organization's corporate social policy has been developed, crises will occur and must be managed. These short-term focused approaches must be embedded in a larger concern for public and ethical issues if they are to be successful. The public affairs division of a corporation is the unit in which principal responsibility for these approaches will reside, but top management will find it necessary to fully embrace public affairs efforts if the firm's total goals are to be maximized.

MULTINATIONAL PERSPECTIVE

Business today lives in an increasingly multinational world. Peter Drucker has called this new world the "transnational economy." Drucker argues that for business to maintain a leadership position in any one developed country, a firm increasingly has to attain and hold such a position in all developed markets worldwide. This applies not only to large firms but also more and more to medium and small firms. The transnational base has become a key factor in business success.[14]

As international business becomes a more critical factor in the competitiveness of American firms, a multinational perspective on business ethics, corporate public policy, and public affairs inevitably must follow. Over the years, several major social issues have found their birth in the international arena. One was the infant-formula controversy that involved the United States, Switzerland, and a number of underdeveloped countries. A second issue has been the role of U.S. business in South Africa.[15] Although many U.S. firms began disinvesting their South African operations in 1986 and 1987, the issue has by no means gone away. This remains true even though South Africa in 1990 officially ended its policy of apartheid.

Even in their departure from South Africa, a number of firms still want to make a public policy statement. A good example is the Atlanta-based Coca-Cola Company. When Coca-Cola pulled out in 1986, it made an unusual promise—to seek out black investors to take over the bottling unit. This was not an easy promise to keep in a country where blacks had limited rights to property. In 1987, however, Coca-Cola announced that it was selling a third of its shares to a group that was 60 percent black, Indian, or racially mixed. Coca-Cola is the first departing company to sell a stake directly to blacks and was thus breaking new ground by bringing small entrepreneurs into the mainstream.[16]

The 1984 Union Carbide Bhopal tragedy in which 2,500 people were killed, considered the worst industrial disaster ever, startled the American and world business communities and brought into sharp focus the responsibilities of firms to international stockholders. There was a time when this event would not have been a headline story, but those days are past, and Union Carbide has been attempting to cope with this disaster ever since.

Just as American managers increasingly have to be concerned with their ethical behavior in other countries, U.S. society is realizing that it too must deal with the social consequences of foreign-based multinational corporations that have affiliates located in the United States. Although many questions have been raised about the practices, policies, and impacts of foreign investors into the United States, T. S. Pinkston conducted a research study in which she found no significant differences in the corporate citizenship orientations of executives from six countries and those of U.S. executives. Her conclusion is that foreign affiliates have effectively conformed to U.S. market behavior and demands.[17]

There is a revived concern for the study of business ethics that crosses cultures. To date, the academic community appears more interested in business ethics than the business community, but this will have to change. The need to develop corporatewide positions on ethical issues will be one of business's greatest challenges in the next few years.[18]

RECONCILING ECONOMIC AND SOCIAL GOALS

Earlier we discussed the need to reconcile economic and social goals, but it is an important one to reiterate because it will continue to run through everything we have dealt with up to this point. A complex challenge for business stems from the expectation that, though social and ethical values are increasing in importance, the demand for higher levels of material comfort and more jobs will continue to strengthen also.[19] The major consequence of this condition is that business cannot relax its economic and technological progress while also continuing to perform successfully in the social arena. One way of depicting this new condition for business is seen in Figure E-1, which shows that business's future survival and success lie in quadrant 2. In this quadrant, business will have to invest an enormous amount of time and effort into creating not only traditional economic outputs but social outputs as well. Fortunately, these social outputs are economically achievable if business focuses on the ethical realm. Managing ethically does not have to measurably increase out-of-pocket costs, and it promises to facilitate the reconciliation of economic and social values in the years to come.

SUMMARY

There are many challenges for business in the near future. Five of these challenges reside in the issues of corporate governance, organizational ethics, business in the political sphere, strategic management, and multinational perspective. There are other ways of grouping future issues for business, but these capture the central concerns we have been developing in this book.

FIGURE E-1   The Growing Importance of Economic and Social Values

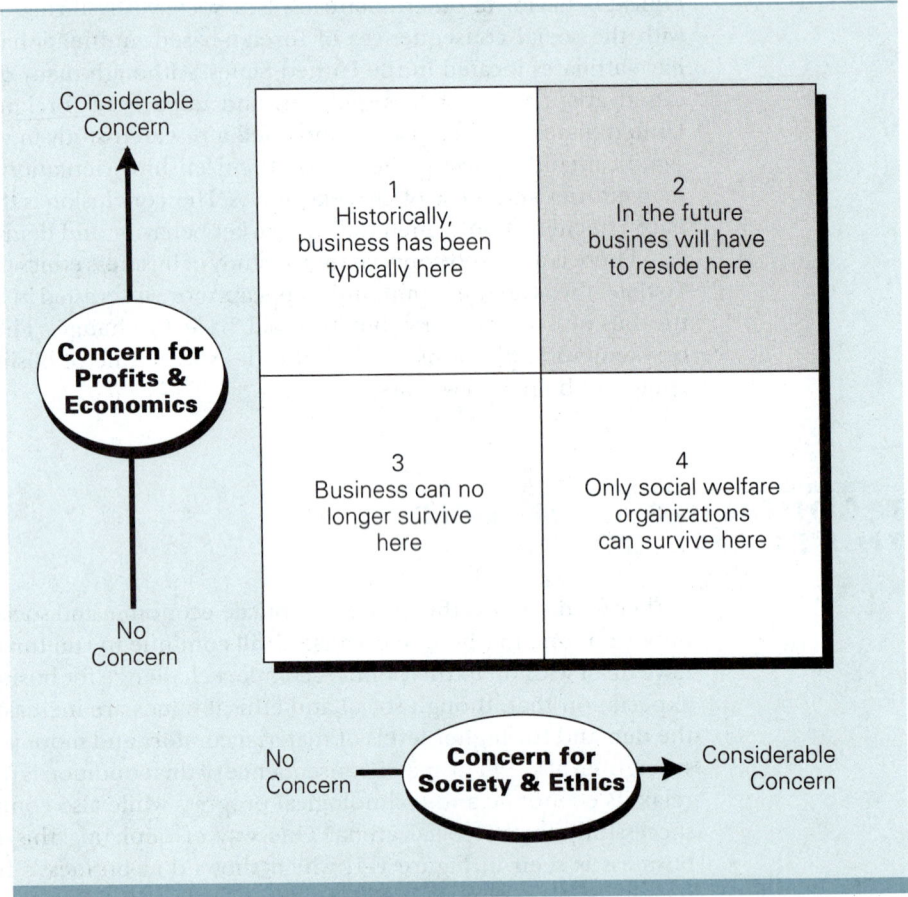

Finally, and perhaps most important from the strict management perspective, there is the need for managers to reconcile their economic goals with their social pursuits. This is achievable, and we think we have presented a convincing case for it in this book. With public expectations ranging from economic performance to social performance, business faces the challenge of how to do all these things for all these people.

As the "societized corporation"—one that stakeholders expect to be a multi-purpose social organization—continues to emerge, some of the most significant challenges managers have ever faced loom on the horizon. Business looks to these challenges with the full realization that public mistrust of business continues. Can the management of any other institution in society say that it faces the future with such uncertainty? Probably not. In any event, perhaps the most difficult task for an organization in the next few years will be the managing of its social performance while maintaining economic survival and competence. If business fails in this pursuit, it will not be a viable institution in our society. Management must and will respond to this challenge.

DISCUSSION QUESTIONS

1. Convert each of the following topics or issues into a question format that would be posed to managers to capture its essence: (1) corporate governance, (2) organizational ethics, (3) business in politics, (4) strategic management, (5) multinational perspective, and (6) reconciliation of economic and social goals.

2. Rank the six major topics in this epilogue posed as challenges to management in terms of most fundamental or important to management; provide a brief explanation as to why you ranked them the way you did.

3. Regarding the multinational perspective, what issues do you think will be most important to managers and businesses over the next 5 years? Briefly explain.

ENDNOTES

1. Lee E. Preston, "Business and Public Policy," *Journal of Management* (Vol. 12, No. 2, 1986), 261–275.
2. Donna J. Wood, "Social Issues in Management: Theory and Research in Corporate Social Performance," *Journal of Management* (June, 1991), 400.
3. Ibid. See also Donna J. Wood, "Corporate Social Performance Revisited," *Academy of Management Review* (October, 1991), 691–718.
4. Preston, 264.
5. Barry M. Mitnick, "Loose Connections," Keynote address, Research Workshop, Social issues in Management Division, 46th Annual Meeting of the Academy of Management, Chicago, IL, August 13, 1986.
6. Robert L. Bartley, "Business Ethics and the Ethics Business," *The Wall Street Journal* (May 18, 1987), 30.
7. "A Nation of Liars?" *U.S. News & World Report* (February 23, 1987), 54.
8. Thomas J. Murray, "Can Business Schools Teach Ethics?" *Business Month* (April, 1987), 24.
9. Beth Brophy, "Ethics 101: Can the Good Guys Win?" *U.S. News & World Report* (April 13, 1987), 54.
10. "Is Congress Ready to Bite the Hands That Feed It?" *Business Week* (June 1, 1987), 102.
11. Alvin Toffler, *The Adaptive Corporation* (New York: McGraw-Hill, 1985), 67–75.
12. Archie B. Carroll and Frank Hoy, "Integrating Corporate Social Policy into Strategic Management," *Journal of Business Strategy* (Winter, 1984), 48–57.
13. Archie B. Carroll, Frank Hoy, and John Hall, "The Integration of Corporate Social Policy into Strategic Management," in S. Prakash Sethi and Cecilia M. Falbe (eds.), *Business and Society: Dimensions of Conflict and Cooperation* (Lexington, MA: Lexington Books, 1987), 466–468.
14. Peter F. Drucker, "The Transnational Economy," *The Wall Street Journal* (August 25, 1987), 38.
15. Lee E. Preston, "Social Issues and Public Policy in Business and Management: Retrospect and Prospect" (College Park, MD: Center for Business and Public Policy, August, 1986), 36–37.
16. "If Coke Has Its Way, Blacks Will Soon Own the 'Real Thing,'" *Business Week* (March 23, 1987), 56.
17. T. S. Pinkston, *"Corporate Citizenship": A Comparative Analysis of Foreign Affiliates, Located in the U.S. and Their Domestic Counterparts* (Unpublished doctoral dissertation, University of Georgia, 1991).
18. Helmut Becker and David Fritzsche, "Business Ethics: A Cross-Cultural Comparison of Managers' Attitudes," *Journal of Business Ethics* (May, 1987), 289–295.
19. Gerald F. Cavanagh, *American Business Values*, 2d ed. (Englewood Cliffs, NJ: Prentice-Hall, 1984).

CASES

Case Studies

GUIDELINES FOR ANALYZING CASES

The guidelines presented below are to be helpful in analyzing the cases. The guidelines are not intended to be a rigid format, however, that the student just mechanically goes through. Each question is intended to surface information that will be helpful in analyzing and resolving the case. Each case is different, and some parts of the guidelines may not apply in every case. Also, the student should be attentive to the questions for discussion at the end of each case. These questions should be answered in any complete case analysis. The heart of any case analysis is the set of recommendations made. The Problem/Issue Identification and Analysis/Evaluation steps should be focused on generating and defending the most effective set of recommendations possible.

Problem/Issue Identification

1. What are the *central facts of the case* and *assumptions* you are making based on these facts?
2. What is the *major overriding issue* in this case? (What major question/issue does this case address that merits its study in this course and in connection with the chapter/material you are now covering?)
3. What *subissues or related issues* in the case merit consideration and discussion?

Analysis/Evaluation

4. Who are the *stakeholders* in the case and *what are their stakes?* (Create a stakeholder map if this is helpful.) What challenges/threats/opportunities are posed by these stakeholders?
5. *What economic/legal/ethical/discretionary responsibilities* does the company have, and what exactly is the nature and extent of the responsibilities?
6. If the case involves a company's actions, *evaluate what the company did or did not do* in handling the issue affecting it.

Recommendations

7. What recommendations do you have for this case? If a company's strategies or actions are involved, should the company have acted the way it did? What actions should the company take now and why? Be as specific as possible, and include a discussion of *alternatives* you have considered but decided not to pursue. Mention and discuss any important *implementation considerations*.

CASE 1 THE MAIN STREET MERCHANT OF DOOM*

The small town was in need of a hired gun. The people were tired of dealing with the local price-fixing merchant scum who ran the town like a company store. This low-life bunch held the people of the town in a death grip and were perceived by the town's people to overcharge on every purchase. In spite of what appeared to be a case of collusion, the law was powerless to do anything. What competition there was had been effectively eliminated.

Suddenly, coming over the rise and wearing white, their hired man came riding. The women and children buzzed with excitement. The men were happy. Although his methods of getting the job done turned some people's stomachs, the local watering hole buzzed with tales of how this hired gun would change their world for the better. How some day soon they would have the benefits long afforded the big city. But, others asked, at what price change?

The 1990s Version of the "Hired Gun"

At age 73, this man appeared to be somewhat frail to handle the enormous job that lay ahead. Yet, the courage and self-confidence that radiated from his presence put to rest their fears. Sam had come to town.

Sam Walton, founder, owner,. and mastermind behind Wal-Mart, was seen by many small communities as a friend to the consumer. On the flip side, many a small-town merchant has been the victim of Sam's blazing merchandising tactics. So what is Wal-Mart to the communities it services? Is Wal-Mart the consumer's best friend, the purveyor of the free enterprise system, the "Mother of All Discount Stores," or conversely, is Wal-Mart really the "Main Street Merchant of Doom"?

The Man Named Sam

Samuel Moore Walton was born March 29, 1918 near Kingfisher, Kansas. His father was a salesman in the insurance, real estate, and mortgage businesses. The family moved often. Sam was a strong lean boy who learned to work hard in order to help the family. He attended the University of Missouri starting in the fall of 1936 and graduated with a degree in business administration. During his time at the University of Missouri, he was a member of the Beta Theta Phi fraternity, was president of the senior class, played various sports, and taught what was believed to be the largest Sunday School class in the world, numbering over 1,200 Missouri students.[1]

At age 22, Sam joined J. C. Penney. One of his first tasks was to memorize and practice the "Penney Idea." Adopted in 1913, it exhorts the associate to serve the public; to not demand all the profit the traffic will bear; to pack the customer's dollar full of value, quality, and satisfaction; to continue to be trained; to reward men and women in the organization through participation in what the business produces; and to test every policy, method, and act against the question "Does it square with what is right and just?"[2]

---

* This case was prepared by William T. Rupp.

In 1962, at 44 years of age, Sam Walton opened his first Wal-Mart store. He took all the money and expertise he could gather and applied the J. C. Penney Idea to middle America. Sam first targeted small underserved rural towns with populations at or below 10,000 people. The people responded, and Wal-Mart soon developed a core of loyal customers who loved the fast friendly service coupled with consistently low prices.

The Store That Sam Built

By 1981, Wal-Mart's rapid growth was evident to all and was especially disturbing to Sears, J. C. Penney's, Target, and K-Mart, for Wal-Mart had become America's largest retailer. The most telling figures are those of overhead expenses and sales per employee. Sears' overhead expenses run 29 percent of sales and K-Mart's 23 percent, while Wal-Mart's overhead expenses run 16 percent of sales. The average Sears employee generates $85,000 in sales per year, while the average Wal-Mart employee generates $95,000.[3]

By the end of the third quarter of 1991, Sam had opened 1,652 Wal-Mart stores, 194 Sam's Clubs, and 4 Hypermarts. Joseph Ronning, an analyst with Brown Brothers Harriman, Inc., said, "The customers are responding to Wal-Mart's low-price image. They have the right product at the right price at the right time."[4]

Sam, the motivational wizard and cheerleader, promoted the associate, the hourly employee, to a new level of participation within the organization. He offered profit-sharing, incentive bonuses, and stock options in an effort to have his Wal-Mart associates share in the wealth. Sam, as the head cheerleader, saw his job as the chief proponent of the "Wal-Mart Way."

Sam, the courageous, borrowed and borrowed, sometimes just to pay other creditors. Arkansas banks that at one time turned him down now compete with banks Sam himself owned.

Sam, the CEO, hired the best managers he could find. He let them talk him into buying an extensive computer network system. This network is a corporate satellite system that enables Sam to use round the clock inventory control, credit card sales control, and total sales on what products where and when. This computer control center is about the size of a football field and uses a Hughes satellite for up-linking and down-linking to each store.

In 1992 Sam, the mortal, died of incurable bone cancer. At age 73, Sam Walton said that if he had to do it over again he would not change a thing. He said:

> This is still the most important thing I do, going around to the stores, and I'd rather do it than anything I know of. I know I'm helping our folks when I get out to the stores. I learn a lot about who's doing good things in the office, and I also see things that need fixing, and I help fix them. Any good management person in retail has got to do what I do in order to keep his finger on what's going on. You've got to have the right chemistry and the right attitude on the part of the folks who deal with the customers.[5]

Sam, the innovator, developed the "store within a store." This concept trains people to be merchants, not employees. These "store within a store" managers have all the numbers for their department, a breakdown of how they are doing in relation to the store and the company as a whole. The concept provides a big opportunity by providing big responsibility. Sam set the goal of visiting every Wal-Mart store every year. To do this he flew his own twin-prop Cessna and visited up to five or six stores per day. Two innovative programs that are changing the whole of retailing are Wal-Mart's "Buy American" campaign and the commitment to the environment.

Sam and Social Awareness: The "Buy American" Plan

The "Buy American" program is a result of a phone call with Arkansas Governor Clinton in 1984. The program was a response to Sam's own enlightenment: Wal-Mart was adding to the loss of American jobs by buying cheaper foreign goods. What a dichotomy! Everything Sam stood for came out of his heartfelt obligation to supply the customer with low-cost quality goods, but running counter to this inner driving force was the realization that he was responsible for the loss of American jobs. This dilemma drove him to find a solution. The phone call with Governor Clinton inspired Sam to do something about the problem. The following is the story of the Farris Borroughs Corporation:

> Farris Borroughs operated Farris Fashions, a clothing manufacturer in Brinkley, Arkansas (population 5,000). The plant employed ninety people and had been making flannel shirts for Van Heusen. The shirts were distributed through J.C. Penney and Sears but now, due to the cost advantages of foreign competitors, they had lost the ability to be competitive. The factory would probably close and ninety Arkansas people would be out of work.
>
> Sam listened to Governor Clinton's story and replied, "I'd hate to see an Arkansas plant shut down. I'll call you back." He knew he had to try and save Farris Fashions. It seemed the "Buy American" bug had infected Sam's decision making mind-set and it was full-steam ahead.
>
> Farris Borroughs and Farris Fashions needed big help. Financing problems and a lack of a supply of "American Made" flannel material had to be overcome. Sam called in representatives from big textile firms to discuss the problems of "Made in America." There was no answer to the raw flannel manufacturing problem. It was explained that American companies simply could not make a profit producing the flannel material. A compromise allowed Farris Fashions to buy foreign flannel material but all construction of the shirts would be done at the Brinkley factory. Sam also guaranteed Farris Fashions a $612,000 order, scheduling help, and a fast payment arrangement.[6]

Sam wanted other manufacturers to join him in the "Buy American" plan. He wrote to 3,000 American manufacturers and solicited them to sell Wal-Mart items they were currently buying from overseas suppliers. Wal-Mart's competitors did not meet the challenge to "Buy American." K-Mart stated they would rather buy American-made goods, but they were looking for the best deal for the customer. Target said they were for free trade and that as the customer's representative they just wanted the best deal for the customer. Wall Street analysts responded positively, saying it was possibly the beginning of a change of direction for American retailers.[7]

In February 1986, about 12 months after the "Buy American" plan had begun, Sam held a press conference. He showed off all the merchandise Wal-Mart was now buying domestically. He estimated that Wal-Mart's "Buy American" plan had restored 4,538 jobs to the American economy and its people.[8]

Sam and Social Concerns: The "Environmental Awareness" Campaign

The American awareness of the environment was on the rise, and Sam looked for a way to involve Wal-Mart in the environmental movement. In August 1989, an ad in *The Wall Street Journal* proclaimed Wal-Mart's "commitment to our land, air, and water." Sam envisioned Wal-Mart as a leader among American companies in the struggle to clean up the environment. John Lowne, corporate vice-president and division manager for Reynolds Metals Company, stated, "Wal-Mart's move will indeed set a precedent for the entire retail industry. I'm surprised it has taken other retailers this long to follow suit."[9]

Wal-Mart wanted to use its tremendous buying power to aid in the implementation of the campaign. Wal-Mart sent a booklet to manufacturers stating the following:

> At Wal-Mart we're committed to help improve our environment. Our customers are concerned about the quality of our land, air and water, and want the opportunity to do something positive. We believe it is our responsibility to step up to their challenge.[10]

In the store, shelf tags made from 100 percent recycled paper inform customers as to the environmental friendliness of the highlighted product. As a result of these shelf tags and Wal-Mart's advertising, customer awareness has increased and some environmentally safe product manufacturers are reaping the reward of increased Wal-Mart orders. Linda Downs, administrative manager of Duraflame/California said Duraflame logs have been proven to burn cleaner than wood and that Wal-Mart's campaign has helped Duraflame to deliver this message. She goes on to say, "Wal-Mart has helped drive home the message we have been trying to promote for years. They have really given us great publicity."[11]

In Wal-Mart's Associates Handbook, new associates are indoctrinated with the "Wal-Mart spirit." The section entitled "Our Commitments" begins with this statement:

> We feel a moral obligation not only to our customers, but to our communities in which our stores are located.

A personal comment from Sam states:

> We live in such a great country, this land of ours, and I'm afraid we all take our freedoms, opportunities and many blessings for granted at times. All of us in our Wal-Mart family should count our blessings daily and do all we can to help others, both within our company and outside, who are less fortunate and in need. Our associates have done just that in our communities. They have shown their willingness to share so generously in 100,000 instances and more. I'm so proud of all you hard-working, dedicated, loyal Wal-Mart associate-partners. You personify, most of all, our Wal-Mart spirit because you care about others![12]

The section on the environment says:

> As a responsible member of the community, Wal-Mart's commitments go beyond simply selling merchandise. With environmental concerns mounting world-wide, Wal-Mart has taken action.
>
> Home office and store associates are taking decisive steps to help the environment by making community recycling bins available on our facility parking lots. Other action plans include "Adopt-a-Highway" and "Adopt-a-Beach" programs, tree planting and community clean up and beautification. By forming a partnership with our associates, our manufacturers and our customers, we're convinced we can make the world a better place to live.[13]

Sam and the Merchants of Main Street

Not everyone is excited to see Sam and his mechanized Wal-Mart army succeed. Small merchants across America shudder when the winds of the "Wal-Mart Way" begin to blow. Kennedy Smith of the *National Main Street Center* in Washington, DC, says, "The first thing towns usually do is panic." Once Wal-Mart comes to a town Smith says, "Downtowns will never again be the providers of basic consumer goods and services they once were."[14]

Some towns have learned to "just say No" to the Wal-Mart overtures. Steamboat Springs, Colorado, is one such city. Colorado newspapers called it the "Shootout at Steamboat Springs." Wal-Mart was denied permission to build on a 9-acre parcel along U.S. 40. Owners of up-scale shops and condos were very concerned with the image of their resort community, and a Wal-Mart and its low-cost reputation just did not fit. The shootout lasted for 2 years, and finally Wal-Mart filed a damage suit against the city. Counter-suits followed. A petition was circulated to hold a referendum on the matter. This was the shot that made Wal-Mart blink and back down. Just before the election in April 1989, Don Shinkle, corporate affairs vice-president, said, "A vote would not be good for Steamboat Springs, and it would not be good for Wal-Mart. I truly believe Wal-Mart is a kinder, gentler, company, and, while we have the votes to win, an election would only split the town more."[15]

In Iowa City, Iowa (population 50,000+), Wal-Mart was planning an 87,000-square-foot store on the outskirts of town. A group of citizens gathered enough signatures during a petition drive to put a referendum on the ballot to block Wal-Mart and the city council (the city council had approved the rezoning of the land Wal-Mart wanted) from building the new store. Jim Clayton, a downtown merchant said, "Wal-Mart is a freight train going full steam in the opposite direction of this town's philosophy." If businesses wind up going down, Clayton says, "you lose their involvement in the community, involvement I promise you won't get with some assistant manager over at Wal-Mart."[16] Wal-Mart spokesperson Brenda Lockhart commented that downtown merchants can only benefit from the increase in customer traffic provided "they offer superior service and aren't gouging their customers."[17] Efforts to stop Wal-Mart and the Iowa City Council were not successful. Wal-Mart opened its Iowa City store November 5, 1991.

Meanwhile, in Pawhuska, Oklahoma, Wal-Mart's entry in 1983, along with other local factors, saw the local five-and-dime, J. C. Penney, Western Auto, and a whole block of other stores close their doors. Dave Story, the general manager in 1987 at the local *Pawhuska Daily Journal Capital,* wrote that Wal-Mart was a "billion-dollar parasite" and a "national retail ogre."[18]

Wal-Mart managers have become very active in Pawhuska and surrounding communities since 1987. A conversation with the current (1991) editor of the Pawhuska paper, Jody Smith, and her advertising editor, Suzy Burns, revealed that Wal-Mart sponsored the local rodeo, gave gloves to the local coat drive, and was involved with the local cerebral palsy and multiple sclerosis fund raisers. On the other hand, Fred Wright, former owner of a TV and record store, said, "Wal-Mart really craters a little town's downtown."[19]

Shift to Kinder, Louisiana (population 2,608). Wal-Mart moved into this small Louisiana town in 1981. On December 31, 1990 the store was closed. During the time Wal-Mart operated in Kinder, one-third of the downtown stores closed. The downtown has become three blocks of mostly run-down red brick buildings. The closest place to buy shoes or sewing thread is 30 miles away in Oakdale, Louisiana, another Wal-Mart.

A major problem arose for the city because of the loss of $55,000 dollars of tax revenues per year. This tax revenue was 10 percent of the total revenues for the city.

The tactics Wal-Mart employed during its 10-year tenure left a bad taste in the mouths of some small retailers. Soon after Wal-Mart's arrival, a price war broke out between Wal-Mart and the downtown retailers. The retailers told *The Atlanta Journal-Constitution* in November 1990, "Wal-Mart sent employees, wearing name tags and smocks, into their stores to scribble down prices and list merchandise." Lou Pearl, owner of Kinder Jewelry and Gifts, stated Wal-Mart associates came to her store and noted the type of art supplies she was carrying. Shortly thereafter, Wal-Mart began carrying the same merchandise at a discount. Sales at the Kinder Jewelry and Gifts dropped drastically, and she dropped the merchandise line. Within several weeks, so did Wal-Mart.[20] Perhaps Troy Marcantel, a 29-year-old downtown clothing merchant, said it best, "What really rankled me was that they used people we have known all our lives. I still don't understand how our own people could do that to us."[21]

Epilogue

The hired gun learned his lessons well. The people who bought at his store were well satisfied. The downtown merchants who survived learned to coexist with the hired gun's associates. But things would never be the same. The changes had come rapidly. The social fabric of the small town was forever changed.

The hired gun rode on, searching for that next town that needed to be liberated from the downtown price-fixing bad-guys.

QUESTIONS FOR DISCUSSION

1. What are the major issues in this case? Assess Wal-Mart's corporate social responsibility using the four-part CSR model. Is Wal-Mart socially responsible for its devastating impact on small merchants? What responsibility, if any, does the company have to these merchants or to the communities it enters?

2. Most of Wal-Mart's success has come at the expense of the small merchant. Research has shown that the average Wal-Mart generates $10 million per year with $8 million coming at the expense of other businesses. What should Wal-Mart do, if anything, to help other vital businesses in the community survive? Why?

3. Sam Walton has been called a motivational genius. After reading this case and with what you have observed at your local Wal-Mart store, explain how this motivational genius empowered the employee. What is the "Wal-Mart Way?" Explain its impact on the associate and on the community. What will happen now that Sam is no longer the motivational leader?

4. Some regard Wal-Mart as a leader in the area of corporate social responsibility. How do the "Buy American" program and the "Environmental Awareness" program illustrate this? Are these programs really examples of corporate social responsibility or are they gimmicks to entice customers into the stores? Are these programs' benefits offset by the company's devastating impact on merchants?

5. Wal-Mart has closed five stores in its short history. What responsibility, if any, does Wal-Mart have to the employees that are let go? What about its loyal customers and the community? Are your answers consistent with Wal-Mart's stated position?

6. In the case of Kinder, Louisiana, Wal-Mart left town without any type of reciprocity. Given Wal-Mart's commitment statements, did they owe a debt to the city of Kinder? Why or why not?

CASE ENDNOTES

1. Vance H. Trimble, *Sam Walton: The Inside Story of America's Richest Man* (New York: Penguin Books, 1990), 30.
2. *Ibid.*, 34.
3. Janice Castro, "Mr. Sam Stuns Goliath," *Time* (February 25, 1991), 62.
4. "Net Up 25% at Wal-Mart," *New York Times* (November 8, 1991), C6.
5. John Huey, "America's Most Successful Merchant," *Fortune* (September 23, 1991), 50.
6. Trimble, 259.
7. *Ibid.*, 260.
8. *Ibid.*, 261.
9. Richard Turcsik, "A New Environment Evolves at Wal-Mart," *Supermarket News* (January 15, 1990), 10.
10. *Ibid.*, 10.
11. *Ibid.*, 11.
12. *Wal-Mart Associates Handbook* (July, 1991), 14.
13. *Ibid.*, 14.
14. Dan Koeppel, "Wal-Mart Finds New Rivals on Main Street," *Adweek's Marketing Week* (November 10, 1990), 5.
15. Trimble, 255.
16. "Just Saying No to Wal-Mart," *Newsweek* (November 13, 1989), 65.
17. *Ibid.*, 65.
18. Karen Blumenthal, "Arrival of Discounter Tears the Civic Fabric of Small-Town Life," *The Wall Street Journal* (April 14, 1987), 1, 23.
19. *Ibid.*, 23.
20. Charles Haddad, "Wal-Mart Leaves Town 'High, Dry,'" *The Atlanta Journal-Constitution* (November 26, 1990), A4.
21. *Ibid.*, A4.

CASE 2   **THE BODY SHOP INTERNATIONAL PLC***

When North American consumers are asked to describe the cosmetics industry, they often respond with words like "glamour" and "beauty." Beginning in 1976, The Body Shop provided a contrast to this image by selling a range of 400 products designed to "cleanse and polish the skin and hair." The product line included such items as "Honeyed Beeswax, Almond, and Jojoba Oil Cleanser" and "Carrot Facial Oil." Women's cosmetics and men's toiletries were also available. They were all produced without the use of animal testing and packaged in plain-looking, recyclable packages.[1] The primary channel of distribution was a network of over 600 franchised retail outlets in Europe, Australia, Asia, and North America.[2] The company had experienced annual growth rates of approximately 50 percent until 1990 when net income began to level off. Few questions were raised in the media about this decline in performance, as the firm's social agenda and exotic product line captured most of the public's interest.

Managing director and founder, Anita Roddick, was responsible for creating and maintaining much of the company's marketing strategy and product development.[3] Roddick believed that The Body Shop was fundamentally different from other firms in the cosmetic industry because "we don't claim that our products will make you look younger; we say they will only help you look your best."[4] She regularly assailed her competitors: "We loathe the cosmetic industry with a passion. It's run by men who create needs that don't exist."[5] During the 1980s Anita Roddick became one of the richest women in the United Kingdom by challenging the well-established firms and rewriting the rules of the cosmetic industry.

Anita Roddick became admired within the business community for the conviction of her beliefs and the success of her company. She had received many honors and awards, including UK Businesswoman of the Year in 1985, British Retailer of the Year in 1989, and the Order of the British Empire.[6] The firm's customers included several celebrities, including Princess Diana of Wales, Sting, and Bob Weir of the Grateful Dead. Ben Cohen, cofounder and chairman of Ben & Jerry's, described her as:

> . . . an incredibly dynamic, passionate, humorous and intelligent individual who believes it's the responsibility of a business to give back to the community. . . . She understands that a business has the power to influence the world in a positive way.[7]

Mrs. Roddick opened the first Body Shop store in Brighton, England, as a means to support her family while her husband was taking a year-long sabbatical in America. Her husband, Gordon Roddick, a chartered accountant by trade, was using much of their savings to finance his trip. Anita Roddick had little money to open a store or to develop products or purchase packaging materials.[8]

---

* This case was prepared by William A. Sodeman using publicly available information.

She called on her previous experiences as a resource. She had been a United Nations researcher for several years in the 1960s, and her field expeditions gave her many opportunities to see how men and women in Africa, Asia, and Australia used locally grown plants and extracts, such as beeswax, rice grains, almonds, bananas, and jojoba, as grooming products. Roddick knew that these materials were inexpensive and readily obtainable. With some library research, she found a number of recipes, some centuries-old, that used these same ingredients to make cosmetics and skin cleansers. With the addition of inexpensive bottles and handwritten labels, Roddick quickly developed a line of products for sale in her first Body Shop. She soon opened a second store in a nearby town. When Gordon Roddick returned to the U.K. in 1977, The Body Shop was recording a sizable profit. At Anita's request, he joined the company as its chief executive officer.[9]

The Body Shop's strategy grew out of the company's early reliance on cost-containment. Roddick was able to afford only 600 bottles when she opened her first store. Customers were offered a small discount to encourage the return of empty bottles for product refills. This offer was extended to both retail and mail order customers.[10] The Body Shop could not afford advertising, so Roddick resolved to do without it.[11]

The Body Shop's retail stores were somewhat different from the cosmetic salons and counters familiar to shoppers in highly industrialized nations. The typical retail sales counter relied on high-pressure tactics that included promotions, makeovers, and an unspoken contract with the customer that virtually required a purchase in order to receive any advice or consultations from a sales counter employee.[12] Body Shop employees were taught to wait for the customer to ask questions, to be forthright and helpful, and not to press for a sale.[13]

Store employees were paid a half-day's wages every week to perform community service activities. At the headquarters facility in Littlehampton, England, the company employed an anthropologist, six herbalists, and a variety of others in similar fields. There was nothing that resembled a marketing department. Husbands and wives frequently worked together and could visit their children during the work day at the on-site day care center.[14] The company's hiring procedures included questions about the applicant's personal heroes and literary tastes, as well as their individual beliefs on certain social issues. At one time, Roddick was ready to hire a retail director but refused to do so when he professed his fondness for hunting, a sport that Roddick despised because of her support for animal rights.[15]

As the company prospered, Anita Roddick used her enthusiasm and growing influence on her suppliers and customers. The Body Shop began to produce products in the country of origin when it was feasible and paid these workers wages comparable to those in the European Community.[16] Customers were asked to sign petitions and join activist groups that The Body Shop endorsed, mostly in the areas of animal rights and environmental causes. The Body Shop contributed significant portions of its earnings to these groups, including Amnesty International and People for the Ethical Treatment of Animals (PETA). Roddick was careful to choose causes that were "easy to understand"[17] and could be communicated quickly to a customer during a visit to a Body Shop store.

An example of this corporate activism was The Body Shop's opposition to a practice that had become common in the cosmetics industry. Cosmetics firms were not required to perform animal testing of their products to comply with product-safety and health regulations. Rather, companies voluntarily adopted animal-based testing procedures to guard against product liability lawsuits.[18]

The Body Shop was not worried about such lawsuits, as the product ingredients Roddick chose had been used safely for centuries. In addition, the older recipes had been used for many decades without incident. These circumstances led to the company's rejection of animal-based product testing. Suppliers wishing to do business with The Body Shop had to sign a statement guaranteeing that no animal testing had been performed by their company for the previous 5 years, nor would such testing ever be performed again by the firm. The Body Shop used human volunteers from its own staff and the University Hospital of Wales to test new and current products under normal use. The Body Shop has also volunteered to share its testing results on individual ingredients with other cosmetics manufacturers.[19]

Most other cosmetics firms used a variety of procedures to determine the safety of cosmetics products, with two animal-based tests becoming the standard procedures. The Draize test involved dripping the substance in question, such as shampoo or a detergent paste, into the eyes of conscious, restrained rabbits and measuring the resultant damage over the course of several days. Rabbits cannot cry, thus allowing researchers to complete the tests quickly. Another test required researchers to force-feed large quantities of a substance to a sample of laboratory animals. The substance may be a solid such as lipstick or shaving cream. Pastes or liquids may also be used. The lethal dose of a substance was determined by the amount that had been ingested by an individual surviving animal when 50 percent of the sample had died, hence the name of the test, LD50.[20] Beginning in the 1970s, animal rights groups such as the Human Society and PETA had protested the use of these tests by the cosmetics industry. The Body Shop lent its support to these groups' efforts, labeling all animal testing as "cruel and unnecessary." By 1991, alternative procedures that involved far less cruelty to animals had already been developed but were yet to be approved for industry use.[21]

In the United States, The Body Shop's market share was limited by two factors. Its prices were significantly higher than those charged for mass-marketed products in drug stores. They were, however, generally comparable with the prices charged for cosmetics and cleansers at department store sales counters. The Body Shop was further constrained by the number of stores it had opened in the United States. By 1991, only 40 stores had been opened in a dozen metropolitan areas across the country. A mail-order catalog and telephone order line were used to supplement the American retail stores, but they were inadequate substitutes for the product sampling and advice that were readily available in The Body Shop's stores. Roddick maintained that those consumers who sampled Body Shop products became loyal customers: "Once they walk into one of our stores or buy from our catalogue, they're hooked."[22]

The Body Shop was taken public in 1984, with the Roddicks owning a combined 30 percent share of the outstanding stock. The firm's subsequent sales and net income figures are as follows (figures for 1988 were not available):[23]

Year	Sales Revenue	Net Income (both in millions)
1985	$15.3	$1.4
1986	28.4	3.4
1987	46.4	6.2
1989	119.0	14.6
1990	137.7	14.7

Without The Body Shop's monetary donations to various social causes, the net income figures would all be higher than reported in the financial statements. Estimates of the company's annual contributions to outside organizations varied between several hundred thousand and several million dollars.

Industry analysts considered The Body Shop to be a strong performer with the potential to prosper even in an economic downturn. The exotic nature of products such as hair conditioner made with 10 percent real bananas and a peppermint foot lotion would attract consumers who desired an affordable luxury. Analysts regarded the public's desire for personal care products as "insatiable," especially in North America.[24] The addition of the strong emotional appeal of social issues formed the basis of one of the most successful marketing concepts in the cosmetic industry in decades.

The 20th anniversary of Earth Day, celebrated in 1990, focused media attention on many of the environmental issues that Roddick and The Body Shop regularly addressed. Further, it spurred interest in environmental issues in the commercial sector. Several new entrants and existing competitors challenged The Body Shop in the United States and Europe. Among the largest of these firms were Estee Lauder and Revlon. The Limited had opened 50 Bath & Body Works stores, patterned after The Body Shop's outlets and located in shopping malls across the United States. In addition, an English competitor, Crabtree & Evelyn, had held a significant presence in North America and Europe since the mid-1970s.

By 1991, The Body Shop was a successful and profitable firm that had attracted a number of well-financed competitors. The company faced a real threat from these firms, as they were all well-financed and had a broad range of experience in marketing cosmetics. Each of these firms was well-established in the United States, yet no one firm dominated the new product segment that The Body Shop had helped create.

In addition, there were indications that the environmental concerns that attracted customers to The Body Shop might not have a permanent drawing power. Roddick had vowed never to sell anything but environmentally friendly cosmetics and grooming products in her stores, but the industry was growing and changing faster than anyone had anticipated. It seemed that The Body Shop needed to take action to assure its long-term survival.

When asked about her role in the company, Anita Roddick stated:

> The purpose of a business isn't just to generate profits to create an ever-large empire. It's to have the power to affect social change, to make the world a better place. I have always been an activist; I have always been incredibly impassioned about human rights and environmental issues. The Body Shop is simply my stage.[25]

QUESTIONS FOR DISCUSSION

1. How does The Body Shop address the four components of corporate social responsibility?
2. Anita Roddick claims that her firm does not advertise, yet it receives free media exposure and publicity through the social causes it champions. Is this approach appropriate for a business to follow?
3. What is your assessment of Anita Roddick's philosophy regarding the "purpose of a business"? Can this philosophy survive long term?
4. The Body Shop asks potential employees questions about "personal heroes" and individual beliefs. Is it ethical to ask such questions of applicants? Are these questions legitimate ones to ask in the first place? Are such questions fair to the applicants?
5. What are Anita Roddick's strengths and weaknesses as a leader? Should she stay on in a managing role or step aside and allow a more experienced person to run the marketing operations?
6. Should The Body Shop enter the mass market and retail its products in drug stores and supermarkets? How would this affect its operations and direction?

CASE ENDNOTES

1. Catalog, *The Body Shop* (Fall 1990).
2. Laura Zinn, "Whales, Human Rights, Rain Forests—and the Heady Smell of Profits," *Business Week* (July 15, 1991), 114.
3. Zinn, 114.
4. Samuel Greengard, "Face Values," *USAir Magazine* (November, 1990), 89.
5. Zinn, 114.
6. Greengard, 93.
7. Greengard, 97.
8. Zinn, 115.
9. Greengard, 94.
10. Greengard, 94.
11. Zinn, 114.
12. Greengard, 90.
13. Maria Koklanaris, "Trio of Retailers Finds Soap and Social Concern an Easy Sell," *The Washington Post* (April 27, 1991).
14. Greengard, 90.
15. Zinn, 115.
16. The Body Shop promotional literature, 1991.
17. Zinn, 115.
18. Body Shop promotional literature, 1991.
19. Body Shop promotional literature, 1991.
20. Peter Singer, *Animal Liberation: A New Ethics for Treatment of Animals* (New York: Avon Books, 1975), 48.
21. The Body Shop promotional literature, 1991.
22. Greengard, 89.
23. Compact Disclosure database, 1991.
24. Koklanaris.
25. Greengard, 97.

CASE 3

CONTROL DATA CORPORATION AND THE NORRIS ERA

At the heart of the corporate social responsibility movement is the debate over the fundamental roles of the public sector and the private sector in addressing the needs of society. Traditionally, the public sector has seen its role as providing public services and meeting the unmet needs of society. Business, on the other hand, has traditionally viewed its role as producing goods and services and selling them for a profit. Many companies today pursue their own version of corporate social responsibility. Very few, however, have pursued it the way Control Data Corporation (CDC) did while William C. Norris was at the helm.

Control Data Corporation was founded in Minneapolis in 1957 by William Norris. Today it is a billion-dollar company that has been a major force in the computer industry for three decades. The firm was founded as a manufacturer of supercomputers. Its *Cyber 205* was among the world's most powerful computers. The company adjusted to miniaturization by becoming the world's largest supplier of computer peripherals—storage disks, printers, memories, and terminals. The growth, development, and business strategy of CDC is a fascinating story by itself. Here, however, we wish to focus on its unique perspective on corporate social responsibility.

It is really Norris's philosophy and zeal that we will discuss because it would take an individual such as Norris to pursue things the way CDC has. Norris retired at age 75 in January 1986 and was succeeded by Robert M. Price. As of 1987, Price was preoccupied with getting CDC back on sound financial footing after 2 consecutive years of losses. It is generally believed that Control Data's financial problems were a result of business decisions, yet one cannot help but wonder whether Norris's preoccupation with social programs was a contributing factor.

The Norris View of Business's Social Role

Norris's philosophy was that business needed to identify unmet social needs and turn them into profitable business opportunities. One of the major areas where he initially sought to pursue this philosophy was inner-city revitalization. His first experiment was in his own city of Minneapolis, which was torn by riots in 1967, as were many cities across the United States. In 1968, Norris decided to help rebuild a Minneapolis ghetto by locating its first inner-city plant there.

Norris's view was that building a plant in the ghetto was not philanthropy but rather a business decision. He laid down three rules for the new corporate investment: "Make the plant new and modern. Make it profitable. Make us dependent on it so that we will have to make it work." Accordingly, the plant was designed to manufacture intricate components.[1] In approaching the project, Norris went to local black leaders and got their street-smart advice. Part of the advice was (1) to build a day care center for working mothers, (2) to offer to put them on flexible working hours, and (3) not to ask job applicants whether they had ever been arrested. In the beginning, absenteeism and quitting were problems. Norris and his managers hung on, sometimes prodding, sometimes training, and sometimes bailing someone out of jail after a long weekend. A decade later, the average worker had been with CDC for 5 years, building skills and moving up.

CDC built other plants in inner-city areas in Washington, DC, San Antonio, and Toledo. By 1982, the company had six inner-city facilities. Norris noted that other CEOs who had attempted to build in ghettos had failed. His response: "They figured it was just philanthropy. They sent in their money but not their smarts or their guts."[2] In the late 1970s, the company expanded on the idea of developing and revitalizing inner-city areas by organizing two consortiums—Rural Ventures, Inc., and City Venture Corporation—to create agricultural and inner-city jobs. Norris's idea for these projects was that the consortiums would make money from consulting fees, and CDC would make money selling computers and services. By 1982, the ventures were both still losing money.[3] Norris thought that ultimately American cities would be rebuilt by large consortiums of private businesses joining together with government, churches, and universities. The object would not be just to remake neighborhoods but to provide jobs, to help small entrepreneurs, and, yes, to make money. He argued: "Rebuilding the cities will be one of the great growth industries of the future. It will replace the auto as the big provider of jobs—if we Americans can ever get ourselves organized."[4]

Other Novel Ventures

Norris's self-proclaimed mission of "addressing society's major unmet needs as profitable business opportunities" led the company into a number of novel ventures. In the early 1980s, the company dabbled in a variety of projects that perennially lost money. The company grew vegetables hydroponically, imported Yugoslavian wine, drew up urban renewal plans, and provided health care on Indian reservations. At one point CDC had the idea of helping ex-convicts. The plan was to help them get jobs by financing used cars at low rates for former inmates, but it didn't work out. Some of the ex-cons took cars and disappeared. A former inmate hired to run the program stole some of the money himself. By the time he was caught, 34 cars and $137,000 were missing. The "cars for cons" program, as some critics dubbed it, was a classic example of the kind of venture that most firms would view skeptically but CDC pursued zealously.[5]

In 1983, the Labor Department gave CDC a corporate responsibility award. The award was for helping women and minorities get better jobs and develop managerial skills. It also applauded the firm's role in developing low-cost housing and day care centers for employees and inner-city plants. Critics looked at the bottom line and maintained that the profitability of Norris's approach just wasn't there. They argued that most of his projects made money slowly, if at all. Norris maintained that profit was his motive and that his business approach could and did succeed in places where both government and charity had failed.[6]

The Business Front

CDC's troubles began appearing on the financial statements in 1984 as net income plunged from $161 million to $31 million. Because of technical problems and lengthy product delays in its attempts to make large disk drives that were "plug compatible" with the latest generation of IBM machines, CDC had to report an overall loss in its third quarter of 1984—its first loss in a decade. In addition to the disk-drive problem, the company had to pull back from a number of loss-plagued business centers that were being run by Commercial Credit Co., the financial services subsidiary it acquired in 1968. These business centers were among Norris's favorite projects.[7]

The basic problem the company faced in the 1980s was whether it could turn business around and come back from its huge losses in 1985 and 1986. CDC's net income for the 10-year period 1976 to 1986 was as follows:

Year	Amount
1986	$(264,500,000) deficit
1985	(567,500,000) deficit
1984	31,600,000
1983	161,700,000
1982	155,100,000
1981	170,600,000
1980	150,600,000
1979	124,200,000
1978	89,464,000
1977	62,995,000
1976	44,240,000

Although many consider Norris a visionary, others think he contributed to CDC's problems by his preoccupation with pet projects. One former employee said that product development decisions were made based on what Norris wanted rather than what customers wanted. For example, for 20 years CDC spent hundreds of millions of dollars developing Plato, a computer-based educational system that did not earn a profit until 1983 and then only a small one. Plato is a self-teaching, computer-based program initially designed to train inner-city workers but that is now used in business and public schools.[8] One Plato program was designed to teach Ojibwa, an ancient Indian language, to Chippewa Indians. The company was involved in computer-based education long before schools actually began work in this area. Critics say, however, that computer education has caught on but Plato hasn't. They say Plato is too expensive and that the microcomputer revolution has passed CDC by. The company eventually came out with a microcomputer, but it was double the price of the Apple computers that schools were beginning to adopt. Plato has fared somewhat better in the smaller industrial-training market.[9]

Some former CDC executives say that the company scrimped on new-product spending for several years while it was putting money into Norris's special projects, a charge the company refutes. Although Norris has denied that his pet businesses have drained investments away from the company's profitable ventures, this criticism of him remains. In 1984, CDC began a painful retrenchment. *Business Week* noted that Norris had to back away from at least some of his cherished but costly ideas of social responsibility. He had always promised his full-time workers that they would never be laid off, for example, but the financial pressures besetting the company forced sizable cutbacks.[10]

In 1983, William C. Norris published a book that contained close to 200 pages of his visionary thoughts for American business. The book was entitled *New Frontiers for Business Leadership*. The closing paragraph of the book summarized his thinking and feeling about American business:

> We are at a crossroad: We can either choose to continue in our traditional mode of surveillance over the status quo, or we can provide the leadership needed to create a new business culture characterized by innovation and cooperation. We can sit back and wait and eventually find ourselves facing a hodgepodge of bureaucratically imposed national planning, or we can act like the industrial statesmen we are supposed to be. If we opt to behave as leaders, I am confident that together we will be able to revitalize American industry in an intelligent and democratic way.[11]

The Post-Norris Period

In 1986, Robert M. Price succeeded Norris as chairman. During the period 1983 to 1988, CDC lost $1.3 billion. From 1988 to 1991 the company experienced mixed financial results. In 1991, Price resigned as chairman and the company was undergoing a major turnaround coordinated by president and CEO Lawrence Perlman. Rather than appoint Perlman CEO, the company chose to form a search committee. Analysts said that the company's failure to appoint Perlman was typical of the poor judgment that caused CDC to lose money between 1983 and 1988. Perlman encountered political opposition from board members. Perlman took radical action to stop the company's losses, laying off 3,100 employees and shutting down the company's supercomputer subsidiary.[12]

Also in 1991, William C. Norris announced his resignation from the CDC board.[13]

QUESTIONS FOR DISCUSSION

1. In your own words, state Norris's philosophy of corporate social responsibility. Also, state and evaluate it in terms of the four-part social responsibility model.
2. What is your assessment of Norris's strengths and weaknesses as a visionary and as a CEO?
3. Who are the stakeholders in this case, and what are their stakes?
4. What is your appraisal of Norris's basic philosophy that business should identify unmet social needs and turn them into profitable business opportunities? Is this philosophy compatible with the role of American business? From a practical point of view, is it feasible? Discuss.
5. In 1987, a number of entrepreneurs and venture capitalists began pouncing on different ways to diagnose, treat, prevent, or cure AIDS and make money

in the process. Is this the kind of project you think Norris might pursue if he were still active, or is it different?

6. Do library research and update the situation at Control Data.

CASE ENDNOTES

1. Marshall Loeb, "Planting in the Ghettos," *Time* (April 3, 1978), 61.
2. *Ibid.*
3. Lawrence Ingrassia, "Far Out Firm: Seeking to Aid Society, Control Data Takes on Many Novel Ventures," *The Wall Street Journal* (December 22, 1982), 1, 10.
4. Loeb, 61.
5. Ingrassia, 1.
6. "Executives Who Look Beyond the Bottom Line," *U.S. News & World Report* (October 22, 1984), 61.
7. "Control Data Starts a Painful Retrenchment," *Business Week* (October 22, 1984), 94.
8. Ford Worthy, "Does Control Data Have a Future?" *Fortune* (December 23, 1985), 24–26.
9. Ingrassia, 10.
10. *Business Week,* 96.
11. William C. Norris, *New Frontiers for Business Leadership* (Minneapolis: Dorn Books, 1983), 190.
12. K. D. Goodman, "Control Data—Company Report," *Market Guide, Inc.* (September 27, 1991).
13. "William C. Norris to Retire from Control Data's Board," *The Wall Street Journal* (April 1, 1991), B4.

CASE 4 LAKEWOOD BANK & TRUST*

Introduction

In 1973, Mr. George Elliot, President and Chief Executive Officer of Lakewood Bank & Trust, faced a critical decision about the bank's development. The older neighborhood in which the bank was located was beginning to deteriorate rapidly, a situation that could have an adverse impact on deposit growth and loan activity and risk. Elliot debated whether or not the bank should make a financial commitment to the neighborhood in the form of admittedly risky residential and commercial rehabilitation and purchase loans. If such a commitment were made, he had to decide also on its form and extent.

History

Lakewood Bank & Trust was one of the largest state-chartered banks in the Dallas metropolitan area in 1973. It ranked tenth among all city banks in total deposits ($63.4 million). Total ownership was held by some 400 individual stockholders. The bank was opened in 1942 near its present location some three miles east of Dallas's central business district. The East Dallas area at that time was stable and growing, providing substantial support for deposit growth and local lending opportunities. To the west of the bank were the older middle- to upper-income subdivisions of Munger Place and Junius Heights, with heavy concentrations of large prairie-style and smaller bungalow-style frame homes built in the first three decades of the twentieth century. Adjoining these subdivisions on the north was the Swiss Avenue district, a neighborhood of distinction, traditionally the residence of Dallas's elite. To the north and east of the bank was the newer Lakewood upper-middle-income subdivision. The Lakewood Country Club to the immediate east of the bank, opened in 1913, completed the area's prestigious image. The bank was located within Lakewood Shopping Center, which was designed to serve the surrounding affluent population.

Lakewood Bank prospered in the 1940s and 1950s, along with its neighborhood. However, in the 1960s several changes began taking place that threatened its position. The city in the 1950s rezoned most of the older East Dallas area to multifamily dwellings in the expectation that there would be considerable demand for close-in, luxury-apartment living. This had the effect of reducing expectations of a single-family character for these neighborhoods. High rates of home-building on the suburban fringe and new expressways shifted upper-middle-income housing demand away from the older, more established areas. The older prairie-style frame architecture was no longer in vogue, being replaced by the newer brick, ranch-style homes. Maintenance costs on the older structures were increasing.

---

*This case was prepared by Kerry D. Vandell and Sydney C. Reagan of the School of Business Administration, Southern Methodist University. It is designed to be used as a basis for class discussion rather than to illustrate either effective or ineffective handling of an administrative situation. Presented at a Case Workshop. Reprinted with permission of the authors. *Not to be duplicated without permission of the author and publisher.*

Finally, civil rights activity generated white flight through fears of racial transition to black or Mexican-American occupancy of the area. Large concentrations of black and Mexican-American households resided to the south of the East Dallas neighborhoods.

These factors created a generally perceived state of decline in the old East Dallas area by the early 1970s. Racial transition to largely Mexican-American occupancy was advancing from the southwest. Median incomes and property values in the area were dropping. Larger single-family homes were being partitioned into apartments and rooming houses.

Physical conditions rapidly degenerated. By 1973, even property values in the more isolated Lakewood area were stabilizing or dropping, and considerable fears were expressed that decline there was imminent. To complement residential decline, Lakewood Shopping Center was being supplanted by the newer shopping malls in the suburbs; its design was considered outdated, accessibility was relatively difficult, and congestion was increasing. The older shops catering to an upper-middle-income clientele were being replaced by thrift shops, liquor stores, record shops, bars, and other commercial establishments oriented more toward the incoming lower-income population.

Bank Profile

This change in conditions of the surrounding neighborhood had not as yet seriously affected the bank's profitability or growth by 1973. Profitability had consistently remained comparable to that of other banks of a similar size in Dallas. Deposits since 1960 had been rising at an average annual rate of 14.5 percent. The bank's growth in deposits was historically higher than average for the city of Dallas, although there were indications it might be falling below the average in the 1970s. Elliot attributed this growth to aggressive loan and deposit development programs that actively sought loans and deposits beyond the bank's neighborhood. In the mid 1960s, the bank began searching for additional lending opportunities in the real estate market. It had had some prior limited experience with financing the purchase of a few homes and commercial properties, largely as favors to regular customers, but no significant real estate investment effort had ever been made. A Real Estate Loan Department was established in 1967. In 1968, the bank expanded into construction financing in the profitable apartment and shopping center markets in Dallas. During the late 1960s and early 1970s, the bank's real estate loan portfolio increased as a share of total assets, largely due to the higher yields available in real estate at that time.

Changes

Although the bank enjoyed continuing financial strength in the 1960s and early 1970s, Elliot observed certain changes in bank operating conditions that appeared to be related to the changes that were taking place in the surrounding neighborhood:

1. *Inability to Generate Installment Loans.* One type loan that was very profitable but that Lakewood was increasingly unable to generate in large volumes was consumer installment loans. Elliot felt this lack of success was in part attributable to the bank's neighborhood, which was composed of mature households rather than young couples, many of whom did relatively little borrowing.

2. *Declining Deposit Potential.* The bank had for a number of years competed with four other banks in the area for deposits and lending opportunities. Elliot's aggressive development programs were successful at increasing the bank's size from fourth to first place in only a few years. In fact, one of the competing institutions moved out of the area entirely, relocating to a newer suburban market. Elliot regarded this as a victory of sorts but also as a warning of the declining potential of the area.

3. *Heavy Financial Commitment to New Building.* In 1963, Elliot recommended, and the board of directors agreed to, the construction of a new $700,000 building that would replace the existing rented quarters. Although there was some talk of relocating, the decision was made with little debate to again locate in the same neighborhood in Lakewood Shopping Center, less than one block away from the old structure. Deterioration of the surrounding area had not advanced far enough at this time to arouse concern about the future of the bank in the East Dallas area. However, the decision of Elliot and the board to build in the same area meant to Elliot the bank had a substantial long-term financial stake in the community and was increasingly vulnerable to adverse change in the area. The new structure was opened in 1965 and an addition was completed in 1971. It was the first new commercial construction in the area in 30 years.

4. *Dispersal of Loan and Deposit Sources and Lowered Local Creditworthiness.* Most new lending and deposit sources were increasingly originating from outside the bank's area. Since Texas does not allow branch banking, the bank could not expand physically into surrounding areas. Elliot surmised that his geographical anchor would ultimately prevent the bank from penetrating more distant markets much more deeply than it already had through the development programs. In addition, those loan applications for commercial credit, installment credit, and construction and repair credit that did originate in the immediate area were increasingly of lower quality. Credit records of applicants were worse and loan security was generally less satisfactory.

The bank had established a goal in 1968 of $75 million in total resources by 1975. Elliot, with the support of long-term projections completed by the bank, by the early 1970s came to the conclusion that the growth trend the bank had enjoyed in the past could not continue, and this goal would not be met if current trends in migration, deterioration, and current bank attitudes and policies continued. At some point a decision would have to be made on a strategy designed to achieve this goal, with the most obvious strategies being a substantial redevelopment effort in the immediate area or relocation to a more profitable suburban location.

Arguments in Favor of Redevelopment

Several factors provided support to a redevelopment strategy. First, several officers, including Elliot, and several board members, including Conway Walker, a former Dallas mayor and very active board member, lived in the East Dallas or Lakewood areas and had a substantial personal commitment to the area. Walker was a long-time resident of the Swiss Avenue district that was being immediately threatened by change. Second, the bank already had some experience with community involvement. Elliot, as early as 1964, had emphasized community involvement by the bank, although more at the individual volunteer service level than at the institutional financial support level. Several officers and other employees had been active in organizations such as the local Chamber of Commerce, the Boy Scouts, and local business and professional associations. The bank had also been active in supporting enlargement and modernization of the shopping center, street-widening programs, and the attraction of new business.

The most active involvement by Lakewood Bank in the redevelopment of the area had come recently, since 1972, in the form of over $800,000 worth of home improvement and home purchase loans on Swiss Avenue. Elliot had decided that default risks on such loans would not be excessive in view of the unique character of the area and the limited scope of lending activity. He was strongly supported in his decision by Walker and several other board members. The project was given impetus in the summer of 1973 with the creation of the Swiss Avenue Historic District by the city of Dallas, an act that reestablished the future of the area as a prestigious single-family neighborhood and brought with it increased city services and development controls. The eleven loans made by Lakewood Bank on Swiss in 1972–1973 acted as a catalyst for other lenders to return to the area. By late 1973 it was clear that Swiss Avenue would remain a stable upper- and upper-middle-income enclave.

Elliot enjoyed the success of the Swiss Avenue experience, and it encouraged him toward a redevelopment strategy. However, he realized several factors mitigated this success as a portent of future broader success in "revitalizing" East Dallas. First, the Swiss Avenue homes were large stately mansions—very unique and with a high degree of architectural quality. Such was not the case with all of East Dallas. Second, although some of the homes had been converted to rooming houses, the Swiss Avenue area had not declined to the extent that other neighborhoods, such as Munger Place and Junius Heights, had. Third, he had some doubt as to whether there would be sufficient demand for older homes in close-in deteriorated neighborhoods by middle- and upper-middle-income families to significantly impact the area.

Arguments Opposed to Redevelopment

There was also considerable skepticism from within and without the bank over expanding redevelopment lending activities in the East Dallas area. This skepticism originated from some lending officers and appraisers in the marketplace—individuals who should have expertise on market potential. None of them resided in the East Dallas-Lakewood area and thus were not influenced by personal commitments to the area. These individuals advanced several arguments against a further commitment, which Elliot seriously evaluated.

First, they said that physical and functional depreciation of the housing stock in older East Dallas (besides Swiss Avenue) was already far advanced and was irreversible. Any expectation of rising property values was pure speculation and not justified by appraisal practices. Only a limited number of younger households felt favorably toward older, deteriorated structures and even these households would move to the suburbs when their children reached school age, in view of the inferior reputation of Dallas public schools. There were few amenities in the area for such households. City services were minimal in most areas, and the crime rate was increasing. Racial transition to Mexican-American and some black occupancy was now past the "tipping point" and extended to within a few blocks of Lakewood Shopping Center, further reducing middle-income white demand. Finally, many of the structures were of questionable architectural quality anyway, especially in the Heights area, lacking the "uniqueness" necessary to revitalize an area.

A second point of skepticism related to the expansiveness of the area and the limited resources of the bank. To turn an area around, they reasoned, would require substantial resources. Property values were in the $10–16,000 range for most of the rundown homes in the area. To bring most structures up to code would require roughly equivalent expenditures. Thus a combined home purchase-home repair loan would require an average commitment (and in some cases more) by bank and borrower of $20–32,000 or more. If the purchase and repair of 30 percent of the 22,000 units in East Dallas were assumed to provide a suitable critical mass for revitalization, to be successful the bank would have to commit itself to almost $150 million worth of such loan activity, an amount obviously far beyond its capability, especially since it was a commercial bank and not primarily in the business of long-term residential mortgage lending. The danger of making fewer than a critical number of loans in the area was that the loan program would have little impact and result in substantial losses in view of the low property values and high per-loan loss exposure. Reducing the area for lending to allow intensive lending would mean the neighborhood would be subject to adverse external forces hastening decay. Committing too large a portion of the bank's assets to such lending would unwisely expose the bank to high risks without compensating returns.

Rather than increasing commitment to the local area, these individuals advocated further loan and deposit development on a metropolitan-wide basis and gradual withdrawal from the area along with eventual relocation in more stable surroundings after finding a replacement tenant for the bank building.

[Postscript and editor's note: The Lakewood Bank case is an actual case developed from a single Dallas bank. Many banks in the United States have encountered parallel circumstances. An interesting case about the South Shore National Bank of Chicago, Illinois, was published in *Chicago* (February, 1977).]

QUESTIONS FOR DISCUSSION

1. What is the major overriding issue in this case?
2. Who are the stakeholders in this case, and what are their stakes? Carefully evaluate and rank their stakes.
3. What economic/legal/ethical/discretionary responsibilities does the bank have, and what is the nature and extent of these responsibilities?
4. State the options you think the bank has at this point. What are the advantages and disadvantages of each option? What course of action should the bank take and why?

CASE 5   THE BILL COLLECTOR[1]

Paula Ross, a 40-year-old social worker by training and previous experience, is now a bill collector for New York State Electric and Gas Corporation (NYSEG). She is the key person in a unique corporate responsibility program aimed at helping NYSEG's customers navigate the social welfare system and get their bills paid at the same time. The program has kept thousands of customers off the bad-debt list. Mrs. Ross, along with 12 other company consumer representatives who were also formerly social workers, in 1 month helped 200 families obtain about $90,000 in public assistance, including 160 families who received approximately $45,000 to pay their utility bills.

Mrs. Ross visits with customers who are delinquent in their utility bills and tells them about public assistance programs for which they may qualify. Her major goal is to stress programs that will help pay their utility bills, but she goes beyond this and provides information about medical, educational, and other plans. For example, on one occasion she convinced the state to pay for the vocational training of a child with a learning disability. On another occasion she convinced the American Cancer Society to pay for a customer's travel to the hospital for radiation treatments. She also talked a hospital into using some of its federal funds to pay the bill for an indigent customer who didn't have medical insurance.

Mrs. Ross enjoys a good reputation with most customers because she helps them solve their problems. The Boudreaus, for example, are a family that speaks highly of Mrs. Ross. "If we go in (to a social service agency), we're peons. But Paula's NYSEG. She's got *power*," says Mr. Boudreau. NYSEG apparently agrees that she has power. The company has agreed not to turn a person's lights off if she says no. This power with the company gives her enormous trust with the customers. They know that she has the motivation and ability to get them social service money they can't get on their own.

Mrs. Ross will seldom take no for an answer when she contacts a delinquent account. One utility customer with a past-due account refused to see her. Mrs. Ross talked the customer into meeting her at a nearby parking lot. She told the customer: "I'm here to see if we can't find you money from somewhere." It turned out that the customer got behind on her payments because of her husband's illness and doctor bills. Mrs. Ross offered to get the customer a "Project Share" grant that is administered by the Red Cross and funded by the utility and also to contact the cancer society to see what other help the customer could get.

William Tabbert, NYSEG's consumer-affairs supervisor, has advocated that utilities, banks, retailers, and insurance companies hire trained social workers. These workers help not only customers who are elderly or indigent but also middle-class and more affluent customers who have gotten behind in their utility, mortgage, or credit-card bill payments. Only a few other power companies have adopted the NYSEG social worker approach, though its write-off rate for uncollected bills runs about 20 percent below the national electric utility average.

Despite its apparent economic and public relations success, the NYSEG program has stirred some controversy. In 1983, the company sued the Chemung County social service agency, charging that the agency failed to pay $340,500 owed NYSEG on behalf of people who had qualified for public assistance. The company won the suit, but bad feelings remain. Some social service agencies have disparaged the company's motives for usurping their role. The Chemung County social service administrator asserted: "In the long run, NYSEG is only interested in serving itself." Some of Mrs. Ross's own fellow employees think she is conducting a "giveaway."

QUESTIONS FOR DISCUSSION

1. What is your assessment of the NYSEG program? Is it proper to call this a corporate social responsibility effort? Who are the stakeholders, and what are their stakes? Evaluate the program from the standpoint of the economic/legal/ethical/philanthropic social responsibility model.
2. Does it matter whether the company is in this program for personal as well as social reasons? Do you think it is? Discuss.
3. Identify the major problems with this rather unique program.
4. Assume you've been hired as a consultant to advise NYSEG on the advisability of continuing versus discontinuing this program. What is your recommendation and why?

CASE ENDNOTE

1. The materials for this case are based on Bill Paul, "Utility Aids Customers' Welfare Needs," *The Wall Street Journal* (July 8, 1987), 6.

CASE 6   HOME OF THE BRAVES?*

Since moving from Milwaukee to Atlanta in 1966 the Braves had been a perennial disappointment to their fans. The high expectations that greeted the new arrivals were replaced after several years with the resignation that accompanied the recognition that having a major league team did not ensure a winning team.

The 1991 season began as had all of the others, with assurances that if their hitters and pitchers produced, anything could happen. What set the 1991 season apart from the previous ones, however, was that in 1991 the hitters and pitchers actually did produce. By mid-June of seasons past the destiny of the Braves had become painfully obvious: They were to dwell in or near the cellar of the Western Division of the National League. In mid-June of the 1991 season, the Braves were contending for the division lead.

As the unexpected respectability of the Braves dawned on their fans, the fans responded by turning out in droves for the games. Attending baseball games became the thing to do in Atlanta. Throughout June and July, the thinking seemed to be that no matter where the Braves finished in their division, it would have been a successful season. The conventional wisdom was that the Braves would eventually fizzle, since they were thought not to have manpower adequate for a season-long pennant race.

In addition to awakening the long-dormant spirit in Atlanta, the newly energized Braves were having a similar effect on their nationwide television audience. The Braves had long been a staple on WTBS, the "Superstation," a cable television station that transmitted Braves games to much of the United States. Long billed as "America's Team," the games were often sandwiched in between reruns of programs such as "Leave It to Beaver" and "My Little Margie." The comedic value of the Braves' games was often thought to be on a par with, if not superior to, the other offerings of the station. Suddenly, however, there was a tremendous outpouring of support from across the nation. The television ratings for the games skyrocketed in 1991 as the Braves proceeded to truly become "America's Team." It was indeed a banner year for Ted Turner, the eccentric multimillionaire who seemed to be doubly blessed since he owned both the Braves and WTBS.

As the season progressed through August and into September, the Braves basked in the glow of both national and international attention. The mass media had adopted the Braves, and their successes and failures were widely chronicled. Not all of the attention focused on the Braves was of a positive nature, however.

By the time the Braves won the playoffs, the American Indian Movement (AIM) had mounted a concerted drive to urge management to change the team's name. AIM was founded in 1928 to represent the interests of Native Americans. The group has been especially vigilant in establishing recognition of Native American treaty rights.

The push intensified with the World Series. Demonstrations were staged by AIM and by other Native American groups outside of the ballparks in Atlanta and Minneapolis during the World Series, demonstrations that exacerbated crowd

---

* This case was prepared by James M. Lahiff, Management Department, Terry College of Business, University of Georgia.

control problems. More important, these demonstrations garnered invaluable worldwide publicity for AIM and for its protests.

By the end of the baseball season, a great deal of support had been generated for this Native American movement. News columnists and civil rights organizations publically sided with the drive to do away with team names such as the Braves, Cleveland Indians, and Washington Redskins, names that were thought to offend Native Americans.

While the main thrust of AIM at present is to get the management of the Braves to change the team's name, the name change is simply the first step in a number of changes being sought. Clyde Bellecourt, AIM national director, expresses his organization's feelings in this way: "The name has got to go. Nothing is going to change, the behavior ain't going to change until the name changes. And even then, it's going to take a while after that before it will change completely."[1]

Braves president Stan Kasten said that the Braves's name had never been an issue prior to Atlanta's success, but he doesn't hold that against the Native Americans. He says, "I fully understand that any cause is in need of a platform and attention, and I don't think anyone here will deny that they used the available platform in the World Series to their best advantage—something I might do if I were in their shoes. I don't have any problem with that." Kasten also said that the Braves is a business that would face "complicated and multifaceted" economic issues if it were to change its logo or name.[2]

AIM is especially distressed with the fans' use of the "tomahawk chop" and chants before, during, and after the ballgames. As the season progressed, the Atlanta fans adopted more and more the behaviors of stereotypical Indians. Novelty tomahawks made of foam rubber became a popular souvenir at the ballpark, where the fans waved them in rhythm to the beat of a tom-tom. Some fans began appearing for the ballgames wearing full Indian headdress. Some, especially those who hoped to be shown on television, would come wearing warpaint, or a reasonable facsimile thereof. Many Native Americans feel that such acts stereotype them as warlike savages or laughable cartoon figures. As *USA Today* editorialized, "Some feel it puts them on the level of animals, a more common source for team names."[3]

One month after the baseball season ended, Ted Turner stated that he had "no intention of changing the name of the Atlanta Braves to pacify the American Indian Movement." He stated that he considered the name a "compliment" because "Braves are warriors." He added, however, that he "would like to see something done to get rid of the chop."[4]

As the controversy unfolded, it appeared that most of the fans, at least the more vocal ones, opposed any name change. Some have vowed to never again attend a Braves game if the name is changed. Fans appear to be equally resistant to the suggestion that the tomahawk chop be put to rest. There has been talk about the formation of a "Chop 'Til You Drop Club."

In recent years, there has been increased sensitivity regarding such matters. The number of major colleges using Native American names has been reduced to six. Stanford University changed their name long ago from the Indians to the Cardinal in 1972; Dartmouth changed from Indians to Big Green in the mid-1970s.

Not even all Native American groups, however, are in complete agreement on this matter. Eastern Michigan University, following a state Department of Civil Rights recommendation, changed its team name from the Hurons to the Eagles in May of 1991. In November of the same year a Huron Indian group requested that the university reinstate the Huron name. Robert Bennett, a member of Huron Restoration, Inc., explained, "These symbols are the way we pass on our history.... We want it (the Huron name) to be in the public's eye so they can know the history of the Huron people and how it is involved with the American history."[5]

Another example of Indian approval for the use of an Indian name is Florida State University. The football team has been called the Seminoles ever since the start of their football program in 1947. Seminole Indian officials not only endorse the use of the name but participate in activities surrounding the football games. The use of the tomahawk chop at athletic events is reported to have begun at Florida State University.

As a member of the Board of Directors of the Atlanta Braves, you must decide how to respond to the request of AIM.

QUESTIONS FOR DISCUSSION

1. Who are the stakeholders in this case and what are their stakes? Discuss the legitimacy and power of the stakeholders.

2. What corporate social responsibility does the Atlanta Braves, a multimillion dollar corporation, have to AIM? What ethical issues, in particular, have a bearing on the resolution of this case?

3. What do you consider to be the main arguments in favor of the desired name change? What are the main arguments against such a change?

4. What are some examples of the "complicated and multifaceted economic issues" Stan Kasten referred to?

5. Of what importance is the fact that AIM never pressed this matter until the Braves began to do well?

6. How, exactly, should Braves' management respond to AIM? What actions other than a team name change might be attempted in order to resolve the problem?

CASE ENDNOTES

1. "Stopping the Chop," *Athens Banner-Herald* (November 22, 1991), 9.
2. *Ibid.*
3. "Redskins, Braves: Listen to Those You've Offended," *USA Today* (November 25, 1991), 12A.
4. "Turner Won't Change Braves' Name, but Wouldn't Mind Stopping the Chop," *Atlanta Journal* (December 3, 1991), F8.
5. "Huron Indian Group: Reinstate Nickname," *USA Today* (November 25, 1991), 2C.

CASE 7 THOMAS BRANDT'S JOB SEARCH (A)*

The phone woke Thomas Brandt on Friday morning, March 27, 1991. Matthew Walsh, Sales Manager at Genetic Development (GD), was calling to receive verbal acceptance of a job offer with GD as sales representative in Durham, North Carolina. The specifics were: company car with unlimited personal use, opportunity to purchase a personal computer and write it off as a company expense, and annual salary expected to be at least $42,000 with significant upside potential. The range of salaries for the company's five sales representatives was $38,000 to $100,000. At that time the Durham area was the geographical location of choice for Thomas, as he found the low cost of living, high growth, and moderate climate quite appealing. Another plus for Thomas was that a sales job would allow him to structure his daily schedule and not be confined to a nine-to-five regimen.

The offer was very acceptable, but three days earlier Thomas had his first interview with Abbott Laboratories for a management development position, described as affording the new employee the opportunity to spend time in each functional department of the Agriculture and Chemical Division of Abbott. This position seemed in line with typical MBA offers and had a strong potential for international placement after three to six years, which Thomas found favorable. Despite the bitter winters, Chicago had advantages since the girl he was dating grew up there.

Thomas explained to Matthew that he was still interested in the job with GD but would like to have the chance to see this opportunity to its end. Matthew seemed disturbed upon hearing this and further defined his offer, concluded the phone conversation by saying that he wanted to hear whether or not Thomas would accept the job on Monday, and said he didn't want to play games.

Background

Prior to starting the MBA program, Thomas interviewed with Genetic Development for its inside sales job. GD was a small biotechnology firm located just outside of Boston. The inside sales position was historically used to train people to go into the field. GD eventually offered Thomas the job, but he decided to enter business school instead.

In his search for a summer position, he contacted GD. Matthew arranged for Thomas to go to Boston to perform marketing research for the summer. Thomas was primarily assigned two tasks: market analysis of the uncovered Southwest area and new product surveys for the 25 new products planned for introduction in the next year. GD anticipated placing its first sales representative in the Southwest in June. Matthew's primary reason for bringing Thomas to GD for the summer was to allow both parties to get a feel for each other. This employment time would

---

*This case (Parts A, B, and C) was written by Beau H. Brock under the supervision of Professor Jeffrey A. Barach as a basis for class discussion rather than to illustrate effective or ineffective administration practices.

Copyright © 1991 by Jeffrey A. Barach, A. B. Freeman School of Business, Tulane University, New Orleans, LA 70118. Reproduced with permission.

serve as the three-month evaluation period which was a part of each employee's employment process.

Matthew viewed Thomas as the "right" person for the Southwest territory because Thomas's parents were born and raised in Ft. Worth, Texas, and because Thomas graduated from high school in Central Louisiana and finished his undergraduate studies at Louisiana State University in Baton Rouge. Not only was Thomas familiar with this area's general culture, he could also easily assimilate the New England culture since he had spent his first two years of college in Connecticut and had lived in New England for the first six years of grammar school. Matthew voiced concerns to Thomas about sending a New Englander to the Southwest region because through all of his travels, even abroad, the Southwest was the only area that Matthew had felt prejudice against him as a person.

When Thomas left at the end of the summer, Matthew told Thomas that he was 99 percent sure that GD was going to offer the Southwest regional representative position to Thomas. Upon his exit, Matthew encouraged Thomas to interview with other companies so that he could get a feel for what opportunities existed and be comfortable taking the GD offer.

As his second year at school progressed, Thomas did some on-campus interviewing to hone his interview skills but did not speak to any biotechnology companies. He maintained contact with GD and used one of its new products as a basis for an assignment in a Consumer Behavior class.

Thomas did attend a job fair in New York during Christmas break where he spoke to Pfizer and to Siemens Biomedical Company. Both these interviews were for sales positions, and the products of these firms were less interesting to Thomas than those of GD.

In February, Thomas received a phone call from GD's sales representative in North Carolina, a friend Thomas made during the summer. The sales rep was aware of Thomas's interest in North Carolina and told Thomas that he was being moved to Washington D.C. He suggested that Thomas let Matthew know that he (Thomas) would like that territory. Thomas contacted Matthew, who said he wasn't sure if it would work, but that it did sound reasonable for Thomas to cover the North Carolina territory.

Guidance?

After overcoming the surprise given him by the early morning phone call from Matthew, Thomas called his parents, hoping to reach his father. But his father was out, so Thomas explained the situation to his mother who suggested he try to stall for time but offered no real feasible means of doing this. She did feel that, if pushed, Thomas should take the offer in North Carolina. Next, Thomas called Juan Columbus, a recent graduate of the MBA program and current employee in the job being offered by Abbott. Juan was one of the interviewers Abbott brought to New Orleans, and he confided that Thomas was one of the five students that Abbott wanted for a second interview.

With this information Thomas went to school and discussed his problem first with one of the A.B. Freeman's career counselors and then with his former policy teacher. Janet Donaldson, the career counselor, said that now was the only opportunity he would have to be hired for his degree, and that after this he would be hired based on his work experiences. She also said that the GD job brought with it the risk of being labeled a "salesman" and that it was still not a management job. She also suggested that he personally reconcile for himself what he was looking for—apparent immediate returns with GD or what seemed to be a more management, career-oriented opportunity with Abbott. When questioned about whether he should take the offer from GD but continue talking with Abbott, Janet said that wasn't ethical and advised Thomas against doing it.

After tracking down Jonathan Bennett, his policy professor, Professor Bennett advised "pushing the system a bit." He suggested that Thomas find out from Abbott just how much time Abbott needed to make the final hiring decision. He suggested that knowing this, Thomas should call GD and try to get a feel for how much Matthew was willing to budge on his original stand. Professor Bennett thought that Thomas could use his past positive work experience with GD to his favor. Thomas agreed that Matthew should find some value in already knowing Thomas, considering the fact that he had once been pleased enough with Thomas to offer him a position. Professor Bennett emphasized that Thomas needed to get a feel for Matthew's attitude and push for as much time as he felt possible. With these suggestions in mind, Thomas had a good idea of where he stood, but he was not exactly sure what he would say on Monday, or what he should do if Matthew required an answer immediately.

When Thomas got back to his apartment, he called the Personnel Recruitment office at Abbott. They told him they expected the hiring decision to be made within two weeks. Sunday evening Thomas spoke with his father. His father agreed with Professor Bennett's suggestions, adding that Thomas emphasize that he has enjoyed the relationship that he maintained with Matthew and GD, but emphasizing to Matthew that, if he did receive the other offer, Thomas was not sure which he would choose. When Thomas asked his father what to do if forced to make a decision, his father's first answer was to turn down the GD offer. Thomas was surprised with this answer because he had almost resolved that the game was hardball, that he could play too, and that he should accept the offer but continue talks with Abbott. Thomas asked his father again: Should he give up the sure thing for something that looked good but was certainly less than certain? This time, as expected, his usually hard-line businessman father advised him to take the GD offer but continue talking with Abbott.

QUESTIONS FOR DISCUSSION

1. What should Thomas do? What would you do? What ethical issues are involved?
2. What should Thomas do if pressed to give an immediate answer to Matthew?

3. Should Thomas have given Matthew a commitment on Friday, never revealing the developing opportunity?
4. Which job should Thomas take?

THOMAS BRANDT'S JOB SEARCH (B)

As Thomas dialed GD Monday afternoon, he reviewed what he would say to Matthew. Thomas would start talking about the mutually beneficial working relationship he had maintained with GD. He planned to emphasize his positive feelings for the company in an effort to gain a decision-making grace period of three weeks. But he felt that if pressed he would make the verbal commitment to GD, continue to interview with Abbott, and cross any bridges that might develop, if and when he came to them.

Thomas started the phone conversation by explaining to Matthew his continued interest in the GD sales position and tried to emphasize the fact that, if he did receive the other offer, he was not sure which job he would take. Thomas commented that he liked both jobs but for different reasons. He also stated that he had enjoyed their past working relationship and sensed that Matthew felt the same about Thomas. He continued by saying that he thought Matthew should find some value in already knowing Thomas as opposed to looking for a new employee whom he did not know. Thomas then suggested that value might be expressed in the form of granting the three weeks needed by Thomas to make a final decision.

Matthew responded with what seemed to be a prepared idea. He told Thomas to take as much time as he needed but that he was going to start interviewing to fill the North Carolina position. If Thomas got back to Matthew in time, then he would be considered along with other candidates for the position. If the North Carolina position was filled by the time Matthew heard from Thomas, then Thomas would be a strong candidate for the Texas position, but that he was no longer a sure thing for that position.

The conversation ended with the understanding that Thomas would contact GD when he had come to a conclusion about GD's offer. However, during this time GD would start looking to fill the vacant North Carolina position and then begin looking to fill the Texas position. Thomas's status in these candidate evaluations depended on both his availability and his relative credentials. After hanging up, Thomas wondered if he should have gone ahead and given Matthew a verbal commitment in order to secure the North Carolina position.

QUESTIONS FOR DISCUSSION

1. What is your assessment of Thomas's decision to verbally commit to GD but continue interviewing with Abbott? Why did he not do this?
2. Would you have made a verbal commitment to GD and then gone ahead with your interviewing at Abbott? Why? Why not?

3. Do you think Matthew's position was a fair and reasonable one?

THOMAS BRANDT'S JOB SEARCH (C)

After what seemed to be a positive set of second interviews with Abbott, Thomas learned that Abbott was going to offer the job to another candidate. Disappointed, but somewhat relieved that the decision was made for him, Thomas called GD that afternoon, two weeks after his Monday afternoon phone call. Thomas spoke to Matthew and explained to him that after considering his alternatives he was excited to go to work for GD.

Matthew then told Thomas the North Carolina position had been filled and they had already started the search process for the Texas position. Matthew came across being quite cool, and continued to say that Thomas would be considered for the Texas position. Matthew said that he expected to have a decision made by the middle of May.

During this entire encounter, Thomas began to question some of Matthew's business practices. Thomas did not expect to have a party thrown for him by GD when he called that afternoon, but he did not expect the ice box treatment that was afforded to him. Thomas wondered what might await him in the future if he ended up with GD. With this bad taste remaining in his mouth, he put his job search in high gear.

QUESTIONS FOR DISCUSSION

1. Do you think Thomas is right in questioning Matthew's business practices? Do you think Matthew was reasonable, given what Thomas was attempting to do?

2. If you were Thomas, would you call Matthew back and tell him you did not appreciate his treatment of you? Or would you begin your job search anew, just as Thomas had done?

3. What ethical issues, trade-offs, and implications enter your mind based on Thomas Brandt's Job Search (A, B, and C)?

CASE 8 END OF THE LINE*

The Weather-Wide Company has been one of the major employers in Cantonville, a small midwestern town, since 1935. With a permanent work force of approximately 300 hourly employees, the company has survived roller-coaster economic conditions without ever having laid off an employee. This record has been a point of pride with Weather-Wide, and it helps explain an employee turnover rate of only 5 percent, the lowest of any employer in the community and one of the lowest in the clothing industry.

The manner in which Weather-Wide has been run also helps explain the low turnover rate. The company was started by Franklin Allen and has been run by the same family ever since. The pay, benefits, and working conditions have been such that there has never been any effort to introduce a union.

Five years ago, RPR Industries, based in New York City, purchased Weather-Wide from the Allen family, but the change in ownership has had little impact on day-to-day operations. Bob Allen, president for the past 15 years, is still running the business with very little direction from New York. Bob has been assured that as long as things go well, New York will "stay out of the way."

Ever since its beginning, the company has produced outdoor clothing for three distinct price ranges. Its Warmweave line is intended for those consumers for whom price is of special concern. Wofford is the medium-price label, and Harris Trent is the upscale line. Each line has its own work force, since the technology involved is somewhat different for each, as is the training required to function therein. While the demand for the three lines has always been affected somewhat by the state of the economy, all three offerings have remained profitable, at least until recently.

For the past 2 years there had been a softening in sales of the Wofford line. The turnaround predicted by top management had begun to seem somewhat unlikely when the informal word came that the home office was considering discontinuing the Wofford line unless there would be a significant upturn in business. The top management team was told to treat this information as they would treat any other rumor and to deny having any knowledge of it should they be asked.

Two more months of continued gradual decline preceded the formal notification of discontinuation, which, when it arrived on March 15, seemed to ease some of the tension that the managers had been experiencing. When the management team met to discuss the matter, they realized that they would be operating in uncharted waters. Never before had the company had to deal with such a situation; for that reason there was no policy to invoke. Early in the meeting, Bob Allen assured the team members that their jobs were "safe" and that they could expect on-site transfers following the shutdown of Wofford.

The management team unanimously agreed that it would be important to proceed cautiously. Even though the Wofford line was to be terminated, the company would first fill all of the outstanding orders. It was estimated that this

---

* This case was prepared by James M. Lahiff, Management Department, Terry College of Business, University of Georgia.

would take approximately 20 weeks, following which approximately 90 employees, the entire Wofford plant crew, would be laid off with little likelihood of being recalled.

All of the managers agreed that it was imperative that the present work force be retained in order to avoid the expense of training new employees for such a short period of time. Because of differences in the respective manufacturing processes, it would not be possible to transfer employees from Warmweave or Harris Trent to Wofford without considerable training. The managers agreed to "keep a lid" on the news about the pending mass layoff in order to avoid triggering the departure of large numbers of employees before the completion of the existing orders. "Besides," as Bob Allen, president and eternal optimist explained it, "things might pick up, and Wofford might not have to close down after all."

Because it was already common knowledge that sales of the Wofford line had been sluggish, employees had grown concerned and had been asking questions about the future for some time. Questions raised by the line supervisors were dismissed by managers with a "You know as much as I do." It was easy for management to rationalize the decision not to tell the truth, since there were few other jobs available in the community at this time.

On May 10, Cascade Sportswear announced that it had signed a long-term contract with a major discount chain and was seeking to hire 40 workers. Experience in the clothing industry would be helpful. Cascade, located in a rural area 20 miles from Cantonville, was a large manufacturer of low-cost casual wear. As soon as that news broke, Bob Allen hurriedly convened a meeting of the management team and reassured them of the security of their own jobs. He also reminded them not to inform anyone of the layoff, which was then estimated to be approximately 12 weeks away. The plan, he said, was to give the Wofford employees 60 days' notice, as required by the Worker Adjustment and Retraining Notification Act.

QUESTIONS FOR DISCUSSION

1. Describe the social responsibility that the management of Weather-Wide has toward its employees.
2. Was it appropriate for management to deny having any knowledge concerning the first rumors of a shutdown? Why or why not?
3. Did management's obligation change after the shutdown of Wofford became definite?
4. Was the obligation of Weather-Wide's management to its employees affected in any way by Cascade's attempt to enlarge its work force?
5. What sort of policy might Weather-Wide create for handling such situations in the future?

CASE 9 THE HIGH COST OF PRINCIPLES[1]

Wymodak, a Denver-based firm, acquired seventy-one 7-Eleven convenience stores in the West and Midwest in 1985. Mark Norek was a merchandising manager from the Denver office who visited the various 7-Eleven stores as part of his job. In April 1986, the Southland Corporation, the parent company of most 7-Elevens in the United States, decided to discontinue stocking *Playboy* and *Penthouse* magazines. Wymodak, however, decided to continue stocking the magazines in the stores it owned.

Dean Krych was manager of a Wymodak-owned 7-Eleven in the area of Superior, Wisconsin. In October 1986, Norek fired Krych because Krych refused to sell *Playboy* and *Penthouse* magazines as Wymodak's company policy and Norek had instructed him to. A couple of days later, Krych's assistant manager was also fired for refusing to stock the magazine. Krych's wife, Diane, resigned from her position as store auditor.

Dean Krych, age 37 at the time of the incident, had served for 7 years as manager. He was a frequent winner of performance awards. He was twice named as his district's manager of the year and won other performance awards as well. Krych noted, after his firing, that "my store had just had the most profitable year it had ever had."

The vice-president of Wymodak was Gary Nelson. Nelson noted that refusal to stock certain specified "core items" such as bread, soft drinks, potato chips, and the two magazines was grounds for dismissal.

Speaking to an Associated Press reporter in a telephone interview, Krych explained why he took the stand that cost him and his wife their jobs. "We Americans have got to stand up for decency. It's a patriotic cause." Krych explained how he felt about recent trends that have moved from soft-porn magazines to x-rated movies and then to x-rated home videos. "If we allow it to continue, the nation will not be a fit place to live." He went on to say, "It's personally not just a religious issue (he is a member of the Assemblies of God church), but it is in the interest of community standards." He continued by saying that the philosophy behind the two magazines was "very destructive." "Basically it is that marriage and constancy are not important, that the family is not so important." He added, "It turns women into sex objects. It has begun using children in its cartoons. We're giving up our livelihood in the cause of decency, in the cause of women and children who have suffered abuse, letting them know there are people who care." Diane, Krych's wife, added, "It was something we had to do. Money isn't everything. We're willing to take the consequences."

Christmas of 1986 was tough on the Krych family household. Their income was cut off, as was their medical insurance that covered the $1,000 monthly cost of caring for their infant son suffering from cerebral palsy. They thought they could get by for a while on their savings and 3 weeks' vacation pay that was owed Dean on dismissal. He said, "We know in our hearts we did what was right."

QUESTIONS FOR DISCUSSION

1. What is your assessment of Krych's decision to refuse to carry *Playboy* or *Penthouse*? What level of ethical analysis does this decision represent (personal, organizational, societal)? Do you think he really understood the consequences of his actions?

2. In light of all the awards Krych won for superior performance, assess the firm's decision to fire him. Was it a wise decision? Was it an ethical or socially responsible decision?

3. Can you think of any more creative ways in which Wymodak and Norek might have dealt with this case?

CASE ENDNOTE

1. The materials for this case are based on "Man Gives Up His Job, Sticks to His Principles," *Athens Banner-Herald* (December 20, 1986), 13.

CASE 10   WELL LOGGING, INC. (A)*

Background: Offshore Oil Industry

The search for oil brought drilling rigs to the Gulf of Mexico following World War II. The offshore environment was vastly more expensive than drilling and exploration on land. This was largely due to the expense of having to drill in varying water depths. With the oil embargo of the 1970s and the increase in worldwide demand for oil and natural gas, the price of oil skyrocketed. The increased drilling activity also resulted in increased oil rig lease rates and an overall increase in the cost of finding and producing oil. The cost to lease and operate a typical drilling rig in 1982 was about $2,000 per hour.

Well Logging, Inc.

Well Logging, Inc., a division of Large Company Limited, was an oil field service company that acquired and interpreted data from oil and gas wells.

In their search for oil, oil companies periodically needed to know information about the geological formations they had drilled through. This information, which was acquired by instruments lowered into the well by a Well Logging engineer and crew of two operators, was crucial in determining future hydrocarbon production potential and well-completion techniques. In addition to acquiring data from oil and gas wells, the Well Logging crew was involved in performing completion services such as running cement bond logs, setting plugs and packers, and perforating the well.

The well itself was drilled with a specifically designed bit (7"–12" in diameter) attached to a series of 33-foot lengths of steel pipe called "drill pipe" (3"–5" in diameter). After the well was drilled through the targeted hydrocarbon reservoir, a steel pipe called "casing" (5"–10" in diameter) was lowered into the well. The casing had a much larger diameter than the drill pipe and served to hold back the formulation wall from collapsing and plugging the hole. Cement was pumped into the space, or "annulus," between the outside of the casing and the formation wall. The cement supported the casing in addition to preventing water from migrating along the "annulus" and polluting nearby hydrocarbon reservoirs. Typically the well was plugged below the potential production zone before explosive charges were used to puncture the casing at precisely the right depth to allow the production of oil or gas. After the well was perforated, a metal pipe or "tubing" (2"–4" in diameter) was lowered to the production zone where it was used to transport the oil or gas to the surface.

A typical well completion would involve first running the cement bond log. The cement bond log used acoustical measurements to determine how well cement filled the annulus between the formation and the outside of the casing.

---

* This case (Parts A and B) was prepared by Todd D. Wohler under the direction of Professor Jeffrey A. Barach as a basis for class discussion rather than to illustrate either effective or ineffective administrative practices.

Copyright © 1987 by J. Barach, A. B. Freeman School of Business, Tulane University, New Orleans, LA 70118. Reproduced with permission.

In conjunction with the acoustic transmitter and receiver was a gamma ray tool and a casing collar locator. The gamma ray tool measured the natural background radiation associated with the formation. The measurement was used to differentiate sandstone zones from shale zones and could be correlated with previously run measurements. The casing collar locator detected the unions between the joints of the metal casing in the well. Each well had a unique spacing associated with the casing collars due to the fact that the casing joints varied in length.

After the cement bond log, gamma ray, and casing collar locator had been run, a plug was set in the casing about 30 feet below the bottom of the production zone. The plug formed the bottom of the well and was set in the proper position by correlating the collar locator measurements from the plug with those from the cement bond log. The same method was used to position the perforating guns which were used to blast holes in the metal casing by using explosive charges. The holes in the casing permitted the oil to flow into the metal casing and then to the surface via metal tubing. The proper positioning of the perforating guns was crucial to the future performance of the well.

The Dilemma of a Field Engineer

Don Toller was a recently hired field engineer working out of the Lafayette, Louisiana, Offshore District in February, 1982. After seven months of intensive training under the tutelage of Randy Fear, an experienced field engineer, Don now felt he was ready to perform his first job offshore on his own.

Don's first solo job offshore presented some minor problems as he had difficulty setting a plug in the well. After one unsuccessful attempt and three hours of downtime, the plug was finally set. Don and his crew, Rodney and George, were flown back to the shore and they were anticipating some badly needed rest. They had been working for nearly 30 hours without sleep. Unfortunately, upon arrival at the district office, Don discovered that he and his crew were going back offshore in four hours. After loading the equipment on a truck, Don, Rodney, and George drove to the dock in Intercoastal City where they were put on a crew boat for the trip to the rig. The boat ride enabled them to get about four hours of sleep before arriving at the rig.

Once at the rig, Don introduced himself to the company man (oil company representative who was responsible for all operations on the rig) while Rodney and George supervised the unloading of equipment from the boat. The company man informed Don that he wanted to run the cement bond log with a gamma ray and casing collar locator, set a plug, and perforate a 20-foot hydrocarbon zone. He also told Don that they would be ready to run the logs in four hours. Don went to the logging unit where he began testing the equipment to ensure everything was working correctly. After testing the equipment, Don and his crew were able to get about two hours of sleep before they were awakened to begin work. After rigging up the necessary equipment, Don ran the cement bond log, gamma ray, and casing collar locator. While running the log, Don experienced some electrical problems that resulted in about four hours of downtime. Don was very conscious of this downtime as he knew it was costing the oil company about $2,000 per hour while he attempted to solve the electrical problems. The company man was also very concerned about the problems Don was experiencing, and this created a pressure-filled environment for the young field engineer. After solving the electrical problems, Don successfully completed the cement bond log and set a plug 50 feet below the production zone. Then Don perforated a 20-foot zone with perforating guns. The positioning of the guns was rather critical because, if the guns were too high, a shale zone would be perforated resulting in no hydrocarbon production. If the guns were too low, hydrocarbon production would result, but the well would begin producing water after some time, thus reducing the well output. Because of this, the company man requested to be present to ensure the job was properly accomplished.

After being awake for nearly 24 hours since arriving at the rig, the crew had fired the last perforating gun. All that was left to do before some badly needed sleep was about three hours of work rigging down the equipment. It was now about 2:00 a. m., and Don figured they would be finished by 5:00 a.m., just in time to catch the morning helicopter back to Intercoastal City. As Rodney was pulling the last perforating gun out of the well, Don was reviewing his logs and discovered what he felt was a problem with the correlation logs. It appeared that because a particular switch was in the wrong position, the gamma ray curve was memorized improperly. After reviewing the logs for nearly an hour, Don realized that the mistake he had made with the memory switch resulted in the well being perforated 15 feet below where it should have been. Don's stomach began to churn. He knew that other field engineers had been fired for similar actions. He feared losing his job because he had recently been married and had financial obligations that depended on his salary. He felt that the oil company might never notice the mistake he had made. After all, he was only 15 feet off depth in a 12,000-foot well, and it would be rather difficult to prove he had made a mistake.

Don also feared waking the company man up at 3:00 a.m. to tell him the bad news. Don knew that his mistake would more than likely cause the oil company to cement up the bottom portion of the well, thus plugging the misplaced holes. After cementing the well, the oil company would have to drill it out again before re-perforating. Don estimated that this would cost the oil company about $200,000 to plug the misplaced holes.

Don also had a conscience to contend with. He felt that as a professional and as a Well Logging field engineer, it was his duty to inform the company man of the mistake he had made. Well Logging's reputation was also at stake and, as a loyal Well Logging employee with the client's best interest in mind, Don knew he should not cover up his mistake.

What a dilemma—Don was self-admittedly in a lose-lose situation!

QUESTIONS FOR DISCUSSION

1. Identify the stakeholders and their interests in this case. What are the pros and cons of the two basic choices Don faces (to conceal the error or to wake the company man and disclose the error)?
2. If you were Don, what action would you take in this dilemma? Justify your decision.

WELL LOGGING, INC. (B)

Don swallowed the large lump in his throat and decided to wake the company man. While the company man dressed and grabbed a cup of coffee, Don waited in the office. As the company man, still a little groggy, entered the office, Don told him of the situation. The company man responded, "You couldn't have made a mistake. I watched you correlate the perforating guns and you were right on depth."

"No, you don't understand what I mean," Don said.

After thoroughly explaining the situation, Don convinced the company man that there was a problem. The company man asked Don to rig down the Well Logging equipment while he informed his boss of the problem. Before leaving the office, Don asked if he could call his manager and let him know what was going on. Don's manager was expectedly bothered by the problem and immediately sent Raul Gamer, the most experienced field engineer in the district, to the rig to help bail Don out of trouble.

Raul arrived at the rig at noon to awaken Don and his crew from their badly needed sleep. Don and Raul reenacted the logging operation, confirming that the well had been perforated 15 feet too deep.

Two days later, after relogging and reperforating the well, Don and the crew were sent back to the Well Logging district office. When Don arrived, he was immediately summoned to his manager's office where the job was discussed for about two hours. Raul Gamer was present and was very supportive of Don. When Don left the office, he was unsure of what was in store for him. He fully expected to be fired, but wondered why it had not happened yet.

The next day, Don's manager informed him that he was on probation for two months and that any slip-ups during that time meant his job. Don was surprised and relieved. The oil company later praised Don's honesty and expressed its appreciation that he had revealed the mistake. Two months later, Don was promoted from a junior field engineer to the position of field engineer. He has since been promoted several times and has enjoyed a rather successful career with Well Logging. Maybe honesty is the best policy.

QUESTIONS FOR DISCUSSION

1. Do you think that Don's job was saved because Raul was supportive of him, or was it for some other reason?
2. In light of the praise Don received for his honesty, why do you suppose he was placed on probation and told that further slip-ups would mean his job?
3. Is honesty the best policy or did it just work out well for Don in this case?

CASE 11 WHAT SHOULD A MANAGER DO?

What should a manager do when faced with an ethical dilemma in his or her organization? Much has been written about the tough choices managers face. Barbara Ley Toffler wrote a book entitled *Tough Choices: Managers Talk Ethics* in which she interviewed executives who described the ethical situations they have faced at work and the ways they handled these situations.[1] Others have proposed various models of the ethical decision-making process that are helpful in describing the steps a manager should go through or the questions a manager should ask to help arrive at an ethical decision.[2]

Another approach to help managers when they experience a conflict between their own personal ethics or standards and those of the organization is to consider the alternatives available for resolving the conflict. Such an approach has been set forth by Richard P. Nielsen, who argued that there are essentially seven types of strategic responses or alternatives based on everyday pragmatics, philosophy, and game theory that the manager may consider when faced with an ethical dilemma.[3] Nielsen's seven alternatives are:

1. Don't think about the ethical dilemma.
2. Obey orders from above.
3. Leave the organization.
4. Conscientiously object.
5. Secretly go outside the company to the press or the government.
6. Publicly go outside the company to the press or the government.
7. Negotiate and build consensus for a change in strategic management.

QUESTIONS FOR DISCUSSION

1. Identify the advantages and disadvantages to you and your organization of each of the seven alternatives listed.
2. Identify the circumstances, factors, or situations that stand out in your mind that would point you toward each of the above seven alternatives.
3. On balance, which strategy(s) stands out as the most promising for dealing with a conflict between your personal standards and what you perceive is being expected of you as a manager by your organization? Explain.
4. Are there any alternatives available that are not addressed by the above seven? Identify and explain. What are their advantages and disadvantages?

CASE ENDNOTES

1. Barbara Ley Toffler, *Tough Choices: Managers Talk Ethics* (New York: John Wiley & Sons, 1986).
2. See for example, Archie B. Carroll, "Linking Business Ethics to Behavior in Organizations," *SAM Advanced Management Journal* (Summer, 1978), 411; Linda K. Trevino, "Ethical Decision Making in Organizations: A Person-Situation Interactional Model," *Academy of Management Review* (July, 1986), 601–617; and Manuel Valesquez, Gerald F. Cavanagh, and Dennis Moberg, "Organizational Statesmanship and Dirty Politics: Ethical Guidelines for the Organizational Politician," *Organizational Dynamics* (Fall, 1983).
3. Richard P. Nielsen, "Alternative Managerial Responses to Ethical Dilemmas," *Planning Review* (November, 1985), 24–29.

CASE 12

THE PLASTICHEM CORPORATION*

Background

The Plastichem Corporation is a plastics and chemicals firm, employing about 12,000 people worldwide, with its main headquarters in Chicago. One of the firm's plants produces isocyanate, a reactive component used in the manufacture of polyurethanes. Plastichem's isocyanate production plant is relatively old by industry standards; while it is not considered to be obsolete, neither is it state of the art. This particular plant is located in Termonia, Illinois, a small company town about 85 miles southwest of Chicago.

The plant employs 300 people—about 20 percent of the town's population—and runs on a continuous three-shift basis every day of the year. Though geared primarily for production, a small technical service group is assigned to the plant with five professionals (chemists/engineers). The plant is run quite independently of Chicago, and minimal communication exists between Termonia and the home office.

Termonia is a tightly knit community in which everyone seems to know each other. In the past few months, rumors have been circulating around town that the main office is considering closing the Termonia operations and building a larger, more efficient facility somewhere in the South. Termonia's citizens are quite concerned about the likelihood of this occurrence and its effect on the town's economy. Workers at the plant know very well that they cannot afford any downtime, since the operation is being evaluated for production efficiency (pounds of isocyanate produced per day) by the home office. Plant expenses also must be maintained at the bare minimum to convince the Chicago office of the utility of the plant.

Precautions in the Use of Isocyanates

The Termonia plant produces TDI, or toluene diisocyanate, which is considered to present the greatest hazard of the commonly used industrial isocyanates. Through the application of suitable safety measures, no apparent harmful effects should result. Occupational Safety and Health Administration (OSHA) regulations govern the industrial usage of this chemical. The American Conference of Governmental Industrial Hygienists (ACGIH) and the American Standards Association have determined the threshold limit values (TLVs) and maximum acceptable concentrations for isocyanates. OSHA has agreed with these values and is responsible for publishing them. A TLV is the level under which all workers may be continuously exposed without the occurrence of adverse physiological effects. The maximum acceptable concentration is a ceiling level not to be surpassed under any circumstances. The TLV for TDI has been set at 0.005 parts per million (PPM) for a time-weighted average eight-hour working day, while the maximum acceptable level concentration is 0.02 ppm for any continuous 20-minute

---

* From Aram's *Managing Business and Public Policy: Concepts, Issues, and Cases,* Second Edition, Copyright © 1986 by John D. Aram. Reprinted with permission from Ballinger Publishing Company.

exposure. Tests have determined that the least detectable odor of TDI occurs at 0.5 ppm, indicating that if a worker smells the TDI, a hazardous condition already exists.

Since the odor cannot be detected at low concentrations, elaborate monitoring systems have been developed by two companies: ADM Scientific and MER Incorporated. These systems are coupled with alarm units that trigger a loud horn when the TLV is exceeded and shut the entire production line down when the maximum acceptable concentration is exceeded for more than 20 continuous minutes. The Plastichem plant has such a monitoring/alarm system.

Inhalation of TDI vapors normally results in severe irritation of the mucous membranes in the respiratory tract. Short exposure at concentrations near the ceiling value can cause progressive disabling illness (analogous to breathlessness or reduced pulmonary functioning). Massive exposure has led to bronchitis, bronchial spasm, and/or pulmonary edema. Liquid TDI splashed directly in the eye can result in irritation or possible damage to the cornea. Contact with the skin due to liquid spills can result in reddening, swelling, and blistering.

Adequate mechanical ventilation is mandatory to control TDI vapor levels. Periodic maintenance of the exhaust system should be done according to OSHA and local air pollution regulations. The Termonia plant has a system that is enclosed and ventilated as specified by OSHA. Termonia also requires that chemical safety goggles and adequate skin protection be used in areas where there is a potential for spills or line ruptures. In addition, the Termonia plant has eyewash fountains and safety showers strategically located about the plant in case of an emergency. Personnel are trained in basic safety procedures.

Finally, TDI is not considered a serious fire hazard, but in the presence of an open flame or extreme heat, it can burn. TDI is sensitive to moisture. It is possible for uncontrollable isocyanate polymerization to occur in the presence of water, resulting in extreme heat generation and pressure buildup, with the possibility of an explosion if it is sealed in a container.

Schnall's Dilemma

Jared Schnall, a chemist in the technical service lab, is well aware of the plant closing rumors. Actually, they are more than rumors. At a recent meeting held three months ago with his supervisor (the head of the lab), a few of the top manufacturing officials, and the liaison from the Chicago office, the corporate liaison explained that the threat of closing down the plant was real. The liaison mentioned that the day-to-day operating data were being monitored carefully so that the main office could make a decision. The key variables were plant expenditures and output rates. They were also told that a decision would be made eight months from the time of the meeting.

In the three months since the meeting with the Chicago liaison, Schnall had become aware of some questionable activities at the production plant. He felt these activities were a direct result of the cost-cutting and output-increasing efforts of the production workers. Owing to their fear of the plant closing, they had undertaken measures that would be considered questionable under normal operating circumstances.

The first activity noticed by Schnall initially occurred two months ago and was repeated on three subsequent occasions. One morning as he was walking back to the tech-service lab through the plant control room, the MER monitoring system began to signal, indicating the TLV had been exceeded. Under normal circumstances, the horn would blow until the TDI leak was found and secured. If the ceiling level was reached during this period and persisted for 20 minutes, the plant would be automatically shut down and evacuated. However, on this occasion and the other three that Schnall witnessed, a worker in the control room "tripped" a circuit to stop the horn's blowing and to prevent the automatic shutdown of the plant, even if the ceiling level was reached. Having been there when the alarm had gone off on a few occasions, Schnall had always heard the continual blowing of the horn, and he had even witnessed a few temporary plant shutdowns. Plant shutdowns are extremely undesirable because it can take anywhere from two to eight hours to locate the leak, to secure the leak, to restart the line, and to reach equilibrium acceptable output conditions.

Wondering why the practice of "tripping" had begun, he asked a friend of his in the control room about it after work. His friend explained to him that this practice had begun when they found out about the possibility of the plant closing. Instead of letting the alarm system shut the plant down temporarily and lower output data, the workers in the control room felt it was better to "trip" the circuit and fix the leak while the system continued to run. They believed their jobs were on the line, and they were willing to take the risk. Schnall was not sure if all of the plant workers were aware of the tripping practice.

Schnall asked his friend if he was concerned about the health conditions on the plant floor during these situations. His friend declared, "Sure I'm concerned, but what else can we do? Besides, the worst thing that has happened so far is a few guys coughed a little and a couple of 'em had to step outside and get some fresh air 'cause their eyes were burning. Listen, Jared, our jobs are on the line. Once we get the word from Chicago that they'll keep the plant open, things'll get back to normal. You'll see!"

Another questionable activity that Schnall discovered pertained to inspection and maintenance procedures. In an effort to keep costs down, two inspection practices had been "temporarily" eliminated. The first was the inspection of waterlines leading into the safety showers and the eye-washes as well as to the actual showers and washes. Schnall was worried that should these fixtures become unknowingly inoperative, owing to lack of inspection and maintenance, someone could have irreparable harm done to them in an emergency situation.

Inspection and maintenance of the air ventilation and circulation system was the other practice that had become nonexistent over the past few months, also in an effort to reduce expenses. In this case, Schnall strongly believed that a steady deterioration of the exhaust system could lead to ineffective removal of dangerous vapors in the event of an emergency. In addition, he knew that an inferior exhaust unit would cause the alarm system to be triggered more often than in normal circumstances. In any case, the lack of inspection and maintenance was in direct violation of OSHA regulations and local air pollution standards.

Schnall was not sure if other questionable practices were being carried out besides the ones he knew about, nor was he sure exactly what he should or could do about this situation. He first consulted with his supervisor, the head of the lab, but his boss did not give him a direct answer. By the time he finished talking with his boss, he realized that his boss was already aware of the situation but was willing to "ride it out" like his friend in the control room.

Still being confused, Schnall began to weigh his alternatives:

1. Ignore it, like his boss.
2. Question or complain to the top management in the production facility. However, Schnall was concerned about how his questions or complaints might affect his permanent working relationship with the production people. His own work schedule was very dependent on the availability of production people and their equipment for trial runs. If they wanted to make work difficult for him, they could. Schnall was especially afraid of confronting the top management because he felt they were probably the ones who initiated the activities in the first place.
3. Go over the production people's heads and contact the Chicago liaison. In this case, working conditions would probably become unbearable for Schnall. He might have to be transferred, but he still feared being stuck with the label of a "spy" wherever he might go in the company. He could contact the Chicago office anonymously and hope that something is done about the safety situation.
4. Contact OSHA if alternatives (2) and (3) are undesirable or are proven fruitless. This alternative could be dangerous, too. Schnall knows that, on the one hand, the home office may have to close Termonia if OSHA is brought in and the normal output levels are determined to be unacceptable. On the other hand, even if OSHA decides to keep the plant running, it might be an uncomfortable working environment for him. Schnall also knows that he is protected by at least three governmental acts. For example, OSHA regulations contain the following statement about employee rights and protection:

> No person shall discharge or in any manner discriminate against any employee because such employee has filed any complaint or instituted or caused to be instituted any proceeding under or related to this Act or has testified or is about to testify in any such proceeding or because of the exercise by such employee on behalf of himself or others or any rights afforded by this Act.[1]

It goes on to say in the following section: "Any employee who believes that he has been discharged or otherwise discriminated against by any person in violation of this subsection may, within thirty days after such violation occurs, file a complaint with the Secretary alleging such discrimination."[2] In a final section the following statement is made: "Within 90 days of the receipt of a complaint filed under this subsection, the Secretary shall notify the complainant of his determination.[3]

5. Quit. That is, refuse to be a part of these activities but let the workers take the risk if they so desire.

There were a few other items that bothered Schnall. First, he felt that there was no opportunity within the company for someone like himself to question or complain about company practices. He did not feel it was safe for an employee to speak out. In essence, there was no neutral office or third party within the company with whom he could speak.

Second, he knew his job was at stake in more ways than one. Almost no matter what choice he made, other than ignoring the situation, he felt he would end up fired, transferred with a negative label attached to him, laid off, or working under undesirable or uncomfortable conditions. He was not pleased with the choices.

The third question that concerned him was the reality of the threat of closure. Was the Chicago liaison using this threat as a ploy to improve the Termonia plant output and efficiency? Was he trying to scare them into working harder? Was he doing this without his supervisor's knowledge?

A final dilemma that perplexed Schnall regarded what would happen if he remained quiet and the home office did decide to keep the plant running. Was it fair for him to withhold information from the main office that would reveal that Termonia people were artificially keeping output high and costs lower under potentially dangerous health conditions? Could this false information lead to the home office making the wrong choice? Also, is the home office not responsible for the safety of the Termonia people whether they are aware of the triggering activities? Should Termonia be run so independently of the home office? Should there be more communication than just through the liaison?

QUESTIONS FOR DISCUSSION

1. What actions would you recommend to Jared Schnall and why? What factors should he weigh in coming to a decision about what to do?
2. What action would you as chief executive officer of Plastichem Corporation want Jared Schnall to take? What is the likelihood that Jared would act in this manner?
3. Is Jared's dilemma likely to be a significant issue in American industry either now or in the future? What are the lessons for managers of United States cor-

porations from experiences like Jared's? What reservations might managers have about reacting to problems such as his?

CASE ENDNOTES

1. The Occupational Safety and Health Act of 1970, Section 11(c)," *Labor Relations Expediter* (Washington, DC: The Bureau of National Affairs, 1971), 6213.
2. *Ibid.*
3. *Ibid.*

CASE 13

MULTITYPE CORPORATION: DOING BUSINESS IN THE CARIBBEAN*

Like many United States manufacturers saddled with high labor costs, Multitype Corporation, a manufacturer of office equipment, transferred many of its operations overseas. Yet Multitype finds itself the focus of demonstrations in the United States because of the host country's domestic policies.

In Multitype's case, the host country is a small Caribbean nation, the Swan Island Republic, which consists of one large island and several smaller islets. In the late 1700s, the British began colonizing these small, desolate islands and tried to establish plantation agriculture as they had in Barbados and Jamaica. But the ground was too swampy, and eventually the plantations were abandoned. The British departed, leaving the islands in the hands of the black laborers who had been transported from Africa to work the plantations. The blacks turned to subsistence agriculture, raising barely enough fruit and vegetables to feed themselves.

For over a century, the Swan Islands were a forgotten backwater within the British Empire. Civil servants from Great Britain were used to staff the small administrative office and hospital in the capital town, New Liverpool; and the British willingly carried the expense of maintaining these services. The black Swan Islanders barely managed to scrape by, living on hand-to-mouth existence generation to generation.

Yet the black Swan Islanders were not alone. In the interior of the island lived a small number—about 200 or so—of Carib Indians, a tribe related to the American Indians. The Caribs were content to live in the forested center of the island, and the blacks were content to live along the shore, so the two groups rarely came into contact. In situations where they did meet, violence was the inevitable result. The Caribs, despite their primitive spears and hatchets, had a tradition of militancy and rebellion against outsiders. The Caribs continued the same lifestyle they had before European exploration and settlement, living much the same as they had in the centuries before Columbus. The Caribs and the blacks were tied for the dubious distinction of being the most impoverished people of the Caribbean.

In spite of the islands' poverty and lack of economic development, independence seemed inevitable as other nations pressured Great Britain to dismember its colonial empire. The Swan Islands were not exempt from this pressure. Finally, in 1977, the British flag was lowered in front of Government House in New Liverpool for the last time, and the bright red and green flag of the Swan Islands Republic was raised.

John Bailey, the black Chief of Police under the British, promptly appointed himself President of the Swan Islands and began to seek ways of improving the economy of the new nation. The soil was too wet for commercial agriculture, and the swarms of mosquitoes made tourism impossible.

Thus, when Multitype was seeking a location with cheap labor for a new manufacturing plant, the Swan Islands seemed ideal. The government of John

---

* This case was written by Marc S. Mentzer. Reproduced with permission. *Not to be duplicated without permission of the author and publisher.*

Bailey welcomed Multitype enthusiastically, and the impoverished population of New Liverpool flocked to the new factory in search of jobs. Even at a wage of $5.00 a day (U.S. currency was used in the Swan Islands), Multitype could choose whomever it wanted from the hundreds of eager job-seekers. Its local employees, entirely black, spoke English, so communication problems were minimal. And due to the workers' motivation and enthusiasm, the plant was extremely profitable for Multitype and enabled the firm to maintain its competitive position in the United States.

Back in the United States, Multitype's top management was shocked to find a group of American Indians picketing the company's headquarters one morning, protesting on behalf of the Carib Indians in the Swan Islands. A malaria epidemic was sweeping the Carib community in the interior of the Swan Islands. For some reason, the black population of the Swan Islands seemed to be immune, but the Carib Indians were not. Drugs for both preventing and treating malaria were available, but the government claimed it didn't have the funds to eradicate the disease among the Caribs. As a result, the Caribs were rapidly dying of malaria; and if nothing was done, the small group would be completely wiped out in a few years.

At Multitype's United States headquarters, the initial response was to ignore the pickets, but they didn't go away. Day after day for months, employees were greeted by the Indians' placards reading "Multitype—Partner in Genocide" and "Get Out of the Swan Islands." Multitype's top management spent more and more of its time discussing the Swan Island situation, especially when it became apparent that the United States demonstrators were hampering Multitype's sales to universities and government agencies.

After doing nothing for two months, Multitype's management decided it would pay for a treatment program among the Swan Island Caribs. But the Bailey government in the Swan Islands stonewalled Multitype's efforts at every turn. First, it declared that the Carib areas were quarantined and therefore off limits—even to medical personnel. When Multitype tried to bring in a team of doctors and nurses anyway, the medical team was arrested at the airport and sent back home on the next plane out. It was only then that Multitype's management became aware of the deep, centuries-long animosity between the Swan Island blacks and the Caribs and realized what was behind the Swan Island government's stubbornness.

The Swan Island government seemed determined to block any aid effort. Even when Multitype's President, Jean Gardner, made a personal appeal to Bailey and politely reminded him of Multitype's role in the economy, she was curtly told to mind her own business, followed by a lecture from President Bailey on how Americans always like to interfere in the domestic affairs of other nations.

Meanwhile, the United States television networks began to give the story a great deal of attention, and the issue even made the covers of the national news magazines. Like it or not, Multitype was in the limelight.

"Look, we've done all we can," Jean Gardner explained at a meeting of her top management. "Bailey has a point. Who are we to tell him how to run his country? How would we feel if a foreign government started telling us how to deal with the American Indians in our own country? We're here to make office equipment and sell it at a profit. Life is unfair: some of the countries we operate in have serious problems. But does that make it our fault?"

"I couldn't agree more," replied the corporate treasurer. "We have to keep this in perspective. All of Swan Islands have only about 25,000 people. These Carib Indians make up less than 1 percent of the population. And let's not forget the good we've done in that pathetic little country. Five dollars a day isn't much, but it's a lot to those people—enough to make the difference between starving and eating!"

"Absolutely right!" agreed Gardner. "These bleeding heart liberals want us to pull out of the Swan Islands entirely. How does that help anybody?"

"That's all well and fine, but what do I tell my customers?" remarked the vice-president of sales, who was normally a quiet fellow but now was visibly agitated. "On every sales call, that's all our reps hear about—those dying Indians in the Swan Islands. I tell you, we're losing sales, and it's going to get worse. We have to do something."

QUESTIONS FOR DISCUSSION

1. Who are the stakeholders in this case and what are their stakes?
2. What is your appraisal of the attitudes that seem to be developing on the part of Multitype's top management?
3. Identify the ethical issues facing Multitype Corporation.
4. Suppose Multitype had the opportunity of putting together a coup d'etat that would replace Bailey with a leader more compassionate toward the Caribs. Would it be the right thing to do?
5. To fulfill its ethical responsibilities to parties involved, and also to address its own economic interests, what position and actions should Multitype take?

CASE 14   THE EARLY CPSC GETS THE WORM GETT'R!*

Fishermen have for centuries used worms to fish. The slithery brown earthworm, lowly as it is, looks delicious to the hungry fish, but little does he know that lurking underneath that tempting morsel is a razor-sharp hook waiting to lift him into the frying pan. Phil and Marilyn Dye, small business people, always thought they were helping the fishermen by supplying them with the elements of fishing success.

Phil and Marilyn produced a product called the "Worm Gett'r." It worked by passing electric current through the ground via two metal probes. These probes were pushed into the ground in a likely "worm spot." The electricity is then applied, resulting in the worms squirming to the surface. Probably, they feel like they are escaping the executioner only to wind up being collected for fish bait. Little did Phil and Marilyn know that soon *they* would become the "shocked" as the Consumer Product Safety Commission (CPSC) descended on them with a probe of its own.

The Company

P&M Enterprises, the name of the Dye's company, produced only one product, the Worm Gett'r. The company was started in 1982 in Caldwell, Idaho. By the time the CPSC descended on P&M, 30,000 Worm Gett'rs had been manufactured, sold, and distributed.

Phil Dye was a respected and responsible local businessman who wanted to make a difference in his town. To accomplish this, he hired 14 people from the local program for the unskilled and disabled. Phil Dye was a shining example of one of the "thousand points of light" President Bush had referred to so many times. But, with a phone call from a CPSC attorney named William Moore, this light was covered and, eventually, extinguished.

The CPSC

The Consumer Product Safety Commission was established in 1973 as a result of an outcry of consumer advocacy groups. As a new agency, it was encouraged by zealous administrators and an enthusiastic political environment. An outgrowth of the newness of the agency is revealed in the lack of routines, slow implementation of programs, and many errors. Research by Cathy Johnson found that the early years of the CPSC were plagued by uncertainty, lack of experience, and a lack of knowledge to carry out effective action.[1]

By 1977, a pattern of priorities among projects began to emerge. A study by Lacy Thomas indicated that the CPSC preferred projects in the following areas:[2]

1. Projects requiring mandatory standards.
2. Projects that consider safety more important than consumer costs.
3. Projects involving the hazards of using a product.

---

* This case was prepared by William T. Rupp.

An additional finding by Thomas indicated that the CPSC failed to recognize resource constraints and timeliness in a project's completion. In other words, the CPSC does not consider the cost to the company or the time necessary to make the changes. Thomas also observed that the CPSC had established nine criteria they used to identify products against which to take action:

1. The frequency of the action (number of complaints)
2. The severity of accidents
3. The amenability to regulatory action
4. The chronic nature of the risk
5. The benefit/cost ratio
6. The unforeseen nature of the risk
7. The probability of exposure
8. The vulnerability of the population to risk
9. The agency's resource risk

Thomas goes on to note that these priorities are actually an aggregation of the individual preferences of the five CPSC commissioners.

The Action Against the "Worm Gett'r"

In 1987, the assault by the CPSC on the Dyes began. Armed with staff attorneys and the backing of the U.S. Treasury, the CPSC started legal action to have the product withdrawn from the market. Over the next $2\frac{1}{2}$ years, the business was bankrupt and the Dyes found themselves in debt for over $60,000 in attorney fees.

The first step of this process started with a charge that the product was dangerous. The Dyes never received a complaint that their product had caused harm to anyone. There simply was no documented evidence that the Worm Gett'r was dangerous. On the other hand, William Moore, the attorney for CPSC, produced documents indicating 28 people had died from use of *similar* products since 1971. The Dyes pointed out that these were all homemade devices made from golf club shafts or barbecue prongs. Many had exposed wiring. One person had fashioned worm probes from coat hangers, plugged them in, put them in his mouth, and attempted to climb over a chain-link fence. Despite the facts, the commission staff decided that the Worm Gett'r must be removed from the market, since it was "functionally identical"[3] to the homemade devices. Phil Dye made a video showing how even misuse of the device, such as holding the probes in his bare hands with the device plugged in and activated, did not cause harm. Phil offered to add a shield and a stronger warning label but was told by CPSC that the Worm Gett'r was "defective by design."[4]

An injunction filed in U.S District court by the CPSC sought to halt the sales of the Worm Gett'r. Judge Marion Callister denied the request stating, "A detailed review of the facts demonstrate that no such threat [of injury or death] is currently present."⁵ He went on to say that more people would probably make the homemade devices if the Worm Gett'r were taken off the market.

William Moore, refusing to give up, argued that the danger was real and the Worm Gett'r's worm-getting utility was marginal at best. The Dyes encouraged the CPSC to compare it with accident statistics from other electrical devices (drills, saws, appliances, and so on). Moore's reported response was "We don't have a body count and we don't need a body count."⁶

Having failed to get the injunction, the CPSC went after the Dye's customers. The Dyes refused to turn over their customer list. Undaunted, the CPSC went to United Parcel Service, used its muscle, and walked away with a listing of the Dye's customers. The CPSC then issued a national press release warning of the danger of the Worm Gett'r. This was done without any testing of the product or a single hazardous complaint.

The Dyes turned to their U.S. Senators from Idaho, Steve Symms and James McClure. Symms stated:

> The CPSC, sitting down here in Washington D.C., on fat cushy, bureaucratic salaries, where they don't have to take any risk for the decisions they make, cost this little company. A company that was at risk, providing a product the public wanted to buy, a product that was safe. Yet, in the most extreme imagination of a bureaucrat, they could figure out that this might not be safe for people to use in every possible instance, therefore they put them out of business.
>
> It's pretty tough fighting the government when they have all the lawyers and all the time and all the patience and money. They can last forever. But the Dyes out in Idaho, Phil Dye, he didn't have any money to start with. He was out there with his life savings on the line. A small, hardworking entrepreneur on a shoestring budget had a good idea, had a product that sold, and the federal government put him out of business. It's just that simple.⁷

When the CPSC voted on the matter, only the now departed chairman, Terrence Scanlon, voted against proceeding to withdraw the Worm Gett'r from the market. His reply to the action: "It's a perfect example of abuse by a regulatory agency."⁸

QUESTIONS FOR DISCUSSION

1. What are the major issues in this case? How do you assess this case as an example of government regulation?
2. Do you believe this is an abuse of an effective use of a United States agency's power? Is there a hidden agenda driving the CPSC? If so, what is its source and its motivation?
3. What should be the role of the CPSC as a regulatory agency?

4. If you were in Phil and Marilyn's position, what would have been done differently in the beginning? How about later in your dealings with the CPSC?

CASE ENDNOTES

1. Cathy Marie Johnson, "New Wine in New Bottles: The Case of the Consumer Product Safety Commission," *Public Administration Review* (January/February, 1990), 74–81.
2. Lacy Glenn Thomas, "Revealed Bureaucratic Preferences: Priorities of the Consumer Product Safety Commission," *Rand Journal of Economics* (Spring, 1988), 102–113.
3. "Washington Takes on the Worm Gett'r," *Insight on the News,* Washington, DC (December 18, 1989), 16–17.
4. *Ibid.,* 16.
5. *Ibid.,* 16.
6. *Ibid.,* 16.
7. *Ibid.,* 17.
8. *Ibid.,* 17.

CASE 15   LOBBYING ETHICS

One of the United States's most serious environmental problems over the years has been air pollution. After more than a decade of efforts to improve the nation's air quality, it has become apparent that the air pollution problems we have extend beyond what federal legislators envisioned in the early 1970s when the *Clean Air Act* was passed. Of concern to many has been the increased use of coal. From 1983 to 1984, the use of coal increased 7 percent. It was expected to increase another 5 percent in 1985. Among the problems that arise when coal is burned is the increase in sulphur dioxide and nitrogen dioxide emissions, which are the key ingredients in the formation of acid rain and sulfate haze. New studies in 1985 confirmed that acid rain threatened the purity and life of thousands of streams and lakes all across the nation.[1] Acid rain has become a battleground between those companies that create it and emit it into the atmosphere and environmentalists who think it is one of the nation's most serious ecological hazards and should be strictly regulated.

Citizens for Sensible Control of Acid Rain

For controversial issues like acid rain, there is considerable lobbying of Congress by the polluting firms that are opposed to additional regulations and by social activist groups that support such legislation. Recently proposed acid rain legislation would require coal-burning power plants to install special equipment or use more expensive low-sulphur coal to reduce pollutants. One of the major lobbying groups that has taken a stand on this issue is "Citizens for Sensible Control of Acid Rain." A recent letter sent out by this group on its letterhead went to thousands of households warning that Congress is considering legislation against acid rain "that would cost $110 billion" and "would mean up to 30 percent higher electric bills." Recipients of the letter were urged to write their congressional representatives and encourage them to vote down such legislation.[2]

An organization known as the U.S. Public Interest Research Group, which supports acid rain legislation, is outraged by the lobbying efforts of the so-called citizens group. It turns out that the "Citizens for Sensible Control of Acid Rain" is not a citizens group at all, at least not in the traditional grassroots sense. The organization is funded by coal and power companies that are major contributors to the acid rain problem.[3] As is the case with many lobbying campaigns, the group is run by a Washington-based public relations firm. Thomas Buckmaster, the public relations executive who runs the campaign, says that his organization generates letters from citizens and, therefore, it is a citizens group. Since the group was founded in 1983, it has spent $4 million sending 800,000 letters to citizens asking them to write their representatives. Buckmaster says that 135,000 people, who he calls "citizen volunteers," have written letters as a result of the campaign. He goes on to add: "Form letter or not, each letter was signed by an individual citizen who has taken the time to read our letter, decided it accurately reflects their point of view, and took the extraordinary step of signing their name and sending to their elected representatives."

Public Interest Research Group (PIRG)

PIRG, which describes itself as a nonpartisan, nonprofit consumer and environmental advocacy group, has taken the position that the lobbying done by the Citizens for Sensible Control of Acid Rain is misleading and deceptive. Alexandra Allen, a lawyer for PIRG, says that sponsors of the citizens group had a vested interest in the issue.[4] Apparently PIRG is concerned because the citizens group did not communicate to people it wrote that it was being funded by the power and coal companies. Others in the lobbying business said that they find such efforts questionable. One head of a large public relations firm admitted that he had organized a number of what he called "phony coalitions" but no longer engages in this practice because he found it to be "personally disturbing." One legislator, Representative James J. Florio (D-New Jersey), said that there is confusion. He cited the case of a constituent who wrote him that he did not realize that the acid rain group was an industry effort. Florio added, "The group purports to be disinterested but clearly is not." Allen, of PIRG, stated, "As Congress considers acid rain legislation this year, we hope that every member is fully aware that Citizens for Sensible Control of Acid Rain is in fact an industry lobby masquerading as a citizens organization."

Buckmaster, from the citizens group, says that what he is doing is not deceptive. He says, "We have been and will continue to be candid about who we are, where our funding comes from, and what the purpose of the organization is." In 1987, the group's stationery was changed to include a line at the bottom indicating that funding for the group was provided by electric, coal, and manufacturing companies.[5]

QUESTIONS FOR DISCUSSION

1. Do you find the practice of the citizens group questionable? Would you go so far as to say that it constituted an unethical lobbying practice? Do you find the practice defensible? Explain.

2. If you disapprove of the citizens group's lobbying practice, what changes do you recommend it make to improve on these practices? What minimal changes should it implement? What, ideally, should this group do?

3. Because lobbying is frequently seen as a practice of wielding influence or power, is it reasonable to think that certain ethical guidelines should be applied to lobbying? Could and should a code of conduct or ethics be developed for lobbyists?

CASE ENDNOTES

1. *The World Almanac and Book of Facts—1987* (New York: Pharos Books, 1986), 149.
2. Philip Shabecoff, "Corporate Acid Rain Lobbying Deceptive, Foes Say," *The Times-Picayune* (August 9, 1987), F-2.
3. Ibid.
4. Ibid.
5. Ibid.

CASE 16 THE BIG MAC ATTACK

Communities are extremely protective of the kinds of commercial developments they permit in historic districts. It was not surprising, therefore, that in 1990 the Zoning Appeals Board (ZAB) in Boston unanimously turned down McDonald's request to build a restaurant in the city's cobble-stoned Blackstone Block District.

After all, the district is listed in the National Register of Historic Places. It contains the last surviving 17th-century street pattern in town. Across the street stands historic Faneuil Hall where the colonists once met to protest British taxes. Nearby are Paul Revere's house and the Old North Church in the North End community. Benjamin Franklin spent some of his childhood near the Blackstone District, and John Hancock once owned land there.

McDonald's had done a good job of getting some area residents on its side for the proposed restaurant. It had promised to sponsor a youth athletic team, provide free beverages for senior citizens, and provide a daily sweep-up of the neighborhood. In addition, the company consented to meeting with local school leaders to sponsor educational programs on topics like drug awareness and ecology. McDonald's offered community organizations in the North End the opportunity to apply for grants from Ronald McDonald's Children's Charities. What McDonald's failed to do was to take some of these residents along for support when it appeared before the Zoning Board.

Initial resistance to the idea of a McDonald's in the district came from merchants and preservation groups. These groups, for different reasons, objected to a fast-food restaurant in the historic district. They spoke out against the idea at a public hearing. The Boston Redevelopment Authority, a watchdog for all development in the city, denounced the plan and recommended a denial. The Zoning Board of Appeals voted 5–0 to deny McDonald's request.

In what Suzanne Alexander, a writer for *The Wall Street Journal*, termed the Big Mac Attack, McDonald's went on the offensive to reverse the Zoning Board's decision. The fast-food giant lined up its own community groups and gathered 500 signatures on a petition. The company hired consultants and also gave out goodies in the neighborhood. Nine months later, the new restaurant proposal came up again before the Zoning Board, but this time the outcome was in McDonald's favor. In a 4–1 decision, the proposed restaurant was approved.[1]

A key factor in the second hearing was that McDonald's had mobilized its grassroots support by bringing more than 50 supporters to the hearing. Residents who could not attend the meeting wrote letters of support on McDonald's behalf. McDonald's supporters spoke up at the hearing and made it clear that they wanted the restaurant and that it would be good for the community.

Commenting on the board's reversal of its decision, the owner of the Union Oyster House Restaurant, a Boston tradition dating back to the early 1800s, commented, "McDonald's hired guns worked on this for a long time. They did what they had to do—outreach and political networking." He continued, "We were sleepy. We were aware of McDonald's interest but we were deceived into believing it would never fly."

Critics of the turn of events maintained that there were some curious circumstances surrounding the Zoning Board's second vote. It was noted that the Zoning

Board's chairman also was a member of a separate committee for a nearby Holocaust Memorial, whose surroundings McDonald's has agreed to keep up. In his defense, the Zoning Board's chairman insisted that he didn't know anything about McDonald's promise to provide upkeep for the memorial when he voted affirmative on McDonald's request before the Zoning Board. The chairman, who opposed McDonald's proposal in the initial vote, said he didn't remember voting on the issue the first time it came up.

It was also noted that three other members of the five-person Zoning Board were absent for the second vote but that their substitutes, who were permitted to vote their own consciences, all voted in favor of McDonald's proposed restaurant.

A McDonald's spokesperson said that the company did nothing wrong in seeking local support for its cause and that the restaurant is committed to being good neighbors.[2]

QUESTIONS FOR DISCUSSION

1. What are the major social or ethical issues in this case? Who are the relevant stakeholders and what are their stakes?
2. How appropriate was McDonald's lobbying effort on its own behalf in this case? Was the public interest served? Do you have any concerns with their approach? What are they?
3. Did McDonald's act in a socially responsible way in this case? Defend your point of view.

CASE ENDNOTE

1. Suzanne Alexander, "McDonald's Moves Into Historic Boston District Using Grass-Roots Lobby to Reverse Zoning Vote," *The Wall Street Journal* (October 28, 1991), B6B.

2. *Ibid.*

CASE 17   **PRODUCT PERFORMANCE AND WARRANTIES: CONSUMER AND PRODUCER OBLIGATIONS***

It was January 16, 1981, when Gary Husel, a traveling service representative for the National Motor Company in the Indianapolis District Office, found a letter in his mailbox from a Mr. and Mrs. Schmidt, asking for assistance in getting their 1976 Lifestyle van repaired. The letter claimed that the vehicle had a problem with the carrier bearing. (The carrier bearing holds together the two-piece driveshaft that is typical of this type of vehicle.) According to the letter, the carrier bearing had failed, allowing the driveshafts to separate, leaving the vehicle inoperable. The letter also claimed that this problem had occurred numerous times while the vehicle was under warranty. Husel thought nothing surprising about the letter other than that the owners claimed the problem had occurred while the vehicle was under warranty. Being the person responsible for customer relations in the part of the state the Schmidts were from and the fact that good company policy required an investigation into any problem supposedly similar to a problem that occurred while a vehicle was under warranty, Husel placed the letter along with about a dozen others into his owner-relations folder for further action. Normally Husel would have taken a complaint letter on a five-year old vehicle and had his assistant send a "Sorry, we cannot assist you in this matter" letter.

Within a few days Husel called the Schmidts to find out additional information about the problem. He spoke with Mrs. Schmidt, and she claimed that the vehicle had never worked properly for very long because of continued carrier bearing problems and that the bearing had failed again. She also said that National Motor had paid for all the repairs and the National dealer in DeMotte, Indiana, had been the one working on them. Husel asked her if they had any repair orders as verification of the prior works being completed. Mrs. Schmidt said National and the dealer had all the paperwork. Before hanging up, Husel said he wanted to check his office records and the dealer's records for verification of a prior problem and he would then recontact her to tell her his findings. If he could verify prior problems as she claimed, he would make arrangements for the vehicle to be inspected to determine if the current problem was related. If it was related, he would then decide what, if anything, National would do toward paying for the needed repair.

Following the conversation with Mrs. Schmidt, Husel went to his office files to look for past correspondence relating to the Schmidts. The current files containing information from 1981, 1980, and 1979 held nothing. Husel then searched the older files in the storage room and found a copy of a complaint form National uses to record phone conversations between customers and National employees. This particular form was dated February 5, 1978, and was between Mrs. Schmidt and a Miss David, a National employee. The form revealed that the van currently had 12,891 miles on it, was purchased June 17, 1976, and had been into a dealer at least five times over the last year and a half for carrier-bearing problems that started shortly after the vehicle was purchased. On the bottom of the form was a space provided for the service representative to write in his or her comments

---

*From Aram's *Managing Business and Public Policy: Concepts, Issues, and Cases,* Second Edition, Copyright © 1986 by John D. Aram. Reprinted with permission from Ballinger Publishing Company.

and actions. On this form was stated: "10-5-78, Problem Resolved—Customer Happy. A. Brown." Attached to the form was a questionnaire sent from the home office in Detroit after the phone call complaint form was turned in by the service representative asking numerous questions about the handling of the reported problem. One question of interest asked: "Was the problem you reported to us resolved to your satisfaction?" It was answered: "No."

By the end of January 1981, Husel had made a visit to the National dealer in DeMotte, Indiana. While there he asked the service and parts managers if they recalled the Schmidts' vehicle and the problems they encountered with it. Surprisingly, both people who had always appeared sharp and as having good memories to Husel could remember nothing of the vehicle or the customers. Husel assumed they had forgotten the incident because it had occurred over two years ago. Fortunately, within a minute the owner arrived and Husel asked him if he recalled the vehicle and the customers. Immediately the dealer recalled the situation. He said that he did not sell the vehicle—the closed dealer in Roselawn, Indiana, had—and that the service representative at the time, Miss Brown, had asked him to have his people work on the vehicle because the selling dealer could not repair it properly. The dealer also said that when his people worked on it, it was already out of warranty. They worked on it a couple of times, and once the Schmidts last picked it up, he assumed it must have been fixed because he never heard from them again.

Husel then asked for copies of the repair orders. As in the situation in his office, 1978 records were in storage. Husel and the service manager went into the storeroom, searched the files, and could find nothing. Husel had no access to the repair orders of the closed dealer and was disappointed not to find any here to substantiate prior work. Even without repair orders he felt the dealer's statement and the complaint form he found were enough evidence to prove that the problem had occurred under warranty and that if the same problem occurred again, he had better authorize a repair to keep out of trouble with the law. Indiana's interpretation of the law did not require an extension of a written warranty for the time a vehicle was inoperable as some states did, but past experience told Husel that Indiana courts generally take the opinion that a component of a vehicle had better give at least one full year or more of problem-free service. The "or more" depended on the frequency of the problem and the expected cost of repair. Husel knew it was well over one year since the vehicle had been repaired last, but it apparently had failed numerous times and he figured he should play it safe by having National pay for the repair.

Husel called the Schmidts thinking he had good news to tell them as long as the current problem turned out to be the same as the old one. When he spoke with Mrs. Schmidt and told her what National was going to do, he recalled that she did not sound the least bit happy. First of all, she said that she could not bring the vehicle to the dealer for an inspection because it was not drivable, which Husel said would be no problem. He would drive out with someone and inspect it. Second, Mrs. Schmidt wanted to know if National was going to reimburse them for the car they had to rent for the last two years. Astonished, Husel said: "What do you mean reimburse you for two years of a rental car?" Mrs. Schmidt then proceeded to tell him that the vehicle had been inoperable for over two years. It had been broken since a few weeks after they last had it in at the DeMotte dealer in October 1978, and they had to rent a car for transportation. Never having heard anything so incredible, Husel asked why they had waited two years to contact National or the dealer about the problem. Husel recalled never getting an answer to this question—just silence.

Husel became irritated and told Mrs. Schmidt that he thought National's offer to fix the vehicle was extremely fair considering that the vehicle was over five years old, that it had been sitting for two years with no action on their part, and that rental assistance was out of the question. Mrs. Schmidt then asked if his decision was final. After confirming that it was, she said, "I'll see you in court." Then she hung up.

Following this conversation, Husel wrote a short report describing the events up through his conversation with Mrs. Schmidt and then discussed the matter with his two supervisors. His supervisor agreed that the offer to repair the vehicle was fair and that the rental request absurd, and the issue was dropped.

In June 1981, the office Husel worked out of received a court summons from Indiana State Court, Valparaiso, Indiana, charging National Motor Company in breach of warranty for failure to abide by the requirements of the *Magnuson-Moss Warranty Act.*[1] It was filed by Mr. and Mrs. Robert Schmidt and asked for $20,000. Included in the $20,000 was the price of the van, financing charges, insurance, and legal fees. Trial was set for early May 1982.

In September 1981, Mr. Robert DeBerg, a Valparaiso attorney hired by National to defend them in the case, contacted Husel to set up a time to discuss the situation and make a joint inspection of the Schmidts' vehicle, which he had already cleared with the Schmidts' attorney.

When they met, Husel told DeBerg all the events as described so far, DeBerg asking questions as they proceeded. When the questioning was over, they went to Schmidt's house, met the Schmidts, and proceeded to look at the vehicle. The vehicle looked as if it had been sitting a long time: flat tires, cobwebs all over it, bird excrement everywhere, and very dirty. Crawling underneath the vehicle, Husel identified the broken carrier bearing, pointing it out to DeBerg. When asked by DeBerg if they had driven the vehicle lately, Mr. Schmidt said the vehicle had been sitting in that exact spot for almost three years. Husel noticed the mileage at 14,628, not much more than the 12,891 reported to National in February 1978. DeBerg also asked the Schmidts why they had not made any further attempts to get the vehicle fixed until January 1981. Mr. Schmidt said they had fooled around with the van for over two years after they bought it and could never get it fixed properly. They had called National in Detroit for assistance and spoken to a Miss Davis, had met a Miss Brown from National out of Indianapolis, and had had it to two dealers and never had the problem resolved. Finally, he said they did not know what else to do, so they just parked it. In late 1980 they were convinced by a friend to see an attorney about the problem, and that started the whole process.

Following this inspection, Husel did not hear anything about the case until early April 1982, when DeBerg called him requesting that they meet again and prepare for the trial. When they met a few weeks later, DeBerg asked a few questions and said he had asked National's legal staff in Detroit to settle the case out of court. He told them National would lose the trial because numerous attempts had been made at fixing the vehicle, starting shortly after it was purchased, and it was still disabled—an issue that was in direct violation of federal warranty law. DeBerg felt that if National offered to settle now, they could bargain for a lower settlement, save legal fees, and avoid the bad publicity. He went on to say that the trial would be by jury, always sympathetic to a consumer complaint, and the issue was basically "explosive." This opinion also emanated from one of the partners of his law firm who told him to "get rid of the case." Husel was surprised to hear these statements from the attorney who was supposedly going to defend his corporation. Husel felt the company would win the case because the customers had made an absurd demand for two years of rental assistance after making no attempt to get the vehicle fixed during that time. Besides, the vehicle was almost six years old now.

Following the conversation with DeBerg, Husel discussed the pending trial with the two supervisors and told them of his recent conversation with DeBerg. The supervisors were aware of DeBerg's request for an outside settlement, and he had tried recruiting them to push his position with the Detroit legal staff. Both supervisors agreed with Husel that National would win the case, and they were not going to make an attempt to influence the legal staff. The supervisors and Husel called the legal staff in Detroit, and had a four-way conversation with Ms. Henderson—she was the person in charge of handling the case there. Ms. Henderson pointed out that the management did not like the warranty law and wanted no precedents set from its successful application. When the conversation ended, all agreed that National would win the case because the customers did nothing for over two years and then demanded rental assistance—both grounds for dismissal.

QUESTIONS FOR DISCUSSION

1. Review the facts of the case as presented. Would you advocate, as Gary Husel did, that National pursue the case in court?
2. As a corporate executive, what action would you support? Why?
3. How would you be inclined to decide this case as a juror? What would be your primary considerations?
4. Finally, how would you speculate that the jury decided the case?

CASE ENDNOTE

1. The *Magnuson-Moss Warranty Act* was passed into law January 4, 1975. In terms of warranties, this act (a) requires manufacturers who issue written warranties on products costing more than $10 to label each with warranty as "full" if it meets federal minimum standards or "limited" if it fails to meet those standards and (b) sets federal minimum standards requiring that full warranties commit the firm issuing the warranty to repair any defect within a reasonable time frame and without charge; to allow the consumer to file suit in state or federal courts for damages from a company's failure to comply with a warranty; and to allow the consumer to recover court costs if he or she won.

   It should be noted that automobile warranties are termed *limited* because certain repairs are considered maintenance and the tires are warrantied by the tire manufacturer. In the court case described in this case, the court determined that the warranty involved would still be subject to treatment as a "full" warranty because the item of concern, the carrier bearing, would be included in a full warranty if the vehicle had one. Also, the intention of the law was not to let manufacturers off the hook by classifying all their warranties as limited, thus excluding themselves from federal regulations.

CASE 18 A VIEW OF THE ALPS*

Introduction

During the winter of 1988, a leading manufacturer of consumer dental products, Dental Inc., found itself the target of several large consumer groups in the United States, including the American Association of Retired People. These groups levied severe allegations against the company's principle product, "Dentu-grip." "Dentu-grip," a world leader in the denture cream market was alleged by these groups to contribute to the accelerated spread of gum disease as well as contributing to the greater long-term danger of mouth cancer. In addition, the Food and Drug Administration (FDA) was rumored to be investigating these claims against "Dentu-grip," although no one at the FDA would confirm these rumors. Two lawsuits had been filed on behalf of persons who had died from some form of mouth cancer alleged to be caused by, among other things, "Dentu-grip."

Dental Inc. vehemently opposed these allegations which had appeared in the news media across the nation. Dental Inc. contacted the primary members of its distribution network with news of the bad publicity it was receiving in the United States. It assured them of the quality of "Dentu-grip" and informed them that the FDA and other U.S. governmental regulatory agencies had made no effort to remove the product from the shelves. Included in Dental Inc.'s distribution network was Schwarzkopf Ges.m.b.H. (translated loosely as Inc. in the United States) & Company of Austria, the only European distributor of "Dentu-grip."

Schwarzkopf Ges.m.b.H. & Company

Schwarzkopf Ges.m.b.H. & Company is the Austrian subsidiary of Schwarzkopf Inc., which began as a manufacturer of hair products and related consumer health/beauty products just outside of Munich, West Germany, in 1904. Schwarzkopf Ges.m.b.H. & Company is located in Kematen in Tirol, a small village of less than 2,000 people, approximately 10 kilometers from Innsbruck. When the facility was constructed in this small community, the owner developed plans to have 15 meters (approximately 18 feet) of its storage area put underground so that the residents' view of the Austrian Alps would not be obstructed by the building.

Over its thirty-five year existence, this subsidiary has developed into the market leader in the Austrian hair and related consumer beauty product market, with strong positions in several other European markets. Schwarzkopf products also hold the number one import position in the Japanese market and are planning to enter the U.S. market in the near future. In addition, this subsidiary is the sole distributor of "Dentu-grip" throughout the European market. For the past 9 years, Schwarzkopf Ges.m.b.H. & Co. has participated in a licensing arrangement which allows the Austrian subsidiary to imprint its own name and symbol on the pre-packaged product which is imported from the United States.

---

*This case was written by Tammie S. Pinkston, University of Oklahoma. Reproduced with permission.

Klaus Schwarzkopf, the grandson of the company's founder, is the President and CEO of Schwarzkopf Ges.m.b.H. Schwarzkopf himself is Canadian-born and received his M.B.A. from Stanford University. When he received the correspondence from Dental Inc. concerning its current situation in the United States with "Dentu-grip," he knew that a multitude of potential actions could be undertaken by all those involved. Schwarzkopf knew from his graduate school experience how easily issues in the social arena spilled over into the U.S. business community.

He called his management team together to discuss the issue concerning "Dentu-grip." After some discussion of potential actions that might be taken by the consumer groups, Dental Inc., and Schwarzkopf Ges.m.b.H. & Co., the management team decided to dismiss the issue for the time being noting that it "wasn't their product" and that no similar concerns or allegations had been expressed in any of the European markets. Still, Schwarzkopf himself couldn't totally dismiss the feeling that potential problems were looming on the horizon.

A Matter of Timing

During the time period that the allegations against "Dentu-grip" were hitting the national media in the United States, a large contingency of college students from the University of Innsbruck were in California, participating in an educational exchange program at the University of Southern California. At the end of the semester of study, when the Austrian students returned home, the situation in the United States with "Dentu-grip" still had not been resolved.

Several of the Austrian students returned to their homes only to find that this product which was "under fire" in the United States was being used by their parents and grandparents. Although they knew from the recent media attention that "Dentu-grip" was an American product, they also knew that Schwarzkopf, a company in their own backyard, was in some way tied to the product. The company's name and symbol could be readily seen on the package. A group of these concerned students, including one individual whose grandfather was currently on the Board of Directors of Schwarzkopf Ges.m.b.H. & Co., decided to take their questions to the company directly and to investigate its relationship with "Dentu-grip." The student approached his grandfather, Walter Freytag, with the disturbing news from the United States Freytag assured his grandson that he would make the Board aware of the situation in the United States with "Dentu-grip."

At the same time, these concerned students were determined to educate the Austrian population on the dangers associated with "Dentu-grip" as indicated in the U.S. media. The students approached a student group at the University of Innsbruck known as "SHERP" (Students for Human and Environmentally Responsible Products) and asked that "Dentu-grip" be added to their list of "PRODUCTS NOT TO PURCHASE." This list appeared in the regional newspapers as well as a special edition printed by the student group on the University campus. Several students also saw to it that the list was posted as notices at prominent locations throughout the city.

Schwarzkopf's Response

Klaus Schwarzkopf and other members of this management team met with the students and acknowledged up front that they were aware of the difficulties facing "Dentu-grip" in the U.S. market. They also readily pointed out that conclusive evidence was still not available on whether or not the allegations were accurate. It was also mentioned that the management team understood research to be ongoing to determine if the product could be tied to the health problems. Schwarzkopf also assured the students that they had experienced no similar complaints in the European markets.

"It is very important to us that you understand the values under which our company is operated," continued Schwarzkopf. "Our corporate principles state that it is our aim to realize and fulfill current and future needs by modern production and customer-oriented services. This can be translated into a set of corporate goals that provide direction for our daily operations. These goals include: (1) reaching our profitability objectives, (2) providing the most effective benefit for our customers, (3) offering efficiency in a 'nice' way, (4) protecting the environment actively, and (5) exhibiting exemplary performance."

"We feel like we live-out these principles on a daily basis," the marketing and production vice-president, Manfred Kessler, added. Kessler continued, "Our product packaging area has made tremendous strides in the area of responsible packaging over the last 2 years. We're packaging our products in half cartons instead of full box cartons and even these can be returned to this facility at no cost for recycling." "We even recycle our energy," commented the plant manager. "The water by-product in our production rooms is carried by pipes to the basement where it recycles into our air conditioning units." "What we're trying to say here is that we are totally committed to the highest goals in being a responsible producer of consumer beauty products, specializing in hair care products."

Schwarzkopf proceeded to explain his company's relationship with Dental Inc. as a licensing arrangement whereby the product arrived pre-packaged. The Schwarzkopf label was then added before the product was exported to other European markets. A small portion of the profits went to Schwarzkopf Ges.m.b.H. while the bulk of profits were remitted back to Dental Inc. in the United States.

The students left the Schwarzkopf facility with a much better feel for its business philosophy. However, they were still resolved to do something in their home market about the "Dentu-grip" problem. The students agreed that there was no justification for removing "Dentu-grip" from the list of "PRODUCTS NOT TO PURCHASE" until there was substantial evidence that there was no danger of gum disease or cancer of the mouth caused by using the product.

In the meantime, Freytag had fueled the interest of the Board of Directors. The Board requested a meeting with Schwarzkopf's top management and expressed their real concerns over the "Dentu-grip" allegations circulating in the U.S. market. Although the Board of Directors could not reach a unanimous decision on what alternatives Schwarzkopf Ges.m.b.H. could reasonably exercise, they urged top management to act—not to simply wait out the storm.

Klaus Schwarzkopf and his management team faced a crucial dilemma. They had illustrated from the day that their facility was constructed their commitment to ethical and responsible business behavior above what was legally mandated. They also knew that this particular situation was at the heart of such resolution. Schwarzkopf feared that the concern over "Dentu-grip" could possibly continue to gain interest and support. However, he also knew, as did the Board of Directors, that the subsidiary's licensing arrangement with Dental Inc. remained a critical link in its strategy to enter the lucrative U.S. market.

QUESTIONS FOR DISCUSSION

1. What is the central issue in this case? What are the related issues in the case?
2. Who are the primary and secondary stakeholders involved in the case? What are the responsibilities that these groups have to other groups involved? What responsibilities (economic, legal, ethical, philanthropic), if any, does the Schwarzkopf subsidiary have relative to its licensing agreement with Dental Inc. for the distribution of "Dentu-grip"?
3. What options do you think that Schwarzkopf and his management team have available to them at this point? What are the benefits and costs associated with each option?
4. What option do you recommend for Schwarzkopf Ges.m.b.H.? Why?
5. What issue(s) does this case raise that may be unique to international corporations in their corporate social responsibility efforts?

CASE 19: ALL-TERRAIN VEHICLES AND THE CONSUMER PRODUCT SAFETY COMMISSION

The first all-terrain vehicles (ATVs) were three-wheeled. In recent years, four-wheeled versions have become popular. ATVs are small motorized vehicles with fat balloon-like tires designed to track through rugged terrain at speeds sometimes up to 50 m.p.h. Riding ATVs has become a very popular recreational sport, and an estimated 2.5 million of the "fun machines" have been sold in the United States since the early 1980s.[1]

The ATVs, viewed by some as cousins to dirt bikes and snowmobiles, have become one of the most controversial leisure products ever produced. The controversy has stemmed from the rapidly rising number of deaths and accidents attributable to the machines. More than 600 people have been killed in ATV accidents, and some 275,000 have been injured—some of these crippled for life. Almost half the casualties have involved children under 16.[2] Year-to-year statistics gathered by the Consumer Product Safety Commission (CPSC) depicted a death pattern from 1982 to 1986 as follows:[3]

1982	25 deaths
1983	75 deaths
1984	130 deaths
1985	240 deaths
1986	235 deaths (estimate)

Critics of the ATVs point to many reasons why the machines need to be outlawed outright. They claim that the machines are inherently unsafe in terms of their design and safety features and that there should be regulations governing who can ride them. The alleged design flaws include a center of gravity that is too high for proper balance, a solid rear axle that makes turning difficult and unsafe, an inadequate suspension system, and a tripod design that is inherently unstable.[4]

The severest criticism has been against allowing youth and children to drive the machines. One San Diego attorney said that letting a child ride an ATV "is like giving him a loaded gun." The case of Wendy Molitor illustrates the reason for the debate. Wendy was an active 10-year-old when she hopped onto a three-wheeled ATV in 1982. Today she is a quadriplegic living on a respirator. She broke her neck when the ATV rolled over on her. But who was at fault here? The company that made the ATV or her parents who permitted her to ride it? Her attorney argued that the company had manufactured and sold a vehicle that was dangerous and had inadequate warnings. But the company maintained in its defense that Miss Molitor was riding as a passenger on an ATV driven by a 12-year-old boy and that the machine was designed to carry only one person.[5]

The companies that have been making ATVs include Honda (which has almost 60 percent market share), Kawasaki, Suzuki, and Yamaha. Children's units are priced at about $800, while adult models run as high as $3,500. The companies, their industry association—the American All-Terrain Vehicle Association—and other defenders say that ATVs are being singled out unfairly and that "gross misuse" by a small minority of riders is the real problem. The director of the Specialty Vehicle Institute of America, another trade group, said, "There has been a horrible lack of parental supervision" in many of the accidents in which children were involved. The manufacturers claimed that other driver abuses included riding with passengers, driving on paved roads, driving too fast, driving while drinking, and not wearing safety accessories such as helmets and boots.

In addition to alleged design flaws, critics of ATVs are strongly against the way ATVs are advertised. They point to TV ads that depict the machines going fast and then jumping through the air. Children, they claim, find these depictions exciting and glamorous and are bound to try to emulate them. Another problem is that dealers promote the products deceptively and incorrectly. Salespersons have been observed trying to sell a prospective buyer an adult-sized machine for an 8-year-old even though the makers say the machines shouldn't be used by anyone under 14. Another salesperson has said that a child could ride as a passenger of an adult even though this was clearly not recommended.[6]

What has the CPSC been doing about the dangers, deaths, and injury statistics being reported regarding ATVs? In 1985, the CPSC created an ATV task force and published an advance notice of proposed rule making, its first in several years. The federal agency also adopted a seven-step plan of action. The seven steps included:

1. Creating the ATV task force
2. Compiling detailed information on ATV use
3. Preparing a hazard analysis as well as an engineering, human factors, and medical analysis of ATVs and their use
4. Holding a series of public hearings around the country to receive consumer input
5. Monitoring the development of voluntary standards for ATV use
6. Sharing information with local, state, and federal officials and user groups
7. Monitoring the ATV industry's education and training effort while reserving the right to assist or strengthen this effort[7]

In December 1986, a year and a half and $2 million worth of study later, the CPSC announced decisions that did not please critics. The federal agency urged manufacturers to *voluntarily* stop selling ATVs for children under 12 years old, called for improved danger warnings on the machines, requested better training programs for beginning riders, urged state governments to adopt rules requiring helmets for riders, and directed its staff to begin working on possible mandatory safety standards.[8]

According to John Emshwiller, simultaneous to its public announcement, the CPSC voted in closed session to take a far tougher stand. It declared ATVs an "imminent and unreasonable risk" to the public and backed a mandatory refund program that could result in the manufacturers having to repurchase hundreds of thousands of the machines from consumers. In addition, the CPSC voted to require new public warnings about product dangers and free training programs.

Word of the closed session leaked out as the commission was seeking Justice Department assistance in preparing a suit to force compliance. Not surprisingly, federal efforts to mandate actions by the makers were going to meet strong resistance.[9] One Honda spokesperson responded, "We don't see any need for any kind of recall or refund program."

In 1987, more questions were being raised about the CPSC's role, particularly in the ATV issue. Jeanne Saddler observed that the commission had not issued a new product safety regulation since 1984. Defenders of the CPSC and its chairman, Terrence Scanlon, said that there was just a philosophical difference between the then current Reagan-appointed commission and its critics. It appeared that the commission's philosophy was to rely on voluntary safety standards whenever possible. David Pittle, a former commission member who is now with Consumers Union, said that the commission "spends years considering safety standards that industry offers and then doesn't just defer to them but grovels to them."[10]

There were also charges that Chairman Scanlon was creating an atmosphere in which the commissioners were caught up in internal battles, thereby delaying one of the agency's major actions—litigation against the makers of ATVs. Critics were also saying that actions involving baby pacifiers, swimming pool covers, and disposable cigarette lighters were being delayed.

One major criticism against Scanlon was that he was making staff changes that were delaying action on ATVs. In June 1987, Scanlon removed the two lead lawyers who were developing the commission's case. These two were replaced by four others who, it was said, weren't as familiar with the case and consequently slowed down any action. Chairman Scanlon said the new attorneys were more experienced. Scanlon also transferred to another project one attorney who was regarded as a leading advocate of tougher regulation. One of the CPSC's commissioners sent a memo to the chairman saying that the transfer was "another attempt to censor the free flow of information and intimidate the staff." The other commissioner responded with a memo that said, "You've got to be kidding."[11]

There was some evidence that Congress was upset and ready to step in. Congressman James J. Florio (D-New Jersey), chairman of the consumer-protection panel of the House Energy and Commerce Committee, introduced a bill that would limit the commission chairman's power. The bill required quicker decisions about regulatory matters, in general, and even ordered the regulation of ATVs. Since 1985, a group representing ATV makers had been working on a set of voluntary standards. The group still had not developed a set of standards the commission considered to be effective. Meanwhile, the commission said that ATVs were responsible for about 20 deaths and 7,000 injuries per month.[12]

The Consumer Federation of America complained that in 1986 the CPSC concluded that voluntary industry standards for disposable cigarette lighters were inadequate but decided to study the problem rather than issue a regulation. One lawyer who often defends clients against the agency summarized the feelings of many: "Part of my living comes from protecting people" [in my industry from the CPSC], "but, I'd rather have a strong and mighty adversary that knows what a good case is instead of one that stumbles around in the dark and hits anything that's warm."

In 1981, President Reagan wanted to abolish the Consumer Product Safety Commission. Later he wanted to transfer it to the Department of Health and Human Services under one administrator.[13]

In January 1988, the CPSC announced a preliminary settlement of a suit it had against the ATV makers. The following decisions were reached regarding ATVs:

1. The three-wheeled ATVs would be banned. They could no longer be produced and sold in the United States.
2. ATV dealers would have to prominently notify consumers of the dangers of the ATVs.
3. The dealers would have to provide hands-on training to purchasers, including those who purchased ATVs during the preceding year.

Critics of the ATV settlement say that it does not do enough. They say that the ATV makers themselves had already reached the decision they needed to discontinue the three-wheeled models; therefore, the government action was not very significant. Apparently sales of the three-wheeled models have declined sharply as a result of adverse publicity, and the four-wheelers have now captured the market. Opponents want a complete ban on all ATVs. Some want refunds to be given to all 1.7 million owners of three-wheelers. Others want refunds only to parents who bought the ATVs for their children. It is clear that the opponents of ATVs will continue their push to have the machines outlawed completely.[14]

QUESTIONS FOR DISCUSSION

1. Is it possible that a manufacturer could be making a product that is so inherently dangerous that it should be completely outlawed? Is the ATV such a product? Discuss the reasons on both sides of this issue. What are manufacturer-distributors' responsibilities and what are users' responsibilities with respect to this product?
2. Who are the stakeholders in this case, and what are their stakes? In the textbook we say that the consumer has a right to safety. How far does that right go in the case of the ATVs?
3. Assuming that four-wheeled ATVs continue to be sold, what *actions* or *strategy* regarding them should be taken by the (a) manufacturers, (b) trade associations, (c) retailers, (d) CPSC, (e) states, (f) consumers?
4. What is your assessment of the 1988 actions taken by the CPSC?

5. What is your assessment of the CPSC and its chairman's apparent philosophy and practices? What should be done when a federal regulatory agency does not do its job?
6. Should manufacturers now be required to recall all the now-illegal three wheel ATVs and give them their money back? Discuss.

CASE ENDNOTES

1. Frederick M. Maynard, "Peril in the Path of All-Terrain Vehicles," *Business and Society Review* (Winter, 1987), 48.
2. John R. Emshwiller, "All-Terrain Vehicles Spark Debate as User Deaths and Injuries Mount," *The Wall Street Journal* (February 11, 1987), 29.
3. *Ibid.*
4. *Ibid.*
5. *Ibid.*
6. *Ibid.*
7. Allan J. Ryan, "What Future for ATVs?" *The Physician and Sports Medicine* (July, 1985), 36.
8. "Makers of All-Terrain Vehicles Asked to End Sales for Young," *The New York Times* (December 19, 1986), A24.
9. Emshwiller, 29.
10. Jeanne Saddler, "Consumer Safety Agency's Role Is Questioned Amid Charges Over Its Chairman's Leadership," *The Wall Street Journal* (September 23, 1987), 76.
11. *Ibid.*
12. *Ibid.*
13. *Ibid.*
14. "The Debate: All-Terrain Menace," *USA Today* (January 5, 1988), 8A.

CASE 20 HOOKER CHEMICAL AND LOVE CANAL*

The History of Love Canal

Love Canal is named for William T. Love, a businessman and visionary who in the late nineteenth century attempted to create a model industrial city near Niagara Falls. Love proposed to build a canal that would facilitate the generation and transmission of hydroelectric power from the falls to the city's industries. The combination of an economic recession that made financing difficult and the development of cheaper methods of transmitting electricity destroyed Love's vision, and the partially dug canal in what is now the southeast corner in the city of Niagara Falls remains the project's sole tangible legacy.

However, the area still attracted industrial development, because it provided easy access to transportation, cheap electricity, and abundant water for industrial processes. Several chemical companies joined other corporations in taking advantage of the region's natural resources. The Hooker Electrochemical Company, now Hooker Chemical & Plastics Corporation, built its first plant in the area in 1905. An Occidental Petroleum Corporation subsidiary since 1968, Hooker manufactures plastics, pesticides, chlorine, caustic soda, fertilizers, and a variety of other chemical products. With over 3,000 employees, Hooker remains one of the region's largest employers and a Niagara Falls area economic force.[1]

In the early 1940s Love Canal's abandoned section—for many years a summer swimming hole—became a dump for barrels of waste materials produced by the various area chemical companies. Hooker received state permission in 1942 to use the site for chemical dumping. It is estimated, although no accurate records were kept, that between the early dumping period and 1953, when this tract of land was sold, these corporations deposited approximately 21,000 tons of different kinds of chemical wastes, some extremely toxic, in the old canal. The companies stored the chemicals in drums, and considered the site ideal for chemical dumping. Located in an undeveloped, largely unpopulated area, the canal featured highly impermeable clay walls that retained liquid chemical materials with virtually no penetration. Research indicated that the canal's walls permitted water penetration at the rate of a third of an inch over a 25-year period.

In 1953 Hooker closed the dump and covered it with an impermeable clay top. The Niagara Falls School Board then acquired the land encompassing and surrounding the dump for $1.00.[2] Hooker advised against the acquisition, and warned the school board of the toxic wastes. However, the board persisted and started condemnation proceedings to acquire land in the area. The city subsequently built an elementary school and a tract of houses adjacent to the site. The constructors removed thousands of cubic yards of top soil. The construction apparently damaged the integrity of the clay covering. Water from rain and heavy snows then seeped through the covering and entered the chemical-filled, clay-lined basin. The basin eventually overflowed on the unfortunate residents, who

---

* This case was prepared by Martha W. Elliott and Tom L. Beauchamp and revised by Joanne L. Jurmu, Anna Pinedo, and John Cuddihy. Not to be duplicated without the permission of the holder of the copyright, © 1989, 1992, Tom L. Beauchamp.

were treated to the noxious smell and unwholesome sight of chemicals seeping into their basements and surfacing to the ground.

In 1978 evidence of toxic chemicals was found in the living area of several homes, and the state health commissioner ordered an investigation, which brought a number of health hazards to light. Several adults showed incipient liver damage; young women in certain areas experienced three times the normal incidence of miscarriage; and the area had three and one half times the normal incidence of birth defects. The investigation also uncovered epilepsy, suicide, rectal bleeding, hyperactivity, and a variety of other ills.

Upon review of these findings, the health commissioner recommended that the elementary school be temporarily closed and that pregnant women and children under the age of two be temporarily evacuated. Shortly thereafter the Governor of New York announced that the state would purchase the 235 houses nearest the canal and would assist in the relocation of dispossessed families. President Carter declared Love Canal a disaster area, qualifying the affected families for federal assistance.[3] However, families in the adjacent ring of houses did not receive federal assistance, although they believed that the canal chemicals endangered their health. Early studies tended to confirm this view, but in mid-July 1982 the EPA released a study that concluded there was "no evidence that Love Canal has contributed to environmental contamination" in the outer ring of 400 homes. This report focused on health hazards and did not address documented symptoms of stress. For example, the divorce rate among remaining families soared as wives and children fled the area, while husbands tried to hold onto their houses and jobs.[4]

Since the investigation first began more than 100 different chemicals, some of them mutagens, teratogens, and carcinogens, have been identified. A number of investigations are continuing to resolve unanswered questions, including the long-range effects of chemical exposure. Cancer, for instance, often does not develop for 20 to 25 years after exposure to the cancer-producing agent. Chromosomal damage may appear only in subsequent generations. Unanswered questions involve determining how to clean up the pollution and who should be held responsible for it.

Criticisms of Hooker

The Hooker Chemical company figures in both of these questions. In 1977 the city of Niagara Falls employed an engineering consulting firm to study Love Canal and make cleanup recommendations. Hooker supplied technical assistance, information, and personnel. The cost of a second study was shared equally by Hooker, the city, and the school board that had originally purchased the land from Hooker. Hooker also offered to pay one-third of the estimated $850,000 cost of cleanup.[5]

In 1980 Hooker faced over $2 billion in lawsuits stemming from its activities at Love Canal and other locations. Thirteen hundred private suits had been filed by mid-1982. The additional complaints and suits stemmed from past and current activities in other states as well as from additional New York sites. In addition, in 1976, Virginia employees of Life Sciences who had been exposed to Kepone, a highly toxic chemical known to cause trembling and sterility in humans filed suits totaling more than $100 million. The suits named Hooker as a supplier of some of the raw materials used in the Virginia manufacturing process. (The parties ultimately settled the suit out of court.) In 1977 Hooker was ordered to pay $176,000 for discharging HCCPD, a chemical used in the manufacture of Kepone and Mirex, which had caused cancer in laboratory animals, into Michigan's White Lake. In 1979 that state's officials sued Hooker for a $200 million cleanup due to air, water, and land pollution around its White Lake plant.[6]

While Hooker was defending its actions in Virginia and Michigan, the state of California investigated the company and ultimately brought suit on charges that Hooker's Occidental Chemical plant at Lathrop, California, had for years violated state law by dumping toxic pesticides, thereby polluting nearby ground water. Hooker officials denied the charges, but a series of memos written by Robert Edson, Occidental's environmental engineer at Lathrop, suggests that the company knew of the hazard as early as 1975 but chose to ignore it until pressured by the state investigation. In April 1975 Edson wrote, "Our laboratory records indicate that we are slowly contaminating all wells in our area, and two of our own wells are contaminated to the point of being toxic to animals and humans...." A year later he wrote, "To date, we have been discharging waste water... containing about five tons of pesticide per year to the ground.... I believed we have fooled around long enough and already over-pressed our luck." Another year later, Edson reiterated his charges and added that "if anyone should complain, we could be the party named in an action by the Water Quality Control Board.... Do we correct the situation before we have a problem or do we hold off until action is taken against us?"[7]

Other complaints about Hooker stemmed from the same area of Love Canal. In 1976 the New York Department of Environmental Conservation banned consumption of seven species of fish taken from Lake Ontario, claiming that they were contaminated with chemicals, including Mirex. The DEP alleged that Hooker's Niagara Falls plant had discharged the Mirex. A Hooker-sponsored study of Lake Ontario fish disputed this allegation of Mirex contamination. While this study has not been accepted by the state, the ban has, for the most part, been lifted.

Hooker's Hyde Park chemical waste dump, located in the Niagara Falls area, has also been a source of continuing concern and dispute to residents and government officials. In 1972 the manager of a plant adjacent to the dump complained to Hooker about "an extremely dangerous condition affecting our plant and employees . . . our midnight shift workers has [sic] complained of coughing and sore throats from the obnoxious and corrosive permeating fumes from the disposal site."[8] The dangerous condition was not adequately rectified, and in 1979 Hooker's Hyde Park landfill became the subject of a nearly $26 million lawsuit seeking filed by the town of Niagara Falls. New York State also filed a suit for more than $200 million for alleged damages at the Hyde Park site.

In 1980 the Environmental Protection Agency (EPA) filed four additional suits against Hooker for $124.5 million in remedial work. The EPA explained that the actions against Hooker involved: (1) litigation under "imminent hazard" provisions of existing EPA laws, and (2) the creation of programs, financed by government and industry, to clean up hazardous waste sites. EPA Administrator Barbara Blum described the imminent hazard litigation as follows: "This program seeks to halt dangerous disposal practices and to force privately-funded cleanup. This approach gets results, of course, only where a responsible party can be identified and has adequate financial resources to carry some or all of the cleanup costs."[9]

Blum also detailed the specific statutes the EPA is acting under and discusses the EPA's collaboration with the Justice Department in enforcing the statutes.

> Sections of the Resource Conservation and Recovery Act, Safe Drinking Water Act, Toxic Substances Control Act, Clean Water Act, and Clean Air Act all authorize EPA to ask the court for injunctive relief in situations which pose threats to public health or the environment. Section 309 of the Clean Water Act levies a penalty of up to $10,000 a day for unpermitted discharges to navigable waters (a leaking dump can be considered a discharge). . . .
>
> People are frightened by Love Canal and by the emergence of threatening hazardous waste sites in their local communities. They are demanding action—and they are getting it.[10]

The EPA has estimated that only 10 percent of all hazardous wastes are disposed of in strict compliance with federal regulations. According to Thomas H. Maugh, II, "Nearly 50 percent is disposed of by lagooning in unlined surface impoundments, 30 percent in nonsecure landfills, and about 10 percent by dumping into sewers, spreading on roads, injection into deep wells, and incineration under uncontrolled conditions."[11] Maugh argues that "legal dump sites gone awry" are a lesser problem than the growing problem of illegally dumped wastes in unsecured dump sites, often in the middle of cities.[12] In October 1981 the EPA announced that "There are at least twenty-nine toxic waste disposal sites around the country as dangerous or more so than Love Canal. . . ."[13]

Hooker's Defense Against the Charges

Hooker Chemical believes that its role and position have been misunderstood. While the company neither denies using the canal as a chemical dump nor denies that the dump has created a serious problem, company officials contend that: (1) the company's efforts to prevent first the public and then the canal area private development are general unrecognized; (2) the company has been in industry leader in safety; (3) Hooker is being unfairly singled out for waste disposal practices that were then almost universal throughout the chemical industry; and (4) a certain level of risk is an inevitable hazard in an industrial society.

Hooker has marshalled data to support these contentions. In the first place, Hooker believes that its efforts to warn the school board and city against interfering with the waste disposal area have gone unappreciated. When the Niagara Falls School Board expressed an interest in selling a portion of the Love Canal tract to a developer, Hooker representatives argued against the plan in a public meeting and later reiterated to the board its warnings of possible hazards. When the school board persisted in its plans and began to obtain adjacent parcels of land through condemnation proceedings, Hooker, in the school board's deed, again referred to the property's past use and stipulated that all future risks and liabilities be passed to the school board. One part of the deed stipulated:

> Prior to the delivery of this instrument of conveyance, the grantee herein has been advised by the grantor that the premises above described have been filled, in whole or in part, to the present grade level thereof with waste products resulting from the manufacturing of chemicals by the grantor at its plant in the City of Niagara Falls, New York, and the grantee assumes all risk and liability incident to the use thereof. It is, therefore, understood and agreed that, as a part of the consideration for this conveyance and as a condition thereof, no claim, suit, action or demand of any nature whatsoever shall ever be made by the grantee, its successors or assigns, against the grantor, its successors or assigns, for injury to a person or persons, including the death resulting therefrom, or loss of or damage to property caused by, in connection with or by reason of the presence of said industrial wastes.[14]

When the school board later sold part of the land to a private developer who planned to build houses, Hooker officials protested the sale both verbally and in writing. Executives contend that the company has been unjustly blamed for others' imprudence. Hooker also claims that it has no legal responsibility for the Love Canal problem and that it has more than met its social and moral obligations in time and money spent on the cleanup effort. Through its Love Canal experiences, Hooker environmental health and safety specialists have developed knowledge and skills that have enabled the company to take a leadership role in problems of underground pollution.

Hooker officials also argue that their past practices satisfied and even exceeded the then-operative industry standards for waste disposal. During the 1942 to 1953 period, when Hooker filled Love Canal with barrels of chemical wastes, neither the industries involved nor the health and regulatory professions recognized the long-term environmental and personal hazards of these industrial "leftovers." Storing the chemical wastes into a clay canal at the time represented an improvement on common methods of disposal in unlined and unsecured landfills.

The company's defense of its behavior in the Love Canal situation parallels in some respects the reaction of certain Love Canal residents. They directed the major thrust of their antagonism not toward Hooker Chemical, but toward the New York State Health Department, which had failed to provide open access to the results of state-conducted health studies and experienced unexplained delays in admitting that a health problem existed. The health department attempted to discourage and actively thwarted independent researchers whose reports indicated more widespread risks to the community's health than the Department was willing to admit or was prepared to pay to rectify. Given these premises, residents have concluded that the health department, not Hooker Chemical, failed to meet its obligations to the community.[15]

Hooker supports the common industry position that society will have to learn to accept a certain level of risk in order to enjoy the products of industrial society. Environmental hazards are one form of industrial "tradeoff." Industrialists cite persons such as Margery W. Shaw, an independent scientist who reviewed a chromosomal study of Love Canal residents. She points out that the level of acceptable risk is a more general societal problem.

> In our democratic society, perhaps we will decide that 500,000 deaths per year is an acceptable price for toxic chemicals in our environment, just as we have decided that 50,000 traffic deaths per year is an acceptable price for automobile travel. On the other hand, we may say that 5,000 deaths per year is an unacceptable price for toxic chemicals.[16]

The Continuing Controversy over Hooker and the Canal Cleanup

Over the years, Hooker has been among the heavily criticized corporations for its environmental policies. Ralph Nader attacked Hooker as a "callous corporation" leaving toxic "cesspools." An ABC news documentary harshly criticized the company, focusing on the increased incidence of disease at Love Canal. Nonetheless, Hooker has won a number of defenders. A *Fortune* magazine editorial defended the corporation for having explicitly conformed to government waste disposal standards, for resisting the canal area construction, and for being the victim of exaggerated and irresponsible reports about the regional incidence of disease.[17] A *Discover* magazine editorial laid the blame for the Love Canal on the school board (but argued that Hooker did act irresponsibly in waste dumpage at a number of other sites).[18] The 1982 EPA study blunted some federal efforts and some lawsuits.

In 1983 the U.S. Center for Disease Control (CDC) conducted a study of Love Canal residents. CDC examined forty-four residents and compared them to a control group chosen from Niagara Falls residents living at least one mile from the evacuated area. The CDC concluded the residents of Love Canal do not show increased incidence of cancer or reproductive abnormalities when compared to residents of other Niagara Falls neighborhoods. CDC critics claim the study was too small to be conclusive. Health officials and state legislators called for more conclusive information.[19]

Amidst the controversy, Niagara Falls city officials had a list of over 100 families from the Love Canal neighborhood who were waiting for housing.[20] Many people eagerly awaited the final word on Love Canal's conditions. While the 1982 EPA study contended that adjacent neighborhoods met safety requirements, New York state health officials reported that they found dioxin (one of the world's most toxic chemicals) at levels eight times higher than the legal dose.[21] The U.S. Office of Technology Assessment undertook an evaluation of all available evidence, but its report shed no additional light on the conditions at Love Canal. It stated that "with available information it is possible either that unsafe levels of toxic contamination exist or that they do not exist."[22]

Voles (field mice common to the Love Canal area) were the subject of another 1983 study. The mice were ideal for the study because they are sedentary, rarely moving appreciable distances. The number of voles found living in the canal area was less than in the control area. (The study placed the control area one mile from the canal area.) Mice living near the canal evidenced liver damage. Life expectancies varied significantly. Any vole in the canal area that reached an age of 30 days could only be expected to live an additional 54 days. A similar vole in the control area would be expected to live 100 days past the 30-day mark. The life expectancy thus was cut in half for those mice living near the canal.[23]

Another study of live birth weights of children born to Love Canal women has also provided cause for concern. Children born to women who lived near chemical swales had significantly lower birth weights in the years 1940–1978 than the state average. A swale is a natural low area along water drainage pathways where chemicals might collect. Several drainage pathways pass through the Love Canal region. Researchers found that 12.1 percent of the children born to women who had lived near one of the swales showed lower than average birth weights as compared to a 6.9 percent average for the state of New York (excluding New York City).[24]

Citizens and health officials have mobilized in an attempt to force the cleanup of Love Canal and keep area inhabitants informed of new findings and projects. Local citizens have grown weary of the problems and want the area cleaned up as soon as possible. Progress has been made, but efforts will continue late into the 1990s. The complex cleanup project began in the spring of 1987 with the dredging of three local creeks. The site, which had remained covered with plastic sheeting and earth, was uncovered. Officials began to dredge dioxin-contaminated mud and tainted sediment from the creeks. The creeks were dewatered and waste removed. The EPA and the state Department of Environmental Conservation stored the wastes in a temporary landfill and storage facility near the site.

Citizens opposed the storage, fearing that it would delay possible rehabilitation of the area. They charged the EPA with negligence and undue delay. In October 1987 the EPA announced plans to complete the cleanup. The EPA planned to incinerate the stored wastes at an expected cost of $26 to $31 million. The incineration process, while costly, is considered a permanent solution. Buried wastes or other disposal methods, such as deep well injection, are considered hazardous.[25] A Technical Review Committee (TRC) oversees testing of Love Canal air and soil samples and will compare its findings to those from other neighborhoods. The TRC also develops criteria for making a final Love Canal resettlement decision. Under the TRC plan, parts of Love Canal will be converted to a reforested park.[26]

In February 1988, a new court decision altered the circumstance of legal liability for Love Canal. Federal Judge John Curtin of the U.S. District Court for the Western District of New York ruled that Occidental Petroleum Corporation's chemicals unit is responsible for the costs of cleaning up Love Canal—costs estimated at $250 million. Curtin found Occidental "at least partially responsible" for the initially inadequate storage and for leakage that has occurred over the years. Occidental argued in the case that the city of Niagara Falls was solely responsible for release of the toxic wastes because city officials ignored warnings about the site and then disrupted its hydrology. But Judge Curtin rejected this "third-party defense" because Hooker Chemical had brought the wastes to the site.[27] New York State Attorney General Robert Abrams said the judge's opinion constitutes "a tremendous victory for the state and federal governments and a resounding defeat for Occidental's strenuous and expensive public-relations campaign to shift the entire blame for Love Canal to the city of Niagara Falls, the board of education, the state of New York, and even the people who were forced to abandon their homes."[28]

The Current Situation

In May 1990, Environmental Protection Agency (EPA) Chief William K. Reilly announced that the government had opened the Love Canal neighborhoods for resettlement. After a 12-year, $250-million cleanup, the EPA concluded that four of the area's seven districts are habitable. The other three will be converted to parkland and industrial areas.[29] At this writing, sixty of the area's 2,500 original residents remain. However, James Carr, planning director of the Love Canal Area Revitalization Agency, placed 236 houses on sale on August 15, 1990 at 20% below market value. Armed with a list of over 200 eager potential Love Canal home-buyers, Carr predicts that the area will quickly regain residents. Given the enormous government cleanup and protection programs, Love Canal's environmental dangers appear to have been eradicated. Carr maintained that, "A child runs far, far greater health risks if his parents smoke or drink than he does living in Love Canal."[30]

The canal now has a state-of-the-art containment system, with two 3-foot-thick caps over the dumpsite. The authorities razed the roughly 240 houses nearest the site, and enclosed the entire area within chain-link fence. Potential home-buyers appear ready to reinhabit Love Canal and put their faith in the cleanup process, despite environmentalists' continuing fears, which spring from inconclusive studies and uncertain conditions. One environmentalist, National Resources Defense Council attorney Rebecca Todd, commented, "Love Canal is a ticking time bomb."[31]

Although Love Canal itself may be slowly regaining normalcy, the disaster continues to haunt Occidental. Recently, New York State filed a $250-million lawsuit against the company, charging that Hooker Electrochemical "recklessly disregarded public health risks" when it operated the dumpsite. Final arguments were heard in a Buffalo, N.Y. federal court in January 1992. Some in industry fear that after it runs its course through the courts, the case will set a precedent, allowing states to sue corporations for punitive damages for actions taken by then-independent subsidiaries years ago. One industry lawyer commented on the suit's inappropriateness, saying, "If the wrongdoers are no longer around, then punitive damages no longer make sense."[32]

CASE ENDNOTES

1. John F. Steiner, "Love Can Be Dangerous to Your Health," in George A. Steiner and John F. Steiner, *Casebook for Business, Government and Society*, 2d ed. (New York: Random House, 1980), 108–109.
2. Sam Borenkind, "Environmental Laws: How Far-Reaching?" *NPN—National Petroleum News* (March, 1991), 60.
3. Thomas H. Maugh, II, "Toxic Waste Disposal a Gnawing Problem," *Science* 204 (May, 1979), 820.
4. Constance Holden, "Love Canal Residents Under Stress," *Science* 208 (June 13, 1980), 1242–1244; and Sandra Sugawara, "Some Love Canal Areas Safe, a New EPA Study Concludes," *Washington Post* (July 15, 1982, Sec. A), 1, 9. See also Beverly Paigen in note 16 on the earlier data.
5. Steiner, 112.
6. Michael H. Brown, "Love Canal, U.S.A.," *New York Times Magazine* (January 21, 1979), 23, *passim*, and Gary Whitney, "Hooker Chemical and Plastics" (HBS Case Services, Harvard Business School, 1979), 3.
7. "The Hooker Memos," in Robert J. Baum, ed., *Ethical Problems in Engineering*, 2d ed. (Troy, NY): Center for the Study of the Human Dimensions of Science and Technology, Rensselaer Polytechnic Institute, 1980), Vol. 2; *Cases*, 38, and "An Occidental Unit Knowingly Polluted California Water, House Panel Charges," *The Wall Street Journal* (June 20, 1979), 14.
8. Whitney, "Hooker Chemical and Plastics."
9. *Ibid.*
10. *Ibid.*, 8.
11. Maugh, 819–821.
12. Steiner, "Love Can Be Dangerous."
13. Joanne Omong, "EPA Names 115 Toxic Waste Dump Sites for Cleanup" *Washington Post* (October 24, 1981), 4.
14. Steiner, 110.
15. Beverly Paigen, "Controversy at Love Canal," *Hastings Center Report* 12 (June, 1982), 29–37.
16. Margery W. Shaw, "Love Canal Chromosome Study," *Science* 209 (August 15, 1980), 752.
17. *Fortune* (July 27, 1981), 30–31.
18. *Discover* 2, no. 4 (April, 1981), 8.
19. "CDC Finds No Excess Illness at Love Canal," *Science* 220 (June 17, 1983), 1254.
20. "Love Canal: Still a Battleground," *U.S. News and World Report* 93 (July 26, 1982), 6.
21. *Ibid.*
22. "Hazards in Love Canal Monitoring," *Science News* 124 (July 9, 1983), 29.
23. John J. Christian, "Love Canal's Unhealthy Voles," *Natural History* 92 (October, 1983), 8–14.
24. Nicholas J. Vianna and Adele K. Polan, "Incidence of Low Birth Weights among Love Canal Residents," *Science* 226 (December 7, 1983), 1217–1219.
25. "EPA Will Burn Sediment to Clean Love Canal Area," *The Wall Street Journal* (October 27, 1987), 72.
26. Carolyn Kuma, "Resampling Could Delay Canal Revitalization Effort," *Niagara Gazette* (November 8, 1986), 1.
27. *U.S.A v. Hooker Chemicals*, U.S. District Court, Western District of New York, CIV-79-990c (February 23, 1988).
28. Roy J. Harris, Jr., "Occidental Unit Is Ruled Liable in Waste Case," *The Wall Street Journal* (February 24, 1988), 2; and Michael Weisskopf, "Company Ruled Liable for Love Canal Costs," *Washington Post* (February 24, 1988), A10.
29. Anne Underwood, "The Return to Love Canal: Would You Live There?" *Newsweek* (July 30, 1990), 25.
30. *Ibid.*
31. *Ibid.*
32. Borenkind, 60.

CASE 21

UPDATE OF HOOKER CHEMICAL AND LOVE CANAL CASE*

Thirteen years after Love Canal acquired its initial notoriety and several hundreds of millions of dollars of cleanup and court costs later, the case was still unresolved. The canal itself was covered with a plastic liner and grassy sod as part of the cleanup or remediation of the area. A barrier drain and a leachate collection, treatment, and monitoring system were installed at the expense and direction of the New York Department of Environmental Conservation and the U.S. Environmental Protection Agency.[1] In addition, an 8-foot chain link fence surrounded the 16-acre canal site and the neighborhoods immediately adjacent to it, and several vertical fluorescent orange well pipes were sunk to depths of 20 to 200 feet as part of the monitoring effort. The buried chemicals, 44 million pounds of lindane, benzene, and other toxic wastes, were intended to be entombed in perpetuity.[2]

The neighborhood immediately surrounding the canal was divided into two categories of habitability by the New York Department of Health. On the north and west sides, the Love Canal Revitalization Agency received permission to renovate as many as 400 of the abandoned homes to prepare them for sale. Several environmental groups sued unsuccessfully to prevent these sales.[3] More than 200 people were on the agency's waiting list, anxious to take advantage of the housing bargains, which averaged 20 percent below market prices.[4] Many of these prospective residents, who were predominantly from the Niagara Falls area, shared the perception that, regardless of Love Canal, living in Niagara Falls, which had a number of other toxic waste dumps and significant chemical operations, was a risky, yet acceptable proposition.[5] The neighborhood on the east side of the canal, an area the state health commissioner determined was uninhabitable, was planned for commercial and industrial development.[6]

The legal battles over who was ultimately responsible for the tragedy continued into a second decade of litigation. In 1988, the federal government won its case in District court to establish that Occidental was legally partially liable for the costs of cleaning up Love Canal under CERCLA (Superfund) legislation. Occidental appealed this decision, which was pending as of mid-1991. As of that time, responsibility for $700 million of cleanup cost and damages, including punitive damages of $250 million requested by the State of New York, had not yet been determined.[7] The state argued that Hooker's practices were not state of the art, that it knew of some chemical migration, and that it should never have let Love Canal out of its control.[8] In addition, the state produced evidence supporting their argument that the company was repeatedly warned by its own employees that the site was a disaster waiting to happen.[9]

Occidental's main defense continued to center on arguments supporting its conformance to industry standards at the time and its purported leadership in responsibly handling wastes compared to then-existing industry standards.[10] Occidental also charged that the U.S. Army was involved in the dumping of hazardous wastes in Love Canal and should be responsible for some of the costs. They also argued that the alleged Army actions were further evidence that toxic

---

* This case was written by Mark Starik of George Washington University.

dumping was acceptable at the time, and, therefore, punitive damages sought by the state, which were typically awarded only in cases of severe violations, were not appropriate in this case.[11]

In 1989, Occidental signed a partial consent decree with the State of New York and the U.S. Government assigning the company the responsibility of taking over storage and destruction (incineration) of Love Canal wastes, which included contaminated sewer and creek sediment, materials stored in barrels on-site, and sludge from the treatment plant.[12] In addition, Occidental, Niagara County, and the Board of Education settled more than 1,300 personal injury suits for about $20 million, with several hundred more pending, as of this writing.[13] On the other hand, Occidental continued to refuse to accept responsibility for the relocation costs of former Love Canal residents. The company did, however, sue dozens of its own liability insurers for coverage of its defense and cleanup costs[14] and has filed counterclaims against the State of New York and the U.S. Government, as well as cross-claims against the City of Niagara Falls and the School Board for cost-sharing purposes.

QUESTIONS FOR DISCUSSION

1. What is your assessment of permitting the 400 abandoned homes to be renovated and sold? What are your arguments?
2. Why do legal battles such as those described in this update take so long? What are the implications for companies and managements?
3. At this point, how do you feel about Occidental's responsibility for the cleanup? Niagara County's responsibility? The school board's responsibility? The Army's responsibility?
4. What major lessons may be learned from the Hooker Chemical and Love Canal tragedy?

CASE ENDNOTES

1. M. Kalecek, "Love Canal—10 Years Later," *The Conservationist* (November/December, 1988), 40–43.
2. C. B. MacKerron, "Superfund Cleanup: The Lessons of Love Canal and Stringfellow," *Chemical Week* (September 2, 1987), 36–40.
3. V. Klinkenborg, "Back to Love Canal," *Harper's Magazine* (March, 1991), 71–78.
4. D. L. Boroughs, "Letter from Love Canal," *U.S. News & World Report.* (May 28, 1990), 18.
5. L. Goodstein, "Back to Love Canal: Resettling a Symbol of Toxic Waste Hazards," *Time* (June 12, 1990), A1, 3.
6. Klinkenborg, 73.
7. A. Flippen, "Love Canal," *The Associated Press* (April 8, 1991), 1559.
8. K. Sternberg, "OxyChem Faces a Dredging Up of the Past," *Chemical Week* (November 7, 1990), 9.
9. Flippin, 1559.
10. Sternberg, 9.
11. A. D. Marcus, "Occidental Sees Hope in Love Canal Memo," *The Wall Street Journal* (May, 15, 1991).
12. *Chemical Marketing Reporter.* Love Canal order signed by Occidental. June 5: 9, 17.
13. MacKerron, 38.
14. D. McLeod, "Pollution: Oxy Told to Pay Love Canal Cleanup," *Business Insurance* (Vol. 22, No. 9, 1988), 1, 29.

CASE 22

COMMUNITY-CORPORATE RELATIONSHIPS: WHEN COMPANIES SAY "GOOD-BYE"*

One of the most significant changes in the Twentieth Century in American economic life is the evolving relationship between the corporation and the community in which it resides. Three years ago *The Wall Street Journal* highlighted what may be a sign of more change in this relationship with the headline "Factory Towns Start to Fight Back Angrily When Firms Pull Out." The article's main point was that after years of "throwing money and favors at companies to win or preserve jobs, these communities now want their due."

Indeed, University of California professor of labor, Harley Shaiken, describes the issue in *The Wall Street Journal* article as: "Companies used to seek incentives to move into an area. Now, they're paying incentives to move out."[1]

In the three years since the issue of community retribution for corporate departures first received national attention, events have evolved which may be indicative of this process of change. Three examples can serve as the basis for review of the importance of the changing phenomena in community-corporate relationships: Norwood, Ohio, and General Motors; Clarksburg, West Virginia, and Anchor Hocking; and Kenosha, Wisconsin, and Chrysler.

Norwood, Ohio

Norwood is a small city of just over 26,000, located about 10 minutes from the center of Cincinnati. The General Motors facility was part of this community for 64 years until the fall of 1986 when, with a decreasing market share, General Motors decided to close this aging plant. At that time the Norwood facility employed 4,200 workers, most of whom did not live in the city limits. It occupied 48 acres of land, with all but 10 of these acres in buildings. Revenues from General Motors comprised nearly 40 percent of the Norwood city taxes.[2]

When General Motors decided to close the Norwood plant, it proceeded as it had in other plant closings around the country: paying benefits to workers and establishing task forces both to provide workers with information on aid programs and to help communities determine the best use for empty plants.

The company's actions, however, did not satisfy Norwood civic leaders. They felt that Norwood had always sought to be a good host for General Motors and that Norwood had done everything that General Motors had requested. It had granted tax abatements and other benefits to General Motors on the assumption that the plant would remain open. It had built an underpass and vacated several streets for the benefit of General Motors.

Thus, a seven-count law suit for breach of contract was filed for the city of Norwood by Stanley M. Chesley, a prominent Cincinnati lawyer known for his suits on behalf of plaintiffs claiming damage from Agent Orange and the chemical leak in Bhopal, India, who had volunteered his efforts to sue General Motors. The suit asked for damages and asked that the plant be reopened. On August 19, 1988, all but one claim was dismissed. The presiding judge ruled that the company had to

---

* This case was written by Carolyn J. Fausnaugh. Reproduced with permission.

continue paying their proportionate share of police and fire protection costs at the site of the closed plant, but rejected the city's efforts to reopen the plant.[3]

Mr. Chesley advised the city to appeal. "We're on the cutting edge of these types of cases, and it's going to take appellate review," Mr. Chesley said, noting that Norwood was one of the first cities to sue a company over a plant closing.[4]

Norwood did not take Mr. Chesley's advice. Once the ruling by the court was made in favor of the company, additional negotiations resulted in accommodations to Norwood, which community leaders found acceptable. General Motors donated two parking garages to the city, and demolished all the buildings on the site except one that the city requested they not demolish. The city has proceeded to arrange the construction of "Central Parke," a mixed use industrial complex on the site.

In a conversation with the author of this case, Mayor Joseph E. Sanker said the transition was proceeding positively. Although the city lost the suit and decided not to appeal, he feels the positive outcome can be attributed to the city's willingness to explore through legal channels the boundaries of public-private cooperation.[5]

Clarkesburg, West Virginia

In 1979, leaders of the city of Clarkesburg and the state of West Virginia worked long and hard on behalf of the Anchor Hocking plant in Clarkesburg. By combining a Federal UDAG grant sponsored by the city of Clarkesburg with Economic Development Bonds issued by the West Virginia Economic Development Authority, political leaders were able to assemble a financing package for improvements and retrofitting the plant. Interest rates on a portion of the funds loaned were as low as 1.126 percent for 20 years.[6]

Anchor Hocking, the manufacturer of a variety of products including plastic laundry detergent bottles, metal caps for baby food jars, decorative hardware, and glassware, was acquired by Newell Co. in a hostile takeover in February, 1987. Seven months later Newell Co. announced it was consolidating the Clarkesburg, W. Va., glassmaking operations with the Lancaster, Ohio, facility. The Clarkesburg plant would be closed.

Under the governor's personal leadership, the state took the position that the understanding behind the loan was that Anchor Hocking would provide jobs for 20 years. A suit was filed against Newell Co. by the State of West Virginia for breach-of-contract. The $614 million damage request was based on the state's estimate of the dollars the plant would have brought into the State's economy between the scheduled closing date and 1999. Close review of the written loan documents revealed targets for employment levels but no specific dates for their attainment. Employment at the plant had reached the levels specified in the agreements. There was also no penalty in the agreements for early payment of outstanding balances.

Clarkesburg City Manager Dan Boroff describes the governor of West Virginia at the time of the announced closing as "charismatic, able to rally people behind him."[7] *The Wall Street Journal* describes him as "politically nimble."[8] Dan Boroff thinks Governor Moore's style and personal involvement led to the tactical maneuvering which followed the filing of the suit. Perhaps the most embarrassing display of such maneuvering was Newell's attempt to discharge its loan obligations. Checks sent to the state were cashed before Governor Moore could have them intercepted. The governor ordered the money be returned to Newell. Another example of the maneuvering is that workers watched the plant to make sure the company didn't remove equipment. Later, the state won a federal court injunction prohibiting Newell from transferring equipment to its other plant. With the equipment impounded, Newell was unable to expand its glassmaking capacity at the Lancaster, Ohio, location. Newell requested the case be moved to state court. In a two-hour gap between federal and state injunctions, the company removed some $500,000 worth of equipment.[9]

Governor Moore was not re-elected. He was succeeded by Governor Caperton who worked hard to reach a compromise agreement outside the court. City Manager Dan Boroff describes the events as "a little embarrassing." He says Newell had the impressive side of the arguments. "Company representatives were honest and didn't disguise anything."[10]

Newell's chief executive officer, Daniel C. Ferguson, is quoted in *The Wall Street Journal* as saying, "We didn't anticipate the reaction we got. We weren't prepared for it."[11] It seemed clear to company decision makers that closing down the Clarkesburg facility and moving equipment elsewhere would greatly enhance the newly acquired unit's efficiency.

Kenosha, Wisconsin

When Chrysler Corporation announced in January 1988 that it planned to close its Kenosha, Wisconsin, assembly and stamping parts facilities which employed about 5,500 people, Governor Tommy Thompson threatened to sue Chrysler for breach of contract almost immediately. Wisconsin Governor Tommy Thompson is reported to have gotten the lawsuit idea from Virginia Governor Moore.[12] The Chrysler acquisition of American Motors Corp. in 1987 was aided by the State of Wisconsin with pollution waivers worth $10 million. In exchange, the state felt it got a promise of three to five more years for the Kenosha complex.

While the merits of suing Chrysler were being bandied about, public pressure was steadily increasing and causing Chrysler considerable embarrassment. At a press conference in New York, Chrysler Chairman Lee Iacocca announced the fourth best earnings achievement in Chrysler's history. Reporters glossed over the good news and proceeded to query Iacocca about Kenosha and the reported $1.3 million local governments had spent on public improvements to help keep the plant open.[13] Around Kenosha, sales of Chrysler products fell sharply.[14] A state senator tried to scuttle a $3.8 million state order for 393 new Chrysler automobiles.[15] Public sentiment was running high against Chrysler.

Chrysler Corp. reached an accord with Wisconsin officials in late September 1988. The total package was estimated to be worth $250 million. Among its more unusual provisions was a pledge from Chrysler to contribute six acres of land to the Kenosha municipal golf course and to provide an option on land that could be used for a dog racing track. Earlier in the negotiations Chrysler had announced that it would contribute the profits from sales of its products in Wisconsin to a trust fund to help meet housing, education and welfare needs of families affected by the closing. The value of this commitment was estimated at $20 million. Other provisions included $60 million to repay more than 10,000 current and former Kenosha workers who took part in an American Motors investment plan in exchange for agreeing to delay certain wage and benefit increases. Among other provisions Chrysler committed to provide financing to an aircraft company to build single-engine planes in Kenosha and to contribute a total of $1 million to the United Way in Kenosha during the next four years.[16]

Governor Thompson described the settlement as "the best achievable under the circumstances. While a lawsuit would establish that Chrysler made commitments, it would be futile in producing any jobs."[17]

QUESTIONS FOR DISCUSSION

1. Identify the stakeholder groups affected by the plant closings in each community.
2. What specific social responsibilities (economic, legal, ethical, or philanthropic) do you think the individual firms involved had to the affected communities? Were some firms more responsible than others? Explain.
3. Is a "legal contract" entered into when a major corporation decides to locate in a community? Discuss.
4. Describe the level of responsibility initially exhibited by each company for mitigating the social and economic impacts on each of the stakeholder groups identified in question 1.
5. What types of company actions may have averted the public nature of the disputes and the filing of suits in Norwood and Clarkesburg?
6. In each community, the conflict was ultimately resolved out of court. Why are such out-of-court settlements attractive to the company? Why are they attractive to the community?
7. What do these incidents portend for the future of business-community relationships? Discuss.

CASE ENDNOTES

1. Joseph B. White, "Factory Towns Start to Fight Back Angrily When Firms Pull Out," *The Wall Street Journal* (March 8, 1988), 1.
2. "GM Sued by Town for $318.3 Million Over Breakup of 64-Year 'Marriage,'" *The Wall Street Journal* (August 21, 1987), 4.
3. "GM Cleared in Shutdown," *New York Times* (August 20, 1988), 45.
4. "GM Wins Dismissal of Most of a Lawsuit Against Plant Closing," *The Wall Street Journal* (August 22, 1988), 7.
5. Telephone conversation, September 3, 1991.
6. "Moore's Anchor Suit Worries Businesses," *Charleston Gazette* (October 13, 1987), F13.
7. Telephone conversation, August 29, 1991.
8. White, 1.
9. *Ibid.*, 1.
10. Telephone conversation, August 29, 1991.
11. White, 1.
12. *Ibid.*, 1.
13. William Mathewson, "Shop Talk," *The Wall Street Journal* (February 23, 1988), 33.
14. "Chrysler to Donate Wisconsin Profits to Fund for Workers from Closed Plant," *The Wall Street Journal* (February 17, 1988), 4.
15. White, 1.
16. "Chrysler to Pay $250 Million to Settle Dispute Over Wisconsin Plant Closing," *The Wall Street Journal* (September 26, 1988), 4.
17. *Ibid.*, 4.

CASE 23 EMPLOYMENT-AT-WILL?

Betty Brewer was fired from her position as a nurse's helper at the Watkinsville Nursing Home (WNH) in Birmingham, Alabama. Betty believed that the employee handbook that had been given to her when she was hired constituted a contract of employment. Not only did she feel she was wrongfully discharged, but she also felt that her termination constituted extreme and outrageous conduct that intentionally or recklessly caused severe emotional distress.

Betty maintained that she was being dismissed for a reason not specifically listed in the employee handbook. Further, she felt that the choice WNH had given her of resigning or being fired caused severe emotional strain.

In defending its position, the nursing home pointed out that the general common law rule is that an employee may be terminated at will. It also stated that under Alabama law an employment contract may be terminated by either party for a good reason, a wrong reason, or no reason at all. As for the handbook, WNH presented several excerpts. First, on the inside cover of the handbook was the following statement:

> This handbook and the policies contained herein do not in any way constitute, and should not be construed as, a contract of employment between the employer and the employee, or a promise of employment.

WNH went on to argue that there is no evidence anywhere that the employee was told that she could be terminated only for the reasons listed on page 20 of the handbook. It stated that this must have been the employee's assumption. In fact, WNH pointed out that page 20 of the handbook clearly states that the reasons for dismissal "include, but are not limited to the following. . . ." Then a list of reasons followed. The company further added, and Betty agreed, that there was no agreement as to the length or duration of employment and that it was indefinite.

QUESTIONS FOR DISCUSSION

1. Do you think Betty was wrongly discharged or was she legitimately dismissed under the notion of employment-at-will?
2. Do you think, based on the evidence presented, that the company did enough to clearly establish that an employee could be fired for reasons not listed in the employee handbook?
3. In your opinion, did the fact that the nursing home gave her the option of resigning or being fired constitute outrageous conduct that intentionally or recklessly caused severe emotional distress?
4. What implications does this case have for the relationship between employer and employee?

CASE 24 WAS DUE PROCESS RENDERED?

Charles Edwards, an employee of Johnson Aircraft, was suspended from his job on Wednesday afternoon, July 24, 1985, pending further investigation.[1] When suspended, he did not request union representation as was permitted by the labor contract between Johnson Aircraft and Edwards's union—the Teamsters. Management made the decision to discharge him 2 days later, on Friday, July 26. On Saturday, July 27, Edwards received written notice in the mail of his discharge.

The letter Edwards received from management stated the following:

> An investigation into employee charges against you of harassment, intimidation, and interference with productive activity, as well as use of vulgar, suggestive language to female employees has been completed. This follows similar reports and investigations resulting in your receiving a written warning and five-day suspension on October 30, 1984. That warning stated that any further substantiated reports of this nature would result in immediate termination.

Edwards filed a grievance against the company, saying he was unjustly discharged. Following is a summary of what was presented at the arbitration hearing.

Johnson Aircraft's Side of the Story

The company felt justified in suspending and then discharging Edwards, pointing to a clause in the bargaining agreement that said that the company shall have the right to suspend and/or discharge for just cause. During the arbitration hearing, the company cited three specific instances in which Edwards committed acts that constituted reasons for discharge. These acts were of the type mentioned in the letter Edwards received on July 27. The company also testified that it had considered facts from employees directly involved in two prior disciplinary incidents. Two female employees testified at this arbitration hearing about these prior incidents.

Edwards's Side of the Story

Edwards's pitch at the arbitration hearing was that he was unjustly discharged because company management never sought nor received his side of the story before firing him. He had no major argument with the suspension but thought it was unjust for the company to discharge him without hearing his explanation. Company management admitted that it had no contact with him about the dispute after it occurred and before they discharged him. On his behalf, his attorney argued that before administering discipline to an employee, the company should make an effort to determine whether the employee really did in fact disobey a rule or order of management. The attorney went on to say that this is the employee's "day in court" principle and that an employee has the right to know the precise charges being made against him and have an opportunity to respond to the charges. Further, the attorney said that it was grossly unfair for management to accept without question the testimony of the women, while assuming the other party to the dispute would not tell the truth. The attorney further criticized management for using the testimony of the women who were involved in earlier disputes for which Edwards had already paid his penalty. The bottom line, Edwards's attorney argued, was that his client had not been given due process; therefore, the discharge was unjust.

QUESTIONS FOR DISCUSSION

1. Did Edwards receive "due process" in this case? Wasn't the arbitration hearing an adequate "day in court"? Explain why.
2. As arbitrator, would you uphold Johnson Aircraft's discharge of Edwards or set it aside? Explain.
3. Discuss the ramifications of your decision for management and employees alike.

CASE ENDNOTE

1. Some of the facts in this case were taken from an actual arbitration case: *Labor Arbitration Awards* (Chicago: Commerce Clearing House, 1986), 3852–3854.

CASE 25 THE LETTER TO THE EDITOR

One of the most significant tensions between employers and employees is an employee's freedom or right to speak out. In some extreme cases, the employee "blows the whistle" on his or her employer by going to a government agency or a newspaper and reporting some alleged wrongdoing. One view is that employees have a right to blow the whistle and should be protected against employer retaliation.[1] Many management groups, however, think employees owe loyalty to their employers. Some writers on this subject think that First Amendment rights need to be watched closely and that they do not give employees the right to thwart the boss.[2] Another writer has stated the issue as follows: "Where does a corporate employee's duty to the firm end and his right of free speech as a citizen begin?"[3]

The Incident

John Cox, a 14-year postal clerk in his mid-30s, was angered by an editorial he read in the newspaper.[4] The editorial was critical of the U.S. Postal Service. He was so upset that he sat down and typed out a letter to the editor in which he sought to defend his employer.

His superiors at the Van Nuys, California, postal branch were pleased on reading the letter, which was published, until they got to the last paragraph. Cox concluded his letter as follows: "Despite some of the worst management in industrial society, postal workers move more mail faster and cheaper than anywhere else in the world." This paragraph wiped the smiles off his superiors' faces.[5]

Management's Response

Twelve days later, Cox received an official disciplinary letter of warning from his boss. The charge against him was "disloyalty to the Postal Service." The warning letter was placed in his personnel file. This meant that it could affect future promotions or other personnel decisions if he committed other infractions. Other such infractions could eventually result in his being fired. The warning also accused him of violating a Postal Service Code of Ethics that required employees to conduct themselves in a manner that reflects favorably on the Postal Service.[6]

Cox Fights Back

Cox, who has also served as a union shop steward, decided to fight back. He filed a complaint with the National Labor Relations Board. He filed a grievance with his union, the San Fernando Valley local of the American Postal Workers Union, and also with the Equal Employment Opportunity office. In explaining his actions, he said that all he was trying to do was defend the Postal Service because he was tired of people criticizing it and blaming it for rate hikes. Cox thought that the warning letter was in retaliation for his union activities and two previous disputes he had had with his superiors. He added that he was only trying to state what was obvious to him and that he did not refer to any single individual in the letter. He also said he didn't expect the *Los Angeles Times* to publish the letter.

Cox's coworkers seemed almost gleeful about the dispute. One clerk said, "We're all getting a lot of laughs because this is going to come back and hurt management."[7]

QUESTIONS FOR DISCUSSION

1. Do you think Cox went too far in making the statement critical of Postal Service management?
2. In your opinion, was Cox disloyal or did he engage in behavior that violated the Code of Ethics? Was this a reasonable expectation to be placed in a code of ethics?
3. What is your assessment of the supervisor's action in giving Cox an official disciplinary letter of warning?
4. How would you have handled this case if you had been Cox's supervisor?

CASE ENDNOTES

1. Nancy Hauserman, "Whistle-Blowing: Individual Morality in a Corporate Society," *Business Horizons* (March-April, 1986), 4.
2. Charles G. Bakaly, Jr. and Joel M. Grossman, "Does First Amendment Let Employees Thwart the Boss?" *The Wall Street Journal* (December 8, 1983), 30.
3. Alan F. Westin, "Employee Free Speech," *The Wall Street Journal* (November 10, 1980), 28.
4. Names have been changed, but all other case facts remain the same as they were reported.
5. "'Disloyal' Post Office Worker Reprimanded for Critical Letter," *Atlanta Journal* (April 23, 1985).
6. *Ibid.*
7. *Ibid.*

CASE 26: THE ZELLERBACH SEVEN[1]

During July 1979, seven black employees of the Zellerbach Paper Company sent a letter to the Los Angeles school board. In the letter they protested an award given to their employer. The award had been for an affirmative action project in which the company brought minority students into the plant. One goal of the project was to interest the youth in jobs.

In the letter, the employees pointed out that charges of discrimination against the company had been filed with the EEOC and were now in the courts. The employees also condemned the corporation's personnel director, who was to receive the award, as "the standard-bearer of the bigoted position of racism at Zellerbach." The letter writers demanded an "immediate reply" as to why the school board had "failed to look at Zellerbach's total affirmative action picture." The employees sent copies of the letter to Los Angeles mayor Tom Bradley, company managers, and the local chapters of several black organizations.

The Company Response

Executive consultations over the letter-writing incident were extensive. The discussion even reached Bill Zellerbach, the company president. The employees were dismissed for "disloyalty." The company took the position that employees could file complaints with appropriate federal and state agencies and it would take no reprisals, even if it was determined that the charges were not correct. However, the company went on to say that employees do not have the right to injure the company and its reputation and relationships with customers by spreading "unfounded defamatory statements about the company," such as this complaint to one of the company's major customers.

The Employees File Grievance

The seven employees, members of the United Paperworkers Union, filed a grievance as permitted by their labor contract, contending there was no just cause for their dismissal. Not only did their union support them but so did the local chapter of the American Civil Liberties Union and a black community organization.

One of the major differences between the case of the Zellerbach Seven and many other cases is that in the Zellerbach Seven a union was present and the employees filed a grievance. Often, no union is present and employees are at the mercy of managerial judgment.

QUESTIONS FOR DISCUSSION

1. What exactly did the Zellerbach Seven do and why did they do it? What issue is at stake in this case?
2. What exactly did the company do and why?
3. Do you think the employees were justified in their action? How else might they have handled their discontent?
4. Was the company justified in the action it took? How else might it have handled the situation?
5. How do you think the labor arbitrator will rule in this case? Why?

CASE ENDNOTE

1. The materials for this case are based on Alan F. Westin, "Employee Free Speech," *The Wall Street Journal* (November 10, 1980), 28.

CASE 27: THE CASE OF THE QUESTIONABLE ORDER

Pauline Gossett had been working for Southwestern Color Lithographers for a year and a half and had proved to be a very capable employee. Southwestern specialized in commercial printing and handled many different types of printing jobs such as booklets, business cards, certificates, church bulletins, labels, letterheads, newsletters, wedding invitations, and so on. Pauline started out with Southwestern as a secretary, but in the last 9 months she began taking on other responsibilities because several other female employees were out due to pregnancies.

The major responsibility she had just taken on was that of providing information about the range of printing services and prices available at Southwestern. It was common in the printing industry for potential customers to seek pricing and service information over the phone. Much to Pauline's dismay, she learned that it had been the practice of her superior, James Smith, to require that such phone inquiries be recorded. His statement to Pauline was, "Do not let customers know that we are recording their phone calls. This information is for our sales and product analyses and there is no need for callers to know about it."

The night that she learned of the recording practice she went home feeling very uneasy. After a short discussion with her husband, Leonard, they both agreed that it wasn't right and that she ought to talk with her boss about it. The next day she tried to bring the topic up gently with Smith, but he obviously did not want to talk about it and quickly retorted, "There is nothing wrong with what we are doing, so don't you worry your little head about it. Anyway, we checked with the state attorney general's office and we were assured that we are not violating either state or federal law with our practice."

Pauline reported her brief discussion with Smith to her husband that evening, and he was not pleased with Smith's reaction. The two discussed her options at this point and concluded that she could not ignore the issue and should bring it up with Smith's boss, the owner of Southwestern Color Lithographers. The next morning she made an appointment with Mr. Allen Kirby, owner of the company. She explained to Kirby how she was very happy at the company and was especially pleased that her job duties had been expanded to include handling telephone inquiries. She liked this role because she firmly believed that the person explaining services and prices was very influential in landing new accounts. Then she got to her concern about the phone calls being recorded. After briefly explaining why she did not think it was right, she exploded in a burst of tears, "I would rather quit my job than do something I think is wrong!" After the brief outburst, Pauline ran out of the office before Kirby had a chance to respond.

QUESTIONS FOR DISCUSSION

1. Identify the social and or ethical issues that are present in this case. What was wrong with what Smith was asking Pauline to do?
2. Put yourself in the position of Kirby. What available options do you see at this point? What are the arguments for and against each option?
3. Still in the role of Kirby, what course of action will you take and why?

CASE 28   E-MAIL AND EMPLOYEE PRIVACY

Ethical issues involving computers are complex and numerous. Major issues that society needs to address include, but are not limited to, the following:

- Should the concept of freedom of the press be extended to electronic bulletin boards?
- Under what circumstances is information to be treated as a good such that unauthorized access to it is to be treated as theft and therefore defined as a criminal act?[1]
- Do employees of an organization have a right to expect their electronic mail (E-mail) is private and not to be read by their employers and others?

It is with this third issue that the current situation is concerned.

Much to her surprise, Alana Shoars arrived to her office at Epson America, Inc. one morning in 1990 only to find her supervisor reading and printing out her E-mail. The E-mail messages were between her and other employees of the firm. Ms. Shoars was especially appalled because, as Electronic Mail Administrator, she trained and taught other employees not to access or read other people's E-mail because she wanted to protect each employee's privacy. Now, she encountered a member of management engaging in the practice that she taught was inappropriate.[2]

Ms. Shoars questioned the practice and was basically told that it was not her business. The next day she was fired for insubordination. She later filed a $1 million lawsuit against the company for wrongful termination.[3]

According to Glenn Rifkin, a commentator on this topic, Epson America declined to discuss Ms. Shoars' termination but did say that her discharge was unrelated to her questioning of the E-mail practice. A company spokesman denied that the company had a policy regarding the monitoring of E-mail.[4]

Without question, computers have introduced a whole host of new ethical issues into the workplace, just as technology has raised numerous questions in the fields of science and medicine. According to Richard O. Mason, there are four major ethical issues in the information age: privacy, accuracy, property and accessibility.[5] The Shoars-Epson case has implications for at least two of these—privacy and accessibility. Privacy has to do with what information people can keep to themselves and not reveal to others. Accessibility has to do with what information a person or an organization has a right to obtain and under what conditions.[6]

Although Ms. Shoars is now employed in a new firm, she still reacts strongly to her episode at Epson. She says, "You don't read other people's mail, just as you don't listen to their phone conversations. Right is right and wrong is wrong."[7]

As someone once said, however, there are always two sides to any story.

The chief information officer at Bank of Boston, Michael Simmons, disagrees with Ms. Shoars' conclusion. He says, "If the corporation owns the equipment and pays for the network, that asset belongs to the company, and it has a right to look and see if people are using it for purposes other than running the business."[8]

Simmons cites cases that he encountered in a previous place of employment. He discovered that an employee was handicapping horse races with the company's computer. Another employee was discovered to be running his Amway business on the firm's computer. Both employees were immediately fired.[9]

Some companies have stated policies on E-mail. Federal Express, American Airlines, United Parcel Service, and Pacific Bell, for example, all employ information systems that automatically inform employees that the company reserves the right to monitor messages. Other companies either don't have formulated policies or don't inform employees of those policies.

Eugene Spafford, a computer science professor at Purdue University, argues that monitoring is wrong even if the company does notify the employees that it may be occurring. Says he, "Even if a company does post notice, is that something it should do? The legal question may be answered, but is it ethical? The company may say it is, but the employees say it isn't, and there's a conflict."[10]

Regarding the legality of such matters, the Federal Electronic Communications Act of 1986 protects the privacy of messages sent through such public networks as Compuserve and MCI mail. However, the law does not apply to internal E-mail systems within corporations.

Two trends seem to be colliding. First, there is a proliferation of E-mail taking place today. Second, advanced technology is making it easier and less expensive for companies to monitor their employees' communications and actions. Mitchell Kapor is the founder of the Electronic Frontier Foundation, which was formed in 1990 to serve as a watchdog over information technology and public policy issues. In regard to E-mail, he thinks the issue is a "hard case" because it falls in between a telephone call on one hand and written correspondence on the other. He observes that most business people would feel comfortable with the employer's right to examine written materials but would not approve listening in on phone conversations.[11]

Only time will tell whether Alana Shoars will eventually get the kind of retribution she thinks she deserves. Her former employer, on the other hand, thinks it is justified in the action taken.

In the meantime, the question remains as Glenn Rifkin so aptly put it: "Do employees have a right to electronic privacy?"

Completely independent of the case described above, the Data Processing Management Association has developed a Code of Ethics and Standards of Conduct to deal with ethical issues in the information systems industry. But this code is designed primarily for information system specialists.[12] What about ordinary employees who work outside the information systems industry but use E-mail and computers in their work?

QUESTIONS FOR DISCUSSION

1. What rights to privacy do E-mail users have? What limits or conditions affect these rights?

2. What rights do employers have in terms of monitoring E-mail or other computer-assisted communications? What limits or conditions affect these rights?
3. Analyze the "employer monitoring E-mail" scenario from the perspective of the four-part corporate social responsibility model.
4. What ethical principles might help us resolve the ethics of E-mail monitoring?
5. Does the fact that a company has an expressly stated policy informing employees that E-mail may be monitored affect how you feel about it? Discuss.
6. What policies should a company develop regarding the issues discussed in this case?
7. Conduct research to discover the outcome of Alana Shoars's lawsuit. Do you agree with the findings? Why? Why not?

CASE ENDNOTES

1. David Kelsey, "Computer Ethics: An Overview of the Issues," *Ethics: Easier Said Than Done* (Issue 15, November, 1991), 32.
2. Glenn Rifkin, "Do Employees Have a Right to Electronic Privacy," *New York Times* (December 8, 1991), 8F.
3. *Ibid.*
4. *Ibid.*
5. Richard O. Mason, "Four Ethical Issues of the Information Age," *MIS Quarterly* (Vol. 10, No. 1, January, 1986).
6. *Ibid.*
7. Rifkin, 8F.
8. *Ibid.*
9. *Ibid.*
10. *Ibid.*
11. *Ibid.*
12. Bruce Spiro, "Ethics in the Information Age," *Information Executive* (Fall, 1989), 38–41.

CASE 29 **YOU OWE ME A SMOKE-FREE WORKPLACE**

In July 1984, Karen Schaefer filed a complaint against her employer, the Walters Corporation, arguing that the terms and conditions of her contract with the company had been violated. She said that the company had a duty to provide her with a smoke-free workplace, and when it didn't it had inflicted emotional distress on her. Karen argued that she is allergic to tobacco smoke and that her employer knew this. She was seeking damages from the courts in the amount of $75,000 and reinstatement in her former office location, which was smoke free.

In presenting her case, Karen said that her employer had provided her with a smoke-free work area up until January of 1983 but then moved her to a work area where smoking was permitted. After a brief time, Karen left her job without notice, and the Walters Corporation then filed a complaint against her for breach of contract.

Karen's Case

In arguing her case that her employer had broken its contract with her to provide her with a smoke-free workplace, Karen presented the following evidence, which she believed, at a minimum, constituted an implied contract. She said that she submitted a résumé to the company noting that she had left one previous position because she was allergic to tobacco smoke and dust. She also said that she had a letter from an allergist substantiating this point and that the letter was available on request. Another point she made was that she had a "Thank You for Not Smoking" sign on her desk before and after the time at which her contract with Walters was executed. She added that before she was moved to the larger area where smoking was permitted, she did work in a smoke-free setting—a private office—that Walters had provided her.

Walters Corporation's Case

The company took the position that the employment contract it had with Karen contained no express provisions requiring that she be provided with a smoke-free workplace. The company believed, therefore, that it was up to Karen to prove that such an understanding was an implied part of the contract. The company's position was that Karen had not proved and could not prove that such an implied contract existed between them based on the evidence presented above.

The Walters Corporation argued that, at most, Karen's evidence showed was that she does not *want* to work in a smoking environment, that she was provided with a smoke-free environment *for a time*, and that the company was *aware* of her preference. The company said that she had not proved that she had raised her preference for a smoke-free environment at the time the contract was agreed on and that there was no such agreement explicitly or implicitly entered into.

As for its duty to provide her with a smoke-free workplace, Karen argued that Walters Corporation had a common-law duty to provide her with a safe workplace and to protect people on its premises from harm. The company's response was that in her complaint she did not argue that second-hand smoke created an unsafe working condition. The company argued that all she had shown was that she personally had problems with such smoke.

Regarding the charge of emotional distress, the company pointed out that she made no claims of being physically injured and therefore cannot recover damages for negligent infliction of emotional distress. The company said that the only thing clear from her charge is that she was required to work in part of a 1,000-square-foot room where smoking by two coworkers was permitted.

QUESTIONS FOR DISCUSSION

1. Based on the case facts presented, do you think Karen had a contract with the Walters Corporation to provide her with a smoke-free workplace? Explain.
2. Do you think the Walters Corporation has an ethical responsibility to provide Karen with a smoke-free workplace? What exactly are Karen's rights in this case?
3. If your answer to question 1 was yes, do you think she is owed damages by the company? Explain.
4. What other issues or implications for management do you find in this case? Discuss.

CASE 30 DISCRIMINATION CASES

In each of the following eight cases, determine whether illegal discrimination has occurred. If you think it has, indicate what kind of discrimination and why. If you think discrimination has not occurred, explain why.

The Airline Attendant

An airline refused to hire men as flight attendants. When challenged in court by a male applicant, the airline pointed to section 703(e) of Title VII of the Civil Rights Act and claimed that sex was a "bona fide occupational qualification" for the position of flight attendant. As evidence, the airline offered the following:

1. Passenger preference: surveys showed that passengers preferred women to men as cabin attendants.

2. Psychological needs: a clinical psychologist testified that women, simply because they were women, could provide comfort and reassurance to passengers better than men could.

3. Feasibility: an industrial psychologist testified that sex was the best practicable screening device to use in determining whom to hire for the position.

The Applicant

A manager was confronted with a large room packed with applicants for only a handful of openings. To screen out some of the people, he announced that all the women with preschool age children should go home. One of those sent home filed a charge of sex discrimination. The company responded by saying that it did not discriminate against women; in fact, many women worked at the facility in question. It was only women with young children that the company preferred not to hire because child-care responsibilities often interfered with work responsibilities. Therefore, the company said that since it did not discriminate because of sex, it had not violated Title VII of the Civil Rights Act.

The Partner

The partners in an office of a national accounting firm proposed that one of its female assistant managers be offered a partnership. They pointed to her outstanding performance in winning major new accounts. None of the other partnership candidates that year had a comparable record. The partners, however, also criticized the manager for being overly aggressive, unduly harsh, difficult to work with, and impatient with staff. Some of the partners reacted negatively to her

---

*From James Ledvinka and Vida Scarpello, *Federal Regulation of Personnel and Human Resource Management* (Boston: Kent Publishing Co., 1991), 60–61, 96–97. © by Wadsworth, Inc. Reprinted by permission of PWS-KENT Publishing Co., a division of Wadsworth, Inc.

personality because she was a woman. One partner described her as "macho"; another said she "overcompensated for being a woman"; a third suggested that she take "a course at charm school." The national policy board of the firm decided not to offer her the partnership. When she discussed the decision with the head partner at her office, she was advised to "walk more femininely, talk more femininely, dress more femininely, wear make-up, have her hair styled, and wear jewelry."

The Retirement Fund

Because women live longer than men, a city government required its women employees to contribute more each month to its retirement fund than men. The contributions were arranged so that women contributed in proportion to their expected benefits, as did men. The resulting system allowed equal monthly retirement benefits for men and women without having either sex subsidize the other. Several women employees complained that the unequal contributions constituted sex discrimination.

Over Forty

A bus company refused to hire intercity drivers over 40 years of age, and an applicant who was turned down because he was over 40 charged the company with age discrimination. In its defense, the company argued that, for most people, physical changes that begin around age 35 have an adverse effect on driving skills. Because the company could not practically determine when such changes take place in an individual applicant, it used chronological age as an indicator. Also, the company presented evidence that experience tended to offset the adverse effects of age. Its safest drivers had a particular blend of age and driving experience with the company—ages between 50 and 55 with experience of about 20 years. Any driver hired past age 40 would not be able to attain that optimal blend.

The Handicapped

A woman with a serious hearing impairment was denied admission to a training program to become a registered nurse. The reason for the rejection was that, even with lip reading, she would have had difficulty performing certain duties such as working with staff wearing surgical masks. She filed charges of discrimination against the handicapped.

The Church Member

An airline's shift assignments were based on seniority, and one employee assigned to Saturday shifts did not have enough seniority to change his shift. This employee was a member of the Worldwide Church of God, which forbids its members to work on Saturdays. At the employee's request, the airline agreed to look for someone to trade shifts with the employee voluntarily, but no one stepped forward to do so. The union refused to make the trade forcibly, for that would have violated the collective bargaining agreement. The company refused to allow the employee to work only four days a week because the employee's job was essential to operations.

Finally, the employee failed to report for work on Saturday and was fired. He filed charges of religious discrimination against the company, pointing out that the airline could have filled his position by assigning a supervisor to it or by giving another employee overtime pay to do it.

The High School Teacher

A male high school teacher "came out of the closet" and proclaimed his homosexuality. The incident was well publicized as the teacher appeared on television talk shows and gave interviews to reporters. Finally, the public controversy was disruptive enough that the school board dismissed him. The teacher made his case public, discussing it on television repeatedly and noting that there was little factual basis for concern that homosexuals have an adverse effect on the children they teach. The school board's response was that, in any event, the teacher's notoriety since his dismissal made any reinstatement out of the question. The teacher filed suit in court, charging that the school board had violated his rights to due process and equal protection of the law by discriminating against him because of his homosexuality.

CASE 31   PROPMORE CORPORATION*

Overview

Don Bradford was on the fast track at the Propmore Corporation. But he wished he could slow things down a bit, given several hard choices he had to make.

Propmore Corporation was a good place to work. It had sales of about $500 million per year, a net profit margin of 5 percent, and a return on equity of 15 percent. Propmore made several key components used by the aerospace industry and consumer goods market. It was a leader in its field. The company was organized by product divisions, each reporting to the Executive Vice-President. Its operations were decentralized, with broad decisionmaking capability at the divisional level. However, at the corporate level functional departments (Purchasing, R&D, Personnel, and Marketing) set company policy and coordinated divisional activities in these areas. Propmore was financially successful, and it treated its people well, as Don Bradford's experience showed.

After earning his MBA four years ago from a respected state university, Don quickly rose through the ranks in Purchasing. At age 31, he holds the prestigious position of Manager. (See organizational chart, Figure C-31) Before joining Propmore, Don earned a B.S. in engineering and worked for three years in the aerospace industry as a design engineer. During his first three years at Propmore, Don was a buyer and received "excellent" ratings in all his performance appraisals. As Purchasing Manager, Don enjoyed good working relationships with superiors and subordinates. He was accountable directly to the Division General Manager and, functionally, to the Corporate Vice-President of Procurement, Mr. Stewart. His dealings with these people were always amiable and he came to count on them for technical guidance, as he learned the role of Divisional Purchasing Manager. Don had several staff assistants who knew the business of buying and were loyal employees. He had done a good job of handling the resentment of those passed over by his promotion to manager, and he had developed a good deal of trust with the buying staff. At least he thought he had—until Jane Thompson presented him with the first in a series of dilemmas. Jane Thompson, age 34, had been with Propmore for ten years. She had a B.A. in English Literature and two years experience as a material expediter before coming to Propmore. Initially hired as a purchasing assistant, Jane became a buyer after two years. She enjoyed her job and the people she worked with at Propmore. In four years of working with Don, Jane had come to admire and respect his approach to management. She appreciated his sensitive yet strong leadership and saw him as an honest person who could be trusted to look after the interests of his subordinates.

But the dilemma with which Jane now presented Don made him wonder whether he had the skill to be a manager in a major division.

---

* This case was developed by Dr. Peter Madsen and Dr. John Fleming for Arthur Andersen & Co., SC. Used by permission of Arthur Andersen & Co., SC.

FIGURE C-31 The Propmore Corporation (Partial Organization Chart)

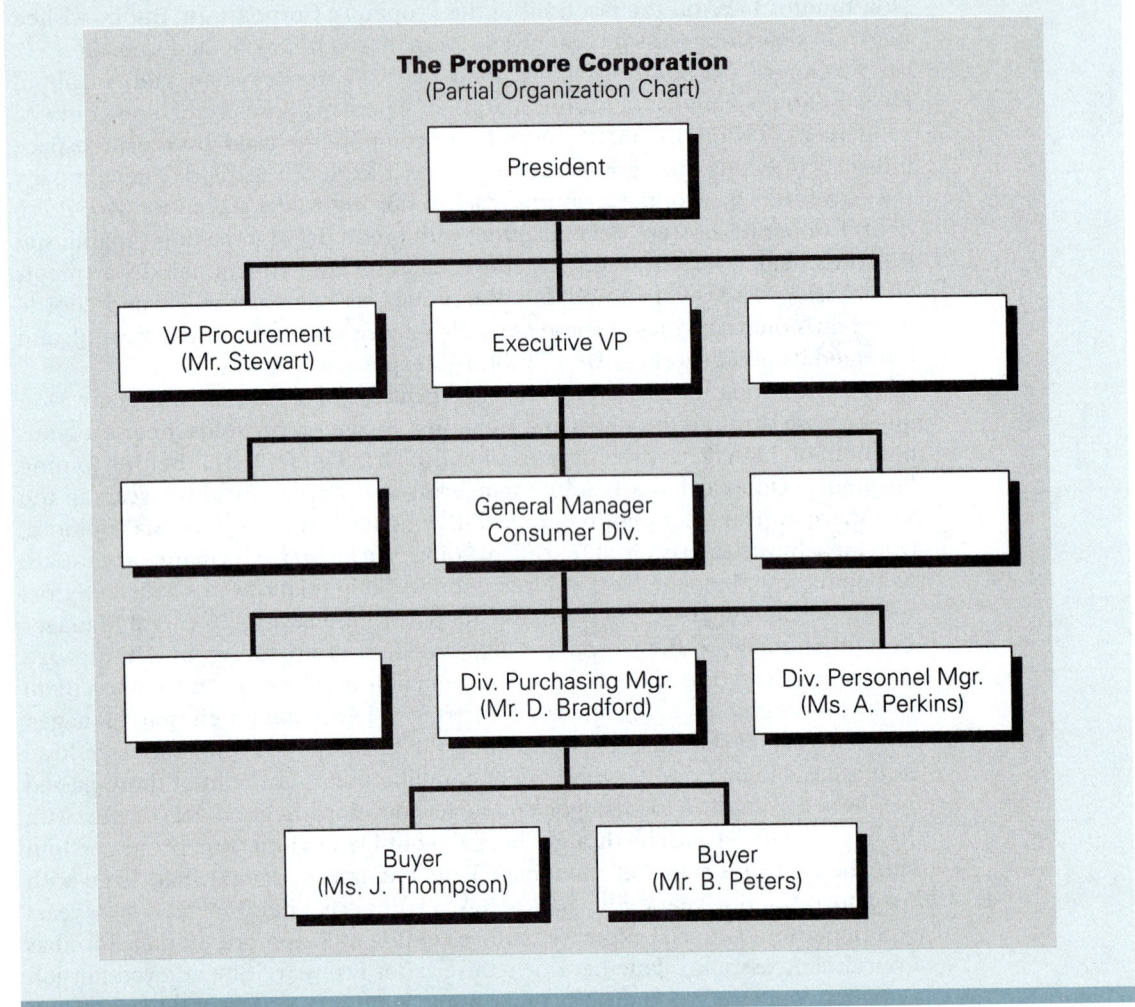

SITUATION I

A LUNCHEON HARASSMENT

After a two hour purchasing meeting in the morning, Bill Smith, an Airgoods Corporation Sales Representative, had invited Jane Thompson to lunch. They left at noon. An hour and a half later, Jane stormed into Don Bradford's office, obviously upset. When Don asked what was wrong, Jane told him in very strong terms that Bill Smith had sexually harassed her during and after the luncheon.

According to Jane, Bill made some sexual comments and suggestions toward the end of the meal. She considered this to be offensive and unwelcome. Jane, however, told Bill to take her back to the office. He attempted to make light of the situation and said he was only joking, but on the way back he made some further comments and several casual physical contacts to which she objected. When they arrived at the company, Bill was embarrassed and tried to apologize. But Jane entered the office before he could finish.

Jane demanded that the Airgoods Corporation be taken off the bidder list for the raw material contract and that Airgoods' President be informed of the unseemingly and illegal behavior of one of his salesmen. She would also consider taking legal action against Bill Smith through the Equal Employment Opportunity Commission for sexual harassment. Also, Jane stated she would investigate suing the Propmore Corporation for failure to protect her from this form of discrimination while she was performing her duties as an employee of the company. At the end of this outburst, Jane abruptly left Don's office.

Don was significantly troubled. Jane played a critical role in getting bids for the raw material contract. He needed her. Yet he knew that if he kept Airgoods on the bidder list, it might be difficult for her to view this vendor objectively.

Don was somewhat concerned about Jane's threat to sue Propmore but doubted that she had a very good case. Still, such an action would be costly in legal fees, management time, and damage to the company's image.

Don wasn't sure what to do about the bidder list. Airgoods had an excellent record as a reliable vendor for similar contracts. Propmore might be at a disadvantage if Airgoods was eliminated. On the other hand, Don firmly believed in standing behind his subordinates.

At this point, he needed more information on what constitutes sexual harassment and what policy guidelines his company had established. He examined two documents: the EEOC Definition of Sexual Harassment (Appendix 1) and the Propmore Corporation's Policy HR-13, on Sexual Harassment (Appendix 2).

QUESTIONS FOR DISCUSSION

1. What are the major issues in this case?
2. How should Don Bradford react to Jane Thompson's emotional allegation against Bill Smith?
3. What should Don do about Jane's threats to sue Propmore and her demand that the Airgoods Corp. be removed from the bidding list? What would be the ethical justification for those actions?
4. According to your interpretation of what constitutes sexual harassment as defined in Appendix 1, has it occurred in this case?
5. How should Don investigate this incident as required by company policy? What additional information does he need?

APPENDIX 1

EQUAL EMPLOYMENT OPPORTUNITY COMMISSION DEFINITION OF SEXUAL HARASSMENT

"Unwelcome sexual advances, requests for sexual favors and other verbal or physical contact of a sexual nature constitute sexual harassment when (1) submission to such conduct is made either explicitly or implicitly a term or condition of an individual's employment, (2) submission to or rejection of such conduct by an individual is used as the basis for employment decisions affecting such individual, or (3) such conduct has the purpose or effect of unreasonably interfering with an individual's work performance or creating an intimidating, hostile or offensive working environment."

"Applying general Title VII principles, an employer, employment agency, joint apprenticeship committee or labor organization (hereinafter collectively referred to as 'employer') is responsible for its acts and those of its agents and supervisory employees with respect to sexual harassment regardless of whether the employer knew or should have known of their occurrence."

—*EEOC guideline based on the Civil Rights Act of 1964, Title V~I*

APPENDIX 2

THE PROPMORE CORPORATION POLICY HR-13

Policy area: Sexual Harassment

Purpose: The purpose of Policy HR-13 is to inform employees of the company that The Propmore Corporation forbids practices of sexual harassment on the job and that disciplinary action may be taken against those who violate this policy.

Policy statement: In keeping with its long-standing tradition of abiding by pertinent laws and regulations, The Propmore Corporation forbids practices of sexual harassment on the job which violate Title VII of the Civil Rights Act of 1964. Sexual harassment on the job, regardless of its intent, is against the law. Employees who nevertheless engage in sexual harassment practices face possible disciplinary action which includes dismissal from the company.

Policy implementation: Those who wish to report violations of Policy HR-13 shall file a written grievance with their immediate supervisors within two weeks of the alleged violation. In conjunction with the Legal Department, the supervisor will investigate the alleged violation and issue his or her decision based upon the findings of this investigation within 30 days of receiving the written grievance.

SITUATION II

GATHERING MORE INFORMATION

Don Bradford had met Bill Smith, the Airgoods Corporation Salesman, on several occasions but did not feel he really knew him. To learn more about Bill, Don talked with his other key buyer, Bob Peters. Bob had dealt with Bill on many contracts in the past. After Don finished recounting the incident concerning Jane, Bob smiled. In his opinion, it was just a "boys will be boys" situation that got blown out of proportion. It may have been more than a joke, but Bob did not think Bill would do something "too far out." He pointed out that Bill had been selling for ten years and knew how to treat a customer.

Don's next step was a visit to the division personnel office. In addition to going through Jane's file, he wanted to discuss the matter with Ann Perkins, the division's Human Resource Manager. Fortunately, Ann was in her office and had time to see him immediately.

Don went over the whole situation with Ann. When he had finished his account, Ann was silent for a minute. Then she pointed out that this was a strange sexual harassment situation: it did not happen at the company, and the alleged harasser was not a member of the Propmore organization. The extent of the company's responsibility was not clear.

She had heard of cases where employees held their companies responsible for protecting them from sexual harassment by employees of other organizations. But the harassment had taken place on company premises, where some degree of direct supervision and protection could have been expected.

Ann filled out a slip authorizing Don to see Jane's personnel file. He took the file to an empty office and went through its contents. There were the expected hiring and annual evaluation forms, which revealed nothing unusual and only confirmed his own high opinion of Jane.

Then Don came to an informal note at the back of the file. It summarized a telephone reference check with the personnel manager of Jane's former employer. The note indicated that Jane had complained of being sexually harassed by her supervisor. The personnel manager had "checked it out" with the supervisor, who claimed "there was nothing to it." The note also indicated that Jane was terminated two months after this incident for "unsatisfactory work."

Don returned to his office and called his functional superior, Mr. Stewart, to inform him of the situation. Mr. Stewart was the Corporate Vice-President of Procurement. He had known Bill Smith personally for a number of years. He told Don that Bill's wife had abandoned him and their three children several years ago. Although Bill had a reputation for occasional odd behavior, he was known in the industry as a hard-working salesperson who provided excellent service and follow-through on his accounts.

QUESTIONS FOR DISCUSSION

1. Should Don have talked with Bob Peters about Jane's allegations? What is the ethical justification for doing so? For not doing so?
2. Is the Propmore Corporation responsible in this incident even though Bill Smith is not one of its employees? What moral responsibilities and obligations does the company have in relation to Jane?
3. What is the significance of the "informal note" that Don found in Jane's personnel file? Should he place credence in it? How should this information be used in appraising Jane's current allegation?
4. What significance should Don attach to the information he received from Mr. Stewart? Should he place credence in it? How should Don use this information in appraising Bill Smith?

SITUATION III

A TELEPHONE CALL

Don felt he needed more information to make a thorough investigation. He contemplated calling Bill Smith. In fairness to Bill, he should hear his version of what happened during the luncheon. But he knew he was not responsible for the actions of a non-employee. Furthermore, he wondered if talking to Bill would upset Jane even more if she found out. And would it be a proper part of an investigation mandated by company policy?

As Don considered his options, the phone rang. It was Bill Smith's boss, Joe Maxwell. He and Bill had talked about the luncheon, he said, and wanted to know if Jane had reported anything.

"Don, I don't know what you know about that meeting," said Joe, "but Bill has told me all the facts, and I thought we could put our heads together and nip this thing in the bud."

Don wasn't sure if this call was going to help or hinder him in his decision making. At first, he felt Joe was trying to unduly influence him. Also, he wasn't sure if the call was a violation of Jane's right to confidentiality. "Joe, I'm not sure we should be discussing this matter at all," said Don. "We might be jumping the gun. And what if Jane—"

"Wait, wait," Joe interrupted. "This thing can be put to rest if you just hear what really happened. We've been a good supplier for some time now. Give us the benefit of the doubt. We can talk 'off the record' if you want. But don't close the door on us."

"Okay," said Don, "let's talk off the record. I'll hear Bill's version, but I won't reach a conclusion over the phone. Our policy requires an investigation, and when that's complete, I'll let you know our position."

"Gee, Don," said Joe, "I don't think you even need an investigation. Bill says the only thing that went on at lunch was some innocent flirtation. Jane was giving him the old 'come on,' you know. She was more than friendly to him, smiling a lot and laughing at his jokes. Bill saw all the signals and just responded like a full-blooded male."

"You mean Jane was the cause of his harassing her?" Don asked.

"No, he didn't harass her," Joe said with urgency in his voice. "He only flirted with her because he thought she was flirting with him. It was all very innocent. These things happen every day. He didn't mean any harm. Just the opposite. He thought there was a chance for a nice relationship. He likes her very much and thought the feeling was mutual. No need to make a federal case out of it. These things happen—that's all. Remember when you asked out one of my saleswomen, Don? She said 'no,' but she didn't suggest sexual harassment. Isn't this the same thing?"

"I don't know. Jane was really upset when she came to me. She didn't see it as just flirting that went on," said Don.

"Come on, Don," insisted Joe. "Give her some time to calm down. You know how women can be sometimes. Maybe she has PMS. Why don't you let things just settle down before you do anything rash and start that unnecessary investigation? I bet in a couple days, you can talk to Jane and convince her it was just a misunderstanding. I'll put someone else on this contract, and we'll forget the whole thing ever happened. We've got to think about business first, right?"

Joe Maxwell's phone call put things in a new light for Don. If it was only innocent flirtation, why should good relations between Propmore and Airgoods be damaged? Yet he knew he had an obligation to Jane. He just wasn't sure how far that obligation went.

QUESTIONS FOR DISCUSSION

1. What are Bill Smith's moral rights in this case?
2. In his investigation of the incident, how should Don Bradford regard Bill Smith's rights?
3. Should Don have talked with Joe Maxwell about the case? Why or why not?
4. What is the difference between "flirtation" and "sexual harassment"?
5. How should Don evaluate what Joe told him? What role should this information play in his investigation? What effect does Joe's reminder of the time Don asked out one of Joe's saleswomen have on Don's course of action?
6. What should Don recommend after his investigation is complete? What is your ethical justification for this recommendation? Can all parties be treated fairly?

CASE 32: THE "SWEDISH BIKINI TEAM" AND SEXUAL HARASSMENT

In 1990, the Stroh Brewery Company spent $19.1 million on advertising. One of the many television commercials produced by the firm was an ad for Old Milwaukee beer, which is made by Stroh's. The commercial became known as the "It does get better" ad.

The television commercial picks up on many years of Old Milwaukee ads wherein a group of men are out on a camping or fishing trip and end their day around a campfire drinking cold Old Milwaukee beer. At one point near the end of the commercial, one of the men proclaims "It just doesn't get any better than this!" In the new TV ad, which first appeared in 1991, the commercial is modified to include a scantily clad bevy of attractive gyrating women, the "Swedish Bikini Team," who parachute into the men's campsite. The revised punchline: "It *does* get better."[1]

The "Stroh Five"

Five women employees of the Stroh Brewery created a national controversy after they filed lawsuits against the firm. The women claim that the company's television ads featuring the Swedish Bikini Team have contributed toward their sexual harassment in the workplace in St. Paul, Minnesota. One of the lawsuits asserts, "The conduct of Stroh's is so extreme and outrageous that it passes the bounds of decency and is utterly intolerable in the civilized community."[2] The five women claim that the ads foster a hostile work environment that encourages sexual harassment. The attorney for the women, Lori Peterson, says, "These ads tell Stroh's male employees that women are stupid, panting playthings."[3]

The "Stroh Five" are seeking a ban on the advertisement and money damages for the harm they claim has been done to them. They say they also have to put up with abusive language and sexually explicit language in the brewery.[4] These work conditions have resulted in severe mental and physical stress. Some of the lawsuits claim Stroh has produced "sexist, degrading promotion posters and advertisements."[5]

The lawsuits are based on the 1986 U.S. Supreme Court ruling (*Meritor Savings Bank* v. *Vinson*) that workplace conduct ranging from grabbing and touching to subtle hints and suggestions can contribute to a hostile work environment and are, therefore, a violation of federal antidiscrimination law.[6]

Lawyers for the American Civil Liberties Union (ACLU) and other free-speech advocates claim that the women are trying to ban a television commercial that no court has found obscene, indecent, or illegal in its purposes or harmful to the audience. The ACLU president, Nadine Strossen, claims "On grounds of feminism, on grounds of free speech, censorship is not the way to go." Lori Peterson, attorney for the plaintiffs, counters that "all kinds of speech are limited." Examples include obscenity, fighting words, and direct threats of violence, when the dangers of speech outweigh the benefits. She charges that the Stroh ad "produces, encourages and condones the [hostile] workshop environment."[7]

The Corporate Response

George Kuehn, senior vice-president for the Detroit-based Stroh's Brewery, said he couldn't comment on the lawsuits. He added, however, "I can say Stroh for upward of 10 years has maintained and enforced a definite policy against discrimination, including sexual harassment." He also said that company officials were not aware of any previous lawsuits that "link advertising to a hostile environment."[8]

DeWitt Helm, president of the Association of National Advertisers in New York, said that he thinks these were the first lawsuits of this type: "To associate sexual harassment with the advertising of an employer's product, I think, is a little far-fetched and bizarre. I just don't see a cause and effect in this whole scenario."[9]

Ms. Peterson and others who support the Stroh's suit argue that the suit is reasonable because the commercial is part of a pattern of behavior under which management also allows abusive language and sexually explicit photos in the workplace. Therefore, they argue, the link is direct enough and the harm is great enough to overcome First Amendment concerns.[10]

Weeks after the lawsuits of the Stroh Five captured the nation's attention with national television coverage, members of the "Swedish Bikini Team" got in on the act and claimed they thought what they were doing was harmless. At about the same time, it was announced in *Time* magazine that *Playboy* planned to feature the Bikini Team in its next issue.[11]

QUESTIONS FOR DISCUSSION

1. Who are the stakeholders in this case and what are their stakes? What are the major and minor issues?

2. Based on what you have read in the case and the text material on sexual harassment, does it seem likely that the company might be found guilty?

3. Do you see a linkage between the kind of television commercial described and the possible perception that a "hostile work environment" might be substantiated?

4. How does a "reasonable man" see this case? How does a "reasonable woman" see this case?

5. Where and how do you draw the line between ads that are "sexy" and those that are "sexist" and contributory toward gender resentment?

6. Conduct library research to follow up on this case. What additional information came to light? How were the lawsuits resolved?

CASE ENDNOTES

1. "Workers File Lawsuits Linking Ads, Harassment," *The Atlanta Journal* (November 15, 1991).
2. *Ibid.*
3. "Battling the Bimbo Factor," *Time* (November 25, 1991), 70.
4. Arthur S. Hayes, "Stroh's Case Pits Feminists Against ACLU," *The Wall Street Journal* (November 14, 1991), B6.
5. *Atlanta Journal* (November 15, 1991).
6. Hayes, B6.
7. *Ibid.*
8. *Atlanta Journal* (November 15, 1991).
9. *Ibid.*
10. Hayes, B6.
11. *Time* (November 25, 1991).

CASE 33 RETHINKING CORPORATE GOVERNANCE

Item: In New York, Saloman, Inc. is regrouping under new management after it was revealed that employees had engaged in illegal bidding in Treasury security auctions. The board of directors at Saloman was kept in the dark long after the former chairman and CEO John H. Gutfreund learned of these illegalities. In fact, the board members learned of these transgressions only shortly before the public.[1]

Item: In Houston, the board of directors of Compaq Computer Corp. ousted its chief executive, Rod Canion, for failing to pull the personal-computer manufacturer out of a sales-and-profit tailspin. The company was able to take speedy action because it had a separate board chairman.[2]

In managing corporations, should the chairman of the board and the CEO of the firm be one and the same person? In most U.S. corporations, they function more like the incident at Saloman than the one at Compaq Computers. A look at *Business Week*'s roster of the 1,000 most valued corporations in America shows that at 80 percent of these firms one person occupies both positions and "rules the roost" at these firms. These combined chairmen/CEOs control the board of directors' meetings where, theoretically at least, these directors are monitoring and appraising the CEO's performance on behalf of shareholders. As someone once said, it's much like the fox guarding the henhouse.

John Nash, president of the National Association of Corporate Directors, commented on the attitude of chairmen/CEOs: "Their attitude is, 'It's my company and it's my board.' They just don't get it that it's not."[3] Harold Williams, former chairman of the Securities and Exchange Commission, says, "The CEO should not be Chairman of the Board." One major problem is that in this dual role, the chairman/CEO controls the agenda and pace of the meeting and this represents powerful control.[4]

Jay W. Lorsch, a professor at the Harvard Business School, argues for a split between the two roles. He calls such a split "the single most significant thing to do." Such a change, he posits, would enhance the director's independence, help prevent corporate crises, and emphasize that the CEO serves at the pleasure of the board, not vice versa.[5]

Getting CEOs to give up their dual roles would not come easily. It's like asking members of Congress to limit the PAC money they receive or to vote term limits for themselves. There is a lot of self-interest involved. Judith Dobrzynski, a commentator on this topic, thinks it would be especially difficult to get CEOs to give up the dual role because there is no research suggesting that companies would work better with nonexecutive chairmen.[6]

Separating the two roles makes sense. Having one person occupy both roles creates a significant conflict of interest. The board is supposed to hire and fire and determine the salary for the CEO, but the CEO is the chairman of the board that is making these decisions. It is little wonder that executive compensation is so high and that board members are so well paid and have such nice perks. There is a lot of mutual reciprocity going on.

The role of nonexecutive chairman would be different from the combined chairman/CEO. The nonexecutive chairman would manage board business, consult with the CEO to set meeting agendas, ensure that board members get the information they need to make their decisions, and regularly conduct an objective assessment of the CEO's performance.[7]

A comparison of the experience at Compaq Computer with that of Saloman, described above, does raise the question of whether a major change is needed in the typical corporation today. The fact that 80 percent of major firms use the combined chairman/CEO position does not, in itself, indicate that it is the desired or best approach for corporate governance in the 1990s. As Dobrzynski puts it, Is chairman and CEO "one hat too many"?

QUESTIONS FOR DISCUSSION

1. What are the arguments supporting the concept of a combined chairman/CEO? What are the problems with such an approach?
2. What are the arguments supporting the concept of separating the chairman's position from the CEO's position? What are the problems with such an approach?
3. Why do you think 80 percent of the major corporations use the combined chairman/CEO position in spite of its many weaknesses?
4. Based on all the arguments presented, which do you think is best for corporate governance in the 1990s? What factors make your choice especially appropriate?

CASE ENDNOTES

1. Judith H. Dobrzynski, "Chairman and CEO: One Hat Too Many," *Business Week* (November 18, 1991), 124.
2. *Ibid.*
3. *Ibid.*
4. *Ibid.*
5. Jay W. Lorsch, *Pawns or Potentates: The Reality of America's Corporate Boards* (Boston: Harvard Business School Press), 1989.
6. Dobrzynski, 124.
7. *Ibid.*

CASE 34

MAYDAY FOR MARINE LIFE:
THE WRECK OF THE EXXON *VALDEZ*

"Yeah, Valdez traffic, Exxon *Valdez*, over. Yeah, should be on your radar there. We've fetched up hard aground north of Goose Island off Bligh Reef. And, uh, evidently we're leaking some oil, and, we're gonna be here for awhile."[1]

This distress call began the record of one of the most infamous environmental events in the United States in the 1980s—the wrecking of the oil supertanker Exxon *Valdez* off the southern coast of Alaska on March 24, 1989. Running aground on Bligh Reef in Prince William Sound, the ship spilled more than 240,000 barrels, 11 million gallons, of crude oil into waters that, up to that point, were considered by many to be part of an unspoiled wilderness. The events leading up to the spill, the spill's effects, and the industry and government response to the spill raised many questions about business's and society's environmental responsibility for conserving and protecting the nation's natural resources for current and future generations of Americans.

Before the Spill: An Accident Waiting to Happen?

In 1970, the Exxon Corporation joined six other major oil companies to form a consortium called the Alyeska Pipeline Service Company, to build, manage, and use the Trans-Alaska Pipeline (TAP), an 800-mile-long, $8 billion oil pipeline designed to transport crude oil from Alaska's North Slope to the southern Alaskan port of Valdez. Alyeska effected many changes to the pipeline design to address various environmental objections and made a number of commitments to the U.S. and Alaskan governments that, in the unlikely event of a major oil spill, Alyeska would mount an effective response to prevent large-scale environmental damage. This response was to include the provision of effective chemicals to disperse the oil; trained, on-site emergency spill response teams; and adequate spill recovery supplies and equipment. In addition, commitments were made to use only double-hulled ships, to prevent as much oil as possible from spilling in the surrounding waters.[2]

Although oil prices were rising in the 1970s when the pipeline was planned, in the 1980s oil prices began falling, becoming a serious concern for the oil industry. Alyeska looked for ways to reduce costs to keep profit margins up and decided to cut significantly or drop completely the programs in its TAP spill response commitments.[3]

The State of Alaska and the U.S. Government had their own oil spill response problems. Although the state received 25 percent of the revenue from each barrel of North Slope oil, it decided to spend these receipts on non-oil-related programs. In addition, the state never required Alyeska to include a worse-case scenario such as a spill of the magnitude of the Exxon *Valdez* in its environmental impact statements as part of the TAP decision.

---

* This case was written by Mark Starik of George Washington University.

As for the federal government's spill response capability, the U.S. Coast Guard and other federal agencies potentially involved in oil spill crisis management were negatively affected by the budget cuts during the Reagan administration. Budgetary considerations were preeminent in the Coast Guard's decision against improvements in the radar systems in Prince William Sound and in its reduction in staff from 37 to 24 during the 1980s. Budget cuts also shut down the national oil spill research center and reduced the federal government's oil spill contingency fund to less than $5 million. Finally, although the federal government was aware that building supertankers with double bottoms or complete double hulls could reduce spills up to 60 percent, it did not require them because the increased costs associated with these safety improvements were seen to put the U.S. shipbuilding industry at a potential competitive global disadvantage.[4]

All of these reductions in institutional capacities to prevent or respond to a large oil spill off Alaska's coast were said to be the result of complacency or, retrospectively, unwarranted complacency. Over 8,800 tanker trips had occurred in the sound since 1977 without a collision or grounding, ensuring the smooth transfer of 2 million barrels per day from Valdez to ports down the West Coast.[5] However, at least 6,000 oil spills from all causes occurred on an average annual basis in U.S. waters each year,[6] nearly a thousand on Alaska's North Slope in some years, 43 along Alaska's southern coast, and 2 in Valdez itself the January prior to the Exxon *Valdez* spill.[7]

The channel negotiated by each tanker, Prince William Sound, was known for narrow passages and submerged reefs and regularly experienced storms and drifting ice from a receding glacier.[8] Outside the Alaskan region, ships making the Valdez run totaled only 13 percent of U.S. tanker traffic but accounted for more than half of the accidents.[9] Although it was only single-hulled, the Exxon *Valdez* was Exxon's most modern supertanker, and Exxon continuously upgraded its ships with advanced automation. However, reports from the shrinking crews of boredom, stress, and excessive hours were apparently never given serious attention.[10] Nevertheless, prior to the Valdez spill, Exxon was thought to have one of the best safety and pollution control records in the industry.[11]

The Spill: Waves of Death

On the evening of March 23, 1989, after loading a full 50 million gallons of crude oil from the Valdez pipeline terminal, Captain Joseph Hazelwood, the captain of the Exxon *Valdez*, and his small, tired crew set out through Prince William Sound. To steer clear of ice in the outbound traffic lane, the ship veered toward Bligh Reef, 25 miles out of Valdez. Hazelwood, who had consumed alcohol just before embarking, illegally and contrary to Exxon regulations left the bridge to his third mate and returned to his quarters. For reasons that are still unclear, the Exxon *Valdez* never veered back to avoid Bligh Reef, and at full or sea speed the tanker ran into the reef's rocky surface, rupturing 8 of the ship's 13 cargo compartments.[12]

Twenty-two minutes later, Captain Hazelwood made his now infamous call for help, the first time the Coast Guard was alerted to any problem with the ship or its journey. While oil gushed through dozens of gaping holes for several hours, an Alyeska observation tug was launched to remove the crew from danger, and other vessels began pumping oil still in the grounded ship hull into another tanker. However, because of communication and preparedness problems, including confusion between Alyeska and Exxon on which one was responsible for an initial oil spill response, the first vessel with containment equipment, one of Exxon's, did not reach the wrecked tanker until 14 hours after the crash.[13] This vessel and others that came later in the days following the spill did not carry enough dispersants, skimmers, booms, or personnel to handle a spill the size of the Exxon Valdez.[14] These delays and shortages were critical, since, during the first few hours of the spill, water and weather conditions were only briefly amenable to oil spill recovery.

In all, Alyeska, Exxon, and Exxon's spill recovery contractor, VECO, Inc., recovered only 3 percent to 13 percent of the spilled oil, far below the 100,000 barrels Alyeska claimed to be able to recover in its contingency plan. The rest of the 11 million gallons either remained in the sound's ecosystem or evaporated and dispersed to others.[15] The immediate damage to the ecosystems on the southern Alaska coast were obvious and significant, but the exact dimensions of the devastation were difficult to assess at the time. Carcasses of tens of thousands of oil-soaked sea otters, sea birds, and other animals that migrated through or used the sound during the spill were found by volunteer rescue teams. Hundreds more animals were cleaned and saved, in part, through the financial assistance of Exxon. Within a week of the spill, the fishing industry was hurt badly by drastic reductions in shell fish, herring, and salmon catches. The secondary (eggs and progeny) effects and long-term (cumulative) effects were also considered significant but undetermined during the spill. One projection made was that roughly 25 percent of the phytoplankton in that part of the sound, at the base of the area's food chain, had been killed.[16] The reactions of one rescuer perhaps best characterized the sense of horror and futility of those involved in this rescue effort experience:

> We cried a lot. All of us did, at least once, maybe twice a day. You'd just have to stop and sit down. People would come up and say, "We can't catch any more birds," and they'd break out sobbing. It's just beyond imagination. Oil everywhere. Dead otters. Dead deer. Dead birds.

After the Spill: A Wake Without a Celebration

Exxon and its subcontractor, VECO, continued to attempt to treat the surface waters and more than 1,000 miles of shoreline of Prince William Sound until mid-September 1989. As many as 11,000 workers were involved in the effort, substantially financed by Exxon, which estimated the total price tag at over $2 billion. However, in addition to its apparent lack of preparedness in preventing the spill and in responding to it effectively, Exxon was criticized for three other major problems. First, the treatment of the beaches involved the use of questionable techniques and materials. Highly pressurized hot water and toxic solvents were used to scour not only the oil but also most living things from the shoreline rocks. These practices and other environmental damage done by the cleanup crews, many of whom were virtually untrained, appeared to indicate a lack of sensitivity for the ultimate purpose of the treatment activity.

Second, Exxon was noncommittal in its plan for returning to the sound in the spring of 1990, though the state and federal governments and many environmental groups believed that further treatment was necessary. The Coast Guard ordered Exxon to resume its treatment that spring, and Exxon complied.

Finally, Exxon was criticized for its less-than-effective public affairs efforts. For example, Exxon's CEO didn't arrive in Valdez until 3 weeks after the spill, and, shortly thereafter, was in Washington, DC, reportedly lobbying against legislation to require double-hulled tankers.[17]

To its credit, Exxon did establish a claims resolution process and made initial payments to fisherman and others who were directly affected by the spill. However, as of mid-1991, 150 civil cases, involving more than $50 billion in damage claims, and several criminal cases were pending related to the spill, including the federal government's five criminal charges against Exxon (two felonies and three misdemeanors under five different environmental laws), but the question of overall responsibility was still to be determined.[18] The State of Alaska brought suit against Exxon for understaffing its supertanker and against Alyeska for overstating its ability to handle a large oil spill. In early 1991, negotiators for the state and federal governments reached a $1 billion out-of-court settlement with Exxon, which included four guilty pleas, but the Alaska House rejected the deal, causing the state and Exxon to withdraw from the settlement.

In part because of charges against income resulting from the spill, Exxon's profits fell from $5.3 billion in 1988 to $3.5 billion in 1989. Exxon's reputation also suffered, falling from 6th to 110th place on *Fortune*'s list of the most admired U.S. companies.[19]

Conclusion or Harbinger?

A number of measures were taken by the principals in the Exxon *Valdez* case to address the possible reoccurrence of such a massive oil spill, both in Alaska and elsewhere. These involved legislation and voluntary programs that included increases in the numbers of available barges and booms, tanker crew alcohol tests, tug accompaniment procedures, and upgrades to the Coast Guard tracking equipment.[20] In 1990, Congress established the Oil Pollution Act, which provided $1 billion for spill cleanup funded from a five-cent-per-barrel fee on oil revenues. It also required all new supertankers to have double hulls and for all currently operating tankers to be retrofitted with double hulls.[21]

However, problems in the U.S. oil transportation system remained. A mid-1991 General Accounting Office (GAO) report found significant operational problems with the TAP, including an ineffective leak detection system and faulty coolant devices designed to prevent the pipeline from buckling.[22] More than 6,000 oil spills took place within the next year after the Valdez spill.[23] And, on January 1, 1990, an Exxon pipeline between New York and New Jersey broke, dumping more than a half million gallons of oil into New York harbor and the surrounding wetlands.[24]

Joseph Hazelwood, who had a history of excessive drinking, was fired by Exxon for violating Coast Guard blood alcohol levels and turned himself in to New York authorities. The State of Alaska pressed criminal charges against him for criminal mischief, reckless endangerment, negligent discharge of oil, and operation of a vessel while intoxicated. A jury found him guilty of negligent discharge of oil, but he was acquitted of the other, more serious, charges. He was fined and in lieu of a suspended jail sentence, he was required to do 1,000 hours of environment-related community service.[25]

Exxon did make a few gestures toward environmental responsibility by adding an environmentalist to its board and by establishing an in-house watchdog position of vice-president for Environment and Safety. However, at a stockholders' meeting after the spill, Exxon refused to commit to develop less-damaging sources of energy and technologies that conserved energy.[26] Exxon did return to the Prince William Sound cleanup for a third and final year in the spring of 1991. This was necessitated by the continuing presence of oil, which was still seen seeping back into the sound from the shore. One government report said that the oil would remain for a decade or more.[27]

Another report released in April 1991, which summarized 58 government science studies in the sound, found that 2 years after the wreck, the spilled oil was a continuing threat to wildlife and that it killed many more animals than were first reported. Five times more otters and several times more seabirds and bald eagles actually died as a result of the spill than the number of carcasses collected in 1989.[28]

In response to the Persian Gulf crisis that flared up in mid-1990, a debate was renewed in the United States about the nation's long-term energy supply and demand. The Bush administration and some members of Congress developed a number of initiatives including measures to open up the Alaska National Wildlife Reserve (ANWR) for oil exploration and drilling (with the chances of a large find projected at 1 in 5), while other groups focused on the need to dramatically increase automobile efficiency standards. One projection indicated that a $1\frac{1}{2}$ mile per gallon efficiency improvement in U.S. cars would save as much oil as was optimistically projected to be under ANWR. The Exxon *Valdez* was repaired at a cost of $30 million, its name was changed to the Exxon *Mediterranean*, and, ironically, it was reassigned to the Persian Gulf in July 1990.[29]

Several days prior to the opening of the federal trial against Exxon in October 1991, the company and the U.S. government plea-bargained a $1.03 billion settlement, in which Exxon and its shipping company pleaded guilty to four environmental law misdemeanors and agreed to pay a criminal fine of $150 million, one-third of which was dedicated to future efforts to restore Prince William Sound.[30] This settlement did not affect the hundreds of lawsuits Exxon still faced from private litigants, such as fisherman and native groups, nor did it affect Exxon's suit filed later that month against the Sperry Marine company for the alleged malfunction of the steering system used on the Exxon *Valdez*.[31]

The main actors in the Exxon *Valdez* case each had different perspectives on the past, present, and future of the events surrounding the Exxon *Valdez* catastrophe. In their own words, these statements were capsulizations of their perspectives:

> ... our memories are short. Everyone's hurting over the spilled oil now. But in a year, five years? We forget. It's the limit of our memory that frightens me. If we don't remember what happened in Prince William Sound, it will happen again. *Volunteer rescue worker*
>
> Exxon and Alyeska simply didn't have enough equipment, dispersant, and trained men on hand to handle the spill. They didn't have enough booms. They didn't have enough skimmers and collection barges. They didn't produce the results they had promised. *Alaska Department of Environmental Conservation spokesman*
>
> Those beaches in Alaska are never going to be clean. This oil is tenacious stuff. We're never going to get it all off the rocks. And, we're not going to call these beaches pristine again in this lifetime. *U.S. Coast Guard spokesman*
>
> The industry has neither the equipment nor the response personnel in place and ready to deal with catastrophic tanker spills.... the industry is not prepared anywhere along the coastal U.S. to deal with a spill of this size. *American Petroleum Institute report, June, 1990*[32]
>
> We believe that Exxon has moved swiftly and competently to minimize the effect this oil will have on the environment, fish and other wildlife. We cannot, of course, undo what has been done. But I can assure you that since March 24, the accident has been receiving our full attention and will continue to do so. *CEO, Exxon Corp.*[33]

QUESTIONS FOR DISCUSSION

1. Who are the stakeholders in this case, what are their stakes, and who is responsible for what in the *Valdez* accident and its aftermath? How were the stakeholders managed?
2. How would you state the major and minor issues in this case?
3. Where would Exxon's situation fit in the three-dimensional corporate social response model (Chapter 2)? Did this position remain constant from 1989 to 1991? Discuss.
4. What is your assessment of Exxon's immediate and later responses to the oil spill? Did the firm meet its social responsibilities as you understand them? Was the firm environmentally responsible?
5. What are the major lessons to be learned from the Exxon *Valdez* oil spill? For students of management? For students of business ethics? For students of public administration and government?

6. What advice regarding crisis management (Chapter 19) would you give to all parties (stakeholders) involved in the spill and its aftermath?

CASE ENDNOTES

1. D. Delanni & M. Davis. "*Nova: The Big Spill*" (March 24, 1990).
2. J. Keeble, *Out of the Channel* (New York: Harper Collins, 1991), 17–23.
3. *Ibid.*
4. A. Davidson, *In the Wake of the Exxon* Valdez (San Francisco: Sierra Club, 1990), xiv, 12, 93–96.
5. M. Tobias, "Black Tide," The Discovery Channel (March 23, 1990).
6. Delanni and Davis.
7. Tobias.
8. Davidson, xii.
9. Davidson, 7.
10. M. Myrondorf, "*Frontline: Anatomy of an Oil Spill*" (March 20, 1990).
11. A. K. Delehunt, "Exxon Corporation: Trouble at Valdez" (Harvard Business School, 1989), Case 9-390-024.
12. Keeble, 30–49.
13. Delehunt, 3.
14. Delanni and Davis.
15. Davidson, 20, 80, 297.
16. Tobias.
17. Davidson, 24, 188–189, 204–205.
18. Myrondorf.
19. P. Nulty, "Exxon's Problem: Not What You Think," *Fortune* (April 23, 1990), 202–204.
20. Myrondorf.
21. Keeble, 265.
22. A. Sullivan, "GAO Criticizes Government's Role in Alaska Pipeline," *The Wall Street Journal* (August 5, 1991), C13.
23. Delanni and Davis.
24. Davidson, 313.
25. Keeble, 46.
26. Davidson, 309.
27. Advanced Technology, Inc. An evaluation of cleanup technologies potentially applicable to Exxon *Valdez* oil spill cleanup operations in 1990. Prepared for the Hazardous Waste Response Branch, National Oceanic and Atmospheric Administration (July, 1990).
28. M. Weisskopf, "Larger Environmental Toll Revealed in U.S. Report," *Washington Post* (April 10, 1991).
29. Keeble, 260.
30. C. McCoy, "Exxon Corp.'s Settlement Gets Court Approval," *The Wall Street Journal.* (October 9, 1991), A3.
31. A. Sullivan, "Exxon, in Suit, Ties Sperry Marine to Valdez Spill," *The Wall Street Journal* (October 31, 1991), A8.
32. Davidson, 119, 165, 216–217, 297–298.
33. Delehunt, 23.

CASE 35

THE CHRYSLER ODOMETER EPISODE AND CRISIS MANAGEMENT

In June 1987, two Chrysler Corporation executives were charged with conspiracy to commit odometer fraud. They pleaded innocent. At about the same time, two class-action suits were filed against the No. 3 automaker. The suits were the aftermath of a Justice Department investigation that resulted in a 16-count indictment against the company. It was charged that a Chrysler unit had sold as "new" more than 60,000 cars and trucks that company employees had allegedly driven, sometimes as much as 400 miles, with the odometers disconnected.[1] An odometer is the gauge that records how many miles a vehicle has been driven.

According to the *Federal Odometer Act of 1974*, it is against the law to roll back, disconnect, or tamper with an odometer with the intent to defraud. The law provides a minimum penalty of $1,500 plus costs and legal fees against those who break it. A Washington lawyer stated that a "customer can recover the minimum penalty without proving any actual damages." According to a Chrysler attorney, the odometer act had so far been applied only to cases involving used-car dealers turning back odometers. Although the company did not believe it broke any laws, it was extremely concerned about the public's perception. One spokesman said, "If there's a perception that we are misleading the public, we have to address that."[2] The company faces about $120 million in total maximum fines.

Chrysler's initial position was that it had not done anything wrong. It claimed that the odometers were disconnected while the cars were being test-driven as part of a quality control program. Further, the company said the disengagement of the odometers was for the purpose of not reducing the warranty protection (which is partially based on miles driven) of customers.[3]

There was considerable public outrage by customers on learning of the alleged Chrysler actions. In addition, a number of Chrysler dealers were very worried about consumer reactions. Everyone agreed that it was a public relations nightmare. Some dealers were disappointed to learn of the alleged occurrences and even held meetings with their salespeople to plot their own crisis strategy.[4] The story developed to such a level that *The Wall Street Journal* published an article in which it summarized the recommendations of a number of public relations specialists as to what Chrysler ought to do.[5]

Iacocca's Response

Within a week after the news broke about the indictments against Chrysler, chairman of the board, Lee Iacocca, held a news conference in which he acknowledged that the company had made "mistakes" in judgment and said that the fact that customers were not informed was "just dumb." He added that the company decision to sell as new some cars that had been damaged during testing and later repaired, "went beyond dumb and reached all the way out to stupid. . . . the only law we broke was the law of common sense."[6] He added, "Did we screw up? You bet we did. I'm damned sorry it happened and it won't happen again." Iacocca still maintained that no laws were broken.

Iacocca also announced a sweeping program that was promoted by way of full-page ads in the major news magazines and newspapers. One headline ad read as follows: "Testing cars is a good idea. Disconnecting odometers is a bad idea. That's a mistake we won't make again at Chrysler. Period."[7] In another full-page ad, Iacocca attempted to set the record straight on the corporate practice and to lay out what the company was doing to make things right. The proposed remedy had four parts: (1) The company agreed to replace with a new 1987 model any vehicle that their records indicated was damaged in the test program, repaired, and then sold as new; (2) the company would send a letter to all owners of vehicles that were in the test program, offering a free inspection and to correct any product deficiencies; (3) the company agreed to extend its present 5-year/50,000 mile protection plan on engine and powertrain to 7 years/70,000 miles; and (4) the company agreed to extend to 7 years/70,000 miles the warranty on all major systems—brakes, suspension, air conditioning, electrical, and steering.[8]

Iacocca closed out the ad by saying how proud he is of Chrysler's products but that he is "not proud of this episode." He then repeated President Harry Truman's famous slogan, "The buck stops here." "It just stopped. Period," Iacocca concluded.

QUESTIONS FOR DISCUSSION

1. What is your appraisal of the Chrysler odometer-disconnecting practice? Was it unfair? Misleading? Unethical? Or just a bad business decision?

2. This case posed a legitimate "crisis" for Chrysler. Identify the crisis stages. Discuss the advantages and disadvantages of how Chrysler and Iacocca handled it. On a 10-point scale where 10 is the best, give Iacocca a grade for crisis management. Defend your grade.

3. What should Iacocca have done, if anything, that he did not? What, if anything, did he do that he should not have done?

CASE ENDNOTES

1. John Bussey, "Chrysler Executives Both Plead Innocent in Odometer Case; 2 Related Suits Filed," *The Wall Street Journal* (June 29, 1987), 5.
2. Melinda Grenier Guiles and Amal Kumar Naj, "Baffled Dealers Seek Ways to Placate Worried Buyers," *The Wall Street Journal* (June 26, 1987), 21.
3. "Dear Chrysler: Outsiders' Advice on Handling the Odometer Charge, " *The Wall Street Journal* (June 26, 1987), 21.
4. Guiles and Naj, 21.
5. "Dear Chrysler . . ."
6. John Bussey, "Lee Iacocca Calls Odometer Policy 'Dumb,'" *The Wall Street Journal* (July 2, 1987), 2.
7. Chrysler advertisement, 1987.
8. *Ibid.*

CASE 36 WHEN *PUSH* COMES TO SHOVE

Operation PUSH (People United to Save Humanity) was founded by the Reverend Jesse Jackson in 1971. It was an outgrowth of Operation Breadbasket, a project Jackson had started while active in the Southern Christian Leadership Conference.[1] The 1988 *Encyclopedia of Associations* describes Operation PUSH as a national and international human rights organization and movement directed toward educational and economic parity for all, particularly black, Hispanic, and poor people. The organization seeks to create an ethical atmosphere and encourages self and community motivation and social responsibility.[2] From the beginning, Operation PUSH used pressure techniques to get white businesses to show greater social responsibility toward the black community. If business people hired too few blacks or sold shoddy products at high prices, Operation PUSH spread the word through the black community not to patronize their businesses.

In the early 1980s, Jesse Jackson began rising to prominence as a civil rights leader. Next to the Reverend Martin Luther King, he clearly became the most visible spokesman for the black community. Also early in the 1980s, Jackson began an upgraded effort to lever concessions for blacks out of major corporations such as Coca-Cola and Heublein's Kentucky Fried Chicken.

PUSH began putting pressure on Coca-Cola and Kentucky Fried Chicken in the early 1980s. One reason these firms were chosen was their high visibility and the fact that large numbers of blacks consume their products. Blacks spent at least $300 million on Coca-Cola's soft drinks in 1980, and they accounted for about 15 percent of sales at Kentucky Fried Chicken (KFC). In spite of this, there was only one black wholesaler among 4,000 who distributed Coke syrup. There were only seven black KFC franchises owned by blacks among a total of 800. For these reasons PUSH began its plan to "renegotiate" black America's relations with corporate America with these two well-known firms.[3]

The boycott became PUSH's primary weapon in attempting to win concessions for blacks with major companies. Jackson called the boycotts a "withdrawal of enthusiasm." Boycotts were used quite often by civil-rights leaders in the 1960s to force political and social changes. Now they are being used to improve economic conditions. In a case involving an NAACP-sponsored boycott, the U.S. Supreme Court ruled that boycotts are protected under the First Amendment. This decision paved the way for boycotts to be employed for a variety of social purposes. Jackson noted that blacks had an estimated gross annual income of $145 billion and said, "We have something that corporations can't do without: big appetites and money."[4]

"Don't Choke on Coke"

Coca-Cola was approached as one of PUSH's first targets late in 1980. Mr. Keough, president and CEO, said that the company entered the talks eagerly and that it had already planned to carry out its own minority participation plan. Inside sources indicated, however, that Coca-Cola was ambivalent and wary. PUSH's demands included a program in which blacks would gain 40 syrup wholesale operations within 10 years and 5 bottling companies in 5 years; the selection of a black advertising firm to handle a Coca-Cola brand; a major hike in black-media advertising; and the endowment of professional chairs at black colleges.

Coca-Cola said it saw no immediate prospects in bottling franchises, since those had already been granted to cover all territories, and the last one was awarded at the turn of the century. The company did agree to select 20 black wholesalers immediately, however. In addition, Coca-Cola loaned $1.5 million to black entrepreneurs just entering the beverage industry. It also agreed to increase its advertising in black-audience publications and to increase its business with black-owned vendors and banks. Coca-Cola's program was valued at $30 million. During the talks with Coca-Cola, PUSH called for a month-long boycott of Coca-Cola products. Jackson coined the expression "Don't Choke on Coke" to be part of its boycott.

Keough later said that the boycott had no financial effect on the company. Furthermore, Keough wanted to make it clear that the company did not bow to pressure from PUSH. He said, "We don't respond to those kinds of (boycott) threats," and reiterated that the company had already decided to pursue the minority participation program before PUSH approached the company.[5]

PUSH was also quite successful with Kentucky Fried Chicken. KFC agreed to a program valued at $180 million that included a pledge to add 105 black franchisers by 1987 and to provide $10 million in financing for 24 of them.[6]

"Bud Is a Dud"

In 1982, Jesse Jackson and PUSH targeted Anheuser-Busch. Jackson accused the company of not hiring, promoting, or doing business with enough minorities. At one of his dramatic media events leading up to a planned boycott of a Tampa brewery, he popped the top off a Budweiser, turned it over, and let it spill on the ground as he proclaimed "Bud is a dud." The boycott of Anheuser-Busch beers began in October 1982, but neither side agreed on the real impact of the boycott. Jackson's attacks on Anheuser-Busch drew him into constant debates with Wayman F. Smith, III, a black vice-president of corporate affairs from the company. Whenever Mr. Jackson went to a brewery to urge a boycott, Mr. Smith came along too and set up his own press conference, offering statistics as to what the company was doing for minorities. Their confrontations became a traveling road show, with a predictable script.[7]

When Anheuser-Busch increased its number of black beer distributors from 1 to 3, Jackson and Smith found themselves at odds with one another once again: Jackson wanted to claim credit for the increase, but Smith argued that it had been planned months before the boycott.[8]

The TV Networks

In 1986, PUSH took on as its target the television networks. In particular, PUSH singled out CBS-owned WBBM-TV in Chicago, PUSH's home town. The incident that sparked the PUSH boycott was WBBM's demotion of Harry Porterfield, a black newsman who co-anchored the 6:00 p.m. evening news. Porterfield was transferred to the less prestigious weekend anchor role to make room for Bill Kurtis, a former WBBM anchor who had served a stint on the CBS Morning News. In spite of the fact that Porterfield left and went to a higher-paying position, PUSH began picketing WBBM's offices and asking blacks to discontinue watching that station.

PUSH's demands of the station were as follows: (1) hire two male black or Hispanic anchors, (2) establish a 40 percent employment quota for minorities, (3) conduct 35 percent of its banking with black-owned businesses, (4) assign 25 percent of its legal business to black law firms, and (5) donate $10 million to the United Negro College Fund and $1 million to "black organizations designated by PUSH."[9]

Soon thereafter, CBS named Jonathan Rodgers to be the new WBBM station manager. Rodgers, a black, did not like the fact that PUSH viewed his appointment as a partial capitulation to PUSH's demand. Furthermore, he did not want to enter into any agreements with PUSH that would take away his prerogative of making many of these changes on his own. Jackson agreed to a grace period for Rodgers. It is unclear whether the boycott hurt the station. The station did slip from first to second place, but the slippage had begun several years prior.[10]

"Bury Revlon"

One of PUSH's more recent battle cries was to "Bury Revlon." A nationwide boycott against the cosmetics giant accused the company of racism. In October 1986, Irving Bottner, head of Revlon's professional-products division, commented on the growing presence of white companies in the ethnic hair care market: "In the next couple of years, the black-owned businesses will disappear. They'll all be sold to white companies."[11] Bottner's remarks enraged many blacks, including Jesse Jackson. To dramatize its boycott against Revlon, PUSH organized a mock-funeral demonstration, complete with a casket with Revlon's name on it. The coffin, it was said, contained Revlon beauty products.

Revlon issued an apology for the Bottner statement, claiming that his comments were "taken out of context," but PUSH was unimpressed and retained the boycott. Black magazines such as *Ebony, Essence,* and *Jet* refused to accept Revlon advertisements. The company did promote a black to vice-president, pledged more minority hiring, and increased contributions to black organizations. It also agreed to sell its manufacturing plant in South Africa, ensuring that it be purchased by blacks there.[12] Revlon would not comment on the impact of the boycott on its sales. Efforts on Revlon's part to appease backfired. For example, the company tried to place an ad in black newspapers saluting Dr. Martin Luther King, Jr. The ad included a large picture of King with a small credit to Revlon's hair-care division at the bottom. Most of the papers rejected this ad. One black commentator said, "People don't think King should be used to gloss over the fact they aren't doing the right thing."

In addition to its agreements levered out of the companies discussed, PUSH has reached agreements with a number of other firms, including Seven-Up and Burger King. A common theme espoused by PUSH is that white companies such as Revlon, Coca-Cola, Miller, Coors, and Burger King exploit black consumers. For its part, PUSH sees its uses of economic leverage as a prime way in which the economic equality issue for blacks can be addressed.[13]

"Say No to Nike"

In 1990, Operation PUSH sat down with executives of Nike, the athletic shoemaker, to discuss economic opportunities for blacks. PUSH asked for detailed market information from Nike, but the company refused, claiming that the information was proprietary. Nike countered with a request for sensitive financial data from PUSH. Two days later, receptionists at PUSH headquarters were answering phones, "Say no to Nike." Amid charges by Nike that PUSH was prompted into action by its competitor, Reebok, the boycott was on.[14]

According to a trade publication, blacks spend more than $260 billion on goods and services annually. PUSH is upset because it estimates that blacks account for 30 percent of Nike's $2.23 billion in revenues. PUSH thinks it should get 30 percent of Nike's business. Reverend Tyrone Crider, national executive director of PUSH in 1990, says, "We want 30 percent of everything." Nike disputes PUSH's estimates (it claims 14 percent is more accurate) but admits it has no black vice-presidents, no money in black-owned banks, and no contracts with black ad agencies. Nike responds, however, that it has plowed profits back into the minority community, especially through minority hiring and on commercials featuring minorities (such as Spike Lee, Michael Jordan, and Bo Jackson) and women.[15]

Black columnist William Raspberry argues that Operation PUSH is focused on the wrong kind of expectation of Nike. Raspberry argues that PUSH is criticizing Nike for exploiting black inner-city youth who favor Nike's high-priced shoes but then are making demands of Nike that do not help the problem in the inner cities. Raspberry claims that PUSH's demands for more black executives in upper management just help the already well-off blacks. He argues that PUSH ought to be demanding scholarships for inner-city children, gym equipment for neighborhoods, or anything else that would really help the inner-city poor.[16]

For its part, Nike has reason to be sensitive to some of the claims of PUSH because the entire athletic footwear industry has been accused of having a role in growing urban violence. It has been reported that in some city neighborhoods, youth have been known to kill one another for a prized pair of shoes.[17]

Nike was doubly upset with the PUSH boycott because it believed rival Reebok was operating in association with PUSH. Nike, which had a 29 percent market share compared to Reebok's 22 percent, grew suspicious when a $5,950 ad from Reebok appeared in Operation PUSH's magazine. PUSH denied any connection.[18]

Nike's aggressive strategy against Operation PUSH appeared to be working, as there were no significant indications that the company was being hurt by the boycott. In spite of this, Nike did announce that it had plans to name a minority to its board of directors, though it claimed this was already in the works before the boycott.[19]

QUESTIONS FOR DISCUSSION

1. What is your assessment of the effectiveness of Operation PUSH? What are the downside risks of their tactics? Are PUSH's tactics ethical?
2. What overall posture should companies take toward social activist groups such as PUSH that choose to use economic boycotts as their primary weapon?
3. In the Revlon case, do you think the company deserved the reaction it got from PUSH for the comments made? What should it have done that it didn't do?
4. In the Nike boycott, do you think it is fair to argue that Nike is exploiting black inner-city youth because of its shoe sales there?
5. What lessons for management about corporate social response can be extracted from this case?
6. Do you think Jesse Jackson's connection with an activist group such as PUSH helps him, hurts him, or does not affect his national political aspirations?

CASE ENDNOTES

1. E. L. Schapsmeier and F. H. Schapsmeier, *Political Parties and Civic Action Groups* (Westport, CT: Greenwood Press, 1981), 346.
2. *Encyclopedia of Associations* 1988 (Detroit, MI: Gale Research Co., 1987), 1036.
3. Johnnie L. Roberts, "Threatening Boycotts, Jesse Jackson's PUSH Wins Gains for Blacks," *The Wall Street Journal* (July 21, 1982), 1.
4. *Ibid.*
5. *Ibid.*
6. *Ibid.*
7. David P. Garino, "Anheuser-Busch Fights Boycott of Its Beer, Promoting a Traveling Debate with Critic," *The Wall Street Journal* (February 1, 1983), 35.
8. *Ibid.*
9. James Kelly, "When PUSH Gives a Shove," *Time* (April 14, 1986), 8.
10. *Ibid.*
11. Penelope Wang and Maggie Malone, "Can Revlon Repair Its Image?" *Newsweek* (February 23, 1987), 53.
12. *Ibid.*
13. *Ibid.*
14. Todd Barrett and Daniel Glick, "When Games Turn Nasty," *Newsweek* (August 27, 1990), 44–45.
15. *Ibid.*, 44.
16. William Raspberry, "PUSHed and Pulled," *The Washington Post Weekly Edition* (September 3–9, 1990), 28.
17. Barrett and Glick, 45.
18. *Ibid.*
19. *Ibid.*

CASE 37   THE GERBER GLASS SCARE

The Gerber Products Company produces and sells baby food. Hardly any infant gets past the baby food stage without consuming food from those little jars with the lovable image on the label. The company claims that the Gerber baby is the second most recognized corporate image in the world. The first is the Coke logo. As one writer observed, the Gerber baby is "a symbol of caring that has etched itself in the memories of generations in this country and abroad."[1] In 1985, Gerber's market share of baby food was 68 percent, followed by Beech-Nut (17 percent), and Heinz (15 percent). Baby food is Gerber's major line of business. Its main businesses include baby food (54 percent), clothing (16 percent), trucking (15 percent), furniture (10 percent), and other (5 percent).[2]

The Gerber Products Company, the nation's largest baby food company, was founded about 60 years ago when Frank Gerber developed a way to strain vegetables at the family cannery for his 7-month-old daughter, Sally. The company was a family business until the 1940s, when the firm went public.[3] The company had a relatively stable and uneventful history until 1984.

The First Glass Scare

In October 1984, some consumers in Vermont and Rhode Island reported finding glass shards (fragments) in Gerber apple-plum and apple-cherry juice. The company studied the situation along with the Food and Drug Administration (FDA) but was not able to find a manufacturing cause for the glass. Nevertheless, the company promptly recalled about 550,000 jars of juice from a 15-state region. In the next quarter, overall sales declined by about 4 percent and then recovered.[4] As it turned out, grocers had apparently dropped cases of unopened baby food, causing damage that was unnoticeable at the time. The consequences were glass splinters drawn into the food when parents opened the vacuum-sealed jars.[5]

The Second Glass Scare

The height of the second glass scare was in early 1986. Consumers again began claiming they were finding glass shards in Gerber's baby food. Over 200 incidents were reported in at least 30 states in February and March of 1986. The FDA and several states investigated many of the incidents, and some retailers even removed Gerber products from their shelves.[6] The governor of Maryland even ordered that Gerber strained peaches could not be sold in the state for a brief period. The FDA said that its investigations had turned up nothing that would justify a recall. In March 1986, the FDA reported that it had inspected 36,000 jars of various brands of baby foods, randomly taken from warehouses around the country, but it only found eight jars with "harmless specs (of glass) the size of a grain of salt." Officials speculated that some of the complaints came from publicity seekers or people conjuring up lawsuits.[7]

The Gerber Response

To fully appreciate the Gerber management response to this crisis, it is helpful to be aware of the context in which this second glass scare occurred. First, it should be recalled that Procter & Gamble (P&G) withdrew its Rely tampon from the market in 1981 when the Center for Disease Control associated this product with a greater-than-average incidence of toxic shock syndrome (TSS). P&G's highly visible product recall cost the company in excess of $20 million, and a number of deaths were associated with TSS and the tampon.[8] P&G received considerable favorable publicity for its fast actions and responsiveness. Second, and more relevant because it occurred during the same period as the Gerber scare, was the Johnson & Johnson (J&J) response to its Tylenol crisis. For the second time in four years, cyanide-laced bottles of Extra-Strength Tylenol had been linked to a poisoning death. In an unprecedented corporate response, J&J "demarketed" Extra-Strength Tylenol at an expense of over $150 million.[9] James Burke, chairman of J&J, held hourly press conferences and appeared on national television news and talk shows explaining why and how J&J was withdrawing Extra-Strength Tylenol from the marketplace.

This is the environment in which Gerber chairman and CEO William L. McKinley had to decide how to handle the second Gerber glass scare. Unlike the more open approach taken during the first Gerber glass scare, McKinley and Gerber executives decided not to recall their products and pursued what some have variously called a low profile, hard-line, tough-it-out strategy. Gerber executives stayed off the airwaves, did not participate in interviews, and in some instances did not return phone calls to the media. In addition, the company sued the state of Maryland for $150 million when the state ordered that strained peaches had to be withdrawn from sale.[10]

Gerber did form a crisis management team under the direction of Robert Johnston, the vice-president over all Gerber-brand food and infant products. The glass-crisis task force was composed of 14 high-echelon executives from sales, administration, quality control, public relations, and other departments. During 3 weeks of the crisis, the group met daily for meetings that lasted a couple of hours or more. The view from the outside world was that company management was doing nothing. One executive remarked, "People kept telling us we weren't doing anything. In fact, we were determined not to do anything." A consensus against a recall had developed among the group. The task force saw their current situation as quite different from the Tylenol case because a death was not involved. Furthermore, they were still remembering their 1984 recall, when they had pulled the product to calm customers, but it hadn't stopped the complaints.[11] McKinley stated, "When we tried to quiet the press with an unjustified recall, it didn't work. So why should we do it again?"[12] In addition, the 1984 recall caused a sales drop.

Reactions to the Gerber Response

Reactions by both critics and supporters to the Gerber approach to handling its crisis were abundant. Inevitably, much of the criticism centered around the comparison of the apparent "do nothing" strategy of Gerber as contrasted to J&J's proactive, high-profile public handling of the Tylenol episode. The contrast invited criticism because it appeared that Gerber was not caring enough to go to the maximum degree to protect consumers.

Critics made it quite clear that the J&J response in the Tylenol case was more nearly the model Gerber should have followed. Gerald C. Meyers, former chairman of American Motors Corp., commented, "Now they've not only got a glass problem, they've got a public-perception problem." The chairman of another major food company said that Gerber should have been as responsive as J&J. He argued, "You must err on the side of going overboard to do what's right in the view of the public." Another marketing executive said that customers will support a company that is under attack if they come clean with the facts. This executive thinks he knows from experience because in 1982, sales of his firm's hot dogs plummeted when complaints of finding razor blades and nails in them came in. He said sales picked up when the company opened up to the media and permitted TV cameras and access to the plants.[13]

There were also many supporters of Gerber's strategy. One investment analyst said, "You don't go pulling products if there's no evidence." Charles S. Goodman, a marketing professor at the Wharton School, said, "If you push the recall button any time someone calls a newspaper, you open yourself up to blackmail." He added, "Some crazy will say 'If you want to stay off the 10 o'clock news, write me a check.'"[14] A marketing professor at the University of Chicago, Harry L. Davis, commented on the failure of Gerber to discuss its recall decision: "In an unfavorable kind of situation, it's better not to talk about it. People tend to remember the negative rather than what the company is doing about it." Thomas Kinnear, a University of Michigan professor, saw it differently: "The company should have been more open. By not saying more they exposed themselves to more accusations and rumors. All the behavioral evidence underlines the wisdom in presenting your case."[15]

As the crisis began to subside, McKinley began making some moves to quiet the criticism against him and his company's strategy in the glass scare. The president of Gerber, Leo D. Goulet, appeared on a television commercial and said that the FDA had never found anything wrong with the company's manufacturing processes and, therefore, consumers had no reason to lose faith in the company. In addition, a four-page form letter was mailed to 900,000 homes with small children. Within two weeks the company planned to reach 2.5 million homes—70 percent of all United States homes with babies—with copies of the letter. Gerber's stock traded late in this same week near its 52-week high of $44.63.

On September 18, 1987, about a year and a half later, Gerber Products' stock closed at $49 with a 52-week (from that date) high of $63 and a low of $39.50.

QUESTIONS FOR DISCUSSION

1. Identify all the social and ethical issues present in the glass-scare episode.
2. Was the Gerber approach to crisis management an ethical approach? Discuss.
3. Do you think Gerber received unfair criticism just because it pursued such a different strategy from that of J&J in the Tylenol crisis?
4. What is your evaluation of the approach Gerber used in its second glass scare? What are its strengths and weaknesses? How would you have handled this crisis?
5. What lessons for crisis management and corporate social response can be extracted from this case?

CASE ENDNOTES

1. Grant Pick, "Gerber's Baby Under Stress," *Across the Board* (July/August, 1986), 9.
2. James Barron, "Gerber's McKinley Starts to Relax," *The New York Times* (March 23, 1986), 31F.
3. *Ibid.*
4. Pick, 10.
5. Barron, 1F.
6. "Why Gerber Is Standing Its Ground," *Business Week* (March 17, 1986), 50.
7. "Gerber Balks at a Recall," *Newsweek* (March 17, 1986), 48.
8. Elizabeth Gatewood and Archie B. Carroll, "The Anatomy of Corporate Social Response: The Rely, Firestone 500, and Pinto Cases," *Business Horizons* (September-October, 1981), 9–16.
9. Stephen Koepp, "A Hard Decision to Swallow," *Time* (March, 1986), 59.
10. *Business Week* (March 17, 1986), 50.
11. Pick, 11–12.
12. *Business Week* (March 17, 1986), 50.
13. *Ibid.*
14. Pick, 12.
15. *Ibid.*, 12–13.

NAME INDEX

A

Abrams, Bill, 288
Abbott Laboratories, 78, 528
Ace Hardware, 353
Ackerman, Robert, 40, 57
ACLU. *See* American Civil Liberties Union.
A. C. Nielson Company, 11
Action for Children's Television (ACT), 270
Act III Communications, 53
Adair, John E., 155, 158
Administrative Management Society, 457
Administrative Procedures Act, 204
Advocacy Institute, 276
Aetna, 374
AFL-CIO, 8
African Development Bank, 349
African National Congress (ANC), 178
Agee, William M., 519
Aharoni, Yair, 310
Ahlberg, B., 367
A. H. Robins, 3, 295
AHS. *See* American Hospital Supply.
Alabama State Police, 495
Allen, Fred T., 144, 152, 158
Allen, Michael, 464
Allen, Richard, 228
Alexander, Charles, 572
Alexander, Herbert E., 249
ALCOA (Aluminum Company of America), 398, 554, 556
Allis Chalmers, 181
All Nippon Airways, 174
Alka-Seltzer, 5
Alyeska, 360-361
American Advertising Federation, 284
American Assembly, 525, 527
American Association of Advertising Agencies, 284
American Bakers Association, 358
American Bar Association, 510
American Business Conference, 233
American Civil Liberties Union (ACLU), 448
American Council of Life Insurance, 372
American Express (AmEx), 247, 397
American Home Products, 170
American Hospital Supply (AHS), 408-409
American Jewish Congress, 534
American Management Association, 445
American Motors Corporation, 595
American Paper Institute, 358
American Red Cross, 459
American Tobacco Company, 192
American Trucking Association (ATA), 240
AMF Inc., 267
Amnesty International, 397
Amoco, 328, 358, 380
Amparano, Julie, 545
Amtrak, 201
Amway, 730
Anchor Hocking, 391
Anderson, Charles, 526, 545
Andreason, Allen R., 287
Andrews, Frederick, 157
Andrews, Kenneth, 551, 559, 572
Anheuser-Busch, 46, 269, 435
Ansoff, H. Igor, 552, 572, 576, 599
Anthony, Robert, 526, 545
Apple Computer, 353, 516
Apcar, Leonard, 545
Aram, John D., 674, 691
Aranson, Peter H., 546
ARCO, 228, 587
Aristotle, 112
Arthur D. Little (firm), 177
Arthur, W., 335
Asian Development Bank, 349
Assael, Henry, 288
Association of National Advertisers, 284
Atchison, Charles, 431
AT&T, 4, 53, 85, 214, 215, 266, 455, 459, 487
Avon Products, 529

B

Bacon, Jeremy, 545
Baer, Donald, 544
Baig, Edward C.,
Bakaly, Jr., Charles C., 438
Baker, Emily L., 463
Baker, James C., 187

Bakke case, 493
Baldridge, Malcolm, 404
Bank of America, 85, 428, 459, 592
Bank of Boston, 549
Barach, Jeffery A., 658, 667
Barclay, William, 111-112, 119
Barnett, Tom, 528
Barry, Vincent, 157, 263, 288
Bartley, Robert L., 621, 626
Bass Brothers, 518
Bassiry, G. R., 188
Bauer, Raymond, 27, 30, 40, 57
Baum, Laurie, 545
Baumen, W. Scott, 149
Baumhart, R. C., 85, 119, 135, 137
BCA. *See* Business Committee for the Arts.
B. Dalton Bookseller, 374
Bean, Ed, 463
Bean, L. L., 279
Beauchamp, Tom L., 83, 501, 705
Becker, Gary S., 221, 496-497, 500
Beech-Nut, 260
Behavior Research Center, 156
Behrman, Jack, 172
Beiler, George W., 566, 572
Bell and Howell, 178
Bell, Daniel, 195, 220
Bell, Martin L., 287
Bell South, 228
Bell Telephone, 381
Bendix Corporation, 91, 519
Beneficial Corporation, 520
Ben & Jerry's Homemade, 353, 354, 357
Bennett, Amanda, 415, 437
Bentsen, Lloyd, 242
Bentham, Jeremy, 112, 125
Bere, James F., 554
Bergenstein, Sigrid, 246, 247, 249, 250
Bergerac, Michel C., 519
Berenbeim, Ronald E., 30, 57, 119
Berle, Adolph, 38, 522, 544
Berkshire Hathaway, 53, 541
Best, Arthur, 287
Better Business Bureau, 267
Bethlehem Steel Corporation, 141
Better Environment Awards for Industry, 357
Bianco, Anthony, 544
Biederman, Daniel, 396, 414
Birdsell, L. Earle, 220
Blair, John D., 79, 83

767

Blake, David H., 188, 572
Blanchard, Kenneth, 147, 158
Block, J. R., 382, 413
Blomstrom, L., 7
Blomstrom, Robert L., 18, 31, 41, 42, 57, 75
Bloom, Paul, 259, 288
Blue Angel, 352
Bluestone, Barry, 399, 414
Blumberg, Phillip, 153, 158
Blumenthal, W. Michael, 91, 119
Boddewyn, J. J., 284, 285, 289
Body Shop, 357
Bodywares, 358
Boeing Vertol, 426
Boesky, Ivan, 85, 260, 521
Bolling, Richard, 238
Bonner, Raymond
Booth, Laurence D., 187
Borg-Warner, 428, 554, 555
"Born Loser," 96
Boulton, William R., 545
Bowen, Howard R., 565, 573
Bowie, Norman E., 501
Bowling, James C., 616
Boy Scouts, 391
Branch, Taylor, 437
Brewer, Otto, 97, 119
Brennan, Edward A., 529
Brennan, William, 493, 496
Brenner, Steven, 135, 137, 143, 157, 158, 252, 287
Breyer, Stephen, 221
Brine, William H., 297
Brinkley, Christie, 269
British Airways, 201
British Gas, 201
British Petroleum Chemicals, 357
British Steel Corporation, 408
Brock, William, 247
Brock, Beau H., 658
Broder, David S., 250
Brody, Michael, 438
Branstein, Scott, 464
Brookings, 391
Brophey, Beth, 501, 626
Brower, M., 335
Brown, Barbara B., 500
Brown, Courtney, 513
Brown, James K., 582, 599
Brown, L. R., 335
Brown, Michael H., 713
Brown & Root, 102, 431
Brown, Terry, 545

BSC, Ltd., 408
Byrne, John A., 544, 545
Buchanan, Bruce, 267, 288
Buchholz, Rogene A., 187, 582
Budde, Neil, 545
Budweiser, 5
Buffett, Warren E., 531, 541
Buntrock, Dean L., 516
Bureau of Labor Statistics, 454
Bureau of National Affairs, 456
Burger King, 395-396
Burke, James E., 53, 298
Bush, George, 216, 217, 218, 292, 339, 432, 476, 490
Business Committee for the Arts (BCA), 392
Business Enterprise Trust, 49, 53, 353, 357
Business Ethics Advisory Council, 85
Business Roundtable, 232-233, 244
Business Week, 19, 453, 459, 498, 515, 516, 517
Business Week 1000, 603
Buss, Terry F., 414

Cabot Corporation, 389
Cabot, Louis W., 389, 413
Caesar, Patricia, 414
Cahan, Vicky, 545
Calfee, John E., 289
California Public Employees Retirement System, 517
Call, Barbara Jo, 463
Callenbach, E., 336
Calvert Ariel Growth Fund, 54
Calvert Ariel Appreciation Fund, 54
Campaign GM (Campaign to Make General Motors Responsible), 53
Campbell Soup, 264, 278
Canadian Broadcasting Corporation, 593
Canon, 292
Carey, John, 289
Carnation, 172, 265, 278
Carnegie, Andrew, 30
Carson, Rachel, 590
Carter, Jimmy, 216, 232
Carter, Stephen L., 492, 501
Cary, William L., 542, 545

Cash, Sarah, 311
Castro, Janice, 310, 544
Caterpillar Tractor Company, 142, 181
Caudron, Sheri, 464
Cavanagh, Gerald F., 626
CBS, 275, 485
CDC. *See* Control Data Corporation.
Center for Corporate Public Involvement, 372, 375
Center for Policy Alternatives, 211
Center for Public Integrity, 240
Center for Science in the Public Interest, 271, 283
Center for the Study of American Businesses, 217
Century Council, 271
CEP (Council on Economic Priorities), 49-51, 57
CEQ, 357, 367
CERES, 355
Chain Saw Manufacturers Association, 103-104
Challenger, 85
Chamber of Commerce of the United States, 9, 13, 227, 230-231, 244
Chandran, Rajan, 311
Charan, Ram, 572
Charter Company, 515
Chase, Thomas Howard, 582
Chavez, Linda, 502
Chemical Manufacturers of America, 358
Chesebrough-Pond, 267
Chevrolet, 138, 539
Chevron, 357
Children's Advertising Review Unit (CARU), 270-271
Chilton, Kenneth, 221
Chrisman, James J., 221, 400, 403, 414, 572
Chrysler Corporation, 200, 203, 593
Church, George J., 311
Ciba-Geigy, 359
CIGNA, 375, 428
Cincinnati Gas and Electric, 525
Circle K Corporation, 528
Citicorp, 428
Citizens and Southern National Bank of Georgia, 391
Civil Aeronautics Board (CAB), 207

Clark, Timothy B., 221
Clay, Gerald, 593-594
Clorox, 2, 5
Coates, Joseph F., 582, 599
Coates, Vary T., 582, 599
Coca-Cola, 178, 182, 516, 623
Cochran, Phillip, 47, 48, 57, 519, 544
Cody, E., 335
Coffin, T., 335
Cohen, D., 311
Coil, James A., III, 463, 502
Colgate-Palmolive, 264
College Football Association (CFA), 18
Comanche Peak Nuclear Plant, 431
Common Cause, 5, 8, 9, 242
Common Situs, 244
Commission on Civil Rights, 482
Committee for Economic Development, 391
Community Relations Committee of Salem, N.J., 391
Comp, T. A., 346
Condon, T. J., 437
Confederation of British Industry, 357
Conference Board, 11, 17, 123, 259, 382, 386, 446, 526
Conrail, 201
Conservation Law Foundation, 350, 351
Consolidated Gas Company, 531
Consumer Product Safety Commission, 103
Continental Airlines, 49
Control Data Corporation (CDC), 427, 428, 435, 459
Conventional Approach, 147
Conway, John A., 413
Cooper, Michael, 414, 616
Cook, Alice H., 501
Cook, T., 336
Coors, 275
Corley, Robert N., 502
Corning, Inc., 392, 485
Corporate Conscience Awards, 53
Corporate Ombudsman Association, 435
Corson, Ben, 288
Corson, E. H., 367
Corson, John J., 573
Corson, W. H., 335

Cosin, Elizabeth M., 463
Council for Aid to Education, 384
Council for Financial Aid to Education, 387
Council for Better Business, 270, 284
Council of Institutional Investigators (CII), 532
Council of Economic Priorities (CEP), 49, 55, 260
Council on Environmental Quality (CEQ), 335
Cousins, D. C., 289
Cox, Eli P., 288
CPSC, 206, 208, 260, 281, 300-303
Cranston, Alan, 243
Cressey, Donald R., 158
Crittenden, Ann, 515, 544
Crowe, Lisa, 157
Crystal, Graef S., 530
Cuddihy, John, 705
Cullen, John B., 157
Cummins Engine, 53
"A Current Affair," 91
Cushman, Robert, 370-371
C. W. Post Center, 254

Daiei Supermarket, 359
Daly, Herman, 339
Das, T. K., 130
Data General Corporation, 528
Dairs, Keith, 31, 39, 41, 42, 56, 57
Dairs, Kristen, 57
Dalton Booksellers, B., 374
Davis, Keith, 7, 18, 25
Dayton Hudson, 374
Dean, T., 367
Deaver, Michael, 228
deButts, John, 232
DEC. See Digital Equipment Corporation.
DeGeorge, Richard, 119, 157, 164, 180, 182, 187, 188
De Klerk, F. W., 178
Delaware, state of, 542
Dellaverson, Joanne, 501
Delta Air Lines, 50, 52, 228
Dentzer, Susan, 157
Denzau, Arthur T., 220
DesJardins, Joseph R., 463
DeStefanos, Linda, 25

Diamond, Stuart, 172, 187
Dickie, Robert B., 616
Digital Equipment Corporations, 428, 455, 485
Dill, William, 505, 544
DiPerna, P., 367
Disney. See Walt Disney.
Dobrzynski, Judith H., 544, 545
Dole, Robert, 238
Donaldson, Thomas, 183, 188
Dow Canada, 596
Dow Chemical, 596
Dow Corning Corporation, 610
Downs, Linda, 632
Draper, E., 335
Drexel Burnham Lambert, 3, 38, 521
Dreyfus Third Century Fund, 55
Drucker, Peter, 38, 160, 187, 252, 287, 401, 406, 414, 545, 626
Duke, Lynne, 500
Duke Power, 479
Dunlap, 367
Dunn, David J., 511, 544
DuPont, 49, 357, 398
Durning, A., 368
Dworkin, Terry Morehead, 311
Dwyer, Paula, 502

Eagle-Picher Industries, 516
Eagleton, Thomas, 243
Eastman Kodak, 353
Eaton, 459
Eberts, Mike, 249
Ecotech Autoworks, 349
Edsall, Thomas B., 501
Eells, Richard, 392, 413
EEOC. See Equal Employment Opportunity Commission.
E. F. Hutton, 3, 85, 140, 141, 549, 593
Egan, T., 367
Eliker, Paul H., 393, 414
Eli Lilly and Company, 358, 391-392
Elkington, John, 288
Elliott, Martha W., 83, 705
Ellis, Dorsey, 299-300, 311
Ellis, James E., 501
Emory, C. William, 287
Englade, Kenneth F., 463

Environmental Defense Fund (EDF), 350, 351
Environmental Media Association, 357
Environmental Protection Agency (EPA), 76, 183, 208, 318, 319, 322, 323, 326, 327, 328, 343, 344, 345, 350, 358, 409, 454
Epstein, Edwin M.,17, 25, 32, 57, 502, 534, 544
EPA. *See* Environmental Protection Agency
Equal Employment Opportunity Commission (EEOC), 208, 470, 472, 473, 475, 476, 477, 484, 485, 487, 488
Ermann, M. David, 393
Estes, Robert, 288
Estes, Ralph, 572
Ethics Resource Center, 148, 150, 153, 155, 156
European Economic Community, 349
Evans, Fred J., 25
Evans, William D., 187
Ewing, David W., 417, 420, 425, 428, 434, 438
Exxon, 85, 260, 360-361, 527, 534, 549
Exxon *Valdez*, 549
Ezorsky, Gertrude, 437

Fahey, Liam, 6, 25, 567, 569, 573, 576, 599
Falk, Carol H., 502
Farmer, Richard N., 187
Fausnaugh, Carolyn J., 716
Fay, John, 463
Foreign Corrupt Practices Act (FCPA), 181
FDA. *See* Food and Drug Administration.
Federal Aviation Administration (FAA), 205, 216
Federal Communications Commission (FCC), 205, 207
Federal Election Commission, 235
Federal Express Corporation, 428
Federalist Papers, 7
Federal Merit System Protection Board, 484-485

Federal Reserve System, 203
Federal Trade Commission (FTC), 8, 192, 240, 258, 260, 265, 266, 267, 270, 277, 280, 281-283
Fedo, David, 187
Ferry, Richard M., 544
Fetterolf, C. Fred, 554
Fialka, John J., 250
Film Recovery Systems, 451-452
Financial Accounting Standards Board, 519
Financial Times, 357
Fink, Steven, 594-595, 599
Finn, Chester E., 481, 501
Fireman, Paul, 516
Firestone, 549
First National Bank of Boston, 593
Fischer, D. W., 42
Fisher, Anne B., 502
Fitzgerald, Ernest, 431
Flavin, C., 335, 336, 367
Fleming, John E., 614, 616, 737
FMC Corporation, 390
Food and Drug Administration (FDA), 213, 277, 278, 280, 281-283, 300, 303-306
Forbes, John B., 413
Ford, Gerald, 216
Ford, Henry, II, 17
Ford Motor Company, 228, 295, 404, 515, 549
Fossedal, Gregory A., 501
Fox, Marvin, 119
Fox, L. W., 158
Frederick, William, 41, 57, 116, 188, 572
Freedman, Alix M., 187, 464
Freeman, Harry, 247
Freeman, R. Edward, 83, 551, 552, 572
Friedman, Milton, 37, 57, 119
Friedman, Robert, 289
Friedrich, Otto, 464
Friends of the Earth, 5, 76
Frigitemp Corporation, 102
Fritzche, David, 626
Fry, Fred L., 221
Fry, Louis W., 3, 85, 413
Fulda, Carl D., 119

GAF, 520

Galen, Michelle, 311, 463
Gallagher, John E., 289
Gallup, George, Jr., 25, 464
Gallup Opinion Index, 119
Gallup Poll, 11, 86, 89
GAO. *See* General Accounting Office
Garland, John, 187
Garrison, Sharon H., 599
Garvin, David, 293, 310
GASP. *See* Group Against Smoking Pollution.
Gatewood, Elizabeth I., 400, 403, 414
Geewax, M., 335
Gendell, Gerald S., 395
Geneen, Harold G., 512, 544
General Accounting Office (GAO), 176
General Dynamics, 3, 85, 181, 549, 593
General Electric (GE), 4, 85, 178, 375, 426, 428, 549, 568
General Motors (GM), 5, 17, 85, 139, 177, 178, 254, 357, 404, 515, 534
General Public Utilities, 528
Gerber Products Company, 763-765
Gest, Ted, 311, 502
Getschow, George, 157
Ghoshal, Sumantra, 572
Gilbert, Daniel R., 557, 572
Gilbert, Lewis, 531
Gillespie, Kate, 176, 187
Girl Scouts, 391, 397
Giroud, Cynthia D., 414
Gissen, Jay, 311
Gittles, Harvey, 158
Gladwell, Malcolm, 289, 311
Gladwin, Thomas M., 172, 187
Glueck, William, 406, 500
G.M. *See* General Motors.
Golab, Stefan, 451
Goldman Sachs, 353, 521
Goldome, 49
Goldstein, Robert C., 464
Goodman, Norman, 382, 413
Goodpaster, Kenneth, 63, 67, 83
Goodyear Tire and Rubber, 172, 528
Gorman, Christine, 288, 289
Gottlieb, Martin, 414
Gottschalk, Earl C., 599

Government Accountability Project, 433
Graham, John L., 176
Granholm, Axel R., 437
Gray, Peter S., 463
Green Cross, 352
Greenblatt, David, 446
Greengard, Samuel, 641
Greene, Mark, 276, 283, 289, 406, 414, 546
Greene, Richard, 437
GreenPeace, 349, 350
Green Seal, 352
Greyhound, 528
Greyser, Stephen, 259, 288
Grossman, Joel M., 438
Group Against Smoking Pollution (GASP), 457
Grover, Ronald, 288
Grumman Corporation, 528
Gulf Oil Corporation, 85, 153

Haas, Robert D., 142
Hacker, Andrew, 311
Hall, John, 182, 188, 626
Hamilton, Joan, 437
Hammonds, Keith H., 413
Hampton Inn, 293
Hancock, Robert S., 288
Hands Across America, 397
Hanes Hosiery, 262
Hansen, J., 335
Hanson, Kirk, 53, 153, 158
Harris, James F., 386
Harrison, Bennett, 399, 414
Harrison, Matthew C., 157
Haxtman, Edwin, 572
Harvard Business Review, 85, 135
Harvard Business School, 13, 621
Hasbro-Bradley, Inc., 103
Hayek, F. A., 38, 57
Hayes, Arthur S., 311, 501
Heald, Morrell, 30, 56, 413
Health Insurance Association of America, 372
Heard, James E., 537, 539
Heidrick and Struggles, Inc., 525
Heinz, H. J., 398, 593-594, 596
Heinz, Lisa, 582, 599
Henry, William A., III, 501
Hequet, Mark, 464

Herman Miller Company, 354
Herrmann, Robert O., 288
Hertzberg, David, 544
Herzel, Leo, 545
Hewlett-Packard, 398
Hildreth, James W., 413
Hilton Hotel, 392
Hinksey Centre (Oxford, England), 184, 185
Hirsch, Leon C., 516
Hirschhorn, J. S., 335
H. J. Heinz, 398, 593-594, 596
Hoewing, Raymond, 233, 244, 605, 616
Hofer, Charles, 556, 572
Hoffman, W. Michael, 187
Hollie, Pamela, 119
Holloway, Robert J., 253, 288
Holmes, Sandra, 44, 57
Holocaust Memorial, 690
Holsendolph, Ernest, 502
Holtzman, Elizabeth, 464
Hoy, Frank, 182, 188, 626
Honda, 161
Honeywell, 178, 428, 485
Hood, Paul C., 311
Hooker Chemical Company, 68-70, 73-75
Hosmer, LaRue T., 145, 158
Howard, Donald G., 187
Howard, Robert, 158
Hrebenar, Ronald, 249
Huey, John, 636
Humane Society, 397
Human Resources Network, 585
Human Rights Now!, 397
Hunt, Albert R., 249
Hunt, Avery, 414
Hunt, J., 368
Husqvarna, Inc., 104
Hutchins, Dexter, 464
Huwa, Randy, 249
Hymowitz, Carol, 501

Iacocca, Lee, 17
IBM, 17, 85, 178, 182, 398, 419, 428, 446, 610, 644
Icahn, Carl, 518, 544
ICC, 207
ICH, 458
Imperial Chemicals Industry, 357

Independent Petroleum Asssociation, 236
Infant Formula Action Coalition (INFACT), 169-170
Information Technology Group (ITG), 426-427
Ingersoll, Bruce, 119, 289
Ingrassia, Lawrence, 545
Institutional Shareholder Services, 516
Inter-American Development Bank, 349
Interfaith Center on Corporate Responsibility (ICCR), 169-170, 532
Internal Revenue Service (IRS), 203, 384, 441
International Rivers Network, 335
Interstate Commerce Commission (ICC), 192, 205
Investor Responsibility Research Center (IRRC), 178, 531, 537
Irvine, S., 340, 367
Issues Management Association, 589, 591
ITG. *See* Information Technology Group.
ITT, 512, 513
Isaak Walton League, 350

Jackson, Brooks, 250
Jacobs, Richard O., 530
Jacobsen, J., 336
Jacobsen, Michael F., 289
Jacoby, Neil H., 25
Jalisco Cheese, 593
Japanese Automobile Manufacturers Association, 359
Jarratt, Jennifer, 582, 599
Jasinowski, Jerry, 231, 232
Jenen, Tamila C., 437
Jenkins, McKay, 500
Jhally, Sut, 288
J & J. *See* Johnson & Johnson.
Joint Council on Economic Education, 393
John Hancock, 375, 428
Johns Manville Corporation, 295
Johnson, Cathy Marie, 683
Johnson, Dirk, 413

Johnson, F. Ross, 517
Johnson, Julie, 464
Johnson, Lyndon B., 489
Johnson, Paul, 495
Johnson & Johnson (J & J), 49, 77, 135, 298, 549, 554, 593
Johnson & Sons, S. C., 592
Johnston, Phillip D., 414
Jones, Mary Gardner, 307, 311
Jones, Patricia E., 79, 83, 244, 250, 599
Jones, Reginald, 232
Jones, Thomas M., 155, 158
Jones-Smith, Jacqueline, 302
Jordan, Michael, 397
Josephson Institute, 86, 88, 130
Joss, Eric H., 440
Joyce, Diane, 445
Junior Achievement, 393
Jurmu, Joanne L., 705
Jury Verdict Research, Inc., 440

Kaiser Aluminum, 493
Kahn, Joseph P., 464
Kansas City Life Insurance, 375
Kapstein, Jonathan, 414
Karmin, Monroe W., 221
Kaut, Immanuel, 112
Katz, Leo, 545
Kavanagh, John P., 402, 414
Kearns, David, 292
Keating, Charles H., 86, 243
Keim, Gerald, 42, 223, 245, 249, 250, 385, 413
Keith, Robert J., 253, 287
Kelly, Orr, 119
Kelley, Patricia C., 607, 616
Kellogg's, 259
Kennedy, John F., 253
Kessler, David, 304
Key, Wilson Bryan, 266
Keynes, John Maynard, 38
Kiam, Victor, 17
Kidder Peabody, 446, 521
Kilmann, Ralph H., 187
King, Martin Luther, Jr., 467
King, William R., 569, 576, 582, 585, 599
Kirkpatrick, Miles, 281
Kleinfield, N. R., 437
Kleinmuntz, Benjamin, 463

Klepper, Anne, 384, 386, 413
Kline, Stephen, 288
Klingner, Donald, 464
K-Mart, 85
Koch, Frank, 377, 413
Koepp, Stephen, 310
Kohlberg, Lawrence, 108, 110, 119, 341
Kolderie, Ted, 221
Konrad, Walecia, 464
Koop, C. Everett, 456
Koral, Alan M., 501
Korn, Lester B., 544
Kosters, Marvin H., 221
Koten, John, 288
Kotler, Phillip, 254, 255, 288
Kramer, Andrew M., 437
Krattenmaker, Thomas G., 281, 289
Kreps, Theodore J., 564, 572
Kristol, Irving, 390, 413
Kroger, Inc., 614
Kwasniewski, Sandra, 442

Labich, Kenneth, 221
Laczniak, Gene, 180, 187, 188
Ladd, Dwight R., 187
Lahiff, James M., 663
Lange, Ann E., 187
LA Times, 357
Lave, Lester B., 311
Laxalt, Paul, 243
Leach, Jim, 238
Leadership Conference on Civil Rights, 492
Lear, Norman, 53
Lecraw, Donald J., 187
Ledvinka, James, 466, 479, 500, 501, 734
Leefeldt, Ed, 544
Lehner, Urban C., 502
Leiss, William, 288
Levi Strauss & Co., 142-143
Levine, Dennis B., 521, 544
Lichter, Linda S., 25
Lichter, S. Robert, 25
Lilly and Company, Eli, 391-392
LIN Broadcasting, 516
Lincoln Federal Savings and Loan Association of California, 86, 243
Linden, Fabian, 75

Linneman, Robert, 311
Linowes, David F., 441, 442
Lipman, Joanne, 289
Lippett, Jordan L., 157
Lippman, T. W., 335, 368
Lipset, Seymour Martin, 249
Litschert, Robert J., 414
Little, Arthur D., 177
Live Aid, 397
Livengood, Anne, 431
L. L. Bean, 279
Lochheed, Carolyn, 221, 311, 464
Locke, John, 112, 126
Lockhead, 172, 174, 181, 431
Lorange, Peter, 572
Lorsch, 528
Low, Charlotte, 75, 502
Lublin, Joan S., 437, 464, 545
Luther, Martin, 129
Lutheran Church in America, 534
Lewis, Phillip V., 134, 157
Lybrand, 414
Lydenberg, Steven D., 57
Lyle, 408

Mabry, Marcus, 289
Mace, Myles L., 158
Machlowitz, David, 501
Machlowitz, Marilyn, 501
MacMillan, Ian C., 79, 83, 244, 250, 599
MADD. *See* Mothers Against Drunk Driving.
Madden, Carl, 113, 119
Madsen, Peter, 737
Madison, James, 87
Magaziner, Ira C., 221
Magnet, Myran, 599
Magnusson, Paul, 220
Mahood, H. R., 227, 249
Mahon, John, 589, 599, 616
Mahoney, Richard J., 527
Maitland, Ian, 233-234, 249
Makinson, Larry, 249
Makower, Joel, 288, 367
Mallary, Maria, 414
Malott, Robert H., 390, 413
Management Institute for Environmental Business, 314
Mandrake, 276
Manning, Bayless, 542

Name Index ◆ 773

Marcus, Ruth, 501
Marcus, Sumner, 542, 545
Martin, Alice Tepper, 57
Mars, Inc., 267
Marshall, Thurgood, 476, 487
Marx, Thomas G., 590, 599
Mason, R. O., 367
Mathews, J., 335
Mathews, Marilynn Cash, 149
Maugh, Thomas H., 83
Max Ways, 119
Mayville, Gail, 353
McAdam, Terry W., 41, 42, 57
McAdams, 367
McAllister, Bill, 501
McCarthy, Eugene, 590
McCloy, John, 153
McCulloch Corporation, 103-104
McDonald's, 357, 380, 395, 435
McGill, Linda D., 437
McGinley, Laura, 221
McGuire, E. Patrick, 259, 288, 311
McGuire, Joseph W., 7, 25, 32, 57
MCI, 266
McKenna, Regis, 253, 287
McKie, James W., 29, 30, 56
McKersie, Robert B., 414
McNeil Laboratories, 135
Means, Gardiner, 522, 544
Mecia, Tony, 501
Medicare, 201
Meese, Edwin, 494
Meier, Barry, 464
Meiners, Roger E., 385, 413
Mentzer, Marc S., 680
Merck, 49, 357
Meritor Savings Bank, 49
Meritor Savings Bank v. Vinson, 744
Merit System Protection Board, 432
Merrill Dow, 297
Mescan, Timothy, 395, 414
Meyer, Priscilla S., 311
Meyers, Gerald C., 595
Morris, Phillip, 516
Miceli, Marcia P., 437
Michalove, Steve, 83
Miles, Robert H., 42, 572, 611, 616
Milkin, Michael, 521
Mill, John Stuart, 125
Miller, Arjay, 526, 545
Miller, James C., III, 221, 282, 289
Miller, Norman C., 250
Miller, Roger Leroy, 311
Mills, Claudia, 269, 288

Ministry of International Trade and Industry (MITI), 200
Minsky, Terri, 414
Mitchell, Neil J., 30, 57
Mitnick, Barry, 626
Mitroff, Ian I., 187, 367, 599
Mitsubishi, 161, 359
Mobil, 85
Molander, Earl, 135, 137, 157, 252, 281
Molitor, T. Graham, 584, 585
Monks, Robert A. G., 529
Monsanto, 527, 587
Moore, Charles R., 158
Morgan, Lee L., 158
Morris, Richard, 396, 414
Morton, Michael F. Scott, 572
Morton Thiokol, 85, 431
Mothers Against Drunk Driving (MADD), 5, 395
Motorola, Inc., 150-152
Mulladay, Sarah F., 463
Multilateral Development Banks (MDBs), 349
Murphey, Thomas, 232
Murray, Alan, 249
Murray, Charles, 481, 501
Murray, Edwin A., Jr., 616
Murray, Thomas J., 626
Myers, Mildred S., 188, 572

Naar, J., 335, 367
Nabisco, R. J. R., 517
Nader, Ralph, 5, 238, 239, 247, 254, 255-256, 288, 406, 531, 542, 546, 590
Nagel, Thomas, 501
Naisbitt, John, 568, 582, 583
Namiki, Nobuaki, 242, 250
Naor, Jacob, 180, 187, 188
Narayanan, V. K., 6, 567, 569, 573
Nash, Laura L., 158
NAM. See National Association of Manufacturers.
NARB. See National Advertising Review Board.
NASA, 85
National Academy of Science, 456
National Advertising Division of Council of Better Business Bureaus, 267, 284

National Advertising Review Board (NARB), 284, 286
National Airlines, 268
National Association of Home Builders, 227
National Association of Manufacturers (NAM), 5, 227, 231-232
National Association of Realtors, 113, 228
National Association of Wholesalers, 230
National Audubon Society, 350
National Automobile Dealers Association (NADA), 227, 240
National Cancer Institute, 277
National Center for Employee Ownership, 404, 405
National Commission of Product Safety (NCPS), 301
National Council of Churches, 169
National Directory of Corporate Charity, 382
National Electronic Injury Surveillance System (NEISS), 296
National Football League, 272
National Life Insurance Company, 375
National Parks Foundation (Costa Rica), 398
National Resources Defense Council (NRDC), 303, 350, 351
National Science Foundation, 269
National Semiconductor Corporation, 455
National Steel, 404, 407
National Urban League, 397
Nazario, S. L., 335, 367
NBA, 397
NBC, 275, 428
NCAA, 18, 19
NCR, 371
Near, Janet P., 437
Neff, Thames J., 545
Nestlé, 69, 105, 169, 278
Newgreen, Kenneth E., 569-570, 573
Newport, Frank, 25, 464
New York Stock Exchange (NYSE), 525
New York Telephone, 374
New York Times, 449

Niagara Falls School Board, 71
Niagara Power and Development Company, 71
Nicholson, Edward A., 414
Nielson Company, A. C., 11
Nike, 397
Nintendo, 283
Nippon Eco Life Center, 359
Nix, Timothy W., 79, 83
Nixon, Richard, 301
Nolan, Joseph, 25
Nolan, Richard L., 464
Northrop, 172
Norton Company, 370, 376
Nuclear Regulatory Commission (NRC), 102
Nulty, P., 335
Nussbaum, Bruce, 545
Nye, David, 449, 463
NYSE. *See* New York Stock Exchange.

O'Boyle, Thomas F., 437
Occidental Petroleum Company, 71
Occupational Safety and Health Administration (OSHA), 208, 451, 452, 453-455
O'Connell, Philip R., 545
Odum, E. P., 335
Office of Federal Contract Compliance Programs (OFCCP), 494
Office of General Counsel, 432
Office of Management and Budget (OMB), 217
Ohio Public Interest Campaign, 411
Oldenburg, K. U., 335
Olin Corporation, 409
Oliver Machinery Co., 297
Oliver, Daniel, 282
Olson, Fred C., 437
Olson, R. L., 336
Olson, Walter, 249
O'Neill, Nancy G., 464
O'Neill, Paul L., 554
OPEC [Organization of Oil Producing Countries], 17, 166
Oregon Plant Closure Organizing Committee, 411
O'Reilly, James T., 464

Ornstein, Norman, 250
OSHA. *See* Occupational Safety and Health Administration.
O'Toole, James, 367

Pace, Eric, 25
Pacific Telesis, 459
Pacific Gas & Electric, 357
Packard, Vance, 265-266, 288
Palmieri, Victor H., 544
Paluszek, John L., 56
Pantry Pride, 519
Park (Korean president), 172
Parks, Rosa, 467
Parrish, Michael, 545
Parsons, Talcott, 504
Partridge, Jack W., 616
Pastin, Mark, 142, 143, 158
Patten, D. Kenneth, 401-402
Paulson, Morton C., 25
Payton, Robert L., 381, 413
PBS. *See* Public Broadcasting System.
Peale, Norman Vincent, 147, 158
Pearl, Daniel, 310
Peat, Marwick, Mitchell, & Co., 537
Pel, Donald A., 516
Pennsylvania Environmental Protection Division, 76
Pennsylvanians Against Smokestack Emissions (PASE), 77
Pentagon, 3, 85
PepsiCo, 105, 374, 516
Pergue, Frank, 269
Perritt, Harry H., Jr., 500
Pertschuk, Michael, 258, 281-282
Peters, Charles, 437
Peters, Thomas J.,, 292, 308, 311, 572
Petit, Thanes A., 38, 57
Pets for People, 397
Petzke, Dianne, 288
Phillip Morris, 393, 516
Phillips, Don, 249
Phillips, Julien R., 572
Phillips Petroleum, 178
Pickens, T. Boone, 518, 532
Pickering, J. F., 289
Pillsbury Company, 253
Pinedo, Anna, 705

Pinkston, Tammie S., 624, 626, 696
Pitney Bowes, 53
Pitts, Robert A., 572
Pizza Hut, 374
Poe, Randall, 463, 464
Polaroid, 358, 428
Pontius, H. Jackson, 119
Porter, D., 368
Posner, Barry Z., 135, 137, 138
Post Center, C. W., 254
Post, James E., 41, 42, 57, 69, 187, 605, 607, 616
Postel, S., 335, 336, 367
Potts, Mark, 289
Pound, Edward T., 119
Pouton, A., 340, 367
Power, Christopher, 545
Powers, Charles, 114, 116, 119
PPG Industries, 586, 614
Preston, Lee E., 57, 620, 626
Price, Robert M., 642, 645
Price, Tom, 250
Prime Computer, 511
"PrimeTime Live," 91
Procter & Gamble (P & G), 4, 17, 77, 178, 277, 278, 549, 593, 597
Project SMART (Stop Marketing Alcohol on Radio and Television), 271
Prokesch, Steven E., 544
Public Affairs Council, 233, 249, 591, 603, 605, 607, 608
Public Broadcasting System (PBS), 393
Public Citizen, 238, 239
Public Relations Society, 15, 113
Pullman, Illinois, 29
Purcell, Theodore, 153, 158, 501

Quaker Oats, 278
Quebec Logging Association, 104
Queenan, Joe, 544

Rackleff, R. B., 335
Radelet, Ana, 432, 437
Ralston Purina, 397
Raspberry, William, 492-493, 502
Rath Packing Co., 404

Name Index

Rating America's Corporate Conscience, 49
Rawls, John, 128, 134, 157
RCA, 520
Reagan, Ronald, 55, 177, 191, 216, 232, 301, 382, 449, 454, 476
Reagan, Sydney C., 647
Real Estate Board of New York, 401
Redburn, F. Stevens, 414
Reebok, 397, 516
Reed, O. Lee, 268, 288, 367, 502
Reibstein, Larry, 437, 464
Reich, Robert, 199, 220, 221
Reilly, William, 350
Remington, 17
Renew America, 347, 348, 357, 367
Reuter, Peter, 308, 311
Revlon, 519
Rexnord, 181
Rich, B. M., 367
Richards, Bill, 545
Richman, B., 335
Richman, Barry, 175, 187
R. J. Reynolds, 276
R. J. R. Nabisco, 517
Robins, A. H., 3, 295
Robinson, James, 247
Robinson, Richard D., 161, 167, 187, 188
Rockefeller, John D., III, 301, 382, 415
Rogman, Alan M., 187
Rolls-Royce, 201
Ronald McDonald Houses, 380, 395
Rose, R. A., 367
Rosebush, James, 396, 414
Rosen, Cary, 414
Rosenthal, Benjamin, 406
Ross, Steven J., 516
Ross Laboratories, 78
Rothfelder, Jeffery, 463
Rothman, Stanley, 25
Rowan, Roy, 157
Rude, Robert, 591, 599
Rudolph, Barbara, 464
Rupp, William T., 629, 683
Russel, George, 544
Ryans, John C., Jr., 187

Sabato, Larry, 241, 249
Saddler, Jeanne, 288, 368

Sagedy, Andria, 249
Samuelson, Robert J., 288
Santa Clara County Transportation Agency, 495
Sanyo, 359
Sara Lee, 516
Savage, Grant T., 78, 79, 83
Savannah Visitors Center, 391
Savings and Loan Association, 219
Scan, 587
Scarpello, Vida, 479, 734
Schachter, Victor, 501
Schellhardt, Timothy D., 545
Schiller, Zachary, 464
Schendel, 556
Schmidt, Warren H., 135, 137, 138
Schmiedeskamp, Jay, 310
Schmitt, Richard B., 545
Schroeder, Michael, 414
Schwadel, Francine, 311
Schwartz, Donald, 542, 545, 546
S. C. Johnson & Sons, 592
SCM Corporation, 393
Scott, Ruth K., 249
Scott Paper, 397
Scoville Manufacturing, 404
Sculley, John, 516
Sculnick, Michael W., 437
Seager, J., 335
Sears, 4, 85, 293, 529, 587
Securities and Exchange Commission (SEC), 102, 176, 205, 521, 525, 532, 533, 621
Seelye, Alfred L., 220
Seligman, Daniel, 57, 490, 501
Seligman, Joel, 546
Seminole Indians, 657
Sethi, S. Prakash, 40, 42, 57, 242, 246, 249, 250
Seventh Generation, 352
Shad, John, 621
Shapiro, Irving, 232, 233
Shaw, William, 263, 288
Shayon, Diane R., 395
Sheffet, Mary Jane, 311
Shepro, Richard W., 545
Shribman, David, 250
Shrivastava, Paul, 357, 368, 599
Siegel, Martin, 521
Sierra Club, 350, 351
Simison, Robert L., 414, 464
Simon, J. L., 336
Simon, (Senator) Paul, 166, 187
Simon, Robert, 501

Simon, Ruth, 544
Simon, Stephanie, 311
Sitomer, Curtis J., 463
"60 Minutes," 12, 91
Smith, Adam, 29, 116
Smith, Lee, 501
Snow, C., 572
Social Investment Forum, 54
Social Security Service, 441
Sodeman, William A., 637
Soeken, Donald, 431
Sokolof, Phil, 259
Soloman, Jolie, 463
Sonat, 374
Sony, 161
Southland Corporation, 102
Sowell, Thomas, 492
S & P, 55, 500
Sperry Rand, 404
Spiegel, David R., 464
Sprint, 266
Stalmaker, Armand, 514
Standard Oil Company, 192
Standard Oil of California, 610
Stanford Business School, 154
Stanford University, 53
Starik, Mark, 313, 338, 714, 749
Star-Kist Foods, 593
Starling, Grover, 414
Staroba, K., 368
Staudohar, Paul D., 414
Stead, Jean Garner, 158
Stead, W. Edward, 158
Steiger, Janet D., 283
Stem, Peter M., 463
Steiner, George A., 111, 119, 220, 377, 413, 573
Stephens, Carroll, 157
Stepp, Laura Sessions, 572
Sterne, D., 367
Sternberg, Sam, 388, 413
Sternberg, William, 157
Stewart, James B., 187, 544
Stone, Christopher D., 57
Stroup, Margaret, 589
Strout, Jeff, 414
Strub, Sean O'Brian, 57
Sturdivant, Frederick, 513, 544
Sullivan, Leon, 177, 178, 531
Sullivan, Louis, 275-276
Sun Company, 541
Sun Oil Company, 235
SunPAC, 235
Susser, Peter, 469

Swasy, Alecia, 289
Swift, Al, 242

Tainer, Lauren, 545
Tanaka, Kakuei, 174
Tarmaking, Bob, 500
Tate, 408
Taylor, Jerry, 289
Temporary National Economic Committee, 564
Tennessee Valley Authority (TVA), 201, 203
Texaco, 518, 593
Texas Instruments, 374, 458
Texas Utilities Electric Co., 102, 431
Thayer, Frederick C., 221
Therrien, Lois, 464
Thomas, Clarence, 476-478, 485, 489
Thomas, Evan, 249
Thompson, A., 367
3M Corporation, 343, 353, 356-357, 365
Three Mile Island, 534
Tilles, Seymour, 572
Tilson, Donn, 395, 414
Time Warner, 516, 529
Tobacco Institute, 228, 457
Toffler, Alvin, 622, 626
Tolba, M. K., 336
Tolchin, Martin, 288, 289
Tolchin, Susan J., 288, 289
Toth, Robert, 414
Toyota, 161
Transamerica, 459
Trans Union Corporation, 525, 537
Tri Star airplanes, 174
Trost, Cathy, 501
Trowbridge, Alexander, 231-232
Troy, Kathryn, 413
Trump, Donald, 17
Tufts New England Medical Center, 446
Tulloch, Henry W., 149
Turner, Ted, 17
TVA. *See* Tennessee Valley Authority.
"20/20," 12, 91
Tylenol, 78

UAL, 516
UAW. *See* United Auto Workers.
Udwadia, Firdaus, 599
U-Haul International, 458
Ullman, Arieh, 245, 250
UNICEF, 169
Union Carbide, 3, 77, 168-169, 170-172, 297, 370, 451, 520, 593
Uniroyal, 260
Unsell, Lloyd, 236, 249
United Auto Workers (UAW), 139
United Church of Christ, 539
United Fruit Company, 163
United Methodists, 534
United Nations (U.N.), 69, 181
United Nations Environment Programme (UNEP), 319, 335, 348-349, 354, 367
United Negro College Fund, 387
United Presbyterian Church, 534
United Shareholders Association (USA), 532, 533
U.S. Brewers Association, 273, 275
U.S. Census Bureau, 418
U.S. Constitution, 15
U.S. Council on Environmental Quality (CEQ), 323
U.S. Department of Commerce, 85, 384
U.S. Department of Education, 372
U.S. Government Printing Office, 203
U.S. Interior Department, 347
U.S. Justice Department, 459, 475, 476, 500
U.S. Postal Service, 202, 203
U.S. Senate Government Affairs Committee, 204
U.S. Supreme Court, 15, 455, 459, 478, 487, 488, 489
 and affirmative action, 493-499
U.S. Surgical, 516
United Technologies, 374
United Way, 390, 397
Upjohn, 435
Urban League, 391
Urofsky, Melvin I., 502
USG Corporation, 457
Usinor Sacilor S.A., 359

U.S. News & World Report, 85, 418, 621
USX Corporation, 454

Valdez, Exxon, 549. *See also* Exxon.
Vandell, Kerry D., 647
Velasquez, Manuel C., 157
Vesper International, 184, 185
Vianna, Nichols J., 713
Vicker, Ray, 119
Victor, Bart, 157
Viner Brothers, 404
Virginia Water Control Board, 409
Vlasic, 299
Vogel, David, 114, 116, 119
Volvo, 264
Votaw, Dow, 505, 544

Wagley, Robert Q., 187
Wagner, Barbara, 463
Wagner, Richard, 39, 149
Waldholz, Michael, 463
Waldman, Steven, 464
Waldman, Peter, 311
Waldron, Hicks B., 529
Walmart, 17, 293
Walt Disney, 518
Walter, Ingo, 172, 187
Walters, Kenneth D., 434, 438, 542, 545
Warner, Joan, 57
Warren, Melinda, 221
Wartick, Steven L., 47, 48, 57, 519, 544, 591, 599
Wartzman, Rick, 158
Waste Management, Inc., 354, 516
Watergate, 91, 137
Waterman, Richard, 240
Waterman, Robert H., 308, 311, 572
Wayne, Leslie, 249, 545
Ways, Max, 90
Weatherhead, Leslie, 99
Weber, Brian, 493
Wedtech fraud, 140-141
Weidenbaum, Murray l., 221, 510, 524, 544
Weight Watchers, 305

Weihenmayer, Edwin, 446
Weirton Steel, 404-405, 407
Weiss, Gary, 544
Weisskopf, M., 367
Weissman, George, 393
Welling, Brentan, 289
Werhane, Patricia, 437, 440-442, 463
Wernham, Roy, 599
West, Nedra, 25
Westin, Alan, 433, 437, 458
Whalen, Bill, 250
White, Eileen, 311
Whitehead, Carlton J., 79, 83
Whitley, J. P., 335
WHO (World Health Organization), 78, 169, 170
Whyte, William H., 419
Wildavsky, Ben, 289
Wilderness Society, 77
Wiley, Harvey W., 303
Wilkerson, Isabel, 501
Williams, Marci Jo, 414

Williams, Oliver, 187
Williams, Walter, 501
Wilson, Graham K., 221
Wilson, Ian, 41, 42, 57, 360, 568, 573
Wilson, Marilyn, 249
Winn, Marie, 288
Winslow, Ron, 119
Witkins, Gordon, 464
Wohler, Todd D., 667
Wolf, Stephen M., 516
Wolverine, 404
Women Against Pornography, 268-269
Wood, Donna J., 47, 48, 57
Work, Clemens P., 311
Working Group on Corporate Governance, 530
World Bank, 349
World Health Organization (WHO), 78, 169, 170
World Resources Institute, 350

World Wildlife Fund, 350
Worrell, Dan l., 158

Xerox, 53, 292, 426-427, 585

Yankelovich, Skelly, and White (YSW), 582, 583
YMCA, 29, 391
Yoffie, David, 246, 247, 249, 250
Young, James S., 303

Zeithami, Carl, 245
Zenke, Ron, 158

SUBJECT INDEX

absolute liability, 298
accommodation strategy, 41
accountability principle, 132
accelerationists, 199
acid rain, 326. *See also* air pollution.
acquisitions, 518-519
acute crisis stage, 594
ADA. *See* Americans with Disabilities Act.
advertising, 262-278
affirmative action, 469, 489-499. *See also* discrimination, Title VII.
age discrimination, 470, 473-475, 487
Age Discrimination in Employment Act, 470, 473, 474, 475
Agent Orange, 297
AIDS, 3, 15, 458-462
airline industry, 216
air pollution, 325-326. *See also* Clean Air Act.
Alar, 260, 294, 303
alcohol advertising, 271-275
ambiguity, tolerance of, 115
American Psychological Association, 445
Americans with Disabilities Act (ADA), 218, 472
Amoco, 328
amoral management, 100, 104, 105, 106-107,139
apartheid, 54, 105, 176-180. *See also* South Africa.
Army contracts, 140-141
asbestos, 171
Asian-Americans, 482
Asians, 469, 481-482
assessing stakeholder environment, 567
auditing roles, 525-526, 528
AUDIT software, 449
authority, hierarchy of corporate, 113, 506-509
Automobile Workers v. Johnson Controls, Inc., 455
autonomous moral development, 110

balance-of-payments deficit, 161
Bendectin, 297
Beshada v. Johns Manville Corporation, 298
BFOQ (bona fide occupational qualification), 470
Bhopal, India, 3, 168-169, 173, 382. *See also* Union Carbide.
Bill of Rights, 15
biological diversity, 325
black underclass, 480-481. *See also* civil rights, discrimination, ghetto poverty.
"bottom line." *See* profitability, profits.
"bottom-line" mentality, 139
boards of directors, 507
  improving, 522-528
  ineffective, 509-515
bona fide occupational qualification (BFOQ), 470
bottle-feeding, 67, 169-170. *See also* Nestlé
Bowen social audit, 565
breach of good faith, 423
bribery, 168, 172-176
bubble concept, 343
bus boycott, 467
Bush administration, 257
business
  and society, 4, 38-39
  development, 365-366
  environmentalism, 356-365
  exposure to social environment, 611-612
  public image of, 11-14
  stake in community, 376
  ethics, 22, 85, 86, 89, 90, 92-93
  offices, 153
  training, 121

candor, 144
Capital Cities-ABC, 283
Carroll's corporate social performance model, 46, 47, 57, 119, 157, 182, 188, 400, 403, 413, 414, 566, 572
categorical imperative, 129

cause-related marketing, 397-398
CEO compensation, 515-517
CERCLA (Comprehensive Environmental Response, Compensation and Liability Act of 1980), 345
chain saw safety, 103-104
Challenger, 431
Chapter 11 bankruptcy, 516, 593
"Chelsea" beer, 46
chemicals, handling, 451-453. *See also* safety, toxic substances.
Chernobyl meltdown, 328
children and advertising, 269-270. *See also* kid-vid.
choice, right to, 254
chronic crisis stage, 595
church activism, 531
cigarette ads, 275-276
cigarettes, 105, 276, 456-458
Circus Fun Cereal, 269
Citrus Hill juice, 277
City of Richmond v. J. A. Crosen 1989, 496
civil rights, 15, 176. *See also* Title VII.
  and social benefits, 482
  movement, 466-469
Civil Rights Act, 94, 178, 193, 208, 455, 466, 467, 468, 475-476, 493. *See also* Title VII.
Civil War, 29
claim, defined, 60
classical economic model, 29
Clayton Antitrust Act, 192
Clean Air Act, 217, 218, 257, 343, 344
Clean Water Act, 257, 344
closing plants (close-downs), 405-408
  and decision factors, 410-411
  impact on community, 399-401
coalition building, 244-245
Code of Conduct for Transnational Corporations, 181
codes of ethics, 148-150, 151
  global, 180-182
collaborative problem solving, 611
collectivistic ethic of government, 194
commitment to excellence, 132
common sense (test), 133

779

communicating ethics codes, 151-152
community
  action programs, 376
  impact analysis, 406
  involvement, 29, 370-372, 373, 374-401
  knowledge of, 376-377
  needs assessment, 378-379
  programs, selecting, 377
  projects, monitoring, 380
  stakeholders and job losses, 399-401
Community Chest movements, 30, 390
comparable worth policy, 483-484
comparison advertising, 266-267
compensation committee, 526
compensatory justice, 127-128, 491
competition, excessive, 207
Comprehensive Anti-Apartheid Act, 178
computer surveillance, 418, 449. *See also* employee rights movement.
concern-for-others principle, 132
confidentiality, 144
conformance of product, 293
conformity, 113
conscience, 93
consent decree, 521
consequences of decisions, 145
consumer affairs offices, 306-308
consumerism, 254-256, 260
consumer rights, 253-254
Consumer Product Safety Act of 1972, 193, 300
conventional approach to ethics, 93-94, 129
conventional level of moral development, 108-109
Corporate Democracy Act, 406, 407
corporate
  due process, 425
  ethics. *See* business ethics.
  governance, 506, 620
  legitimacy, 163
  philanthropy, 383-390
  public affairs, 601, 602-604
  public policy, 549-551
corporate social performance models, 46, 48
corporate social responsibility (CSR), 41
Costa Rica wilderness reserves, 346

Crisco corn oil, 278
crisis management, 593-598
Critical Technologies Act of 1991, 199
criticism/response cycle, 10
CSR. *See* corporate social responsibility.
culture, 112, 160, 165. *See also* diversity in ethics, MNCs.
custom, ethical, 116
commerce clause of U.S. Constitution, 205
commercials (TV), 13, 14. *See also* advertising.

Daisy shaver, 268-269
Dakota cigarettes, 276
Dalkon shield, 3, 295
"Dallas," 12, 94
DDT, 171, 328
decentralization, 7
Declaration of Independence, 126
defense strategy, 41
deforestation, 324
Deficit Reduction Act, 520
Delaney Amendment, 304
Delphi technique, 587
democratization of Congress, 224
deregulation, 166, 213-216
DES, 298
descriptive ethics, 92-93, 97. *See also* ethics.
Die Hard Batteries, 5
directing role of board, 528
disagreement, tolerance of, 115
disciplining ethics code violators, 152-153
disclosure rule, 129, 134
discretionary responsibilities, 33-34
discrimination, 105, 466-468, 478-479
  federal law and, 469-478
  right to freedom from, 183
disinvestment, 177. *See also* apartheid, South Africa.
disparate treatment and impact, 478-479
dissidence, acts of, 419
distributive justice, 126, 127
diversity in ethics, 111
doctrine of the mean, 112

Dominant Social Paradigm (DSP), 341
Domini Social Index (DSI), 55
Draize test, 539
Drug-Free Workplace Act of 1988, 448
drugs, illegal, 215-216
Drug Price Competition and Patent Restoration Act, 304
drug testing, 445-448. *See also* employee rights movement, Food and Drug Act.
due process, 424-425

EAP. *See* Employee Assistance Programs.
economic
  inequality, 467
  regulation, 207-209
  responsibilities, 32, 76
Ecotopia, 332
educational opportunity, 183, 466. *See also* discrimination.
egalitarian movement, 126. *See also* rights, rights movement.
EIS, 183. *See* environmental impact statement, ethical impact statement.
Electronic Communications Privacy Act, 449
"electronic sweatshop," 449
Emergency Planning and Community Right-to-Know Act of 1986, 345
Employee Assistance Programs (EAPs), 448
employee
  constitutionalism, 425
  ownership, 404-405
  rights movement, 417, 440-441
Employee Polygraph Protection Act of 1988, 442
employees, 419, 507
employment-at-will doctrine, 421-422
Endangered Species Act, 346, 347
ends-means conflicts, 126
energy inefficiency, 327
enterprise-level strategy, 552, 601
environment and global warming, 320-321

environmental
  analysis, 565-568
  concerns, 313-316
  cost-benefit analysis, 361
  crisis, 329-332
  ethics, 340-342
  issues, responsibility for, 338
  risk management, 362-363
environmental impact statements (EISs), 183, 342
environmentalism, business, 356-365
Equal Credit Opportunity Act, 280, 281
Equal Employment Opportunity Act of 1972, 470
equal opportunity, 490. *See also* Title VII.
Equal Pay Act of 1963, 470, 473, 474, 483
Essence magazine, 760
ethical
  custom, 116
  decision making, 125-126, 144, 146
  diversity, 111
  issues and social change, 91
  judgments, 95
  leadership, 115-116, 139, 141-142
  problems and media, 91
  responsibilities, 33
  role models, 124, 528
  tests, 132-133, 147
ethical impact statements (EISs), 183
ethics, 3, 20-21, 22, 92, 94-95, 97
  and global strategy, 182
  and strategic management, 551
  in multinational environment, 168
ethics advocate role, 153
ethics codes, 148-150, 151
ethics screen, 145-146
European reconstruction, 161
executive loan programs, 374-375
Executive Order 11246, 489, 494
Executive Order 12044, 217
expropriation of business, 164
external affairs. *See* public affairs.
external sources of manager's values, 109, 111
external stakeholders, 22
Exxon *Valdez*, 75, 328, 354

Fair Credit Reporting Act, 280, 281
Fair Debt Collection Practices Act, 280, 281
fairness principle, 131
Fair Packaging and Labeling Act of 1966, 304
fair value, 293
federal chartering, 541-543
Federal Election Campaign Act (FECA), 234, 235
Federal Packaging and Labeling Act of 1967, 280
Federal Water Polution Control Act. *See* Clean Water Act.
fetal health, 455
fidelity as principle, 144
fixed exchange rate, 161
Food and Drug Act, 303
Food, Drug and Cosmetics Act of 1938, 304
forecasting, 567-568
Foreign Corrupt Practices Act (FCPA), 174-176
formal policies, inadequate, 140
Fortune magazine rankings, 49, 50, 149, 278, 382, 442, 498, 594, 603
"Frank and Ernest," 73
freedom for business, 39
Freedom of Information Act, 257
freedom of speech and association, 183, 434
Frito Corn Chips, 105
Full Employment Act, 193
functional-level strategy, 552

gag (test), 134
Gallup poll, 217, 291, 456
"gap analysis," 99
GATT, 353
gender discrimination. *See* sex discrimination.
generic stakeholder group, 67
German marks, 161
ghetto poverty, 467. *See also* blacks, discrimination.
Ghostbusters, 269

glass ceiling, 482-483. *See also* Title VII, women.
global
  business, 165-168
  ethics, 180, 182
  markets, 162
  philanthropy, 397-398
  strategy, 182
  warming, 320-321
goal formulation, 559
golden parachutes, 519-520
Golden Rule, 112, 128-129, 134
Golden Rule of Politics, 234
"The Gospel of Wealth" (Andrew Carnegie), 30
government
  and business, 194-196, 197-198
  and environment, 347-348
  as stakeholder, 202
governments of host countries, 166
grassroots lobbying, 228-229
grease payments, 174-176. *See also* bribery.
The Green Consumer, 352
"green" consumers, 351-352
Green Lights program, 358
greenmail, 518-519
Green Point Average (GPA), 313
"The Green Report II," 278
Gresham's Law, 542
grievance procedures, 426. *See also* Title VII.
Griggs V. Duke Power Company, 478
Group Areas Act, 178
group immorality, 126
growth years, 161

Harris poll, 459
Hazard Communication Standard, 452
hazardous chemicals, 451-453. *See also* chemicals, handling, toxic substances, toxic wastes.
HCCPD, 707
hearing, right to a, 254
hedonistic ethic, 129
health
  and advertising, 277-278
  and ozone depletion, 320
  and welfare giving, 390

in workplace. *See* fetal health, safety.
  right to, 456-462
high ethics, principles of, 143
"high-tech anxiety," 418
Hispanics, 469
Honduras, 163
honesty principle, 131
honesty tests, 444-445
host countries, 163, 165. *See also* LDCs, MNCs.
hostile LDCs, 164
hostile work environment, 484. *See also* Title VII.
human resource management in MNCs, 167
human rights and nature, 339
Hush Puppies, 404

image, business, 376. *See also* public affairs.
immoral management, 102-103
impact of MNC products, 167
income gap, 516
indigenization laws, 164
individual/adversarial strategy, 611
individualistic ethic of business, 194-196
industry environment, 567
industry-level ethical challenges, 123-124
industrial policy of government, 198-199, 200-202
inequality. *See* discrimination, Title VII.
infant formula, 67, 76, 105, 169-170. *See also* bottle-feeding, Nestlé
information, right to, 253-254, 452.
inside directors, 507, 524
insider trading, 520-522
interest groups, 5. *See also* PACs, stakeholders.
internal stockholders, 23
international business ethics, 104-105, 124, 160, 180-182. *See also* MNCs.
intuition ethic, 129
Inventory of Ethical Issues in Business, 86, 87, 88

investments in social consciousness, 54-55. *See also* disinvestments.
Iron Law of Responsibility, 18
issues analysis, 585
issues management, 47
  process, 578-579, 581
  approaches to, 575-576
  in practice, 591-592

Japanese reconstruction, 161
job losses, 399-401. *See also* closings, termination.
Johnson v. Transportation Agency, Santa Clara County, California, 495-496
Johnson's Wax, 181
justice, as a principle, 127-128

Kellogg's All-Bran, 277
kid-vid, 270-274, 281. *See also* advertising.
Kreps audit, 564

labeling hazardous contents, 453
labor-creating technology, 164
Land Acts, 178
land degradation, 324
law-and-order morality, 109-110
law and corporations, 19, 95, 132. *See also* individual laws and legal cases.
layoffs, 494. *See also* closings.
LBOs (leveraged buyouts), 518
LDCs (less developed countries), 67, 163
  and infant formula, 169. *See also* Nestlé
  and pesticides, 171
  ethical problems in, 168, 170
leadership, 132, 141
Least Cost Utility Planning, 351
legal model, 29, 32-33, 41
legal system, 110-113
legality standard of ethics, 139

Legislative Reorganization Act, 229
legitimacy, 504-506, 528
  of stockholders, 71, 74
less-developed countries. *See* LDCs.
leveraged buyouts (LBOs), 518
Levi Strauss Aspirations Statement, 142-143
liability, 193, 279-280, 297-299
lie detectors, 442-445
limited warranty, 279
Listerine, 305
literacy programs, 372-373, 374
litigation increase, 295-296
loan guarantees, 203
lobbying, 227-234. *See also* interest groups, PACs.
Local 28, Sheetmetal Workers International Association v. EEOC, 495
Local 93, International Association of Firefighters v. City of Cleveland, 495
losing (sunset) industries, 199
Love Canal, 68-70
loyalty, 113, 131
  to employers, 418-419
Lysol, 261

macroenvironment, 6, 567
macro level of corporate power, 17
Magnuson-Moss Warranty Act of 1975, 275, 282
Maine Protection, Research and Sanctuaries Act of 1972, 344
making something public (test), 133
Malcolm Baldridge National Quality Award, 292
management grievance committee, 426
managerial view of the firm, 61, 63
mark (German), 161
market ethic, 139
market-oriented MNCs, 164
market share liability, 298
Martin v. Wilkes, 496
material safety data sheets (MSDSs), 452
McKinsey 7S framework, 363, 365, 561
means-ends ethic, 130

Memphis Fire Department v. Shotts, 494
mergers, 518-519
Meritor Savings Bank v. Vinson, 485
Mexican-Americans, 105
Michigan Whistle-Blowers Protection Act of 1981, 433
micro level, 17
"milk nurses," 169
Minnesota and pay equity, 483-484
MNCs (multinational corporations), 163-164
  and double standards
  and ethics abroad, 183-184, 185
MNC-host country challenges, 165
MNC suspensions, 182-183
monitoring
  employees, 448-449
  environment, 567-568
mobility of employees, 419
modifying MNC products, 167
money making as criterion, 101-102
monopoly, 192
Montreal Protocol, 348, 351
Motor Vehicle Safety Act, 591
moral
  climate, 115, 135, 137
  consciousness, 142
  development research, 108-111
  disagreement, 115
  evaluation, 115
  imagination, 114
  judgment, elements of, 117
  management, 98, 100, 102-104, 107
  obligation, 99-100, 116
  right, 60
MSDSs. *See* material safety data sheets.
multifiduciary approach, 62, 64-65
multinational corporations. *See* MNCs.
multinational perspective, 163, 623-624
multistakeholder consultation, 184
murder charges, 452

National Environmental Policy Act (NEPA), 342
National Pollutant Discharge Elimination System, 344

National Traffic Auto Safety Act, 591
"natural law," 129
natural monopolies, 205
negative externalities, 205-206, 211
NEPA. *See* National Environmental Policy Act.
New Environmental Paradigm (NEP), 341
New Breed, 265
new international order, 162. *See also* global business, MNCs.
news shows, 12
Niagara Falls, New York, 68
NIMBY problem, 338-339
900 telephone numbers, 283
noise pollution, 328-329
nominating committee, 526
nonregulatory government influence, 198
normative ethics, 93
Norris-LaGuardia Act, 193
North American Free Trade Agreement, 353
Northern spotted owl, 347

Occupational Safety and Health Act of 1970, 193
Oekogenda (Eco-Agenda), 359
oil crisis, 161, 207
Olympics, 380
ombudsperson, 426-427
"one's best self" test, 133
open-door management policy, 426
organizational ethics, 621-622
organizational structure in MNCs, 167
organization-level ethical challenges, 123
outplacement, 408
ownership as stakeholder claim, 74
ozone depletion, 320

P.A. *See* Public Affairs.
PACs (political action committees), 234-243, 622
passive nondiscrimination, 490

PCBs (polychlorinated biphenyls), 418
peer review, 427
performance of product, 293
permanent employees, 423
personal ethics, 121-123, 124-125, 145
Persian Gulf War, 11
phaseouts versus closings, 408-409
philanthropy, 29, 33-34, 381, 383-390
  strategic, 394-398
  to arts and culture, 392-393
  to health and welfare, 390-391
  to universities, 389-390
philosophical conflict in MNCs, 164
philosophy as source of values, 112
philosophy of entitlement, 15
physical movement, right to, 183
Pintos, 295, 549
planning-oriented countries, 164
plant closings, 399-401, 405-408, 409
Plax, 305
pluralism, 7, 8, 111
political action committees (PACs), 234-243, 622
political
  economy, 567
  environment, 6, 223-226
  involvement of business, 226-227
  participation, right to, 183
  splits, 12
  vulnerability of MNCs, 167
Polycal, 262
polychlorinated biphenyls (PCBs), 418
polygraph tests, 442-445
poison pill, 519
Population Registration Act, 178
postconventional moral development, 110
post-World War II reconstruction, 161
power and respectability, 16, 18-19
poverty in ghettos, 180, 469
P.R. *See* public relations.
preconventional moral development, 108
preferential treatment, 490. *See also* Title VII.
Pregnancy Discrimination Act, 470, 487
prescriptive ethics, 98-99

prime-time TV, 72
principles approach to ethics, 110, 125-126, 147
principle of justice, 126-128
principle of justice (Rawls), 134
principle of rights, 126
Privacy Act of 1974, 441
privacy, 450-451
　and AIDS, 461-462
　invasion of, 413
　on the job, 448-449
　planning, 450, 451
　right to, 440
privacy impact statement, 450
privatization, 201-202
pro-action strategy, 39-41
probability-impact matrix, 571, 586
procedural justice, 128
prodromal crisis stage, 594
production view of the firm, 61, 63
product liability reform, 299
product safety and local conditions, 171. *See also* health, safety.
professional ethics, 123-124, 130, 418-419
profitability, 101-102, 113-114, 139
　and amorality, 106-107
profits, excess, 207
profits repatriation limits, 164
"Project Hometown America," 397
promise-keeping, 131, 420
property, right to, 183
prosecuting unsafe managers, 452
protected groups, 466. *See also* Title VII.
proxy machinery, 509
public affairs (P.A.), 603
　in each manager's job, 613
　strategy, 601
　success record, 615
　international program of, 609
public-government relationship, 197
Public Health Service Act, 304
public issues committee, 527
publics, multiple, 9. *See also* stakeholders.
public opinion polls, 86-87
public policy, corporate, 549-551
public policy exceptions (to employment at will), 422
public relations approach, 41, 603

punishment and reward morality, 108
purified idea (test), 134
Pyramid of Corporate Social Responsibility (CSR), 34-35

quid pro quo harassment, 484. *See also* Title VII.
quota system, 490. *See also* Title VII.

racial inequality, 391, 466-468, 480-481. *See also* Title VII.
radon, 328-329
Railway Labor Act, 193
Rapid Shave, 264
reaction strategy, 41
Reagan administration, 2, 217, 256, 257, 259, 260, 270, 494, 498
redesigning MNC products, 167
Regents of the University of California v. Bakke, 493
regulatory federal agencies, 210-211
regulation, 198, 204-213
Rehabilitation Act of 1973, 459
religious discrimination, 489
religious values, 111-112
relocation, 408
Rely tampons, 77, 549, 597
replacement industry, 410
reproductive health, 455. *See also* fetal health, Title VII.
reputation-and-morale principle, 132
Research Conservation and Recovery Act, 345
respect-for-others principle,132
responsiveness, 40
Responsible Care program, 358
responsibility of business, 40, 143
　for shutdowns, 401-404
revelation ethic, 130
reverse discrimination, 491. *See also* Title VII.
rights, 60, 126-127. *See also* Civil Rights Act.
　not to be fired without just cause, 421

　fundamental international, 183-184
rights movement, 15
right-to-know laws, 452
risk arbitrage, 521
Roper Survey, 313
rubber-stamp boards, 513

safety issues, 170-171, 183, 253, 294-295, 451-455. *See also* health, OSHA.
Savings and Loan (S & L) scandal, 3, 85-86
Securities Act of 1933, 193
self-interest, business, 376
self-regulation of advertising, 284-286
selling versus closing, 404
separation of ownership and control, 507-509
7S framework, 562
sex discrimination, 482-488. *See also* Title VII.
sexual harassment, 94, 484-487. *See also* Title VII.
shareholders, 507, 531-532
Sherman Antitrust Act, 192
shutdowns, 399-401. *See also* closings, layoffs..
Slimer, 269
smoking in the workplace, 456-458
Snicker bars, 269
social
　audit, 562, 564
　contract, 19-20, 28, 110
　ethics, 3
　environment, 6, 11-17, 19
　goals of regulation, 206-207
　involvement, selecting, 44
　problems, 5, 15, 21
　regulation, 208-209
social responsibility, 27-32. *See also* corporate ethics.
　and functional performance, 53-54
　investing, 54-55
　and privacy, 451
　arguments regarding, 37-38, 38-39
societal level of ethical challenges, 124, 126
sociopolitical forecasting, 568
soft drink product chart, 51

Solid Waste Disposal Act of 1965, 344
South Africa, 3, 50, 54, 55, 105, 168, 176-180, 521, 532, 533, 534, 536
special interest groups 9, 224. *See also* stakeholders
species interaction, 315
serviceability of product, 293
stakeholder
  issues, 45, 47, 567
  management, 20-21, 77-78, 80
  view of the firm, 61-62, 65, 66
stakeholders, 22, 59, 60, 165
  types of, 78-79
stakes, types of, 60, 61, 74
stockholders, 59. *See also* shareholders.
strategic
  approach, 62, 64
  control, 562
  environmental management, 363-365
  movement, 550, 622-623
  philanthropy, 394-398
strategy
  education, 561
  formulation, 559-561
  implementation, 561-562
strict liability, 297-299
subsistence, right to, 183
subliminal advertising, 265-266
Sudafed, 299
Sullivan Principles, 177. *See also* disinvestment.
Summeralls, 262
Superfund law, 71, 345
superior's influence, 136-139
superminority, 481-482
suspension of business, 182-183. *See also* closings, MNCs, shutdowns.
Syntex, 459

takeovers, 518-519
Tang, 397
task environment, 567
television, 11-14
technological environment, 6
technological hazards, 418
Teenage Mutant Ninja Turtles, 269

terminations, 420-424. *See also* employee rights movement.
Three Mile Island, 328
"third sector," 382
Third World, 67, 76, 167, 170, 325. *See also* LDCs.
Time magazine, 489
Title VII (Civil Rights Act), 94, 469-470, 471, 472, 475, 476, 478, 480, 485, 487, 488, 489, 491. *See also* affirmative action, equal opportunity.
Tyson Chick'n Quick, 262
tort law, 293-299
torture, right to freedom from, 183
toxic shock syndrome, 75
toxic substances, 328
toxic wastes, 69-71, 345
trade association lobbying, 230-234
transfer payments, 202, 408
transitional economy, 160
trend information service, 582
trial, right to fair, 183
trucking industry, 215-216
trust, organization, corporate, 192
Truth in Lending Act, 280, 281
Tylenol, 298, 299, 549

UAW v. Johnson Controls, Inc., 487
UDAG grant, 717
umbrella organizations, 227, 230-233
unemployment and discrimination, 466, 467
unethical behavior, 137-138
universal ethical principle, 110
Uptown cigarettes, 276
U.S. dollar value, 161
utilitarianism, 125-126, 130

Valdez principles, 354, 355, 358
value judgments, 95-96, 111-114
ventilation (test), 133
Viadent, 305
Vietnam Era Veterans Readjustment Assistance Act of 1974, 470
Vietnam War, 161, 225

voluntary responsibilities, 33-34
voter participation, 225

Wagner Act, 193
Wall Street (movie), 365, 520
WARN. *See* Worker Adjustment and Retraining Notification Act.
Warranty Act of 1975, 193
warranties, 279-280
Wartick and Cochran's corporate social performance model, 48
wastes, solid and hazardous, 321-323. *See also* toxic wastes.
water environments, 323-324. *See also* Clean Water Act.
Watergate, 91, 137, 234
Water Quality Act of 1965, 193
weasel words, 264
Whistle-Blower Protection Act, 432
whistle-blowing, 153, 429-435
winning (sunrise) industries, 199
withdrawal strategy, 41
women
  and advertising, 268-269
  and poverty, 469
  as managers, 482-483
  and environmental issues, 354
women-headed households, 469
women's movement, 468
Wood's corporate social performance model, 48
Worker Adjustment and Retraining Act Notification (WARN), 407
workforce, changes in, 417-420
workplace hazards, 418. *See also* health, OSHA.
workplace privacy, 440-441, 448-449, 461-462
Wygant v. Jackson Board of Education, 495

Y

Yankelovich "Corporate Priorities" service, 568
yen, 161